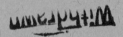

Sixteen Modern American Authors

Volume 2: A Survey of Research and
Criticism Since 1972

Sixteen Modern American Authors

Volume 2: A Survey of Research and Criticism

Since 1972   *Edited by Jackson R. Bryer*

Duke University Press   Durham and London 1990

© 1989 Duke University Press
All rights reserved
Printed in the United States of America on acid-free paper ∞
Library of Congress Cataloging-in-Publication data appear
on the last page of this book.

BERNICE SLOTE (1911–1983)

. . . that is happiness; to be dissolved into something complete and great.—Willa Cather, *My Ántonia*

REGINALD L. COOK (1903–1984)

They would not find me changed from him they knew—
Only more sure of all I thought was true.
—Robert Frost, "Into My Own"

Contents

Preface

In the sixteen years since the last edition of this book appeared, scholarship and criticism on modern American writers has continued unabated. When it came time to plan this third incarnation of *Sixteen* (originally *Fifteen*) *Modern American Authors*, it seemed best simply to ask each contributor to prepare a new essay, updating the version in the 1973 edition and incorporating material inadvertently omitted earlier. At a time when it is not unusual for T. S. Eliot, William Faulkner, and Ernest Hemingway each to be the subject of over a hundred entries in the annual *PMLA* Bibliography, these updates obviously fill out a sizable volume.

Aside from the directive to update the last version of his essay, each contributor was given total freedom as to how he chose to do so. As a result, some of the essays here are more exhaustive than others; some place their emphasis on book-length studies, others try to cover periodical articles as well. In each case the aim was the same: to give a full and comprehensive picture of research and scholarship during the period covered. In general, the starting point of that period is 1972, although as noted above contributors were encouraged to pick up stray pre-1972 items which had not been mentioned earlier. Because completion of the Faulkner essay was unavoidably delayed, the terminal dates vary somewhat. Virtually all of the essays include significant material through 1985; in addition, most contributors supplied Supplements to their essays to bring coverage of book-length studies through mid-1988.

The one exception is Reginald L. Cook's Frost chapter. This essay was the last piece of writing Cook was able to complete before becoming incapacitated by his final illness in 1984. In a tragically ironic echo of the situation with Frederick J. Hoffman's Hemingway essay in the 1969 edition of this book, Cook was not able to do the polishing and updating which the other contributors did. We elected to leave his essay as submitted rather than presume to add material in his name. His widow and his former Middlebury College colleague John McWilliams were of great help in editing the Frost essay, and McWilliams generously agreed to add a very brief Supplement to it.

Cook's death brings to four the number of original contributors to this series who have died. Bernice Slote died in 1983 and thus could not update her Cather chapter; C. Hugh Holman, who died in 1981, could not prepare the new Wolfe essay. In both cases, we were fortunate to find scholars of the highest distinction to step in—James Woodress on Cather and Richard S. Kennedy on Wolfe. Our roster also includes six others new to the project—James L. W. West III on Dreiser, Stuart Y. McDougal on Eliot, Philip G. Cohen, David Krause, and Karl F. Zender on Faulkner, and Bruce Stark on Hemingway. The editor is grateful to them and to those stalwarts who have been with the series since its inception for making this volume possible.

College Park, Maryland
April 13, 1989

Acknowledgments

Certain contributors wish to thank individuals and institutions that have been especially helpful to them as they prepared their essays for this book.

Mr. Rideout thanks Martha Mitten Allen, David D. Anderson, Claire Bruyère, Hilbert E. Campbell, Nicole Cawley-Perkins, Herbert Channick, Gene H. Dent, Frank Gado, Harvey Goldberg, Barry Gross, Sylvia A. Holladay, Mario Maffi, James B. Meriwether, William V. Miller, Charles E. Modlin, Kichinosuke Ohashi, Anthony F. Palmieri, Damon Persiani, Paul P. Somers, Jr., David Stouck, Welford Dunaway Taylor, R. C. Townsend, Richard L. Wentworth, Ray Lewis White, and Iwao Yamamoto.

Mr. Woodress thanks former contributors to *American Literary Scholarship*, Warren French, David Stouck, and John J. Murphy, whose comprehensive reviews of Cather scholarship greatly facilitated the preparation of his essay.

Mr. Weber thanks James Bense, Kevin Hancock, and Kate Mawdsley, Assistant University Librarian, University of California at Davis.

Mr. West thanks Neda M. Westlake, Frederic E. Rusch, G. L. McMullen, and the staff of the Interlibrary Loan Department, Newman Library, Virginia Polytechnic Institute and State University.

Mr. McDougal thanks Jean Jones and Warren Johnson.

Mr. Bryer thanks Ruth M. Alvarez, Matthew J. Bruccoli, Beatriz Dailey, Drew Eisenhauer, Alan Margolies, and Duke University Press for permission to reuse portions of his chapters on F. Scott Fitzgerald in *American Literary Scholarship* for 1973–78 and 1983.

Mr. Cohen thanks James Hinkle, Thomas L. McHaney, Noel Polk, and the Interlibrary Loan staff at the University of Texas at Arlington Library.

Mr. Zender thanks Duke University Press for permission to reuse portions of his chapters on William Faulkner in *American Literary Scholarship* for 1974, 1975, 1980, 1981, 1982, and 1985.

Mr. Krause thanks Bruccoli-Clark Publishers for permission to reuse portions of his essay "William Faulkner" in *Dictionary of Literary Biography Yearbook: 1986*.

Mr. Stark thanks Melvin J. Friedman.

Mr. Raleigh thanks Mary Ann O'Farrell and Alex Siskin.

Mr. Espey thanks Mary Ryan, Charlotte Spens, and Ann Hinckley of the UCLA Research Library staff, the entire staff of the Department of Special Collections of the UCLA Library, James Laughlin and Peggy Fox of New Directions, Carroll F. Terrell of *Paideuma*, James Kubeck of the Los Angeles office of the University of California Press, the editors of the Black Swan Press, George Bornstein, Marjorie Perloff, Kay Davis, Archie Henderson, Christine Froula, Terri Brint Joseph, Carolyn See, and Jordan Espey.

Mr. French thanks the staff of the Ohio University Library and Robert DeMott.

Mr. Riddel thanks the Research Committee of the UCLA Faculty Senate, Mark Bauerlein, Sharada Nair, and Jeanette Gilkenson.

Mr. Kennedy thanks Aldo P. Magi, John S. Phillipson, and Andrea Brown.

Key to Abbreviations

AAus	Americana-Austriaca
ABC	American Book Collector
Adam	Adam International Review
AI	American Imago
AL	American Literature
ALitASH	Acta Litteraria Academiae Scientiarum Hungaricae
ALM	Archives des Lettres Modernes
ALR	American Literary Realism
Amer. Poetry	American Poetry
AmerS	American Studies
AmLS	American Literary Scholarship: An Annual
Amst	Amerikastudien/American Studies
AN&Q	American Notes and Queries
AntigR	Antigonish Review
AppalH	Appalachian Heritage
AppalJ	Appalachian Journal
APR	American Poetry Review
AQ	American Quarterly
ArAA	Arbeiten aus Anglistik und Amerikanistik
Archiv	Archiv für das Studium der Neueren Sprachen und Literaturen
ArielE	Ariel: A Review of International English Literature
ArQ	Arizona Quarterly
ASch	American Scholar
AtM	Atlantic Monthly
BALF	Black American Literature Forum
BB	Bulletin of Bibliography
BC	Book Collector
BCM	Book Collector's Market
BForum	Book Forum

BMMLA	*Bulletin of the Midwest Modern Language Association*
BNYPL	*Bulletin of the New York Public Library*
BRH	*Bulletin of Research in the Humanities*
BSUF	*Ball State University Forum*
BUJ	*Boston University Journal*
BuR	*Bucknell Review*
C&L	*Christianity and Literature*
CB	*Classical Bulletin*
CCR	*Claflin College Review*
CE	*College English*
CEA	*CEA Critic*
CEAmL	Critical Essays on American Literature
CentR	*Centennial Review*
ChiR	*Chicago Review*
CHum	*Computers and the Humanities*
CimR	*Cimarron Review*
CL	*Comparative Literature* (Eugene, Oreg.)
CLAJ	*College Language Association Journal*
CLQ	*Colby Library Quarterly*
CLS	*Comparative Literature Studies*
CML	*Classical and Modern Literature: A Quarterly*
CollL	*College Literature*
ColQ	*Colorado Quarterly*
CompD	*Comparative Drama*
ConL	*Contemporary Literature*
ConnR	*Connecticut Review*
ConP	*Contemporary Poetry*
ContempR	*Contemporary Review*
CP	*Concerning Poetry*
CQ	*Cambridge Quarterly*
CRCL	*Canadian Review of Comparative Literature*
CRevAS	*Canadian Review of American Studies*
Crit	*Critique: Studies in Modern Fiction*
CritI	*Critical Inquiry*
CritQ	*Critical Quarterly*
DAI	*Dissertation Abstracts International*
DLB	*Dictionary of Literary Biography*
DQ	*Denver Quarterly*
DQR	*Dutch Quarterly Review of Anglo-American Letters*
DR	*Dalhousie Review*
DrN	*Dreiser Newsletter*
DrS	*Dreiser Studies*
EA	*Études Anglaises*
EAL	*Early American Literature*
EAS	*Essays in Arts and Sciences*

EIC	*Essays in Criticism*
Éire	*Éire-Ireland* (St. Paul, Minn.)
EJ	English Journal
ELH	ELH [formerly *Journal of English Literary History*]
ELit	*Études Littéraires*
ELN	*English Language Notes*
ELUD	*Essays in Literature* (University of Denver)
ELWIU	*Essays in Literature* (Macomb, Ill.)
English	*English: The Journal of the English Association*
EngR	*English Record*
EON	*Eugene O'Neill Newsletter*
ES	*English Studies*
ESA	*English Studies in Africa*
ESC	*English Studies in Canada*
ESColl	*English Studies Collection*
ESQ	*ESQ: A Journal of the American Renaissance*
ESRS	*Emporia State Research Studies*
ETJ	*Educational Theatre Journal*
Expl	*Explicator*
FaSt	*Faulkner Studies: An Annual of Research, Criticism, and Reviews*
FDP	*Four Decades of Poetry 1890–1930*
FHA	*Fitzgerald/Hemingway Annual*
FJ	*Faulkner Journal*
FJS	*Fu Jen Studies: Literature and Linguistics*
ForumH	*Forum* (Houston, Tex.)
GaR	*Georgia Review*
GeoR	*Geographical Review*
GL&L	*German Life and Letters*
GPQ	*Great Plains Quarterly*
GrLR	*Great Lakes Review*
GyS	*Gypsy Scholar*
HAB	*Humanities Association Bulletin*
Harvard Mag.	*Harvard Magazine*
HCN	*Hart Crane Newsletter*
HK	*Heritage of the Great Plains*
HLB	*Harvard Library Bulletin*
Hn	*Hemingway Newsletter*
HN	*Hemingway Notes*
HR	*Hemingway Review*
HSL	*University of Hartford Studies in Literature*
HSN	*Hawthorne Society Newsletter*
HudR	*Hudson Review*
HUSL	*Hebrew University Studies in Literature and the Arts*
ICarbS	*ICarbS* (Carbondale, Ill.)

IEY	Iowa English Bulletin
IJAS	Indian Journal of American Studies
IJWS	International Journal of Women's Studies
IowaR	Iowa Review
IQ	Italian Quarterly
JAAC	Journal of Aesthetics and Art Criticism
JAAR	Journal of the American Academy of Religion
JAC	Journal of American Culture
JAmS	Journal of American Studies
JCF	Journal of Canadian Fiction
JEGP	Journal of English and Germanic Philology
JGE	JGE: The Journal of General Education
JML	Journal of Modern Literature
JNT	Journal of Narrative Technique
JOHJ	John O'Hara Journal
Jour. of the West	Journal of the West
JPC	Journal of Popular Culture
KAL	Kyushu American Literature
KanQ	Kansas Quarterly
KN	Kwartalnik Neofilologiczny
KR	Kenyon Review
L&P	Literature and Psychology
Lang&L	Language and Literature
Lang&S	Language and Style
LC	Library Chronicle
LCUT	Library Chronicle of the University of Texas
LFQ	Literature/Film Quarterly
LGJ	Lost Generation Journal
LH	Literature and History
LHY	Literary Half-Yearly
LitR	Literary Review
LMonog	Literary Monographs
LNL	Linguistics in Literature
LOS	Literary Onomastics Studies
LT	Levende Talen
LWU	Literatur in Wissenschaft und Unterricht
MarkhamR	Markham Review
MCLR	Mississippi College Law Review
McNR	McNeese Review
MD	Modern Drama
MFS	Modern Fiction Studies
MHLS	Mid-Hudson Language Studies
MichA	Michigan Academician
MinnH	Minnesota History
MinnR	Minnesota Review

MissQ	Mississippi Quarterly
MissR	Missouri Review
MLM	Modern Literature Monographs
MLN	Modern Language Notes
MLR	Modern Language Review
MLS	Modern Language Studies
MMisc	Midwestern Miscellany
MP	Modern Philology
MPS	Modern Poetry Studies
MQ	Midwest Quarterly
MQR	Michigan Quarterly Review
MR	Massachusetts Review
MSE	Massachusetts Studies in English
MSEx	Melville Society Extracts
MSLC	Modernist Studies: Literature and Culture 1920–1940
MSS	Manuscripts
MTJ	Mark Twain Journal
MuK	Maske und Kothurn
NAL	New American Library
NALF	Negro American Literature Forum
N&Q	Notes and Queries
NBR	New Boston Review
NConL	Notes on Contemporary Literature
NDEJ	Notre Dame English Journal: A Journal of Religion and Literature
NDQ	North Dakota Quarterly
Negro Hist. Bull.	Negro History Bulletin
NEQ	New England Quarterly: A Historical Review of New England Life and Letters
NER	New England Review and Bread Loaf Quarterly
NewC	New Criterion
NG	National Geographic
NLB	Newberry Library Bulletin
NLH	New Literary History
NM	Neuphilologische Mitteilungen
NMAL	NMAL: Notes on Modern American Literature
NMW	Notes on Mississippi Writers
NOR	New Orleans Review
NR	New Republic
NsM	Neusprachliche Mitteilungen aus Wissenschaft und Praxis
NYer	New Yorker
NYFQ	New York Folklore Quarterly
NYRB	New York Review of Books
NYTBR	New York Times Book Review

NYTM	*New York Times Magazine*
OhR	*Ohio Review*
OJES	*Osmania Journal of English Studies*
OL	*Orbis Litterarum*
OLR	*Oxford Literary Review*
ON	*Old Northwest*
OQ	*Ohioana Quarterly*
OralEng	*Oral English*
Pacific Hist. Rev.	*Pacific Historical Review*
P&L	*Philosophy and Literature*
ParR	*Paris Review*
PBSA	*Papers of the Bibliographical Society of America*
PCL	*Perspectives on Contemporary Literature*
PCP	*Pacific Coast Philology*
PLL	*Papers on Language and Literature*
PMLA	*Publications of the Modern Language Association*
PMPA	*Publications of the Missouri Philological Association*
PNotes	*Pynchon Notes*
PoT	*Poetics Today* (Jerusalem, Israel)
PQ	*Philological Quarterly* (Iowa City, Iowa)
PR	*Partisan Review*
PrS	*Prairie Schooner*
PsychocultR	*Psychocultural Review*
PULC	*Princeton University Library Chronicle*
PVR	*Platte Valley Review*
QJLC	*Quarterly Journal of the Library of Congress*
QJS	*Quarterly Journal of Speech*
QQ	*Queen's Quarterly*
RALS	*Resources for American Literary Study*
RANAM	*Recherches Anglaises et Américaines*
RES	*Review of English Studies*
Rev.	*Review*
RFEA	*Revue Française d'Études Américaines*
RFI	*Regionalism and the Female Imagination*
RHM	*Revista Hispánica Moderna: Columbia University Hispanic Studies*
RLC	*Revue de Littérature Comparée*
RLM	*Revue des Lettres Modernes*
RLV	*Revue des Langues Vivantes*
RMR	*Rocky Mountain Review of Language and Literature*
RMS	*Renaissance & Modern Studies*
RNL	*Review of National Literatures*
RomN	*Romance Notes*
RS	*Research Studies* (Pullman, Wash.)
RUCR	*Revista de la Universidad de Costa Rica*

SAB	South Atlantic Bulletin
SAF	Studies in American Fiction
SALit	Studies in American Literature (Kyoto, Japan)
SAQ	South Atlantic Quarterly
SARev	South Atlantic Review
SatR	Saturday Review
SB	Studies in Bibliography
SCR	South Carolina Review
SDR	South Dakota Review
SELit	Studies in English Literature (Tokyo, Japan)
SEA	Studies in English and American
SES	Steinbeck Essay Series
SFQ	Southern Folklore Quarterly
SHR	Southern Humanities Review
SJS	San Jose Studies
SLitI	Studies in the Literary Imagination
SLJ	Southern Literary Journal
SMS	Steinbeck Monograph Series
SN	Studia Neophilologia
SNNTS	Studies in the Novel
SoQ	Southern Quarterly
SoR	Southern Review
SoRA	Southern Review (Adelaide, Australia)
SoSt	Southern Studies
SR	Sewanee Review
SSF	Studies in Short Fiction
SSMLN	Society for the Study of Midwestern Literature Newsletter
StAH	Studies in American Humor
StAR	St. Andrews Review
STC	Studies in the Twentieth Century
StCS	Studies in Contemporary Satire
StQ	Steinbeck Quarterly
StTCL	Studies in Twentieth Century Literature
Studies	Studies: An Irish Quarterly Review
SwAL	Southwestern American Literature
SWR	Southwest Review
TCEL	Thought Currents in English Literature
TCI	Twentieth Century Interpretations
TCL	Twentieth Century Literature
TCV	Twentieth Century Views
TFSB	Tennessee Folklore Society Bulletin
TJ	Theatre Journal
TJQ	Thoreau Journal Quarterly
TLOP	The Language of Poems

TLS	[London] *Times Literary Supplement*
TQ	*Texas Quarterly*
TriQ	*TriQuarterly*
TSE	*TSE: Tulane Studies in English*
TSL	*Tennessee Studies in Literature*
TSLL	*Texas Studies in Literature and Language*
TUSAS	Twayne's United States Authors Series
TWN	*Thomas Wolfe Newsletter* or *Thomas Wolfe Review*
UDQ	*University of Denver Quarterly*
UES	*UNISA English Studies*
UTQ	*University of Toronto Quarterly*
UWR	*University of Windsor Review*
VC	*Virginia Cavalcade*
Vermont Hist.	*Vermont History*
VLit	*Voprosy Literatury*
VQR	*Virginia Quarterly Review*
WAL	*Western American Literature*
W&L	*Women & Literature*
WCPMN	*Willa Cather Pioneer Memorial Newsletter*
WCR	*West Coast Review*
WCWN	*William Carlos Williams Newsletter*
WCWR	*William Carlos Williams Review*
WE	*Winesburg Eagle*
WHR	*Western Humanities Review*
WiF	*William Faulkner: Materials, Studies, Criticism*
WLB	*Wilson Library Bulletin*
WSJour	*Wallace Stevens Journal*
WVUPP	*West Virginia University Philological Papers*
YER	*Yeats Eliot Review*
YES	*Yearbook of English Studies*
YFS	*Yale French Studies*
YR	*Yale Review*
YULG	*Yale University Library Gazette*
ZAA	*Zeitschrift für Anglistik und Amerikanistik*

Sherwood Anderson

Walter B. Rideout

I BIBLIOGRAPHY

By far the most important bibliographical work published during the last dozen or so years is Ray Lewis White's *Sherwood Anderson: A Reference Guide* (Boston, 1977). This volume's 2,550 entries, all references to writings about Anderson, not by him, are arranged by year from 1916 through 1975. Within each year are listed items such as books, pamphlets, dissertations, newspaper items, reviews, and articles. Entries are from many foreign-language as well as English publications. Each item is briefly summarized, cross-references are supplied for reprintings and translations, and there is a full index. This volume, which exhibits an extraordinarily high degree of inclusiveness and accuracy, is indispensable for every Anderson scholar and often helpful for the general reader. The *Guide* supersedes White's "Checklist of Sherwood Anderson Studies, 1959–1969" (*NLB*, July 1971) and his three succeeding checklists covering 1970 to 1975 in the *Winesburg Eagle* (Nov. 1975, Apr. 1976, Nov. 1976), except that these four lists also itemize editions and reprints of works by Anderson. White's *Guide* and checklists are now supplemented by annual listings from 1976 to, at present, 1985, scrupulously prepared by Diana Haskell of the Newberry Library and published in each April issue of the *Winesburg Eagle* beginning with 1978.

Less inclusive but useful bibliographies of publications by or about Anderson are Douglas G. Rogers's *Sherwood Anderson: A Selective, Annotated Bibliography* (Metuchen, N.J., 1976), which features summaries, often extended, of each of 256 books and articles about him, and David D. Anderson's "Sherwood Anderson (1876–1941)," in *A Bibliographical Guide to Midwestern Literature* (ed. Gerald Nemanic, Iowa City, 1981). James B. Meriwether's "Sherwood Anderson," in *First Printings of American Authors: Contributions Toward Descriptive Checklists* (ed. Matthew J. Bruccoli, Detroit, 1978), is of special interest for reproducing the title pages of twelve of Anderson's books, including several English editions. The twenty-four books by Anderson and thirty books about him "currently available" in 1977 are listed by Douglas G. Rogers and Ray Lewis White in "Sherwood Anderson in Print" (*WE*, Apr. 1977).

Minor additions to Eugene P. Sheehy and Kenneth A. Lohf's basic *Sherwood Anderson: A Bibliography* (1960) are noted by Richard Colles Johnson in "Addenda to Sheehy and Lohf's Bibliography of Sherwood Anderson" (*PBSA*, First Quarter 1972) and by Johnson and G. Thomas Tanselle in "Addenda to Bibliographies of Sherwood Anderson [et al.]" (*PBSA*, First Quarter 1972). More significant is Tanselle's "Addenda to Sheehy and Lohf's *Sherwood Anderson*: Copyright Information and Later Printings," in *Sherwood Anderson: Centennial Studies* (ed. Hilbert H. Campbell and Charles E. Modlin, Troy, N.Y., 1976; hereinafter referred to as Campbell and Modlin), which from copyright records provides "the official publication date of each book (by law the copyright date)" and "the dates of some of the later printings of the books," and for the first time confirms that Anderson did publish a pamphlet entitled *An Idea to Establish a Commercial Democracy* in Elyria, Ohio, on 22 October 1909, although no copies have as yet been found. Ray Lewis White's "Sherwood Anderson: Fugitive Pamphlets and Broadsides, 1918–1940" (*SB*, 1978) gives detailed bibliographic citations for seventeen items "too fugitive or ephemeral to have been noted or described" by Sheehy and Lohf; and in "Anderson in Chicago Newspapers: A Supplementary List" (*WE*, Nov. 1977), White and Diana Haskell list ninety-seven previously uncited entries concerning the author from 1916 through 1969.

Of Anderson's books, *Winesburg, Ohio* has received by far the most bibliographic attention. In his "Winesburg Revisited" (*Serif*, Sept. 1970), Josiah Q. Bennett confirms most of William L. Phillips's original distinctions between the first and second impressions of that book; and in "The Editions of *Winesburg, Ohio*" (Campbell and Modlin), Phillips confidently identifies the "points which characterize the first impression . . . : orange or yellow cloth; top edge stained orange-yellow or yellow; a perfect title page frame; extraneous 'of' p. 4, second line from the bottom; 'lay,' p. 86, l. 5; perfect type in 'his,' p. 196, l. 9; and perfect type in 'cutting,' p. 260, l. 9." Ray Lewis White has contributed four more notes on the book in "*Winesburg, Ohio*: First-Impression Errors" (*PBSA*, Second Quarter 1977), listing sixteen "misprints or authorial errors"; "Winesburg in Translation: Ohio in the World" (*OQ*, Summer 1976), giving "a chronological bibliography of the 40 editions in 23 non-English languages from 1924 through 1970"; "*Winesburg* in 1919: The Publisher's Catalog Copy" (*WE*, Apr. 1978), reprinting two pieces, probably by Huebsch, praising the book in the publisher's mimeographed circular, "Notes from B. W. Huebsch"; and "*Winesburg, Ohio*: The Story Titles" (*WE*, Nov. 1984), providing "a chart that shows the progression or development of the *Winesburg* titles from (1) the earliest extant manuscript, to (2) the revised manuscript readings, to (3) the periodical titles for the ten stories so published, to (4) the stories on a draft table of contents, to (5) the final titles as published in Anderson's book in May of 1919." Finally, in "The Achievement of Sherwood Anderson" (*NLB*, July 1971), Richard Colles Johnson provides a descriptive list of 134 items in an Anderson exhibit at the Newberry Library honoring the fiftieth anniversary of the publication of *Winesburg* and the presentation of the manuscript of it to the Library's Anderson Collection by the Newberry Library Associates.

The definitive article on the unpublished manuscript of another book is "*Mary Cochran*: Sherwood Anderson's Ten-Year Novel" (*SB*, 1978), in which William S. Pfeiffer cogently argues that Anderson "began *Mary Cochran* between 1909 and 1912 in Ohio, continued work on it during the teens in Chicago, and stopped working on the novel" by 1921. As for the publishers of his completed works, information about Benjamin W. Huebsch is supplied by Ann Catherine McCullough in her unpublished dissertation, "A History of B. W. Huebsch, Publisher" (Univ. of Wisconsin-Madison, 1979), chapter four of which is a full description of "Publishing Sherwood Anderson" based on the Huebsch Papers at the Library of Congress; and relevant information about Horace Liveright of Boni & Liveright is contained in Walker Gilmer's *Horace Liveright: Publisher of the Twenties* (New York, 1970), especially the well-researched chapter, "Sherwood Anderson." In "Sherwood Anderson and the Viking Press, 1925–1941" (*RALS*, Autumn 1980), Hilbert H. Campbell traces the steady decline in sales of the six Anderson books originally published by Huebsch after 1925, when Anderson went to Liveright and Huebsch merged with Viking.

Another kind of aid to Anderson scholarship is Campbell and Modlin's "A Catalog of Sherwood Anderson's Library" (Campbell and Modlin), which itemizes the 837 books Anderson left "at Ripshin Farm, Troutdale, Virginia, or at Rosemont, his wife Eleanor's home in Marion, Virginia, at the time of his death in 1941." Two pieces of more tangential interest are Campbell's "The *Washington County Forum*: A Minor Anderson Connection" (*WE*, Apr. 1978), which notes his identification as "Associate Editor" of an Abingdon, Virginia, weekly newspaper published in 1935 by his son Robert and the reprinting in that paper of certain of his "What Say!" columns; and " 'Implications of Obscenity': The English Trial of *Many Marriages*" (*JML*, Mar. 1983), in which prolific Anderson scholar Ray Lewis White quotes the English review of that novel which resulted in the court trial of the editor of the *Sporting Times* for publishing obscenity and his sentence to four months in prison.

A particularly helpful article on a foreign country's reception of Anderson's work is MarySue Schriber's "Sherwood Anderson in France: 1919–1939" (*TCL*, Feb. 1977), which states that during these years "French periodicals carried some thirty-five notices of Anderson and his work, most of them short reviews but a few of them of greater length, and chapters of three French studies of American literature were devoted to Anderson." French critics and reviewers tended to praise his language but to find his narratives disorderly; to praise, with some reservation, his psychological penetration and his revolt against an American civilization marked by materialism and puritanism; to see him as the preserver of earlier spiritual values in his country. Schriber's model article concludes with "A Checklist of French Commentary on Sherwood Anderson: 1919–1939."

Despite this considerable bibliographic activity, a different kind of trial and a much longer sentence in time than that of the unlucky English editor still await the person or persons dedicated enough to compile the "complete and accurate descriptive bibliography" noted in the original publication of *Fifteen Modern American Authors* as still "among the desiderata of Anderson scholarship."

II EDITIONS

The outstanding event in this area of Anderson scholarship has been the appearance in 1982 of the Rinsen Edition of *The Complete Works of Sherwood Anderson* under the editorship of Kichinosuke Ohashi, Professor of American Literature at Keio University in Tokyo and one of Japan's leading authorities on twentieth-century American literature. That the first uniform edition of all the writings of Anderson published in book form has been issued by the Rinsen Book Company of Kyoto, Japan, instead of by an American firm should be the occasion of some national embarrassment to us, but it is the occasion much more of gratitude that such an edition, complete in twenty-one handsome volumes, is now in print. The arrangement of the individual volumes in the set is by genre and within the genre by year of publication; so, for example, the eight novels, including the hybrid *Winesburg*, comprise volumes 1 through 8, followed by the volumes of short stories, volume 11 containing the brief *Alice and The Lost Novel* and *Death in the Woods*. Included in series thereafter are the semi-autobiographical books, the nonfiction volumes, the poems and plays together, and finally the *Memoirs* and *The Sherwood Anderson Reader*. Volume 21 is an appendix containing many photographs of and documents about "Clyde as Winesburg," twenty stories by Anderson previously published in magazines and anthologies but now collected for the first time, and an index of titles.

Faced with the present unsatisfactory textual situation of Anderson's works, Ohashi sensibly decided to use for his texts "photocopied reproductions of first editions, first printings, or limited editions." Although "typographical blurs and broken types" have been emended, the unrevised "lay" on p. 86, l. 5 of *Winesburg*, by which Phillips originally identified the first impression, therefore remains. One notes, however, that the first impression's extraneous "of" on p. 4 has been silently corrected. But these are hardly serious matters, and Ohashi settles a more serious one by printing both the original ending of *Windy McPher-*

son's Son in the 1916 John Lane edition and the revised ending of the 1922 Huebsch one. An added benefit is that following a uniform title page for each work is a reproduction of the original title page. With typical Japanese taste Rinsen has also reproduced certain first edition design elements such as the map of Winesburg and the pale blue covers of *Alice and The Lost Novel*. Both Ohashi and Rinsen deserve highest praise for their accomplishment.

Although one might wish that Ohashi had incorporated into several of his texts the few corrections made by Anderson or by editors subsequent to first impressions, that he did make a sensible decision as to texts is clearly demonstrated by G. Thomas Tanselle's "The Case Western Reserve Edition of Sherwood Anderson: A Review Article" in *Proof* (1975). Here Tanselle examines carefully and at length the editorial plan and its execution in the three volumes of the edition of the oddly titled *The Major Fiction of Sherwood Anderson*, edited by Ray Lewis White: *A Story Teller's Story* (1968), *Tar: A Midwest Childhood* (1969), and *Marching Men* (1972). Tanselle finds that the plan "leaves much to be desired, and the execution of that plan is both inconsistent and inaccurate." He concludes that these three volumes "stand in greater need of editing now than they did before Mr. White embarked on his task" and that "Meanwhile, Anderson scholars face an awkward situation and will have to decide whether the better course at present may not be to make their quotations from the original editions." More recently, Hilbert H. Campbell, in "The Perils of False Assumptions: Editing Sherwood Anderson's *Tar*" (*PBSA*, Third Quarter 1981), has confirmed that "the original BL [Boni & Liveright] text of *Tar*, whatever its shortcomings, is far better than the CWR [Press of Case Western Reserve] 'critical text' edition," partly because of the "somewhat confusing and inconsistent principles employed in editing the CWR text," but mainly because "an extensively revised typescript of *Tar*," obtained by the Newberry Library in 1981, "proves to be surprisingly close to the BL text." This typescript shows, for example, that in most cases material "restored" by White to the CWR text as being intended by Anderson had in fact been deleted by him before a final setting copy went to the publisher.

Given the evidence produced by Tanselle and Campbell, it is fortunate that White has dropped his project for a series of "critical editions," but the large task of re-editing Anderson's work in accordance with the guidelines established by the Center for Scholarly Editions needs to be undertaken. Douglas G. Rogers takes a step in that direction in his critical edition of *Many Marriages* (Metuchen, N.J., 1978). Rogers reproduces the text of the novel's first edition—but, without explanation, the text of the third impression rather than of the first—and provides twenty-five pages of textual notes listing variants among the texts of the published book (1923), that of the shorter version serialized in the *Dial* from October 1922 through March 1923, and those of the setting copies of the book and of the serial version. Most encouraging among editing ventures at present is William V. Miller's continued progress on a complete (excluding *Winesburg*) authoritative edition of Anderson's seventy-eight collected and uncollected short stories following Center for Scholarly Editions guidelines.

Two pieces from Anderson books have been edited by Ray Lewis White in "Winesburg, Ohio: The Unique Alternate Draft of 'Nobody Knows'" (*WE*, Nov. 1982) and by Charles E. Modlin in "'In a Field': A Story from *A Story Teller's Story*" (*WE*, Apr. 1983). The former prints "the only extant alternate draft of any *Winesburg* story," a manuscript version of "Nobody Knows," which differs only in minor points from the printed version; the latter reproduces a typescript made from Anderson's penciled revisions of the tale concluding book 3 of *A Story Teller's Story*, given the title "In a Field," sent to his literary agent in January 1940 but not published. In "'Death in the Woods': Anderson's Earliest Version" (*WE*, Apr. 1982), Ray Lewis White prints excerpts, connected by summary, from "an almost complete narrative of a death in the woods," probably typed by Anderson around 1916. The narrative is on the backs of pages of the *Winesburg, Ohio* manuscript in the Newberry Library. As White suggests, it is essential that the material on the backs of these manuscript pages be fully catalogued and analyzed.

Two more extended selections from Anderson's unpublished works have been edited by Martha Mulroy Curry in *Sherwood Anderson's "The Writer's Book": A Critical Edition* (Metuchen, N.J., 1975) and William S. Pfeiffer in his dissertation, "An Edition of Sherwood Anderson's *Mary Cochran*" (Kent State Univ., 1975). Anderson apparently conceived *The Writer's Book* as a textbook on the craft of writing, but left the 267-page manuscript unfinished at his death. Curry prints its seven parts, probably composed between 1933 and 1939, sections of which were included, much revised, in Paul Rosenfeld's edition of *Sherwood Anderson's Memoirs* but which Curry restores to original form in the ninety-two printed pages of Anderson text. Her own lengthy "Commentary" cites parallels between passages in *The Writer's Book* and passages from Anderson's other works. Pfeiffer's dissertation, which deserves publication in book form, presents independently the three Newberry Library texts of Anderson's early novel—see the comment on Pfeiffer's article above—which is of considerable interest as reflecting Anderson's concern in 1913 with feminism and new marital arrangements.

There have been a number of reprints of different Anderson works in the past dozen years, the most important of which is *Sherwood Anderson, The Writer at His Craft* (Mamaroneck, N.Y., 1979), compiled by Jack Salzman, David D. Anderson, and Kichinosuke Ohashi and published by Paul P. Appel. This volume brings together sixty-nine previously uncollected contributions by Anderson to periodicals during his literary career. Many of these were published in the 1930s, the compilers point out, have received little critical attention, and, taken together, will be helpful in a reappraisal of Anderson's total work. Also under the Appel imprint is a reissue of *Home Town* (1975), with an introduction by David D. Anderson which summarizes Sherwood Anderson's view of the small town, in this last book he published during his lifetime, as "America in microcosm and in reality." Taking over from Viking, Penguin has re-issued the Malcolm Cowley text of *Winesburg, Ohio* (1976), Horace Gregory's revised edition of *The Portable Sherwood Anderson* (1977), and John H. Ferres's useful volume, *Sherwood Anderson "Winesburg, Ohio": Text and Criticism* (1977).

Reprint houses have tended to specialize rather monotonously in the less central, shorter books, especially *Alice and The Lost Novel* and *Mid-American Chants*. Arden Library reprinted the former in 1978 along with *The Modern Writer* and *Nearer the Grass Roots*. Folcroft reprinted *Alice* and the *Chants* (1978) along with, likewise, *The Modern Writer* (1976) and *Nearer the Grass Roots* (1977). Frontier Press in 1972 and Norwood Editions in 1980 reprinted the *Chants*, while Bern Porter reprinted *Alice and The Lost Novel* in 1979. It is refreshing that from time to time the *Winesburg Eagle*, the official publication of the Sherwood Anderson Society, reprints less available earlier discussions of Anderson or short pieces by him, such as William A. Sutton's presentation, in the November 1977 issue, of Anderson's article "The Future of Japanese and American Writing," written in the autumn of 1927 and first published, in Japanese transla-tion, in the 1 and 3 January 1928 issues of the Tokyo newspaper *Jiji Shimpo* (*Current News*). Furthermore, in 1985 Arbor House broke "tradi-tion" by very sensibly reprinting Anderson's last novel, *Kit Brandon*, out of print since 1936, with an introduction by Christopher Sergel describing the origin of the character Kit and warmly recording some of his memories of Anderson, a close friend of his father and mother, Roger and Ruth Sergel. It is also pleasant to note Caedmon's release in 1983 of a three-record stereo set in which E. G. Marshall reads, with some dramatization of scenes by a cast, a number of the *Winesburg* tales in a "compound narrative" composed by the writer Theodore Sturgeon. Most recently, W. W. Norton in 1986 reprinted *Death in the Woods and Other Stories*, Anderson's last collection of tales originally published in 1933.

III MANUSCRIPTS AND LETTERS

Anderson's centennial year of 1976 was an appropriate time for an updating of information on the Newberry Library's splendid Sherwood Anderson Collection. In "The Sherwood Anderson Collection Comes to the Newberry Library" (Campbell and Modlin), the late Amy Wood Nyholm, who was devoted to the collection and to the many scholars who used it, describes how she solved the problem of organizing Eleanor Anderson's generous gift to the Newberry of her husband's letters and manuscripts. Nyholm's fundamental decision was to divide the enormous mass of material into three major categories: "Out" (letters from Anderson to others, arranged chronologically); "In" (letters from others to Anderson, arranged alphabetically by name of correspondent); "Works" (manuscripts, arranged by title in alphabetical order). In a companion article, "The Sherwood Anderson Papers at the Newberry Library" (Campbell and Modlin), Diana Haskell, Nyholm's very able successor, provides an overview of the contents of the collection, which numbered 12,941 items in 1949 and 16,926 items in 1976, and continues to grow through gift and purchase.

Another centennial publication was Michael Fanning's *France and Sherwood Anderson: Paris Notebook, 1921* (Baton Rouge, La., 1976). The book begins with a chapter, "Anderson's Summer in France," which gives the facts of his first European visit; and it concludes with a chapter, "France and *A Story-Teller's Story*," which discusses the sympathetic attitudes he brought to France and yet his visit's confirmation of his Americanness. The forty-eight-page central part of the book is the printing of the "Paris Notebook, 1921," the journal-workbook Anderson kept during his visit. This contains not only accounts of his reactions to French people, life, and culture as well as of meetings with Joyce and Stein, but also a number of drafts of pieces he worked on during the visit, including what seems to be an abortive attempt at "Death in the Woods." Hence the Notebook is important both biographically and critically. Yet another 1976 publication was William A. Sutton's monograph in the Ball State University series, *The Revision of "Seeds"* (Muncie, Ind.). Through a careful study of the revisions of the manuscript of Anderson's tale "Seeds," Sutton shows that "Sherwood Anderson was not customarily a spontaneous writer, as he liked to present himself in romanticizing the impulse-inspired aspect of the writer, even though he was unconcerned with formal study of either writing technique or language convention."

A very important publication in the category of letters is Charles E. Modlin's edition, *Sherwood Anderson: Selected Letters* (Knoxville, Tenn., 1984). This excellently edited volume contains 201 letters, most of which have never been published elsewhere and none of which duplicate the principal other publications of Anderson's letters. Selected "on the basis of their unusual interest in revealing Anderson's literary and personal concerns," this collection includes, among those of special note, three letters to Hemingway, fourteen to Anderson's patron Burton Emmett, and sixteen to his long-time friend Roger Sergel. A number of letters are either recent acquisitions of the Newberry Library or part of a "reserved" group not available for publication until now. Incidentally, the publication of the letters to Hemingway supplants Ray Lewis White's "Anderson's Private Reaction to *The Torrents of Spring*" (*MFS*, Winter 1980–81), in which White supplements his paraphrase of Hemingway's letters to Anderson concerning that parody of *Dark Laughter* (*MFS*, Summer 1967) by paraphrasing Anderson's three replies. The entire correspondence about *Torrents* is thus now available in Modlin's edition and in Carlos Baker's *Ernest Hemingway: Selected Letters, 1917–1961* (New York, 1981). The year 1985 was likewise an outstanding one for the publication of Anderson correspondence, since the University of Illinois Press issued William A. Sutton's edition of *Letters to Bab: Sherwood Anderson to Marietta D. Finley, 1916–33*, a series of 309 letters Anderson wrote to this close friend which have extraordinary interest for their detailed revelation of his literary and personal development during these essential years. Sutton's article, "Anderson's Letters to Marietta D. Finley Hahn: A Literary Chronicle," in *Sherwood Anderson: Dimensions of His Literary Art: A Collection of Critical Essays* (ed. David D. Anderson, East Lansing, Mich., 1976; hereinafter referred to as Anderson, *Dimensions*), provides a detailed explanation of how Sutton located and obtained for the Newberry Library these very important letters, together with the manuscripts of *Marching Men* and "Seeds."

Three other groups of Anderson's letters were published during the 1970s. The largest is a collection of fifty-four letters printed with brief annotation by Hilbert H. Campbell and Charles E. Modlin in their *Sherwood Anderson: Centennial Studies*. These were "selected for their importance in revealing some of Anderson's attitudes, activities and relationships during the twenty years (1920–40) that they span. Four groups of letters reflect his close friendships with Jerome and Lucile Blum, Burton and Mary Emmett, Laura Copenhaver, and J. J. Lankes. Darwin T. Turner's "An Intersection of Paths: Correspondence Between Jean Toomer and Sherwood Anderson" (*CLAJ*, June 1974) prints from the Jean Toomer Collection at Fisk University the letters exchanged between the two writers running mostly from 1922, when Anderson first praised Toomer for expressing the "black consciousness" in his art, to 1924. Turner's commentary on the exchange analyzes Anderson's semi-primitivistic attitude toward blacks. In Cathy Harvey's "Dear Lyle/Sherwood Anderson" (*SoSt*, Fall 1979), a brief introduction precedes the printing of the correspondence between Anderson and the New Orleans writer Lyle Saxon from fall 1924 to fall 1927, eight letters being from Anderson, seven from Saxon. This interchange records both mutual praise and Anderson's generous efforts to get Saxon's early work published.

Four articles have made other unpublished letters available in print. Thaddeus B. Hurd's "Two New Anderson Letters" (*WE*, Nov. 1981) gives the background and the texts of two brief notes written by Anderson in February 1893 inviting a Clyde girl, Mabel Supner, to go to dancing class with him. *Literary America, 1903–1934: The Mary Austin Letters* (ed. T. M. Pearce, Westport, Conn., 1979) includes a letter of summer 1923 from Anderson to Austin. "Sherwood Anderson to David

Karsner" (*WE*, Apr. 1982) is a letter of 5 April 1926 from Anderson providing an autobiographical sketch for Karsner's use in preparing an article on the author for the *New York Herald-Tribune*. In "Sherwood Anderson in Japan: The Early Period" (*TCL*, Feb. 1977), Kichinosuke Ohashi prints and discusses the correspondence in the mid-1920s between Anderson and three Japanese figures: Shinkichi Takahashi (Dadaist poet) and Kinetaro Yoshida and Matsuo Takagaki ("the earliest scholars to deal with American literature in Japan"). Included are translations back into English of two letters from Anderson to Yoshida up to now available only in Japanese translations. Nearly the first half of Ohashi's book (title translated), *Sherwood Anderson and Three Japanese: American Literature in Japan in the Late 1920s* (Tokyo, 1984), which deals with the Japanese reception of Anderson and his contemporaries, consists of a more extensive explication and discussion of this article. Like a number of other items on Anderson in Japanese, this book should be translated into English, or Andersonians should learn Japanese.

IV BIOGRAPHY

Unlike the situation in the previous three areas of scholarship, no outstanding achievement in the last dozen years can be reported, although many lesser items, some very valuable, have appeared. Walter B. Rideout continues to work on his critical biography of Anderson, and Kim Townsend has recently begun a "biographical study" designed, in his words, to "present the Anderson that I imagine to be there in his life and works that is of special relevance at the present time." Among the shorter biographical pieces are Rideout's extended account of Anderson's life and literary career in *American Novelists, 1910–1945, Part I: Dictionary of Literary Biography*, vol. 9 (ed. James J. Martine, Detroit, 1981), and Claire Bruyère's compact, yet perceptive entry, "Sherwood Anderson (1876–1941)," in volume 18 of the *Encyclopaedia Universalis* (Paris, 1974). Margaret A. Van Antwerp, with the editorial advice of Diana Haskell, has compiled a well-chosen selection of documentary materials concerning Anderson's life and career in the *Dictionary of Literary Biography: Documentary Series: An Illustrated Chronicle*, vol. 1 (Detroit, 1982), a selection including, as the volume's subhead states, "Photographs, Manuscripts, Facsimiles, Letters, Notebooks, Interviews, And Contemporary Assessments."

David D. Anderson's "Sherwood Anderson: A Photographic Gallery" (*TCL*, Feb. 1977) reproduces an excellent series of photographs covering Anderson's Clyde years, his business career, his years of artistic success, and his period of involvement with the life of a Virginia town and the Depression. These are selected from David D. Anderson's extensive collection which he is preparing for book publication as *The Four States of a Man's Life: A Photo Biography of Sherwood Anderson*. "Sherwood Anderson's First Century," also by David D. Anderson (*SSMLN*, Fall 1976 and *OQ*, Fall 1976), briefly summarizes Anderson's life and his creation of an "American myth"—"the rejection of material values and the search for permanent human values." More speculative is Mia Klein's "Sherwood Anderson: The Artist's Struggle for Self-Respect" (*TCL*, Feb. 1977). Using a psychoanalytic approach, Klein postulates a struggle within Anderson between the artist's self-hatred because of his rebellion against "the Collective Father (society's laws, its code, its standards, its truth)" and his self-respect because of his devotion to "the Spirit Father (the individual's private, independent truth, his personal God.)" The argument would be stronger if Klein did not rely on all of Anderson's longer works as equally valid sources of literal evidence for such a struggle.

A variety of articles have dealt with Anderson's Clyde background. In the few pages of "Sherwood Anderson's Clyde, Ohio" (Campbell and Modlin), Thaddeus B. Hurd, son of Anderson's best boyhood friend, Herman Hurd, concentrates a detailed history of the founding and development of the town from the settlement around 1827 of "Hamer's Corners," through the coming of the railroads in 1852, to the building up, over the next few decades, of the town to which Anderson's family came in 1884. In "Fun in Winesburg" (*MMisc XI*, 1983), this same well-informed historian of Clyde draws on the files of the local newspaper, the *Clyde Enterprise*, to describe town life in the early 1880s, a time before the advent of the movies, radio, and television when, in the words of Hurd's father, "'We made our own good times.'" Stephanie Kraft's "Sherwood Anderson's Vanishing Winesburg," in her *No Castles on Main Street: American Authors and Their Homes* (Chicago, 1979), is a brief, pleasant description of Clyde and Anderson's life there which relies somewhat uncritically on his own writings. In "Sherwood Anderson's Sentimental Journey" (*RALS*, Spring 1982), Hilbert H. Campbell prints the entries in Eleanor Anderson's journal concerning a two-day visit (11–12 Nov. 1934) she and her husband paid to Ohio towns where the Anderson family had lived. On the twelfth, they drove to Clyde, "where Sherwood knows and loves and remembers everything," and to Elyria, where he "reluctantly" showed her the factory and "the street he thought he lived in."

Three articles describe another approach to recreating Clyde-Winesburg. Gene H. Dent's "Sherwood Anderson/A Story Teller's Town: The Filming of a Documentary" (*MMisc III*, 1975) emphasizes the considerable extent to which Anderson's Winesburg still corresponds physically to present-day Clyde, and discusses problems Dent was then meeting prior to making his very moving videotape documentary for television, *A Story Teller's Town*. Harry Forrest Lupold and Dent's "Sherwood Anderson on Videotape" (*OQ*, Winter 1980) and Dent's "Sherwood Anderson on Video: *A Story Teller's Town* and *Sherwood Anderson's Blue Ridge Country*" (*GrLR*, Summer 1981) discuss the making of Dent's two tele-

vision documentaries, *Town* being first aired in March 1976 and subsequently shown at the Sherwood Anderson Centenary celebrations,
the equally fine *Blue Ridge* being first aired in March 1979.

More recently, Bill Osinski's "Sherwood Anderson's Clyde, Ohio," a
feature article in the *Akron Beacon Journal's Beacon Magazine* (19 Feb.
1984), based on recent interviews with Clyde residents, suggests that
Anderson's achievement continues to be relatively ignored locally partly
because the older citizens had been shocked by *Winesburg*, and partly
because, as the former town librarian told Osinski resignedly, "'Clyde
just isn't a very literary community.'" Thaddeus Hurd and another
townsman, Glen Giffen, are working through the Clyde Heritage League
to ensure that "Clyde acknowledges its hometown author." An interesting specialized article is Herbert Channick's "The Great Adventure: Sherwood Anderson and Harness Racing" (*Hoof Beats*, Dec. 1971). Channick,
a Chicago attorney and "harness horseman," brings together from various of Anderson's works the evidence of his life-long love of harness
horses and racing, a love which began in Clyde.

The best piece on Anderson's early life is William Baker's "Sherwood
Anderson in Springfield" (*ALR*, Spring 1982), an admirably informed
account of Anderson's year (1899–1900) at Wittenberg Academy. On
the basis of careful research in local documents and a manuscript fragment, Baker argues that, more than by his Academy work, Anderson
was directed eventually toward writing by his acquaintance with persons
associated with "The Oaks," the boarding house where he lived with
his brother Karl. In "Sherwood Anderson's Ohio" (*ON*, Summer 1979),
David D. Anderson indicates the importance to Anderson of his native
state by detailing the Ohio settings for *Windy McPherson's Son, Winesburg,
Ohio, Poor White*, about half the stories in *The Triumph of the Egg* and
Horses and Men, A Story Teller's Story, Tar, the satirical sketch, "Ohio: I'll
Say We've Done Well," and the late fragment, "Buckeye Blues." In a
note connecting Anderson's early with his later life, "Sherwood Anderson's Middle Name" (*AN&Q*, Sept. 1976), Hilbert H. Campbell reports
that although the author's middle name was presumably "Berton," he
once told a friend that it was "Beale," and he twice used the pseudonym
"Beal Anderson" to "disguise his identity."

A few articles have considered, with varying success, Anderson's
relationships with several persons early in his literary career. John H.
and Margaret M. Wrenn's "'T.M.': The Forgotten Muse of Sherwood
Anderson and Edgar Lee Masters" (Campbell and Modlin) compares
the relationships of Tennessee Mitchell to the two writers as lover of
Masters and second wife of Anderson, but though making a case for
her as "the forgotten muse" behind Masters's *Spoon River Anthology*, fails
to prove that she similarly "molded" Anderson's writing of *Winesburg,
Ohio* and his literary career. Likewise Ray Lewis White, in "Sherwood
Anderson, Ben Hecht, and *Eric* [sic] *Dorn*" (*AL*, May 1977), claims that

the friendship between the two men ended in 1921 because Hecht's characterization of Anderson in *Erik Dorn* under the name of "Warren Lockwood" was "not flattering"; yet a reading of Hecht's novel indicates rather that Dorn is an often scathing self-portrait while Lockwood, aside from being called "unsophisticated," is presented fairly favorably.

More persuasively, David D. Anderson's "Sherwood Anderson and *The Seven Arts*" (*SSMLN*, Spring 1980) surveys the relations between Anderson and the editors of the magazine which in its one year of life (1916–17) published four of his Winesburg stories and praised him as the type of the new American artist, while in " 'From East-Side to South-Side with Love': The Friendship of Sherwood Anderson and Paul Rosenfeld" (*MMisc VII*, 1979), David D. Anderson traces in detail the mostly warm relationship between the two men from 1917 to 1941. Leland H. Cox, Jr.'s "Sherwood Anderson" in *American Writers in Paris, 1920–1939: Dictionary of Literary Biography*, vol. 4 (ed. Karen Lane Rood, Detroit, 1980) deals primarily with Anderson's first visit to Paris in 1921 and his relationship with Gertrude Stein. Possible evidence for the influence of Stein's style on Anderson's is provided by Ray Lewis White's "The Chicago Renaissance Discovers Gertrude Stein" (*AN&Q*, Mar.–Apr. 1982), which summarizes and quotes from four Chicago newspaper reviews of *Tender Buttons* in the summer of 1914, reviews Anderson and other Chicago Renaissance writers "could have seen."

Robert E. Ned Haines has contributed two articles on Anderson and Alfred Stieglitz. The first, "Anderson and Stieglitz: A Fellowship of Sayer and Seer" (Campbell and Modlin), draws on the correspondence between the two men to show judiciously the similarities in the intuitive aesthetics of each, especially as Stieglitz reveals his aesthetics in his admiring comments on Anderson's writings and the latter reveals his in his admiring comments on Stieglitz's devotion to modernist art and artists. (This article, slightly revised, is reprinted in Haines's *The Inner Eye of Alfred Stieglitz* [Washington, D.C., 1982].) On the other hand, Haines's "Turning Point: Sherwood Anderson Encounters Alfred Stieglitz" (*MarkhamR*, Fall 1976) reductively asserts that Stieglitz's influence was responsible for turning the author from what Haines considers the "pessimism" of *Poor White* to the "optimism" of his post-1924 work. Obviously what each of the two men got from their friendship has yet to be described satisfactorily, as is further illustrated by F. Richard Thomas's chapter on Anderson in *Literary Admirers of Alfred Stieglitz* (Carbondale, Ill., 1983), which may be noted here though it is more critical than biographical in nature. Thomas cites interesting parallels between Anderson's tales and Stieglitz's theory and practice of photography, but he cannot substantiate his claim that Stieglitz influenced Anderson to adopt a "photographic" style since many of the *Winesburg* stories, from which Thomas draws a number of his parallels, had been written before the writer even met the photographer. A safer, and more significant, conclusion by Thomas is that "Anderson learned through Stieglitz that it was possible for the machine [the camera] to produce good effects [beauty] in a world that was becoming more standardized."

Information about other of Anderson's relationships has been made available, particularly that with Hemingway. Paul Somers, Jr., whose "Sherwood and Me" (*Great River Review*, No. 2, 1980) finds amusing parallels between two Ohioans, summarizes, in "Sherwood Anderson Introduces His Friend Ernest Hemingway" (*LGJ*, Fall 1975), Hemingway's subsequent personal and literary relations with the Paris literary figures to whom Anderson wrote letters of introduction for him in 1921. In "The Hemingway-Anderson Feud: A Letter from Boni" (*HN*, Fall 1981), Anthony F. Palmieri prints and comments on a letter he received from Albert Boni of Boni & Liveright supporting Anderson's statement that he had personally urged Liveright to accept *In Our Time* for publication, while in "A Note on the Hemingway-Anderson Rupture" (*FHA*, 1978), Palmieri reports Eleanor Anderson's statement to him concerning the rupture over *The Torrents of Spring*: "One of the last things Sherwood told me [before he died] was that Hemingway had sent him word that he was sorry." Aside from the correspondence between Hemingway and Anderson discussed above, the most important information concerning their relationship is contained in R. L. Samsell's "Paris Days with Ralph Church" and the accompanying memoir by Church, "Sherwood Comes to Town" (*FHA*, 1972). The latter piece is unusually valuable since it carefully records conversations between Anderson and Ralph Church, a trained philosopher who knew him well, in Paris in the winter of 1926–27. The conversations cover such matters as Anderson's irritated-amused reaction to *The Torrents of Spring*, his assessment of Hemingway's strengths and weaknesses as a writer, and his own writing methods. Unfortunately, Church's account concludes by reprinting, without confirmation or denial, Anderson's own description in the *Memoirs* of a single brusque meeting with Hemingway in Paris in 1927.

A less often discussed relationship is surveyed in David D. Anderson's "Sherwood Anderson and Edmund Wilson" (*SSMLN*, Spring 1981), which primarily uses the rather sparse correspondence between the two men to trace their generally admiring but desultory friendship. Useful for understanding a different sort of relationship is William A. Sutton's "Elizabeth Prall Anderson (1884–1976)" (*WE*, Apr. 1976), which, drawing on her own account in *Miss Elizabeth* but correcting her factual inaccuracies, summarizes the life of Anderson's third wife with emphasis on her marriage to Anderson from 1924 to 1932. The effect of residence in New Orleans, where Sherwood and Elizabeth settled in 1924, is discussed in two articles. In "Julius Weis Friend's History of the *Double Dealer*" (*MissQ*, Fall 1978), Leland H. Cox, Jr., prints Friend's typescript essay, "The Double Dealer: Career of a 'Little' Magazine," which includes observant comment on Anderson as a person and on his relationship with the magazine in his earlier residence in the city in 1922. Michael Fanning's "New Orleans and Sherwood Anderson" (*SoSt*, Summer 1978) argues somewhat reductively, and with a number of factual errors, that Anderson considered New Orleans "civilized" because the "sensualism" of the black and French cultures in the city appealed to the sensual side of his nature. Further information on Anderson in New Orleans and his relationship with Faulkner in 1924–25 is contained in Joseph Blotner's *Faulkner: A Biography* (New York, 1974), especially pp. 366–72, 400–31.

As has been suggested earlier, there has been increasing interest in the last decade and a half of Anderson's life and work after his move to Virginia in 1926. Welford Dunaway Taylor's "Journey with an American Adventurer" (*UR* [Univ. of Richmond] *Magazine*, Summer 1976), like his earlier "Sherwood Anderson" (*VC*, Spring 1970), is a brief summary of Anderson's career with emphasis on his Virginia connection. William Terrell Cornett's "Anderson's Appalachian Years" (*Iron Mountain Review*, Spring 1983) argues that Anderson's move to Virginia was both an escape from cities and "a way of coming home"; while native Virginian Ray Lewis White recalls in the same periodical issue his twenty years of scholarly involvement with Anderson, adopted Virginian. Robert F. Williams, once an employee on Anderson's newspapers and later Superintendent of Schools of Smyth County, Virginia, recalls in "The Great Train Ride" (*WE*, Apr. 1976) his first meeting with Anderson on the one passenger car of the logging train running between Marion and Troutdale, Virginia.

In "Two Dismounted Men: Sherwood Anderson and J. J. Lankes" (Campbell and Modlin), Welford Dunaway Taylor skillfully summarizes the life, work, and attitudes of J. J. Lankes (1884–1960), Virginia woodcut artist, who admired Anderson's writings as Anderson admired Lankes's designs. Although the two men met infrequently, they corresponded from 1927 to 1940, drawn together by a mutual interest in "authentic American subjects" and "the life of the common man." A supplement to this article is Taylor's *Sherwood Anderson, J. J. Lankes and the Illustration of "Perhaps Women,"* a handsomely designed and printed pamphlet by the Waves Press (Richmond, Va., 1981), which describes the circumstances of Lankes's making, in the spring of 1931, the memorable woodcut-frontispiece of Anderson's collection of essays concerning the differing effects of factory machines on men and on women. This piece has been reprinted in *Midamerica X* (1983), under the title "Sherwood Anderson's *Perhaps Women*: The 'Story in Brief.'"

Two quite differing articles deal with Anderson's first years in Virginia. According to Tony J. Owens's carefully analytic article, "Faulkner, Anderson, and 'Artist at Home'" (*MissQ*, Summer 1979), Faulkner for his short story "Artist at Home," written in 1931, drew on a hostile perception of Anderson's personality and career in creating his protagonist, Roger Howes, a burned-out writer through whose manipulative behavior, in part, the story comes to represent, in Owens's words, "the dissociation and debasement of art and experience in a diminished, wasteland setting." (The identification of Howes and his wife Anne with Sherwood and Elizabeth Anderson was originally made by Richard F. Peterson in "An Early Judgment of Anderson and Joyce in Faulkner's 'Artist at Home'" [KAL, Oct. 1977].) A much more attractive picture of Anderson emerges from Charles E. Modlin and Hilbert H. Campbell's "An Interview with Mrs. Sherwood Anderson" (Campbell and Modlin), which provides essential factual information about Eleanor Copenhaver's life before her marriage to Anderson in 1933 and about their subsequent life together. Campbell's "Dreiser in New York: A Diary Source" (DrN, Fall 1982) prints brief but informative entries from Eleanor Anderson's diary concerning Anderson's meetings with Theodore Dreiser in New York during 1933–34, the one period in which the two writers saw each other with some frequency.

Several pieces deal with other aspects of Anderson's life in the 1930s, three being notes by Ray Lewis White. In "Sherwood Anderson and *The American Spectator Conference*: Dictators and Drinks" (AN&Q, Sept. 1976), White finds that an October 1933 conference on the subject of dictatorship among the editors of the *American Spectator* (Theodore Dreiser, George Jean Nathan, Ernest Boyd, and Anderson) produced such inferior results that a transcript of the proceedings was not after all published in that periodical. In "Query" (AN&Q, Sept. 1976), White quotes Anderson's note that on 10 August 1937 he had his voice recorded at the University of Colorado Writers' Conference, but unfortunately the recording has not been located. And in "Sherwood Anderson Meets John Steinbeck: 1939" (StQ, Winter 1978), White reports Anderson's diary entry for 14 November 1939 indicating that he had spent the day with Steinbeck at the latter's ranch near Los Gatos, California, and in this one meeting between the two writers had liked him.

Much more significant is Gil Wilson's "A Mural Portrait of Sherwood Anderson" (WE, Apr. and Nov. 1976, Apr. 1977), a lengthy, revealing memoir of the acquaintance of Wilson, then a young mural painter, with Anderson in 1938–39. The "Portrait," an essential biographical piece, includes long, informative conversations with Anderson about art and writing, politics, people, the times. Additional impressions of Anderson by Wilson appear in Philip L. Gerber's "A Voice from the Thirties (VI): An Interview with Gilbert Wilson" (SSMLN, Fall 1984). Likewise very interesting is Pendleton Hogan's charming account, in "The Big White Portico of Sherwood Anderson" (WE, Apr. and Nov. 1980), of hearing Anderson deliver the address on 20 September 1939, at the Opening Exercises at Roanoke College in Salem, Virginia. Hogan summarizes the address, "The Modern Writer in a World of Realism," and the conversation at a subsequent luncheon, during which Anderson gave his definition of the novel, described his settling in Troutdale, Virginia, and maintained that he wished—at least at that pleasant moment—he "'might have been born a Southern Gentleman.'" Finally, Davis T. Ratcliffe's "A Blessing on the Hilltop" (*WE*, Apr. 1984) reprints a letter he wrote to the Richmond *Times-Dispatch* briefly describing the burial ceremony for Anderson he witnessed on 26 March 1941.

V CRITICISM

Criticism of Anderson's work has been marked both by its relative quantity and by its generally high quality. Although, as with any literary figure, a considerable amount of this criticism is at best undistinguished, again and again one is struck by a freshness of approach, an acuteness of insight, and a persuasiveness of argument or analysis.

1 Book-length Studies

Three book-length studies of Anderson and a pamphlet have appeared, the fact that two of the books were published in Germany suggesting, along with the work done in France and Japan, a renewal of interest in the author abroad as well as at home. The one book in English is Welford Dunaway Taylor's *Sherwood Anderson* (*MLM*, New York, 1977), which for the most part copes ingeniously with the restrictions imposed by the format of Ungar's Modern Literature Monographs Series. A compact summary of Anderson's life in chapter 1 is followed by a chapter entirely on *Winesburg, Ohio* and a third which, after a fine introductory analysis of the poem-tale "The Dumb Man" as illustrative of Anderson's perception of his story material, organizes eight of his best stories under four thematic rubrics: "Frustration," "The Unlived Life," "Initiation," and "Realization." The fourth chapter, on the novels, treats only *Poor White* and *Kit Brandon*, a bracketing which obviously omits consideration of the other five long fictions but does sharply define Anderson's developing attitude toward the machine age. The final chapter deals with the major nonfictional volumes and thus emphasizes the often overlooked work of the last decade and a half of Anderson's career. There is one curious flaw in this compressed survey—the treatment of the term "grotesque." On his first page, Taylor limits the term to "Those who were most assertive and who showed the least regard for the concerns of others and for human values in general," surely an inaccurate simplification, and his categorization of the grotesques in the chapter on *Winesburg* is at variance with the parable in "The Book of the Grotesque." Otherwise, this brief volume is an admirable introduction to Anderson's work.

Gerard M. Sweeney's very sensible pamphlet, *Sherwood Anderson: Wanderer and Myth-Maker* (Columbus, Ohio, 1979), begins like Taylor's book with a succinct summary of Anderson's life and then discusses his weaknesses as a novelist, his strengths as a short story writer, and some of his major subjects and themes. Sweeney is particularly interesting in his analysis of Anderson's theme of escape, which is best understood, not as physical flight, but as transcendence of the self through personal relations or social consciousness. "Life for Anderson," he concludes, "was not a problem which could be solved, but rather a mystery which at best could be symbolically probed."

In his informed and thorough *Sherwood Anderson: Ästhetizismus als Kulturphilosophie* (Heidelberg, 1982), Walter Göbel argues that Anderson's thought has a definite aesthetic-cultural basis. Beginning with Anderson's relation to the "cultural nationalists" of the *Seven Arts*—Van Wyck Brooks, Waldo Frank, and Paul Rosenfeld—and ending with a comparison of his ideas to some of Emerson's, Göbel presents Anderson's theories concerning the nature of art and of the artist. Anderson rejects the world of fact for that of the "fancy," the imagination, and holds that the world of the latter is characterized by the qualities of order, beauty, and morality. The artist should combine the "bohemian," the handicraftsman, and the lover, and should, like Whitman's "divine literatus," function as a quasi-religious prophet and seer who should attack industrialism and materialism because they are ugly in themselves and deform the human spirit and should create a vision of individual and social renewal. The longest chapter in the book deals with manifestations of this aesthetic outlook in many of Anderson's works, which show his concern for the moment of experience and the epiphany, his attraction to nature and the pastoral, and his "aestheticizing" of horses, blacks, and eventually the machine, this last under the influence of Alfred Stieglitz. Anderson, Göbel concludes, is in the tradition of Romanticism and Transcendentalism. Göbel's article, "Sherwood Anderson: Das Transzendieren der Wirklichkeit" (*Sprachkunst*, No. 2, 1982), condenses some of his book's argument and conclusion, while his "Sherwood Anderson and Ben Hecht: Fancy and Fact" (*WE*, Nov. 1982) emphasizes Anderson's imaginative treatment of reality by comparing his account of an odd incident in Chicago with Hecht's journalistic one.

Alfons Klein's *Figurenkonzeption und Erzählform in den Kurzgeschichten Sherwood Andersons* (Göttingen, 1978) is more narrowly focused but very detailed. Using an approach he describes as combining the New Criticism and "aesthetically orientated content analysis," Klein examines Anderson's theory and practice of short fiction, giving primary attention, as his title indicates, to "the relationship between Anderson's conception of literary characters and narrative form in his stories." He identifies the author's "two most important categories" of characters as the "common man" and the "grotesque," and asserts that in presenting both he "celebrates the vital importance of [man's] imaginative faculties." In his social views, Klein explains, Anderson is not a reformer or a radical but more generally an opponent of capitalist materialism as perverting human values; in his psychological views, Anderson is not a Freudian, though he shows the distorting effects on his characters of repressed sexuality. Rather, "depictions of human isolation and loneliness appear to constitute the central thematic interest in Anderson's short stories"; hence, the "core of Anderson's conception of literary characters may thus be seen in the attempt to confront the individual figures and the reader with this existential situation in order to free them from ambitious self-interest and the illusory promises of the American dream, and to teach, in the author's phrase, 'the right use of the imagination.'" In fleshing out these abstractions, Klein discusses many of Anderson's stories, including a number of the early, the late, and the often-overlooked tales.

An important doctoral dissertation should be cited here. In her 693-page "L'oeuvre de Sherwood Anderson: sentiment d'impuissance et création littéraire" (Université de Paris-Sorbonne, 1982), Claire Bruyère approaches Anderson's complete work, in her words, "thematically and aesthetically from the angle of their author's creative problems." Her thesis is that

> a feeling of artistic impotence, partly due to his ideal of perfection in art, was in Anderson an obsession which paradoxically turned out to be his main artistic asset.
>
> This obsession coincides with a peculiar sensitivity to certain aspects of human relationships and of American life in its continuity and change. Given that subject matter, his best works are writings in which the narrative posture is one of uncertainty as to the "truth" of whatever is represented.
>
> Once presented and discussed in the light of this and related obsessions, namely that of disorder, that of immaturity and that of escape, the works of Sherwood Anderson, taken as a whole, appear to constitute a major body of American literature (of particular interest to the European reader) which deserves to be treated with everything but condescension.

In somewhat shortened form this dissertation was published as a book with the title *Sherwood Anderson: L'Impuissance créatrice* (Paris, 1985).

2 Collections

Four volumes of essays on Anderson by various hands have been published. Walter B. Rideout's *Sherwood Anderson: A Collection of Critical Essays* (TCV, Englewood Cliffs, N.J., 1974) has some overlap in contents with Ray Lewis White's earlier (1966) *The Achievement of Sherwood Anderson: Essays in Criticism*; but nine of its fifteen articles differ, including T. K. Whipple's chapter on Anderson in *Spokesmen* (1928) and Benjamin T. Spencer's "Sherwood Anderson: American Mythopoeist" (*AL*, Mar. 1969). David D. Anderson's *Critical Essays on Sherwood Anderson* (CEAmL, Boston 1981; hereinafter referred to as Anderson, *Critical Essays*) is a larger volume. It contains fifteen contemporary reviews of Anderson's books and twenty-one articles, many of them published from 1962 onward and three specifically written for this book. Included also are facsimiles of the five typescript pages of "Buckeye Blues," an unpublished example of Anderson's Depression reporting, and two 1939 letters from Anderson to Sidney Hook. The introductions of both the Rideout and David D. Anderson collections trace the rise, the decline, and the gradual renewal of Anderson's critical reputation.

The two other edited volumes, which have been cited earlier, were published in 1976 as part of the Sherwood Anderson Centennial celebrations. *Sherwood Anderson: Dimensions of His Literary Art: A Collection of Critical Essays*, which contains eight original essays on various aspects of Anderson's work, was edited by David D. Anderson, who not only was deeply involved in the preparation of the celebrations but has been from its founding the major force in the Society for the Study of Midwestern Literature and editor of its *Newsletter* and annuals. Campbell and Modlin's *Sherwood Anderson: Centennial Studies*, the more substantial volume, is divided into two sections, "Sources" and "Critical Essays," though two in the latter section are bibliographical, four biographical. The individual essays in each volume are discussed in the relevant categories of this survey.

Four periodicals have published issues devoted to Anderson, the three latest of these in connection with the Centennial celebrations. In order of publication these are: "Special Sherwood Anderson Number" (*NLB*, July 1971), edited by James M. Wells; "Sherwood Anderson Centenary Number" (*AN&Q*, Sept. 1976), Hilbert H. Campbell and Charles E. Modlin, guest editors; "Sherwood Anderson Issue" (*TCL*, Feb. 1977), Jack Salzman, guest editor; "Sherwood Anderson Commemorative Edition" (*Smyth County Va. News*, 12 Nov. 1978). The Anderson Centennial proceedings at Michigan State University, 9–11 September 1976, are charmingly summarized by Margaret Anderson Stuart, daughter of Anderson's older son Robert and herself a writer, in "Centennial Impressions" (*WE*, Nov. 1976).

3 Articles

A number of articles have been concerned with Anderson's work as a whole or with major aspects of it. For two decades or more and especially within the last dozen years, David D. Anderson has been conducting a revaluation of Anderson. One element of this revaluation is perhaps best expressed in his introduction to his *Critical Essays on Sherwood Anderson*. Rejecting what he sees as a fixed critical assumption from the mid-1920s to the early 1960s, that Anderson was a minor writer with "one relatively successful book," *Winesburg*, he asserts that Anderson's "later direction and later works are . . . substantial, provocative works in their own right, that Anderson remained a profound, provocative, and perceptive writer to the end, and that he has much to say to those of us who live in the last quarter of the twentieth century." Although in his enthusiasm David D. Anderson may be claiming too much for all of Anderson's uneven later productions, his rejection of the minor writer-one book assumption is sound and is necessary for righting the critical balance.

The second aspect of the revaluation is most fully expressed in David D. Anderson's "Anderson and Myth" (Anderson, *Dimensions*; reprinted in Anderson, *Critical Essays*). Here he postulates that central to much of Anderson's work is his creation of a "fundamental myth . . . of escape and fulfillment," which he believed to be the essence of his own and of America's experience. In its best known form, the myth in Anderson's early work depicted the rejection of materialism for the vision of the artist, but in the mid-1920s he began to emphasize the endlessness of the search for an ultimate truth. In the work of the late 1920s and the 1930s, especially in his depiction of strong women, he projected a third form of the myth as the renewal of America through individual rededication to the dignity and freedom of the self. In several other articles, David D. Anderson restates or amplifies his conceptions of the importance of Anderson's later writings and of the unity of his work as a whole because of an underlying myth: "The Real World of Sherwood Anderson" (*OQ*, Autumn 1973); "The Search for a Living Past" (Campbell and Modlin); "Sherwood Anderson and the Editors of *Time*" (*AN&Q*, Sept. 1976); "Dispersion and Direction: Sherwood Anderson, the Chicago Renaissance, and the American Mainstream" (*Midamerica V*, 1978); "Sherwood Anderson and the Two Faces of America" (*WE*, Nov. 1979); "Midwestern Writers and the Myth of the Search" (*GaR*, Spring 1980).

Other scholars have taken other approaches to Anderson's work and his beliefs, often revising or qualifying earlier interpretations and assessments. Among the best of these is Glen A. Love, who has contributed two pieces: "Horses or Men: Primitive and Pastoral Elements in Sherwood Anderson" (Campbell and Modlin) and "Sherwood Anderson: Stilling the Machine," a chapter in his *New Americans: The Westerner and the Modern Experience in the American Novel* (Lewisburg, Pa., 1982). In the former, Love examines Anderson's work and beliefs and concludes that the label of "primitivist" distorts both. Instead of expressing a simple desire to escape from the industrial age into mindlessness, the "representative note" of Anderson's writings "is one of a struggle toward resolution between the character [in any of his typical fictions] and a threatening society. If there is rejection or escape, it is typically undertaken so that the individual can somehow bring himself to cope with an inescapable and complex urban present. The essential tone in Anderson is reconciliatory, and in this sense his work may be seen as a contemporary version of pastoral." In support of his argument, Love gives an extended, sensitive reading of "I Want to Know Why." In the chapter from his book, Love demonstrates, through a shrewd analysis of primarily the novels,

Anderson's persistent ambivalence toward modern technology. His early works "present a range of tentative but uneasy responses to the machine age," while his "continuing attempt to posit still new responses to the technological present during the thirties is convincing testimony to the seriousness with which he accepted his role as communal artist, as well as to his unending ordeal with the machine, his inability to either accept it or leave it alone." Love's chapter is a definitive statement concerning Anderson's attitudes toward the machine age.

Concerned also with Anderson's ambivalence in his long fiction is Nancy L. Bunge, who argues provocatively in "The Ambiguous Endings of Sherwood Anderson's Novels" (Campbell and Modlin) that his novels end ambiguously, not because he had a deficient aesthetic sense, but because he attempted to deal truthfully with his characters and their decisions, usually to begin a liberating relationship with a loved one. Although he wanted to end each novel hopefully, he nevertheless undercut the hope by questioning in various ways the possibility that such a relationship can persist. In "Anderson's Theories on Writing Fiction" (Anderson, *Dimensions*), on the other hand, Martha Mulroy Curry contrasts Anderson's distinction between the short story—in Anderson's words in *The Writer's Book* "an idea grasped whole as one would pick an apple in an orchard"—and the novel, a genre in which he was less successful, Curry indicates, because he was unable to maintain extended control over theme, character, and form. A similar assessment is made by David Stouck in his compact entry on Anderson in *Great Writers of the English Language: Novelists and Prose Writers* (ed. James Vinson, New York, 1979), which summarizes some of Anderson's major themes and concludes that his "influence and reputation . . . outweigh his actual achievement as a writer" except for *Winesburg* and a few "first rate" tales.

A quite different approach to Anderson and his work is taken by Charles I. Glicksberg in "Sherwood Anderson: The Phallic Chekhov," a chapter in his book *The Sexual Revolution in Modern American Literature* (The Hague, 1971). On the basis of his reading of the *Memoirs*, *Winesburg*, and *Many Marriages*, Glicksberg asserts, "One theme that repeats itself with obsessive insistence in Anderson's work focuses on the traumatic effect of sexual frustration on the individual, the spiritual tragedy caused by the culturally imposed necessity for the repression of instinct." As its subtitle may suggest, Glicksberg's chapter is less illuminating about Anderson and Freudianism than the standard discussion by Frederick J. Hoffman, which was overlooked—a Freudian slip, perhaps?—in the original essay on Anderson in *Fifteen Modern American Authors*. In *Freudianism and the Literary Mind* (Baton Rouge, La., 1957), it should belatedly be pointed out, Hoffman argues convincingly that Anderson was not directly influenced by Freudianism, as some earlier critics asserted; rather, he developed his themes independently, especially the distortive effects of repression, "but with such a startling likeness of approach" that these critics were self-deceived. Where Freud had concerned himself with "neurosis through repression," Anderson held that "frustration has two causes: external pressures against an active search for normal happiness—that is, conventionality and 'the morality of the average'; and the timidity and weakness of the individual." Hoffman concludes that there is "some justification in noting the parallel courses of psychoanalysis and Anderson's fiction, but there is little evidence to prove that those two courses intersected at any vital points."

Special recognition should also be given seven other general assessments of Anderson, six of them by non-Americans. In his "Sherwood Anderson's Transcendentalist Aesthetics," a chapter in his book *The Transcendentalist Constant in American Literature* (New York, 1980), the distinguished French scholar Roger Asselineau provides a fine summary of Anderson's aesthetics, demonstrating by explications of several story details that his art is not simple realism but a mode of realism allied to symbolism and expressionism. Thus his stories "are lyric poetry in the form of fiction." Here it must be confessed that another regrettable omission in the original essay on Anderson was reference to Asselineau's landmark contributions to Anderson scholarship: "Réalisme, rêve et expressionnisme dans 'Winesburg, Ohio'" (*ALM*, Apr. 1957) and "Langue et Style de Sherwood Anderson dans *Winesburg, Ohio*" (*RLM*, No. 78–80, 1963), part of the collection of essays on Anderson, *Configuration Critique de Sherwood Anderson*, edited by Asselineau. One last omission was Tony Tanner's "Sherwood Anderson's Little Things" in his *The Reign of Wonder: Naivety and Reality in American Literature* (Cambridge, England, 1965), in which this usually astute English scholar-critic records his near total aversion to Anderson's work. Anderson, Tanner contends, immersed himself in "little things," random observed details, without any "apparent principle of selection and omission at work." Hence he "does not bring us a life; he brings us a moment. It is a fragmentary view of life, and it is clear that Anderson's approach can only lead to fragmentation. His vision permits of no plot developments or notable dramatic crises: there are no gestures of summarizing significance, nor do the individual details accumulate to the point of revealing larger meanings."

Following a quite different approach to a quite different conclusion, Robert Rougé, in his "Sh. Anderson—La Recherche de L'Amour" in *L'Inquiétude Religieuse dans le Roman Américain Moderne* (Paris, 1974), draws on several of Anderson's works to argue that the author sees the artist as playing a Christlike role, imaging in fiction a transcendent universal love uniting mankind despite the solitude each individual inevitably suffers. Alfred Weber's "Sherwood Andersons Reflexionen über die Dichtung" in *Amerikanische Literatur im 20. Jahrhundert/American Literature in the 20th Century* (ed. Alfred Weber and Dietmar Haack, Göttingen, 1971) is more secular in outlook but equally admiring. Anderson, he admits, was not a systematic theorist of prose writing, but was nevertheless consistently concerned with the relation between factual reality and the creative imagination: "In bringing together elements from naturalism and romanticism, in his use of imaginative sympathy to confront the conditions of existence, in his moral sense, and most importantly in his creative consciousness, he shares and to a certain extent predicates the most pressing considerations of 20th century literature."

An often perceptive but ambivalent attempt at a "balanced" assessment of Anderson's work is "Sherwood Anderson" by the late English scholar Brian Way in *The American Novel and the Nineteen Twenties* (ed. Malcolm Bradbury and David Palmer, London, 1971). On the one hand, Way rejects the views of Anderson as merely "an influence on other writers" or as "a one-book writer," and asserts that "What matters most is . . . that he is one of the great masters of the American short story," giving evidence for this judgment from expert appraisals of certain *Winesburg* tales, "Unlighted Lamps," "Death in the Woods," and "The Corn Planting." On the other hand, Way dismisses "the bulk of [Anderson's] work" as being "characterized by extremes of foolishness, sentimentality and technical incompetence." In his compact, illuminating survey, *The Modern American Novel* (New York, 1983), Malcolm Bradbury, English scholar and novelist, considers *Winesburg, Ohio* to be Anderson's "one outright triumph" but relates his development as a writer to that of modernism: "One essential way to perceive modernism is to see it as an art that insists on its internal frame, on the active presence of the medium used, on the 'foregrounding' of the artistic activity, so that the achievement of the story's form becomes part of the story. That was how Anderson's work now developed, in an endeavor to render the intuitive, the unspoken, the unconscious as essential realms of experience both *within* the story and in the *making* of the story." A somewhat similar observation underlies American Frank Gado's introduction to his collection, *The Teller's Tales: Short Stories by Sherwood Anderson* (Schenectady, N.Y., 1983), a most useful paperback text now that Maxwell Geismar's *Sherwood Anderson: Short Stories* is unfortunately out of print. In one of the best discussions of Anderson's short story technique ever published, Gado explains that Anderson's tales proceed, not by *ambi*guity either of meaning or of authorial purpose, but by a conscious "method of *antiguity*"; that is, the telling of the tale "creates a form by 'unresolving' what the content (i.e., the narrator's construction of an objective reality) seems to have resolved." Gado supports his point by analyzing each of the thirteen stories in his collection.

Several other general articles deserve mention. In "The Midwestern Novel: Walt Whitman Transplanted" (*ON*, Sept. 1977), Nancy L. Bunge groups Anderson, Sinclair Lewis, Hemingway, and Saul Bellow as sharing "a Midwestern background" and "strikingly similar literary goals." Jürgen Dierking, in "Ein verdrängtes Dilemma: Sherwood Anderson (1876–1941)" (*Gulliver*, 1981), "emphasizes [Anderson's] central interest in the 'common man' and stresses his function as chronicler of the machine age." Welford Dunaway Taylor's "Anderson and the Problem of Belonging" (Anderson, *Dimensions*) asserts that Anderson has certain affinities with the New Humanism of Paul Elmer More and should be judged, not as a deficient intellectual, but as an intuitive, poetic humanist. In "The Warmth of Desire: Sex in Anderson's Novels" (Anderson, *Dimensions*), Ray Lewis White rather self-contradictorily argues that Anderson's seven novels are weakened by his sentimental, moralistic presentation of sexuality, but that four of them reveal "realistic sexual attitudes" on his part.

Finally, three articles should be mentioned with a warning. Prema Nandakumar's "Sherwood Anderson: 1876–1941" (*Triveni*, Apr.–June 1977) is a pleasant but brief and sometimes inaccurate appreciation of Anderson's life and work. Frank Baldanza's "Northern Gothic" (*SoR*, July 1974) compares the two Ohio writers, Anderson and James Purdy, and rather insistently finds the former inferior in technique and outlook to the latter, whom Baldanza does describe well. (Interestingly, Purdy in an interview with Bradford Morrow [*Conjunctions*, No. 3, 1982] says that Anderson influenced him by "the isolation in his work, the small town vernacular.") In "The Liberation of the Short Story: Sherwood Anderson," a chapter in his book, *The American Short Story: A Critical Survey* (Norman, Okla., 1973), Arthur Voss assigns Anderson "a prominent place in the history of the short story" but for the most part presents plot summaries in support of his judgment.

There has been considerable interest in Anderson's treatment of particular categories of characters in his fiction. Among the best informed of such pieces are three articles by William V. Miller on major character types in the short stories: mountain people in "In Defense of Mountaineers: Sherwood Anderson's Hill Stories" (*BSUF*, Spring 1974); women in "Earth-Mothers, Succubi, and Other Ectoplasmic Spirits: The Women in Sherwood Anderson's Short Stories" (*Midamerica I*, 1974; reprinted in Anderson, *Critical Essays*); artists, the most frequently appearing type according to Miller, in "Portraits of the Artist: Anderson's Fictional Storytellers" (Anderson, *Dimensions*).

Given the increasing interest in women's studies, it is not surprising that Anderson's complex attitudes toward women in his life and in his fiction are examined by four articles in addition to Miller's. In "Gender Reconsiderations in Three of Sherwood Anderson's Novels" (*MSE*, Fall 1978), Joyce R. Ladenson praises his "primitive androgynous concerns," radical for his time, in creating the central women figures in *Poor White* and *Kit Brandon*, but deplores his romantic, gender-stereotyped view of marriage as the solution to their needs. Nancy Bunge's "Women in Sherwood Anderson's Fiction" (Anderson, *Critical Essays*) mostly summarizes Anderson's views on the differing effects of the machine on men and on women; but both her "Women as Social Critics in *Sister*

Carrie, Winesburg, Ohio, and *Main Street"* (*Midamerica III,* 1976) and Marilyn Judith Atlas's "Sherwood Anderson and the Women of Winesburg" (Anderson, *Critical Essays*) astutely point out that, in Atlas's words: "*Winesburg, Ohio* does not satisfactorily portray the possibility of an active, independent, and creative woman who is also a survivor, but at least it portrays the women whose lives are limited because they live within a system which was never created for their benefit."

Anderson's attitudes toward blacks in life and in his fiction are examined in six articles, most of them negative in conclusion. The first in date of publication is Anneliese H. Smith's "Part of the Problem: Student Responses to Sherwood Anderson's 'I Want to Know Why'" (*NALF,* Spring 1973), which reports that her class questionnaires revealed the inability of white students to perceive the stereotyping of blacks in that story. Similarly, George C. Matthews's "Ohio's *Beulah Land* or Plantation Blacks in the Fiction of Sherwood Anderson" (*CLAJ,* June 1982) finds that Anderson perpetuates certain stereotypes in his black characters in "Out of Nowhere Into Nothing" and "I Want to Know Why." In "Black Mystics, French Cynics, Sherwood Anderson" (*BALF,* Summer 1977), Michael Fanning draws skillfully on Anderson's "Paris Notebook, 1921" to suggest that in *Dark Laughter* the knowing laughter of the blacks at the end of the novel is directed at both the repressed deserted white husband and the adulterous white lovers, who are futilely attempting to escape "repressed industrial white America." David M. Lockwood's "Writers of a New Spirit: Jean Toomer, Sherwood Anderson, and William Faulkner" (*SSMLN,* Fall 1981) adds little to our knowledge of any of these writers; but Mary Jane Dickerson's "Sherwood Anderson and Jean Toomer: A Literary Relationship" (*SAF,* Autumn 1973), though somewhat disorganized, makes a fair case for the influence of *Winesburg* on *Cane,* a less convincing one for the influence of *Cane* on *Dark Laughter.* The most cogent of the articles is Mark Helbling's "Sherwood Anderson and Jean Toomer" (*NALF,* Summer 1975), which examines the reasons for Anderson's encouragement of Toomer to remain specifically a black writer and finds them to be an "aesthetic fascination for another's creative talent," a manifestation of white superiority, and most importantly a conviction that blacks possess a "primitive vitality" and, like any true artist, live in opposition to the industrialization and standardization of the dominant white society, which has lost contact with its inner self.

In the last dozen years, scholars of Anderson have begun to reexamine and reevaluate several of his individual books, beginning with his first novel, *Windy McPherson's Son.* In "'Borne Back Ceaselessly Into the Past': The Autobiographical Fiction of Sherwood Anderson" (*MMisc IX,* 1981), Roger J. Bresnahan traces in *Windy, Winesburg,* and *Tar* the author's increasing success in "shaping [his] memories," while in "Sherwood Anderson's Technologically Displaced Persons" (*SSMLN,* Fall 1982), David D. Anderson discusses Windy of *Windy McPherson's Son* and Joe

Wainsworth of *Poor White* as examples of men unable to cope with the machine age. Carl S. Smith's detailed section on *Windy* in his *Chicago and the American Literary Imagination, 1880–1920* (Chicago, 1984) analyzes the novel as offering "a highly developed and sympathetic portrait of the businessman as artist," and points out Anderson's shifting views of his subject within the book. With equal persuasiveness, J. R. Scafidel, in "Sexuality in *Windy McPherson's Son*" (*TCL*, Feb. 1977), demonstrates that a "major theme in the novel is impotence"; that various characters illustrate this theme; that Sam McPherson in particular illustrates it both in his substitution of a desire to make money for his "natural sexual drive" and in his ultimate failure to find "Truth"; and that the endings of both the original 1916 edition and the revised 1922 one reinforce this major theme, which Anderson handles "with the understanding of a psychologist and the facility of an artist."

Anderson's second and third books have received less notice. John Ditsky's "Sherwood Anderson's *Marching Men*: Unnatural Disorder and the Art of Force" (*TCL*, Feb. 1977) is a close reading of the novel and has occasional insights but suffers from too much plot summary. A more analytic discussion is Mario Maffi's chapter on *Marching Men* in his *La giungla e il grattacielo: Gli scrittori e il sogno americano 1865/1920* (Bari, 1981). Maffi views the book as neither a political nor a radical novel but as a romance of moral reform noteworthy for its vision of the modern industrial world as a chaos to which the book's protagonist seeks to bring order. As for Anderson's third book, Philip Greasley's "Myth and the Midwestern Landscape: Sherwood Anderson's *Mid-American Chants*" (*Midamerica VI*, 1979; reprinted in Anderson, *Critical Essays*) identifies a theme unifying the poems: "Using Mid-American land- and city-scapes as the focus of his vision, he forged an optimistic myth for twentieth century urban-industrial man." More recently, in a very well-written article, " 'Beauty Breaking through the Husks of Life': Sherwood Anderson and James Wright" (*Midamerica X*, 1983), Leland Krauth compares the themes in Wright's poems to those in *Mid-American Chants*, noting that both Ohioans are repelled by the ugliness inflicted by industrialism on the Midwest landscape, yet have sudden perceptions of visionary beauty.

Far more than any other of Anderson's books, *Winesburg, Ohio*, of course, continues to attract the most critical attention. The one volume wholly concerned with his masterpiece is Ray Lewis White's *The Merrill Studies in "Winesburg, Ohio"* (Columbus, Ohio, 1971), a collection of pieces divided into four sections: "Composition" (one article), "Reviews" (seven), "Aspects" (five articles), "Achievement" (four articles). In *"Winesburg, Ohio*: The Table of Contents" (*NMAL*, Autumn 1984), White documents four tentative orderings of the stories by Anderson before he settled on the final one; and White has also ferreted out four previously unlocated reviews: "*Winesburg, Ohio*: A Lost Chicago Review" (*WE*, Apr.

1977); "Mencken's Lost Review of *Winesburg, Ohio*" (*NMAL*, Spring 1978); "*Winesburg, Ohio*: The Earliest Non-English Language Review" (*WE*, Apr. 1978); and "*Winesburg, Ohio*: A Unique 1919 Ohio Review" (*OQ*, Spring 1979). In "E. Haldeman-Julius on Sherwood Anderson" (*WE*, Nov. 1978), William F. Ryan reports that the publisher praised *Winesburg* and *Poor White* in print for their "realism" and selected tales from *Winesburg* for two of his Little Blue Books, but felt that the later writings contained too much "mystical groping."

A more recent, foreign appraisal of *Winesburg* is contained in G. H. S. Mueller's "Hans Erich Nossak and Sherwood Anderson's *Winesburg, Ohio*" (*WE*, Nov. 1977), which summarizes a 1958 essay on the book by the German novelist Nossak, who in that year published his translation of *Winesburg*, and notes that Nossak especially praises Anderson's "subtle poetic quality" and his "compassionate tenderness" towards his youthful characters.

Possible influences on the writing of *Winesburg* have been considered in several articles. Walter B. Rideout's "Talbot Whittingham and Anderson: A Passage to *Winesburg, Ohio*" (Anderson, *Dimensions*) analyzes Anderson's unpublished novel *Talbot Whittingham* to show how it foreshadows the composition of *Winesburg* in its concern with the development of a writer, its examination of the idea of the "grotesque," and its use of small town setting and characters in book two of the novel. In "Dubliners in Winesburg, Ohio: A Note on Joyce's 'The Sisters' and Anderson's 'The Philosopher'" (*SSF*, Fall 1975), Joan Zlotnick argues that resemblances between the two stories make the influence of *Dubliners* on *Winesburg* "particularly evident"; but in "Of Dubliners and Ohioans: A Comparative Study of Two Works" (*BSUF*, Autumn 1976), while extending her list of "striking similarities" to two more pairs of stories, she admits that "there is no evidence to prove the direct influence of *Dubliners* (1914) on *Winesburg, Ohio* (1919)." Sister Martha Curry settles the matter in her "Sherwood Anderson and James Joyce" (*AL*, May 1980) by assembling the evidence indicating that Anderson had not read *Dubliners* before writing *Winesburg* and by comparing the two books to show nevertheless important similarities between them. A persuasive case for the influence of Turgenev's *The Hunting Sketches*, one of Anderson's favorite books, on the composition of *Winesburg* is made, however, by Forrest L. Ingram's "American Short Story Cycles: Foreign Influences and Parallels" in *Proceedings of the Comparative Literature Symposium*, vol. 5: *Modern American Fiction* (ed. Wolodymyr T. Zyla and Wendell M. Aycock, Lubbock, Tex., 1972).

Ingram is also the author of the longest, most detailed discussion of *Winesburg* to be noted in this survey, the perceptive and judicious "Sherwood Anderson: *Winesburg, Ohio*," the climactic chapter in his book *Representative Short Story Cycles of the Twentieth Century: Studies in a Literary Genre* (The Hague, 1971). Having begun his book by defining a "story cycle" as "a set of stories so linked to one another that the reader's experience of each one is modified by his experience of the others," Ingram critiques previous scholarship on *Winesburg* and then argues that "the chief unifying forces" of the book are (1) a single narrator who "controls the tone, mood, direction, and presentation of the stories"; (2) a set of "thematic patterns or motif-rhythms" which by association "thread through the stories"; and (3) Anderson's "cyclic method of handling symbols." Ingram's chapter is a major contribution to the study of *Winesburg*. In addition, his "The Dynamics of Short Story Cycles" (*NOR*, Spring 1970) summarizes his argument that such cycles constitute a genre and notes of *Winesburg* that "one discovers in [Anderson's] handling of setting, action, theme, time, character, and symbol the typical pattern of story cycles—the pattern of recurrence and development of a single integrated movement."

Several articles have discussed *Winesburg* in a general way. John H. Ferres's "The Nostalgia of *Winesburg, Ohio*" (*NLB*, July 1971) asserts that the book "is now more than ever a culture symbol for the ideal [American] past." In "The Arts of Winesburg and Bidwell, Ohio" (*TCL*, Feb. 1977), Jon S. Lawry conducts a complex, occasionally unclear argument to the effect that in *Winesburg*, the Bidwell tales, and the city novels Anderson describes and yet "bends . . . back upon itself" the American social movement from village to town to city. More straightforwardly, Park Dixon Goist, in "The Ideal Questioned But Not Abandoned: Sherwood Anderson, Sinclair Lewis, and Floyd Dell" in his book *From Main Street to State Street* (Port Washington, N.Y., 1977), views Winesburg as "a town where community is almost totally lacking" and the Bidwell of *Poor White* as a town where community is shattered by industrialism.

In "The Revolt That Wasn't: The Legacies of Critical Myopia" (*CEA*, Jan. 1977), Barry Gross sensibly points out that Edgar Lee Masters and Anderson "*were* in revolt, but not from the village." Rather, Anderson wrote in *Winesburg* as an elegist of "an already vanished America, a time when 'the factories had not yet come.'" An especially discerning discussion of *Winesburg* is Ann Massa's "Sherwood Anderson" in her *American Literature in Context, IV: 1900–1930* (London, 1982). Although her placing of the book in the socio-historical context of 1919 is somewhat forced, she skillfully uses the tale "Paper Pills" to show how the other stories as well emphasize such themes as that "For Anderson the significant truth is not that of individual philosophy or individual probity but the shared and fundamental truth of love and an accompanying tolerance."

A number of articles deal, often extremely well, with major aspects of *Winesburg*. In "Sherwood Anderson and the Lyric Story" in *The Twenties: Fiction, Poetry, Drama* (ed. Warren French, Deland, Fla., 1975), Eileen Baldeshwiler identifies certain "lyric" elements in the book and then demonstrates how they appear in several of the tales. In "Something in the Elders: The Recurrent Imagery in *Winesburg, Ohio*" (*WE*, Nov. 1983),

Robert Allen Papinchak traces the book's recurrent images and themes through a number of the tales and shows how they coalesce into a significant pattern. Likewise concerned with recurrent images is David Stouck's fine article, "*Winesburg, Ohio* As a Dance of Death" (*AL*, Jan. 1977; reprinted in Anderson, *Critical Essays*), which tellingly observes that the book's death imagery "directs us to something dark and pessimistic in the book that recent critics, unlike the early reviewers, have either ignored or explained away."

Another important article is Raymond Wilson's "Rhythm in *Winesburg, Ohio*" (*GrLR*, Spring 1982), which demonstrates that the repetition of "hands" functions in three ways in the book: as "objective correlative to express the characters' inner needs," as motivation, and as description. All three functions combine to make "hands" a "rhythm" fulfilling E. M. Forster's suggestion that a novel "can be stitched together internally because it contains rhythm." Sally Adair Rigsbee's "The Feminine in *Winesburg, Ohio*" (*SAF*, Autumn 1981) argues very perceptively that the tales are unified by the themes of "the failure of communication and the development of the artist," both themes being "closely related to Anderson's focus on the meaning of the feminine." *Winesburg*, she concludes, "is intended to be a prophetic statement about the quality of the relationships of men and women in the modern world."

Special mention should also be made of retrospective readings of Anderson's book by two quite different present-day writers. In the "Sherwood Anderson" chapter of his *Earthly Delights, Unearthly Adornments: American Writers as Image Makers* (New York, 1978), Wright Morris, a Midwesterner by birth, presents *Winesburg* as revealing "an original American blend of craft, sophistication, and naïveté," while an appreciation by the non-Midwestern John Updike, "Twisted Apples" (*Harper's*, Mar. 1984), concludes that "Though *Winesburg* accumulates external facts . . . as it gropes along, its burden is a spiritual essence, a certain tart sweet taste to life as it passes in America's lonely lamplit homes" and that the book "imparts this penetrating taste—the wine hidden in its title—as freshly today as yesterday."

Considerable attention has been directed to the role of George Willard in *Winesburg*. In "The 'New' Realism: A Study of the Structure of *Winesburg, Ohio*" (*CEA*, Mar. 1979), Sylvia A. Holladay disputes the charge that the book lacks order and unity and asserts that George's "mental associations" provide the "order of the parts," while "his movement toward maturity" provides unity. Two articles, Douglas G. Rogers's "Development of the Artist in *Winesburg, Ohio*" (*STC*, Fall 1972) and Samuel Pickering's occasionally inaccurate "*Winesburg, Ohio*: A Portrait of the Artist as a Young Man" (*SoQ*, Oct. 1977), read the book as primarily a *Kunstlerroman*. Ray Lewis White, in "Of Time and *Winesberg* [sic], *Ohio*: An Experiment in Chronology" (*MFS*, Winter 1979–80), proposes a time scheme for the events of the stories concerning George, running from

July 1894 to April 1896 when he leaves the town. Perhaps trapped by his book's thesis, Sam Bluefarb, in "George Willard: Death and Resurrection" in *The Escape Motif in the American Novel: Mark Twain to Richard Wright* (Columbus, Ohio, 1972), mistakenly sees George as eagerly escaping from a town filled with people whom he regards with a "mixture of pity and scorn." More convincingly, David D. Anderson, in "The Midwestern Town in Midwestern Fiction" (*Midamerica VI*, 1979), views George as "the archetypal young Midwesterner" leaving town in search of fulfillment "in a society he was convinced was open for him in Chicago as it had been in Winesburg."

Other special aspects of *Winesburg* have been examined as well. One of these is the book's style, which is discussed by Ahmad K. Ardat in "The Prose Style of Selected Works by Ernest Hemingway, Sherwood Anderson, and Gertrude Stein" (*Style*, Winter 1980) and by Linda W. Wagner in "Sherwood, Stein, the Sentence, and Grape Sugar and Oranges" (Anderson, *Dimensions*). Where Ardat's linguistic analysis finds both similarities and sharp differences in style among the three writers, Wagner sees Stein's *Three Lives* as having "contributed toward Anderson's presentation" of *Winesburg* in both style and subject matter. In "'A Great Deal of Wonder in Me': Inspiration and Transformation in *Winesburg, Ohio*" (*MarkhamR*, Summer 1977), Martin J. Fertig cites several instances where a character's inspired self-revelation produces "an actual transformation in the physical constitution of [the] character," such being an expression "of Anderson's effort to convey his conception of transcendent reality." In a somewhat quirky essay, "'An Aching, Hurting Thing': The Aesthetic of Ritualistic Reenactment" (Anderson, *Critical Essays*), Roger J. Bresnahan maintains that the "only salvation [for the characters in *Winesburg*] is that their stories get out through ritualistic reenactment in the imagination of the reader"; and in "The 'Old Hands' of Winesburg" (*MMisc XI*, 1983), Bresnahan makes the interesting observation that the town's leading citizens do not in fact give "direction to the town."

Several articles make connections between *Winesburg* and another work, writer, or subject. M. R. Satyanarayana compares *Winesburg* to Steinbeck's *The Long Valley*, in his article "From Winesburg to Salinas Valley in Search of Love" (*OJES*, No. 1, 1971) and likewise identifies "striking common features—the theme of loneliness, an atmosphere of melancholy, and a complete absence of humour." Jeff Campbell, in "Winesburg, Texas: The Last Picture Show" (*Journal of the American Studies Association of Texas*, 1977), finds convincing parallels between Larry McMurtry's novel *The Last Picture Show* and *Winesburg*. In "Deux contes nord-américains considérés comme actes de langage narratifs" (*ELit*, Apr. 1975), Marie Francoeur and Louis Francoeur apply communication theory to *Winesburg*, especially to "The Book of the Grotesque" as narrative introduction, and to *Contes pour un homme seul* by the Canadian writer Yves Theriault, analyzing the various recurring textual signals by observation of which a reader of either book may become its "ideal reader." Unfortunately, Albert Waldinger is not an "ideal reader" in his "Folk Ethics and the Village Tale: *Winesburg, Ohio* and Berdichevsky's Jewish Ukraine" (*SSMLN*, Spring 1980), for he misreads *Winesburg* by treating the grotesques as examples of "moral perversion."

Other scholars have been better informed, or sometimes only more provocative, about the grotesques. The purpose of David D. Anderson's "*The Little Review* and Sherwood Anderson" (*MMisc VIII*, 1980) is to trace the development of Anderson's concept of the grotesque through his first contributions to that magazine; Hirotada Ohara's "An Essay on Anderson's Imagery of Grotesque" (*Journal of Human and Cultural Sciences* [Musashi Univ., Tokyo], 1982) is a suggestive but "preliminary" examination of how Impressionist and Expressionist painting may have influenced that concept; and James Schevill's "Notes on the Grotesque: Anderson, Brecht, and Williams" (*TCL*, May 1977) assembles a collage of elements within American society that he calls American Grotesque, in the "mythology" of which, he maintains, Anderson pioneered.

In "Anderson's Twisted Apples and Hemingway's Crips" (*Midamerica I*, 1974), Paul P. Somers, Jr. defines Anderson's term and posits an influence by Anderson on Hemingway in the latter's portrayal of men turned into grotesques by some "shattering initiatory experience"; and in "Distorted Matter and Disjunctive Forms: The Grotesque as Modernist Genre" (*ArQ*, Winter 1977), Joseph R. Millichap uses the examples of *Winesburg, The Sound and the Fury*, and *The Heart Is a Lonely Hunter* to theorize that in "the Grotesque the Modernist writer discerned disjunctive forms capable of reflecting the fragmentation and alienation of the modern world." Anderson's use of the term in "The Book of the Grotesque" is related to Emerson's essay "Intellect" by William L. Phillips in "Emerson in Anderson" (*AN&Q*, Sept. 1976) and by Martha M. Park in "How Far from Emerson's Man of One Idea to Anderson's Grotesques?" (*CLAJ*, March 1977), while in "The Futile Pursuit of Truth in Twain's 'What Is Man?' and Anderson's 'The Book of the Grotesque'" (*MTJ*, Winter 1975), Eberhard Alsen argues that Anderson's parable of the grotesque derives from Twain's essay. More evocative than scholarly is Alexandre Mavrocordato's "Le Prisonnier de Winesburg: Réflexions sur le 'Livre des Grotesques'" (*EA*, July–Sept. 1976), which postulates that the old writer is a mask for Anderson himself.

A few articles deal with individual stories in *Winesburg*. Jim Elledge's "Dante's Lovers in Sherwood Anderson's 'Hands'" (*SSF*, Winter 1984) has some insights but strays from its subject, the possible "specific parallels" between "Hands" and the Paolo-Francesca episode in Dante's *Inferno*. In "The Eclectic Dr. Reefy" (*AN&Q*, Sept. 1976), William L. Phillips suggests that the Dr. Reefy of "Paper Pills" was probably based on a Dr. Philip D. Reefy, who practiced "Eclectic" medicine in Elyria, Ohio, at the time Anderson lived there; while in "The Identity of Anderson's

Fanatical Farmer" (*SSF*, Winter 1981), Robert H. Sykes finds striking parallels between Jesse Bentley of "Godliness" and Joseph F. Glidden, a prosperous farmer-inventor of DeKalb, Illinois. John O'Neill's persuasive "Anderson Writ Large: 'Godliness' in *Winesburg, Ohio*" (*TCL*, Feb. 1977) argues that this four-part tale has a three-fold relation to the book as a whole. Keith Carabine's "Sherwood Anderson's 'Adventure': An Appreciation" (*SSMLN*, Spring 1980) is a close reading which supports his claim that the story "merits inclusion in the small canon of Anderson's best work." Luther S. Luedtke's excellent "Sherwood Anderson, Thomas Hardy, and 'Tandy'" (*MFS*, Winter 1974–75) traces the relations between the young stranger in "Tandy" and Jude Fawley in *Jude the Obscure*, and between Hardy's and Anderson's visions of the failure of love in the modern industrialized world. In "Langage et point de vue dans la nouvelle de Sherwood Anderson: 'The Strength of God'" (*EA*, Apr.–June 1973), Christiane Johnson provides a detailed analysis of Anderson's use of repeated words and phrases in this tale with the result that throughout "c'est un vocabulaire limité mais très révélateur qui est utilisé." In "'The Tale of Perfect Balance': Sherwood Anderson's 'The Untold Lie'" (*NLB*, July 1971), Walter B. Rideout explains how the form and content of this story produce "an absolute balance of opposites," making this one of Anderson's finest tales.

Some interest has been shown in books Anderson published after *Winesburg*. The most valuable piece on *Poor White* is "Sherwood Anderson on *Poor White*" (Campbell and Modlin), an interview conducted with Anderson in 1931 by Eleanor Copenhaver, whom he was to marry in 1933, which emphasizes the economic-historical background of the book. Anderson's use of Lincoln in creating Hugh McVey in *Poor White* and in writing "Father Abraham: A Lincoln Fragment" is examined by David D. Anderson in "The Uncritical Critics: American Realists and the Lincoln Myth" (*Midamerica II*, 1975). Less useful is Daniel R. Hoeber's "The 'Unkinging' of Man: Intellectual Background as Structural Device in Sherwood Anderson's *Poor White*" (*SDR*, Spring 1977), which asserts that Anderson relied on his knowledge of scientific materialism to give his novel "unity and continuity." On the other hand, in "Anderson's *Poor White* and Faulkner's *Absalom, Absalom!*" (*MissQ*, Summer 1976), John B. Rosenman makes a provocative connection between the killing of Jim Gibson in Anderson's novel and that of Thomas Sutpen in Faulkner's. Shigeo Hayashi's "On the Theme and Ending of *Poor White*" (*Studies in Foreign Literature* [Ritsumeikan Univ., Kyoto, Japan], 1978) emphasizes the symbolism of the "brightly colored stones" as projecting Hugh McVey's future self-realization as a poet.

Many Marriages has attracted three pieces. Douglas G. Rogers's "Sherwood Anderson's Writing of *Many Marriages*" (*OQ*, Summer 1981) places the composition of this novel within the context of Anderson's life; Mia Klein's "Sherwood Anderson's *Many Marriages*: A Model of the Most

Perilous Journey" (*Midamerica VII*, 1980) approaches the book through certain concepts from R. D. Laing and Jung; and William A. Sutton's "A Question of Legibility" (*WE*, Apr. 1977) notes Anderson's correction of a book shop catalog which quoted him as having stated that he wrote *Many Marriages* "to flush my purse" when he had actually written in his occasionally opaque scrawl, "to flesh my prose." A thorough reappraisal of this unusual novel is needed.

A Story Teller's Story has fared better. In a section entitled "The Next Generation: Then As Now: Sherwood Anderson" in his book *Educated Lives: The Rise of Modern Autobiography in America* (Columbus, Ohio, 1976), Thomas Cooley rightly places Anderson among the modernists because, though *Story* is partly structured chronologically, it also is developed through the fluid "ordering" of psychological time. John W. Crowley's "The Education of Sherwood Anderson" (Campbell and Modlin) is a first-rate analysis of the subtle argument Anderson conducts in *Story*, one of his best and least understood books. "Anderson, like [Henry] Adams," Crowley declares, "raises his own existence to the level of myth; he uses his education, the learning process through which he became a writer, as a paradigm of the life of the modern American artist."

Some aspect of Anderson's one popular success, *Dark Laughter*, has been considered in five articles. David M. Lockwood's "Sherwood Anderson and *Dark Laughter*: Discovery and Rebellion" (*SSMLN*, Summer 1981) is a rather disorganized discussion of the novel's themes, while in "*Dark Laughter* and *Rabbit, Run*: Studies in Instinctive Behavior" (*SN*, No. 1, 1977), Rolf Lundén draws a series of parallels between the two novels, showing that "these books have in common an interest in man's refusal to conform and his attempt to seek fulfillment in a life of the senses." In "Anderson's Satiric Portrait of William Faulkner in *Dark Laughter*" (*NMW*, Summer 1979), Jeffrey J. Folks identifies as being based on Faulkner the young poet in *Dark Laughter* whose "effeminate romanticism" offends the protagonist Bruce Dudley and attracts Bernice, the wife he shortly leaves. This portrait, Folks proposes, was added during Anderson's final revision of the novel in the spring of 1925 and represented Anderson's change of attitude toward Faulkner. Stefania Buccini's "Pavese 'suggestionato' da *Dark Laughter* di Sherwood Anderson" (*Critica Letteraria*, No. 40, 1983) briefly examines Cesare Pavese's translation into Italian of Anderson's novel, which he much admired for its poetic style. An unusually important article is William Holtz's "Sherwood Anderson and Rose Wilder Lane: Source and Method in *Dark Laughter*" (*JML*, Mar. 1985). Basing his argument on newly available documentary evidence that the original for "Rose Frank" in this novel was the American journalist Rose Wilder Lane, whom Anderson met in Paris in 1921, Holtz demonstrates how Anderson's aesthetic of imaginative truth as opposed to factual truth accounts for "the special power of his fiction."

Despite the recent interest in Anderson's Virginia years relatively few articles explore his later books. David D. Anderson's "From Memory to Meaning: The Boys' Stories of William Dean Howells, Clarence Darrow, and Sherwood Anderson" (*Midamerica X*, 1983) views *Tar* as defining "the origins of the Midwestern American experience" and as completing a cycle, begun by Howells's *A Boy's Town*, depicting the growth, maturity, and decline of the Midwestern town. One of the rare analyses of the content and form of *Hello Towns!* is David D. Anderson's "Sherwood Anderson, Virginia Journalist" (*NLB*, July 1971), which demonstrates how Anderson applied an artist's understanding and technique to produce a new kind of journalism, presenting in this book "a picture of human life particularized in the town's life." Also concerned with Anderson's editing of his newspapers is Welford Dunaway Taylor's "Buck Fever and His Kin" (*Iron Mountain Review*, Spring 1983), which traces some of the newspaper forebears of "Buck Fever," the reporter Anderson created, from Franklin's "Silence Dogood" through "Mr. Dooley" and others, but finds no evidence to link Buck specifically to any of these imagined reporter-commentators. Sylvia Cook's "Gastonia: The Literary Reverberations of the Strike" (*SLJ*, Fall 1974) contains only two brief passages on *Beyond Desire*; but Kenichi Takada adds considerably to our knowledge of Anderson's political attitudes in 1932 in his article, "*Beyond Desire*: Sherwood Anderson's Unpublished 'Introduction' and 'Review'" (*Bulletin of the Faculty of General Education, Utsunomiya University*, Dec. 1984), which consists of an introductory note and transcriptions of Anderson's typescripts of an introduction to the novel and his own review of it. For an understanding of Anderson's last collection of stories, Mary Anne Ferguson's "Sherwood Anderson's *Death in the Woods*: Toward a New Realism" (*Midamerica VII*, 1980; reprinted in Anderson, *Critical Essays*) is fundamental. Not only does she follow the development of the title story through its several forms, but she makes a convincing case that the book is an organized whole, not simply a collection of tales, and she has excellent insights into Anderson's "later" method.

As for Anderson's last novel, in "Sherwood Anderson's *Kit Brandon*: A Study in Oral Form" (*GrLR*, Summer 1978), Philip A. Greasley makes detailed reference to this book to illustrate the elements of the oral style, which he considers characteristic of much Midwestern fiction; Welford D. Taylor's "Kit Brandon: A Reidentification" (*NLB*, July 1971) gives conclusive evidence that the actual woman rumrunner on whom Anderson modeled his protagonist was not Mamie Palmer, who had died in 1928, but Willie Carter Sharpe, with whom he talked many times in the spring of 1935. In "Kit Brandon: Androgynous Heroine" (*WE*, Nov. 1984), Karyn Riedell argues that Anderson in his works displayed "confused feelings concerning women's 'role,'" but that in *Kit Brandon* he "seems to have an understanding of their struggle for freedom."

With few exceptions the articles on individual stories deal with the much-anthologized ones, a favorite tale for discussion still being "The Egg." Stewart A. Kingsbury's "A Structural Semantic Analysis of the 'Punch Line' of Sherwood Anderson's Short Story, 'The Egg,'" in *Papers from the Michigan Linguistic Society Meeting, October 3, 1970* (ed. David Lawton, Mount Pleasant, Mich., 1971), is a technical analysis of one sentence in the story and is more useful to the linguist than to the literary scholar. In "Personal Failure in 'The Egg' and 'A Hunger Artist'" (*WE*, Apr. 1983), Donald E. Arbuckle and James B. Misenheimer, Jr. compare Anderson's and Kafka's protagonists as victims of ambition who "try to make their bleak existences important to others and fail miserably," while the effects of American ambition are also considered by Horst Groene in "The American Idea of Success in Sherwood Anderson's 'The Egg'" (*NsM*, Fall 1975). Three other pieces not only are more searching in analysis but also focus on connections between the narrator of "The Egg" and his father. In "Anderson's 'The Egg'" (*Expl*, Fall 1981), Patrick Bassett and Barbara Bassett contend that for the father eggs represent personal failures while for the narrator son they represent "cosmic failure, that is, the futility of life itself." David R. Mesher's "A Triumph of the Ego in Anderson's 'The Egg'" (*SSF*, Spring 1980) makes the persuasive argument that "The Egg" is about "not the father but the son who, as narrator-turned-creator, projects the reality of his own psychology onto the history of his subject"; and in his penetrating "Coming Full Circle: Sherwood Anderson's 'The Egg'" (*SSF*, Fall 1981), Mark Savin argues subtly and convincingly that beneath "the surface text of the story—the sometimes maddening desire of parents to provide a better life for their children"—lies a "subtext—the awkward and troubling recognition of a son's deep similarity to his father," for the "public performances of the father are enacted as well in the narrative performances of the son."

There has been little unity of approach or conclusion about another favorite, "I Want to Know Why." Glen Love's fine reading of the story in his "Horses or Men: Primitive and Pastoral Elements in Sherwood Anderson" has already been referred to in this section. Peter Bischoff, in "Zur Genese der modernen amerikanischen Short Story: Sherwood Andersons 'I Want to Know Why'" (*ArAA*, No. 2, 1981), locates the modernity of the tale in its combination of two traditions, the initiation story and the oral style. Siegfried Neuweiler's "Sherwood Anderson's 'I Want to Know Why': Die Strukturelle Eigenart einer 'Story of Initiation,'" in *Studien und Materialen zur Short Story* (ed. Paul Goetsch, Frankfurt, 1971), proposes that this example of psychological realism deals with the narrator's rejection of his expected social role and then his acceptance of it.

In "The Mark of Sherwood Anderson on Hemingway: A Look at the Texts" (*SAQ*, Autumn 1974), Paul P. Somers, Jr. closely compares

"I Want to Know Why" and "My Old Man." He finds that in several characteristics of the colloquial style Anderson is more formal than Hemingway, suggests that in the matter of repetition both writers owed more to Stein than Hemingway may have owed to Anderson, and concludes that Hemingway was significantly indebted to Anderson only in their common use of the "*subjective descriptive technique*," the use of "vague adjectives [such as 'lovely' and 'good'] which convey states of feeling rather than concrete details." Helen H. Naugle, in "The Name 'Bildad'" (*MFS*, Winter 1976–77), "scrutinizes" the name of the black cook in the story in terms of "anagramatic dissection" and biblical allusion, and decides that Bil*dad* is a "father image worthy of emulation" by the boy narrator.

In his learned "'Rising in the World' and 'Wanting to Know Why': The Socialization Process as Theme of the American Short Story" (*Archiv*, No. 2, 1981), Peter Freese groups Anderson's tale with Hawthorne's "My Kinsman, Major Molineux" and Robert Penn Warren's "Blackberry Winter" as peculiarly American stories of adolescent initiation, in which "Puritan pessimism" and "romantic optimism" merge in a fictional resolution "stressing the ambiguity of gain and loss as the dominant characteristic of this phase of [the adolescent's] development." To a limited extent Freese's analysis resembles that of Frederick Krotz in "Sherwood Andersons 'I Want to Know Why'" in his *Interpretationen amerikanischer Prosa unserer Zeit: Anderson, Hemingway, Faulkner, Steinbeck* (Bonn, 1979). Except for a minor slip in its first sentence—Anderson's tale was published in 1919, not 1918—Krotz provides a careful close reading emphasizing, with frequent reference to texts on child-youth development, the story's accurate portrayal of adolescence, in this case that of a youthful idealist from a Midwest puritanical background who undergoes an erotically tinged disillusionment. In the section entitled "Growing Up Male in America: 'I Want to Know Why,'" in her book *The Resisting Reader: A Feminist Approach to American Fiction* (Bloomington, Ind., 1978), Judith Fetterley uses a valuable perspective to present a generally very acute reading of the tale.

"Death in the Woods" has attracted somewhat less attention and, surprisingly, with exceptions, much less admiration. A. R. Coulthard, in "The Failure of Sherwood Anderson's 'Death in the Woods'" (*Interpretations*, Spring 1983), in fact will have none of it. He charges that the story is flawed by violation of point of view, forced coincidence and pointless repetition, and "the thematic infelicity . . . in the story's denouement," while William J. Scheick, in "Compulsion Toward Repetition: Sherwood Anderson's 'Death in the Woods'" (*SSF*, Spring 1974), employs Freud's definition of the term as "a tendency to repeat an unpleasant incident in order to gain mastery over it" to propose that the narrator's first encounter with sex through the sight of the half-naked body of the old woman in the snow arrests his development, with the result that "death rather than participation in life becomes for him the ideal condition, a state of suspension whereby he can maintain youth and innocence." The argument is more ingenious than convincing. Robert A. Martin's "Primitivism in Stories by Willa Cather and Sherwood Anderson" (*Midamerica III*, 1976) insists that Cather's "Neighbour Rosicky" is an illustration of cultural primitivism, "Death in the Woods" of psychological primitivism. One recalls with some relief Mary Anne Ferguson's sympathetic discussion of the tale in her "Sherwood Anderson's *Death in the Woods*."

Two articles treat the film version of "I'm a Fool," one of the nine films in the *American Short Story* television series first shown in 1977. Jordan Pecile's "On Sherwood Anderson and 'I'm a Fool'" in *The American Short Story* (ed. Calvin Skaggs, New York, 1977), examines a scene from Ron Owen's film script, while Gregory S. Sojka's "'I'm a Fool' on Film: Humor and Irony in Sherwood Anderson" (*WE*, Nov. 1979) is an informed discussion of the content and technique of the film version, concluding that it "makes the craft of Sherwood Anderson's art apparent and accessible to a popular contemporary viewing audience."

Three articles deal with other Anderson tales. Although she occasionally forces the evidence, Lonna M. Malmsheimer, in "Sexual Metaphor and Social Criticism in Anderson's *The Man Who Became a Woman*" (*SAF*, Spring 1979), greatly enriches the debate over this extraordinary story by proposing that the narrator's "clinically hysterical" behavior stems from no unwillingness "to accept his biological role as male," but rather from his inability "to accept his role in terms of maleness as socially defined." Walter B. Rideout's "A Borrowing from Borrow" (Campbell and Modlin) shows how in creating the character Tom Edwards of "An Ohio Pagan" and his mythopoeic visions Anderson drew on his reading in George Borrow's *Wild Wales* (1862) about the historical Thomas Edwards (1739–1810), Welsh poet and dramatist, whom young Tom names as his grandfather. By analyzing three of Anderson's less well-known stories, "There She Is—She Is Taking Her Bath," "The Yellow Gown," and "The Triumph of a Modern," Paul P. Somers, Jr. demonstrates, in "Sherwood Anderson's Mastery of Narrative Distance" (*TCL*, Feb. 1977), that the author "is able to create enough narrative distance between the 'implied author' and the narrator to achieve irony by means of which the reader can judge the character without authorial intrusion," thus revealing an unexpected resemblance to Henry James in the latter's management of certain stories.

One article has appeared on Anderson's involvement with the drama, William A. Sutton's "Sherwood Anderson's First Posthumous 'Publication'" (*AN&Q*, Sept. 1976), which explains that his anti-Fascist radio play *Above Suspicion* was actually only a rough draft made in January 1941. The Free Company revised it after his death for broadcast on 4 May 1941.

More work has been done on literary relationships, direct and indirect, between Anderson and other writers. One of the most interesting pieces is James B. Meriwether's "Faulkner's Essays on Anderson," in *Faulkner: Fifty Years After "The Marble Faun"* (ed. George H. Wolfe, University, Ala., 1976). In a searching analysis of Faulkner's two surviving essays on Anderson—that published in the *Dallas Morning News* on 26 April 1925 and that in the *Atlantic* for February 1953—Meriwether proposes that the latter is essentially a parable of which the significance "lies not so much in what Sherwood Anderson taught, but in what William Faulkner learned," the lessons, that is, he himself had to learn in order to become an artist. In "Les Oeuvres croisées de Sherwood Anderson et de William Faulkner" (*SUD*, No. 48/49, 1983), Claire Bruyère first outlines the personal relationships of Anderson and Faulkner and then skillfully explores the deeper connections of their work and of their attitudes toward art, concluding that "these two idealists in search of the absolute" were indirect descendants of English romanticism, conjoined in such Keatsian beliefs as that art arrests time and prolongs the moment. Another relationship is explored in M. Landor's "M. Gor'kij o Šervude Andersone" (*VLit*, Sept. 1973), which records the long-term interest in Anderson's work shown by Maxim Gorky paralleling the American's long-term interest in the Russian's work.

The influence of Anderson's writings on yet other writers has been discussed in several articles. In Jac Tharpe's "Interview with Erskine Caldwell" (*SoQ*, Fall 1981), Caldwell states that he became interested in being a writer himself from reading *Winesburg, Ohio* and Anderson's stories in little magazines. He liked Anderson's "attitude and approach to the story" and considers him "a natural born writer." E. W. F. Tomlin's "T. S. Eliot, Wyndham Lewis and Sherwood Anderson" (*N&Q*, June 1980) suggests that Eliot may have drawn his description of the river in "The Dry Salvages" from the quotations about the Mississippi in *Dark Laughter* included in Lewis's discussion of Anderson in *Paleface*. James Bryan's "Sherwood Anderson and *The Catcher in the Rye*: A Possible Influence" (*NConL*, Nov. 1971) notes certain similarities in style and tone between the first published Holden Caulfield story, "I'm Crazy," and Anderson's "I'm a Fool" and "I Want to Know Why." In "Some Notes on the Influence of American Authors upon Filipino Writers" (*CLS*, June 1976), Miguel Anselmo Bernad reports that the poet and fiction writer Jose Garcia Villa has stated that "the turning point in his literary career was his reading of Sherwood Anderson's *Winesburg, Ohio*."

Closer to home are the four papers making up a program, "Sherwood Anderson and Modern American Fiction," arranged by David D. Anderson for the Division on Twentieth-Century American Literature at the Modern Language Association meeting of December 1983: David D. Anderson's "Sherwood Anderson's Grotesques and Recent American Fiction"; Walter B. Rideout's "'I Want to Know Why' as Biography and

Fiction"; David Stouck's "Sherwood Anderson and Post-Modernism"; and Kenny J. Williams's "Disorderly Realism, or the Reality of the Unreal." The first two of these papers, along with two others, were published in 1984 in *Midwestern Miscellany XII*, the first issue of this annual "devoted to a single Midwestern writer." David D. Anderson's paper proposes that Sherwood Anderson's "greatest accomplishment" was his definition of the "grotesque" as an aspect of the American character generally and then compares and contrasts his work with that of one of his admirers, Saul Bellow. Rideout's paper shows the considerable extent to which Anderson's tale incorporates his personal experience in 1919, when it was written, and briefly suggests ways in which the tale prefigures later American fiction. In "The Revisions in *Windy McPherson's Son*, Sherwood Anderson's First Novel," Ray Lewis White yet again contributes helpfully to bibliographic scholarship on Anderson by reporting his collation of the 1916 version of *Windy* and the 1922 revision. He lists thirty-nine instances of minor revision in the first 334 pages of the novel; prints in oblique type the substantial revisions from page 335 onward, paralleling this text with that of the 1916 version in regular type, and summarizes the import of the changed ending. In *"Many Marriages* as a Postmodern Novel," David Stouck shrewdly identifies elements in Anderson's experimental novel which are also found in certain postmodernist fictions—the mixture of realism and fantasy, the fablelike quality of the narrative, the intrusions of the author directing "the reader to the activity of the artist," and the "very stylized, self-reflexive writing where words have something akin to a plastic function." Stouck's excellent MLA paper, which points out these elements in other Anderson fictions as well, was later published as "Sherwood Anderson and the Postmodern Novel" (*ConL*, Fall 1985). These five pieces give further evidence of the continuing influence of Sherwood Anderson's writing within modernist and contemporary fiction.

VI SUPPLEMENT

Bibliography. As a contribution toward "the establishment of the complete canon of Anderson's published writings," Charles E. Modlin, Hilbert H. Campbell, and Kenichi Takada, in "Sherwood Anderson: Additions to the Bibliography" (*SB*, 1986), have compiled a list of thirty-six unnoted publications, mostly in periodicals.

Editions. Four Walls Eight Windows Publishing Company (New York) reprinted *The Triumph of the Egg* in paperback in 1988 with, as introduction, Herbert Gold's revision of his 1958 essay, "The Purity and Cunning of Sherwood Anderson."

Manuscripts and Letters. Especially noteworthy is Hilbert H. Campbell's edition of *The Sherwood Anderson Diaries, 1936–1941* (Athens, Ga., 1987), a meticulously edited transcription of the diaries Anderson kept from

January 1, 1936, until February 28, 1941. "Although individual entries can be fairly pedestrian," Campbell points out, "taken together they provide an interesting record of the patterns and routines of his life and work."

Biography. The most important book on Anderson to be published since 1985 is Kim Townsend's *Sherwood Anderson* (Boston, 1987). Although it contains some factual errors and insufficiently evaluates Anderson's experimental works of the mid-1920s, this well-written, well-proportioned "life" is a sympathetic but not uncritical portrait of a complex man, one who, as Townsend rightly observes, "constantly renewed, remade himself—after every failure, but after every success as well." This biography very capably supplants the much earlier ones by James Schevill and Irving Howe. An excerpt from Walter B. Rideout's biography in progress appeared as " 'The Most Cultural Town in America': Sherwood Anderson and New Orleans" (*SoR*, Winter 1988).

Criticism. Among a number of critical articles two stand out. Paying close analytic attention to the narrator's emphasis on the creative process of the story, Clare Colquitt, in "The Reader as Voyeur: Complicitous Transformations in 'Death in the Woods' " (*MFS*, Summer 1986), concludes that the narrator "proceeds to dehistoricize" the dead woman "by objectifying her into art" and implicates the unwary reader in the same "masculinist convention." In "Sherwood Anderson's American Higher Realism" (*The Plough*, Sherwood Anderson Issue, Spring/Summer 1988), Larry Smith describes the writer's highly personal narrative methods resulting from his "compassion for subject and character" and from "his intuitive trust in the imaginative life."

In Memoriam: Eleanor Copenhaver Anderson, 1896–1985. Anderson's fourth wife and his widow not only donated her husband's papers to the Newberry Library but also gave generous, unselfish assistance to Anderson scholars. We are lastingly in her debt.

Willa Cather

James Woodress

I BIBLIOGRAPHY

One of the most important events in the past decade of Cather scholarship was the appearance of Joan Crane's *Willa Cather: A Bibliography*
(Lincoln, Nebr., 1982). For the first time we have full bibliographic
descriptions of Cather's works: quasi-facsimile title pages, collation for-
mulas, notes on paper, bindings, dust jackets, publication, translations.
There are historical notes, notes on illustrations, details supplied by
cooperating publishers on press runs and printings, listings of appearances of stories and other pieces in anthologies. The bibliography is put
together with meticulous care. It is accurate, authoritative, and definitive
and establishes the canon of Cather's works with one important exception,
Georgine Milmine's *The Life of Mary Baker Eddy*. L. Brent Bohlke found
in the New York Public Library a letter in which Cather, despite many
previous denials, confessed to writing all but the first installment (*AL*,
May 1982). JoAnne Lathrop's *Willa Cather: A Checklist of Her Published Writings* (Lincoln, Nebr., 1975) has been superseded by Crane's bibliography.

A valuable and complementary volume to Crane's bibliography of
primary works is Marilyn Arnold's *Willa Cather: A Reference Guide* (Boston,
1986). With this compilation we now have an up-to-date and exhaustive
annotated list of writings about Cather from 1895 through 1984. Arnold
has done a fine job of collecting, organizing, describing, and indexing
(both by subject and author) this 415-page volume. Besides providing
scholars with the sources of Cather criticism, this gathering of data charts
the growth of the subject's reputation. She was extensively written about
during the late 1920s and early 1930s when she was at the peak of her
career, but by the early 1940s she was being ignored. There is not one
item in Arnold's compilation dated 1945, but by 1984 there were ninety-
seven, and it is likely that there will be more books written about her
in the 1980s than in all the previous years put together.

A survey of forty-two dissertations on Cather alone and six more
dealing with Cather and others may be found in *American Literary Realism*

(Summer 1975) by Charlotte S. McClure. The first was Yvonne Handy's French thesis at the University of Rennes in 1940, the first of only three written during Cather's life. There was one more in the late 1940s, ten more in the 1950s, and fifteen in the 1960s.

II EDITIONS

Although there have been several reprintings of Cather titles, some with scholarly introductions, since 1973, there has been only one important new edition. This is James Woodress's definitive edition of *The Troll Garden* (Lincoln, Nebr., 1983), which establishes an authoritative text for Cather's first collection of stories and is equipped with introduction, notes, textual commentary, emendations, and tables of revisions. This edition follows the editorial principles established by the MLA's Center for Editions of American Authors. It provides in its tables of revisions a record of all the emendations, cuts, and sometimes additions that Cather made in four of the stories ("The Sculptor's Funeral," "'A Death in the Desert,'" "A Wagner Matinee," and "Paul's Case") as they underwent successive revisions from serial version to *The Troll Garden* to *Youth and the Bright Medusa* to *The Novels and Stories*. The tables offer a rare glimpse of the artist at work in pruning and polishing her fiction. The introduction deals extensively with the origin, writing, publication, and reception of this early work.

The most important reprinting was a new edition of *Alexander's Bridge* (Lincoln, Nebr., 1977) with an introduction by Bernice Slote, who documents some of the sources for Cather's first novel and demonstrates through theme and imagery the connection between this early work and the rest of the canon. Although Cather disparaged *Alexander's Bridge*, it employs some of her favorite image patterns, and the theme of the divided self that threads its way through her fiction to its most important use in *The Professor's House* appears here thirteen years before. The University of Nebraska Press also brought out a new edition of *The Song of the Lark* (1978), reproduced by photo-offset from the original Houghton Mifflin printing in 1915. It contains an unsigned introduction by Virginia Faulkner.

Other important reprintings are *The Early Novels and Stories*, edited by Sharon O'Brien, for the Library of America (New York, 1987). Included are stories from *The Troll Garden*, *O Pioneers!*, *The Song of the Lark*, *My Ántonia*, and *One of Ours*. By now Houghton Mifflin and Knopf have relaxed their tight hold on Cather copyrights, and reprintings of her more popular works are beginning to proliferate. There now are five editions of *My Ántonia* listed in *Books in Print* and four of *Death Comes for the Archbishop*, as well as listings of additional reprintings of *April Twilights*, *Alexander's Bridge*, *The Song of the Lark*, and *The Troll Garden*. Further, Penguin is planning an edition of *O Pioneers!* to be edited by Blanche Gelfant, and

Houghton Mifflin has reissued *O Pioneers!* with a foreword by Doris Grumbach.

A handful of previously uncollected pieces of Cather's journalistic career have been reprinted in the *Willa Cather Pioneer Memorial Newsletter*, which devotes two of its annual issues to literary material: uncollected writings, interviews, notes, short articles, reviews. Issues of Spring and Summer 1972, Fall 1977, and Summer 1979 reprinted reviews from the Pittsburgh *Leader*, both of drama and music, and the issue of Summer 1973 reprinted a story for children and a Christmas memory of Jim and Elsie found in the *National Stockman and Farmer* (1896). A more ambitious early essay was reprinted in the *Prairie Schooner* (Spring–Summer 1981): "The Case of Richard Strauss," edited by Virginia Faulkner. This nine-page essay in music criticism, found by Bernice Slote, originally appeared in the Pittsburgh *Gazette* on 6 March 1904. Susan Rosowski brought out in the *Prairie Schooner* (Winter 1984) an article that she was working on with the late Bernice Slote, "Willa Cather's 1916 Mesa Verde Essay: The Genesis of *The Professor's House*." This essay reprints a previously unknown newspaper piece that Cather wrote about her visit to the national park. Since this essay was written, a slightly shorter version of the same essay has turned up in *Book News Monthly* (Jan. 1916). There still are a good many uncollected early pieces (see Crane's bibliography).

Textual studies of Cather's work are rare, though this is an area that is sure to receive more attention as time goes on. Three articles focus on textual matters. Joan Crane's "Willa Cather's Corrections in the Text of *Death Comes for the Archbishop*, 1927 to 1945" (*PBSA*, Second Quarter 1980) shows Cather's passion for accuracy in her text. Crane's bibliography also contains a good deal of material on emendations of this novel as well as revisions of the introduction to *My Ántonia*. The second article is by Robin Hayeck and James Woodress, "Willa Cather's Cuts and Revisions in *The Song of the Lark*" (*MFS*, Winter 1979–80). This essay establishes that Cather cut 5 percent of her 1915 text for the Houghton Mifflin library edition of her works, mostly from Books 5 and 6, and it studies the emendations as a measure of Cather's growing artistic maturity. The third piece is John Hinz's "The Hand of the Artist in *Shadows on the Rock*" (*SAF*, Autumn 1977), which examines the page of Cather's manuscript with corrections that appears as a frontispiece to the library edition of the novel. Hinz shows Cather composing her narrative spontaneously then pruning away excess verbiage. (See also V.2.b under Cary.)

Two books that fit no category in this essay but which Cather aficionados will like are *Willa Cather: A Pictorial Memoir* (Lincoln, Nebr., 1973; repr. 1986) and Roger and Linda K. Welsch's *Cather's Kitchens* (Lincoln, Nebr., 1987). The former has text by Bernice Slote and many original photos by Lucia Woods. It's a handsome tribute and documents Cather's life in Nebraska, Virginia, New England, the Southwest, and Canada. The latter is an anthropologist and folklorist's book about plains cooking inspired by the large amount of food and cooking lore in Cather's fiction. Full of recipes and anecdotes, it is, as Susan Rosowski says in a foreword, an entry into Cather's writing via a neglected avenue, the kitchen.

III MANUSCRIPTS AND LETTERS

Cather's prohibition in her will against the publication of her letters still stands, but occasionally through ignorance or intention her letters find their way into print. Yehudi Menuhin in his autobiography, *Unfinished Journey* (New York, 1977), reprints two letters written to him, and the back cover of the *Mark Twain Journal* (Winter 1973–74) reproduces in facsimile a letter from Cather to Cyril Clemens written about 1938 regarding *Huckleberry Finn*. One letter to Mary Austin (20 June 1926) from the Huntington Library collection is paraphrased in *Literary America, 1903–1934: The Mary Austin Letters* (ed. T. M. Pearce, Westport, Conn., 1977), and twelve others are briefly described. Approximately fifteen hundred letters are now in libraries and may be used by scholars. Margaret Anne O'Connor, in "A Guide to the Letters of Willa Cather" (*RALS*, Autumn 1974), catalogues one thousand of these letters, scattered from Maine to California, which went to 184 different correspondents.

Many of Cather's letters, along with letters to her, were destroyed by Cather herself or Edith Lewis in the interest of privacy and to the impoverishment of scholarship; but three letters written by Isabelle McClung to Cather have come to light in Marion Marsh Brown and Ruth Crone's *Only One Point of the Compass: Willa Cather in the Northeast* (Danbury, Conn., 1980). In "The Friendship of Willa Cather and Dorothy Canfield" (*Vermont History*, Summer 1980), Joseph P. Lovering describes the friendship and the collection of Cather letters in the University of Vermont Library. Since O'Connor's calendar of letters was compiled, Harvard has acquired Cather's thirty-five-year correspondence with Houghton Mifflin, and the University of Texas (Austin) has acquired Cather's correspondence with Alfred and Blanche Knopf.

During the past decade, five Cather letters to Louise Pound owned by the Duke University Library have become available to scholars (see IV under Robinson). These letters make clear that Cather had a strong romantic attachment to Louise that was only partially reciprocated. In one dated 15 June 1892, Cather complains that it is manifestly unfair that feminine friendships should be considered unnatural.

IV BIOGRAPHY

Two very different biographies of Cather appeared in 1987: Sharon O'Brien's *Willa Cather: The Emergent Voice* (New York) and James Woodress's *Willa Cather: A Literary Life* (Lincoln, Nebr.). The former is a detailed feminist biography of Cather down to the publication of *O Pioneers!* It has aroused considerable controversy, but it is well researched, ably written (despite being overly long and often repetitious), and a significant contribution to Cather scholarship. Focusing on Cather's childhood, adolescence, and literary apprenticeship, it argues a clear thesis: because Cather as adolescent rejected her gender and masqueraded as male and as a beginning writer embraced values of the male literary tradition, her apprenticeship was a long struggle to resolve the culturally imposed contradictions between femininity and creativity. As long as she devalued women, she devalued herself, and it was not until she accepted her female ancestry (both biological and literary) that she could write with the unique voice we hear in her major novels. What will not convince many Cather scholars is O'Brien's argument that Cather not only was lesbian but considered herself lesbian, and having to conceal this socially unacceptable sexual orientation, her apprenticeship was doubly difficult. O'Brien does a lot of speculating and finds much hidden agenda in the early fiction, but backs her theories with reading in psychology, psychoanalysis, and feminist theory and criticism.

Woodress's biography, the first full-length life, covers Cather's entire canon and career, makes use of the 1,500 letters now in institutional collections, adds a great deal of new biographical detail, corrects errors in previous works (including his own *Willa Cather: Her Life and Art* [1970]) and misrepresentations made by Cather herself. It is extensively documented, rides no thesis, and lets Cather speak for herself where she can be quoted and paraphrases where she may not be quoted. It also uses judiciously Cather's large amount of autobiographical fiction to supplement the external evidence and to build a portrait of an extraordinary writer who lived for art and left an oeuvre that contains a handful of undeniable classics. It takes account of the best Cather criticism (including feminist) of the past two decades and confronts the lesbian issue. A number of reviewers have called the biography definitive. David S. Reynolds in the *New York Times Book Review* (11 Oct. 1987) wrote: "Mr. Woodress does not try to superimpose on Cather's life any theories— feminist, Freudian, Lacanian, or otherwise. Instead, he recounts in straightforward and lively prose the life of a remarkable woman. . . . By avoiding psychoanalytic guesswork, however, he lends a new objectivity to the study of Cather." Earl Rovit in the *Library Journal* (1 Feb. 1988) wrote: "Well-written, unflagging in its interest, and warmly sympathetic, this biography is a worthy complement to Cather's distinguished work. Highly recommended."

Also in the period covered by this essay another biography appeared: Phyllis C. Robinson's *Willa: The Life of Willa Cather* (Garden City, N.Y., 1983). Although the title is irritating, the book is lively reading and based on a good bit of research, but not always documented; it is not addressed to scholars or students of Cather. A disproportionate amount of space is devoted to Cather's life down to the time she published her first novel, and her novels and stories get short shrift. Since there is little excuse for a literary biography if it does not illuminate the writer's art, this book will be of small value for scholars and students. This was the first Cather biography to call her a lesbian, but there are very few new biographical facts. The biography is marred by many unsupported assertions and inferences stated as fact and makes no use of the large amount of criticism reviewed in this essay. Reviews of this book were generally unfavorable.

There have been two other books that deal in partial biography: the Brown-Crone book just mentioned treats Cather's summers spent on Grand Manan Island but is written without documentation and contains a good bit of fiction. It does present a picture of Cather's summer cottage and the ambience of the New Brunswick setting that Cather loved. It is based on conversations with local people who remembered Cather during the 1930s and early 1940s. The other biographical work is Kathleen D. Byrne and Richard C. Snyder's *Chrysalis: Willa Cather in Pittsburgh* (Pittsburgh, 1980). Although this work does not contain much new information about the decade that Cather spent in Pittsburgh, it supplies augmented detail and pulls together the previously known facts about that period. The book provides more information than we have had on Cather's Pittsburgh friends.

Cather's niece, Helen C. Southwick, in "Willa Cather's Early Career: the Origins of Legend" (*Western Pennsylvania History Magazine*, April 1982), also tried to damp down the current reading of lesbianism in the Cather-McClung relationship. She disputes the testimony in Elizabeth Moorhead's *These Two Were Here* (1950) as the faulty recollections of a woman in her eighties of events that had occurred half a century before. She marshals evidence that Isabelle McClung never threatened to leave home if Cather could not live with her and believes it is likely that Judge McClung himself invited her to become a part of the McClung household. She argues convincingly that Cather never would have gone to the McClungs if she could not have had a room of her own. She points out numerous errors in Moorhead's book and rightly takes previous biographers to task for not questioning her accuracy. This article was inspired perhaps by such recent speculations as Jane Rule's *Lesbian Images* (New York, 1975), which contains a chapter on Cather that assumes her lesbianism. Rule, however, finds that what distinguishes Cather is not a masculine sensibility but a capacity to transcend the sexuality of her characters. The Pittsburgh era is also dealt with by Peter Benson in "Willa Cather at *Home Monthly*" (*Biography*, Summer 1981), which surveys the history of that magazine and Cather's brief tenure as editor.

An important contribution to Cather biography is found in Patricia L. Yongue's two-part essay, "Willa Cather's Aristocrats" (*SHR*, Winter,

Spring 1980). Yongue has investigated Cather's friendship with the young English aristocrat Stephen Tennant by way of demonstrating her definite attraction to the grace and charm of wealth and position and her desire to be a Virginia lady like her mother.

A volume of great utility for Cather scholars is L. Brent Bohlke's *Willa Cather in Person: Interviews, Speeches, and Letters* (Lincoln, Nebr., 1986). For a writer who had a reputation of being very private and inaccessible, Cather actually left a well-blazed trail. Bohlke has collected some three dozen interviews given between 1897 and 1940, fifteen speeches (none later than 1933), and ten letters that were published during her lifetime. These documents were not previously unknown, and biographers and critics have been using them right along, but the sources often were obscure, many of them from files of newspapers long defunct. Thus it is a significant service to scholarship to have these materials conveniently assembled within the covers of one book.

A special issue of the *Great Plains Quarterly* (Fall 1982) contains several articles of biographical interest. James Woodress, in "The Uses of Biography: The Case of Willa Cather," discusses the autobiographical aspects of several novels, especially *The Professor's House*. Mildred Bennett, in "The Childhood Worlds of Willa Cather," introduces the scenes of Cather's infancy and early years, the persons and places she knew in Virginia and Red Cloud. Bernice Slote, in "An Exploration of Cather's Early Writing," traces Cather's ideas about art, music, and literature from her journalistic youth to her mature work. David Stouck, in "Marriage and friendship in *My Ántonia*," approaches this novel from an autobiographical perspective, seeing it as growing out of Cather's reaction to Isabelle McClung's marriage. Of slight biographical interest is A. L. Rouse's two-part article, "On the Track of Willa Cather" (*Blackwood's Magazine*, Aug., Sept. 1980), a pleasantly discursive appreciation that recounts two visits to Nebraska some twenty years apart. Rouse interviewed both Elsie Cather and Louise Pound.

Four final biographical items are Alfred Knopf's reminiscence, "Miss Cather," in *The Art of Willa Cather* (ed. Bernice Slote and Virginia Faulkner, Lincoln, Nebr., 1974; hereinafter referred to as Slote and Faulkner), an account of Cather's switch from Houghton Mifflin to Alfred A. Knopf, which is quite inaccurate (see Woodress, *Willa Cather: A Literary Life*, pp. 316–18, for the real story); and three dictionary items: a 12,000-word essay on Cather in *American Novelists, 1910–1945, Part I: Dictionary of Literary Biography*, vol. 9 (Detroit, 1981), by James Woodress; a nine-page essay in *Fifty Western Writers* (ed. Fred Erisman and Richard E. Etulain, Westport, Conn., 1982) by John J. Murphy; and a fifty-page spread on Cather in *Dictionary of Literary Biography: Documentary Series: An Illustrated Chronicle*, vol. 1 (Detroit, 1982), edited by Margaret A. Van Antwerp. The last contains a generous selection of photographs, manuscript facsimiles, letters, reviews, interviews, facsimiles of corrected galley proof, and the *New York Herald Tribune* obituary.

V CRITICISM

This section is divided into general studies, special studies, and studies of individual works. The first treats entire books devoted to Cather as well as chapters from books and individual essays that deal with her work from a broad perspective. The second surveys articles focusing on a narrow aspect of the canon; and the third discusses essays devoted to a specific novel or story. Some of these pieces have been hard to classify, and their location in the following pages may be open to question. In addition, articles of trivial importance have been given the silent treatment. Articles written after 1984 are covered in the Supplement.

1 General Studies

a. Books. A good place for a beginner to approach Cather is through Philip Gerber's *Willa Cather* (TUSAS, Boston, 1975). Brief as the volumes in this series are, this book nonetheless is a well-organized, well-thought-out survey that treats both life and works. The discussion of the works is organized thematically into "The Bright Challenge" (youth's struggle towards accomplishment) and "The Reign of Mammon" (America in the clutches of materialism). These opposing perspectives provide a very good way of looking at the entire canon. The appendix contains a well-selected brief annotated bibliography.

The best book on Cather in eleven years is Susan Rosowski's *The Voyage Perilous* (Lincoln, Nebr., 1986), a remarkably lucid, thoughtful, and convincing study of a subject that has been waiting for treatment. It has been a long while since critics have lumped Cather with other twentieth-century realists, but Cather's romanticism has never before been examined comprehensively. *The Voyage Perilous* contains a great deal of excellent scholarship that relates Cather to the entire Romantic tradition, and it treats in depth her novels and stories from her apprenticeship to her final work. Rosowski defines the essential characteristic of Romanticism as the concern with "a mode of perception by which the imagination is used in its synthesizing or creative powers to transform and give meaning to an alien or meaningless world." Her thesis, which she pursues successfully, is that Cather early took up the Romantic challenge to vindicate imaginative thought in a world threatened by materialism and carried it out with remarkable consistency throughout her career. The study is particularly interesting and breaks new ground in tracing gothicism, that dark underside of Romanticism, throughout Cather's work from college days to her last two novels, *Lucy Gayheart* and *Sapphira and the Slave Girl*, which she reads as modern gothics.

The other book of this period that compares in quality to Rosowski's is David Stouck's *Willa Cather's Imagination* (Lincoln, Nebr., 1975), an illuminating study full of insight and good judgment. Part 1 shows the breadth of Cather's imagination by considering the various modes through which her fiction moves: epic, pastoral, and satiric. Part 2 explores the depth of Cather's moral vision and the literary forms she found to express it. *My Mortal Enemy* is an inferno of hate; *Shadows on the Rock* a purgatorial quest through sin and suffering; *Death Comes for the Archbishop* a paradisiacal vision of life, to use Dante's *Divina Commedia* as a loose organizing principle. Part 3 looks at art's relation to life, a theme running throughout Cather's fiction. *The Song of the Lark* is contrasted with the last four books in which Cather seems to doubt art's redemptive power and gives supremacy to life values. This study is felicitously written and the scholarship is impeccable.

A third book which also appeared in 1975 is Mona Pers's *Willa Cather's Children* (Uppsala), a Swedish dissertation that extracts one of the central threads from Cather's art. In Cather's fiction, Pers finds, characters who like children are invariably sympathetic, and children are always a source of love and hope. The study goes on to show how Cather recreated her own childhood in the lives of many fictional characters. It concludes with an analysis of the fictional ramifications of Cather's fondness for childhood: unhappy marriages, disillusioned adults, artistic weakness in treating mature artists. Pers believes that Cather's strongest appeal is to those who cherish memories of their childhood.

Another recent book-length study of Cather is Marilyn Arnold's *Willa Cather's Short Fiction* (Athens, Ohio, 1984), the first detailed account of Cather's rather large production of short stories. This is a competent, reliable work that provides much criticism of stories that previously have had little attention. The sensible chronological organization "preserves the natural linear design Cather created in writing the stories and gives the reader a sense of biographical continuity." Except for "The Sculptor's Funeral" and "Paul's Case," the only two stories that Cather for most of her career would allow to be anthologized, her short fiction is not well known. Arnold rescues some excellent stories from oblivion with her readings of "Coming, Aphrodite!," "Uncle Valentine," and "Double Birthday," and she also gives deserved attention to the very late tales, "The Best Years" and "Before Breakfast."

A book by various hands is *The Art of Willa Cather* (see IV), which came out of the Cather Centennial held at the University of Nebraska in 1973. Four of the essays here belong under the heading of general studies: "The House of Willa Cather" by Eudora Welty (reprinted in Murphy; see below), "The Two Worlds of Willa Cather" by Marcus Cunliffe, "Willa Cather: American Experience and European Tradition" by James Woodress, and "Willa Cather and the Art of Fiction" by James E. Miller, Jr.

Welty writes of Cather from the point of view of a fellow artist whom she much admires and finds the great thing, the vital principle, in her work to be passion, which is every artist's secret, as Thea Kronborg's teacher explains in *The Song of the Lark*. Cunliffe, a British historian, addresses himself to the question of why Cather has been neglected by historians and the extent to which she sheds light on her age. Woodress argues that her great strength is the ability to blend her American experience with Old World knowledge and tradition. Miller assesses Cather's achievement in the light of James's theory of fiction and finds her best work to be novels in which, like James, she uses an observer to tell a story or creates a drama of consciousness in one character.

A second book-length collection of essays, *Five Essays on Willa Cather: The Merrimack Symposium* (North Andover, Mass., 1974), resulted from a pre-celebration of the Centennial held at Merrimack College in October 1972. Four of the essays belong here: Bernice Slote's "Willa Cather: The Secret Web"; Richard Giannone's "Willa Cather and the Human Voice"; John J. Murphy's "Willa Cather: The Widening Gyre"; and Lillian D. Bloom's "The Poetics of Willa Cather." Slote demonstrates the way casual references in Cather's fiction often reveal subtle associations and inferences that open up the pattern and meaning of a work. Giannone argues that Cather felt the need to restore to fiction the human voice and advanced the art by returning it to its oral, classic origins. Murphy develops the thesis that male characters in the Nebraska novels fail to establish fruitful relationships with women because they insist on idealizing them or rejecting them as fallen women, while in the later Catholic novels the ideal and the real are joined in the Virgin. Bloom believes that Cather's critical principles were formed by her organic view of art. She rejected invention or manipulation of her materials, for she thought that a novel had its own inevitable design.

A recent study that devotes half of its space to Cather is Judith Fryer's *Felicitous Space: The Imaginative Structures of Edith Wharton and Willa Cather* (Chapel Hill, N.C., 1986). Taking its title from Gaston Bachelard's *Poetics of Space*, Fryer has written a "woman-centered inquiry," focusing on the connection between space and the female imagination. Although feminist theory is brought to bear on the subject, the individual readings of the novels seem not unlike those of other Cather critics of either sex. There are some nice *aperçus*, such as the discussion of Cather's debt to Millet's paintings or the comparison of Cather's response to the Southwest with that of Georgia O'Keeffe; but there also are assertions that other feminists may take exception to, such as Fryer's notion that only male critics see Cather as a "pastoral" writer. This is not an easy book to use. The continual moving back and forth among Cather's works will leave the reader in a state of exasperated confusion. Fryer calls her chapters meditations to explain why her book follows a logic of its own (i.e., has no formal structure) and contains a great deal of the author as well as her subject. Fryer's chapter on Cather in *The Desert is No Lady: Southwestern Landscapes in Women's Writing* (ed. Vera Norwood and Janice Monk, New Haven, Conn., 1987) is a condensed version of this book.

b. *Chapters in Books.* John J. Murphy has edited *Critical Essays on Willa Cather* (CEAmL, Boston, 1984; hereinafter referred to as Murphy), reprinting some of the best Cather criticism of the past generation plus a number of contemporary reviews of Cather's work. There are in addition five original essays: Murphy and Kevin Synott's "The Recognition of Willa Cather's Art," which is a concise survey of the growth of Cather's reputation; Stouck's "Willa Cather and the Impressionistic Novel," which is an important study of Cather's roots in the French novel and the critical theory of impressionism and symbolism that helped shape those works Cather admired and chose as models for her own work; Woodress's "Cather and Her Friends"; Murphy's "A Comprehensive View of Cather's *O Pioneers!,*" which pulls together the various threads of criticism that others have commented on *passim*; and Paul Comeau's "*The Professor's House* and Anatole France" (see V.3.b.vii). Harold Bloom's *Modern Critical Views: Willa Cather* (New York, 1985) contains only reprinted items.

Ellen Moers, in *Literary Women* (New York, 1976), treats Cather as one of the great women writers. She believes that *The Song of the Lark*, which may owe a debt to George Sand's *Consuelo*, contains in the Panther Canyon section "the most thoroughly elaborated female landscape in literature." There are interesting insights scattered throughout Moers's book: she thinks *A Lost Lady* is "an Electra story, raw and barbarous"; the image of the dressmaker's forms in *The Professor's House* is "a brilliant symbolic summary of everything Willa Cather's generation of women writers had to say . . . about Motherhood"; her landscapes are something like the Yorkshire moors of the Brontës or the African highlands of Isak Dinesen. Linda Huf, in "*The Song of the Lark* (1915): The Exception of Willa Cather," in *A Portrait of the Artist as a Young Woman* (New York, 1983), which treats the *bildungsroman* of half a dozen women writers, gives Cather's novel a perceptive reading from this point of view.

Chapters on Cather in books on various subjects have been written by Bernice Slote, James Lilienfeld, Sharon O'Brien, Ann Douglas, Glen A. Love, Herbie Butterfield, and Phyllis Rose. Slote's "An Appointment with the Future: Willa Cather," in *The Twenties: Fiction, Poetry, Drama* (ed. Warren French, Deland, Fla., 1975), discusses Cather's work in terms of the wasteland theme of the decade. She finds it embedded in *One of Ours* and *The Professor's House*, but in other novels of the same era the images of sterility are balanced with affirmations of life. In another essay, probably the last thing she wrote before her death, "Willa Cather and Plains Culture," contributed to *Vision and Refuge: Essays on the Literature of the Great Plains* (ed. Virginia Faulkner and Frederick C. Luebke, Lincoln, Nebr., 1982), Slote elaborates on Cather's familiar thesis that "human history is a record of an emigration, an exodus from barbarism to civilization."

Lilienfeld's essay, "Reentering Paradise: Cather, Colette, Woolf, and Their Mothers," appears in *The Lost Tradition: Mothers and Daughters in Literature* (ed. Cathy N. Davidson and E. M. Broner, New York, 1980). Lilienfeld explores and speculates on the relationship between Cather and her mother, examining known biographical facts and two fictional works, "Old Mrs. Harris" and *Sapphira and the Slave Girl*. O'Brien's contribution to *American Novelists Revisited: Essays in Feminist Criticism* (ed. Fritz Fleischmann, Boston, 1982) is also concerned with mothers and daughters: "Mothers, Daughters, and the 'Art Necessity': Willa Cather and the Creative Process." This is a well-constructed analysis of Cather's struggle to combine the roles of woman and artist and her relationship with her mother and the other women she loved. O'Brien finds *O Pioneers!* and *The Song of the Lark* early feminist novels and successful examples of the creation of an autonomous female hero. The male perspectives of *My Ántonia* and *A Lost Lady*, she believes, reflect the usually male viewer's needs and preoccupations and make these novels as sexist as Faulkner's *Light in August*. O'Brien also has contributed "Tomboyism and Adolescent Conflict: Three Nineteenth-Century Case Studies" in *Woman's Being, Women's Place: Female Identity and Vocation in American History* (ed. Mary Kelly, Boston, 1979). She examines the ramifications of Cather's rejection of her femininity during her Red Cloud adolescence. This resulted from her inability to see any way in her society that she could combine being a woman with the goals she wanted to achieve. Only later, after she began meeting opera singers and actresses, did she realize that "women could reject Victorian definitions of woman's role and nature without rejecting their sex." These articles are subsumed in O'Brien's *Willa Cather: The Emergent Voice*.

Douglas's article is "Willa Cather: A Problematic Ideal," in *Women, the Arts, and the 1920s in Paris and New York* (ed. Kenneth W. Wheeler and Virginia Lee Lussier, New Brunswick, N.J., 1982). This is a curious essay that begins by conceding that Cather is "perhaps the most influential woman writer of this century"; but Douglas is disturbed that "Cather did not sleep with monsters, as Adrienne Rich has said a thinking woman must do. Cather was liberated from certain torture chambers which have confined her equally talented sisters." Love's "The Cowboy in the Laboratory" is part of his *New Americans: The Westerner and the Modern Experience in the American Novel* (Lewisburg, Pa., 1982), which treats Cather along with Norris, Garland, Anderson, and Lewis. These writers were attempting to "accommodate the mechanized present and future without denying the organic past." Love points out that in Cather's novels from *Alexander's Bridge* to *The Professor's House* we are given a procession of contemporary westerners—bridge-builder, opera star, railroad lawyer, soldier, scholar, and cowboy turned scientist. Butterfield's essay, "Willa

Cather," in *American Fiction: New Readings* (ed. Richard Gray, London, 1983), does not contain new readings but rather a brief though appreciative summary of Cather's entire canon. Phyllis Rose studies Cather from the standpoint of "Modernism: the Case of Willa Cather" in *Modernism Reconsidered* (ed. Robert Kiely and John Hildebidle, Cambridge, Mass., 1983): "In modernist critical writings, including Cather's, certain themes recur: an urge to shake loose of clutter, a refusal to accept the mimetic function of art as previously defined, a feeling that a certain 'spirit' was escaping the older forms, an urge toward anonymity. The vessel is emphasized rather than the content; art is imagined as a fragile container for the ineffable substance of life." This important article is reprinted in Rose's *Writing of Women: Essays in a Renaissance* (Middletown, Conn., 1985).

   c. General Articles. General articles from periodicals, arranged chronologically, begin with Sister Lucy Schneider's "Artistry and Instinct: Willa Cather's 'Land Philosophy'" (*CLAJ*, June 1973), the concluding and summarizing essay of a series that she began writing in 1968. This philosophy views the land as "a symbol for essences," "good by nature" but sometimes seemingly evil in operation, a blending of "the elemental and the traditional," "a force actively operating on man," the "source of harvests," the source of "openness and breadth of vision," and a force fostering transcendence. A related article is John Ditsky's "Nature and Character in the Novels of Willa Cather" (*CLQ*, Sept. 1974), which examines all twelve novels three times according to Cather's use of the land: as "the embodiment of history," a "source of hope," and the "shaper of individual character."

   A more successful discussion of Cather's art appears in Margaret H. Freydberg's "Willa Cather: The Light Behind Her Books" (*ASch*, Spring 1974), an essay arguing that the essence of Cather's artistry derives from the fusion of her detailed observation of life with her profound moral integrity. A good article on two central configurations in Cather's art is Frank W. Shelton's "The Image of the Rock and the Family in the Novels of Willa Cather" (*MarkhamR*, Fall 1976), which argues that Cather's protagonists often forsake the family, which they see as a "trap," to seek refuge in the rock, the symbol (though often illusory) of community. Only in *Shadows on the Rock* does Cather combine in the rock both the support of the nuclear family and the satisfactions of the extended family. Another treatment of recurring patterns is Mona Pers's "Through the Looking-Glass with Willa Cather" (*SN*, No. 1, 1976), which argues that the various window scenes in the fiction present the author's longing for the unattainable. Pers examines window scenes in which outsiders wish to get inside and insiders yearn to get outside to freedom and independence.

   A perceptive essay on Cather's use of the Southwest is David Stouck's "Willa Cather and the Indian Heritage" (*TCL*, Dec. 1976), a discussion probing a side of Cather that views art "not as the product of self-expression but as a process of sympathy for people, places, and events." This aspect of Cather's art found its highest expression in her interest in the Indians of the Southwest. James R. Bash, in "Willa Cather and the Anathema of Materialism" (*CLQ*, Sept. 1973), returns to a topic familiar in Cather scholarship: detestation of the "ugly crest of materialism" that manifested itself in mechanization and standardization, misuse of the land, and devotion to making money.

There were seven general articles in 1981, three by Susan J. Rosowski, others by Judith Fryer, Michael A. Klug, Paul Comeau, and Marilyn Arnold. Rosowski's "Willa Cather—A Pioneer in Art: *O Pioneers!* and *My Ántonia*" (*PrS*, Spring–Summer 1981) applies a theory of response to the landscape involving loss and recovery of the self and emphatic union with space to explain Cather's approach to Nebraska in these novels. Fryer, in "Cather's Felicitous Space" (*PrS*, Spring–Summer 1981), anticipates ideas incorporated in her later book (see V.1.a) in discussing *The Song of the Lark*, *The Professor's House*, and *Death Comes for the Archbishop*. Thea emerges from and St. Peter retreats to intimate space, while Archbishop Latour balances both inner and outer landscapes.

Three of the 1981 essays dealt with psychological dualism. In "The Patterns of Willa Cather's Novels" (*WAL*, Winter 1981), Rosowski views Cather's characters from the perspective of personal and second selves, and in "Willa Cather's Women" (*SAF*, Autumn 1981), she looks at "how a woman encounters contradictions between the human pattern of two selves and cultural myths that would limit her to only one of them." Rosowski finds the emotional pattern of two selves running throughout Cather's fiction. The early novels involve a synthesis with the outward self rooted in the personal self, and the later novels present increasingly complex treatments of the social roles assigned to women. Klug's essay, "Willa Cather Between Red Cloud and Byzantium" (*CRevAS*, Winter 1981), finds Cather a representative figure in modern American fiction: "Her conflict is the essential conflict of the modern artist . . . the conflict which inevitably frustrates an increasing number of citizens in every modern society that places a high value on individual freedom."

Paul Comeau, in "The Fool Figure in Willa Cather's Fiction" (*WAL*, Winter 1981), follows this character type from "Lou, the Prophet" through Crazy Ivar and Tillie Kronborg to *One of Ours* in which the fool becomes protagonist in a world of lapsed values. Arnold, in "Willa Cather's Nostalgia: A Study of Ambivalence" (*RS*, Mar. 1981), uses "Eleanor's House," "On the Gull's Road," "The Old Beauty," and profiles in *Not Under Forty* to demonstrate that Cather is not the purveyor of nostalgia that some have claimed.

An article which deals with theme in more than one novel is John J. Murphy's "Willa Cather and Catholic Themes" (*WAL*, May 1982), which sees Cather as seeking refuge in Catholic subjects. The spiritual mystery residing in otherwise mundane events romanticizes the world for Cather and her characters, enabling them to believe "in the mystery and importance of their own little lives." John Ditsky's "Listening with Supersensual Ear: Music in the Novels of Willa Cather" (*JNT*, Fall ·1983) is a footnote to Richard Giannone's *Music in Willa Cather's Fiction* (1968).

Marilyn Arnold, in a contribution to volume 2 of *Critical Survey of Long Fiction* (ed. Frank Magill, Pasadena, Calif., 1983), surveys three conflicts in Cather's fiction: East versus West, civilization or art versus land, and materialism versus innate values. Robert W. Cherny, in "Willa Cather and the Populists" (*GPQ*, Fall 1983), looks at Cather's early anti-Populist and pro-Republican sentiments in her early journalism and her prairie novels.

A special double issue of *Women's Studies* (No. 3, 1984), edited by Margaret Anne O'Connor, contained nine articles on Cather, two of which are general in nature. Linda Pannill, in "Willa Cather's Artist-Heroines," looks at early critical writings and fiction; and Ned Ryerson, in "From the Tree House," reviews Cather's career and responds to critics who continue to call her work escapist.

A second special Cather issue of the *Great Plains Quarterly* (Fall 1984) carried four general articles. John Murphy's "Cather's Nebraska Grotesques and Jamesian Frames" is a significant study of the Jamesian influences; Lucia Woods's "Light and Shadow in the Cather World: A Personal Essay" comments on the photographs she took for *Willa Cather: A Pictorial Memoir*; James E. Miller, Jr., reflects on "Willa Cather Today"; and Mona Pers presents the results of her investigations in "Willa Cather's Scandinavian Connection."

2 Special Studies

Studies of Cather with a narrow focus range widely, and some articles included here may seem rather arbitrarily selected. The following essays deal with Cather from a feminist standpoint, sex and marriage, influences and analogues, Cather's view of history, her use of the classics, her reputation abroad, and other topics.

a. Feminist Criticism, Sex, Marriage (see also IV, V.1.a). Feminist criticism of Cather begins in the period under review in this updated essay. Susan Rosowski, in "Willa Cather's Female Landscapes: *The Song of the Lark* and *Lucy Gayheart*" (*WS*, No. 3, 1984), reads these novels from a feminist perspective, and in "Willa Cather's Pioneer Women: A Feminist Interpretation," in *Where the West Begins: Essays on Middle Border and Siouxland Writing in Honor of Herbert Krause* (ed. Arthur R. Huseboe and William Geyer, Sioux Falls, S.Dak., 1978), she argues that Cather avoids sexist roles in presenting pioneer women and that a woman like Alexandra Bergson synthesizes the expansiveness attributed to the male pioneer with the stability of the female. Jennifer Bailey, in "The Dangers of Femininity in Willa Cather's Fiction" (*JAmS*, Dec. 1982), believes that Cather felt that conventional relationships between men and women were undesirable, and therefore they are absent in her major novels (*O Pioneers!*, *A Lost Lady*, *The Professor's House*). Sharon O'Brien's "The Limits of Passion: Willa Cather's Review of *The Awakening*" (*W&L*, Fall 1975) relates Cather's negative review of Kate Chopin's novel to her distrust of sexual love in her own fiction. Edna Pontellier's passion is subjective and self-gratifying, whereas Cather believed that happiness could only come through self-abnegation, by identifying with something greater than oneself. O'Brien's recent article, " 'The Thing Not Named': Willa Cather as a Lesbian Writer" (*Signs*, Summer 1984), is a thoughtful, cogent essay that is sure to arouse controversy. Laying considerable stress on Cather's indiscreet letters to Louise Pound, O'Brien argues that Cather possessed a lesbian sense of self in the 1890s that resulted from severe psychological and social processes that occurred during her adolescence and college years.

Also on the subject of sex and marriage is Doris Grumbach's "Heroes and Victims: Willa Cather's Marriage Theme" (*QJLC*, Fall 1982). Grumbach discusses the "coruscating view" of marriage in *A Lost Lady* and *My Mortal Enemy* and sees both Captain Forrester and Oswald Henshawe as wronged by their wives. She wonders if Cather's moral is misogamist. Although it deals with only one novel, Deborah Lambert's "The Defeat of a Hero: Autonomy and Sexuality in *My Ántonia*" (*AL*, Jan. 1982) is primarily concerned with Cather's sexual nature and appropriately belongs here. Lambert assumes Cather's lesbianism and argues that as a result she transformed her emotional life and experience into acceptable heterosexual forms and guises. She includes Ántonia's prototype as one of Cather's loves. The argument is unconvincing and ignores the androgynous nature of Cather's writing from the viewpoint of the entire canon. Loretta Wasserman is more restrained in "The Lovely Storm: Sexual Initiation in Two Early Cather Novels" (*SNNTS*, Winter 1982). Any argument from life, she believes, has to be made tentatively, but she thinks the Julio episode in Cather's first trip to the Southwest is important, and she argues that Cather is not an asexual novelist. She cites the affairs between Fred and Thea in *The Song of the Lark* and between Jim and Lena in *My Ántonia*. Within the context of the times Cather ran some risk "in describing two illicit affairs as fully as she did."

b. Sources, Influences, Analogues. Sources and analogues have been a fertile ground for Cather critics during the past decade. No less than twenty-seven such articles have appeared in this period, many of which are of minor importance and will be treated briefly.

Sarah Orne Jewett's relationship with Cather is well known, and two articles deal with it. Richard Cary's "The Sculptor and the Spinster: Jewett's 'Influence' on Cather" (*CLQ*, Sept. 1973) looks at revisions made in "The Sculptor's Funeral" to conclude that Jewett's advice had no influence on the touching up of this tale. James Woodress's "Sarah Orne Jewett and Willa Cather: Anti-Realists," in *English Studies Today*, Fifth Series (ed. Spencer Tongue, Istanbul, 1973), argues that Cather and Jewett were both anti-realists and shared an Emersonian view of man's relation to nature. William M. Curtin, in "Willa Cather and The Varieties of Religious Experience" (*Renascence*, Spring 1975), speculates on the possible influence of William James. In "The Sculptor of the Beautiful" (*CLQ*, Mar. 1978), Eben Bass argues that Hawthorne's "The Artist of the Beautiful" provided a theme and images, including the butterfly as a symbol of beauty, for "The Sculptor's Funeral." John J. Murphy, also interested in Cather's connection to Hawthorne, in "Willa Cather and Hawthorne: Significant Resemblances" (*Renascence*, Spring 1975), looks at Cather in the context of American literature and compares the way Cather and Hawthorne handle perennial American themes.

Parallels between Cooper's Leatherstocking Tales and Littlepage novels and Cather's western fiction occupy Murphy in "Cooper, Cather, and the Downward Path to Progress" (*PrS*, Spring–Summer 1981). Both novelists, he writes, saw the business ethic and destruction of heroic context as the outcome of the American experience. In " 'Presumptuous Girls' of Cather, Dreiser, and James" (*PVR*, Apr. 1981), Murphy again compares similarities, this time among the protagonists of *The Song of the Lark*, *Sister Carrie*, and *The Portrait of a Lady*. In "*The Professor's House* and 'Rip Van Winkle'" (*WAL*, Feb. 1984), Patricia Lee Yongue finds parallels in character, action, and structure between Irving's story and Cather's novel. In *Women in Western Literature* (ed. Helen Stauffer, Troy, N.Y., 1982), Murphy's essay, "*The Virginian* and *My Ántonia*: Different Sides of the Western Coin," sees various points of similarity between Owen Wister's novel and Cather's. In "Poe's Shadow on *Alexander's Bridge*" (*MissQ*, Fall 1982), Merrill M. Skaggs argues that Cather rejected her first novel because Poe influenced the writing of it. She sees parallels between the novel and "The Fall of the House of Usher."

Cather's relationship with her contemporaries has furnished material for eleven essays. Tom Quirk's important article, "Fitzgerald and Cather: *The Great Gatsby*" (*AL*, Dec. 1982), adds "Paul's Case" and *Alexander's Bridge* to *My Ántonia* and *A Lost Lady* as influences on Fitzgerald's novel. See also Matthew Bruccoli's " 'An Instance of Apparent Plagiarism' " (*PULC*, Spring 1978), which prints a letter Fitzgerald wrote Cather explaining that he had already written a description of Daisy for *Gatsby* when he read a similar description of Marian Forrester in *A Lost Lady*. This letter is also in *Correspondence of F. Scott Fitzgerald* (ed. Matthew J. Bruccoli and Margaret M. Duggan, New York, 1980). Cather's possible influence on Ellen Glasgow is the subject of Debra D. Munn's "A Probable Source for Glasgow's *Barren Ground*" (*MarkhamR*, Winter 1982). Munn thinks it is "almost as though Glasgow took a basic outline of *O Pioneers!* and reworked the story to make it her own." Pei-Tzu Hsu's "Love of

Land in [Pearl] Buck and Cather" (*FJS*, 1979) compares the importance of landscape and the farm in the two writers.

Robert A. Martin looks at "Neighbour Rosicky" and "Death in the Woods" in "Primitivism in Stories by Willa Cather and Sherwood Anderson" (*Midamerica III*, 1976); and Randall L. Popken, in "From Innocence to Experience in *My Ántonia* and *Boy Life on the Prairie*" (*NDQ*, Spring 1978), compares Cather and Garland. Virgil Albertini once again notes that Cather's harsh pictures of Nebraska life in her early stories invite comparison with E. W. Howe and Garland in "Willa Cather's Early Short Stories: A Link to the Agrarian Realists" (*MarkhamR*, Summer 1979). Lillian D. Bloom sees similarities between Cather and Wharton in "On Daring to Look Back with Wharton and Cather" (*Novel*, Winter 1977). David Stouck, in "Mary Austin and Willa Cather" (*WCPMN*, No. 2, 1979), briefly compares these two western writers; Michael Peterman, in "'The Good Game': The Charm of Willa Cather's *My Ántonia* and [Canadian novelist] W. O. Mitchell's *Who Has Seen the Wind*" (*Mosaic*, Spring 1981), sees similarities between these two novels. Finally, Robert A. McGill's "Heartbreak: Western Enchantment and Western Fact in *The Professor's House*" (*SDR*, Autumn 1978) identifies the ideas of letting go with the heart and feeling the ground under one's feet as having their sources in Frost's "Wild Grapes."

Articles on Cather's debts to or comparison with writers other than American range over four national literatures. Paul Comeau, in "The Importance of *Hamlet* to Cather's *A Lost Lady*" (*MarkhamR*, Fall 1981), analyzes likenesses between Shakespeare and Cather. He starts with the epigraph from Ophelia's mad speech and explores similarities between Niel Herbert and Hamlet. The play is not Cather's novel, but Comeau notes that association with world literature was an intrinsic part of Cather's creative process. (See also V.3.b.viii under Eichorn; V.3.b.vi under Nichols). Another of Cather's literary passions, Carlyle, is the subject of two articles. Patricia L. Yongue's "Willa Cather on Heroes and Hero-Worship" (*NM*, No. 1, 1978) suggests that one of the contexts in which *Death Comes for the Archbishop* may be read is Carlyle's *On Heroes, Hero-Worship, and the Heroic in History*, for both writers believed that significant human history came through the accomplishments of great men; Meredith R. Machen's "Carlyle's Presence in *The Professor's House*" (*WAL*, Winter 1980) sees structural and thematic parallels between Cather's novel and *Sartor Resartus*. Another article by Yongue, "Marion Forrester and Moll Flanders" in *Women in Western American Literature* (ed. Helen Stauffer, Troy, N.Y., 1982), sees similarities between Defoe and Cather. Frank W. Shelton, in "The Wild Duck Image in Willa Cather and Henrik Ibsen" (*AN&Q*, Oct. 1976), discusses the different ways in which the image is used in Ibsen's play and in *O Pioneers!*

Because of Cather's passion for French literature, one might expect articles on her French connections, and there were two: Michel Gervaud's "A Note on Willa Cather and Flaubert" (*WCPMN*, Fall 1979) connects Flaubert's belief that art should *faire rêver* with Cather's concern in art for the thing felt on the page but not named; Alice B. Salo's "*The Professor's House* and *Le mannequin d'osier*: A Note on Willa Cather's Narrative Technique" (*SAF*, Autumn 1980) tentatively outlines connections between Cather and Anatole France. (See also V.1.b under Moers for George Sand; V.2.d under Gervaud; V.3.b.vii under Comeau.) Finally, Richard Chadbourne, in "Two Visions of the Prairies: Willa Cather and Gabrielle Roy" in *The New Land: Studies in a Literary Theme* (ed. Richard Chadbourne and Hallvard Dahlie, Waterloo, Ontario, 1978), compares Cather to the Canadian novelist, who also grew up on the prairie; and Catherine McLay sees similarities between *My Ántonia, A Lost Lady*, and Ethel Wilson's Canadian novel, *Hetty Dorval*, in "Ethel Wilson's Lost Lady: *Hetty Dorval* and Willa Cather" (*JCF*, 1981–82). (For a biblical analogue see V.3.a under Giannone; for a possible use of Turgenev see V.3.a under Bohlke.)

  c. Use of Classics and History. Cather's use of the classics, a subject that is still far from exhausted, provided material for four articles. An outstanding one is Donald Sutherland's "Willa Cather: The Classic Voice" (Slote and Faulkner), in which a classicist explores Greek and Latin influences on her fiction. Sutherland finds that the greatest influence is in the expressive quality of voice, the vocal mode of her fiction, which also was the classical. He compares Cather to Virgil, who also wrote of farming and of life's brevity. (See also V.1.a under Giannone.) John H. Randall III, in *Five Essays on Willa Cather* (see V.1.a), deals with "Willa Cather and the Pastoral Tradition," in which he links Cather's prairie novels to the idyls of Theocritus and the eclogues and georgics of Virgil. Paul Olson, in "The Epic and Great Plains Literature: Rolvaag, Cather, and Neihardt" (*PrS*, Spring–Summer 1981), argues for Cather's use of the *Aeneid*. An important article by John J. Murphy, "Euripides' Hippolytus and Cather's *A Lost Lady*" (*AL*, Mar. 1981), examines the Greek play as a possible source for the novel. Parallels and similarities abound, among which "Niel Herbert, the principal point-of-view figure, . . . resembles Hippolytus in temperament and outlook." The changes Cather made in Euripides, however, provide "a provocative indication of Cather's creative process." (See also V.3.b.ix under Murphy.)

  Two articles inquire into Cather's view of history. Bernice Slote's "Willa Cather and the Sense of History," in *Women, Women Writers, and the West* (ed. L. L. Lee and Merrill Lewis, Troy, N.Y., 1980), notes that Cather was concerned with truth of feeling and belief rather than literal fact so that her historical novels are only loosely accurate. James Woodress, in "Willa Cather and History" (*ArQ*, Autumn 1978), surveys Cather's interest in historical fiction and her own historical novels. He argues that she dropped her early view of history based on faith in the idea of progress (as espoused by the romantic historians) for a view of history as a series of disconnected episodes each to be dealt with separately.

d. Cather Abroad. Three papers dealing with Cather abroad were presented at the Cather Centennial and published in Slote and Faulkner's *The Art of Willa Cather.* Hiroko Sato, in "Willa Cather in Japan," summarizes Cather's reception in Japan where readers are particularly attracted to her love of nature and emphasis on family relationships and tradition. Sato followed up this essay with a book on Cather: *Cather: Bi No Saishi [Cather: A Devotee of Beauty]* (Tokyo, 1977), one of two studies of Cather written in Japanese, the other being Mamoru Ohmori's *Willa Cather no Shosetsu: Hitotsi no Ikikata no Tanyku [The Novels of Willa Cather: An Exploration of a Way of Life]* (Tokyo, 1976). Michel Gervaud, in "Willa Cather and France: Elective Affinities," considers Cather's love affair with France and French culture and French influence on her life and writings. Aldo Celli, in "Italian Perspectives," surveys Cather's references to and reception in Italy, then applies structuralist critical principles popular in Italy to her work.

e. Miscellaneous. And finally there were four miscellaneous articles on special topics. Fred Erisman's "Western Regional Writers and the Uses of Place" (*Journal of the West,* Jan. 1980) treats Cather as a western writer; Warren French, in "Directions: Additional Commentary" (Slote and Faulkner), outlines a subject that someone should study fully: the connection between Cather's art and modern painting; S. M. Bennett's "Ornament and Environment: Uses of Folklore in Willa Cather's Fiction" (*TFSB,* Sept. 1974) surveys Cather's use of folk materials from the immigrant neighbors of her childhood and from her travels in the Southwest and Quebec; Susan J. Rosowski, in "Discovering Symbolic Meaning: Teaching with Willa Cather" (*EJ,* Dec. 1982), suggests that Cather's fiction has a valuable place in the high school curriculum.

3 Individual Works

a. Stories. Although a significant portion of the Cather canon is short fiction, only a miniscule amount of critical attention in journals is devoted to her stories. (See also V.1.a under Arnold.) Of the early tales, except for a brief general essay (see V.2.b under Albertini), only "The Clemency of the Court" has elicited an article: L. Brent Bohlke's "Beginnings: Willa Cather and 'The Clemency of the Court'" (*PrS,* Summer 1974), which locates the story's probable source in a scandalous incident at the Nebraska State Penitentiary in Lincoln in 1893 and possible additional sources in stories by Turgenev. In addition to the introduction to the University of Nebraska Press's edition of *The Troll Garden* (see II), three essays appeared on stories in that collection: Larry Rubin, in "The Homosexual Motif in Willa Cather's 'Paul's Case'" (*SSF,* Spring 1975), praises Cather for making clear Paul's sexual orientation through physical description, dress, and relations with others without violating taboos of the period; the other story treated is "The Sculptor's Funeral" (see V.2.b under Bass and Cary).

Two stories from *Obscure Destinies* and one late tale have received attention. Edward J. Piacentino, in "The Agrarian Mode in Cather's 'Neighbour Rosicky'" (*MarkhamR*, Spring 1979), studies the way the images in the story connect Rosicky with the land he loves. (See also V.2.b under Martin and V.3.b.iv under Bohling.) In "Willa Cather as Psalmist" (*NDEJ*, Fall 1980), Richard Giannone argues that Psalm 23 "provides a fitting correlative" for Mrs. Harris's "pilgrimage to innocence in 'Old Mrs. Harris,'" while Sister Lucy Schneider, in "Willa Cather's 'Best Years': The Essence of Her Land Philosophy" (*MQ*, Oct. 1973), applies her special point of view to this story from *The Old Beauty and Others*. Marilyn Arnold, in "Coming, Willa Cather" (*WS*, No. 3, 1984), argues that Cather's short fiction is underrated, and in "Cather's Last Three Stories: A Testament of Life and Endurance" (*GPQ*, Fall 1984), she reads this late work perceptively, especially "The Old Beauty." (For a discussion in another context of "Eleanor's House," "On the Gull's Road," and "The Old Beauty" see V.1.c under Arnold; for "Lou the Prophet" see V.1.c under Comeau; for "The Enchanted Bluff" see V.3.b.vii under Chaliff.)

b. Novels. Many of the novels discussed in this section are also treated in the books, chapters, and articles dealt with in Sections V.1 under general criticism and V.2 under special topics. As one might expect, the novels which have received the most attention over the past decade are *My Ántonia, Death Comes for the Archbishop, The Professor's House,* and *A Lost Lady.*

i. Alexander's Bridge. Except for essays previously discussed (see II under Slote and V.2.b under Skaggs), Cather's first novel was left undisturbed through 1984 (see Supplement).

ii. O Pioneers! In "Symbolic Representation in Willa Cather's *O Pioneers!*" (*WAL*, Fall 1974), Maynard Fox shows how early scenes often foreshadow later relationships and how imagery is tied to plot "more than it is in any other Cather novel." L. Brent Bohlke sees an analogy between Alexandra's erotic dream and the vision of St. Teresa of Avila in "The Ecstasy of Alexandra Bergson" (*CLQ*, Sept. 1975). In "The Unity of Willa Cather's 'Two-Part Pastoral': Passion in *O Pioneers!*" (*SAF*, Autumn 1978), Sharon O'Brien suggests that the two stories combined in the novel are both parables about passion: Alexandra's taming of the soil is passion regulated; the deaths of Marie and Emil represent the destructive outcome of sexual passion unleashed. Bruce P. Baker II's "*O Pioneers!*: The Problem of Structure" (*GPQ*, Fall 1982) analyzes Cather's epigraph poem "Prairie Spring" as a key to the relationship between the two parts of the novel. (See also V.1.b under Murphy.)

iii. The Song of the Lark. Although there was a new printing of the 1915 edition and a textual study (see II), this novel by itself inspired only three articles. In "The Contrapuntal Complexity of Willa Cather's *The Song of the Lark*" (*MQ*, Apr. 1976), Robert Roulston sees an imagination of Wagnerian power informing the novel and shows how basic themes introduced at the outset undergo permutations like Wagnerian leitmotifs during the course of the story. Ann Moseley, in "The Dual Nature of Art in *The Song of the Lark*" (*WAL*, Spring 1979), argues that the Dionysian-Apollonian polarities of passion and discipline are internalized in Thea Kronborg and their balance is the key to her artistic success. David Stineback examines the novel in "No Stone Unturned: Popular Versus Professional Evaluations" (*Prospects*, 1982).

iv. My Ántonia. A wide variety of topics interested critics of this novel. John J. Murphy, in "The Respectable Romantic and the Unwed Mother: Class Consciousness in *My Ántonia*" (*CLQ*, Sept. 1973), suggests that "Jim Burden's inability to rise above class distinctions renders the novel a hauntingly sad testimony to the unfulfilled potential of Jim Burden and the American West." Mary E. Rucker's "Prospective Focus in *My Ántonia*" (*ArQ*, Winter 1973) concentrates on Jim Burden, who moves from a childhood desire to merge with nature to an adult desire for "love and community" and back to the early impulse. Her emphasis is not on Jim's memory but on the conflicts of his growing up. A more important article is James E. Miller, Jr.'s "*My Ántonia* and The American Dream" (*PrS*, Summer 1974), which argues that Jim Burden's failure to find happiness as an adult is another example, like Jay Gatsby's, in American literature of the failure of the American dream.

One of the best recent articles on this novel is Evelyn Helmick's "The Mysteries of Ántonia" (*MQ*, Jan. 1976), which gives a mythic reading. Cather's ability to evoke strong responses lies in the conscious connection of her art with the eternal themes of myth. This Helmick demonstrates with examples. Floyd C. Watkins, in a chapter on *My Ántonia* in *In Time and Place: Some Origins of American Fiction* (Athens, Ga., 1977), studies the Nebraska landscape and the ethnic backgrounds of the immigrants in the novel. He believes that landscape determines culture and shapes lives. Two short articles concerned with literary conventions are "The Iconography of Vice in Willa Cather's *My Ántonia*" (*CLQ*, June 1978) by Evelyn H. Haller, which argues that the minor characters are described not so much in terms of personality as in terms of morality, and "Renaissance Pastoral Conventions and the Ending of *My Ántonia*" (*MarkhamR*, Fall 1978) by Richard C. Harris, who compares the enclosure of fence and hedges of Ántonia's orchard in Book 5 with the sort of geography found in Renaissance pastorals. This implies that Jim in the end finds peace, not loss. Edward J. Piacentino analyzes through imagery the way Cather carries out her precept that "in writing novels as in poetry the

thing, the feeling is everything." In "Another Angle of Willa
rtistic Prism: Impressionistic Character Portraiture in *My Án-*
america IX, 1982), he is mainly concerned with Ántonia and
ormer defined by images of earth, the latter by images of light.

rticles on *My Ántonia* appeared in 1983. Charlotte Goodman's
"The ᴸᵒˢᵗ Brother, the Twin: Women Novelists and the Male-Female
Double *Bildungsroman*" (*Novel*, Fall) finds Cather's novel a lament that a
single person cannot experience the maternal fulfillment of Ántonia and
the intellectual attainments of Jim Burden. Mary Kemper Sternshein's
"The Land of Nebraska and Ántonia Shimerda" (*HK*, Spring) sees the
setting of *My Ántonia* as paralleling and foreshadowing the growth of
the heroine. Paul Schlach's "Russian Wolves in Folktales and Literature
of the Plains: A Question of Origins" (*GPQ*, Spring) assigns the wolf
story in the novel to the folklore of the Germans who emigrated to
America from Russia. Finally, Beth Bohling, in "The Husband of *My
Ántonia*" (*WAL*, May 1984), gathers biographical data on John Pavelka,
the prototype of Anton Cuzak and Neighbour Rosicky, and compares
the fictional treatment in this novel and the story from *Obscure Destinies*.
(See also IV under Stouck, V.2.a under Lambert, and V.2.b under
Murphy.)

v. One of Ours. There were four articles on this novel. Marilyn Arnold's
"Willa Cather's Losing Battle" (*WAL*, Fall 1978) sees it as a failure because
of the weak protagonist for whom no clear values are provided. Claude
glorifies war because it frees him from the bonds of a materialistic society,
but because Cather makes clear that war is a false ideal Claude emerges
a pathetic victim. John J. Murphy, in "*One of Ours* as American
Naturalism" (*GPQ*, Fall 1982), discusses the novel as Cather's only attempt to deal directly with large contemporary issues within the tradition
of American realism and naturalism. Jean Schwind, in "The 'Beautiful'
War in *One of Ours*" (*MFS*, Spring 1984), argues convincingly that deni-
grators of the novel incorrectly assume Claude's romantic illusions are
Cather's, that the ending, though brief, makes clear Cather's final view
of the war is deeply pessimistic. Frederick T. Griffiths, a classics scholar,
in "The Woman Warrior: Willa Cather and *One of Ours*" (*WS*, No. 3,
1984), reads the novel as Cather's recasting of classical and medieval
myth to reflect her female consciousness. (See also V.1.c under Comeau.)

vi. A Lost Lady. Another good essay by Evelyn Helmick, "The Broken
World: Medievalism in *A Lost Lady*" (*Renascence*, Autumn 1975; reprinted
in Murphy), continues her study of myth and archetypes. Here she
shows how Cather's treatment of the Midwest has parallels with the
decline of feudal society and how the novel has the characteristics of a
courtly romance. Dalma H. Brunauer, in "The Problem of Point of View
in *A Lost Lady*" (*Renascence*, Autumn 1975), argues that Niel Herbert is
blind to love and that Marian Forrester is only "lost" in the eyes of the
prudish Niel. Eugénie L. Hamner, in "Affirmations in Willa Cather's

A Lost Lady" (*MQ*, Apr. 1976), believes that Captain Forrester's values survive because both Niel and the captain accept rather than judge Marian's behavior. A clearer argument is found in Susan J. Rosowski's "Willa Cather's *A Lost Lady*: The Paradoxes of Change" (*Novel*, Fall 1977), which argues that the theme is human adaptation to change and shows how Marian's flexibility allows her to move forward while Niel's pride and idealism threaten to isolate him from the present. In "Willa Cather's *A Lost Lady*: Art Versus the Closing Frontier" (*GPR*, Fall 1982), Rosowski analyzes the tensions between possibility and loss on the frontier, as reflected in the novel. (See also Rosowski's *The Voyage Perilous*.)

The relation between Niel and Marian also interests Anneliese H. Smith in "Finding Marian Forrester: A Restorative Reading of Cather's *A Lost Lady*" (*CLQ*, Dec. 1978). Smith finds Marian repeatedly betrayed by male ignorance and self-interest, including that of the point-of-view character Niel. Kathleen L. Nichols's "The Celibate Male in *A Lost Lady*: The Unreliable Center of Consciousness" (*RFI*, No. 1, 1978; reprinted in Murphy) is a Freudian reading, which argues that Niel views Marian as a surrogate mother and accordingly is dismayed and embittered by the revelation of her sexual nature. Nichols shows that oedipal conflict is central to the allusions in the novel, particularly from *Hamlet*.

Two articles on *A Lost Lady* appeared in the *Women's Studies* special Cather issue (No. 3, 1984). Nancy Morrow, in "Willa Cather's *A Lost Lady* and the Nineteenth Century Novel of Adultery," finds the frequent comparisons of the novel to *Madame Bovary* not very appropriate. Where Flaubert (and also Tolstoy in *Anna Karenina*) were concerned with moral issues and the impact of adultery on family stability, Cather went in another direction. She chose "a narrative situation laden with moral implications" but refused to address moral questions in traditional ways. "In *A Lost Lady* she has, in a sense, 'unfurnished' the nineteenth century adultery novel of its moral purpose." Diane Cousineau, in "Division and Difference in *A Lost Lady*," draws on Jacques Lacan to explain the effect of a discontinuity she sees between the authorial stance and the central male consciousness of Niel Herbert. (See also discussions of this novel in V.2.b under Comeau, V.2.c under Murphy.)

vii. The Professor's House. Critics never tire of writing on this novel. Hardly a year goes by without at least one article on this novel. David C. Stineback's "Willa Cather's Ironic Masterpiece" (*ArQ*, Winter 1973) argues that it is Cather's renunciation of nostalgia, that the professor, in order to survive, must give up his idea of the past embodied in Tom Outland for the dull realities of the present represented by Augusta. This article is reprinted in Stineback's *Shifting World: Social Change and Nostalgia in the American Novel* (Lewisburg, Pa., 1976). In "The Function of Structure in Cather's *The Professor's House*" (*CLQ*, Sept. 1975), Marilyn Arnold examines the three parts of the novel as dramatizing a conflict between society and solitude. Barbara Wild, in " 'The Thing Not Named' in *The Professor's House*" (*WAL*, Winter 1978), believes the novel's deep theme is the friendship between Tom Outland and St. Peter. She thinks the relationship of Christ and Peter may have been in Cather's mind. On the other hand, Cynthia Chaliff, in "The Art of Willa Cather's Craft" (*PLL*, Winter 1978), writes perceptively that *The Professor's House*, whose form has bothered critics, is the culmination of Cather's method of linking two stories that fired her imagination. She traces this method back to "The Enchanted Bluff" and concludes that "one stratagem of unconscious disguise that occurs frequently in [Cather's] work is the omitted connection between the two plots that go to make up her story."

Two articles deal with the novel in terms of painting. Patricia L. Yongue's "Willa Cather's *The Professor's House* and Dutch Genre Painting" (*Renascence*, Spring 1979) relates scenes in the novel to different types and periods of Dutch art, and L. Brent Bohlke's "Godfrey St. Peter and Eugene Delacroix: A Portrait of the Artist in *The Professor's House*" (*WAL*, May 1982) argues from parallels found in Delacroix's journal that the French artist may have been the prototype of the professor. In two other articles, Missy D. Kubitschek, in "St. Peter and the World All before Him" (*WAL*, May 1982), reads both the professor's and Tom Outland's stories as Edenic myths in which the protagonists have to adapt to a post-lapsarian world, and John J. Murphy, in "The Mesa Verde Story and Cather's Tom Outland's Story" (*NMAL*, Spring 1981), compares the historical account of the discovery of Mesa Verde and Cather's alteration of the facts for artistic purposes. (See also V.2.b under Machen, Yongue, McGill, and Salo.)

Glen Lich, in "Tom Outland: A Central Problem" (*SwAL*, No. 1, 1982), concludes that young Tom is the ordering principle of the novel, and Margaret Doane, in "The Reliability of Godfrey St. Peter: Self-Knowledge and Isolation in *The Professor's House*" (*SwAL*, No. 2, 1983), sees the isolation of the professor and Tom as essential for their self-knowledge and return to the human family. Doane, in another article, "A Defense of Lillian St. Peter: Men's Perceptions of Women in *The Professor's House*" (*WAL*, Feb. 1984), catalogues many disparaging comments on women to conclude that Cather makes anti-female bias a dominant characteristic of the novel, and James C. Work's "Confounded Conundrums in *The Professor's House*" (*WAL*, Feb. 1984) is a spoof on Cather's novel in the manner of Twain's "Fenimore Cooper's Literary Offenses." James F. Maxfield, in "Strategies of Self-Deception in Willa Cather's *Professor's House* [sic]" (*SNNTS*, Spring 1984), challenges Leon Edel's view that the professor's alienation can best be explained in terms of Cather's biography. He believes that there is adequate motivation in the novel to account for the professor's rejection of life.

Paul Comeau, in "*The Professor's House* and Anatole France" (Murphy), has used the four references in the novel to Anatole France "to show how they function in the professor's story, how they are artfully incorporated into Tom Outland's narrative, and how they finally serve as a psychological and emotional annotation to St. Peter's brush with death at the end of the book." This is a significant article. Doris Grumbach, in "The Room in *The Professor's House*" (*WS*, No. 3, 1984), explains the professor's problem in terms of "his late and blinding realization that the life he had been leading, the life of father and husband, is, and always has been, a false one for him, that his existence within these roles is no longer bearable." Finally, it should be noted that Leon Edel's psychoanalytic reading of the novel originally published in *Literary Biography* (1957) has been revised with new material added in *The Stuff of Sleep and Dreams: Experiments in Literary Psychology* (New York, 1982; reprinted in Murphy). The new material previously had been omitted "out of deference to the wishes of the late Edith Lewis."

viii. My Mortal Enemy. A handful of articles on this novel appeared in the mid-1970s, but it was neglected from 1978 until 1986. Harry Eichorn's "A Falling Out with Love: *My Mortal Enemy*" (*CLQ*, Sept. 1973; reprinted in Murphy) analyzes ably the references to Shakespeare and Bellini's *Norma*. The former allow Cather to "bypass Nellie and to see into the mind of Myra Henshawe herself." For Nellie, Myra "suggests . . . the tragic heroine of an Italian opera." Shakespeare is used to reveal the life that Myra would have liked, Bellini to suggest the life that Nellie would have preferred for her. Elizabeth Gates Whalley, in "Willa Cather's *My Mortal Enemy*" (*PrS*, Summer 1974), argues that the novel's purpose is "to show the tragedy of the misspent life where love did not last." She sees, as other critics have previously, something of Cather herself in Myra.

Dalma H. Brunauer and June D. Klamecki, in "Myra Henshawe's Mortal Enemy" (*C&L*, Fall 1975), look at style, imagery, point of view, and characterization to conclude that Myra is her own enemy. The most recent essays are Susan J. Rosowski's "Narrative Technique in Cather's *My Mortal Enemy*" (*JNT*, Spring 1978), which traces the way the romantic myth of young Myra gives way in the eyes of the narrator to the older, disillusioned woman of the ending, and Michael W. Murphy's "Willa Cather's Mortal Affirmation" (*Greyfriar*, 1978), which argues that the novel is not the reflection of Cather's pessimism that some critics have seen. Rather it is another treatment of a central theme in Cather's work: the influence of the past on the present, in this case "the devastating allurement of a sentimentalized past." (See also Supplement.)

ix. Death Comes for the Archbishop. The novel that Cather thought her best is a perennial source of interest to critics. Mary-Ann and David Stouck, in "Art and Religion in *Death Comes for the Archbishop*" (*ArQ*, Winter 1973), suggest that the vision informing the novel is the "renunciation of earthly power and ambition" and that in the latter part of her career Cather saw religion and religious art as the only possible sources of enduring happiness. David Stouck's essay, "Willa Cather's Last Four

Books" (*Novel*, Fall 1973), is subsumed in his book (see V.1). Another chapter in *In Time and Place* (see V.3.b.iv) is devoted to this novel, in which Floyd C. Watkins explores the authenticity of Cather's materials and shows that, though sometimes she alters facts for artistic effect, her story is based on actual geography, history, and culture. A very significant contribution to the study of this novel is found in John J. Murphy's "Willa Cather's Archbishop: A Western and Classical Perspective" (*WAL*, Aug. 1978; reprinted in Murphy). Murphy sees Father Latour as hero in both the American manner, like Natty Bumppo, and in the classical manner, like Virgil's Aeneas, "whose destiny was to shape a new culture in Italy by transplanting the home gods of Troy."

In a minor article, "The Genesis of the Prologue of *Death Comes for the Archbishop*" (*AL*, Nov. 1978), James Woodress finds a pictorial source, acknowledged by Cather, for the prologue of this novel in the French painter Jehan George Vibert's "The Missionary's Story." A tangential article is Robert F. Gish's "Paul Horgan and the Biography of Place" (*PrS*, Spring–Summer 1981), which compares the response to New Mexico of Cather and Horgan: both identified with Archbishop Lamy, who was educated in the East and felt exile in the West. Another essay linking the archbishop to Aeneas is Jeanny R. Pontrelli's "The Archetypal Hero in *Death Comes for the Archbishop*" (*HK*, Spring 1982). Pontrelli also compares the archbishop and his vicar to knights in quest of the Holy Grail.

In an article on this novel by David Stouck, "Cather's *Archbishop* and Travel Writing" (*WAL*, May 1982), the novel is set in the context of travel writing by nineteenth-century authors like Thoreau, Melville, and Howells. Its structure not only resembles the oldest form of narrative in North America, but it also is in its other-worldly aspects a journey to the next world. Ann Moseley's "The Pueblo Emergence Myth in Cather's *Death Comes for the Archbishop*" (*SwAL*, No. 1, 1982) studies the cavern scene, Indian myth, and Latour's emergence toward mystical union. Finally, Brent Bohlke's "The Spiritual Quest of Willa Cather" (*GPQ*, Fall 1984) suggests that Bishop Beecher, the Episcopal bishop of Nebraska and an old friend of Cather's, contributed partially to the portrait of the fictional archbishop.

x. Shadows on the Rock. Essays exclusively on this novel are rare—only three in the last decade and none since 1976. The most significant is John J. Murphy's "The Art of *Shadows on the Rock*" (*PrS*, Spring 1976), which compares the novel to a six-part musical composition with each book containing "all the major themes in varying degrees and developing one to its dramatic height": order, family, self-denial, the wilderness, national identity, and maturity. Dramatic intensity is achieved by interweaving comparisons and contrasts. In "The French-Canadian Connection: Willa Cather as a Canadian Writer" (*WAL*, Fall 1976; reprinted in Murphy), Benjamin George draws from the novel Canadian-American cultural contrasts. He sees Cather's concern for tradition, her view of nature as a threat to civilization, and her picture of the woodsman hero who maintains his ties to society, all as characteristics of the Canadian cultural experience. A slight article is Sister Lucy Schneider's "Permanence and Promise: Cather's *Shadows on the Rock*" (*Renascence*, Winter 1974).

xi. Lucy Gayheart. Sister Lucy Schneider also is the author of one of the four articles on this novel. "Of Land and Light: Willa Cather's *Lucy Gayheart*" (*KanQ*, Fall 1973) again applies her ideas on land philosophy (see V.1.b) to Cather's fiction. In "'Lucy's Case': An Interpretation of *Lucy Gayheart*" (*MarkhamR*, Winter 1980), John J. Murphy views the heroine as turning to art as an escape from the confines of reality. He finds it a novel about the process whereby people become symbols and legends. Paul Comeau, in "Willa Cather's *Lucy Gayheart*: A Long Perspective" (*PrS*, Spring–Summer 1981), believes that the novel is a "philosophical work in which . . . the processes of art and life are shown to be the same creative process of memory." An important essay on this novel is "Movement and Melody: The Disembodiment of Lucy Gayheart" in Blanche Gelfant's *Women Writing on America: Voices in Collage* (Hanover, N.H., 1984). Gelfant sees Cather taking the risk of using "as a pre-text for *Lucy Gayheart* the conventional love story whose traces she had tried to expunge from her earlier fiction." She hoped to effect a magical transmutation by turning the popular romance into an allegory of Romantic desire. If she failed, "her attempt was revealing, interesting, and, I believe, significant enough to warrant a serious reconsideration of the novel."

xii. Sapphira and the Slave Girl. Cather's last novel also gets sparse critical attention. In "Cather's Last Stand" (*RS*, Dec. 1975), Marilyn Arnold argues that the novel is wholly escapist and that Cather turned to her Virginia childhood as a refuge. Richard Giannone has written "Willa Cather and the Unfinished Drama of Deliverance" (*PrS*, Spring 1978), which sees the novel as a paradigm of all of Cather's fictions, which "tell the story of human striving for freedom experienced as inner wholeness." Paul Borgman, in "The Dialectic of Willa Cather's Moral Vision" (*Renascence*, Spring 1975), sees a pattern in Cather's fiction embodying Dionysian and Apollonian principles that culminates in the marriage relationship of Sapphira and Henry Colbert. Merrill M. Skaggs, in "Willa Cather's Experimental Southern Novel" (*MissQ*, Winter 1981–82), believes that "Cather returned to the scenes of her childhood in order first to assault standard literary assumptions about antebellum life, then to challenge the widely accepted stereotype of the Southern lady, and finally to try out a new . . . narrative form."

Two recent articles on Cather's final book perhaps signal a kindling of interest in *Sapphira*. Eugénie L. Hamner, in "The Unknown, Well-Known Child in Cather's Last Novel" (*WS*, No. 3, 1984), is fascinated by the conclusion of the novel in which Cather introduces herself as narrator. She speculates on why Cather did this, but believes the introduction of five-year-old Willa jeopardizes the novel's cohesiveness. Susan Rosowski, in "Willa Cather's American Gothic: *Sapphira and the Slave Girl*" (*GPQ*, Fall 1984), writes an important essay later incorporated into *The Voyage Perilous* (see V.1.a).

VI SUPPLEMENT

Although essays and notes on Cather run to several dozen per year, I will treat in this supplement only those that seem the most significant. Cather scholarship has reached such proportions that many writers don't bother to find out if their discoveries or *aperçus* have been published previously, and thus many articles replow old ground. The bulk of the recent criticism deals with single novels, but there have been some useful essays on general topics. Loretta Wasserman addressed herself to a topic that needed attention: "The Music of Time: Henri Bergson and Willa Cather" (*AL*, May 1985), in which she argues persuasively that Cather was much influenced by Bergson's ideas on unconscious memory and his two notions of time: chronological time and lived time. They are important in understanding *My Ántonia* and *The Professor's House*. John Murphy, in "Willa Cather and Religion: Highway to the World and Beyond" (*Literature and Belief*, No. 4, 1984), is concerned with scriptural dimensions of the frontier novels plus *The Professor's House, My Mortal Enemy, Death Comes for the Archbishop*, and *Shadows on the Rock*. He sees Cather moving in these works from romantic egotism to self-denial. Murphy also contributed a good essay focused on Cather's western fiction to *A Literary History of the American West* (ed. J. Golden, Fort Worth, Tex., 1987). George Dekker, in an excellent book, *The American Historical Romance* (New York, 1987), links Cather to the inaugurator of the historical genre, Sir Walter Scott. Scott and Cather, says Dekker, display moral compassion greater than any other writers.

An illuminating article on an unexpected topic is Jean Schwind's "The Benda Illustrations to *My Ántonia*: Cather's 'Silent' Supplement to Jim Burden's Narrative" (*PMLA*, Jan. 1985). Schwind argues convincingly that the stark black-and-white drawings by W. T. Benda, who knew the Midwest, provide a realistic counterpoint for Jim's romantic memoir. One of the most perceptive readers of Cather in a handful of recent articles is Merrill Maguire Skaggs, whose "*Death Comes for the Archbishop*: Cather's Mystery and Manners" (*AL*, Oct. 1985) explains Cather's ability to pull herself up after *My Mortal Enemy* and write *Death*. Skaggs argues that in the latter novel Cather for the first time successfully combined religion and art. In "A Good Girl in Her Place: Cather's *Shadows on the Rock*" (*R&L*, Autumn 1985), Skaggs finds the protagonist Cécile to be the embodiment of cultural continuity and community. A more recent article, "A Glance into *The Professor's House*: Inward and Outward Bound" (*Renascence*, Spring 1987), is an impressive reading of the novel, in which Skaggs focuses on the characters of Tom Outland and Augusta to explain the professor's midlife crisis and his salvation, the letting go with the heart, as Cather called it.

The Professor's House now has outdistanced all other Cather novels in the amount of critical exegesis. Besides Skaggs's essay, there have been at least eleven other articles devoted to this book since 1984. Among them are Thomas F. Strychacz's "The Ambiguities of Escape in Willa Cather's *The Professor's House*" (*SAF*, Spring 1986), which illustrates the complexities of the novel by arguing that many of the supposed opposites are in reality correspondences. John B. Gleason, in "The 'Case' of Willa Cather" (*WAL*, Feb. 1986), offers a rebuttal to Leon Edel's well-known psychoanalysis of the novel (see V.3.b.vii). John N. Swift's "Memory, Myth, and *The Professor's House*" (*WAL*, Feb. 1986) is a Freudian reading, and Alice Hall Petry's "In the Name of the Self: Cather's *Professor's House*" (*CLQ*, Mar. 1987) is concerned with the denouement, in which Petry sees the novel ending on a note "insistently affirmative." Two illuminating articles treating the professor and another work are David Laird's "Willa Cather and the Deceptions of Art," in *Interface: Essays on History, Myth and Art in American Literature* (ed. Daniel Royot, Montpellier, France, 1985), and Eileen T. Bender's "Pioneer or Gadgeteer: Bergsonian Metaphor in the Work of Willa Cather" (*MQ*, Autumn 1986). Laird thinks that *The Professor's House* and *My Ántonia* both show life being sacrificed to the artistic patterning of it, while Bender finds Cather opposed to technology rather than to science.

Discussions of the neglected nouvelle *My Mortal Enemy* filled most of the literary issue of the *Willa Cather Pioneer Memorial Newsletter* (Summer 1986). Five essays by John Murphy, Merrill Skaggs, Mildred Bennett, Kathryn T. Stofer, and Jean Tsien explored various dimensions of the work. For Murphy religion is the key to the story; for Skaggs the narrator is crucial. Bennett focuses on Myra's marriage, Stofer on gems and jewelry, and Tsien sees the novel as an indictment of money.

Elizabeth Ammons takes an American Studies approach in "The Engineer as Cultural Hero and Willa Cather's First Novel, *Alexander's Bridge*" (*AQ*, Winter 1986) and projects the novel against literature about engineers and the Progressive Era. Fritz Oehlschlaeger, in "Willa Cather's 'Consequences' and *Alexander's Bridge*: An Approach through R. D. Laing and Ernest Becker" (*MFS*, Summer 1986), uses the ideas of these psychoanalysts to explicate the works.

The literary number of the *Willa Cather Pioneer Memorial Newsletter* (Summer 1987) is a substantial issue with three articles on *Death Comes for the Archbishop*, one on *The Song of the Lark*, and two on Cather and possible influences. Kevin Synott, in " 'The Color of Adventure': Pictorial Dimensions in Cather's Archbishop," studies Cather's painterly techniques in the novel; Marilee Lindemann, in "Con-Quest or In-Quest? Cather's Mythic Impulse in *Death Comes for the Archbishop*," reads the novel as a feminist work that revises the traditional patriarchal formula for American romance; and Lance Larsen, in "The Howlett Basis of Vaillant and Latour's Friendship," compares the novel with W. J. Howlett's *The Life of the Right Reverend Joseph P. Machebeuf*, the book that inspired the novel. (Incidentally, this rare work was reprinted by Regis College, Denver, in 1987.) "Word Music in 'The Ancient People,' Part IV of *The Song of the Lark*" is Stephen Tatum's stylistic study of the novel to show how Cather's use of language blends visual and aural effects. Finally, Joseph Murphy, in "*Shadows on the Rock* and *To the Lighthouse*—A Bakhtinian Perspective," sees affinities between Cather and Woolf, while John Murphy, in "Cather's 'Two Friends' as a Western 'Out of the Cradle,'" finds interesting parallels between Cather's story and Whitman's poem.

O Pioneers! and *A Lost Lady* continue to get their share of critical attention. Cynthia K. Briggs, in "The Language of Flowers in *O Pioneers!*" (*WCPMN*, Summer 1986), has written a valuable guide to Cather's use of all kinds of flora in the novel. Edward J. Piacentino, in "Flower Imagery in a Willa Cather Novel" (*PVR*, Spring 1984), does a similar job for *A Lost Lady*. Bruce Baker's "From Region to the World: Two Allusions in Cather's *A Lost Lady*" (*MidAmerica*, 1986) points out references to Ovid's *Metamorphoses* and to Shakespeare's Sonnet No. 94, from which Cather quotes the last line.

Finally, there have been two recent articles on Cather's last novel: Minrose C. Gwin's essay on *Sapphira and the Slave Girl* in *Black and White Women of the Old South* (Knoxville, Tenn., 1985) and Marilyn Arnold's "'Of Human Bondage': Cather's Sub-narrative in *Sapphira and the Slave Girl*" (*MissQ*, Summer 1987). Gwin compares Cather's novel to Faulkner's *Absalom, Absalom!* in its inconsistency of character and narrative techniques. Arnold analyzes the way in which the novel operates on two levels: first as a narrative winding through stories, places, and characterizations based on Cather's memories and second as an explanation of the troublesome aspects of Cather's personal and historic Virginia. The institution of slavery is symbolic of a whole culture in bondage to its own artificial code of conduct, a code based on degrees of privilege that shackle everyone regardless of color or station.

Hart Crane

Brom Weber

I BIBLIOGRAPHY

The major, new, and henceforth essential contribution in this area is Joseph Schwartz's invaluable *Hart Crane: A Reference Guide* (Boston, 1983), which updates and expands Schwartz's *Hart Crane: An Annotated Critical Bibliography* (1970). Works dealing wholly or partially with Crane are itemized and succinctly described in chronologically ordered sections for the years 1919 through 1980. It is no discredit to this invaluable work to note that there are some minor errors—for example, Robert Creeley may be discomfited to learn that Brom Weber is cited erroneously as editor of Creeley's *A Quick Graph: Collected Notes and Essays* (San Francisco, 1970) and Weber may not be pleased either—but this gaffe and some others do not impair the book's general reliability and usefulness.

An important complementary project that Schwartz might consider undertaking (of all Crane scholars he is best prepared for it) is the compilation of a thematic index of Crane criticism from its earliest appearance in published form, with themes and sub-themes cross-referenced to poems and prose. After almost sixty years of commentary, the welter of materials and the need to be published have combined to make redundancy less discernible and originality less frequent.

Joseph Schwartz and Robert C. Schweik's "A Supplement to HART CRANE: A DESCRIPTIVE BIBLIOGRAPHY" (*HCN*, Summer 1978) updates their *Hart Crane: A Descriptive Bibliography* (Pittsburgh, Pa., 1972); both the 1972 volume and its 1978 update hereinafter will be cited as Schwartz and Schweik.

Kevin J. Harty's "Hart Crane in Translation: An Expanded Annotated Checklist" (*Visionary Company*, Spring 1982) augments Schwartz and Schweik with expanded annotations of four "volumes containing translations of Crane's poetry only . . . and adds two additional volume-length translations of Crane—one in Japanese and one in Spanish." Another item to be added to Schwartz and Schweik is Yu Kwang-Chung's translation into Chinese of "At Melville's Tomb," accompanied by Yu's commentary in Chinese, in his *Rain on the Cactus* (Taiwan, 1964, 1967). A large representative selection of Crane's poems has been translated into German by Jürgen Muck (*Akzente*, Dec. 1982).

Two concordances, each correlated with Brom Weber's edition of *The Complete Poems and Selected Letters and Prose of Hart Crane* (1966), are useful for those studying the poet's language and substance. Gary Lane's *A Concordance to the Poems of Hart Crane* (New York, 1972; hereinafter cited as Lane) and Hilton Landry, Elaine Landry, and Robert DeMott's *A Concordance to the Poems of Hart Crane* (Metuchen, N.J., 1973; hereinafter cited as Landry-DeMott) are essentially similar; for example, neither records the occurrence of frequently recurrent parts of speech such as articles and pronouns. However, the two concordances differ in some respects. Lane provides a list of "suppressed words" and Landry-DeMott a list of "words omitted or merely illustrated." These lists reveal that Landry-DeMott omit more of Crane's words than Lane; the latter also accounts for words that appear in the titles of Crane's poems and books. Finally, Lane, though not Landry-DeMott, offers a table listing the numerical frequency of words occurring in the poetry.

Books owned by Crane were scattered during his peripatetic life and afterward; many presumably are lost or tucked away in private collections. Fortunately, "154 titles in 162 volumes" in the Hart Crane Collection in the Columbia University Libraries, as well as two volumes in the Southern Illinois University Library, have been identified as Crane's and cataloged in Kenneth A. Lohf's "The Library of Hart Crane" (*Proof*, 1973). The largest number of titles (eighty-four) fall into the category of American and English language and literature, the remainder (foreign language, English translation, or English) fall into the categories of non-English language and literature (Danish, French, Greek, Italian, Russian, Spanish), the arts, history and travel, and philosophy. Lohf's bibliographical details are helpful, especially his data on Crane's annotations (writing, underscorings, check marks, etc.). However, scholars will find it necessary to scrutinize the books directly. Space limitations in *Proof* required that "significant markings, underscorings, and notations [be] enumerated . . . [only when] feasible and applicable" and, "except in a few significant instances, Crane's notations have not been quoted either in part or in full."

II EDITIONS

Three new editions of Crane's poetry have been published: (1) a reissue (1970) of the third impression of the second (New York) edition of *The Bridge* (1930), with a new introduction by Thomas A. Vogler and Waldo Frank's introduction to *The Collected Poems of Hart Crane* (1933); (2) a third impression (New York, 1972) of the first edition of *White Buildings* (1926), with the original foreword by Allen Tate and a new foreword by John

Logan; (3) a third collected edition, *The Poems of Hart Crane* (New York, 1986), edited by Marc Simon with an introduction by John Unterecker.

The Poems of Hart Crane (1986) is a "reader's edition" containing the texts of (1) *White Buildings* and (2) *The Bridge*, followed by six additional sections: (3) *"KEY WEST An Island Sheaf"*; (4) *"KEY WEST* Folder Subsection"; (5) "Poems Uncollected but Published by Crane"; (6) "Poems Unpublished by Crane"; (7) "Incomplete Works"; and (8) "Fragments." According to Simon, who is an able, assiduous editor steeped in the theory and methodology of contemporary textual scholarship, "such a sequence comes closest to how H[art] C[rane] would have intended his editor to present his extant compositions to future readers eager to have for the first time the complete canon of all his ninety-two poems (besides those in HC's two books published in his lifetime) available in one volume."

Each earlier collected edition has increased our knowledge of Crane's poetry and Marc Simon's is no exception. For example, "In a Court" was excluded from Weber's 1966 edition because, although the poem was posthumously published and attributed to Crane in the periodical *Literary America*, Weber had not found any manuscript or other independent, reliable documentary evidence of Crane's authorship. "In a Court" now is included in Simon's 1986 edition because he has discovered that the poem was "composed c. March 1924" and that Crane "had originally sent [it] to *The Dial*, which rejected it." Even so, the matter of attribution has not yet been settled definitively, for Simon has depended for copy-text upon "the only surviving version of this poem . . . namely, *Literary America*, 1 (September 1934), p. 14," to which Crane, who died in 1932, apparently had never submitted the poem.

Probably not all Crane scholars will agree with Simon's determination of the states of completion of certain poems as evidenced by their placement in one of his edition's categories (6, 7, 8) of poems unpublished by Crane. However, such questions generally had best be postponed until after publication of what Simon describes as "an already prepared variant textual edition of the poems of HC," presumably a second volume containing the edition's complete textual apparatus and other items related to the edition. It is not too early to express doubt that the self-critical Crane, whose last work submitted by him for publication shortly before his death was the dense, meticulously polished "The Broken Tower" (1932), ever would have authorized publication of most of the complete and incomplete poems, as well as fragmentary lines, in *The Poems of Hart Crane* (1986) or any other general "reader's edition" such as *White Buildings* and *The Bridge*. It is commendable biographically to "humanize" Crane and rescue him from stereotypical images of gloom and disorder, as Unterecker's introduction so vividly does, by setting forth evidence of the poet's lively comic sense, affection for family and friends, playfulness, and the like. It is an entirely different matter to present, in a "reader's edition," poems and lines that tend to encourage misconceptions of Crane's deepest literary intentions for himself and that belong, more appropriately, in a format such as the new collected edition's second volume containing data primarily of interest to scholars.

III MANUSCRIPTS AND LETTERS

Kenneth A. Lohf's *The Literary Manuscripts of Hart Crane* (1967; hereinafter cited as Lohf) has been supplemented by three new addenda. Dean H. Keller's "CALM Addendum No. 2: Hart Crane" (*PBSA*, First Quarter 1970) announces acquisition by Kent State University of the Charles Harris collection of manuscripts of "The Bridge of Estador," "For the Marriage of Faustus and Helen," and "Stark Major," none itemized in Lohf, and of Crane's letters to Harris.

In "CALM Addendum No. 3: The Literary Manuscripts of Hart Crane" (*PBSA*, First Quarter 1972), Joseph Schwartz and Robert C. Schweik argue the need for two corrections of Lohf. The first of these involves seven poems—"Echoes," "Exile," "Love and a Lamp," "Meditation," "Medusa," "Naiad of Memory," and "To Earth"—identified in Lohf as having constituted the group of seven poems sent by Crane to Charles C. Bubb in a letter dated 13 November 1918 (no. 15, *The Letters of Hart Crane, 1916–1932* [1952]). Schwartz and Schweik note that the letter implies that only six poems were transmitted and, because Crane advised Bubb that the poems had "been published mostly in the *Pagan*, one in *The Little Review* of December last," the six poems had to include "North Labrador" and probably any five other poems drawn from among nine that had been published in *The Pagan* before the letter's date. Schwartz and Schweik's reasonable speculation should be expanded to include three more possible choices, each published prior to the crucial date: "C 33," "Carmen de Boheme," and "Postscript." Another matter dealt with in "CALM Addendum No. 3" centers on Lohf's identification of "Voyages I–VI" as the manuscript version of the poems published in the *Little Review* (Spring–Summer 1926). Schwartz and Schweik question the validity of the identification. Marc Simon's "CALM Addendum No. 4: Hart Crane" (*PBSA*, First Quarter 1974) directs attention to the existence of an unpublished manuscript version of "Faustus and Helen III."

"Hart Crane Letters" (*Bancroftiana*, Feb. 1975) notes without specification that poetry manuscripts Crane sent Yvor Winters bear emendations by both men. The manuscripts have been acquired by the University of California at Berkeley. Until such time as they are listed in a new edition of Lohf, scholars can use references to them in Thomas Parkinson's *Hart Crane and Yvor Winters: Their Literary Correspondence* (Berkeley, Calif., 1978).

"The Prose Manuscripts of Hart Crane: An Editorial Portfolio" (*Proof*, 1972) is another valuable contribution by Kenneth A. Lohf. Available in it, reproduced from manuscripts in the libraries of Columbia and Southern Illinois Universities and accompanied by Lohf's expert commentary, are facsimiles of "Note on the Paintings of David Siqueiros," two versions of "A pure approach to any art . . . ," "From Haunts of Proserpine," notes and drafts of an unfinished review of Phelps Putnam's *Green River*, pages from "Vocabulary" notebook, and pages from "Note Book." At this point it is appropriate to note, belatedly, that Lohf's *The Literary Manuscripts of Hart Crane* (1967) contains facsimiles of drafts and worksheets of "Voyages II," "Ave Maria," "The River" and "Van Winkle," "Quaker Hill," "Key West," and "Euclid Avenue."

P. J. Croft's *Autograph Poetry in the English Language: Facsimiles of Original Manuscripts from the Fourteenth to the Twentieth Century* (London, 1973) provides a facsimile of a typescript and holograph worksheet of "Cape Hatteras" (not listed in Lohf), accompanied by Croft's transcript of the worksheet, commentary on Crane's method of composition, and brief analysis of Crane's handwriting as deduced from the worksheet.

Poetry not published by Crane, nor included in posthumous editions, is now available in printings from manuscripts: (1) "What Nots?" ("An Unpublished Crane Poem" [*HCN*, Winter 1977]); (2) "After Jonah" (*HCN*, Fall 1977); (3) "Supplication to the Muses on a Trying Day" (*HCN*, Fall 1977); (4) "An Untitled Poetic Fragment" (*HCN*, Summer 1978). Some of these items are manifestly works in progress; others are occasional pieces lightly dashed off which successfully embody humorous and convivial aspects of Crane's personality too often subdued by his "serious" high rhetoric and oblique imagery. "Supplication . . ." is an unfinished prose poem of special interest because it possesses some of the brilliant surrealistic associationalism of "Havana Rose" and like it probably was written in Mexico. Malcolm Cowley, in "A Response from Malcolm Cowley" (*HCN*, Summer 1978), recalls being given the manuscript after Crane's death by Peggy Baird (Cowley), Crane's companion during his last days in Mexico. Cowley believes the poem "is eloquent, fanciful, sonorous, funny, and means nothing whatsoever."

Thomas S. W. Lewis's *Letters of Hart Crane and His Family* (New York, 1974) is an ably edited complement to Brom Weber's *The Letters of Hart Crane, 1916–1932* (1952), whose editor did not have access to many of the manuscripts available to Lewis. His edition includes: (1) letters by Crane to his mother, grandmother, father, and the latter's third wife; (2) letters by Crane's relatives to him; and (3) three letters to Crane by, respectively, Waldo Frank, B. W. Huebsch, and Eugene Jolas. This collection has stimulated renewed biographical interest in Crane, and it has much of literary interest as well.

Crane's poetry first appeared in the *Little Review* in 1917 and he later served the magazine briefly as an advertising salesman. Dennis M. Read's "Hart Crane's Letters to *The Little Review*" (*BRH*, Summer 1979) is primarily a historical account of Crane's relations with the magazine's editors (Margaret Anderson and Jane Heap) which includes six previously unpublished letters Crane wrote them from 1923–29.

Crane's letters (1923–30) to Kenneth Burke, the literary critic and theorist who was Crane's long-time friend, have been edited with annotations by R[obert] Y. Zachary in *"Hart Crane to Kenneth Burke*: Ten Unpublished Letters" (*Sulfur*, No. 2, 1981). As Zachary observes, the letters are primarily of biographical interest. In one, Crane comments on Spengler's *Decline of the West* and in another expresses appreciation for comments on his poetry by Burke.

Crane's more self-revelatory letters to Wilbur Underwood (1876–1935), finally published free of previously restrictive constraints, swell the number of the poet's letters in print. Underwood befriended Crane in Washington, D.C., in 1920; the two corresponded thereafter until not long before Crane's death. Underwood's private career as a writer and his public career as a clerical-administrative bureaucrat in the State Department until 1933 are briefly reviewed in Philip K. Jason's "Wilbur Underwood: Hart Crane's Confidant" (*MarkhamR*, Feb. 1974). Underwood's posthumous *Selected Poems*, stylistically unlike Crane's poetry, was published in 1949; most of his papers, which Jason used, are housed in the Library of Congress. Because of "restrictions" imposed after Underwood's death by Philip Horton, to whom Underwood had loaned Crane's letters, and the apprehensions of others who feared that publication of the letters would be unwise because they contained potentially embarrassing and/or libelous invasions of privacy, Underwood's name and identifying references to him and certain other individuals were deleted so that some of the letters might be published even partially in *The Letters of Hart Crane, 1916–1932* (1952). "Wind-blown Flames: Letters of Hart Crane to Wilbur Underwood" (*SoR*, Apr. 1980) subsumes "A Last Letter from Mexico" (*HCN*, Spring 1979) and is an uncensored compilation of correspondence selected and edited from the collection at Yale University by Warren Herendeen and Donald G. Parker, who promise a complete collection in the future. Underwood was a stimulating friend and correspondent; some of Crane's letters to him rank with the most revealing and evocative the poet ever composed. Herendeen and Parker describe and evaluate Underwood's neglected poetry and argue that much of it, especially his early work, was "a more significant and potent influence upon Crane than . . . the poetry of Samuel B. Greenberg."

The editor of *The Letters of Hart Crane, 1916–1932* (1952), while collecting items for that volume, queried Yvor Winters (1900–68) about whether he possessed any letters Crane had written him. Winters replied that the letters had been burned. Consequently, only one of Crane's letters to Winters (29 May 1927), a carbon copy of which Crane had preserved in his files, appeared in the collection. According to Thomas Parkinson's impressive *Hart Crane and Yvor Winters: Their Literary Corre-*

spondence (Berkeley, Calif., 1978), immolation at Winters's behest was the fate not only of letters sent to Winters, but also of letters he himself wrote to others. Fortunately, Winters was mistaken about Crane's case, for most of the letters, poetry manuscripts, and other materials Crane sent Winters actually survived. A substantial number of extant documents composed from mid-1926 until late in January 1930 were acquired from the Winters estate by the University of California at Berkeley ("Hart Crane Letters" [*Bancroftiana*, Feb. 1975]). Ironically, none of Winters's letters to Crane are known to have survived. Forty-eight of Crane's letters from the Winters collection, woven together by Parkinson into a judicious and informative literary-historical chronicle, appear in *Hart Crane and Yvor Winters: Their Literary Correspondence*, which subsumes Parkinson's "The Hart Crane-Yvor Winters Correspondence" (*OhR*, Fall 1974), "Hart Crane and Yvor Winters: A Meeting of Minds" (*SR*, July 1975), and "Hart Crane and Yvor Winters" (*SR*, Apr. 1976). As a collection, they provide a firm basis for reexamining one of Crane's most vital literary friendships and also reveal his literary intelligence and self-awareness at keen heights.

"'My dear Father': An Unpublished Crane Letter" (*HCN*, Winter 1977) discusses and prints a letter to Crane's father, dated 1 April 1917, in which Crane writes reassuringly of his serious preparations for entering Columbia University and of his postponement of "versifying" for "the future." An eloquent letter dated 19 January 1923 from Crane to poet-anthologist Louis Untermeyer appears in Richard Allan Davison's "Hart Crane, Louis Untermeyer, and T. S. Eliot: A New Crane Letter" (*AL*, Mar. 1972). Davison provides a helpful context for the letter, wherein Crane sets forth his aesthetic aims and ambivalent attitude to Eliot. Crane's discussion of his letter will be found in his subsequent letter of 6 February 1923 to Gorham Munson. Crane wrote an angry letter on 4 June 1930 to Yvor Winters after reading the latter's review of *The Bridge*. Crane accused Winters of misreading, "misrepresentation," "exaggeration," and "public" reversal of private opinions expressed in Winters's letters to Crane. The letter, whose manuscript location is not given, appears for the first time in Vivian Pemberton's "Hart Crane and Yvor Winters, Rebuttal and Review: A New Crane Letter" (*AL*, May 1978).

Crane's admiration for Washington A. Roebling, the engineer chiefly responsible for successful construction of the Brooklyn Bridge, led him to send Washington's son John A. Roebling a copy of *The Bridge* and a letter dated 18 August 1930 ("'In Hommage to' the Roeblings: An Unpublished Letter" [*HCN*, Spring 1979]). Crane wrote that his "devotion to the Brooklyn Bridge as the matchless symbol of America and its destiny" had inspired the poem "which, in its way, is as ambitious and complicated as was the original engineering project." An enthusiastic letter by Margaret Shippen Roebling acknowledging Crane's gift is included in Vivian Pemberton's "The Roebling Response to Hart Crane's

The Bridge" (*OQ*, Winter 1977). A biographically important letter written by Crane in Mexico on 17 February 1932 to Bessie M. Crane, his step-mother, has hitherto been available only in part. Vivian H. Pemberton's "'On the side of Life': A 'Lost' Letter Fragment" (*HCN*, Summer 1978) prints the letter in toto.

IV BIOGRAPHY

"An Interview with Philip C. Horton" (*HCN*, Spring 1979), by Warren Herendeen and Donald G. Parker, is informative about the writer of the first book devoted wholly to Crane (*Hart Crane: The Life of an American Poet* [1937]), the genesis of the work, and many of his Crane-related thoughts and feelings. Horton's accounts and judgments of Crane's mother, father, and friends (Lorna Dietz, Emil Opffer, Peggy Babcock, Peggy Cowley) whom Horton encountered or learned about during the writing of his biography are vivid, his responses to his interlocutors candid, and their questions and responses acute.

Carol Schloss, in "The Lives of Hart Crane: Revision of Biography" (*Biography*, Spring 1980), compares Philip Horton's *Hart Crane: The Life of An American Poet* (1937) and John Unterecker's *Voyager: A Life of Hart Crane* (1969) in order to consider some theoretic and analytic problems of biography. Though Crane is not Shloss's primary concern, her scrutiny of both books is specific and will alert their readers to the imaginative nature of biographical exposition, the essentially different though at times similar Crane patterns which the two biographies proffer, and the consequences of those patterns for subsequent Crane criticism and scholarship. Shloss's explicit and implicit "cultural assumptions" make her more sympathetic to Unterecker's book than to Horton's, but she writes equitably about both.

Vivian H. Pemberton's "'Broken Intervals'—The Continuing Biography of Hart Crane" (*Visionary Company*, Spring 1982) announces her discovery of "previously unpublished letters, memorabilia and photographs" and "new information" which she believes will help her "correct some misconceptions and provide some fresh perceptions of Crane's life and works." Some of her discoveries and revisions have appeared earlier in print (see III and IV), appear to be preliminary unveilings of a larger work in progress, and proffer revelations of varying importance and accuracy. In "Broken Intervals . . ." (see above), she "correct[s] some misconceptions" in Crane books by Philip Horton (1937), Brom Weber (1948), and John Unterecker (1969), as well as in shorter works by others.

A stage in Crane's continuing metamorphosis as cultural symbol is revealed in Peter J. Sheehan's "Hart Crane and the Contemporary Search" (*EJ*, Dec. 1971), which postulates that Crane, many of whose works are liked by students, is relevant for classroom study "at a time of great cultural unrest such as America is now experiencing. . . . Crane was a rebel who attempted to go beyond those social limits of his time which grieved him in order to find its lasting values, delineate and celebrate them, and then establish their rhythm as a pattern for succeeding generations." Crane is especially useful for pedagogy because "he chose to cop out, as our students put it, by committing suicide. If our students can be shown the tremendous creative gifts that Crane possessed, as well as their attendant problems, they can come to realize that copping out is a disastrous waste of the unique and sometimes painful wonder which each person possesses."

Crane's steeping in William James's *Varieties of Religious Experience* and the issue of Crane's mysticism are explored further in Victor Strandberg's "Hart Crane and William James: The Psychology of Mysticism" (*McNR*, 1975–76). Strandberg holds that "the central feature of Crane's poetic vision [is] his mysticism" and that James's book provides an important "understanding" of Crane's mysticism and its effects on his "poems— their relation to psychedelic stimuli, their fire and water imagery, their mood of mingled fear and welcome towards annihilation of the ego, and above all, their striving to express monistic insight." Of the poems discussed by Strandberg, "Possessions" receives most attention. Strandberg also suggests that James's comments on religious "conversions and backslidings" enable us to comprehend "Crane's tragic end" within the process of mystical experience.

It is now generally believed that Crane wrote "The Broken Tower" in Mexico in 1932, not long before he died, though in the 1930s there were some who thought the poem had been created earlier. Because "The Broken Tower" is one of his most masterful poems, conclusively dating the poem as a 1932 piece strengthens the argument that, contrary to Crane's own belief and the assertions of some critics, he had not lost all his poetic powers after completing *The Bridge*. Vivian H. Pemberton's "The Composition of 'The Broken Tower'" (*HCN*, Spring 1979) provides hitherto unpublished evidence (two postcards mailed by Crane in Mexico on 27 January 1932) that the bell-tower experience which generated composition of "The Broken Tower" occurred in 1932.

Carol Johnson's "Hart Crane's Unimproved Infancy," in *The Disappearance of Literature* (Amsterdam, 1980), acknowledges the poet's "authentic and superior gifts—he was at least Keats' equal—but [proceeds] to suggest how such gifts failed to issue in more nearly perfect poems" such as "At Melville's Tomb" and "Voyages." Because neither Crane's parents nor society helped nurture him to a stage of satisfactory selfhood, "obliterating" rather than "expanding [his] consciousness" became Crane's dominant behavioral pattern in life as well as in art: "Crane employed poetry . . . in the simplest romantic mode: to escape an indelible psychic reality, to embrace a fantasmal alternative, an abstract ideal of 'absolute beauty.'" However, "wanting to be a public poet when his material was so intensely private was his greatest mistake," for the "compulsive and priggish optimism" with which he conceived and executed *The Bridge* sustained neither the poem nor the poet.

After publication of John Unterecker's biography, as well as a resurgence of critical interest in psychologically oriented modes of literary study, it was inevitable that concern with Crane's role as an important figure in American literary history would be augmented by an interest in elucidating and evaluating his formative familial and midwestern backgrounds. Vivian H. Pemberton has been the leading figure in this recent development. In "Hart Crane's Heritage," included in *Artful Thunder: Versions of the Romantic Tradition* (ed. Robert J. DeMott and Sanford E. Marovitz, Kent, Ohio, 1975), and "Hart Crane's Ancestor, Ohio's Poet of Politics: Jason Streator" (*OQ*, Summer 1976), Pemberton compensates for what she believes has been insufficient attention by Crane's biographers to his familial and regional backgrounds, with consequent unawareness of their significant relevancy to his initial interest in the arts and his subsequent growth as a literary artist. Not all of Pemberton's data is new, and she is more attentive to the paternal (Crane) side of the poet's family than to the maternal (Hart) side, but she succeeds in illuminating the cultural contexts which positively nurtured Crane's youthful aestheticism. Many of his family members "seem to have been active, publicly and privately, in cultural activities" such as the practice and appreciation of literature, music, visual art, and drama, though none of Crane's familial ancestors or contemporaries ever achieved more than local fame or were avant-gardists. Some were writers and journalists; an aunt, Alice Crane Williams, was a composer, teacher, and performer of music who apparently inspired "The Fernery," which Pemberton explicates. She also reveals that the originals of some of the geographical and other physical details in "The Dance" can be traced back to the Garrettsville, Ohio, locale in which Crane was born and to which he frequently returned in his youth. In "Poetry and Portraits" (*HCN*, Fall 1977), Pemberton discusses Crane's friendship with his maternal cousin Helen Hart Hurlbert (whom he often visited when in Ohio) and prints an unpublished letter (20 Sept. 1931) he wrote from Mexico to Mrs. Hurlbert and her husband. Pemberton's "Bessie Crane Hise (1893–1977)" (*HCN*, Summer 1978) is an obituary of Crane's last stepmother and "the last surviving member of [his] immediate family."

Francis O. Mattson's "Hart Crane and Roy Campbell" (*BNYPL*, 1972) corrects a misconception that the Campbell family offended Crane so gravely during his 1929 visit at their Martigues, France, home that Crane, after two weeks, fled the Campbell ménage under mysterious circumstances. Two documents—an unpublished Campbell letter "written close to the event" and an unpublished carbon typescript of Campbell's autobiography, as well as the published autobiography (*Light on a Dark Horse*, London, 1951) itself—have led Mattson to conclude that the

Campbells apparently were so embarrassed and annoyed by Crane's sexual sorties, unrestrained drunkenness, and chauvinistic boasting that they compelled him to leave for nearby Marseille after only one week.

Alfred Galpin's "A Boat in the Tower: Rimbaud in Cleveland, 1922" (*Renascence*, Autumn 1972) contends that Crane read French adequately, though not fluently, with the aid of a French-English dictionary, and recounts Galpin's friendship with Crane in Cleveland, Ohio, during the summer of 1922, when the two young men "discussed or read together . . . French poetry from Victor Hugo to Rimbaud." Galpin praises Crane's "Locutions des Pierrots" as "light verse which is not too unworthy of the light originals [of Laforgue]" and seeks to demonstrate that, after 1922, Crane was more than superficially acquainted with Rimbaud's poetry in the original French as well as in English translation. Galpin's article would have been more definitive if he had made use of Crane's volumes of French materials now in Columbia University.

Until an extended study of Crane's long, intimate friendship with Allen Tate appears—there should be one comparable to Thomas Parkinson's of the Crane-Winters friendship—Radcliffe Squires's *Allen Tate: A Literary Biography* (New York, 1971) and *The Literary Correspondence of Donald Davidson and Allen Tate* (ed. John Tyree Fain and Thomas Daniel Young, Athens, Ga., 1974) will fill some of the gap. Particularly interesting in the latter volume is Tate's letter of 24 March 1927, to Davidson, which sympathetically elucidates lines from "For the Marriage of Faustus and Helen" whose "meanings" Davidson's review of *White Buildings* (*Nashville Tennessean*, 3 Apr. 1927) had declared were "insoluble."

Malcolm Cowley's *A Second Flowering: Works and Days of the Lost Generation* (New York, 1973) offers the most comprehensive account he has yet published of his long friendship (1923–31) with Crane. Though some of the material has appeared in Cowley's earlier writings, he here weaves new and old details together with great verve. The few pages on Crane in Cowley's *–And I Worked at the Writer's Trade: Chapters of Literary History, 1918–1978* (New York, 1978) fuse materials from his "Hart Crane: The Evidence in the Case" (*SR*, Mar. 1970) and "Laforgue in America: A Testimony" (*SR*, Winter 1963).

The posthumously published *Memoirs of Waldo Frank*, edited by Alan Trachtenberg (Amherst, Mass., 1973), disappointingly fails to provide the full story of Frank's long, intimate association with Crane. In addition, Frank's critical remarks do not significantly augment his earlier discussions of the poet beyond an assertion that Crane had veered politically to Communism while in Mexico. Frank's chapter on Crane is part of a section of the manuscript which, the editor advises, Frank left "incomplete and unrevised."

In 1923 and 1924, novelist John Dos Passos lived in the same Brooklyn rooming house inhabited by Crane, and the latter's letters indicate that he and Dos Passos had mutual friends. Townsend Ludington's *John Dos*

Passos: A Twentieth-Century Odyssey (New York, 1980) indicates that the men became "good friends," but does not provide enough information about the friendship. Dos Passos "tried to calm" Crane during his "emotional, often alcoholic, frenzies" and "urge[d] him to go home to bed instead of roaming, as Crane frequently did."

Crane's friendship with poet-critic Yvor Winters is placed in a proper perspective in Dick Davis's *Wisdom and Wilderness: The Achievement of Yvor Winters* (Athens, Ga., 1983) which subsumes "Turning Metaphysician: Winters' Change of Direction" (*SoR*, Oct. 1981). Davis emphasizes that Winters's progressive changes of critical attitude to Crane were neither capricious nor malevolent. Instead, Winters's movement from full approbation to approbation mixed with negation reflected Winters's own development as a poet and critic who initially had been sympathetic to Imagism and "a pantheistic and ecstatic ideology," then rejected them both and finally embraced a moralism which led him to use "Crane's work, life, and death" as the core of a "moral tract . . . warn[ing] against the dangers" of Crane's "beliefs" while not repressing "admiration for Crane's having had the courage of his convictions, his 'sanctity'" in carrying out the logical (for Crane) act of suicide. In the same publication (*SoR*, Oct. 1981) in which the extract from Davis's book appeared, John Baxter's joint review of *The Collected Poems of Yvor Winters* (Manchester, 1978) and Thomas Parkinson's *Hart Crane and Yvor Winters: Their Literary Correspondence* (Berkeley, Calif., 1978) stresses what unmodified emphasis on their final rupture may obscure, namely, that the two writers had similar concerns and enjoyed a profound "collaboration."

One of Crane's earliest young literary friends, whom he met in New York in 1919, is the subject of David E. Shi's candid *Matthew Josephson: Bourgeois Bohemian* (New Haven, Conn., 1981). Shi makes good use of Crane's letters to help round out the portrait of a literary modernist of the 1920s and, in turn, provides other materials helpful for evaluation of Crane's judgments of Josephson. Shi also offers an amusing account of Crane's imbroglio with James Thurber at a party.

Alan M. Wald's *The Revolutionary Imagination: The Poetry and Politics of John B. Wheelwright and Sherry Mangan* (Chapel Hill, N.C., 1983) contains scattered references to Wheelwright's conjunctions with Crane during the 1920s. Wald believes that modernist writers such as "Eliot, Pound, Crane, Joyce, and others were never unconcerned with the public world; their tendency was to aestheticize their social views, transforming political realities into private languages, myths, and symbolic paradigms that were intellectually more manageable for them."

Crane met Harry and Caresse Crosby in France in January 1929 and, though *The Bridge* was still in progress, the wealthy young couple undertook to publish his poem under their Black Sun Press imprint as soon as it was completed. After Harry Crosby's suicide in December 1929, the first edition (Paris, 1930) of *The Bridge* was published under Caresse Crosby's direction. Harry Crosby, a poet of lesser accomplishment than Crane, expressed his admiration for the latter's writing and made other references to Crane in his diaries, now available in a new edition, edited by Edward Germain (*Shadows of the Sun*, Santa Barbara, Calif., 1977), who claims his text for the year 1929 is more reliable than that of the edition published earlier (Paris, 1930). Crosby's diary entries provide informative background for Crane's "To the Cloud Juggler," the memorial poem for Harry Crosby; Caresse Crosby's autobiography, *The Passionate Years* (New York, 1953), is similarly helpful. Sy Kahn, in "Hart Crane and Harry Crosby: A Transit of Poets" (*JML*, No. 1, 1970), concludes that, despite minor differences between poet and patron, their professional and personal relations were based on important literary, intellectual, and emotional parallels and similarities. Geoffrey Wolff, in *Black Sun: The Brief Transit and Violent Eclipse of Harry Crosby* (New York, 1976), is more critical of Harry Crosby than Sy Kahn and offers less reverent portrayals of both Crosbys.

Though Crane had many friends who, like Waldo Frank, helped him emotionally, financially, and otherwise during the years devoted to the writing of *The Bridge*, its first edition (Paris, 1930) was dedicated to financier and philanthropist Otto H. Kahn, whose patronage of Crane is noted in Frank's *Memoirs* (1973). Frank, who seems to have known Kahn fairly well, portrays him as "an American Maecenas" who decried "banking," supported "radical and aesthetically revolutionary plays," and predicted that the demise of capitalism would occur in the early 1980s, "a true gentlemen" who "was no lover of the 'Genteel Tradition'" . . . an "entrepreneur" of whom one "had only to see the gleam of his cool blue eyes, to watch his blunt, powerful acquisitive hands to know that he knew exactly what he was doing." Kahn's impact on Crane is explored in Gregory R. Zeck's "'The Chan's Great Continent': Otto Kahn and the Bridge" (*MarkhamR*, Summer 1978) and Miriam Fuchs's "Poet & Patron: Hart Crane & Otto Kahn" (*BForum*, No. 1, 1982). From December 1925 through April 1930 Kahn intermittently gave Crane cash gifts amounting to $2400 (Zeck) and possibly $2600 (Fuchs). Fuchs does not cite Zeck's earlier article; unlike him, she cites Kahn's files, housed in Princeton University, which contain correspondence to and from Kahn, Crane, and the latter's mother.

Both Zeck and Fuchs agree, to cite the latter, that "encouragement was denied [Crane] from family as well as from those in a position to judge his work and to reward him with payment or publication," that Kahn's largesse filled the vacuum, and that Crane used Kahn's generosity to compensate for what Crane regarded as familial hostility and neglect. Zeck probes Crane's mind and behavior more profoundly than Fuchs, who is more concerned with the issue of art patronage. Highlighting some of the subtle ways in which Crane's "Ave Maria" poetically acknowledges the poet's indebtedness to his patron, Zeck freshly enlarges our understanding of Crane's artistry, most notably his skilled punning. Fuchs reveals that, according to documents in Kahn's files, the banker maintained an increasingly cool distance from Crane as the latter's requests for funds became more importunate. Crane, apparently stung by Kahn's perfunctory, business-like, abstract remarks about his poetry, pleaded unsuccessfully with Kahn for specific responses; Kahn also managed to resist Crane's plea for a weekly stipend of $25. However, Kahn graciously recommended Crane as a worthy candidate for a Guggenheim Fellowship.

Acknowledging that "both Philip Horton and John Unterecker, in their biographies of Crane, have described [the] relationship [between Crane and Emil Opffer] and analyzed its effect on Crane's life and poetry, [so that] the main outlines of it seem quite well established at this point," Helge Normann Nilsen, in "Memories of Hart Crane: A Talk with Emil Opffer" (*HCN*, Summer 1978), freshly expands existing knowledge with his sensitive report of a meeting and conversation with Opffer in Denmark. The latter, born in 1896, was "nearly eighty-two" at the time. Additional biographical information about Opffer and Crane will be found in Alex Gildzen's "A Walk in the Starlight: Emil Opffer and James Broughton" (*Visionary Company*, Spring 1982), which quotes from the Broughton papers in the Kent State University Libraries.

Malcolm Cowley has written brief, personal obituaries of three of Crane's friends: "Matthew Josephson (1899–1978)" and "Hannah Josephson (1900–1976)" (*HCN*, Summer 1978), and "A Memorial" for Susan Jenkins Brown (*Visionary Company*, Spring 1982). Deference to Ms. Brown's wishes had led the editor of *The Letters of Hart Crane, 1916–1932* (1952) reluctantly to omit identification of the addressees of letters written to her and William Slater Brown.

Lincoln Kirstein ("Crane and Carlsen: A Memoir, 1926–1934" [*Raritan*, Winter 1982]) admittedly "never knew Crane personally" and apparently saw him mostly at large social gatherings. However, Kirstein was familiar with Crane's poetry, had participated in *Hound & Horn*'s editorial rejection of "The Tunnel" (which Kirstein now regrets), and knew a number of Crane's acquaintances (including Walker Evans, E. E. Cummings, Archibald MacLeish, Allen Tate). During this period, Kirstein became intimate with an obscure friend of Crane's named Carl Carlsen (ex-seaman, unsuccessful writer, Crane's great admirer, "chum" of Eugene O'Neill and the brothers Emil and Ivan Opffer), to whom most of Kirstein's candid, animated memoir is devoted. Kirstein conveys a vivid sense of the atmospherics of Crane's life in New York City during the late 1920s and early 1930s. Kirstein is more favorably inclined to Crane's poetry in 1982 than he was then, especially impressed with Crane's "alchemy of the word" which Kirstein believes has made Crane superior in "verbal" power to all Americans "before or since." According to Kirstein, the "roots" of Crane's "dysfunction, tension, torment, terror, and hysteria" were twofold: first, "Cleveland," the locus of his divided parents and his father's Philistinism; second, the religion of Crane's mother, "Christian Science," which encouraged him to "embrace a stupendous falsity: Cleveland, Chagrin Falls, according to Christian Science, don't exist, . . . [the kind of] denial [that] precipitates a terrible burden on the vulnerable lyric mechanism through the solipsism of unmeasured fantasy."

The following art by Crane has been reproduced: (1) portrait of Samuel Loveman, in "'Sam Loveman from Hart Crane': A Drawing by Hart Crane" (*HCN*, Winter 1977); (2) portrait of Susan Jenkins Brown (*Visionary Company*, Spring 1982); (3) a portrait, presumably of Paul Rosenfeld (originally published in the *Little Review* for Winter 1922) in Dennis Read's "Hart Crane's Letters to *The Little Review*" (*BRH*, Winter 1979 and *Visionary Company*, Spring 1982).

The Ohio painter whose work Crane championed ("Bill" in the poem "Sunday Morning Apples") is recalled, with some references to the poet, in Philip Kaplan's "'Look for the Miracle!' Some Early Memories of William Sommer, From 1924 to 1936" (*Serif*, June 1971). Sommer's portrait of Crane appears in the *Hart Crane Newsletter* (Winter 1977).

Painter Peter Blume's 1976 comments about Crane are presented in Slater Brown's "A Letter from Peter Blume" (*HCN*, Winter 1977). "A Letter from Peter Blume" (*HCN*, Summer 1978) gives the painter's recollections of Crane in Connecticut and Brooklyn from mid-1929 through early 1931. Warren Herendeen and Donald G. Parker, in "Commentary" (*HCN*, Fall 1977), discuss Crane's involvement with Blume and the latter's painting, "Parade," which is reproduced on the cover of the *Hart Crane Newsletter* (Fall 1977).

A major American photographer's relations with Crane and mutual friends and associates are documented and analyzed in Robert E. Haines's *The Inner Eye of Alfred Stieglitz* (Washington, D.C., 1982), which subsumes "Alfred Stieglitz and the New Order of Consciousness in American Literature" (*PCP*, Apr. 1971). Crane was a member of a briefly unified, informal group of writers—Sherwood Anderson, Waldo Frank, Gorham Munson, Paul Rosenfeld, Jean Toomer—who in the early 1920s espoused varieties of romantic nationalism and were inspired by Stieglitz's artistry, ideas, and enthusiasm. Stieglitz's photographs excited Crane's admiration, and he began a never-completed essay on Stieglitz's art. They corresponded intermittently but warmly, most frequently during the early 1920s; Stieglitz generously and non-critically praised Crane's poetry, thereby greatly bolstering the latter's self-confidence.

V CRITICISM

1 About Crane Criticism

Eugene Paul Nassar, in *The Rape of Cinderella: Essays in Literary Continuity* (Bloomington, Ind., 1970), uses Crane didactically in his last two chapters to illustrate the vagaries of some modern criticism. In the penultimate chapter analyzing *The Bridge* (see below), Nassar aims to show that true "criticism" is that action which "is concerned with evaluation of the continuity of tone of an author's work by a critic who uses as his basis of judgment the unique body of attitudes created in the work." In his last chapter, Nassar sharply evaluates other "critiques" of *The Bridge* in order to distinguish "criticism" and its practice from "metacriticism," defined as "the assessment of the view of life of a work or its author by a critic who uses as his basis of judgment his own or other views of life." Nassar believes that most critics of Crane and *The Bridge* have been metacritics in critical disguise, thus susceptible to the lure of non-literary, interdisciplinary areas and the interpretation of poetry "through biography, letters, history of ideas, philosophy, psychology, religion, sociology, etc.," whereas the true critic must "read only the poem till you feel you have caught its central attitudes, its tone."

Karl T. Piculin's "The Critics and Hart Crane's THE BRIDGE: An Interview with John Unterecker" (*HCN*, Summer 1978) is an animated conversation between generally like-minded critics who, after noting and explaining the regrettable errors perpetrated by other critics who have misunderstood or misrepresented Crane and *The Bridge*, compensatorily provide the salvational basis for forming correct responses to the poet and the work. *The Bridge* is here regarded as if it were a divine work received and sung by a gifted but helpless mortal, one not always more competent to understand the nature of his work than his earliest critics, most of whom were inadequate because they practiced New Criticism or other questionable forms of criticism.

Joseph Schwartz's "The Recognition of Hart Crane, 1916–1934" (*Visionary Company*, Spring 1982) is the first comprehensive review of Crane's literary reputation and covers the years 1916–34. Schwartz dispels many misunderstandings, for he has exhaustively scrutinized "notices, articles, and reviews in periodicals and newspapers of the time . . . [and] criticism of Crane's work found in contemporaneous books and anthologies—in short, everything published in his lifetime . . . concerned with his reputation as a writer and in immediate response to his work." It appears that Crane was highly appreciated during his lifetime and "managed to publish without much difficulty almost everything he submitted." Schwartz establishes several stages in the constant expansion of Crane's literary prestige: (1) "By the fall of 1922 . . . had a reputation as a minor poet"; (2) at age 25 (1924) "regarded . . . as a significant, emerging poet"; (3) despite some "reservations about obscurity," reviews of *White Buildings* (1927) were predominantly favorable and "few first volumes of poetry of our major writers have had a better initial reception"; (4) with the publication of *The Bridge* (1930), had "'arrived' as a standard American poet"; (5) at the time of his death (1932), was acknowledged to be "a major American poet." Schwartz's study incorporates such pertinent matters as Crane's responses to negative and mixed criticism, objective judgments about classic critical reviews of Crane which sparked literary controversies, and sensible observations about misconceptions such as the critical neglect of *White Buildings*.

2 Collections

Two volumes of collected critical documents are available: David R. Clark's *Critical Essays on Hart Crane* (CEAmL, Boston, 1982; hereinafter cited as Clark) and Alan Trachtenberg's *Hart Crane: A Collection of Critical Essays* (TCV, Englewood Cliffs, N.J., 1982; hereinafter cited as Trachtenberg). All items in Trachtenberg are reprints; Clark contains two hitherto unpublished selections by Mary Jean Butts and Donald Pease. There is some overlap—the same early pieces by Allen Tate (1926), Yvor Winters (1930), and Waldo Frank (1933) appear in both—but otherwise the contents are different. Each provides some relatively inaccessible printed materials, Elliott Carter in Clark and William Carlos Williams and Derek Savage in Trachtenberg. For what they contain, both volumes are useful and eliminate the time and expense involved in acquiring separate copies of their contents. However, in view of continuing critical argument over general and particular aspects of Crane's achievement, an ideal collection of critical documents might well be structured differently than either of these two collections. Editors, of course, have every right to manifest their critical biases; the contents and structures of both Clark and Trachtenberg generate the impression that, after critical negations of Crane in the 1920s, 1930s, and 1940s, a shift to affirmation occurred and there now exists only a yea-saying critical consensus. The impression created is erroneous because, although the post-1940s assuredly witnessed an increase in the number of critics who extol Crane's poetry, commentary with serious reservations about Crane's achievement and poetics continued (and continues) to appear. Under the circumstances, convenient and inexpensive though one-volume compilations may be, those concerned with developing rounded perspectives on any aspect of Crane scholarship and criticism must supplement Clark and Trachtenberg with extensive scrutiny of unrepresented materials. Fortunately, these operations are easily managed with the aid of Joseph Schwartz's annotated critical bibliography (1983; see I).

3 General

a. Full-length Studies. Sherman Paul's *Hart's Bridge* (Urbana, Ill., 1972), which subsumes "Lyricism and Modernism: The Example of Hart Crane" in *English Symposium Papers III* (Fredonia, N.Y., 1972), recounts the history of Crane's self in the process of adjustment to increasing differentiation between itself and the external world. Paul believes that Crane's "imagination" was not "religious or visionary . . . ; for him the poem is not to be judged by anything external to it: its form is organic in the primary sense of self-originating and its 'truth' is nothing absolute but the coherence of meanings generated by its 'language.'" Accordingly, Paul offers phenomenological readings of Crane's poetry, though he does not ignore his prose and the criticism evoked by his poetry. Crane's milieu and biography also receive limited attention, the former all too often as tantalizing speculations which Paul fails to support or probe. Paul reads Crane's poetry and prose *"admiratively"* and *"vigilantly,"* informing us that the first term comes from Gaston Bachelard, who proposed "'the maxim of our admirative critique of poets; admire first, then you will understand.'" *Hart's Bridge*, not unexpectedly, is a work of generously enthusiastic approbation which does not always specify the bases for meanings assigned to poetic lines and phrases. Regrettably, generosity and literary history sometimes are abandoned when Paul considers the poetry's treatment by critics. Nonetheless, it is stimulating to read Paul's view of Crane as a radical American modernist similar to Williams, of Crane's "logic of metaphor" as "Cubist" rather than "symbolist . . . not used to evoke a reality beyond the senses but to present an object clearly to the senses by way of simultaneous perspectives of meaning." These and other insights, however, will be most enriching to a reader who comes equipped with a rather full preliminary knowledge of Crane's poetry and prose, as well as of the critical literature devoted to it since the mid-1920s.

M. D. Uroff's *Hart Crane: The Patterns of His Poetry* (Urbana, Ill., 1974) is a lucid, major work which bypasses Crane's biography and his poetry's critical history to focus wholly on his poetic art. This proves to be a productive approach because the special drama of the poet's brief life and the widely diverse judgments aroused by his poetry have generated a critical literature which, in varying degree, often has generated as many misconceptions as it had hoped to clear away. Probably because Uroff deals with all of Crane's poetry, she is the first critic to have explored in depth Crane's uncollected West Indian poems as the unified group he intended them to be. She interestingly organizes her book on the principle that "it is impossible to separate Crane's poetry into strict periods and to regard *The Bridge* as his mature work for which the lyrics [collected in *White Buildings* and left uncollected at his death] were the preparation." Having discerned that there "are certain imaginative patterns that are repeated throughout his poetry and thus may be said to typify it," Uroff traces the interrelated flow of five different, yet related, imaginative patterns and their subpatterns: "violence," "possession," "flight," "stasis," and "mastery." The results splendidly illumine difficult poems for, as Uroff puts it, Crane "uses particular words, images, and metaphors again and again, and rearticulates whole patterns. These recurrent elements in his work reveal the coherence as well as the complexity of his imaginative activity." Nor, as it happens, does Uroff slight *The Bridge*: "Crane's earliest critics assumed that his long poem lacked a logical framework, but they missed the imaginative framework evident in his poetry as a whole."

Samuel Hazo's *Smithereened Apart: A Critique of Hart Crane* (Athens, Ohio, 1977) is a reprint, with new preface and updated bibliography, of Hazo's *Hart Crane: An Introduction and Interpretation* (1963).

Robert Combs, in *Vision of the Voyage: Hart Crane and the Psychology of Romanticism* (Memphis, 1978), argues that Crane was not a visionary "poet-priest," a "heroic redeemer" bringing a "special Truth, a Word" to this world from some world "beyond," rather a Romantic, to wit, a Hegelian phenomenologist who nondogmatically scrutinized the normative psychological and intellectual explanations with which society and the individual organize and control experience. Unlike Romantic idealists, however, Crane did not search for ideal forms. Instead, he concerned himself with human existence and the process of scrutinizing it; he aimed "in his poetry to dissolve the objectivity of experience, its thing-quality, by assuming a relentlessly self-critical attitude toward his own perceptions and feelings." Thus, in consistency with Crane's mindset, he resolved matters in the mode of Romantic irony as, for example, in "The Broken Tower" (Combs does not discuss any of Crane's other uncollected poems). In the second and third parts of *Vision of the Voyage*, Combs, with his theory of Crane's particular romanticism always in the foreground, explicates *White Buildings* and *The Bridge* and attempts to elucidate Crane's poetics. Combs's explications, like his book itself, are dominated by his overwhelming desire to explore and confirm his theory of Crane's romanticism; explications too often are not correlated with earlier critical explications nor is Combs exhaustive. He does respond overtly to earlier judgments of the poetry when they conflict with his own ideas. Ironically, an ideological straightjacket such as Combs pictures Crane trying to escape from seems to confine Combs himself.

b. Shorter Studies. Crane's relation to Symbolism is intensively analyzed and evaluated in James L. Kugel's *The Techniques of Strangeness in Symbolist Poetry* (New Haven, Conn., 1971). Kugel believes that Eliot and Pound, and those like Crane whom they influenced, did not comprise a neo-Symbolist school nor did they share with "'traditional' Symbolist aesthetic . . . many of its preoccupations: anti-Positivism, the German idealistic thinkers, the inroads of science and technology on the modern world." Furthermore, reversing "Symbolism's disregard for the reader," Crane and other modernists actually were concerned with the existence and nature of an audience for their works. Nevertheless, Kugel persuasively argues, these modernist poets derived "the stylistic basis of their writing" from Symbolism.

What Crane did with language, why, and the outcome are major concerns in Crane studies. Arthur Oberg, in "The Modern British and American Lyric: What Will Suffice" (*PLL*, Winter 1972), observes that Crane, like other modern lyric poets (for example, Eliot, Pound, Stevens, Williams), was "dissatisf[ied] with the limits of human language." Invoking "the purer arts of music, dance, and painting," Crane created an "imagery of the machine and of language (grammar, syntax, speech) [that] draws attention to the image-making process in the most basic sense of questioning whether any image can suffice." The cumulative progression of images, though it establishes patterns, finally "is one of imagistic profusion and extremity threatening the integrity of the work."

Edwin Fussell contends in *Lucifer in Harness: American Meter, Metaphor, and Diction* (Princeton, N.J., 1973) that Crane, unlike Whitman, Eliot, and Pound, failed to resolve "his linguistic problem" adequately. Like Bryant in the early nineteenth century, a conservative Crane chose to embrace English poetic tradition, isolating himself "from the radical tradition of American poetry, dialectic and pluralism." His poetry is riddled with Emerson and Dickinson's poetic weaknesses and vices instead of Whitman's virtues. However, "at his simplest, Crane can write with absolute perfection, as in the final stanza of 'Praise for an Urn.'" Fussell himself writes with colloquial Poundian verve as he objects to such matters as Crane's "nominalistic" rhetoric, his "perpetual Emersonian metaphorical fussing with the single word, [his] over-strained mixing of metaphors in the British mode."

Yvor Winters's published comments on Crane, in sources other than his own books, are conveniently available in the posthumous *Yvor Winters: Uncollected Essays and Reviews* (ed. Francis Murphy, Chicago, 1973). Included are Winters's classic reviews (1927 and 1930, respectively) of *White Buildings* and *The Bridge*, as well as other statements. Winters's judgments about Crane are cursorily outlined in less than one page of René Wellek's extensive review of Winter's critical theories and practice ("Yvor Winters Rehearsed and Reconsidered" [*DQ*, Autumn 1975]), which Wellek pithily summarizes as follows: "Winters admired Crane greatly but considered him the prime example of the corrupting influence of Emerson and Whitman logically leading to madness and suicide." For evidence, Wellek relies almost entirely upon Winters's "The Significance of *The Bridge* by Hart Crane, or What Are We to Think of Professor X?," the concluding section of Winters's *In Defense of Reason* (1947). This essay is also explored, painstakingly and lengthily, in Richard J. Sexton's *The Complex of Yvor Winters' Criticism* (The Hague, 1973). Sexton reminds us that the essay deals not only with Crane, but also with then "current practices in the teaching of literature in American higher education," that is, proponents of Emerson and Whitman avoid the logical consequences of Emersonian-Whitmanian doctrines while encouraging others to emulate Crane's example. Those who have not read the essay will find Sexton's *explication de texte* an enlightening introduction to the intellectual qualities which Winters brought to bear upon what, for him, was a painfully personal issue as well as a symbol of crucial flaws in American culture.

Crane is accorded incisive yet comprehensive consideration in Donald Barlow Stauffer's *A Short History of American Poetry* (New York, 1974), which says that Crane's "tortured career" and "visionary poetry" reflect "two aspects of the American romantic tradition": (1) Poe's concept of "pure poetry" created by one who finds himself "in a fallen world" to which he is hostile, from which he is alienated, and from which he finds relief by exacerbating his senses with "various stimulants," and (2) "a Whitmanesque vision of spiritual fulfillment through a mystical belief in man's ability to transform himself into a transcendent being." Stauffer analyzes several poems in *White Buildings* and compares "Voyages" with *The Bridge*, then concludes that "'Voyages' is not an exercise in preparation for *The Bridge*; it confronts more directly and without that poem's added complexities of history, modern technology, and epic aspiration the central issue of Crane's mature work: the transcendence of space and time and the union of love and poetic vision in the one redeeming Word." However, Stauffer praises *The Bridge* for "the greatness of many of its incomparably brilliant passages" despite the "static . . . inert" nature of its central symbol, its "formlessness," and its "failure . . . to achieve an impossible goal," i.e., "transform modern America into a self-defining and self-sustaining myth."

Dougald McMillan's *"transition": The History of a Literary Era, 1927–1938* (London, 1975; New York, 1976) devotes a chapter to Crane as a major *transition* figure like Beckett, Stein, and Joyce, and other chapters to aesthetic theories and movements such as surrealism, expressionism, dadaism, and verticalism with which Crane was familiar and his poetry demonstrates affinities. McMillan also recounts the history of *transition*'s favorable critical treatment and frequent publication of Crane's poetry and traces similarities between the "American romanticism" of Crane's ideas and those of Eugene Jolas, *transition*'s founding editor who introduced Crane to his patrons Harry and Caresse Crosby.

Richard Strier's "The Poetics of Surrender: An Exposition and Critique of New Critical Poetics" (*CritI*, Autumn 1975) uses the example of Crane's "logic of metaphor" theory to explore the implications of New Criticism upon those who, like Crane, were its conscious or unconscious adherents. Strier argues persuasively that Crane's New Critical belief in explication as the proper way in which to read his poetry often encouraged him to write poetry in which "the absence of a clear syntax leaves *all* the meaning of a poem or passage potential; richness replaces definiteness and the images . . . become heaps of meaning to which their specific words in particular positions is almost irrelevant. The result is a poetry . . . supremely eloquent and fundamentally inarticulate: it must be explicated to speak." Strier demonstrates that this is the case of "At Melville's Tomb." On the other hand, Strier argues that Crane's "logic of metaphor" is applicable to "Voyages II," whose explication supports the validity of Crane's poetic theory.

Unlike Strier, John T. Irwin ("Naming Names: Hart Crane's Logic of Metaphor" [*SoR*, Apr. 1975]) holds that Crane's "logic of metaphor" poetry is not vitiated because of its dependence upon explication. Crane's "aristocratic" poetics and his propensity for nominalization properly require explication by an "experienced reader," for "in Crane the principal thrust of metaphor is the production, on the level of surface form, of elliptical noun phrases or complex names, new words with which to create in the poem a new embodiment of the imaginative logos." Despite its seemingly elitist linguistic complexity, the poetry creates a "counterworld" with radical implications: "For Crane, the absolute of the imagination is reached by dissolving the preconceptions embodied in traditional linguistic structure. This human imaginative order that opposes itself to the moral chaos of the external world is then in turn embodied in the associative structure of the poem. This opposing of the ordered world of the poem to the chaotic external world forms the central meaning of both *The Bridge* and 'Voyages.'"

Paul Ramsey's deeply pondered evaluation, "The Biding Place: Reflections on Hart Crane" (*Parnassus*, Fall–Winter 1976), concludes that, despite weaknesses, Crane is "a major poet" because of his remarkable artistry and his "magnificent romantic lyrics" which have an enduring, "profound, evocative, resonating, unifying effect." Crane (in "O Carib Isle!") achieved "one of the greatest visions in twentieth-century poetry of moral and metaphysical evil." Nevertheless, after considering poems embodying Crane's religious vision, Ramsey qualifies his general judgment: Crane's "poetry [is] primarily of experience rather than understanding." This characteristic, in Ramsey's opinion, damages *The Bridge* as also does the "lack of transition between sections." Crane's "belief that suffering precedes and somehow leads to salvation (holiness, reconciliation, joy) . . . is a major structural element" of the work, but the poem's two crucial final sections do not complete the pattern. Nevertheless, as a set of lyric "poems rather than a fulfilled poem," five of *The Bridge*-poems ("To Brooklyn Bridge," "Ave Maria," "The River," "The Dance," and "Cutty Sark") "alone would entitle Crane to rank with the best American poets."

Though Crane's indebtedness to poet Samuel B. Greenberg (1893–

1917) led Philip Horton in the 1930s to rescue Greenberg from general obscurity, Crane plays a relatively small role in Marc Simon's *Samuel Greenberg, Hart Crane and the Lost Manuscripts* (Atlantic Highlands, N.J., 1978), which subsumes "Hart Crane and Samuel B. Greenberg: An Emblematic Interlude" (*ConL*, Spring 1971) and "Hart Crane's 'Greenberg Mss' and the Launching of 'Voyages II'" (*JML*, Sept. 1976). However, Simon's study of the life, sensibility, and poetry of Greenberg, a Jewish-American immigrant who lived in New York City, is an important contribution to American sociocultural history. Of the book's 149 pages, many given over to voluminous documentation, about a third of the text usefully assembles existing knowledge of the origins, progress, and results of the Greenberg-Crane connection and extends it somewhat. The history of Greenberg's manuscripts, from which Crane made typescripts for himself in the 1920s, is recounted exhaustively. The poems Crane selected are helpfully presented in a twenty-three-page appendix.

Three psychologically oriented studies by Eric J. Sundquist, Gregory R. Zeck, and David Bleich fruitfully explore correlations between Crane's life and work of the kind he indignantly deplored when Gorham B. Munson first found them critically useful in the mid-1920s. Sundquist's "Bringing Home the Word: Magic, Lies, and Silence in Hart Crane" (*ELH*, Summer 1977) reconstructs Crane's quest for the "Word," that is, (1) the cultural "tradition" that would redeem "the fallen American community in which an insane American technology has usurped the poetic throne of belief," and (2) the personal genealogy that would "locate and stabilize" him. Sundquist's complex prose follows the quester's consciousness to its journey's end: "When Crane found his bringing *home* of the Word to be the endlessly criminal plundering of an authority which fell apart in his hands, the only possible scene of an original, unindebted performance had to become the exultant suicide of silence."

Gregory Zeck's "Identity and Form in Hart Crane" (*MichA*, Summer 1978) argues that Crane's inability "to synthesize the male and female elements of [his] human identity" and his "ambivalence toward the values of his culture" saddled him with a life-long identity crisis that harmed both his life and his poetry. Neglecting the open-form poetry of Whitman, ostensibly one of his masters, Crane developed a defensive, closed form which exalted "respectable masculine intellect," repressed "feminine" feeling, and concealed homosexuality, thus obscuring his troubled self from the world in "obscure poetry." But this proved not to be an escape for Crane. Because he "[felt] his interior [metaphoric] language and homosexual love as a mystical experience," they might have enabled him to transcend his predicament. But "he was a divided mystic at best. . . . *The Bridge* ends in radical anxiety, [a] transcendence hysterically declared but not completed. . . . [which] comes to represent the confusion rather than the synthesis of America and its sexual roles."

At the end, the "tight and untrusting form" of "The Broken Tower" foiled Crane's attempt to celebrate his newly acquired heterosexuality and his "more inclusive identity based on trust and love."

David Bleich's "Symbolmaking and Suicide: Hart Crane (1899–1932)" (*HSL*, Nos. 1, 2, 3, 1978) argues that Crane's poetry is explicable, but no explication can be profoundly perceptive unless supported by perceptive knowledge of his life. Bleich expounds the increasingly common bivalent view of the life as an extreme case of psychosocial agony that brought him to an early death, of the poetry as the vehicle of his imagination's therapeutic power. The argument hinges on Bleich's subsumption of the poetic process within the general symbolmaking process, which for most people "begins in infancy with the onset of syntactical language and *psychologically serves the function of climaxing and realizing the process of self-object differentiation.*" Early growth of Crane's self-awareness was stunted by destructive parental behavior, later growth by self-destructive, narcissistic defense mechanisms including a poetry which at times was unable to help him maintain psychic health.

Allen Grossman's "Hart Crane and Poetry: A Consideration of Crane's Intense Poetics with Reference to 'The Return'" (*ELH*, Winter 1981) admittedly "is in accord with the analyses" in the essays of Irwin, Sundquist, and Bleich noted above, "but differs . . . in its interpretation." Like these writers, Grossman believes that the fact of Crane's suicide is symptomatic of the failure of his life, but does not mean that his poetry also failed. Grossman probes the relation further by suggesting that Crane's suicide was a form of creative self-birthing consonant with his central poetic theme: "Crane's subject was the establishment, not of culture, but of existence itself, the reconstruction of the primal scene with the intention of undoing the dismemberment of birth by the 'transmemberment' of song which traces 'the visionary company of love' back to the hurricane kiss of beginning (which might be any moment of experience)—and then to begin again. There will be 'a new threshold' (a new birth) and 'a new anatomy' (a new body)." Grossman argues at length that Crane was neither a modern nor an experimental poet. Instead, he was part of the Miltonic "high style" tradition.

Crane's relation to the Miltonic tradition is reviewed in "Influence for the Worse? Hart Crane Rethinks Milton" (*Visionary Company*, Spring 1982) by John T. Shawcross, who believes "Crane became part of the Miltonic stream of poetry by his acceptance of his role as *vates*." In 1921, Crane expressed dislike of Milton. However, Shawcross notes that "the subject matter, the diction, the language, and the metric of [Crane's] poem on Eve ['Garden Abstract' (1920)] are Miltonic" and that "*Paradise Lost* is there in the fabric of Crane's ['For the Marriage of Faustus and Helen' (1923)], in its fundament, and in its language." Even so, Shawcross says, a more significant sign of Crane's indebtedness to Milton is that, like him, Crane neither rejected tradition nor followed it slavishly.

He holds that *The Bridge* has been misunderstood by "myopic" critics who write "opaque criticism" of the kind in which one discovers "that even *Paradise Lost* has been labelled an antiepic." He contends *The Bridge* is an epic with "a mixed form, *genera mista*, with all the implications for structure, tone, characteristics, style that the term *genre* predicates"; he makes his point with an unpersuasive explication of the oft-disparaged "Indiana" as a well-conceived, well-executed poem contributing effectively to the success of *The Bridge*.

According to Bernard Duffey, in *Poetry in America: Expression and Its Values in the Times of Bryant, Whitman, and Pound* (Durham, N.C., 1978), Crane "alter[ed] a . . . traditional sense of transcendence into verbal or aesthetic intricacy . . . that moved toward the transforming of experience by language . . . [and resulted in] an experience or even a testimony of revelation . . . without definite substance." There is a profusion of action "verbs and verbal nouns" in Crane's poetry "in contrast to the plainer noun predominance and reliance on linking verbs in Pound and Eliot." Crane's poetics and linguistic preference served him well in "Voyages," but not equally well in *The Bridge*.

Robert K. Martin's *The Homosexual Tradition in American Literature* (Austin, Tex., 1979) demonstrates in a candid, impressive chapter that Crane's homosexuality played a central role in his life and work. Martin carefully traces the extent to which the juvenile and mature poetry, from "C 33" through later poems, including *The Bridge*, is striated with two dominant themes: "a strong, almost obsessive belief in the miraculous powers of love, and a sense of despair brought on by the impossibility of experiencing that love" freely and fully as a homosexual. Martin believes that only in two poems was Crane able to articulate the "full spiritual relationship" he sought: cryptically in the "Voyages" sequence dealing with his love affair with Emil Opffer, openly in "Cape Hatteras," centered on Whitman. John T. Shawcross's "A Note on 'The Bridge'" (*HCN*, Fall 1977) anticipates Martin by noting that "Cape Hatteras" marks Crane's public assumption of his homosexual role and, Shawcross argues, is linguistically and thematically indebted to the idea of bridging Whitman had expressed overtly and metaphorically in "A Noiseless, Patient Spider," a poem not cited by Martin.

Several critics have concerned themselves, in depth, with visual and kinetic elements in Crane's poetry. George Knox's "Crane and Stella: Conjunction of Painterly and Poetic Worlds" (*TSLL*, Winter 1971) augments earlier accounts of the poet's and painter's interaction with additional detail. Knox notes that their aesthetic mutuality and different arts were interestingly celebrated in Robert Indiana's *The Bridge* (1964), a "four-paneled" work: "Each of the four diamond panels has an image of the Brooklyn Bridge (adapted from Stella's versions) enclosed in a circle . . . each circular image (enclosed in a diamond) has a line from Crane's *The Bridge* written around the bottom arc."

Crane also responded with great enthusiasm to his conjunction with Alfred Stieglitz's "photographic" aesthetics because, as F. Richard Thomas demonstrates in "Hart Crane, Alfred Stieglitz, and Camera Photography" (*CentR*, Summer 1977), the photographer's prints embodied and invigorated tendencies of Crane's that survived as important characteristics of his literary aesthetics. A virtue of Thomas's article is its critical attention to some generally neglected poems: "The Bridge of Estador," "Garden Abstract," "Episode of Hands," and "Moment Fugue."

Robert K. Martin ("Painting and Primitivism: Hart Crane and the Development of an American Expressionist Esthetic" [*Mosaic*, Winter 1981]) makes a strong case for the hypothesis that it was the visual arts which moved Crane's poetry "away from Impressionism and toward Expressionism, giving new form to his Symbolist bent in the search for 'spiritual harmony.'" Among contributory factors Martin adduces were Crane's knowledge of post-Impressionist aesthetic criticism, his familiarity with Expressionist visual art, theater, and music, and probably also the special influence of Expressionist painter Marsden Hartley, whom Crane may have met in the early 1920s and whom he subsequently met intermittently. Martin speculates that Hartley's poetry, which is inferior to Crane's, may have influenced the latter's "attempt to render the material of American experience from an Expressionist perspective" in works such as "The Dance." The kinetic energy in that poem was matched by Crane's life and by the dancing which he liked to engage in as well as to observe. Audrey T. Rodgers, in *The Universal Drum: Dance Imagery in the Poetry of Eliot, Crane, Roethke, and Williams* (University Park, Pa., 1979), synthesizes an interesting, coherent portrait of Crane's interest in the kinetic as expressed in his life, letters, and poetry.

David E. Lavery's brief, phenomenological "The Eye as Inspiration in Modern Poetry" (*NOR*, Winter 1981) notes that though Crane, on the one hand, implied in his poetry that "inspiration springs from the movements of the physical eye," on the other hand he also, contradictorily, asserted in prose that vision was attainable only in a state of ecstatic, mystical transcendence.

William H. Pritchard's *Lives of the Modern Poets* (New York, 1980) is more concerned with poetry than with biography. He is aware that "with the exception of Robinson's work . . . there is less agreement about the importance and success of Hart Crane's poetry than about that of any other poet [Hardy, Yeats, Frost, Pound, Eliot, Stevens, Williams] considered" in the book. Accordingly, Pritchard's chapter on Crane mediates between "admirers" prone to "ecstatic affirmations and approvals" and "detractors, or at least nonsupporters—cold and sober." Acknowledging his indebtedness to Warner Berthoff's view "that for the most part Crane's poems do not have a narrative structure, even though there are moments of narrative in *The Bridge*," Pritchard argues, with the aid of perceptive readings, "that Crane's virtues are such as ask to be admired in lines and passages, rather than in whole, sequential poems." He proposes a moratorium on the question of whether or not *The Bridge* fails or succeeds if judgment depends on the presence or absence of coherence, for this criterion is not particularly pertinent in an epoch in which such dubiously coherent poems as Williams's *Paterson* and Pound's *Cantos* also were created.

Crane is neither in Whitman's visionary tradition nor in Blake's, according to Hyatt Howe Waggoner (*American Visionary Poetry* [Baton Rouge, La., 1982]). Crane achieved vision and beauty in "Voyages II," "Voyages VI," "Cape Hatteras," and other sections of *The Bridge*, but not in the latter as a whole and not too often in other poems. Waggoner says several factors led Crane often to envision, but only rarely to vision: fear and distrust of reality, disordering of the senses, lack of secular or religious belief, and a "pervasively oxymoronic style" which "denies meaning."

Harold Bloom, in "Hart Crane's Gnosis" (*Agon: Towards a Theory of Revisionism*, New York, 1982), which subsumes "Hart Crane's Gnosis" (*Akzente*, Dec. 1982), regards Crane as "a prophet of American Orphism, of the Emersonian and Whitmanian Native Strain in our national literature," and studies him from that perspective. Those who have mastered Bloom's vocabulary and style will be enriched by his perceptive criticism of "The Broken Tower" and of poetry collected in *White Buildings* and *The Bridge*.

M. L. Rosenthal and Sally M. Gall, in *The Modern Poetic Sequence: The Genius of Modern Poetry* (New York, 1983), which subsumes Rosenthal's "On Four Poems by Hart Crane" (*Visionary Company*, Spring 1982), impressively scrutinize Crane's major sequences and conclude that "Voyages" is more successful than *The Bridge*. Both are "efforts toward visionary transcendence over the limitations of the empirical moment, but 'Voyages'—shorter [than *The Bridge*], more inwardly centered, and intellectually less ambitious—was easier for him to handle." Rosenthal and Gall also compare *The Bridge* with major sequences by two of Crane's older contemporaries, again finding it wanting. It "does not *discover* American life and memories as Williams does in [*Paterson*]" and though, like Eliot's *The Waste Land*, "it affirms a vision of redemption against" depression and fragmentation, unlike Eliot's "Christian frame of 'positive reference'" for his vision, Crane's referential frame is an insubstantial "public" one weakened by "false inspirationalism" and "lapses into bombast." Rosenthal and Gall acutely observe that parts of *The Bridge* suggest that it "might have become a sequence whose main organic body resembled that of 'Voyages' . . . much more centered on successive states of feeling and awareness and much less on public symbols and values."

Gorham Munson's *The Awakening Twenties: A Memoir—History of a Literary Period* (Baton Rouge, La., 1985) is a vital document for Crane students. Munson was Crane's first important literary friend from his own generation, and *The Awakening Twenties* offers a hitherto untold view of the 1920s from the perspective of an American literary intellectual more serious and thoughtful than most other young Americans who, during that period, participated in the turbulent literary life of expatriate Europe and New York City. One of the book's chapters, "'On Perilous Seas Forlorn'—The Untold Story of Hart Crane," is Munson's first extended critical and biographical study of the poet since publication of Munson's early pioneering essay in his *Destinations* (1928). This new and more detailed account of his personal friendship and literary association with the poet, as well as Munson's final critical judgments of Crane's poetics and poetry, constitutes an essential corollary perspective to portraits of Crane by other contemporaries, some of whom strangely neglect such significant matters as Crane's religious experience and superficially scrutinize his poetry.

4 Individual Works

a. White Buildings

i. Full-length Studies. Alfred Hanley's *Hart Crane's Holy Vision: "White Buildings"* (Pittsburgh, 1981) is the second full-length work dealing wholly with *White Buildings*, the first being Konrad Hopkins's (1957). Oddly, Hopkins is unmentioned either in Hanley's relatively few footnotes or his sparse "Selective Bibliography," though he does provide a few textual references to other Crane scholars. In Hanley's opinion, the only critic who had anticipated his view of Crane as an "incarnational" poet was R. W. B. Lewis in *The Poetry of Hart Crane: A Critical Study* (1967). Hanley regards *White Buildings* as a collection of "religious verse" possessing "thematic unity and structural design . . . analogous to the integrity and cyclic structure of *The Bridge*"; that is, "the 'perfect cry' of 'some constant harmony' aspired to in the book's first poem is answered by the 'unbetrayable reply' of the last. *White Buildings* is about the pained pursuit of that holy truth that begins in quiet speculation and passes through the clamor and fire of experience to tranquil illumination." Though Crane used imagery and concepts of Judeo-Christian origin, Hanley believes *White Buildings* embraces neither orthodox Christianity nor Transcendentalist or neoplatonist versions: "Crane's faith as a poet is not in a purely transcendent or abstract ideality, but in a beauty, unity, trust and love—a permanence—incarnated paradoxically within the impermanent . . . [and that] through sacrificial immolation and a radical transformation of the perception of the poet, this Ideal is transubstantiated from the often unlovely, fragmented, and suffering life of humankind."

ii. Shorter Studies. In his foreword to the third impression of the first edition of *White Buildings* (New York, 1972), John Logan sympathetically discusses "My Grandmother's Love Letters," "Garden Abstract," "Sunday Morning Apples," and "Voyages" as exemplifications of the "motif of *bi*sexuality in Crane's life and work." Logan finds the motif important because, firstly, it "helps to account for the difficulty his poetry had in being accepted by an earlier generation" and, secondly, it explains the presence of some linguistic "obscurity" in the poetry as a consequence of "the fact that Crane felt compelled to hide and/or transform his sexuality in his language" despite the already obscuring effect of his "then avant garde symbolist or surrealist mode of expression." Logan believes that "in *White Buildings*, more than in any other first-rate American poetry (the possible exception would be Whitman), there is so much to be learned . . . about the dynamics of human sexuality, particularly about the balancing of feminine and masculine aspects of the personality."

John T. Shawcross's "An Inquiry into the Metric of Names: Sound and Rhythm of Names in Hart Crane's *White Buildings*" (*LOS*, 1978) is primarily a detailed examination of the "effect of names in [Crane's] poetry through their contextual sounds and rhythms," which deliberately gives relatively less attention to the names' denotative, allusive, and etymological evocations without denying their importance. Shawcross's onomastic approach to Crane's metrics is fruitful and should be extended to names this essay does not examine.

Gregory R. Zeck's "The Logic of Metaphor" (*TSLL*, Fall 1975) and Reid Maynard's "A Defense of Hart Crane's Poetic License" (*LWU*, Oct. 1976) consider the validity and significance of Crane's comments about "At Melville's Tomb" in his well-known letter to Harriet Monroe (*Poetry*, Oct. 1926) written in response to her challenging queries (also in *Poetry*, Oct. 1926). Crane's letter propounds his theory of the "logic of metaphor" and explicates the poem. The implications of the interchange, of course, are pertinent to Crane's poetics in general. Maynard finds that the poem "contains definite allusions to Melville's *Moby-Dick*" which justify Crane's explications. Zeck also evaluates Crane's responses, but is more concerned with Crane's poetics. In Zeck's opinion, Crane—who "more than once presents his poetics confusingly"—did not articulate them correctly to Monroe. Crane "rejects and so locates himself between logic and illogic as structuring aesthetic principles." However, "the 'apparent illogic' which his theory of metaphor defines is actually . . . an *alogicality*, an equivocal cognitive mode opposed to the univocal dimensions of logic but not therefore merely or mainly emotive." Philip Furia, in "Crane's 'At Melville's Tomb'" (*Expl*, May 1975), suggests that the poem's last line, if interpreted as a reference "to the Christian pattern of death and resurrection," makes it possible that "Melville in this poem enacts the same symbolic pattern of transcendence" to the heavens that Columbus, Whitman, and "Maquokeeta" enact in *The Bridge*.

Both Richard Hutson ("Hart Crane's 'Black Tambourine'" [*LWU*, No. 1, 1970]) and Edward Kessler ("Crane's 'Black Tambourine'" [*Expl*, Sept. 1970]) agree that the poem expresses Crane's sense of his sociocultural isolation by its transmutation of similar black American experience. Hutson explicates the poem at greater length, emphasizing its importance in Crane's development as "his first really successful exercise in transforming his humiliation and frustration into art" and deepening his "identification with the exiled and downtrodden" visible earlier in "Porphyro in Akron" and later in *The Bridge*. Whether or not the black American novelist-poet Jean Toomer ever read "Black Tambourine" and was influenced by it while creating his novel *Cane* (1923) are unresolved questions, according to Victor A. Kramer's "The 'Mid-Kingdom' of Crane's 'Black Tambourine' and Toomer's *Cane*" (*CLAJ*, June 1974). Kramer reports that, though Toomer never acknowledged any indebtedness either to Crane or "Black Tambourine," such mutual friends as Gorham Munson or Waldo Frank actually may have provided Toomer with a copy of the poem before he had completed *Cane*. Whatever the case, Kramer has discovered several thematic similarities in both poem and novel, the use of a cellar setting in *Cane* which resembles the poem's setting, and cockroach "images similar to the poem's roach which 'spans a crevice' effectively employed" in *Cane*.

Robert L. Perry's "Critical Problems in Hart Crane's 'Chaplinesque'" (*CP*, Fall 1975) reviews and adjudicates several critical controversies over the poem's tone and the meaning of some of its words and lines. Perry agrees that the poem, especially the "kitten' symbol but not its "central metaphor" of "poet as clown," is sentimental. However, he rejects charges that some controversy-stirring "parts of the poem [are] indecipherable," reviews divergent views of their meanings, explicates the text, and finally provides his own resolutions of critical disagreements.

Marc Simon's "Carlyle, Samuel B. Greenberg, and Hart Crane: An Original Source" (*AN&Q*, Mar. 1979) oddly justifies the title's inclusion of Crane's name: "Hart Crane's 'Emblems of Conduct' retains the original Carlyle influence through Greenberg in [two] lines. . . . However, it is only in Greenberg's piece that Carlyle's salient landscape figures so sharply as the original source of Crane's poem from the Greenberg Manuscripts." Earlier, Simon says that "Thomas Carlyle's book [*On Heroes, Hero-Worship and the Heroic in History*] served as the original source, through Greenberg, of Crane's poem, though Crane was not aware of Greenberg's source, nor was Fisher [who introduced Crane to Geeenberg's unpublished poetry]." A footnote explains that "there is no evidence that Crane knew of Carlyle's influence," nor, it might be added, does Simon indicate that Crane had read Carlyle's book.

"Critical Problems in Hart Crane's 'The Fernery'" (*Expl*, Fall 1976) is Robert L. Perry's effort to impose a coherent order of meaning on a poem subjected to the analyses of six critics who "differ markedly" about aspects of the poem. In turn, Nat Henry, in "Crane's 'The Fernery'" (*Expl*, Summer 1978), summarizes Perry's thematic synthesis of the poem ("the poet's desire for, and his aunt's dread of, the fresh but potentially splintering light of self-knowledge") and rejects it. Henry conjectures that Crane's metric may have led him to make the poem's final line "a *runover* line," a supposition strengthened by the absence of a concluding punctuation mark, instead of the *"endstopped"* line which Perry and other critics assume it to be. This syntactic speculation enables Henry to develop a plausible naturalistic pattern of meaning in which the aunt, "far from having 'lost touch with reality,' . . . has maintained a constant awareness of it in suppressing any expression of it."

Bruce Bassoff's "Rhetorical Pressures in 'For the Marriage of Faustus and Helen'" (*CP*, Fall 1972) argues that part 1 of the sequence fulfills Crane's statements about the poem and justifies the ideas about his poetics he set forth in "General Aims and Theories." Crane wished "to promulgate an order for the world through language" and to emulate William Blake's rejection of poetry written "'only with the eye and for the readiest surface of the consciousness.'" Bassoff regards part 1 as a nontraditional "meditation" in which Crane, engaged in "evolv[ing] his own ritual for [transcendence]," apparently succeeds in creating the "'absolute poetry'" he desired by forsaking "social speech . . . shared understandings or . . . a socially placed personality" and replacing "the poet as person" with "the poet as priest or pray-er." The principal danger in Crane's poetry is hallucination (defined earlier by Bassoff as "the mistaking of the projections of self for perceptions of reality, or the dissociation of rhetoric from content"): "oblique predication, displacement of parts of speech, indefinite comparison, and paratactic style generate multiple relationships but can yield a sense of dissociated rhetoric." In "Crane's 'For the Marriage of Faustus and Helen,' III, 1–23" (*Expl*, Mar. 1973), Bassoff turns his attention to "problems of indefinite address and confused reference that pervade Crane's poetry. The primary difficulty in this section . . . is the anaphoric use of 'we' and 'you' . . . accentuated by the typographic foregrounding of 'religious gunman' and 'We even' (lines 5 and 10 . . .). . . ." Part 2 of the same sequence is clarified by Roger Dickinson-Brown ("Crane's 'For the Marriage of Faustus and Helen,' II, 7–8 and 11–12" [*Expl*, Apr. 1973]), who proposes that two cultural phenomena of the 1920s were Crane's sources for four lines: (ll. 7–8) "a billboard advertisement for Gold Dust Cleanser" in New York's Times Square which contained "two rotating black babies 'scouring' the billboard" and (ll. 11–12) "'Tiffany Ball' . . . a large, rotating, suspended globe, made of many flat little mirrors which, when spotlighted, throw a phantasmagoria of vague and shifting blobs of light on the dance floor."

Philip R. Yannella's "'Inventive Dust': The Metamorphoses of 'For the Marriage of Faustus and Helen'" (*ConL*, Winter 1974) argues that the poem effectively realizes most of Crane's intentions for it, even though it is "a poem . . . deeply flawed and at times rhetorically pompous," because it is "the first distinctively Blakean poem published in the United States," repudiated Eliot, and thus made "the historically 'right choice'" confirmed by postmodernist American poetry. The sequence articulates "renewed hope in the American city, . . . establish[ing], through the central metaphor of Helen, an urbanism and an accessory technology . . . which is the last hope of modern man" and replaces Newtonian aesthetics and metaphysics with systems "probably best characterized as relativistic and atomist, . . . non-Aristotelian, non-Newtonian, and non-Euclidean." Consequently, negative criticism of *The Bridge*'s structure as nonrational is based on "a stance toward reality not shared by" Crane and other poets such as Williams and Olson.

Robert K. Martin ("Hart Crane's 'For the Marriage of Faustus and Helen': Myth and Alchemy" [*CP*, Spring 1976]), unlike Yanella (whom Martin does not cite), believes that Crane consciously utilized classical mythology; Martin delineates its presence in part 2, lines 24–26. He and Yanella agree that the troubling parodic epigraph of Crane's poem, spoken by the whore Dol Common in Jonson's *The Alchemist*, functions effectively. Both Martin and Yanella also argue that alchemical transformation is present in the poem's imagery and development. Martin's major contribution probably is his discussion of Crane's rewriting of the Faust legend, "eliminat[ing] the damnation of Faust and conclud[ing] it with an epithalamium . . . demonstrat[ing] [Crane's] belief in transformation and his faith in poetry as a magic art."

Mary Ann Caws shares Crane's belief about "Passage," written in a letter dated 19 August 1925, that "it is still the most interesting and conjectural thing I have written." In "On One Crossing-Over: Valéry's Sea into Hart Crane's Scene," included in *The Analysis of Literary Texts: Current Trends in Methodology* (ed. Randolph D. Pope, Ypsilanti, Mich., 1980), Caws first reads "Passage," then extracts from Paul Valéry's *Le Cimetière marin*, and finally provides a re-reading of "Passage" affected by the fact that "these two poems echo together like steps not lost, 'pas perdus' and not meant to be, in the mental resonance of the corridor of reading, along the threshold between two perceptions, and toward one sensitivity to borders and exchange." Crane did not actually visit Provence until mid-1929, but Caws suggests that in "Passage," written several years earlier, he imaginatively "exchanged the farm at Patterson [New York] on which he is in fact living—thus the pears and bushels—for the black and red 'vine-stanchioned' valleys of Provence."

An interesting hypothesis is propounded in the first sentence of Gregory R. Zeck's psychoanalytic "Hart Crane's 'The Wine Menagerie': The Logic of Metaphor" (*AI*, Fall 1979). Zeck hypothesizes that the poem "dramatizes, more fully than in any other lyric, the familial context of [Crane's] struggle for identity and demonstrates how his particular esthetic, the 'logic of metaphor,' solves poetically the problem of who he is." Zeck is aware of the difficulties involved in psychoanalysis of a poem as intricate as "The Wine Menagerie" (for example, it presents a "filter of intense and even hallucinatory metaphors . . . in a secretive language"), but his critiques nevertheless seem appropriate, for they set off fascinating speculations about the poem and Crane.

Yvor Winters's insight that the "I" in "Repose of Rivers" is a river, instead of the poet or any other human being, has been expanded by David R. Clark ("Hart Crane: 'Repose of Rivers,'" in Clark's *Lyric Resonance*, Amherst, Mass., 1972) and Francis Fike ("Symbolic Strategy in 'Repose of Rivers'" [*HCN*, Winter 1977]), who provide a coherent structural pattern in which a dead river, immersed in the sea, reviews its past. Fike's reading is more detailed than Clark's, augmented with consideration of Crane's "working in a symbolist mode which requires not that each literal detail carry particularized symbolic meaning, but that some details may function in a supportive, non-symbolic way, and that the main symbolic meaning issues from the situation of the whole poem." Fike perceives the dead river to be a symbol of "the individual human life, [which] after passage through death, finds not dissolution and loss, but continued existence on a high plane of fulfillment . . . [in] the sea . . . symbol of Crane's view of God, the ocean of Being which receives human life into itself with beatific fulfillment and without dissolving individual identity."

Robert L. Perry's "Critical Problems in Hart Crane's 'Sunday Morning Apples'" (*Rendezvous*, Fall 1975) reviews and evaluates the critical literature dealing with the poem's "general character," its relation to Stevens's "Sunday Morning," and "the meaning of particular lines."

Elliott Carter's analytical "A Commentary on the Poem by the Composer" introduces the score of his musical setting, for voice and piano, of "Voyages III," entitled *Voyage (Hart Crane)* (South Hadley & Northampton, Mass., 1945; reprinted, with an informative editorial note on Carter's efforts over the years to render Crane's poetry in music, in Clark). The composer's sensitive comments, intended to assist a singer preparing to perform the song, provide a sequential account of the interaction between "three protagonists: the Sea (which is the medium through which everything in the poem moves and changes and to which every idea is referred), Love (to whom the poem is addressed) and the Poet."

b. *The Bridge*

i. *Full-length Studies.* Richard P. Sugg's *Hart Crane's "The Bridge": A Description of Its Life* (University, Ala., 1976) seeks to rescue the poem from the depredations of critics antipathetic to romanticism, sympathetic to moralism, or disturbed by the work's tendency to straddle and blur rather than to sharpen polarities (for example, history and legend, pessimism and optimism, faith and despair, tradition and innovation, etc.). Despite a bibliography listing Crane scholarship and criticism from the 1930s onward, Sugg's book is shaped with hagiological serenity to accord with his assumption that "the 'continuous and eloquent span' of *The Bridge* must be described within the context of Crane's poetic beliefs and practices, for its very structure depends upon the movement of the imagination, the hero of this 'epic of the modern consciousness,' towards the creation of a poem, the fulfillment of its dream of act." The result may be considered critical solipsism which abjures objectivity and elucidates elements related to one another by virtue of their coexistence in the poem or their rationalization by Crane's theoretical statements. Even so, perhaps because Sugg's method may well be a proper way to approach as complex a work as *The Bridge*, his book provides a substantial number of enlightening readings. Sugg's critical stance recurs frequently in many essays on Crane's poetry.

Helge Normann Nilsen's *Hart Crane's Divided Vision: An Analysis of "The Bridge"* (Oslo, Norway, 1980), which subsumes "Hart Crane's Indian Poem" (*NM*, No. 1, 1971), "Hart Crane's 'Atlantis': An Analysis" (*DQR*, No. 4, 1973), "Hart Crane's *The Bridge* and the Poetics of Faith" (*Edda*, No. 4, 1977), "Crane and Frank: Images of America" (*HCN*, Winter 1977), and " 'Surrender to the Sensations of Urban Life': A Note on the Poetry of Hart Crane" (*EA*, July–Sept. 1981), is a major contribution to Crane studies. Nilsen argues that *The Bridge* should not be read "in terms of Platonic idealism," for it is actually in the mystic, romantic, nationalist tradition of Whitman, brought up to date in the 1920s by Waldo Frank and transmitted by him and Gorham Munson to Crane. His "aim was to present a revelation of spiritual unity in America, a sense of 'the Whole.'" *The Bridge* "contains a 'myth of America' in the sense that it reveals a divine spirit in the works of America, past and present." However, because Crane's attitude during composition was "divided" rather than whole, affirmative and also pessimistic, *The Bridge* "expresses both absolute faith and absolute doubt, . . . a pattern that is repetitive rather than evolving, changing, maturing." Though on the whole "an impressive poetic performance," not all of *The Bridge*'s sections are successful. "Indiana" and "Quaker Hill" are weak because "large parts of these poems are prosaic and pedestrian and lack the richness and tension of the texture that more successful sections present." These ("To Brooklyn Bridge," "Ave Maria," "The Harbor Dawn," "Van Winkle," "The River," "Cutty Sark," and "The Tunnel") "are superb examples of romantic American poetry of the modern age, and that in itself is a rare achievement."

Edward Brunner's *Splendid Failure: Hart Crane and the Making of "The Bridge"* (Urbana, Ill., 1985), which subsumes " 'Your Hands Within My Hands Are Deeds': Poems of Love in *The Bridge*" (*IowaR*, Winter 1973), is a major addition to Crane studies. The book is actually more wide-ranging than its title implies, for Brunner expertly scrutinizes and explicates Crane's poetry and poetics, with occasional reference to his biography, from the composition of "For the Marriage of Faustus and Helen" in 1923, the year Crane first conceived of a Bridge poem, to 1932 and his last poem, "The Broken Tower," thus encompassing not only *The Bridge*, but also *White Buildings* and the uncollected poems. Many issues dividing Crane's critics are reasonably resolved by Brunner, who is generously tender to the poet himself and discriminatingly enthusiastic about his art. The book's title merely dramatizes Brunner's central argument that there are actually two Bridge poems instead of merely one: (1) an unpublished exploration of consciousness, demonstrably of high quality, completed in 1926; (2) an expansion of the 1926 sequence, containing five additional poems ("The River," "Indiana," "Cape Hatteras," "Quaker Hill," and "Atlantis"), the whole arranged in an order vitiating the 1926 sequence. The 1930 Bridge poem, in Brunner's judgment, is a relatively conventional cultural epic, less true to Crane's deepest concerns than the 1926 epic; circumstances after 1926 created problems which led him to write at less than his best in some of the added poems, generally to weaken the unity and integrity of the 1926 poem. Brunner argues that Crane, having been spurred on in 1923 by ambition and friends to write public poetry refuting Eliot, responded with "For the Marriage of Faustus and Helen" plus the concept and early lines of the 1930 Bridge poem, all enthusiastically received and personally gratifying. However, after 1923 Crane veered back and forth between private poetry, such as he had written before 1923, and public poetry. Ironically, as Brunner makes clear, the 1926 Bridge poem Crane set aside actually was an epic of consciousness, a cultural epic devoted thematically to Crane's concern with the difficulties experienced by love in the modern world; the 1926 Bridge refuted Eliot more effectively than the 1930 version.

Paul Giles's *Hart Crane: The Contexts of "The Bridge"* (New York, 1986) is another major addition to Crane studies, providing an intensive focus on *The Bridge* and also a wide-ranging study of the outer worlds of Crane's poetry. Giles, for example, provides chapter-length considerations of the pertinence of such topics as homosexuality and capitalism when reading and evaluating the poem. Though some critics regard Crane's dense rhetoric as predominantly linguistic noise or ineffable expression, Giles discerns substantial meaning in the rhetoric because, as he demonstrates, it is replete with complex verbal punning. Giles argues that it is relatively unimportant whether or not Crane punned consciously all or most of the time; the mere presence of such linguistic subtlety is sufficient justification for a critic to claim, as Giles does, that it is a result of Crane's poetic genius. There are some critics who may dispute all or a few of Giles's revelations of Crane's verbal ambiguities. Probably few critics will deny that *Hart Crane: The Contexts of "The Bridge"* is a sophisticated, illuminating book whose analyses are supported by modestly wielded though impressively detailed knowledge of Crane's life, works, and archival remains, as well as of the pertinent contexts—literary, historical, psychological, social—which encouraged Crane to create *The Bridge*, a work Giles describes as "witty, ironic, sacrilegious and erotic . . . the nearest thing to *Finnegan's* [sic] *Wake* that we have . . .

a poem of radical scepticism where every proposition is susceptible of contradiction as the pun swings eternally between opposites . . . [and] words seem to dance together in a gleeful circle of equivocation, liberated from the moralistic business of sedentary denotation."

ii. Shorter Studies. The chapter on Crane in Thomas A. Vogler's *Preludes to Vision: The Epic Venture in Blake, Wordsworth, Keats, and Hart Crane* (Berkeley, Calif., 1971), which subsumes Vogler's introduction to Crane's *The Bridge* (1970; see II), has been influential in Crane studies and the whole book expresses many of the ideas animating much, though not all, Crane criticism in the 1970s and early 1980s. Vogler's linkage of Crane to Blake and Milton, for example, is an approach being developed by other critics, and echoes of Vogler's phrasing in later works suggest that elements of *Preludes to Vision* have permeated a segment of the collective critical unconscious. Vogler argues that the epic theme of man in relation to his world survives, even if epic's traditional forms have become obsolete. His reading of *The Bridge*, allegedly "free of pre-commitment to Crane's own statements," finds in the work "a theme that provides a high degree of organic unity . . . a search or quest for a mythic vision, not the fixed, symbolic expression of a vision held firmly in the poet's mind." Vogler holds that prophetic vision was not attained: "*The Bridge* is a record of the poet's attempt 'to hold each desperate choice' and is an outpouring of the poet's own 'word' rather than the reception of an ultimate 'Word.'"

James C. Cowan ("The Theory of Relativity and *The Bridge*" [*HSL*, No. 2, 1971]) "suggest[s] a significant parallel between Crane's poetic statement and the most important scientific theory of his day, perhaps even of the century," namely, Einstein's theory of relativity and its modification in Alfred North Whitehead's *Science and the Modern World* (a copy of which Crane owned in early 1926). Cowan analyzes several poems in *The Bridge* in order to illustrate how, in his judgment, a scientifically oriented Crane used metaphor, symbol, light, and motion (curvilinear and straight-line) to obliterate conventional time and space, to unite technological and natural imagery into new patterns (unities) of meaning, to achieve simultaneity of events, and to unite the sections and subsections of *The Bridge*.

According to Edwin Fussell ("The Genesis of Hart Crane's *The Bridge*," in his *Lucifer in Harness: American Meter, Metaphor, and Diction*, Princeton, N.J., 1973), the poem's creation was drawn-out and confused because Crane began with a "constituting metaphor and title, but he [did] not know what poetic matter might be thereby constituted." The impulse had been "a powerful poetic intuition, felt as a metaphorical form that [would] yield the structure of the poem as soon as the metaphorical import of the intuition [could] be determined." Crane had difficulty writing the poem until 1926, when his constituting metaphor was "transformed from a mystical synthesis of past-future America to a reflexive analogue of the very act of the poem in the process of building itself toward its metaphorical span." Fussell concludes that *The Bridge* is "a brilliantly concatenated series of lyric poems of uneven quality, which clearly relate to each other but never entirely coalesce."

Ian S. MacNiven's "Hart Crane and T. S. Eliot on the Modern City" (*RUCR*, Dec. 1973) explicates *The Bridge* in order to show that Crane infused it with optimistic content about American urban life in an effort to controvert Eliot's pessimism about twentieth-century urban life in *The Waste Land*. Still, because Crane shared some of Eliot's despair about the city, *The Bridge* at times handles the theme ambivalently. Ultimately, however, the poem rises above the "mechanical hell" of New York City, for "Crane was willing to tolerate the real city in the faith that it was serving in man's quest for individual salvation." In passing, MacNiven cites a number of verbal echoes of Eliot, Keats, Blake, and Omar Khayyám in *The Bridge* and also notes, without specification, that "Crane's fifteen uses [in the poem] of the word *dream* in various forms are evidence of the importance of dreams in his concept of poetic vision."

Though Crane declared that *The Bridge* was "a symphony with an epic theme," A. G. Ullyatt, in "Hart Crane: *The Bridge*" (*UES*, June 1975), holds that a more accurate analogy can be made with the orchestral "rhapsody" which, in contrast to the symphony's "more restricted structure," has no fixed structure, appears to be improvised, encompasses "'sharply contrasted feelings . . . [and] popular or folk melodies,'" and "does not preclude themes of epic proportions." Ullyat argues that the poem is held together by its transformation of apparently disparate though related images into complex symbols, as well as by the design of "To Brooklyn Bridge" as a thematic overture whose preliminary themes are developed from varying perspectives in the sections which follow.

A more rigorous and elaborate correlation of Crane's poem with music can be found in Michael Sharp's "Theme and Free Variation: The Scoring of Hart Crane's *The Bridge*" (*ArQ*, Autumn 1981), which reads the poem as a musical score ("a motet for eight voices," its parts variously prelude, aubade, ritual folk chant, fugue, nocturne, and serenade) and argues that its structure resembles that of d'Indy's *Istar Variations* (1897), where the composer "modified the variation, as a restatement of a musical theme, by transferring the theme from its usual place at the beginning of a composition to the end." The pertinence of comparing *The Bridge* with music is emphasized by Sharp's revelation that the poem contains "nearly two hundred direct or indirect references to sound and music; over ten musical instruments are mentioned specifically by name." Sharp also explores Crane's general familiarity with music and composers and clarifies Crane's poetic concerns in the perspective of similar concerns in modern music.

There is only one chapter ("Hart Crane and the Machine") devoted to the poet in Dickran Tashjian's *Skyscraper Primitives: Dada and the American Avant-Garde, 1910–1925* (Middletown, Conn., 1975), but the book as a whole expands the attention given by earlier Crane scholars to the formative intellectual, aesthetic, social, and personal content of Crane's world (magazines, literature, visual art, friends, editors, writers, painters, New York Bohemia, etc.) during the 1910s and early 1920s which encouraged him to assume prophetic responsibility for coping with modern technology. Tashjian holds that Crane initially was ambivalent about technology and the American culture which extolled it. However, his doubts about technology were resolved for him by his confidence in the transformative powers of visionary poetry such as *The Bridge*.

Donald Pease's "*The Bridge*: Emotional Dynamics of an Epic of Consciousness," in *The Twenties: Fiction, Poetry, Drama* (ed. Warren French, Deland, Fla., 1975), argues that the poem attains and embodies its prophetic vision if a reader, as Crane wished, participates with the poet in the poem's action "through the emotional dynamics of individual lyrics," for Crane "experiences the world in all of its fragmentation and through powerful emotion rides the experience to its limits until frustration becomes ecstasy." The "inclusive quality of the epic form" harmoniously integrates the lyrics.

Kingsley Widmer, whose essay "*The Waste Land* and the American Breakdown" appears with Pease's in Warren French's *The Twenties* (see immediately above), disagrees with Pease's argument. Widmer emphatically doubts the success of *The Bridge* in "overcom[ing] the dominant disconnections of our sensibility" and procreating "a visionary image of, somehow, the prophetic and redemptive word . . . ; the whole effort shows 'intellectual schizophrenia,' with the mystical intent and the naturalistic perceptions, the affirmative myths and the tormented personal details, pervasively contradicting each other." Furthermore, "though sensitive to urban anguish and outcast suffering, Crane quite lacks a social morality and a political side to his vision."

Donald Pease further develops his concept of *The Bridge* as epic prophecy in "Hart Crane and the Tradition of Epic Prophecy" (Clark; this essay subsumes Pease's "Blake, Crane, Whitman, and Modernism: A Poetics of Pure Possibility," *PMLA*, Jan. 1981). Pease's definition of the prophetic vision, relatively amorphous in his 1975 essay, is explicitly set forth here as "an epiphanic act of longing" arising during and after the experience of "The Tunnel"; that is, "it is not the fulfillment of the desire [for vision] that confers the visions, it is a despair over their never being fulfilled which finally opens into vision [of 'Atlantis']. . . . Crane increases the distance between the actual and the possible, the desire and its object until only the span of longing between them remains, and this longing itself generates a world." In this special "moment" is resolved the "contrariety constituting the form of the epic prophecy," for "an epic brings the ways of the world into a fully realized form, while a prophecy returns that actualized world where everything seems complete—even final—back to the status of a renewed possibility, where everything seems once again about to begin." Pease holds that *The Bridge*, using precedents of epic prophecy provided by Blake and Whitman and a methodology akin to dreaming, is a counter-response to Eliot's *The Waste Land*.

Karl T. Piculin's "The Critics and Hart Crane's THE BRIDGE: An Interview with John Unterecker" (*HCN*, Summer 1978) aims to counter the errors of many other critics of Crane. Unterecker, author of the most recent Crane biography, gives his views on *The Bridge*'s genre, style, unity, structure, etc.

Ware Smith, in "Strands of *The Bridge*" (*HCN*, Spring 1979), provides corrections, with frequent reference to particular sections, of "misleading assumptions" about two of *The Bridge*'s components—its narrator and its women—and explores the nature of its religious vision. The narrator of *The Bridge* is an "epic poet voicing a vision of his culture" which is "a radical critique of America." Crane's female characterizations are "a compendium of various forms of a denying mother, . . . an ever-changing form who frustrates, infuriates, and deludes the epic voyager—forcing him ever onward, accelerating and focusing his 'beyonding' impulse while remaining the still center to which he can return, in whom he can find sustenance." The religious vision projected in *The Bridge* consists of "two mythic configurations, Christian and Indian . . . linked or bridged by a series of unifying ideas and images."

Joseph Schwartz's "A Divided Self: The Poetic Sensibility of Hart Crane with Respect to *The Bridge*" (*MSLC*, Nos. 1, 2, 3, 1979) presents a comprehensive, extended study of Crane's mind, psyche, and experience which concludes that his "search for unity without an adequate base in some certitude that went beyond his own invention of it [was] a failure. . . . The bridging metaphor, where he was most at home poetically, was not the organizing center of a comprehensive philosophy." Crane tried to write a national epic on a cosmic scale despite his recurrent doubts about the project and his inclination toward a private poetry. His divided attitudes and his swings between animating belief and deflating despair prevented *The Bridge* from becoming a harmonious entity; many sections of the poem are individually brilliant. Schwartz believes the factor most instrumental in leading Crane to complete *The Bridge* for publication was romantic nationalist Waldo Frank, the friend to whom Crane dedicated the second edition of the work.

Valid readings of *The Bridge* have not been forthcoming heretofore, according to "A Poetics for *The Bridge*" (*TCL*, Fall 1980), by Roger Ramsey, because (1) critics have paid excessive attention to Crane's expressions of intent in his letters ("they are not to be trusted as guide or gloss") and therefore have become involved in fruitless discussions of epic, myth, and vision, and (2) critics have failed to recognize that the poem, viewed in the light of terms as defined in Northrop Frye's *Anatomy of Criticism* (1957), is a Longinian lyric rather than an Aristotelian work. Ramsey holds that readers must identify themselves with both poem and poet, become aware that *The Bridge* is a "transubstantiative" lyric whose "moments are characterized not by understanding . . . but by intensity. . . . not emotional . . . but rather spiritual, which it will be allowed often seems to transcend the understandable." Thus, the language of such moments may involve the reader in ways he cannot entirely explain; the resultant "'obscurity' . . . is thereby a necessity, not an excrescence." Drawing additionally upon Frye's definition of lyric ("an associative rhetorical process, most of it below the threshold of consciousness, a chaos of paranomasia, sound-links, ambiguous sense-links, and memory-links very like that of the dream"), Ramsey argues that there are no important similarities between Crane's language and that of Whitman.

According to John T. Irwin's "Figurations of the Writer's Death: Freud and Hart Crane," in *The Literary Freud: Mechanisms of Defense and the Poetic Will* (ed. Joseph H. Smith, New Haven, Conn., 1980), Crane suffered from an "originality neurosis," whose "threat . . . is that the writings of an older man . . . , through their similarity and priority, preempt the possibility of originality for the younger man's writings and thus threaten the survival of the younger man's work—that is, they prefigure the death of the younger man's written corpus." Although there are echoes of Bryant's death poem "Thanatopsis" and "The Fountain" in *The Bridge*, Crane apostrophized Whitman and Poe in the poem and made no reference to Bryant. Nevertheless, Irwin argues, it was Eliot whom Crane actually repressed: "Setting out to confute Eliot's pessimistic rule, Crane found himself in danger of becoming an example of that rule. Crane simply had to free himself and his poem from Eliot, but the problem was, that in terms of both technique and antithetical content, *The Waste Land* was so much a part of *The Bridge* that to repress Eliot directly, to psychically kill him, would destroy *The Bridge* and finish Crane as a poet." The solution was repression of Bryant superimposed over, and thus concealing, repression of Eliot.

According to Stephen Fender's comparative study, "Ezra Pound and the Words Off the Page: Historical Allusions in Some American Long Poems" (*YES*, 1978), allusions to American history in Whitman and Crane are "public" and "comforting" whereas in Pound and Williams allusions are "hidden" and "subversive." Crane and Whitman emphasize "American public school history," that is, "simplified tales of individual enterprise, glamorous exploration, discovery, and invention" which are comforting because each poet alludes "to what [he] knows his audience must share; the common denominator of information disseminated by, say, folk wisdom, the popular press, and free public education." In contrast, Pound and Williams's historical allusions are "private," shaped by their personal attitudes towards such matters as financial policy and industrialization. Their historical sources usually were esoteric primary sources, generally impossible to find in most public libraries. Their history, consequently, is subversive because it makes "no *immediate* appeal to shared knowledge" and, "in true Socratic fashion, sends us back to the original documents."

John Carlos Rowe, who also considers Crane's handling of history in "The 'Super-Historical' Sense of Hart Crane's *The Bridge*" (*Genre*, Winter 1978), finds it "ironic" that Crane has been charged with "being insufficiently 'historical,' because Crane's very effort to transform American history is also an attempt to destroy the hold of that history on contemporary man." Crane set about doing what American history and historians had neglected, namely, building a "living 'bridge' of the present that would measure the relations of past and future, man and the gods." *The Bridge*, therefore, must not be read "according to traditional models for an historical or mythic consciousness," but as "an extended attack on the very idea of American history, whose obsession with the past or future has exhausted the synergy of the present." *The Bridge* does not progress toward a concluding "mythic vision"; instead, "each of the individual poems has its visionary moment," even those "most concerned with modern America's corruptions such as 'National Winter Garden' or 'The Tunnel.'"

Sidney B. Poger's "Crane and Montague: 'The Pattern History Weaves'" (*Éire*, Winter 1981) compares *The Bridge* and *The Rough Field* (1972), by contemporary Irish poet John Montague, finding significant similarities and differences between them. The form of both poems is a fusion of the lyric and the epic. Montague wrote about Ireland in the 1960s, Crane about the United States in the 1920s. Both poets sought to combine time (present and past) with space: "Although Ireland seems to have little in the way of space or geography, it has plenty of history. America has tremendous space, but a history inchoate, still malleable." History in *The Bridge* is lyric (personal) and epic (the nation), using "autobiographical details with a submerged personality; a composite female figure to represent the nation and what one derives from a relationship with it; and the counters of both space and time."

"Originality, Quotation, and Crane's Poetry," a chapter in Joseph G. Kronick's *American Poetics of History: From Emerson to the Moderns* (Baton Rouge, La., 1984), scrutinizes Crane's theoretical statements in prose as carefully as those he expressed in poetry. Crane rejected "a belief in originality along with a genetic view of history that considers the present an evolutionary product of the past." He "looked upon myth not as a totalizing system but as a purely linguistic structure without a transcendent referent"; his "bridge is a trope for the power of language over history." Although *The Bridge* encompasses both past and future, Crane is searching for "some vision of eternity"; his chief interest in such "historical figures of America's past" as "Columbus, Pocahontas, and the pioneer" is "as abstract signs, the symbols of the future he foresees."

That Crane was a cultural revisionist, seeking to create a new present by revising America's consciousness of its past, is a major theme in essays by Alan Trachtenberg and Suzanne Clark Doeren which place special emphasis on the concept of culture. Trachtenberg's "Cultural Revision in the Twenties: Brooklyn Bridge as 'Usable Past,'" in *The American Self: Myth, Ideology, and Popular Culture* (ed. Sam B. Girgus, Albuquerque, N. Mex., 1981) sets Crane in the tradition of other cultural critics of the 1920s, such as Waldo Frank, Van Wyck Brooks, and Lewis Mumford, who sought not merely to compel an inhospitable American culture to provide cultural "space" for art, but also "to alter the larger culture itself, to revise its sense of itself, its dominant values, and especially its idea of its history." *The Bridge*, then, "is a rethinking and recasting of the past into a future represented by the poet's present." Like other 1920s artists and intellectuals, Crane conceived of his need for the transformation of his fragmented existence into wholeness as similar to the problem facing all of American society; the Brooklyn Bridge became a symbol of bridging, connection; the act of crossing the bridge, of connecting, became *The Bridge*, the transformed present and the culture of the future.

Suzanne Clark Doeren's "Theory of Culture, Brooklyn Bridge, and Hart Crane's Rhetoric of Memory" (*BMMLA*, Spring 1982) helpfully illuminates ideas active in some recent criticism of Crane, and encourages equally sophisticated theoretical self-consciousness in other critical ventures, by tracing the way in which ideas drawn from such sociocultural thinkers as Arnold, Marx, Nietzsche, Freud, and Benjamin, and from such fields as semiotics and American Studies, can fruitfully be applied. The critic must have "a theory of language and culture that can accommodate the shattering of codes as well as their repetition." Heuristically applying the elements of such a theory, Doeren seeks to show that *The Bridge* can be read "without either overemphasizing the creative machinery of the poem, as a destruction of history, or reducing [Crane's] effort to a nostalgia for a lost American past."

In "Two Views of *The Bridge*" (*SR*, Spring 1981), Malcolm Cowley mediates between critics who find *The Bridge* wholly successful and those who don't. Cowley ranks the poem above all "longer [American] poetic works" except Whitman's "Song of Myself," but concludes that Crane's intention to "create a myth of America" was not realized nor could it be. Crane's virtues included "vision, energy, obdurate patience—genius . . . a magnificent sense of rhythm"; his weaknesses were "limited knowledge" and insufficient "stamina" to sustain him during the concurrent progress of his poetic "task" and his "debaucheries."

Tom Chaffin's "Toward a Poetics of Technology: Hart Crane and the American Sublime" (*SoR*, Winter 1984) argues "that much of the confusion surrounding *The Bridge* can be resolved if the poem is read not as a failed epic but as a poem that, for good or ill, derives much of its force from the tradition of the sublime." However, the sublime has been viewed too narrowly by critics such as Josephine Miles, who formulated a theory of an American sublime whose "poetry of praise" of American life and landscape she has traced in a line from Bradstreet in the seventeenth century through Whitman in the nineteenth to Crane in the twentieth. According to Chaffin, Miles and her critical cohorts seem to have overlooked Edmund Burke's earlier pertinent view of the sublime, namely, that it is a secular "phenomenal act, . . . a function not of nature but of the mind" and, as Burke put it, a "terror that naturally arises from a force which nothing can withstand." Chaffin grants that sections of *The Bridge* exemplify the Milesian concept of the American sublime, but emphasizes that Burke's theory of the sublime also is pertinent; the poem's fear of technology and urbanism is so strong that it is inaccurate to term *The Bridge* a work of unalloyed "praise."

Mary Jean Butts's "Art as Affirmation: A Study of Hart Crane's 'Atlantis'" (Clark) is a detailed analysis of *The Bridge*'s concluding section, regarded by some critics as one of the less successful segments of the poem. Butts's careful exegesis is based on the belief that *The Bridge*'s theme is the "affirmation of art, the process of life, and the artist" and that the poem is based on Platonic theory. The best parts of this extract from a 1967 dissertation are those dealing with Crane's handling of language (ambiguities, archaisms, conceits, sound, word order, and sentence patterns) and imagery, though the explanatory application of Crane's "logic of metaphor" may not be persuasive to all readers.

In "The Two Cranes and 'Blind Baggage'" (*HCN*, Summer 1978), Joseph E. Brogunier interestingly discusses Crane's metaphoric transformation in "The River" (l. 33) of the phrase "blind baggage," an imaginative bit of railroading slang.

Three critics have analyzed aspects of "The Tunnel," one of the most problematic sections of *The Bridge*. George S. Lensing, in "Hart Crane's Tunnel from *The Waste Land*" (*ArielE*, Apr. 1975), reviews Crane's ambivalent feelings about T. S. Eliot and carefully compares and contrasts "The Tunnel" and *The Waste Land*. Crane early in the 1920s condemned "Eliot's moral landscape" though acknowledging his poetic genius, but was compelled to "assimilate" Eliot's pessimistic "perspective" before *The Bridge* could be concluded with the optimistic "Atlantis." Lensing argues that Crane discovered "that the affirmations of the poem could only be made by the direct confrontation with the waste land of American society which surrounded him." Accordingly, "The Tunnel" "does not share the visionary optimism one finds elsewhere in the poem" and "totally undisguises the sustained horrors of modern American society."

Douglas Messerli's " 'Out of the Square, the Circle': Vision in Nightmare in Crane's 'Tunnel' " (*FDP*, Jan. 1977) argues that Crane's return to *The Bridge*, after he had slumped into bitter pessimism in June 1926, paradoxically was the result of reading Spengler's *The Decline of the West*, the experience to which Crane attributed the onset of his despair with the idea of the poem. Spengler believed that one of the reasons for the West's decline was its view of "past, present and future merely as progression"; Crane understood that in order properly to unite space and time in myth, to articulate his vision of the future, he had to find the past in the present. Messerli notes that the protagonist's initial desire to achieve circular harmony by walking northward from Times Square to Columbus Circle is frustrated with such harmony attained only by riding the excruciating underground subway in the opposite direction, to Brooklyn.

In "Crane's *The Bridge*, 'The Tunnel,' 58–60" (*Expl*, Oct. 1975), Robert K. Martin explicates three lines frequently cited by critics as conveying the nightmare qualities of modern life and love. The three lines form "a compound sentence composed of two metaphors." The first metaphor links subway tunnels with phonograph records so that the "hellish sounds which the poet hears . . . form part of his interior vision, his realization of the darkness of self." Thus "Crane's terrors are not of Manhattan . . . but of the soul." The second metaphor ("love / A burnt match skating in a urinal") implies "a sexual encounter in a subway men's room," but "the match is an important symbol of rebirth, because it will not be drowned, but will be tossed up to the surface . . . ; love, even in its most reduced, transitory form of anonymous sexual encounter, is an experience of regeneration." Martin relates both metaphors to the persona's downward and upward motion in "The Tunnel."

c. Uncollected Poems. George Knox's " 'Sight, Sound and Flesh': Synoptic View from Crane's Tower" (*MarkhamR*, Oct. 1971) reminds us that explication, of "The Broken Tower" in this instance, need not be a brief, wearisome plodding between a gauntlet of earlier critical comments, only occasionally enlivened by an original critical observation. Focusing on the visual, auditory, and sexual elements of "The Broken Tower," Knox reviews earlier criticism, sets forth the poem's biographical context, and explicates in depth. He also reasonably relates his data to pertinent data from the full Crane canon and life, as well as from pagan and Christian sources. Knox concludes that Crane's "bell-ringing was a summational symbolic act, bringing into a hermetically fused metaphor associations that had been accumulating throughout his poetic career—that visionary moment when once more sight, sound and flesh became charismatically metamorphosed in symbolic action," the poem finally a "mythic

prefiguration of imminent death." Sharon Cameron's insightful explication of "The Broken Tower," in *Lyric Time: Dickinson and the Limits of
Genre* (Baltimore, Md., 1979), focus wholly on the poem. The sense of
the "ephemeral presence" of God, "a spiritual whole," promises relief
for the poem's "speaker" from the temporal-spatial chaos of the "broken
world" and its "broken intervals." The last four stanzas realize the necessary alternative: love unifies and creates wholeness. However, the "syntactically troubled" character of these stanzas "dissuade[s] us from mistaking the ease of any such resolution, for in brokenness there is plurality,
connection, life."

In "Crane's 'The Mango Tree'" (*Expl*, Nov. 1973), Bernie Leggett
qualifies and augments earlier explication of the poem. He correlates
details from the poem with data about the tree in its native habitat,
declaring that, "though Crane thought of the mango as the tree of Eden,
he *saw* it (explicitly in line 2) as like the Christmas tree." In addition,
Leggett denies that "the poem realizes the 'divine light'. . . . [T]he
mango guides the way to love, but the source behind its light remains
mysterious."

Peter J. Sheehan's "Crane's 'Moment Fugue'" (*Expl*, May 1973) is a
compact, intricate, absorbing analysis of a complex, "seldom noticed"
poem Sheehan terms "an ironic masterpiece," one with a setting similar
to "The Tunnel" section of *The Bridge*. "The structure of ['Moment Fugue']
is fugal, depicting the five impressions that flood the mind of the speaker
the moment he sees the flower seller." These impressions, Sheehan
shows, "are blended with a series of oppositions, both gradually losing
their clear outlines as the poem builds to a crescendo [l. 12] and then
modulates down into a last line of numerous vowels and soft 's' sounds."
Significantly, "the flowers, though beautiful, are dead because they have
been cut." The speaker's concluding "vision" is of "the inevitability of
the cut of death" for himself and for the "syphilitic" flower merchant
and his customers.

Norman Hinton and Lise Rodgers, in "Hart Crane's 'The Moth that
God Made Blind'" (*PLL*, Summer 1980), have given us an extensive
analysis of one of Crane's poems of the 1910s. Investigations of paper
and handwriting suggest Crane may have written the poem in 1915 and
revised it in 1918 or shortly thereafter, when under the influence of Carl
Schmitt, who encouraged him to balance dualities. Hinton and Rodgers
effectively reject "psychoanalysis of the poem as revolt against" his father
and the poem's dismissal as a latter-day echo of "Swinburne and Dow-
son, Johnson and Wilde." Their detailed reading uncovers insoluble
"ambiguities or inconsistencies" which suggest that, as in real life Crane
sought to balance his own desires with the conflicting desires of his
father, so in "The Moth that God Made Blind" he evinced an incipient
literary modernism which "speaks to the emerging spirit of Pound and

Eliot." The poem's "aesthetic[,] which he never outgrew, . . . [is] one of equilibrium between opposing forces, refusing to produce confident answers to major questions about existence, truth, beauty, and the like . . . often identified with the 'modern (i.e., 20th century) sensibility.'"

The major contribution of Z. Zatkin-Dresner's "Levels of Meaning in Hart Crane's 'Royal Palm'" (*Thoth*, Winter 1974–75) is its discussion of the poem's prosody, too often bypassed by critics who prefer to explore Crane's meanings. The essay evaluates the applicability of numerous critical judgments of the poem, which has attracted attention for its own sake as well as because Crane dedicated it to his mother.

John R. Scarlett's "Crane's 'The Sad Indian'" (*Expl*, April 1971) is a brief, carefully researched, critically perceptive study of a late work which Scarlett regards as "a protest on behalf of Hart Crane and the Indian and a strategy for helping Crane find identity and purpose." "The Sad Indian" fuses elements of Aztec culture and history with Crane's obser-vations of contemporary Mexico and its "deracinated Indians" and, Scar-lett argues, reflects self-identification with the Indian similar to that appearing earlier in "The Dance" section of *The Bridge*.

5 Crane's Influence

Robert K. Martin's *The Homosexual Tradition in American Literature* (Austin, Tex., 1979) discusses Crane's literary influence on three younger poets: Alfred Corn, Robert Duncan, and Richard Howard.

Crane's life and works impressed themselves durably in the imagina-tion of Caroline Gordon, wife of poet-critic Allen Tate, both of whom knew Crane personally and, for a brief period in 1926, lived with him. Ashley Brown's "Caroline Gordon and Hart Crane: A Literary Relation-ship" (*Visionary Company*, Spring 1982) traces the forms and contexts of the appearance of Crane in Gordon's fiction: initially as a real-life figure in the novel *The Women on the Porch* (1944), then as a latter-day Dantesque Arnaut Daniel named Horne Watts in the novel *The Malefactors* (1956) and, finally, once again as himself in "A Visit to the Grove" (1972), a section of a "long autobiographical novel" left unfinished at Gordon's death. Because Brown's absorbing essay admittedly does not attempt to crystallize a coherent, composite portrait of Crane in Gordon's fiction, that task remains to be done.

Those familiar with Tennessee Williams's works, which include a re-corded reading (Caedmon, 1965) of Crane's poetry and its accompanying jacket commentary, have long been aware that Williams, who did not know Crane personally, was profoundly influenced by him aesthetically and emotionally. Gilbert Debusscher's "'Minting their Separate Wills': Tennessee Williams and Hart Crane" (*MD*, Dec. 1983) comprehensively explores the relationship. "'I feel that he stands with Keats and Shake-speare and Whitman,'" Williams wrote of Crane and, as Debusscher reveals, for Williams the dead poet was virtually a ubiquitous concern, appearing overtly and covertly in Williams's prose and drama: "Williams molded Hart Crane, both as a man and as a poet, into a heightened image of himself, an idealized alter ego and a tutelary power. Through Crane, Williams succeeded in 'looking out, not in,' in transcending his immediate self and formulating a compelling statement about the artist in the modern world."

Theodore Dreiser

James L. W. West III

I   BIBLIOGRAPHY

Theodore Dreiser: A Primary and Secondary Bibliography, compiled by Donald Pizer, Richard W. Dowell, and Frederic E. Rusch (Boston, 1975), is the most ambitious bibliography of the author yet published. Its makers tell us that it is the first bibliography to "bring together in one book all that is known of primary and secondary materials concerning Dreiser." Pizer is responsible for the primary entries, Dowell and Rusch for the secondary sections and for the interviews.

Of the two kinds of material treated, the secondary is the better handled. Dowell and Rusch, working with the extensive files at the University of Pennsylvania and with the materials they have gathered as editors of the *Dreiser Newsletter*, are able to provide admirably thorough coverage. Their annotations, though nonevaluative, are useful and concise, and the index is excellent. If there is a problem, it is with the sheer size of these secondary listings. Scholars and students needing a more manageable compilation might turn initially to Jack Salzman's unannotated "Criticism of Theodore Dreiser: A Selected Checklist" in Salzman's special *Modern Fiction Studies* issue on Dreiser (Autumn 1977). Yearly annotated checklists of work in the Dreiser field appear in the *Dreiser Newsletter*, published at Indiana State University, Terre Haute.

The primary entries in this Dreiser bibliography are ineptly done. The preface to the volume is defensive, implying that full descriptive entries would be of interest only to a rarefied breed of "professional bibliographer." But to judge from the amateurishness with which the entries in section A of this volume have been handled, these listings will not be of much use even to those "scholars and critics of Dreiser whose interests are not professionally bibliographical"—the group for which section A was apparently prepared.

There is confusion over such simple concepts as "edition" and "impression." Reimpressions and subeditions printed from the first American plates are intermixed with true new editions, with only ambiguous asterisks to indicate kinship. It is impossible to trace the British publication histories of Dreiser's books; some of the items noted are true new editions while others are only issues of the American sheets. To add to the confusion, translations are placed in section A rather than in a section to themselves, making it difficult to follow the chronological pattern of Dreiser's career. Section A in a primary bibliography can function as many things. It can be a guidebook for scholars, a handbook for collectors, or a sourcebook for historians of the publishing industry, but above all it must be a usable account of the shape and pattern of an author's career, a history of the forms in which his books have been presented to the public. Section A in this bibliography does not fulfill that need for the Dreiser scholar.

Section B lists only previously unpublished contributions to books and ignores "first book appearances"—initial republications of the author's work in anthologies or other collections. Section C is better: it is a listing of Dreiser's newspaper and periodical appearances, based on the checklist published by Pizer in *Proof* (1971). Yet even these C listings, as Pizer recognizes, are incomplete. Some indication of the lacunae (and some notion of Dreiser's prolific output) can be seen in Stanton Garner's "Dreiser and the *New York Times Illustrated Magazine:* A Bibliographical Supplement" (*PBSA*, First Quarter, 1975). By checking the actual run of this periodical rather than relying on the *New York Times Index*, Garner turned up eight additional items from the period immediately after Dreiser left *Ev'ry Month*. Theodore Nostwich, whose edition of Dreiser's early newspaper work is complete in manuscript, has made a thorough search of the newspapers for which Dreiser wrote before 1900 and has expanded the number of items that can be attributed to him by about one-third over Pizer's listings.

A purely secondary bibliography on Dreiser has recently appeared: Jeanetta Boswell's *Theodore Dreiser and the Critics, 1911–1982* (Metuchen, N.J., 1986). In almost all respects this bibliography is disappointing. Boswell relies uncritically on the work of some previous Dreiser bibliographers but, paradoxically, seems to make little use of the listings compiled by Dowell and Rusch. Her coverage is spotty, and her citations and annotations are frequently inaccurate. The cutoff date for the Dowell/ Rusch listings is 1973; to locate subsequent work, scholars would be best advised to consult the semiannual listings in the *Dreiser Newsletter*, not Boswell's volume.

Louis Oldani's "Bibliographical Description of Dreiser's *The 'Genius'*" (*LC*, Winter 1973) shows the high level of sophistication at which a descriptive bibliography of Dreiser should be executed. Another example of bibliographical research is James L. W. West III's "Dreiser and the B. W. Dodge *Sister Carrie*" (*SB*, 1982), a reconstruction of the textual and commercial history of this pivotal "edition" of *Carrie*.

II EDITIONS

The most important and controversial edition published in the Dreiser field during the past decade is the Pennsylvania Edition of *Sister Carrie*: historical editors, John C. Berkey and Alice M. Winters; textual editor, James L. W. West III; general editor, Neda M. Westlake (Philadelphia, 1981). This scholarly edition presents a clear text based on the holograph manuscript at the New York Public Library. The edition includes a preface by Westlake and a historical essay written by West, maps and explanatory notes prepared by Berkey and Winters, a defense of editorial principles by West, a selected textual apparatus, and various appendixes. The historical essay, entitled *"Sister Carrie:* From Manuscript to Print," corrects errors in previously published scholarship, especially some misconceptions about the roles played in the composition of the novel by Dreiser's wife Sallie (or "Jug") and by his friend Arthur Henry. This essay adds information and detail to what Dreiser scholars previously knew. Of special interest is the reconstruction of the process by which Dreiser altered the ending of the novel and, with Henry's help, cut some 36,000 words from the typescript.

The text of the Pennsylvania Edition is different from that of the 1900 Doubleday, Page and Co. edition, the typesetting on which all editions have been based since 1900. The Pennsylvania text is much closer to the manuscript; nearly all of the 36,000 words removed by Henry and Dreiser are restored, as are Dreiser's original endings for the last two chapters. The Pennsylvania Edition concludes with Hurstwood committing suicide, not with Carrie musing in her rocking chair. The restoration of this material, according to the editors, alters characterization in the novel. Carrie is tougher and more resourceful, and she is a better actress. Drouet is less admirable, Hurstwood is more of a philanderer, Ames is more vulnerable to Carrie's charms. The editors believe that the Pennsylvania *Sister Carrie* is "a new work of art, heretofore unknown, which must be approached freshly and interpreted anew." "In its expanded form," they add, *"Sister Carrie* is infinitely richer, more complex, and more tragic than it was before." West stipulates at the end of the editorial essay, however, that the Pennsylvania text "should not be thought of as 'definitive.' There will never be a 'definitive' text of *Sister Carrie*. Its textual history is so complicated and, in places, so conjectural, that the ideal of a 'definitive' text will never be achieved." In the editing of Dreiser's texts, just as in the interpretation of his writings, one must develop a tolerance for ambiguity and irresolution.

There are other differences between the Pennsylvania Edition and previous texts. The Pennsylvania *Sister Carrie* is free of the typist and compositorial error that crept into the first edition; the anapestic chapter titles are gone; the original fifty-chapter structure has been restored. Real names of businesses, hotels, actors, theaters, and literary works have been reinstated, as have sections from Augustin Daly's melodrama *Under the Gaslight*, in which Carrie makes her theatrical debut in Chicago. Appendixes supply the chapter titles and the alternate endings for chapters 49 and 50. A scaled-down textual apparatus includes major emendations and other significant editorial data. A full typescript apparatus is on deposit for the record at the University of Pennsylvania Library, the Lilly Library, the Library of Congress, and the Huntington Library. The text of the Pennsylvania *Sister Carrie* has been published as a classroom paperback by the Penguin American Library, with an introduction by Alfred Kazin and a brief note on the text by West. Kazin's introduction was prepublished in the *New York Review of Books* (19 Feb. 1981).

The Pennsylvania *Sister Carrie* has drawn much attention and has sparked some disagreement. The edition was announced in a lengthy article by book critic Herbert Mitgang on the front page of the *New York Times* (17 Apr. 1981); that account was syndicated by both AP and UPI, and the wide exposure resulted in several other notices in major review organs. Noteworthy among these subsequent reviews were Justin Kaplan's (*NYTBR*, 31 May 1981), Richard Lingeman's (*Nation*, 11–18 July 1981), and Richard H. Brodhead's (*YR*, Summer 1982). There was also a broadcast on National Public Radio and an article in *People* magazine (6 July 1981).

Scholarly reactions have been both highly favorable and decidedly negative. Chief among the negative responses is Donald Pizer's lengthy attack on the Pennsylvania Edition (*AL*, Jan. 1982). Pizer contends that almost all changes to which an author acquiesces must remain in a text. A scholar should read and critique that first-published text because it is the end product of a collaborative creative act involving author, editor(s), and publisher. Pizer argues that the 1900 *Sister Carrie* is preferable because it "emerged out of the personal tensions, conflicting motives, and cultural complexities of its moment." Hershel Parker has challenged Pizer's position in a long review (*RALS*, Autumn 1981). Parker believes that the editorial theory behind the Pennsylvania *Sister Carrie* is sound and sees its text as far superior to the "maimed" text of the 1900 edition. Parker writes, "Now that we know what Dreiser really wrote, thanks to the Pennsylvania editors, we can see many places in the text as we knew it where passages are syntactically dangling, with referents lost, topics skewed." "Reading *Sister Carrie* as Dreiser wrote it," concludes Parker, "has transformed my opinion of the book and greatly enhanced my opinion of the author."

A spinoff publication from the Pennsylvania *Sister Carrie* is West's *A "Sister Carrie" Portfolio* (Charlottesville, Va., 1985), a pictorial history of the composition, publication, and suppression of Dreiser's novel. This volume presents the visual dimension of the *Carrie* project—an aspect missing from the Pennsylvania edition, which contains only eight small illustrations. The *Portfolio* includes facsimiles of leaves from the

manuscript and typescript, reproductions of correspondence and contracts, and photographs of Dreiser and others involved in the *Sister Carrie*
story. These images are brought together with captions and a running
commentary.

Another "edition" of *Sister Carrie*, not mentioned in Elias's 1973 supplement, is a photo-offset reissue of the abridged 1901 Heinemann "Dollar Library" text with an introduction by Jack Salzman (New York, 1969).
According to Salzman, Arthur Henry reduced the first 195 pages of the
novel by over half and in the process lessened the importance of Carrie's
role. As a result, Hurstwood's tragedy dominates the Heinemann text.
Salzman gives Henry title-page credit in this reissue, but in 1969 Salzman
did not have positive proof of Henry's role in the abridgement. That
proof is provided by John C. Berkey and Alice M. Winters in "The
Heinemann Edition of *Sister Carrie*" (*LC*, Spring 1979), one of several
articles in a special *Library Chronicle* issue devoted to *Sister Carrie*.

The second volume in the Pennsylvania Edition is Dreiser's *American
Diaries, 1902–1926*, edited by Thomas P. Riggio, with West serving as
textual editor and Westlake as general editor (Philadelphia, 1982). The
edition contains Dreiser's seven extant "American" diaries—those he
kept while living or traveling in the United States. These diaries, previously unpublished, cover Dreiser's most active and productive years.
They take him from his neurasthenic period in Philadelphia (1902–3),
when he considered giving up the writing game, through publication
of *An American Tragedy* in 1925, after which he began to enjoy the greatest
success of his career. Dreiser was an intermittent diarist, usually keeping
these journals in periods of intellectual ferment or emotional turmoil.
The entries are not especially introspective or self-revelatory, but
throughout one senses Dreiser's great energy and commitment to his
profession and his sheer pleasure in the act of writing. Among the most
sensational passages are those treating his sexual escapades, which were
frequent, and which often overlapped. Riggio, in his introduction,
supplies the background for each diary and demonstrates the biographical importance of the material. He also makes a persuasive case for
linking the writing and the varietism. The diary texts are rendered as
"private" documents, with nearly all misspellings, grammatical errors,
and other verbal idiosyncrasies preserved. There is an abbreviated apparatus at the rear of the volume and a complete record of emendation
on deposit at Pennsylvania. There are extensive explanatory and historical notes by Riggio, a full index, and twenty-six illustrations.

Many reviewers took the publication of these diaries as an occasion
for lengthy reassessments of Dreiser's career and reappraisals of his
importance in the history of American literature. Among the more penetrating of these reviews are the anonymous notice in the *New Yorker* (28
June 1982) and the reviews by Alfred Kazin (*NYTBR*, 22 Aug. 1982),

Richard Lingeman (*Nation*, 18 Sept. 1982), Pearl K. Bell (*TLS*, 24 Sept. 1982), and Kenneth S. Lynn (*ASch*, Fall 1982).

The third of the volumes produced by the Pennsylvania Dreiser Edition is the previously unpublished *An Amateur Laborer*, edited by Richard W. Dowell with West and Westlake again serving as textual and general editors (Philadelphia, 1983). The *Laborer* is an unfinished autobiographical account of Dreiser's bout with neurasthenia in 1902–3. We follow the author from a difficult period in Brooklyn, during which he literally came down to his last few cents, to his rescue by his brother Paul, who sent him to Muldoon's Sanitarium for rest and repair. Dreiser then took a job on the New York Central Railroad and worked in the carpentry shop at Spuyten Duyvil. There are twenty-four finished chapters, followed by a large group of fragments and false starts which testify to the trouble Dreiser was having with the book. The editors speculate that he had difficulty reconciling his contempt for the rich dissipators at Muldoon's with his dismay at the ignorance and stolidity of his comrades in labor on the railroad. Dreiser left the book unfinished but returned to the material repeatedly to quarry out essays, short fiction, and even some parts of *The "Genius."* In his introduction, Dowell scrupulously traces these patterns and relates the laboring experience to Dreiser's later career. In a textual note, West dates the extant manuscript, housed at the University of Pennsylvania Library, and explains editorial principles. (For an explanation of the technique used to date the manuscript, see West's "Mirrors and Microfilm: The Dating of Dreiser's *An Amateur Laborer*" [*MSS*, Winter 1983].) All twenty-four finished chapters are presented as "public" texts; some 15,000 words, selected from the fragments, are included as "private" texts. There are ten illustrations and an abbreviated textual apparatus, with a complete record of emendation on deposit at Pennsylvania. Among the noteworthy reviews of *An Amateur Laborer* are those by Herbert Mitgang (*New York Times*, 8 Sept. 1983); W. A. Swanberg (*Chicago Tribune Book World*, 27 Nov. 1983); and E. L. Doctorow (*NYTBR*, 4 Dec. 1983).

The other important unfinished book left by Dreiser at his death was a huge philosophical and mystical treatise on which he had been working for more than twenty years. In 1965, Marguerite Tjader received permission from the Dreiser estate to put the material into publishable form. Her edition is entitled *Notes on Life* (University, Ala., 1974); it is edited by Tjader and John J. McAleer, with a foreword by John Cowper Powys. Dreiser left a great amount of writing, but Tjader makes it clear that her edition "is not a finished philosophical study." Rather, it is "a vast brooding reaction to the Universe." Among Dreiser's materials were some lengthy essays and chapters, some shorter essays, and some paragraphs and notes. This edition presents all of the longer essays and a selection of the shorter items. Dreiser's ordering of topics is followed, with some rearrangement toward the end. The introduction is brief; the account of the handling of texts is vague; and there is no apparatus or index.

The title of Donald Pizer's *Theodore Dreiser: A Selection of Uncollected Prose* (Detroit, Mich., 1977) suggests that the collection is a miscellany, but it is actually a selection of philosophical writings from various periods of Dreiser's career. It is therefore a kind of companion volume to *Notes on Life*. There are essays, commentaries, occasional pieces, and a few interviews. Much of the early philosophical writing from *Ev'ry Month* is here. Pizer discerns a pattern: Dreiser shifts from "a stress on the destructiveness, turmoil, and impersonality of the 'formula' which is life to an emphasis on its wonder, beauty, and beneficence." Pizer has chosen to reproduce only published texts, even though manuscripts and typescripts of some of these writings do survive among Dreiser's papers at Pennsylvania. There is some minor silent emending and some slightly more significant emending within square brackets.

Yoshinobu Hakutani's edition of *Selected Magazine Articles of Theodore Dreiser: Life and Art in the American 1890s* (Cranbury, N.J., 1985) is a worthy project rendered confusing by its manner of publication. The prefatory matter of the book was written for a one-volume selection of some fifty-four of Dreiser's roughly 120 early magazine articles, but the 288-page book at hand contains only half of this material. Nothing on the title page or binding of the book indicates that it is the first volume of a two-volume set; that fact is mentioned in only one place—on the rear flap of the dust jacket. Did the publisher perhaps decide, late in the game, to divide the material into two volumes but then neglect to make appropriate changes in the front matter and on the binding? One presumes that the remaining material will be published eventually in a second volume. To judge from this first installment, Hakutani has made a judicious selection from Dreiser's early magazine work, and he has handled the texts responsibly, correcting only demonstrable errors and preserving most other features of the original periodical texts. The articles themselves, heretofore virtually unavailable, are of much interest both to Dreiserians and to students of the American 1890s. Dreiser writes about many public figures and topics of the period; especially welcome are his interviews, for the magazine *Success*, with such men as Philip D. Armour, Marshall Field, Andrew Carnegie, and Thomas A. Edison. Hakutani has also included some of the illustrative material which accompanied the original articles.

Jennie Gerhardt is finally back in print, with an introduction by Helen Yglesias (New York, 1982). The introduction urges us to consider *Sister Carrie* and *Jennie Gerhardt* together from a feminist perspective because "our present feminist sensibilities create a need to so arrange these sisterly books in our minds." Yglesias gives a good account of Jennie's strength and womanliness but does not mention Letty Gerald, who in her way is as interesting a female character as Jennie. The publisher of this edition chose to photo-offset the text of the corrupt 1928 Constable "New Uniform Edition," presumably because at 367 pages this British text was cheaper to reprint than the 433-page Harpers 1911 first American edition.

A one-volume edition of the Trilogy of Desire, with a good general introduction by Philip L. Gerber, was published by World in 1972, shortly before that firm was absorbed by a conglomerate. The novels in the trilogy were then issued separately by Thomas Y. Crowell in its large paperback Apollo series, with Gerber's entire introduction in each volume. These World and Crowell "editions" are photo-offset reproductions of the 1927 revised *Financier*, the 1914 *Titan*, and the 1947 *Stoic*. Both the World and the Crowell issues are now out of print, but in 1981 New American Library published the trilogy, in separate volumes, in its Signet Classics series. Ten paperback and four clothbound editions of *Sister Carrie* were listed in *Books in Print* for 1983–84, but there is no edition of either *The "Genius"* or *The Bulwark* currently available in this country.

III MANUSCRIPTS AND LETTERS

Thomas P. Riggio's "Europe without Baedeker: The Omitted Hanscha Jower Story—from *A Traveler at Forty*" (*MFS*, Autumn 1977) prints for the first time the texts of two chapters omitted from *Traveler* by the Century editors. These chapters describe a German streetwalker whom Dreiser met and by whose plight he was moved. Riggio reveals that the Century editors cut over forty chapters from Dreiser's typescript; some of it was "woman stuff," the rest was descriptions of low-class urban life or autobiographical revelations judged too intimate for public consumption. The manuscript of *Traveler* does not survive, but fortunately we have the typescript. Someday Dreiserians should be able to read the text whole.

Neda M. Westlake and Jack Salzman have resurrected "An Unpublished Chapter from *An American Tragedy*" in the first volume of *Prospects* (1975). This item is one of three pieces in a special section entitled "*An American Tragedy*: A 50th Anniversary." The title of this first item is slightly misleading, since this is not a chapter removed from the finished typescript Dreiser sent to Liveright. Rather, it appears to be an early draft in which Dreiser is trying to work out the basics of Clyde's character. The editors give an unemended text, with inconsistencies and illogicalities untouched. The draft tells us some interesting things about Dreiser's methods of composition. "Dreiser was obviously writing rapidly," the editors note, "feeling his way into the early life of Clyde Griffiths, as though trying several possible tunes before the melody would become clear to him." Also reproduced in this section of *Prospects* are some of the plates from *The Symbolic Drawings of Hubert Davis for "An American Tragedy" by Theodore Dreiser* (New York, 1930).

Robert A. Morace's article, "Dreiser's Contract for *Sister Carrie*: More Fact and Fiction" (*JML*, May 1982), is in effect a footnote to the Pennsylvania Edition of *Carrie*. Morace wishes to defend Frank Norris from Jack Salzman's contention that he backed out on Dreiser and refused to fight Frank Doubleday over *Sister Carrie* (Salzman, "The Publication of *Sister Carrie:* Fact and Fiction" [*LC*, Spring 1967]). Certainly Morace is correct; Norris had no real leverage in the firm, and it would have mattered little had he gone to the wall for Dreiser. A second and more important matter concerns the contract between Doubleday and Dreiser for publication of the novel. Morace has seen the Doubleday copy of the contract, which still survives in that publisher's files. The escalating royalty clause has not been excised on the Doubleday copy; but it has been struck out on Dreiser's copy, which is among his papers at Pennsylvania. Morace makes much of the difference and puts together fanciful explanations for the strikeovers on Dreiser's copy. He imagines a confrontation between Dreiser and Doubleday in the latter's office in which Doubleday becomes angry and marks through the clause. A more plausible explanation is that the clause was struck because it had become pointless. The escalating royalties would have begun only after 1,500 copies had been sold, but Doubleday printed only 1,008 sets of sheets and did not have them all bound up. Perhaps Dreiser, who saw how the numbers were going to work out when he received his royalty statements, struck the clause himself on his copy. One thing is certain: the clause was not excised by mutual agreement because it was not initialed by the signatories.

Yoshinobu Hakutani, in "Dreiser and Rose White" (*LC*, Spring 1979), uses manuscript evidence to identify Rose, Jug's sister, as the original of "Rella" in *A Gallery of Women*. Dreiser tried to conceal the autobiographical basis of the sketch with a short foreword, but Hakutani shows the foreword to have been an obvious subterfuge.

Three articles growing out of the Pennsylvania *Sister Carrie* project deal with unpublished manuscript material; all three appear in the special *Library Chronicle* issue devoted to *Carrie* (Spring 1979). Neda M. Westlake, in "The *Sister Carrie* Scrapbook," describes a book of *Sister Carrie* memorabilia kept by Dreiser. This scrapbook contains numerous letters from persons who read *Carrie*, along with other important materials. In "*Nicholas Blood* and *Sister Carrie*," James L. W. West III reprints a four-part item on Dreiser and Arthur Henry from the March 1902 *Bookman* and follows up some of the clues in the piece. "John Paul Dreiser's Copy of *Sister Carrie*," also by West, is a description of the most spectacular copy of the 1900 *Sister Carrie* at Pennsylvania, a copy inscribed by Dreiser jointly to his father and to his sister Mame and her husband Austin Brennan. The copy contains penciled revisions by Dreiser throughout the first six chapters. West speculates about the nature of these changes and asks why Dreiser stopped making them after chapter 6.

Several new Dreiser letters have appeared in print. In "Dreiser to Sandburg: Three Unpublished Letters" (*LC*, Winter 1976), Robert Carringer and Scott Bennett document Dreiser's support of young Carl Sandburg in 1915. William J. Heim, in "Letters from Young Dreiser" (*ALR*, Spring 1975), publishes three letters from a very green Theodore Dreiser to his Warsaw friend Judson Morris. These letters, written from Chicago in 1888 and 1889, are earlier than any in the Elias collection. Ezra Pound's support of Dreiser in the battle over *The "Genius"* is revealed in Louis Oldani's "Two Unpublished Pound Letters: Pound's Aid to Dreiser" (*LC*, Spring 1977).

The two volumes of *Dreiser-Mencken Letters*, edited by Thomas P. Riggio (Philadelphia, 1986), have recently appeared and are in every respect a worthy production. Included here are virtually all of the communications that passed between Dreiser and Mencken between 1907 and 1945. This is one of the major literary correspondences of the twentieth century in America; it is also an intriguing portrait of two men who were basically dissimilar in temperament and tastes but who formed an alliance that, in the end, helped both achieve recognition and success. The letters themselves are fascinating: Mencken, witty and pithy, is the better epistoler, but Dreiser is not far behind. Riggio has divided the correspondence into six sections; his introductory remarks for each section provide background and trace the progress of the relationship. (For Riggio's condensed and unified version of these remarks, see the *American Scholar* [Spring 1985].) The textual policy for the letters is sensible, save perhaps for the decision not to add periods to the ends of all of Dreiser's sentences. The annotations are brief and unobtrusive.

IV BIOGRAPHY

The major event here is the recent publication of volume 1 of Richard Lingeman's projected two-volume biography of Dreiser. This first volume, entitled *Theodore Dreiser: At the Gates of the City, 1871–1907* (New York, 1986), takes the story up to the "second debut" of *Sister Carrie*—the B. W. Dodge edition of the novel. Lingeman's account is full, readable, and above all sympathetic. We see Dreiser as Dreiser would have wished us to see him; that is to say, Lingeman accepts the pattern for viewing Dreiser's early life that Dreiser himself provided for us in *Dawn* and *Newspaper Days*. The major shortcoming of this biography is its failure to address or interpret Dreiser's writing in any significant way, but one must still be grateful to Lingeman: his humane, balanced view of Dreiser is an excellent antidote to the damage done by Swanberg.

The only other book-length biographical study of Dreiser to appear since 1973 is Vera Dreiser's *My Uncle Theodore: An Intimate Family Portrait* (New York, 1976). Vera Dreiser, the daughter of Ed, the youngest of the Dreiser children, was attracted to her uncle. Part of the attraction seems to have been sexual and another part seems to have come from Vera's desire to rebel against her mother, Mai, who hated Dreiser. Perhaps because she is a psychologist by profession, Vera seems anxious to categorize her relatives, to pin them sprawling on the wall, often with limited evidence. John Paul Dreiser, Sr., we learn, was suffering from "minimal brain dysfunction," and his wife was so "self-preoccupied" that she did great damage to Theo's masculinity. Theodore himself was an arrested Oedipal: "Every normal little boy loves his mother in a *forbidden* way," explains Vera, "but passes through this phase easily when other family relations are normal. In Theo's case they were not. Sarah burdened Theo as a young child with her dependent and possessive love. His mother was seductive while he was still a young child. He developed a *fixation*." Psychologizing aside, *My Uncle Theodore* is valuable for the information it contains about Dreiser's parents and siblings, and about Jug, Helen Dreiser, and Louise Dresser.

Through what one must assume was a missed connection, there are two lengthy sketches of Dreiser in the *Dictionary of Literary Biography*. The first, by Philip Gerber, is in volume 9, *American Novelists, 1910–1945* (Detroit, Mich., 1981); the second, by Donald Pizer, is in volume 12, *American Realists and Naturalists* (Detroit, Mich., 1982). The accounts differ in the ways one would expect. Pizer sticks more closely to the biographical facts than Gerber and concentrates on *Sister Carrie, Jennie Gerhardt*, and *An American Tragedy*. Gerber gives the better statement of Dreiser's philosophy and is stronger on the trilogy and the short stories.

Terre Haute historian Augustus R. Markle conducted research during the 1940s and 1950s on Dreiser's boyhood years, and he challenged the accuracy of many of Dreiser's statements in *Dawn*. But in "Ask Mr. Markle?" (*DrN*, Spring 1977), Richard W. Dowell demonstrates that Markle himself was casual and biased in his work. Thomas P. Riggio, in "The Dreisers in Sullivan: A Biographical Revision" (*DrN*, Fall 1979), uses Sullivan County newspaper files and materials at the Indiana State Library to expose other errors by Markle. Riggio clears up several important points about the fire which destroyed John Paul Dreiser's mill and about the senior Dreiser's support of the local Catholic church.

"The Curious History of Dreiser's *The Bulwark*" (*Proof*, 1973), by Jack Salzman, is a tangled story that begins in 1914 and ends only after Dreiser's death. Dreiser had advanced far enough with the manuscript of *The Bulwark* by 1916 for John Lane Co. to prepare promotional dummies and trial dust jackets, but thereafter Dreiser's interest in the novel lapsed. For thirty years he used *The Bulwark* as bait whenever he negotiated with a new publisher, and at various times the book was under contract to Lane, Liveright, Simon and Schuster, Putnam's, and Doubleday. The various typescripts were edited or influenced by Louise Campbell, James T. Farrell, Marguerite Tjader Harris, and Helen Dreiser; the final published text is a conflation by Doubleday editor Donald Elder, who served as a kind of mediator. One of the Lane dummies is facsimiled in Salzman's informative article, along with the Putnam's contract.

If Philip L. Gerber's book on the trilogy is up to the level of "Dreiser's *Stoic*: A Study in Literary Frustration" (*LMonog*, 1975), then Dreiser scholars can look forward to a very useful volume. Gerber's monograph on Dreiser's last novel is essentially a biographical account to which have been added some perceptive comments about the ways Dreiser transformed fact into fiction.

"Theodore Dreiser Visits Toronto" (*CRevAS*, Spring 1983), by Joseph Griffin, is a well-researched account of Dreiser's September 1942 trip to the Canadian city, where he was to give an address entitled "Democracy on the Offensive." Because Dreiser unwisely made anti-British statements to the local press, his speech was canceled and he had to hurry out of Toronto. There were repercussions: Dreiser was censured by the Writers' War Board and had to prepare a public explanation of his behavior for the League of American Writers.

Rolf Lundén's "Theodore Dreiser and the Nobel Prize" (*AL*, May 1978) is a summary of Dreiser's efforts to win the award and an account of his disappointment when he failed. The Swedish judges, says Lundén, probably gave the prize to Sinclair Lewis because, like most Swedes, they had great contempt for American materialism. Of the two authors, Lewis was the more critical of American acquisitiveness; by voting the award to him, the judges gave a backhanded slap to America. Lundén's monograph *Dreiser Looks at Scandinavia* (Stockholm, 1977) is an account of the author's visit to Scandinavia with Helen in the summer of 1926. Lundén's narrative is essentially an expansion of the unpublished diary Dreiser kept during the trip. An appendix entitled "Scandinavia Looks at Dreiser" is a sketch of his critical reception in Sweden, Denmark, and Norway; Lundén had published most of this material earlier (*DrN*, Spring 1975).

The chapter on Dreiser in Charles A. Madison's *Irving to Irving: Author-Publisher Relations, 1800–1974* (New York, 1974) is predictably entitled "Dreiser's Troubles with Publishers." The chapter is not footnoted or otherwise documented, but most of the facts about Dreiser's difficulties with the tribe of Barabbas come from Swanberg's biography, from Salzman's "The Publication of *Sister Carrie*: Fact and Fiction," and from Walker Gilmer's 1970 book on Horace Liveright. One of the many publishers who did not like Dreiser was Bennett Cerf. *At Random: The Reminiscences of Bennett Cerf* (New York, 1977) includes Cerf's recollections about Dreiser, whom he remembered as churlish and disagreeable.

Dreiser's friendship with Sherwood Anderson is illuminated by Hilbert H. Campbell in "Dreiser in New York: A Diary Source" (*DrN*, Fall 1982). This note includes previously unpublished passages from Anderson's 1933 and 1934 diaries, with explanatory annotations by Campbell. Vincent Fitzpatrick's "Mencken, Dreiser, and the Baltimore *Evening Sun*"

(*Menckeniana*, Winter 1976) reveals nothing new about the Dreiser-Mencken relationship, but Fitzpatrick has gone through Mencken's *Evening Sun* columns and extracted all references to Dreiser. The most interesting are those from 1916, when the suppression of *The "Genius"* was a hot item. In "Gratitude and Grievances: Dreiser's Inscriptions to Mencken" (*DrN*, Fall 1981), Fitzpatrick demonstrates how these inscriptions reflect the progress and deterioration of the Dreiser-Mencken friendship.

Of significant value is Ulrich Halfmann's "Dreiser and Howells: New Light on their Relationship" (*Amst*, Feb. 1975; abstracted in *ALR*, Autumn 1975). Halfmann concludes that Dreiser's first article on Howells for *Success* was not based on a face-to-face interview but instead on a questionnaire that Dreiser submitted to Howells. Many of the quotations attributed to Howells are actually taken from *My Literary Passions* (1895). Howells may have disapproved of Dreiser's "interviewing" methods; that would help explain his reluctance to endorse the younger author's novels in later years.

Dreiser's early attraction to Japanese life and culture is chronicled in Yoshinobu Hakutani's "Theodore Dreiser, Japan, and World War II" (*RALS*, Fall 1978). In the late 1930s, Dreiser turned against Japan as his own loyalties shifted away from Germany toward America and Russia. Hakutani reproduces, from the University of Pennsylvania collection, Dreiser's June 1941 contribution to a newspaper symposium on Japanese-American relations.

One of the more interesting articles of the decade is Margaret B. McDowell's "The Children's Feature: A Guide to the Editors' Perceptions of Adult Readers of Women's Magazines" (*MQ*, Oct. 1977). McDowell argues that "in periods of alarmist shifts toward conservatism in regard to the woman's role in the family, articles for adults in women's magazines tend to become more sentimental and limited to domestic concerns." Articles for children often reflect this same tendency. McDowell chooses two magazines to illustrate her point: the *Delineator* after 1906 and *McCall's* after 1954. Dreiser was editor of the *Delineator* during much of the period studied by McDowell; his editorial policy aimed, among other things, at decreasing the national divorce rate. One cringes at the picture of the author of *Sister Carrie* soliciting articles on "The Well-Arranged Living Room" or "How You Can Develop Your Chest."

The point of "*Sister Carrie* Again" by Christopher P. Wilson (*AL*, May 1981) is not clear. Wilson appears to be saying that after about 1900, publishing houses began trying to sew up authors for their entire careers. Walter Hines Page, he feels, really had Dreiser's best interests in mind when he tried to dissuade him from publishing *Sister Carrie*. Doubleday, Page and Co. would have "signed" Dreiser had he written a second, more acceptable novel. Wilson is hampered by having read only the selections from the Doubleday-Dreiser correspondence that Donald Pizer included in his Norton Critical Edition of *Sister Carrie* (New York, 1970). Wilson should read the entire correspondence at Pennsylvania and read it more skeptically than he has read the letters in Pizer's edition.

Two final items in this section concern Dreiser biographer W. A. Swanberg. Dennis W. Petrie, in *Ultimately Fiction: Design in Modern American Literary Biography* (West Lafayette, Ind., 1981), gives an extended critique of Swanberg's biography as part of a larger examination of prominent biographies of modern American authors. Petrie contrasts Swanberg's *Dreiser* with Andrew Turnbull's *Scott Fitzgerald*: Turnbull is sympathetic to his author, Swanberg antipathetic to his. Swanberg views Dreiser as a child and sees himself as the parent, ferreting out Dreiser's malefactions and administering punishment. Swanberg's failure to analyze Dreiser's writing, according to Petrie, "weakens his endeavors immeasurably." Support for Petrie's assessment comes from Burroughs Mitchell, the editor at Scribner's who handled Swanberg's books. In his memoirs, entitled *The Education of an Editor* (Garden City, N.Y., 1980), Mitchell reveals that the editors at Scribner's proposed the biography to Swanberg, who initially had no interest in Dreiser. Swanberg was looking for another rogue to tackle after finishing *Citizen Hearst*. The editors' suggestion was a mistake; Mitchell admits that the Swanberg-Dreiser match was a classic case of incompatibility between author and subject. "By a notable exercise of will," notes Mitchell, "[Swanberg] managed to control his dislike of Dreiser" and finish the book.

V CRITICISM

1 Full-length Studies

The major book here is Donald Pizer's *The Novels of Theodore Dreiser: A Critical Study* (Minneapolis, 1976). Pizer's two aims in the book are "to establish the facts of the sources and composition of each of Dreiser's novels and to study the themes and form of the completed work." Pizer has "sought to avoid a schematized view of Dreiser which posits a single overriding theme or direction in his work. Much Dreiser criticism of the past," he believes, "has been weakened by a tendency to sacrifice the distinctiveness of particular novels for a symmetrical interpretation of his career as a whole." Some of Pizer's reviewers faulted him for not pursuing a pattern—see, for example, Riggio (*SNNTS*, Summer 1977)— but Pizer's decision not to do so may have been wise, given what we are beginning to find out about the composition of *The Bulwark* and *The Stoic*. It is difficult to know whose ideas of resolution one is reading in those last two novels.

Among general studies of modern American writers, *The Novels of Theodore Dreiser* most nearly resembles Michael Millgate's *The Achievement of William Faulkner* (1966). For each novel Pizer, like Millgate, has attempted to summarize the circumstances under which the book was written, revised, edited, and published. Pizer has made use of the surviving manuscripts and correspondence at Pennsylvania, the Lilly Library, and elsewhere. In the second half of each chapter he has essayed a general interpretation of the novel, often working from what he knows of its composition, and thus his interpretations are closely tied to his reconstructions of the compositional histories of the books. Therein lies the problem. The making of each novel was so complex that Pizer is able only to sketch in the broad outlines of what happened. Inevitably he misses important details that a scholar concentrating only on one novel would note. For example, he fails to differentiate Jug's handwriting in the manuscript of *Sister Carrie* from Arthur Henry's and therefore misses her crucial role in the making of that novel. Her changes are all ascribed to Henry—a major blunder. (See Stephen C. Brennan, "The Composition of *Sister Carrie*: A Reconsideration" [*DrN*, Fall 1978].) In the chapter on *Jennie Gerhardt*, Pizer downplays the enormous importance of Ripley Hitchcock's editing of the novel, and for *The Bulwark* he appears to ignore Salzman's discoveries, even though Salzman's *Proof* article was available to him.

Pizer's most serious problem is his predisposition to approve of the editing and cutting of each novel, no matter who did it or what was done. In some ways the approach resembles Swanberg's: Dreiser is seen as an unlettered, childish writer who was incapable of putting his material into proper shape. His various editors, rather after the manner of disciplinarians, caught the errors and identified the overwritten passages, then administered chastisement with the blue pencil. Of course, Pizer *must* approve the editing of each novel if he is to interpret the published document—else how can his interpretation have validity? Pizer's book shows why immensely detailed research into the textual histories of Dreiser's novels is needed. We may discover that meanings exist in these novels in a kind of shifting continuum, that intentionality was infused by Dreiser in a series of steps, and that important, fugitive meanings survive in prepublication versions, in manuscripts and typescripts untouched by the Ripley Hitchcocks and the Donald Elders.

Pizer constructed no pattern for Dreiser's career, but Lawrence E. Hussman, Jr., in *Dreiser and His Fiction: A Twentieth-Century Quest* (Philadelphia, 1983), does see a pattern and pursue a thesis. He argues that Dreiser's first five novels are weak and confused because of internally warring elements (determinism, idealism, romanticism, sentimentalism). In the later novels Dreiser resolves his problems and reaches a resolution in *The Bulwark*. One does not have to agree with Hussman's thesis to profit from his book. He distorts his interpretations slightly in order to make the early novels look confused, but there is good handling of abstract ideas throughout this book, and the writing is excellent. The best chapter is on *An American Tragedy*, and there is a good chapter on seven of Dreiser's short stories which Hussman brings together and labels the "marriage group." *Dreiser and His Fiction* contains the first extended interpretation of the new Pennsylvania *Sister Carrie*.

Yoshinobu Hakutani's *Young Dreiser: A Critical Study* (Madison, N.J., 1980) is a "French biography" of the author. Hakutani worked on this project for some seventeen years; four of the eight chapters were previously published (one each in 1964 and 1967, and two in 1978). That background might explain why the chapters in this book seem to be discrete essays rather than parts of an integrated whole, and it might also reveal why many of the critical issues raised are old ones. (For an elaboration of these criticisms, see Riggio, "Dreiser in the Making" [*Rev.*, 1981].) Hakutani argues that Dreiser's thinking and writing come less from his reading of Huxley, Spencer, and Hardy than from his difficult childhood and his later journalistic apprenticeship. Hakutani has the advantage of having read *Dawn* and *Newspaper Days* in the uncut typescript versions. This is a useful introduction to Dreiser, with good chapters on the editorial and free-lance work.

Rolf Lundén's *The Inevitable Equation: The Antithetic Pattern of Theodore Dreiser's Thought and Art* (Uppsala, 1973) addresses the contrast, the antithetic pattern, embodied in an author who was at once "a Babbitt and a Shelley." Dreiser had the mind of a deterministic philosopher but the heart of an emotional idealist. In part 1 of his book Lundén discusses the basic philosophical pattern of *Notes on Life*, which he has studied in its unpublished form. He then traces that pattern back into Dreiser's life as far as possible, into the 1890s, just as Hakutani does. In part 2 of the study, Lundén moves forward, showing how the antithetic pattern is present in the novels, short fiction, and poetry. His book is as much a study of Dreiser's philosophical beliefs as it is an interpretation of his fiction, and it is most valuable for what it tells us about *Notes*. Lundén's remarks are more extensive than any of the commentary in the Tjader-McAleer edition.

R. N. Mookerjee's *Theodore Dreiser: His Thought and Social Criticism* (Delhi, 1974) is a biographical study which concentrates on Dreiser's role as social critic during his last twenty years. Mookerjee discusses various early influences on Dreiser (his family, religious training, education, and newspaper work), then examines the published oeuvre to show how Dreiser's social consciousness emerged. This study includes discussions of such neglected volumes as *Tragic America* and *America Can Be Saved*.

Among guides and handbooks, Philip L. Gerber's *Plots and Characters in the Fiction of Theodore Dreiser* (Hamden, Conn., 1977) deserves mention. The book includes a chronology of Dreiser's career, a preface for the nonspecialist, and plot summaries of the novels and the stories in *Free* and *Chains*. These summaries are given in alphabetical order by title—an unfortunate arrangement presumably dictated by the requirements of the Archon series in which this book was published. A chronological ordering would have shown the pattern of Dreiser's career more clearly. Still, one can discern trends in the fiction and a fondness for certain kinds of characters and situations. Gerber notes the frequency with which Dreiser's characters adopt aliases, and he comments on their rootlessness and constant movement.

James Lundquist's *Theodore Dreiser* (MLM, New York, 1974) is an introduction for the general reader or undergraduate. The initial chapter, a biographical account entitled "Dreiser Himself," suffers from an uncritical acceptance of information from the autobiographies. There is an oddly full account (for this type of book) of Dreiser's difficulties with Hollywood over the movie version of *An American Tragedy*. Perhaps the emphasis at Ungar on film studies influenced this section. Fortunately, Lundquist was able to rely on good earlier work by Richard Lehan and Ellen Moers. He alerts the undergraduate to the contradictions in Dreiser's writings and tells him not to be disturbed.

2 Collections

Jack Salzman's *Theodore Dreiser: The Critical Reception* (New York, 1972) is a 742-page assemblage of contemporary reviews of Dreiser's work. In his introduction Salzman gives a summary of Dreiser's career, then sketches in the reception of each book and comments on the battles that raged around some of the novels. The organization is chronological by book. The texts are faithfully reproduced; plot summaries in the reviews have been deleted. Most of these notices were sent to Dreiser by clipping services, and the clippings are today stored in two large filing cabinets at the University of Pennsylvania Library. Salzman has saved Dreiser scholars hours of hunting through those cabinets. One disappointment is that the only British reviews included are those for *Sister Carrie*, but one can understand the omission, given the already hefty size of the book.

Donald Pizer has edited *Critical Essays on Theodore Dreiser* (CEAmL, Boston, 1981). This is the third such collection to appear in the Dreiser field; the other two are *The Stature of Theodore Dreiser* (ed. Alfred Kazin and Charles Shapiro, Bloomington, Ind., 1955) and *Dreiser: A Collection of Critical Essays* (ed. John Lydenberg, TCV, Englewood Cliffs, N.J., 1971). The Pizer volume contains more reviews and more material generally than either of its predecessors, though almost one-third of Pizer's selections (twelve out of thirty-seven items) were also included either in Kazin-Shapiro or Lydenberg. Some of the selections have been cut, and there are no previously unpublished contributions, as there often are in the other volumes in the Critical Essays series. In his introduction, Pizer divides Dreiser criticism into three phases. He also notes, "From the appearance of *Sister Carrie* to the present, an opportunity to examine

Dreiser also has meant an opportunity to press the claims of a particular view of American life and a specific concept about the nature of fiction."

3 General Essays

Donald Pizer's essay, "American Literary Naturalism: The Example of Dreiser" (*SAF*, Spring 1977; reprinted in *American Fiction: Historical and Critical Essays*, ed. James Nagel, Boston, 1977), may be a partial answer to those critics of *The Novels of Theodore Dreiser* who complained that the book had no unifying theme. American literary naturalism, according to Pizer, has almost always been viewed with hostility in this country. Many critics find naturalistic belief "both objectionable in its own right and incompatible with fictional quality." Pizer argues that one does not have to penetrate beyond the "tainted" philosophical beliefs of the naturalists to find what is good in their work, and he points to Dreiser as his example. He uses some of his comments on *Jennie Gerhardt* and *An American Tragedy* from *Novels* to show the complexity and wholeness of Dreiser's vision. A related essay by Pizer is "Nineteenth-Century American Naturalism: An Approach through Form" (*ForumH*, Winter 1976). Here he takes as his starting point Edwin Cady's essay "Three Sensibilities: Romancer, Realist, Naturalist" from *The Light of Common Day* (Bloomington, Ind., 1971). Cady had difficulty characterizing the naturalistic sensibility because the ideas which the naturalist should espouse were frequently contradicted by his fiction. Pizer attempts to render a definition by approaching naturalistic fiction through form. Naturalistic writing is often circular; the value of experience is not necessarily affirmed. Though life leads nowhere, the naturalistic novelist still believes in the importance of a curious, questioning temperament.

Philip L. Gerber's "Dreiser: 'Extreme and Bloody Individualism,'" in *American Literary Naturalism: A Reassessment* (ed. Yoshinobu Hakutani and Lewis Fried, Heidelberg, 1975), summarizes the common objections to Dreiser's style and subject matter. Gerber suggests that critics miss the point: Dreiser's real purpose is to draw a "portrait of a society whose potential for greatness has been 'betrayed by money.'"

In "Dreiser and the Prophetic Tradition" (*AmerS*, Fall 1974), Robert Forrey investigates the religious element in Dreiser's writing from the beginning of his career to the end. Dreiser's religious impulse was "prophetic," that is, "more concerned with the now than the hereafter; with social justice, rather than salvation; and with the spirit, rather than the letter of religious law."

The last chapter of Ronald E. Martin's *American Literature and the Universe of Force* (Durham, N.C., 1981) is on Dreiser, whom Martin sees as comfortably "at home" with turn-of-the-century ideas about systems of force. The Cowperwood trilogy is a good example; in those novels, "fate could virtually be diagrammed as a complex system of vectors." Dreiser's shortcomings as a philosopher get the usual thumping.

Wilbur M. Frohock's "The State of Dreiser Criticism on His Centenary," in *Geschichte und Gesellschaft in der amerikanischen Literatur* (ed. Karl Schubert and Ursula Müller-Richter, Heidelberg, 1975), notes a recent improvement in the tone of critical writing on Dreiser. Frohock believes that part of the change grows out of a broader conception among American critics of what the novel can be. No longer must an author have written Jamesian narratives accessible to New Critics. Frohock's assessment includes a useful sketch of the history of Dreiser criticism; one wishes his essay had appeared in a more accessible publication.

One of the more intriguing general essays is Robert Forrey's "Theodore Dreiser: Oedipus Redivivus" (*MFS*, Autumn 1977), an "attempt to apply some of the insights of the French Freudians to Dreiser's work." Forrey discerns an Oedipal structure in Dreiser's life and work; instead of passing through anal, oral, and phallic stages, "Dreiser remained essentially oral in his psycho-sexual orientation." The idea is in some ways persuasive, but Forrey is selective about choosing evidence, and his arguments become vague at the end of his article. Another stimulating essay is Philip Fisher's "Looking Around to See Who I Am: Dreiser's Territory of the Self" (*ELH*, Winter 1977). Fisher locates Dreiser in a tradition of character development with Zola, Joyce, and Dos Passos—as opposed to the tradition of James, Conrad, Proust, and Faulkner. Fisher's frenchified jargon obscures the ideas in the early part of his article, but his statements about Clyde in the *Tragedy* are sound. According to Fisher, Dreiser often pictures societies that are made up of small social units; Clyde's identity is defined by the successive units to which he attaches himself.

An essay by Ellen Moers, "The Survivors: Into the Twentieth Century" (*TCL*, Jan. 1974), is a contemplative piece inspired by the centenary celebration of Dreiser's birth held in Terre Haute in 1971. Moers honors the "middle-aged makers of modern"—Proust, Thomas Mann, Yeats, Valéry, Stravinsky, Rilke, Joyce, Frank Lloyd Wright, Shaw, and Picasso. She sees much similarity between Proust and Dreiser and calls both men "canny old artificers . . . whose radical experiments issued from their maturity."

Gary Stephens's "Haunted Americana: The Endurance of American Realism" (*PR*, Spring 1977) is a general essay about the strength of American realistic fiction. Twain, Howells, James, and Dreiser are the examples, and the ideas are familiar. Stephens sees Dreiser as the most successful of these four writers. In "Dreiser at the World's Fair: The City Without Limits" (*MFS*, Autumn 1977), Guy Szuberla discusses Dreiser's view of the city as a place of infinite possibility. Szuberla shows how the Chicago World's Fair of 1893 was meant to convey a sense of infinitude; Dreiser caught the idea, as his reports for the *St. Louis Republic* attest. This is an excellent article. Szuberla has even done research in Frederick Law Olmsted's papers at the Library of Congress to study

Olmsted's original conception of the "White City" he wanted to create at the Chicago Fair.

George M. Spangler's "Suicide and Social Criticism: Durkheim, Dreiser, Wharton, and London" (*AQ*, Fall 1979) takes sociologist Emile Durkheim's three categories of suicide (egotistic, altruistic, and anomic) and applies them to the three novelists mentioned in his title. Hurstwood's suicide in *Sister Carrie* is a good example of the "egotistic," in which the individual cannot integrate with society. In "The Image of Women in Dreiser's Fiction" (*PCP*, Apr. 1972), Sybil B. Weir presents Dreiser as "the first, and perhaps the only, major American novelist who refuses to present women only as symbols of the American ideal." The sexual careers of Dreiser's female characters do not make them immoral in his eyes. Weir examines Dreiser's heroines in succession and at length, finding Roberta Alden and Sondra Finchley his most successful creations.

In "Literary Discourse, 'Ordinary Discourse,' and Intentions: David Lodge and the Language of *Sister Carrie*," a chapter in *Worlds from Words: A Theory of Language in Fiction* (Chicago, 1981), James Phelan begins with Lodge's belief in the nonparaphrasability of literary language, disagrees with that stance, and shows convincingly how, in *Sister Carrie*, Dreiser's intention remains constant despite "improvements" and paraphrases. Phelan concludes with an amusing rewrite of a passage from *Sister Carrie* in the style of Henry James.

Thomas P. Riggio's "Dreiser on Society and Literature: The San Francisco Exposition Interview" (*ALR*, Autumn 1978) is transcribed from an unmarked recording at Pennsylvania, but internal evidence indicates that the interview took place during the 1939 Golden Gate International Exposition. The interview prompted Dreiser "to a rare public discussion of his reading and his aesthetics," which were still heavily influenced by nineteenth-century ideals, even at this late date. For Dreiser, art should reflect life, not distort it.

Joseph J. Kwiat undertakes a thorough examination of this same subject in "Theodore Dreiser's Creative Quest: Early 'Philosophical' Beliefs and Artistic Values" (*ArQ*, Autumn 1981). Dreiser's philosophy was "sophomoric and experimental," his artistic ideas "haphazard and contradictory." Nevertheless, "the critic is impressed with Dreiser's struggle to discover a rationale for his early labors as a practicing novelist." Some of these ideas come up again in two other articles, with similar titles, both by Kwiat: "The Social Responsibilities of the American Painter and Writer: Robert Henri and John Sloan; Frank Norris and Theodore Dreiser" (*CentR*, Winter 1977) and "The American Painter and Writer's Credo of 'Art for Truth's Sake': Robert Henri and John Sloan; Frank Norris and Theodore Dreiser" (*JAC*, Summer 1978). These painters and writers have similar ideas about the artist and his relation to society, about politics, activism, and leftist movement. A very good examination of specific similarities between Dreiser's work and Sloan's is Joel C. Mickelson's "Correlations between Art and Literature in Interpreting the American City: Theodore Dreiser and John Sloan," in *Images of the American City in the Arts* (ed. Joel C. Mickelson, Dubuque, Iowa, 1978). Sloan, one of the original eight painters in the "Ashcan School," was a partial model for Eugene Witla.

Dreiser's philosophical essay, "A Counsel to Perfection," from *Hey Rub-a-Dub-Dub*, is analyzed by Lester H. Cohen in "Locating One's Self: The Problematics of Dreiser's Social World" (*MFS*, Autumn 1977). Dreiser's essay reveals a contradiction also found in his fiction: one should live willfully but should be aware that he is only a pawn at the mercy of random forces. Dreiser believes in a pluralistic universe of multiple realities in which nothing is absolute, even determinism.

4   Sources and Influences

The best article in this category is Thomas P. Riggio's "Notes on the Origins of 'Sister Carrie'" (*LC*, Spring 1979), an excellent blend of bio-graphical, critical, and archival scholarship. Riggio's purpose is to explore the origins in Dreiser's mind of the two-word title of his first novel. Carrie is a "sister" biologically and also in her kinship to the sisterhood of all women. Riggio comments on Dreiser's own sisters and on Louise Kerlin, who was informally adopted by Paul Dresser as his sister and protégé. As a source for the name "Carrie," Riggio unveils Carrie Rutter, a young girl who figured strongly in Dreiser's sexual awakening. This Carrie appears in the manuscript of *Dawn*, where she is also called "Cad." Riggio skillfully recreates the complex web of association and memory that lay behind Dreiser's writing "Sister Carrie" at the top of that blank sheet of paper.

Another good influence study is Stephen C. Brennan's "*Sister Carrie* and the Tolstoyan Artist" (*RS*, Mar. 1979). Some years ago, Ellen Moers pointed out Dreiser's debt to Tolstoy's *What to Do?* In this article, Brennan shows influence on Dreiser from Tolstoy's *What Is Art?*, first published in America in the fall of 1898. Brennan uses evidence from the manuscript of *Sister Carrie* to show that the Tolstoyan aspect of the novel was stronger before Henry and Dreiser cut the text.

In "Dreiser and Balzac: A Literary Source for Hurstwood and Carrie" (*AN&Q*, Sept. 1978), Brennan suggests that the source for Hurstwood's wanderings, before he commits suicide, is Balzac's *The Wild Ass's Skin*, which Dreiser read in the Carnegie Library in Pittsburgh and from which he borrowed for one of his "Reflections" columns in *Ev'ry Month*. The crib in the column is undeniable, but the parallels between the Balzac passage and Hurstwood's last scenes are not especially strong. Even less convincing is Charles N. Watson, Jr.'s "The 'Accidental' Drownings in *Daniel Deronda* and *An American Tragedy*" (*ELN*, June 1976).

Lawrence E. Hussman, Jr.'s "Thomas Edison and *Sister Carrie*: A Source for Character and Theme" (*ALR*, Spring 1975) is subsumed in *Dreiser and His Fiction: A Twentieth-Century Quest*, but it deserves separate mention here. Hussman points to convincing parallels between Ames and Edison; he also draws on the manuscript of *Carrie* for supporting evidence from the original ending of chapter 49. D. B. Graham's "Dreiser's Maggie" (*ALR*, Spring 1974) is a footnote to earlier research by Ellen Moers and Joseph Katz on Dreiser's debt to Stephen Crane. Graham analyzes the passage early in *Carrie* in which a rude youth calls Carrie by the name "Maggie." Duane J. MacMillan also sees Crane's presence in Dreiser's first novel. In *"Sister Carrie*, 'Chapter IV': Theodore Dreiser's 'Tip-of-the-Hat' to Stephen Crane" (*DrN*, Spring 1979), he maintains that the fourth chapter of *Carrie* is "an almost perfect paradigm of the style consistently exemplified by Crane's serious fiction." One last source study for Dreiser's first novel is Allen F. Stein's *"Sister Carrie*: A Possible Source for the Title" (*ALR*, Spring 1974), an attempt to trace Dreiser's title to a popular Civil War song by A. P. Peck. The lyrics urge "Sister Carrie" (a reference to South Carolina) not to leave home (the Union).

In "Mark Twain and Theodore Dreiser: Two Boys Lost in a Cave" (*MTJ*, Summer 1978), Thomas P. Riggio reconstructs, from Dreiser's correspondence and journalism, "a long and serious interest in Twain." Then Riggio shows in detail how Dreiser drew heavily on chapters 31 and 32 of *Tom Sawyer* (the McDougal Cave episode) for a scene in chapter 71 of *Dawn*. D. B. Graham sees Thoreau's mark on "The Shining Slave Makers" in "Dreiser and Thoreau: An Early Influence" (*DrN*, Spring 1976). Graham draws parallels between the ant war in *Walden* and the battle of the ants in Dreiser's short story.

Eugene L. Huddleston's *"Herndon's Lincoln* and Theodore Dreiser's *An American Tragedy*" (*MQ*, Spring 1981) points out similarities between the biographical portrait of Lincoln by his law partner and Dreiser's depiction of Clyde Griffiths. The implication, that Clyde might have ended up like Lincoln had events taken a different turn, is hard to accept. Huddleston backs off at the end of his article and admits that the parallels are typical ones in American literature and cultural myth. In "Griffin's Irish Tragedy, *The Collegians*, and Dreiser's *American Tragedy*" (*Éire 19* [Univ. of Florida], 3 Aug. 1977), Grace Eckley argues that Irish novelist Gerald Griffin's obscure 1829 novel had direct influence on Dreiser's masterpiece. So convinced is she of her case that she finally comes to believe "that Dreiser's critics, centering the mass of their analyses in his theme of social ambition, can scarcely utter a phrase which is true of Dreiser and not true of Griffin."

T. D. Nostwich is on firm ground in "The Source of Dreiser's 'Nigger Jeff'" (*RALS*, Fall 1978). Previous Dreiser scholars had traced the story to a newspaper account in the *St. Louis Republic* for 17 September 1893;

Nostwich, however, has found a much more likely source in two news stories, published in the *Republic* for 17 and 18 January 1894 and almost surely written by Dreiser.

Cathy N. and Arnold E. Davidson, in "Carrie's Sisters: The Popular Prototypes for Dreiser's Heroine" (*MFS*, Autumn 1977), argue that Dreiser's depiction of Carrie Meeber is in part a satire of literary conventions now entirely forgotten. Dreiser sets up situations exactly as they would be presented in sentimental fiction of his day, then turns things upside down in order to shock or offend his reader. The Davidsons, who have bravely read through a good bit of late nineteenth-century sentimental fiction, show how *Sister Carrie* violates established conventions of the "working girl novel," the "costume novel," and the "role reversal novel."

In "Lily Bart and Carrie Meeber: Cultural Sisters" (*ALR*, Autumn 1980), Alan Price points out similarities between the Dreiser and Wharton heroines. Both are encouraged to be decorative in order to win material things; neither is allowed truly to develop herself. Carrie charms Hurstwood with a performance on stage, just as Lily does Selden (who resembles Ames). Both women are displaced, alienated, and unfulfilled in America of the late 1800s. Price's article is stimulating; one wishes he had pursued the parallels between Lily in the late chapters of *The House of Mirth* and Hurstwood during his final decline.

While he was working on the *Tragedy* in 1921, Dreiser read a psychobiography of Poe by John W. Robertson. In "American Gothic: Poe and *An American Tragedy*" (*AL*, Jan. 1978), Thomas P. Riggio discusses the results of that reading. Poe gave Dreiser models for handling criminal obsessions, mental disorders, and ambivalent guilt in murderers. Del G. Kehl's "*An American Tragedy* and Dreiser's Cousin, Mr. Poe" (*RMR*, Autumn 1978) explores similar territory and offers a revealing comparison between "Ligeia" and parts of Dreiser's novel.

5 Individual Works

a. Sister Carrie. It is probably not correct to say, as Jack Salzman does, that, "in effect, Dreiser has become *Sister Carrie*" ("Dreiser Then and Now" [*JML*, Mar. 1971]). Still, Salzman is uncomfortably close to the truth—especially if one thinks of which Dreiser novel is most commonly taught in American college classrooms. The pedagogical emphasis on *Sister Carrie* may explain why the great preponderance of Dreiser criticism deals with his famous first novel. Dreiserians need to teach and write on other novels, and on the short fiction and autobiography.

The past decade's crop of articles on *Carrie* is not especially impressive. The most stimulating piece is an attack on the novel by Leon F. Seltzer entitled "*Sister Carrie* and the Hidden Longing for Love: Sublimation or Subterfuge?" (*TCL*, May 1976). Seltzer's anger is sparked by his frustration with Carrie as a character; Dreiser seems to be urging more emotional capacity for her than the character he portrays actually has. Seltzer's biggest error is that he regards Dreiser as a thoroughgoing mechanist. Then he attacks Dreiser because his depiction of Carrie is partly romantic and melodramatic. Seasoned readers of Dreiser have always recognized these contradictions. Seltzer, however, concludes that Carrie is empty, "deficient in her capacity to love," and he argues for a similar deficiency in Dreiser's own character—citing biographical evidence from Swanberg, of course.

Mary A. Burgan, in "*Sister Carrie* and the Pathos of Naturalism" (*Criticism*, Fall 1973), is also dissatisfied with the 1900 *Carrie*, in which authorial pity is an overlay not sufficiently integrated into the text. Some of Burgan's best comments are on Dreiser's documentation: "The sheer mass of the work," she concludes, "is more important and satisfying than any of its parts." Terence J. Matheson's "The Two Faces of Sister Carrie: The Characterization of Dreiser's First Heroine" (*ArielE*, Oct. 1980) is an examination of "two separate persons, both named Carrie Meeber, who, though inhabiting the same body, nevertheless possess entirely different personalities." One Carrie is sympathetic, naive, earnest; the other is cunning, hard, and ambitious. The favorable impression, according to Matheson, comes from Dreiser's rhetorical devices and the unfavorable impression from Carrie's actual behavior.

Max Westbrook, in "Dreiser's Defense of Carrie Meeber" (*MFS*, Autumn 1977), takes the ideals and values of Theodore Roosevelt as a good example of what Dreiser was rebelling against in 1900. Roosevelt's mixture of racism and liberalism might be called Lamarckian; Dreiser's combination of determinism and idealism could be termed Darwinian. Roosevelt argued that there was a single standard to which all people were accountable, but Dreiser felt that values shifted and were unstable.

Hurstwood takes his lumps in Jacqueline Tavernier-Courbin's "Hurstwood Achieved: A Study of Dreiser's Reluctant Art" (*DrN*, Fall 1978). Concentrating on chapter 27 of the 1900 text, Tavernier-Courbin argues that "the potential for Hurstwood's downfall is already complete and the downward process already broached by the time he steals the money." Poor Hurstwood "has the instincts of a knave but neither the brains, the self-discipline nor the ability to forestall possible consequences." So much for pity.

Harold Kaplan's *Power and Order: Henry Adams and the Naturalist Tradition in American Fiction* (Chicago, 1981) is an investigation of power, order, and force in American naturalistic writing. He focuses on *Sister Carrie* for its picture of money and sex and for its "complete subordination of the human sensibility to the power process"—a tendency which causes the peculiar flatness of some of the best scenes in the novel.

The poststructuralists have discovered *Sister Carrie*, and the results are mixed. In "*Sister Carrie*'s Popular Economy" (*CritI*, Winter 1980), Walter Benn Michaels argues that Dreiser's novel appears on the surface to be a condemnation of capitalism. A working out of the economic principles espoused in the text, however, shows Dreiser to be pro-capitalist. That might be true. Certainly Michaels could have marshalled biographical evidence to support his point, had he cared to, but biographical evidence is against the rules. One can barely discern the point of Fred G. See's "The Text as Mirror: *Sister Carrie* and the Lost Language of the Heart" (*Criticism*, Spring 1978). The language is almost impenetrable, and that is ironic because the article itself is about Dreiser's use of language. See appears to be contrasting Dreiser's use of language with that of Jonathan Edwards, Hawthorne, and Emerson. For Dreiser, language has limits; because his is a language of material surfaces, it can only reflect itself and result in the intensification of desire for what it already describes.

Another article on the shortcomings of *Sister Carrie* is Sandy Petrey's "The Language of Realism, the Language of False Consciousness: A Reading of *Sister Carrie*" (*Novel*, Winter 1977). Petrey is attempting to interpret the tension between the language of flat realism in the novel, which dominates the text, and the "hypotactic passages of moral speculation." Petrey's article, essentially an attack on Dreiser's rhetorical flights and philosophical asides, is itself attacked by Ellen Moers in a subsequent issue of *Novel* (Fall 1977). Moers takes the passage Petrey judged among the worst in the book and explicates it, showing that it contains references to the central philosophical and thematic concerns of the novel.

Dreiser is one of the authors treated in Nicolaus Mills's "Class and Crowd in American Fiction" (*CentR*, Spring 1980). Dreiser's depiction of the strike in *Sister Carrie*, according to Mills, shows his fundamental sympathy with the working man and his approval of violence as a means of countering the power of organized capitalism. Strength is with the crowd; Hurstwood feels it and is attracted by it but remains alone and alienated.

Philip Fisher's "Acting, Reading, Fortune's Wheel: *Sister Carrie* and the Life History of Objects," in *American Realism: New Essays* (ed. Eric J. Sundquist, Baltimore, 1982), is the best examination of imagery in *Sister Carrie* yet published. Fisher first examines images of motion, then discusses windows, stages, names, clothes, hotels, newspapers, and cities. He is adept at relating these images to the larger thematic concerns of Dreiser's novel. There is an excellent section on Rousseau's ideas about the popular theatre and the damage it can do to a democracy. Portions of this essay, and of Fisher's earlier general essay on Dreiser from the Winter 1977 issue of *ELH*, are included in chapter 3 of his book *Hard Facts: Setting and Form in the American Novel* (New York, 1985).

A good study focusing only on images of motion in Dreiser's first novel is "Movement in Dreiser's *Sister Carrie*" (*DrN*, Spring 1980), by Robert James Butler. More limited but nevertheless illuminating is John C. Hirsh's "The Printed Ephemera of *Sister Carrie*" (*ALR*, Spring 1974), an examination of such items as newspapers, paper money, tickets, menus, and theatre programs in Dreiser's novel.

"*Sister Carrie*: Dreiser's Wasteland" (*AmerS*, Fall 1975), by Clark Griffith, is essentially an examination of imagery in *Carrie*, especially in the scene between Carrie and Hurstwood in Jefferson Park. In that Eden-like setting, the two show their potential for love, but their love cannot survive and flower outside the garden. Emily Toth's "Timely and Timeless: The Treatment of Time in *The Awakening* and *Sister Carrie*" (*SoSt*, Fall 1977) argues that time differs between the two novels, though in other respects they are similar. Dreiser's novel is masculine, incremental, linear; Chopin's is lyrical, epiphanic, feminine. *Sister Carrie* is located in historical and social time, while *The Awakening* has a timeless quality, and its chronology is vague.

b. *The Trilogy of Desire*. Philip L. Gerber's massive study of Dreiser's trilogy is nearing completion, and some finished parts of the project have begun to appear. "The Financier Himself: Dreiser and C. T. Yerkes" (*PMLA*, Jan. 1973) is an engagingly written general article explaining why Dreiser chose Yerkes as a model for his fictional financier. In "Dreiser's Debt to *Jay Cooke*" (*LC*, Winter 1972), Gerber details Dreiser's borrowings from Ellis Paxson Oberholtzer's 1907 biography of the financier Cooke. A more extensive exploration of Dreiser's sources for the trilogy is Gerber's "Frank Cowperwood: Boy Financier" (*SAF*, Autumn 1974). Working here from the Oberholtzer book, from a privately published history of the Yerkes family, and from archival materials at Pennsylvania, Gerber shows how Dreiser drew on a variety of sources to construct the early life of his hero. Two briefer pieces by Gerber that treat other Dreiser source material for the trilogy are "Hyde's Tabbs and Dreiser's Butlers" (*DrN*, Spring 1975) and "The Financier Orders His Tomb" (*DrN*, Spring 1979). Gerber describes Rella Armstrong's unsuccessful efforts to adapt *The Financier* to the stage in "Cowperwood Treads the Boards" (*DrN*, Fall 1982).

An eccentric but attractive interpretation of *The Financier* and *The Titan* is Jack E. Wallace's "The Comic Voice in Dreiser's Cowperwood Narrative" (*AL*, Mar. 1981). Wallace argues that most critics read these two novels as tragedies because of an anti-urban, anti-financier bias among liberal American academics. Seeing Cowperwood as a tragic hero makes him ideologically respectable. Wallace believes that the first two novels of the trilogy should instead be seen as comic. We know that Cowperwood will recover from his setbacks and amass more money. The narrative voice in both novels is predominantly comic; whenever it begins to seem tragic, it takes on an ironic pitch. Wallace adds another possible model for Cowperwood—the financier Joseph G. Robin, about whom Dreiser wrote in *Twelve Men*. Robert Roulston's "The Libidinous Lobster: The Semi-Flaw in Dreiser's Superman" (*Rendezvous*, Winter 1974–75) also urges us not to see Cowperwood as a tragic hero. He was not typical of most nineteenth-century American financiers, who were moralistic and prudish. The novels in the trilogy are "elephantine critiques of American sexual and religious mores," and Cowperwood is usually defeated by moralistic adversaries.

C. R. B. Dunlop, an attorney, examines "Human Law and Natural Law in the Novels of Theodore Dreiser" in the *American Journal of Jurisprudence* (1974). Dunlop concentrates on *The Financier* and *The Titan*; he sees Dreiser as an author "torn between a view of the world as disordered and amoral, and a yearning for a fundamental law which can be used to measure and judge modern society and human law." In "Dreiser's *Financier*: The Man of Business as a Man of Letters," in *American Realism: New Essays* (ed. Eric J. Sundquist, Baltimore, 1982), Walter Benn Michaels compares Cowperwood's taste for financial speculation with his taste in women. Unlike John D. Rockefeller, who liked stability in his business dealings, Cowperwood is attracted by the flux and chance of monetary speculation. That is why in private life he prefers his unpredictable mistress to his steady wife.

The best part of Carl S. Smith's "Dreiser's *Trilogy of Desire*: The Financier as Artist" (*CRevAS*, Fall 1976) is the first half, in which he views Cowperwood as the ultimate creative artist of his period, a man who uses the raw materials of cities to transform the lives of the people there. In the second half of the article, Smith attempts to link this artistic behavior with Cowperwood's pursuit of women and his acquisition of art, but the effort is not entirely successful. In "The Disproportion of Sadness: Dreiser's *The Financier* and *The Titan*" (*MFS*, Autumn 1977), John O'Neill examines the first two novels of the trilogy in light of "the disproportion between man and the world"—a phrase he borrows from Alfred Kazin. *The Financier*, according to O'Neill, is only a limited success and *The Titan* a failure.

Mary Anne Lindborg, in "Dreiser's Sentimental Heroine, Aileen Butler" (*AL*, Jan. 1977), compares Aileen to Emma Bovary. Both women take their conceptions of life from fiction, but most of the novels read by Aileen in *The Financier* were published years after she was supposed to have read them. Dreiser seems to have sacrificed accuracy for the association value of the titles.

c. An American Tragedy. James T. Farrell's essay, "Dreiser's *Tragedy*: The Distortion of American Values" (*Prospects*, 1975), is a thoughtful treatment of Dreiser as determinist and of determinism itself. Clyde's tragedy is that his values are distorted by society; what he absorbs from his surroundings is not knowledge but simply an expansion of his desires. Ironically, Clyde remains isolated and without identity until the media take up his case and brand him a murderer, a role he eventually accepts. Robert H. Elias also concentrates on Clyde's character in "Theodore Dreiser and the Tragedy of the Twenties," in the same volume of *Prospects* (1975). Elias sees Clyde as a product of the American 1920s, a period during which self-realization was widely believed to be incompatible with social involvement or commitment to others. Clyde has been conditioned by society to swim away from the drowning Roberta—and to endure the subsequent pathos.

Paul A. Orlov's "The Subversion of the Self: Anti-Naturalistic Crux in *An American Tragedy*" (*MFS*, Autumn 1977) is a wide-ranging though syntactically opaque essay which argues that the *Tragedy* is fundamentally not naturalistic. Instead it is "an anti-naturalistic statement about the self's intrinsic importance." In a briefer treatment entitled "Plot as Parody: Dreiser's Attack on the Alger Theme in *An American Tragedy*" (*ALR*, Autumn 1982), Orlov suggests that certain plot elements in Dreiser's novel are meant deliberately to mirror or invert those in a typical rags-to-riches Alger book.

C. R. B. Dunlop, the attorney who wrote thoughtfully about *The Financier* and *The Titan*, tackles Dreiser's greatest novel in "Law and Justice in Dreiser's *An American Tragedy*" (*University of British Columbia Law Review*, Dec. 1971). Dunlop's article is heavy on plot summary, but there are intelligent considerations of the courtroom and death-row scenes. Another legal treatment is Mona G. Rosenman's "*An American Tragedy*: Constitutional Violations" (*DrN*, Spring 1978). In this carefully researched piece, Rosenman demonstrates that numerous constitutional guarantees were ignored in the Chester Gillette trial and in Dreiser's fictional reworking of it.

The theme of Michael Spindler's "Youth, Class, and Consumerism in Dreiser's *An American Tragedy*" (*JAmS*, Apr. 1978) is that Clyde falls victim to the youth-oriented consumerism of the 1920s, to the appeal of things. That point, one would think, is obvious to a perceptive reader, as is the theme of Carla Mulford Micklus's "*An American Tragedy*; or, the Tragedy of the Adamic Myth" (*ALR*, Spring 1981). In the *Tragedy*, according to Micklus, Dreiser explodes the hopeful myth of the American Adam and shows how one cannot escape his own past. Martin Bucco's "The East-West Theme in Dreiser's *An American Tragedy*" (*WAL*, Nov. 1977) traces a pattern of references to East-West movement in the novel; these references show finally that all movement is futile. Dan Vogel offers a narrow consideration of the *Tragedy* in *The Three Masks of American Tragedy* (Baton Rouge, La., 1974). He argues that "Dreiser's modernization of Greek fate into scientific naturalism is so monolithic that it becomes naive." One senses that Vogel dislikes the *Tragedy* because it does not fit readily into any of the categories he has fashioned for American tragedy, categories he has adapted from Greek thought and drama.

An American Tragedy has been usefully compared to a number of other literary works during the past decade, not to establish influence but to illuminate technique and theme. In "A Question of Choice in the Naturalistic Novel: Zola's *Thérèse Raquin* and Dreiser's *An American Tragedy*," in *Proceedings of the Comparative Literature Symposium* (ed.

Wolodymyr T. Zyla and Wendell M. Aycock, Lubbock, Tex., 1972), Lilian R. Furst sees the murderers in these two novels as heavily influenced by milieu and conditioning. There is, however, some free will at work. In the second half of her article, Furst mentions other naturalistic novels in which free will operates, and she finishes by questioning certain assumptions about the naturalistic movement as a whole. In "Strange Bedfellows: *The Waste Land* and *An American Tragedy*," in *The Twenties: Fiction, Poetry, Drama* (ed. Warren French, Deland, Fla., 1975), Carol Clancy Harter concedes that there is no evidence to suggest Dreiser read Eliot, or that either writer was much aware of the other. Still their two great modernist works, growing out of the same times, share certain themes and images. Both deal with the corrupting force of materialism, though Eliot's narrator is more aware of the sterility of modern life than is Dreiser's Clyde.

Two critics have independently compared *An American Tragedy* with Truman Capote's *In Cold Blood*. John J. McAleer, in *"An American Tragedy and In Cold Blood" (Thought*, Winter 1972), notes the autobiographical kinship between the authors and their heroes and also points out similarities between Clyde and each of Capote's two murderers. Both books condemn the American Dream, but Dreiser's novel is the better work of art. Capote is shackled to facts and must consciously manipulate techniques and styles, while Dreiser is free to create details and emphasize situations as his imagination moves him. A similar conclusion is reached by Ivo Vidan in "The Capitulation of Literature? The Scope of the 'Nonfiction Novel,'" in *Yugoslav Perspectives on American Literature: An Anthology* (ed. James L. Thorson, Ann Arbor, Mich., 1980). Vidan feels that Capote's book has no interior structure and that it urges no particular world view. *An American Tragedy*, by contrast, exhibits "logical conception of a narrative and plot" and offers a "complete perspective on the world." Yoshinobu Hakutani's *"Native Son* and *An American Tragedy*: Two Different Interpretations of Crime and Guilt" (*CentR*, Spring 1979) is an extended comparison which demonstrates that, despite superficial similarities, the two novels are profoundly different. *Native Son*, Hakutani believes, does not truly belong in the naturalistic tradition.

d. Other Dreiser Books. The first full-length article ever published on *Jennie Gerhardt* (yes, that's correct) is a disappointment. In "Loneliness, Death, and Fulfillment in *Jennie Gerhardt*" (*SAF*, Spring 1979), Mordecai Marcus attacks Lester Kane as hypocritical and barbaric; Lester is characterized by "Oedipal immaturity"—principally because he does not marry Jennie. Marcus judges Lester by standards of behavior and morality that Dreiser almost surely would not have used. Marcus does make illuminating comparisons between the Kane and Gerhardt families, and he recognizes the importance of the death-bed scenes in the novel.

Thomas P. Riggio's "Another Two Dreisers: The Artist as 'Genius'" (*SNNTS*, Summer 1977) is a strong article informed by study of the manuscript of The "Genius." Riggio finds Dreiser's fifth novel largely a failure but argues that in composing the book, Dreiser discovered "a character and a set of issues that would dominate his writing for the next decade." Dreiser's subject would be the place and role of the artist in society, and the sources of his creativity and inspiration. Dorothy Klopf, in "Theodore Dreiser's The 'Genius': Much Matter and More Art" (MFS, Autumn 1977), asserts that in the novel "Dreiser assumes the mantle of Emerson and Thoreau as the twentieth-century prophet of American Transcendentalism." Dreiser recognizes that the ideal exists but knows that human beings cannot fulfill it.

Almost the first attention ever paid to Dreiser's dramatic writings is Helene Keyssar's "Theodore Dreiser's Dramas: American Folk Drama and Its Limits" (TJ, Oct. 1981). Keyssar sees Dreiser's published plays as folk dramas in which ordinary persons are treated as important and potentially tragic figures. The plays are so bizarre and discomforting, and their subject matter is so repellent, that they did not fare well on the American stage. Frederic E. Rusch calls The Hand of the Potter "Dreiser's Other Tragedy" (MFS, Autumn 1977) and traces the play to its source—the 1912 sex murder of an adolescent girl in the Bronx by a man named Nathan Swartz. The resemblances between the Swartz case and the play are close, but, according to Rusch, Hand is more than a documentary account.

Yoshinobu Hakutani, in "The Dream of Success in Dreiser's A Gallery of Women" (ZAA, No. 3, 1979), maintains that Gallery has been neglected because it has been improperly compared to Twelve Men. Though the women in Gallery differ from one another in many ways, all dream of success in a male world. Most fail because they lack "a stable and independent philosophy that transcends the narrow confines of feminine mentality."

e. Short Fiction. Three book chapters should be noted here: Donald Pizer's "A Summer at Maumee" in The Novels of Theodore Dreiser; Yoshinobu Hakutani's "The Making of Dreiser's Early Short Stories" in Young Dreiser; and Lawrence E. Hussman, Jr.'s chapter on Dreiser's "marriage group" in Dreiser and His Fiction. The Pizer chapter appeared previously in Essays Mostly on Periodical Publishing in America: A Collection in Honor of Clarence Gohdes (ed. James Woodress, Durham, N.C., 1973); the Hakutani chapter was previously published in Studies in American Fiction (Spring 1978).

The only article to treat the entire corpus of short fiction is Joseph Griffin's "Dreiser's Short Stories and the Dream of Success" (EA, July–Dec. 1978). According to Griffin, the "dream of success" is a dominant theme in Dreiser's short fiction, but there are always "antithetical forces at work . . . that make fulfillment difficult or impossible." Griffin recognizes that the short stories are related in unexpected ways to the novels; often they are miniature versions of (or interesting variations upon) those novels. Griffin takes up "Dreiser's Later Short Stories" (*DrN*, Spring 1978) and finds that in his mature short fiction Dreiser began to blur the distinction between the short story and other forms such as the personal sketch and the documentary narrative. Several of these later performances are more mellow, and two or three appear to have been tailored for the slick magazine market. Griffin's "'When the Old Century Was New': An Early Dreiser Parody" (*SSF*, Summer 1980) treats this story as a spoof of the costume romances popular in mass-circulation magazines of the late 1890s and early 1900s.

In "Dreiser Experiments with Form: Five Stories from *Chains*" (*ESC*, June 1982), Griffin discusses some of Dreiser's efforts with interior monologue in his second collection of short stories. Dreiser was attempting to create a "cumulative, often non-chronological, 'incremental progression' that is repetitive, circuitous, disorganized—because that is the actual progression of the protagonist's meditation in the circumstances." None of the experiments, according to Griffin, is entirely successful, but all are interesting examples of Dreiser's commitment to fictional innovation.

Much of the material from these four articles is incorporated into Griffin's *The Small Canvas: An Introduction to Dreiser's Short Stories* (Cranbury, N.J., 1985). Griffin analyzes the stories in *Free* (1918) and *Chains* (1927); he also gives attention to five uncollected stories which appeared between 1929 and 1938. There is a discussion of the two editions of *The Best Short Stories of Theodore Dreiser* (1947 and 1956) and a chapter on the corpus of short fiction as a whole. Griffin's comments throughout are informed and perceptive—especially when he deals with Dreiser's experimental work.

D. B. Graham has published three articles on Dreiser's revisions of individual stories: "'The Cruise of the "Idlewild"': Dreiser's Revisions of a 'Rather Light' Story" (*ALR*, Winter 1975); "Dreiser's Ant Tragedy: The Revision of 'The Shining Slave Makers'" (*SSF*, Winter 1977); and "Psychological Veracity in 'The Lost Phoebe': Dreiser's Revisions" (*SAF*, Spring 1978). In each article, Graham compares the magazine text of the story to its collected appearance in *Free* and comments on Dreiser's changes. These three articles would have been stronger had Graham used evidence from the manuscripts, and it is difficult to agree with his assertion, in all three pieces, that stylistic revisions from one version to another are so unimportant as to be beneath notice. But in each article Graham goes well beyond simple textual comparison and makes perceptive critical comments.

An article similar to the three by Graham is "Unquiet Anchorage: Dreiser's Revisions of 'When the Sails are Furled'" (*RS*, June 1980) by Willis J. Buckingham and Barnett Shepherd. Three versions of this sketch of a retired sailors' home are compared—*Ainslee's* (Jan. 1899), the *New York Tribune* (22 May 1904), and *The Color of a Great City* (1923).

6 Motion Picture Adaptations

The three movie "versions" of *An American Tragedy* have drawn much attention over the past decade. "Eisenstein's Subversive Adaptation," Keith Cohen's contribution to *The Classic American Novel and the Movies* (ed. Gerald Peary and Roger Shatzkin, New York, 1977), pronounces Serge Eisenstein's unproduced screenplay of the *Tragedy* a "stillborn masterpiece." The treatment was technically innovative, calling for new effects such as sound montage; but Eisenstein's screenplay put the blame for Clyde's misdeeds squarely on society, thus "deconstructing" Dreiser's more ambiguous novel. Eisenstein's adaptation was judged subversive by the Paramount executives, and they refused to produce it.

Three other critics compare Eisenstein's script to the two versions of *An American Tragedy* that were eventually shot—Josef von Sternberg's in 1931 and George Stevens's in 1951—and come to different conclusions. Bernice Kiliman, in *"An American Tragedy*: Novel, Scenario, and Films" (*LFQ*, Summer 1977), sees the Stevens version as a limited success, a "unified emotional experience." By contrast, in "Sociological Treatise, Detective Story, Love Affair: The Film Versions of *An American Tragedy*" (*CRevAS*, Fall 1977), Barrie Hayne judges von Sternberg's film the most successful of the three treatments at capturing Dreiser's meaning, though superficially it was the least faithful to his novel. Lilian R. Furst believes all three versions to be failures in "Innocent or Guilty? Problems in Filming Dreiser's *An American Tragedy*" (*ConnR*, May 1976). The problem, she thinks, was the technical difficulty of rendering the murder scene ambivalently. Finally, in chapter 9 of *The Cinematic Imagination: Writers and the Motion Pictures* (New York, 1972), Edward Murray argues that Eisenstein's script does not measure up to Dreiser's novel in psychological complexity. Murray sees both of the produced films as romanticized hooey.

Carolyn Geduld's "Wyler's Suburban Sister: *Carrie* 1952," in *The Classic American Novel and the Movies*, reveals that Dreiser's original story was considered immoral and un-American by the Hollywood money men. Director William Wyler therefore transformed it into a parable of a young woman punished for making the wrong choices in men—specifically for choosing males who would not or could not marry her. What Wyler's Carrie really wants is matrimony, 1950s style. Hurstwood's suicide was filmed, but the footage was cut before the film was released; in 1952 it was thought improper to show a man who represented the American virtues of solidity, wealth, and success killing himself. Robert E. Morsberger's "'In Elf Land Disporting': *Sister Carrie* in Hollywood" (*BRMMLA*, Dec. 1973) is a comparison of Wyler's film with Dreiser's book. Wyler, according to Morsberger, turned the novel into a soap opera and drenched the sound track with gushy, romantic music. Hurstwood became "Rhett Butler on Skid Row." Morsberger had access to an early draft of Wyler's script at the Academy of Motion Picture Arts and Sciences; this draft helps him account for the problems found in the eventual film. Morsberger investigates Twentieth Century-Fox's 1942 motion picture *My Gal Sal* in "Dreiser's Frivolous Sal" (*DrN*, Spring 1976). The film, based on "My Brother Paul" from *Twelve Men*, is a glossy, sentimental musical comedy bearing small resemblance to Paul's life or Dreiser's sketch. Dreiser's major motive was apparently financial: Fox paid him some $50,000 for the film rights to Paul's story.

VI   SUPPLEMENT

The *Dreiser Newsletter* is now *Dreiser Studies*. The journal has been expanded and redesigned in order to print longer articles and more substantial unpublished or resurrected materials than it did previously. Among the recent findings are "Dreiser: Autobiographical Fragment, 1911" (*DrS*, Spring 1987), edited from the original at the Alderman Library by Thomas P. Riggio, and "Dreiser's 'Poet of Potter's Field'" (*DrS*, Fall 1987), reprinted from the *St. Louis Republic* with commentary by T. D. Nostwich.

Nostwich has edited *Theodore Dreiser's "Heard in the Corridors": Articles and Related Writings* (Ames, Iowa, 1988), a small but useful collection of the author's quasi-fictional inventions for various newspapers during the 1890s. This collection was quarried from Nostwich's original manuscript for his edition of Dreiser's *Newspaper Writings, 1892–1895* (Philadelphia, 1988), the first of the volumes of journalism to be issued by the Pennsylvania Dreiser Edition. The materials in this initial volume are fascinating; they tell us much about the apprenticeship of the author of *Sister Carrie*, and they help clear up some mysteries about *Dawn*. The second volume of Yoshinobu Hakutani's edition of *Selected Magazine Articles of Theodore Dreiser* has appeared (Cranbury, N.J., 1987); this time it is clearly identified on the title page as volume 2. Thomas Riggio and Speer Morgan have edited Dreiser's previously unpublished short story "The Total Stranger" (*MissR*, No. 3, 1987) from the surviving typescript at the Humanities Research Center at the University of Texas. This tale of marital incompatibility between working-class characters is surprisingly sentimental and moralistic.

Shelley Fisher Fishkin's chapter on Dreiser in *From Fact to Fiction: Journalism and Imaginative Writing in America* (Baltimore, 1985) is excellent; particularly interesting is her work on *An American Tragedy*. Susan L. Mizruchi also concentrates on the *Tragedy* in her chapter on Dreiser in *The Power of Historical Knowledge: Narrating the Past in Hawthorne, James, and Dreiser* (Princeton, N.J., 1988), a theoretically sophisticated study of narrative reconstructions of the past in four American novels. Recent articles of note are Stephen C. Brennan's "The Two Endings of *Sister Carrie*" (*SAF*, Spring 1988); Philip L. Gerber's "A Star Is Born: Celebrity in *Sister Carrie*" (*DrS*, Spring 1988); James M. Hutchisson's "The Composition and Publication of 'Another American Tragedy': Dreiser's 'Typhoon'" (*PBSA*, No. 1, 1987); and James L. W. West III's "Double Quotes and Double Meanings in *Jennie Gerhardt*" (*DrS*, Spring 1987).

T. S. Eliot

Stuart Y. McDougal

I BIBLIOGRAPHY

Scholars of T. S. Eliot's work are fortunate in having at their disposal the monumental study by Donald Gallup, *T. S. Eliot: A Bibliography* (1969). This bibliography is a model of its kind and serves as the point of departure for any examination of Eliot's work. Several more recent supplements should be noted. George Monteiro has added three items to the section on translations in "Addenda to Gallup's *Eliot*" (*PBSA*, First Quarter 1972), and A. S. G. Edwards has attributed six anonymous letters to Eliot in "Addenda to Gallup: T. S. Eliot" (*PBSA*, First Quarter 1981). Alan M. Cohn and Elizabeth R. Eames identify seven book reviews and three reviews of journal articles that Eliot contributed to the *Monist* during 1917 and 1918 in "Some Early Reviews by T. S. Eliot: Addenda to Gallup" (*PBSA*, Third Quarter 1976). Louis Menand and Sanford Schwartz attribute to T. S. Eliot an anonymous review of Émile Durkheim's *The Elementary Forms of the Religious Life*, translated by J. W. Swain, that appeared in *Westminster Gazette* (Aug. 1916) in "T. S. Eliot on Durkheim: A New Attribution" (*MP*, Feb. 1982). Menand and Schwartz explain their reasons for attributing to Eliot this review of a book that Eliot reviewed again in 1918 and they reprint the piece in full. John J. Soldo discusses *Fireside*, a magazine the poet began at the age of ten, in "Jovial Juvenilia: T. S. Eliot's First Magazine" (*Biography*, Winter 1982; reprinted in his study, *The Tempering of T. S. Eliot* [Ann Arbor, Mich., 1983]). "Disjecta Membra," Eliot's review of Amy Lowell's *Tendencies in Modern American Poetry*, has been reprinted in *Parnassus* (Fall/Winter 1976).

Several bibliographies of secondary materials have appeared in the last two decades. The earliest of these, Mildred Martin's *A Half-Century of Eliot Criticism: An Annotated Bibliography of Books and Articles in English, 1916–1965* (1972), has been supplemented by a special issue of the *T. S. Eliot Newsletter* (Nos. 1 and 2, 1977), compiled by Mechthild and Armin Paul Frank and K. P. S. Jochum and containing an additional

1,300 items between 1911 and 1965. Two other bibliographical aids have appeared more recently: Beatrice Ricks's *T. S. Eliot: A Bibliography of Secondary Works* (Metuchen, N.J., 1980) and Alistair Davies's *An Annotated Critical Bibliography of Modernism* (Totowa, N.J., 1972). Although Ricks's work brings us closer to the present, her organization is quixotic and her annotations are uneven. More helpful is Alistair Davies's work, which contains a substantial chapter on Eliot criticism through 1981. Davies's superior organization and helpful annotations make his volume more useful than those cited above. A specialized work is Armin Paul Frank's "T. S. Eliot in Germany, 1965 to the Present: An Estimate and a Bibliography" (*YER*, Nos. 1 and 2, 1982), which covers the years 1965–76.

Robert H. Canary's *T. S. Eliot: The Poet and His Critics* (Chicago, 1982) is a detailed review-essay of nearly four hundred pages covering the major criticism of Eliot with an emphasis on the work of the 1960s and 1970s. Canary organizes his material topically, with chapters on "The Personal Poet," "The Impersonal Poet," "The Social Critic," "The Religious Poet," "The Traditional Poet," and "The Modern Poet." Although his categories overlap and at times seem arbitrary, they do bring order to a complex field. This is an extremely helpful introduction to the secondary materials.

An informative and varied sampling of critical responses to Eliot's poetry and drama is contained in *T. S. Eliot: The Critical Heritage* (ed. Michael Grant, London, 1982). This two-volume collection of reviews, arranged chronologically, documents the extraordinary impact of Eliot on his contemporaries. Taken together, these reviews present a vivid picture of the changing tastes of the period. A companion volume on the reception of Eliot's essays and critical works would be a welcome addition to the record.

II EDITIONS

Although Faber and Faber published a one-volume edition of *The Complete Poems and Plays of T. S. Eliot* in 1969, no similar volume has appeared in America. The American edition of *The Complete Poems and Plays: 1909–1950* (1958) lacks the *Poems Written in Early Youth*, the "occasional verses," and Eliot's last two plays. A complete American edition is long overdue.

The publication of *Selected Prose of T. S. Eliot* (New York, 1975), edited with an introduction by Frank Kermode, at last makes possible an inexpensive, carefully edited selection of Eliot's critical work for the student and general reader. Kermode has chosen well for his selection, although the reader expecting to find hitherto unpublished material here will be disappointed.

With the publication of Helen Gardner's *The Composition of "Four Quar-*

tets" (New York, 1978), the reader is able to examine the "intolerable wrestle / With words and meanings" that occupied Eliot over a long period of years and through an extensive series of drafts. Although less dramatic than the manuscripts for *The Waste Land*, these drafts nonetheless provide considerable help in understanding Eliot's last major poem. Three incisive essays by Gardner precede and clarify her annotated texts of the poems: "The Documents in the Case," "The Growth of *Four Quartets*," and "The Sources of *Four Quartets*." This volume is a fine companion to her early study, *"Four Quartets": The Art of T. S. Eliot* (1950).

Nevill Coghill's student edition of *The Cocktail Party* (London, 1974) reprints the text with editorial commentary, notes, and an interpretative study of the play. The volume should prove very useful in undergraduate courses.

III MANUSCRIPTS AND LETTERS

The most important publication of new Eliot materials since the poet's death in 1967 is *"The Waste Land": A Facsimile and Transcript of the Original Drafts* (New York, 1972), edited by the poet's widow, Valerie Eliot. Publication of this material confirmed and clarified stories of Ezra Pound's important role in the revisions. The manuscript also revealed the deeply personal origins of much of the material in the poem and has provided source material for biographers and psychological critics. It has stimulated a considerable body of criticism.

According to *Publishers Weekly* (20 July 1984), the long-awaited collection of her husband's letters being edited by Mrs. Eliot will be published by Harcourt Brace Jovanovich in four volumes, with the first scheduled for 1985. Although as this essay goes to press early in 1988, the first volume has not yet been published, when it does appear it should provide a mine of critical and biographical information.

IV BIOGRAPHY

In a memorandum dated 30 September 1963 attached to his will, T. S. Eliot noted: "I do not wish my Executors to facilitate or countenance the writing of any biography of me." This is hardly surprising coming from the poet who wrote of the need to "extinguish" one's personality in one's work. As a result of Eliot's insistence on privacy (*Tace et Fac*, "Be Silent and Act," was the family motto), an attitude shared by his widow, several unauthorized and highly speculative works have appeared that do his reputation a profound disservice. The most notorious of these is T. S. Matthews's *Great Tom: Notes Toward the Definition of T. S. Eliot* (New York, 1974). These "notes" are primarily conjectures, deriving from the author's professed empathy for Eliot, based on what the author suggests are similarities of "background and upbringing" as well as a shared first name and middle initial. Where concrete evidence is unobtainable, Matthews creates scenes and engages in speculation. Where facts are available, he all too often either misinterprets or distorts them. In his discussion of *The Waste Land*, for example, Matthews quotes the comments Vivienne scrawled in the margin by the conversation between the neurasthenic young woman and the cryptic young man in "A Game of Chess": "she pencilled W O N D E R F U L and then again *wonderful wonderful*—quite disregarding Pound's denigrating and picky grumbles about the same passage." Pound had marked "photography" by these lines, indicating their closeness to Eliot's own conversations with Vivienne. Viewed in this light, Vivienne's comments are quite horrifying. There is material in these notes for a biographer, but T. S. Matthews has overlooked it.

Eliot's Early Years (New York, 1977) by Lyndall Gordon is a perceptive biographical and critical study that demonstrates by contrast just how much can be done with existing manuscript material. Although Gordon is hampered by restrictions against direct citation of unpublished materials, she succeeds in eliciting "the autobiographical element in Eliot's poetry by measuring the poetry against the life." Her discussions of Eliot's early religious experiences (Eliot's "consuming search for salvation") are particularly revealing, although she overstates the role of Eliot's religious experience in *The Waste Land*. But she does demonstrate the extent to which Eliot drew upon personal feelings in his early verse, just as he did in *The Waste Land*. Her book does much to dispel the notions of impersonality that Eliot sought to establish and that critics have dutifully accepted for all too long.

T. S. Eliot is one of the subjects of Louis Simpson's *Three on the Tower: The Lives and Works of Ezra Pound, T. S. Eliot, and William Carlos Williams* (New York, 1975). "T. S. Eliot, or Religion" is a short, sensitive critical biography that will be welcomed by undergraduates.

John J. Soldo's *The Tempering of T. S. Eliot* (Ann Arbor, Mich., 1983) focuses on Eliot's childhood and adolescence, ending with his graduation from Harvard. Through citation and paraphrase from Eliot's unpublished letters, undergraduate and graduate notebooks and essays, and books with Eliot's marginalia, Soldo vividly reconstructs Eliot's youth. Although Soldo's judgments are often questionable (e.g., "It was the tragedy of Henry's life [Henry Ware Eliot, T. S. Eliot's father] that he was born with extremely prominent ears"), he presents a body of information for which future biographers can be thankful.

An "intellectual biography" of the years 1909–22 is offered by Piers Gray in *T. S. Eliot's Intellectual and Poetic Development: 1909–1922* (Atlantic Highlands, N.J., 1982). Gray's study has somewhat more ambitious aims than John D. Margolis's fine earlier study *T. S. Eliot's Intellectual Development: 1922–39* (1972), but the two books complement each other well. Gray charts the development of Eliot's intellect by examining a host of thinkers and writers whose work influenced him, including Jules Laforgue, Henri Bergson, Josiah Royce, F. H. Bradley, George Santayana, James G. Frazer, Émile Durkheim, Lucien Lévy-Bruhl and Ezra Pound. Of particular interest is Gray's detailed analysis of an essay on "The Interpretation of Primitive Ritual" that Eliot wrote for Royce's seminar at Harvard. His lengthy citations and paraphrase convey the essence of this important document. Gray emphasizes the unity of Eliot's intellectual *and* poetic development during the period that culminated in *The Waste Land*.

George Whiteside has organized a descriptive catalogue of "T. S. Eliot's Doctoral Studies" (*AN&Q*, Feb. 1973) that will be helpful to Eliot's future biographers. A later stage in T. S. Eliot's intellectual life is reconstructed by Ronald Schuchard in "T. S. Eliot as an Extension Lecturer, 1916–1919" (*RES*, May and Aug. 1974). Schuchard provides syllabi for Eliot's courses that enable one to chart Eliot's intellectual concerns during a crucial stage of his career. A fine account of the journal that published much of Eliot's early verse is presented in Ellen Williams's fascinating literary history, *Harriet Monroe and the Poetry Renaissance: The First Ten Years of "Poetry," 1912–22* (Urbana, Ill., 1977). These same years are covered from a different standpoint by Robert H. Bell in "Bertrand Russell and the Eliots" (*ASch*, Summer 1983). Bell chronicles this relationship from its beginnings at Harvard University, through a period of intimacy in London during the war, to the estrangement that resulted from Russell's sexual involvement with Vivienne. Bell's tactful, well-documented discussion of the complicated relationship among the three is "revealing in the deepest sense . . . [by] providing significant glimpses of three complex personalities."

Leon Edel adumbrates Eliot's "early *rite de passage*, relying . . . on the supreme evidence available to us, the emotions expressed in his poems and plays." In "Abulia and the Journey to Lausanne," a chapter of his *Stuff of Sleep and Dreams: Experiments in Literary Psychology* (New York, 1982), Edel analyzes Eliot's "aboulie" with the help of terms provided by Ernest Schachtel in his book *Metamorphosis*. Edel suggests that Eliot was one of those individuals "who refuse to accept a relatively separate existence from their paradisial past" and who become afflicted with "loss of the will, despair and apathy," characteristics that abound in the poetry. Edel draws upon Schachtel selectively to sketch a sensitive psychological portrait of Eliot (that at one point refutes the hypothesis of Eliot's homosexuality). Edel also provides a well-informed and illuminating discussion of the therapeutic methods of Dr. Roger Vittoz, the Swiss psychiatrist whom Eliot consulted in Lausanne.

A figure in Eliot's life who has provoked much speculation over the years is Jean Verdenal, to whom Eliot dedicated his first volume of poems. John Peter was the first to suggest that *The Waste Land* was a lament for a lost male love who had died by drowning, the dead lover being Jean Verdenal ("A New Interpretation of *The Waste Land*" [*EIC*, July 1952]). Although the essay provoked an immediate outcry from Eliot and others, the matter did not surface again until George Watson's attempt to refute the thesis. In "Quest for a Frenchman" (*SR*, Summer 1976), Watson argues that Verdenal was merely a friend in Paris who shared Eliot's intellectual and literary interests and who was able to introduce Eliot to the cultural life of that city. Moreover, his death during World War I occurred on land, not at sea. "The sexual explanation, in short, is reductive," Watson declares, "and I object to it not only because it is unproven but because it is trivial."

Watson's refutation, however, did not put the matter to rest. The publication of the facsimile edition of *The Waste Land* in 1972 encouraged scholars to turn again to the personal sources of Eliot's art. In his review of this edition, William Empson offered some interesting biographical speculations (*EIC*, Oct. 1972; reprinted in *Using Biography* [London, 1984]). Empson suggests that the "central theme" of the poem is "a father," and he supports this assertion with an engaging analysis. Other critics found more than a strained father-son relationship in the poem. In 1977 James E. Miller, Jr. resurrected Jean Verdenal and reopened the controversy about his relationship to Eliot. *T. S. Eliot's Personal Waste Land: Exorcism of the Demons* (University Park, Pa., 1977) is an insightful, provocative, and maddening book. Miller identifies Phlebas with Verdenal and the unhappily married couple in the poem with Eliot and his first wife, Vivienne. Although Miller warns against a simplistic biographical reading of Eliot's poem, he does not skirt this danger himself. At the same time he presents some extremely suggestive readings of Eliot's poetry.

Miller modified his thesis in *The American Quest for a Supreme Fiction: Whitman's Legacy in the Personal Epic* (Chicago, 1979). He still views *The Waste Land* as a confessional poem, but the "validity" of his reading no longer hangs "on identification of Phlebas the Phoenician in Eliot's life." Miller relates the confessional aspect of the poem to the tradition of *Leaves of Grass* and then demonstrates the great lengths to which Eliot went to efface personal elements from the published version of the poem. Although Miller errs in attributing too many of these changes to Pound, he does present a convincing case for a biographical interpretation of the poem.

Interesting corroboration for Miller's biographical reading is provided by Erwin R. Steinberg in "*Mrs. Dalloway* and T. S. Eliot's Personal Waste Land" (*JML*, Mar. 1983). Steinberg examines Eliot's friendship with the Woolfs during the early 1920s when, on the testimony of Leonard Woolf, the relationship deepened significantly. He then shows how the materials of Eliot's life were transmuted by Virginia Woolf into fiction. Steinberg suggests that the story of Septimus Smith in *Mrs. Dalloway* "not only reflected many of the aspects of T. S. Eliot's life from 1909 through

1921 as James Miller and others sketched it . . . but also echoed many of the ideas and images in Eliot's *The Waste Land.*"

William E. Meyer, Jr. adopts the methods of Miller for an examination of the personal sources of Eliot's work after *The Waste Land* in "T. S. Eliot: Biography, Poetry, and Anglo-Catholicism" (*ArQ*, Autumn 1979). After brief biographical readings of *Ash Wednesday* and *Four Quartets*, Meyer notes that "to some extent Eliot's famous 'impersonal theory of poetry' and all that follows from it may be a kind of defensive maneuver for the sake of screening his own intensely personal poetry from the biographical or psychological intrusions of insensitive critics."

A number of shorter biographical studies over the last decade have examined Eliot's relations with other writers. Keath Fraser considers the friendship between Eliot and Richard Aldington in "*Stepping Heavenward*: The Canonization of T. S. Eliot" (*UWR*, Fall–Winter 1977). Fraser attributes the cooling of this friendship to Aldington's satiric portrayal of Eliot in his novel *Stepping Heavenward*, a book Fraser calls Eliot's "unofficial life." Michael B. Thompson provides a useful summary of Aldington's published observations on Eliot and then cites fundamental differences of "vision, temperament, ambition, and procedure" as the reasons for the rupture between the two writers in "Richard Aldington and T. S. Eliot" (*YER*, No. 1, 1979). Jeffrey Meyers discusses a more lasting relationship from the early London period in "Wyndham Lewis and T. S. Eliot: A Friendship" (*VQR*, Summer 1980). Over the years Eliot gave moral and financial support to Lewis, and the two remained friends until Lewis's death in 1957.

Another early and lifelong friendship was that between Eliot and his former Harvard classmate, Conrad Aiken. Ted R. Spivey draws upon his conversations with Aiken from 1965 to 1969 to document "Aiken's Eliot: Toward a Revision" (*SoQ*, Fall 1978). A less important but extremely interesting figure in Eliot's life was William Force Stead, the clergyman who baptized Eliot in 1927. In "William Force Stead's Friendship with Yeats and Eliot" (*MR*, Spring 1980), George Mills Harper chronicles the unusual life of this minor poet who gave up a career in the Foreign Service and became a clergyman. Harper reprints an interesting short essay by Stead, "Some Personal Impressions on Mr. T. S. Eliot," with annotations by Eliot. Eliot's relationship with Igor Stravinsky is discussed by Robert Craft in "Stravinsky and Eliot: 'Renard' and 'Old Possum'" (*Encounter*, Jan. 1978). The two artists who had long admired each other's work first met in 1956 and quickly became good friends. Although the collaboration they discussed never occurred, Stravinsky based his anthem *The Dove Descending* (1962) on "Little Gidding."

Ezra Pound's "shadow boxin' with the possum" in 1934 is vividly chronicled by Christina C. Stough in "The Skirmish of Pound and Eliot in *The New English Weekly*: A Glimpse of Their Later Literary Relationship" (*JML*, June 1983). Stough traces the split between the two writers after publication of *The Waste Land* and then focuses on their exchange in the *New English Weekly*. This began with Pound's negative review of Eliot's *After Strange Gods* ("Mr Eliot's Mare's Nest"), which inaugurated almost weekly ripostes in the pages of that journal, punctuated by Pound's essays (a favorable review of *The Use of Poetry and the Use of Criticism* and "Mr. Eliot's Solid Merit"). Stough presents a humorous and instructive summary with copious quotation.

Several acquaintances and friends have recorded their own impressions of Eliot. E. W. F. Tomlin draws upon a long friendship (thirty-four years) to make some telling observations about Eliot's character and business demeanor ("T. S. Eliot: A Friendship," *Listener*, 28 Apr. 1977). Donald Hall recounts some very illuminating anecdotes about Eliot in his "Notes on T. S. Eliot" in *Remembering Poets* (New York, 1978). He handles the details of Eliot's life with a tact that other biographers would do well to emulate. Like Hall, B. L. Reid relates his own encounters with a number of modern poets, Eliot among them, in "Four Winds" (*SR*, Apr.–June 1979) but his comments add disappointingly little to the record. Eliot's former secretary and junior editor at Faber and Faber, Ann Ridler, paints an affectionate portrait of her former boss in "Working for T. S. Eliot—A Personal Reminiscence" (*PR*, Mar. 1983). Whether describing his habits of dictation or his attack on the *Times* crossword puzzle during the weekly business meeting at Faber and Faber, Ridler reveals the person beneath the persona. John Malcolm Brinnin discusses his meetings with Eliot between 1950, when Brinnin invited Eliot to read at the Poetry Center in New York City, and 1957, the year Eliot married Valerie Fletcher in *Sestet: T. S. Eliot and Truman Capote and Others* (New York, 1981). Brinnin's Eliot is largely the public Eliot, the éminence grise of English letters. Brinnin includes a statement written by Eliot in 1955 expressing his opposition to the treatment of Jewish intellectuals in Russia.

A useful reference work is Caroline Behr's *T. S. Eliot: A Chronology of his Life and Works* (London, 1983). Behr arranges the events and publications of Eliot's life in chronological order with brief but helpful commentaries, and provides a bibliography of source materials for the study of Eliot's life.

In *T. S. Eliot: A Life* (New York, 1984), Peter Ackroyd has written what will no doubt remain the standard Eliot biography for years to come. Anything like a definitive life is impossible, due to the many restrictions on the publication of letters and manuscripts imposed by Eliot's estate. (Some crucial documents, like Eliot's correspondence with Emily Hale, will remain unavailable to scholars until well into the twenty-first century.) In spite of these obstacles, Ackroyd ably chronicles the works and days of Eliot's rather quotidian existence, although he pays less attention to Eliot's interior life. Ackroyd has a better understanding of the English environment of Eliot's maturity than of the American environment of his youth, and he is frequently given to generalizations that may annoy American readers. For example, in describing Eliot's reading in his final year at prep school, Ackroyd states that "it may not go very deep, but it goes extraordinarily wide and confirms the American predilection for cross-cultural references on a gigantic scale." And, even in as thorough a biography as this, there are lacunae: for example, Eliot's relationship with Bertrand Russell is covered with more detail and under-standing by Robert H. Bell (see above). But in general, Ackroyd's biography is a careful and gracefully written study for which all students of Eliot can be grateful.

V   CRITICISM

Until recently, criticism of Eliot's work has been guided largely by the principles enunciated by Eliot himself. His own critical strictures, out-lined so early in his career, helped shape the New Criticism which dominated Anglo-American letters for so long. We have already noted the challenges to Eliot's theory of the impersonality of the artist in section IV, above, stimulated in part by the publication of the facsimile edition of *The Waste Land*. Other recent developments in literary theory have begun to have an impact on Eliot studies as well.

1   General Studies

The last fifteen years have witnessed the appearance of a number of studies of Eliot intended for the general reader. In *T. S. Eliot: Poet and Dramatist* (New York, 1972), Joseph Chiari has written a descriptive study of "a great poet as well as . . . a great human being." Chiari knew Eliot personally for nearly twenty years, and this study pays tribute to that friendship. Although suffused with admiration for Eliot, the book is impersonal and presents little biographical material. Neither does the criticism break new ground.

Stephen Spender has contributed a volume, *T. S. Eliot* (New York, 1976), to the Modern Masters Series edited by Frank Kermode. This is the best general study of Eliot since Bernard Bergonzi's *T. S. Eliot* (1971) and it should find a wide audience. Spender draws upon a lifetime's acquaintance with the work and a personal knowledge of the poet to provide a stimulating, incisive, and illuminating survey of Eliot's poetry, prose, plays, and politics. For students seeking a single introduction to Eliot, this is an excellent choice.

In *T. S. Eliot: Revised Edition* (TUSAS, Boston, 1982), Philip R. Headings has added five new chapters to his earlier general study of Eliot (1964) primarily to expand his excellent remarks on the Dantean contexts of Eliot's work. Burton Raffel's introductory study, *T. S. Eliot* (New York, 1982), adds nothing of note to the record and is marred by Raffel's obvious lack of sympathy for Eliot's later work.

B. C. Southam's *A Student's Guide to the Selected Poems of T. S. Eliot* (London, 1974) is a compilation of annotations keyed to this collection of Eliot's poetry. Although useful, this volume, like other such handbooks, conveys the misleading view that a mastery of minutiae will forever unlock the mysteries of the poetry. It should be recommended to students with caution.

A representative sampling of approaches to Eliot is gathered by Linda W. Wagner in *T. S. Eliot: A Collection of Criticism* (New York, 1974). This volume contains nine essays, most of them then of recent vintage. Such works are useful but have a limited lifespan; it is clearly time for a new collection reflecting the critical ferment of the last decade.

A number of scholarly studies include general assessments of Eliot's work. In his *Lives of the Modern Poets* (New York, 1980), William Pritchard presents an intelligent introduction to Eliot's work that expands his earlier and more restricted treatment of Eliot in *Seeing Through Everything: English Writers, 1918–1940* (New York, 1977). Pritchard speculates as to whether poetry lovers at the end of the century "will continue to read, argue about, share their pleasure in 'Prufrock,' *The Waste Land, Four Quartets*, and a few of his other poems" and his fine discussion of these works suggests an affirmative answer.

Donald E. Stanford devotes a chapter to T. S. Eliot in his eccentric *Revolution and Convention in Modern Poetry: Studies in Ezra Pound, T. S. Eliot, Wallace Stevens, Edwin Arlington Robinson, and Yvor Winters* (Newark, Del., 1983). Stanford contends that "the revolutionary movement [represented by the work of Pound, Eliot, and Stevens] will pass into history as an interesting, provocative, and sometimes brilliant deviation from the main line of poetry in English written since the sixteenth century." The major poetic accomplishments of this century are represented instead by the mature work of Yeats, Hardy, Bridges, Robinson, Frost, Winters, "and perhaps a few others." Stanford's thesis is weakened by his excessive praise for the "classicists," Robinson and Winters, and his unusual literary judgments. For example, he dislikes "Eliot's scissors-and-paste technique, of using the language of other writers better than himself" and suggests that *The Waste Land* will "eventually [be] numbered among the curiosities of literature." *Four Quartets* is "not a successful major poem," Stanford declares, adding that "any attempt to define an ineffable experience in words is bound to be somewhat unsatisfactory." Perhaps, but by this criterion many of the major poems in the language will be found wanting.

Helen Gardner provides an eloquent and personal overview of Eliot's career in "T. S. Eliot," in *Harvard English Studies 2: Twentieth-Century Literature in Retrospect* (ed. Reuben A. Brower, Cambridge, Mass., 1971). Gardner attributes the power of much of Eliot's work to the fact that "again and again he touches the raw nerve of experience, experience that is often painful and disturbing but which is transformed by his

expression of it into something that can be contemplated and understood." Her essay is a moving testimony to the importance of Eliot in
one critic's life: "He remains the poet who made sense to me of my own
experience of life and of the age I lived in."

David Perkins assesses Eliot's contribution to the development of modern poetry in *A History of Modern Poetry: From the 1890s to the High
Modernist Mode* (Cambridge, Mass., 1976). Perkins addresses his book
to the general reader and student and aims to be inclusive, treating a
multitude of writers within a variety of historical and social contexts.
He scants Eliot's early work to concentrate on *The Waste Land* and demonstrate its signal importance in the development of modern poetry.
Specialists will encounter familiar territory here but may nonetheless
value the extensive treatment of minor authors and the ambitious scope
of the work. Alfred Kazin briefly surveys Eliot's early work in *An American
Procession* (New York, 1984), with a focus on his expatriation and his
experience of World War I. He provides a vivid picture of the contexts
of Eliot's art.

A number of general studies have appeared that are intended for a
more scholarly audience. In *T. S. Eliot: The Longer Poems* (New York,
1976), Derek Traversi seeks "to establish the essential continuity of Eliot's
work," but he creates difficulties for himself by limiting his study to *The
Waste Land*, *Ash Wednesday*, and *Four Quartets*. His line-by-line explications of the poems are detailed and thorough, but his method contributes
to an emphasis on the particular at the expense of the larger pattern and
robs the poetry of all mystery and passion.

In *T. S. Eliot Between Two Worlds: A Reading of T. S. Eliot's Poetry and
Plays* (London and Boston, 1973), David Ward traces the effects of Eliot
having begun his career at a time when an "old world . . . ceased to
be." Adopting for his title lines from Matthew Arnold's "Stanzas from
the Grande Chartreuse" ("Wandering between two worlds, one dead, /
The other powerless to be born"), Ward argues that Eliot's work is in
part a reflection of the extraordinary tensions of this transitory period.
Ward examines the effects of these profound historical changes, including the end of "the kind of philosophy . . . which engaged Eliot's interest," and suggests that what had once "been considered respectable
material for speculative and ratiocinative debate" now sought its expression in creative activity. Ward explicates Eliot's work within the context
of this artistic and cultural climate.

A. D. Moody's *Thomas Stearns Eliot: Poet* (Cambridge, England, 1979)
is a comprehensive and intelligent chronological study of Eliot's oeuvre
and of "the author within his own poems." Moody makes full use of
published and unpublished manuscript material to chronicle the steady
development of Eliot's career from the early experimental poetry to the
conservative and consolidating achievements of *Four Quartets* and the
plays. Moody's study is limited by his acceptance of Eliot's critical pro-

nouncements as a means of elucidating the poetry and by his conviction that Eliot is a "true voice of our Western world" and hence an accurate reflection of the western malaise. For all of its many virtues, then, this book remains an Eliotic study, enclosed within a framework constructed by the master himself.

The focus of Gertrude Patterson's *T. S. Eliot: Poems in the Making* (New York, 1971) is upon Eliot's methods of composition and their relationship to the modernist experimentation in the arts. Until late in his career Eliot was to compose in fragments that he then assembled into poetic form. Patterson demonstrates Eliot's affinities with the short, precise lyrics of Imagism and the larger structures of symbolism. Her attention to Eliot's methods of composition represented a welcome (although quite preliminary) change in Eliot criticism in 1971.

In *These Fragments I Have Shored: Collage and Montage in Early Modernist Poetry* (Ann Arbor, Mich., 1984), Andrew M. Clearfield examines the forms of modern poetry in an attempt to "establish a typology of poetic structure." Pound is the "montage poet par excellence" while Eliot is "the best example in English (at least before the postmodern period of renewed French influence) of a collage poet." Clearfield focuses primarily upon poetry written in English from about 1912 to 1920, with useful chapters on "Construction of the Lyric Poem to the Time of the Symbolists" and "Discontinuous and Asyntactic Poetry on the Continent." He develops these distinctions in extended discussions of the early work of each poet.

Cleanth Brooks is also concerned with clarifying the nature of Eliot's modernism, and he argues that T. S. Eliot's pervasive "concern with the divided psyche" is precisely what defines him as a "modernist" poet. In "T. S. Eliot as a 'Modernist' Poet," in *Literary Theory and Structure: Essays in Honor of William K. Wimsatt* (ed. Frank Brady, John Palmer, and Martin Price, New Haven, Conn., 1973), Brooks reviews the "history of the question" of the divided psyche in Western culture, and then examines Eliot's attempts to create an "authentic poetry" that would "bring thought and feeling together once more," rather than merely mirror this fragmentation. "Just as in proportion as the culture is seen to lack unity," Brooks suggests, "unity is demanded of poetry." And for Eliot, "poetry was order."

In "The Concept of Private Meaning in Modern Criticism" (*CritI*, Summer 1981), Frederic K. Hargreaves, Jr. attacks the notion that "private meaning" is the exclusive province of poetry. Using Wittgenstein for support, Hargreaves argues at length against this concept and the voluminous criticism which it has produced. His essay is a stimulating call for a revision of our views of modernism.

"We look, in a poet as well as in a novelist," Eliot noted in his essay on Kipling, "for what Henry James called the Figure in the Carpet." In *T. S. Eliot: The Pattern in the Carpet* (Berkeley, Calif., 1975), Elisabeth W.

Schneider examines Eliot's work with the aim of demonstrating "the continuity persisting beneath development and change." Within the self-imposed limitations of her study (she does not consider either the plays or the critical essays), she does an excellent job explicating Eliot's poetry and revealing certain constants throughout his career. Another study that focuses on patterns in Eliot's work is Balachandra Rajan's *The Overwhelming Question: A Study of the Poetry of T. S. Eliot* (Toronto, 1976), an elegant and carefully crafted examination of the "remarkable power of wholeness" in Eliot's major poems. Rajan identifies two forces as determining the "shape" of Eliot's poetry: "The spiral of process and the circle of design. Each necessitates the other and both stipulate the search for reality as a condition of man's being." This search continues throughout Eliot's work; each poem "represents a step forward, or upward, building on the position won in the previous poem." Rajan concludes his allusive study by offering his own very positive assessment of Eliot's poetry.

Eloise Knapp Hay stresses the unity of Eliot's oeuvre by emphasizing the ways his philosophical and religious views inform his literary works. In *T. S. Eliot's Negative Way* (Cambridge, Mass., 1982), Hay argues that Eliot's work is characterized by a pervasive pattern of negation. Hay distinguishes between two different "negative ways," although she does not connect them convincingly: Eliot's early intellectual skepticism and negativity (reinforced by his studies of Bradley, primitive religions, and Buddhist thought at Harvard) and his later turn toward the "Christian *via negativa*." Images of "void" and "path" allow Hay "to trace one significant pattern, certified by Eliot, that illuminates important features of his individual poems and also the design of his whole creative work." But without demonstrating connections between these two "ways" and without showing that a rhetoric of negation leads to a pursuit of "negative ways," Hay's thesis remains unconvincing, in spite of her many excellent discussions of individual works.

Anthony Libby has written a study of "hymns to negation" in *Mythologies of Nothing: Mystical Death in American Poetry, 1940–70* (Urbana, Ill., 1984). Like Hay (although without the benefit of her work), Libby argues that Eliot "offers the clearest example of the *via negativa* to appear in modern poetry." However, Libby stresses only the religious pattern of negativity in Eliot's work. He distinguishes "two mysticisms, transcendent and imminent, [that] combine and often struggle with each other." Libby clarifies this struggle in Eliot's poetry and shows that it characterizes the work of Stevens and Williams as well; from these "giants" this current flows through the works of the more recent poets to whom he devotes most of his study.

"Eliot's lifelong quest was in search of form adequate to his rich experience," Alan Weinblatt asserts in the preface to *T. S. Eliot and the Myth of Adequation* (Ann Arbor, Mich., 1984). Weinblatt proposes "to use the concept of adequation as a critical X-ray to disclose this quest as the underlying purpose that unifies and explains Eliot's diverse undertakings." The concept is adopted from the writings of the French philosopher Maurice Merleau-Ponty; the word "adequation" appears nowhere in Eliot's writings, although he does employ the German *Adäquatheit* in his dissertation on Bradley. Weinblatt's study also began as a dissertation and all too often still reads like one. In defending his use of the term "adequation" he notes that "if this study succeeds in unifying the various facets of Eliot's quest and in rendering Eliot . . . visible, I suspect that the term adequation may well be exorcised." Weinblatt's study does succeed in demonstrating the unity of Eliot's work in novel and important ways, but in spite of his terminology rather than because of it.

M. K. Naik's *Mighty Voices: Studies in T. S. Eliot* (Atlantic Highlands, N.J., 1980) is a rather uneven collection of essays on a variety of "comparative studies, neglected areas and unexplored approaches." The best of them are "T. S. Eliot Among the Cats: *Old Possum's Book of Practical Cats*" and "Songs Terrestial and Celestial: The 'Four Quartets' and *The Bhagavad Gita*."

In "The Possum in the Cave," in *Allegory and Representation* (ed. Stephen J. Greenblatt, Baltimore, Md., 1981), Hugh Kenner recounts how Pound and Eliot separated while on their walking tour of Provence in 1918, with Eliot descending to view the prehistoric drawings in a cave and Pound mounting the hill to explore Montségur. Kenner employs this "exemplum" to create a contrasting "poetics of the cave" (Eliot) and a "poetics of sunlight" (Pound), the former a "post-symbolist signification of ineffabilities, controlled by allusion and acoustic nuance" and the latter a poetics where words "point, and the arranger of the words works in trust that we shall find their connection validated outside the poem." Kenner responds to J. Hillis Miller's reflections on "nihilism, metaphysics' alien guest" by affirming the "physical" nature of Pound's poetics over and against the metaphysical.

Kenner's definition of Eliot's poetics is implicitly contested by Marjorie Perloff in the opening chapter of her fine study of *The Poetics of Indeterminacy: Rimbaud to Cage* (Princeton, N.J., 1981). Perloff distinguishes between two "separate though often interwoven strands" of modernism, "the Symbolist mode that Lowell inherited from Eliot and Baudelaire and, beyond them, from the great Romantic poets, and the 'anti-Symbolist' mode of indeterminacy or 'undecidability.'" She begins her study by contrasting John Ashbery's "These Lacustrine Cities" with Eliot's treatment of the city in *The Waste Land* in order to show that "Eliot's Unreal City is, first and foremost, a very real fog-bound London." For Perloff, "*The Waste Land* has, despite its temporal and spatial dislocutions and its collage form, a perfectly coherent symbolic structure." She concludes her discussion of *The Waste Land* by noting that "however difficult it may be to decode this complex poem, the relationship of the word to its referents, of signifier to signified, remains essentially intact."

In a stimulating exploration of Eliot's use of foreign language phrases, Denis Donoghue reflects "On the Limits of a Language" and the uses of tradition (*SR*, Summer 1977). Donoghue's examination of the poet's "recourse to elements outside his own language" clarifies an extremely important aspect of Eliot's works. His observations on *The Waste Land* and *Four Quartets* are particularly apt.

Eliot's critics continue to ponder Eliot's fascination with time. C. A. Patrides examines Eliot's obsession against the background of changing historical attitudes toward time and contemporary interest in the subject. In "The Renascence of the Renaissance: T. S. Eliot and the Pattern of Time" (*MQR*, Spring 1973; reprinted in *Aspects of Time*, ed. C. A. Patrides, Manchester, England, 1976), Patrides argues that Eliot subjects the Christian view of time and history to negative presentation in *The Waste Land* and positive treatment in *Four Quartets*. Patrides suggests further that Eliot's fascination with the nature of time can be demonstrated by his translation and publication in the *Criterion* of Charles Mauron's essay "On reading Einstein" (also reprinted in *Aspects of Time*). Vincent Miller also considers how Eliot's Christian views shape his notions of time and concludes that time, for Eliot, "exists as an essential and unending purgation" ("Eliot's Submission to Time" [*SR*, Summer 1976]). In *"The Waste Land* and *The Sound and the Fury*: To Apprehend the Human Process Moving in Time" (*SLJ*, Fall 1976), Mary E. McGann compares the treatment by both writers of "time and death as concurrent tensions in the human process," but her study suffers from excessive generality.

Although the focus of Paul G. Stanwood's essay "Time and Liturgy in Donne, Crashaw, and T. S. Eliot" (*Mosaic*, Winter 1979) is the poetry of Donne and Crashaw, his comments on the aesthetic function of liturgy illuminate Eliot's poetry as well. In *Time in the Poetry of T. S. Eliot: A Study in Structure and Theme* (Totowa, N.J., 1981), Nancy Gish seeks to prove that "mood, tone and structure as well as theme are largely determined by ideas of time." Although at one point in her study Gish criticizes scholars for often "taking the part for the whole," she frequently does the same herself. As earlier books and the articles discussed directly above have amply demonstrated, Eliot was obsessed with time; however, time forms but one of many strands in the complex pattern of his work.

In *Landscape as Symbol in the Poetry of T. S. Eliot* (Jackson, Miss., 1978), Nancy Duvall Hargrove discusses Eliot's use of landscape for descriptive settings and as complex symbols for "emotional, moral, and spiritual states that are difficult to portray." She demonstrates this familiar thesis with a rather pedestrian tour of Eliot's poetry. The book is illustrated with nearly fifty photographs which confirm the accuracy of Eliot's powers of observation. A footnote to Hargrove's book is offered by John N.

Serio, who charts a shift from the early "biblical, literary and symbolic landscapes" to "one grounded firmly in actual places," and who observes that Eliot's poetic voice became "more personal" in the later poetry as the landscapes became more "natural" ("Landscape and Voice in T. S. Eliot's Poetry" [*CentR*, Winter 1982]).

Critics have long taught us to appreciate Eliot's powers of sight and sound. Now Harvey Gross adds to the record by sniffing out the olfactory images in Eliot's poetry and demonstrating their importance. His "The Wild Thyme Unseen: Notes on Mr. Eliot's Remarkable Nose" (*Antaeus*, Winter/Spring 1981) is a witty paean to Eliot's power of smell.

Jewel Spears Brooker suggests that Eliot's art depended on the collaboration of his readers or spectators and hence could not be considered "elitist." In "Common Ground and Collaboration in T. S. Eliot" (*CentR*, Summer 1981), Brooker conveys Eliot's despair at what he perceived to be a "dissolution of common ground" for art, and she discusses those techniques Eliot employed to assure the reader's participation.

Dana Gioia examines the business careers of a number of distinguished American poets including Wallace Stevens, T. S. Eliot, A. R. Ammons, Richard Eberhart, James Dickey, and Archibald MacLeish in "Business and Poetry" (*HudR*, Spring 1983). Gioia argues that these writers learned a very important lesson from their business experience—"that poetry is only one part of life, that there are some things more important than writing poetry"—a lesson that may have helped them "survive."

Two other studies examine the American aspects of Eliot's work. In *Poetry in America: Expression and Its Values in the Times of Bryant, Whitman, and Pound* (Durham, N.C., 1978), Bernard Duffey considers Eliot's work (with emphasis on *The Waste Land, Ash Wednesday*, and *Four Quartets*) within the context of an American tradition of literary expression. Eliot's work is seen to be characteristic of the third of Duffey's "phases" of American poetry, one that "shifted from the mind of incoherence [stage two] to more private sophistications of feeling and thought." In "T. S. Eliot as an American Poet" (*CentR*, Spring 1982), Sam S. Baskett examines Eliot's claim of 1959 "to being, among other things, a New England poet." Baskett essays a topic of considerable interest and importance, but his uninformed survey of Eliot's responses to the American scene results in little new information or insights.

In *The Universal Drum: Dance Imagery in the Poetry of Eliot, Crane, Roethke, and Williams* (University Park, Pa., 1979), Audrey T. Rodgers explores the appeal of dance to this disparate group of poets. In her first chapter, "The Poet as Dancer," Rodgers suggests that the dance, considered as "rhythmic patterns of movement," acquired in the works of these writers a range of associations with parallels "in primitive ritual, in formal ballet, and in the fresh new interpretations by the dancers in the late nineteenth and early twentieth centuries." Rodgers examines the first of these parallels in Eliot's poetry and finds that "the dance in Eliot's poetry turns on the duality of its fundamental references: as apotheosis and dance of death."

Although Eliot's cats have received considerable attention on the stages of England and America recently, the other beasts in his menagerie are the focus of Marianne Thormählen's *Eliot's Animals* (Lund, Sweden, 1984). Thormählen suggests that Eliot's "animals are apt to serve as metaphorical indicators of man's predicament, not of his nature as such." Thus, her analyses concentrate more on the context of the image than on the "symbolic image as a recurring motif." With the help of Eliot's animals, Thormählen leads us to fresh perspectives on some of the central concerns of Eliot's poetry.

A. C. Partridge devotes three chapters to a rhetorical analysis of Eliot's poetry in his ambitious study *The Language of Modern Poetry: Yeats, Eliot, Auden* (London, 1976). Jacob Korg briefly explores the linguistic experimentation of Eliot in *Language in Modern Literature: Innovation and Experiment* (New York, 1979). And Charles D. Hartman has some very fine pages on Eliot's metrical structures in *Free Verse: An Essay on Prosody* (Princeton, N.J., 1980).

Ann P. Brady's *Lyricism in the Poetry of T. S. Eliot* (Port Washington, N.Y., 1978) suffers from its self-imposed limitations. Brady's declared preference for Eliot's lyric poetry causes her to neglect other forms in Eliot's work and to give highest marks to those poems she deems most lyrical (for example, "Marina"). This emphasis leads to distorted readings of the long poems where Eliot balances both lyrical *and* discursive passages.

Joyce Meeks Jones has ambitious aims in *Jungian Psychology in Literary Analysis: A Demonstration Using T. S. Eliot's Poetry* (Washington, D.C., 1979), but she cannot hope to do justice to them in a work of fifty pages. She simplifies Jungian theories and demonstrates an insufficient knowledge of Eliot's poetry and of Eliot scholarship.

A more successful psychological exploration of Eliot's work is Tony Pinkney's limited but highly revealing *Women in the Poetry of T. S. Eliot: A Psychoanalytic Approach* (Salem, N.H., 1984). Pinkney draws upon the psychoanalytic work of Melanie Klein, D. W. Winnicott, and, to a lesser extent, Jacques Lacan, to analyze the aggressive impulses directed toward women in Eliot's work. His reading is "guided throughout by a maxim enunciated neither by Klein nor Winnicott but by Eliot's own imaginative creation, Sweeney: 'Any man has to, needs to, wants to / Once in a lifetime, do a girl in.'" Pinkney focuses upon the pre-Oedipal and pregenital work of Klein and Winnicott, particularly the "schizoid defences" of the infant (including "omnipotent denial, splitting, projection and idealisation") in order to "'open up' the texts, to focus on the apparently marginal and to defamilarise the well known." Although many of Pinkney's assertions are highly debatable (for example, "the absent centre of *The Waste Land* is precisely an Oresteian phantasy of attack on the mother"), his study is valuable for the crucial issues it raises and for the central questions it poses. Pinkney succeeds in returning us to the texts with fresh insights.

M. L. Rosenthal's *Sailing into the Unknown: Yeats, Pound and Eliot* (New York, 1978) contains two illuminating chapters on Eliot. In "Uncomfortable Choices: Eliot's 'Little Gidding,'" Rosenthal presents a balanced assessment of Eliot's achievement in that poem. "Eliot: Essences and Open Forms" draws upon the material in his *Mosaic* article (discussed below) and shows how Eliot developed the "extended lyric structure in sequence form" by combining fragments written at different times. Rosenthal's book makes an important contribution to our understanding of the work of these three poets.

Rosenthal extends his suggestive comments on form in a major study, coauthored with Sally M. Gall, *The Modern Poetic Sequence: The Genius of Modern Poetry* (New York, 1983). In their informative discussion of *The Waste Land*, Rosenthal and Gall demonstrate that Eliot "used language, not for narrative or dramatic purposes of character illustration or suspense or resolution, but first and foremost to build the poem's tonal centers." They show how Eliot's success at achieving this resulted in a "breakthrough" for himself as well as for others. The achievements of the later poems, however, and especially *Four Quartets*, were of a different order. In *Four Quartets*, Eliot's "strong meditative bent, together with directly personal self-scrutiny," resulted in the "modern meditative sequence" that opened the way to Williams, Stevens, and Olson, among others.

T. S. Eliot and the Poetics of Literary History by Gregory S. Jay (Baton Rouge, La., 1983) is the first book-length study of Eliot's work to be decisively shaped by the theoretical developments of the 1960s and 1970s. Jay rightly argues that "many of the issues now debated in theoretical circles—influence, originality, authority, genealogy, repetition, difference, structure—are the very problems that generate Eliot's poetics." Yet, except for the recent studies of Eliot's relations to Romantic and Victorian poetry, a handful of deconstructive studies of the drama, and the renewed interest in biographical criticism, Eliot's work has not been subject to the sort of extensive reevaluation that has reshaped our perceptions of other modern writers. Jay proposes such a reevaluation in an extremely ambitious book that is at once "a reading of Eliot and . . . a work in critical theory." Jay suggests that "refiguration and transfiguration appear to be the best analytical terms for naming the way poetic or critical identities take shape in Eliot's work," and he combines psychoanalytic and deconstructive approaches to explore these aspects of Eliot's work. Jay elucidates Eliot's struggle to rewrite his poetic past through an examination of the complex phenomena of prefiguration/refiguration/transfiguration, of figures (rhetorical, paternal, and poetic) and *figurae*, of literary corpora and corpus delicti. His provocative and polemical study should reintroduce Eliot into the critical debates of today and bring him new readers.

The most comprehensive study of Eliot to appear in the last decade is Ronald Bush's *T. S. Eliot: A Study in Character and Style* (New York, 1984). Bush brings to this study an extensive knowledge of Eliot's work, including unpublished lectures, manuscripts, and letters from which he quotes copiously (or paraphrases, where quotation was prohibited by the estate) in order to examine "the motives not only of Eliot's writing but of his life." For, Bush argues, "style, like character is a habitual mode of bringing our preconscious impulses into harmony. And just as it is impossible to recognize a man's character unless we understand the internal pressures he lives with, so it is impossible to understand his style unless we first recognize the impulses it serves to repress, channel and adapt." Bush deftly, tactfully, and sympathetically weaves these two elements together to give us a more complete understanding of Eliot's work than we have heretofore possessed. In addition, by tracing Eliot's development as a poet, Bush illuminates the nature of the modernist movement, "why it flourished and why it eventually became a lifeless fossil rising over the landscape of contemporary literature." His study is essential reading for all students of Eliot.

2   Sources and Influences

Both the highly allusive nature of Eliots' work and his own interest in literary tradition have given rise to many studies devoted to questions of literary influence. These range from the identification of sources to psychological studies of Eliot's relationships with his precursors.

In *Eliot's Compound Ghost: Influence and Confluence* (University Park, Pa., 1981), Leonard Unger addresses the nature of literary influence directly. Unger begins his study with a quote (1948) from Eliot discussing different categories of literary influence, categories that determine the parameters of Unger's own work. Following Eliot's lead, Unger elucidates a "dynamics of correspondence by which a variety of sources becomes both a confluence and an influence" upon a poet's work. Among the "sources" Unger discusses are Edward FitzGerald, A. C. Benson, Joseph Conrad, John Milton, and Frances Hodgson Burnett. His remarks reflect a lifetime's acquaintance with Eliot's work and a preference for Eliot's theories of influence over more contemporary and influential models.

Eliot's abiding interest in the classics is the subject of several essays. Using Eliot's "Dialogue on Dramatic Poetry" as a model, William Arrowsmith examines "Daedal Harmonies: A Dialogue on Eliot and the Classics" (*SoR*, Winter 1977). With wit and erudition, Arrowsmith demonstrates the importance of understanding the contexts of Eliot's allusions through his analyses of well-chosen examples from Eliot's verse. Gareth L.

Schmeling and David R. Rebmann discuss Eliot's fondness for the *Satyricon* of Petronius in "T. S. Eliot and Petronius" (*CLS*, Dec. 1975). They attribute this in part to Eliot's penchant for well-written erotica and note that he quotes from Petronius at least ten times in his published writings. They suggest that the epigraph to *The Waste Land* is at least in part a dig at the Society for the Suppression of Vice. John J. Soldo summarizes Eliot's course work in the classics and includes Eliot's previously unpublished note to John Hayward on the subject of Petronius in "T. S. Eliot and the Classics: The Influence of Petronius" (*MarkhamR*, Winter 1982; reprinted in his *The Tempering of T. S. Eliot*).

The most important study of Eliot's classical inheritance is Lillian Feder's *Ancient Myth in Modern Poetry* (Princeton, N.J., 1971). Feder concentrates on the work of four modern poets, Yeats, Pound, Eliot, and Auden, with the twofold aim of developing "a definition of myth as a continuous and evolving mode of expression" and of indicating "how classical myth functions in modern English and American poetry as an aesthetic device which reaches into the deepest layers of personal, religious, social, and political life." Feder demonstrates the resilience of myth for the modern sensibility and the very significant (although different) ways it functions in the works of each poet.

Eliot began to read Dante at Harvard in 1910 and continued all his life. In "Dante Through the Looking Glass: Rossetti, Pound, and Eliot" (*CL*, Spring 1972), Ron D. K. Banerjee focuses on the ways Rossetti's "Blessed Damozel" mediated between Dante and the early work of these two modernists. Graham Hough praises Eliot's *Dante* (1929) as "the clearest path to Dante for an English reader" in "Dante and Eliot" (*CritQ*, Winter 1974). Hough calls Eliot's absorption of the lines and lessons of Dante an act of "cultural blood-transfusion—the importing of a whole order of feeling from a different civilisation." His study, a fine example of the uses a major poet can make of a precursor, has been reprinted in his *Selected Essays* (London, 1978). John J. Soldo provides valuable information on "Eliot's Dantean Vision, and His Markings in His Copy of the *Divina Commedia*" (*YER*, Nos. 1 and 2, 1982; reprinted in his *The Tempering of T. S. Eliot*) by listing those passages Eliot underlined in his edition of Dante's poem.

Two essays on Dante and Eliot touch upon the rediscovery of Dante by the Romantic poets. In "New Verse, Ancient Rhyme: T. S. Eliot and Dante" (*Parnassus*, Fall/Winter 1976), Thomas Vance discusses the impact of Dante on Shelley, Eliot, and Pound. Glenn O'Malley compares Shelley and Eliot as translators of Dante in "Dante, Shelley, and T. S. Eliot," in *Romantic and Modern: Revaluations of Literary Tradition* (ed. George Bornstein, Pittsburgh, 1977). In "T. S. Eliot's Metaphysical Dante," in *Dante Among the Moderns* (ed. Stuart Y. McDougal, Chapel Hill, N.C., 1985), Stuart Y. McDougal discusses Eliot's creation of a "metaphysical" Dante, able to fuse the realms of intellect and feeling. McDougal shows how

Eliot profited from the example of Dante at crucial stages of his own career. A. C. Charity contributes a penetrating examination, "T. S. Eliot: The Dantean Recognitions," to the volume *"The Waste Land" in Different Voices* (reviewed below). And finally, in *Dante and English Poetry: Shelley to T. S. Eliot* (Cambridge, England, 1983), Steve Ellis provides an outstanding survey of nineteenth- and twentieth-century responses to Dante's work. He begins with the Romantic rediscovery of Dante and thus provides a context for our understanding of the modernists' works. His essays on Yeats, Pound, and Eliot are shaped in part by the continuities (Yeats) or absence of continuities (Pound and Eliot) Ellis sees between their work and the Romantic tradition. Ellis's fine chapter on "T. S. Eliot: the Return to Reality" concentrates on Eliot's reading of the *Vita Nuova* and its importance in *Dante, Ash Wednesday,* and *Four Quartets.* In confirming the significance of Dante in nineteenth- and twentieth-century literature, Ellis clarifies our understanding of the literary history of this period and demonstrates the central role Dante played in the imaginations of the poets he examines.

The number of Ph.D. dissertations that find their way into print is surely small, but smaller yet is the number of published dissertations by scholars who never complete their doctorates. Because of World War I, Eliot was unable to return to Harvard to defend his dissertation and hence never received his degree. His dissertation, *Knowledge and Experience in the Philosophy of F. H. Bradley,* was published in 1964, and a number of subsequent studies have examined the impact of Bradley's work on Eliot's poetry and prose.

In *A Common Sky: Philosophy and the Literary Imagination* (Berkeley, Calif., 1974), A. D. Nuttall considers the "rise, obvious in philosophy, less obvious perhaps in literature, of solipsistic unease" in writers as diverse as Laurence Sterne, Jean-Paul Sartre, and Eliot. His witty and wide-ranging chapter on Eliot examines Eliot's conversion to British Anglicanism from the idealism of Bradley and provides extremely provocative insights into Eliot's personality and poetry.

Lewis Freed builds a detailed case for the importance of Bradley to Eliot's criticism in *T. S. Eliot: The Critic as Philosopher* (West Lafayette, Ind., 1979). Freed marshals much convincing evidence for his thesis, but he ultimately weakens his case by seeing everything through Bradleyan glasses. A more modest and moderate assessment of Bradley's impact on Eliot's poetry is provided by Jewel Spears Brooker in "The Structure of Eliot's 'Gerontion': An Interpretation Based on Bradley's Doctrine of the Systematic Nature of Truth" (*ELH,* Summer 1979). Brooker's Bradleyan-based analysis of the fragmentary structure of "Gerontion" could profitably be applied to other early poems by Eliot. Thomas J. Morrissey argues along similar lines in "'Intimate and Unidentifiable': The Voices of Fragmented Reality in the Poetry of T. S. Eliot" (*CentR,* Winter 1978). He attributes Eliot's belief in the "fragmentary nature of human experience" to the study of Bradley and suggests that this notion shaped his conception of the poetic voice. These studies complement Anne C. Bolgan's *What the Thunder Really Said* (see below).

Some of the best pages in Timothy Materer's *Vortex: Pound, Eliot, and Lewis* (Ithaca, N.Y., 1979) concern Bradley's impact on Eliot. Although the focus of his study is on the personal and artistic relationships of the Vorticists, Materer also succeeds in illuminating the historical, artistic, and cultural contexts of this movement and in clarifying the roles of Joyce, Gaudier-Brzeska, and others. But a more detailed comparative study remains to be made of the unusually close collaborations between these artists who read, discussed, and edited each other's work and who, in the process, created modernism.

Although scholars have examined the impact of T. E. Hulme's work on Eliot, Ronald Schuchard is the first to document this influence as early as 1914. In "Eliot and Hulme in 1916: Toward a Revaluation of Eliot's Critical and Spiritual Development" (*PMLA*, Oct. 1973), Schuchard suggests that by 1916 Eliot knew Hulme's work well and had already formulated a "classicist, royalist, anglo-catholic" point of view that was strongly indebted to Hulme. Throughout the next decade, Hulme continued to shape Eliot's views. Michael Gillum argues that Hulme's influence on Eliot extended through *Four Quartets*. In "T. E. Hulme and Eliot's *Four Quartets*" (*EL*, Spring 1983), Gillum states that Eliot was "more interested in Hulme as a religious, rather than a political or literary thinker," and suggests that a "figure of thought" ("the pursuit of desires as a series of dead end journeys, horizontal movements away from a central point") from Hulme's *Speculations*, a volume well known to Eliot, "entered into the imaginative process that produced *Four Quartets*."

Two years after the publication of *The Waste Land*, Eliot called Sir James Frazer's *The Golden Bough* "a work of no less importance for our own time than the complementary work of Freud—throwing its light on the obscurities of the soul from a different angle." John B. Vickery convincingly demonstrates the extraordinary influence of Frazer's work on modern writers in *The Literary Impact of "The Golden Bough"* (Princeton, N.J., 1973). Vickery makes an excellent case for the importance of Frazer's work by analyzing its place within nineteenth-century thought before considering its impact on the work of Yeats, Eliot, Lawrence, and Joyce. His chapter on "T. S. Eliot: The Anthropology of Religious Consciousness" elucidates Eliot's "well-developed and persistent interest in psychology and anthropology, particularly as they applied to comparative religion," and demonstrates the significance of these interests for Eliot's poetry. This is an important book for all students of modernism.

Eliot's debt to Lewis Carroll and Edward Lear is discussed by James Rother in "Modernism and the Nonsense Style" (*ConL*, Spring 1974). Rother posits a relationship between the nonsense style and Symbolism and suggests the appropriateness of the nonsense style in a world where communication has become increasingly difficult. William Baker provides interesting documentation for this view in "T. S. Eliot on Edward Lear: An Unnotated Attribution" (*ES*, Dec. 1983). Baker discusses an unrecorded "Lecture on Edward Lear and Modern Poetry" that Eliot delivered at Scripps College, Claremont, California, when he was visiting his friend Emily Hale during the Christmas holidays of 1933. Baker reprints a contemporary report on the lecture that appeared in *The Scripture*.

James Torrens, S.J. analyzes the strong impact of the French monarchist Charles Maurras on Eliot's thinking and writing in the late 1920s ("Charles Maurras and Eliot's 'New Life'" [*PMLA*, Mar. 1974]). Eliot had known the work of Maurras since his first stay in Paris (1910–11) and he strongly admired Maurras's sense of order and his anti-Romantic stance. Long before Eliot's 1928 declaration of his political and religious sympathies, Maurras's newspaper, *L'Action Française*, had announced its program as *classique, catholique,* and *monarchique.* Eliot defended Maurras in the pages of the *Criterion* and dedicated *Dante* (1929) to him. Torrens discusses the influence of Maurras's aesthetic theories on Eliot and notes that this influence culminates with *Ash Wednesday.*

Two essays posit the impact of the British novelist May Sinclair on Eliot. In "'New Mysticism' in the Writings of May Sinclair and T. S. Eliot" (*TCL*, Spring 1980), Rebeccah Kinnamon Neff surveys Eliot's work and concludes that Sinclair's influence was "pervasive and positive." A more moderate and more convincing argument is presented by P. S. Padmanabhan in "The Irritant and the Pearl: 'Jones's Karma' and the Poetry and Drama of T. S. Eliot" (*CRCL*, June 1982). Padmanabhan suggests that the publication of May Sinclair's short story "Jones's Karma" in the *Criterion* of October 1923 influenced Eliot's later use of Hindu themes.

In *The Great Circle: American Writers and the Orient* (Detroit, Mich., 1983), Beongcheon Yu devotes a chapter to Eliot's abiding fascination with Eastern thought. Yu provides a useful summary of Eliot's training in Indian thought at Harvard and then surveys the impact of these studies on *The Waste Land, Four Quartets,* and the plays. Although his study does not break new ground, it is a good introduction to an important subject.

In his essay "Date Line" (1934), Ezra Pound outlined five categories of criticism, one of which was "criticism by translation." Joan Fillmore Hooker demonstrates the truth of Pound's proposition in *T. S. Eliot's Poems in French Translation: Pierre Leyris and Others* (Ann Arbor, Mich., 1983) by analyzing the considerable body of Eliot's work that exists in French translation. Hooker compares these versions with the originals and, where more than one version exists, with each other. In the process she reveals a great deal about the craft of translation as well as about Eliot's own work.

In 1930 Eliot published a translation of a work he much admired, *Anabasis* by Saint-John Perse. Richard Abel argues that Perse's work had a marked influence on the poems Eliot wrote between 1927 and 1932. In "The Influence of St.-John Perse on T. S. Eliot" (*ConL*, Spring 1973), Abel establishes this with an examination of "Journey of the Magi," where Eliot's choice of narrator and use of imagery are strongly shaped by Perse's example. In another essay, "Saint-John Perse Encounters T. S. Eliot" (*RLC*, July–Sept. 1975), Abel suggests that the influence was reciprocal. He examines Perse's French published version of "The Hollow Men, I" in *Commerce* and concludes that it affected Perse's later poetry.

Claire Huffman attempts to correct earlier assessments of Eliot's influence on Eugenio Montale in "T. S. Eliot, Eugenio Montale, and the Vagaries of Influence" (*CL*, Summer 1975). She concludes that Montale's "highly eclectic" view of Eliot tells us more about Montale than about Eliot. In a later essay, "Montale, Eliot and the Poetic Object" (*IQ*, Summer 1980), Huffman suggests that Montale established a distance from Eliot by redefining much of Eliot's terminology.

Many recent studies have begun to reexamine the relationship between the great modernists and their Romantic and Victorian predecessors. P. G. Ellis suggests that Eliot's dissatisfaction with Matthew Arnold's view of literary tradition caused him to adopt and modify the evolutionary theories of Wilde, Pater, and Bergson in his own work ("The Development of T. S. Eliot's Historical Sense" [*RES*, Aug. 1972]). Eliot was thus much closer to his immediate predecessors than critics have acknowledged. In "Clough's *Amours de Voyage*: A Possible Source for 'The Love Song of J. Alfred Prufrock'" (*WHR*, Winter 1975), James R. Locke conjectures about parallels between the two works, but in the absence of specific evidence these seem rather forced.

Two complementary studies by Marion Montgomery suggest lines of continuity between the Romantics and Eliot. *The Reflective Journey Toward Order* (Athens, Ga., 1973) posits a kinship between Wordsworth and Eliot which Eliot eventually recognized. "Through a Glass Darkly: Eliot and the Romantic Critics" (*SWR*, Autumn 1973) explains Eliot's change of attitude toward Wordsworth because of his discovery of "counter-romantic" elements in the earlier poet. In "T. S. Eliot and Byron" (*ELH*, Fall 1978), Alice Levine eschews questions of direct influence and examines instead the "unconscious, sub-surface relationship between the poets." Through an extended comparison of *The Waste Land* and *Childe Harold's Pilgrimage* as quest poems, Levine succeeds in clarifying the "relationship between the nineteenth- and twentieth-century [poetic] sensibilities" in spite of Eliot's generally negative assessments of Byron's achievement.

The strongest impulse to redefine the Romantic and Victorian legacy to modernism has come from Princeton, New Jersey, where several generations of scholars have pressed for a reexamination of the nature of modernism in terms of its nineteenth-century inheritance. The most comprehensive study to date of the "main lines of actual convergence between the romantic and the modernist generations" is by one of the senior scholars of the group, Carlos Baker, late professor emeritus. Baker's *The Echoing Green: Romanticism, Modernism, and the Phenomena of Transference in Poetry* (Princeton, N.J., 1984) is divided into two parts: "Ancestral Voices," a reassessment of the work of the Romantic poets, and "Modern Echoes," a carefully documented and well-informed study of the impact of the Romantics on Yeats, Frost, Pound, Eliot, Stevens, and Auden. Baker proves to be a superb if selective guide to nearly two centuries of Anglo-American poetry as well as an able elucidator of "the variant phenomena of literary transference from one generation to another."

A. Walton Litz, one of Baker's colleagues, chronicles a shift from repugnance to rapprochement in Eliot's attitude toward Victorian poetry in "'That Strange Abstraction, "Nature"': T. S. Eliot's Victorian Inheritance," in *Nature and the Victorian Imagination* (ed. U. C. Knoepflmacher and G. B. Tennyson, Berkeley, Calif., 1977). Litz demonstrates that Eliot's feelings toward his immediate predecessors were much more complex than earlier critics have acknowledged. In *The Presence of the Past: T. S. Eliot's Victorian Inheritance* (Ann Arbor, Mich., 1983), David Ned Tobin, one of Litz's former students, attempts to "place Eliot more clearly in the English poetic tradition and to see how his poetry grew from what Victorian poets had done." He begins his study with a chapter on "the Victorian poet most closely related to Eliot," Eliot's mother, Charlotte Champe Stearns, and then proceeds to consider Eliot's relations with Arnold, Newman, and finally Tennyson, who, "more than any other Victorian . . . is in the background of Eliot's work." Tobin traces Eliot's changing attitudes toward Tennyson through his early criticism and then turns to Eliot's introduction to a 1936 edition of the *Poems of Tennyson* in which his earlier "strategies of defense" vis-à-vis Tennyson fall away and Eliot acknowledges Tennyson's greatness. Tobin convincingly elucidates the many poetic strategies shared by the two poets and in general makes a good case for Tennyson's abiding importance to Eliot.

A convincing argument for the continuities of romanticism and modernism is adduced by George Bornstein, a former student of Baker and Litz, in his *Transformations of Romanticism in Yeats, Eliot and Stevens* (Chicago, 1976). Bornstein suggests that we can properly understand the romantic legacy to modernism by shifting our focus of attention from the content of a poem to the "mental action" of the poem's speaker. Using this approach, he rereads the major works of his chosen poets with illuminating results. In his chapter on Eliot, "The Anti-Romanticism of T. S. Eliot," Bornstein notes a tension between the "anti-romantic thrust of [Eliot's] intellect" and Eliot's imagination. Bornstein demonstrates that Eliot "was a romantic against the grain, illustrating in his own career the contention of his essay on Baudelaire that in a romantic age a poet could not be anti-romantic except in tendency."

David Spurr reads Eliot's poetry and criticism in terms of an unresolved rivalry between a rational intellect and the disorderly forces of the imagination and intuition. In *Conflicts in Consciousness: T. S. Eliot's Poetry and Criticism* (Urbana, Ill., 1984), Spurr examines "the sources of structural tension in Eliot's poems and the problem of relating these tensions to a developing poetic consciousness." Spurr traces the evolution of Eliot's "embattled sensibility" from those early works, where the "ironic persona . . . eventually disintegrates under the pressure of the poet's inner conflicts," through a second stage where the poet "adopts an external set of values rather than an ironic persona." But the new role also "serves somewhat the same function by providing a structure to combat the forces of a visionary imagination." Spurr discovers the same tensions in Eliot's critical writings. His sympathetic study contributes to our understanding of the poet and his work, while corroborating the view of Eliot's relationship to Romanticism advanced by Bornstein and others.

In "T. S. Eliot and the Cubists" (*TCL*, Spring 1980), David Tomlinson suggests that modern art had a greater importance for Eliot than we have recognized. He speculates on the possibility that Eliot's writer's "'block' on the 'Waste Land' material" may have been released by visiting the Picasso exhibition in London between January and February of 1921. His discussion of the London art scene of this period is better informed than his views on Eliot's poetry. This essay should be read with Timothy Materer's *Vortex* (see above) and John Dixon Hunt's "'Broken images': T. S. Eliot and Modern Painting" (see below).

In addition to Timothy Materer's *Vortex*, several studies focus on Eliot's relationships with his peers. Terence Diggory analyzes the changing relationship between the work of Yeats and Eliot in *Yeats & American Poetry: The Tradition of the Self* (Princeton, N.J., 1983). Diggory argues that Yeats was strongly influenced by early American writers (particularly Whitman) in the development of a literature that "discovered in the self an alternative to tradition that was at the same time a new source of tradition." He shows how Yeats then became a decisive force in the development of later American writers. Diggory reviews Eliot's responses to Yeats's work and clarifies the impact of Yeats on Eliot, particularly in "Little Gidding."

George A. Panichas examines the problematic relationship between Eliot and D. H. Lawrence in a chapter of *The Reverent Discipline: Essays in Literary Criticism and Culture* (Knoxville, Tenn., 1974). Panichas argues that in spite of their expressed animosity toward each other, Eliot and Lawrence shared "an underlying sympathy of religious vision." He points to the apocalyptic visions of *Women in Love* (1920) and *The Waste Land* (1922) as evidence of this, but surely their later works underscore more radical differences.

And finally, Eliot's long and problematic relationship with Pound is the subject of a detailed study by Robert Langbaum in *Pound Among the Poets* (ed. George Bornstein, Chicago, Ill., 1985).

3 The Poetry

a. The Early Work. As previously unpublished poems by Eliot come to light, we begin to form a more complete sense of his oeuvre. In "'The Death of Saint Narcissus' and 'Ode': Two Suppressed Poems by T. S. Eliot" (*AL*, Jan. 1979), Vicki Mahaffey discusses these "confessional" poems in detail and suggests that Eliot withheld them in order to emphasize "the rational aesthetic attitude" of his criticism. In a complementary essay, "From Narcissus to Tiresias: T. S. Eliot's Use of Metamorphosis" (*MLR*, Apr. 1979), Nancy R. Comley examines Eliot's revisions of "The Death of Saint Narcissus" in *The Waste Land* and concludes that the "hermaphroditism of Narcissus is absorbed into the more powerful figure of Tiresias."

In "Eliot's 'Prufrock' and the Form of Modern Poetry" (*ArQ*, Spring 1974), James F. Knapp asserts that Eliot developed techniques in "Prufrock" that are strikingly similar to the psychological processes of avoidance, distortion, regression, wish-play, and rationalization. Knapp suggests that new conceptions of human experience have helped determine the technical innovations of modern poetry. Barbara Everett goes "In Search of Prufrock" (*CritQ*, Summer 1974) and finds a poem that is exploratory. Her own explorations lead her to new sources, including Turgenev's "The Diary of a Superfluous Man," Whitman's "Song of the Open Road," and W. S. Gilbert, among others. Everett's ingenuity here seems rather strained at times, but her emphasis on the process of discovery in the poem is salutary.

In "'Prufrock': An Absurdist View of the Poem" (*ESC*, Winter 1980), Shyamal Bagchee attempts to demonstrate the contemporaneousness of "Prufrock" by analyzing that "special feeling of the absurd [that] arises from Prufrock's, and our, apprehension that although the world is amoral and illogical, we are not yet prepared to accept it as such." Those readers who do not accept Bagchee's thesis at the outset will not be persuaded by his laborious analysis of the poem. In "T. S. Eliot's 'Companion' Poems: Eternal Question, Temporal Response" (*ContempR*, Aug. 1975), Joyce Hamilton Rochat suggests that Prufrock and Gerontion are essentially "the same character at different stages of development." However, Nancy K. Gish argues more convincingly for a strong break between the early poems and "Gerontion," with "Gerontion" looking forward to Eliot's "poetry of thought," rather than backward to the early poetry ("Thought, Feeling and Form: The Dual Meaning of 'Gerontion'" [*ES*, June 1978]).

Using Ignatian and Augustinian models of meditative techniques, Zohreh Tawakuli Sullivan examines questions of "Memory and Meditative Structure in T. S. Eliot's Early Poetry" (*Renascence*, Winter 1977). Sullivan's understanding of Eliot's early monologues seems excessively shaped by her knowledge of his later conversion.

Three short essays suggest sources for Eliot's early poems. On the basis of her examination of Eliot's marginalia in his copy of René Taupin's *L'Influence du symbolisme français sur la poésie américaine, 1910–20*, Patricia Clements establishes a source for Eliot's "Rhapsody" in one of Thomas Dekker's prose pamphlets, "The Belman of London" ("Thomas Dekker and Eliot's 'Rhapsody on a Windy Night'" [*N&Q*, June 1980]). Clayton C. Reeve suggests that Hawthorne's *The Marble Faun* offers a parallel for Eliot's use of a fifteenth-century Italian painting in "Mr. Eliot's Sunday Morning Service" ("A Possible Borrowing by Eliot from Nathaniel Hawthorne" [*YER*, No. 1, 1979]). Eleanor Cook identifies the source of the quotation "false note" in Eliot's "Portrait of a Lady" as chapter 10 of Henry James's *The Portrait of a Lady* and ably clarifies its meaning within Eliot's poem ("Portraits of Ladies" [*N&Q*, Dec. 1980]).

In "A Freudian Dream Analysis of 'Sweeney Among the Nightingales'" (*YER*, No. 1, 1978), George Whiteside discusses Eliot's enigmatic work as Sweeney's nightmare of "male desire and fear of alluring females' retaliation for it." Malcolm Pittock examines the important issue of "Poet and Narrator in 'Sweeney Among the Nightingales'" (*EIC*, Jan. 1980), but with rather limited success. By contrast, William Arrowsmith's "The Poem as Palimpsest: A Dialogue on Eliot's 'Sweeney Erect'" (*SoR*, Winter 1981) is original in conception and brilliant in execution. Arrowsmith argues for the importance of this poem by noting that it combines two of Eliot's "most obsessive" themes, "seduction and abandonment . . . and the death of a father." His discussion clarifies this difficult poem and reveals new ways of considering the other quatrain poems.

b. The Waste Land. Helen Williams's useful student guide to *The Waste Land* has been reprinted with a new chapter on the facsimile edition (*T. S. Eliot: "The Waste Land,"* London, 1973). A more valuable addition to Eliot scholarship is Grover Smith's *"The Waste Land"* (London, 1983). Smith aims to "set forth the relation between *The Waste Land* and its author's prior work and poetic aims, reconstruct something of the process of its composition, and trace its fortunes among the critics." He accomplishes these aims, and much more, with the meticulous attention to details and sources we have come to expect from the author of *T. S. Eliot's Poetry and Plays: A Study in Sources and Meaning* (2nd ed.; Chicago, 1974). This is an admirably concise and informative work.

Two studies examine possible Germanic influences on the poem. John Barry builds a strong case for the influence of Oswald Spengler's *Decline of the West* on *The Waste Land* ("*The Waste Land*: A Possible German Source" [*CLS*, Dec. 1972]). Stoddard Martin eschews questions of "influence" and examines instead Eliot's "relationship" to Wagner in *Wagner to "The Waste Land": A Study of the Relationship of Wagner to English Literature*

(Totowa, N.J., 1982). Martin attempts to demonstrate "how the poem [*The Waste Land*] might be read as a version of *Parsifal* with which it shares the Grail-legend framework."

Vincent Daly identifies a brief version of the Thunder Fable in English in an essay by Eliot's Sanskrit professor at Harvard that is a more likely source than the German edition cited by Eliot in the notes to *The Waste Land* ("The Immediate Source of The Thunder Fable: *The Waste Land*, ll. 396–423" [*YER*, No. 2, 1978]).

A comparative study of "*The Waste Land* and the *Aeneid*" by Marjorie Donker clarifies the many themes and literary devices shared by those two works (*PMLA*, Jan. 1974). Bernard F. Dick also draws upon the *Aeneid* in his more specialized discussion of "*The Waste Land* and the *Descensus ad Infernos*" (*CRCL*, Winter 1975). Dick examines the descent to the underworld in *Odyssey* XI and *Aeneid* VI and then analyzes the pervasiveness of this motif in Eliot's poem. On a slighter scale, Marion Perret shows Eliot's indebtedness to John Day's *The Parliament of Bees* in "The Fire Sermon" ("Eliot, the Naked Lady, and the Missing Link" [*AL*, Nov. 1974]). Michael Hancher's excellent comparative study, "The Adventures of Tiresias: France, Gourmont, Eliot" (*MLR*, Jan. 1978), challenges the view that Eliot's conception of Tiresias was solely influenced by classical sources by providing contemporary models as well.

John Pikoulis, in "Palgrave and Eliot" (*N&Q*, Oct. 1981), directs us to two "songs" that Palgrave published together in his *Golden Treasury*, Shakespeare's "Full fathom five thy father lies" (entitled "A Sea Dirge") and Webster's "Call for the robin-redbreast and the wren" (entitled "A Land Dirge"), which ends with the lines "For keep the wolf far hence, that's foe to men / For with his nails he'll dig them up again." Pikoulis suggests that Palgrave's collection may have provided Eliot with the inspiration for using these lines.

Peter A. Martin's "'Son of Man' in the Book of Ezekiel and T. S. Eliot's *The Waste Land*" (*ArQ*, Autumn 1977) is a painstaking study of Eliot's use of this biblical phrase. Martin also demonstrates the similarities between Ezekiel's waste land and Eliot's, thereby underscoring the extent of Eliot's general indebtedness to this book. In "Dry Bones Can Harm No One: Ezekiel XXXVII in *The Waste Land* V and *Ash Wednesday* II" (*ES*, Feb. 1984), Marianne Thormählen concentrates on *The Waste Land*, ll. 385–95, and *Ash Wednesday* II to demonstrate that "the symbolic image of dry bones in a barren place has entirely different functions, while both instances share an indebtedness to Ezekiel's prophecy." Her discussion serves as a "warning not to neglect the all important individual context."

Jeffrey L. Spear discusses the question of "spiritual renewal" in the concluding lines of part 1 in "'The Burial of the Dead': Eliot's Corpse in the Garden in a Christian Context" (*AL*, May 1978). Spears sees little hope of renewal at this point in the poem but points toward "additional promise in the rain that comes at last at the end of the poem." In "Life by Water: Characterization and Salvation in *The Waste Land*" (*Mosaic*, Summer 1978), Paul Lewis argues that Phlebas is the first "character" in Eliot's poetry to achieve "spiritual renewal." He attains this through an "extinction of personality and an escape from time" (terms Lewis draws from "Tradition and the Individual Talent"). Although Phlebas does undergo such an experience, he is not sufficiently realized as a character to be considered the "highest level of consciousness in the poem."

Tom Gibbons identifies Madame Sosostris's wicked pack of cards as the tarot pack designed by Pamela Coleman Smith according to the specifications of the English occultist, A. E. Waite ("The *Waste Land* Tarot Identified" [*JML*, Nov. 1972]). Dean Schnetzer confirms the identification of "The Man with Three Staves in *The Waste Land*" (*BNYPL*, Spring 1975) with the picture of the Fisher King on the Waite/Smith tarot cards. Robert Currie suggests that Eliot was also familiar with Waite's book *The Pictorial Key to the Tarot* and shows that Eliot's general knowledge of the tarot was extensive ("Eliot and the Tarot" [*ELH*, Winter 1979]). In "The Tarot Fortune in *The Waste Land*" (*ELH*, Winter 1982), Betsey B. Creekmore asserts that Madame Sosostris employs the "Ancient Celtic Method of Divination" explained by Waite to provide a "coherent fortune" in response to the question: "May I die?" Applying this method herself, Creekmore ingeniously—if not always plausibly—duplicates the fortune, card by card. Using the same method, Max Nänny arrives at a different conclusion in "'Cards are Queer': A New Reading of the Tarot in *The Waste Land*" (*ES*, Aug. 1981). Nänny demonstrates that "the Tarot passage is one of the crucial nodes in *The Waste Land* in which the personal and the mythical meet," and his reading illuminates the poem as a whole.

Three volumes commemorated the fiftieth anniversary of the publication of *The Waste Land*—*Eliot in His Time: Essays on the Occasion of the Fiftieth Anniversary of "The Waste Land"* (ed. A. Walton Litz, Princeton, N.J., 1972), *"Ulysses" and "The Waste Land": Fifty Years After* (ed. R. G. Collins and Kenneth McRobbie [*Mosaic*, Fall 1972]), and *"The Waste Land" in Different Voices* (ed. A. D. Moody, London, 1974). Taken together, these volumes constitute a broad range of approaches to the study of Eliot's poem.

Eliot in His Time consists of eight essays, most of which focus on *The Waste Land*. "*The Waste Land* Fifty Years After," by A. Walton Litz, emphasizes the importance of considering Eliot's poem within the general context of modernist literary experimentation and underlines the significance of Eliot's affinities with Henry James, Bradley, Conrad, Joyce, Pound, and Frazer. In "The Urban Apocalypse," Hugh Kenner attempts to date the stages of composition of the poem, demonstrates the autobiographical nature of the original conception of the poem, and stresses the importance of London (and Dryden's *Annus Mirabilis*) within Eliot's original design. Richard Ellmann reconstructs the events of Eliot's life which contributed to his "ode to dejection" in "The First *Waste Land*." The role of Ezra Pound in editing the manuscript is analyzed by Helen Gardner in "The Waste Land: Paris, 1922." In "New Modes of Characterization in *The Waste Land*," Robert Langbaum, drawing upon Eliot's doctoral dissertation on Bradley and the drafts of *The Waste Land*, demonstrates that the poem is "organized around new concepts of identity and new modes of characterization, concepts and modes that Eliot had been working toward" in his early poems. Robert M. Adams assesses the nature of the "revolution" set in motion by Pound and Eliot in "Precipitating Eliot." Michael Goldman examines Eliot's drama from the standpoint of stagecraft, rather than versification or Christian doctrine, in "Fear in the Way: The Design of Eliot's Drama." Donald Davie's consideration of *Four Quartets* as the product of the "Anglican Eliot" concludes the volume.

The essays in *"The Waste Land" in Different Voices* were first delivered at the University of York in 1972. B. Rajan's allusive essay on "The Dialect of the Tribe" opens the volume, followed by D. W. Harding's sensitive examination of the personal sources of the poem ("What the Thunder Said"). Richard Drain suggests that the "isolated sensibility" of *The Waste Land* cannot escape from the prison of its solitude ("'The Waste Land': The Prison and the Key"). A. D. Moody considers "the poet within the poem" in "'To fill all the desert with inviolable voice.'" Moody demonstrates that the poem "*is* the expression of intense personal feeling, but only in an impersonal form." In a perceptive comparative study of "Pope, Eliot, and 'The Mind of Europe,'" J. S. Cunningham argues that "*The Waste Land* and *The Dunciad* can make us feel what it would be like to redeem the time by redeeming the heritage." Nicole Ward examines Baudelaire's impact on *The Waste Land* in "'Fourmillante Cité': Baudelaire and 'The Waste Land,'" while Bernard Harris identifies the presence of Shakespeare and Wagner in *The Waste Land* in "'This music crept by me': Shakespeare and Wagner." In one of the longest and best essays in the volume, A. C. Charity discusses "T. S. Eliot: The Dantean Recognitions." Charity begins with a detailed consideration of "the art, and of the impulses behind the art, of Dante," followed by a close analysis of the impact of Dante's work on *The Waste Land*, the "limbo" poetry, and "Little Gidding." Charity's discussion confirms Eliot's statement of 1950 that Dante had been the "most persistent and deepest influence" on his verse. John Dixon Hunt's "'Broken images': T. S. Eliot and Modern Painting" succeeds more as "an exercise in cultural history" than as an elucidation of Eliot's work. Although parallels may be found between Eliot's techniques and those of modern painters, in the absence of any biographical evidence or expressed critical interest, we can only speculate about Eliot's knowledge of modern art. In "'The

Word within a Word,'" Denis Donoghue approaches *The Waste Land* as "a distinctly American work" which he calls (using Hawthorne's term) a "romance." Donoghue demonstrates that Eliot places "inordinate burdens upon language and the poetic imagination" and concludes that "language commands the otherwise empty space between consciousness and experience, consciousness and action, consciousness and the earth." In "Ideology and Poetry," Kathleen Nott surveys Eliot's "beliefs and opinions" and attempts to "isolate a structure" in them, an objective which is far too ambitious for an essay of this length. Donald Davie concludes the collection with a moving essay on "Eliot in One Poet's Life," the poet being Davie himself.

The *Mosaic* collection represents an equally wide range of critical approaches. Grover Smith analyzes "The Making of *The Waste Land*" with careful attention to the drafts of the poem. Harvey Gross explores Eliot's sense of alienation as "Metoikos in London." The Greek term, meaning "resident alien," is one Eliot had applied to himself with irony in 1945; it points to a personal characteristic which shapes much of his poetry. In "T. S. E. on *The Waste Land*," Leonard Unger reviews Eliot's own comments on his poem, as a way of illuminating the "private-public writer-reader problem." D. E. S. Maxwell composes a portrait of the Eliot of the London years in "He do the Police in Different Voices" and then demonstrates how Eliot's early poems "act out the manner of Eliot's life." M. L. Rosenthal defines *"The Waste Land* as an Open Structure" and examines both "the dynamics of the poem's movement as an extended lyric structure in sequence form" and the "undeveloped potentialities suggested by excised portions of the earlier draft." Glauco Cambon asks us "to appreciate the tentativeness of *The Waste Land* as an initial project and the significance of the solutions reached by editorial consent" in *"The Waste Land* as Work in Progress." William T. Moynihan discusses *Four Quartets* as a "dramatic meditation," which "does not so much set forth a belief" as tell us "how a believer feels." His emphasis on "Character and Action in 'The Four Quartets'" is a welcome corrective to the many studies of Eliot's beliefs in this poem. The collection ends with a reprint of Donald Davie's fine essay, "Eliot in One Poet's Life."

A controversy over the meaning of *The Waste Land* and the extent of the Buddhist influence in the poem broke out in the pages of the *Times Literary Supplement*. Craig Raine began with an essay entitled "Met him Pikehoses: *The Waste Land* as a Buddhist Poem" (*TLS*, 4 May 1973), in which he argued that *"The Waste Land* remains the one work [of Eliot's] in which Buddhist ideas assert their absolute primacy." An immediate rejoinder came from Jayanta Padmanabha (*TLS*, 18 May 1973), followed by P. Malekin (*TLS*, 25 May 1973), both of whom opposed Raine's interpretation. Raine responded on 15 June, with Malekin having the final—but certainly not the last—word on 29 June.

A detailed examination of *The Waste Land* in the context of the drafts

of the poem is provided by Marianne Thormählen in *"The Waste Land":
A Fragmentary Wholeness* (Lund, Sweden, 1978). Her carefully documented study also includes an excellent critical survey of earlier work
on *The Waste Land* and is thus a good place for students of the poem to
begin. Although at times excessively schematic, Thormählen's examination yields fresh insights.

In "St. Magnus Visited" (*MR*, Spring 1980), Elizabeth Huberman records how her feelings upon visiting this church and perceiving the
contrasts between the dark, gloomy exterior and the radiant interior
enhanced her understanding of Eliot's use of the church in *The Waste
Land*. Her essay supports the argument of Nancy Duvall Hargrove in
Landscape as Symbol in the Poetry of T. S. Eliot (see above) and articulates
the feelings of many visitors to the sites of Eliot's poems.

Charles Sanders has chosen an important and hitherto unexamined
topic for *"The Waste Land*: The Last Minstrel Show" (*JML*, No. 1, 1980).
Noting the simultaneous decay of the American minstrel show and the
British music-hall, Sanders suggests that these form "a 'familiar compound ghost' behind the many-textured arras of *The Waste Land."* Sanders
reiterates this point excessively, speculates wildly, and fails to develop
the potential of his interesting subject.

The publication of the facsimile edition of *The Waste Land* has resulted
in new attention to the composition, editing, and personal origins of
the poem. In *What the Thunder Really Said: A Retrospective Essay on the
Making of "The Waste Land"* (Toronto, 1973), Anne C. Bolgan, who helped
edit Eliot's dissertation on Bradley for publication, makes large claims
for the importance of Bradley to *The Waste Land*. She argues that "it is
in Bradley's philosophy that we shall find the source not only for every
major critical concept appearing in Eliot's literary criticism but also for
that informing ideology which gives rise to the controlling images and
symbols of his poetry." This is a position Bolgan had articulated earlier
in "The Philosophy of F. H. Bradley and the Mind and Art of T. S. Eliot:
An Introduction," in *English Literature and British Philosophy* (ed. S. P.
Rosenbaum, Chicago, 1971). Drawing upon the distinctions among
voices that Eliot makes in "The Three Voices of Poetry," Bolgan identifies
the voices—personal, literary, and philosophical—that went into the
making of *The Waste Land*. After examining these in detail, Bolgan concludes that although the tension among them is never resolved, the
poem is a "failure only in Bradley's sense of the word—relative, that is,
to the attainment of the Absolute."

The most convincing study of the order of composition of *The Waste
Land* is offered by Lyndall Gordon in *"The Waste Land* Manuscript" (*AL*,
Jan. 1974 and published as an appendix in *Eliot's Early Years* [see IV,
above]). With the care of a master sleuth, Gordon tracks down clues
and creates hypotheses. Gordon suggests that the arrangement of the
fragments indicates that Eliot first viewed the work as "a dirge for aspects

of [his own] identity that he had lost." It was only at Lausanne, where he wrote the final part of the poem in a single sitting, that Eliot "shifted the emphasis from personal case history to cultural disease." The deletions heightened the "cultural" aspect of the poem.

Chester G. Anderson decides on the basis of the manuscripts that the "'Waste' in the title refers to feces as well as to desert or ruined land." In "On the Sublime and Its Anal-Urethral Sources in Pope, Eliot, and Joyce," in *Modern Irish Literature: Essays in Honor of William York Tindall* (ed. Raymond J. Porter and James D. Brophy, New York, 1972), Anderson moves from the anal imagery in the deleted "Fresca" passage to an assertion of the anality of Eliot's work through "The Hollow Men." In fact, Anderson declares, "the poems of Eliot's first bitter and neurotic decade are filled with oedipal guilt, impotence, decapitation, castration, and anal regression." These provocative assertions remain undeveloped and unsubstantiated.

Barbara Everett takes up the question of the unity of *The Waste Land* in "Eliot In and Out of *The Waste Land*" (*CQ*, Spring 1975). She argues that *The Waste Land* "has neither 'story' nor 'narrator' nor 'protagonist' nor 'myth' nor 'themes' nor 'music' nor 'locale': these are exact and technical terms deriving from conventions which the poem includes only to fragment and deny." The poem is, however, united by the presence of a single sensibility, although it cannot be identified with a single person or persona. Eleanor Cook's superb essay on "T. S. Eliot and the Carthaginian Peace" (*ELH*, Summer 1979) works from "the hypothesis that a vision of Rome and the Roman Empire lies behind Eliot's conception of London and the British Empire." Cook's delineation of Eliot's vision of "imperial apocalypse" complements Hugh Kenner's earlier essay on Eliot's "urban apocalypse."

Laurel Boone reexamines the relationship between Eliot and Dickens in the light of *The Waste Land* manuscripts. In "Tiresias and The Man from Somewhere" (*SAQ*, Autumn 1980), Boone compares *The Waste Land* with *Our Mutual Friend* and concludes that Dickens is the source for the symbolic use of the river Thames and the dust, as well as the "*modus operandi*" of Tiresias. Although Boone's specific parallels seem strained, her case for Dickens's influence on Eliot is convincing.

Sister M. Christopher Pecheux examines the original "Death by Water" section of *The Waste Land* in the context of the manuscript of the poem ("In Defense of 'Death by Water'" [*ConL*, Summer 1979]) and suggests that the deleted lines had introduced the "theme of redemption" early in the poem. This, she argues unconvincingly, is much more effective than the final version, where there is no redemption until the voice of the thunder speaks at the end of the poem. Michael Holt examines the same passage with a view toward reevaluating the poem as a whole. In "Hope and Fear: Tension in *The Waste Land*" (*CollL*, Winter 1981), Holt finds a "paradox of conversion" in the original "Death by Water" section.

Because of Pound's lack of sympathy for Eliot's religious interests, Holt argues, he urged Eliot to cut these lines, and the resulting poem bears little trace of Eliot's original aims. Holt's argument is weakened by his failure to consider any aesthetic criteria for the changes in this passage.

Several other studies consider Pound's role in the editing of *The Waste Land*. In "Pound, Eliot, and the Rhetoric of *The Waste Land*" (*NLH*, Spring 1979), Marshall McLuhan argues that Pound imposed a "five division pattern of classical oratory" on a poem which Eliot had organized according to principles that anticipated "the four divisions of *Four Quartets* in respect to the four seasons, four elements and four anagogical levels of exegesis." Although McLuhan's thesis seems forced, his passing observations on the two poets merit close attention. A more sympathetic view of Pound's role is presented by Lewis Turco in "*The Waste Land* Reconsidered" (*SR*, Spring 1979). Turco suggests that Pound perceived an "indwelling musical structure" in the manuscripts which he was able to heighten through his deletions. Barbara Everett moves from a tiny detail (Pound's marginal gloss "Marianne") to larger questions of style in her informative note on "Eliot's Marianne: *The Waste Land* and its Poetry of Europe" (*RES*, Feb. 1980).

Several new readings of *The Waste Land* have been undertaken in poststructural or deconstructionist modes. William V. Spanos essays an ambitious reevaluation of *The Waste Land* in "Repetition in *The Waste Land*: A Phenomenological De-Struction" (*Boundary 2*, Spring 1979). Although Spanos aspires to retrieve the poem from oblivion, he ends by obfuscating it with imprecise jargon and convoluted syntax. A more successful reading is Margaret Dickie Uroff's "*The Waste Land*: Metatext" (*CentR*, Spring 1980). Uroff demonstrates that Eliot's poem can be considered profitably as "both a text and a metatext, a poem and a commentary on poetry." She attributes the "revolutionary" quality of the poem to its having made possible "a new understanding of language as a system that creates rather than imitates reality." In "*The Waste Land*: Ur-Text of Deconstruction" (*NLH*, Spring 1982), Ruth Nevo presents *The Waste Land* as a "Deconstructionist Manifesto," with "disunification, desedimentation or dissemination" as the "*raison d'être* of the poem." Assertions abound (for example, Eliot's "mythical method" is "the identical twin to Harari's account of Derrida's deconstruction") but they are not supported by verification. Nevo concludes by considering the role of the notes: "If they are supplementary, what do they supplement?" Mutlu Konuk Blasing addresses this issue in "*The Waste Land*: Gloss and Glossary" (*ELWIU*, Spring 1982). Blasing points out the "coexistence of a poem and a set of notes in the same text" and then stresses the tension between these two parts: "The critical sensibility responsible for the Notes, however, attempts to analyze and rearrange the poem according to different, alien, and rather conventional ideas of wholeness and coherence." As a result, the notes "fragment further the sensibility of the poem."

Although it appeared too late for review here, Harriet Davidson's *T. S. Eliot and Hermeneutics: Absence and Interpretation in "The Waste Land"* (Baton Rouge, La., 1985) will surely be the most detailed poststructural analysis of *The Waste Land* to date. Davidson draws on the work of Saussure, Ricoeur, Derrida, Lacan, and Heidegger not merely to explicate Eliot's poem, but rather "to display the larger principles of a hermeneutic view of world and self."

Anthony Easthope examines "*The Waste Land* as a Dramatic Monologue" (*ES*, Aug. 1983). Easthope argues that the poem is "unified *in the first place* as the voice of a single unnamed speaker identifiable within an area of psychological consistency whose consciousness develops through definable phases" and thus "goes far beyond any traditional dramatic monologue." His discussion of the "mimetic" and "textual" aspects of the poem is particularly useful. In "'He Do the Police in Different Voices': The Design of *The Waste Land*" (*CollL*, Aug. 1983), Audrey T. Rodgers uncovers a "design" in the poem which "is conceived, emerges, and takes final shape from the perspective of the poet as seer." This is a surprisingly uninformed essay, marred by inaccurate identifications and a very simplified scheme of the poem. Sherlyn Abdoo examines "Women as Grail in T. S. Eliot's *The Waste Land*" (*CentR*, Winter 1984). Abdoo suggests that the dual role of woman in the Grail myth, both as "the giver of mortal life" and as "the temptress," is also "integral to Eliot's patterns of imagery and theme," and she discovers in the poem "a heavily defended but unmistakable longing for erotic as well as spiritual fulfillment."

Scholars are beginning to elucidate the influence of Eliot's contemporaries on *The Waste Land*. Eliot's admiration for the work of Igor Stravinsky is well known, and, in "Musical and Poetic Analogues in T. S. Eliot's *The Waste Land* and Igor Stravinsky's *The Rite of Spring*" (*CentR*, Spring 1980), Mildred Meyer Boaz clarifies the parallels between these two seminal compositions, but her essay is weakened by generalities. A more focused exploration of the achievements of these two artists occurs in W. Bronzwaer's "Igor Stravinsky and T. S. Eliot: A Comparison of their Modernist Poetics," in *Comparative Criticism: A Yearbook. Volume 4* (ed. E. S. Shaffer, Cambridge, England, 1982). Bronzwaer cites many interesting connections between these two but overemphasizes the break between their modernism and Romanticism, apparently in ignorance of the recent work on the subject cited above. Fred D. Crawford examines Eliot's relationship with Conrad Aiken and suggests that *The Waste Land* is filled with echoes of Aiken's early work ("Conrad Aiken's Cancelled Debt to T. S. Eliot" [*JML*, Sept. 1979]). Crawford acknowledges that a comparison of these two versions of a similar theme "demonstrates the superior poetic genius" of Eliot.

In *"Ulysses," "The Waste Land," and Modernism* (Port Washington, N.Y., 1977), Stanley Sultan attempts (in less than a hundred pages) to define modernism "as an event and a condition of Western culture" in order to clarify the relationship between the "supreme exempla of the modernist novel and poem in the language" and to elucidate the nature of *The Waste Land*. He is most successful at demonstrating "confluences" between the two works and in showing the impact of *Ulysses* on the drafts of Eliot's poem. Shari Benstock also examines these two works in "1922 and After: The Poetic Landscapes of Joyce and Eliot" (*CentR*, Fall 1976). Benstock presents an exhausting catalogue of similarities and differences between the two writers and then shows how their landscapes diverge as Eliot's work becomes increasingly religious.

The extraordinary impact of *The Waste Land* on Eliot's contemporaries has not gone unnoticed. Although *The Waste Land* had a demonstrable influence on F. Scott Fitzgerald's *The Great Gatsby* (1925), Letha Audhuy vastly overstates the case in "*The Waste Land*: Myth and Symbols in *The Great Gatsby*" (*EA*, Jan.–Mar. 1980). She sees traces of Eliot everywhere; her case is further undermined by her ignorance of Eliot scholarship. In "Thomas Wolfe and T. S. Eliot: The Hippopotamus and the Old Possum: (*SLJ*, Spring 1981), John L. Idol, Jr. surveys Wolfe's generally negative reactions to Eliot's work and discusses some of Wolfe's parodies of Eliot. Idol's limited understanding of Eliot weakens an interesting essay. Bruce Bailey includes Thomas Wolfe in his amusing survey of humorous ripostes to *The Waste Land* by authors as different as James Joyce, Richard Aldington, F. Hodgson Burnett, Christopher Morley, and Amy Lowell in "T. S. Eliot's *The Waste Land* in Parody, Travesty, and Satire" (*YER*, No. 1, 1978). Although Bailey's survey would have been enlivened by more direct citation, it forms a nice supplement to Michael Grant's *T. S. Eliot: The Critical Heritage*. The reactions of younger poets to *The Waste Land* are appraised by John R. Boly in "W. H. Auden's *The Orators*: Portraits of the Artist in the Thirties" (*TCL*, Fall 1981). Boly argues that *The Orators* liberated the poets of Auden's generation from the stifling influence of *The Waste Land*.

The most extensive study of Eliot's impact on British novelists is Fred D. Crawford's *Mixing Memory and Desire: "The Waste Land" and British Novels* (University Park, Pa., 1982). Crawford considers allusions, themes, and images in the work of seventeen novelists, whom he divides into three groups: those writers who were well established when *The Waste Land* appeared, those who achieved prominence before World War II, and a younger generation of postwar writers. Although Crawford acknowledges the difficulties of establishing the "influence" of a work as allusive as Eliot's poem, he himself fails to posit a satisfactory theory of influence. Hence, some of the examples Crawford adduces seem strained or far too general to be convincing. Crawford does better when he sticks closer to documented sources, as in his discussion of the mutual misunderstandings of Eliot and Richard Aldington.

    c. The Middle Period: 1922–1937. Following his religious conversion in 1927, Eliot became increasingly interested in the Anglican liturgy. In "T. S. Eliot and the Language of Liturgy" (*Renascence*, Spring 1972), Karen T. Romer examines the impact of this language on Eliot's poetry, particularly the Ariel Poems, "Coriolan," and *Ash Wednesday*, and demonstrates that an awareness of the liturgical language enriches our understanding of the poetry. Similarly, Nancy K. D. Gish considers "The Meaning of the Incarnation in Two 'Ariel Poems'" (*MichA*, Summer 1973). Both "Journey of the Magi" and "A Song for Simeon" underscore the necessity of death to this life as a precondition to rebirth. The nature of the enlightment achieved by the Magus at Bethlehem is clarified by R. D. Brown in "Revelation in T. S. Eliot's 'Journey of the Magi'" (*Renascence*, Spring 1982). Brown explains that the term "satisfactory" has a precise theological meaning in the work of Lancelot Andrewes and is not simply an example of Eliot's poetic understatement.

In "Language, History and Text in Eliot's Journey of the Magi'" (*PMLA*, Oct. 1980), Daniel A. Harris argues that this undervalued poem actually occupies "a central position in [Eliot's] poetic development." Through a sophisticated application of contemporary literary theory, Harris provides an innovative reassessment of "Journey of the Magi" and opens up new directions in Eliot criticism. Neil Taylor suggests "A Possible Source for T. S. Eliot's 'Journey of the Magi'" (*N&Q*, Aug. 1982) in R. B. Cunninghame-Graham's story "The Fourth Magus" (1910). Having "lingered on the road" for thirty-three years, Graham's magus arrives at Golgotha in time to witness Christ's death. He observes that "birth and death are not so very different after all."

Rebeccah A. Kinnamon examines the parallels between *Ash Wednesday* and Jacques Maritain's essay "Poetry and Religion," which Eliot had translated anonymously and published in the *Criterion* in 1927 ("Eliot's 'Ash Wednesday' and Maritain's Ideal for Poetry" [*GaR*, Summer 1973]). Kinnamon suggests that *Ash Wednesday* exemplifies the principles enunciated by Maritain in his essay. In another examination of this poem, E. Peter Dzwonkowski, Jr. compares Eliot's depiction of the plight of man in a time-bound world in "'The Hollow Men' and *Ash Wednesday*: Two Dark Nights" (*ArQ*, Spring 1974). Lacking will, the hollow men remain trapped in the world of time. The speaker of *Ash Wednesday*, by contrast, wills to enter the dark night of the soul and achieves a vision that remains beyond the grasp of the hollow men.

d. Four Quartets. Barbara Everett pays "A Visit to Burnt Norton" (*CritQ*, Autumn 1974) and finds in the opening section of Eliot's poem "an experience of terror" which she analyzes in terms of the genre of the ghost story. Her examples include two authors much admired by Eliot, Henry James and Charles Dickens, as well as other works by Eliot himself ("The Death of Saint Narcissus," "East Coker," and "Little Gidding"). Her emphasis on the experience of the reader is salutary.

Two essays on "The Dry Salvages" enunciate the obvious. In "The

Mythic Perspective of Eliot's 'The Dry Salvages'" (*ArQ*, Spring 1974), Audrey T. Rodgers solemnly declares that "T. S. Eliot is seldom thought of as a mythic poet, yet all his poetry reflects the pattern of the quest—an essential ingredient of the mythic perspective." She then attempts to show how the "mythic perspective" provides a unifying force for the disparate elements of each quartet and for the series as a whole. F. Peter Dzwonkoski, Jr. argues that the poem is one of Eliot's "most heart felt expressions of compassion for a weakwilled and fallen humanity which simply will not see God at the heart of time" ("Time and the River, Time and the Sea: A Study of T. S. Eliot's 'Dry Salvages'" [*CimR*, Jan. 1975]). His narrow focus on the theology and his evangelical tone result in a very partial reading of the poem. In a short but useful essay on the same poem, Stephen J. Adams identifies the "sestina" which opens "Dry Salvages II" as a *coblas estrampas* with *rimas cars*, a form developed by Arnaut Daniel and known to Eliot through Pound ("T. S. Eliot's So-called Sestina: A Note on 'The Dry Salvages II'" [*ELN*, Mar. 1978]).

In "A Note on 'Little Gidding'" (*EIC*, Jan. 1975), Christopher Ricks discusses two of Eliot's less well known essays, "Note sur Mallarmé et Poe" (1926) and "Charybde et Scylla" (1952), and suggests that they demonstrate "Eliot's own aftersight and foresight about 'Little Gidding.'" J. Barton Rollins also examines the "Note sur Mallarmé et Poe" and finds Eliot repeating views on metaphysical poetry which he had expressed earlier to English audiences in "Andrew Marvell" and "The Metaphysical Poets" ("T. S. Eliot on Mallarmé and Poe" [*MarkhamR*, Fall 1981]).

Barry Spurr offers interesting speculation on "The Genesis of 'Little Gidding'" (*YER*, No. 1, 1979). He notes that several months before visiting Little Gidding, Eliot had examined and annotated a liturgical drama, *Stalemate—The King at Little Gidding*, by a lay brother of an Anglican house that Eliot frequented. Both these activities, he suggests, are "commemorated" in Eliot's poem. In "Gide, Translation, and 'Little Gidding,'" Catharine Savage Brosman provides a sensitive analysis of Gide's version of Eliot's poem that illuminates both works (*FR*, Apr. 1981). This version is also discussed at length by Joan Fillmore Hooker (see above).

Four Quartets, like *The Waste Land*, provides seemingly endless possibilities for source studies. Duane Voskuil suggests that Eliot's answers to the philosophical and religious questions posed in *Four Quartets* owe much to Hinduism and Buddhism ("Some Philosophical Ideas in T. S. Eliot's *Four Quartets*" [*NDQ*, Summer 1972]). G. Schmidt offers independent confirmation with "An Echo of Buddhism in T. S. Eliot's 'Little Gidding'" (*N&Q*, Sept. 1973). Narsingh Srivastava reviews "The Ideas of the *Bhagavad-Gita* in *Four Quartets*" (*CL*, Spring 1977). C. T. Thomas posits an "analogy from Hindu mythology" in "Eliot's *Burnt Norton*, II, 16–23" (*Expl*, Spring 1980).

Sister Corona Sharp establishes the indebtedness of the poem to sources of Western mysticism in "'The Unheard Music': T. S. Eliot's *Four Quartets* and John of the Cross" (*UTQ*, Spring 1982). Eliot discovered the writings of St. John of the Cross while at Harvard, cited them in "Lancelot Andrewes" (1926), quoted them "ironically" as epigraph to *Sweeney Agonistes* (1926–27), and was reading them in a translation by E. Allison Peers during the composition of "East Coker" (1940). Sharp demonstrates that the influence extends "beyond the obvious allusions made by the poet to the Spanish mystic." This essay supplements the books by Hay and Libby (see above). Classical models are considered by Andrew V. Ettin in "Milton, T. S. Eliot, and the Virgilian Vision: Some Versions of Georgic" (*Genre*, Summer 1977). Ettin examines Virgil's *Georgics*, Milton's *Paradise Regained*, and Eliot's *Four Quartets* as examples of "generic analogues," with thematic and stylistic similarities. Linda Bradley Salaman traces the relationship between Eliot and his ancestor, Sir Thomas Elyot, in "A Gloss on 'Daunsinge': Sir Thomas Elyot and T. S. Eliot's *Four Quartets*" (*ELH*, Winter 1973). Although faint, Elyot's influence is present in the earthly values of "human piety, labor, and wisdom."

The continuities between *Four Quartets* and eighteenth- and nine-teenth-century poetry form the focus for several recent essays. In "Eliot Written in a Country Churchyard: The *Elegy* and *Four Quartets*" (*ELH*, Summer 1976), George T. Wright demonstrates through a detailed analysis that Gray's *Elegy* is a "possible base from which Eliot evolved *Four Quartets*." This fine essay complements Hugh Kenner's "The Urban Apocalypse" (see above) in confirming the importance of eighteenth-century poetry for Eliot. Building upon a reference to Arthur Hugh Clough in a letter from Eliot to his friend John Hayward in 1940, Paul Murray seeks to find traces of the Victorian poet in *Four Quartets*. In "The Unidentified Ghost: Arthur Hugh Clough and T. S. Eliot's *Four Quartets*" (*Studies*, Spring 1981), Murray attempts to identify echoes from the work of the poet Eliot never mentioned in essays or reviews and never alluded to in his other poetry. Murray's efforts, like those of James R. Locke (see above), remain unconvincing.

Christopher Clausen emphasizes the Romantic inheritance of *Four Quartets* in "Tintern Abbey to Little Gidding: The Past Recaptured" (*SR*, Summer 1976), but Clausen's comparisons are too general to be compelling. Barbara Everett examines Eliot's "struggle" with French Symbolism in "Eliot's *Four Quartets* and French Symbolism" (*English*, Spring 1980). She views *Burnt Norton* as the culmination of a decade of labor to create a "philosophical style" modeled after the example of the Symbolists. Her discussion of Eliot's development during this period is more convincing than her exaggerated claims for the impact of Symbolism. A more temperate discussion of the Symbolist heritage in *Four Quartets* is presented by Stephen Spender in "Rilke and Eliot," in *Rilke: The Alchemy of Alienation* (ed. Frank Baron, Ernst S. Dick, Warren R. Maurer,

Lawrence, Kans., 1980). Spender views *Four Quartets* and the *Duino Elegies* as works that realize "the aims of symbolism and the aesthetic movement" and fuse "pure poetry" with religious meanings. And, in "T. S. Eliot and the Leçon de Valéry" (*CritQ*, Spring 1982), Tony Pinkney argues that Eliot could have profited more from his own criticism of Valéry. *Four Quartets*, Pinkney suggests, suffers from the same "rigid dualisms" for which Eliot had criticized Valéry.

The "musicality" of the *Quartets* continues to fascinate critics. In *Eliot's "Four Quartets": Poetry as Chamber Music* (London, 1978), Keith Alldritt considers Eliot's "pre-eminently verbal" achievement in terms of principles of musicality. Alldritt attributes Eliot's interest in the relations between poetry and music to the Symbolists before examining *Four Quartets* as a Symbolist work in sonata form. Alldritt is most successful in demonstrating how the various voices of the poems form effective counterpoints with each other, and least successful in naming those voices (for example, lecturer, prophet, conversationalist, and conjuror). Andrew Kennedy argues that the voices of *Four Quartets* should not be considered as distinctly different, but rather as versions of a single voice. In "The Speaking 'I' in *Four Quartets*" (*ES*, April 1979), Kennedy provides a detailed examination of the many complex modulations of voice in Eliot's poem.

Brian Hatton correctly insists that many of the earlier discussions of the musicality of *Four Quartets* have been reductive and suggests a new approach in "'Musical Form' in Poetry: *Four Quartets* and Beethoven" (*YER*, No. 2, 1979). Arguing that "the logic of music lies in its harmonic and rhythmic relationships" and "not [in] the emotional response of its readers," he proposes to examine the logical musical structure of Eliot's poem. The diagrams and classifications he provides, however, are variations on an old theme in Eliot criticism and contribute little that is new to our understanding of the poem.

Nancy Anne Cluck reprints many fine essays on Eliot and music (including several criticized by Brian Hatton, above) in *Literature and Music: Essays in Form* (Provo, Utah, 1981). This volume includes Paul Chancellor's "The Music of *The Waste Land*," Helen Gardner's "The Music of *Four Quartets*," D. Bosley Brotman's "T. S. Eliot: 'The Music of Ideas,'" Herbert Howarth's "Eliot, Beethoven, and J. W. N. Sullivan," Harvey Gross's "Music and the Analogue of Feeling: Notes on Eliot and Beethoven," and Thomas R. Rees's "The Orchestration of Meaning in T. S. Eliot's *Four Quartets*."

Julia Maniates Reibetanz undertakes a detailed metrical analysis of *Four Quartets* in *A Reading of Eliot's "Four Quartets"* (Ann Arbor, Mich., 1983), based on Eliot's declared attempt to create a new accentual meter in these poems. She traces the development of this meter in *The Hollow Men, Ash Wednesday*, and the five short poems called *Landscapes* before considering the "far more complex and extended music of sounds and rhythms, of words, lines, and verse paragraphs" that characterizes *Four Quartets*. Through a close reading of these poems, Reibetanz convincingly demonstrates how "the metrical patterns of each line, paragraph, or section contribute to the argument of the poem," thereby enhancing our understanding of the work.

Frances O. Austin suggests that Eliot employed present participles and gerunds in *Four Quartets* to represent "flux and action that is continuous" ("*Ing* Forms in *Four Quartets*" [*ES*, Feb. 1982]). Thus Eliot "conveys his themes through the grammar." Peter Barry contests this thesis in "Making Sense of Syntax, Perhaps: A Reply Note to Frances Austin's '*Ing* Forms in *Four Quartets*'" (*ES*, Feb. 1984). Barry examines the functions of different tenses in English and concludes that "there is no inherent connection between the *ing* form of the verb and either present or continuous time." Hence, "it is difficult to see how . . . Eliot can be said to be conveying his themes through grammar."

Eugene Webb devotes a chapter to *Ash Wednesday* and *Four Quartets* in *The Dark Dove: The Sacred and Secular in Modern Literature* (Seattle, Wash., 1975). Webb suggests that it took Eliot more than a decade after his conversion to bring "the immanent and transcendent poles of the sacred . . . into balance in his poetry." Webb complains of the "obscurity" of the theological allusions of *Ash Wednesday* and of its "desolate" portrait of the secular world. Greater clarity and balance are achieved in *Four Quartets*, a poem addressed "both to those inside the church and to those outside it" and concerned with "the relationship between time and eternity, which, as the poem presents it, is a version of the problem of the relationship between the secular and the sacred." Webb's general observations are more suggestive than his rather sketchy explications of these poems.

Rajendra Verma's *Time and Poetry in Eliot's "Four Quartets"* (Atlantic Highlands, N.J., 1979) is an impressionistic and critically uninformed study of "Time Concepts and Philosophical Poetry" in Eliot's poem. Verma presents a section-by-section reading of each of the *Quartets*, moving from exposition to an examination of the sources. Verma offers little that is new except perhaps comments on Eliot's indebtedness to the *Bhagavad-Gita* in "The Dry Salvages." Kathleen Woodward profitably compares the late work of American modernists in *At Last, the Real Distinguished Thing: The Late Poems of Eliot, Pound, Stevens, and Williams* (Columbus, Ohio, 1980). Although at times reductive, Woodward's study provides an unusual perspective on "T. S. Eliot and the *Four Quartets*: The Still Point, Aging, and the Social Bond."

F. R. Leavis devotes over a hundred pages to a reading of *Four Quartets* in *The Living Principle: 'English' as a Discipline of Thought* (New York, 1975). While never neglecting the poetry as such, Leavis is carefully attuned to the unfolding argument of the sequence. The Eliot of *Four Quartets*, Leavis argues, is a "divided man," "imprisoned" in "self-contradiction." Leavis delineates these contradictions in detail and questions many of the assumptions underlying the poem. His forceful and elucidative essay is an important one. Leavis's changing views of Eliot's work are ably discussed by R. P. Bilan in "F. R. Leavis's Revaluation of T. S. Eliot" (*UTQ*, Winter 1978).

Another discursive, personal, and compelling reading of *Four Quartets* is A. E. Dyson's in *Yeats, Eliot, and R. S. Thomas: Riding the Echo* (London, 1981). Dyson's subtitle stresses the importance of "the poems discussed being *heard*." In his chapter on *Four Quartets*, Dyson asserts that this poem is "neither more or less Christian than *The Waste Land*. . . . The difference is mainly tonal, and the challenge for the reader is defined by this." Dyson's comments illuminate this "last, and perhaps most teasing, enigma that the poet left."

James Olney offers a Jungian reading of *Four Quartets* in *Metaphors of Self: The Meaning of Autobiography* (Princeton, N.J., 1972). Olney approaches autobiography "in relation to the vital impulse to order that has always caused man to create and that, in the end, determines both the nature and the form of what he creates." He suggests that Eliot "treats his own experience as representative and symbolic" in *Four Quartets*, with the result being a work that is, "in effect, an autobiography of and for Everyman as a philosophic and spiritual being." Olney carefully delineates the symbolic patterns of the poem and then characterizes the subject of the poem as "the whole self-in-becoming." He demonstrates how in *Four Quartets* "the poet combines the intuitive depth of the mystic's vision with the sensory delicacy of the scientist's observation and the structural inevitability of the logician's syllogism, the complete consort dancing together to the rhythm of the emotions and of the unconscious, to realize the complete pattern of self."

William V. Spanos offers a Heideggerian reading of the poem in "Hermeneutics and Memory: Destroying T. S. Eliot's *Four Quartets*" (*Genre*, Winter 1978). Spanos contends that the poem was not shaped by a predetermined doctrine but remained rather a poetry of exploration. As the *Quartets* appear to move toward closure, they continue to assert the openness of experience. In fact, Spanos views the "decreative" aspects of the poem as definitive.

One of the most challenging discussions of *Four Quartets* appears in Frank Burch Brown's *Transfiguration: Poetic Metaphor and the Languages of Religious Belief* (Chapel Hill, N.C., 1983). Brown draws heavily upon current literary theories and particularly theories of metaphor to elucidate the languages of religious experience. He views metaphor "as having the capacity to provide highly significant transformations of language, thought, and experience—transformations of a kind not duplicated by other linguistic strategies." These transformations, of course, have considerable consequences: "What makes a poetic transformation significant, and therefore transfigurative," Brown states, "is simply that the metaphoric process it involves does in some way alter one's ordinary experience in such a way as to engage and address what is essentially one's whole self." Brown confirms this hypothesis with a probing examination of *Four Quartets*. He argues that "the purpose of *Four Quartets* is to offer a significant transformation of experience that will cause one to become, in a very particular way, alive to one's whole being—including one's being in relation to a whole larger than oneself." His analysis reveals some of the important ways in which *Four Quartets* is able "to affect us wholly, as human beings."

e. *Old Possum's Book of Practical Cats*. Molly Best Tinsley writes with appropriate wit about "T. S. Eliot's Book of Practical Cats" (*StAH*, Jan. 1975), which she considers "an oblique commentary on human society and its conventions." Lest that sound too dull, she discovers in the book "the mischief and muddle that could find no place in the ordered universe of a classicist, royalist, and Anglo-Catholic." Robert F. Fleissner has provided a comic reading of Eliot's book in "About the Mews: Catching Up with Eliot's Cats" (*Thalia*, 1982).

4   The Plays

Although *Cats*, the musical based on *Old Possum's Book of Practical Cats*, has been a great success on Broadway, and Michael Hastings's play *Tom and Viv* has achieved a certain notoriety for its depiction of Eliot's marriage to his first wife, Eliot's own drama has received surprisingly little attention in the last decade.

Edna G. Sharoni examines the complex sources of *Murder in the Cathedral* (including Epictetus, Seneca, Dante, and Milton) and suggests that the play provided Eliot with the opportunity to unite hitherto theoretical interests in dramaturgy with his personal religious struggles ("'Peace' and 'Unbar the door': T. S. Eliot's *Murder in the Cathedral* and Some Stoic Forebears" [*CompD*, Summer 1972]). Sharoni provides an informative analysis of Eliot's Christian transformation of Stoic symbols in the character of Thomas à Becket. A study which focuses exclusively on Becket's character is John Cutts's "Evidence for Ambivalence of Motives in *Murder in the Cathedral*" (*CompD*, Summer 1974). Cutts explains this "ambivalence" in Becket and argues that finally Becket "commands his own martyrdom." Carol Billman examines "History Versus Mystery: The Test of Time in *Murder in the Cathedral*" (*Clio*, Fall 1970) and praises Eliot for maintaining a tension between "temporal history and unchanging transcendence."

Edith Pankow considers "The 'Eternal Design' of *Murder in the Cathedral*" (*PLL*, Winter 1973) and suggests that Eliot succeeds in fusing conventions from classical drama (including the tragic flaw), medieval liturgy, and medieval allegory to create a complexly unified work. In "Liturgy and Time in Counterpoint: A View of T. S. Eliot's *Murder in the Cathedral*" (*MD*, Sept. 1980), Lionel J. Pike asserts that medieval liturgy is the definitive element in Eliot's play. In its use of ritual and liturgy and in its form, which draws on the mass, Eliot's play is closer to medieval drama than to modern theater. William J. McGill provides insights on aspects of the staging of Eliot's play in "Voices in the Cathedral: The Chorus in Eliot's *Murder in the Cathedral*" (*MD*, Sept. 1980). In a strongly Derridean reading of *Murder in the Cathedral*, Michael Beehler argues that the play "traces Eliot's desire for a presence which would authorize the signs of history by halting their recessive play, but it is at the same time a gesture which forever defers the return of presence, marking it as always already absent" ("*Murder in the Cathedral*: The Countersacramental Play of Signs" [*Genre*, Fall 1977]).

Eliot's successful blending of "high moral seriousness" and light comedy in *The Cocktail Party* is capably discussed by Gary T. Davenport in "Eliot's *The Cocktail Party*: Comic Perspective as Salvation" (*MD*, Sept. 1974). P. G. Mudford analyzes Eliot's last four plays in terms of their development of a tradition of "high comedy" that would include such works as *A Midsummer Night's Dream*, *The Marriage of Figaro*, and *Don Juan* ("T. S. Eliot's Plays and the Tradition of 'High Comedy'" [*CritQ*, Summer 1974]).

Hazel E. Barnes reexamines the relationship between Euripides's *Alcestis* and *The Cocktail Party* with interesting results. In "Death and Cocktails: The Alcestis Theme in Euripides and T. S. Eliot," in *The Meddling Gods: Four Essays on Classical Themes* (Lincoln, Nebr., 1974), Barnes argues that the "myth of Alcestis and Euripides' dramatic treatment of it provide the overtones and even part of the harmonic material for the musical order which Eliot seeks in his own drama." After discussing each play individually and then surveying previous scholarship on the relationships between them, she suggests that the "most significant link" between the two works can be found in the "key word," *daimon* ("an intermediate between human and god"), a term which Eliot had been persuaded to change to "guardian" by E. Martin Browne, the play's director. Barnes argues that Eliot's play is a reply to existentialism, and her analysis of the roles of the daimons/guardians supports an interesting interpretation of the ending of Eliot's play in these terms.

Hildegard Hammerschmidt also considers "The Role of the 'Guardians' in T. S. Eliot's *Cocktail Party*" (*MD*, Mar. 1981), and she suggests that we regard the guardians as "magicians or even magi" who perform a type of "ritual magic." This is an interesting, although rather limited, reading. Vimela Rao argues that the *Bhagavad-Gita* has been overlooked as a source for *The Cocktail Party* and he attempts to correct this oversight in "T. S. Eliot's *The Cocktail Party* and the *Bhagavad-Gita*" (*CLS*, June 1981). Rao notes many parallels but weakens his case through generalizations.

In an essay which complements his study of "New Modes of Characterization in *The Waste Land*" (see above), Robert Langbaum analyzes

"The Mysteries of Identity as a Theme in T. S. Eliot's Plays" (*VQR*, Autumn 1973). Langbaum views Eliot's final three plays as dramatizations of the Christian paradox that man must lose himself in order to find himself. These two essays have been combined and reprinted, with slight revisions, as "Eliot: the Walking Dead" in Langbaum's *The Mysteries of Identity: A Theme in Modern Literature* (New York, 1977).

Michael T. Beehler undertakes a reevaluation of *The Family Reunion* in "Troping the Topic: Dis-Closing the Circle of *The Family Reunion*" (*Boundary 2*, Spring 1980). He moves from an examination of "the central *topos* of the play" ("The book as house and the house as book") to a consideration of the other tropes. Beehler's ingenuity often strains the credulity of this reader, but his essay as a whole is suggestive.

5   The Critical Prose

In the late 1910s and early 1920s, Eliot effected a revolution in literary taste through a series of periodical essays and reviews. Louis K. MacKendrick provides an informative survey of the early essays, reviews, and letters Eliot wrote for the *Egoist* in "T. S. Eliot and the *Egoist*: The Critical Preparation" (*DR*, Spring 1975). MacKendrick cites three dominant themes in Eliot's pieces: "the nature and function of the critic, the role of tradition, and literature's needs for cross-cultural fertilization," themes which coalesced in his last essay for the *Egoist*, "Tradition and the Individual Talent." Another critic who focuses on Eliot's early work is B. L. Reid, who argues in "T. S. Eliot and *The Sacred Wood*" (*SR*, Spring 1982) that Eliot arranged the essays in his book with the same attention to structure evident in his groupings of poems. Nicholas Joost and Ann Risdon examine the "London Letters" Eliot published in *The Dial* from 1921–22 and show how "the major preoccupations—themes, images, [and] revelations of hints that inspired and directed [Eliot] as poet and critic"—found fuller treatment in *The Waste Land* ("Sketches and Preludes: T. S. Eliot's 'London Letters' in the *Dial*" [*PLL*, Fall 1976]). J. I. Morse explores the same period in Eliot's life from a psychological standpoint in "T. S. Eliot in 1921: Toward Dissociation of Sensibility" (*WHR*, Winter 1976). Morse attempts to prove that Eliot formulated this idea in order "to transcend his anguish," an anguish caused largely by his "professional oedipus complex" with Matthew Arnold.

Mowbray Allen's *T. S. Eliot's Impersonal Theory of Poetry* (Lewisburg, Pa., 1978) is an elementary survey of one aspect of Eliot's work. More recent criticism has demonstrated that Eliot's dicta were not as rigidly held as Allen maintains. For example, Ronald Schuchard suggests, in "'Our mad poetics to confute': The Personal Voice in T. S. Eliot's Early Poetry and Criticism" (*OL*, No. 3, 1976), that Eliot's development of a theory of impersonality for the poetic process occurred simultaneously with his development of a "method of repersonalization" for the critical process. Richard Shusterman argues that "Eliot's critical theory, for all its polemics of objectivity, contains and recognizes a significant aspect of subjectivity" ("Objectivity and Subjectivity in Eliot's Critical Theory" [*OL*, No. 3, 1982]). Shusterman also demonstrates that the "subjective" element in Eliot's criticism became more pronounced in the later writings.

In *T. S. Eliot and Education* (London, 1970), the British educator G. H. Bantock provides a helpful but uncritical survey of Eliot's views on society and education. Bancock's own convictions have been strongly influenced by Eliot's, and he is writing for an audience whom he expects to share these views. Some of the same flaws mar Brian Lee's *Theory and Personality: The Significance of T. S. Eliot's Criticism* (London, 1979). Lee undertakes a close but selective reading of Eliot's essays with particular attention to "two central terms, expressive of a central interest: Impersonality and Personality." Focusing upon "Tradition and the Individual Talent" and then radiating outward, Lee makes a good case for the importance of the tension between these two terms in Eliot's work. But his approach is largely untouched by recent developments in literary theory. Lee calls Eliot "the founder of our criticism," and Lee himself seems unwilling to step outside Eliot's world and bring new perspectives to bear on the work.

A sympathetic analysis of Eliot's later criticism is provided by Roger Kojecky in *T. S. Eliot's Social Criticism* (New York, 1972). Kojecky argues that "Eliot's social criticism, like his poetry, lies nearer the centre of the modern tradition than has sometimes been thought." His "expository and biographical" approach does much to clarify Eliot's views and the British intellectual milieu in which they were formulated. However, Kojecky skirts the issues of Eliot's fascism and anti-Semitism and is altogether too defensive of Eliot. His conclusion, that "any opinion of Eliot's social criticism, as such, will depend largely on individual attitudes towards Conservatism," hardly settles the matter. An even more apologetic study is Russell Kirk's *Eliot and His Age: T. S. Eliot's Moral Imagination in the Twentieth Century* (New York, 1971). Kirk writes from the standpoint of a fellow conservative who lauds Eliot as a "champion of the moral imagination" and a "critic of the civil social order." Although Kirk's discussion of the early life and works is commonplace, he does offer an informed (if biased) defense of Eliot's political and social views.

A thoroughgoing and passionate attack on Eliot's critical and theoretical work was launched by James Smith in "Notes on the Criticism of T. S. Eliot" (*EIC*, Oct. 1972). Smith decries Eliot's ignorance and arrogance; Eliot's prose is a "huge gallimaufry." Such famous concepts as the "objective correlative" or the "dissociation of sensibility . . . apply . . . to facts which cannot do other than shatter the theories." Smith treats these concepts as though they were eternal verities to be proved or disproved, thus giving them more significance than Eliot would have ascribed to them. His essay is an example of critical overkill.

The political views of many of the great modernist writers have long been the subject of controversy and commentary, but until recently they have not been scrutinized impartially. In *The Political Identities of Ezra Pound and T. S. Eliot* (Stanford, Calif., 1973), William M. Chace examines dispassionately the politics of these two artists in order to demonstrate that an understanding of their politics is necessary for an assessment of their literary achievements. Chace shows us that although Pound and Eliot were not unique in their views, they can be viewed as "cognate expressions of an extreme revulsion against liberal democracy and an elitism paralleled in few other writers of the century." Chace examines the sources and nature of this revulsion and elitism, and the manifold ways in which it pervades their works. His book makes an important contribution to our understanding of the artistic achievements of these two men and of the age in which they lived.

Cairns Craig's study, *Yeats, Eliot, Pound and the Politics of Poetry: Richest to the Richest* (Pittsburgh, 1982), attempts to provide answers to a question he asks of these authors early in his book: "is there a deep-seated relationship between the modernity of their art and the reactionary nature of their politics?" Others, like Chace, have asked this question before. But Craig's answer is grounded in an examination of the British philosophical tradition of associationism, rather than in cultural or political theory. Craig defines the purpose of associationist "reverie" as "an inward journeying, a discovery of the logic that has been secretly stored by the mind in the patterns of its own associational resources, in the memory." He attributes the attraction to fascism of Yeats, Pound, and Eliot to their need to maintain forms of society "which preserved and promulgated the kinds of memory on which their poetry relied." This leads to suggestive readings of the poetry but less persuasive discussions of the politics.

An extremely penetrating analysis of the ways in which social and political assumptions can shape an entire literary canon is undertaken by John Guillory in "The Ideology of Canon-Formation: T. S. Eliot and Cleanth Brooks" (*CritI*, Sept. 1983). Guillory examines the ideology of the canon that "emerged in T. S. Eliot's earlier criticism, was presented as a canon by Cleanth Brooks in *The Well Wrought Urn*, and has since been institutionalized to a greater or lesser extent in the curricula of university English departments." Guillory analyzes the canon as the product of a "literary culture, a marginal elite" and demonstrates that "the authority of the culture . . . is not to be distinguished from the authority of the canon." Guillory concludes by asserting "the permanent difficulty of forming a canon acceptable to a consensus of the literary culture" given our political and social diversity.

In 1934 Eliot noted that "the views of Shakespeare taken by different men at different times in different places form an integral part of the development and change of European civilization during the past 300 years." Eliot's own views on Shakespeare have been subjected to critical scrutiny by G. K. Hunter in "T. S. Eliot and the Creation of a Symbolist

Shakespeare," in *Harvard English Studies 2: Twentieth-Century Literature in Retrospect* (ed. Reuben A. Brower, Cambridge, Mass., 1971). Hunter argues that we must consider the close association between the development of the "new criticism" and "the most powerful movement in the poetry of the same time . . . the domestication of French Symbolism." He suggests that Shakespeare, "too large to be ignored, too great to be dismissed . . . seemed also too antipathetic to be accommodated inside the Symbolist aesthetic." However, Eliot read Shakespeare on his own terms, and the results were most fruitful for Shakespeare criticism. Hunter traces the development of Eliot's Shakespeare criticism with particular attention to his observations on Shakespeare's last plays. "The revaluation of the last plays as Symbolist masterpieces," he writes, "is one of the great achievements of twentieth-century Shakespeare criticism. But the mode of criticism which discovered the pattern of the last plays could not stop at this point." Hunter concludes by tracing the enormous impact of Eliot's work on later Shakespeare criticism. In *"Hamlet" and the New Poetic: James Joyce and T. S. Eliot* (Ann Arbor, Mich., 1983), William H. Quillian analyzes the literary response to *Hamlet* in the decade from 1911 to 1922. Quillian demonstrates the enormous and positive hold that *Hamlet* exerted on the literary imagination of the nineteenth century before examining the "fundamental shift in the orientation of critical inquiry" represented by the "condemnation of the play as an artistic failure by Eliot and Joyce." In his chapter on "Mr. Eliot and the 'Disintegration' of Hamlet," Quillian presents an informative reading of Eliot's essay of 1919 "Hamlet and His Problems" and chronicles Eliot's changing attitudes toward this play in his later work.

Eliot's views of history are compared with other nineteenth- and twentieth-century historians by Grania Jones in "Eliot and History" (*CritQ*, Autumn 1976). Jones concludes that Eliot avoided the "modern disease of obsessive historiography by returning to the simplicity of exemplary history, as it was told and perceived by all traditional societies." In another examination of the same general subject, Alan Weinblatt explores Eliot's development of a "poetics of feeling" in his later critical writings ("T. S. Eliot and the Historical Sense" [*SAQ*, Summer 1978]). Weinblatt uncovers a tension in Eliot's writings between this "poetics of feeling" and a "poetics of neoclassicism . . . and compensation" that accords with those explorations of Eliot's relations to Romanticism discussed above.

In his preface to *The Literary Criticism of T. S. Eliot: New Essays* (London, 1977), David Newton-De Molina suggests that "now may be a time to expect some fresh historical revaluations and reassessments." This promise is fulfilled by the excellent essays of this collection, which consider Eliot's work with dispassionate rigor, alert to its strengths and weaknesses, and able to evaluate the work in terms other than Eliot's own. The collection opens with F. W. Bateson's argument that Eliot's criticism, like his poetry, suffered a serious decline after 1922 ("Criticism's Lost Leader"). Denis Donoghue considers the failure of *The Criterion*, a failure which cannot be "explained as one small instance of the immense failure of Europe in the years between 1922 and 1939" ("Eliot and the *Criterion*"). Rather, the "failure is more immediate and personal" and can be traced to the tensions in Eliot's "strained, willed, and therefore grim" public life. In "The Poet as Critic," Graham Hough explores the tension within Eliot between the "incautious literary condottiere" and the "well-balanced man of letters." Samuel Hynes records "The Trials of a Christian Critic" and concludes that Eliot failed as a Christian critic because he made his Christianity "visible," rather than invisible, and "so made his religion seem a way of being reactionary, ungenerous and cold." R. Peacock provides a survey of "Eliot's Contribution to Criticism of Drama," a criticism that has as its impulse Eliot's "desire to write plays and, indeed, to initiate a general revival of verse drama." In "The 'Philosophical Critic,'" William Righter presents an Eliot "caught between two languages and two traditions," whose thought reflects a conflict "between schematic ordering and centrifugal pressures." W. W. Robson analyzes "A Poet's Notebook: *The Use of Poetry and the Use of Criticism*" both for its biographical and critical interest. Roger Sharrock discusses the "elusive question" of "Eliot's 'Tone'" and claims that "In arguing for the substantiality and integrity of poetry as itself and not another thing Eliot is returning to the chief Romantic doctrine of poetic uniqueness in order to criticize later aberrations of that doctrine." C. K. Stead concludes the volume by making a strong case for the continuities between Romantic and Victorian prose and Eliot's work: "That Eliot in *The Waste Land* was more truly the heir of the Romantic movement than his Georgian contemporaries who laid claim to the inheritance is something I suspect many more critics would now be willing to recognize than was the case ten or fifteen years ago" ("Eliot, Arnold, and the English Poetic Tradition").

In an essay which complements W. W. Robson's "A Poet's Notebook: *The Use of Poetry and the Use of Criticism*" (see above), Sheldon W. Liebman presents a strong case for the significance of Eliot's Harvard Lectures of 1932–33. In "The Turning Point: Eliot's *The Use of Poetry and the Use of Criticism*" (*Boundary 2*, Winter 1981), Liebman shows that Eliot seized the occasion of these lectures for a revaluation of earlier critical positions. The lectures are important, Liebman notes, "not only as a personal testament revealing the extent to which Eliot changed his mind about his own critical principles but also as a public document raising compelling questions about the institution Eliot's critical theory and practice helped to establish: modern literary criticism." A recognition of this revisionary tendency within Eliot supports the general reexamination of Eliot's work that has begun to take place.

Eugene Goodheart considers "The Reality of Disillusion in T. S. Eliot" in his provocative study *The Failure of Criticism* (Cambridge, Mass., 1978). Goodheart discusses the rigorous moral authority of nineteenth-century criticism and argues that "the rise of modernism is the defeat of criticism" in this sense. Eliot's criticism, Goodheart demonstrates, lacks the "dynamic principle of change" that informed the beliefs of Carlyle, Ruskin, and Arnold. Instead, Eliot is drawn to "a religious ideal which has already been realized both institutionally and doctrinally in a dead past" and thus "is continually tempted by despair." Goodheart's closely argued polemical study makes an important contribution to our understanding of the development of criticism from the nineteenth century to the present.

The tendency in recent criticism of Eliot's poetry to reconsider Eliot's relationship to Romantic and Victorian poetry and to stress continuity rather than rupture has extended to Eliot's critical work as well. Several of the essays in David Newton-De Molina's *The Literary Criticism of T. S. Eliot* (see above) move in this direction, but the first extended consideration of this topic is Edward Lobb's *T. S. Eliot and the Romantic Critical Tradition* (London, 1981). Lobb reassesses Eliot's criticism, both from the standpoint of its view of literary history (which is "basically Romantic in its nostalgia for a lost golden age") and its view of language and use of rhetoric. Lobb argues that Eliot's criticism takes its place "in the Romantic tradition of historiography and rhetorical persuasion." Lobb draws support from Eliot's unpublished materials, particularly the important Clark Lectures of 1926. He presents a valuable service by extensively quoting and summarizing these otherwise inaccessible materials, but his study is marred by an imprecise use of language and a rather limited notion of literary influence.

Daniel O'Hara offers a different view of Eliot's critical heritage in "'The Unsummoned Image': T. S. Eliot's Unclassic Criticism" (*Boundary 2*, Fall 1981). Eliot's criticism, O'Hara suggests, belongs "neither to the Romantic, nor to the pseudo-neo-classic schools of modern criticism. . . . Rather it continues the elaboration, the tracing of difference between the two schools right up to the 'post-modern' breaking point." O'Hara is instructive on "the interpretive play of [Eliot's] characteristic figures of speech," but his general thesis would be strengthened if he tempered Derrida with Bornstein and Stead. More convincing is Walter Benn Michaels's "Philosophy in Kinkanja: Eliot's Pragmatism" (*Glyph*, 1981). Michaels charts the development of Eliot's gradual break with a "classical conception of philosophy" and shows that Eliot's hard-won "pragmatism" is a "way of understanding the identity of relative and absolute and denying them both."

Bertrand Russell is posited as an influence on Eliot's early criticism by Richard Shusterman in "Eliot and Logical Atomism" (*ELH*, Spring 1982). Although Russell would seem to be a likely influence on the young Eliot, the philosophical assumptions that Schusterman attributes to Russell are far too general and could easily have come from other sources as well.

Carol T. Christ focuses on Eliot's nineteenth-century predecessors in "T. S. Eliot and the Victorians" (*MP*, Nov. 1981), examining Eliot's early work in the light of the achievements of Victorian poetry. Christ demonstrates that many of Eliot's early pronouncements (the objective correlative, notions of impersonality, the reunification of sensibility) derive from developments in Victorian poetry, as do many of Eliot's poetic themes and techniques. Christ has extended the context and scope of this study in *Victorian & Modern Poetics* (Chicago, 1984). In a succinct and clearly written study, Christ argues that the modernists and the Victorians transformed their Romantic inheritance in similar ways. Thus, "each of the major Victorian and Modernist poets reacts against the subjectivism which he associated with Romanticism by attempting to objectify the materials of poetry," and each devises similar poetic strategies to do so. Christ very ably analyzes these strategies and convincingly reasserts the importance for the modernists of the Victorian responses to the Romantics. Her book enhances our understanding of nineteenth- and twentieth-century poetics and contributes substantially to our knowledge of the history of modernism.

VI SUPPLEMENT

Manuscripts and Letters. The long-awaited first volume of Eliot's correspondence—*The Letters of T. S. Eliot, Volume I, 1898–1922* (ed. Valerie Eliot, New York, 1988)—appeared on the hundredth anniversary of the poet's birth. Not surprisingly, Old Possum was nearly as guarded in his correspondence as in his poems and essays. But the letters do help fill out the record, and provide many insights into Eliot's relationships with others. Perhaps the most revealing are those letters to his mother in which the carefully crafted persona is dropped momentarily to reveal the insecure voice of Mrs. Eliot's youngest child. These letters were well worth the long wait.

Biography. In *Eliot's New Life* (New York, 1988), Lyndall Gordon explores the period of Eliot's life beginning in the 1930s when Eliot, after his separation from his first wife, became increasingly involved in the church. Gordon displays the tact, sensitivity, and intelligence that characterized her study of *Eliot's Early Years*. Her discussions of Eliot's relationships with Emily Hale, Mary Trevelyan, and finally Valerie Fletcher, whom Eliot married at age sixty-eight, are particularly informative. She moves deftly between the life and work and illuminates both.

Rich material for the biographer may be found in Burton Raffel's entertaining volume, *Possum and Ole Ez in the Public Eye: Contemporaries and Peers on T. S. Eliot and Ezra Pound, 1892–1972* (Hamden, Conn., 1985). Raffel presents a chronologically arranged collection of comments about

206

Eliot and Pound by writers, "some friendly, some unfriendly," as they reacted to the personalities and works of these two important figures. One only wishes this collection were twice as long.

Criticism. Three general critical studies have appeared recently. F. B. Pinion scrutinizes Eliot in *A T. S. Eliot Companion: Life and Works* (Totowa, N.J., 1986). After a fifty-page overview of Eliot's life, Pinion offers a chronological survey of the poetry, plays, and essays. Although Pinion's work is fairly comprehensive, it is highly derivative. He seems to read the poems literally, and his paraphrases have an odd and unintentionally comic effect of flattening out the poems. His paraphrases of the essays are more constructive for the beginning reader.

Angus Calder attempts a "bifocal reading" of Eliot's work in *T. S. Eliot* (Sussex, England, 1987), a volume in the Harvester "New Readings" series. Such a reading attempts to "place" the poetry historically and also to "try to evaluate the possible worth of its meanings for us now in our present historical moment." Although Calder presents interesting insights into Eliot's poetry, his study does not lead to a general reevaluation of Eliot's work as a whole.

Martin Scofield's avowedly "introductory critical study" of *T. S. Eliot: The Poems* (Cambridge, England, 1988) is sensible (if somewhat old-fashioned), thorough, and generally well informed. Scofield presents a concise overview of Eliot's life before turning to the poetry. He draws heavily upon Eliot's prose to elucidate the poetry, and his remarks should prove extremely useful to readers approaching Eliot for the first time.

Several general studies of modernism include extended treatments of Eliot's work. In *The Tradition of Return: The Implicit History of Modern Literature* (Princeton, N.J., 1984), Jeffrey M. Perl posits a historical pattern based on the conflict of "progress" and "return" that he argues accounts for the concerns and obsessions of modern literature. Perl considers the poetry of Eliot in this context, focusing upon *Four Quartets* as the "ultimate document" of high modernism. He reads *Four Quartets* as a work exemplifying the pattern of recurrence that he defined as characterizing modernism as a whole. His analysis is clever but unconvincing.

In Michael H. Levenson's *A Genealogy of Modernism: A Study of English Literary Doctrine 1908–1922* (Cambridge, England, 1984), the focus is not upon the "elucidation of texts" but rather upon an analysis of "some transformations in modernist thought" during the crucial years of this movement (1908–14). After considering some of the precursors of modernism, Levenson examines the development of such doctrines as Impressionism, Imagism, Vorticism, and classicism. His book concludes with an excellent chapter on the "most celebrated work" of modernism, *The Waste Land*, in which he details how the poem "revised, even as it consolidated, the [theoretical] work of two decades."

Sanford Schwartz considers the "affiliations between Modernist poetics and contemporaneous developments in philosophy" in his impressive study of *The Matrix of Modernism: Pound, Eliot, and Early Twentieth-Century Thought* (Princeton, N.J., 1985). Schwartz is well read in Anglo-American and continental philosophy; he shows how the work of such philosophers as Bergson, James, Bradley, Nietzsche, and Husserl decisively shaped the theory and practice of the modernists. His study enables us to reconsider the poetry of Pound and Eliot in a new light.

James Longenbach investigates the historicism of Pound and Eliot in *Modernist Poetics of History: Pound, Eliot, and the Sense of the Past* (Princeton, N.J., 1987). Longenbach's focus is on the formative work of Pound and Eliot culminating in the early cantos and *The Waste Land*. Longenbach presents illuminating discussions of the historical contexts of modernism as well as the "philosophical underpinnings" of Pound's and Eliot's historicism. He examines with sensitivity the question of the direct influence of historians on their work (Burckhardt on Pound, Bradley on Eliot) and the less direct "continuities" (Croce and Pound, Dilthey and Eliot). He succeeds in clarifying the "status of historical knowledge in their works." It is regrettable that this thoughtful and intelligent study halts at the frontier marked 1922.

Perry Meisel examines Eliot's work in *The Myth of the Modern: A Study in British Literature and Criticism after 1850* (New Haven, Conn., 1987). "The will to modernity," he suggests in an argument indebted to Harold Bloom, "is largely a defensive response to the increasingly intolerable burdens of coming late in a tradition." His "revisionist" study is an attempt to "elucidate the structure of modernism at large" and to "reformulate some of our normative canonical arrangements as well." Meisel offers three probing and provocative chapters on Eliot's repression of the "reality of influence": "Repression and the Individual Talent," "*The Waste Land*: The Flight from Lucifer," and "Art and Ideology in the *Four Quartets*."

A less anxious view of modernism is Stanley Sultan's *Eliot, Joyce and Company* (New York, 1987). Although Sultan's study concentrates ostensibly upon three works, "The Love Song of J. Alfred Prufrock," *The Waste Land*, and *Ulysses*, "probably . . . the most famous English short poem, long poem, and novel written during the century," his book is in fact a wide-ranging and critically well-informed overview of modernism. Sultan does an excellent job of analyzing "these three historical documents/artifacts of Modernism" and considering "their relations—with antecedents, with each other, and with us, the literary culture of which they were exemplary shapers."

Three recent books concentrate on aspects of Eliot's philosophical training. In *The Philosophy of T. S. Eliot: From Skepticism to a Surrealist Poetic, 1909–1927* (Philadelphia, 1986), William Skaff examines Eliot's "unique synthesis of contemporary philosophy, psychology, anthropology, and studies in mysticism" with the aim of demonstrating how this synthesis shaped his religious beliefs, his literary theory, and his poetic and dramatic practice. Although Skaff clarifies Eliot's own philosophic development through a careful examination of Eliot's eclectic reading during the teens and twenties, he makes far too great a claim for the influence of Eliot's philosophical studies on his development as a poet and critic.

Cleo McNelly Kearns provides a detailed examination of Eliot's extensive work with Indic philosophy in *T. S. Eliot and Indic Traditions: A Study in Poetry and Belief* (Cambridge, England, 1987). Kearns argues convincingly that Eliot found "perspectives" in the major classics of Hindu and Buddhist traditions "that intersected at crucial points with his own growing religious convictions, his work in philosophy, and his interest in techniques of meditation and their relation to writing." Kearns carefully documents Eliot's knowledge of Indic texts and traditions and offers a sophisticated analysis of the points of connection between these traditions and Eliot's readings in Western philosophy. In the final section of the book, she provides illuminating interpretations of Eliot's poetry in the context of his knowledge of Indic traditions.

A study that is sure to enhance our understanding of Eliot's development as a critic is Richard Shusterman's *T. S. Eliot and the Philosophy of Criticism* (New York, 1988). Shusterman offers a persuasive analysis of Eliot's connection with the tradition of Anglo-American analytic philosophy, thus providing an important corrective to the studies that overstate the influence of Bradley on Eliot. Shusterman also demonstrates how Eliot's "later theory anticipates and converges with certain currents in contemporary continental philosophy, most strikingly with the hermeneutic philosophy of Gadamer on the topics of interpretation and tradition." This cogently argued and well-informed study will significantly revise our understanding of Eliot's development as a critic.

Agha Shahid Ali examines Eliot as a critic during the period *l'entre deux guerres* when Eliot devoted considerable effort to editing *The Criterion*. In *T. S. Eliot as Editor* (Ann Arbor, Mich., 1986), Ali chronicles in detail the history of *The Criterion* in order to demonstrate "how Eliot's selection of contributions reveals his priorities—literary, social, and political—as an editor." To read this study is to gain a greater understanding of how the mind of Eliot—and the mind of Europe—developed during these crucial years.

The Waste Land is the focus of several recent books. Harold Bloom, whose antipathy to Eliot is well known, has edited a volume of essays on *The Waste Land* in the "Modern Critical Interpretations" series (*T. S. Eliot's "The Waste Land"* [New York, 1986]). This outstanding collection includes an introduction by Bloom and recent essays by Hugh Kenner, Graham Hough, Richard Ellmann, Bernard F. Dick, Eleanor Cook, Grover Smith, Gregory S. Jay, and Cleo McNelly Kearns, most of which are reviewed above.

Calvin Bedient has produced a very closely argued and highly suggestive study of Eliot's poem in *He Do the Police in Different Voices: "The
Waste Land" and Its Protagonist* (Chicago, 1986). Bedient confronts the
problem of the narrator in Eliot's poem by suggesting that "the voices
in the poem are the performances of a single protagonist—not Tiresias
but a nameless stand-in for Eliot himself—performances, indeed, of a
distinctly theatrical kind." Through a very careful working out of the
play of voices in the poem, Bedient is able to clarify the "emotional,
intellectual, and cultural disposition of the poem." This critically informed study demands a great deal of its readers, but its rewards are
considerable. It will help shape future discussions of *The Waste Land*.

Informative, but less ambitious, is John Xiros Cooper's *T. S. Eliot
and the Politics of Voice: The Argument of "The Waste Land"* (Ann Arbor,
Mich., 1987). Cooper considers *The Waste Land* as a "signifying practice, rather than as a discrete textual object," or, for that matter, as "fragments of Eliot's psychobiography." He clarifies the argument of the
poem (an argument whose "discursive markers" have been "systematically erased") by examining the poem within the "sociohistorical present
in which it was composed and published."

An important tension in Eliot's work is illuminated by Robert Crawford's *The Savage and the City in the Work of T. S. Eliot* (Oxford, England,
1987). Crawford argues that "meetings of polar opposites are vital to
the pattern of Eliot's work," and he examines one of these—Eliot's
"linking of the most primitive and barbaric with the most sophisticatedly
urban"—in considerable detail. As Crawford admits at the outset, his
study opens doors in Eliot's poetry "which lead to predictable and less
predictable destinations, including Mendelian heredity, evolution,
blood-and-thunder stories, Melanesia, and Lloyds Bank." I encourage
readers to "go and make [the] visit," for they are sure to return from
this fascinating voyage with a significantly enlarged understanding of
the terrain covered.

William Faulkner

Philip G. Cohen, David Krause, and Karl F. Zender

I BIBLIOGRAPHY

William Faulkner is one of the few major twentieth-century American authors for whom no complete primary bibliography exists. In both previous versions of this essay (1969, 1973), James B. Meriwether noted the pressing need for such a volume. No comprehensive bibliography of Faulkner's published and unpublished work has yet appeared, and Faulknerians still need one just as badly. Until such a bibliography appears, one should consult Meriwether's essential *William Faulkner: A Checklist* (1957) which lists the textually significant forms of Faulkner's writings published in America. This pamphlet should be supplemented with Meriwether's *The Literary Career of William Faulkner* (1961, 1971).

Meriwether's "The Short Fiction of William Faulkner: A Bibliography" (*Proof*, 1971) includes manuscript, typescript, and proof versions in its listing of "all textually significant forms of Faulkner's works of fiction shorter than full-length novels" and provides useful bibliographical information. Readers should know that five of the stories listed under "Lost Stories" have since been located and four of these appear in Joseph Blotner's edition of *Uncollected Stories of William Faulkner* (New York, 1979).

Until recently, Keen Butterworth's "Census of Manuscripts and Typescripts of William Faulkner's Poetry" (*MissQ*, Summer 1973) was the best (albeit incomplete) bibliography of Faulkner's poetry. Doubtless it will be superseded by Judith Sensibar's *Faulkner's Poetry: A Bibliographical Guide to Texts and Criticism*, due out in late 1988. Sensibar will provide a complete listing of Faulkner's poetry—manuscripts and typescripts, published and unpublished, complete and fragmentary—along with an annotated bibliography of secondary criticism on the poetry.

Cohen prepared the sections of this essay dealing with Bibliography, Editions, and Manuscripts. Zender was responsible for Letters, Biography, and Criticism, 1973–1979. Krause prepared Criticism, 1980–1988.

For translations of Faulkner's fiction into other languages, one may consult Petra Gallert's bibliographies: "German-Language Translations of Faulkner" (*MissQ*, Summer 1982), "Italian Translations of Faulkner" (*MissQ*, Summer 1983), and "Dutch and Belgian Translations of Faulkner: A Checklist" (*MissQ*, Summer 1984); all are updatings of Meriwether's listing in his *Literary Career*. Finally, Doreen Fowler and Ann J. Abadie's *Faulkner: International Perspectives—Faulkner and Yoknapatawpha, 1982* (Jackson, Miss., 1984; hereinafter referred to as *International Perspectives*) contains the following checklists of translations: Myriam Díaz-Diocaretz's "Faulkner in Spanish," Monika Brückner's "Faulkner in German," M. Thomas Inge's "A Chronology of Faulkner Translations Into Russian," H. R. Stoneback's "A Checklist of Faulkner Translations into Chinese," and Kenzaburo Ohashi's "Faulkner in Japanese."

John Earl Bassett's *William Faulkner: An Annotated Checklist of Criticism* (New York, 1972) is a descriptive secondary bibliography listing and cross-referencing its entries under several headings: Books about Faulkner; Studies of Individual Novels; Studies of Short Stories, Poetry, and Miscellaneous Writings; Topical Studies; and Other Materials (reviews of books about Faulkner, magazine and journal articles, newspaper articles, books, doctoral dissertations, and British theses and dissertations). Restricted to work in or translated into English, the volume lists reviews alphabetically and later criticism chronologically within each section. An appendix of late items and an author index complete the volume, covering Faulkner criticism up to the beginning of 1972. While his organization occasionally renders the volume difficult to use, Bassett is especially good at listing American and British reviews from little magazines and political magazines along with those from more mainstream publications.

Thomas L. McHaney's *William Faulkner: A Reference Guide* (Boston, 1976) covers much of the same ground. Beginning with 1924 and ending with 1973, the volume is organized chronologically and lists and describes all serious and substantial writings on Faulkner's life and work. Less repetitious than Bassett, McHaney's volume provides very useful indexes of its entries by authors, titles, titles of Faulkner's works, names of people and places, and by subject, theme, and type of critical approach. Coupled with excellent cross-referencing, this sophisticated indexing makes it difficult to miss anything. Although McHaney does not annotate as many reviews as Bassett, he covers a large amount of criticism in languages other than English and his annotations are both lengthier and more reliable. McHaney is under contract to G. K. Hall to do a second *Guide* covering the years 1974 to 1987.

Bassett's *Faulkner: An Annotated Checklist of Recent Criticism* (Kent, Ohio, 1983) extends his coverage from "about 1971" to 1982, mentions some 1983 items, and includes errata for his first volume. He conflates entries from McHaney and Beatrice Ricks (see below) under the same headings of his earlier arrangement. An important new section, Commentary in Other Languages, begins its coverage in 1966 and provides little or no annotation. With the exception of book reviews, Bassett now omits journalistic pieces but still indexes his entries by author only. This new volume is a little more difficult to use than his earlier effort because the alphabetical listing by author under each section has been abandoned in favor of listing entries by month or season of publication. Furthermore, the placement of items in individual categories and the cross-referencing cannot always be relied upon. Nevertheless, the compilation is thorough, again especially in its listing of reviews. One would do best to consult McHaney up to 1973 and then cross over to Bassett, also using the latter's first volume for locating reviews and other items not in McHaney.

Much less useful is Beatrice Ricks's *William Faulkner: A Bibliography of Secondary Works* (Metuchen, N.J., 1981). Entries are listed alphabetically with a minimum of description under the headings Biography, Works (novels, stories, articles-essays-sketches, interviews, letters, poetry, speeches), General Criticism, and Bibliography. The volume's coverage extends to the end of 1978, and it includes criticism in foreign languages and author and subject indexes. Because each section is developed independently to eliminate cross-referencing, much repetition occurs. Ricks may also be safely ignored due to the idiosyncratic placement of many entries under her headings.

Patricia Sweeney's *William Faulkner's Women Characters: An Annotated Bibliography of Criticism, 1930–1983* (Santa Barbara, Calif., 1985) arranges criticism on Faulkner's female characters alphabetically under headings of Faulkner's novels and some of his short stories, listed chronologically. The volume is cross-referenced with an appendix of items received too late to be annotated and indexes for character names, authors, titles, and subjects. Dissertations, reviews of Faulkner's books, and Faulkner's own comments on his female characters are excluded. Extremely repetitious without being comprehensive on its avowed subject, the volume is a tool of limited use.

Several publications contain yearly surveys of criticism and scholarship on Faulkner. *Mississippi Quarterly*'s "Annual Checklist of Southern Literature" in the Spring number contains complete secondary and some primary bibliography with brief descriptions of the previous year's work on Faulkner. The first checklist appeared in 1969 for the year 1968, and the initial eight appear with supplemental entries in Jerry T. Williams's *Southern Literature 1968–1975: A Checklist of Scholarship* (Boston, 1978). Beginning in 1978, *Mississippi Quarterly*'s annual Faulkner Summer issue, edited by Meriwether, contains a Faulkner "Survey of Research and Criticism," a selective descriptive and evaluative bibliography of the previous year's primary and secondary work on Faulkner. Since 1979's survey of the year's work in 1978, the reviewing committee has discussed all book-length studies but only commented on articles and excerpts from books considered to be sound in scholarship and reasoning. The Summer 1987 Faulkner issue was the last annual Faulkner number; *Mississippi Quarterly* will publish special Faulkner issues occasionally but has no plans to continue the survey.

The descriptive and evaluative review-essays on Faulkner in the annual *American Literary Scholarship* (Durham, N.C.) survey each year's primary and secondary work on Faulkner, aiming for comprehensiveness. These reviews tend to be more balanced and avoid the occasionally idiosyncratic judgments of the *Mississippi Quarterly* survey. Faulkner scholars such as Meriwether, Karl F. Zender, Panthea Reid Broughton, and Linda Wagner-Martin have provided these surveys in the past; M. Thomas Inge is slated for the 1986 and 1987 volumes.

A number of guides to writing on Faulkner in other languages exist. *International Perspectives* contains Mick Gidley's "Selected Recent British Writing on Faulkner" and Myriam Díaz-Diocaretz's "Spanish Criticism of Faulkner 1932–59." In "The Reception and Reputation of William Faulkner in Norway, 1932–1982" (*NMW*, Nos. 1 and 2, 1984), Hans Skei lists and discusses translations of Faulkner's books into Norwegian, their prefaces, the journalistic reviews they elicited, general assessments, and scholarly work and theses. Catherine Georgoudaki's "The Greek Reception of William Faulkner" and Jan Nordby Gretlund's "William Faulkner's Strange Career in Danish" (*NMW*, No. 1, 1986) describe Greek and Danish translations of Faulkner and some of the critical responses they generated. For an introduction to writing in Japanese on Faulkner, one should consult Kiyoyuki Ono's "The Japanese Reception of William Faulkner" (*NMW*, No. 1, 1984). The first six installments in the series "William Faulkner: An Annotated Checklist of Research and Criticism in Japan" may be found in *William Faulkner: Materials, Studies, and Criticism* (Oct. 1978; June 1979; Dec. 1979; July 1980; Apr. 1981; Dec. 1981; No. 2, 1982; No. 1, 1983; No. 2, 1983). Unfortunately for western scholars, most of these checklists are in Japanese.

Several other useful tools deserve mention. Bassett's *William Faulkner: The Critical Heritage* (London, 1975) reprints a number of important American and English reviews of Faulkner's books beginning with *The Marble Faun*. Curiously, Bassett omits reviews of *These 13*, *A Green Bough*, *Doctor Martino and Other Stories*, and *Knight's Gambit*, and reviews for the volumes which followed *Collected Stories*. Tetsumaro Hayashi's *William Faulkner: Research Opportunities and Dissertation Abstracts* (Jefferson, N.C., 1982) lists most of the English-language dissertations from 1941 to 1979 that include discussions of Faulkner, reprinting their abstracts when available. Indexed by author, director, title, university, and subject, the volume has more than the occasional omission and error. James B. Lloyd's *The Oxford "Eagle," 1900–1962: An Annotated Checklist of Material on William Faulkner and the History of Lafayette County* (Mississippi State,

Miss., 1977) is a useful guide to biographical and historical material contained in the files of Faulkner's hometown newspaper.

Two excellent new journals devoted to Faulkner studies must also be noted: the *Faulkner Journal*, which began with a Fall 1985 issue, and the Japanese journal *William Faulkner: Materials, Studies, and Criticism* (1978–85). The *Faulkner Newsletter* and *Yoknapatawpha Review*, edited by William Boozer, a quarterly newsletter which began publication in 1981, includes a brief checklist of new Faulkner editions and secondary work on Faulkner, as well as brief items, reviews, and news stories.

II EDITIONS

For years textual scholars have grumbled about Random House's treatment of Faulkner's novels, citing the absence of an explicitly stated editorial rationale, its policies of silent regularization and standardization, and the high incidence of errors and changes introduced by compositors, proofreaders, and editors during initial publication, reissues, and new editions, especially in the Vintage paperback series. Clearly, numerous problems exist in many of the Random House editions published during Faulkner's lifetime and after his death. Since Random House is understandably not in the business of publishing scholarly editions, those interested in reliable editorial apparatus and commentary on individual works frequently have resorted to the steady stream of textual-critical dissertations pouring forth from James B. Meriwether's students at the University of South Carolina.

The best succinct summary of the issues involved in editing Faulkner may be found in Meriwether's remarks about Faulkner's "Editions and Manuscripts" in *Sixteen Modern American Authors* (1973). While Faulkner read proof more carefully for earlier books, his later published texts, beginning with *Pylon* and *Absalom, Absalom!*, reveal more Random House copy-editing and house-styling. At times Faulkner rejected this intervention; at times he accepted it. Editing his novels is made difficult by the absence, in some cases, of important documents like setting copy, galleys, and page proofs. One cannot know conclusively in many instances if a particular change was introduced by Faulkner, an editor, or a compositor. Furthermore, these different authorial and editorial changes, some of which have general or specific authorial approval, raise difficult theoretical issues which cannot be resolved conclusively.

In the 1980s, Random House and the Library of America have attempted to remedy this situation by sponsoring a major effort to produce a series of corrected Faulkner texts under Noel Polk's supervision. Editor, critic, and scholar of Faulkner's texts, Polk is well trained to head this carefully planned project. Over the next several years, he will edit all the fiction for the Library of America. As these texts become available, Random House/Vintage will then pick them up for paperback publication. Although Polk edited *"Sanctuary": The Original Text* (New York, 1981), *"The Sound and the Fury": New Corrected Edition* (New York, 1984), and *"Absalom, Absalom!": The Corrected Text* (New York, 1986) directly for Random House, from now on Library of America texts will have precedence. These volumes will feature Polk's editorial notes and Joseph Blotner's page and line annotations, and the Vintage paperback reissues will include these notes. In the absence of compelling evidence to the contrary, Polk generally prefers what Faulkner wrote to what his editors and house-styling produced. Consequently, copy-text is usually a pre-publication document like a typescript, with corrections frequently made from manuscript. Because these are scholar-edited but not definitive texts, one must still use the relevant University of South Carolina dissertations, the Faulkner Concordances, and the Garland Faulkner Manuscript Series (see below) to reconstruct alternative texts.

Polk's *"The Sound and the Fury": New Corrected Edition* takes Faulkner's carbon typescript as copy-text and concludes with a brief editorial note and a selective list of significant variations between the carbon typescript, the 1929 Cape and Smith first edition, and the present text. A new Vintage paperback edition appeared in 1987. In *An Editorial Handbook for William Faulkner's "The Sound and the Fury"* (New York, 1985), Polk sets forth his editorial assumptions and practices, discusses the issues involved in editing the novel as a whole and each of the four sections, and provides an introduction recounting what we know and, more importantly, what we do not know about the composition, revision, editing, and proofing of the novel, along with appendixes of variants which carefully record the differences between the three texts cited above. Because the setting copy and galleys have not survived, it remains impossible to know with certainty whether a variant represents a change by Faulkner, an editor, or a compositor. Consequently, Polk also scrupulously provides the reasoning behind his emendations of copy-text. Since he distrusts first edition variants that seem to explain or clarify, his text is much closer to the typescript than to the first edition.

Perhaps Polk's most controversial decision was to violate the author's explicit final intentions by omitting from the text the Compson Appendix which Faulkner wrote in 1945 for Malcolm Cowley's *Portable Faulkner* and which he then instructed Random House to place at the beginning of the Modern Library dual edition of *The Sound and the Fury* and *As I Lay Dying* (1946). It appeared at the end of the Vintage reissue of the novel in 1962. Polk argues persuasively on biographical, psychological, and aesthetic grounds that the Appendix is a separate and distinct work of art. One may agree with this position but still wish the Appendix had been included and surrounded by caveats.

The Appendix does appear in the "Backgrounds and Contexts" section of David Minter's Norton Critical Edition, *William Faulkner: "The Sound and the Fury"* (New York, 1987). Minter reproduces a slightly revised version of Polk's text and a selective list of textual variations and includes the two versions of Faulkner's unpublished introduction to the novel, letters to and from Faulkner about the novel, and his remarks in interviews about it. With its excellent selection of criticism and reasonable price, this volume deserves to become a basic classroom text.

Except for some corrections and regularizations, Polk's handsome *"Absalom, Absalom!": The Corrected Text* reproduces as faithfully as possible the novel's original typescript, which Faulkner prepared for publication; it is a clear text, complete except for the chronology and genealogy. Some textual problems in the typescript are solved by consulting the holograph manuscript and the corrected galleys of the first edition, and Polk once more provides a brief editorial note and a selective list of significant variations between the text and the ribbon typescript setting copy. Vintage issued this new edition in paperback in 1987.

The first Library of America volume, *William Faulkner: Novels, 1930–1935—"As I Lay Dying," "Sanctuary," "Light in August," and "Pylon"* (New York, 1985), contains a chronology of Faulkner's life, Polk's excellent textual note, a selective bibliography, Blotner's line and page notes, and Faulkner's notorious introduction to the 1932 Modern Library edition of *Sanctuary*. As with his texts of *The Sound and the Fury* and *Absalom, Absalom!*, Polk seeks the texts Faulkner wanted in print at the time of their original publication, so his conservative editorial policies "attempt to reproduce Faulkner's typescripts as he presented them to his publishers before editorial intervention." Consequently, he takes for his copy-texts Faulkner's own ribbon typescript setting copies, which he typed and proofread "with varying degrees of care." Polk emends the copy-texts only with "those revisions on typescript or proof that Faulkner seems to have initiated himself as a response to his own text, not those he made in response to a revision or correction suggested by an editor." He concedes that this distinction is not always so easily drawn. With some exceptions, Polk preserves Faulkner's spelling, punctuation, capitalization, and wording of the texts as faithfully as possible. To help evaluate these texts and enable scholars to construct other versions of the novels, one wishes Garland would publish the scholarly apparatuses for these texts. Such a possibility seems unlikely.

Due in 1989, Library of America's volume 2 will contain *Absalom, Absalom!, The Unvanquished, The Wild Palms*, and *The Hamlet*, while the third volume will probably go back and cover *Soldiers' Pay, Mosquitoes, Flags in the Dust*, and *The Sound and the Fury*. Succeeding volumes will each contain four novels, except for one which will have three. How many volumes the short stories will require and what the principle of selection will be has not yet been decided.

Using the Library of America computer tapes, Polk also prepared new Vintage paperback editions of four texts in 1987. *"Pylon": The Corrected Text, "Light in August": The Corrected Text, "Sanctuary": The Corrected Text,* and *"As I Lay Dying": The Corrected Text* (New York, 1987) are accompanied by Polk's editorial notes and Blotner's line and page annotations. As with the Library of America volume, the Vintage *Sanctuary* also prints Faulkner's notorious introduction to the 1932 Modern Library edition.

For a concise guide to Faulkner's texts in general, one should consult Meriwether's "The Books of William Faulkner: A Revised Guide for Students and Scholars" (*MissQ*, Summer 1982), which provides essential textual information and comments on the relative reliability of books published during and after Faulkner's lifetime. Because his guide was published before Polk's editorial effort began, one should also see "Abbreviations for Texts to be Cited in *The Faulkner Journal*" at the back of that journal's most recent issue. This note lists the soundest texts in hardcover and paperback currently available and is updated as the newly edited texts become available.

Given the understandable reluctance on the part of commercial publishers to produce texts according to scholarly criteria, the Library of America and Random House's massive effort seemed unlikely at the beginning of the 1970s. As a result, Meriwether suggested in "A Proposal for a CEAA Edition of William Faulkner" (*Editing Twentieth-Century Texts*, ed. Francess G. Halpenny, Toronto, 1972) that Faulkner scholars should produce independent scholarly apparatuses with all the necessary corrections and emendations but keyed to existing texts. Under his direction, University of South Carolina graduate students have produced a series of textual-critical dissertations on individual Faulkner novels; they include discussions of the composition, revision, editing, proofing, and publication of the novels. More important are the appendixes containing annotated bibliographies of criticism, chronologies of events in the novels, and historical collations with lists of corrections, emendations, and explanations keyed to the then most reliable Random House texts. Essentially these appendixes provide apparatuses for scholarly editions produced according to CEAA and CSE guidelines. Scholars should consult these theses along with the Garland Facsimiles and Concordances for the variants needed to reconstruct other texts according to their own theoretical orientations.

The relevant dissertations are Thomas L. McHaney's "William Faulkner's *The Wild Palms*: A Textual and Critical Study" (1968); Abner Keen Butterworth's "A Critical and Textual Study of William Faulkner's *A Fable*" (1970; reprinted in his 1983 UMI Research Press volume of the same name); James E. Kibler, Jr.'s "A Study of the Text of William Faulkner's *The Hamlet*" (1970); Noel Polk's "A Textual and Critical Study of William Faulkner's *Requiem for a Nun*" (1970); Carl Ficken's "A Critical and Textual Study of William Faulkner's *Light in August*" (1972); Leland Cox's "Sinbad in New Orleans: Early Short Fiction by William Faulkner— An Annotated Edition" (1977; Faulkner's fiction which appeared in the New Orleans *Times-Picayune* and *The Double Dealer*); Edwin T. Arnold III's

"William Faulkner's *Mosquitoes*: An Introduction and Annotations to the Novel" (1978); George F. Hayhoe's "A Critical and Textual Study of William Faulkner's *Flags in the Dust*" (1979); Diane L. Cox's "William Faulkner's *As I Lay Dying*: A Critical and Textual Study" (1980); and Gail M. Morrison's "William Faulkner's *The Sound and the Fury*: A Critical and Textual Study" (1980; 2 vols.).

In the 1970s and 1980s a steady stream of juvenilia, different versions of texts, unpublished texts, fragments, drafts, and reviews appeared in print. Random House, for example, published Douglas Day's edition of *Flags in the Dust* (New York, 1973), the novel Faulkner reluctantly allowed Ben Wasson to cut by 15 percent in 1928 to create his third published novel, *Sartoris*. Day's introduction and editing are problematic, and the 1974 Vintage paperback edition introduces a number of new errors. For a sound review of Day's edition, see George F. Hayhoe's "William Faulkner's *Flags in the Dust*" (*MissQ*, Summer 1975). Joseph Blotner's essential *Uncollected Stories of William Faulkner* (New York, 1979) contains forty-five stories under three headings: stories revised for later books, uncollected stories, and unpublished stories. Despite some omissions and problems with the volume's organization, it makes available a number of hitherto inaccessible stories along with biographical and bibliographical notes on each entry. Vintage published a paperback edition in 1981.

Polk's edition of *"Sanctuary": The Original Text* reproduces the typescript which Faulkner prepared for publication. After editing at Cape and Smith, the typescript was then used as printer's copy for the original typesetting that Faulkner reordered and revised so heavily in galleys. Polk provides an especially illuminating afterword, a textual note, and a list of some emendations of the typescript. Diane L. Cox has edited *Elmer* and provided a textual note with a table of emendations (*MissQ*, Summer 1983); the same text is available in a 1984 limited edition from the Seajay Society. Essential reading for any Faulknerian, *Elmer* is the unfinished novel Faulkner began during his European trip in 1925 before he abandoned it for work on *Mosquitoes*. Random House has also made another key Faulkner text available by reproducing the Red Ozier Press's beautiful 1983 limited edition of *Father Abraham*, edited by Meriwether (New York, 1984). Faulkner probably wrote *Father Abraham* late in 1926 and abandoned it by early 1927 to work on *Flags in the Dust*. For fourteen years until the publication of *The Hamlet* in 1940, he repeatedly rewrote, revised, and drew upon this material. The text reproduces with a minimum of editorial alteration the holograph manuscript in the Arents Collection of the New York Public Library and is accompanied by Meriwether's introduction and textual note.

For some time now, Carvel Collins has been preparing for Random House an edition of Faulkner's early publications from 1917 to 1926. This welcome edition will reprint the material Collins earlier gathered in *William Faulkner: "New Orleans Sketches"* (1958) and *William Faulkner:*

Early Prose and Poetry (1962), add works which have surfaced more recently, and feature Collins's lengthy background essay. Since new texts have surfaced and parts of some texts could be updated, a new edition of *Essays, Speeches and Public Letters* (1965) would also be welcome.

Faulkner scholars have also been busy reissuing editions of the hand-bound and often hand-lettered booklets which Faulkner produced and illustrated in the early 1920s. Four such hand-bound copies survive of Faulkner's striking one-act Symbolist dream play, *The Marionettes*, which he hand-lettered, illustrated, and bound into pamphlets in 1920. The University Press of Virginia reissued its 1975 limited edition facsimile reproduction of one of the booklets, along with Polk's model introduction and textual appendixes, which include descriptions of the extant copies, a historical collation, and alterations in the manuscripts (Charlottesville, 1977).

The University of Notre Dame Press published a new edition in type of its 1977 facsimile of Faulkner's 1926 booklet *Mayday*, which he lettered, illustrated with watercolors, and bound by hand (Notre Dame, Ind., 1980). In his thorough introduction, Carvel Collins provides a provocative Freudian interpretation of this allegorical medieval tale and sees it as a testing ground for themes and techniques Faulkner would later employ in *The Sound and the Fury*. *"Helen: A Courtship" and "Mississippi Poems"* (New Orleans and Oxford, Miss., 1981) is a new edition in type of two earlier limited editions which reproduced by offset Faulkner's hand-lettered and hand-bound sonnet sequence *Helen: A Courtship* and a sequence of twelve typed poems, along with a seven-page carbon typescript of his 1925 *Double Dealer* essay "Verse, Old and Nascent: A Pilgrimage." Faulkner presented *Helen* to Helen Baird in 1926, and *Mississippi Poems* to Myrtle Ramey in 1924. Collins again provides a very useful biographical and critical introduction to *Helen* and Blotner does the same for *Mississippi Poems*. Judith Sensibar's edition of *Vision in Spring* (Austin, Tex., 1984) presents another of Faulkner's early poem sequences, a cycle of fourteen poems in type, some of which appeared elsewhere. The original eighty-eight-page carbon typescript which Faulkner hand-bound and presented to his wife Estelle in 1921 has disappeared, and this edition is based on a surviving photocopy, which makes editing the text difficult. Sensibar provides a thorough introduction, an appendix listing known versions of the *Vision of Spring* poems, and an appendix containing photographs of the *Vision in Spring* fragments. Finally, Dean Faulkner Wells has recounted three of her uncle's ghost stories in *The Ghosts of Rowan Oak: William Faulkner's Ghost Stories for Children* (Oxford, Miss., 1980).

Much of Faulkner's work for Hollywood also became available during the 1980s. Bruce Kawin, the author of the useful *Faulkner and Film* (New York, 1977), has edited *Faulkner's MGM Screenplays* (Knoxville, Tenn., 1982). With two exceptions, the volume "contains facsimiles of every surviving manuscript William Faulkner wrote for MGM studios (1932–33)." Kawin's perceptive introduction accompanies the four treatments and three screenplays and demonstrates a number of connections between Faulkner's fiction and his film work. In volumes 3 and 4 of *Faulkner: A Comprehensive Guide to the Brodsky Collection* (see below), Louis Daniel Brodsky and Robert W. Hamblin present *The De Gaulle Story* and *Battle-Cry* (Jackson, Miss., 1984, 1985). The volumes also contain a number of documents surrounding these two unproduced screenplays which Faulkner wrote during the 1940s for Lt. Col. Jack Warner as his contribution to the war effort. Brodsky and Hamblin's meticulous introductions guide us through the complex textual thickets of the materials and make a number of valuable connections between these texts and the fiction Faulkner wrote after World War II. The two have also edited *"Country Lawyer" and Other Stories for the Screen* (Jackson, Miss., 1987), which presents three more story outlines Faulkner wrote for Warner Brothers in the early 1940s: "Country Lawyer," "The Life and Death of a Bomber," and "The Damned Don't Cry."

Brodsky and Hamblin's *Comprehensive Guide* will run to seven volumes, and *Volume V: Manuscripts and Documents* will appear in 1988. This new installment will contain drawings, poetry, fiction, nonfiction, plays, last wills and testaments, and biographical documents. Some documents Faulknerians can look forward to seeing include forty-one poems, holograph and typescript drafts of *Requiem* and *A Fable*, several versions of "Wash," a chapter of *Absalom*, all but one of Faulkner's fourteen major speeches, a version of *Requiem for a Nun* and a one-act comedy called "Innocent's Return," written with Joan Williams. The volume will also contain a number of Faulkner texts which Brodsky has published in scholarly journals in the 1980s.

An essential piece of reading in terms of Faulkner's sense of his own literary beginnings is Joseph Blotner's edition of "William Faulkner's Essay on the Composition of *Sartoris*" (*YULG*, Jan. 1973). Max Putzel's variant transcription of this key essay, probably written in 1931, appears in the *Publications of the Bibliographical Society of America* (Fourth Quarter 1980). Even more important are the two versions of Faulkner's introduction to an aborted 1933 new edition of *The Sound and the Fury*. In "An Introduction to *The Sound and the Fury*" (*MissQ*, Summer 1973), Meriwether presents the longer version, reprinted in his *A Faulkner Miscellany* (Jackson, Miss., 1974). The shorter version appears along with an account of the introduction's genesis in Meriwether's "An Introduction for *The Sound and the Fury*" (*SoR*, Autumn 1972). It now appears that the shorter version predates the longer one.

The annual Summer Faulkner issue of *Mississippi Quarterly* printed a number of previously published and unpublished Faulkner texts. Meriwether's *A Faulkner Miscellany* reprints some miscellaneous Faulkner items from the Summer 1973 issue: Millgate's "Faulkner [One-Page Note] on the Literature of the First World War," Polk's "'Hong Li' and *Royal Street*: The New Orleans Sketches in Manuscript," "And Now What's To Do," "Nympholepsy," the longer version of "An Introduction to *The Sound and the Fury*," "A Note on *A Fable*," and "Faulkner's Acceptance Speech for the Andres Bello Award, Caracas, 1961."

Other pieces by Faulkner published in *Mississippi Quarterly* include his satirical poem "Ode to the Louver" (Summer 1974) and "Faulkner's Speech at the Teatro Municipal, Caracas, in 1961" (Summer 1974). Faulkner's 1934 *Memphis Commercial Appeal* article on the son of John McGavock Grider, whose diary became the basis for Elliott White Springs's *War Birds: Diary of an Unknown Aviator* (1926), appears in the Summer 1975 issue. Faulkner's 1925 *Times-Picayune* review of John Cowper Powys's *Ducdame* appears in Carvel Collins's "A Fourth Book Review by Faulkner" (Summer 1975). From the Brodsky Collection comes "Eunice" (Summer 1978), a narrative poem Faulkner wrote some time between 1920 and 1922. Judith Sensibar's "Pierrot and the Marble Faun: Another Fragment" (Summer 1979) prints an early poetic fragment which Faulkner wrote on three blank pages at the end of his 1917 first edition of Ralph Hodgson's *Poems*. Deborah Thompson's "*Light in August*: A Manuscript Fragment" appears in the same issue (Summer 1979). "An Unpublished Episode from 'A Mountain Victory'" (Summer 1979) prints a section cut from the story by Faulkner at the request of the *Saturday Evening Post* when they published it in 1930. The uncut and unedited typescript of his 1935 *American Mercury* piece on Jimmy Collins's *Test Pilot* appears in "The Uncut Text of Faulkner's Review of *Test Pilot*" (Summer 1980).

An important fragment is George F. Hayhoe's "The Rejected Manuscript Opening of *Flags in the Dust*" (Summer 1980). Gail M. Morrison's "A Manuscript Fragment" (Summer 1981) appears on the verso of a page of the *Sanctuary* carbon typescript. "Pierrot, Sitting Beside the Body of Colombine, Suddenly Sees Himself in a Mirror" (Summer 1982) prints a poem which Faulkner presented to Ben Wasson's mother possibly in 1921. Joseph Blotner's "Faulkner's Speech at Nagano, August 5, 1955" appears in the Summer 1982 issue. More important is Gail M. Morrison's "Never Done No Weeping When You Wanted To Laugh" (Summer 1983), which prints an incomplete manuscript early version of Faulkner's 1931 *American Mercury* story "That Evening Sun Go Down." He then revised the story for inclusion in *These 13* as "That Evening Sun." "The Manuscript of Faulkner's Introduction to *Sanctuary*" may be found in the Summer 1983 issue. Finally, "As I Lay Dying" (Summer 1986) is one of Faulkner's various attempts to write the story of Flem Snopes's spotted horse auction. Probably written in 1928, this version is one of two with the same title. The other was rejected by *Scribner's Magazine* in 1928. Unless otherwise mentioned, all pieces have been edited by Meriwether.

Also useful to Faulknerians are the Faulkner Concordances, a massive project published by the Faulkner Concordance Advisory Board with the support of the United States Military Academy at West Point and distributed by UMI Research Press. Under each individual word, entries are made up of complete sentences, clauses, phrases. These grammatical "sense units" have been selected "to give the best contextual reading of words within the single-line limitation of the concordance format." Essential appendixes in each volume contain a statistical summary of usages, a vocabulary alphabetically arranged with frequency of usage, and a vocabulary arranged according to frequency of usage. Each volume also features an introduction by a Faulkner scholar who makes critical use of the findings.

Since the editors chose the most reliable texts in existence at the time, the earlier concordances are unfortunately but unavoidably keyed to older Random House editions, not the new ones. With a minimum of difficulty, one can still use these concordances with the new editions. Because variant lines from Faulkner's manuscripts and typescripts appear in the first "sense unit" under each heading, one can also use concordances to look at some of the variations between prepublication documents and the editions used. Collations have been done carefully once, however, so one can be reasonably certain only that variations in words have been recorded. For a more complete investigation, one should still consult the Garland facsimiles and appendixes in the relevant University of South Carolina dissertations.

Of the volumes produced to date and distributed by UMI Research Press (Ann Arbor, Mich.), Jack L. Capps has edited *As I Lay Dying* (1977), *Go Down, Moses* (1977, 2 vols.), and *Light in August* (1979, 2 vols.). Noel Polk has edited *Requiem for a Nun* (1979) and *Intruder in the Dust* (1983). Noel Polk and Kenneth L. Privratsky have edited *The Sound and the Fury* (1980, 2 vols.) and *A Fable* (1981, 2 vols.). Privratsky has edited *The Wild Palms* (1983) and Polk and Lawrence Z. Pizzi have edited *The Town* (1988). *The Mansion* is scheduled for publication next, and *Absalom, Absalom!*, *Pylon*, *The Unvanquished*, and *The Hamlet* will be set from the Library of America and Random House computer tapes. *Sanctuary* will be a conflated concordance to both the revised and unrevised texts. *The Reivers* is also being prepared. Although there will be two volumes of collected stories and uncollected stories, each of Faulkner's short stories will be concorded separately, treating each text as a novel.

III   MANUSCRIPTS AND LETTERS

During the 1970s and 1980s a number of exhibition catalogs and descriptive bibliographies of public and private Faulkner collections were published. With its formidable William Faulkner Collections, the University of Virginia's Alderman Library remains the most important holder of Faulkner manuscripts, typescripts, galley proofs, and page proofs, and also owns a rich assortment of letters, photographs, drawings, and other Faulkneriana. A recent major acquisition is a forty-five-page manuscript corresponding to pages 13–151 of the 1927 Boni and Liveright first edition of *Mosquitoes*. The manuscript differs significantly from the printed version. The University Press of Virginia plans to publish a facsimile edition with a full transcription of the text. To save wear and tear, many of the manuscripts have been microfilmed and are accessible via interlibrary loan to qualified researchers who have been granted access to the collection.

Linton Massey's *William Faulkner, Man Working, 1919–1962* (1968) and Joan St. C. Crane and Anne Freudenberg's *Man Collecting: Manuscripts and Printed Works of William Faulkner in the University of Virginia Library* (Charlottesville, 1975) may be consulted as guides, albeit intentionally incomplete ones, to the collections. Crane and Freudenberg's excellent catalog describes their 1975–76 exhibition of the Faulkner manuscripts and printed works in the "Massey/Faulkner" Collection. It is not a full representation of Virginia's published and unpublished holdings but a listing of its most important manuscripts, letters, and books, the latter being limited to first editions and first printings. Each entry is accompanied by a bibliographical description and an informal historical note. Although it would be a Herculean task, a complete descriptive bibliography of Virginia's current holdings would be most welcome.

George F. Hayhoe's "Faulkner in Hollywood: A Checklist of His Film Scripts at the University of Virginia" (*MissQ*, Summer 1978) and "Faulkner in Hollywood: A Checklist of his Filmscripts at the University of Virginia: A Correction and Additions" (*MissQ*, Summer 1979) present a descriptive bibliography of many of Faulkner's MGM and Twentieth-Century Fox scripts at Virginia. In the New York Public Library's Arents Collection is Faulkner's *Father Abraham* manuscript, while its Berg Collection has the first typescript draft of *Soldiers' Pay*, among other Faulkner papers.

Garland Publishing Company's *William Faulkner Manuscripts* (New York, 1986 and 1987) is an essential series which provides in its forty-four volumes facsimile reproductions of the manuscripts, typescripts, and significant proof stages of Faulkner's fictions in the collections of the New York Public Library and the University of Virginia Library, with the vast majority of documents coming from the latter. "Included are all typescripts, manuscripts, and proofs from these collections that document the composition, editing, and publication of Faulkner's novels and short stories, as well as a few related materials. Excluded are those carbon typescripts and galley- and page-proofs which are not significantly different from the ribbon typescripts and published texts." Each volume is arranged and introduced by one of the four series editors,

Blotner, McHaney, Millgate, and Polk, and the first volume containing *Elmer* features a general essay by the four editors and Polk's useful "Some Notes on Reading Faulkner's Hand." McHaney has edited *"Elmer"* and *"A Portrait of Elmer," "Father Abraham"* and *"The Wishing Tree," As I Lay Dying, "Doctor Martino" and Other Stories, The Wild Palms* (2 vols.), *The Hamlet* (2 vols.), *Go Down, Moses, Knight's Gambit,* and *"Unpublished Stories,"* which includes an index to the short fiction in the series. Blotner has edited *Soldiers' Pay* (2 vols.), *Mosquitoes, Flags in the Dust* (2 vols.), *Light in August* (2 vols.), and *Short Stories*. Polk has edited *The Sound and the Fury* (2 vols.), *Sanctuary* (2 vols.), *These 13, Pylon, Absalom, Absalom!, Intruder in the Dust,* and *Requiem for a Nun* (4 vols.). Millgate has edited *A Fable* (4 vols.), *The Town* (2 vols.), *The Mansion* (4 vols.), and *The Reivers* (2 vols.).

The Harry Ransom Humanities Research Center at the University of Texas at Austin houses an important Faulkner collection which includes the holograph manuscript of *Absalom, Absalom!* and the corrected galleys of *Absalom, Absalom!* and *Sanctuary*. A number of Phil Stone's papers are also on deposit here. Although no complete bibliography of the collection exists, one may consult Meriwether's catalog for his *William Faulkner: An Exhibition of Manuscripts* (1959). One may also obtain at cost from the Center a xerox of the card catalog's inventory of Faulkner holdings.

In 1971 four boxes of Faulkner manuscripts and typescripts were discovered in a stairwell closet of Faulkner's Oxford home, Rowan Oak. The Rowan Oak Papers are now on deposit at the Special Collections Department of the University of Mississippi. This cache includes such finds as the incomplete manuscript of *Pylon*, the setting copy of *The Unvanquished*, the ribbon typescript setting copy of *Sanctuary*, many passages of preliminary materials for *Absalom, Absalom!*, and numerous early treatments of the "Spotted Horses" material. Arthur F. Kinney and Doreen Fowler's "Faulkner's Rowan Oak Papers: A Census" (*JML*, June 1983) is a bibliography of these papers. In 1983 the library acquired the Lelia and Douglas Wynn Collection of William Faulkner Poetry Manuscripts, which includes typescripts of two poem sequences, *Mississippi Poems*, and a number of Swinburnian lyrics, light verse, and love lyrics.

The Princeton University Library owns a small number of Faulkner manuscripts and related materials, such as eight Faulkner letters and eleven typed manuscripts of essays, speeches, and short stories, many of which have Faulkner's holographic corrections. A list of these holdings may be obtained by writing to the Curator of Manuscripts. Tulane University's Howard-Tilton Memorial Library houses the William B. Wisdom Collection of Faulkneriana, which includes the two manuscript books *Mayday* and *Helen: A Courtship*, manuscripts and typescripts of some short stories and poems, and letters. For a listing of the collection, consult Thomas Bonner, Jr.'s *William Faulkner: The William B. Wisdom Collection: A Descriptive Catalogue* (New Orleans, 1980). The Library of Congress's small cache of Faulkner materials includes a handful of Faulkner letters in its Wesley Stout Papers and Joseph Wood Krutch Papers.

In 1982 Faulkner collector Louis Daniel Brodsky and Robert W. Hamblin initiated *Faulkner: A Comprehensive Guide to the Brodsky Collection* with *Volume I: The Biobibliography* (Jackson, Miss., 1982), a descriptive bibliography of Brodsky's impressive Faulkner Collection, which includes the carbon typescripts and galley proofs of *The Hamlet*, preliminary typescripts of sections of *A Fable* and *Requiem for a Nun*, numerous filmscripts, and many poems in manuscript and typescript. This volume offers full descriptive comments and facsimile reproductions of some entries. Since then, four more volumes have appeared and two more are planned. The last volume will contain a supplement to the *Biobibliography* which will be larger than the initial volume. Although the *Biobibliography* and its supplement will supersede Brodsky and Hamblin's *Selections from the William Faulkner Collection of Louis Daniel Brodsky: A Descriptive Catalogue* (Charlottesville, Va., 1979), they are cross-referenced to this earlier volume, which contains extended commentary on some entries and facsimile reproductions of many items.

Carl Petersen's *Each in Its Ordered Place: A Faulkner Collector's Notebook* (Ann Arbor, Mich., 1975) describes many but not all the items Petersen has amassed in twenty-five years of collecting "books, magazines, pamphlets, broadsides, press releases, photographs, and drawings, clippings, phonograph records, posters, telegrams, and theater programs." Manuscript leaves, letters, and inscribed books are also included along with a listing of secondary background and critical material. In *On The Track of the Dixie Limited: Further Notes of a Faulkner Collector* (La Grange, Ill., 1979), Petersen identifies important material he has acquired since 1974 and provides photographic reproductions of some entries and annotates many of them.

Faulkner's letters are housed in various repositories, most notably the Alderman Library of the University of Virginia, the Humanities Research Center of the University of Texas at Austin, the Beinecke Library of Yale University, and the Berg Collection of the New York City Public Library. No comprehensive edition of the letters exists, and none is to be expected in the near future, because many letters are sequestered. One wishes that this unfortunate circumstance would change, for full access to the letters could help students of Faulkner arrive at a better understanding of both his life and his art. Even if some letters need to remain unavailable to protect the feelings of people mentioned in them, there would seem to be no excuse for continuing to limit access to large numbers of letters to a single scholar, as is the case at one major repository. This sort of academic imperialism has bedeviled Faulkner studies for years, to its detriment.

In the present circumstance, scholars must patch together their knowledge of Faulkner's letters from a variety of sources. Foremost among these is Joseph Blotner's edition of *Selected Letters of William Faulkner* (New York, 1977; hereinafter referred to as *Selected Letters*). This generous sampling sheds invaluable light on Faulkner's life and career, especially on his relations with his publishers and agents, his economic circumstances, and his understanding of himself as an artist. It is not, however, a fully representative collection, for, as Panthea Reid Broughton notes, Blotner seems intent on preserving "Faulkner's distinction between public and private selves" (*AmLS*, 1976). Blotner's circumspection is most evident in the areas of Faulkner's relations with his family and of his romantic involvements. The collection affords little evidence of the tensions (partly known, be it acknowledged, through Blotner's biographical work) between Faulkner and his wife Estelle, and between Faulkner and other members of his family. Also absent is much indication of the intensity, duration, and significance—at times, even of the existence—of Faulkner's affairs with Meta Carpenter, Joan Williams, and Jean Stein.

A partial corrective to Blotner's emphasis on the public and professional side of Faulkner's career as a letter writer can be found in Louis Daniel Brodsky and Robert W. Hamblin's *Faulkner: A Comprehensive Guide to the Brodsky Collection, Volume II: The Letters* (Jackson, Miss., 1984). This important volume contains nearly 500 letters from Brodsky's collection of Faulkneriana, over 100 of them by Faulkner himself and the remainder by family members (including Estelle Faulkner), friends, and business associates. It is especially strong on the last decades of Faulkner's life. A further corrective can be found in several works discussed more fully below: Meta Carpenter Wilde and Orin Borsten's *A Loving Gentleman* (New York, 1976), the two versions of Joseph Blotner's *Faulkner: A Biography* (New York, 1974 and 1984), and Malcolm Franklin's *Bitterweeds: Life with William Faulkner at Rowan Oak* (Irving, Tex., 1977). The first of these books contains intriguing excerpts from Faulkner's erotic and romantic letters to Wilde, which are sequestered in the Berg collection until 2039. The two-volume version of Blotner's biography contains fuller versions of several letters reprinted in excerpted form in *Selected Letters*; the one-volume version (New York, 1984) reprints several never-before-published letters, including an extremely important letter Faulkner wrote to his publisher on the eve of his marriage. The final volume, *Bitterweeds*, reprints, although in garbled form, a number of letters from Faulkner to his stepson Malcolm Franklin; some of these also appear in *Selected Letters*.

More specialized compilations of Faulkner's correspondence also exist. James B. Meriwether's *Essays, Speeches and Public Letters* (1965) reprints the various letters, most of them from late in his career, that Faulkner wrote for publication. Also by Meriwether are the descriptively titled "Faulkner's Correspondence with *The Saturday Evening Post*" (*MissQ*, Summer 1977) and "Faulkner's Correspondence with *Scribner's Magazine*"

(*Proof*, 1973). Richard Lyons's *Faulkner on Love: A Letter to Marjorie Lyons* (Fargo, N.D., 1974) and Doreen Fowler and Campbell McCool's "On Suffering: A Letter from William Faulkner" (*AL*, Dec. 1985) reprint with commentary individual letters by Faulkner. James G. Watson's *William Faulkner, Letters & Fictions* (Austin, Tex., 1987) is an illuminating study of the interconnections between Faulkner's careers as letter writer and as writer of fiction (see below).

IV BIOGRAPHY

Our understanding of the relevance of Faulkner's biography to his fiction has undergone radical transformation since the last edition of *Sixteen Modern American Authors*. Himself desirous of personal anonymity, Faulkner seemed to the first generation of his critics to have created a body of fiction fully (or at least sufficiently) explicable by impersonal modes of analysis. But we now see that his novels have a full and intense personal dimension— more so, perhaps, than the works of any of his contemporaries. The main cause of this shift in understanding— indeed, the most important event in the history of Faulkner studies—was the appearance of the two-volume version of Joseph Blotner's *Faulkner: A Biography* (1974). A dozen years in the making, the book was worth the wait. Massive in intention and accomplishment, it chronicles with an incredible wealth of detail the course of Faulkner's life and career. On matters as widely divergent as Faulkner's ancestry, his Hollywood career, his relations with his literary contemporaries, his reading, his travels, and the genesis, revision, and publication of his fiction, the book shows whole and clear what had formerly been known only in fragment or in error.

This is not to say that the book is without its defects. As James B. Meriwether demonstrates in "Blotner's *Faulkner*" (*MissQ*, Summer 1975), *Faulkner: A Biography* contains a large number of errors, especially in the transcription of quotations and the footnoting of sources. In addition, a central problem in judgment bothers some readers of the book. Blotner mainly eschews interpretation in favor of a narrative account of the events of Faulkner's life. Unfortunately, his disavowal is incomplete; interpretation slips in the side door, often in unsophisticated forms. It is hardly instructive, for example, to see Blotner repeatedly discuss Faulkner's alcoholism merely as a way of escaping social obligations and as an anodyne for physical pain, or to see him rely on "shyness" as a categorical explanation for many of the mysterious (and frequently cruel) aspects of Faulkner's behavior. Also, even when the book is read simply as a narrative, one finds occasional grounds for disquietude. Something—either personal adulation for his subject or a desire to protect the feelings of Faulkner's close relatives—led Blotner into discretions and evasions, especially in the area of Faulkner's sexual life. As David

Minter says in "Faulkner and the Uses of Biography" (*GaR*, Fall 1974), "There is no way . . . to justify devoting several pages to the history of New Orleans and but a few lines to Estelle Faulkner's highly theatrical attempt to drown herself in the Gulf of Mexico on a honeymoon following a long-delayed marriage." Some questions are not asked, some answers not given.

Many of these problems are corrected in the one-volume version of *Faulkner: A Biography* (1984). In this version, which is both a condensation and a revision, Blotner eliminates many of the plot summaries, summaries of early reviews, and accounts of family and regional history that slowed the narrative flow of the earlier version. He also corrects factual errors, cites important new documents and letters, and makes assiduous use of criticism and scholarship published since 1974. Most importantly, he approaches his subject with greater candor and a more questioning attitude, giving due weight and prominence to aspects of Faulkner's life that were ignored or glancingly presented in the earlier version. Despite these virtues, though, students of Faulkner's life would not be well advised to rely on this version alone, for the book's one-volume length is achieved at the expense of omitting occasional significant details. Both versions deserve a place on any Faulkner scholar's shelf.

The years since 1974 have seen several other additions to our knowledge of Faulkner's life, in the form of memoirs, interviews, biographical essays, and introductions. Foremost among the memoirs is Meta Carpenter Wilde and Orin Borsten's *A Loving Gentleman*, an account of Faulkner and Wilde's extended love affair. Although romanticized and not always factually reliable, the book sheds valuable light on Faulkner's personality and on his life (particularly his Hollywood experiences) during the 1930s and 1940s. It should be supplemented with Panthea Reid Broughton's interview with Wilde (*SoR*, Fall 1982), with Joan Williams's brief reminiscence of her later relationship with Faulkner in "Twenty Will Not Come Again" (*AtM*, May 1980), and with Williams's intriguing *roman à clef*, *The Wintering* (New York, 1971).

Other useful memoirs are *Count No 'Count: Flashbacks to Faulkner* (Jackson, Miss., 1983), by Ben Wasson, a longtime acquaintance of Faulkner's who served briefly as his literary agent; *What is an Editor? Saxe Commins at Work* (Chicago, 1978), by Dorothy Commins, wife of Faulkner's editor at Random House; and *Bitterweeds: Life with William Faulkner at Rowan Oak*, an amateurishly written and printed but occasionally revealing reminiscence by Malcolm Franklin, Faulkner's stepson. Brief anecdotal reminiscences can be found in Murry C. Falkner's "The Coming of the Motor Car" (*SoR*, Winter 1974); Malcolm Franklin's "A Christmas in Columbus" (*MissQ*, Summer 1974); Dean Faulkner Wells's *The Ghosts of Rowan Oak: William Faulkner's Ghost Stories for Children* (Oxford, Miss., 1980); and three items by Jim Faulkner: "Memories of Brother Will" (*SoR*, Autumn 1980), "No Pistol Pocket" (*SoR*, Spring 1981), and

Across the Creek: Faulkner Family Stories (Jackson, Miss., 1986). Also useful are *The Making of William Faulkner's Books 1929–37: An Interview with Evelyn Harter Glick* (Columbia, S.C., 1979); Louis Daniel Brodsky's "Reflections on William Faulkner: An Interview with Albert I. Bezzerides" (*SoR*, Spring 1985); and James Dahl's "A Faulkner Reminiscence: Conversations with Mrs. Maud Faulkner" (*JML*, Apr. 1974). The interview with Bezzerides, a colleague of Faulkner's at Warner Brothers in the early 1940s, contains especially valuable information and insights. Bezzerides is also the author of the script of a PBS documentary on Faulkner aired in 1979; the script has been published as *William Faulkner: A Life on Paper* (ed. Ann Abadie, Jackson, Miss., 1980).

The list of biographical essays and biographically based introductions begins with several items by Carvel Collins: "Faulkner and Mississippi" and "Faulkner, the Man and the Artist" (*UMSE*, 1975 [published 1978]); "Introduction to Faulkner's *Mayday*" (South Bend, Ind., 1980); "Biographical Background for Faulkner's *Helen*" (*"Helen: A Courtship" and "Mississippi Poems,"* Oxford, Miss., 1981); and "A Memoir—William B. Wisdom, Collector," in *William Faulkner: The William B. Wisdom Collection, a Descriptive Catalogue*. Filled with biographical fact and inference, suggestive, reticent, and quarrelsome by turns, these items (a selective list) are by-blows of Collins's long-promised critical biography. No one can read these studies, or hear Collins speak, without realizing that he possesses a treasure trove of knowledge about Faulkner; nor can one seriously doubt that a career as complex, various, and commanding as Faulkner's can sustain more than one major biography. But when Collins's book will be finished remains (as it has for so long) uncertain.

Brief contributions to our knowledge of Faulkner's life can also be found in Cleanth Brooks's "The Image of Helen Baird in Faulkner's Early Poetry and Fiction" (*SR*, Spring 1977); Bruce Kawin's "Faulkner's Film Career: The Years with Hawks" (*Faulkner, Modernism, and Film: Faulkner and Yoknapatawpha, 1978*, ed. Evans Harrington and Ann J. Abadie, Jackson, Miss., 1979; hereinafter referred to as *Faulkner, Modernism, and Film*); Susan Snell's "William Faulkner, Phil Stone, and Katrina Carter: A Biographical Footnote to the Summer of 1914" (*SLJ*, Spring 1983); and Robert W. Hamblin's "Lucas Beauchamp, Ned Barnett, and William Faulkner's 1940 Will" (*SB*, 1979). Joseph Blotner adds occasional insights to those contained in the two versions of his biography in "Introduction to *Mississippi Poems*" (*"Helen: A Courtship" and "Mississippi Poems"*) and in four essays: "Continuity and Change in Faulkner's Life and Art" (*Faulkner and Idealism*, ed. Michel Gresset and Patrick Samway, S.J., Jackson, Miss., 1983); "Did You See Him Plain?" (*Fifty Years of Yoknapatawpha: Faulkner and Yoknapatawpha, 1979*, ed. Doreen Fowler and Ann J. Abadie, Jackson, Miss., 1980; hereinafter referred to as *Fifty Years of Yoknapatawpha*); "The Falkners and the Fictional Families" (*GaR*, Fall 1976); and (with Chester A. McLarty) "Faulkner's Last Days" (*AL*, Dec.

1985). Also worth consulting are Susan Snell's unpublished doctoral dissertation, "Phil Stone of Yoknapatawpha" (Univ. of North Carolina, 1978), a biography of Faulkner's friend and mentor; Dean Faulkner Wells's unpublished M.A. thesis, "Dean Swift Faulkner: A Biographical Study" (Univ. of Mississippi, 1975), a biography of her father by Faulkner's niece; and Michel Gresset's *A Faulkner Chronology* (Jackson, Miss., 1985). Gresset's book is an accurate but selective log of Faulkner's life and career; it can be used to advantage in conjunction with Blotner's biography. By contrast, Stephen Oates's *William Faulkner: The Man and the Artist* (New York, 1987) is a fictionalized biography, based almost entirely on published materials; it contains nothing of use to the Faulkner specialist. Finally, mention should be made of Michael Millgate's *The Achievement of William Faulkner* (1965). Even after twenty years, the first chapter of this book remains the best compact account of Faulkner's life and career.

The outpouring of biographical information during the last fifteen years has produced a corresponding outpouring of biographically based critical studies—most notably Judith Bryant Wittenberg's *William Faulkner: The Transfiguration of Biography* (Lincoln, Neb., 1979) and David Minter's *William Faulkner: His Life and Work* (Baltimore, Md., 1980). Each book has its virtues. Wittenberg's, although less theoretically sophisticated than Minter's and less thorough in its research and documentation, is sometimes more provocative in its insights and interpretations. In the words of Panthea Reid Broughton, "Wittenberg is good on the relation between Faulkner's personal anxieties and his early work," and she "helps us see how Faulkner's gradual (and belated) maturation was embodied in his fiction" (*AmLS*, 1979). Especially noteworthy is Wittenberg's account of the relation between Faulkner's impending marriage and his composition of *Sanctuary*—an account whose shrewd insights are largely confirmed by Blotner's one-volume *Faulkner: A Biography*. Minter's book, by comparison, provides a more carefully reasoned, coherent, and comprehensive interpretation of Faulkner's career. It is more alert to aesthetic implications and more observant of the conscious, intellectual dimension of Faulkner's artistic development. Especially to be admired are Minter's analyses of Faulkner's move from poetry to prose, of the evolution of Faulkner's artist figures between *Flags in the Dust* and *As I Lay Dying*, and of the influence on Faulkner's art of his relationships with women.

Several shorter studies also apply biographical information to the fiction in insightful ways. Lewis P. Simpson's "The Loneliness of William Faulkner" (*SLJ*, Fall 1975) and Louis D. Rubin, Jr.'s "William Faulkner: The Discovery of a Man's Vocation" (*Faulkner: Fifty Years After "The Marble Faun,"* ed. George H. Wolfe, University, Ala., 1976; hereinafter referred to as *Fifty Years*) are exemplary early instances of the kind of speculation and interpretation Blotner's biography made possible. Taking Faulkner's own distinction between a "writer" and a "literary man" as a basis for discussion, Simpson engages in a sensitive demonstration of Faulkner's slow, reluctant, and self-denied movement from the one term to the other. (This essay has been reprinted in altered form in Simpson's *The Brazen Face of History* [Baton Rouge, La., 1980].) Equally valuable are two psychoanalytically oriented studies, Jay Martin's "'The Whole Burden of Man's History of His Impossible Heart's Desire': The Early Life of William Faulkner" (*AL*, Jan. 1982) and David M. Wyatt's "Faulkner and the Burdens of the Past" in his *Prodigal Sons: A Study in Authorship and Authority* (Baltimore, Md., 1980). Finally, two more recent studies— Louis Daniel Brodsky's "Faulkner's Life Masks" (*SoR*, Autumn 1986) and Michel Gresset's "Faulkner's Self-Portraits" (*FJ*, Fall 1986)—also reward attention.

V CRITICISM

1 General Estimates: Books

a. 1973–1979. Armed with the advantages of hindsight, we can see that the biographical revolution discussed above was merely one part of a much larger critical revolution. Under the multiple pressures of structuralism, poststructuralism, deconstruction, feminism, reader-response theory, and French Freud, the New Critical verities—the iconic text, the primacy of unity, irony, and ambiguity as aesthetic values, the alliance between literature and Christian Humanism—have been called into question. But in the 1970s most Faulknerians, like most other critics, knew of these impending developments only in the way Jake Barnes knows of the troubles awaiting him in Pamplona—as "an ignored tension, and [as] a feeling of things coming that you could not prevent happening." Understandably, then, the best work of the time—among both general and particular studies—cannot be divided into "good" Moderns and "bad" Ancients (or vice versa). Some of the best work of the time anticipates the new directions of the 1980s; but other of it continues the lines of investigation laid down by the first generation of Faulkner critics.

The list of book-length studies anticipatory of new methods and directions is headed by John T. Irwin's *Doubling and Incest/Repetition and Revenge: A Speculative Reading of Faulkner* (Baltimore, Md., 1975). As its title implies, this extremely important study is concerned with certain recurrent motifs. Part of the value of the book lies in the care and subtlety with which Irwin examines the occurrences of these motifs in individual novels—mainly *The Sound and the Fury* and *Absalom, Absalom!*, but also *Mosquitoes, Sartoris, As I Lay Dying*, and *A Fable*. Its greater value, though, lies in setting a new direction for psychoanalytic criticism of Faulkner's fiction, in providing a new, less formally restrictive way of understanding

Faulkner's intertextual references, and in opening Faulkner criticism to French structuralist and psycholinguistic theory. Not surprisingly, the book has begun to show some signs of age, most notably in the exclusivity of its emphasis on Oedipal patterns of development and on male models for literary indebtedness. But it remains a landmark study, fully worthy of the serious attention of all students of Faulkner's fiction.

Three other books also anticipate later directions of study. Myra Jehlen's *Class and Character in Faulkner's South* (New York, 1976) offers many grounds for criticism. It is factually inaccurate and reductive in its readings, it understates the importance of Faulkner's modernist affiliations and epistemological interests, and it applies its Marxist critical method in sometimes facile ways. But the book also offered the first direct challenge to the communitarian and agrarian reading, deriving mainly from Cleanth Brooks's *William Faulkner: The Yoknapatawpha Country* (1963) that dominated Faulkner studies in the 1970s, and it prepared the way for later and more convincing Marxist and new literary historical studies (e.g., Eric J. Sundquist's *Faulkner: The House Divided*). The second book, Gary Lee Stonum's *Faulkner's Career: An Internal Literary History* (Ithaca, N.Y., 1979), anticipates the current interest in the dynamics of Faulkner's career. Arguing that Faulkner "develops by expressly questioning the assumptions on which [his] earlier work depends," Stonum offers a strong reading of the shape of Faulkner's career, but one that assumes too often that only ideas create ideas. The book would have benefited from attention to a wider range of themes and to the influence on Faulkner's artistic development of biographical and historical factors. Finally, Albert J. Guerard's *The Triumph of the Novel: Dickens, Dostoevsky, Faulkner* (New York, 1976) uses traditional methods to explore new themes. The book contains the first substantial, evenhanded discussion of the misogynistic elements in Faulkner's art; in its insistence on the importance of transgression to Faulkner's imagination, it offers a welcome alternative to the moralizing emphasis characteristic of much Faulkner criticism in the 1970s.

The list of traditionally oriented studies is headed by Cleanth Brooks's *William Faulkner: Toward Yoknapatawpha and Beyond* (New Haven, Conn., 1978), which applies the method of Brooks's *William Faulkner: The Yoknapatawpha Country* to the non-Yoknapatawpha fiction. The book displays Brooks's characteristic virtues of humane sympathy, critical acumen, and rhetorical polish. It contains a very strong chapter on *Soldiers' Pay*, and it provides important historical contexts in which to view *Mosquitoes*, *Pylon*, *The Wild Palms*, and Faulkner's early poetry and prose. If the book is less satisfactory than *The Yoknapatawpha Country*, this is partly a result of the relative lack of artistic merit of some of the material discussed; but it arises more generally from the capacity of the non-Yoknapatawpha fiction to reveal limitations inherent in Brooks's approach to Faulkner. (For a trenchant discussion of this issue, see Thomas L. McHaney's review-essay, "Brooks on Faulkner: The End of the Long View" [*Rev.*, 1979].)

Two other important traditionally oriented studies are Panthea Reid Broughton's *William Faulkner: The Abstract and the Actual* (Baton Rouge, La., 1974) and Bruce Kawin's *Faulkner and Film* (New York, 1977). Broughton's book provides a welcome corrective to earlier devaluations of the role of abstraction in Faulkner's fiction; Kawin's book is the first thorough and fully informed study of Faulkner's relations with the film industry and of the place of cinematic structures and techniques in his fiction. Several other books on general topics are of less value. Warren Beck's *Faulkner* (Madison, Wis., 1976) combines Beck's influential early essays with a large quantity of later work, much of it printed here for the first time. Diffuse and repetitive, the later work threatens to submerge the seminal early essays. Elizabeth Kerr's *William Faulkner's Gothic Domain* (New York, 1979) also suffers from diffuseness and lack of organization. It treats the concept of Gothicism so broadly that, as Panthea Reid Broughton says, "almost everything Faulkner wrote can become either Gothicism or truncated Gothicism" (*AmLS*, 1979). Lynn Levins's thematic study, *Faulkner's Heroic Design: The Yoknapatawpha Novels* (Athens, Ga., 1976), defines heroism in an unimaginative way and lacks argumentative subtlety. Lewis Dabney's *The Indians of Yoknapatawpha* (Baton Rouge, La., 1974) is a weakly argued treatment of an interesting topic.

The 1970s saw the beginning of the important Faulkner and Yoknapatawpha series, which reprints the proceedings of the conference held annually at the University of Mississippi. The first volume to appear, *The South and Faulkner's Yoknapatawpha: The Actual and the Apocryphal* (ed. Evans Harrington and Ann J. Abadie, Jackson, Miss., 1977; hereinafter referred to as *The Actual and the Apocryphal*), actually reprints the proceedings of the third conference. The next year saw the publication of the proceedings of the first two conferences (*UMSE*, 1974 and 1975) and of the fourth conference (*The Maker and the Myth: Faulkner and Yoknapatawpha, 1977*, ed. Evans Harrington and Ann J. Abadie, Jackson, Miss., 1978; hereinafter referred to as *The Maker and the Myth*). The final volume to appear in the 1970s was *Faulkner, Modernism, and Film*. Essays from these volumes will be commented on in the appropriate sections elsewhere in this chapter. Also worthy of note are *A Faulkner Miscellany* and *Faulkner: Fifty Years After "The Marble Faun."* The first of these volumes reprints selected items from the annual Faulkner number of *Mississippi Quarterly* (Summer 1973). The second reprints the proceedings of a conference held at the University of Alabama in 1974; it contains important essays, commented on elsewhere in this chapter.

b. 1980–1988. In 1988 all of Faulkner's best books and stories continue to address their readers in the way Horace Benbow addresses his sister Narcissa near the end of *Flags in the Dust*: "I dare say you cannot read this as usual, or reading it, it will not mean anything to you." Faulkner's professional readers, the critics, keep trying so variously and so relentlessly to make Faulkner readable and meaningful—to make something *usual* of him—that it is tempting to borrow Mr. Compson's cynical words about physicians to describe them: "They make their livings advising people to do whatever they are not doing at the time, which is the extent of anyone's knowledge of the degenerate ape" (*The Sound and the Fury*). Richard Brodhead and André Bleikasten have recently called upon both new and experienced readers of Faulkner to (re)learn how to read him. Reminding us that "the Faulkner we possess . . . is always and necessarily one his readers have helped to make," Brodhead encourages continued rethinking, reimagining, and remaking—continued repossessing—of Faulkner's texts: "There is still as great a need as ever for Faulkner to be known anew" (*Faulkner: New Perspectives*, ed. Richard H. Brodhead, TCV, Englewood Cliffs, N.J., 1983; hereinafter referred to as Brodhead). Bleikasten redefines and reaffirms (in the spirit of Roland Barthes) an erotics of reading Faulkner, celebrating the bursts of ideas and feelings, desires and delights, oppressions and repressions that constitute the work of reading ("Reading Faulkner," in *New Directions in Faulkner Studies: Faulkner and Yoknapatawpha, 1983*, ed. Doreen Fowler and Ann J. Abadie, Jackson, Miss., 1984; hereinafter referred to as *New Directions*). In "For/Against an Ideological Reading of Faulkner's Novels," Bleikasten begins the complex process of articulating not only a poetics, but also a politics and an ethics of reading Faulkner. "The real question," Bleikasten writes, "is whether Faulkner's work ever manages to gain distance from ideology or whether it simply mirrors the perplexities and confusions of a disaffiliated bourgeois intellectual" (*Faulkner and Idealism: Perspectives from Paris*, ed. Michel Gresset and Patrick Samway, S.J., Jackson, Miss., 1983; hereinafter referred to as *Faulkner and Idealism*).

In two new books Cleanth Brooks never manages or even attempts to gain any critical distance from his perceptions of Faulkner's implicit ideologies, but prefers to replicate, explicate, and rationalize them. Faulkner's current and future readers must remain grateful to Brooks for being among the first to open up the strange world of Yoknapatawpha to the general public; yet some may be legitimately disappointed that at this juncture in his long and generous career, Brooks has not risked reseeing, rethinking, reimagining, has not risked remapping any corner of the topography of Faulkner's imagination. *On the Prejudices, Predilections, and Firm Beliefs of William Faulkner* (Baton Rouge, La., 1987), in fact, reprints a dozen essays (lectures, actually) composed by Brooks between 1971 and 1985, acknowledging that "a man doesn't change his convictions from year to year simply to be sure of presenting something fresh." The essays, all graced by Brooks's characteristic sanity and gentility, will provide convenient touchstones for less tradition-bound critics, who have already begun the challenging project of rehistoricizing and repoliticizing Faulkner's achievements. Among the essays most likely in the present critical climate to stir up controversy are "Faulkner and the Fugitive-Agrarians," "Faulkner and Christianity," "Faulkner and the Community," and the intrepid "Faulkner's Ultimate Values." (For an excellent example of how critics have already begun to question Brooks's ideological assumptions, see John N. Duvall's "Murder and the Communities: Ideology In and Around *Light in August*" [*Novel*, Winter 1987].)

William Faulkner: First Encounters (New Haven, Conn., 1983), though "not intended for the Faulkner specialist," demands serious consideration because it distills more than twenty years of Brooks's distinguished scholarship into readings of the major works which will influence another generation of Faulkner readers. In *First Encounters* Brooks shows no inclination to question any of his old New Critical assumptions about how and why to read Faulkner. He remains surprisingly defensive about Faulkner's southernness. And he remains satisfied to describe theme, characters, and plot—in his own words—"undistracted by too much critical apparatus." Alternately disarming and disconcerting, Brooks tends to rely on his own intuitive way of making sense of Faulkner, when instead he might teach readers something new about how to make sense (and how to stop making sense?) of Faulkner for themselves. Brooks's (dis-)ingenuous dismissal of any need for a theory, poetics, or at least methodology of reading reveals the very ideological biases and limitations it apparently intends to conceal or displace. Despite obvious good intentions, Brooks unfortunately tries to compromise, stabilize, and normalize encounters with texts written by Faulkner to resist compromise, simplification, stabilization, and—above all—normalization.

Three other books seem aimed primarily at readers encountering Faulkner for the first time: Alan Warren Friedman's *William Faulkner* (New York, 1984), John Pikoulis's *The Art of William Faulkner* (Totowa, N.J., 1982), and John Pilkington's *The Heart of Yoknapatawpha* (Jackson, Miss., 1981). Of the three, Friedman offers the most satisfactory introduction, Pilkington the most disappointing, and Pikoulis the most quirky. Both Friedman and Pilkington write under the powerful influence of Brooks (as well as Irving Howe, Olga Vickery, and Michael Millgate); Friedman, however, proves much more independently authoritative, generating unusually well-written interpretations of canonical novels, while quietly, subtly, and convincingly interrogating conventional thematic and formalist assumptions, admirably resisting the pressure to impose easily paraphrasable meanings on Faulkner's texts. Pilkington announces his objective of presenting "balanced, even-tempered, perhaps slightly conservative studies of nine of Faulkner's best novels," and, for the most part, merely repeats earlier, outmoded studies, as he presses toward the unobjectionable conclusion that "at the heart of Yoknapatawpha lies Faulkner's vision of man in a moral universe." Pilkington's impatience with Faulkner's structural experiment in *Go Down, Moses*, coupled with a barely restrained lack of sympathy for Faulkner's treatment of black-white relations in that novel, *is* objectionable. Many will object even more strenuously to Pikoulis's casual and confident dismissal of *As I Lay Dying* and *Light in August*: "These are usually regarded as major works but I cannot share that opinion and so have had no choice but to leave them out." While other idiosyncratic, if more defensible, judgments shape *The Art of William Faulkner*—Pikoulis finds *The Hamlet* "the most impressively written and organised" of all Faulkner's works, and considers *The Unvanquished* a "difficult masterpiece of implication . . . the nearest Faulkner came to writing a novel of sustained and subtle moral enquiry"—it may serve quite well as a generally level-headed and attractive introduction to Faulkner's art for the British audience to whom it is, most directly, addressed. One might reasonably wish that Pikoulis demonstrated a bit more familiarity with the traditions of American Faulkner criticism, and Pilkington a bit less.

In *The Play of Faulkner's Language* (Ithaca, N.Y., 1982), John T. Matthews pays extraordinary attention to significant excesses, blurs, breaks, leaks, remainders, and holes in Faulkner's writings. Matthews deftly uses language about language to write about Faulkner writing and to engage precisely those moments in Faulkner's texts which have until now proven most resistant to theory and to reading. With sophistication and tact, he appropriates the deconstructive theories of Jacques Derrida; his fundamental strategy, however, depends on sensitive, close readings of Faulkner's language. Matthews employs New Critical strategies of textual analysis to reopen the texts, to reopen the work of reading, and to reopen theoretical assumptions about textuality, reading, and theory. Not since John T. Irwin's *Doubling and Incest/Repetition and Revenge: A Speculative Reading of Faulkner* (1975) has a critical study of Faulkner made so much difference. And because Matthews *reads* rather than speculates (unlike Irwin, who speculates more than he reads), *The Play of Faulkner's Language* has been at once more widely influential and less controversial than Irwin's book.

Some readers may remain uncomfortable with Matthews's emphasis on Faulknerian makings rather than Faulknerian meanings, on Faulknerian poetics rather than mimetics. Even those who fail to recognize in Faulkner exactly the kind of elevations, confrontations, grievings, and celebrations of (and in) language disclosed by Matthews should acknowledge the brilliance and power of his elegant argument. *The Play of Faulkner's Language* clearly emerges as the most original and important study of Faulkner's writing this decade. It also stands as one of the best recent books on *any* American author and represents the kind of humane and generous literary criticism that may encourage a sustained reevaluation of the continued possibilities of poststructuralist theory.

Warwick Wadlington's *Reading Faulknerian Tragedy* (Ithaca, N.Y., 1987) remains openly suspicious of some of the strategies of reading practiced by Matthews (and others), so much so that he appends a brief caveat called "Some Limitations of Deconstructive 'Reading.'" For Wadlington, who pleads for a "reunderstanding of reading as an element of humanly creative culture," reading becomes "not only an interpretive but a comprehensive performative act, engaging the unfolding possibilities of literary role-enactment and giving full reality to the perceived authorial performances." In his highly stimulating first chapter, Wadlington "offers an anthropology of rhetoric centered on the terms *performance*, *persons*, and *reproduction*," contending that "to understand reading, we need a conception of persons which is psychosocial or anthropological."

Wadlington explains that his "subject is less Faulknerian tragedy as a static product, a finished achievement, than it is the process of scripting and actualizing tragic possibilities in the act of writing and reading"; he wants to illuminate "the diverse ways audiences can take in reading Faulknerian tragedy, and the various consequences of role-taking which they enjoy or suffer, ranging from sensuous pleasure and possible affront to daunting entanglement with otherness." If this sounds promising enough in theory, Wadlington's applications of his ways of reading to *The Sound and the Fury*, *As I Lay Dying*, *Light in August*, and *Absalom, Absalom!* disappoint and confuse, despite occasional fine observations. Although at least one accomplished Faulkner scholar, Gary Lee Stonum, welcomed *Reading Faulknerian Tragedy* as possibly "the best Faulkner study of the decade" (in a dust jacket blurb), it may take some time for Wadlington's ambitious and original theories of reading Faulkner's tragedies to be appropriated and tested fully by other experienced readers. Wadlington has, nonetheless, written a challenging and important book.

Robert Dale Parker begins *Faulkner and the Novelistic Imagination* (Urbana, Ill., 1985) asking: "What is it like to read a Faulkner novel?" Parker does especially well in explaining what it is like to read *Sanctuary*, and he also writes with welcome common sense about the fragmented experience of reading *As I Lay Dying*. Although he never quite says so, the novelistic imagination referred to in Parker's title must be that of the reader, who must recognize and cope with Faulkner's elusive and evasive narrative strategies: "The main thing we know reading Faulkner is that we don't know the main thing." This refreshingly sane book should somehow reassure both new and seasoned travelers in Yoknapatawpha that reading a Faulkner novel is often like crossing unfamiliar borders without a map.

Victor Strandberg reads Faulkner from six different perspectives in *A Faulknerian Overview* (Port Washington, N.Y., 1981); collectively the six independent essays establish Strandberg as a well-informed and imaginative reader. In "Liebestod: The Lessons of Eros," Strandberg advances some provocative if potentially reductive "speculations relating to sexual biopsychology" in Faulkner's life and art. In "Faulkner's God," Strandberg argues that "Faulkner's achievement as a religious writer may be best understood through its correlations to the broad-reaching, empirical system of William James." And in perhaps the most expansive and thought-provoking of the six essays, "Transition: From Freud to Marx," Strandberg situates Faulkner responsibly within dominant intellectual trends of his culture. Strandberg's perspectives offer such a compelling overview of Faulkner that one (almost?) wishes that his book were longer so that it could accommodate more detailed close analyses.

No one could possibly wish that *Heart in Conflict: Faulkner's Struggles with Vocation* (Athens, Ga., 1987), by Michael Grimwood, were any longer than its ample 378 pages, although some skilled editing could have shaped and tightened his worthwhile material into a more coherent argument. In Part One of his book Grimwood applies Freudian and Eriksonian theories of personality to Faulkner's apprenticeship, arguing "that the psychological sources of Faulkner's vocation contained the seeds of its potential undoing." In Part Two Grimwood shifts from a basically psychological to a basically sociological investigation of Faulkner's vocation and argues "that the degeneration many readers attribute to Faulkner's writing in the forties resulted not from superficial difficulties imposed upon him from the outside but from psychic and social pressures that are inherent in pastoralism." When working with specific Faulkner texts or when contextualizing Faulkner through precise historical, political, literary, and cinematic references, Grimwood sometimes proceeds with brilliance and authority. And his conception of Faulkner's struggles allows him to propose attractive possibilities. But *Heart in Conflict* makes even its best points obliquely, erratically, and diffusely.

Martin Kreiswirth and Max Putzel both attempt to explain Faulkner's discovery and acceptance of his vocation as writer of fiction (see also Judith Sensibar's *The Origins of Faulkner's Art*, discussed below). Kreiswirth's *William Faulkner: The Making of a Novelist* (Athens, Ga., 1983) argues—probably overargues—that *The Sound and the Fury* "marks the crucial point in Faulkner's career at which he revisited his past, saw it afresh, and reworked it into his future." Kreiswirth writes with considerable specificity and assurance about Faulkner's first three novels, especially about *Soldiers' Pay*. Economically and reasonably, he shows that *Soldiers' Pay* "more clearly and closely anticipates the structural organization and formal adventurousness of *The Sound and the Fury* than any of the books written in between." He then, somewhat less successfully, treats *Mosquitoes* "as a kind of compendium or anthology of [Faulkner's] past" and *Flags in the Dust* as "in effect a prospectus for his future." Kreiswirth probably has more to say about the beginnings of Faulkner's career than does Judith Sensibar, but he encounters at least as much trouble as she does accounting for the mysterious origins of Faulkner's art. *William Faulkner: The Making of a Novelist* should be read, but not with any unrealistic expectations that it can finally account for the mysteries of how Faulkner helped make himself into a great novelist.

Putzel, in *Genius of Place: William Faulkner's Triumphant Beginnings* (Baton Rouge, La., 1985), claims more but accomplishes less than Kreiswirth. Downplaying Faulkner's lengthy apprenticeship in poetry (in contrast to Sensibar's overemphasis), Putzel sets out to write "about young William Faulkner and how he learned his craft and proved himself an artist." Putzel wants to explain "how the ambience of his home place inspired Faulkner's best work, particularly the flair for comic effect." Unfortunately, he explains very little about Faulkner's development as an artist and still less about his genius, his comedy, or (even) his sense of place. Putzel's generally shapeless and self-indulgent discussions—he disarmingly admits that his book is "not a thesis or a monograph but an explorer's log," and allows that a "shifting angle of vision and . . . changes of mood . . . robbed [his] journal of the unity you have a right to expect"—nonetheless merit some attention. Despite (or, perhaps, because of) a certain anti-academic bias—he dismisses "any such explication of the discourse [of *The Sound and the Fury*] as teachers commonly use to make this book an instrument of classroom torture"—Putzel occasionally proves himself a wise and affectionate reader of Faulkner's stories and novels.

In *William Faulkner, Letters & Fictions* (Austin, Tex., 1987), James G. Watson explores analogous epistolary forms and conventions deployed in Faulkner's personal and fictional correspondence. The result is a lively and literate—if at times overly cautious—study of textuality and reflexivity. Watson opens up the canon in interesting ways by reading Faulkner's published letters as fictional representations of self well worth juxtaposing with representations of letter-writing and letter-reading within the fictions. While no startlingly new interpretations of novels result from Watson's approach, it does afford moments of illumination. Some readers, for example, may be surprised by Watson's disclosure that "in *The Sound and the Fury* there are twenty-one specific letters and telegrams, and the delays, misdirections, and interceptions to which they are subject portray characters, move the plots of the novel, and convey the themes of failed communication and broken identity proposed by the sound and the fury in the title." For others, Watson's remarks on *The Unvanquished* may recomplicate that underrated novel: "In the broken world of the Civil War, letter writers and readers appeal for order to epistolary conventions of the lost past and struggle with departures from epistolary custom and usage that derive from and express the exigencies of the present." *William Faulkner, Letters and Fictions* deserves attention and respect for its fresh and sensible discussions of familiar material, even as it raises legitimate questions about what a more ambitious and sophisticated theoretical approach might reveal about Faulkner's letters and fictions.

Two books address the question of what Grimwood calls "Faulkner's supposed conversion from nihilism to affirmation" between 1928 and

1950: Doreen Fowler's *Faulkner's Changing Vision: From Outrage to Affirmation* (Ann Arbor, Mich., 1983) and Lyall H. Powers's *Faulkner's Yoknapatawpha Comedy* (Ann Arbor, Mich., 1980). Fowler's book, a revision of her 1974 Brown University dissertation directed by Hyatt H. Waggoner, unpretentiously describes the change proclaimed in its title (and adumbrated in Waggoner's *William Faulkner: From Jefferson to the World* [1966]). For Fowler, the change begins in 1932: "All of Faulkner's earlier novels concluded in despair. In *Light in August*, Faulkner offers alternatives to despair which will reappear repeatedly in his later works: faith, commitment, and suffering." Powers minimizes any change in Faulkner's vision. For him, "the Yoknapatawpha Saga is a unified opus, very like the old traditional sagas," and the "main thrust of [Faulkner's] major fiction has, in truth, always been optimistic, hopeful, encouraging." Powers reads Faulkner's works attending to three patterns or themes: the self-destructiveness of evil, the second chance, and the saving remnant. He reaches the predictable and forced conclusion, announced by his title, that "the Yoknapatawpha Saga is our modern American divine comedy."

Cataclysm as Catalyst: The Theme of War in William Faulkner's Fiction (Stockholm, 1983), by Thomas Nordanberg, contributes to our understanding of Faulkner's developing imaginative vision. Prompted by Faulkner's own observation (Philippines, 1956) that "war or disaster gives a release to the impulse to write," Nordanberg examines three phases of Faulkner's literary engagements with war: 1925–1932, during which Faulkner engages World War I; 1931–1942, during which Faulkner turns to the American Civil War; and 1941–1959, when Faulkner writes about World War II. Although Nordanberg's inquiry limits itself because of its rather odd organization—character by character—it consistently demonstrates intelligence and good sense. Nordanberg does especially well with *The Unvanquished* and *A Fable*, but also has worthwhile points to make about *Soldiers' Pay*, *Sartoris*, and a number of short stories. Not everyone will agree with Nordanberg's conclusion that "an understanding of Faulkner's use of the theme of war may . . . be essential to the larger and often discussed problem of reconciling the pessimism of his early works with the optimism expressed in the Nobel Prize address, of how the nightmare world of *The Sound and the Fury* and *Sanctuary* can change into the affirmative vision of *The Mansion* and the unreserved comedy of *The Reivers*." But Nordanberg will convince most open-minded readers that Faulkner's imaginative response to war matures and complicates the moral visions of his fictions.

Robert Harrison's *Aviation Lore in Faulkner* (Philadelphia, 1985) surprises and delights. Harrison lucidly and helpfully glosses references to flying and airplanes in Faulkner's work, against the background of an apparently authoritative exposition of the basic principles of flight and a brief account of Faulkner's own career as an aviator. Harrison's notes open up and enrich the underrated *Pylon* in striking and unexpected ways; they also illuminate *Flags in the Dust* and several interesting stories, notably "Turnabout" and "All the Dead Pilots." His impressive scholarship helps us better understand not only how well Faulkner understood aviation, but how flying figured in his imagination.

Although more broadly and ambitiously conceived than either Nordanberg's or Harrison's study, Carl E. Rollyson's *Uses of the Past in the Novels of William Faulkner* (Ann Arbor, Mich., 1984) remains considerably less interesting and less valuable. Rollyson presents thoroughly competent but pedestrian readings of *Flags in the Dust*, *The Unvanquished*, *Absalom, Absalom!*, and *Go Down, Moses* in support of his thesis that "in his best work Faulkner goes beyond most historians and historical novelists in making the past and present, historical fact and human imagination, the inseparable parts of a single process: the understanding of the meaning of history." Rollyson's subject is an important one and his book, whatever its limitations, could well become a touchstone as the so-called New Historicism begins to influence Faulkner studies.

Faulkner's Fictive Architecture: The Meaning of Place in the Yoknapatawpha Novels (Ann Arbor, Mich., 1987) helps open up the important study of space and place in Faulkner's texts. William T. Ruzicka uses a sensible and modest methodology of architectural phenomenology to explain how Faulkner imagines structures and places in his books and stories. Ruzicka looks, for instance, at mansions and cabins, the wilderness, as well as Jefferson's courthouse and the town square. Informed by Heidegger, Ruzicka's account uses Faulkner to illustrate that "by reading and witnessing to the significances of both fictive and actual, natural and manmade places, men can dwell fully—that is to say poetically—in the world." Readers of Ruzicka will also want to consult James G. Watson's fine essay, "Faulkner: The House of Fiction" (*Fifty Years of Yoknapatawpha*).

For Constance Hill Hall, in *Incest in Faulkner: A Metaphor for the Fall* (Ann Arbor, Mich., 1986), Milton rather than Dante (as for Powers) provides the appropriate literary and cultural contexts within which to read Faulkner. Pretty much dismissing John T. Irwin's *Doubling and Incest/Repetition and Revenge* as "narrowly Freudian and highly speculative," Hall argues that Faulkner's representations of incest are literary and moralistic rather than anthropological or even psychological. Her claim that "both Milton and Faulkner conceive of incest as a metaphor for original sin," makes some sense, as far as it goes, but it doesn't go very far: "In its realistic depiction, one that accords with the findings of nonliterary studies, and in its use as a metaphor for the original sin, incest brings home the horror of evil and announces the need for change." This kind of conclusion doesn't seem to help us much with Horace and Narcissa Benbow, or Quentin and Caddy Compson, or Charles Bon and Henry and Judith Sutpen. Something more than metaphor seems to figure in these relationships.

Elizabeth M. Kerr wants "to arrive at the total meaning of the myth of Yoknapatawpha County, to answer the basic questions" in *William Faulkner's Yoknapatawpha: "A Kind of Keystone in the Universe"* (New York, 1983). "What is Faulkner's fundamental concept of man and society?" she inquires. "Can one derive from the myth any positive concept of man and the life worth living? Is there any redemptive vision of how man may overcome the evil in life and his own errors and weakness and bring himself closer to the authentic life?" Kerr's extravagant book raises important, if unfashionable, questions. If *William Faulkner's Yoknapatawpha* advances any thesis at all, it must be that Faulkner wrote as a Christian humanist and existentialist: "In his humanist concept of man as endowed with freedom as an individual, Faulkner was in essential agreement with the most pervasive literary philosophy of the century, existentialism." Because Kerr has so obviously immersed herself long and lovingly and wisely in Faulkner's fictional cosmos, and because so much trendier criticism tends to diminish Faulkner's humane vision, this book may, at first, appeal to some readers. Paragraph by paragraph, however, it becomes more and more excruciating to read.

Publication of a good book about Faulkner's techniques of characterization would be welcome indeed. *Recollection and Discovery: The Rhetoric of Character in William Faulkner's Novels* (Bern, 1983), by Cathy Waegner, is not a good book, but can be welcomed as a reminder of how badly we need a study of character and identity in Faulkner's fictions, accommodating both a supple understanding of modernism and a sophisticated use of postmodernist poetics. Waegner misappropriates Wolfgang Iser's concepts of "repertoire" and "implied reader." She claims to "link Iser's concepts more specifically to the spheres of language and structures of self in a new notion of rhetoric" and further claims that "recollection and discovery provide a way of talking not only about the rhetorical strategies of the novels, but also about my construct of the reader, which is more specific than Iser's 'implied reader.'" Nothing in *Recollection and Discovery* even comes close to justifying Waegner's boldly revisionist claims. It's hard to say just what she means by either rhetoric or reader. She dismisses Wayne Booth in a note, although she could have learned much from *The Rhetoric of Fiction* and could have borrowed a workable notion of rhetoric as simply "the author's means of controlling his reader." If Waegner constructs any reader at all for Faulkner, it can only be herself.

Eight volumes of the proceedings of the annual Faulkner conference at the University of Mississippi have been published since 1980 (all by the University Press of Mississippi, in Jackson). All eight volumes have been expertly edited by Doreen Fowler and Ann J. Abadie. In 1985 and 1986 the conference topics were, respectively, "Faulkner and Women" and "Faulkner and Race"; these two volumes will be discussed in the sections of this essay labeled, respectively, "Gender" and "Race." The remaining six volumes, covering the years 1979–1984, will be described here, with special attention to general essays; important essays on individual works will be noted in appropriate categories below.

In *Fifty Years of Yoknapatawpha*, the two most impressive essays are both by Michael Millgate. In "'A Cosmos of My Own': The Evolution of Yoknapatawpha," Millgate offers the intriguing speculation "that Faulkner at some point had the idea of Quentin as a dying narrator before whose eyes his whole world would pass in almost instantaneous review." The same essay also proposes two crucial moments of discovery for Faulkner: the first, when he perceived the possibility of his own fictional cosmos; the second, when he perceived the endless possibilities for experimenting with fictional techniques to represent Yoknapatawpha. Millgate argues in "Faulkner's First Trilogy" not only that there are complex patterns connecting *Sartoris* (1929), *Sanctuary* (1931), and *Requiem for a Nun* (1951), but also, even more vigorously, that "each Faulkner text must be considered a unique, independent, and self-sufficient work of art, not only capable of being read and contemplated in isolation but actually demanding such treatment." Millgate consistently brings to his discussions of Faulkner's work an uncanny—perhaps unmatched—balance of critical qualities: a wise understanding of Faulkner's literary, cultural, and personal backgrounds; an intimate knowledge of Faulkner's manuscripts and their composition; and shrewd, humane instincts for both analysis and synthesis. Both of his essays in *Fifty Years of Yoknapatawpha* demonstrate, moreover, an impressive power of generalization. Sometimes he asserts or suggests somewhat more than he can fully substantiate or illustrate within the compass of an article, but he always does so with such obvious authority and tact that one tends to trust him. One also tends to trust Joseph Blotner in "The Sources of Faulkner's Genius," Thomas L. McHaney in "Faulkner's Curious Tools," and Noel Polk in "'I Taken an Oath of Office Too': Faulkner and the Law." And one can admire the way James G. Watson uses the poetics of space articulated by Gaston Bachelard to explore the architecture of Faulkner's imagination in "Faulkner: The House of Fiction."

The best essays in *"A Cosmos of My Own": Faulkner and Yoknapatawpha, 1980* (1981; hereinafter referred to as *"A Cosmos of My Own"*)—Robert W. Hamblin's "'Saying No to Death': Toward William Faulkner's Theory of Fiction," James B. Carothers's "The Myriad Heart: The Evolution of the Faulkner Hero," and Panthea Reid Broughton's "The Cubist Novel: Toward Defining the Genre" and "Faulkner's Cubist Novels"—all intelligently accomplish pretty much what their titles promise.

Faulkner and the Southern Renaissance: Faulkner and Yoknapatawpha, 1981 (1982; hereinafter referred to as *Southern Renaissance*) reprints papers read at the 1981 Faulkner conference by Richard H. King, David Minter, Cleanth Brooks, Louis D. Rubin, Jr., Floyd C. Watkins, and others. The superficially old-fashioned topic of Faulkner and the Agrarians may have inhibited many of the participants, who resist genuinely revisionist historical or political readings of Faulkner's work. The single best paper is probably Richard H. King's "Memory and Tradition," which uses Nietzsche and Freud to frame the problems Faulkner's characters tend to have learning to forget the past. David Minter's "'Truths More Intense than Knowledge': Notes on Faulkner and Creativity" instructively evaluates a conservative/radical or modernist/postmodernist dialectic shaping Faulkner's imagination.

The proceedings of the 1982 conference were published in 1984 as *Faulkner: International Perspectives*; in this volume Faulkner's reception and reputation throughout the world are reassessed, with special attention to the Soviet Union. In "From Vignette to Vision: The 'Old, Fine Name of France' or Faulkner's 'Western Front' from 'Crevasse' to *A Fable*," Michel Gresset deftly surveys Faulkner's imaginative appropriation of France. Also especially interesting are the essays by Kenzaburo Ohashi ("'Native Soil' and the World Beyond: William Faulkner and Japanese Novelists"), Alexandre Vashchenko ("The Perception of William Faulkner in the USSR"), and Sergei Chakovsky ("William Faulkner and Soviet Literary Criticism"). The volume's most durable work comes from Calvin Brown, who surprises us with what he knows about what Faulkner knew (and did not know) in "From Jefferson to the World."

New Directions in Faulkner Studies (1984) includes some fine work by Michael Millgate, André Bleikasten, Thomas L. McHaney, Noel Polk, and James Hinkle, but the volume's ultimate value may reside in its rather dramatic, not to say distressing, exposure of the conservative and timid legacy of New Criticism still directing mainstream Faulkner scholarship as recently as 1983–1984. (Some welcome and overdue new directions were to emerge in *Faulkner and Women* [1986] and *Faulkner and Race* [1987].) Like Millgate's contributions to *Fifty Years of Yoknapatawpha*, his *New Directions* paper stands as a model of superbly imaginative scholarship, demonstrating a continuity and originality of purpose (both aesthetic and ethical) all too rare in contemporary criticism. In "William Faulkner: The Shape of a Career," Millgate responds to the implications of Gary Lee Stonum's work, cautioning that "Faulkner's career may have very imperfectly embodied his ambitions for it." In a fascinating and useful paper, "Some Yoknapatawpha Names," James Hinkle reports and assesses what he learned about Faulkner's pronunciation of names (like Sartoris) from listening to hours of tapes of Faulkner reading and speaking. Thomas L. McHaney writes very well, if perhaps a bit too insistently, about Faulkner's place in the modernist canon in "Faulkner and Modernism: Why Does It Matter?" Noel Polk continues his learned, literate, and moderate Freudian readings of Faulkner's career in a sometimes moving essay, "'And the Dungeon was Mother Herself': William Faulkner: 1927–1931." Judith Bryant Wittenberg's "The Art of Ending" appropriately concludes *New Directions* with a sensible consideration of Faulkner's ways of ending his novels and his career (*The Reivers*).

James M. Cox's accomplished performance, "Humor as Vision in Faulkner," nicely opens *Faulkner and Humor: Faulkner and Yoknapatawpha, 1984* (1986; hereinafter referred to as *Faulkner and Humor*). Cox wryly observes that "meaning is, after all, antithetical to humor," so perhaps it is inevitable that the rest of the papers in this weak collection have trouble finding meanings in Faulkner's humor or humor in Faulkner's meanings. The most successful performances, after Cox's, are traditional but solidly informative papers by Thomas L. McHaney ("What Faulkner Learned from the Tall Tale") and M. Thomas Inge ("Faulkner Reads the Funny Papers"). James M. Mellard's "Lacan and Faulkner: A Post-Freudian Analysis of Humor in the Fiction" is about as humorless as its title warns it could be.

Papers from the first and second International Faulkner Colloquia (held in Paris in 1980 and 1982) have also been published by the University Press of Mississippi: *Faulkner and Idealism* and *Intertextuality in Faulkner* (ed. Michel Gresset and Noel Polk, Jackson, Miss., 1985). Once again comments on papers concerned with individual novels (all of *Intertextuality*'s) will be withheld until the appropriate point in this essay. The rest of *Faulkner and Idealism* never quite lives up to the promise of André Bleikasten's "For/Against an Ideological Reading of Faulkner's Novels" and Gresset's "The 'God' of Faulkner's Fiction," but Thomas L. McHaney's "The Development of Faulkner's Idealism: Hands, Horses, Whores" studies an engaging configuration of imagery.

McHaney has edited *Faulkner Studies in Japan* (Athens, Ga., 1985; hereinafter referred to as McHaney), a graceful collection of essays representing the longstanding Japanese artistic and scholarly interest in Faulkner. As McHaney indicates in his introduction, the collection stands as "a showcase of recent work on Faulkner in Japan," as "both a reflection of Faulkner's universality and a contribution to the important international critical discussion of his work."

Faulkner: The Unappeased Imagination (ed. Glenn O. Carey, Troy, N.Y., 1980; hereinafter referred to as Carey) contains fifteen essays of uneven, but mostly low, quality. Among the few essays of high quality, two address general topics: Richard A. Milum's "Continuity and Change: The Horse, the Automobile, and the Airplane in Faulkner's Fiction," and Carolyn Porter's "Faulkner and His Reader." Although Porter might profitably have focused more directly on the roles of Faulkner's readers than she in fact does, her essay raises some important questions about what it's like to read Faulkner, especially *Absalom, Absalom!*

In keeping with the format of Twentieth Century Views, only Richard H. Brodhead's introduction to *Faulkner: New Perspectives* is new. But Brodhead's introduction is a smart and lively reflection on reading Faulkner and, in general, his selection of essays—by Cleanth Brooks, Irving

Howe, Donald M. Kartiganer, David M. Wyatt, Calvin Bedient, among others—makes good sense. Whether or not the collection presents, as it intends, the best new writing on Faulkner published since Robert Penn Warren's Twentieth Century Views volume (1966) remains open to question. Unquestionably *New Perspectives* is a better buy for students and teachers than Harold Bloom's critical anthology, *William Faulkner* (New York, 1986).

Only one volume of *Faulkner Studies: An Annual of Research, Criticism, and Reviews* (ed. Barnett Guttenberg, Miami, Fla., 1980) has been released. The best general essay is Ilse Dusoir Lind's "Faulkner and Nature," which must be read with some caution. The apparent demise of *Faulkner Studies* makes the emergence of *The Faulkner Journal*, under the strong editorship of James Carothers and John T. Matthews, all the more significant and timely.

2 General Estimates: Articles

a. 1973–1979. In the 1981 Faulkner chapter of *American Literary Scholarship*, it was said that most essay-length general studies of Faulkner's fiction remind one of H. G. Wells's mind, as described by Aldous Huxley: miles and miles wide, but only an inch deep. Exceptions to this observation are two essays by Lewis P. Simpson, "Faulkner and the Southern Symbolism of Pastoral" (*MissQ*, Summer 1975) and "Sex & History: Origins of Faulkner's Apocrypha" (*The Maker and the Myth*). The first applies to Faulkner an argument about the distinctive character of southern pastoralism that Simpson develops at greater length in *The Dispossessed Garden: Pastoral and History in Southern Literature* (Athens, Ga., 1975); the second examines sexuality as the locus for Faulkner's exploration of the conflict between myth and history. Both are learned and stimulating essays.

Also of value are Joan S. Korenman's "Faulkner and 'That Undying Mark'" (*SAF*, Spring 1976), a discussion of the development of Faulkner's craving for immortality, and Mary Jane Dickerson's "Faulkner's Golden Steed" (*MissQ*, Summer 1978), a study of the role of horses in Faulkner's fiction. Although marred by an assumption that Faulkner began *Sanctuary* before writing *The Sound and the Fury*, Philip M. Weinstein's "Precarious Sanctuaries: Protection and Exposure in Faulkner's Fiction" (*SAF*, Autumn 1978) provides some real insight into the role of protected spaces (both literal and metaphoric) in Faulkner's fiction. Weinstein's essay merits comparison with Karl Zink's seminal early study, "Flux and the Frozen Moment" (1956). Finally, James G. Watson's "If *Was* Existed: Faulkner's Prophets and the Patterns of History" (*MFS*, Winter 1975) offers insight into how the past and the future are related in the minds of Faulkner's protagonists.

b. 1980–1988. Donald M. Kartiganer has written a superb entry on Faulkner for the authoritative *Columbia Literary History of the United States* (ed. Emory Elliott, New York, 1987); less noteworthy are Cleanth Brooks's Faulkner entry for *The History of Southern Literature* (Baton Rouge, La., 1985) and Lewis P. Simpson's "William Faulkner of Yoknapatawpha," in *The American South: Portrait of a Culture* (ed. Louis D. Rubin, Jr., Baton Rouge, La., 1980). Richard Gray offers a succinct account of Faulkner's literary career as "an imaginative recovery of the South," in "From Oxford: The Novels of William Faulkner," in his edition of *American Fictions: New Readings* (London, 1983). Gray reflects responsibly on Faulkner's self-consciousness about his position as a southern writer: "The deliberate construction of a landscape, a sense of place; an urgent, dramatized recreation of the past; and the rediscovery, and the very personal and self-critical exploration, of an inherited name for evil." Less effectively, Daniel Joseph Singal, in *The War Within: From Victorian to Modernist Thought in the South, 1919–1945* (Chapel Hill, N.C., 1982), tries to situate Faulkner "at the center of an immense cultural change that had taken place in the region between the two world wars" by arguing that, "far more than any other writer of his generation, Faulkner made southern evil visible."

In "William Faulkner: The Two Voices" (*Southern Literature in Transition: Heritage and Promise*, ed. Philip Castille and William Osborne, Memphis, Tenn., 1983), Michael Millgate responds to those who, along with Walter Slatoff, have found debilitating oppositions, contradictions, and ambivalences in Faulkner's work: "I would . . . see that kind of patterning as conscious and controlled rather than simply obsessive or schizoid. And I would argue that it operated for Faulkner as a kind of exploratory device, directed toward the expression or (better, perhaps) the exposition of complexities that he believed to be inherent in his own experience as a human being who happened to inhabit a particular society and region." Elmo Howell's "Southern Fiction and the Pattern of Failure: The Example of Faulkner" (*GaR*, Winter 1982) reworks a failed argument about Faulkner's moral and artistic limitations.

Richard H. King devotes three chapters of *A Southern Renaissance: The Cultural Awakening of the American South, 1930–1955* (New York, 1980) to Faulkner. King writes at some length about *Flags in the Dust, The Sound and the Fury,* and *Absalom, Absalom!,* but writes most originally and most persuasively about *Go Down, Moses.* King's central concern is "the dialectic between weak sons and strong fathers in Faulkner's work." He claims that "the family metaphor implicates Faulkner's view of the history of the South as well as his rendition of the family drama; that the incest theme is closely connected with the problem of miscegenation; that both signal Faulkner's meditations on the nature of the cultural order, particularly as it threatens to collapse; and that finally [John T.] Irwin's pessimistic reading of Freud's notion of repetition distorts his reading of Faulkner." Covering much the same ground as *A Southern Renaissance* are Lucinda Hardwick MacKethan's "Faulkner's Sons of the Fathers: How to Inherit the Past" (in *The Dream of Arcady: Place and Time in Southern Literature*, Baton Rouge, La., 1980) and André Bleikasten's "Fathers in Faulkner" (in *The Fictional Father: Lacanian Readings of the Text*, ed. Robert Con Davis, Amherst, Mass., 1981). Bleikasten offers a surprisingly un-exciting survey of Faulkner's representations of paternal and patriarchal authority; Lacan does not really help him bring alive "the haunting question of fatherhood, in its psychoethical as well as in its wider cultural implications." Of somewhat more interest, at least for those who read French, are Bleikasten's "Faulkner descripteur" (*RANAM*, 1986) and "Temps, mythe et historie chez Faulkner" (in *Age d'or et apocalypse*, ed. Robert Ellrodt, Paris, 1986).

In Faulkner's frequent representations of sound—and silence—Karl F. Zender hears "a sustained meditation on the artist's power." In "Faulk-ner and the Power of Sound" (*PMLA*, Jan. 1984), Zender writes with real insight about Quentin Compson in *The Sound and the Fury*, Linda Snopes Kohl in *The Mansion*, and "The Jail" section of *Requiem for a Nun*. Zender writes even more interestingly about the style of *The Mansion*, explaining how, "by deafening Linda, Faulkner forces the world to aban-don its allegiance to sound and to resume its dependence on reading." "Faulkner and the Power of Sound," then, suggests a great deal about Faulkner's conception of the relative powers of writing and reading, his conceptions about the power of his style, the power of his art. Zender argues that Faulkner's confidence both in sound and in his own artistic style fluctuates during the course of his career.

Focusing on such apprentice work as *The Marble Faun* and *Mayday*, James G. Watson suggests that "Faulkner's criticism of his fiction in his fiction measures more accurately than any retrospective statements of his the developing self-assurance and reconciliation to his art and life" necessary for the creation of his masterworks ("Literary Self-Criticism: Faulkner in Fiction on Fiction" [*SoQ*, Fall 1981]). Michel Gresset writes beautifully about Faulkner's lyrical, dramatic, and "signed representa-tion" of himself in his work in "Faulkner's Self-Portraits" (*FJ*, Fall 1986) and movingly about problems of belonging in "Home and Homelessness in Faulkner's World and Life" (*WiF*, May 1983).

Elizabeth Duvert's adventurous "Faulkner's Map of Time" (*FJ*, Fall 1986) discovers "an icon of Faulkner's vision of landscape as spatialized time" in his famous drawing(s) of Yoknapatawpha. Wesley A. Kort writes perceptively about Faulkner's polyphonic time in *Modern Fiction and Human Time: A Study in Narrative and Belief* (Tampa, Fla., 1985): "The separation of culture from nature and of present from past is characteristic of a society that also divides men from women, centered from peripheral, and white from black. . . . The rift between actions that produce change and those that are determined by the meaning and value of the estab-lished society is a defining characteristic of Yoknapatawpha time." Martin Kreiswirth nicely illuminates "certain primary features of Faulkner's literary imagination, certain narrative preoccupations and common ways of shaping fictional wholes" in "Centers, Openings, and Endings: Some Faulknerian Constants" (*AL*, Mar. 1984). Michael Oriard's "The Ludic Vision of William Faulkner" (*MFS*, Summer 1982) explicates some literal and figurative connections between game-playing and freedom in Faulkner's work.

In a pair of important and provocative articles, Lawrence Schwartz explores the political, economic, and cultural conditions which helped to secure Faulkner's place in the literary canon after World War II. "Malcolm Cowley's Path to William Faulkner" (*JAmSt*, Aug. 1982) documents how Cowley came to endorse Faulkner's modernist vision only after repudiating his own commitment to the heritage of naturalism and social realism, but then, disturbingly, concludes reductively that "Faulkner's work was patronized and canonized because his supremely individualistic themes and technically difficult prose served an ideological cause. He produced, intended or not, a commodity of enormous political value." In "Publishing William Faulkner: The 1940's" (*SoQ*, Winter 1984), Schwartz "analyzes the actual demand for and sales of [Faulkner's] books, during a decade when he had little commercial or cultural value, and was essentially saved from extinction by a few marginal critics and chary publishers." The University of Tennessee Press published an amplified version of Schwartz's argument, *Creating Faulkner's Reputation: The Politics of Modern Literary Criticism*, in late 1988. Presumably Schwartz's book intends to provide what he calls for at the end of "Publishing William Faulkner": "a further analysis that sets the post-war changes in the book trade into the context of Cold War cultural politics where the new aestheticism led to the Nobel Prize, and coalesced with commercial publishing to make Faulkner's reputation."

Cheryl Lester also looks at what Malcolm Cowley did for or to Faulkner as he constructed "an author who is portable, who has produced a *whole* that can be decoded and transmitted to others." Despite its rather juvenile title, Lester's "To Market, To Market: *The Portable Faulkner*" (*Criticism*, Summer 1987) presents a strikingly mature and original argument about Faulkner's strategies for subverting his own portability through the Compson Appendix. Lester raises the fascinating and attractive possibility that Cowley didn't really understand Faulkner and that "two different approaches to language, literature, and the genealogy of meaning" resulted in the problematic book we know as *The Portable Faulkner*.

3 Sources, Influences, Intellectual Backgrounds

a. 1973–1979. The 1970s saw the publication of a number of contributions to our knowledge of the regional backgrounds of Faulkner's fiction. Foremost among these is Calvin S. Brown's *A Glossary of Faulkner's South* (New Haven, Conn., 1976). In Panthea Reid Broughton's words, Brown's intention is "to gloss every reference in the Yoknapatawpha fiction unclear to readers in times and places other than Faulkner's" (*AmLS*, 1976). Although Brown occasionally explains widely familiar expressions (e.g., "fence picket," "feed lot"), most of the terms he glosses are either unclear or have variant regional meanings. The book also contains, as an appendix, an updated version of Brown's "Faulkner's Geography and Topography" (1962), a valuable exploration of points of correspondence between Yoknapatawpha County and Lafayette County, Mississippi. This appendix should be read in conjunction with "Faulkner's Localism," an essay by Brown in *The Maker and the Myth*, and with three essays by Charles S. Aiken: "Faulkner's Yoknapatawpha County: Geographical Fact into Fiction" (*GeoR*, Jan. 1978); "Faulkner's Yoknapatawpha: A Place in the American South" (*GeoR*, July 1979); and "A Geographical Approach to William Faulkner's 'The Bear'" (Proceedings of the Southeastern Division, Association of American Geographers, Memphis, Tenn., 1979). Writing as a geographer, Aiken brings interesting maps, photographs, and historical descriptions to bear on the fiction. Finally, Hubert McAlexander, Jr.'s "General Earl Van Dorn and Faulkner's Use of History" (*JMH*, Nov. 1977), Matthew O'Brien's "William Faulkner and the Civil War in Oxford, Mississippi" (*JMH*, May 1973), and Richard T. Dillon's "Some Sources for Faulkner's Version of the First Air War" (*AL*, Jan. 1973) shed light on the topics identified in their titles.

Influence studies during the period under review ran the gamut from broadly based discussions of Faulkner's relation to major schools of thought and literary movements to attributions of specific sources for phrases, images, and motifs. Although the broadly based studies are often too general to be of interest, some afford moments of real insight. Heading the list of works of this sort is Hugh Kenner's "Faulkner and the Avant-Garde" (*Faulkner, Modernism, and Film*), an impressionistic but judicious and knowledgeable attempt to distinguish Faulkner's stylistic and structural innovations from the programmatic aims of the avant-garde movement of the 1920s. Also of value are three studies that examine Faulkner's fiction in relation to nineteenth- and twentieth-century writers: David Jarrett's "Eustacia Vye and Eula Varner, Olympians: The Worlds of Thomas Hardy and William Faulkner" (*Novel*, Winter 1973); Arthur F. Kinney's "Faulkner and Flaubert" (*JML*, Apr. 1977); and John M. Ditsky's "'Dark, Darker than Fire': Thematic Parallels in Lawrence and Faulkner" (*SHR*, Fall 1974). Kinney's essay invites comparison with André Bleikasten's later work on the same topic. Less interesting but still of value are Joseph Blotner's "Romantic Elements in Faulkner" (*Romantic and Modern: Reevaluations of Literary Traditions*, ed. George Bornstein, Pittsburgh, 1977), a catalog of prominent romantic tropes and themes in Faulkner's fiction, and Mary Dell Fletcher's "William Faulkner and Residual Calvinism" (*SoSt*, Summer 1979), a sometimes predictable but comprehensive survey of a familiar theme.

The list of studies of specific sources includes two items from Mick Gidley's continuing series of explorations of Faulkner's reading. The first, "William Faulkner and Willard Huntington Wright's *The Creative Will*" (*CRevAS*, Fall 1978), discusses one of the few works of literary theory Faulkner is definitely known to have read. The second, "William Faulkner and Some Designs of Naturalism" (*SAF*, Spring 1979), traces connections between Faulkner's ideas and those of Rémy de Gourmont and Joseph Wood Krutch. Three other informative studies, two of them by Ilse Dusoir Lind and the other by Hugh Kenner, appeared in *Faulkner, Modernism, and Film*. Lind's first essay, "Faulkner's Uses of Poetic Drama," provides useful information about Faulkner's early interest in drama and traces connections between Eugene O'Neill's *All God's Chillun Got Wings* and *Light in August*. Her second, "The Effect of Painting on Faulkner's Poetic Form," examines Faulkner's interest in a number of painters, ranging from Aubrey Beardsley to Rembrandt (cf. Timothy K. Conley's less successful study, "Beardsley and Faulkner" [*JML*, Sept. 1976]). Kenner's essay, "Faulkner and Joyce," traces some of Faulkner's stylistic debts to Joyce. Kenner is especially persuasive on Faulkner's and Joyce's relation to the class-based orthography of earlier literature. Also worth mentioning are Joan S. Korenman's "Faulkner's Grecian Urn" (*SLJ*, Fall 1974), an overview of Faulkner's debt to Keats's poem, and Joel M. Grossman's "The Source of Faulkner's 'Less Oft is Peace'" (*AL*, Nov. 1975), which demonstrates that the phrase quoted in its title derives from Shelley's "To Jane: The Recollection."

Another substantial body of studies explores Faulkner's influence on later writers. Because the likeliest route to these studies is through bibliographies and reviews of the influenced authors, they will not be discussed here.

b. *1980–1988*. Joan M. Serafin's *Faulkner's Uses of the Classics* (Ann Arbor, Mich., 1983) and Jessie McGuire Coffee's *Faulkner's Un-Christlike Christians: Biblical Allusions in the Novels* (Ann Arbor, Mich., 1983) both deliver what their titles promise with reasonable competence and efficiency: catalogs of Faulkner's references, respectively, to classical and biblical texts (both, however, remain limited by their origins as dissertations written about twenty years ago). Linda W. Wagner (*AmLS*, 1983) described Serafin's study as a "model of information giving"; it seems more helpful and satisfying than Coffee's work with the Bible, partly because it presents its glosses with a minimum of interpretive comment or contextualization. *Faulkner's Un-Christlike Christians* prefaces its useful concordance with forty pages of needlessly reductive commentary.

Timothy Kevin Conley's "Resounding Fury: Faulkner's Shakespeare, Shakespeare's Faulkner" (*Shakespeare and Southern Writers: A Study in Influence*, ed. Philip C. Kolin, Jackson, Miss., 1985) misses too many opportunities to score big points, but surprises with some keen suggestions about Faulkner's use of Shakespearean comic strategies in *Soldiers'*

Pay and *Pylon*. K. J. Phillips, in "Faulkner in the Garden of Eden" (*SHR*, Winter 1985), writes imaginatively but narrowly about Faulkner's tree imagery. John M. Howell generates a very fine discussion of Faulkner's poetic appropriation of T. S. Eliot (and others) in "Faulkner, Prufrock, and Agamemnon: Horses, Hell, and Highwater" (Carey). Alexander Marshall III reconsiders Faulkner's appropriations of Verlaine, Laforgue, Mallarmé, and others in "William Faulkner: The Symbolist Connection" (*AL*, Oct. 1987). Judith Bryant Wittenberg speculates intelligently about what *Mourning Becomes Electra* might have meant to Faulkner in "Faulkner and Eugene O'Neill" (*MissQ*, Summer 1980).

Michael Kreyling's chapter on Faulkner in his *Figures of the Hero in Southern Narrative* (Baton Rouge, La., 1987) argues that "the figure of Pierrot was and perhaps still is the gravitational center of a system of images, attitudes, allusions, and style that collided, in Faulkner's case, with the heroic aesthetic of his community and narrative tradition." It's hard to be sure just what we learn about Faulkner's art from "Faulkner's Pierrotic Hero: Stranger in Yoknapatawpha," but Kreyling's point is apparently compressed in the chapter's final sentence: "Faulkner prized failure in other writers and esteemed his own works by the magnitude of his failure in them, and he saw the human race as a *commedia dell'arte* troupe in which only Pierrot could believe, or act as if he believed, in heroism, the purity of motive, the truths of the human heart." Charlie Chaplin as inspiration for Faulknerian personae, themes, and techniques is the delightful subject of Jeffrey J. Folks's "William Faulkner and the Silent Film" (*SoQ*, Spring–Summer 1981).

With characteristic savvy, Thomas L. McHaney evaluates what Faulkner may have meant to those who followed him in "Waiting for the Dixie Limited: Faulkner's Impact upon the Creative Writer" (*Fifty Years of Yoknapatawpha*). Faulkner's impact on South American fiction has been profitably addressed in a number of new studies, including Harley D. Oberhelman's *The Presence of Faulkner in the Writings of Garcia Marquez* (Lubbock, Tex., 1980) and Nancy Lester's "A General View of Faulkner's Influence on Gabriel García Márquez" (*SALit*, June 1985). Among other specialized studies of influence are: Allan Chavkin's "Faulkner's Secular Romanticism" (*McNR*, 1980–1981); Martin Bidney's "Faulkner's Variations on Romantic Themes: Blake, Wordsworth, Byron, and Shelley in *Light in August*" (*MissQ*, Summer 1985); Ronald Wesley Hoag's "Expanding the Influence: Faulkner and Four Melville Tales" (*SARev*, Nov. 1985); André Bleikasten's "Bloom and Quentin" and François L. Pitavy's "Joyce's and Faulkner's 'Twining Stresses': A Textual Comparison" (both in *The Seventh of Joyce*, ed. Bernard Benstock, Bloomington, Ind., 1982).

4 Style and Structure

a. 1973–1979. The 1970s saw the publication of three important books on style and structure: Donald M. Kartiganer's *The Fragile Thread: The*

Meaning of Form in Faulkner's Novels (Amherst, Mass., 1979), Arthur F. Kinney's *Faulkner's Narrative Poetics: Style as Vision* (Amherst, Mass., 1978), and Joseph W. Reed's *Faulkner's Narrative* (New Haven, Conn., 1973). Of the three, *The Fragile Thread* most often addresses current issues and concerns; in its assertion of a positive aesthetic value for "the fragmentariness of Faulkner's novels," the book anticipates the challenge mounted by deconstruction to the aesthetics of unity. (Paul de Man, Ihab Hassan, Jacques Derrida, and Joseph N. Riddel [misspelled Riddell by Kartiganer] are all cited in the book's preface.) Regrettably, *The Fragile Thread* achieves its break with tradition more in its theoretical orientation than in its practice. Although insightful, Kartiganer's chapters on individual novels at times revert to a traditional modernist mode of interpretation, in which fragmentation symptomizes the breakdown of western culture. There is little sense given in his readings that fragmentation might be a democratizing process, a healthy challenge to established authority.

Kinney's study is more traditional than Kartiganer's, but not less interesting. Essentially a rhetorical study, *Faulkner's Narrative Poetics* asserts that Faulkner's fragmentary structures and multiple points of view reach completion (and, presumably, achieve unity) in the "constitutive consciousness" of the reader. Whether we agree with this view or not, we can be grateful to Kinney for demonstrating, in Panthea Reid Broughton's words, "how [Faulkner's] novels are structured by analogy, synecdoche, image chains, correlatives, juxtaposition, counterpointing" and a long list of other techniques (*AmLS*, 1978). The oldest of the three books, Reed's *Faulkner's Narrative* shows the most signs of age. Occasionally quirky in method, stylistically self-indulgent, and too quick to dismiss the post-World War II fiction, the book nonetheless contains a number of interesting insights.

Two other books should be briefly mentioned. Joanne V. Creighton's *William Faulkner's Craft of Revision: The Snopes Trilogy, "The Unvanquished," and "Go Down, Moses"* (Detroit, 1977) is a workmanlike but unremarkable study of the subject identified in its title. It demonstrates how Faulkner transformed short stories into novels, but its worth as literary criticism is limited by the conventionality and predictability of its readings. Edwin R. Hunter's *William Faulkner: Narrative Practice and Prose Style* (Washington, D.C., 1973) is a bit of an oddity. The work of a Faulkner aficionado, idiosyncratic in style and structure, the book contains occasional comments of interest; especially noteworthy are two appendixes cataloging the "sense units" of the first and second sections of *The Sound and the Fury*.

Some shorter studies also deserve attention. "The Faulknerian Voice" and "Faulkner the Innovator," Albert J. Guerard's two contributions to *The Maker and the Myth*, extend the comments on style in his *Triumph of the Novel* (see above). In "Caddy and Addie: Speakers of Faulkner's

Impeccable Language" (*JNT*, Sept. 1973), Paul R. Lilly, Jr. provides a thoughtful and well-documented demonstration of Faulkner's attraction to the symbolist view of silence as the purest form of speech. James G. Watson's "Faulkner: Short Story Structures and Reflexive Forms" (*Mosaic*, Summer 1978) is a suggestive but too brief discussion of reflexivity in Faulkner's short fiction. Two other studies, Calvin S. Brown's "Faulkner as Aphorist" (*RLC*, July–Sept. 1979) and Bruce Kawin's "The Montage Element in Faulkner's Fiction" (*Faulkner, Modernism, and Film*), offer insight into the topics named in their titles. Essentially a Lukácsian critique of Faulkner for his "defective" sense of social change, Brent Harold's "The Value and Limitations of Faulkner's Fictional Method" (*AL*, May 1975) makes valuable observations about the relation between Faulkner's style and primitivism, positivism, and the art-for-art's-sake movement.

 b. 1980–1988. Lothar Hönnighausen's *William Faulkner: The Art of Stylization* (New York, 1987) "takes Faulkner's artwork as a starting-point to approach his early poetry and prose" and aims at "a more intimate acquaintance with that element of Faulkner's imagination which added a Symbolist dimension to the realism of his novels." The result is a well-written and elegantly produced volume (more than 100 stylish reproductions) which makes a solid and original contribution to our understanding of the development of the prose style we recognize as "Faulknerian." Hönnighausen illuminates the origins of Faulkner's art more brightly than Sensibar, Kreiswirth, or Putzel (discussed elsewhere in this essay), even if his disclosures may not be quite as "astounding" as Thomas L. McHaney promised a few years ago they would be (see "Faulkner and Modernism" in *New Directions*). Hönnighausen's masterly analysis does support McHaney's contention that Faulkner must be read—like Eliot and Joyce—as a fundamentally modernist writer.

 Gail L. Mortimer's well-conceived purpose in *Faulkner's Rhetoric of Loss: A Study in Perception and Meaning* (Austin, Tex., 1983) is "to draw connections among various rhetorical choices that Faulkner makes—choices that we refer to collectively and recognize instinctively as his style—and to show how these choices reflect Faulkner's unique ways of organizing experience." Because Mortimer recognizes that Faulkner's "rhetorical choices, as forms of self-expression, have psychological import," she inevitably explores the borders between rhetoric and psychology, between art and life, and between male and female expressions of selfhood. In her pivotal chapter, "Significant Absences," Mortimer impressively establishes that "Faulkner's world is a world sustained among tensions about loss: loss of the self, loss of control, loss of desired objects through the passage of time." She also explains "how Faulkner's structuring of his narrators' and characters' perceptions expresses a particular way of being in the world and a particular set of expectations about that world." In Faulkner's world as in ours men and women exist, perceive, and expect differently. Her final chapter presents a temperate feminist account of Faulkner's masculine representations of "ontological and psychological anxiety," significantly advancing the difficult project of rethinking Faulknerian perceptions and representations of sexual difference.

Several other recent critics might reasonably have borrowed Mortimer's subtitle, *A Study in Perception and Meaning*. Hugh M. Ruppersburg's *Voice and Eye in Faulkner's Fiction* (Athens, Ga., 1983), Carolyn Porter's *Seeing and Being: The Plight of the Participant-Observer in Emerson, James, Adams, and Faulkner* (Middletown, Conn., 1981), and Michel Gresset's *Faulkner ou la Fascination: Poétique du Regard* (Paris, 1982) all in one way or another study problems of perception and meaning. Collectively, these critics make possible continued reevaluation of how we know what's in Faulkner's books, of how we see and hear what Faulkner's style represents his characters (and sometimes himself, at least as narrator) as seeing and hearing.

Ruppersburg takes a modest but clear-sighted and revealing look at Faulknerian strategies of point of view, employing a traditional critical vocabulary—narrative, perspective, audience, distance—to present a very sensible and readable account of how point of view determines (or makes indeterminate) a novel's themes and meanings. In 1988 some readers will have trouble accepting Ruppersburg's assertion that the "key to [Faulkner's] meanings resides in the minds of his characters, and the minds of his characters compose the foundation of his fiction." But with his problematic "key" tightly in hand, Ruppersburg opens up *Pylon* and *Requiem for a Nun* in unusually worthwhile ways. (He is less successful with the more familiar *Light in August* and *Absalom, Absalom!*)

In *Seeing and Being*, Carolyn Porter articulates a moderate Marxist strategy for seeing what can be known through the history of writing and the writing of history. She balances the structures of society against the structures of language, fusing ideological and semiotic analysis. Porter's two chapters about Faulkner—"Faulkner's America" and "The Reified Reader"—demonstrate her power as a close reader of both Faulkner's writing and its historical situation. She often reads the margins between political, philosophical, and literary economies, exposing Faulkner's own exposures (and concealments) of contradictions inherent within American capitalism. Her analysis of *Absalom, Absalom!*, for example, convincingly insists on understanding Thomas Sutpen as "a register of American history," specifically the history of capitalism's complicity with slaveholding. Even more importantly, Porter explains how Faulkner disrupts his own and his readers' most cherished ideological preconceptions and perceptions.

Although this survey has, for the most part, restricted itself to Faulkner scholarship published in English, Michel Gresset's *Faulkner ou la Fascination: Poétique du Regard* makes such an important contribution that its publication in France must be called to the attention of all serious students of Faulkner. Until the English translation is published by Duke University Press in 1989, the conscientious or curious English-speaking reader should at least consult "The 'God' of Faulkner's Fiction" (*Faulkner and Idealism*) in which Gresset rehearses some of the central concerns of his book: "Indeed, the *glance*, by putting the object of desire into a focus, leads to the confusion of the real and the imaginary; it creates a conjunction of desire and want: a sign of all power and powerlessness. As a consequence, it is bound to be the geometric place of that rarest of contradictions which must be called an absolute relationship, and which, in Faulkner's works, is clearly exemplified by the overbearing importance assumed by the phenomenon of fascination." Gresset's innovative book establishes him as among the very best readers (not just one of the best *French* readers) of Faulkner.

In *Three American Originals: John Ford, William Faulkner, and Charles Ives* (Middletown, Conn., 1984), Joseph W. Reed begins with big questions: "what does America do to its artists? what does being American mean to an artist?" His eccentric and suggestive answers emerge through fascinating experiments in comparative biography and cultural history. According to Reed, the films of John Ford, the fiction of William Faulkner, and the music of Charles Ives all engage common values of originality and community and common structures of genre and canon. At the stylistic heart of all three artists' work, Reed finds what he calls *suspension* (not noting that *suspension* happens to be one of Faulkner's favorite words): "The Americans swing between any two qualities, any adjectival epithets, and the suspension in that tethered movement allows for uncertainty of identity." Reed's own thought-provoking essays constitute not so much an argument or even a sustained meditation on suspension and originality, but rather an original and suspended meditation on the place (and displacement) of the artist in America. In "Faulkner's Narrative Styles" (*AL*, Nov. 1981), J. E. Bunselmeyer illustrates some of the uses of speech act theory.

5 Race

a. 1973–1979. Race was not a frequent topic of discussion in Faulkner criticism during the period under review, but valuable comments can be found in Darwin T. Turner's "Faulkner and Slavery" (*The Actual and the Apocryphal*), Marjorie Pryse's *The Mark and the Knowledge: Social Stigma in Classic American Fiction* (Columbus, Ohio, 1979), and Blyden Jackson's two contributions to the proceedings of the first Faulkner and Yoknapatawpha Conference, "Faulkner's Depiction of the Negro" and "Two Mississippi Writers: Wright and Faulkner" (*UMSE*, 1974). Turner's essay sometimes confuses Faulkner with his characters, but it also describes succinctly one important boundary of Faulkner's imagination. Pryse's book examines the role of social stigma in the maintenance of community;

it provides a forceful counterstatement to the idealization of community in much Faulkner criticism. Other studies of some value are George E. Kent's two-part essay, "The Black Woman in Faulkner's Works, with the Exclusion of Dilsey" (*Phylon*, Dec. 1974 and Mar. 1975); Donald A. Petesch's "Faulkner on Negroes: The Conflict Between the Public Man and the Private Art" (*SHR*, Winter 1976); Margaret Walker Alexander's "Faulkner and Race" (*The Maker and the Myth*); and the sometimes rancorous exchange between Darwin T. Turner, Shelby Foote, and Evans Harrington in *The Actual and the Apocryphal*. The period also saw the publication of essays by Lee Jenkins and Walter Taylor that were later incorporated into book-length studies.

b. *1980–1988*. Writing in 1946, Ralph Ellison suggested that Faulkner "explored perhaps more successfully than anyone else, either white or black, certain forms of Negro humanity," and then went on to propose that Faulkner might be "the example for our writers to follow, for in his work technique has been put once more to the task of creating value" (*Shadow and Act*). In *Faulkner's "Negro": Art and the Southern Context* (Baton Rouge, La., 1983), Thadious M. Davis stimulates a responsible and necessary reconsideration of the complex dialectic between verbal strategies and moral imperatives, between techniques and values, in Faulkner's best novels. Davis sees Faulkner's art as an "effort to transcend the tensions and divisions emanating from his cultural heritage, as well as from his position as artist within that culture, that divided world." Looking at the southern context, she observes that "for the southerner of either race, there is usually present the alternative side and the opposite point of view, or simply put, another way of seeing, doing, living, being, thinking." Looking at Faulkner's art, Davis tries to discover "what the Negro reveals about the novels and the process of creating them." Her balanced point of view works to accommodate and to explain the kind of tensions and divisions between art and its contexts that empower Faulkner's techniques and values.

What Davis sees, especially in *The Sound and the Fury* and *Absalom, Absalom!*, frequently startles, if only because earlier critics do not seem to have noticed what her focus makes so obvious and significant. Although Davis insists that she does "not attempt to isolate Faulkner's attitude toward Negro characters and to glean from this his attitude toward black people outside his fiction," she repeatedly evaluates the quality of Faulkner's representations of black experience and "the South's irresponsible and selective morality." Davis wants more realism and more sociology than her New Critical methodology can admit or handle.

Walter Taylor's *Faulkner's Search for a South* (Urbana, Ill., 1983) and Lee Jenkins's *Faulkner and Black-White Relations: A Psychoanalytic Approach* (New York, 1981) both contribute to the important task of reevaluating Faulkner's representations of racial difference. Taylor and Jenkins, however, lack Davis's gifts as a sensitive reader; both have troublesome axes to grind, both want even more realism and sociology than Davis does, and both find considerably less to say about Faulkner's art than Davis. And both express impatience and frustration at not finding what they think they ought to find in Faulkner's black and white fictions. Taylor has written a more interesting account of his frustrations with Faulkner than has Jenkins. Taylor asserts that "the image of 'perfection' Faulkner was seeking was usually—perhaps always—something that could be described as 'the South': some cluster of images, experiences, and fantasies inherited from the world of his youth." Taylor's thesis, however, is not simply that an obsessive search for a South motivates and shapes everything about Faulkner's life and work. He argues, rather, that because the South that Faulkner desires can exist only in imaginings and fantasies about the past, Faulkner refused any unmediated dealings with the *real* South (real, as perceived, but never defined, by Taylor himself), and consequently dooms himself to "a kind of social schizophrenia" and a compulsive pattern of failure (both artistic and moral).

Taylor tries to write an exposé of what he calls Faulkner's "lifelong psycho-drama" in black and white, but suppresses an explicitly psychoanalytic method and vocabulary. Lee Jenkins, as his subtitle announces, intends to take "a psychoanalytic approach" to what he perceives as Faulkner's "fundamental sense of the otherness of blacks." Claiming that "the problem is not one of holding Faulkner to a mimetic representation of reality when such is not his intention," Jenkins admits that he has serious problems with Faulkner's "intention, his narrative technique, and the kind of knowledge it yields." Jenkins would require of Faulkner's imaginative creation a "faithfulness to social and historical reality," at least whenever Jenkins determines that Faulkner should have intended such faithfulness. His contention that Faulkner "distort[s] the reality of black life for his own aesthetic effects," insofar as it insinuates racism, results mostly from his confusion about Faulknerian mimesis and intentionality. Readers like Jenkins and Taylor—and sometimes Davis— remain suspicious of the mysteries of sublimation and creation; they do not like to grant Faulkner his world elsewhere because they cannot quite imagine it. So they look only for whatever actuality they can recognize in Faulkner's apocrypha. For a restatement of Jenkins's views on Faulkner and race, see "Mythic Time and the Shadow Figure in Faulkner" (*CUNY English Forum, Vol. 1*, ed. Saul N. Brody and Harold Schecter, New York, 1985).

Unhappy that other studies of Faulkner and race have been "one-dimensional," Erskine Peters declares that *William Faulkner: The Yoknapatawpha World and Black Being* (Darby, Penn., 1983) "has been designed to be comprehensive": "Every aspect, from his use of imagery to his use of character, must be considered in order to apprehend the whole." Peters, not unlike Davis, begins with the premise that "if we are to undertake a thorough investigation of black being, that is, the realm and essence of black life as it is filtered through the whites in William Faulkner's Yoknapatawpha world, we must first establish a historical and cultural context." But he has less success than Davis in doing so in any meaningful way. Peters's first and last chapters do glance at the contexts, recording bits of the cultural legacy Faulkner inherited and the one that he bequeathed in spite of periodic repudiations. And from beginning to end Peters teases by flashing some intriguing possibilities about Faulkner's literary affinities with Jefferson, Cooper, Cable, Chesnutt, Toomer, Fauset, Wright, O'Connor, Ellison, and Gaines. But he refuses to develop any comparisons; he gives no explanation, no analysis, no extended illustration of the affinities and affiliations he perceives.

None of the books assessed so far remains as committed to a coherent poetics, politics, and ethics of reading as does Eric J. Sundquist's *Faulkner: The House Divided* (Baltimore, Md., 1983). Matthews, in *The Play of Faulkner's Language*, has helped readers to resee Faulkner's language and its play; Sundquist has helped us to reconceive the place of language and the play of art within cultural and political structures. In *Faulkner: The House Divided*, he presents an unusually intense meditation on writing and race, writing and difference. According to Sundquist, Faulkner managed to make something great of his writing only by reassociating himself with the color of his skin, only became an important writer when he admitted within his fictions the burdensome worries and pressures of being white, male, and from Mississippi. "Faulkner's best work," Sundquist claims, "reflects a turbulent search for fictional forms in which to contain and express the ambivalent feelings and projected passions that were his as an author and as an American in the South." His thesis that "Faulkner's career up to *Light in August* might well be considered an extended repression of the Negro" at times seems needlessly reductive, even when allowing, as Sundquist seems to intend, for the full metaphorical implications of the word "figure." He never really persuades us that Faulkner's only genuine subject is always (or should always have been) miscegenation. Always literate and provocative, Sundquist's chapters on *The Sound and the Fury* and *Sanctuary* remain only marginally relevant to his thesis and only partially successful as coherent readings of the novels; and his reading of *As I Lay Dying*, simply by making an eloquent case for the novel's greatness, paradoxically subverts his thesis that genuinely great writing only followed Faulkner's discovery of the theme of miscegenation. For Sundquist, Faulkner discovers the horrors and possibilities of miscegenation in *Light in August*. His formidable chapter on that novel, along with those on *Absalom, Absalom!* and *Go Down, Moses* make *Faulkner: The House Divided* a distinguished contribution to Faulkner studies.

Figures of Division (New York, 1986), by James M. Snead, also attends—with intermittent brilliance—to matters of "style and reality" and argues that "the futility of applying strictly binary categories to human affairs is the main lesson of Faulkner's novels, which dramatize the problematics of division." According to Snead, "Faulkner's challenge to reigning figures of division emerges in a style that mixes and connects entities as much as their social function tends to divide and distinguish them." Through his rereadings of Faulkner's major novels, Snead attempts to illustrate just how "Faulkner's narratives are accurate reconstructions and dismantlings of linguistic and social classifications, proving that some extraordinary human beings struggle against overwhelming odds, to reverse a separation that rhetoric has tried to make into a permanent reality." Not surprisingly, he traces a falling off in Faulkner's mastery of figures of division: "Faulkner in his later years had to strike a difficult balance between experimentation and declamation. In the end, he packaged a self-referential principle of rhetorical complexity to signify value rather than using that complexity to unmask society's betrayals of its self-professed values." Snead seems more comfortable deconstructing Faulkner's style than his cultural realities.

Craig Werner's essay, "Tell Old Pharaoh: The Afro-American Response to Faulkner" (*SoR*, Autumn 1983), rereads Faulkner through the dark and skeptical eyes of Richard Wright, James Baldwin, Toni Morrison, Alice Walker, and several other black writers. Werner finds that "Faulkner is one of the few white writers who adapts aspects of the Afro-American voice, rather than expecting the common language to be essentially Euro-American in structure and content." With careful attention to narrative structures, Werner demonstrates that "in his most profound moments, Faulkner . . . revoices standard Afro-American scenes in terms of Euro-American experience." Acknowledging Faulkner's "limited understanding of Afro-American culture," Werner hears in Faulkner's voice as well as in Afro-American voices responding to Faulkner "a profound statement of the need for a common black-white vocabulary in American literature." Ladell Payne, in *Black Novelists and the Southern Literary Tradition* (Athens, Ga., 1981), emphasizes the common cultural legacies of black and white Southern writers.

Faulkner and Race: Faulkner and Yoknapatawpha, 1986 (ed. Doreen Fowler and Ann J. Abadie, Jackson, Miss., 1987; hereinafter referred to as *Faulkner and Race*) publishes papers delivered at the 1986 Faulkner and Yoknapatawpha Conference and effectively documents the current state of scholarship on this subject, while testifying to the profound need for continued dialogue. The most significant contributions are by Eric J. Sundquist, Philip M. Weinstein, and Thadious M. Davis. In "Faulkner, Race, and the Forms of American Fiction," Sundquist situates Faulkner's canon within the contexts of other novels by blacks and whites that give "clearer voice to black lives and to the cultural traditions of race in America." Brief glances at works ranging from Melville's *Benito Cereno* to Alice Walker's *The Color Purple* enable Sundquist to articulate penetrating questions about some of the "ways in which the central themes of miscegenation, rebellion, sacrificial justice, and gothic histori-cism have found expressive form in some key works of fiction that themselves explore the question of canon," questions, in short, about the "relation between love and literacy."

Weinstein's "Marginalia: Faulkner's Black Lives" brilliantly meditates on "the covert relations between marginal black and central white, the menace the black 'draws off' as well as the central longings it may conceal, the various ways in which Faulkner construes black in order to imagine its intermingling with white, and finally the subliminal images of blackness the reader experiences in the act of absorbing Faulkner's Black Lives." Davis, in "From Jazz Syncopation to Blues Elegy: Faulkner's Development of Black Characterization," moves outside the assumptions of her *Faulkner's "Negro"* and traces Faulkner's cultural borrowings from black music in his styles of characterization, a movement from structures of rhythm (jazz) to structures of emotion (blues). Two other general essays in *Faulkner and Race* also deserve serious attention: Craig Werner's "Minstrel Nightmares: Black Dreams of Faulkner's Dreams of Blacks" and Noel Polk's "Man in the Middle: Faulkner and the Southern White Moderate."

John C. Inscoe shows in "Faulkner, Race, and Appalachia" (*SAQ,* Summer 1987) that "Faulkner owed much to current literary and histor-ical treatments of the Appalachians in his depiction (especially in 'Moun-tain Victory' and *Absalom, Absalom!*) of an exclusively white society which remained free of the stratification and oppression of the plantation South and yet was as racially prejudiced as, if not more so than, any other segment of the South."

Many will disagree with John R. Cooley's assertion in *Savages and Naturals: Black Portraits By White Writers in Modern American Literature* (Newark, Del., 1982) that "Faulkner probably fails to give Dilsey a mind and to record her thoughts because . . . [he] must have felt it necessary to keep Dilsey innocent of history and racial consciousness," and with Cooley's more generalized indictment of Faulkner on the grounds that "he could and should have produced a black character rebellious and verbal enough to anticipate the growing independence and demand for social justice among southern blacks." Even if Cooley's critical voice sounds familiar or tiresome or self-limiting, even if it sounds a bit dated or out of place among the best contemporary dialogue about Faulkner and race, it articulates legitimate and lingering concerns.

6 Gender

a. 1973–1979. Reading the few gender-oriented studies produced in the 1970s offers little intimation of the revolution in criticism that was even then being effected by feminist critics. (An exception is Josephine Donovan's "Feminism and Aesthetics" [*CritI,* Spring 1977], which draws on Faulkner's fiction for examples of undesirable depictions of women.)

The one book on the topic, David Williams's *Faulkner's Women: The Myth and the Muse* (Montreal, 1977), stands in almost polar opposition to current directions in feminist criticism. A Jungian study, the book treats "woman" as "an awesome and wonderful 'otherness'" and Faulkner's fiction as "testimony to the artist's inspiriting encounter with godhead." This approach, which exalts women at the expense of ignoring their real role in society and history, would not be particularly bothersome if it produced valuable insights into the fiction. But unfortunately, as Panthea Reid Broughton says, "Williams's turgid prose so obfuscates whatever insights he may have to offer that we tend to lose them and he us" (*AmLS*, 1977). Furthermore, when Williams argues that Faulkner's later female characters are less interesting than his earlier ones because they are "the end product of feminine individuation," he seems, as Broughton also says, "to be making a moral judgment on [these characters] rather than an aesthetic judgment on Faulkner."

Of the remaining three significant studies (all by women) only one— Annette Kolodny's *The Lay of the Land: Metaphor as Experience and History in American Life and Letters* (Chapel Hill, N.C., 1975)—is founded on a fully articulated feminist theory of literature. In this ground-breaking study, Kolodny applies her understanding of the significance of feminine metaphors for the American landscape to *Go Down, Moses*. The other two studies, Ilse Dusoir Lind's "Faulkner's Women" (*The Maker and the Myth*) and Linda Welshimer Wagner's "Faulkner and (Southern) Women" (*The Actual and the Apocryphal*), emphasize the positive aspects of Faulkner's depictions of women. Lind makes the valuable historical point that Faulkner is the first major American writer to depict "the functioning of the [female] organs of reproduction." Finally, mention should be made here of the chapter entitled "Faulkner's Misogyny" in Albert J. Guerard's *The Triumph of the Novel*.

   b. 1980–1988. Perhaps the best general introduction to the continuing study of questions of gender in Faulkner's art and life is provided by Judith Bryant Wittenberg in "William Faulkner: A Feminist Considera- tion" (*American Novelists Revisited*, ed. Fritz Fleischmann, Boston, 1982). According to Wittenberg, "at least three psychoanalytical precepts are relevant to a feminist assessment of Faulkner's work: the idea that any individual has the potential to contain traits of both sexes, the belief that a person's character is largely formed by his or her early experiences and family relationships, and the concept of projection, of one's 'reality' as constructed out of one's own desires and fears."

   Wittenberg contributes "Faulkner and Women Writers," a paper on Faulkner's possible female precursors, to *Faulkner and Women: Faulkner and Yoknapatawpha, 1985* (ed. Doreen Fowler and Ann J. Abadie, Jackson, Miss., 1986; hereinafter referred to as *Faulkner and Women*). Ilse Dusoir Lind's illuminating "The Mutual Relevance of Faulkner Studies and Women's Studies: An Interdisciplinary Inquiry" appropriately sets the agenda for this collection of papers from the 1985 Faulkner and Yoknapa-tawpha Conference, but the most sophisticated feminist inquiries are provided by John N. Duvall and Philip M. Weinstein. Suggestively juxta-posing work by André Bleikasten, Myra Jehlen, Anne Goodwyn Jones, and Nancy Chodorow, Lind asks that Faulkner criticism become "more self-consciously ideological." Duvall and Weinstein, as if on cue, respond.

Duvall, using the publications of Cleanth Brooks as his main example, argues convincingly that "what the discourse of Faulkner studies so often lacks . . . is a self-reflexivity that would call into question its as-sumptions when speaking about gender." In his eloquent "Faulkner's Critics and Women: The Voice of the Community," Duvall indicts "inter-pretive paternalism . . . within a discourse that privileges 'community' and 'family'" and suggests a way out of "the prisonhouse of masculin-ist ideology" through a "critical historicizing of the interpretive con-text." Weinstein's "Meditations on the Other: Faulkner's Rendering of Women" looks for another way to transcend paternalistic, masculinist discourse: "Faulkner approaches his women differently from his men: only a New Critical insistence on universality, on the work of art as heroically complete in itself, could have blinded us to the differences made by gender. Seen for the most part from outside, deprived both vertically in time and horizontally in space of their own subjective history, Faulkner's women move through their world as 'wonderful' creatures, but considerably handicapped, from a narrative perspective, when com-pared with his men." Weinstein's elegant essay nicely complements—aesthetically *and* ethically (and ideologically)—his "Marginalia: Faulk-ner's Black Lives" (*Faulkner and Race*).

Gail L. Mortimer's *Faulkner's Rhetoric of Loss* should be mentioned again here; Mortimer amplifies some of her perceptions of Faulkner's percep-tions of women and writes sensitively about the significance of urns and liquids in "The Smooth, Suave Shape of Desire: Paradox in Faulknerian Imagery of Women" (*WS*, Nos. 1 and 2, 1986).

Mimi Reisel Gladstein concludes *The Indestructible Woman in Faulkner, Hemingway, and Steinbeck* (Ann Arbor, Mich., 1986) with a rhetorical question: "For men with dependent and self-destructive personalities, longing for a simpler world, woman personifies what he is not, the *other*. The dependent man, then, would project a dependable other; the self-destructive man, an indestructible other. For men who all had terrible bouts with depression, is it not appropriate that the *other* should also serve as a symbol of optimism?" The query raises further questions about the quality of reasoning shaping Gladstein's reading of Faulkner's art and life. Although supposedly revised for publication, *The Indestructible Woman* cannot transcend its origins as a 1973 University of New Mexico dissertation: developments in both feminist criticism and Faulkner scholarship during the past fifteen years have drained Gladstein's study of whatever originality or relevance it may once have possessed.

In *The Southern Belle in the American Novel* (Tampa, Fla., 1985), Kathryn Lee Seidel devotes a brief chapter to "William Faulkner and the Destruction of Narcissus." According to Seidel, "Faulkner's belles are unique because he realizes that the relationship of narcissism, repression, and masochism . . . forms the controlling matrix of the belle's personality." Seidel's book has considerable merit, but—despite some suggestive observations about Cecily in *Soldiers' Pay*, Narcissa in *Sartoris*, Temple Drake in *Sanctuary*, and Caroline Compson in *The Sound and the Fury*—her treatment of women in Faulkner seems weak and sometimes suspect (why, for example, label Caddy Compson a "prostitute"?).

Ellen Douglas's "Faulkner's Women" (*"A Cosmos of My Own"*) is still worth reading. Less well-conceived and less temperate, though still of considerable interest, is Joyce Carol Oates's "'At Least I Have Made a Woman of Her': Images of Women in Twentieth-Century Literature" (*GaR*, Summer 1983). Focusing on *Light in August* and employing a rather naive conception of projection, Oates makes the simplistic assumption that "the distinction between male protagonist and male author is often negligible."

7 Studies of Individual Works

a. Poetry and Early Prose

1973–1979. The short list of items on Faulkner's poetry and early prose is headed by Noel Polk's "William Faulkner's *Marionettes*" (*MissQ*, Summer 1973). Later revised to serve as the introduction to Polk's edition of *The Marionettes*, this essay is a model of literary and historical detective work. Michel Gresset's "Faulkner's 'The Hill'" (*SLJ*, Spring 1974) displays similar scholarly virtues. Gresset subjects the early prose sketch named in his title to a careful, thorough examination and shows that it contains in embryo a number of Faulkner's central themes and motifs. A second essay on "The Hill" in the same journal, Philip Momberger's "A Reading of Faulkner's 'The Hill'" (*SLJ*, Spring 1977), arrives at essentially similar conclusions.

The remaining items in this category consist of three studies published in the annual Faulkner issue of *Mississippi Quarterly*. After fifteen years, Thomas L. McHaney's "The Elmer Papers: Faulkner's Comic Portraits of the Artist" (Summer 1973) remains the best introduction to Faulkner's unpublished early novel and to the short story salvaged from it in the 1930s. (Other valuable comments on the Elmer material can be found in Brooks's *Toward Yoknapatawpha and Beyond*.) The second study, Gail Moore Morrison's "'Time, Tide, and Twilight': *Mayday* and Faulkner's Quest Toward *The Sound and the Fury*" (Summer 1978), is a careful examination of an important precursor to Faulkner's first undisputed masterpiece. The essay should be compared with Carvel Collins's introduction to his edition of *Mayday*, which explores related issues. The final item, Margaret Yonce's "'Shot Down Last Spring': The Wounded Aviators of

Faulkner's Wasteland" (Summer 1978), concentrates primarily on an early poem, "The Lilacs."

1980–1988. Judith L. Sensibar, both in her introduction to *Vision in Spring* and in her companion study *The Origins of Faulkner's Art* (Austin, Tex., 1984), unfortunately exaggerates the importance of this modest fourteen-poem sequence in Faulkner's development. According to Sensibar, studying the forms and voice of *Vision in Spring* "can resolve questions of authorial intention in much of Faulkner's fiction." Despite her conscientious attention to Faulkner's poetry, Sensibar cannot persuade that such resolutions could or should occur. In its best moments, her study can reveal something about the beginnings of Faulkner's writing, but little if anything about the genuine origins of his art. Nonetheless, Sensibar has earned the gratitude of Faulknerians for her responsible editing of *Vision in Spring.* Even if this sequence can never be wholly assimilated into the central Faulkner canon, it commands attention, if only because Faulkner wanted to be a great poet before he wanted to be a great novelist. *The Origins of Faulkner's Art*, it should be noted, contains several intriguing remarks about Faulkner's personal life made by his daughter Jill during a series of private interviews with Sensibar between 1979 and 1983.

Patrick J. Samway, S.J., provides a descriptive account of Faulkner's poetry in "Faulkner's Poetic Vision" (*Southern Renaissance*); Robert W. Hamblin and Louis Daniel Brodsky carefully reconstruct a history of the process through which Faulkner seems to have composed his first published poem in "Faulkner's 'L'Apres-Midi d'un Faune': The Evolution of a Poem" (*SB*, 1980).

Panthea Reid Broughton's "An Amazing Gift: The Early Essays and Faulkner's Apprenticeship in Aesthetics and Criticism" (*New Directions*) authoritatively assesses the gift and apprenticeship described in its title. And it should be remembered that Martin Kreiswirth's *William Faulkner: The Making of a Novelist* responsibly treats some of this apprentice work.

b. Soldiers' Pay

1973–1979. The fullest study of *Soldiers' Pay* to appear in the 1970s is the chapter on the novel in Brooks's *Toward Yoknapatawpha and Beyond.* This richly laden chapter demonstrates convincingly the not-inconsiderable literary merit of Faulkner's first novel. It also shows in precise detail the nature of the novel's indebtedness to Eliot's "The Waste Land," to Joyce's *Ulysses*, and, more generally, to fin de siècle aestheticism. A second historically oriented study, Michael Millgate's "Starting Out in the Twenties: Reflections on *Soldiers' Pay*" (*Mosaic*, Fall 1973), is also rich in insight and information. Less filled with information but still worthy of attention are Philip Castille's "Women and Myth in Faulkner's First Novel" (*TSE*, 1978) and James M. Mellard's "*Soldiers' Pay* and the Growth of Faulkner's Comedy" (*American Humor: Essays Presented to John C. Gerber*, ed. O M Brack, Jr., Scottsdale, Ariz., 1977). A narrowly focused note by Emily K. Dalgarno, "Faulkner and Gibbon: A Note on *Soldiers' Pay*" (*NMW*, Summer 1979), sheds some light on Faulkner's references to *The Decline and Fall of the Roman Empire*. Less valuable, because concerned with inconsequential points of resemblance, is Dalgarno's "*Soldiers' Pay* and Virginia Woolf" (*MissQ*, Summer 1976).

1980–1988. Margaret J. Yonce has written a complex but sound genetic study of the novel: "The Composition of *Soldiers' Pay*" (*MissQ*, Summer 1980); Thomas L. McHaney's "The Modernism of *Soldiers' Pay*" (*WiF*, July 1980) carefully situates Faulkner's first novel within its intellectual and cultural circumstances; and John Earl Bassett, in "*Soldiers' Pay*: Towards a Self-Image of the Artist" (*MarkhamR*, Fall–Winter 1985–1986), approximates Kreiswirth's approach to the novel (in *William Faulkner: The Making of a Novelist*).

c. Mosquitoes

1973–1979. As with *Soldiers' Pay*, the fullest study of *Mosquitoes* to appear in the 1970s is the chapter on the novel in Brooks's *Toward Yoknapatawpha and Beyond*. Although less informative than the chapter on *Soldiers' Pay*, the chapter on *Mosquitoes* nonetheless provides a useful discussion of themes and of the New Orleans background of the action. Brooks's discussion of the theories of art and creativity discussed in the novel should be compared with John T. Irwin's exploration of the same topic in *Doubling and Incest/Repetition and Revenge*. The only other two items of note on *Mosquitoes* are both by Edwin T. Arnold. The first, "Freedom and Stasis in Faulkner's *Mosquitoes*" (*MissQ*, Summer 1975), is a competent thematic study, too often diverted by evaluative questions. The second, "Faulkner and Huxley: A Note on *Mosquitoes* and *Crome Yellow*" (*MissQ*, Summer 1977), lists a considerable number of parallels between the works named in its title.

1980–1988. The most helpful new reading of the novel is probably that of Kreiswirth in *William Faulkner: The Making of a Novelist*, not that of Ilse Dusoir Lind in "Faulkner's *Mosquitoes*: A New Reading" (*WiF*, July 1982), which, despite its title, isn't really new. John Earl Bassett's "Faulkner's *Mosquitoes*: Towards a Self-Image of the Artist" (*SLJ*, Spring 1980) is a readable companion to his piece on *Soldiers' Pay*.

d. Sartoris/Flags in the Dust

1973–1979. Other than the landmark event of the publication of *Flags in the Dust*, little significant work was done during the 1970s on Faulkner's first Yoknapatawpha novel. In "'The Germ of My Apocrypha': *Sartoris* and the Search for Form" (*Mosaic*, Fall 1973), James G. Watson engages in a study that really should have awaited the availability of *Flags in the Dust*. T. H. Adamowski's "Bayard Sartoris: Mourning and Melancholia" (*L&P*, No. 4, 1973) is a good, relatively jargon-free application of Freud's "Mourning and Melancholia" and Otto Fenichel's "Depression and Mania" to *Sartoris*. The few remaining studies, all of *Flags in the Dust*, include Richard P. Adams's review-essay, "At Long Last,

Flags in the Dust" (*SoR*, Fall 1974), which provides a balanced assessment of the novel's literary merits. In the words of Panthea Reid Broughton, Kerry McSweeney's "The Subjective Intensities of Faulkner's *Flags in the Dust"* (*CRevAS*, Fall 1977) "does a great deal to explain the difference between Faulkner's control and his lack of control of his art" (*AmLS*, 1977). The "subjective intensities" mentioned in the title are sexuality and a sense of the past. The final item, Katherine C. Hodgin's "Horace Benbow and Bayard Sartoris: Two Romantic Figures in Faulkner's *Flags in the Dust"* (*AL*, Jan. 1979), explores the Keatsian and Byronic qualities of the characters named in its title.

1980–1988. Arthur F. Kinney's *Critical Essays on William Faulkner: The Sartoris Family* (CEAmL, Boston, 1985; hereinafter referred to as *The Sartoris Family*) pulls together diverse materials relevant to a continuing reassessment of *Sartoris/Flags in the Dust* (as well as *The Unvanquished*, several short stories, and an unproduced film script called *War Birds*): historical backgrounds, comments by Faulkner, documents surrounding the controversial publication histories of *Sartoris* and *Flags in the Dust*, a selection of early reviews, and nineteen critical essays (nine of them written for this volume). Among the new essays, Bruce Kawin's *"War Birds* and the Politics of Refusal" clearly ranks as the best, partly because it encourages a reconsideration of Faulkner's evolving attitudes toward revenge. Also new and of interest are François Pitavy's "'Anything but Earth': The Disastrous and Necessary Sartoris Game" and Andrea Dimino's "The Dream of the Present: Time, Creativity, and the Sartoris Family." Kinney's introduction and his editorial choices try too hard to ground *Sartoris* and the Sartoris family in history and biography and also underestimate Faulkner's compulsively revisionist approaches toward this material. While serious students of *Sartoris/Flags in the Dust* cannot comfortably ignore this anthology, neither can they comfortably trust it.

The textual controversy regarding the novel is reflected in the brief exchange between Thomas L. McHaney and Albert Erskine republished in *The Sartoris Family*. Philip Cohen takes another look at it in "Textual Anomalies in Faulkner's *Flags in the Dust"* (*NMW*, No. 1, 1985). Cohen has published six additional pieces on *Flags in the Dust* within the last few years; all apparently derive from his 1984 University of Delaware dissertation, and all are thoroughly professional contributions to scholarship, although it seems fair to wonder why a few of the pieces could not have been consolidated, and even fairer to ask why Cohen rather fussily refuses to quote from the Random House edition of *Flags in the Dust* available to the reading public. Cohen demonstrates an especially sound sense of French influences on Faulkner and of narrative structures: "Balzac and Faulkner: The Influence of *La Comédie humaine* on *Flags in the Dust* and the Snopes Trilogy" (*MissQ*, Summer 1984); "The Composition of *Flags in the Dust* and Faulkner's Narrative Technique of Juxtaposition" (*JML*, July 1985); "Faulkner's Early Narrative Techniques and *Flags in the Dust*" (*SoSt*, Summer 1985); "The Last Sartoris: Benbow Sartoris' Birth in *Flags in the Dust*" (*SLJ*, Fall 1985); "*Madame Bovary* and *Flags in the Dust*: Flaubert's Influence on Faulkner" (*CLS*, Fall 1985); and "Horace Benbow and Faulkner's Other Failed Idealists" (*SCR*, Spring 1986).

Cohen did not quite hold a monopoly on publications on *Flags in the Dust*. Pamela E. Rhodes, in her provocative essay, "Who Killed Simon Strother, and Why? Race and Counterplot in *Flags in the Dust*" (*Faulkner and Race*), shows that "in the jarring of the two modes in which he presents [Simon Strother]—the comic stereotype and the more complexly independent figure who pursues opportunities for self-definition—Faulkner is engaged with a problem of characterization and style that derives directly from his problems in confronting social change." John Earl Bassett examines family structures in "Faulkner, Sartoris, Benbow: Shifting Conflict in *Flags in the Dust*" (*SoSt*, Spring 1981); in a pair of articles, Linda E. McDaniel evaluates the presence of Keats in *Flags in the Dust*: "Horace Benbow: Faulkner's Endymion" (*MissQ*, Summer 1980) and "Keats's Hyperion Myth: A Source for the Sartoris Myth" (*MissQ*, Summer 1981). Also worth mentioning are Nancy Drew Taylor's "Moral Housecleaning and Colonel Sartoris's Dream" (*MissQ*, Summer 1984) and Dexter Westrum's "Faulkner's Sense of Twins and the Code: Why Young Bayard Died" (*ArQ*, Winter 1984).

e. The Sound and the Fury

1973–1979. In the first edition of *Sixteen Modern American Authors*, James B. Meriwether noted "the continuing proliferation of article-length studies [of *The Sound and the Fury*]" and asked "when will we have a full-scale, comprehensive study of the book which will bring together and integrate the results of forty years of critical comment and scholarly investigation?" Meriwether's question was answered in 1976, with the appearance of André Bleikasten's *The Most Splendid Failure: Faulkner's "The Sound and the Fury"* (Bloomington, Ind.). Like Irwin's *Doubling and Incest/Repetition and Revenge*, this fine study helped to open Faulkner criticism to contemporary directions in literary theory. By discussing Caddy's absence as a "primal gap" that the Compson brothers try either to heal or to obscure, Bleikasten anticipates later deconstructive and Lacanian readings of the novel. Unlike some of these readings, though, Bleikasten combines his interest in contemporary theory with an accessible style, a scrupulous regard for the text, a full knowledge of prior criticism, and a fine sense of literary nuance. After twelve years, one sees areas where the book could be improved—most notably in its treatment of Quentin Compson, which is oddly moralistic, and in its discussion of the novel's language, especially the Reverend Shegog's sermon. (As is the case with much psychoanalytically based work of the 1970s, the book would also benefit from a less exclusive emphasis on Oedipal patterns of development.) The book's deficiencies are minor, though, in comparison with its many virtues. It remains the one indispensable study of *The Sound and the Fury*.

The list of good articles on *The Sound and the Fury* is headed by a series of stylistic studies. In the first two, "The 'Loud World' of Quentin Compson" (*SNNTS*, Summer 1975) and "Jason Compson and Sut Lovingood: Southwestern Humor as Stream of Consciousness" (*SNNTS*, Fall 1976), Stephen M. Ross begins his searching, theoretically sophisticated study—soon to culminate in a book entitled *Fiction's Inexhaustible Voice*—of voice as theme and technique in Faulkner's fiction. In "Quentin's Tunnel Vision: Modes of Perception and Their Stylistic Realization in *The Sound and the Fury*" (*L&P*, No. 1, 1977), Judith Slater demonstrates the relation between imagery, syntax, and Quentin Compson's habitual patterns of perception. A more narrowly focused study, Roger Ramsey's "Light Imagery in *The Sound and the Fury*: April 7, 1928" (*JNT*, Winter 1976), traces the association between images of light and experiences of death and loss in the first section of the novel. Also of value is the chapter (a seminal reader-response study) on *The Sound and the Fury* in Wolfgang Iser's *The Implied Reader: Patterns of Communication in Prose Fiction from Bunyan to Beckett* (Baltimore, Md., 1974). One comes away from this body of work, and from similar later studies, with the sense that the topic of the novel's style is far from exhausted.

Other articles on the novel pursue a variety of emphases. Douglas B. Hill, Jr.'s "Faulkner's Caddy" (*CRevAs*, Spring 1976), a scrupulous character study, anticipates later gender-oriented criticism. Another study focused on Caddy, Boyd Davis's "Caddy Compson's Eden" (*MissQ*, Summer 1977), explores mythic and literary associations of the garden and tree imagery in the novel and in Faulkner's early fiction. In "Profane Time, Sacred Time, and Confederate Time in *The Sound and the Fury*" (*SAF*, Autumn 1974), Arthur Geffen explores the varieties of time named in his title ("profane time" is northern, liberal, progressive time) and concludes that the Compson family is imprisoned in confederate time. In pursuit of his argument, Geffen engages in a forced attempt to associate the dates in the novel with significant dates in southern history. Also of value are Wayne W. Westbrook's "Jason Compson and the Costs of Speculation: A Second Look" (*MissQ*, Summer 1977) and Mary Jane Dickerson's "'The Magician's Wand': Faulkner's Compson Appendix" (*MissQ*, Summer 1975). Westbrook's brief note clarifies some puzzling aspects of Jason Compson's cotton market speculations. Although tendentious and overly long, Dickerson's essay offers an informative reading of the Compson Appendix as a semi-autonomous work of fiction, showing how it is related to the other work Faulkner was doing in the 1940s.

A few other items deserve mention. Philip M. Weinstein's "Caddy *Disparue*: Exploring an Episode Common to Proust and Faulkner" (*CLS*, Mar. 1976) is a well-written comparative study. John L. Longley, Jr.'s

"'Who Never Had a Sister': A Reading of *The Sound and the Fury*" (*Mosaic*, Fall 1973) suffers from attempting too much in too brief a compass. Douglas Messerli's "The Problem of Time in *The Sound and the Fury*: A Critical Reassessment and Reinterpretation" (*SLJ*, Spring 1974) reviews past discussions of the theme of time and proposes an alternative based on the work of Eugene Minkowski. Three other studies—M. D. Faber's "Faulkner's *The Sound and the Fury*: Object Relations and Narrative Structure" (*AI*, Winter 1977); Charles D. Peavy's "'If I Just Had a Mother': Faulkner's Quentin Compson" (*L&P*, No. 3, 1973); and J. C. Cowan's "Dream-Work in the Quentin Section of *The Sound and the Fury*" (*L&P*, No. 3, 1974)—approach the novel from traditional psychoanalytic perspectives and arrive at predictable conclusions. Finally, David Minter's "Faulkner, Childhood, and the Making of *The Sound and the Fury*" (*AL*, Nov. 1979) anticipates arguments developed more fully in *William Faulkner: His Life and Work*.

1980–1988. With the exception of John T. Matthews's chapter, "The Discovery of Loss in *The Sound and the Fury*" (*The Play of Faulkner's Language*), it is surprisingly hard to find unequivocally first-rate work on *The Sound and the Fury* since 1980. Critics have seemed unusually slow and cautious about moving beyond André Bleikasten's 1976 benchmark—and temporarily, at least, preemptive—study, *The Most Splendid Failure*. One suspects, indeed hopes, that some major revisionist readings are (over-)due. Elegant and impressive as Bleikasten's accomplishment may remain, it surely does not pretend to be the last word on *The Sound and the Fury*. Bleikasten himself takes a retrospective look at the novel in his edition of the Garland Critical Casebook, *William Faulkner's "The Sound and the Fury"* (New York, 1982), but it would probably be unrealistic—and ungenerous—to expect that he should be the one to point the ways beyond *The Most Splendid Failure*. His introduction to this casebook is characteristically graceful, but not much of a departure for him. The most useful essay in the collection—and the only other new one—also looks back: Gail M. Morrison's "The Composition of *The Sound and the Fury*." Reprinted essays by Stephen M. Ross, François Pitavy, and Margaret Blanchard are quite good, but tend to isolate fragments of the novel; no real attempt is made to place the novel in Faulkner's canon, let alone to question its canonicity.

Arthur F. Kinney's *Critical Essays on William Faulkner: The Compson Family* (CEAmL, Boston, 1982; hereinafter referred to as *The Compson Family*), like his companion volume on the Sartoris family, pulls together an assortment of materials—statements from Faulkner, early reviews, a short story called "Candace," and twenty-three critical essays (only three of which are new). Most of the materials concern *The Sound and the Fury*, although *Absalom, Absalom!* and a few short stories are included. A new essay by Donald M. Kartiganer, "Quentin Compson and Faulkner's Drama of the Generations," commands respect and represents, at least implicitly, an attractive alternative to John Irwin's version of Freud's Oedipal paradigm. Essays by Millgate, Gresset, and John Hagopian remain important but sound dated.

Two essays by James M. Mellard sound current, but both employ jargon-inhibited paradigms to enforce basically sentimental readings of *The Sound and the Fury*. In *The Exploded Form: The Modernist Novel in America* (Urbana, Ill., 1980), Mellard says that "the first three sections of *The Sound and the Fury* are only modes of presentation generated through *imitations* of the features of drama, lyric, and epic within the definite limitations of prose fiction" and insists that "Faulkner explodes the assumption that differences in content somehow finally cause the differences in mode." And in "Faulkner's *Commedia*: Synecdoche and Anagogic Symbolism in *The Sound and the Fury*" (*JEGP*, Oct. 1984), Mellard claims that "it is Dilsey . . . who is the synecdochic image embodying the anagogic meaning and form of the novel, for it is she who contains the whole range of experience—plenitude and vacancy, comedy and tragedy—presented in *The Sound and the Fury*." Bernhard Radloff, in a pair of fairly dense but rewarding essays, uses Heidegger to help reconceptualize Faulknerian notions of time: "Time and Time-Field: The Structure of Anticipation and Recollection in the Quentin Section of *The Sound and the Fury*" (*DR*, Spring 1985) and "The Unity of Time in *The Sound and the Fury*" (*FJ*, Spring 1986). See also John C. Hampsey's "Checking in on Time in *The Sound and the Fury*" (*ArQ*, Summer 1987). Julie M. Johnson suggests in "The Theory of Relativity in Modern Literature: An Overview and *The Sound and the Fury*" (*JML*, June 1983) that popularized distortions of Einstein's theory find their way to Quentin's Harvard in 1909–10 and inform the novel's discourses about space and time.

Thadious Davis's rereading of *The Sound and the Fury* in *Faulkner's "Negro"* reveals how the entire Gibson family, not just Dilsey, "serve[s] structural, thematic, and symbolic functions." It revoices Faulkner's text, making the Gibsons, especially Luster, much more audible (that is, more visible and legible, more meaningful) than they may have been for many readers—at least many *white* readers—until now. Stephen M. Ross extends his excellent studies of Faulknerian voices in "Rev. Shegog's Powerful Voice" (*FJ*, Fall 1985); François L. Pitavy reflects on Benjy's voice in "Idiocy and Idealism: A Reflection on the Faulknerian Idiot" (*Faulkner and Idealism*). May Cameron Brown listens attentively to Quentin's voice in "The Language of Chaos: Quentin Compson in *The Sound and the Fury*" (*AL*, Jan. 1980) and Linda W. Wagner reconsiders the apparent voicelessness of Caddy in "Language and Act: Caddy Compson" (*SLJ*, Spring 1982). John Earl Bassett analyzes domestic structures in "Family Conflict in *The Sound and the Fury*" (*SAF*, Spring 1981); Austin M. Wright tries to use *The Sound and the Fury* as an example of what he calls a "Disclosure Plot" in *The Formal Principle in the Novel* (Ithaca, N.Y., 1982);

and John J. Conder tries to force the novel into a naturalist mold in *Naturalism in American Fiction: The Classic Phase* (Lexington, Ky., 1984).

f. *As I Lay Dying*

1973–1979. As with *The Sound and the Fury*, the list of significant work on *As I Lay Dying* is headed by a book by André Bleikasten. A translation of a study first published in France in 1970, *Faulkner's "As I Lay Dying"* (Bloomington, Ind., 1973) displays its author's characteristic virtues of subtlety, literary sensitivity, and freedom from dogmatism. It devotes thorough and judicious chapters to sources, language and style, techniques, character, setting, themes, and critical reception. If the book is not as indispensable as *The Most Splendid Failure*, this is so for two reasons. First, it still shows traces of its original purpose, of serving the needs of French students of the novel; the chapter on language and style, for example, is more an introduction to southern country idioms than a study of the novel's style. Second, and more importantly, at this stage in his career Bleikasten seems not to have acquired a theoretical frame of reference adequate to the quality of his insights. He sees that *As I Lay Dying* cannot be confined within a single genre and that it evades assimilation by either "humanist or antihumanist ideologies"; but he does not locate these refusals and evasions in the deconstructive and Barthesian frame of reference of his later work, a context that allows them to be understood as having large cultural, philosophical, and aesthetic implications.

In another resemblance to *The Sound and the Fury*, the good article-length work on *As I Lay Dying* is headed by a number of studies of style, two of them by Stephen M. Ross. The first of Ross's studies, "Shapes of Time and Consciousness in *As I Lay Dying*" (*TSLL*, Winter 1975), is a convincing rejoinder to R. W. Franklin's claim, in "Narrative Management in *As I Lay Dying*" (*MFS*, Spring 1967), that Faulkner lost control of verb tense in the novel. Ross shows how Faulkner uses variations in tense to indicate changes in the degree of engagement of the narrators with the material they narrate. Ross's second study, "'Voice' in Narrative Texts: The Example of *As I Lay Dying*" (*PMLA*, Mar. 1979), is a major contribution to his continuing exploration of the concept of voice in Faulkner's fiction. Distinguishing between "mimetic" and "textual" voice, Ross shows how Faulkner problematizes representational notions of voice in *As I Lay Dying*.

Three other studies add to our understanding of the novel's style. In "Yoknapatawphan Baroque: A Stylistic Analysis of *As I Lay Dying*" (*Style*, Spring 1973), E. Pauline Degenfelder uses an analytic method derived from Francis Christensen's rhetorical studies and from transformational grammar to dissect the novel's two main styles, which she calls "baroque" and "colloquial." In "Perception, Language, and Reality in *As I Lay Dying*" (*ArQ*, Spring 1976), Joseph M. Garrison uses a close analysis of language to demonstrate how Darl fails to distinguish between "those perceptual faculties which tyrannize and those which liberate." His comments have implications for our understanding of the novel as a whole. In "William Faulkner, Addie Bundren, and Language" (*UMSE*, 1975 [published 1978]; also *Essays in Poetics*, 1978), Richard Godden engages in a philosophically rich demonstration of the inadequacy of Addie Bundren's separation of words and doing as a model for Faulkner's understanding of language.

The studies of theme, structure, and historical backgrounds that appeared in the 1970s are not of much interest. In "Darl Bundren's 'Cubistic' Vision" (*TSLL*, Spring 1977), Watson G. Branch explains the peculiarities of Darl's character as effects of his wartime experiences in France, which are presumed to include an exposure to cubism. This essay is an extreme example of the need, evinced by many critics, to confine the novel within a representational frame of reference. Equally eager to save the novel for mimesis are Charles Palliser's "Fate and Madness: The Determinist Vision of Darl Bundren" (*AL*, Jan. 1978) and George Rooks's "Vardaman's Journey in *As I Lay Dying*" (*ArQ*, Summer 1979). Palliser argues that "Darl's apparent 'second sight' . . . is nothing more nor less than the exercise of intuition . . . combined with an . . . all-pervasive acceptance of determinism"; Rooks traces Vardaman's supposed psychological deterioration. A richer representational study, because it is based on an intimate knowledge of southern burial customs, is Floyd C. Watkins's "*As I Lay Dying*: The Dignity of Earth," in his *In Time and Place: Some Origins of American Fiction* (Athens, Ga., 1977). Finally, notice should be given here of Calvin Bedient's "Pride and Nakedness: *As I Lay Dying*" (*MLQ*, Mar. 1965). Overlooked in previous versions of this survey, Bedient's essay offers a brilliant discussion of the "defamiliarizing" qualities of the novel. By honoring Faulkner's refusal to provide either "a moral or a morality," Bedient has written a landmark study.

1980–1988. "Death, Grief, and Analogous Form: *As I Lay Dying*," in Eric J. Sundquist's *Faulkner: The House Divided*, clearly represents the best new work on the novel; it is a breathtaking piece of analysis, even if it seems to compromise the thesis of Sundquist's book. Nearly as stunning and well worth comparing with Sundquist's piece, despite a certain tendency toward the precious and pretentious, is Ann Leclercle-Sweet's "The Chip and the Chink: The Dying of the 'I' in *As I Lay Dying*" (*FJ*, Fall 1986). Robert Dale Parker's chapter in *Faulkner and the Novelistic Imagination*, "Something Secret and Selfish: *As I Lay Dying*," also impresses, but in a very different way; it commonsensically addresses frequent misreadings of the novel, opening a space for rereading.

Dixie M. Turner's monograph, *A Jungian Psychoanalytic Interpretation of William Faulkner's "As I Lay Dying"* (Washington, D.C., 1981), is an amateurish and reductive application of Jungian archetypes to the Bundren family and should be ignored. Diane L. Cox's Garland Casebook,

William Faulkner's "As I Lay Dying" (New York, 1985), is a thoroughly professional and discriminating collection of essays and should be consulted for Cox's well-informed introduction and annotated critical bibliography, as well as for such classic essays as Calvin Bedient's "Pride and Nakedness in *As I Lay Dying*" (1965) and Stephen M. Ross's "Shapes of Time and Consciousness in *As I Lay Dying*" (1975). Still, one wishes that Cox had chosen even more varied approaches (her choices focus mostly on matters of style and characterization) and had been more forthcoming about the publishing history of the essays (apparently only essays by Gail Moore Morrison and Catherine Patten are new).

Fred Miller Robinson reads *As I Lay Dying* quite well in *The Comedy of Language* (Amherst, Mass., 1980), although he pays attention, despite his book's title, to the social rather than linguistic sources and shapes of comedy in *As I Lay Dying*. Less convincing is Patricia M. Schroeder's "The Comic World of *As I Lay Dying*" (*Faulkner and Humor*). John Tucker locates the novel within currents of modernism in "William Faulkner's *As I Lay Dying*: Working Out the Cubistic Bugs" (*TSLL*, Winter 1984); while John T. Matthews, in both "Intertextuality and Originality: Hawthorne, Faulkner, and Updike" (*Intertextuality*) and "'The Word as Scandal': Updike's *A Month of Sundays*" (*ArQ*, Winter 1983), locates *As I Lay Dying* within a tradition of writing about adultery going back to Christ's cryptic tracings on the ground in the New Testament. Like Matthews, Kiyoyuki Ono, in "Faulkner and History: *As I Lay Dying* and *The Scarlet Letter*" (*WiF*, Apr. 1985), sees the presence of Hawthorne in Faulkner's text. Charles Palliser's "Predestination and Freedom in *As I Lay Dying*" (*AL*, Dec. 1986) stands as one of the best studies of Faulkner's uses of Calvinism.

Three complementary studies look at the significances of eyes and vision in *As I Lay Dying*: Michiko Yoshida's poetic "The Act of Looking in *As I Lay Dying*" (McHaney); Robert J. Kloss's "Addie Bundren's Eyes and the Difference They Make" (*SCR*, Fall 1981); and François L. Pitavy's "Through Darl's Eyes Darkly: The Vision of the Poet in *As I Lay Dying*" (*WiF*, July 1982). Although too long and repetitious, Patrick O'Donnell's "The Spectral Road: Metaphors of Transference in Faulkner's *As I Lay Dying*" (*PLL*, Winter 1984) has something important to say about "the ironic and complex metaphorical motions of the novel" and how they "define its subject as a reflection upon the meaning of both funereal and metaphorical journeys." Wesley Morris also says something important about *As I Lay Dying* in "The Irrepressible Real: Jacques Lacan and Poststructuralism" (*American Criticism in the Poststructuralist Age*, ed. Ira Konigsberg, Ann Arbor, Mich., 1981).

Psychoanalytically inclined readers will find points of interest in T. H. Adamowski's "'Meet Mrs. Bundren': *As I Lay Dying*—Gentility, Tact, and Psychoanalysis" (*UTQ*, Spring 1980); Melvin Backman's "Addie Bundren and William Faulkner" (Carey); Robert J. Kloss's "Faulkner's *As I Lay Dying"* (*AI*, Winter 1981); and David Kleinbard's *"As I Lay Dying*: Literary Imagination, the Child's Mind, and Mental Illness" (*SoR*, Winter 1986). Like some of his other work on Faulkner's representations of families, John Earl Bassett's *"As I Lay Dying*: Family Conflict and Verbal Fictions" (*JNT*, Spring 1981) limits itself through some questionable biographical and psychological assumptions.

Other dimensions of verbal fictions in *As I Lay Dying* are studied by Constance Pierce in "Being, Knowing, and Saying in the 'Addie' Section of Faulkner's *As I Lay Dying"* (*TCL*, Fall 1980); by Linda Mathews in "Shaping the Life of Man: Darl Bundren as Supplementary Narrator in *As I Lay Dying"* (*JNT*, Fall 1986); by Frederik N. Smith in "Telepathic Diction: Verbal Repetition in *As I Lay Dying"* (*Style*, Spring 1985); by William Rodney Allen in "The Imagist and Symbolist Views of the Function of Language: Addie and Darl Bundren in *As I Lay Dying"* (*SAF*, Autumn 1982); and by Judith Lockyer in "Language and the Process of Narration in Faulkner's *As I Lay Dying"* (*ArQ*, Summer 1987).

g. Sanctuary

1973–1979. Faulkner's sixth novel received almost no important attention during the period under review. An exception is T. H. Adamowski's "Faulkner's Popeye: The 'Other' as Self" (*CRevAs*, Spring 1977), a philosophically and psychologically sophisticated study of Popeye's role in the novel. Also of value, Donald A. Petesch's "Temple Drake: Faulkner's Mirror for the Social Order" (*SAF*, Spring 1979) examines the social symbolism of Temple's behavior. Although Petesch says that Faulkner is judging society, not Temple, some of his comments blur this distinction. Two other studies, James E. Miller, Jr.'s *"Sanctuary*: Yoknapatawpha's Waste Land" (*Individual and Community: Variations on a Theme in American Fiction*, ed. Kenneth H. Baldwin and David K. Kirby, Durham, N.C., 1975) and Calvin S. Brown's *"Sanctuary*: From Confrontation to Peaceful Void" (*Mosaic*, Fall 1973), are competent but explore familiar ground. Finally, Linda Kauffman's "The Madam and the Midwife: Reba Rivers and Sairey Gamp" (*MissQ*, Summer 1977) suggests some interesting parallels between *Sanctuary* and *Martin Chuzzlewit*.

1980–1988. J. Douglas Canfield sorts the essays he has selected for *Twentieth Century Interpretations of "Sanctuary"* (TCI, Englewood Cliffs, N.J., 1982) into sociological, psychological, imagistic, mythopoeic, and structuralist categories. Five of the eleven essays were published before 1970 and have been superseded in one way or another; in fact, in light of the approaches to *Sanctuary* to be evaluated here, only two of Canfield's choices seem of permanent value—Thomas L. McHaney's classic *"Sanctuary* and Frazer's Slain Kings" (1971) and Philip M. Weinstein's "Precarious Sanctuaries: Protection and Exposure in Faulkner's Fiction" (1978)—and, like all the essays in the volume, even these are compromised by ruthless editing.

In "The Space between *Sanctuary"* (*Intertextuality*), Noel Polk explores

Faulkner's writing and rewriting of what he called his "most horrific tale," as well as the extraordinary significance of Faulkner's literary accomplishments in the eighteen months (1929–30) between the two versions of *Sanctuary*. Polk makes a persuasive case "that the first *Sanctuary* is, at least for the time being, in so many ways a more interesting book than the second, and that taken together, in their inter- and intratextual relationships with each other and with the other novels and stories in the space between, the two versions form a single literary text that is far more significant than either of the versions taken singly. We cannot now pretend to understand either *Sanctuary* without also coming to terms with the other." Polk also makes use of Freud, especially the "Wolf Man" case history, to help explain how and why *Sanctuary* was originally about Horace Benbow rather than about Temple Drake. In a companion essay, "Law in Faulkner's *Sanctuary*" (*MCLR*, Spring 1984), Polk again uses Freud, demonstrating the centrality of the Oedipus complex to *Sanctuary*'s representations of authority, sexuality, and guilt.

John T. Matthews's "The Elliptical Nature of *Sanctuary*" (*Novel*, Spring 1984) accepts Polk's judgment that the two versions should be treated as a single text. Matthews, in probably the most original and impressive contemporary study of the novel, discloses that "the figure of ellipsis pervades the rhetorical, psychological, narrative, and thematic structures of *Sanctuary*." He generates his dense, highly theoretical argument through close textual analysis, powerfully sustaining his thesis that "the text's elliptical texture indicates the unrepresentability of the passage from nature to culture, from mating to the family, from lawlessness to social organization." Matthews nicely explains just how "Temple's story is an elaborate transmogrification of Horace's story," and just how "the two plots of the story, like the two versions of the novel, are more intimately related than earlier criticism has granted." Two essays by André Bleikasten on *Sanctuary* also deserve to be read carefully. One illuminates the shadowy presence of "Emma Bovary's Ghost in *Sanctuary*" (*Intertextuality*); the other studies the language of the body in the novel, reveals "terror and nausea exorcised in the very act of writing" ("Terror and Nausea: Bodies in *Sanctuary*" [*FJ*, Fall 1985]), and should be compared with Terry Heller's "Terror and Empathy in Faulkner's *Sanctuary*" (*ArQ*, Winter 1984). George Toles's "'The Space Between': A Study of Faulkner's *Sanctuary*" (*TSLL*, Spring 1980) should be compared with, but not confused with, Polk's similarly titled—and superior—essay.

Joseph R. Urgo believes that *Sanctuary* is "a novel concerned with the forms of human interaction and the limits of responsibility," and urges a somewhat more sympathetic reconsideration of Temple's victimization in "Temple Drake's Truthful Perjury: Rethinking Faulkner's *Sanctuary*" (*AL*, Oct. 1983). Diane Luce Cox and Elisabeth Muhlenfeld agree with Urgo that Temple deserves a fresh look: Muhlenfeld's "Bewildered Witness: Temple Drake in *Sanctuary*" (*FJ*, Spring 1986) persuades more than

Cox's "A Measure of Innocence in *Sanctuary*" (*MissQ*, Summer 1986). And, finally, see John Earl Bassett's "*Sanctuary*: Personal Fantasies and Social Fictions" (*SCR*, Fall 1981), as well as Parker's chapter on *Sanctuary* in *Faulkner and the Novelistic Imagination*.

h. Light in August

1973–1979. The 1970s saw the publication of two important books on *Light in August*. The first, François Pitavy's *Faulkner's "Light in August"* (Bloomington, Ind., 1973), was originally published in France in conjunction with André Bleikasten's *Faulkner's "As I Lay Dying."* Like Bleikasten's book, Pitavy's is thorough, sensitive to nuance, and knowledgeable about prior work on the novel. Individual chapters are devoted to structure and technique, character, setting, theme, style, and critical reception; the study is particularly strong on the novel's language and imagery. The book shows its age, though, in the amount of time Pitavy spends defending *Light in August* against negative criticism. Also, his central argument is not convincing. He promotes Gail Hightower to an unwarranted position of prominence, and he sees in Hightower's final moments (in contrast to most contemporary readings) an unequivocal endorsement of compassion and love.

The second book, Regina K. Fadiman's *Faulkner's "Light in August": A Description and Interpretation of the Revisions* (Charlottesville, Va., 1975), is a careful, detailed study whose purpose is sufficiently described in its title. Because of gaps in the textual history, Fadiman is forced to function more as a detective than as a bibliographical critic. Fortunately, she is a good one. On the basis of such evidence as paper thickness, ink color, and the sequences of crossed-out page numbers, she constructs a hypothesis as to the genesis of the novel. In her view, Faulkner first wrote a present-tense narrative focusing on Byron Bunch, Lena Grove, and Gail Hightower. When he saw the importance of Joe Christmas (a minor figure in this narrative), he wrote the long flashback account of Christmas's life. Too speculative ever to compel more than qualified assent, Fadiman's argument is nonetheless plausible and well-presented.

Several important essays also appeared during the period under review. Walter E. Johnston's "The Shepherdess in the City" (*CL*, Spring 1974) displays the benefits of bringing a broad knowledge of prior literature to bear on Faulkner's novel. Johnston's study of *Light in August*, Robert Musil's "Tonka," and Joyce's *Ulysses* in the context of Virgilian and Wordsworthian pastoralism is especially convincing in its analysis of the tonal complexity of Faulkner's opening presentation of Lena Grove. Franklin G. Burroughs, Jr.'s "God the Father and Motherless Children: *Light in August*" (*TCL*, July 1973) is one of the better attempts to claim that the novel is unified at the level of theme; Burroughs sees the heart of the novel as a struggle between a masculine, Manichaean religiosity and a feminine, subversive eroticism. C. Hugh Holman's "Faulkner's August Avatars," in his *Windows on the World: Essays on*

American Social Fiction (Knoxville, Tenn., 1979), provides a good discussion of the novel's modernist qualities. Overly long and uneven, R. G. Collins's "*Light in August*: Faulkner's Stained Glass Triptych" (*Mosaic*, Fall 1973) argues that the novel's three plots offer three views of life in the contemporary South. Finally, Ilse Dusoir Lind's "Apocalyptic Vision as Key to *Light in August*" (*SAF*, Autumn 1975) argues with perhaps excessive assurance that *Light in August* was influenced by Jewish and Christian apocalyptic writings.

Some brief studies add to our factual knowledge regarding the novel. Useful, but not free of error, Sally Padgett Wheeler's "Chronology in *Light in August*" (*SLJ*, Fall 1973) should be supplemented with Stephen Meats's "The Chronology of *Light in August*" (*William Faulkner's "Light in August": A Critical Casebook*, ed. François Pitavy, New York, 1982; see below). Also concerned with chronology is Cleanth Brooks's "When Did Joanna Burden Die?: A Note" (*SLJ*, Fall 1973), which appears in expanded form in *Toward Yoknapatawpha and Beyond*. In "Faulkner's Small Debt to Dos Passos: A Source for the Percy Grimm Episode" (*MissQ*, Summer 1974), Don Graham and Barbara Shaw make a convincing case for the influence of an early version of a scene in *1919* on Faulkner's novel. Jackson W. Heimer's "Faulkner's Misogynous Novel: *Light in August*" (*BSUF*, Summer 1973) broaches an important topic, but in a reductive and unconvincing way.

1980–1988. Two recent anthologies of criticism help establish the important problems now facing students of *Light in August*. François Pitavy has edited and introduced the Garland Critical Casebook, *William Faulkner's "Light in August"* (New York, 1982), and Michael Millgate has edited and introduced *New Essays on "Light in August"* for the new Cambridge series on the American novel (New York, 1987). Given the distinguished accomplishments of both editors and the high standards of both series, it is especially disappointing to report that neither anthology is as good as it should be. There are no new essays in this Garland Casebook (although Pitavy's introduction is fresh and helpful and Stephen Meats provides an appended chronology); the twelve essays were originally published between 1949 and 1980, most in the 1970s; the best are by Pitavy, Donald M. Kartiganer, and Carole Anne Taylor, who analyzes problems of language and self-knowledge in "*Light in August*: The Epistemology of Tragic Paradox" (*TSLL*, Spring 1980).

The Cambridge essays are, of course, all new, but none of them really offers the kind of revisionary reading *Light in August* so clearly deserves. Millgate's introduction is characteristically well-informed and well-expressed, but his essay, "'A Novel: Not an Anecdote': Faulkner's *Light in August*," never catches fire; neither does Martin Kreiswirth's competent "Plots and Counterplots: The Structure of *Light in August*." In the collection's most thought-provoking piece, "*Light in August*: The Closed Society and Its Subjects," André Bleikasten interrogates some assumptions about Faulkner and community inherited from Cleanth Brooks. Neither Judith Bryant Wittenberg's "The Women of *Light in August*" nor Alexander Welsh's "On the Difference between Prevailing and Enduring" stimulate as much rethinking as they could.

Aside from the relevant chapters of Eric J. Sundquist's *Faulkner: The House Divided* and Walter Taylor's *Faulkner's Search for a South* (both illuminating readings of Joe Christmas constitute the high points of their respective books), the most stimulating new piece on *Light in August* may be John N. Duvall's "Murder and the Communities: Ideology In and Around *Light in August*" (*Novel*, Winter 1987). Duvall asks what it means to say that Joe Christmas murders Joanna Burden (and McEachern) because he wants readers to be more self-conscious about their implicit ideologies, wants the interpretive communities to avoid replicating the racist (and sexist) ideology of Jefferson. Any critic who rigorously pursues Duvall's interrogation of communal ideologies in the novel and its criticism will resist Doreen Fowler's neat formulation that "Faulkner's message" in *Light in August* is that, "however attractive the darkness of solitude and alienation may seem, human beings have a responsibility to admit the light. Only by actively participating in the human community can we build a public world that will nurture rather than maim life." Fowler's assertion, in "Faulkner's *Light in August*: A Novel in Black and White" (*ArQ*, Winter 1984), results from her "effort to find a consistent pattern of meaning" in the novel's light and dark imagery. Her "Joe Christmas and 'Womanshenegro'" (*Faulkner and Women*) takes a complementary approach to another configuration of imagery.

According to Harold Hungerford, in "Past and Present in *Light in August*" (*AL*, May 1983), "the time-scheme, and the characters' perception of their relationship to and responsibility for the past, *are* the moral structure." Whether or not this is necessarily so, Timothy P. Martin's "The Art and Rhetoric of Chronology in Faulkner's *Light in August*" (*CollL*, Spring 1980) makes an important contribution to our understanding of time in *Light in August*; so does Hungerford's article. And so, in a different way, does Eileen T. Bender, in "Faulkner as Surrealist: The Persistence of Memory in *Light in August*" (*SLJ*, Fall 1985).

Arnold Weinstein's "Fusion and Confusion in *Light in August*" (*FJ*, Spring 1986) deserves a serious reading; according to Weinstein, "ultimately *Light in August* is a peculiarly seasonal Passion Play, a spectacular meditation on what lives and what dies, what is separate and what is connected." James Leo Spenko, in "The Death of Joe Christmas and the Power of Words" (*TCL*, Fall 1982), and Louis G. Ceci, in "The Case for Syntactic Imagery" (*CE*, Sept. 1983), write well about the language of *Light in August*. Richard Godden's promisingly conceived essay, "Call Me Nigger! Race and Speech in Faulkner's *Light in August*" (*JAmS*, Aug. 1980), disappoints. So do the more-or-less structuralist readings by John Tucker, Mariana Torgovnick, and Ronald Wesley Hoag; still, Tucker's

"William Faulkner's *Light in August*: Toward a Structuralist Reading" (*MLQ*, June 1982), Torgovnick's "Story-Telling as Affirmation at the End of *Light in August*" (in *Closure in the Novel*, Princeton, N.J., 1982), and Hoag's "Ends and Loose Ends: The Triptych Conclusion of *Light in August*" (*MFS*, Winter 1985) should not be overlooked by the serious student of Faulknerian design. Neither should the sensitive reading Kenzaburo Ohashi gives the novel in "*Light in August*: The Spell of the 'Window' and the Tragedy of the 'Earth'" (McHaney).

Virginia V. Hlavsa's relentless efforts to establish modernist biblical analogues in *Light in August* must be considered—skeptically: "The Mirror, the Lamp, and the Bed: Faulkner and the Modernists" (*AL*, Mar. 1985); "St. John and Frazer in *Light in August*: Biblical Form and Mythic Function" (*BRH*, Spring 1980); and "The Levity of *Light in August*" (*Faulkner and Humor*). Also worth reading, with varying degrees of skepticism, are: Richard Pascal's "Faulkner's Debt to Keats in *Light in August*: A Reconsideration" (*SoR*, July 1981); Stephen Hahn's "'What Leaf-Fring'd Legend Haunts About Thy Shape?': *Light in August* and Southern Pastoral" (*FJ*, Fall 1985); Debra A. Moddelmog's "Faulkner's Theban Saga: *Light in August*" (*SLJ*, Fall 1985); André Bleikasten's "In Praise of Helen" (*Faulkner and Women*); and Judith Halden's "Sexual Ambiguities in *Light in August*" (*SAF*, Autumn 1982).

i. Pylon

1973–1979. In the 1970s, more good work on *Pylon* appeared in French than in English. Students of the novel are advised to consult André Bleikasten's "*Pylon*: Ou L'Enfer des signes" (*EA*, July–Sept. 1976); Michel Gresset's "Théorème" (*RANAM*, Summer 1976); and François Pitavy's "Le Reporter: Tentation et derision de l'écriture" (*RANAM*, Summer 1976). All three essays emphasize the role of language in the novel; Pitavy and Gresset argue that the reporter discovers and affirms the power of art. Of the two essays to appear in English—Duane MacMillan's "*Pylon*: From Short Stories to Major Work" (*Mosaic*, Fall 1973) and Joseph McElrath, Jr.'s "*Pylon*: The Portrait of a Lady" (*MissQ*, Summer 1974)— only McElrath's is of much value. It offers an alternative to the censure of Laverne Shumann evident in much earlier (and later) criticism.

1980–1988. Ruppersburg offers the best new general reading of *Pylon* in *Voice and Eye*. In an original and important essay, "Money and Matter in *Pylon* and *The Wild Palms*" (*FJ*, Spring 1986), Karl F. Zender shows how "*Pylon* reveals itself to be a searching reflection on the emotional and artistic dangers arising from the need for money." Marta Paul Johnson reminds us in "'I Have Decided Now': Laverne's Transformation in *Pylon*" (*MissQ*, Summer 1983) that the reader sees Laverne only through the Reporter, Jack, and Jiggs; Johnson's "*Pylon*: Faulkner's Waste Land" (*MissQ*, Summer 1985) seems moralistic and less helpful, but her "The Killer in *Pylon*" (*MissQ*, Fall 1987) is worthwhile. Robert Harrison's *Aviation Lore in Faulkner* becomes indispensable.

j. Absalom, Absalom!

1973–1979. As a glance at the annual volumes of *American Literary Scholarship* will show, the popularity of *Absalom, Absalom!* as a subject for study had its beginnings in the 1970s. The single book among the mass of material from the period—Estella Schoenberg's *Old Tales and Talking: Quentin Compson in William Faulkner's "Absalom, Absalom!" and Related Works* (Jackson, Miss., 1977)—reminds one of Coleridge's distinction between genius and talent. Although not uncommon now, Schoenberg's central idea—that "Quentin's working out of the story of Sutpen's children . . . is Faulkner's means of retelling Quentin's story and explaining Quentin's suicide"—was a stroke of genius in the 1970s. But Schoenberg's development of the idea displays less than satisfactory command of the talents of literary criticism. Unlike John T. Irwin, who also challenges the hegemony of the unitary text, Schoenberg shows little tolerance for the notion that literary data may signify in more than one structure simultaneously, or even (*vide* Irwin) in the "space" between determinant structures. She instead treats *The Sound and the Fury* and *Absalom, Absalom!* as if they were a single novel, with events in the one also existing in the other. Because Quentin comes home for Christmas in *The Sound and the Fury*, for example, he must be in Jefferson when Rosa Coldfield takes an ambulance to Sutpen's Hundred in *Absalom, Absalom!* Furthermore, Schoenberg's inattention to Faulkner's other novels deprives her of an important resource. That the two portrayals of Quentin Compson are stages in the evolution of Faulkner's attitude toward suicide seems indisputable; but so are the portrayals of Harry Wilbourne and Lieutenant Levine and Eula Varner. Fully to see how Faulkner retells the story of Quentin Compson and explains his suicide requires placing *The Sound and the Fury* and *Absalom, Absalom!* in the context of the career as a whole.

The long list of essays on *Absalom, Absalom!* is headed by several studies of Faulkner's narrative method and its epistemological implications. Despite the considerable differences among these studies, they create an impression of sameness. This is so because they do not anticipate the decisive challenge posed by deconstruction to the aesthetics of closure. Those that do not find closure in the plot of the novel find it in the mind of either the narrators or the reader. The small group of studies committed to finding closure in the novel's plot includes two essays by Cleanth Brooks: "On *Absalom, Absalom!*" (*Mosaic*, Fall 1973) and "The Narrative Structure of *Absalom, Absalom!*" (*GaR*, Summer 1975). Both essays, especially the second, attempt to determine what "really happens" when Quentin visits Sutpen's Hundred. A similar study is Hershel Parker's "What Quentin Saw 'Out There'" (*MissQ*, Summer 1974), which argues that Quentin learns the secret of Charles Bon's birth by noticing Jim Bond's physiognomic resemblance to other members of the Sutpen family. In "Collapse of Dynasty: The Thematic Center of

Absalom, Absalom!" (*PMLA*, Jan. 1974), Ralph Behrens seems to want one right interpretation of the meaning of Sutpen's design. After reviewing previous interpretations, he opts for one based on the analogy, implied by the novel's title, to the rise and fall of biblical dynasties.

Those whose sympathies incline more toward studies that argue for closure in the narrators' minds or the mind of the reader can find a particularly well-argued version of the mind-of-the-reader view in Arnold Weinstein's *Vision and Response in Modern Fiction* (Ithaca, N.Y., 1974). Other valuable studies along these lines are Carl E. Rollyson, Jr.'s "The Recreation of the Past in *Absalom, Absalom!"* (*MissQ*, Summer 1976); John Middleton's "Shreve McCannon and Sutpen's Legacy" (*SoR*, Winter 1974); Claudia Brodsky's "The Working of Narrative in *Absalom, Absalom!*: A Textual Analysis" (*AmSt*, No. 2, 1978); Richard Forrer's *"Absalom, Absalom!*: Story-telling as a Mode of Transcendence" (*SLJ*, Fall 1976); and James H. Matlack's "The Voices of Time: Narrative Structure in *Absalom, Absalom!"* (*SoR*, Spring 1979). Rollyson and Middleton focus on Quentin and Shreve's performance as narrators, Brodsky and Forrer on the third-person narrator, and Matlack on the novel's indebtedness to an oral tradition of storytelling. Of more limited interest are J. Gary Williams's "Quentin Finally Sees Miss Rosa" (*Criticism*, Fall 1979); Susan Resneck Parr's "The Fourteenth Image of the Blackbird: Another Look at Truth in *Absalom, Absalom!"* (*ArQ*, Summer 1979); and Margaret Dickie Uroff's "The Fictions of *Absalom, Absalom!"* (*SNNTS*, Winter 1979). Williams argues that the central action of the novel consists of the emergence of Quentin's ability to "see" Rosa Coldfield. Parr argues that we do not know whether Charles Bon has black blood and that it would diminish the novel if we did. Uroff makes the questionable assertion that Faulkner's ambivalence about fiction-making in *Absalom, Absalom!* anticipates his decline as a novelist. Finally, Shlomith Rimmon-Kenan's structuralist analysis, "From Reproduction to Production: The Status of Narration in Faulkner's *Absalom, Absalom!"* (*Degrés*, Winter 1978), deserves mention for its discussion of the ways Faulkner undermines narratorial reliability.

As might be expected, thematically oriented studies include several explorations of the theme of history. In the chapter on the novel in the posthumously published *Versions of the Past: The Historical Imagination in American Fiction* (New York, 1974), Harry B. Henderson III depicts Quentin Compson as caught between "holistic" and "progressivist" views of history. Carl E. Rollyson, Jr.'s *"Absalom, Absalom!*: The Novel as Historiography" (*LH*, Spring 1977) argues for the importance of imaginative truth, such as Quentin and Shreve achieve, to historians as well as novelists. In "The Time of Myth and History in *Absalom, Absalom!"* (*AL*, May 1973), Patricia Tobin anticipates later directions of study by reading *Absalom, Absalom!* as a critique of patriarchal structures. This essay was reprinted in revised form in *Time and the Novel: The Genealogical Imperative* (Princeton, N.J., 1978). John V. Hagopian's *"Absalom, Absalom!* and the Negro Question" (*MFS*, Summer 1973) concludes that "the novel as a whole clearly repudiates Southern racism."

The remaining studies take a variety of approaches. Terrence Doody's "Shreve McCannon and the Confessions of *Absalom, Absalom!*" (*SNNTS*, Winter 1974), T. H. Adamowski's "Children of the Idea: Heroes and Family Romances in *Absalom, Absalom!*" (*Mosaic*, Fall 1976), and Paul Rosenzweig's "The Narrative Frames in *Absalom, Absalom!*: Faulkner's Involuted Commentary on Art" (*ArQ*, Summer 1979) all address psychological issues. Doody's and Adamowski's studies are particularly valuable—Doody's for its analysis of the psychodynamics of Quentin's relationships with Rosa and Shreve, and Adamowski's for its examination of Thomas Sutpen's career in terms of the Freudian paradigm of the family romance. In "The Metaphor of Family in *Absalom, Absalom!*" (*SoR*, Winter 1975), George S. Lensing provides a more conventional approach to the role of family in the novel. Elisabeth Muhlenfeld's "'We Have Waited Long Enough': Judith Sutpen and Charles Bon" (*SoR*, Winter 1978) argues that Judith Sutpen and Charles Bon actually loved one another. Muhlenfeld shows how Quentin and Shreve (not just Mr. Compson) interpret the Judith-Charles relationship to suit their convenience.

The three remaining studies include Arthur F. Kinney's "Form and Function in *Absalom, Absalom!*" (*SoR*, Autumn 1978); despite its title, this essay is primarily a study of some of the novel's sources. Stephen M. Ross's "Conrad's Influence on Faulkner's *Absalom, Absalom!*" (*SAF*, Summer 1974) examines the topic identified in its title in a commonsensical fashion. Finally, Virginia V. Hlavsa's "The Vision of the Advocate in *Absalom, Absalom!*" (*Novel*, Fall 1974) is based on the fanciful notion that the novel has the structure of a nine-part trial. The first four parts of the trial turn out to be parodic.

1980–1988. More critics continue to write about *Absalom, Absalom!* than any other single Faulkner text, no doubt largely because "this novel questions what few do, the sources of the discursive power that not only allows narrators to talk but also allows a novel to dramatize narrators narrating" (Stephen M. Ross, "The Evocation of Voice in *Absalom, Absalom!*" [*ELWIU*, Fall 1981]). *Absalom, Absalom!* asks: why tell (and retell) stories? why listen to stories over and over again? and *how* should we tell and listen to stories? John T. Matthews's "Marriages of Speaking and Hearing in *Absalom, Absalom!*" (*The Play of Faulkner's Language*) holds up as the most stimulating critical essay on the novel since 1980; but a considerable body of important work has been done. In *Faulkner's "Absalom, Absalom!" and Interpretability: The Inexplicable Unseen* (Bern, 1985), Christine de Montauzon uses Jean Piaget's work on epistemology in a thoughtful attempt to explain how and why we should attend to *Absalom, Absalom!* De Montauzon cares about what it means to read *Absalom, Absalom!* rather than about what *Absalom, Absalom!* means. She considers how the cognitive processes of reading—strategies of assimilation and accommodation, desires for recognizability and totalization, responses to style and symbolism—determine our experience of Faulkner's difficult text. De Montauzon concludes that *Absalom, Absalom!* is "an extreme example of the 'open' text," a text which "transmutes hermeneutics into poetics, meaning into being." Her book is valuable less for its rather predictable conclusions than for its clear-headed, patient, and sensitive exposition of the "various forms of elusiveness, suspension, indeterminacy and disruption . . . which draw the reader into setting up endlessly multiplied accommodations."

Elisabeth Muhlenfeld has edited Garland's Critical Casebook, *William Faulkner's "Absalom, Absalom!"* (New York, 1984); only Muhlenfeld's splendid introduction, her impeccable bibliography, and a good essay by François Pitavy, called "The Narrative Voice and Function of Shreve: Remarks on the Production of Meaning in *Absalom, Absalom!*," are new. Of the scores of essays on *Absalom, Absalom!* published within the past decade, Muhlenfeld's scrupulous and lucid account of the novel's genesis and development, the history of its composition and recomposition (in her introduction), will almost certainly be valued most highly by future scholars. Muhlenfeld meticulously and interestingly situates *Absalom, Absalom!*'s writing and rewriting within the biographical patterns of a particularly intense two and a half years of Faulkner's life (early 1934 to mid-1936). She also unfolds the extraordinary process through which Faulkner struggled to make decisions about his book's structure, design, and modes of telling.

Among the many compelling observations about how the tale of *Absalom, Absalom!* finally got itself told is Muhlenfeld's discovery that "Faulkner considered beginning his novel with a draft of Mr. Compson's complete letter, the text of which varies only slightly from the printed text in *Absalom, Absalom!* bracketing Chapters VI through IX." This compositional fact would seem to support David Krause's argument, presented in three interrelated essays, that letters within the text—Compson's letter, Bon's letter, as well as several invented by Shreve—provoke characters to read them in ways that significantly determine (or make indeterminate) how and why to read *Absalom, Absalom!* Krause appropriates and tests some theoretical conceptions of the reading process from Derrida, Foucault, and, most helpfully, Barthes: "Opening Pandora's Box: Re-Reading Compson's Letter and Faulkner's *Absalom, Absalom!*" (*CentR*, Summer 1986); "Reading Bon's Letter and Faulkner's *Absalom, Absalom!*" (*PMLA*, Mar. 1984); and "Reading Shreve's Letters and Faulkner's *Absalom, Absalom!*" (*SAF*, Autumn 1983).

Other critics have also found interesting ways to reread Faulkner's *Absalom, Absalom!* through lenses afforded by contemporary literary theory. In "The Evocation of Voice in *Absalom, Absalom!*" (*EL*, Fall 1981), Stephen Ross uses Derridean notions of presence to examine Faulknerian voices. Ross argues that in *Absalom, Absalom!* "voice's power of evocation becomes the text's presumed and unquestioned discursive origin," affirming the novel's "mimetic faith in the created presence which the escape from voice produces." Also worthwhile is Ross's "Oratory and the Dialogical in *Absalom, Absalom!*" (*Intertextuality*). In "Incredulous Narration" (*Reading for the Plot: Design and Intention in Narrative*, New York, 1984), Peter Brooks reads *Absalom, Absalom!* through the "concept of narrative as a coded activity," articulated by Barthes in *S/Z*. For Brooks, the novel "becomes a kind of detective story where the object of investigation—the mystery—is the narrative design, or plot, itself." He does not intend to reduce *Absalom, Absalom!* to a novel about novels, "but rather to contend that narrating is an urgent function in itself, that in the absence of pattern and structure, patterning and structuration remain necessary projects, dynamic intentions." Brooks makes an interesting case that "the attempted recovery of the past makes known the continuing history of past desire as it persists in the present, shaping the project of telling." Linda Kauffman uses Barthes differently and to even better effect in "Devious Channels of Decorous Ordering: A Lover's Discourse in *Absalom, Absalom!*" (*MFS*, Summer 1983).

J. Hillis Miller, Jr., in "The Two Relativisms: Point of View and Indeterminacy in the Novel *Absalom, Absalom!*," presents a restrained and rather subdued deconstructive reading of the novel (in *Relativism in the Arts*, ed. Betty Jean Craige, Athens, Ga., 1983). He focuses "on the relationship between relation as storytelling and relations as the network of family and community ties" and reaches the relatively unthreatening and predictable conclusion that "failure of a narration is, for Faulkner, the evidence of its validity, since only the failed narration, which exposes its loose ends and inconsistencies, can be an adequate representation, figure for what has no literal name, of that unnameable 'it.'" Faulknerians should welcome Miller's thoughtful theoretical discussion but may wish that he (and Peter Brooks as well) showed more familiarity with the history and current state of Faulkner scholarship. Ralph Flores's deconstructive reading, "Half-Breeding: *Absalom, Absalom!*" (in *The Rhetoric of Doubtful Authority: Deconstructive Readings of Self-Questioning Narratives, St. Augustine to Faulkner*, Ithaca, N.Y., 1984), leads him to the thought-provoking conclusion that "the social hegemony's pressure to retain black/white and white/white oppositions (of all sorts) becomes as striking as its monstrousness construed as systematic exclusions of the other as, uncontrollably, what is constructed as itself."

Two interesting essays take fresh looks at Faulkner's sense of the gothic. "The Vampire Motif in *Absalom, Absalom!*" (*SoR*, Summer 1984), by Cheryl B. Torsney, calmly explicates some metaphors of the predatory and the parasitic. "The Gothicism of *Absalom, Absalom!*: Rosa Coldfield Revisited" (*"A Cosmos of My Own"*), an unconventional essay by François L. Pitavy, has much to say about absence and desire and about Faulkner's gothic themes, images, structures, and strategies. Pitavy writes especially well about closed doors and dark houses and about the reader's need for intelligence and imagination. Frederick R. Karl argues that *Absalom, Absalom!* "comes at race through secret passageways, by means of hiding necessary information, by using divulgence as a psychological weapon." Karl's "Race, History, and Technique in *Absalom, Absalom!*" (*Faulkner and Race*) claims that "race *has been absorbed into technique.*"

Minrose C. Gwin's balanced essay, "'Twin Sistered to the Fell Darkness': Clytie, Rosa, and the Mystery of Racism" (in *Black and White Women of the Old South*, Knoxville, Tenn., 1985), situates Faulkner's fictional women within the cultural contexts of women's autobiographies of the Old South and shows how Clytie Sutpen and Rosa Coldfield become "a metaphor for the brutalizing and destructive power of a racist society, and the lingering vestiges of that power in our culture." If at first Thadious Davis's claim that "Clytie reveals the most about Faulkner's art and the Negro" in *Absalom* seems excessive, her rereading of the novel movingly shows that, although Charles Bon "becomes, like the Negro in general, the metaphorical embodiment of all that is invisible in southern life," it is Clytie who deserves most urgently to be seen in her invisibility, heard in her silences (*Faulkner's "Negro"*).

Elizabeth Langland makes brief but pointed remarks about the problematics of constructing, representing, and knowing social realities within and through *Absalom, Absalom!* in her *Society in the Novel* (Chapel Hill, N.C., 1984). Among the essays about Faulkner and the possibilities of historical discourse are Susan Swartzlander's "'That Meager and Fragile Thread': The Artist as Historian in *Absalom, Absalom!*" (*SoSt*, Spring 1986); Suzanne W. Jones's "*Absalom, Absalom!* and the Custom of Storytelling: A Reflection of Southern Social and Literary History" (*SoSt*, Spring 1985); and Norman Markowitz's "William Faulkner's 'Tragic Legend': Southern History and *Absalom, Absalom!*" (*MinnR*, Spring 1981). Stephen M. Ross takes a more expansive view of the novel's engagements with history in "Faulkner's *Absalom, Absalom!* and the David Story: A Speculative Contemplation" (*The David Myth in Western Literature*, ed. Raymond-Jean Frontain and Jan Wojcik, West Lafayette, Ind., 1980). Maxine Rose's more modestly focused "Echoes of the King James Bible in the Prose Style of *Absalom, Absalom!*" (*ArQ*, Summer 1981) finds a specific cultural context for the novel's biblical rhetoric. John McClure's "The Syntax of Decadence in *Absalom, Absalom!*" (*MinnR*, Spring 1981) also studies the novel's intense rhetoric, as, in a more intuitive way, does Deborah Robbins's "The Desperate Eloquence of *Absalom, Absalom!*" (*MissQ*, Summer 1981). Lacanian and structuralist principles inform but cannot enliven Robert Con Davis's "The Symbolic Father in Yoknapatawpha County" (*JNT*, Winter 1980), which argues that Rosa "signifies the impulse of and desire for paternal authority."

Of the dozens of remaining essays on *Absalom, Absalom!*, only four seem worth noting: Deborah L. Clarke's "Familiar and Fantastic: Women in *Absalom, Absalom!*" (*FJ*, Fall 1986); Philip J. Egan's "Embedded Story Structures in *Absalom, Absalom!*" (*AL*, May 1983); Ikuko Fujihira's "From Voice to Silence: Writing in *Absalom, Absalom!*" (*SELit*, Engl. No., 1984); and Bernhard Radloff's "*Absalom, Absalom!* An Ontological Approach to Sutpen's Design" (*Mosaic*, Winter 1986).

k. *The Unvanquished*

1973–1979. The few items on *The Unvanquished* can be briefly treated. Thomas Daniel Young's "Pioneering on Principle: or How a Traditional Society May be Dissolved" (*Faulkner, Modernism, and Film*) is a traditional communitarian analysis, using terminology from John Crowe Ransom to trace Rosa Millard's moral deterioration. In the emergence of the Snopeses, Young says, we see "how Western European civilization may be destroyed." M. E. Bradford's "Faulkner's *The Unvanquished*: The High Cost of Survival" (*SoR*, Summer 1978) offers a similarly apocalyptic reading. As Panthea Reid Broughton says, Bradford's thesis, that the novel's protagonist is "*res publica*, the Commonwealth," "gets lost in his [southern] chauvinism" (*AmLS*, 1978). In "Sartoris Ludens": The Play Element in *The Unvanquished*" (*MissQ*, Summer 1976), A. James Memmott provides a modest but illuminating application of Johan Huizinga's theories of play to the novel. Finally, Richard A. Milum's "Faulkner, Scott, and Another Source for Drusilla" (*MissQ*, Summer 1978) traces associations between *The Unvanquished* and *Rob Roy*.

1980–1988. Alan Holder's chapter, "An Odor of Sartoris: William Faulkner's *The Unvanquished*," in his *The Imagined Past: Portrayals of Our History in Modern American Literature* (Lewisburg, Penn., 1981), is considerably more interesting than his accompanying chapter, "The Doomed Design: William Faulkner's *Absalom, Absalom!*"; still, Holder concludes by merely reaffirming the wrongheaded but firmly entrenched position that *The Unvanquished* "ends up accepting Southern history in a way that *Absalom, Absalom!* does not." By sticking to the party line that Faulkner is guilty of aesthetic and ethical evasions in *The Unvanquished*, Holder evades the subtle and complex demands the novel makes in imagining its historical and cultural past.

Not much real help comes from Kinney's *The Sartoris Family*, but help may be on the way in the form of a projected volume of close textual commentary from James Hinkle, previewed in *College Literature* (Fall 1986). His "Reading Faulkner's *The Unvanquished*" glosses the first two sections of "Ambuscade." Hinkle obviously has a formidable command of information about the Faulkner canon and its historical, cultural, and literary contexts; one has high hopes that his book-length study of *The Unvanquished* will effectively disseminate his knowledge to other readers, making possible a sustained reevaluation of this subtle novel.

For now, the following articles on *The Unvanquished* remain worthy of attention: John Pilkington's "'Strange Times' in Yoknapatawpha" (*Fifty Years of Yoknapatawpha*); Marjorie Pryse's "Miniaturizing Yoknapatawpha: *The Unvanquished* as Faulkner's Theory of Realism" (*MissQ*, Summer 1980), although she overstates her suggestive position that "scale" becomes *the* "theoretical model of Faulkner's technique"; Warren Akin, IV's "'Blood and Raising and Background': The Plot of *The Unvanquished*" (*MLS*, Winter 1980–81); Thomas L. McHaney's well-informed "An Episode of War in *The Unvanquished*" (*FJ*, Spring 1987); and Winifred L. Frazer's original and provocative "Faulkner and Womankind—'No Bloody Moon'" (*Faulkner and Women*).

l. The Wild Palms

1973–1979. Other than a strong chapter in Cleanth Brooks's *William Faulkner: Toward Yoknapatawpha and Beyond*, the only significant study of *The Wild Palms* to appear during the period under review is Thomas L. McHaney's *William Faulkner's "The Wild Palms": A Study* (Jackson, Miss., 1975). One comes away from these and later studies (e.g., Gail L. Mortimer's "The Ironies of Transcendent Love in *The Wild Palms*" and Karl F. Zender's "Money and Matter in *Pylon* and *The Wild Palms*") with the sense that readers of the novel divide into opposed factions, depending on their attitude toward Harry Wilbourne and Charlotte Rittenmeyer's quest for romantic fulfillment. McHaney's book is very strongly committed to an antiromantic reading; it is assiduous (almost relentless) in its exposure of the ironies attendant upon Harry and Charlotte's quest, and it is especially severe in its judgment of Charlotte's character and motives. Within the limits established by this approach, *William Faulkner's "The Wild Palms"* is a strong, insightful study, particularly valuable for its analysis of the novel's philosophical background, for its demonstration of the thematic, symbolic, and imagistic parallels between the alternating stories, and for its discussion of the relation between *The Wild Palms*, Sherwood Anderson's *Dark Laughter*, and Hemingway's fiction. After a dozen years, it remains the best starting place for study of the novel.

1980–1988. Two very different essays in the collection *Faulkner and Intertextuality* mark the place to start with *The Wild Palms* in 1988. In "*The Wild Palms*: Degraded Culture, Devalued Texts," Pamela Rhodes and Richard Godden read the novel, from a moderate and literate Marxist perspective, as Faulkner's Hollywood-provoked meditation on commodity; their stimulating essay should be compared to Karl F. Zender's on *Pylon* and *The Wild Palms*. In "Forgetting Jerusalem: An Ironical Chart for *The Wild Palms*," François Pitavy de-romanticizes the presence of Psalm 137 in the novel. Gail L. Mortimer does a different kind of de-romanticizing as she extends her studies of Faulknerian anxieties about women, especially mothers, in "The Ironies of Transcendent Love in Faulkner's *The Wild Palms*" (*FJ*, Spring 1986). Mortimer's fine essay might profitably be read alongside Dieter Meindl's "Romantic Idealism and *The Wild Palms*" (*Faulkner and Idealism*). Gary Harrington has published a pair of solid, brief articles on *The Wild Palms*: "The Con-Artist in *The Wild Palms*" (*DR*, Spring 1985) and "Distant Mirrors: The Intertextual Relationship of Quentin Compson and Harry Wilbourne" (*FJ*, Fall 1985). Doreen Fowler's brief "Measuring Faulkner's Tall Convict" (*SNNTS*, Fall 1982) tries to rehabilitate the convict as a reluctant hero of "order and responsibility." Douglas Day speculates interestingly about an unacknowledged translation of the novel into Spanish in "Borges, Faulkner, and *The Wild Palms*" (*VQR*, Winter 1980).

   m. The Hamlet, The Town, and The Mansion

   1973–1979. Little significant work on the Snopes trilogy appeared during the 1970s. Heading the short list is Joseph Trimmer's "V. K. Ratliff: A Portrait of the Artist in Motion" (*MFS*, Winter 1974), a welcome reminder of the importance of aesthetic considerations to Ratliff's "Snopes Watching." Trimmer's argument that Ratliff is "symbolic of Faulkner's conception of the role of the artist" is most convincing when applied to *The Town*, least so when applied to *The Hamlet*. Less valuable are Holly McFarland's "'The Mask not Tragic . . . Just Damned': The Women in Faulkner's Trilogy" (*BSUF*, Spring 1977), an overly long study of the topic identified in its title, and Nancy Norris's "*The Hamlet, The Town*, and *The Mansion*: A Psychological Reading of the Snopes Trilogy" (*Mosaic*, Fall 1973), which strains to apply psychological concepts and terminology to a group of novels not particularly receptive to this approach.

   The three remaining items from the period all focus on individual novels. Edwin Moses's "Faulkner's *The Hamlet*: The Passionate Humanity of V. K. Ratliff" (*NDEJ*, Spring 1973) offers an unconvincingly upbeat reading of Ratliff's moral development in *The Hamlet*. The other two studies, both by Eileen Gregory, are "Faulkner's Typescripts of *The Town*" (*MissQ*, Summer 1973) and "The Temerity to Revolt: Mink Snopes and the Dispossessed in *The Mansion*" (*MissQ*, Summer 1976). The first is primarily a genetic study; the second identifies and discusses classical, Christian, and modern analogues for Mink's act of revenge against his cousin.

   1980–1988. Regrettably, little work of genuine substance has been done recently on the Snopes trilogy. Only John T. Matthews's wonderful "*The Hamlet*: Rites of Play" (*The Play of Faulkner's Language*) stands out. Matthews shows that "Flem reflects the arbitrary, deathly foundation of writing as he manipulates the various systems of meaning in the hamlet meaninglessly. Against him, Ratliff promotes an ethics of joy, a playfulness that values improvisation, fantasy, and extravagance in the presence of a revealed and binding mortality." Louise K. Barnett's "The Speech Community of *The Hamlet*" (*CentR*, Summer 1986) seems to play nicely off of Matthews's reading. So does Charlotte Renner's "Talking and Writing in Faulkner's Snopes Trilogy" (*SLJ*, Fall 1982), which doesn't live up to its considerable promise, but does raise interesting points about how the Snopes trilogy documents a movement from oral to print culture and toward "more collaboration than competition among [Faulkner's] narrators." Noel Polk reads *The Mansion* with his usual authority and grace in two related essays: "Idealism in *The Mansion*" (*Faulkner and Idealism*) and "Faulkner and Respectability" (*Fifty Years of Yoknapatawpha*). Philip Cohen continues his fine work on Faulkner and Balzac in "French Peasants and Southern Snopeses: Balzac's *Les Paysans* and Faulkner's *The Hamlet*" (*MissQ*, Fall 1987).

With only moderate reservations, the following can also be recommended: Elizabeth D. Rankin's "Chasing Spotted Horses: The Quest for Human Dignity in the Snopes Trilogy" (Carey); Margaret Dunn's "The Illusion of Freedom in *The Hamlet* and *Go Down, Moses*" (*AL*, Oct. 1985); Gary Lindberg's discussion in *The Confidence Man in American Literature* (New York, 1982); Gail Mortimer's "Evolutionary Theory in Faulkner's Snopes Trilogy" (*RMR*, No. 4, 1986); Dawn Trouard's "Making Labove Cast a Shadow: The Rhetoric of Neurosis" (*L&P*, No. 4, 1981); and Dwight Eddins's "Metahumor in Faulkner's 'Spotted Horses'" (*ArielE*, Jan. 1982).

n. Go Down, Moses

1973–1979. An air of depletion characterized studies of *Go Down, Moses* in the 1970s, as critics continued to bicker over the nearly exhausted topic of how to judge Isaac McCaslin's relinquishment of his inheritance. An exception is Wesley Morris's *Friday's Footprint: Structuralism and the Articulated Text* (Columbus, Ohio, 1979). Although rhetorically and stylistically self-indulgent, this book establishes a valuable new direction for study by taking a structuralist approach to the roles of myth and history in the novel. Also useful are two studies of particular scenes and a brief contribution to our knowledge of the novel's factual background. In "Faulkner as Historian: The Commissary Books in *Go Down, Moses*" (*MarkhamR*, Winter 1978), Carl E. Rollyson, Jr. examines Ike's reading of the ledgers as part of his continuing exploration of Faulkner's understanding of the workings of the historical imagination. Albert J. Devlin's "'How Much It Takes to Compound a Man': A Neglected Scene in *Go Down, Moses*" (*MQ*, Summer 1973) displays the significance to Ike's maturation of Hubert Beauchamp's brief liaison with a quadroon mistress. John T. Hiers's "Faulkner's Lord-to-God Bird in 'The Bear'" (*AL*, Jan. 1976) discusses Faulkner's regional name for the Pileated Woodpecker. Of less value, because mainly concerned with the topic mentioned at the beginning of this paragraph, are R. D. Ackerman's "The Immolation of Isaac McCaslin" (*TSLL*, Fall 1974), T. H. Adamowski's "Isaac McCaslin and the Wilderness of the Imagination" (*CentR*, Winter 1973), and Stuart D. James's "The Ironic Voices of Faulkner's *Go Down, Moses*" (*SDR*, Autumn 1978).

The five remaining studies focus on individual sections of the novel. David Walker's "Out of the Old Time: 'Was' and *Go Down, Moses*" (*JNT*, Winter 1979) examines some of the ways "Was" anticipates themes developed in the rest of the novel. Karl F. Zender's "A Hand of Poker: Game and Ritual in Faulkner's 'Was'" (*SSF*, Winter 1974) explores the conclusion of the same section in terms of the formal requirements of games and rituals. The other three studies—John L. Cleman's "'Pantaloon in Black': Its Place in *Go Down, Moses*" (*TSL*, 1977); Eberhard Alsen's "An Existentialist Reading of Faulkner's 'Pantaloon in Black'" (*SSF*, Spring 1977); and Warren Akin, IV's "'The Normal Human Feelings': An Interpretation of Faulkner's 'Pantaloon in Black'" (*SSF*, Fall 1978)— are competent studies of the third section of the novel (although Alsen rides an anti-Christian perspective rather hard). Finally, mention should be made of Charles S. Aiken's study of the geographical background of the novel and of Joanne V. Creighton's study of its compositional history, both mentioned earlier in this essay.

1980–1988. In *Threads Cable-Strong: William Faulkner's "Go Down, Moses"* (Lewisburg, Penn., 1983), Dirk Kuyk, Jr. tries to teach us how to negotiate "the unfamiliar and therefore hazardous middle ground between novels and collections of stories." Reproducing Faulkner's suspended structure, Kuyk devotes one chapter to each of Faulkner's seven stories while simultaneously proposing a reading which would bind the stories, with threads cable-strong, into a novel. Consequently, none of the individual stories or chapters receives a thorough, self-contained, or satisfying interpretation, nor is the reading of *Go Down, Moses* as a whole consistent in texture or design. Kuyk's well-intentioned strategy begins by not only trying to stick "close to the experience of reading the text," but also by trying to establish the pretense of critic as "a first-time reader." This strategy allows Kuyk to pose a series of sensible, probing questions about the first four paragraphs of "Was," but gets quickly abandoned as he tries to explain what he has "learned from reading *Go Down, Moses* over and over again." When Kuyk remembers his own original impulse to work closely with Faulkner's text, he reveals himself to be a reader of considerable experience and tact. But too often, in offering accurate, well-meaning, and, frankly, helpful reconstructions of chronology (fabula) as he does for "The Bear," Kuyk subverts Faulkner's text and sabotages the experience of reading "The Bear" and *Go Down, Moses* as Faulkner wrote them to be read: "by the heart."

In "The Ritual of Mourning in *Go Down, Moses*" (*The Play of Faulkner's Language*), John T. Matthews reads "by the heart," despite some heavy theoretical baggage. Karl F. Zender reads *Go Down, Moses* biographically in "Faulkner at Forty: The Artist at Home" (*SoR*, Apr. 1981) and opens up the important subject of Faulkner's compulsive representations of scenes of reading within his fictions in "Reading in 'The Bear'" (*FaSt*, 1980). In a sophisticated but not entirely convincing essay, John Limon uses a conception of interpretive communities to question the place of "Pantaloon in Black" within *Go Down, Moses* in "The Integration of Faulkner's *Go Down, Moses*" (*CritI*, Winter 1986). Daniel G. Ford writes quite nicely about what holds the book together in "Mad Pursuit in *Go Down, Moses*" (*CollL*, Spring 1981). Ronald Schleifer seems less self-assured in "Faulkner's Storied Novel: *Go Down, Moses* and the Translation of Time" (*MFS*, Spring 1982).

Patrick McGee argues in his eloquent "Gender and Generation in Faulkner's 'The Bear'" (*FJ*, Fall 1985) that, "in this centerpiece of the novel, history wars with its counterpart—the myth of an original, uncorrupted nature, of a world without writing, without the markings of civilization, without the problematics of interpretation, without the conflicts of sexuality, without death." John H. Schaar uses the principles and vocabularies of political science to open up "The Bear" in "Community or Contract? William Faulkner and the Dual Legacy" (in *The Problem of Authority in America*, ed. John P. Diggins and Mark E. Kann, Philadelphia, 1981). In a different way, Richard Pascal explores some of the same questions in "Love, Rapacity, and Community in *Go Down, Moses*" (*ArielE*, July 1984). Both Thomas C. Foster, in "History, Private Consciousness, and Narrative Form in *Go Down, Moses*" (*CentR*, Winter 1984), and Warren Akin, IV, in "Providence and Structure in *Go Down, Moses*" (*SoR*, Summer 1982), examine how communities construct their histories. Akin is quite good on Part IV of "The Bear," but less convincing about the novel as a whole. Among the better evaluations of Isaac are Susan V. Donaldson's "Isaac McCaslin and the Possibilities of Vision" (*SoR*, Winter 1986) and Laura P. Claridge's "Isaac McCaslin's Failed Bid for Adulthood" (*AL*, May 1983).

A number of useful articles consider influences or analogues. John M. Howell's "Hemingway, Faulkner, and 'The Bear'" (*AL*, Mar. 1980) argues for the possible influence of *For Whom the Bell Tolls*; in a related piece, "McCaslin and Macomber: From *Green Hills* to *Big Woods*" (*FJ*, Fall 1986), Howell considers a different angle of Hemingway's possible influence. Paul S. Stein's "Ike McCaslin: Traumatized in a Hawthornean Wilderness" (*SLJ*, Spring 1980) and J. Douglas Canfield's "Faulkner's Grecian Urn and Ike McCaslin's Empty Legacies" (*ArQ*, Winter 1980) also deserve attention.

The best new discussions of style in *Go Down, Moses* are John Duvall's "Using Greimas' Narrative Semiotics: Signification in Faulkner's 'The Old People'" (*CollL*, Fall 1982) and Michael Toolan's two impressive linguistic analyses, "The Functioning of Progressive Verbal Forms in the Narrative of *Go Down, Moses*" (*Lang&S*, Spring 1983) and "Syntactical Styles as a Means of Characterization in Narrative" (*Style*, Spring 1985).

Finally, two efforts to assess the book's comic elements should be noted: Kathleen Latimer's "Comedy as Order in *Go Down, Moses*" (*PCL*, 1984) and Nancy B. Sederberg's "'A Momentary Anesthesia of the

Heart': A Study of the Comic Elements in Faulkner's *Go Down, Moses*" (*Faulkner and Humor*).

    o. Intruder in the Dust

    1973–1979. The most significant study of *Intruder in the Dust* to appear in the 1970s is less concerned with the novel than with its film adaptation. Literate, thorough, and well-informed, Regina K. Fadiman's *Faulkner's "Intruder in the Dust": Novel into Film* (Knoxville, Tenn., 1978) takes a developmental approach to its topic. After a brief discussion of the novel's genesis and themes, Fadiman discusses the circumstances surrounding the decision to make the film, the writing of the screenplay, and the shooting of the film. The bulk of her book is given over to a reproduction of Ben Maddow's screenplay; Fadiman argues that some revisions of the screenplay may have originated with Faulkner, a point confirmed by Katherine L. Knight in her review (*MissQ*, Summer 1978). The book also contains an extensive set of appendixes, mainly related to the screenplay and to Clarence Brown's career as a director. (Fadiman's book largely supersedes E. Pauline Degenfelder's earlier study, "The Film Adaptation of Faulkner's *Intruder in the Dust*" [*LFQ*, April 1973].)

    Peter J. Rabinowitz's "The Click of the Spring: The Detective Story as Parallel Structure in Dostoyevsky and Faulkner" (*MP*, May 1979) is the best essay-length study to appear in the 1970s. Rabinowitz argues that Faulkner uses detective-story conventions to solve problems inherent in a subgenre called "the discovery novel." Although the essay is generally convincing, one suspects that the problems Rabinowitz identifies are partly of his own making. Although overly concerned with defending the novel against its detractors, Carol R. Rigsby's "Chick Mallison's Expectations and *Intruder in the Dust*" (*MissQ*, Summer 1976) succeeds in providing a good account of Chick Mallison's maturation.

    1980–1988. The most extensive work on this novel during the past decade has been done by Patrick Samway, S.J.: *Faulkner's "Intruder in the Dust": A Critical Study of the Typescripts* (Troy, N.Y., 1980) and "*Intruder in the Dust*: A Re-evaluation" (Carey). Karl F. Zender has dismissed Samway's study of the typescripts as "useless" and his "Re-evaluation" as mostly plot summary (*AmLS*, 1980); unfortunately, little evidence can be marshalled to refute Zender's harsh judgment and redeem Samway's work. The most recent essay on *Intruder in the Dust* is a serious and sound, if conservative and optimistic, reading by John Earl Bassett, "Gradual Progress and *Intruder in the Dust*" (*CollL*, Fall 1986).

    p. Knight's Gambit

    1973–1979. Only one item of significance appeared on *Knight's Gambit*. In "Faulkner's 'Knight's Gambit': Sentimentality and the Creative Imagination" (*MFS*, Summer 1978), Edmond L. Volpe broaches, but does not develop, an intriguing topic when he links Gavin Stevens's image of Mrs. Harriss as an untouched young girl to Faulkner's comments about the genesis of *The Sound and the Fury*.

1980–1988. Patrick J. Samway, S.J., in "Gavin Stevens as Uncle-Creator in *Knight's Gambit*" (*Faulkner and Idealism*), tries to establish that "in this work, we see one aspect of Faulkner's philosophy of composition which focuses on the juxtaposition of stories using the image of the chess game as a controlling device or metaphor." According to Samway, "Faulkner, like Gavin, knew that what is real is often hidden and mysterious, and that the task of the artist is to assist the reader in seeing possible and probable relationships."

q. *Requiem for a Nun*

1973–1979. Only two items of significance appeared on *Requiem for a Nun.* In "The Textual History of Faulkner's *Requiem for a Nun*" (*Proof*, 1975), Noel Polk provides a careful and stimulating analysis of the major changes Faulkner made in the novel after it had been set in galleys. He argues that the changes decrease sympathy for Gavin Stevens and Nancy Mannigoe and increase it for Temple Drake. Portions of Polk's study are reprinted in his book on *Requiem for a Nun* (see below). The second study, Hugh M. Ruppersburg's "The Narrative Structure of Faulkner's *Requiem for a Nun*" (*MissQ*, Summer 1978), has also been reprinted, in Ruppersburg's *Voice and Eye in Faulkner's Fiction*. In an extreme example of the formalist desire for unity of point of view, Ruppersburg argues that the dramatic sections of the novel should be regarded as narratives spoken by the narrator of the prose interludes.

1980–1988. Students of this novel will want to measure their own critical responses against those articulated by Noel Polk, one of Faulkner's most gifted and experienced readers, in his ambitious *Faulkner's "Requiem for a Nun": A Critical Study* (Bloomington, Ind., 1981). Polk sets out to prove that "Nancy's murder of Temple's baby . . . is the act of a madwoman and not of a saint; that Nancy's and Stevens' stated motives are not necessarily their real ones; that Stevens is not at all out to 'save' Temple but rather to crucify her; and that Temple rather than Nancy is at the moral center of the novel." Some will remain unpersuaded by Polk's somewhat tendentious and moralistic argument about suffering and redemption, and some will find his theoretical assumptions—about characterization, for example—problematic and dated. Nonetheless, most will value Polk's passionate, yet generally judicious, recuperation of *Requiem for a Nun*, a novel that makes unusual demands on its best readers and raises unsettling questions.

Although it seems curiously out of place in *Faulkner and Race*, Karl F. Zender's "*Requiem for a Nun* and the Uses of the Imagination" develops a compelling argument about how "the narrative and dramatic sections of *Requiem for a Nun* enact, in different but related ways, Faulkner's attempt to work through the implications of [a] period of creative blockage."

Also helpful with *Requiem for a Nun* are Jacques Pothier's "Jefferson, From Settlement to City: The Making of a Collective Subject" (*WiF*, May

1984) and Doreen Fowler's "Time and Punishment in Faulkner's *Requiem for a Nun*" (*Renascence*, Summer 1986).

r. A Fable

1973–1979. The most significant item to appear on *A Fable*, Lewis P. Simpson's "Yoknapatawpha & Faulkner's Fable of Civilization" (*The Maker and the Myth*), links Faulkner's self-proclaimed "magnum o" to the disappearance of his Yoknapatawpha subject matter. This essay presents a convincing case for viewing *A Fable* as an attempt "to confront . . . and to arrest" "the decline of the . . . cultural rationale of the Yoknapatawphian subject." (The essay is reprinted in revised form in Simpson's *The Brazen Face of History* [Baton Rouge, La., 1980].) Two other helpful studies are Adrienne Bond's "*Eneas Africanus* and Faulkner's Fabulous Racehorse" (*SLJ*, Spring 1977) and Kathryn A. Chittick's "The Fables in William Faulkner's *A Fable*" (*MissQ*, Summer 1977). Bond's essay demonstrates the indebtedness of the "Notes on a Horsethief" chapters of the novel to Harry Stillwell Edwards's *Eneas Africanus*. Chittick's essay works to break interpretation free from excessive reliance on the novel's central Christian allegory. The only remaining significant items—Duane J. MacMillan's "His 'Magnum O': Stoic Humanism in Faulkner's *A Fable*" (*The Stoic Strain in American Literature: Essays in Honor of Marston La France*, ed. Duane J. MacMillan, Toronto, 1979) and Rosemary M. Magee's "*A Fable* and the Gospels: A Study in Contrasts" (*RS*, June 1979)—pursue essentially the same objective.

1980–1988. Keen Butterworth completed his monograph, *A Critical and Textual Study of Faulkner's "A Fable"* (Ann Arbor, Mich., 1983), in 1970 as a dissertation at the University of South Carolina. It is a thoroughly competent and conservative piece of work, with an especially sound compositional history of the novel and table of suggested textual emendations. An appended survey of criticism is useful, despite a tendency to protect Butterworth's perhaps excessively high regard for *A Fable* by defensively discrediting opposing interpretations. A brief, candid preface acknowledges heavy debts to Cleanth Brooks and undercuts Butterworth's critical study: "If . . . I were to begin a study of *A Fable* from scratch today, I would forgo much of the explication, perhaps all of it. I would, rather . . . prepare the reader to read *A Fable*—not tell him how to read it." In the same curious paragraph, nonetheless, Butterworth tell us to read *A Fable* as "an optimistic book, for it trusts in redemption, the possibility of confronting man's fate with dignity and honor."

Richard H. King takes a considerably more skeptical, tough-minded approach in "*A Fable*: Faulkner's Political Novel?" (*SLJ*, Spring 1985), seeing the novel as "a displacement from politics to a vague sort of spiritualized humanism." According to King, "Faulkner's was a politics of privatism," and *A Fable* emerges as "Faulkner's failed political novel." Situating the novel shrewdly within "the political culture of [Faulkner's] state and region," King has written perhaps the most stimulating essay on *A Fable* in many years. Dinnah Pladott takes a promising revisionary approach to biblical analogues in "Faulkner's *A Fable*: A Heresy or a Declaration of Faith?" (*JNT*, Spring 1982). Less revisionary, more recuperative perspectives are afforded by Doreen Fowler's two essays: "The Old Verities in Faulkner's Fable" (*Renascence*, Autumn 1981) and "'In Another Country': Faulkner's *A Fable*" (*SAF*, Spring 1987). In the latter essay, Fowler traces allusions to the New Testament, Christopher Marlowe, and *Sanctuary* in order to assert Faulkner's faith in "the recoverability of all times and all places."

Lothar Hönnighausen's "The Military as Metaphor" (*FJ*, Spring 1987) concludes that a "principle of relentless realism, metaphorically portrayed in the military, arrives at an archetypal dialectical confrontation with the rebellious idealism of the corporal." As Noel Polk notes in an accompanying response, Hönnighausen's fine essay represents an essentially literary—as distinct from philosophical, religious, or biographical—reading of *A Fable*. Polk's contribution to *Faulkner and Women*, "Woman and the Feminine in *A Fable*," forcefully yet gracefully discloses the novel's depiction of "a military world which not only seeks to escape the feminine but also actively fights back, if not at the feminine itself, then at least at certain symbols of femininity which linger around the battlefield."

s. *The Reivers*

1973–1979. The only significant essay on *The Reivers*, Edwin Moses's "Faulkner's *The Reivers*: The Art of Acceptance" (*MissQ*, Summer 1974), offers a welcome inspection of the novel's retrospective qualities; readers may wish to demur when Moses claims for the book the status of a major work. William E. McCarron's brief note, "Shakespeare, Faulkner, and Ned William McCaslin" (*NConL*, Dec. 1977), explains an allusion to *Richard II*.

1980–1988. James B. Carothers's wise essay, "The Road to *The Reivers*" ("*A Cosmos of My Own*"), shows "that when [Faulkner] finally came to write *The Reivers* he drew on imagery, vocabulary, situation, character, and theme from the entire range of his writing, that *The Reivers* is neither a sentimental afterthought, a commercial contradiction, nor a pusillanimous retraction of his great early work, but rather, that *The Reivers* is a fully realized articulation of themes and techniques Faulkner employed throughout his developing career." John Earl Bassett, in "*The Reivers*: Revision and Closure in Faulkner's Career" (*SLJ*, Spring 1986), claims, rather unremarkably, that "two kinds of revision take place—one syntagmatic, the updating of stories through sequels or reanalysis of motivations, one paradigmatic, new treatments of a type of conflict or theme."

In "Faulkner's *Reivers*: How to Change the Joke without Slipping the Yoke" (*Faulkner and Race*), Walter Taylor restates, more bluntly, a position he first put forth in *Faulkner's Search for a South*: "Faulkner's mellow reminiscence beams the very loud political message that Jim Crow was not so bad." Taylor insists that "Ned does not represent black Americans in any significant way; he represents, rather, the distilled essence of the tradition that enslaved them."

t. The Stories

1973–1979. Several writers of the annual review-essays for *American Literary Scholarship* have complained about the proliferation of studies of the short stories indifferent to (or ignorant of) the rest of the Faulkner canon and prior criticism and scholarship. The following comments ignore work of this sort. The list of good, knowledgeable studies from the 1970s is headed by Robert W. Hamblin's "'Carcassonne': Faulkner's Allegory of Art and the Artist" (*SoR*, Spring 1979), a convincing allegorical reading of the story Faulkner placed last in *Collected Stories*. A less successful but still interesting study of the same story is Richard A. Milum's "Faulkner's 'Carcassonne': The Dream and the Reality" (*SSF*, Spring 1978). Both studies should be read in conjunction with Noel Polk's comprehensive analysis of the story (see below). Also of value are two studies of "That Evening Sun" and one of "Red Leaves." In "Faulkner's 'The Village' and 'That Evening Sun': The Tale in Context" (*SLJ*, Fall 1978), Philip Momberger suggests, in Panthea Reid Broughton's words, "that 'The Village' grouping in the *Collected Stories* [is] not just topical but thematic" (*AmLS*, 1978). The second study of "That Evening Sun," May Cameron Brown's "Voice in 'That Evening Sun': A Study of Quentin Compson" (*MissQ*, Summer 1976), draws on the textual history of the story to create a convincing character analysis. Edmond L. Volpe's "Faulkner's 'Red Leaves': The Deciduation of Nature" (*SAF*, Autumn 1975) is a helpful analysis of the story's "life symbols and death symbols."

The period also saw the publication, in the annual Faulkner number of *Mississippi Quarterly*, of several studies of neglected or unpublished stories. Particularly valuable among this group are Sharon Smith Hult's "William Faulkner's 'The Brooch': The Journey to the Riolama" (Summer 1974) and Tony J. Owens's "Faulkner, Anderson, and 'Artist at Home'" (Summer 1979). Both bring interesting historical information to bear on their subjects. Other *Mississippi Quarterly* studies, of varying quality, are Frank Cantrell's "An Unpublished Faulkner Short Story: 'Snow'" (Summer 1973); Beatrice Lang's "An Unpublished Faulkner Story: 'The Big Shot'" (Summer 1973); Giliane Morell's "Prisoners of the Inner World: Mother and Daughter in *Miss Zilphia Gant*" (Summer 1975); Philip Castille's "'There Was a Queen' and Faulkner's Narcissa Sartoris" (Summer 1975); Lisa Paddock's "'Trifles with a Tragic Profundity': The Importance of 'Mistral'" (Summer 1979); and Hans H. Skei's "A Forgotten Faulkner Story: 'Thrift'" (Summer 1979).

1980–1988. William Faulkner's Short Stories (Ann Arbor, Mich., 1985), by James B. Carothers, reminds us of Faulkner's many superb accomplishments in the short story, of his respect for it as "the most demanding form after poetry," and of his belief that "in the novel you can be careless but in the short story you can't." Carothers advances two general arguments: first, that the short stories retain an essential integrity independent of the novels which often absorb them; and second, that the stories document Faulkner's "development from pessimism to optimism," from "ironic determinism to a thoroughly comic artistic vision." Although he does not quite manage to develop either argument satisfactorily in this brief book, Carothers *does* demonstrate that he knows enough about how the short stories work (and about how they were composed and recomposed) to write another more ambitious book. Carothers's 1983 paper, "'And Now What's to Do'" (*New Directions*), proclaims that "we are going to have to question, and to modify or discard some of the prevailing notions, habits, and practices of the past if we are to deal responsibly with the short stories in the future." Carothers's next book should do this and help substantiate his own very credible claim that Faulkner's "short stories deserve the same close reading given his novels." Noel Polk's "William Faulkner's 'Carcassonne'" (*SAF*, Spring 1984) offers a superb example of what remains to be learned from close readings of the short stories.

Like Carothers's book, Hans H. Skei's *William Faulkner: The Novelist as Short Story Writer* (Oslo, 1981) began as a dissertation. Skei tries to cram in a great deal of information about the compositional histories of stories, but gives almost no critical attention to how the stories work or why we should read them. Not only does Skei seem to lack Carothers's respect for Faulkner's artistic accomplishments as a writer of stories, but he also seriously underestimates Faulkner's own respect for the genre, trivializing many stories by seeing them as only the products of a kind of crude economic determinism.

James G. Watson expands our understanding and appreciation of Faulkner's work in this genre in a pair of strong articles: "Short Story Fantasies and the Limits of Modernism" (*FaSt*, 1980) and "Faulkner's Short Stories and the Making of Yoknapatawpha County" (*Fifty Years of Yoknapatawpha*); the latter emphasizes the unity of the *Collected Stories*. Less effectively, Arthur F. Kinney also insists upon the unity of Faulkner's important 1950 collection in "Faulkner's Narrative Poetics and *Collected Stories*" (*FaSt*, 1980). Joseph M. Flora describes one feature of Faulknerian poetics in "The Device of Conspicuous Silence in the Modern Short Story" (*The Teller and the Tale: Aspects of the Short Story*, ed. Wendell M. Aycock, Lubbock, Tex., 1982); giving special attention to "That Evening Sun," Flora shows that "by having the narrator's silence become a major part of his method, Faulkner attunes the reader's ears to other modulations of sound."

"That Evening Sun" remains one of the few Faulkner stories to be read closely in published criticism. None of the following readings surprises or satisfies, but each contributes something to our sense of how this fine story works: Laurence Perrine's "'That Evening Sun': A Skein of Uncertainties" (*SSF*, Summer 1985), which reminds us of just how little we know for certain about what happens in the story; Dirk Kuyk, Jr., Betty M. Kuyk, and James A. Miller's "Black Culture in William Faulkner's 'That Evening Sun'" (*JAmS*, Apr. 1986); Ken Bennett's "The Language of the Blues in Faulkner's 'That Evening Sun'" (*MissQ*, Summer 1985); and Paula Sunderman's "Speech Act Theory and Faulkner's 'That Evening Sun'" (*Lang&S*, Fall 1981).

Only "Dry September," "A Rose for Emily," and "Barn Burning" get as much individual attention as "That Evening Sun." The two most rewarding new articles on "Dry September" are Lawrence Jay Dessner's "William Faulkner's 'Dry September': Decadence Domesticated" (*CollL*, Spring 1984) and John K. Crane's "But the Days Grow Short: A Reinterpretation of Faulkner's 'Dry September'" (*TCL*, Winter 1985). On "A Rose for Emily," see James M. Mellard's rather pretentious "Faulkner's Miss Emily and Blake's 'Sick Rose': 'Invisible Worm,' *Nachträglichkeit*, and Retrospective Gothic" (*FJ*, Fall 1986) and Dennis W. Allen's "Horror and Perverse Delight: Faulkner's 'A Rose for Emily'" (*MFS*, Winter 1984).

While there have been no startling developments in published interpretations of "Barn Burning," something can be learned from each of the following four essays: Jane Hiles's "Kinship and Heredity in Faulkner's 'Barn Burning'" (*MissQ*, Summer 1985); Joseph Comprone's "Literature and the Writing Process: A Pedagogical Reading of William Faulkner's 'Barn Burning'" (*CollL*, Winter 1982); Merrill Maguire Skaggs's "Story and Film of 'Barn Burning': The Difference a Camera Makes" (*SoQ*, Winter 1983); and M. E. Bradford's "Family and Community in Faulkner's 'Barn Burning'" (*SoR*, Spring 1981).

Bradford continues to be about the most prolific critic of Faulkner's short fiction, turning out thoughtful readings of individual stories, advancing a conservative (neo-Agrarian) political and cultural agenda; see especially: "Faulkner's 'A Courtship': An Accommodation of Cultures" (*SAQ*, Summer 1981); "A Late Encounter: Faulkner's 'Mountain Victory'" (*MissQ*, Fall 1987); and "The Anomaly of Faulkner's World War I Stories" (*MissQ*, Summer 1983). Anne Goodwyn Jones looks at a similar cluster of stories, to different effect, in "Gender and the Great War: The Case of Faulkner and Porter" (*WS*, Nos. 1 and 2, 1986); and Jeffrey J. Folks reads a few stories exploring the consequences of war in "Honor in Faulkner's Short Fiction" (*SoR*, Summer 1982).

Finally, it should be remembered that Max Putzel works extensively with Faulkner's short stories in *Genius of Place*. Much important work, obviously, remains to be done: we need more and better close readings of individual stories (and clusters of stories) still outside the popularized canon; and we need more inclusive and theoretical approaches to Faulkner's poetics of short fiction.

u. Nonfiction Prose

1973–1979. James B. Meriwether's "Faulkner's Essays on Anderson" (*Fifty Years of Yoknapatawpha*) applies Faulkner's 1953 essay on Sherwood Anderson to Faulkner's own career in illuminating ways. Also of interest is Michael Grimwood's "The Self-Parodic Context of Faulkner's Nobel Prize Speech" (*SoR*, Spring 1979). Grimwood's comments about Faulkner's uneasiness with his vocation anticipate arguments presented at greater length in his *Heart in Conflict*. Finally, Christof Wegelin's "'Endure' and 'Prevail': Faulkner's Modification of Conrad" (*N&Q*, Oct. 1974) discusses the indebtedness identified in its title.

1980–1988. In "Faulkner's Nobel Prize Address: A Reading" (*SAQ*, Winter 1982), Jerry A. Herndon suggests that the address raises questions about "a sense of existential freedom: a freedom *from* the values and conventions of the past," while simultaneously "challeng[ing] the cult of moral relativism." Herndon also speculates that Faulkner "may have had in mind as models Abraham Lincoln's two most memorable performances, the Gettysburg Address and the Second Inaugural Address."

F. Scott Fitzgerald

Jackson R. Bryer

I BIBLIOGRAPHY

This area, usually one of the most active in Fitzgerald studies, has continued to be so during the past decade. Book-length works—supplements to the two standard bibliographical resources, composition studies of two Fitzgerald novels, a study and bibliography of his foreign critical reception, a concordance to *The Great Gatsby*, a facsimile of the *Gatsby* manuscript, and an apparatus for preparing a definitive edition of *Gatsby*—as well as a number of worthwhile shorter pieces—have appeared.

Matthew J. Bruccoli's *Supplement to "F. Scott Fitzgerald—A Descriptive Bibliography"* (Pittsburgh, 1980) corrects and updates Bruccoli's 1972 work and adds two valuable new sections on translations and republications. The first of these concentrates on foreign-language editions in book-length form; while the second is more comprehensive in including "anthology, magazine, and newspaper republications in the English language of Fitzgerald's stories, poems, essays, interviews, and excerpts from novels—all writings except letters." The length of this volume—219 pages—testifies eloquently to Bruccoli's diligence as well as to the vitality of Fitzgerald's work in the 1970s.

Several briefer items, some published before Bruccoli's *Supplement* and others after it, add important information. Linda Berry's "The Text of *Bits of Paradise*" (*FHA*, 1975) lists the variants between the magazine texts of the stories and the book texts; Michael Adams's "Fitzgerald Filmography" (*FHA*, 1977) provides names of the screenwriters, directors, producers, and casts for the twelve movies made from Fitzgerald's works through 1976; and Jennifer McCabe Atkinson, in "Indeed, 'Lo, the Poor Peacock!'" (*FHA*, 1972), describes the cuts and emendations made in Fitzgerald's story when *Esquire* published it for the first time in its September 1971 issue. In "The Bantam 'Gatsby'" (*BCM*, Nov./Dec. 1978), James L. W. West III looks at the covers and jackets of the 1945, 1946, 1949, and 1951 paperback impressions of the novel as reflections of the changing reputation and image of its author; and West's "The Second Serials of *This Side of Paradise* and *The Beautiful and Damned*" (*PBSA*, First Quarter 1979) discusses the advertising leading up to the newspaper serializations and the "butchered or botched" texts of the novels which for many readers (West estimates 50,000 for *Paradise*, 35,000 for *Damned*) represented either the first or the only form in which they were exposed to the two works.

Fitzgerald's unpublished works also received some attention. In "The Unpublished Stories: Fitzgerald in His Final Stage" (*TCL*, Apr. 1974), Ruth Prigozy provides good summaries of seven stories. While her claims for the literary value of some of these seem excessive, she does well in relating several thematically to the published fiction. Alan Margolies's "A Note on Fitzgerald's Lost and Unpublished Stories" (*FHA*, 1972) locates in the Princeton Library two stories previously called lost, and Margolies, in "F. Scott Fitzgerald's Prison Play" (*PBSA*, First Quarter 1972), briefly describes an apparently uncompleted play, notes for which survive at Princeton.

Four of Fitzgerald's five novels were the subjects of substantial textual studies in the past decade. James L. W. West III's *The Making of "This Side of Paradise"* (Philadelphia, 1983) gives an extremely suggestive summary of the process which Fitzgerald used in, literally, piecing together his first novel from portions of his first draft as well as already published stories and playlets and even letters received from friends. Although West is hampered by having been unfortunately and inexplicably prohibited from quoting letters, typescripts, and manuscripts, he is extremely helpful in accounting for the novel's acknowledged unevenness and cavalier disregard for point of view in book 1 and in tracing the postpublication textual history of Fitzgerald's most carelessly written and sloppily proofread volume.

Matthew J. Bruccoli, in *"The Last of the Novelists": F. Scott Fitzgerald and "The Last Tycoon"* (Carbondale, Ill., 1977), unlike West, had full access to all the surviving notes and manuscripts, and he uses them extensively in providing a detailed reconstruction of the successive drafts. Bruccoli's account is very technical and is difficult to follow without an intimate knowledge of the text; but his conclusion—that Edmund Wilson, in preparing the posthumous edition of the incomplete novel, "obscures the gestational nature of Fitzgerald's work and misleads readers into judging work-in-progress as completed stages"—emerges gracefully and inescapably from his careful scholarship. After his book appeared, Bruccoli located the correspondence between Wilson and Maxwell Perkins of Scribner's while *The Last Tycoon* was being prepared for publication; in "The Perkins/Wilson Correspondence About Publication of *The Last Tycoon*" (*FHA*, 1978), he summarizes the contents of the letters and concludes that Wilson was solely responsible for editing Fitzgerald's drafts.

While *The Great Gatsby* now remains (along with *The Beautiful and Damned*) without a book-length composition study (surely one is long overdue), three very useful textual resources which appeared in the past decade should make that study much easier to prepare. Two are the work of the seemingly indefatigable Matthew J. Bruccoli. *"The Great Gatsby": A Facsimile of the Manuscript* (Washington, D.C., 1973) supplies, besides the facsimile, Bruccoli's introduction which is the best detailed examination of the novel's composition we have. His *Apparatus for F. Scott Fitzgerald's "The Great Gatsby" [Under the Red, White, and Blue]* (Columbia, S.C., 1974) is designed so that anyone who wants to prepare a definitive text of *Gatsby* can do so by marking up his own copy (presumably the widely used Scribner Library edition) based on the collations and emendations and revisions Bruccoli presents. While Bruccoli's *Apparatus* is undeniably useful, it also has elicited some negative responses from reviewers, most notably Denzell S. Smith (*TLS*, 5 Sept. 1975) and James L. W. West III (*Proof*, 1975). Andrew T. Crosland's *A Concordance to F. Scott Fitzgerald's "The Great Gatsby"* (Detroit, 1975), the first concordance of an American novel, uses as its text the 1925 first printing as emended by Bruccoli in his *Apparatus* and is a model of clarity and accuracy. It appeared at a time when scholars and critics were beginning finally to turn their attention to Fitzgerald's style, and it surely facilitated such study and will continue to do so.

There were also several good textual articles. Chief among these is Brian Higgins and Hershel Parker's "Sober Second Thoughts: The 'Author's Final Version' of Fitzgerald's *Tender Is the Night*" (*Proof*, 1975), which stands as the most meticulous examination of the relative merits of the 1934 and 1951 editions of the novel. While one may quarrel with their claim that the 1934 text is clearly superior, the precision with which Higgins and Parker study the thematic and verbal patterns in Fitzgerald's text makes this not only bibliographical scholarship of the highest order but also a valuable close reading of *Tender*. Lucy Buntain, in "A Note on the Editions of *Tender is the Night*" (*SAF*, Autumn 1973), concludes that neither edition is obviously superior and that "the competing editions of *Tender* indicate Fitzgerald's painful indecision about what the novel should ultimately mean." Similarly and more recently, in *"Tender Is the Night*: The Text Itself" (in his edition of *Critical Essays on "Tender Is the Night*," CEAmL, Boston, 1986), Milton R. Stern, after a careful summary of the previous scholarship on the subject and a brief account of the novel's composition history, concludes that "there are too many facts on both sides of the argument to allow for one version and one version only." But Stern also argues strongly and convincingly for the efficacy of Fitzgerald's second thoughts on and revision of the 1934 edition, noting that "the facts *for* the 1934 version are not also facts *against* the 1951 version."

Fitzgerald's short stories and essays have continued to receive textual attention as well. Thomas E. Daniels's "Toward a Definitive Edition of F. Scott Fitzgerald's Short Stories" (*PBSA*, Third Quarter 1977) presents a careful, albeit somewhat unrealistic, formula for preparing an edition which would provide "texts as close to Fitzgerald's intentions as possible." Given the various versions of the stories, this represents an immense task which Daniels acknowledges would involve "a great deal of perception . . . and possibly a little psychic insight." That such an effort is feasible is amply demonstrated by Daniels's own "The Texts of 'Winter Dreams'" (*FHA*, 1977), by James L. W. West III and J. Barclay Inge's "F. Scott Fitzgerald's Revision of 'The Rich Boy'" (*Proof*, 1977), and by West's "Notes on the Text of F. Scott Fitzgerald's 'Early Success'" (*RALS*, Spring 1975). Garry N. Murphy and William C. Slattery's "The Flawed Text of 'Babylon Revisited': A Challenge to Editors, A Warning to Readers" (*SSF*, Summer 1981) notes the continued presence in the story of a paragraph which Fitzgerald wanted deleted because he had used it in *Tender Is the Night*.

That Fitzgerald's work and life have continued to attract a great deal of popular and scholarly attention is graphically demonstrated by Jackson R. Bryer's 542-page *The Critical Reputation of F. Scott Fitzgerald: A Bibliographical Study—Supplement One through 1981* (Hamden, Conn., 1984). Although Bryer does pick up a number of items inadvertently omitted from his 1967 volume and adds new early pieces on film and stage adaptations of Fitzgerald's fiction and a section of reviews of Zelda Fitzgerald's *Save Me the Waltz* (1932), most of his *Supplement* enumerates in annotated form the reviews, articles, books, and book sections which appeared in the fifteen years since his earlier volume. Bryer's unannotated section on dissertations and masters theses should be supplemented by Deborah A. Forczek's "Fitzgerald and Hemingway in the Academy: A Survey of Dissertations" (*FHA*, 1978).

Owing to the 1980 publication of Linda C. Stanley's *The Foreign Critical Reputation of F. Scott Fitzgerald: An Analysis and Annotated Bibliography* (Westport, Conn.), Bryer omits from his *Supplement* a section on foreign-language criticism. As her title indicates, Stanley provides analyses of Fitzgerald's reception abroad as well as heavily annotated listings of works about him and a chronological compilation of translations and editions. Her book is divided into six chapters, with France, Great Britain, Germany, Italy, and Japan receiving full-chapter treatment, while Australia, Canada, Denmark, India, the Low Countries, Norway, Portuguese (Brazil), Russia, South Africa, Spain, and Sweden are grouped together in the final chapter. While one suspects that Stanley has missed some items, her surveys are incisive, and her listings make available much previously inaccessible material. More information on Fitzgerald's reputation in Japan can be found in Kiyohiko Tsuboi's "The Reception of F. Scott Fitzgerald in Japan" (*FHA*, 1979) and in Sadao Nagaoka's "Fitzgerald Bibliographical Center in Japan" (*FHA*, 1979).

The Fitzgerald issue of *Twentieth Century Literature* (Summer 1980) includes two helpful bibliographical surveys. Jackson R. Bryer's "Four Decades of Fitzgerald Studies: The Best and the Brightest" selects the most worthwhile pieces from 1950 to 1980 in various categories; while Sergio Perosa, in "Fitzgerald Studies in the 1970s," restricts himself to some twenty book-length works by and about Fitzgerald. Elaine P. Maimon's "F. Scott Fitzgerald's Book Sales: A Look at the Record" (*FHA*, 1973) supplies valuable documentation on a myth-shrouded topic: the status and sales figures for Fitzgerald's books between 1936 and 1968. While her chart is restricted to titles published by Scribner's, Maimon comes up with some fascinating statistics—Fitzgerald did not die "out of print" (eight of his books were in print in 1940, but they sold only seventy-two copies); but between 1947 and 1950 only one volume (*Gatsby and The Last Tycoon*) was in print, and total sales for the four years were 1,657.

Three restricted surveys add little. One, Malcolm Cowley's "The Fitzgerald Revival, 1941–1953" (*FHA*, 1974), does contain some new information about Cowley's own role in bringing Fitzgerald's works back before the public; but J. J. Fenstermaker's "The Literary Reputation of F. Scott Fitzgerald, 1940–1941: Appraisal and Reappraisal" (*FHA*, 1979) and Andrew Crosland's "Sleeping and Waking—The Literary Reputation of *The Great Gatsby*, 1927–1944" (*FHA*, 1974) simply go over old territory. The annual surveys of Fitzgerald scholarship and criticism in *American Literary Scholarship* (Durham, N.C., 1973–86) are, as always, the places to begin; between 1971 and 1978, they were prepared by Jackson R. Bryer. Scott Donaldson took over from 1979 to 1982, Bryer did the survey in 1983, and Michael S. Reynolds took on the assignment with the 1984 essay. With the demise of the *Fitzgerald/Hemingway Annual* and its "Fitzgerald Checklist" in 1979, *American Literary Scholarship* assumed even greater importance.

II EDITIONS

Just about as many "new" (previously uncollected in book form, previously unpublished, or published in revised form) books by Fitzgerald appeared during the past decade as he saw into print during his lifetime. Three of them collectively brought into book form for the first time sixty-four stories previously unpublished or available only in magazines. Matthew J. Bruccoli's edition of *The Price Was High: The Last Uncollected Stories of F. Scott Fitzgerald* (New York, 1979) includes forty-nine heretofore uncollected stories and one ("On Your Own") never before published, leaving only eight published stories uncollected and nine unpublished. Bruccoli provides helpful concise introductions to each story, giving the date and circumstances of its composition and brief commentary on it. Although most reviewers of the volume agreed with Bruccoli's admission in his introduction that these are "not Fitzgerald's best," many also echoed Malcolm Cowley's comment that "almost all of them contain something to surprise us" and "such moments . . . are a sound reason for preserving even the weaker stories" (*NYTBR*, 4 Mar. 1979).

Bits of Paradise: 21 Uncollected Stories by F. Scott and Zelda Fitzgerald, selected by Scottie Fitzgerald Smith and Matthew J. Bruccoli (London, 1973; New York, 1974) contains, besides a typically graceful and evocative reminiscence-foreword by Scottie Fitzgerald Smith, eleven previously uncollected stories by Scott (one, "The Swimmers," is among his best), nine fictional sketches by Zelda, and one piece written in collaboration. *The Basil and Josephine Stories* (ed. Jackson R. Bryer and John Kuehl, New York, 1973) probably succeed more consistently than the selections in *Bits of Paradise*; and although only three of them have never been collected before, the two series undoubtedly benefit from being issued together as juxtaposed units with recurrent themes and motifs.

Fitzgerald's careers as playwright, poet, and screenwriter also have received increased exposure. *F. Scott Fitzgerald's St. Paul Plays: 1911–1914* (ed. Alan Margolies, Princeton, N.J., 1978) is a carefully prepared first publication of the four dramas he wrote for the Elizabethan Dramatic Club in his hometown. Although they suffer from truncated second acts and an overabundance of terrible puns, they also show a remarkable grasp of dramatic structure, character differentiation, and control of essentially melodramatic situations, considering that their author was in his middle and late teens. Fitzgerald's only professionally produced play, *The Vegetable* (1923), was reissued by Scribner's in 1976 with an excellent introduction by Charles Scribner III tracing the history of the play's composition and appendixes which include scenes cut from the manuscript during its author's final revisions and a list of "corrections and addenda" which he inserted in the final acting script.

Matthew J. Bruccoli's edition of Fitzgerald's *Poems 1911–1940* (Bloomfield Hills, Mich., and Columbia, S.C., 1981) collects 149 poems, jingles, and doggerel verses, plus the fifty-five lyrics he wrote for three Triangle Club musicals at Princeton. James Dickey is certainly correct in asserting, in his fine brief introduction to the volume, that "Fitzgerald's lyric gift . . . needed not the structure and formal manipulations peculiar to versification, but those of the novel and the story"; but Dickey also notes that "the evidences of an unusual mind are never completely worthless, no matter whether the mind is in its true groove or out of it," and this collection does show Fitzgerald to have been a clever writer of light verse.

The 1938 MGM production of *Three Comrades* was the only film assignment of the many Fitzgerald undertook during his three visits to Hollywood for which he received actual screen credit; and it is good to have the full text in print in *F. Scott Fitzgerald's Screenplay for "Three Comrades" by Erich Maria Remarque* (ed. Matthew J. Bruccoli, Carbondale, Ill., 1978). Bruccoli's designation of the script as "a competent job, but too long and rather slowly paced" is accurate; and his afterword and appendixes, telling in detail and showing how producer Joseph Mankiewicz butchered Fitzgerald's work by demanding extensive revisions, are fascinating.

Bruccoli has also given us behind-the-scenes glimpses of Fitzgerald at work in his editions of *The Notebooks of F. Scott Fitzgerald* (New York, 1978) and of *F. Scott Fitzgerald's Ledger: A Facsimile* (Washington, D.C., 1973). About 60 percent of *The Notebooks* is available in Edmund Wilson's 1945 edition of *The Crack-Up*; but here we have them all, divided into sections entitled (by Fitzgerald), to name just a few, "Descriptions of Girls," "Rough Stuff," "Feelings & Emotions (without girls)," and "Moments (What People do)," together with Bruccoli's "Editorial and Explanatory Notes," which do a masterful job of identifying persons and places as well as, where applicable, indicating where Fitzgerald used notebook entries in his fiction. The *Ledger* is less valuable for what it contains—Fitzgerald's records of his publications and of his and Zelda's earnings and an "Outline Chart of my Life" from 1896 to 1935 (all of this has been extensively mined by scholars)—than for its overall tone and for the type of material its compiler chose to include, especially in the "Outline Chart."

Although they were both issued in limited editions, the facsimile reprinting of Scott's humorous true account of *The Cruise of the Rolling Junk* (Bloomfield Hills, Mich., and Columbia, S.C., 1976), which originally appeared in three 1924 issues of *Motor*, and the first publication of Zelda's play *Scandalabra* (Bloomfield Hills, Mich., and Columbia, S.C., 1980) are noteworthy. And in what is surely the most underrated and overlooked Fitzgerald publication of the past fifteen years, *The Romantic Egoists: A Pictorial Autobiography from the Scrapbooks and Albums of Scott and Zelda Fitzgerald* (New York, 1974), editors Matthew J. Bruccoli, Scottie Fitzgerald Smith, and Joan P. Kerr expertly juxtapose clippings, photographs, and other memorabilia from the scrapbooks and albums with passages from letters and from published works. The volume also contains a portfolio, mostly in color, of Zelda's paintings, the first publication of Scott's brief 1924 essay "The Pampered Man," a charming and modest introduction by Smith, and Bruccoli's succinct account of Fitzgerald's "Posthumous Vindication."

Bruccoli has also given us two synopses of movie scenarios which Fitzgerald prepared but apparently never completed, "Ballet Shoes" (*FHA*, 1976) and "The Feather Fan" (*FHA*, 1977), and the full text of "Lipstick," a narrative screenplay which he wrote in 1927 for Constance Talmadge, only to have it rejected by producers John W. Considine (who had commissioned it) and B. P. Schulberg (*FHA*, 1978). Charles Mann's carefully edited text of "F. Scott Fitzgerald's Critique of *A Farewell to Arms*" (*FHA*, 1976) is the first appearance of the harshly critical notes on a late draft of the novel which Fitzgerald sent to Hemingway and which the latter heeded in only one instance. It is an important document in one of the most complex friendships in American literary history.

The other additions to the Fitzgerald canon are less important but worthy of note nonetheless. Margaret M. Duggan has found as a clipping in one of his scrapbooks "A New Fitzgerald Book Review: *The Boy Grew Older*" (*FHA*, 1977); Richard Winslow reprints from the 8 April 1923 *New York Herald* "Fitzgerald's 'Favorite Story'" (*FHA*, 1978), an English drinking tale; Matthew J. Bruccoli, in "Fitzgerald's St. Paul Academy Publications: Possible Addenda" (*FHA*, 1975), republishes four unsigned limericks about his schoolmates from his high school publication, *Now & Then*, which he pasted in his scrapbook, possibly because he had written them; and James L. W. West III establishes, on the basis of Fitzgerald's marked copy at Princeton, Fitzgerald's contributions to Mencken and Nathan's *The American Credo* (*PULC*, Autumn 1972). *F. Scott Fitzgerald on Writing* (ed. Larry W. Phillips, New York, 1986) contains "Fitzgerald's best thoughts on his craft" arranged by subject.

III MANUSCRIPTS AND LETTERS

While we continue to await Alan Margolies's catalogue and description of the Fitzgerald Papers at Princeton, which he is expanding to include significant Fitzgerald collections in other libraries, a few important groups of materials have been acquired by various institutions. Princeton remains far and away the greatest repository, and they have continued to add to their holdings. The most significant of their more recent acquisitions are manuscripts, letters, and memorabilia of Zelda Fitzgerald and the archives of Harold Ober Associates, Fitzgerald's long-time agent. The Ober archives do not include correspondence exchanged between Ober and Fitzgerald; these were retained by the Ober family and given to Indiana University in 1977, along with some manuscripts. Smaller additions to the Princeton collection have been announced periodically in the *Princeton University Library Chronicle* (Autumn 1970, Winter 1972, Autumn 1972, Autumn 1975, Autumn 1978, Winter 1979, Autumn 1980, Autumn 1981, Autumn 1982, Autumn 1983, Autumn 1984).

In 1971, the University of Southern California acquired from Metro-Goldwyn-Mayer a considerable amount of material relating to Fitzgerald's screenwriting career, including drafts of screenplays and treatments and notes from story conferences. The availability of these manuscripts has not as yet produced the sort of detailed examination of Fitzgerald in Hollywood which Aaron Latham and others were prevented from doing earlier because of the restrictions placed by MGM; but Wheeler Winston Dixon has made a good start in this direction with *The Cinematic Vision of F. Scott Fitzgerald* (Ann Arbor, Mich., 1986). Dixon focuses on the two film scripts "which can be conclusively identified as principally the work of F. Scott Fitzgerald," *Infidelity* and *Three Comrades*, and his analysis of them is the fullest we have. He also devotes chapters to *Gatsby*, *Tender*, and *The Last Tycoon* "in order to determine the connections between the style and structure of" the novels and the film scenarios. *Fiction, Film, and F. Scott Fitzgerald* by Gene D. Phillips, S.J. (Chicago, 1986) has the avowed purpose of determining "to what degree the films of Fitzgerald's fiction—all scripted by hands other than his own—are worthy renditions of the stories from which they are derived"; but Phillips's discussions tend to be more descriptive than analytic. He divides his study into three parts: Fitzgerald as screenwriter, films made from Fitzgerald's short stories, and films of his novels.

The Minnesota Historical Society in St. Paul has been building a prom-ising gathering of items. Chief among these is an oral history project of interviews with St. Paul contemporaries of Fitzgerald. In "Fitzgerald in St. Paul: An Oral Portrait" (*FHA*, 1976), Lloyd Hackl briefly describes the project and quotes extensively from an interview with Mrs. C. O. (Xandra) Kalman, a lifelong Fitzgerald friend. The Kalmans also gave to the Minnesota Historical Society their copies of correspondence ex-changed with Scott and Zelda.

Fitzgerald's important friendship with H. L. Mencken is clarified greatly by recently available materials in the New York Public Library. These are described and commented upon by James L. W. West III in "The Mencken-Fitzgerald Papers: An Annotated Checklist" (*PULC*, Au-tumn 1976). His association with Arnold Gingrich, the editor of *Esquire*, the magazine in which, during the last four years of Fitzgerald's life, virtually all of his published fiction appeared, is documented in the Gingrich Papers at the University of Michigan. Fitzgerald's correspond-ence with his St. Paul friend Ruth Howard Sturtevant has been deposited at the University of Virginia.

The fourth collection of Fitzgerald correspondence to appear within the past two decades, *Correspondence of F. Scott Fitzgerald* (ed. Matthew J. Bruccoli and Margaret M. Duggan, with the assistance of Susan Walker, New York, 1980), is the largest and most comprehensive. It does not include any letters published in the earlier volumes and goes well beyond them in printing drafts of letters which may not have been mailed, letters printed in dealer and auction catalogs which are now unlocatable, inscrip-tions in presentation copies, and a generous selection of letters to Fitz-gerald. While a certain amount of this material is ephemeral and of interest only to the most avid Fitzgerald scholar, there is also a good deal to attract more general readers. Those interested in the literary milieu of the 1920s and 1930s will relish the gossip and information in letters exchanged between Fitzgerald and Mencken, Van Wyck Brooks, Ring Lardner, Sherwood Anderson, James Branch Cabell, Gertrude Stein, John Peale Bishop, and others. Above all, the collection is valuable for its presentation of both sides of the correspondence between F. Scott and Zelda Fitzgerald and for the first appearance in print of Zelda's letters, especially an incredible forty-five-page stream-of-consciousness résumé of her marriage which she wrote in 1930 in a Swiss psychiatric clinic.

Further evidence of Zelda's peculiarly lyrical and poetic epistolary style can be found in Taylor Littleton's "A Letter from Zelda Fitzgerald" (*FHA*, 1975) and in "Zelda Fitzgerald's Tribute to F. Scott Fitzgerald" (*FHA*, 1974), the latter an undeniably overwritten but hauntingly poignant and hitherto unpublished obituary memoir. Excerpts from Zelda's letters also form the basis for "Zelda: A Worksheet" (*ParR*, Autumn 1983), a document prepared by actress Lane Yorke for playwright Bill Luce who in turn used it in preparing "Zelda," which was performed at the Spoleto Festival in Charleston, South Carolina, in 1980 with Yorke as the star. These recent appearances of Zelda's letters suggest that a volume of her letters as well as one that would contain both sides of her correspondence with her husband should be published.

Bruccoli and Duggan's collection includes most, but not all, of the smaller gatherings of letters which have been published recently. Of R. L. Samsell's "Six Fitzgerald Letters to Hunt Stromberg" (*FHA*, 1972), three do not appear in Bruccoli and Duggan; one letter from Scott and one from Zelda, first published by Katherine B. Trower in "The Fitzgeralds' Letters to the Hoveys" (*FHA*, 1978), are not reprinted in the later volume; and none of the ten letters from Fitzgerald to Ruth Sturtevant which Roger Lewis published (*FHA*, 1979) appears in Bruccoli and Duggan, although they do include four other letters Fitzgerald wrote to Sturtevant.

As will be seen below, at least one recent Fitzgerald biographer has made good use of letters written to Fitzgerald and letters written about him by his friends. In 1984, Arthur Mizener gave to Princeton papers and correspondence concerning his research on Fitzgerald. Ernest Hemingway's letters to Mizener are owned by the University of Maryland; several are published in Carlos Baker's edition of Hemingway's *Selected Letters: 1917–1961* (New York, 1981), along with many of Hemingway's letters to Fitzgerald and numerous Hemingway letters in which he discusses Fitzgerald. "Edmund Wilson's Letters: To and About F. Scott Fitzgerald" (*NYRB*, 17 Feb. 1977) were later incorporated into Elena Wilson's edition of her husband's *Letters on Literature and Politics: 1912–1972* (New York, 1977), where they joined other Wilson letters in which Fitzgerald is mentioned prominently. *Ring Around Max: The Correspondence of Ring Lardner & Max Perkins* (ed. Clifford M. Caruthers, DeKalb, Ill., 1973) also includes much of interest about Fitzgerald, as do *The Fourteenth Chronicle: Letters and Diaries of John Dos Passos* (ed. Townsend Ludington, Boston, 1973) and *Selected Letters of John O'Hara* (ed. Matthew J. Bruccoli, New York, 1978). Linda Patterson Miller's "'As a Friend You Have Never Failed Me': The Fitzgerald-Murphy Correspondence" (*JML*, Sept. 1976) prints nineteen letters and three telegrams from the Murphys to Fitzgerald and provides a tantalizing small taste of Miller's forthcoming biography of Gerald Murphy and of her edition of Murphy's correspondence with Fitzgerald, Hemingway, Dos Passos, MacLeish, and others, also in preparation. Finally, in "Notes Toward a Corrected Edition of *Dear Scott/Dear Max*" (*FHA*, 1978), Jackson R. Bryer lists corrections in the first printing of his and Kuehl's 1971 collection.

IV BIOGRAPHY

Who could have imagined, in 1973 when the last version of this essay appeared, that in a decade and a half there would be four new major Fitzgerald biographies published, all of which make a contribution? Matthew J. Bruccoli's *Some Sort of Epic Grandeur: The Life of F. Scott Fitzgerald* (New York, 1981) succeeds best as a documentary account of the life which utilizes many new sources both published and unpublished and unavailable to previous biographers. Occasionally Bruccoli fails to indicate his sources; and he tends to place entire documents in his text without comment (the full ten-page letter Fitzgerald wrote Hemingway concerning *The Sun Also Rises* is included, uninterrupted by badly needed explanations of what is being referred to and unsupplemented by any indication of how extensively Hemingway heeded the advice). But, contrary to what some reviewers contended (e.g., Kenneth S. Lynn, *Harper's*, Dec. 1981; Jonathan Yardley, *Washington Post*, 11 Oct. 1981), the book reads easily and contains numerous insights along with its undeniable abundance of factual material. It will be used as a reference for years to come.

André Le Vot's *F. Scott Fitzgerald: A Biography* (Garden City, N.Y., 1983) originally appeared in French in 1979 as *Scott Fitzgerald*. Le Vot's vantage as a European enables him to provide some fresh views of Fitzgerald and his era—his sections on Princeton, on America in 1920, on the corruptness of the Jazz Age, on Prohibition, and on Paris in the 1920s are especially good—but his book is marred by a lengthy and unoriginal critical analysis of *The Great Gatsby* which suddenly and inexplicably interrupts the biographical account and by Le Vot's—or his translator's—occasionally obtrusive overwritten style. But Le Vot spent many years researching this book, and he draws effective connections between the fiction and the life; and, as Veronica A. Makowsky points out (*Rev.*, 1984), the "true strength" of his work stems from "his ability to analyze character within the dynamics of a relationship."

Scott Donaldson, in *Fool for Love: F. Scott Fitzgerald* (New York, 1983), also is concerned with assessing how Fitzgerald interacted with others; his thesis is that he "was driven to please other people, especially rich and prominent people." Donaldson traces this need to Fitzgerald's relationship with his mother (she was "largely responsible for his social insecurity"), and he sees it as satisfied far more successfully with women than with men. His book, which makes extensive use of letters to Fitzgerald, is a mosaic of chapters on various facets of his life and career—his childhood, his years at Princeton, his drinking, his womanizing, his attitudes toward Jews and blacks, his crack-up—combined with sensitive analyses of the fiction (the sections on *Tender Is the Night* and on the short stories are particularly good). The result is an extremely persuasive psychological study interspersed with and inextricably bound to illuminating critical examinations of the fiction.

Invented Lives: F. Scott & Zelda Fitzgerald by James R. Mellow (Boston, 1984) delivers less than it promises. Mellow is concerned, he tells us in his preface, with "what masters of invention" Scott and Zelda became, "creating new versions of themselves, putting themselves into their stories, acting out their stories in real life," and with "the hazards of such invention." But what follows this hopeful beginning is neither a useful psychological investigation of Scott and Zelda's self-dramatizing instinct and its effects on their marriage nor the sort of much-needed corrective to previous scholarship which often has read their fiction as literal autobiography. Instead we get a beautifully written account which effectively brings to life the social and literary worlds inhabited by the Fitzgeralds but has little new to say. Most distressing is Mellow's obvious dislike for his subjects, foreshadowed in his preface when he admits, "I have become less and less sympathetic toward people with major and minor talents . . . who waste their gifts on drugs and drink, egotism and temperamental behavior." Because he is determined "not to let the glamorous Fitzgeralds get away with anything," Mellow accentuates the negative aspects of their personalities and behavior and tends to dismiss, rationalize, or ignore more positive evidence. A more balanced, if less extensive, appraisal of the Scott-Zelda relationship is offered by Jeffrey Meyers in a chapter on the Fitzgeralds in his *Married to Genius* (New York, 1977).

Although it does contain a predictably graceful and authoritative biographical account, Arthur Mizener's *Scott Fitzgerald and His World* (New York, 1972) is more noteworthy for its many contemporary photographs of the Fitzgeralds and of people and places associated with them, carefully chosen to give the unique flavor of the period. Similarly, John J. Koblas's *F. Scott Fitzgerald in Minnesota: His Homes and Haunts* (St. Paul, Minn., 1978) is a modest fifty-page booklet which, after a brief biographical introduction, presents descriptions, discussions, and photographs of thirty-five locations in and near St. Paul with Fitzgerald associations—homes he lived in, places he frequented—or which are mentioned in his fiction.

Aside from his marriage, probably no relationship in Fitzgerald's life was as complex and as troubling to him as that with Ernest Hemingway. In his deceptively slim volume, *Scott and Ernest: The Authority of Failure and the Authority of Success* (New York, 1978), Matthew J. Bruccoli skillfully gathers the available documentary evidence—letters, reminiscences, interviews with mutual friends, published autobiographical accounts, and previously published research—to present what will undoubtedly remain for some time the fullest account we have. Briefer but suggestive analyses of the Hemingway-Fitzgerald friendship are offered by Scott Donaldson in *By Force of Will: The Life and Art of Ernest Hemingway* (New York, 1977), by Ruth Prigozy in "A Matter of Measurement: The Tangled Relationship Between Fitzgerald and Hemingway" (*Commonweal*, 29 Oct. 1971), and by Carlos Baker in "The Sun Rose Differently" (*NYTBR*, 18 Mar. 1979).

One can roughly divide the other biographical items into first-hand reminiscences and scholarly pieces. Carol Irish's scholarly essay "The Myth of Success in Fitzgerald's Boyhood" (*SAF*, Autumn 1973) revises the view of the early years as responsible for Fitzgerald's sense of inferiority and consequent desires for financial success, social position, and athletic glory by discovering that he was actually well-liked and respected by his peers, and that he "grew up in a *milieu* which hymned 'earnest worship of and respect for riches as the first article of its creed' and encouraged fierce competition among its young." Irish interviewed some of Fitzgerald's contemporaries and examined his earliest writings, thus giving her article a firm basis in an understanding of the period. Next to her thoughtful essay, Ernest R. Sandeen's much briefer account in his *St. Paul's Summit Avenue* (St. Paul, Minn., 1978) seems superficial.

Like Irish, William W. Seward, Jr. has researched his piece on "F. Scott Fitzgerald's Associations with Norfolk and Virginia Beach" (*FHA*, 1974) well by interviewing the daughters of Fitzgerald's favorite cousin Ceci; they remember his visits well, and Seward's article is immediate and authentic. Donald Marsden's *The Long Kickline: A History of the Princeton Triangle Club* (Princeton, N.J., 1968) presents a full picture of Fitzgerald's participation in three Triangle Club musicals.

Two of Fitzgerald's most important literary friendships are illuminated significantly in a pair of major biographies. In *Max Perkins: Editor of Genius* (New York, 1978), A. Scott Berg not only gives us the fullest account of Fitzgerald's relationship with his editor and the most detailed discussion of his publications as Perkins saw them into print, but he also deals with Perkins's relationships with his other authors and presents his views about Fitzgerald. Berg's "Hemingway and Fitzgerald— Where Would They Have Been Without Him?" (*NYTBR*, 16 Sept. 1984) distills much of the book's essence into a tribute to Perkins on the centenary of his birth. Jonathan Yardley's "Harmony in Great Neck: The Friendship of Ring Lardner and F. Scott Fitzgerald" (*SatR*, 9 July 1977) likewise is adapted from his *Ring: A Biography of Ring Lardner* (New York, 1977) and discusses the unlikely but deep friendship which developed between the Fitzgeralds and the Lardners in 1922–24, when both families were living in Great Neck.

Fitzgerald's expatriate years are well surveyed by André Le Vot in "Fitzgerald in Paris" (*FHA*, 1973); while his later sojourn in North Carolina is examined carefully by Billy Pritchard in "The Fitzgeralds in Asheville: The Tragic Years" (*Asheville Citizen-Times*, 28 Apr. 1974) and by Dannye Romine in "Tryon Revisited" (*Mountain Living*, Fall 1974). Tom Dardis, in "F. Scott Fitzgerald: What Do You Do When There's Nothing To Do," a chapter in his *Some Time in the Sun* (New York, 1976), traces the last years, in Hollywood, in an effort to show that they were not entirely bleak and sad as they are often depicted but rather were characterized by a good relationship with Sheilah Graham, a return to financial solvency, and a promising novel.

If we turn to the personal reminiscences, one of the best commentators on the Fitzgeralds was their daughter, who recalled them in "Notes About My Now-Famous Father" (*Family Circle*, May 1974) and in an interview with Christiane Johnson (*EA*, Jan.–Mar. 1976). A St. Paul friend, Kitty Milbank, remembers Scott in her *Miscellanea* (New York, 1965); and C. Lawton Campbell, who first met Scott at Princeton in 1914 and then encountered Zelda in Montgomery in 1919, reminisces about his friendships with both in "The Fitzgeralds Were My Friends" (*FHA*, 1978). Another Princeton friend, John D. McMaster, contributes "As I Remember Scott (Memoir)" (*Confrontation*, Fall 1973).

The most important and enduring relationship which Fitzgerald formed at Princeton was with Edmund Wilson; Wilson has written about it throughout his volumes of memoirs, diaries, and notebooks—*A Prelude: Landscapes, Characters and Conversations From the Earlier Years of My Life* (New York, 1967), *The Twenties* (New York, 1975), *The Thirties* (New York, 1980), *The Forties* (New York, 1983), and *The Fifties* (New York, 1986). Ginevra King, the young Chicago debutante with whom Fitzgerald fell madly in love during his first year at Princeton and who is generally thought to be one of the primary models for his heroines, recounts her memories to Elizabeth Friskey in "Visiting the Golden Girl" (*Princeton Alumni Weekly*, 8 Oct. 1974).

Among the Fitzgeralds' closest friends during their years abroad were Gerald and Sara Murphy. Their daughter, Honoria Murphy Donnelly, has written effectively of this friendship in her memoir *Sara & Gerald: Villa America and After* (New York, 1982). Donald Ogden Stewart, also a friend during this period and thereafter, speaks of them in his *By a Stroke of Luck!: An Autobiography* (New York, 1975). In June 1972, the *Fitzgerald/Hemingway Annual* sponsored a conference in Paris on "Fitzgerald and Hemingway in Paris"; the proceedings were later published and include reminiscences by André Chamson, Morrill Cody, Florence Gilliam, and Harold Loeb, an extended essay by André Le Vot, the text of the discussion which followed the papers, and a map of the Montparnasse area of the city marked to indicate twenty-eight places "significant in the lives of Fitzgerald, Hemingway and their friends" (*FHA*, 1973). Fitzgerald's French translator, Victor Llona, recounts details of his friendship with him in 1926–27 in "Days and Nights in Paris With Scott Fitzgerald" (*Voyages*, Winter 1971); Allen Tate, in an interview with Matthew J. Bruccoli (*FHA*, 1974), speaks of Fitzgerald in Paris in 1929; and Herbert Gorman tells of three "Glimpses of F. Scott Fitzgerald" (*FHA*, 1973) in the late 1920s.

Lawrence Lee, in "Tender Was the Man: Memories of F. Scott Fitzgerald" (*Pittsburgh Press*, 14 July 1974), records his recollection of the author in Montgomery and in Charlottesville, Virginia, during the early 1930s. Theodora Gager, who was hired in 1932 for about a month as his nurse to keep him away from gin and cigarettes, has spoken of her recollections in interviews with William Katterjohn (*FHA*, 1974) and Tom Lindley (*Evansville* [Ind.] *Courier and Press*, 11 Jan. 1976).

Tony Buttitta's *After the Good Gay Times: Asheville—Summer of '35: A Season With F. Scott Fitzgerald* (New York, 1974) presents remarkably vivid and full recreations of conversations with Fitzgerald by Buttitta, who was at the time the proprietor of Asheville's Intimate Bookshop. Fitzgerald often stopped in to talk and reminisce, and Buttitta kept careful notes on these occasions, he tells us, on the flyleaves of some sixty books which were then as now in his personal library. While Buttitta sometimes stretches one's faith in his credibility with pages of conversations supposedly quoted faithfully, his is a remarkably sharp portrait of a frequently drunk and consistently pessimistic Fitzgerald, mourning the loss of his talent and his youth, and pursuing an affair with a married woman and a casual flirtation with a local prostitute. That Buttitta's bleak picture is an accurate one is implied in other recollections of Fitzgerald during this period by Edwin A. Peeples (*Mademoiselle*, Nov. 1973), Margaret Culkin Banning (*FHA*, 1973), and J. T. Fain (*FHA*, 1975).

Sheilah Graham's third full book on her relationship with Fitzgerald, *The Real F. Scott Fitzgerald: Thirty-Five Years Later* (New York, 1976), probably doesn't add enough material to that available in the earlier two to justify its publication, but it does arrange it in a novel fashion—rather than retell the story chronologically, she gives us chapters on Scott as husband, Scott as father, Scott as drinker, Scott as lover, Scott as writer, *The Last Tycoon*, Scott as educator of Sheilah (a rehash of *College of One*), and Scott's death. Because they were so close during his last years, anything that Sheilah Graham has to say about Fitzgerald is worthwhile, but this book does go over a lot of old ground.

Other views of Fitzgerald during his last years are provided by Arnold Gingrich in *Nothing But People: The Early Days at "Esquire"—A Personal History 1928–1958* (New York, 1971); by his secretary in Hollywood, Frances Kroll Ring, in "Sisyphus in Hollywood: Refocusing F. Scott Fitzgerald" (*FHA*, 1973) and in *Against the Current: As I Remember F. Scott*

Fitzgerald (Berkeley, Calif., 1985); and by Samuel Marx, former story editor at MGM, in "The Lasts Writes of the 'Eminent Authors'" (*Los Angeles Times*, 13 June 1976).

Two final items worth mentioning in this section are William F. Lewis's "Masculine Inferiority Feelings of F. Scott Fitzgerald" (*Medical Aspects of Human Sexuality*, Apr. 1973) and Richard L. White's "F. Scott Fitzgerald: The Cumulative Portrait" (*Biography*, Spring 1981). Lewis emphasizes Fitzgerald's relationship with Hemingway and the familiar details from *A Moveable Feast* as support for his overly simplistic conclusion that "basic instability, lack of discipline, and strong feelings of masculine inferiority were partly responsible for his tragic life, inconsistent literary output, and suffering at the hands of women." White's essay is a useful survey of the biographical volumes available to 1980 which compares and contrasts the pictures provided by Mizener, Turnbull, Buttitta, Graham, Latham, Milford, and Mayfield. He suggests an intriguing but debatable point when he remarks, "Unlike Hemingway, Fitzgerald never invites his biographers, readers, or public to deal with him in a rough and tumble manner. Rather, he beckons (never demands) his biographers to treat him in careful, sympathetic, gentle, deliberate, and even detached tones."

V CRITICISM

1 Collections

The six collections published since the last version of this essay include two which are entirely composed of reprinted material, two which are made up of new pieces, and two which include a few new items as well as several reprinted ones. Jackson R. Bryer's *F. Scott Fitzgerald: The Critical Reception* (New York, 1978) republishes 318 contemporary reviews of Fitzgerald's books from *This Side of Paradise* to *The Last Tycoon*. Many of the notices appeared in local newspapers, and the book thus makes available much material which would otherwise be very difficult to consult. Bryer provides an introduction which surveys reviewers' responses to Fitzgerald's work; and he also includes several reviews found as clippings in Fitzgerald's scrapbooks at Princeton but which could not be located.

Kenneth E. Eble's *F. Scott Fitzgerald: A Collection of Criticism* (New York, 1973) has the admirable aim to "focus upon recent critical articles, to avoid reprinting articles already available in other collections, and to refrain from using portions of books." Eble does choose his twelve selections from the 1950s and the 1960s; and he manages to include critiques of each of the five novels. But his is a slim volume; one of the few remaining major needs in Fitzgerald studies is for a large and judicious collection which would reprint the best scholarship and criticism of the past three and a half decades.

Of the two collections which include substantial amounts of new material, Jackson R. Bryer's *The Short Stories of F. Scott Fitzgerald: New Approaches in Criticism* (Madison, Wis., 1982; hereinafter referred to as Bryer) contains twenty-two new essays on the stories (the individual essays will be discussed below) and an extensive checklist of criticism on Fitzgerald's short fiction. Matthew J. Bruccoli's *New Essays on "The Great Gatsby"* (New York, 1985; hereinafter referred to as Bruccoli) presents, besides a brief but useful introduction by the editor, new pieces by Richard Anderson, Roger Lewis, Susan Resneck Parr, Kenneth E. Eble, and George Garrett (they will be discussed below).

Scott Donaldson's *Critical Essays on F. Scott Fitzgerald's "The Great Gatsby"* (CEAmL, Boston, 1984; hereinafter referred to as Donaldson) is a well-organized combination of some of the early seminal studies—by Trilling, Eble, Doyno, and Lehan—with a selection of the best more recent essays and five pieces written especially for this volume (these will be discussed below). Donaldson also reprints excerpts from Fitzgerald's letters in which he comments about *Gatsby*, as well as snippets from letters to Fitzgerald (some printed for the first time) in which his contemporaries praise him for the novel. Donaldson's comprehensive and substantial gathering anticipated a similar collection which Milton R. Stern has prepared on *Tender Is the Night. Critical Essays on F. Scott Fitzgerald's "Tender Is the Night"* (CEAmL, Boston, 1986; hereinafter referred to as Stern), like Donaldson's *Gatsby* volume, combines reprinted and original pieces. Stern's graceful and informative introduction charts the decidedly erratic path of the novel's critical reputation, and his selections demonstrate that pattern, beginning with a generous sampling of the mixed reviews it received in 1934, proceeding through the virtual lack of attention it received in the 1940s and 1950s (only six items come from those two decades, as opposed to seventeen reviews), and on to the encouraging appreciation and serious study it has gotten in the past twenty-five years. The volume concludes with Joseph Wenke's helpful "*Tender is the Night*: A Cross-Referenced Bibliography of Criticism," which is an unannotated chronological listing of 305 periodical articles and 141 books which include mention or extensive discussion of *Tender*.

2 Full-length Studies

Considering the number of full-length bibliographical and biographical volumes surveyed above and the torrent of critical articles which will be looked at below, the fact that there have only been eight full-length critical studies in the past decade is astonishing and deplorable. When one adds to this statistic that one of the eight is a superficial study aimed at high school and junior college readers, another is an unrevised doctoral dissertation done at a foreign university, a third is a sixty-four-page pamphlet on *Gatsby*, and a fourth is a brief general account done for a monograph series, the dearth of significant in-depth critical full-length work becomes even more apparent.

The title of Joan M. Allen's *Candles and Carnival Lights: The Catholic Sensibility of F. Scott Fitzgerald* (New York, 1978) suggests its thesis—that Fitzgerald's nature was divided, personally and as a writer, between "the lights of the carnival . . . the apparently glamorous life" and "his profound moralism, the realization of sin and destructiveness which underlie and permeate the temporal world." Allen's concern is with the second of these and with how Fitzgerald's "Roman Catholic early education and family experiences, the complexities of a Catholic upbringing in an atmosphere of inadequate paternity and oppressive maternity and ambivalence about money, formed his moral consciousness." The book is best in documenting the facts of Fitzgerald's Catholic upbringing and influences; when applying this to the fiction, Allen too often overreaches in trying to find evidence of Catholic elements.

A similar over-zealous application of his thesis weakens Thomas J. Stavola's *Scott Fitzgerald: Crisis in An American Identity* (New York, 1979); not surprisingly, both Allen's and Stavola's books began as dissertations. Stavola uses the psychoanalytic theories of Erik Erikson as "a most useful means of relating the identity crisis of Fitzgerald and those of the major male characters in his four completed novels to American culture." After a chapter summarizing Erikson's theories and another depicting the symbiotic relationship between Scott and Zelda, he devotes a chapter apiece to the male protagonists of the first four novels. These readings are hampered by Stavola's tendency to read the fiction as autobiography; Erikson's theories do enable him to make some interesting observations about Fitzgerald the man and about his marriage.

William A. Fahey's *F. Scott Fitzgerald and the American Dream* (New York, 1973), while intended for a young adult audience (as part of Thomas Y. Crowell's Twentieth-Century American Writers series), presents a competent biographical and critical survey, with a chapter on each novel and one devoted to the short stories. *F. Scott Fitzgerald* by Rose Adrienne Gallo (MLM, New York, 1978) also is part of a series. With a brief, choppily written biographical chapter and individual chapters on each of the novels, on the short stories, and (for no apparent reason) on film adaptations of Fitzgerald's works, Gallo gives a good deal of plot summary. But the critical judgments throughout are sound (except for a serious undervaluing of *This Side of Paradise*), and there are particularly good analyses of "Babylon Revisited" and *The Last Tycoon*.

Eugen Huonder's published dissertation, *The Functional Significance of Setting in the Novels of Francis Scott Fitzgerald* (Bern, 1974), is a plodding and workmanlike examination of setting as a means of creating atmosphere, character, meaning, and symbol in the four completed novels, with an emphasis on the development of Fitzgerald's visual imagination. Far more satisfactory and the best critical book on Fitzgerald since Lehan's in 1966 is Brian Way's *F. Scott Fitzgerald and the Art of Social Fiction* (London, 1980; New York, 1980). Way is refreshingly determined not to dwell on the details of Fitzgerald's life, asserting that "his major novels and stories were created by a better self than the one which biography and legend alike have chosen to celebrate." He finds instead "a novelist more subtly responsive to the cultural and historical aura that surrounded him than any American contemporary save Faulkner, a social observer more intelligent and self-aware than any since Henry James." Although Way occasionally depends on secondary sources rather than having consulted the texts or manuscripts themselves, his close readings of the novels and stories are invariably original and informed. He is especially skillful at placing Fitzgerald in the social, historical, and literary contexts of his day and at separating the good from the bad in the fiction.

Dan Seiters's concern, in *Image Patterns in the Novels of F. Scott Fitzgerald* (Ann Arbor, Mich., 1986), is with how "Fitzgerald's use of imagery becomes more sophisticated and more skillfully integrated into his fiction with each succeeding novel." To do this he examines "transportation imagery, communication imagery, light-dark imagery, dirt-disease-decay imagery, and water imagery," concluding that a major reason why the first two novels are less successful than the last three is because, beginning with *Gatsby*, Fitzgerald "switched allegiance from that group of writers who *tell* a tale" to those "who tell what happened, certainly, but more significantly, *show* what it was like to be there," thus subordinating "the intellectual and physical side of experience in favor of the emotional and psychological" and doing so "particularly through the use of imagery." Seiters also notes that after *This Side of Paradise*, "a novel generally devoid of image patterns, Fitzgerald allowed the theme to determine which of the clusters of images would be more important than any other." In *The Beautiful and Damned*, "the main source of cohesion stems from dirt-disease-decay imagery"; in *Gatsby* and *Tender*, water imagery dominates because it best exemplifies the central ironic contrast both novels explore "between the enormous promise life seems to offer and the unromantic reality"; and in *The Last Tycoon*, images of light and shade, "of artificial light and moonlight," predominate in a novel dealing with "the creation of illusion in Hollywood." While Seiters's presentation is often quite mechanical, his approach to Fitzgerald's fiction is one rarely found until very recently and badly needed; surely there is room for additional book-length studies of the style and language of the fiction.

Aside from a slightly revised new edition of Kenneth E. Eble's *F. Scott Fitzgerald* (TUSAS, Boston, 1977), which adds a new final chapter summarizing recent scholarship, the only other full-length works both deal exclusively with *The Great Gatsby*. While some of Robert Emmet Long's *The Achieving of "The Great Gatsby": F. Scott Fitzgerald, 1920–1925* (Lewisburg, Pa., 1979) previously appeared in articles, the book does an excellent job of looking at Fitzgerald's pre-*Gatsby* writing as preparation for the later novel, of showing how Conrad's early fiction was influential on Fitzgerald's conception of *Gatsby*, and, most impressively, of closely examining the novel's "structure of interwoven detail and nuance." John S. Whitley's sixty-four-page pamphlet on *Gatsby* (London, 1976), the first on a modern American novel in the prestigious Studies in English Literature series edited by David Daiches, devotes a chapter each to Nick and to Gatsby. Some of the discussion rehashes familiar material; but Whitley's analyses of parallels between *Gatsby* and Keats's poetry, *Heart of Darkness, Moby-Dick*, and, more briefly, Poe's poetry, are illuminating.

3 General Essays

There has been an abundance recently of good general essays, in the form either of periodical articles or chapters in critical books. Even a topic as seemingly exhausted as Fitzgerald seen in the context of his era has received several fresh readings. One of the best of these is James W. Tuttleton's "F. Scott Fitzgerald: The Romantic Tragedian as Moral Fabulist," in his *The Novel of Manners in America* (Chapel Hill, N.C., 1972). Tuttleton deals at length with *Gatsby* and more briefly with *This Side of Paradise*. He places their author in the novel of manners tradition, calling him the "Social Historian of the Jazz Age"; but he combines close study of the texts with an informed understanding of Fitzgerald within the history of the American novel. For Alfred Kazin, in his typically graceful and insightful section on Fitzgerald in *An American Procession* (New York, 1984), "Fitzgerald became the twenties, and the twenties a version of F. Scott Fitzgerald," and Gatsby "was not a character but an idea of the everlasting self-creation that Americans have mastered."

Other pieces which deal with Fitzgerald in the context of American culture include Robert N. Wilson's "F. Scott Fitzgerald: Personality and Culture," in his *The Writer as Social Seer* (Chapel Hill, N.C., 1979), which suggests that Fitzgerald's behavior and attitudes were consonant with major American values; J. Bakker's unoriginal "F. Scott Fitzgerald and the American Dream" (*LT*, Dec. 1971), which considers *This Side of Paradise* and *Gatsby* in light of the American success myth; Charles I. Glicksberg's "Fitzgerald and the Jazz Age," in his *The Sexual Revolution in Modern American Literature* (The Hague, 1971), which emphasizes the "tug of war" between "the hedonistic and the ascetic" in Fitzgerald's novels; C. W. E. Bigsby's thorough and intelligent "The Two Identities of F. Scott Fitzgerald," in *The American Novel and the Nineteen Twenties* (London, 1971), which concludes that not until *Tender Is the Night* could Fitzgerald bring himself "to establish the irrevocable connection between personal tragedy and cultural decline which formed the basis of his dialectic"; and Michael Spindler's "The Rich Are Different: Scott Fitzgerald and the Leisure Class," in his *American Literature and Social*

Change (Bloomington, Ind., 1983), which discusses the four completed novels as reflections of their author's—as well as middle class Americans'—ambivalent attitudes toward the leisure class of the post-World War I world.

Another popular approach has been to examine Fitzgerald's fiction in terms of a motif or metaphor which runs through it. Robert A. Ferguson's "The Grotesque in the Novels of F. Scott Fitzgerald" (*SAQ*, Autumn 1979) is one of the best and most original of this type of study, as are Ruth Prigozy's "'Poor Butterfly': F. Scott Fitzgerald and Popular Music" (*Prospects*, 1976) and Edwin T. Arnold's "The Motion Picture as Metaphor in the Works of F. Scott Fitzgerald" (*FHA*, 1977). Much less satisfactory are Stephen L. Tanner's redundant "Fitzgerald: 'What to Make of a Diminished Thing'" (*ArQ*, Summer 1978), Edward Marcotte's confusing "Fitzgerald and Nostalgia" (*MQ*, Winter 1976), Douglas Robillard's diffuse "The Paradises of Scott Fitzgerald" (*EAS*, May 1975), and John Ditsky's slight note on "F. Scott Fitzgerald and the Jacob's Ladder" (*JNT*, Fall 1977).

While it may overstate its point, Georges-Michael Sarotte's "Francis Scott Fitzgerald: Self-Virilization and Its Failure," in his *Like a Brother, Like a Lover: Male Homosexuality in the American Novel and Theater* (Garden City, N.Y., 1978), certainly introduces a new topic in its exploration of the latent homosexuality in Fitzgerald and his novels. Less controversial is Robert E. Rhodes's "F. Scott Fitzgerald: 'All My Fathers,'" in his and Daniel J. Casey's collection, *Irish-American Fiction* (New York, 1979), in which Fitzgerald's treatment of the Irish in his fiction is surveyed. Christian K. Messenger's chapter on Fitzgerald's depiction of "The School Sports Hero," in his *Sport and the Sprit of Play in American Fiction* (New York, 1981), traces the evolution of that hero from the romanticized Humbird and Allenby of *This Side of Paradise* to the brutal Tom Buchanan of *Gatsby* and the complex Dick Diver of *Tender Is the Night*. Robert J. Higgs takes a similar tack in his briefer section on Fitzgerald in *Laurel & Thorn: The Athlete in American Literature* (Lexington, Ky., 1981). B. Ramachandra Rao's "Scott Fitzgerald," in his *The American Fictional Hero: An Analysis of the Works of Fitzgerald, Wolfe, Farrell, Dos Passos and John Steinbeck* (Chandigarh, 1979), has little new to say in its discussion of the quests of the heroes of the five novels. Although noteworthy as its author's only published comments on Fitzgerald, James T. Farrell's "F. Scott Fitzgerald and His Romanticism" (*Thought*, 5 May 1973) is no more than a brief overview written for Indian readers.

Richard Lehan's "F. Scott Fitzgerald and Romantic Destiny" (*TCL*, Summer 1980) is a carefully researched and modestly argued exploration of a topic which has too often been dealt with carelessly in the past—Oswald Spengler's influence on Fitzgerald. Lehan draws effectively from his many years of research on Fitzgerald in looking at the Spenglerian elements in *Gatsby, Tender Is the Night, The Last Tycoon* and in the incomplete "Philippe, Count of Darkness." In "Madness and Sexual Mythology in Scott Fitzgerald" (*IJWS*, May/June 1978), Madonna C. Kolbenschlag ranges uncertainly back and forth between discussions of Fitzgerald's fictional heroines and of his relationship with Zelda, relating both fiction and the life to Freud's and Laing's theories of madness and sex role behavior.

Five essays concern the role place plays in Fitzgerald's fiction. Two, Barry Gross's "Fitzgerald's Midwest: 'Something Gorgeous Some-where'—Somewhere *Else*" (*Midamerica*, 1979) and Roger G. Kennedy's section on Fitzgerald in his *Men on the Moving Frontier* (Palo Alto, Calif., 1969), consider him a midwest writer. Gross focuses on *Gatsby* and several short stories in delineating the "two midwests" he sees in the fiction: the "secure and stable one of Basil Duke Lee and Nick Carraway" and the "narrow and constricted country of Randolph Miller . . . and Jimmy Gatz." Kennedy contrasts Fitzgerald and architect William Gray Purcell, arguing that the novelist is a realistic "observer and reporter of aspects of the mid-western experience that preceded the Jazz Age."

Patricia Kane, in "F. Scott Fitzgerald's St. Paul: A Writer's Use of Material" (*MinnH*, Winter 1976), sees Fitzgerald's use of his hometown in his work as more symbolic than actual in that "he freely altered or reinterpreted his perceptions to suit the characters and themes of his fiction." Scott Donaldson's "Scott Fitzgerald's Romance With the South" (*SLJ*, Spring 1973) claims plausibly that his attitude toward the South was shaped by his wife and his father and moved from a portrayal of the southern belle as warm and charming in "The Ice Palace" to vicious and cruel in "The Last of the Belles." In "The Switzerland of Fitzgerald and Hemingway" (*FHA*, 1978), Hans Schmid recounts the details of Fitzgerald's stay in that country in 1930–31 and notes his use of his experiences and observations in *Tender Is the Night* and several short stories.

The emergence during the past decade of an informed and sensitive body of feminist criticism has encouraged increased and fresh attention to Fitzgerald's female characters and to his attitude toward women. A good brief response is James W. Tuttleton's four pages on Fitzgerald in "'Combat in the Erogenous Zone': Women in the American Novel Be-tween the Wars," in *What Manner of Women: Essays on English and American Life and Literature* (ed. Marlene Springer, New York, 1977). David Fedo, in "Women in the Fiction of F. Scott Fitzgerald" (*BSUF*, Spring 1980), examines Fitzgerald's view of Gloria Gilbert, Daisy Buchanan, and Nicole Warren, claiming that their creator saw them as "weak, frail creatures, unfit for the spell of their beauty." In "Fitzgerald's Female Narrators" (*MHLS*, 1979), Fay T. Greenwald focuses on Rosemary Hoyt and Cecilia Brady in concluding that Fitzgerald's "attempts at constructing a female narrative point of view both as technique and as characters were failures." Two other essays are more balanced in their appraisals. Jan Hunt and

John M. Suarez's "The Evasion of Adult Love in Fitzgerald's Fiction" (*CentR*, Spring 1973) looks at Fitzgerald's need to portray women either as "monsters of virtue" or "monsters of bitchery"; while Mary A. McCay, in "Fitzgerald's Women: Beyond Winter Dreams," in *American Novelists Revisited* (ed. F. Fleischmann, Boston, 1982), draws a similar distinction between Fitzgerald's "useless women" for whom he had contempt (Gloria Gilbert, Judy Jones, Jordan Baker, and Daisy Buchanan) and the women of his later fiction (Kathleen and Cecilia of *The Last Tycoon*) who reflect his pride in his daughter and his admiration of Sheilah Graham.

Fitzgerald's later fiction is also Walter Wells's concern in "The Hero and the Hack," in his *Tycoons and Locusts: A Regional Look at Hollywood Fiction of the 1930s* (Carbondale, Ill., 1973), where he traces through the Pat Hobby stories and *The Last Tycoon* many of the elements of Hollywood fiction he has discussed earlier in his study. William R. Anderson likewise looks at the heroes of the later fiction in his "Fitzgerald After *Tender Is the Night*: A Literary Strategy For the 1930s" (*FHA*, 1979), but he tends to mix biography and literary analysis carelessly in his delineation of two Fitzgeralds during the last years—"poor Scott" and a resilient battler who created strong characters in his last work. Sam B. Girgus's chapter on Fitzgerald in his *The Law of the Heart: Individualism and the Modern Self in American Literature* (Austin, Tex., 1979) provides provocative views of Dick Diver and Monroe Stahr.

A long overdue concern with Fitzgerald's style, exemplified in the Seiters book discussed above, is reflected in three general essays, as well as in several of the more specific pieces to be discussed below. Peggy Maki Horodowich's "Linguistics and Literary Style: Deriving F. Scott Fitzgerald's Linguistic Contours," in *Papers from the 1977 Mid-America Linguistics Conference* (ed. Donald M. Lance and Daniel E. Gulstad, Columbia, Mo., 1978), is the first application of modern linguistic theories to a study of Fitzgerald's prose and a very revealing one. Using a tag-memic-generative model of grammar and applying it to the five novels, her principal finding is that the "evocative quality" of *Gatsby* is partially attributable to Fitzgerald's preference for "fluid process verbs and dependent and independent adjectival and adverbial clauses"; while in *The Last Tycoon* "a decline of adjectival clauses" and a shift away from motion clauses causes a bareness in the style. Although not nearly so rooted in linguistic evidence, Donald Monk's "Fitzgerald: The Tissue of Style" (*JAmS*, April 1983) and Dawn Trouard's "Fitzgerald's Missed Moments: Surrealistic Style in His Major Novels" (*FHA*, 1979) are both worthwhile.

Fitzgerald's politics, in particular his brief flirtation with Marxism, is the subject of three essays. Dan Isaac goes the farthest, in "The Other Scott Fitzgerald" (*Nation*, 28 Sept. 1974), by seeing *The Last Tycoon* as a "proto-Marxist novel" and its author as a "sentimental Marxist" who was "desperately striving to become a serious historical and political writer." Scott Donaldson also finds a period of Marxist sympathy, in

"The Political Development of F. Scott Fitzgerald" (*Prospects*, 1981), but his essay traces Fitzgerald's changing political ideas from 1913 to 1940 and sees them reflected differently in many of the works. Ronald J. Gervais, in "The Socialist and the Silk Stockings: Fitzgerald's Double Allegiance" (*Mosaic*, June 1982), also finds in the fiction, especially "May Day" and *The Last Tycoon*, evidence of Fitzgerald's divided political loyalties.

Several general essays suggest the possible influence on Fitzgerald's work of earlier or contemporary writers. In "Scribbling Upward: Fitzgerald's Debt of Honor to Horatio Alger, Jr." (*FHA*, 1978), Gary Scharnhorst shows convincingly how Fitzgerald satirized Alger's Myth of Success in his fiction; and Ralph Curry and Janet Lewis's "Stephen Leacock: An Early Influence on F. Scott Fitzgerald" (*CRevAS*, Spring 1976) is a gently argued piece which finds traces of Leacockian humor in the short stories and implicitly reminds us that we have too few studies of humor in Fitzgerald's work. S. S. Moorty's two essays on Frank Norris's influence on Fitzgerald, in *Proceedings of the Utah Academy of Sciences, Arts, and Letters* (Part 2, 1976) and in *Studies in American Literature: Essays in Honour of William Mulder* (ed. Jagdish Chander and Narindar S. Pradhan, Delhi, 1976), are both oversimplified, as is M. Sivaramakrishna's examination of *Gatsby* and *This Side of Paradise* as influenced by William James's concept of "the will to believe" (*OJES*, No. 1, 1971). William Wasserstrom's "The Goad of Guilt: Henry Adams, Scott and Zelda" (*JML*, Apr. 1977) dwells unoriginally and occasionally incoherently on Adams's influence on Fitzgerald and on the mutually destructive and dependent relationship between Scott and Zelda. Kim Moreland, in "The Education of Scott Fitzgerald: Lessons in the Theory of History" (*SHR*, Winter 1985), gives a much clearer presentation of Adams's influence. In "F. Scott Fitzgerald and Charles G. Norris" (*JML*, Mar. 1983), Richard Allan Davison argues convincingly for the "echoes from Norris's fiction [which] not only remained in Fitzgerald's mind, but found their way into his writings."

Finally, no decade in Fitzgerald studies would be complete without a couple of pieces which analyze and try to account for the extent of those studies. As his title suggests, H. Alan Wycherley's "The Fitzgerald Fad" (*CEA*, Jan. 1974) laments the sentimentalists who have tried "to blurb into immortality a writer of limited talent and scope." In "Paradise Regained: Fitzgerald on Campus" (*GyS*, Fall 1973), Alan Wheelock speculates plausibly about the reasons for "the phenomenal resurgence in popularity" of Fitzgerald on college campuses.

4 Essays on Individual Works

a. The Great Gatsby. By actual count, since the last version of this essay, there have been just about 160 periodical essays, notes, and book chapters devoted solely or primarily to *The Great Gatsby*. That number is roughly three times the total of the essays which deal with the four other novels combined and just about equal to the number of all the other critical essays on Fitzgerald during the past thirteen years. What is more dispiriting than the statistics is that too little of this criticism convincingly breaks new ground or says anything very original about old topics. In fact, while the survey which follows must of necessity be cursory in its descriptions, it rather easily and only occasionally arbitrarily breaks down into a very few all too familiar categories.

There have been a number of solid general essays on *Gatsby*, several of them written by longtime Fitzgerald scholar-critics. In what is the single best piece on the novel during the past decade, James E. Miller, Jr.'s "Fitzgerald's *Gatsby*: The World as Ash Heap," in *The Twenties: Fiction, Poetry, Drama* (ed. Warren French, Deland, Fla., 1975; reprinted in Donaldson), the critic, who was one of the first to deal with Fitzgerald as a literary craftsman, carefully and brilliantly examines such aspects of his artistry as juxtaposed scenes, pervasive image patterns, the use of details from the 1920s, and the novel's broader meaning. Because Miller covers so many elements of *Gatsby* and is invariably authoritative in his analyses, this essay would be a good place to start if one has never read any previous critiques of Fitzgerald's most famous novel. Kenneth E. Eble's "*The Great Gatsby*" (*CollL*, Winter 1974) is also a judicious review of approaches to the novel with a focus on the three elements which Eble, another experienced Fitzgerald commentator, finds to be the bases of its greatness—theme, design, and style. In his "'Would 25-Cent Press Keep Gatsby in the Public Eye—or Is the Book *Unpopular?*'" in *Seasoned Authors For a New Season: The Search for Standards in Popular Writing* (ed. Louis Filler, Bowling Green, Ohio, 1980) and in "Fitzgerald in the Fifties" (*SNNTS*, Fall 1973), Barry Gross speculates intelligently on why *Gatsby* spoke so eloquently to the generation which grew up in the 1950s. By contrast, V. N. Arora's "*The Great Gatsby*: The Predicament of the Dual Vision" (*IJAS*, Jan. 1978) is totally unoriginal.

Kenneth E. Eble is the author also of one of four very useful general essays in Bruccoli's *New Essays on "The Great Gatsby."* Eble's "*The Great Gatsby* and the Great American Novel" examines the book's "relationship to the concept of the 'great American novel'; the substance of the novel . . . ; and the novel's structure and style." He observes that what may be most American about *Gatsby* is its "preoccupation with 'self,' the fictional one focused on Gatsby, the real one lying behind the fascination that the Fitzgerald story continues to have for the American public"; but his essay is most valuable in its trenchant examinations of the novel's style and structure. Style is also poet and novelist George Garrett's concern in "Fire and Freshness: A Matter of Style in *The Great Gatsby*." Garrett begins by asserting that he knows of "no other twentieth-century masterpiece" which is so universally admired by contemporary American writers as *Gatsby* and then seeks to discover why this is so. He dismisses its content and context as "far removed" from most modern readers, and contends that it is "a matter of style, an imperishable style, that has made *Gatsby* a permanent experience." This not very original or surprising observation is followed by a fascinating and detailed study of the time schemes and narrative strategies present in Nick's narration which concludes that, "behind its seemingly bland and polite surface," *Gatsby* is "a complicated composite of several distinct kinds of prose, . . . a composite style whose chief demonstrable point appears to be the inadequacy of any single style (or single means of perception, point of view) by itself to do justice to the story."

The two other general essays in the Bruccoli collection focus on thematic matters and do so through close reading of the text. Roger Lewis's "Money, Love and Aspiration in *The Great Gatsby*" asserts that while "the separation of love and money characterizes serious American fiction," in *Gatsby* the two are linked through the novel's "greater subject— the tragic nature of aspiration." In "The Idea of Order at West Egg," Susan Resneck Parr views the novel through what she sees as Fitzgerald's perception that "the conscious individual can function best if he or she can reconcile and accept 'opposed ideas.'" She looks at the novel's major characters whom she sees "choosing illusions and playing roles as a way of creating a sense of meaning and order in their lives" but discovering in the end that "neither the choice of embracing illusions nor the effort to live without them suffices." Like all the other essays in Bruccoli's excellent volume, Parr's piece is rich in insights based securely on the text.

One of the earliest critical stances on *Gatsby* was to view it as a comment on or criticism of the American experience or to speak of it within the framework of the American success myth. That this approach can still yield fruitful readings is demonstrated by Brian M. Barbour in *"The Great Gatsby and the American Past"* (*SoR*, Spring 1973) and by Giles Gunn in "F. Scott Fitzgerald's *Gatsby* and the Imagination of Wonder" (*JAAR*, June 1973; reprinted in Donaldson). Barbour relates the two opposing forces in the novel to two American dreams as articulated by Franklin and Emerson. The Franklinian dream of "self-validating materialism" is seen in its "least attractive form" in the Buchanans; while Gatsby embodies the Emersonian dream, much of whose power "lies in its promise to free the ordinary self from the materialism, stagnancy, and moral complacency of the enacted Franklinian dream." Gunn perceives the novel as "a story about Gatsby's poetry of desire, his imagination of wonder" that Americans have lost because "we can no longer be so vulnerable." Kermit W. Moyer's thesis, in *"The Great Gatsby: Fitzgerald's Meditation on American History"* (*FHA*, 1972; reprinted in Donaldson), is very close to Barbour's in that he sees the basic opposition in the novel to be between materialism and transcendental vision; he does a good job of relating characters and scenes to one or the other of these forces.

In what is certainly the most provocative but also one of the most original of the recent "American culture" readings of *Gatsby*, Judith Fetterley ("*The Great Gatsby*: Fitzgerald's *droit de seigneur*," in her *The Resisting Reader: A Feminist Approach to American Fiction*, Bloomington, Ind., 1978) sees the novel as "another American 'love story' centered in hostility to women and the concomitant strategy of the scapegoat [Daisy]." Fetterley's piece contains a number of gratuitous extra-literary assertions and is strident in tone, but its discernment and delineation of patterns of "investment/divestment" and "advantage/disadvantage" in *Gatsby* are useful, and her readings are lively and challenging. Stephen Zelnick's approach, in "The Incest Theme in *The Great Gatsby*: An Exploration of the False Poetry of Petty Bourgeois Consciousness," in *Weapons of Criticism: Marxism in America and the Literary Tradition* (ed. Norman Rudich, Palo Alto, Calif., 1976), is as polemical as Fetterley's but much more questionable and less innovative in its assertion that *Gatsby* is "a specific and historically definite portrayal of the American nineteen-twenties" by a writer, "whose theme, although he was finally unable to grasp it firmly, is the tortuous contradictions of his own petty bourgeois class."

In a stimulating essay, "Reflections and Affinities: Aspects of the American Past, the American Dream, and 'The Great Gatsby'" (*ESA*, Mar. 1973), G. F. Hartford views the novel against the background of James Truslow Adams's concept of the American dream (he was the first to use the phrase in print); while Patricia Bizzell's "Pecuniary Emulation of the Mediator in *The Great Gatsby*" (*MLN*, May 1979) draws on the concepts of Thorstein Veblen and René Girard in arguing that, in American ideology, "getting money replaces heroic achievement as a way of living morally in the world" and that Gatsby's death is the inevitable result of pursuing such an ideology. Marcella Taylor calls *Gatsby* "The Unfinished American Epic" in *The Twenties* (Aix-en-Provence, 1982) which focuses "on the passing of the last utopian frontier in Western European Civilization, and suggests the significance of that disappearance in American society and perhaps in contemporary civilization." Taylor's examination of the characteristics of epic present in the novel is far more worthwhile than is her thesis, which is unclear and disjointed. As its title suggests, Vasant A. Shahane's "F. Scott Fitzgerald's Dual Vision in The Great Gatsby," in *Indian Studies in American Fiction* (ed. M. K. Naik, S. K. Desai, S. Mokashi-Punekar, Delhi, 1974), offers little new material.

A variety of symbol patterns and motifs in *Gatsby*—some previously studied, others newly discovered—are the subjects of another group of recent essays. The eyes of Dr. T. J. Eckleburg and the novel's general use of ocular imagery, already well-surveyed, somehow persist as a topic. Sanford Pinsker adds little to earlier research in "Seeing *The Great Gatsby* Eye to Eye" (*CollL*, Winter 1975); and Chris Schroeder's contention, in "The Oculist, the Son, and the Holy Owl Eyes" (*AN&Q*, Feb.

1980), that the oculist who paid for the billboard, Dr. Eckleburg, and Owl Eyes constitute a Holy Trinity is farfetched. But Marie J. Kilker's "'Some Clews' to the Source of Doctor Eckleburg's Eyes and *The Great Gatsby*" (*PMPA*, 1980) and Warren Bennett's "Prefigurations of Gatsby, Eckleburg, Owl Eyes, and Klipspringer" (*FHA*, 1979) are both helpful. Kilker finds in Harry Clews, Jr.'s *Mumbo Jumbo* (1923), a book which Fitzgerald knew, a billboard image much like the one in *Gatsby*. Bennett shows in a careful study how the ocular image of the later novel is prefigured in its author's earlier fiction. Like Bennett, Ruth Prigozy, in "Gatsby's Guest List and Fitzgerald's Technique of Naming" (*FHA*, 1972), shows how a pattern long acknowledged in *Gatsby* can be discerned in Fitzgerald's previous work; another piece on the guest list, by Edward Stone (*FHA*, 1972), relates it to similar passages in Henry James and Wolfe.

Three recent essays offer relatively little new material on another hackneyed topic, the role time plays in *Gatsby*. Barry Gross's major contribution in "Back West: Time and Place in *The Great Gatsby*" (*WAL*, Spring and Summer 1973) is his observation that, in a reversal of the nineteenth-century concept, "West is past, East is future" in the novel; the failure of its transplanted Westerners to live in the East represents their inability to live in the future. In "Time and Time Structure in *The Great Gatsby*" (*RLV*, Bicentennial Issue, 1976), Paul Melebeck dates every event in the novel and then examines how the novel does what Gatsby cannot do, control time. Melebeck sees time in *Gatsby* as both material and visible as well as psychological and emotional. R. Michael Sheffield, in "The Temporal Location of Fitzgerald's Jay Gatsby" (*TQ*, Summer 1975), also finds two different sorts of time operating—quantitative and qualitative—but his discussion of these is often confusing and not original enough to justify trying to follow it.

Another favorite approach has been to impose a pattern or framework on *Gatsby*; such studies invariably succeed or fail on the basis of whether or not they genuinely enhance our understanding of the novel. David Stouck's "White Sheep on Fifth Avenue: *The Great Gatsby* as Pastoral" (*Genre*, Dec. 1971) and John H. Kuhnle's "*The Great Gatsby* as Pastoral Elegy" (*FHA*, 1978) both are original and enlightening, as is Peter L. Hays's "*Gatsby*, Myth, Fairy Tale, and Legend" (*SFQ*, 1977), which argues convincingly that *Gatsby* combines characteristics of the fairy tale with those of the legend, thereby enabling Fitzgerald "to mock the American dream, to show that it is no more than a legend to those who believe in it, and a fairy tale, in the most pejorative sense, for most of us."

Three essays view *Gatsby* through the lens of myth criticism. In a piece which is richly suggestive of the novel's many levels, "*The Great Gatsby*: Apogee of Fitzgerald's Mythopoeia" (*FHA*, 1976), Neila Seshachari develops the thesis that Gatsby is "a minor avatar of the truly great mythic heroes." In "'Boats Against the Current': Mortality and the Myth of

Renewal in *The Great Gatsby*" (*TCL*, Summer 1980), Jeffrey Steinbrink lucidly argues that Gatsby's failure stems from his belief in the myth of rejuvenation in a basically entropic universe. Bruce Michelson's "The Myth of Gatsby" (*MFS*, Winter 1980–81), contending that *Gatsby* is a "modern myth," fruitfully draws parallels between it and a plausible source—Ovid's story of Phaeton.

Two essays which view Gatsby in religious terms are Jeffrey Hart's "Reconsideration: *The Great Gatsby* By F. Scott Fitzgerald" (*NR*, 17 Apr. 1976) and H. Keith Monroe's "Gatsby and the Gods" (*Renascence*, Autumn 1978). Of the two, Monroe's is the more convincing in his claim that "what has, at first glance, seemed a desultory ironic linking of Gatsby with Christ seems, on closer examination, to be an expression of a philosophical dualism that recognizes the chasm between the material vegetative world and the imaginative ideal world." Hart's is a flimsy piece that claims that although the novel is defined in religious terms, they are not those of Christianity but rather of magic and witchcraft. In "Hallucination and History in *The Great Gatsby*" (*SDR*, Spring 1977), David Laird offers little new in his study of a "pastoral romance" imbedded in a "city novel" in which is created, "within its own internal structures, an immediate sense of historical process."

Three essays published in the same year all deal with sexual aspects of *Gatsby*. Patricia Pacey Thornton's "Sexual Roles in *The Great Gatsby*" (*ESC*, Winter 1979) presents the intriguing thesis that the genders of the couples in the novel "seem inextricably confused; they are more like twins than lovers." Keath Fraser is also concerned with sexual ambiguity in "Another Reading of *The Great Gatsby*" (*ESC*, Autumn 1979; reprinted in Donaldson); but where Thornton examines three couples (Tom-Daisy, Gatsby-Myrtle, Nick-Jordan), Fraser focuses on Nick's "uncertain sexuality." Murray J. Levith's note (*Expl*, Spring 1979) ranges widely in finding much sexual imagery in the novel. A related piece, more complex and detailed than these others, is A. S. Paulson's "*The Great Gatsby*: Oral Aggression and Splitting" (*AI*, Fall 1978), which discusses "the text's tendency to double its characters and imagery in terms of a notion Freud employed to understand certain perversions of genital sexuality: the notion of splitting."

Among the discussions of more explicit image patterns and motifs in *Gatsby*, we have two essays which deal with automobiles and two others which concern "technology"—of which cars are one manifestation. Lawrence E. MacPhee, in "*The Great Gatsby*'s 'Romance of Motoring': Nick Carraway and Jordan Baker" (*MFS*, Summer 1972), sees Jordan as embodying the type of disorder and disarray which the automobile symbolizes in the novel and points out that her name is compounded from the names of two of the best-known names in motoring. MacPhee finds several fascinating echoes in Fitzgerald's novel of motifs used in the Jordan Company's advertising for its sportscars. Vincent Kohler's "Somewhere West of Laramie, On the Road to West Egg: Automobiles, Fillies, and the West in *The Great Gatsby*" (*JPC*, Summer 1973; the article is wrongly attributed to R. A. Corrigan in the journal) also notes these echoes, but he expands his coverage to observe that the cars of other characters reflect them.

Of the two essays on technology, Irving S. Saposnik's "The Passion and the Life: Technology as Pattern in *The Great Gatsby*" (*FHA*, 1979) is better than Kenneth S. Knodt's "The Gathering Darkness: A Study of the Effects of Technology in *The Great Gatsby*" (*FHA*, 1976), because, while Knodt discusses the railroad, telephones, motorboats, motorcycles, and guns—as well as automobiles—he does not go as far as Saposnik in exploring the implications of the pattern. Saposnik is impressive in his contention that the use and misuse of technology in the novel reflects "a severe imbalance between outward form and inner dislocation."

One of the decade's most original articles is Lawrence Jay Dessner's "Photography and *The Great Gatsby*" (*ELWIU*, Spring 1979; reprinted in Donaldson), which examines the novel's many references to photography and cinematography as a demonstration of how Fitzgerald "shows us that photography is not merely a means of entertainment, professional or domestic, and a method of documentation, but a way people who are not self-conscious philosophers reinforce their assumptions about the nature of reality and time." Dessner's is an effective close reading, as are B. W. Wilson's "The Theatrical Motif in *The Great Gatsby*" (*FHA*, 1975) and W. T. Lhamon, Jr.'s "The Essential Houses of *The Great Gatsby*" (*MarkhamR*, Spring 1977; reprinted in Donaldson). Wilson is concerned with Gatsby's "dual role as performer and impresario and the significance such a role has for our understanding of the novel," while Lhamon examines the Buchanans' house, Myrtle's New York apartment, and Gatsby's mansion as manifesting "at a subtle, structural level the seeming variety but underlying undimensionality that the novel postulates." Bruce Bawer's note on the musical metaphor in *Gatsby* (*NMAL*, Fall 1981) is much briefer but suggestive in showing how musical references serve to contrast "Gatsby's romanticism with the world's reality."

Two other "pattern studies" also contribute a few new insights. Robert Ian Scott, in "A Sense of Loss: Entropy vs. Ecology in *The Great Gatsby*" (*QQ*, Winter 1975), considers the novel an illustration of the second law of thermodynamics: time and wealth destroy the reality on which human relationships and hope depend; his illustrations of the many forms of entropy in *Gatsby* are too obvious. J. S. Lawry's "Green Light or Square of Light in *The Great Gatsby*" (*DR*, Spring 1975) provides an interesting bridge between the myth criticism which was a staple of the first three decades of Fitzgerald studies and the close stylistic studies which have, happily, begun to appear with refreshing regularity in the 1970s and 1980s. Lawry concentrates on two images in the novel, "a line leading to a green light, and a flat white light fixed and bounded in a square" as comments on "the North American encounter with space, time, and being." But Lawry's study of these "images" only uses them as a point of departure; and they are, after all, not Fitzgerald's images but rather Lawry's rewording of the prose.

Without question, the most important and most innovative work on Fitzgerald in recent years is that which has finally turned away from the glamorous details of his life and from his status as a "Jazz Age novelist" and focused on his style by examining, in most instances, brief passages from his fiction. Several of the best of these pieces deal with *Gatsby*. Two skillfully blend textual research with analysis. Carla Micklus's "Fitzgerald's Revision of *The Great Gatsby*: The Creation of a Textual Anomaly" (*AN&Q*, Oct. 1980) shows how Nick's use of the phrase "men who had cared for her" to describe Daisy is carelessly left over from an earlier version of the novel in which an omniscient narrator and a narrator who knew the Buchanans well were to tell the story; it is inappropriate for Nick who knows them only slightly. In "Fitzgerald, Perkins, and *The Great Gatsby*" (*JNT*, Fall 1982), Carla Mulford argues effectively that the "biography" of Gatsby which, at Perkins's suggestion, Fitzgerald moved forward from chapter 8 to chapter 6, would have been better left at the later position in the novel. In a linguistically oriented essay based on "the arrangement and choice of words," "Structural Imagery in *The Great Gatsby*: Metaphor and Matrix" (*LNL*, Fall 1975), Barbara Gerber Sanders, through detailed and at times highly technical analysis, finds a "birth metaphor at the center of *Gatsby*" and claims further that it is used as "a standard by which to interpret" the characters. Using this interpretation, Nick and his "awakening" become the true subject.

Like Sanders, Leonard A. Podis, in "'The Unreality of Reality': Metaphor in *The Great Gatsby*" (*Style*, Winter 1977), focuses on Nick; but Podis cites a number of metaphors—"dead metaphors," "rationally analogical metaphors," and "radically subjective" metaphors—employed by Nick which he claims destroy the wall between reality and the world of imagination, thereby ideally projecting the romantic/realistic vision of *Gatsby*. In another original close reading, "Nonverbal Communication in *The Great Gatsby*" (*Lang&L*, Nos. 1–3, 1982), Ruth E. Roberts looks at such nonverbal components of Daisy and Gatsby's interaction as body language, tone of voice, and "interactional synchrony" in order to draw a "clearer picture of Daisy's allure for Gatsby"; Roberts also glances briefly at similar elements in the depictions of Tom, Jordan, and George Wilson.

Several recent critics have focused on limited sections of the novel. Edwin Moses, in "Tragic Inevitability in *The Great Gatsby*" (*CLAJ*, Sept. 1977), does a good close examination of the novel's first chapter, contending that "the pattern of the whole is implicit in the part" and that much of the power of Gatsby emanates "from the sense of tragic inevitability which Fitzgerald develops in the very first chapter." Christiane Johnson does a similarly detailed analysis of the famous last page in "*The Great Gatsby:* The Final Vision" (*FHA*, 1976; reprinted in Donaldson).

In "A View From the (Queensboro) Bridge" (*FHA*, 1975), Joan S. Korenman briefly chooses details from the passage in chapter 4 which describes Nick and Gatsby's trip across the bridge and which shows "Fitzgerald's mastery of patterning and his use of irony." Another brief note, Robert A. Martin's "Gatsby's 'Good Night' in Chapter III of *The Great Gatsby*" (*CEA*, May 1977), offers further evidence of Fitzgerald's care in writing the novel by showing that Gatsby's five "good nights" are all addressed to Nick and are evidence of his deliberate and aggressive attempts "to cultivate Nick's friendship to the exclusion of everyone else 'clustered' around him," because he wants Nick to arrange a meeting with Daisy for him.

One of the very best studies of style in *Gatsby* is Bruce R. Stark's "The Intricate Pattern in *The Great Gatsby*" (*FHA*, 1974), which draws on an assortment of seemingly minor details—the colors of Myrtle's dresses, the sounds and colors of Daisy's name, the necklace Tom buys at the end of the novel, the expensive leash Tom buys for Myrtle's dog, the rain at Gatsby's funeral—and ingeniously demonstrates how "the words in *The Great Gatsby* participate in a multitude of complex patterns that link images, anomalous minor scenes, and even rather large units to one another in a variety of complex and subtle ways." Three other essays, like Stark's, deal with patterns of small linguistic units. F. H. Langman's "Style and Shape in *The Great Gatsby*" (*SoRA*, Mar. 1973; reprinted in Donaldson) is an early and somewhat disorganized but nonetheless useful study which occasionally looks at such aspects of the novel's language as its choice of verbs, its use of adverbs and adjectives, its introductions of characters, and its reiterations of images and words.

Jackson R. Bryer, in "Style as Meaning in *The Great Gatsby*: Notes Toward a New Approach" (Donaldson), first rapidly reviews four decades of criticism of *Gatsby* and then offers his own contribution, a study of such small linguistic elements as adjectives and adjective phrases, brief descriptive phrases, and Fitzgerald's use of verbs. One of the patterns Bryer finds is that of "linked ambivalence or oxymorons"; these are also discussed in Takashi Tasaka's "The Meaning of Oxymoron in *The Great Gatsby*" (*Yasuda Joshi Daigaku Kiyō*, Nov. 1977). Alliteration as a stylistic device in *Gatsby* is treated briefly by Charles A. Nicholas in "The G-G-Great Gatsby" (*CEA*, Jan. 1976), while William Baer and Steven McLean Folks, in "Language and Character in *The Great Gatsby*" (*TLOP*, Dec. 1977), present poorly written but right-minded attempts to discern Fitzgerald's attitude toward Daisy and Tom by examining "the language that he gives these characters to say." Ron Neuhaus's "Gatsby and the Failure of the Omniscient 'I'" (*UDQ*, Spring 1977) is an unconvincing piece on a much-discussed topic, the novel's narrative voice.

As always, there are a large number of essays which link *Gatsby* with other literary works. These can in turn be subdivided into those which overtly suggest influence and those which simply place Fitzgerald's novel alongside another work (or works) in order to elucidate the texts. In the first category, the most comprehensive survey of the already-noted literary influences on *Gatsby* and the ideal place to start study of this topic is Robert Roulston's "Something Borrowed, Something New: A Discussion of Literary Influences in *The Great Gatsby*" (Donaldson). Roulston is particularly adept at distinguishing between those influences which are questionable and those which are likely. A similarly wide-ranging piece is Joseph Corso's "One Not-Forgotten Summer Night: Sources for Fictional Symbols of American Character in *The Great Gatsby*" (*FHA*, 1976). Corso's concern is not with literary precursors of *Gatsby* but rather with experiences and persons from Fitzgerald's life which helped shape the novel, especially the figures of Jay Gatsby and Dan Cody; not surprisingly, some of his suggestions seem forced, others quite possible. In *"The Great Gatsby*: Two Versions of the Hero" (*ES*, Feb. 1973), David Parker relates Gatsby to the hero of English Romantic literature (specifically, Browning's Roland) and Nick to the hero of the novel of "sentimental education" (the narrator of *Wuthering Heights* is discussed briefly) in a very illuminating essay.

Of course, Fitzgerald's indebtedness to the English Romantics has long been acknowledged, but it continues to interest. Robert E. Morsberger expands the field considerably in "The Romantic Ancestry of *The Great Gatsby*" (*FHA*, 1973) by noting everyone from Scott through Dumas, Conan Doyle, London, Kingsley, and Sabatini to Dickens as literary analogues which might have influenced Fitzgerald in what is a poorly organized and necessarily highly speculative piece. While overt influence is never claimed, Leslie F. Chard III, in "Outward Forms and the Inner Life: Coleridge and Gatsby" (*FHA*, 1973), draws interesting parallels between *Gatsby* and "Dejection: An Ode," a poem which Fitzgerald surely knew well. Two articles on the familiar Keats connections, George Monteiro's "James Gatz and John Keats" (*FHA*, 1972) and Joseph P. Wagner's "*Gatsby* and John Keats: Another Version" (*FHA*, 1979), offer "The Eve of St. Agnes" and "Endymion," respectively, as sources. By contrast, Tim Sherer, in "Midwestern Influences in F. Scott Fitzgerald's *The Great Gatsby*" (*SSMLN*, Summer 1981), sees Gatsby as not so much a romantic as a product of such midwestern attributes as perseverance, optimism, and individualism.

In a learned and careful essay, "Love, Death and Resurrection in *The Great Gatsby*," in *Aeolian Harps: Essays in Literature in Honor of Maurice Browning Cramer* (ed. Donna G. Fricke and Douglas C. Fricke, Bowling Green, Ohio, 1976), Robert J. Emmitt provides the best study of how Fitzgerald's novel was influenced by the Grail legend, the waste land myth, and "the ancient Semitic and Egyptian resurrection myths." Emmitt's claims may at first appear tenuous; but his application of them to central elements of *Gatsby* such as its use of color, its symbols of seasonal change, and its pattern of death and rebirth are impressive and sensitive to the novel's complexity. By comparison, Christine M. Bird and Thomas L. McHaney's "*The Great Gatsby* and *The Golden Bough*" (*ArQ*, Summer 1978) and Letha Audhuy's "*The Waste Land*: Myth and Symbolism in *The Great Gatsby*" (*EA*, Jan.–Mar. 1980), both serviceable contributions, seem slight, as does Michael Pottorf's note on "*The Great Gatsby*: Myrtle's Dog and Its Relation to the Dog-God of Pound and Eliot" (*AN&Q*, Feb. 1976).

The Conradian influence on *Gatsby* has also been discussed often; but two essays add some to the topic by looking at *The Secret Agent* as a possible source. In "*The Great Gatsby* and *The Secret Agent*" (*FHA*, 1975), Andrew Crosland primarily deals with parallel characters and coincidence of names. Ted Billy, in "Acts of Madness or Despair: A Note on *The Secret Agent* and *The Great Gatsby*" (*SAF*, Spring 1983), amplifies the discussion with a close comparison of the last three chapters of the two novels, which finds similarities in plot, in use of the lunacy motif, in emphasis on blindness and faulty perception, in ironic kitchen scenes following deaths, and in behavior of murderers.

Several good essays have suggested entirely new influences. Two of the best of these are Steven Curry and Peter L. Hays's "Fitzgerald's *Vanity Fair*" (*FHA*, 1977) and Lawrence Thornton's "Ford Madox Ford and *The Great Gatsby*" (*FHA*, 1975). Curry and Hays's thorough study traces likenesses in narrative technique, major characters, settings, in the metaphorical functions of setting, and in each novel's indictment "of the materialism and superficiality of its respective age." Thornton expertly examines similarities in "impressionistic form and romantic theme" and in narrative technique between *Gatsby* and *The Good Soldier*. In another convincing piece, "Traces of *Tono-Bungay* in *The Great Gatsby*" (*JNT*, Winter 1980), Robert Roulston focuses on structure, point of view, plot, and theme. Tom Quirk's "Fitzgerald and Cather: *The Great Gatsby*" (*AL*, Dec. 1982) contends that *Alexander's Bridge* and "Paul's Case," rather than *My Ántonia* and *A Lost Lady*, exercised "the most suggestive influence" on *Gatsby*. Michael A. Peterman (*CRevAS*, Spring 1977) sees Edith Wharton's 1924 novel *The Spark* as a "factor in the shaping and controlling" of *Gatsby* and cites parallels in point of view, narrative mood and tone, and central characters. Finally, a remarkably well-argued case for Chaucer's *Troilus and Criseyde* has been presented in two essays, Nancy Y. Hoffman's "*The Great Gatsby*: *Troilus and Criseyde* Revisited?" (*FHA*, 1971) and F. T. Flahiff's "*The Great Gatsby*: Scott Fitzgerald's Chaucerian Rag," in *Figures in a Ground: Canadian Essays on Modern Literature Collected in Honor of Sheila Watson* (ed. Diane Bessai and David Jackel, Saskatoon, 1978).

Brief notes suggesting influences include D. B. Graham's (*FHA*, 1972), which traces the Valley of Ashes to Norris's *Vandover and the Brute*; Harry Williams's assertion of "strikingly similar" approaches "to the use of money" in *Gatsby* and Pope's *Moral Epistles* (*FHA*, 1972); John Ower's slight piece (*FHA*, 1975), which argues for *The Rubáiyát* as a source for Nick's use of the word "caravansary"; Dorothy M. Webb's relation of details from El Greco's "View of Toledo" to *Gatsby* (*FHA*, 1975); Elizabeth Evans's indication that Fitzgerald may have had a scene from Lardner's *The Big Town* in mind in composing the "shirt scene" (*NConL*, Jan. 1980); Joseph Brogunier's questionable piece on parallels between "An Incident in *The Great Gatsby* and *Huckleberry Finn*" (*MTJ*, Summer 1972); Paul A. Makurath, Jr.'s shaky presentation of a character in Eliot's *The Mill on the Floss* as a source for Gatsby (*FHA*, 1975); Alice Hall Petry's exploration of Fitzgerald's use of the "Will-o'-the-Wisp" folk motif in *Gatsby* (*NMAL*, Autumn 1984); and Karl-Ludwig Selig's "*Don Quixote* and *The Great Gatsby*" (*RHM*, No. 3–4, 1978–79).

Fitzgerald's most famous novel has undoubtedly influenced a number of contemporary writers, and, in the past two decades, we have begun to get articles and notes on this subject, one of the few in Fitzgerald studies which could sustain additional investigation. The most substantial of these is Richard Anderson's "Gatsby's Long Shadow: Influence and Endurance" (Bruccoli), which briefly surveys the novel's critical reputation historically and then focuses on a number of writers and works "touched" by it or which "openly or tacitly acknowledge discipleship," a group he calls "the Gatsby novels." The other recent pieces are notes—Don Graham's "The Common Ground of *Goodbye, Columbus* and *The Great Gatsby*" (*ForumH*, Winter 1976); Robert Emmet Long's "The Image of Gatsby in the Fiction of Louis Auchincloss and C. D. B. Bryan" (*FHA*, 1972); F. A. Rodewald's treatment of "Faulkner's Possible Use of *The Great Gatsby*" (*FHA*, 1975) in *Absalom, Absalom!*; Shyamal Bagchee's comparison of "*The Great Gatsby* and John Fowles's *The Collector*" (*NConL*, Sept. 1980); and Charles Baxter's "Defaced America: *The Great Gatsby* and *The Crying of Lot 49*" (*PNotes*, Oct. 1981).

The articles and notes which link *Gatsby* with other literary works without a suggestion of influence do not, for the most part, offer very surprising or original comparisons. In a typically polished and intelligent monograph, Louis Auchincloss selects *Three "Perfect Novels" and What They Have in Common* (Bloomfield Hills, Mich., and Columbia, S.C., 1981)—*The Scarlet Letter, Wuthering Heights*, and *Gatsby*. John H. Randall III (*Costerus*, 1973) examines *Gatsby* along with *Daisy Miller* and *The House of Mirth*, but not as novels of manners as one might expect. Randall's view is that they all raise a political issue, the "tragi-comic tension in our nation between the aspirations of our founding fathers . . . and our social customs and modes of behavior, which all too often give those ideals the lie."

Essays relating Fitzgerald to Hemingway and Faulkner continue to proliferate. William T. Stafford, in his *Books Speaking to Books: A Contextual Approach to American Fiction* (Chapel Hill, N.C., 1981), considers Nick Carraway, Benjy Compson, and Jake Barnes as "Three 'Innocent' American Narrators of the 1920s"; Ronald J. Gervais (*AAus*, 1980) compares the homecoming scenes in *Gatsby*, *The Sun Also Rises*, and *The Sound and the Fury*. Sister Mary Kathryn Grant, RSM, in "The Search for Celebration in *The Sun Also Rises* and *The Great Gatsby*" (*ArQ*, Summer 1977), looks at "the use and function of dancing" in the two novels; while Peter L. Hays's "Hemingway and Fitzgerald," in *Hemingway in Our Time* (ed. Richard Astro and Jackson J. Benson, Corvallis, Ore., 1974), looks at a variety of similarities between *Gatsby* and *Sun*—both narrators are middle-class veterans of World War I observing the rich and romantic; both novels are influenced by "The Waste Land."

In "From Renegade to Solid Citizen: The Extraordinary Individual in the Community" (*SDR*, Spring 1977), Fran James Polek more originally links *Gatsby* with *Absalom, Absalom!* and *The Godfather* as novels structured around "dynamic" renegades whose initial motivation to "make it" without "benefit of traditional community is tempered by a repressed but equally strong motivation to eventually rejoin the traditional community as a fully accepted leader or power figure." Sidney H. Bremer (*SAQ*, Summer 1980) considers *The Age of Innocence*, *Miss Lonelyhearts*, and *Gatsby* as "historical reflections of a deep postwar pessimism." Terrence Doody's chapter comparing *Gatsby* with *An American Tragedy* in his *Confession and Community in the Novel* (Baton Rouge, La., 1980) also stresses the pessimism of Fitzgerald's novel. Two essays, by Roslyn Kane (*LFQ*, Summer 1974) and Robert L. Carringer (*CritI*, Winter 1975), in apparent ignorance of one another, cite parallels between *Gatsby* and *Citizen Kane*.

Kiyohiko Tsuboi's "Steinbeck's *Cup of Gold* and Fitzgerald's *The Great Gatsby*," in *John Steinbeck: East and West* (ed. Tetsumaro Hayashi, Yasuo Hashiguchi, and Richard F. Peterson, Muncie, Ind., 1978), does little more than restate the obvious in its assertion that both authors were products of the same era and thus subject to like mythic and sociological influences. Equally obvious is Olatubosun Ogunsanwo's claims of parallels between the narrators of George Meredith's *One of Our Conquerors* and *Gatsby* (*Neohelicon*, No. 2, 1981). Jan Bakker's note on "Parallel Water Journeys Into the American Eden in John Davis's *The First Settlers of Virginia* and F. Scott Fitzgerald's *The Great Gatsby*" (*EAL*, Spring 1981) is dubious, as are T. Jeff Evans's brief piece (*NMAL*, Spring 1980) connecting *Gatsby* and *Daisy Miller* and William P. Kean's suggestion of a connection between a phrase in *Gatsby* and Laura Richards's popular children's story "The Golden Windows" (*NMAL*, Winter 1978).

Among the essays on the individual characters in the novel, the greatest number continue to focus on Nick Carraway. Oddly enough, three of the best debate an old issue, Nick's reliability as a narrator. In "'Pandered in Whispers': Narrative Reliability in *The Great Gatsby*" (*CollL*, Spring 1980), Colin S. Cass sees Nick's apparent pandering resulting from Fitzgerald's need to cover up the implausibities in his plot; while Scott Donaldson, in "The Trouble With Nick" (Donaldson), argues that

Nick is "the perfect narrator" for this novel because sometimes and in part just because he is unreliable. Kent Cartwright's "Nick Carraway as an Unreliable Narrator" (*PLL*, Spring 1984) is more critical of Nick, contending that his "final disillusionment . . . derives as much from his own moral dimness, his passivity, and his exaggerated gentility as it does from the facts of Gatsby's life; correspondingly, those qualities sometimes compromise the narration, altering . . . the response . . . that his telling draws from the reader."

Several of the other pieces on Nick deal in some way with his ambivalence and complexity as a narrator and as a character. Closest to the text is Ruth Betsy Tenenbaum's "'The Gray-Turning Gold-Turning Consciousness' of Nick Carraway" (*FHA*, 1975), which carefully examines the images manifested by what Tenenbaum calls Nick's "double consciousness"—his "everyday consciousness" ("rigid, even absolutist, conventional and other-directed, opinionated and prosaic, and, not least, highly literate") and his "poetic consciousness" (aware of "nuances and movement," capable of "whimsical free associations" and of "imaginative configurations of the grotesque, the comic, the surreal, and the absurd"). Eric Nelson's "Commitment and Insight in *The Great Gatsby*" (*RLV*, Summer 1977) is weakened by its insistence on identifying Nick's "divided sensibility" with the "divided sensibility" of American culture; while Susan Resneck Parr's "Individual Responsibility in *The Great Gatsby*" (*VQR*, Autumn 1981) does a good job of exploring the contradictions in Nick's narrative but then explains them by the unnecessary assertion that Fitzgerald shared his narrator's ambivalence. Leonard A. Podis's focus in his note (*Expl*, Summer 1980) is on the ambivalence of Nick's decision to return to the west after Gatsby's death.

Erik S. Lunde's approach, in "Return to Innocence?: The Value of Nick Carraway's Midwestern Perspective in F. Scott Fitzgerald's *The Great Gatsby*" (*SSMLN*, Summer 1980), is fresher in its suggestion that it is Nick's "midwestern perspective, with its critical, moralistic, agrarian overtones," which gives him the "detachment necessary to make judgements on the activities of Eastern compatriots." In "Nick Carraway and the Romance of Art" (*ESC*, June 1984), K. G. Probert sees Nick "operating as a highly self-conscious and manipulative narrator" who uses "norms provided by three types of traditional romance in his attempt to understand the shape and meaning of Gatsby's life": "The Odyssean seafaring romance, the Arthurian quest romance, and the medieval romanticized form of the Troy story." Peter Gregg Slater's "Ethnicity in *The Great Gatsby*" (*TCL*, Jan. 1973) presents the intriguing thesis that "a heightened awareness of ethnic differences" constitutes a "significant element" in *Gatsby*; but his tendency to identify what he calls Nick's "ethnocentric interpretation of the American dream" with Fitzgerald's is superfluous.

Paul A. Scanlon's "The Great Gatsby: Romance and Realism" (*AntigR*, Autumn 1976) is a modestly argued presentation of Jay Gatsby as a medieval chivalric knight; Scanlon is particularly persuasive in his depiction of the courtship of Daisy as being in the best courtly tradition. Ann Massa, in her section on Fitzgerald in *American Literature in Context, IV—1900–1930* (London, 1982), centers on the figure of Gatsby but has little new to add. In notes, Taylor Alderman (*MFS*, Winter 1973–74) and Matthew J. Bruccoli (*FHA*, 1975) speculate, respectively, on the origin of the name Jay Gatsby and on a possible real-life model for the character; Gordon Bordewyck (*AN&Q*, May 1979) plausibly relates three images associated with the Eucharist in chapter 3 to Gatsby as a secular priest overseeing "a pagan bacchanal."

Daisy and Tom Buchanan have been the subjects of several articles. Those on Daisy tend to reflect recent feminist perspectives. Thus, Leland S. Person, Jr., in "'Her story' and Daisy Buchanan" (*AL*, May 1978), sees Daisy as misinterpreted by both Nick and Gatsby, both of whom exhibit "a male tendency to project a self-satisfying, yet ultimately dehumanizing, image on woman." For Person, Daisy is Gatsby's "double," and the novel's theme of the death "of a romantic vision of America" is embodied in the "accelerated dissociation—the mutual alienation—of men and women before the materialistic values of modern society." Sarah Beebe Fryer's "Beneath the Mask: The Plight of Daisy Buchanan" (Donaldson) agrees with Person that Nick's is a distorted view of Daisy, and she carefully examines his observations of her behavior in three key scenes. Fryer feels that Daisy is forced ultimately to choose between her desires for "romantic devotion" and for "stability and social respectability" and is a "victim of a complex network of needs and desires" who "deserves more pity than blame." Joan S. Korenman's provocative "'Only Her Hairdresser . . .': Another Look at Daisy Buchanan" (*AL*, Jan. 1975) notes that Fitzgerald describes Daisy as both a blonde and as a brunette and then traces her "enigmatic charm" to the fact that she has traits both of the fair-haired Romantic heroine (passivity, pragmatism, a desire for security) as well as of the "knowledgeable, experienced dark women" of the Romantic tradition (her "low, thrilling voice" has a "powerful sexual appeal"). Glenn Settle, in "Fitzgerald's Daisy: The Siren Voice" (*AL*, Mar. 1985), is also concerned with Daisy's voice, as well as with "the backdrop against which she is presented," in his close reading of her "as classical Siren."

The one substantial essay on Tom, Robert Roulston's original "Tom Buchanan: Patrician in Motley" (*ArQ*, Summer 1978), also tries to complicate our conception of this character and largely succeeds. Roulston's point is that Tom is "one of the great comic characters in literature"; and he compares him with Falstaff and Twain's Pap Finn and Duke and King, as figures who display "shrewdness," "self-evident fatuousness," "exuberant amorality," a "lack of self-knowledge," and an "earthy, even a coarse nature." Like Twain and Shakespeare, Roulson claims persuasively, Fitzgerald saw Tom as an undeniable force of nature and felt he must exorcise him with laughter, for to rail against him would have been futile. John B. Humma's note, "Edward Russell Thomas: The Prototype for *Gatsby*'s Tom Buchanan?" (*MarkhamR*, Feb. 1974), speculates on similarities between the Buchanans and socialites Edward Russell and Linda Lee Thomas (she later became Mrs. Cole Porter), while Leverett T. Smith, Jr. (*AN&Q*, Jan./Feb. 1982) tries to answer the question of "Why Tom Buchanan Played End at New Haven," explaining that ends during the years when Tom played tried to get downfield quickly under punts and hit the return man before he could get going, and these are qualities that Tom displays in life.

In "Sub Specie Doctor T. J. Eckleburg: Man and God in 'The Great Gatsby'" (*ESA*, Sept. 1972), G. I. Hughes links Gatsby with George Wilson as the only two characters in the novel "who believe in anything"; but his conclusion, that, as "committed idealists in a world which admits only cynical alienation," they appear mad, is much too simplistic. Edward J. Piacentino's note (*NMAL*, Winter 1983) suggests intriguingly that the Dan Cody-Ella Kaye adventure foreshadows the Gatsby-Daisy relationship; and Alice Hall Petry (*CRevAS*, Summer 1985) presents an impressive amount of evidence to support her contention that "what little information Fitzgerald provides about Cody points to his having been directly inspired by" Warren G. Harding. Brief pieces by David Savage (*AN&Q*, Jan. 1975) and Riley V. Hampton (*AL*, May 1976) deal with "Owl Eyes." Savage contrasts him with Dr. Eckleburg, and Hampton offers Ring Lardner as the "real-life prototype" for the character.

Two recent essays locate *Gatsby* within a Marxist dialectic. Richard Godden, in "*The Great Gatsby*: Glamor on the Turn" (*JAmS*, Dec. 1982), invokes not only Marx but Veblen, Brecht, Raymond Williams, and Georg Lukács as well, in an article that alternates between fresh insights and oversimplifications and focuses most of its attention on Nick and Gatsby. Unaware of Godden's work, Ross Posnock's "'A New World, Material Without Being Real': Fitzgerald's Critique of Capitalism in *The Great Gatsby*" (Donaldson) covers much of the same ground but seems slightly less rigid in its application of Marxist doctrine to the novel.

A number of brief notes, some helpful, others redundant or of questionable relevance, continue to appear each year. The matter of the appropriateness of *Hopalong Cassidy* as the book in which young Jimmy Gatz wrote his resolves has been debated by Taylor Alderman (*FHA*, 1975), Peter Valenti (*NMAL*, Fall 1979), and Richard Davison (*FHA*, 1979). The source for Tom's remark about Goddard's *The Rise of the Colored Empires* has occupied James Ellis (*AL*, Nov. 1972), M. Gidley (*JAmS*, Aug. 1973), and Taylor Alderman (*FHA*, 1977). Duane Edwards (*BSUF*, Winter 1982) and David L. Vanderwerken (*NMAL*, Spring 1979) have provocative but ultimately unconvincing answers to the questions of who killed Myrtle Wilson and Jay Gatsby, respectively. Robert Emmet Long (*FHA*, 1972) explains the allusion to Gilda Gray in the novel; James

Ellis (*FHA*, 1978) does the same with references to "the Duke of Buccleuch" and "the Earl of Doncaster"; and Sterling K. Eisiminger (*FHA*, 1974) finds several factual errors in the novel.

The two most helpful notes are Dalton H. Gross's (*N&Q*, Jan. 1976) on Wolfsheim's reference to the death of Rosy Rosenthal as "a chillingly realistic introduction to Gatsby's world," and Robert A. Martin's (*AN&Q*, Dec. 1973), which shows how Fitzgerald's shifting of the Dutch sailors' vision from the end of chapter 1 to the last page of the novel can be seen as the reason for "a number of subsequent references scattered throughout the novel in which Gatsby is closely associated with water and nautical objects connected with water."

The third movie version of *Gatsby*, which premiered in 1974 to a great deal of media hoopla (including *Time* and *Newsweek* cover stories) but very mixed reviews, probably inspired a number of articles on the previous film adaptations of the novel and on the 1926 stage version by Owen Davis. The most comprehensive of these is Alan Margolies's "Novel to Play to Film: Four Versions of *The Great Gatsby*" (Donaldson), which traces in careful detail how each film and the stage play differed from Fitzgerald's novel and how each was received by the critics. Robert E. Morsberger's "Trimalchio in West Egg: *The Great Gatsby* Onstage" (*Prospects*, 1980) and David W. Cheatham's "Owen Davis's Dramatization of *The Great Gatsby*" (*FHA*, 1979) are good full discussions of the play and the circumstances surrounding its production. DeWitt Bodeen, in "F. Scott Fitzgerald and Films" (*Films in Review*, May 1977), deals not only with the three *Gatsby* movies but also with other films made from Fitzgerald's works, including the early silent screen productions of three short stories and *The Beautiful and Damned*, and with a stage adaptation of *Tender Is the Night* which was never produced. Irene Kahn Atkins's "In Search of the Greatest Gatsby" (*LFQ*, Summer 1974) is an interesting comparison of the 1949 and 1974 films which doesn't go as far as Margolies's essay; while Edward T. Jones's "Green Thoughts in a Technicolor Shade: A Revaluation of *The Great Gatsby*" (*LFQ*, Summer 1974) and Louis Giannetti's "The Gatsby Flap" (*LFQ*, Winter 1975) are both defenses of the 1974 adaptation which basically praise its fidelity to the original.

b. Tender Is the Night. Another of the encouraging developments in Fitzgerald studies is the increased critical attention paid to *Tender Is the Night* in recent years. While the attention has not rivalled—and probably never will—that paid to *Gatsby*, it has produced some excellent essays. Ironically, a number of these approaches to *Tender* echo similar pieces on *Gatsby*; but where with the latter they are redundant, with the former—because there is so much less in print—they constitute innovative criticism.

Several of the best recent articles are notable for their assumption that Fitzgerald's last completed novel is a complex and carefully designed work, a viewpoint not present in much earlier commentary. In "The Aesthetic of Forbearance: Fitzgerald's *Tender Is the Night*" (*Novel*, Fall 1977), Maria DiBattista ingeniously considers the novel within the framework of an aesthetic of forbearance, which "implies a suppression of narrative information and as such represents a guiding principle in the construction of plot" and "demands a canny treatment of history, of character, and of appropriate generic and mythic material to insure that the ironic mystery of its fable is protected against sentimental, moralistic readings." DiBattista's fascinating discussion also leads into suggestions of parallels with *The Odyssey*.

Bruce L. Grenberg, in "Fitzgerald's 'Figured Curtain': Personality and History in *Tender Is the Night*" (*FHA*, 1978; reprinted in Stern), sees Fitzgerald as "a 'critical,' a 'philosophical,' and, if you will, a 'moral' historical novelist, intent on comprehending and explaining in rational terms the motives and implications of human events, viewed simultaneously as personal experience and public phenomena." Nicole's schizophrenia thus becomes "metaphorical as well as clinical," typifying "the experience and suffering of an immature America in the opening decades of the twentieth century"; Devereux Warren's rape of his daughter is "an apt metaphor for the intrafamilial self-destructive conflict of World War I." For Grenberg, in what remains one of the seminal essays on *Tender*, the novel as a whole, through Dick Diver, "depicts an America whose ideals, noble in themselves, are becoming untenable, whose idealists, by the very virtue of their ideals, are being corrupted, or crushed and cast out by a new culture progressively giving itself over to material, amoral pleasure." This is an approach which has been applied to *Gatsby*; Grenberg is the first to show its relevance to *Tender*.

Robert Roulston has written two solid essays on the role of place in the novel. His "Slumbering With the Just: A Maryland Lens for *Tender Is the Night*" (*SoQ*, Jan. 1978) contends that Fitzgerald's view of Maryland as combining northern "industriousness" with southern "genteel repose" embodied for him "the scheme of values which pervades *Tender Is the Night*." In a more narrowly focused piece, "Dick Diver's Plunge Into the Roman Void: The Setting of *Tender Is the Night*" (*SAQ*, Winter 1978), Roulston examines the five chapters set in Rome, a locale which he calls "a perfect microcosm of all that has become debased in Western civilization." Rome provides "an x-ray of Dick's psyche—a kind of waking nightmare in which . . . wish fulfillment and punishment combine in a kind of *pas de deux* . . . between the id and the ego."

Roulston's, DiBattista's, and Grenberg's essays all are close readings of the text, another positive aspect of recent *Tender* criticism, and one exemplified as well by John Stark's earlier "The Style of *Tender Is the Night*" (*FHA*, 1972). Stark does a useful analysis of the opening three paragraphs of the 1934 edition, discussing such elements as sound, adjectives, imagery, allusions, and sentence and paragraph construction.

Equally helpful is Jeffrey Berman's *"Tender Is the Night*: Fitzgerald's *A Psychology for Psychiatrists"* (*L&P*, No. 1/2, 1979), which explores Fitzgerald's knowledge of psychiatry, in particular the concept of "transference-love" which is so central to the novel. Berman's conclusions are that Dick is not a very convincing psychiatrist and that Fitzgerald's use of the "psychoanalytic dynamics of transference" is much more vague than Freud's sense of it.

As with *Gatsby*, one of the most common ways of looking at *Tender* is by discerning in it a pattern, motif, prevalent metaphor, or the presence of a literary archetype. Scott Donaldson's "'No, I Am Not Prince Charming': Fairy Tales in *Tender Is the Night*" (*FHA*, 1973) takes note of the references to fairy tales in the novel, claiming that they "suggest the drastic consequences in failure of perception and in moral corruption of swallowing whole the sentimentalized view of the world implicit in this fiction." But Donaldson also carefully points out that Fitzgerald deliberately separates "his book from the sentimental, romantic fairy tale which, it is strongly implied, has been responsible for much of the moral irresponsibility he deplores." In "The Spinning Story: Gothic Motifs in *Tender Is the Night*" (*FHA*, 1976), Judith Wilt finds in Fitzgerald's novel the "peculiarly Gothic narrative strategy . . . of drawing in, often through two or three loops of storytellers, towards the unthinkable act, the unsayable desire, the unbearable bargain, the 'unhuman' mystery that generates the story." Wilt also points to other Gothic elements in a richly rewarding essay.

Ruth Prigozy's provocative "From Griffith's Girls to *Daddy's Girl*: The Masks of Innocence in *Tender Is the Night*" (*TCL*, Summer 1980) traces the daddy's girl motif in the novel to the treatment of the father-daughter relationship in the films of D. W. Griffith. Joan Kirkby's more complex "Spengler and Apocalyptic Typology in F. Scott Fitzgerald's *Tender Is the Night*" (*SoRA*, Nov. 1979) finds in each of Fitzgerald's novels "an end of time feeling" which is most fully developed in *Tender*. Barry V. Qualls, in "Physician in the Counting House: The Religious Motif in *Tender is the Night*" (*ELWIU*, Fall 1975), is on original ground in suggesting that the novel is an inverted pilgrim's progress in which we witness the dissolution of Dick's religious sense in the face of the "fair world of the moneyed leisure class." So too is Rita Gollin, in her "Modes of Travel in *Tender is the Night*" (*STC*, Fall 1971), where she shows how bicycles, cars, trains, and boats "symbolize the values and dilemmas of the twenties, particularly Dick Diver," who commands expensive cars in central sections of the novel but ends, "poignant and ironic," as a bicyclist. In "Vitality and Vampirism in *Tender Is the Night*" (Stern), James W. Tuttleton presents in convincing detail his "lurid thesis" that "there is a motif of female vampirism latent in *Tender Is the Night*," which is "a constant in Fitzgerald's fiction from *This Side of Paradise* onward" and which takes its form from three Keats poems—"Endymion," "La Belle Dame sans Merci," and "Lamia."

The characterization of Dick Diver, which was the subject of intense debate and controversy among reviewers in 1934, has continued to interest recent critics. Most grapple with the question of whether or not Dick's disintegration is plausibly motivated and explained and, if so, how and why. Hallvard Dahlie and Juanita Williams Dudley agree that it is but offer different explanations. In "Alienation and Disintegration in 'Tender Is the Night'" (*HAB*, Fall 1971), Dahlie traces a "pattern of isolation and alienation" which illuminates Dick's downfall, showing how, even at the beginning of the novel, he cannot "give of himself honestly and unselfishly" and is unable to "identify himself honestly with the characters and forces of his world." Dudley, in "Dr. Diver, Vivisectionist" (*CollL*, Spring 1975), also finds a foreshadowing of Dick's fate early in the text, focusing on his remark that he wants to give a "bad party" as prefiguring "the chronicle of a brilliant and promising young man who connived at his own destruction by forces representing wealth and power."

George D. Murphy's "The Unconscious Dimension of *Tender Is the Night*" (*SNNTS*, Fall 1973) also cites an explanation for Dick's collapse— his super-ego's failure "to come effectively to terms with the disruptive, libido-charged impulses of his id and ego"—but his essay is weakened considerably by the tendency to use Fitzgerald's fiction as a touchstone to his life. In "Technical Potential and Achievement in *Tender Is the Night*" (*DQR*, No. 2, 1973), F. G. F. Schulte comes to much more negative conclusions regarding Fitzgerald's depiction of Dick, contending that he suppresses knowledge of his hero's flaws and does not clearly define the forces working against him. Unfortunately, Schulte's study is woodenly written and seems overly simplistic.

Vincent Robson and Robert Merrill, in essays written more than a decade apart, come to similar conclusions about the inevitability of Dick's fate. Robson, in "The Psychosocial Conflict and the Distortion of Time: A Study of Diver's Disintegration in *Tender is the Night*" (*Lang&L*, Winter 1972), sees Diver "trapped" and "unable to break out of his circular motion toward end and beginning; a motion which itself has no termination." In "*Tender Is the Night* as a Tragic Action" (*TSLL*, Winter 1983), Merrill sees the 1951 revised version as superior to the 1934 edition because it establishes the "gradual, 'progressive' character of Dick's alteration" more clearly and because it establishes the "sense of a fatalistic progression so crucial to" a conception of him as a tragic figure. Merrill believes that Dick's fate is sealed from the moment that he makes "the tragic mistake" of marrying Nicole.

Gerald Nelson's chapter on Dick in his *Ten Versions of America* (New York, 1972) mainly consists of a running contrast between Fitzgerald's protagonist and Jake Barnes. A more effective comparison is the more unlikely one which Richard Foster, in "Time's Exile: Dick Diver and the Heroic Idea" (*Mosaic*, Spring 1975), makes between Dick and Hamlet. Foster finds Dick a "tragic hero because he found himself cut off, finally, from both his duty and his fulfillment in it," but he sees the novel ending in a "late Emersonian" "note of affirmation." Another very useful essay, Louis K. Greiff's "Perfect Marriage in *Tender Is the Night*: A Study in the Progress of a Symbol" (*FHA*, 1974), also finds echoes of Emerson in *Tender* but comes to an almost completely opposite position regarding them. Greiff relates the union of Dick and Nicole to passages in Emerson on the union of spirit and matter engendering a "heightened reality," but concludes that the novel celebrates this union in book 1 and traces its destruction in books 2 and 3, providing Fitzgerald's "terminal comment on the entire transcendental question."

Several brief notes also deal with Dick. In "The Divine Dick Diver" (*NMAL*, Fall 1977), Margaret McBride explores the symbolic connotations of the name Diver which suggests both a "tragic fall" and a "god" and discusses Dick as a Christ figure. Thomas Deegan's "Dick Diver's Childishness in *Tender Is the Night*" (*FHA*, 1979) looks at two motifs which delineate Dick's incompleteness—the childlike aspects of his character and the contrast in his mind between light and darkness. John M. Howell, in "Dr. Tom Rennie and *Tender Is the Night*" (*ICarbS*, Spring–Summer 1981), suggests the real-life models for Dick may have been Dr. Rennie, one of Zelda's Baltimore psychiatrists, and James Rennie, the actor who created the title role in the stage version of *Gatsby*. Michael Adams (*FHA*, 1977) deals with the reference in *Tender* to Constance Talmadge's film *Breakfast at Sunrise*, while Allen Shepherd (*FHA*, 1979) studies the influence of Fitzgerald's novel on Robert Penn Warren's *A Place to Come To*.

Another group of recent pieces have dealt with the female characters in the novel. In "Nicole's Gardens" (*FHA*, 1978), Suzanne West skillfully shows how Fitzgerald underlines "the development of Nicole's character by associating her with three different gardens"—the one at Dr. Dohmler's sanitarium ("a romantic Eden"), the one at the Villa Diana ("an enclosed refuge that Dick establishes for his half-cured bride"), and a metaphorical garden that Nicole creates herself. Essays by Marjory Martin and Mary Verity McNicholas, O. P. expand the discussion to the other women in *Tender*. Martin's "Fitzgerald's Image of Woman: Anima Projections in *Tender Is the Night*" (*ESColl*, Sept. 1976) argues that they are aesthetically valid when one sees them as anima projections of Dick and that, as anima projections, they must be analyzed in terms of archetypal associations. Her analysis of various female characters as illustrations of archetypal figures—goddess, priestess, temptress, Kore maiden, Madonna, and purely sexual creature—is highly original and suggestive of fruitful further study. McNicholas's "Fitzgerald's Women in *Tender Is the Night"* (*CollL*, Winter 1977), while not as innovative, is nonetheless a thorough examination of the women in the novel in relation to Dick's dual nature and Fitzgerald's own dual vision of females.

That dual vision is handled far more disputatiously by Judith Fetterley in "Who Killed Dick Diver? The Sexual Politics of *Tender is the Night"* (*Mosaic*, Winter 1984). Fetterley sees Dick's marriage as his assumption of a woman's role—he lives "a woman's life" and becomes a mother and a wife, surrendering his "energy, health, sanity, even identity, from self to the other." Thus, for Fetterley, *Tender* "proposes that American men are driven 'mad' by the feminization of American culture which forces them to live out the lives of women and which purchases the sanity of women at men's expense." But she also finds a subtext "subliminally interwoven with the dominant text, whose message contradicts and subverts that of the dominant text" and implies a "negative attitude toward conventional masculinity." This subtext reveals Fitzgerald's "awareness that his sanity and his career were purchased at the price of Zelda's and purchased by his manipulation of the power accorded men over women." Fetterley's detection of this subtext is extremely dubious.

By contrast, Sarah Beebe Fryer, in "Nicole Warren Diver and Alabama Beggs Knight: Women on the Threshold of Freedom" (*MFS*, Summer 1985), seeks to dispel the notion that Fitzgerald was "extremely unsympathetic toward his female characters" by examining Nicole and Alabama (in Zelda Fitzgerald's novel *Save Me the Waltz*) as figures who "embody ideals of self-realization that their mothers did not share and confront role conflicts characteristic of women on the threshold of a new era of freedom." In Fryer's view, Nicole shows "conflicting ideals of femininity (submissiveness) and independence" while Alabama "nearly succeeds in establishing her own sense of identity, independent of any man's opinion." Jacqueline Tavernier-Courbin's "Sensuality as Key to Characterization in *Tender Is the Night"* (*ESC*, Dec. 1983) is also more restrained than Fryer's essay in its contentions that "sensual desire and consciousness are . . . the most important elements which motivate the characters, further the action, and give the novel its life force" and that "the more basic desire is, the more positive it appears to be" and "the more complex and indefinite it is, the more destructive it becomes."

Several articles link *Tender* with the work of other writers. In "The Limits of Professionalism: A Sociological Approach to Faulkner, Fitzgerald and Hemingway" (*Criticism*, Spring 1973), George Monteiro uses Talcott Parsons's concept of "affective neutrality" in the role of the physician in society as a touchstone to a study of *Tender*, *The Wild Palms*, and three Hemingway short stories. Raymond J. Wilson's "Henry James and F. Scott Fitzgerald: Americans Abroad" (*RS*, June 1977) is a modestly argued suggestion of "startling similarities" between *Tender* and *Daisy Miller* and *The American*. Lewis B. Horne, in "The Gesture of Pity in

'Jude the Obscure' and 'Tender Is the Night'" (*ArielE*, Apr. 1980), compares the protagonists of the two novels who both "suffer the advent of a new era inimical to the qualities with which each man was born and nurtured" and who both dramatize "the waning effectiveness of the altruistic impulse." Alan S. Wheelock's "As Ever, 'Daddy's Girl': Incest Motifs in *Day for Night*" (*GyS*, Spring 1975) argues that Truffault's film was consciously influenced by Fitzgerald's novel.

Among brief notes on *Tender*, George Monteiro (*NConL*, Mar. 1976) anticipates Nelson's longer piece by suggesting *Daisy Miller* as the source for the scene in which Dick, bicycling through Europe, unexpectedly meets Nicole. Peter Doughty notes an apparent error in Fitzgerald's text, in "The Seating Arrangement in *Tender Is the Night*" (*FHA*, 1979); Matthew J. Bruccoli (*FHA*, 1979) cites as a source for Abe North's death the 1928 beating in a speakeasy and subsequent death of a Princeton contemporary of Fitzgerald's (the parallel is mentioned in a 1934 letter from Bennett Cerf to Maxwell Perkins); and Robert Wexelblatt (*NMAL*, Winter 1984) analyzes the novel's four allusions to Ulysses S. Grant.

Between July 1949 and April 1950, novelist Malcolm Lowry and his wife Margerie worked on a movie adaptation of *Tender*, producing a 455-page script (held now by the University of British Columbia Library and for "copyright reasons" unpublishable) which was never filmed and several pages of "Notes." The latter have been published as *Notes on a Screenplay for F. Scott Fitzgerald's "Tender Is the Night"* (Bloomfield Hills, Mich., and Columbia, S.C., 1976). Prefaced with an excellent introduction by Paul Tiessen, which traces the Lowrys' interest in *Tender* and explains the fate of their script, as well as relating it to Lowry's novel *Under the Volcano*, the "Notes" themselves, which were never intended for publication, have been left unedited and uncorrected and, as a result, are presented in a hard-to-follow shorthand stream-of-consciousness style. Further, they contain little analysis of Fitzgerald's novel; more often the comments concern the Lowrys' screenplay itself. These "Notes" should be consulted in conjunction with Ruth Perlmutter's "Malcolm Lowry's Unpublished Filmscript of *Tender Is the Night*" (*AQ*, Winter 1976), which provides an analysis of the script and points out "remarkable affinities between Lowry and Fitzgerald in life and work."

c. *The Other Novels*. Fitzgerald's three other published novels continue to be largely ignored. Each has been the subject of a handful of recent articles and notes. Two pieces identify the numerous obscure and mostly literary references in *This Side of Paradise*—Dorothy Ballweg Good's "'A Romance and a Reading List': The Literary References in *This Side of Paradise*" (*FHA*, 1976) and Lynn Haywood's "Historical Notes for *This Side of Paradise*" (*RALS*, Autumn 1980).

In the best of the two other substantial essays on Fitzgerald's first novel, "*This Side of Paradise*: The Ghost of Rupert Brooke" (*FHA*, 1975), Robert Roulston uses Fitzgerald's fascination with and references to

Brooke in the text to illuminate the novel's merits and defects. Madelyn Hoffman's "This Side of Paradise: A Study of Pathological Narcissism" (L&P, No. 3 and 4, 1978) draws upon the theories of Heinz Kohut and Otto Kernberg in its assertion that Amory Blaine's "ultimate equation of beauty with evil represents an awareness on some level that the narcissistic personality's weakness for charisma in others represents a quest for reunion with the original narcissistic charismatic parent." Robert M. McIlvaine's "Thomas Parke D'Invilliers and Villiers de L'Isle-Adam" (NMAL, Summer 1977) is a brief and questionable suggestion that the name Fitzgerald chose for the character in This Side of Paradise (and for the author of the verses on the title page of Gatsby) "is meant to remind the reader of Villiers de L'Isle-Adam and thus heighten the fin de siècle atmosphere that pervades the Princeton section of the novel."

The Beautiful and Damned, which probably warrants less attention than This Side of Paradise, has received a bit more. None of the essays is truly seminal, but all contribute some useful insights. Leonard A. Podis's "The Beautiful and Damned: Fitzgerald's Test of Youth" (FHA, 1973) seems elementary in its conclusion that Fitzgerald's second novel represents his "first major attempt . . . to reconcile his romantic faith in the magic of youth with his morally ingrained suspicions that life wasn't 'the reckless business' for which he and his creatures had been taking it." In "The Beautiful and Damned: The Alcoholic's Revenge" (L&P, No. 3, 1977), Robert Roulston overuses the details of Fitzgerald's life in his plausible claims that, while writing the novel, he had "marital and professional tribulations which were exacerbated by his growing dependence upon alcohol" and that the novel records "the progress of Fitzgerald's malady."

Wayne W. Westbrook's "Portrait of a Dandy in The Beautiful and Damned" (FHA, 1979) briefly describes Ward McAllister, the real-life model for Anthony Patch's father. In "The Symbolic Function of Food and Eating in F. Scott Fitzgerald's The Beautiful and Damned" (BSUF, Summer 1981), George J. Searles convincingly shows how food imagery "reinforces the fundamentally judgmental, censorious tone of the book, while lending to it an additional artistic dimension." Ronald J. Gervais, in "'Sleepy Hollow's Gone': Pastoral Myth and Artifice in Fitzgerald's The Beautiful and Damned" (BSUF, Summer 1981), sees "the primary symbols" of the novel as "pastoral landscapes of artificial preservation" and the major tension existing "between the pastoral impulse as neurotic withdrawal or as fulfillment of a basic human need for order and stability."

The Last Tycoon is the subject of four worthwhile essays. Kermit W. Moyer's "Fitzgerald's Two Unfinished Novels: The Count and the Tycoon in Spenglerian Perspective" (ConL, Spring 1974) traces the Spenglerian elements in the four published sections of Fitzgerald's abortive and critically ignored novel "The Count of Darkness" and in The Last Tycoon. In "The Last Tycoon: The Dilemma of Maturity for F. Scott

Fitzgerald" (*FHA*, 1979), Wendy Fairey carefully mixes biography and criticism to show how Stahr represents a mature Fitzgerald's view of a hero whose romanticism is mixed with pragmatism. In the love story, we "move beyond Fitzgerald's earlier notion of men being destroyed by their women to a more impartial and judicious sense of life simply being very difficult," but Fairey also points out that to "see fatigue as the crucial development of maturity is a limitation of vision that may have been as destructive as time itself."

Robert Roulston, in "Whistling 'Dixie' in Encino: *The Last Tycoon* and F. Scott Fitzgerald's Two Souths" (*SAQ*, Autumn 1980), presents a close reading of the novel's first chapter in which Fitzgerald "seems to be setting up the Old South as a paradigm for the patterns of disintegration which he would later depict as operating upon . . . Hollywood." Jack Cashill's "The Keeper of the Faith: Mogul as Hero in *The Last Tycoon*" (*RFEA*, Feb. 1984) notes that, alone among many American writers who have depicted capitalists at work, Fitzgerald has "accorded his character heroic status." Cashill sees the book "as much a novel of capitalism as it is a novel of Hollywood"; Stahr is different from other capitalists in his "transcendent sense of 'great purposefulness.'"

In briefer notes, Edward J. Piacentino (*AN&Q*, Sept./Oct. 1981) examines the novel's "recurring moon imagery"; Gabrielle Winkel (*FHA*, 1975) speculates inconsequentially on the real-life source of Prince Agge of Denmark; Neill R. Joy (*NMAL*, Spring 1978) sees the fight scene between Stahr and Brimmer as a "mutation" of the 1937 "Eastman-Hemingway imbroglio" in Maxwell Perkins's office; and T. Jeff Evans (*AN&Q*, April 1979) claims that Fitzgerald parodies the famous love scene in Hemingway's *For Whom the Bell Tolls* when Stahr and Kathleen visit the building site of his new home. Edward Murray's chapter on Fitzgerald in his *The Cinematic Imagination: Writers and the Motion Pictures* (New York, 1972) discusses Fitzgerald's interest in, association with, and use of film in his life and work. Murray calls *The Last Tycoon* "one of the most striking applications of the cinematic imagination to a literary subject that has yet been written."

Several reviewers of and commentators on the 1976 film version of *The Last Tycoon* contributed serious pieces on the relation of movie to novel. Chief among these are Hollis Alpert's "Fitzgerald, Hollywood, and *The Last Tycoon*" (*American Film*, Mar. 1976), Irene Kahn Atkins's "Hollywood Revisited: A Sad Homecoming" (*LFQ*, Spring 1977), Richard Combs's "*The Last Tycoon*" (*Sight and Sound*, Spring 1977), John Callahan's "The Unfinished Business of *The Last Tycoon*" (*LFQ*, Summer 1978), and I. Lloyd Michaels's "Auteurism, Creativity, and Entropy in *The Last Tycoon*" (*LFQ*, No. 2, 1982). In "*Gatsby, Tycoon, Islands*, and the Film Critics" (*FHA*, 1978), Michael Adams surveys reviews of not only the film of *The Last Tycoon* but also of the 1974 version of *Gatsby* and the 1977 adaptation of Hemingway's *Islands in the Stream*.

d. The Short Stories. Within the past decade, as noted earlier, sixty-one Fitzgerald stories hitherto available only in back files of magazines have been collected in book form. While this has not led to the wide-ranging examination of Fitzgerald as short story writer which is needed, it has provided the impetus for Bryer's collection of twenty-two new essays, *The Short Stories of F. Scott Fitzgerald: New Approaches in Criticism*, and to a modest increase in the number of articles and notes devoted to the short fiction. Unfortunately, aside from several of the essays in the Bryer collection, most of these pieces have continued to focus on the most popular and already widely recognized stories (especially those in the popular Scribner Library paperback, *Babylon Revisited and Other Stories*).

The first section of Bryer's collection contains ten general essays or "overviews" of the stories. Scott Donaldson's "Money and Marriage in Fitzgerald's Stories" (some of which reappears in Donaldson's *Fool for Love*) traces how the stories reveal Fitzgerald's "changing attitudes toward money and marriage," dividing them into those which depict "the success, or seeming success, of the poor young man in wooing the rich girl" and those in which "the young man is rejected in his quest or subsequently disappointed" and considering such overlooked stories as "Presumption" and "A Snobbish Story." In "The Romantic Self and the Uses of Place in the Stories of F. Scott Fitzgerald," Richard Lehan groups stories around novels which are contemporaneous with them, discussing how Fitzgerald's sense of place and of the romantic self changed in the course of his career.

Lawrence Buell's "The Significance of Fantasy in Fitzgerald's Short Fiction" finds five "main forms" of fantasy and focuses on "The Diamond as Big as the Ritz." Kenneth E. Eble, in "Touches of Disaster: Alcoholism and Mental Illness in Fitzgerald's Short Stories," observes the similar effects of both diseases on their victims in Fitzgerald's fiction and concentrates on "A New Leaf," "An Alcoholic Case," and "The Crack-Up" essays. In "Fitzgerald's Changes on the Southern Belle: The Tarleton Trilogy," C. Hugh Holman presents a highly informed investigation of the role the South played in Fitzgerald's life and work, with an emphasis on his portrayal of the southern belle in "The Ice Palace," "The Jelly-Bean," and "The Last of the Belles."

In a very persuasive essay, "Fitzgerald's Short Stories and the Depression: An Artistic Crisis," Ruth Prigozy shows, through close examination of the stories written between 1929 and 1935, how Fitzgerald moved beyond "the romantic antics of young lovers" and began to deal with the serious and complex problems of marriage which he addressed in *Tender*. Alan Margolies's equally intriguing "'Kissing, Shooting, and Sacrificing': F. Scott Fitzgerald and the Hollywood Market" notes that, in writing several of the early stories, Fitzgerald had "his eye on sales to Hollywood," demonstrating how the stories in question (especially "The Offshore Pirate" and "Dice, Brass Knuckles & Guitar") reflect this intention.

Two of the general essays in the Bryer collection focus on the fiction of Fitzgerald's later years, although Robert A. Martin clearly demonstrates, in "Hollywood in Fitzgerald: After Paradise," how closely he was tied to Hollywood throughout his career, not just during the last three and a half years. "Jacob's Ladder," "Our Own Movie Queen," and "Magnetism" are among the lesser-known stories which Martin studies. James L. W. West III's "Fitzgerald and *Esquire*" carefully outlines Fitzgerald's association with Arnold Gingrich's new magazine between 1934 and 1941, utilizing previously unpublished correspondence and analyzing "Three Acts of Music" and "The Lost Decade" as stories which "employ a compressed, understated method which is quite unusual in Fitzgerald's fiction."

The other general essay in Bryer's collection, Joseph Mancini's "To Be Both Light and Dark: The Jungian Process of Individuation in Fitzgerald's Basil Duke Lee Stories," traces in great detail through the Basil stories Jung's notion that, in the process of individuation, the "individual learns to distinguish himself from two modes of collective life, the unconscious realm or ground of all being, and the conscious world of society." Rochelle S. Elstein's unoriginal "Fitzgerald's Josephine Stories: The End of the Romantic Illusion" (*AL*, Mar. 1979) claims that in the course of the five-story series, Fitzgerald "worked and reworked the same elements until [in 'Emotional Bankruptcy,' the last of the series] he arrived at a formulation which was antithetical to the original construct of the 'genteel romantic heroine.'"

The two other linked series of stories Fitzgerald wrote have also received some recent commentary. John O. Rees and Thomas E. Daniels have written on the Pat Hobby stories. Rees's "Fitzgerald's Pat Hobby Stories" (*ColQ*, Spring 1975) does little more than give plot summaries and indicate that the stories deserve more attention; but Daniels's "Pat Hobby: Anti-Hero" (*FHA*, 1973) is far more useful in pointing out Fitzgerald's ability "to create a character quite different from what he had done in the past, and then to present [him] in a very objective way." In "Fitzgerald's 'Philippe, Count of Darkness'" (*FHA*, 1975), Janet Lewis ranges intelligently and widely over a variety of aspects of the unfinished novel which survives as a series of connected stories—the details of its composition, summaries of the episodes, Fitzgerald's reworking of the original manuscripts, his plans for its completion, inconsistencies among the published installments and, most worthwhile of all, a close study of the text.

Three other general essays try, with varying degrees of success, to find a pattern in Fitzgerald's short fiction. For Alan Casty, in "'I and It' in the Stories of F. Scott Fitzgerald" (*SSF*, Winter 1972), it is the loss of "I" or self: "the recurrent pattern of relationship is the violation of the other in the mode of I and It" and "the end is always the violation of oneself, the loss of self, as well." Charlotte LeGates's "Dual-Perspective

Irony and the Fitzgerald Short Story" (*IEY*, 1977) somewhat superficially applies to the shorter fiction a view that has often been expressed regarding the novels: "Because he is able to convey, simultaneously, two diametrically opposed views, he creates dual-perspective irony." In "Structural Metaphors in Fitzgerald's Short Fiction" (*KanQ*, Spring 1982), William J. Brondell analyzes "Absolution," "The Freshest Boy," and "Babylon Revisited" as examples of stories which contain superstructures carrying the action of the plot as well as a "deep structure" which portrays "accurately and convincingly the inner life of the characters who inhabit the stories."

Of the five essays and three notes published on "Absolution" in the past decade, three full-length articles deal with the same topic—the relationship between the story and *Gatsby* (for which it was originally intended to be a prologue). Robert A. Martin's "The Hot Madness of Four O'Clock in Fitzgerald's 'Absolution' and *Gatsby*" (*SAF*, Autumn 1974) and Lawrence D. Stewart's "'Absolution' and *The Great Gatsby*" (*FHA*, 1973) take diametrically opposed positions. Stewart contends that the novel and the story are "basically irreconcilable" because "the short story's alleged Gatsby-as-boy is a child who has no awareness of Father Schwartz's dilemma and who uses the priest's behavior as justification for developing quite different notions." Martin, on the other hand, sees the two "linked by numerous parallels" and demonstrates how "some of the original links that would have tied 'Absolution' to *Gatsby* as prologue to novel are still visible beneath the surfaces." Ryan LaHurd, in "'Absolution': *Gatsby*'s Forgotten Front Door" (*CollL*, Spring 1976), seemingly is ignorant of Stewart's and Martin's essays and has little new to offer in his portrait of Rudolph as a pre-adolescent Jimmy Gatz.

Keith Cushman's "Scott Fitzgerald's Scrupulous Meanness: 'Absolution' and 'The Sisters'" (*FHA*, 1979) likewise ignores John Kuehl's 1964 *James Joyce Quarterly* essay on precisely the same subject, the influence of Joyce's story on Fitzgerald's. Irving Malin, in "'Absolution': Absolving Lies" (Bryer), presents a meticulous and valuable explication of a story which "asks whether art itself—that is, imagination, dream, romance—can be as sufficient, helpful, and necessary as religious belief. . . . What is the connection between artistic 'lies' and religious 'truths?'" Two of the three notes on "Absolution," those by J. I. Morse (*FHA*, 1972) and by E. R. Hagemann (*NMAL*, Spring 1980), point to errors in the Latin used in the story. The other, Gail Moore Morrison's "Faulkner's Priests and Fitzgerald's 'Absolution'" (*MissQ*, Summer 1979), finds verbal parallels between Faulkner's "The Priest" and Fitzgerald's story and more general parallels with Faulkner's "Mistral."

"May Day" is the subject of several very good recent pieces. James W. Tuttleton's "Seeing Slightly Red: Fitzgerald's 'May Day'" (Bryer) considers it a story which "combines with uncommon adroitness the social and psychological, the public and the private tensions of Fitzgerald the man and the historical moment, the year 1919." Tuttleton is particularly helpful in giving the details of what actually happened in New York City on 1 May 1919 and in stressing Fitzgerald's politics as important background for the story. In "Fitzgerald's 'May Day': A Prelude to Triumph" (*ELUD*, No. 1, 1973), Michael P. Gruber performs the necessary but hardly very difficult task of identifying themes which are common to the story and Fitzgerald's other works.

Anthony J. Mazzella, in "The Tension of Opposites in Fitzgerald's 'May Day'" (*SSF*, Fall 1977), contributes a full and impressive explication of the story as one "structured on the careful modulation of opposites, of integration and disintegration" and as "a moving expression of order struggling against approaching chaos." Robert K. Martin is on highly original, if debatable, grounds in "Sexual and Group Relationships in 'May Day': Fear and Longing" (*SSF*, Winter 1978), when he asserts that, in Gordon Starrett, Fitzgerald is "treating, albeit covertly and perhaps unconsciously, the problems faced by the repressed homosexual when he is forced to leave a place of relative happiness and security, such as the military or a men's college, and take up a place in a heterosexual world which he fears." Alan Perlis's concern, in "The Narrative Is All: A Study of F. Scott Fitzgerald's *May Day*" (*WHR*, Winter 1979), is with the story's structure, narrative techniques, and handling of point of view. Perlis is effective in demonstrating how the narrator's sympathy for the characters gradually dissolves into indifference as the story progresses.

"Babylon Revisited," previously the most studied of Fitzgerald's stories, continues to attract comment. In "When the Story Ends: 'Babylon Revisited'" (Bryer), Carlos Baker looks at the story's "double theme of freedom and imprisonment, of locking out and locking in" and gracefully relates it to events in Fitzgerald's life in Hollywood. David Toor's "Guilt and Retribution in 'Babylon Revisited'" (*FHA*, 1973) makes the serviceable but obvious observation that the world of the story is one not of "external retribution" but one in which payment for errors is self-punishment which leads to guilt and to "further degeneration of the mind—neurotic reinforcement of behavior that leads eventually to total insanity or a form of suicide."

A logical and well-reasoned reading, James B. Twitchell's "'Babylon Revisited': Chronology and Characters" (*FHA*, 1978), reexamines the story's chronology as a means of exonerating Charlie Wales "from the charge of being a conscious or unconscious coconspirator in his ultimate disappointment." In "The Snow of Twenty-Nine: 'Babylon Revisited' as *ubi sunt* Lament" (*CollL*, Winter 1980), Ronald J. Gervais links the story with Villon's "Ballade of Dead Ladies": both are "farewells to lost ladies, who represent the lost values of love, youth, and beauty that exist now only in the imagination." Elsa Nettels suggests a "striking resemblance" between Howells's "A Circle in the Water" and "Babylon Revisited"

(*SSF*, Summer 1982), but her essay is most noteworthy for stressing the difference in the two writers' attitudes toward their stories, differences which are illuminating.

There are two articles and two notes on "The Ice Palace." In "F. Scott Fitzgerald and the Quest to the Ice Palace" (*CEA*, Jan. 1974), Edwin Moses provides a useful, if not overly innovative, explication which stresses that neither the "static and backward" South nor the "aggressive, militaristic, spiritually dead" North are viewed as ideal in the story; what is "really needed is a synthesis." John Kuehl's "Psychic Geography in 'The Ice Palace'" (Bryer) also deals with the North-South contrasts but adds the further distinction which Fitzgerald makes between the romantic past and "preservation through refrigeration." Ronald J. Gervais's note (*NMAL*, Summer 1981) also mentions that the story does not create a reconciliation of North and South but contends that it does achieve unity "as verbal enactment of the creative process"; Gervais uses Coleridge's literary theories to bolster his argument. Tahita N. Fulkerson's brief piece (*FHA*, 1979) suggests Fitzgerald's debts to Ibsen in the story.

Both recent essays on "Crazy Sunday" are concerned with the fictional methods of the story. Kenneth Johnston's focus, in "Fitzgerald's 'Crazy Sunday': Cinderella in Hollywood" (*LFQ*, Summer 1978), is on Joel Coles's trustworthiness as a narrator. His inability to "distinguish between appearance and reality" provides the "major source of irony" pervading the story; it is Joel's "blunted and uncertain perception which is responsible for the inconsistent portrayal of character, the blurred relationships and motivations, and the 'structural disharmony'" previous critics have found. Sheldon Grebstein's "The Sane Method of 'Crazy Sunday'" (Bryer) concentrates on the story's "'crazy'" motif, on its "emphasis upon the artificiality and theatricality" of the Hollywood party scene as a "microcosm," and on its use of eye imagery and images of seeing.

Two essays on "The Diamond as Big as the Ritz" relate Fitzgerald's story to the work of other writers. Leonard A. Podis finds "strong parallels" between "Fitzgerald's 'The Diamond as Big as the Ritz' and Hawthorne's 'Rappacini's Daughter'" (*SSF*, Summer 1984); both "are concerned with the potential for evil that attends misplaced priorities and with the attractiveness of that evil," and both depict "the entrance of a young man into an enchanted yet poisonous environment," captivation turned to captivity, entrapped young women, and "dominant ruthless fathers." In "Brautigan's *The Hawkline Monster*: As Big as the Ritz" (*Crit*, Winter 1981–82), Lonnie L. Willis shows how Fitzgerald's story provides "a sense of tradition for Brautigan's skepticism and a source for his 'monster.'"

Neither of the two essays on "Winter Dreams" is particularly substantial. Akiko Ishikawa's "From 'Winter Dreams' to *The Great Gatsby*" (*Persica*, Jan. 1978) offers little new in its comparison of the story and novel.

Neil D. Isaacs's "'Winter Dreams' and Summer Sports" (Bryer) implies a fruitful area for future study in its assertion of Fitzgerald's fascination with and use of sports and sports figures in his fiction; but the analysis of the story is too brief and superficial to be of much value.

"The Curious Case of Benjamin Button," a story which has attracted very little attention previously, is the subject of two recent notes. Andrew Crosland (*FHA*, 1979) points out sources for the story in Twain and Samuel Butler but observes that Fitzgerald put his own original stamp on their ideas. In a more analytic piece, John Gery (*SSF*, Fall 1980) maintains that the story, in addition to conveying a "satiric view of the Gilded Age," also portrays the "underlying American social ideal of the unique power of individualism."

Happily, within the past few years several Fitzgerald stories received their first full-essay treatment. Four such pieces appeared in the Bryer collection, along with Peter Wolfe's "Faces in a Dream: Innocence in 'The Rich Boy,'" an excellent new study of a story which has received some previous comment. Wolfe carefully explicates the tale's theme, structure, use of a narrator, and characterization. Alice Hall Petry (*SSF*, Spring 1985) corrects Wolfe's (and other critics') assumption that Anson actually sees Paula Legendre's picture in the Port Washington bedroom where he is about to make love to Dolly Karger. Victor Doyno's "'No Americans Have Any Imagination': 'Rags Martin-Jones and the Pr-nce of W-les'" (Bryer) is a model of how a totally ignored Fitzgerald story can be fruitfully examined from a variety of vantages; Doyno expertly uses stylistic, folkloristic, thematic, structural, genetic, and contextual approaches. In "'The Swimmers': Paris and Virginia Reconciled" (Bryer), Melvin J. Friedman introduces still another approach—a comparatist one which stresses the story's position in a French-American literary sequence that "starts with Edgar Allan Poe and carries to Yves Berger and William Styron."

Christiane Johnson rescues another story from obscurity in "Freedom, Contingency, and Ethics in 'The Adjuster'" (Bryer), which she sees as having no "clear focus" and a "contrived" conclusion, but which, as she shows, "touches on most of the themes dear to the author and foreshadows concerns that he developed in his later work, especially in *Tender Is the Night*." Similarly, in "Rich Boys and Rich Men: 'The Bridal Party'" (Bryer), James J. Martine contrasts that 1930 story with the earlier "May Day" and "Magnetism" to demonstrate that Fitzgerald's "understanding of the rich, the human situation, and the processes of male maturity" deepened. In "Two Sets of Books, One Balance Sheet: 'Financing Finnegan'" (Bryer), George Monteiro offers the intriguing idea that the story is Fitzgerald's response to Hemingway's "poor Scott" remark in "The Snows of Kilimanjaro" in that he portrays Finnegan (Hemingway) as the same sort of scapegoat that Hemingway made Fitzgerald in his story.

Of the nine other items on previously unstudied stories, only three are full articles and two of these are by Alice Hall Petry. Petry's "Love Story: Mock Courtship in F. Scott Fitzgerald's 'The Jelly-Bean'" (*ArQ*, Autumn 1983) claims plausibly that the story's excellence lies in its juxtaposition of "double protagonists," Jim Powell and Nancy Lamar, who represent, respectively, "the best and worst of the Old South and the best and the worst of the New South"; their "mock courtship" thus represents "a couple, a town, a region undergoing a serious identity crisis." In "F. Scott Fitzgerald's 'A Change of Class' and Frank Norris" (*MarkhamR*, Spring 1983), Petry appears unaware of earlier work linking Fitzgerald and Norris but does add slightly to the connection by citing parallels between *The Pit* and Fitzgerald's story. In conjunction with the excellent 1977 television adaptation of "Bernice Bobs Her Hair" for the Public Television series, "The American Short Story," Matthew J. Bruccoli prepared a brief but informative essay on the story for *The American Short Story* (ed. Calvin Skaggs, New York, 1977). In a more recent note, "Bernice's Liberation: Fitzgerald's 'Bernice Bobs Her Hair'" (*NMAL*, Winter 1984), Edward Cifelli contends that the story succeeds best as "a colorful anecdote" but fails badly if it was intended to be "a comment on liberated women in 1920."

In a note on "Diamond Dick and the First Law of Women," Daryl E. Jones (*FHA*, 1978) relates the 1924 story to the pulp fiction Fitzgerald read in his youth and to *Gatsby*. Joan Crane (*ABC*, Sept./Oct. 1980) gives an account of the genesis of "The True Story of Appomatox." Jennifer McCabe Atkinson tells of "The Discarded Ending of 'The Offshore Pirate'" (*FHA*, 1974); it was deleted between typescript and printed story probably at the advice of Fitzgerald's agent, and it is reproduced in facsimile in Atkinson's note. In "'The Camel's Back' and *Conductor 1492*" (*FHA*, 1974), Alan Margolies shows that the story has almost no similarities to the movie, despite Fitzgerald's indication in his *Ledger* that he had sold the story to Warner Brothers and that they had made it into *Conductor 1492*. William Harmon and Susan W. Smock (*AN&Q*, Mar./Apr. 1983) contend that T. S. Eliot may have "'stripped'" a phrase from Fitzgerald's "The Love Boat" and used it in his poem "Animula."

e. The Essays. "The Cruise of the Rolling Junk," as noted earlier, is a slightly fictionalized account of an automobile trip Fitzgerald and his wife took from Westport, Connecticut, to Montgomery, Alabama, in 1920. Published in 1924 in *Motor* and reissued in a limited facsimile edition in 1976, it is the subject of two essays. Roderick S. Speer's "*The Great Gatsby*'s 'Romance of Motoring' and 'The Cruise of the Rolling Junk'" (*MFS*, Winter 1974–75) finds a similar sense of disappointment lurking beneath the surface idealism in *Gatsby* and the essay. In "'The Cruise of the Rolling Junk': The Fictionalized Joys of Motoring" (*FHA*, 1978), Janet Lewis skillfully shows how the article combines "fact and fancy in describing the actions and participants" and how it also anticipates its author's later perception in his fiction that "Southern nostalgia" is "contrived" and that "one cannot, in fact, repeat the past." Lewis convincingly supports her conclusion that this is a piece Fitzgerald "worked on with care and real interest, a genuine attempt to bridge autobiography and storytelling." Stephen L. Tanner suggests a similar blending with respect to "My Lost City" in "Fitzgerald's Lost City" (*RMR*, No. 1, 1981). Tanner characterizes that essay as "a skillfully wrought parable" which "expresses the essence of Fitzgerald's artistic vision" and shows how it utilizes such literary devices as selection, imagery, symbolism, and myth, as well as characteristic Fitzgerald themes. Ronald J. Gervais, in a note on "The Crack-Up" (*AN&Q*, May/June 1983), corrects the *Norton Anthology*'s citation of a source for a reference in the essay.

5 Zelda Fitzgerald

Because no study of Zelda Fitzgerald and her fiction can fail to be of interest to those concerned with her husband and his fiction, it is worth noting here that a number of worthwhile bibliographical, biographical, and critical items have appeared in the past decade. The impetus for these was undoubtedly Nancy Milford's 1970 biography, as well as the dramatic recent upsurge in women's studies and feminist criticism.

In "Zelda Fitzgerald's Lost Stories" (*FHA*, 1979), Matthew J. Bruccoli usefully reprints from the files of Fitzgerald's agent synopses of eight stories Zelda wrote between 1930 and 1932 which were never published and for which no manuscripts survive. Bruccoli has also provided facsimiles of the programs from the 1934 exhibition of Zelda's paintings at Cary Ross's New York gallery listing the paintings exhibited (*FHA*, 1972) and from the 1933 Baltimore production of Zelda's play, *Scandalabra* (*FHA*, 1972). In 1974, the Montgomery (Alabama) Museum of Fine Arts mounted an exhibition of Zelda's work and issued an illustrated catalogue, *Zelda* (Montgomery, 1974), which included a brief foreword by her daughter, Scottie Fitzgerald Smith, and an introduction by Edward Pattilo giving the details of her career as a painter.

Anna Valdine Clemens's "Zelda Fitzgerald: An Unromantic Revision" (*DR*, Summer 1982) examines Mizener's and Turnbull's and Milford's and Mayfield's portrayals of Zelda and calls for a new biography which would "involve a closer examination of Zelda's breakdowns and years of confinement, a reassessment of her skills as a writer, and more pointed emphasis on the nature of the forces that curtailed her freedom." William T. Going's chapter on Zelda and Sara Haardt Mencken, in his *Essays on Alabama Literature* (University, Ala., 1976), is the sort of superficial biographical survey which prompts Clemens's call. William H. Epstein's "Milford's *Zelda* and the Poetics of New Feminist Biography" (*GaR*, Summer 1982), on the other hand, praises Milford's biography for presenting Zelda's life in pretty much the feminist perspective Clemens seems to be seeking.

While there may well be room for a new biography along the lines suggested by Clemens, the "reassessment of [Zelda's] skills as a writer" has surely begun. We have had excellent studies of Zelda's novel *Save Me the Waltz* by Linda W. Wagner (*JNT*, Fall 1982), by Jacqueline Tavernier-Courbin (*SLJ*, Spring 1979), by Victoria Sullivan (*CEA*, Jan. 1979), and by Meredith Cary (*FHA*, 1976). Sullivan and Tavernier-Courbin both emphasize, perhaps a bit too heavily, the relationship between Scott's and Zelda's fiction; Wagner and Cary tend to treat *Save Me the Waltz* more as an independent artistic achievement worthy of study in its own right. In "Rivalry and Partnership: The Short Fiction of Zelda Sayre Fitzgerald" (*FHA*, 1977), W. R. Anderson's two-fold objective is implied in his title: "to trace Zelda Fitzgerald's progress as she moved from her first tentative efforts in fiction through a series of increasingly more ambitious undertakings toward her novel" and "to explore the inter-relationship between her writing and the literary career of her husband." Linda W. Wagner (*NConL*, May 1982), in a brief note on *Scandalabra*, relates the concerns of the play to those of *Save Me the Waltz*, which preceded it.

VI   SUPPLEMENT

Matthew J. Bruccoli's *F. Scott Fitzgerald: A Descriptive Bibliography—Revised Edition* (Pittsburgh, 1987) incorporates additions and corrections made in his *Supplement to "F. Scott Fitzgerald: A Bibliography"* (1980) and includes as well the listings from Bruccoli's original 1972 *Descriptive Bibliography*. But the *Revised Edition* also represents a condensation of the earlier versions in that it eliminates several sections found in them: material quoted in dealer catalogues; movies made from Fitzgerald's work; mimeographed scripts of movies he worked on; braille publications; translations; republications of stories and essays; and book contracts.

The yearly bibliographical essay on "Fitzgerald and Hemingway" in *American Literary Scholarship: An Annual* (Durham, N.C.) continues to provide the best ongoing discussion of secondary materials; the 1985 survey was the work of Michael S. Reynolds, and Gerry Brenner assumed the assignment for 1986 and 1987.

James L. W. West III calls the unpublished 1937 story "The Vanished Girl" "not one of Fitzgerald's better efforts" because the "plotting is artificial and improbable, characters are wooden, and motivations are unclear" ("Fitzgerald Explodes His Heroine" [*PULC*, Winter 1988]). Few readers would dispute West's assessment and one wonders why he chose to exhume and publish this particular story (*PULC*, Winter 1988), hitherto blessedly hidden away in the Princeton University Library. At a time when Fitzgerald's published short fiction remains largely and unfairly neglected by serious scholar-critics, the media attention generated by the first appearance of this inferior piece hardly represented a healthy corrective.

Two Fitzgerald collections are included in Harold Bloom's massive Chelsea House project: *F. Scott Fitzgerald* (New York, 1985) in the Modern Critical Views series, and *F. Scott Fitzgerald's "The Great Gatsby"* (New York, 1986) in the Modern Critical Interpretations series. Both contain—aside from Bloom's brief introduction to each—only reprinted essays.

The one new critical book on Fitzgerald is Sarah Beebe Fryer's *Fitzgerald's New Women: Harbingers of Change* (Ann Arbor, Mich., 1988), which goes well beyond previous examinations of Fitzgerald's female characters. Individual chapters (two of which were published previously as separate essays) deal with Isabelle, Clara, Rosalind, and Eleanor of *This Side of Paradise*; with Gloria Gilbert Patch; with Daisy Buchanan; with Nicole Warren Diver and Alabama Beggs Knight (of Zelda Fitzgerald's *Save Me the Waltz*); with Nicole alone; and with Kathleen Moore and Cecilia Brady of *The Last Tycoon*. Fryer sees these heroines as transitional figures, "a curious blend of confidence and uncertainty . . . [who] live on the threshold of a new era and still feel the influence of the old order, which stubbornly insists on subordinating them to men."

Of the very few recent general essays, the best is Thomas B. Gilmore's "The Winding Road to Pat Hobby: Fitzgerald Confronts Alcoholism," in his *Equivocal Spirits: Alcoholism and Drinking in Twentieth-Century Literature* (Chapel Hill, N.C., 1987). This is a fascinating study of "how Fitzgerald's experience of alcoholism or his attitudes toward it appear in or shape his work" from *The Beautiful and Damned* through *Gatsby* and *Tender* down to later stories like "The Lost Decade," "An Alcoholic Case," "A New Leaf," "Babylon Revisited," "Crazy Sunday," and the Pat Hobby series. By comparison, Julie M. Irwin's similar "F. Scott Fitzgerald's Little Drinking Problem" (*ASch*, Summer 1987) is mechanical and superficial. Robert A. Martin's careful essay on Fitzgerald's use of weather, "Fitzgerald's Climatology" (*LGJ*, Spring 1987), is also worthy of mention.

Four recent examples of the seemingly endless stream of commentary on *Gatsby* merit attention: Arnold Weinstein's "Fiction as Greatness: The Case of *Gatsby*" (*Novel*, Fall 1985), John Skinner's "The Oral and the Written: Kurtz and Gatsby Revisited" (*JNT*, Winter 1987), Ernest Lockridge's "F. Scott Fitzgerald's *Trompe l'Oeil* and *The Great Gatsby*'s Buried Plot" (*JNT*, Spring 1987), and Joyce A. Rowe's "Closing the Circle: *The Great Gatsby*" (in her *Equivocal Endings in Classic American Novels*, Cambridge, England, 1988). Fitzgerald's other novels still attract minimal critical interest, best seen in Richard Godden's "Money Makers Manners Make Man Make Women: *Tender Is the Night*, a Familiar Romance?" (*LH*, Mar. 1986) and in Neill R. Joy's "*The Last Tycoon* and Max Eastman: Fitzgerald's Complete Political Primer" (*Prospects*, 1987).

Critical scrutiny of Fitzgerald's short fiction increases and broadens slowly. Leland S. Person, Jr.'s "Fitzgerald's 'O Russet Witch!': Dangerous Women, Dangerous Art" (*SSF*, Fall 1986) is a good first essay on this story. Substantial new pieces on more popular stories are Patrick D. Murphy's "Illumination and Affection in the Parallel Plots of 'The Rich Boy' and 'The Beast in the Jungle'" (*PLL*, Fall 1986), Gerald Pike's "Four Voices in 'Winter Dreams'" (*SSF*, Summer 1986), and Robert Roulston's "Fitzgerald's 'May Day': The Uses of Irresponsibility" (*MFS*, Summer 1988).

Robert Frost

Reginald L. Cook

I BIBLIOGRAPHY

In the 1970s the appearance of two outstanding bibliographies—Peter Van Egmond's *The Critical Reception of Robert Frost* (Boston, 1974) and *Robert Frost: A Bibliography, 1913–1974*, compiled by Frank and Melissa Christensen Lentricchia (Metuchen, N.J., 1976)—filled an important need for scholars and others interested in the main writings of and about Robert Frost and his poetry. Selective in coverage and orderly in its classifications, Van Egmond's volume aims "to lay the groundwork for further biographical and critical studies," an aim that is more representative than comprehensive. Of its two divisions, the first includes interviews, talks, letters, and news items closely associated with Frost as poet, and the second focuses on books and articles which discuss Frost and his poetry. Relevant memorabilia that reflect the popular and critical reception of Frost's poetry are exceedingly helpful, as are the succinct, informative commentaries.

Although the Lentricchias' bibliography does not include descriptive notes such as appear in Van Egmond's bibliography, it is more comprehensive and detailed in distinguishing between primary and secondary material. It is a valuable working bibliography, particularly useful in its inclusion of selected reviews, its listing of uncollected Frost poems, and its appendix. A bibliographical history of the poems, which every Frost researcher will appreciate, appears in the appendixes. This carefully prepared bibliography represents a substantial base for future bibliographical studies. In time, what will be needed is a standard bibliography which includes both Van Egmond's descriptive notes and the comprehensiveness of the Lentricchias' volume.

Two other distinguished publications appearing in the decade, Donald J. Greiner's *Robert Frost: The Poet and His Critics* (Chicago, 1974) and *Robert Frost 100*, compiled by Edward Connery Lathem (Boston, 1974), add to bibliographical research and to an appreciation of Robert Frost's work. Greiner's study is outstanding in its fair-mindedness and critical acumen. It evaluates Frost criticism from the time of the publication of *A Boy's Will* (1913) until the 1970s. Comprehensive within its limits, it offers an in-depth examination with well-mannered, judicious analyses of representative criticism of Frost and his poetry. Critical texts are never treated either perfunctorily or captiously, but are interrelated so as to achieve a balanced presentation. Greiner's book is a stimulant to further study of Frost's poetry, closely examines relevant critical opinion from a chronological and historical perspective, and suggests further needed studies, especially of Frost's relationship to religion and science. For the general as well as the scholarly reader, Greiner performs a meritorious service in reviewing and analyzing so perceptively the history of Frost literary criticism.

Robert Frost 100 celebrates an outstanding event in the Frost centennial year. One hundred carefully selected Frost items span the poet's lifetime and form the nucleus of a traveling exhibit. In 1974, this exhibit appeared successively at Princeton University, the Newberry Library in Chicago, the libraries of the Universities of Texas, California, and Virginia, the New York Public Library, and finally at Dartmouth College. In the introductory note, Archibald MacLeish contends correctly that a part of Frost's reputation was personal rather than literary and "needs the support of the books." The distinction of the texts is surely commensurate with the excellence of the exhibition. The volume is meticulous in textual scholarship and handsomely printed.

In 1969, Holt, Rinehart and Winston published *The Poetry of Robert Frost*, edited by Edward Connery Lathem, a volume which presently constitutes a standard text. But a publisher's note refers to the time when "a variorum or definitive edition in which it will be appropriate to print every scrap of verse that can be attributed to Frost" will appear. We are assured the present volume for the general reader is "scrupulously edited for textual accuracy." However, Donald Hall, in "Robert Frost Corrupted" (*AtM*, Mar. 1982), challenges the publisher's claim of textual accuracy and describes the present text as "corrupt" since the editor "has altered the rhythm of Frost's poems by repunctuating them." According to Hall's figures, Lathem has made 1,364 emendations, "of which his notes justify 247 by reference to earlier printings. Thus he makes 1,117 changes for which he offers no textual sources." Hall sharply arraigns Lathem's revisions for their ambiguity and Lathem's lack of authorization for making them. When the question of what constitutes a text is raised, Hall opts for a text that represents a poet's "probable intention" rather than one that is "the product of copy-editing designated as official by the poet's estate." Hall recommends the commissioning of a responsible scholar to edit a variorum edition to "re-establish Frost's intended punctuation." It is Frost's sentence-sounds, Hall contends, that "must return to the poet's page." In Hall's quarrel with Lathem's "corrupted" text, only a diffident Frostian would not favor the original idiosyncratic text of such an independent poet.

The texts of two unpublished Frost plays, "In an Art Factory" and "The Guardeen," are closely examined in the third section of Robert D. Sell's *Robert Frost: Four Studies* (Abo, Finland, 1980). The original manuscripts are to be found in the Clifton Waller Barrett Collection at the University of Virginia. In "Robert Frost and the Lockless Door" (*NEQ*, Mar. 1983), Donald G. Sheehy presents an interesting interpretation of "The Guardeen." First written in 1916 and completed in 1941–42, the play is based on a traumatic event in Frost's experience in the summer of 1895. Reflecting a crucial tension between solitude and community, as well as Frost's shifting perspective on the role of the artist in society, Sheehy believes "The Guardeen" combines "the rhetoric of politics with recently re-informed memory of fear to produce a drama of romantic self-justification." Significantly, Sheehy concludes fear is a metaphorical center in Frost's poetry.

II LETTERS

Two important collections of letters were published in the 1970s. The first in order of appearance was *Family Letters of Robert and Elinor Frost* (ed. Arnold Grade, Albany, N.Y., 1972). Of the 183 letters, 133 were written by Robert Frost and fifty by Mrs. Frost. These letters provide "a moving narration of nearly half a century—from 1914 to 1963"—with the exception of gaps in the early 1920s, and, of course, in the later years. One can agree with the editor's emphatic statement: "The letters *do* speak with a commanding voice; they contain mysteries, insights, apparent contradictions, and the essence of considerable drama." Lesley Frost's foreword contains two telling statements. First: "It must be remembered that it was a family fraught with and tempered by the powerful complexities of my father's genius"; secondly, in addition to the dominance of Frost's personality, Lesley Frost remembers the "saving grace of laughter." *Family Letters* contains a five-page family chronology, identifying notes for each letter, a six-page listing of the letters, their dates and place-name origin, an accommodating index, eight pages of facsimiles, and excellent photographs. The editor has anticipated the needs of both general and scholarly readers. Of particular interest will be the role of Elinor Frost as wife and mother.

The second selection of letters is William R. Evans's *Robert Frost and Sidney Cox: Forty Years of Friendship* (Hanover, N.H., 1982). This volume completes the triumvirate of letters to which Frost referred in the dedication of *In the Clearing* (1962). Evans presents a chronologically well-organized and valuable compilation of letters exchanged between Sidney Cox, professor of English, and his poet friend, spanning the years from

1911 to 1951. Evans has contributed reliable factual and biographical introductions to each section of the six-part sequence. A coda from 1952 (when Cox died) to 1957 completes the text. This collection is inferior neither to the informative Bartlett letters nor to the fascinating Unter-meyer correspondence. It contains some of the most characteristic and searching letters Frost ever wrote.

Two other subordinate publications of Frost letters should be noted. The first of these is the engaging, although brief, correspondence of Frost with a student studying at the University of Florida in 1937. In *An Interlude with Robert Frost* (Bloomington, Ind., 1982), J. Albert Robbins publishes the correspondence he had with Frost after posing three in-teresting questions to the poet in 1937. Robbins asked: first, did Frost consider the so-called decadence of his poetry—which Amy Lowell re-ferred to in the phrase "a decaying New England"—as representative of New England? (Frost replied bluntly: "No greater nonsense was ever written about New England and me than by Amy Lowell.") Secondly, which did Frost consider to be predominant in his life and people: nature as friend and benefactor, or nature as foe and destroyer? ("I am glad if the goodness of nature gets more stress in my poems than the bad-ness. . . . I feel under no obligation to make it out in either way," Frost said cagily. "I am fairly cheerful some of the time.") And thirdly: Are his later poems not more didactic and "beyond" New England in outlook? (Frost answered characteristically: "No doubt one's philosophy gets more overt in the give-and-take of a long life. . . . I've been reluctant to bother people with too much thought.")

In Elaine Barry's *Robert Frost on Writing* (New Brunswick, N.J., 1973), previously unpublished letters of Frost to Lewis Gannett, Ashley Thorndike, and Norman Foerster, among others, appear in her text. The appearance of these letters suggests the importance of a more com-prehensive edition of Frost's correspondence.

III BIOGRAPHY

The first two volumes of Lawrance Thompson's official biography—*The Early Years, 1874–1915* (1966) and *The Years of Triumph, 1915–1938* (1970)—have already been discussed. In 1971, Thompson was awarded a Pulitzer Prize for *Robert Frost: The Years of Triumph*. The third volume, *Robert Frost: The Later Years, 1938–1963* (New York, 1976), by Thompson and R. H. Winnick, was highly praised by most reviewers.

The largely unreserved and approving response to Thompson's biog-raphy poses an issue for an unquestioning dependence upon its reliabil-ity. What facts a biographer chooses to use and the particular stress he gives this factual material are of the utmost importance. The severe constraint in the Frost-Thompson relationship—to be amplified below—must be kept in mind whenever the biography is read. Surely, Donald J.

Greiner's unqualified tribute to the biography in *Robert Frost: The Poet and His Critics* is open to modification: "The authority on Frost's life, and official biographer was Lawrance Thompson," he asserts. "Because he had access to the materials necessary to establish as reliably as possible the correct biographical facts and chronology of events, his work will be considered the authoritative source when errors in the other biographies and memoirs are noted." William H. Pritchard, a leading Frost scholar, has in preparation a biography of Frost which should revise some of the questionable facts as they appear in the official biography. Pritchard's important biography is scheduled to appear in 1984.

It should be noted how much the subsequent Frost studies by Greiner, Gerber, Kemp, Lentricchia, Poirier, and Potter have made use of the official biography. Although Frost scholars are greatly indebted to Thompson's research, the unquestioning acceptance by numerous recent scholars of the statements in the official biography is somewhat startling. Only those with inherent independence question some of Thompson's inferences and conclusions. Reuben Brower and Richard Poirier attest to their own undeniable originality of judgment and sensibility in two of the strongest interpretive studies yet published. But their work has in no way diminished the influence of the official biography. That influence is reflected in many of the individual contributions in the *Centennial Essays* of 1974, 1976, and 1978, edited by Jac Tharpe (Jackson, Miss.; hereinafter referred to as *CentE*), and in *Robert Frost: Studies of the Poetry*, edited by Kathryn Gibbs Harris (Boston, 1979; hereinafter referred to as Harris).

A positive response to the official biography should be tempered by the incisive statement of Archibald MacLeish. "Dead a dozen years [Robert Frost] remains something of an enigma to his readers and even to the biographer [i.e., Lawrance Thompson] he himself selected to explain himself to his posterity," MacLeish wrote in "New England and Frost and Frost's New England" (*NG*, Apr. 1976), which is to say that Robert Frost, despite the three-volume official biography, remains a very complex enigma. There are other, even more severe, criticisms of Thompson's handling of his subject. Richard Poirier, in *Robert Frost: The Work of Knowing* (New York, 1977), speaks out sharply. "In his harsh, distorted, and personally resentful view of Frost's manipulative, calculating use of other people," states Poirier, "Thompson sees only the determinations of a man who wanted fully to control his career and his public image." And Peter J. Stanlis, in "Acceptable in Heaven's Sight: Robert Frost at Bread Loaf, 1939–1941" (*CentE*, 1978), is critically emphatic. "It should be clear," he says, "that almost everything in my experience of Frost at Bread Loaf contradicts the view of his [Frost's] psychological nature and emotional temperament presented in Lawrance Thompson's three-volume biography."

In *Robert Frost: The Later Years* (1976)—the third volume of the "official biography"—R. H. Winnick scrupulously follows his mentor's practice in textual procedure. Seventy-seven pages of notes and a thirteen-page excerpt from Lawrance Thompson's introduction to his unpublished "Notes from Conversations with Robert Frost" are included. Altogether, the patiently gathered, exhaustively transcribed, and carefully identified notes in the three volumes total 402 pages. Little wonder Donald J. Greiner refers to Thompson's accomplishment as representing an "incredible knowledge of Frost's life and times."

In the one-volume edition of the authorized biography, *Robert Frost: A Biography* by Lawrance Thompson and R. H. Winnick (New York, 1981), edited by Edward Connery Lathem, appears a five-page appendix, indexing the verse and prose compositions of Frost referred to in the text, and a useful index, but some of the magic has vanished with the omission of Thompson's annotations. A total of approximately 1,843 pages, including the indexes in the three-volume biography, has been reduced to 543 pages. Nor has the omission of the notes and the reduction of the main text modified the points of contention in the Frost enigma. In a pluralistic world, definitiveness as applied to biography is problematic at best.

In a brief significant statement, entitled "Problems of Biography" (Harris), William A. Sutton thinks Lawrance Thompson's "greatest difficulty" was not having the advantage of studying the previous work done by R. S. Newdick in preparation for a biography of Frost. After Newdick's sudden death in July 1939, his papers had remained publicly unavailable. Thompson, a good researcher who wanted to record Frost accurately, took fifteen hundred pages of notes over a span of thirty-seven years. In recording various versions of events, he found Frost's lively imagination at work, "as," according to Sutton, "his attitudes changed." Although Frost's accounts were unreliable, Thompson tended to depend upon them. The reading of the Dismal Swamp episode in November 1894 is a case in point. Frost would claim the latest account given Thompson was accurate and that Thompson's memory was at fault. This was insulting to Thompson and led to a vexing constraint between the biographer and Frost. Sutton's summary oof the facts is valuable in the context of biographical study of so paradoxical and enigmatic a man as Frost: "The result of being demeaned by Frost's lack of respect for his work shows in Thompson's biographical work on Frost through a constantly shifting pattern of inaccuracy, and it finally told on Thompson himself." Thompson, in consequence, began to lose his sense of objectivity. In the 1950s, when Frost turned on Thompson and encouraged Louis Untermeyer to become his biographer, Thompson naturally found this professional affront a "strange betrayal."

In *Newdick's Season of Frost: An Interrupted Biography of Robert Frost* (ed.

William A. Sutton, Albany, N.Y., 1976), R. S. Newdick makes a revealing statement on Frost's relationship to his friends: "Robert Frost, like Dr. Johnson, demanded subjection wherever he went. Also like Johnson, Robert Frost made a kind of confidant of nearly every one with whom he talked, and thereby flattered the listeners into an exaggerated sense of the esteem in which the listener was held." Newdick first became smitten with Frost in 1934 and for the next five years, or until his early death in July 1939, cultivated a close relationship with Frost. Devoted to Frost, he made known his desire to write a biographical study. Yet, as Thompson was later to discover, Frost was a paradoxical man, who both wanted and feared the study and recording of his life. As in the case of Thompson and later Elizabeth Shepley Sergeant, Newdick, with a scholar's thoroughness, began to probe intimately.

But Newdick did not live to finish the biography. Sutton, with scholarly tact and patience, has brought together most of the materials Newdick had at hand. Only approximately a fifth of the text represents Newdick's projected biography, that is, chapters 1 to 14 (inexplicably chapter 13 is omitted). The text of Newdick's *Season of Frost* is eighty-one pages in length and stops with a chapter on the publication of *A Boy's Will* (1913). The remainder of the 454 pages consists of Newdick's voluminous notes transcribed and introduced by Sutton. Like Thompson, Newdick was a competent and assiduous researcher. One suspects Frost would have viewed most of the information as superficial, but like a jigsaw puzzle, once put together it hints tellingly of an unusually complex and temperamental man.

Sutton's presentation of the Newdick material is as revealing of a biographer's problems with Frost as it is of Frost himself. The preliminary chapters of Newdick's text, dealing with Frost's familial background, are strong and cogent. The remainder, because it is incomplete, should be judged with caution. However, one doubts that the availability of the Newdick text will greatly qualify Thompson's work. Moreover, the Newdick volume is not impeccably edited. As Robert Fleissner reports (*NEQ*, June 1977), "It is regrettable to have to mention some shortcomings, but I think it would be churlish to the memory of Frost to avoid pointing out that this book is not exemplary of the best in modern textual editing. Mr. Sutton does not fully explain how he set up his text, what style he used and why, and his critical notes (including interpolations) are sparse."

Augmenting the full-length biographical studies are: (1) essays of biographical importance and (2) those associated with Frost's career as a poet. In the first category, Paul M. Cubeta's admirable "Robert Frost and Edward Thomas" (*NEQ*, June 1979) forthrightly states that "Edward Thomas was the British critic who first brought Frost significant recognition in England, and Frost alone was responsible for Thomas's writing poetry." Aware that later biographies of Edward Thomas by R. George

Thomas and William Cooke play down the influence of Frost's friendship as the reason for Edward Thomas's turning to poetry, Cubeta nevertheless makes out a firm case for an extraordinary "bond of friendship" between Thomas and Frost. He shows that Frost poems pertinent to Edward Thomas—"A Soldier," "Not to Keep," "The Road Not Taken," and especially "Iris by Night"—create "the covenant of friendship remembered two decades later."

R. George Thomas's "Edward Thomas and Robert Frost" (*Poetry Wales*, Spring 1978) views the relationship from the other side of the ocean. "The evidence we have from letters, and the memories of family and friends," he states, "suggests that Edward [Thomas] was the more persistent in fostering the friendship [with Frost] and the greater beneficiary from it, as man and poet." Yet the thrust of the contention is that Thomas's "quickly maturing" poetry moved away from Frost's precepts "and found its own quite different mode" of poetic expression. R. George Thomas also thinks that Frost remained either unaware of Edward Thomas's critical reputation or failed to include it "in his skilfully orchestrated campaign for recognition." The emphasis in this critical judgment indicates how negatively influenced the biographer-critic is by the first two volumes of the official biography. This typifies a partisan tone which resonates throughout the essay.

William R. Evans's "Robert Frost and Carl Burell" (*CentE*, 1974) shows that in the later formative years, "no one except Elinor [Frost] was so influential on Frost" as Carl Burell. Evans thinks that Frost's intellectual curiosity and independence drew him to the unusual Burell, with whom the poet botanized and worked on the Derry farm for two years. They shared a lively sense of humor and common interests in poetry, books (ranging from philosophy to evolution), and religion (tinged with skepticism).

R. J. Sokol's "What Went Wrong Between Robert Frost and Ezra Pound" (*NEQ*, Dec. 1976) traces the disaffection which developed in the relationship of Frost and Pound between the first meeting in March and 17 July 1913. "Robert Frost had to go his own road," Sokol concludes, "and even in the insecurity of his first year in England he knew that meant he could not follow Pound." Pound's review of *A Boy's Will* in *Poetry* (May 1913) bothered Frost on two counts: first, the indirect reference to the family legacy and to being scorned by American editors until the English discovered him incensed Frost; and secondly, the image of Frost as a barnyard poet, to be praised mainly for simplicity and directness, affected his self-pride and independence. Sokol points out acutely that Frost recognized his right to be regarded as a poet at the age of eighteen and that he was a poet of a particular kind, with a natural style and not one imposed upon him by Ezra Pound.

Thomas Daniel Young's "Our Two Worthies: Robert Frost and John Crowe Ransom" (*CentE*, 1976) indicates that, although Ransom often insisted the real value of a Frost poem was seldom enclosed within the apparently innocent simplicity of its paraphrasable content, he couldn't make up his mind about the poet. While Frost regarded Ransom highly as a poet, the latter's preference for a textual richness lacking in his friend's poetry accounts for a diminished, perhaps condescending, appreciation. Ransom thought Frost tended to discharge his debt to a less literate society. This essay hints of a subtle confrontation between the addiction of Southern writing to elegance and the New Englander's preference for deceptive simplicity.

Julian Mason's "The Fellowship of Robert Frost and Lewis Chase," in *Robert Frost: The Man and the Poet* (ed. Earl J. Wilcox, Rock Hill, S.C., 1981; hereinafter referred to as Wilcox), reflects how much time Frost voluntarily gave to correspondents in and out of academia—in this instance, to Chase, for whom he supplied information and copies of his books and to whom he wrote several informative letters. "[Chase] was," as Julian Mason says, "one of the academicians who could appreciate the new accomplishments in poetry and help others to do so too, at a time when this was needed." The essay exemplifies a common practice on Frost's part in the unfolding of his career, as a poet needing a public and as a man requiring a supplementary income; so he annually "barded around" on the collegiate circuit.

In the second category of essays associated with Frost's poetic career, Peter Davison's "'Toward the Source'—The Self-Realization of Robert Frost, 1911–1912," in *Robert Frost: Lectures on the Centennial of His Birth* (Washington, D.C., 1975; hereinafter referred to as *Centennial Lectures*), is illuminating. After distinguishing between the tone in *A Boy's Will* and *North of Boston*, Davison adduces evidence that, following an interior struggle in January 1912, Frost's style changed dramatically. "One thing can be fairly proved: the poems written at this moment [January 1912] were not those later published in *A Boy's Will* but some that would go to make up the more revolutionary *North of Boston*, and some that would furnish Frost's later books." Davison believes it is likely that before the end of 1911, at Plymouth, Frost had already started to make changes in style and craftsmanship.

In "Robert Frost and the Majesty of Stones Upon Stones" (*JML*, No. 1, 1981–82), Lesley Lee Francis indicates how, early and late, her grandfather was fascinated "with pre-Columbian artifacts and the search for man's origin, in the cradle of civilization." Frost's interest in botany, astronomy, and geology have frequently been noted. His interest in archeology, which is well-established in this carefully researched essay, validates how much more than a narrow regionalist the poet really was. The relationship between pre-Columbian and other cultures is reflected in what Francis describes as Frost's "archeological poems": "A Missive Missile," "The Bad Island—Easter," "To an Ancient," "Closed For Good," "A Cliff Dwelling," and, of course, some of Frost's earliest poems. Francis underscores that Frost's inveterate archeological interests found an expression not only in poems, but also in the "customary tales and anecdotes," which he spun when recollecting the "tangible signs of early civilization and man's shadowy origins."

A biographically related study is Nancy Vogel's *Robert Frost, Teacher* (Bloomington, Ind., 1974). As the title indicates, the content stresses the poet's relationship to the classroom, early and late, in a long career. A second volume, *Prose Jottings of Robert Frost* (Lunenburg, Vt., 1982), edited by Edward Connery Lathem and Hyde Cox, presents selections from the poet's notebooks and miscellaneous manuscripts becomingly introduced by Mrs. Kathleen Morrison. This handsome publication also contains an informative editors' preface. For Frostians, the "jottings" are rewarding reading. The deft hand and shrewd mind of the poet are everywhere apparent in this relatively short collection.

The Derry journals of Lesley Frost, entitled *New Hampshire's Child* (Albany, N.Y., 1969), including copious notes and an index by Lawrance Thompson and Arnold Grade, spans the years from early 1905 until the late summer of 1909 when the Frosts lived on the Old Londonderry Turnpike, two miles southeastward from Derry village. The main text, composed of the written exercises Lesley prepared for her parents, not only presents an intimate glimpse of familial life, it also underscores Robert Frost's relationship to his children as a mentor. The botanist, the birder, the reader, the poultryman aspects are revealing, and none more so than Lesley's reactions to her father. Idyllically, Lesley describes life on the Derry Farm as "a long and passionate borning," and refers interestingly to her father: "We didn't know he was 'a poet,' or even one in the making." In the overview of the Frosts, who at this time were very poor and struggled to make ends meet, there is a particular poignance in this reminiscence. In an introductory note Lesley writes of her father, "He was given to self-torture, even taking a certain pride in the idea that God had possibly *chosen* to give him a hard time." Yet God's severity does not appear to have extended from parent to child. *New Hampshire's Child* is a charming and well-edited volume.

Mrs. Kathleen Morrison's *Robert Frost: A Pictorial Chronicle* (New York, 1974) belies its subtitle. Mrs. Morrison had known Frost from her early undergraduate days at Bryn Mawr, and, after Mrs. Frost's death of cancer on 21 March 1938, became indispensable to Frost as a close companion and secretary. Informative and detailed, the memories are deeply felt. The excellence of both the text and the carefully selected seventy-eight black-and-white photographs make this an aesthetically attractive and valuable volume.

Numerous articles and sketches, in which academic associations with Frost were memorialized, have appeared. Of Frost's first association at the University of Michigan, Dorothy Tyler, who knew Frost well, has written an extended account, beginning with "Robert Frost at Michigan"

(*CentE*, 1978); in a second piece, she describes "Frost's Last Three Visits to Michigan" (Ann Arbor and Detroit) in 1962 only a few months before his death (*CentE*, 1974); and, in a final essay, "The Strong Are Saying Nothing" (*CentE*, 1976), Tyler writes movingly of the Frost burial ground at the First Church, Congregational, "in beautiful Old Bennington." As in the two previous essays, Frost is paid an ardent tribute. As yet there has not been a similar spokesman or spokeswoman for Frost's tours of duty at Amherst, Harvard, or Dartmouth.

Some attention has been given to Frost's association with Middlebury College, which honored him with his second doctoral degree in 1924. The Middlebury College connection is mainly at the Bread Loaf Mountain Campus, where Frost first appeared in 1921 at the second year of the founding of the English School, and at the Bread Loaf Writers' Conference in 1926. Throughout his life Frost remained closely associated with both the English School and the Writers' Conference, and detailed accounts of this relationship are documented in two separate publications: George K. Anderson's *Bread Loaf School of English: The First Fifty Years* (Middlebury, Vt., 1969) and Theodore Morrison's *Bread Loaf Writers' Conference: The First Thirty Years—1926–1955* (Middlebury, Vt., 1976). In 1963, the School of English paid a special tribute to Robert Frost on 11 July, when George Anderson, Donald Davidson ("Recollections of Robert Frost"), Cleanth Brooks ("A Meeting with Frost"), and Reginald L. Cook ("The Unspent Spender") spoke in memory of Frost. The tributes were later published in *Robert Frost and Bread Loaf* (Middlebury, Vt., 1964).

During the centennial year of Frost's birth, there was further recognition of Frost's association with the English School at Bread Loaf in Reginald L. Cook's *Robert Frost: A Living Voice* (Amherst, Mass., 1974). This volume includes the transcription of twelve lectures and talks given by Frost at the English School from 1953 until 1962. Peter Stanlis has written a long, reliably reported, and illuminating essay, "Acceptable in Heaven's Sight" (*CentE*, 1978), based on meetings with Robert Frost at Bread Loaf from 1939 to 1941. Charles H. Foster has also written of "an undiminished Robert Frost" in eight selections from a diary record of 1938, kept while attending the Writers' Conference and published as "Robert Frost at Bread Loaf" (*CentE*, 1978).

Among other searching reminiscent glimpses of Frost is Edward Cifelli's interview with John Ciardi, formerly a director of the Writers' Conference and a sharp-eyed critic of Frost ("Ciardi on Frost: An Interview," *CentE*, 1974). T. H. Littlefield has written a brief, lively account of a meeting with Frost at the Homer Noble Farm in "A Ripton Afternoon" (*CentE*, 1978). Clifford Lyons summarizes his memories in "Walks and Talks with Robert Frost" (Wilcox).

Other detailed reminiscences which appear in the *Centennial Essays* include: G. William Gahagan's account of Frost's association with San

Francisco ("A 'Day' in the Life of Robert Lee Frost—1874," *CentE*, 1974); Wade Van Dore's memories of an early association with Frost in "The Subtlety of Robert Frost" (*CentE*, 1974); Victor E. Reichert's affectionate remembrance of meetings with Frost in Cincinnati and Ripton in "The Robert Frost I Knew" (*CentE*, 1978); Luella Nash LeVee's personal memory of the poet's helpfulness to her as a writer in "Per Ardua ad Astra" (*CentE*, 1978); and Reginald L. Cook's "Robert Frost in Context" (*CentE*, 1978), which enlarges on Frost's conversational talent.

In a biting reproach, Alfred Kazin said of Frost: "He could not stop talking" (*New York Jew*, New York, 1978). Robert Francis, a substantial poet in his own right, would hardly wish that Frost had ever stopped talking. In *A Time to Talk* (Amherst, Mass., 1972), Francis records two sets of conversational periods with Frost. The first period (1933–35) reflects the generosity and capacity of Frost as a mentor to a young poet; the second (1950–59) is testimony to a sensitive and expansive friendship. An epilogue adds brief remarks on Frost's eightieth birthday dinner in Amherst, the memorial service at Amherst College's Johnson Chapel following his death, and a closing statement on the poet's career.

Donald Hall, in *Remembering Poets: Reminiscences and Opinions* (New York, 1978), forthrightly describes the Frost he knew from an early Bread Loaf meeting when he was sixteen, through his Harvard experience, in Ann Arbor in April 1962, and on a last visit to the Homer Noble Farm in the fall of 1962. Hall reacts to the poet's personality vividly. "He was vain, he was cruel, he was rivalrous with all other men: but he could also be generous and warm—when he could satisfy himself that his motives were dubious," writes Hall ambivalently. "He was a man possessed by guilt, by knowledge that he was 'bad,' by craving for love, by the necessity to reject love—and by desire for fame which no amount of celebrity could satisfy." Hall, determined to modify Frost's early reputation for benignity by a "new, posthumous reputation for nastiness," turns the screw. "But Frost's character was at least three faced": the one the masses saw, "simple and sweet"; secondly, in private and to his literary acquaintances, "he avowed that he was selfish and cynical." Thirdly, "and least obvious Frost was secretly magnanimous, while accusing himself of being a saint for the Devil's reasons. To get Frost to do something good, you had to convince him that he could do it for a wicked reason."

The impression made by Hall's hard-focused profile is of an acid and testy man but it is similar to Alfred Kazin's corrosive view in *New York Jew*. Frost was eighty years old when Kazin met him while teaching at Amherst College, and it is the poet's egotism and haunting past that stands out in unflattering comments. "Frost wanted his tomb in the form of the biggest and most adulatory biography, and I knew why," writes Kazin. "He could not bear the life he had lived." Kazin adds grimly, "His soul was crowded with ghosts." But he also says perceptively:

"Frost had emotions as well as genius; he was open to America, to everything in its past and to everything in *his* past; he was open to sorrow, and determined to express it all." But despite being "a creature of immense talent, subtlety, force, pride, remorse, and anguish," he was "*the* poet of backward-looking America." Although Kazin does not fail to remark on the poet's critical thinking, original and speculative, it is the excessive ambition, competitiveness, and guilt that repel him.

Stewart L. Udall, Secretary of the Interior in President Kennedy's cabinet, published two articles describing his association with Frost. The first was entitled "'. . . and miles to go before I sleep'" (*NYTM*, 11 June 1972) and a shorter version appeared as "Robert Frost, Kennedy and Khrushchev: A Memoir of Poetry and Power" (*Shenandoah*, Winter 1975). Udall focuses on Frost's appearance at the Kennedy inaugural ceremony and on his "good-will mission" to Russia in the summer of 1962. Of the Russian trip, Udall says: "When the trip was over I realized Frost went because he cared about the future and felt he could make a contribution to peace if he were given the opportunity to talk man-to-man with Nikita Khrushchev. His determination was fierce. . . ." Yet the ultimate result was a strained relationship with President Kennedy over Frost's impolitic remark to reporters that the U.S. was "too liberal to defend itself." Udall notes: "Frost was not invited to Washington for a debriefing; and Kennedy gave him no opportunity to present his personal message from Khrushchev."

IV CRITICISM

In a lecture, "'Inner Weather': Robert Frost as a Metaphysical Poet" (*Centennial Lectures*), Allen Tate raises a familiar question. "Now, eleven years after his death, Frost is in partial eclipse," Tate notes, and he wonders whether such an occasion as the present centenary celebration would help to restore some of the popularity Frost enjoyed for nearly fifty years. "Is the living voice, back of the printed line, necessary?" he inquires, and adds perceptively, "Without the living presence one attends more closely what is said and how Frost says it." Allen Tate's query has received elaborate commentaries. The reaction to Frost's living voice in his own time is explicitly reflected in Linda W. Wagner's *Robert Frost: The Critical Reception* (New York, 1977), and indirect comments on Tate's insight are to be found not only in the scholarly studies of Frank Lentricchia, Richard Poirier, and John Kemp, but also among the essays in the three volumes of the *Centennial Essays* to which reference has already been made.

1 Full-length General Studies

Wagner's *Robert Frost: The Critical Reception* prints selected reviews of Frost's poetry encompassing the forty-nine years of his active publication. Because it is clearly selective, the volume represents a solid frame of reference in which to review the positive and negative aspects of Frost's popularity. The inclusion of dissenting views greatly intensifies the critical discussion. Examined closely these reviews reflect a variety of critical response to the poet as a "humanist," "classicist," "symbolist," "synecdochist," "revisionist," and, of course, "New England rural." Frost's complexity, sophistication in handling form in the great tradition of English verse, an inherent conservatism, and the surfacing of a public and a private image are also noted.

Frank Lentricchia's *Robert Frost: Modern Poetics and the Landscapes of Self* (Durham, N.C., 1975) is a carefully structured book that boldly states the case for Frost both as a major and a modern poet. In the first of two parts—"Landscapes of Self"—Lentricchia both describes and analyzes the relationship of relevant poems to archetypal images. He distinguishes between the "fictive" as reconstitution of reality and "antifiction," which presents the existential reality of the environment. The second part— "Landscapes of Modern Poetics"—discusses the interrelationship of post-Kantian metaphysics and aesthetic theories to Frost's literary art. This section is abstruse, elaborate, and theoretical. Although Santayana and Dewey, Ernst Cassirer and Eliseo Vivas, as well as Coleridge, Schiller, and Nietzsche, are rallied as supportive evidence, the key figure is William James. The influence of his pragmatism, with its emphasis on empirical reality, upon Frost's viewpoint is underscored. Unfortunately, this part is flawed by a specialized terminology. For example, there is a tendency to use such arcane terms as "apocalyptical metaphor," "the phenomenology of mythic imagination," "ontological autonomy," "the anagogic phase of metaphor," and "the monistic thrust of metaphor." Lentricchia's study shows best in the analyses of those "particular intersections of self and place"—the brook, the farmhouse, and the woods— which "represent the personal world, shaped by the poet's consciousness in and through language." Lentricchia clarifies this fact importantly when he states, "the basic human act in Frost . . . is the movement of self across a particular landscape, the encounter of self with the special objects in the landscape and the constitution of self in language against those objects."

Richard Poirier's aim in *Robert Frost: The Work of Knowing* (New York, 1977) is implied in the statement that "there is a Frost who has been missed," or, as he says, "almost lost," by those who were in a position through acquaintance with the poet and his work to contribute much to the interpretation of the poet's work. Poirier himself supplies an explanation when he points out that part of Frost's great popularity consisted in making people feel that "in writing a poem he was being *more* like them rather than less." This conjecture would have been wholly valid had Poirier added that Frost encouraged an ambiguous reaction from his audience. Frost constantly understated, played down, or objected to scholarly probing of his poems for hidden meanings. Yet, paradoxically, he openly decried the critical attention Pound, Eliot, and Yeats received for their profundity while his own poetry was treated superficially.

In an introductory note to the reader, Poirier states that in writing about Frost's work, he hopes his interpretations are saved from inflation and summary. His superb study succeeds in this respect for several reasons. First, he focuses on the poetry rather than on extraneous or correlative matters, like political ideology or social issues. Second, he reads a Frost poem perceptively in the light of the other poems. This approach is shared by other critics like George Monteiro in "Robert Frost's Analogies" (*NEQ*, Sept. 1973) and Richard Foster in "Leaves Compared with Flowers: A Reading in Robert Frost's Poems" (*NEQ*, Sept. 1975). Third, Poirier discusses rewardingly many of the lesser poems, like "Waiting," "In a Vale," and "A Dream Pang," and some of the neglected ones like "A Star in a Stone-Boat." Fourth, he doesn't avoid sensitive aspects, like Frost's sexuality in "Putting In the Seed" and "The Subverted Flower." Fifth, he is thoroughly independent in his judgment. Lentricchia and Poirier would not agree on "Directive." The former favors it; the latter does not. Sixth, he makes adept use of the background resources of English and American literature in discussing both Frost's prose and poetry. And, lastly, Poirier relates Frost to the chief literary movement of the twentieth century, dominated by Joyce, Yeats, Pound, and Eliot.

What distinguishes Poirier's study is its detachment. While sympathetic and admiring of Frost as a poet, Poirier remains objective in setting the record straight concerning the criticism directed against Frost as a man and against the partisans of the man as poet. He is properly concerned mainly with understanding Frost's poetry in its context. In restrained statement and well modulated tone, Poirier's study is outstanding.

The critical studies of Lentricchia and Poirier are chiefly concerned with exemplifying Frost's poetics. John C. Kemp, in *Robert Frost and New England: The Poet as Regionalist* (Princeton, N.J., 1979), is concerned with the myth of Frost as a New England regionalist. The connection between the poet and his region is also discussed by Hayden Carruth in "The New England Tradition" (*American Libraries*, July–Aug. and Oct. 1971), by Perry D. Westbrook in "Robert Frost's New England" (*CentE*, 1974), and by Charles Carmichael in "Robert Frost as a Romantic" (*CentE*, 1974). James R. Vitelli, in "Robert Frost: The Contrarieties of Talent and Tradition" (*NEQ*, Sept. 1975), notes that with the publication of *Selected Letters* (1964) and the official biography, Lawrance Thompson has taken us "a long way towards seeing the distance between man and the myth." Simply stated and persuasively argued, Kemp's thesis contends that Frost's identity as a New England Yankee influenced the development of his art. But rather than beginning as a rural New England poet—the "mythical" Frost role—the early years of Frost's life from 1890 until 1912 represent a period of experimentation. After transitional years from 1912 until 1914, when Frost adopted a New England identity, he became identified with rural New England, not as a provincial but as a cosmopolitan poet.

The "demythicizing" of Frost in the role of an original New England Yankee, as John Kemp shows us, has strong corroborative evidence. "I think that it is a mistake," says Archibald MacLeish in *Riders on the Earth* (Boston, 1978), "to look for the New England mind in Frost's work or the New England feel. It was not New England that produced Robert Frost: it was Robert Frost who chose New England. And the relation of Frost to New England was not the relation of the native son, who can take his country-earth for granted, but of the stranger who falls in love with a land and makes (literally *makes*) his life in it."

Kemp's view of Frost, independently asserted, emphasizes the biographical facts as they are reported in the Thompson biography, which show Frost's early inclination to adopt the role of a Shelleyan Romantic wanderer. Later, during the Derry days as an outsider, he is shown adopting the pose of a New England farmer. Following his return from England in 1915, he is portrayed as a public performer exploiting the pose into prominence. In his later career as one of the most popular poets in the history of our country, he is viewed as the spokesman for the New England region. Although Kemp somewhat neglects Frost's regional sense of humor, he does not fail to confront intelligently the provocative query as to the poet's disputed right to "a more solid position among the first rank of American authors." Kemp's exploratory study is an incisive clarification of Frost's role as a New England poet. He shows clearly that, as a poet, Frost "does not need so much to be better known as to be known better."

Strictly speaking, James L. Potter's *Robert Frost Handbook* (University Park, Pa., 1980) is not a critically interpretive study similar to those of Lentricchia, Poirier, and Kemp. As a handbook, it is intended "to provide the basis for a sound, general comprehension of Frost as a poet." Potter's avowed aim is to understand Frost's poetry "as a whole in the light of all the sophisticated critical work that has been done, especially since 1960." In this respect his book ambitiously extends the scope of Donald J. Greiner's *Robert Frost: The Poet and his Critics* (1974). However, the proportion of subjective comment is far greater in Potter's work than in Greiner's. Potter determinedly advances a personal thesis. He claims there exists "a fundamental tension between two different conceptions of the universe and man's role in [Frost's work]: a secular or even agnostic view, and a more religious one."

Although Potter recapitulates and summarizes a great deal of the current critical opinion on Frost and his poetry, his *Handbook* also offers independent judgments. The linguistic materials, which include reference to the metrical, syntactic, and metaphorical aspects of Frost's poetry, are effectively presented, but there is little on the poet's political views. (See Peter J. Stanlis's *Robert Frost: The Individual and Society* [Rockford, Ill., 1976] and Stanlis's "Robert Frost: Politics in Theory and Practice" [*CentE*, 1976].) Moreover, while Frost's poetry certainly reflects "the darker conception of life," surely some accounting needs to be made of the human hope, resourcefulness, ingenuity, and courage forcefully expressed in Frost's verse. On the whole, however, the *Handbook* is a masterly sorting out of varied opinions and views into an orderly synthesis. Interestingly, Potter decides that the mythic Frost, or, in his own phrasing, "everyone's grandpa," and the "terrifying" poet and "bad" man were both parts of a figure who "was, of course, both and neither myth and/or monster—in other words, he was a complex and contradictory man and poet." This statement indicates the nice balance maintained throughout the *Robert Frost Handbook*.

In the preface to the revised edition of *Robert Frost* (TUSAS, Boston, 1982), Philip L. Gerber notes that he has kept in mind the opinions and analyses of later criticism of Frost since the original appearance of *Robert Frost* in 1966. Gerber's chapters on the poet's craftsmanship, theories, and themes now present revised views. These additions strengthen the discussion without greatly lengthening the text. The pages concerning the Emerson-Frost connection are notably informative. A chapter entitled "Testing Greatness: Frost's Critical Reception" has been added, and the earlier selective bibliography has expanded annotations. Against Yvor Winters's charge that, in his blank verse, Frost's theory of conversational style was at its worst, Gerber argues forcibly and clearly: "While conversation is what Frost aims for . . . in his dialogues, it is not conversation *per se* that results from his efforts, but the *appearance* of it." What is especially commendable in Gerber's *Robert Frost* is such forthrightness of statement. Critical readers may disagree with Gerber's views but they must confront them.

Gerber has put together a recent compilation of carefully selected and genuinely provocative essays and articles arranged in chronological order. *Critical Essays on Robert Frost* (CEAmL, Boston, 1982; hereinafter referred to as Gerber) contains Gerber's informative introduction. This collection complements *Robert Frost: A Collection of Critical Essays* (1962), edited by James M. Cox. Gerber's collection represents a balanced assessment of both critical and appreciative writings and includes an interesting original essay by Donald J. Greiner entitled "The Indispensable Robert Frost," in which eight of Frost's poems are presented and discussed as minimally indispensable to an understanding of the poet.

2 Theory and Method

Elaine Barry's *Robert Frost on Writing* (New Brunswick, N.J., 1973) is a book-length presentation of Frost's practical criticism and critical theory. It assembles and remarks upon Frost's statements about writing collected from his lectures, prefaces, essays, and letters. It aims to give the essence of Frost's aesthetic theories and judgments "while demonstrating the variety of his critical expression." As a critical theorist, Frost is shown to be a sophisticated and self-conscious innovator whose theories range from early ideas about the "sound of sense" and a craftsman's concern for metrics to a later more abstract, conceptual awareness of language and of the meaning of meaning. Frost is described as astute rather than profound in his critical attitude, and Barry decides correctly that his critical approach lacked a philosophical center. In evaluating Elaine Barry's presentation, Richard Foster (*NEQ*, Sept. 1974) points out convincingly that already most of the materials cited by Barry were publicly available. Barry surely exaggerates in her contention that Frost's statements "form one of the most significant bodies of poetical theory by any American poet." This contention would seem to ignore the poetical theories of Poe and Emerson, Pound and Eliot, Williams and Stevens.

In Frank Lentricchia's "Robert Frost and Modern Literary Theory" (*CentE*, 1974), and in part two—"Landscapes of Modern Poetics"—of *Robert Frost: Modern Poetics and the Landscapes of Self*, Frost's theory of poetry is examined in relationship to the nature of consciousness in his poems. Similarly, in James L. Potter's *Robert Frost Handbook*, Frost's theory is referred to in part 2, "Uncertain Balance: Frost's Poetic Stance," and specifically in chapter 10, "Frost's Poetic Techniques." Discussion of Frost's theory is also to be found in Philip L. Gerber's *Robert Frost*.

Among the numerous essays examining particular phases of Frost's poetic theory, the following are representative. Joseph M. Garrison, Jr., in "'Our Singing Strength': The Texture of Voice in the Poetry of Robert Frost" (*CentE*, 1974), stresses the significance of the poet's "sound of sense." Oral content, or intonation, is precisely the aspect that should be and is not being studied or utilized productively by teachers and critics. Readers do not let Frost's richest resource, his ability to capture the spoken word, inform their practices, so Garrison illustrates this resource by informed readings of the poems. Donald J. Greiner's two essays, "Robert Frost's Dark Woods and the Function of Metaphor" (*CentE*, 1974) and "The Difference Made for Prosody" (Harris), consider, respectively, the relevance of metaphor in Frost's theory and Frost's contribution to American poetry through insistence on traditional poetic form, dramatic stress, and varied voice tones. Greiner ably points up one of Frost's major contributions; in effect, by his experiments with prosody, he "rejuvenated the traditional rhythms, meters, and patterns of rhyme," and discovered old ways to be new.

In "Robert Frost's 'Sentence Sounds': Wildness Opposing the Sonnet Form" (*CentE*, 1976), Karen Lane Rood shows that despite deviations all twelve of Frost's Italian sonnets have a clearly recognized formal characteristic. John F. Sears, in "William James, Henri Bergson, and the Poetics of Robert Frost" (*NEQ*, Sept. 1975), makes clear by paralleling passages from James's *Psychology* and Bergson's *Creative Evolution* with passages from Frost's dicta on poetic theory, how much the two thinkers consciously or unconsciously influenced Frost's thinking and method. Sears's essay, a solid contribution, shows how Frost "conceived of the emerging poem both as a figure of the poet reacting upon the world, and as a process—an easy and natural flow to which the poet surrenders himself." Sears concentrates on the unexplored areas of thought and metaphor that link Frost to James and Bergson, and stresses that James's influence was upon the ethical side of the poet's nature, whereas Bergson's impact was on Frost's mystical side (i.e., on his way of dealing with the mysteries of time, creation, and process).

Thomas Vander Ven's "Robert Frost's Dramatic Principle of Under-sound" (*AL*, May 1973) states that even if Frost never published a systematic formulation of dramatic principles, his reflections on a wide range of dramatic concepts form a consistent dramatic theory. Dominant in his attitude was the idea that good writing must be dramatic. "Sound of sense" is distinct from word, idiom, meter, idea, and physical environment; art takes the human voice tones and constructs "out of printed language a vehicle which can carry a precise sound of voice to the reader's ear." Although a poem is not a "sound of sense" in itself, it is the context for one. A poem is effective, therefore, when the reader is capable of recognizing in his own experience the poem's vocal tones, since, according to Frost, "the tones are elemental and universal to the race."

Sheldon W. Liebman, in "Robert Frost: On the Dialectics of Poetry" (*AL*, May 1980), also finds in his *obita dicta* on the origin, nature, and function of poetry sufficient evidence that he should be taken seriously as a critic. The poet's scattered statements are described as a meditation on poetic creation but hardly the formulation of a theory. In the creative process, which is a cognitive experience, the poems appear to begin in the disorder of feelings and move beyond these origins to a clear and orderly end.

Complementing the discussion of the poet's theory are several substantial essays related to his method. Floyd C. Watkins, in "The Poetry of the Unsaid: Robert Frost's Narrative and Dramatic Poems" (*TQ*, Winter 1972), underscores the poet's indirect method, which Watkins calls "the unstated." Convinced that the best of the poems particularizing character in *North of Boston, Mountain Interval*, and *New Hampshire* appeared in the nine years between 1914 and 1923, Watkins asserts, "No other American poet has equaled the quality or quantity of Frost's narrative and dramatic poems of those years." He also claims, "[Frost] caught the humor of human foibles, and he saw deep, deep into the agonies of the mind." And he did it by the dramatic technique of the understated and unsaid; that is, by adapting his poetic form to the dramatic content. Watkins adds significantly, "The art of reading Frost's dramatic poems is based almost as much on knowing what is not said as on knowing what is in the poem."

V. Y. Kantak, in "Poetic Ambiguity in Frost" (*WHR*, Winter 1974), states that Frost avoids "the stance of embroiled complexity" that made Pound and Eliot difficult. He judges that Frost's use of the common mode of ordinary speech suffices for articulating "inner wildness"; he considers the lyrics to be subtly made in the dramatic mode; and he finds Frost's nature poetry sharply opposed to the Romantic commitment to the benignity of nature. Thus Frost's poetry centers in man, and nature is "out there," as in Vergil and Lucretius.

Marion Montgomery, in "Robert Frost: One Who Shrewdly Pretends" (*CentE*, 1976), sees in Frost "fundamentally an allegorist of the alienated Self," and decides he has in fact such a close, careful concern for "the particular and the local," that, despite his celebrity as a public poet, he is *not* a poet of community, but one who, like the wily Odysseus, is shifty and secretive. Frost is interpreted as one for whom poetry is a game one plays: "The game in Frost is typically between fact and fancy, as in 'Birches.'"

Marjorie Cook's "Acceptance in Frost's Poetry: Conflict as Play" (*CentE*, 1976) interprets conflict as challenge to serious play and states that what is characteristic of Frost is the delight he takes in the conflict itself, accepting life's struggle as the element of play in his philosophy. The question is raised concerning how playful one can be before serious responsibilities are abandoned in whimsicality. The charge of whimsical escapism has been leveled against the poems of "strategic retreat." Despite the common view of Frost as a tragic poet, his "essentially comic vision of complex acceptance keeps turning up" in poems like "From Plane to Plane" and "Not Quite Social."

Margaret Edwards, in "The Play of 'Downward Comparisons': Animal Anthropomorphism in the Poems of Robert Frost" (*CentE*, 1976), discusses the idea of poetry as play in the context of the playfulness among creatures in Frost's poetry. Frost is considered as playing the game well according to the rules. Walton Beacham's "Technique and the Sense of Play in the Poetry of Robert Frost" (*CentE*, 1976) suggests that it is dexterity with irony that has established his critical reputation, and that Frost's ironic "playfulness" has contributed greatly to his popular success. Beacham carefully indicates how the poet uses aspects of his technique like stanzas, meter, and rhyme to reinforce the irony established by dramatic situation. "Frost," he contends, "is an amazingly adept metricist whose craft delights anyone who recognizes how his lines operate." Equally informative is Stephen D. Warner's brief essay, "The Control of Play and the Play of Control in Robert Frost's Poetry" (*CentE*, 1976). In the poet's "pragmatic poetic game," Warner shows how the control of form is often confused by the reader with a control of substance. "Mending Wall" shows how metaphor and play can give a false impression of mastery on the part of the persona. "Increasingly," Warner says, "for Frost the play *in* poetry became the play of poetry." Play, for him, is control of metaphors for reality (as in "Mending Wall"); later, the control will be directly in the voice of the poems and the play will be between voice and form.

Marjorie Cook, in "Detachment, Irony, and Commitment" (Harris), distinguishes three of Frost's poetic attitudes: "He objectively presents what he considers an ambiguity inherent to the human situation. But at times he finds ironic contrasts between the expected and the actual event so severe that he can make no commitment. And at other times he moves beyond detachment in objectivity and irony to a commitment that incorporates and transcends the essential ambiguity." Although Frost emphasizes objectivity and ambiguity, he recognizes the risk involved and the necessity of commitment, hence the appearance of irony. Just as commitment is essential for individual direction, and detachment is essential for perspective and balance in a pluralistic world, so is detachment inherent in the ironic perspective, essential to the maintenance of "a working balance among conflicting pressures." Shrewdly, Cook declares that the poet "may be objective, ambiguous, even ironic, and still committed, both to form and to the mystery of belief."

In a related essay, "Dilemmas of Interpretation: Ambiguities and Practicalities" (Wilcox), Cook poses a nagging query: "Does the ambiguity in Frost's poetry stem from evasiveness or from a sensitive perceptiveness about the human condition?" She contends that although Frost is preoccupied with questions of meaning and interpretation, "he subtly weaves all these complexities into the practical situations in his poetry, but he does not always interpret *for* us." She shows that, as a master at including the possibility of various perspectives, the poet succeeds in showing us "the complexities of the world and of ourselves and the difficulties of interpreting."

David M. Wyatt's "Frost and the Grammar of Motion" (*SR*, Jan. 1980) is a well-illustrated essay which reveals how Frost's poetry explores rules governing our movement through time and in space. Wyatt examines nine acts of the mind that correlate with acts of the body: "Reaching Up," "Stooping Down," "Descending Ascent," "Looking Back," "Questing Out," "Stopping," "Turning Back," "Meeting and Passing," and "Returning." Wyatt states: "the grammar within which [Frost] makes his way is the bequest of poetry itself, the whole range of strategies for formulating, retarding, or in any other way shaping the motion of a poem inverted or sanctioned by the tradition. The preferences Frost experiences within the tradition define the kind of poet he becomes."

Allen Tate, in "'Inner Weather': Robert Frost as a Metaphysical Poet" (*Centennial Lectures*), concedes that Frost's "restricted diction" represents "a revolutionary reform contemporaneous with the experiments in poetic diction of Pound and Eliot." Since Frost's powers of observation combined with his "gifts of discovery," he saw "New England nature and the nature of New England man as his own, but both natures had to be discovered. He therefore invented a language for this double imaginative activity. He was much more the conscious technician than some of his critics have thought." However, Tate finds "Mending Walls" a "tiresome" poem and "Birches" a "portentous allegory," and he refers to the poet's "monotonous metrics and a monotony of tone which results from a narrowly calculated vocabulary." Marion Montgomery, in "Robert Frost: One Who Shrewdly Pretends" (*CentE*, 1976), sharply counters Tate's critical objection, especially to "Birches."

Laurence Perrine's "Sound and Sense in Frost" (Wilcox) regards Frost as a master who achieves correspondence between sound and sense in two ways: in "the sound *of* sense," and in the conventional manner described by Pope and practiced by Milton and Tennyson. William H. Pritchard writes persuasively in "Robert Frost: Elevated Play," in his *Lives of the Poets* (New York, 1980): "Our ultimate judgment of how good or even great Frost was will depend on how high we rate 'play' or extravagance as the true or worthy end of all poetry." In the last twenty years of the poet's life, Pritchard admits to a falling off and lessening of intensities in the poetry. He considers *North of Boston* Frost's great book of people, and contends that he is one in whom "the necessity to imagine the speaking voice is inseparable from imagining a life." From beginning to end the elevated play in his poetry depends upon "something heard." And yet, Pritchard concludes, "For all the talk about Frost's marvelous sense of particularity, the concreteness of his speech and image, there is always something abstract, philosophical, bookish even, about the experience of the poem."

Linda Ray Pratt, in "Robert Frost and the Limits of Thought" (*ArQ*, Autumn 1980), raises a formidable question concerning Frost's method of play in "For Once, Then, Something," "The Most of It," "On Looking Up By Chance at the Constellations," and "Design." While recognizing the quality of the poems in form and language, Pratt finds each poem "a riddle of contradictions" because of its ambiguity, which may be the result of inability to resolve a situation, or subterfuge, or complexity of thought. She decides the ambiguities mark Frost's failure to take a position. "Almost always one can enjoy the poetry," she says, "but one learns to distrust the poet." The reason for the limits in his thought, she concludes, is not intellectual slackness, but his excessive delight in dramatic effects, and a vulnerability which he protects by playfully pretending or fooling.

In chapter 10 of his *A History of Modern Poetry* (Cambridge, Mass., 1976), David Perkins identifies Frost's use of irony as an evasive tactic. "It is a means of speaking without affirming or denying," as he explains, "or at least of avoiding full commitment to whatever his words may imply." He finds that what "baffles is how seriously [Frost] means what he says and how much more than he literally says he may mean to imply." Critics favoring Frost call this "balance." "But whatever we think of it," Perkins concludes, "it is undeniably important in the chemistry of his effects." This forthright statement leaves the discussion of Frost's evasiveness where it is likely to remain: in the personal view of each reader.

Underscoring Frost's use of speech imaginatively, Margery Sabin, in "The Fate of the Frost Speaker" (*Raritan*, Fall 1982), points out that the poet succeeded in producing a "double action." First, he shielded private experience behind "the communal front of language," and secondly, he sought to reach out "to a more general human life through speaking gestures." In "Getting Physical" (*Raritan*, Fall 1982), Walter Benn Michaels contends that Frost's insistence on the importance of voice stresses physiology rather than character, personality, or prosody. "A Servant to Servants" is exemplary of his point. He argues that Frost, while following William James, took the experience of the body "to mark the impossibility of ever actually encountering a thing called the self." Then, going beyond James, Frost raises the question "of how a thing called the self could ever actually come into being."

3 Themes

a. Nature. Marie Borroff ("Robert Frost: 'To Earthward'" [*CentE*, 1976]) enlarges on what she calls Frost's "kinesthetic crunch," which is the impact point of the presence of "the linear body against the physical world it emanates from and lives in." "The kinesthetic motif," figured forth in hands, is tellingly illustrated in the poetry. "The engagement of the self in material actuality—the meshing of gears between body and world—is," she says, "an essential part of Frost's experiential vision." She concludes that Frost's greatest gift may be inherent in his method— the ability "to develop symbolic meaning with cumulative force seemingly without art or effort, in naturalistically portrayed scene and action."

In Cleanth Brooks's "Frost and Nature" (Wilcox), the relationship between nature and human nature is examined. Except for "Two Look at Two," which alone among Frost's poems suggests how nature gives "an answering response to the human heart," his poetry shows that "nature is not aware that the human world exists at all: nature is deaf and dumb to all human aspiration." To understand Frost's poetry, Brooks thinks it must be kept clearly in mind that Frost's attitude toward nature is "quite 'romantic.'" Neither worshipping nor fearing nature, he belongs to it and finds it infinitely interesting and lovely, but he knows how little he can ask of it. Nature is quite unconscious of his existence. Meanwhile, man's gift is consciousness; he exists within a sense of history.

Like Brooks, Margaret Edwards, in "Pan's Song, Revised: Robert Frost as the Articulate Backwoodsman" (*CentE*, 1974), indicates that although Frost found his primary metaphors in the natural world he did not share Emerson's Romantic view of nature. Instead he combines nature observations with philosophical abstractions in order to construct a human psychology. "Pan's Song" revises both Wordsworth's faith in returning to the outworn creed and Emerson's drawing inspiration from Pan. In answer to the question "what [role] should he play?" Frost "plays" several interchangeable roles: confronting nature as alien to himself, as a challenge, as an equal partner, or as a phenomenon to be protected and revered.

Samuel Coale's "The Emblematic Encounter of Robert Frost" (*CentE*, 1974) finds Frost more realistic and less tragic than Wordsworth in encountering nature. Coale identifies the relationship between the poet and nature with Frost's notion of Emblemism. "If my poetry has to have a name, I'd prefer to call it Emblemism—it's the viable emblem of things I'm after," Frost stated. "The Wood-Pile" and "Stars" are selected to show that Frost's emblems do represent visible tokens of "the very presence of existence itself."

Robert M. Rechnitz, in "The Tragic Vision of Robert Frost" (*CentE*, 1974), underscores the theme of nature's dualism in Frost's poetry: the seasonal order of life and death. Rechnitz reveals perceptively Frost's acceptance of limitations within the frame of this dualism. Thus his tragic vision, which is an attitude rather than a concept, views the universe as "vast and incomprehensible except for those vague promptings of the sensibility which defy articulation."

In "Lyric Impulse: Birds and Other Voices" (Harris), Kathryn Gibbs Harris shows (1) that in his poetry Frost's birds represent a variety of expression, and (2) that the two people most obviously associated with these references are Edward Thomas and Elinor Frost. Although Frost does not violate the law of verisimilitude in his nature poems, his birds are "fabulously serious, even tragic, actors"; and, occasionally, they also add a comic effect. Richard Foster, in "Leaves Compared with Flowers: A Reading in Robert Frost's Poems" (*NEQ*, Sept 1973), establishes that Frost's nature symbology measures the fragility of man's life and joyous hopes (emblematically experienced in flowers, songbirds, butterflies) against the symbol of man's fate as a mortal being represented by trees and their leaves. Foster believes the question Frost's nature poetry raises is how to understand and manage life in the light of inevitable mortality.

Roberts W. French, in "Robert Frost and the Darkness of Nature" (*EngR*, Winter 1978; reprinted in Gerber), is emphatic in finding Frost at unease in nature, despite some poems—notably "Mowing" or "Two Look at Two"—that express a joy in nature. Those who consider Frost simply as "a celebrant of nature" distort the poetry "by overlooking its dark complexities." French has in mind "An Old Man's Winter Night," "The Hill Wife," "Storm Fear," "Spring Pools," "The Most of It," among other poems. His main point is that "if Frost's poetry insists on anything . . . it insists on the impenetrable barriers between man and nature: we live in a world that we cannot know, for it will not reveal itself; and yet we yearn for some sort of communion."

b. *Politics.* Peter J. Stanlis's *Robert Frost: The Individual and Society* (Rockford, Ill., 1973) is a moderately long, well-documented, two-part discussion of Frost's political views. The first part underscores the Frostian belief that "the individual and society could transcend their conflicts and achieve harmony." Stanlis contends that in Frost's view the individual's relationship to civil society takes precedence over the relationship of human nature to external "physical" nature. In the second part, Stanlis states that although Frost does not construct a systematic political philosophy nor prepare a sustained discourse in politics, he remains consistent in his political convictions. These principles, enumerated and amplified, identify the poet as "certainly one of the most original and unstereotyped Democrats that the Democratic Party ever had." Self-described, he is "a Madisonian-Washingtonian-Jeffersonian Democrat." Stanlis sums up his sympathetically comprehensive discussion by declaring, "in both theory and practice he held fast to a politics that provided the maximum of personal liberty against all the claims of the modern totalitarian State."

Margaret V. Allen's "'The Black Cottage': Robert Frost and the Jeffersonian Ideal of Equality" (*CentE*, 1974) and Laurence Perrine's "The Meaning of Frost's 'Build Soil'" (*CentE*, 1974) also discuss Frost's political views as reflected in the poetry. Allen discusses how Jefferson's "hard mystery" about being born free and equal "troubled" Frost. She states that he distrusted the uncritical liberal mentality in its belief in progress, science, government planning, and in its intolerance of those with whom it disagreed. Although not dealing primarily with political ideas, "The Black Cottage" effectively dramatizes conflicts between these ideas. Perrine, who considers "Build Soil" a parody of Vergil's first eclogue, states its basic theme as "the comparative merits of socialism and individualism." Trenchantly, Perrine decides: "On a spectrum of political opinion, Frost's position was essentially conservative. But his was a responsible conservatism, not a mindless reactionaryism. . . . It was rooted firmly in the tradition of individualism and self-reliance preached by Emerson and Thoreau. One need not agree with it. But one must respect it."

George W. Nitchie, in two well-informed and provocative essays— "Robert Frost: The Imperfect Guru" (*CentE*, 1974) and "Robert Frost: Some Reflections on Poetry and Power" (*CentE*, 1976)—mounts a vigorous counterargument to the partisans and apologists for Frost's political conservatism. In the first essay, he refers to Frost as "a great romantic nihilist," whose popular image should be taken with caution. Nitchie contends that man as a social creature and a political animal gets "little acknowledgement" in Frost; as a guru, or intellectual and moral guide, Frost fails to include labor unions, welfare agencies, social legislation, braintrusting, city planning, mass movements, the literature of social protest, and the New Deal as alternatives to the myth of rugged individualism. Nitchie's two major criticisms are: (1) that Frost believed that efforts in working out social and political problems were "undesirable or unnecessary or ineffective," and (2) Frost entertained "a deep and deviant hostility to ideas of an elaborately social world." In effect, such ideas constituted a threat to the image of rugged individualism by which both he and New England were to be identified. Rexford Stamper, in "Robert Frost: An Assessment of Criticism, Realism, and Modernity" (CentE, 1974), disagrees with Nitchie's negative assessment of Frost as a poet whose work fails to embody social consciousness, and certainly Peter J. Stanlis, as well as Laurence Perrine, have, as noted, stated the other side of the case on Frost's political views.

In "Robert Frost: Some Reflections on Poetry and Power" (CentE, 1976), Nitchie, questioning the political influence of a public poet like Frost, decides that he might be the voice of New England but not of the United States. Nitchie suggests a perversely unconvincing twist in Frost's ardently avowed patriotic stance. Here again Nitchie's views should be examined in the light of Stanlis's documented statements. And the views of both might well be reexamined in the light of John E. Sears's remark (NEQ, Sept. 1977) that Frost treated political matters "at the level of gossip and bad puns, and it seems unlikely that he expected to be taken seriously as a political thinker."

c. Science. In "A Few Touches of Frost" (SoR, Autumn 1966), F. Cudworth Flint remarks, "Indeed, it was never safe to assume that one knew the limits of Frost's knowledge and experience." Nor was it, especially when touching physical and theoretical science. His interest extended from botany and geology through archeology to physics and astronomy. R. L. Cook's Robert Frost: A Living Voice (1974) includes a lecture by Frost entitled "An Interest in Science." Laurence Perrine states in "Robert Frost and the Idea of Immortality" (CentE, 1976): "Frost, after all, had 'a lover's quarrel' with science. He quarreled with it whenever it became over dogmatic. . . . But he also took pains (or rather joy) in keeping up with science; he understood it remarkably well; and he appropriated many of its conclusions for his thinking and his poetry." Validations of Perrine's statement appear in a letter the poet wrote his grandson William Prescott Frost on 1 November 1939 (Family Letters, 1972), describing "the almost total eclipse of the moon."

Kathryn Gibbs Harris, in "Robert Frost's Early Education in Science" (SCR, Nov. 1974), has traced the progress of Frost's growing awareness of science, beginning with his Swedenborgian mother's introducing him to the Swedish mystic's distinction between opposites and a necessary unity and the doctrine of action. She describes his growing interest in botany and astronomy stimulated by the knowledge and enthusiasm of Carl Burell. To these influences in natural science should be added an interest in social science through William James's *Psychology*, and then, in 1911, the reading of Henri Bergson's *Creative Evolution*. "What Bergson did for Frost," according to Harris, "was to make the connection between nature and the aesthetic tendency in man completely coherent. And . . . what he did in relation to James's psychology was to show that the same motion that characterizes mind characterizes all organisms. It is this motion which endures and permits, eventually the evolution of consciousness."

An informed and stimulating examination of Frost's attitude toward science appears in John T. Hiers's "Robert Frost's Quarrel with Science and Technology" (*GaR*, Summer 1971). Using the poetry and Frost's reading in books on science as cogent supporting evidence, Hiers presents Frost's case against science and technology "as the eroding agents of traditional systems of ethical value." If science tends blindly to explore the universe with an empirical approach, Frost's "poignant condemnation" is of its failure to answer the basic question of the heart. Hiers argues that science only heightens ontological mystery by its discoveries, whereas "the initial step for love of and faith in humanity is not inspired through uncertainty, but through the individual's satisfaction with himself as an individual capable of imposing form and meaningful order upon his diverse and ultimately mysterious universe." Hiers clearly believes Frost succeeded in imposing form and order on the chaos of human experience.

d. Religion. In 1967, Howard Mumford Jones ("The Cosmic Loneliness of Robert Frost") contended that Frost's God was to be identified "somewhere between the God of Job and the God of Voltaire." And, in James Potter's *Robert Frost Handbook* (1980), "two different ontological perspectives" are suggested as representative of Frost's religious attitudes: first, that of "an agnostic existentialist" to whom the existence of God is irrelevant, and, second, that of a Puritan for whom God is "harsh and demanding." Potter finds Frost's uncertainty about the existence of God and the fundamental manageability and darkness of the universe attributable not to diffidence but "to an obscurity which the poet found to be inherent in the universe." Potter adds significantly: "Some readers find it strange that [Frost] managed to live such a full and creative life in this state of uncertainty. He did so by means of a deliberately maintained faith, religious, humane, and poetic." But in Yvor Winters's vivid phrase, Frost was a "spiritual drifter," and John F. Sears believes that he "purposely obscured the exact nature of his religious opinions" (*NEQ*, Sept. 1977).

Since Frost's religious views are complex, there have been extensive discussions and little unanimity. Robert Francis, a discreet friend of the poet, says, in *A Time to Talk* (1972), "The God in Frost's poems is always outside humanity and sometimes very far outside. . . ." James M. Cox, in "Robert Frost and the End of the New England Line" (*CentE*, 1974), thinks "God in Frost's skeptical universe, far from ceasing to exist, becomes the very principle of uncertainty—the force that may or could be the condition behind every conditional." Dorothy Judd Hall, in "An Old Testament Christian" (*CentE*, 1978), states that "a comprehensive look at his life-long self-revelations in poetry and prose—however guarded they were—reveals to us a deeply religious man." A well-documented statement supporting Hall's contention is Victor E. Reichert's "The Faith of Robert Frost" (*CentE*, 1974). This essay documents Frost's religious beliefs as they were noted and communicated to Lawrance Thompson. Of particular importance is the account of the sermon Frost gave at Rockdale Avenue Temple in Cincinnati on 10 October 1946, when for "the first time . . . [he] clearly gives his view of religion." Reichert states that although Frost described himself as "an Old Testament Christian," it is a mistake to call his religious beliefs "any more complicated than the whole remarkable and tough texture of his mind and soul." This view appears to agree with Robert Francis's perceptive statement (*A Time to Talk*) that, although Frost was "a profoundly thoughtful man, he was not a thinker. As far as his poetry is concerned it may have been well that he wasn't, for if he had worked out a comprehensive and cohesive pattern or system, his poems might have been prisoners within it."

Many articles relate directly to Frost's religious belief. Alfred R. Ferguson's "Frost and the Paradox of the Fortunate Fall" (*CentE*, 1974) describes the paradox of the fortunate fall as a device by which Frost balances precariously between the polarities of good and evil. "Certainly, by linking, as he does, the fall, the apple tree, the high human virtue of the act of choice, and God's choice of descent into man, [Frost] emphasizes the paradox of *felix culpa*," says Ferguson. "Normally the connection of the fall and the rise is for Frost less a theological concern than a metaphor to suggest a precarious equilibrium between good and evil or stasis and dynamism." Laurence Perrine, in "Robert Frost and the Idea of Immortality" (*CentE*, 1976), finds a general tendency in Frost's thinking toward immortality, grounded in agnosticism, but it does not end there. Frost's acceptance of man's inability to know did not cut off speculation; he found value both in uncertainty about a future life and a faith in it. Although his poetry is thoroughly earth-centered, he leaned toward the conviction that the soul would continue to exist after death in remembrance. Perrine thinks this belief, foreshadowed in *A Boy's Will* (1913), becomes explicit in *In the Clearing* (1962).

Joseph Kau's "'Trust . . . to go by contraries': Incarnation and the Paradox of Belief in the Poetry of Robert Frost" (CentE, 1976) also sees Frost as an agnostic but not a rigid one; that is, he does not whole-heartedly trust God in matters of existence and destiny. Kau detects a tension between complete trust and agnostic skepticism, and he assumes that Frost's belief is "that life is an act of faith, for it begins in mystery and ends in hope." Thomas McClanahan, in "Frost's Theodicy: 'Word I Had No One Left But God'" (CentE, 1976), argues that Frost is con-cerned with the need to justify the ways of God to man. The outcome of this vindication and the manner in which it is accomplished mark him as a sophisticated philosophical poet who developed a theodicy that grew out of an intellectual preoccupation with William James.

In "Robert Frost's New England" (CentE, 1974), Perry D. Westbrook relates Frost's religious belief to his mother's mingled Presbyterianism, Unitarianism, and Swedenborgianism. Although a member of no church, Frost appears extremely close to Calvinism in orthodoxy. Westbrook reaffirms the thrust in Frost's sermon at the Rockdale Avenue Temple: that the offering of his poetry might prove not unacceptable in God's eyes; in effect, that "in harmony with the teachings of his mother's Presbyterian and his father's Congregational forbears," Frost would like to receive grace and salvation. And John F. Sears, in "Frost's Figures of Upright Posture" (Wilcox), remarks: "You could say that Frost's poet is a secularized Calvinist trying to save himself in a difficult universe: his capacity to fulfill his intention is a sign of moral worth." Ronald Bieganowski, in "Sense of Place and Religious Consciousness" (Harris), traces the record of Frost's attachment to New England from A Boy's Will to "Directive," a record that illustrates "the pattern of Frost's deepen-ing sense of place [which] represents his growing religious conscious-ness." In a second article, "North of Boston: Human Dimensions to Robert Frost's Spiritual Readings" (Wilcox), Bieganowski sets forth three signifi-cant movements in Frost's personal growth that are characteristic of his religious consciousness. These movements, as found in North of Boston, are (1) a spiritual disruption of the self, (2) a hesitant growth toward a transcendent vision in some characters, and (3) a religious hope in other characters.

In a discerning interpretation, "Making Sweetbreads Do: Robert Frost and Moral Empiricism" (NEQ, Mar. 1976), Thomas K. Hearn, Jr. illus-trates the convergence of philosophy and poetry. He examines questions in moral philosophy as treated by the empiricist David Hume and related to Frost's poetry. Supporting the Humean stance (1) that denies moral truths as self-evident, and (2) that moral law is not the product of super-natural agents, Hearn shows that in Frost's poetry "our moral awareness is grounded in our attitudes, feelings, or emotions rather than thought or reason." In moral decisions, we "make do" with things less than perfect or ideal. Not a romantic, Frost accepts no kind of moral infallibility. Another equally interesting essay related to the theme of religion is Nancy C. Joyner's "Comic Exegete" (Harris). She discusses knowledgeably Frost's use of the Bible, especially in the juxtaposition of humorous poems and biblical references. His use of the Bible is attributed to two impulses: (1) to show off biblical knowledge, and (2) to use biblical passages humorously in order to gain an aesthetic distance from his subject matter. His reinterpretation of difficult scriptural passages becomes a significant poetic device.

Although Frost's "New England Biblicals"—*A Masque of Reason* (1945) and *A Masque of Mercy* (1947)—have been reviewed and sparingly discussed, the most thorough treatment is that of Peter J. Stanlis in "Robert Frost's Masques and the Classic American Tradition" (*CentE*, 1974). In an informal statement, Stanlis not only shows how the Masques differ from traditional ones but how they are less in debt to any English source and more closely related to "[Frost's] own resources in the classic American tradition of literature." Stanlis contends that Frost called his Masque a play not only because he rejected man's finite reason as insufficient to understand the mystery of God's justice, but even more because his Masque was a satire on faith in reason, "a severe condemnation of modern man's proud and delusive Faustian ways toward God." Stanlis describes *A Masque of Mercy* as "that rarest of literary forms, a city eclogue engrafted upon a dramatic fantasy." He notes Frost's belief that the modern man's main problem is not commutative justice in the courts of equity, but a conflict over social distributive justice and the various means by which it is brought about.

Further studies of the Masques are to be found in Darrel Abel's "Robert Frost's 'True Make-Believe'" (*TSLL*, Winter 1978), Heyward Brock's "Robert Frost's Masques Reconsidered" (*Renascence*, Spring 1978), and particularly in Noam Flinker's "Robert Frost's Masques: The Genre and the Poems" (*PLL*, Winter 1979).

In a more general discussion of Frost's religious attitudes, "Going and Coming Back: Robert Frost's Religious Poetry" (*SAQ*, Autumn 1974), Floyd C. Watkins finds the poet's beliefs in his prose statements often vacillating and enigmatic. In the poetry these beliefs fall into two categories: (1) poems of belief appearing early and late in his life which are both artistically weak and superficial in their religious assertions, and (2) the middle period, beginning with *New Hampshire* (1923), in which Frost inquires significantly into the place of man in the cosmos. Watkins thinks the best poems are based upon disbelief and concludes that the poet was never able to write a poem "at a moment of intense belief." The loss of poetic vision and imagination in the poet's late years corresponds with his declining interest in cosmic questions.

Dorothy Judd Hall, in "The Height of Feeling Free: Frost and Bergson" (*TQ*, Spring 1976), argues that, contrary to the contention of Yvor Winters and George Nitchie, Frost did not hedge on religious matters. She believes that in Bergson's *Creative Evolution* Frost found "a way to justify the Emersonian and Swedenborgian concept of an invisible universe in terms consistent with modern scientific theory—a means, also, of bringing into alignment biblical metaphor and evolutionary hypothesis." Central to Bergson is the concept of an invisible force—*élan vital*—continually being materialized in naturalistic forms and giving the life process purposeful meaning through freedom of choice. Frost, whose vision grew organically by freedom of association, shows affinities with Bergson's belief in a creatively evolving universe. Hall's *Robert Frost: Contours of Belief* (Athens, Ohio, 1984) incorporates her previous views of the poet's treatment of ethics and religion in literature. She focuses in each chapter on poems where "belief is a central concern in his work and the driving force behind it." The two Masques and poems like "West-Running Brook" and "Directive," among others, are testimonials to religious faith. "They are," she correctly insists, "the fruit of spiritual struggle." Not only does Hall's study ask "an appropriate question," whether Frost's reservations in matters of faith arise from being uncommitted, or merely non-committal, it also treats various aspects of Frost's belief—hence the significance of contours—and succeeds impressively in relating the core of his religious belief to the art of poetry. The ten chapters in this well-structured study are carefully researched, notably penetrating, and becomingly compact.

e. Sexuality. In an interview (*CentE*, 1974), John Ciardi states that Frost not only had an intensely strong Puritanical strain, but also "a very strong sexual impulse." Ciardi, while disavowing Freudianism, thinks the two contrary impulses—Puritanism and sexuality—set up "a contest of forces" which produced "the energy and agony out of which the poems came." Ciardi asserts Frost lived his life "at a level of passion not generally sensed."

Richard Poirier, in *Robert Frost* (1977), shows that not only "Putting in the Seed" but as well "Rose Pogonias" and "A Prayer in Spring" implicitly propose "that sexual love can make us aware that we participate in the larger creative processes of nature." Stearns Morse, in "'The Subverted Flower': An Exercise in Triangulation" (*CentE*, 1976), suggests that the poem is autobiographical and that it might be viewed as an example of the repressive effect which results from hatred and fear of the body. Donald J. Greiner is less tentative than Morse. In "The Indispensable Robert Frost" (Gerber), he contends that "The Subverted Flower" recalls "those moments of embarrassment in 1892 when Frost believed that Elinor was shaming him by initially refusing to return his desire for sexual love."

Frost's treatment of the relationship of men and women appears prominently in several essays. Robert H. Swennes, in "Man and Wife: The Dialogue of Contraries in Robert Frost's Poetry" (*AL*, Nov. 1970), points out the prevalence of the dialogue of the contrary sexes throughout

Frost's poetry. In *North of Boston*, each dialogue between men and women reveals a different moment in domestic life, yet "they all suggest the need for visible love and effective communication between individuals to find their lives together." Despite the bleak image of life in "Home Burial," Swennes finds most of the monologues and dialogues represent "constructive" responses to the harsh reality of life. He asserts that Frost "suggests ways by which man can bridge over the gulfs which separate men from one another," and that the reconciliation of the two contraries—man and woman—becomes "the most significant creative act which man can perform. The union is one of love." Thus Frost's poetry is essentially love poetry of which "The Master Speed" is exemplary.

Phebe Shi Chao's "Frost and Women," in *Miscellany Two: Vermont Academy of Arts and Sciences Occasional Paper, No. 13* (Montpelier, Vt., 1974), stresses how well Frost writes about women: "At his best he had the ability to treat as *individuals* the women who appear in his poetry, to be objective when viewing their psychological make-up and seeing what made the individual, who also happened to be a woman, what she was." Chao inquires pertinently whether Frost, in his sympathetic handling of women, was compensating in his art for a dominating attitude toward his wife and daughters in real life. Her supporting evidence is derived from the official biography.

Patricia Wallace, avoiding biography in "The 'Estranged Point of View': The Thematics of Imagination in Frost's Poetry" (*CentE*, 1976), reflects on women characters in poems like "The Hill Wife," "Two Witches," and "Paul's Wife," who are "outsiders" in their relationship to the social fabric. These "outsiders" are the special possessors of an "estranged point of view." Wallace's reaction underscores Marion Montgomery's identification of Frost as "an allegorist of the alienated Self" in his poetry.

4 Explication

This section focuses on representative interpretations of separate volumes of Frost's poetry and the explication of individual poems. The centenary celebration of his birth, the completion of the three-volume official biography, and the availability of expanded source materials greatly increased critical attention. Recent bibliographical studies now enable professional scholar and general reader alike to approach Frost more readily. Critical interpretation has become at once more informed and imaginative, despite the tendency, as Richard Foster has indicated, to consider each poem as though it were "a kind of windowless aesthetic monad whose chief law of being is its enclosed self-completeness" (*NEQ*, Sept. 1975).

Recent valuable assessments of individual volumes include Donald Haynes's "The Narrative Unity of *A Boy's Will*" (*PMLA*, May 1972) and Lewis H. Miller, Jr.'s "Design and Drama in *A Boy's Will*" (*CentE*, 1974);

chapter 4 in John C. Kemp's *Robert Frost and New England* (1974) on *North of Boston*; and Stephen D. Warner's "Robert Frost in the Clearing: The Risk of Spirit in Substantiation" (*CentE*, 1974). Frost's short play *A Way Out* (1929) is briefly discussed in Potter's *Robert Frost Handbook*. In Kemp's *Robert Frost and New England*, James K. Guimond's "*A Way Out:* Pastoral Psychodrama" (Harris), and Donald G. Sheehy's "Robert Frost and the Locked Door" (*NEQ*, Mar. 1983), it is more intensively interpreted.

Numerous analyses and *explications de texte* are to be found in the various volumes of *Explicator*. These brief but ingenious insights indicate the considerable interest of scholars in the precise details of Frost's poetry. Forty-odd explications have appeared in *Explicator* during the last dozen years. They represent the diligence, thoroughness, enthusiasm, and imagination previously accorded Eliot and Pound in poetry, and Faulkner and Hemingway in prose. However, only more extensive interpretive analyses and their sources will be noted here. Preference will be given to essays and articles that deal either with major or more unusual poems. "Directive" is an example of a major poem and "Maple" of an unusual one.

Among the outstanding recent interpretations of "Directive," John F. Lynen's "Du Côté de Chez Frost" (*CentE*, 1974) is both informed and comprehensive. Lynen concludes "Directive" is "a poem that emphasizes the transformation of static objects into dynamic events, of essences into activities, of being into becoming." Another major poem—and one of Frost's great lyrics—"Stopping By Woods"—was given a provenance in N. Arthur Bleau's "Robert Frost's Favorite Poem" (*CentE*, 1978) and supporting evidence in Lesley Frost Ballantine's "In Aladdin's Lamp Light" (*CentE*, 1978). William H. Shurr, in "Once More to the 'Woods': A New Point of Entry Into Frost's Most Famous Poem" (*NEQ*, Dec. 1974), categorizes the interpretive readings of the poem: (1) as an ethical statement concerning social commitment and obligations, (2) as a death-wish, (3) as a symbol related to theological existentialism, and (4) as the record of a religious experience. Shurr interprets the poem as a statement of resistance to an uncongenial religious experience, and he relates it to a cluster of similar "emblematical nights" in Frost's poetry; for example, "An Old Man's Winter Night," "Desert Places," and "Acquainted with the Night."

"The Death of the Hired Man" is linked to modernism and transcendence in Warren French's "'The Death of the Hired Man': Modernism and Transcendence" (*CentE*, 1978) and discussed at length in Nancy Vogel's "A Post Mortem on 'The Death of the Hired Man'" (*CentE*, 1974). "Mending Wall" is variously interpreted by Charles N. Watson, Jr. ("Frost's Wall: The View From the Other Side" [*NEQ*, Dec. 1971]) as a dramatic monologue rather than as a meditative lyric, as Lawrance Thompson contends; by Mordecai Marcus, in "Psychoanalytic Approaches to 'Mending Wall'" (Harris), with Freudian emphases; and by Donald Cunningham ("Mending Wall" [*Pebble*, Nos. 14 & 15, 1976]) as "the inability of the poem's narrator to understand and communicate with the neighbor." "The Road Not Taken" receives a perceptive reading by Russel Speirs in the *Christian Science Monitor* (8 Jan. 1974), by Robert F. Fleissner in "A Road Taken: The Romantically Different Ruelle" (Harris), and by David M. Wyatt in "Choosing in Frost" (*CentE*, 1976), and is warmly considered in Philip Booth's "Frost's Empty Spaces" (*Pebble*, Nos. 14 & 15, 1976). The subjects of James Ellis's "Frost's 'Desert Places' and Hawthorne" (1965) are elaborated upon by Edward Stone's "Other 'Desert Places': Frost and Hawthorne" (*CentE*, 1974). Guy Rotella, in "Metaphor in Frost's 'The Oven Bird'" (Wilcox), establishes a correlation between the bird's fleeting song and the poet's diminished midsummer singing.

"Design" has been carefully analyzed by George Monteiro in "Robert Frost's Metaphysical Sonnet" (*CentE*, 1974), and closely examined by each of the following: Robert M. Rechnitz ("The Tragic Vision of Robert Frost" [*CentE*, 1974]), Joseph M. Garrison, Jr. ("'Our Singing Strength': The Texture of Voice in the Poetry of Robert Frost" [*CentE*, 1974]), Thomas McClanahan ("Frost's Theodicy: 'Word I Had No One Left But God'" [*CentE*, 1976]), Karen Lane Rood ("Robert Frost's 'Sentence Sounds': Wildness Opposing the Sonnet Form" [*CentE*, 1976]), and Dorothy Judd Hall ("An Old Testament Christian" [*CentE*, 1978]).

"The Witch of Coös" receives a brilliant exegesis by Patricia Wallace in "The 'Estranged Point of View': The Thematics of Imagination in Frost's Poetry" (*CentE*, 1976), and "To Earthward" receives an equally illuminating interpretation by Marie Borroff in "Robert Frost: 'To Earthward'" (*CentE*, 1976). "The Draft Horse" is closely discussed by Donald J. Greiner in "Robert Frost's Dark Woods and the Function of Metaphor" (*CentE*, 1974). "After Apple-Picking" is reconsidered in John J. Conder's "'After Apple-Picking': Frost's Troubled Sleep" (*CentE*, 1974). Margaret V. Allen's presentation of "The Black Cottage" in "'The Black Cottage': Robert Frost and the Jeffersonian Ideal of Equality" (*CentE*, 1974) is greatly rewarding. "The Gift Outright" is discussed by Hamida Bosmajian in "'The Gift Outright': Wish and Reality in History and Poetry" (*AQ*, Spring 1970) as "a meditation on America's past; the colonial pregrace state, the mystic moment when identity was achieved, and the historical results of that moment."

Among the lesser recognized poems, several have received exceptionally perceptive interpretations; notably, "Wild Grapes" in Helen Bacon's vivid essay, "For Girls From 'Birches' to 'Wild Grapes'" (*YR*, Oct. 1977), in which Frost's poem is traced to Euripides's *Bacchae*, linking Frost with the classical tradition. Another superior interpretative statement is that of Darrel Abel ("Robert Frost's 'True Make Believe'" [*TSLL*, Winter 1978]) on "Maple."

Other rewarding explications include: Patricia Wallace on "Paul's Wife" in "The 'Estranged Point of View': The Thematics of Imagination in Frost's Poetry" (*CentE*, 1976); Laurence Perrine's "The Meaning of Frost's 'Build Soil'" (*CentE*, 1974); R. F. Fleissner on "The Gold Hesperidee" in "Like 'Pythagoras' Comparison of the Universe with Number': A Frost-Tennyson Parallel" (*CentE*, 1974); Sister Mary Jeremy Finnegan on "Hard Not To Be King" in "Frost Remakes an Ancient Story" (*CentE*, 1974); Marie Borroff on "The Grindstone" in "Robert Frost: 'To Earthward'" (*CentE*, 1976); Alan T. Gaylord's "The Imaginary State of 'New Hampshire'" (*Pebble*, Nos. 14 & 15, 1976); William Meredith's "A Fratricide: Robert Frost's 'The Vanishing Red'" (*Pebble*, Nos. 14 & 15, 1976); Maxine Kumin's "A Note on 'Provide, Provide'" (*Pebble*, Nos. 14 & 15, 1976); "I Will Sing You One-O" in Floyd C. Watkins's "Going and Coming Back: Robert Frost's Religious Poetry" (*SAQ*, Autumn 1974) and John Lynen's "'I Will Sing You One-O'" (*Pebble*, Nos. 14 & 15, 1976); Stearns Morse's "'The Subverted Flower': An Exercise in Triangulation" (*CentE*, 1976); Donald J. Greiner's "The Indispensable Robert Frost" (Gerber); Alfred R. Ferguson's "Frost and the Paradox of the Fortunate Fall" (*CentE*, 1974); John A. Rea's "Language and Form in 'Nothing Gold Can Stay'" (Harris); Linda Ray Pratt's "Prosody as Meaning in Frost's 'The Hill Wife'" (*Pebble*, Nos. 14 & 15, 1976); William S. Waddell, Jr.'s "By Precept and Example: Aphorism in 'The Star-Splitter'" (Wilcox); and "Paul's Wife" and "The Silken Tent" in Herbert Marks's "The Counter-Intelligence of Robert Frost" (*YR*, July 1982).

In "Robert Frost in the Clearing," in *Miscellany Two: Vermont Academy of Arts and Sciences Occasional Paper, No. 13* (Montpelier, Vt., 1974), Richard Eberhart reflects on the perplexing implications of "Away!" "Since man does not know the ultimate secrets or meaning of God, that is, by reason," says Eberhart, "and if reason is the strongest thing in Frost, stronger than any devotional feeling, for any established religious system, why is it not quite human, even humane, for him to praise the living, life itself, and deny death by saying that he may come back from it to the living if he wishes to?"

Robert Pack, in "Robert Frost's 'Enigmatical Reserve': The Poet as Teacher and Preacher" (*Centennial Lectures*), considers Frost's poems as parables. "His poems," according to Pack, "speak most profoundly when they speak by indirection." "The Oven Bird," "The Most of It," and "The Draft Horse" are selected to illustrate this parabolic tendency.

5 Sources and Influences

Frost's relationship to the Hebraic tradition appears in the two Masques and in scattered references throughout his poetry. Nancy C. Joyner's "Comic Exegete" (Harris), previously referred to, notes two categories: the casual reference to the Bible for metaphoric purposes and central biblical metaphors.

Predictably, Frost's interest in the classical world of the Greeks and Romans—early noted by Elizabeth Shepley Sergeant in "Good Greek Out of New England," in *Fire Under the Andes* (1927)—has produced several lively essays. Helen H. Bacon's "'In-and-Out-door Schooling': Robert Frost and the Classics" (*Centennial Lectures*) originated as a lecture at the Library of Congress. She states that "One of the most deeply guarded and cherished secrets of the poetry [of Frost] is the affinities, which are never identities, with classical poetry which the Yankee surface masks." Bacon, distinguishing between georgics, or actual farming, as it is to be found in Vergil's *Georgics*, and the literary poems dealing with rural life described as pastoral, associates Frost with the georgic. "Frost," she says flatly, "is more a georgic than a pastoral poet. His own references to eclogues in connection with the poems is perhaps another characteristic bit of foolery." Frost's georgic tendencies are tellingly illustrated in his poetry. In another important discussion of the classical influence in Frost, "Dialogue of the Poets: *Mens Animi* and the Renewal of Words" (*MR*, Summer 1978), Bacon states that "Frost and Catullus inhabit the same world, outside of space and time, because they recognize the same creative force (*mens animi*), which is the source of poems and thought."

Sister Jeremy Finnegan's "Auditory Memory and Latin Heritage" (Harris) traces the influence of Frost's parents and his educational training to his interest in the classics. Both his remarkable auditory memory, stimulated by his mother's reading, and the Latin heritage helped Frost in the evolution of his style. Since his interest extended to the technical aspects of Latin poetry, the heritage was assimilated "to the totality of his art." James F. Knapp, in "The Greek World and the Mystery of Being" (Harris), aware that Lynen in *The Pastoral Art of Robert Frost* (1960) presents Frost as creating a new myth of rural life and that Helen Bacon stoutly opposes the description of him as a pastoral poet in the classical sense, nevertheless finds his imagination deeply rooted in the ancient world. Knapp remarks significantly: "But if all [of the Greek philosophers'] theories are finally no more than metaphors, Frost still saw the deeper rightness in their bold decision to look to the stars and question the mystery of Being." An ancient speculative attitude, Knapp thinks, was "strangely vital to his own modernity."

Philip L. Gerber (*Robert Frost* [1982]), while conceding that it is now a commonplace to suggest that Frost more nearly resembles Thoreau than Emerson in wit, verbal precision, and command of the ironic mode, nevertheless finds close affinities between the two. Like Emerson, Frost had a direct firsthand perception of "original relation to the universe"; he relied on intuition, possessed a self-reliant individualism, and had a strong sense of national identity as an *American* poet. Gerber, however, believes Frost demonstrated a closer affinity with Whitman than appears on the surface: "For Frost it was heart over head, all the way, even to a seeming distrust of the human mental process." And both Marice C.

Brown's "Introduction: The Quest for 'all creatures great and small'" (*CentE*, 1974) and Jac L. Tharpe's "Afterword: Frost as Representative of the Eidolons" (*CentE*, 1974) respectively notice the connection.

James M. Cox's "Robert Frost and the End of the New England Line" (*CentE*, 1974) is a fine, full-bodied essay which, as Richard Foster notes, "says beautifully what Frost is: Emerson is the father and Thoreau the son (theory and practice) of the New England moral and spiritual tradition, and Frost is its 'memory'" (*NEQ*, Sept. 1975). "What is probably most remarkable about Frost's poetry," says Cox, "is that the self which stands up in all forms is decisively continuous, gaining coherence and singularity by virtue of the variety of play among the forms of poetry."

Lloyd N. Dendinger, in "Emerson's Influence on Frost Through Howells" (*CentE*, 1974), remarks on the affinities between Howells's critical dicta and Frost's poems, "which significantly clarify the nature of Frost's Emersonianism." Frost, as a realist, takes a middle position between the extremes of romantic idealism and naturalistic determinism. Thus Frost is Emersonian in his affirmations but non-Emersonian in his recognition of evil and in the absence of a transcendental rationale. Like Cox, Dendinger recognizes that Frost is in the Emersonian tradition without being properly an Emersonian poet. William Chamberlain, in "The Emersonianism of Robert Frost" (*ESQ*, Spring 1969), probes the emphasis on organicism in "West-Running Brook" and "Directive," as part of Frost's Emersonian heritage.

The influence of Hawthorne upon Frost is remarked upon by both Edward Stone in "Other 'Desert Places': Frost and Hawthorne" (*CentE*, 1974) and by J. Donald Crowley in "Hawthorne and Frost: The Making of a Poem" (*CentE*, 1974). In the former essay, the influence seems more apparent than real, and in the latter the analysis of the connection of "The Wood-Pile" to Hawthorne appears overstated.

The impact of William James on Frost, as described in the forceful essays of Thomas McClanahan and John F. Sears, is neither tentative nor overstated. But Lewis H. Miller, Jr., in "William James, Robert Frost, and 'The Black Cottage'" (*CentE*, 1978), contends rather tenuously that Frost's passion for the "speaking voice" is to be found in James's *Pragmatism*. More convincingly, Miller finds the pragmatic method "explicitly and consecutively realized" in "The Black Cottage," a poem that not only dramatizes but epitomizes the philosophic temperament of William James. William Mulder, in "See 'New Englandly': Planes of Perception in Emily Dickinson and Robert Frost" (*NEQ*, Dec. 1979), illustrates three planes of perception in the two poets: the elementary level of description in which the regional landscape is observed provisionally and pictorially; the moral and didactical level where perception becomes precept; and the symbolical, or inward level reflecting psychic meanings.

Among the essays discussing Frost and his contemporaries is Peter L. Hays's "Two Landscapes: Frost's and Eliot's" (*CentE*, 1974), in which it is contended that Frost structured *New Hampshire* not only to mock Eliot's pedantry and "obscuration," but also to counter the pessimistic tone of *The Waste Land*. By his humor, harmonious music of the blank verse, and belief ("It must be I want life to go on living"), Frost challenges Eliot's despair.

Todd M. Lieber's "Robert Frost and Wallace Stevens: What to Make of a Diminished Thing" (*AL*, Mar. 1975) is an absorbing discussion of two very different contemporaries. Despite lack of interest in each other and their different styles, Frost and Stevens shared a common environment and confronted a world lacking in spiritual significance. Lieber focuses on how both poets dealt with the loss of unity, order, and belief, sought out metaphysical rather than sociological compensations, found alternatives to pessimism, and shared a conception of poetry as a corrective to the malaise of the modern spirit. Lieber's essay is knowledgeable, thoughtful, stimulating, and debatable, especially on Frost. Donald J. Greiner, in "Factual Man and Imaginary Rabbits: Robert Frost and Wallace Stevens" (Wilcox), distinguishes between voice and vision, which he thinks is the principal difference between the two poets. Juxtaposing "An Old Man's Winter Night" and "A Rabbit as King of the Ghosts," Greiner's sprightly essay shows that, in their respective poems, the poets, rather than being at polar extremes, concern themselves with propriety of fact and vision, thereby giving us, unlike Lieber's general view, two sides of one coin. "The two poets," Greiner thinks, "are closer to being relatives than strangers."

In a strong essay—"Frost, Winnicott, Burke" (*Raritan*, Fall 1982)—that is at once sympathetic and speculative, Richard Poirier shows where and how Emerson, Kenneth Burke, and the British psychoanalyst D. W. Winnicott suggest affinities to Frost's poetry. The nub of the affinity is that "things" or "objects" imply a magic and meaning which entitles us to forms of verbal and creative opportunity. For example, in Frost's poems of hiding, retreat, or admitted deception, according to Poirier, the poet pretends to be truthful and available. "The availability, the admission of disguise," Poirier says, "is the ultimate mask of a permanently hidden Frost." Thus, he considers voice in Frost to be a form not of revelation but of deception, and he thinks the poet is essentially unknowable and indefinable. Although Poirier's argument is ingenious and original and his evidence clearly informed, the view leaves unresolved the dichotomy between revelation and deception. Frost's avowed aim in writing was to make "little bits of clarity." Such a view appears at odds with Poirier's presentation of the poet as a furtive noncommunicator—"the Hawthorne of American poetry."

6 Views and Counterviews

Arthur M. Sampley, in "The Myth and the Quest: The Stature of Robert Frost" (*SAQ*, Summer 1971, reprinted in Gerber), raises formidable questions about Frost's stature. "How great is a poet," he asks, "who has no consistent vision of man's place in the universe? What are we to think of one who adopts the tone of a seer and yet is uncertain himself about man's fundamental problems?" "I think," Sampley states flatly, "Frost has . . . a system," although it is "ramshackle like the throne in *A Masque of Reason*." The "system," suggested in "The Most of It" and other poems, is one of man's relation to a world presided over by Divine Intelligence, but without any assurance that this intelligence either rewards or punishes man personally. Man is sustained partly by a belief in a divine purpose but mainly by a stubborn belief that he can somehow wrestle with whatever he does encounter. For Sampley the central meaning of Frost's life is the image of "the lonely, hard-set individual who masters his fears, his weaknesses, even his fate through courage and dogged resolution."

Charles Carmichael, in "Robert Frost as a Romantic" (*CentE*, 1974), argues that considering the poet as a Romantic helps to explain the difference between the widely accepted Frost myth and the Thompson biographical portrait. The periods of isolation, alienation, and terror in the poet's life bring into question the validity of the image of a gregarious folk hero. Carmichael's tenuous point is that as long as Frost maintained the tension between self and role, he wrote great poetry, but his tacit acceptance of the "Frost Myth" led to the loss of a major source of tension in his life. He no longer had to struggle to maintain his identity or a self-created role—and this marks a change and decline. Carmichael's theory is undercut by his imposing upon Frost such Romantic stereotypes as the Byronic hero, the poet-visionary, the Romantic historian, and the virtuoso. Nor does Carmichael's theory satisfactorily explain either the sanguine strain in Frost's poetry or his later preoccupation with spiritual "questing" as in "Directive" or "Kitty Hawk."

Questionings of Frost's stature also emerge from Allen Tate's reactions to specific Frost poems often favored by the poet's popular audience. In "'Inner Weather': Robert Frost as a Metaphysical Poet" (*Centennial Lectures*), Tate, with a bit of one-upmanship on "Marse Robert," objects to "the sententious meiosis of the last line" of "Birches." "The birches," says Tate, "seem too frail to bear such a portentous allegory." In commenting on "Mending Wall," Tate somewhat petulantly remarks, "I hope my rather feckless paraphrase of this poem is at least as tiresome as the poem itself." More pointedly, he says, "Fences good or bad make nothing; but upon the rhetorical trick that attributes causation to them the poem depends."

A more general view of the critical reactions to Frost's poetry will be found in Reginald L. Cook's "The Critics and Robert Frost" (*CentE*, 1974). In "The Two Frosts and the Poetics of Confession" (*CentE*, 1978), Richard Foster distinguishes between the "flawed man" and another Frost, "the important public personage." Foster appears to be overly influenced by the official biographer's viewpoint toward the poet: "Lawrance Thompson has shown how many and how deep were Frost's personal faults, how arrogant and selfish and vain he could be, and how cruel, especially to those closest and dearest to him." But is this allegation truly the whole story? William A. Sutton's "Problems of Biography" (Harris) reviews the vexing problem of biographer Thompson and his paradoxically complex subject with fair-minded objectivity. Sutton's essay is, in large measure, a corrective to Foster's measuring of the poet solely through the lens of Thompson's biography.

7 Frost's Modernity

No consensus prevails on whether Frost is a modern poet or essentially a nineteenth-century one. James R. Vitelli, in "Robert Frost: The Contrarieties of Talent and Tradition" (*NEQ*, Sept. 1974), thoughtfully proposes a searching question: "If Frost seems so unmodern, what, then, has happened to tradition as a result of the presence of his individual talent?" In reflecting on this question, he decides that when we penetrate the contrarieties in the relationship between Frost's talent and American tradition, "and observe how these contrarieties contributed to the strategy of his career, to his attitudes towards his material and to his attitude toward himself, we may find that his poems no less than those of Eliot have pushed modern poetry into new and dramatic explorations of the self—where modern poetry has achieved one of its chief distinctions." This is a cogent point and Vitelli's first-rate essay goes a long way in establishing its validity.

Frank Lentricchia (*Robert Frost: Modern Poetics and the Landscapes of Self*) views Frost as a modern poet and *not* as a post-Georgian. Warren French, in "'The Death of the Hired Man': Modernism and Transcendence" (*CentE*, 1978), thinks that, despite Frost's extraordinary popularity, modernist critics never felt quite comfortable with him. "I think," French states, "the reason was not that he had not caught up with them, but rather that they had not caught up with him." Philip L. Gerber (*Robert Frost* [1982]), in reflecting on Frost's career, relates him to both the past and present—he "faced both ways, backward as well as forward." John Ciardi (*CentE*, 1974) offers a different view on Frost's "modernity." "Frost," says Ciardi, "in a sense, in a true sense, and I imply no denigration, was a nineteenth-century poet who lived a long time into the twentieth century. He had written most of his poems by 1900 or within the next ten years. . . . He went on and kept mining those notebooks he had filled when he was younger and kept publishing them as if he had just written them. . . . I think he tried to become a twentieth-century poet in those poems I have called the editorials and in the bardic poems, 'Kitty Hawk' and 'America Is Hard to See' foremost among them. But he was born in another tradition." It is hard to quarrel with Ciardi's formidable point.

Lloyd N. Dendinger, in "Emerson's Influence on Frost Through Howells" (*CentE*, 1974), finds Nitchie's emphasis on Frost's lack of commitment in *Human Values in the Poetry of Robert Frost* (1960) unsatisfactory because in Frost's "commitment" to "non-commitment" his choice is consonant with his times and makes him "the most modern of poets." And John F. Lynen, in "Du Côté de Chez Frost" (*CentE*, 1974), believes: "Frost is not the less a modernist poet in that he holds the reader's mind within the frame of one of its manifold perceptual systems, the vision of perspective painting, and thus reveals the chaos of conflicting systems as it is seen from this standpoint."

8 Frost's Achievement

In the twenty years since Frost's death two facts stand out: first, his complexity as man and poet, and second, the commanding position which he holds as an American poet. In *Robert Frost: The Poet and His Critics* (1974), Donald Greiner states, Frost "remains one of the three or four most respected American poets of the century, and his work continues to challenge intelligent readers to better and more incisive interpretations." Significantly, he adds, "The case for or against Frost is far from over."

The question remains: how is he to be regarded? In *Robert Frost* (1982), Philip L. Gerber says: "There seems little doubt that Frost will be remembered. But only time will tell whether he is to be recalled as a physician who distributed placebos to his troubled age, or as a good Greek out of New England who drew back the dark curtain of eternity and directed men's eyes into the realm of final mysteries." George W. Nitchie, in "Frost and the Unwritten Epic" (Wilcox), believes the verdict is not in Frost's favor. "Frost," Nitchie asserts, "moves us more deeply . . . at those moments when we see *through* his apparent world of men and events, to professed affirmation and denials, and into those vulnerable privacies that had to do with the difficulty of being Robert Frost living." Nitchie thinks Frost didn't so much want "to *write* epic as to *be* epic," and he failed because he did not make the final identification of himself with his heroic darkness.

"Frost promised nothing that he didn't perform," says William H. Pritchard in "The Grip of Frost" (*HudR*, Summer 1976). But did the audience who heard Frost on the public platform understand the poems they listened to? This query suggests there is a relation between technique and substance, that is, between activation of the speaking voice and those inward impulses of a human being that are not wholly comprehended by superficial listeners. Pritchard, aware of the dual possibilities in understanding Frost, recognizes that he is "the poet of isolation and dread" quite as much as he is "the poet of aspiration, love, remembered fulfillment." Eben Bass, in "Robert Frost: Poetry of Fear" (*AL*, Jan. 1972), shares Pritchard's awareness of the tension between the inner and outer halves n Frost's temperament, and notes that fear is a recurring theme in his poetry both as a private experience and as an intruder into marriage. Similarly, Donald G. Sheehy, in "Robert Frost and the Lockless Door" (*NEQ*, Mar. 1983), stresses fear as a metaphysical center in Frost's poetry. He notes "the fear of the obliteration of self at the hands of an inexplicably malevolent stranger or through the potentially inimical strangeness of nature, the fear of failing to live up to the expectations of others, especially of a loved one, or the more rigorous expectations of self; the fear that the outer threat may be a projection of an inner flaw or evil onto a neutral world. Facing these fears tried the will and resources of the man who lived alone."

In "The Indispensable Robert Frost" (Gerber), Donald J. Greiner enumerates eight poems ("Storm Fear," "Home Burial," "After Apple-Picking," "An Old Man's Winter Night," "Stopping By Woods," "Design," "The Subverted Flower," and "Directive") which represent "the indispensable" Frost. But if Greiner's choices are to stand for Frost's major poetic achievement, what are we to say? Invariably, these poems stress the so-called "dark side" in a poet whose "comic genius" amply confirms his belief and personal demonstration that "the way of understanding is partly mirth." Frost's sense of humor is interstitial in the poetry and not to recognize it is to tip the balance unduly on the dark side. In an eloquent and a most perceptive essay, entitled "The Counter-Intelligence of Robert Frost" (*YR*, Summer 1982), Herbert Marks shows that Frost's vision spanned two poles: the paradoxical alliance of truth and concealment (illustrated by "Paul's Wife") and the mutual dependence of freedom and restraint.

The case for or against Frost extends into categorizing him as a major or minor poet, an area as gray as the "modernity" issue. In "A Polemical Preface" to *Robert Frost: Modern Poetics and the Landscapes of Self*, Frank Lentricchia states unhesitatingly that Frost is "a major poet." This means, according to Lentricchia, "that he has written in enduring language about our enduring conflicts. The price of not knowing him intimately may be our own self-diminishment." And William H. Pritchard, in "Robert Frost: Elevated Play," in *Lives of the Poets*, remarks that there may be a doubt that Frost is either "major" or "modern," because the lyrics "still fall short of the large ambitions and risks of a major writer; and that their old-fashioned contentedness with rhyme, syntax, and stanza pattern, with a sequential or logical mode of thought, disqualify him for a place in the modern pantheon." Pritchard, however, is not plagued by this doubt.

Nor apparently are other knowledgeable readers of Frost's poetry in doubt about the certainty and magnitude of his achievement. John Ciardi (*CentE*, 1974) says, "I would tend to believe, by and large, that [Frost] was not an innovator, though I think he did as much as any man to tune the metrics of the twentieth century to the spoken voice." Marie

Borroff, in "Robert Frost's New Testament: The Use of Simplicity," in *The Language and the Poet* (1979), elevates Frost's contribution to a high plane. She believes, "Despite his exploitation of the Christian tradition in the structure, symbolism, and language of his poems, the supreme bearer of spiritual enlightenment in our time, for Frost, was poetry itself." While Borroff's statement takes note of the alliance between Frost's humility and his dedicated passion to the purposes of poetry, Warren French, in "Frost Country" (*CentE*, 1976), emphasizes the fact that "Frost's choice to live modestly in the country and try to channel some fruits of the better life there back into our polluted cities . . . has today more application to the conservation and replenishment of our physical, intellectual, and moral lives than it had when he made it fifty years ago." The weight of sympathetic and reflective criticism today favors Frost's prescience that he has lodged "a few poems where they will be hard to get rid of."

V SUPPLEMENT

Since Reginald L. Cook's death in 1984, the most important addition to Frost studies has been William H. Pritchard's *Frost: A Literary Life Reconsidered* (New York, 1984). Intent on a critical biography of moderate length, Pritchard makes no attempt to replace Thompson's three volumes, nor does he directly argue against Thompson's biographical facts. Instead, he recasts certain infamous incidents (the "Dismal Swamp" episode, Frost's suicide threat in front of six-year-old Lesley, the touchy rivalries with Robinson and Pound) in the light of a different view of Frost's temperament. Where Thompson saw personal meanness, envy, and a will to dominate, Pritchard sees a poetic mind full of evasive play, measuring its solitary strength against all creation by most any available means. Thompson's biography was written at a time when the world's image of Frost as a kindly rural sage still needed to be challenged. By 1984 Pritchard can simply acknowledge the sad consequences of Frost's needs to control others and promote himself. He writes of Frost's life without dark moralizing and without slighting either Frost's wit or his geniality.

Pritchard's Frost is, first and last, a poet, a voice "fooling my way along," "guessing at myself," and then relishing the beauty of the ways words play over the mind's guessings. Frost's foxy claim to represent a world north of Boston is, for Pritchard, as much a part of this poetic identity as Frost's love of subtly undermining clichés he seemed to affirm. Given Frost's need to be number one, Pritchard's book enables us to see how Frost's poetic manner turned into a public mannerism, how Frost became his audience, and why he raided his "strongbox" of youthful poems in later years. But Pritchard's overall emphasis is on the subtlety of thought and technique which this manner encouraged within individual poems. Familiar tags of Frostian poetics like "the sound of sense," "breaking the meter," and "the old way to be new" are themselves made new because Pritchard shows us how often and how well Frost fulfilled them.

Pritchard's book will probably remain the standard one-volume study of Frost, man and poet, for a good many years. It maintains an engaging balance of biography and criticism. Pritchard's account of the changes between Frost's volumes of poetry, especially between *A Boy's Will* and *North of Boston*, shows us the evolving stages of Frost's career in a wide literary context. Pritchard's eye for lively and important quotations in Frost's letters and speeches seems to be unfailing. There is, in sum, a great deal here both for Frost specialists and for general readers. One wonders only whether Pritchard's very success may not eventually work against Frost's stature. Frost's evasive verbal play, his sly challenge to a world presumed to offer no Answer, may have made for fine poems, but can it finally be the stance of a major poet?

John McWilliams

Ernest Hemingway

Bruce Stark

I BIBLIOGRAPHY

There are now four fundamental books listing works by and about Ernest Hemingway. These are Audre Hanneman's *Ernest Hemingway: A Comprehensive Bibliography* (1967), her *Supplement* (Princeton, N.J., 1975), Linda Wagner's *Ernest Hemingway: A Reference Guide* (Boston, 1977), and Jo August's *Catalog of the Ernest Hemingway Collection at the John F. Kennedy Library* (Boston, 1982). Since August's *Catalog* concerns unpublished material, it will be discussed in section III below.

Needless to say, Hanneman did not catch everything, so that one of the chief tasks of Hemingway bibliographers since 1975 has been to bring forward additions and corrections to the listings in her two thick volumes. The principal vehicle for these addenda has been the *Papers of the Bibliographical Society of America*, in which George Monteiro published four such items (Fourth Quarter 1977, Second Quarter 1978, Fourth Quarter 1979, Second Quarter 1980); William White, surely the male dean of Hemingway bibliographers, published four (Second Quarter 1978, First Quarter 1979, Fourth Quarter 1981, Third Quarter 1982); and James B. Meriwether published one (First Quarter 1983).

Perhaps more substantial than these addenda, or R. H. Miller's note about Scribner's bindery card for *For Whom the Bell Tolls* (*FHA*, 1979), or even the fifty-eight additional reviews of *Islands in the Stream* that Ray Lewis White discovered (*LC*, Spring 1978), are three new pieces of Hemingway-related journalism: a pair of Paris reviews and a Kansas City news story. Both reviews appeared in the European edition of the *Chicago Tribune* in 1923. The one, found by Michael S. Reynolds, is a review by Hemingway of Gertrude Stein's *Geography and Plays* and was published on 5 March 1923 (*AL*, Oct. 1983); the other, discovered by Scott Donaldson, is a review by Gertrude Stein of Hemingway's *Three Stories and Ten Poems*, published 27 November 1923 (*AL*, Mar. 1981). Both of these discoveries are important, but Donaldson's is not as new as it seems. Even though several Hemingway scholars had lost track of

Stein's review, it was mentioned by Linda Wagner in her *Reference Guide* and was reprinted, as Wagner notes, by Hugh Ford in *The Left Bank Revisited: Selections from the "Paris Tribune," 1917–1934* (University Park, Pa., 1972). George Monteiro's discovery (*AL*, Mar. 1982) of a news story written by Hemingway for the *Kansas City Star* added a thirteenth *Star* item to the twelve published by Matthew Bruccoli in his *Ernest Hemingway, Cub Reporter* (1970) and listed by Hanneman in her *Supplement* (none of Hemingway's *Kansas City Star* journalism was included in her first volume).

The authority and usefulness of Hanneman's work is so great that it completely superseded most of the single volume bibliographies that preceded it; the same is true, moreover, of those that followed it, e.g., William F. Nolan's *Hemingway: Last Days of the Lion* (Santa Barbara, Calif., 1974), a slim, rather eccentric volume that appends a checklist of thirty-four books, derived from White and Baker, to an essay on Hemingway's life and a poem about him called "Now Never There." Equally eccentric in a different way is Robert B. Harmon's *Understanding Ernest Hemingway: A Study and Research Guide* (New York, 1977). The title sounds promising, but it is too full of errors and odd misunderstandings to be useful.

Complementary to Hanneman and Baker is Linda Wagner's *Ernest Hemingway: A Reference Guide* (Boston, 1977). Excluding works by Hemingway, Wagner's book annotates writings about him in chronological order from 1923 to 1975. In addition to a brief introduction that surveys the major trends in Hemingway criticism for the years covered, there is also an index that gathers together all the references to each of Hemingway's "major works." One can thus find the references to *A Farewell to Arms* but not to "The Killers" because it is concealed inside *Men Without Women*.

Since Hanneman stopped in 1975 and Wagner in 1977, those who want more up-to-date information on what has been written about Hemingway will have to search out the checklists that appear in the four journals which have concentrated on Hemingway. They are the *Fitzgerald/Hemingway Annual*, published yearly from 1969 to 1979; *Hemingway Notes*, published twice a year from 1971 to 1981; the *Hemingway Review*, published twice yearly since fall 1981; and the *Hemingway Newsletter*, begun in January 1981. Until 1974, the "Hemingway Checklist" in the *Annual* was compiled by Margaret M. Duggan and averaged about seven pages per year; when William White took it over in 1975, the average number of pages doubled to about fifteen per year. This dramatic leap forward probably does not indicate a surge in work on Hemingway (although 1975 was a very big Hemingway year in the *PMLA* bibliography), but suggests instead the exceptional passion for completeness that William White brings to his bibliographical work. It is not unusual to find in his checklists articles and books written in Russian, Japanese, Chinese, Rumanian, Bulgarian, Georgian, and Israeli

Hebrew. Although all of the languages are transliterated, none of the articles were annotated in White's *Annual* checklists. Worthy of note, too, is the carefully researched "Fitzgerald and Hemingway in the Academy: A Survey of Dissertations" by Deborah A. Forczek (*FHA*, 1978). This valuable article annotates seventy-seven Ph.D. dissertations written about Hemingway from 1949 to December 1976.

Overlapping the *Annual* for seven of its issues is *Hemingway Notes*, a twice-yearly publication whose bibliographies are compiled by William White along with the journal's two founding editors, Taylor Alderman and Kenneth Rosen. In addition to being more inclusive than the *Annual* checklists, these bibliographies are also more informative since many of the entries are briefly but helpfully annotated. In spring 1974, *Hemingway Notes* stopped publication, but with the demise of the *Annual* in 1979, it was revived for four numbers in an expanded format under the editorship of Charles M. Oliver and then transformed by him into the *Hemingway Review* in the fall of 1981. When *Hemingway Notes* was revived, William White took over the bibliographical chores, adding a regular column, "For the Collector." This column records a dedication to collecting and bibliography that stuns anyone not so inclined. Because of this dedication, White's checklists for both *Hemingway Notes* and the *Hemingway Review* are most complete but also less informative since he favors technically descriptive notes on printing, first appearance, reissues, new bindings, etc., over summaries of content.

These book-length bibliographies and periodical checklists will certainly provide even the most dedicated student of Hemingway with more information than he can easily assimilate, much less master. To guide him through this mass of information, he will need the help of specialized bibliographies and summary articles reviewing the state of Hemingway studies. Two good examples are the 101-item "Macomber Bibliography" that William White compiled for the "Special 'Macomber' Issue" of *Hemingway Notes* (Spring 1980), and the bibliography of "Hemingway in England" assembled by Graham Clarke for the *Hemingway Review*'s "Special British Issue" (Spring 1982).

The model for White's "Macomber" bibliography was almost certainly the checklist of work on Hemingway's short stories that Jackson J. Benson worked up for his *The Short Stories of Ernest Hemingway: Critical Essays* (Durham, N.C., 1975; hereinafter referred to as Benson). This "Comprehensive Checklist of Hemingway Short Fiction Criticism, Explication, and Commentary" records the complete bibliography for each one of Hemingway's 109 pieces of published and unpublished short fiction; moreover, each of the items is provided with its working title, approximate date of composition, date and place of first publication, and a list of the collections it later appeared in.

For the more historically minded, a valuable review of work on Fitzgerald and Hemingway is made each year in *American Literary Schol-*

arship: An Annual. From 1971 to 1978 this review was written by Jackson R. Bryer; between 1979 and 1982 it was done by Scott Donaldson; Bryer returned for the 1983 essay. In 1984 and 1985 Michael S. Reynolds did the chapter; Gerry Brenner took over for 1986 and 1987.

Another way to get an overview is to seek out review essays by those sages who have gained enough perspective on the field to survey it with perspicacity and proportion. Two such scholars are Jackson J. Benson and Philip Young. Benson gave a farewell address to the 1976 Hemingway conference held in Tuscaloosa, Alabama, that sorted sixty-seven books into comprehensible categories, surveyed 234 critical articles written between 1971 and 1974, and then, in an aside, made some very practical recommendations about which books should be read by students at various levels of sophistication. Benson's address is published as "Hemingway Criticism: Getting at the Hard Questions," in *Hemingway: A Revaluation* (ed. Donald R. Noble, Troy, N.Y., 1983; hereinafter referred to as Noble).

Philip Young's perspective on "Hemingway Studies," a term he dislikes, is more ambiguous. Young began surveying work on Hemingway in 1964; he did it again in 1973 in "Posthumous Hemingway and Nicholas Adams," in *Hemingway: In Our Time* (ed. Richard Astro and Jackson J. Benson, Corvallis, Oreg., 1974; hereinafter referred to as Astro and Benson). Another survey appeared in 1983, "Hemingway: The Writer in Decline" (Noble), and another appeared in an interview with Bruce Morton (*HN*, Fall 1980). Yet another appeared in 1980, "Hemingway Papers, Occasional Remarks," in *Ernest Hemingway: The Papers of a Writer* (ed. Bernard Oldsey, New York, 1981; hereinafter referred to as Oldsey). One of the themes that runs through these very personal reviews is that in an academic field that has become an "industry," production stimulates production because "the more that's written on a subject, the more significant the subject seems, and the more significant it seems the more secondary (tertiary) will be the matters that seem worth going into."

We conclude this section with two books, both published in 1981, that focus on what Hemingway read rather than on what he wrote. Michael S. Reynolds's *Hemingway's Reading 1910–1940: An Inventory* (Princeton, N.J., 1981) is "an inventory of those books, periodicals, and newspapers that Hemingway owned or borrowed between 1910 and 1940," not "a study of literary influences" nor "a compilation of Hemingway's literary allusions." Searching through several libraries, the cards at Sylvia Beach's book store, and his book orders from Scribner's, Reynolds compiled a list of 2,304 items that are printed out and coded for author, title, date, genre, source, subject matter, and comments. Of these 2,304 items, almost half are derived from what Reynolds designates "Key West Book Inventory, 1940" and reproduces in appendix 4. Besides this facsimile, Reynolds also provides five other appendixes that reproduce, first, several records from Hemingway's high school years: a list of his high school courses, descriptions of the English courses offered along with the texts they used, and a list of the high school's acquisition records. Appendix 5 contains something called "Hemingway's Recommended Reading List," a list that Reynolds apparently conflated from several different sources; and, finally, we are given a "User's Guide and Inventory" in appendix 6. Suffixed to these six appendixes are useful subject and title indexes; prefixed to them is an essay called "Hemingway's Bones," the bulk of which is devoted to certain important patterns that emerge from Reynolds's inventories and lists. Reynolds returns to these patterns, with certain additions, in "Unexplored Territory: The Next Ten Years of Hemingway Studies" (Oldsey). The tone of his book is rather flip and its scholarship surprisingly casual; for example, the so-called "Key West Book Inventory, 1940," one of his primary sources, is incorrectly dated and its compiler misidentified (see Stanley Wertheim's review [HR, Fall 1982]; and compare Reynolds's account of it to the one given by Brasch and Sigman in the book discussed below).

We are on much firmer ground with *Hemingway's Library: A Composite Record* by James D. Brasch and Joseph Sigman (New York, 1981), a book that attempts to identify "all the books that Hemingway is known to have owned," a much different and more definable task than speculating on what he may have read. Because Brasch and Sigman are interested in what Hemingway "owned," they exclude books that he may have read or known about; also excluded are periodicals, newspapers, and books mentioned in his works or letters unless it can be proved that he actually owned them. Their volume is "A Composite Record" because it lists books that were located in different places at different times, for example, in his Key West house, and, most importantly, in the library of about six thousand items that is still housed in his Cuban home, the Finca Vigía (for more about that library, see Brasch and Sigman, *FHA,* 1978). The records of these libraries plus their other sources are carefully discussed in their introduction and yield an inventory of 7,368 items for which the title, author, date and place of publication, and source are given, when possible. Their introduction also includes a well-documented discussion of Hemingway's reading habits, his passion for information, his literary pronouncements, and the importance of all of this for our conception of Hemingway as a writer. It is a fascinating essay whose serious tone and careful scholarship establish the value and honesty of their work.

II EDITIONS

There is not much to report on new work by Hemingway and even less on new editions of his already published work. We can add to the list of Hemingway's works a collection of poetry, an essay on the short story, two facsimile editions, one anthology, two new editions of his journalism, several new short stories, and one novel. The collection of poetry is the first authorized edition of Hemingway's poetry, compiled, edited, and annotated by Nicholas Gerogiannis under the title *88 Poems* (New York, 1979; reissued in paperback in 1983 as *Complete Poems*, Lincoln, Nebr.). Gathering together the poems from nine editions, as well as from other sources, Gerogiannis arranges them into four sections according to their probable dates of composition from "Juvenilia 1912–1917" to "Farewells 1944–1956." Elucidating the poems' many topical references, analogues, and background are twenty-six pages of "Explanatory Notes." No editorial apparatus is included; it was published separately (*FHA*, 1979). Gerogiannis provides an informative and intelligent introduction in which he looks back over the whole development of Hemingway's poetry from the short, hard, imagistic poems written in Paris to the long, loosely structured ones of his last period. For a good discussion of the poems' technique, see Judson Jerome's review in *Writer's Digest* (Aug. 1985).

A long, loosely structured, and "painfully self-revealing" piece of prose that Hemingway wrote in May 1959 was not published until 1981 in the *Paris Review* (Spring 1981). Intended as the preface to a student's edition of his more popular short stories, "The Art of the Short Story" proved to be so unsuitable that the whole project was dropped. Assuming the guise of a tough Old Vet lecturing a group of simple-minded and effete young college students, addressed sarcastically as "Gentlemen" and "Jack," Hemingway discourses at length in a very anecdotal and uninformed way that reveals a lot but says very little. In spite of Erik Nakjavani's recent effort to see this essay as "an important text for Hemingway scholarship inasmuch as in it Hemingway deals extensively and for the last time with his theory of omission" (*HR*, Spring 1984), it remains an embarrassing aberration of Hemingway's declining years that amply confirms the picture Philip Young has painted of him (most emphatically in "Hemingway: The Writer in Decline" [Noble]).

In 1977 Bruccoli Clark books published exact facsimile editions, right down to their covers, of Hemingway's first two books, *Three Stories & Ten Poems* (1923) and *in our time* (1924). Although some may wonder why such facsimiles should be published, or purchased, it is a rare delight for a teacher of Hemingway, as well as a visible thrill for his students, to touch such rare books, even if only in facsimile.

Until very recently Scribner's has been content simply to republish Hemingway's fiction untouched or to provide badly made anthologies. *The Enduring Hemingway: An Anthology of a Lifetime of Literature* (New York, 1974), edited with an introduction by Charles Scribner, Jr. simply reprints extracts from Hemingway's major works that follow the course of his life from Paris to Cuba. The only previously uncollected extract is "Miss Mary's Lion" reprinted directly from *Sports Illustrated* (it is the middle part of three articles published by that magazine in 1971–72 under the title *African Journal*). In another Scribner's anthology, *Ernest Hemingway On Writing* (New York, 1984), Larry W. Phillips has collected everything Hemingway said on the subject of writing, cut it out, and then pasted it all together under thirteen very general headings with no comment, no analysis, and no index.

Scribner's focus on Hemingway's well-known and therefore endlessly marketable fiction has seemed unnecessarily limited since hidden away in crumbling and often mutilated periodicals are still uncollected pieces of fiction and nonfiction that should be saved from the dust and put into the public domain. There are, for example, such uncollected short stories as his fable for children "The Faithful Bull," published in *Holiday* (Mar. 1951) and ably discussed by Kenneth G. Johnston (*FHA*, 1977), as well as "Two Tales of Darkness," published in *Atlantic* (Nov. 1951) and discussed at length by Delbert E. Wylder (Astro and Benson). Although Gene Z. Hanrahan (*The Wild Years* [1962]) and William White (*By-Line: Ernest Hemingway* [1957]) have provided us with useful collections, the great mass of Hemingway's nonfiction remains half-submerged in semi-underground publications like Margaret Calien Lewis's M.A. thesis (University of Louisville, 1969) that reprints all twenty-eight of his NANA dispatches "available here and nowhere else," as William White notes in his enthusiastic review (*HN*, Fall 1980); and like the *Uncollected Prose of Ernest Hemingway* (ed. Clinton S. Burhans, Jr., East Lansing, Mich., 1968) that was used extensively by William E. Coté in his keen evaluation of Hemingway's skill as a reporter in "For Whom the Bell Blooms: Hemingway's Spanish Civil War Reporting," in *Up In Michigan* (ed. Joseph J. Waldmeir, East Lansing, Mich., 1983; hereinafter referred to as Waldmeir).

Two signs that Scribner's has finally seen some value in Hemingway's nonfiction are their publication of *Dateline: Toronto—Hemingway's Complete "Toronto Star" Dispatches, 1920–1924* (ed. William White, New York, 1985) and of a new version of *The Dangerous Summer* (New York, 1985). The old version of the latter, edited out of a manuscript of 120,000 words by A. E. Hotchner, appeared in *Life* (5, 12, and 19 Sept. 1960); this one, edited by Michael Pietsch of Scribner's, consists of 45,000 words, and it sounds, on the whole, like very good late Hemingway. For William Kennedy, who wrote a useful review in the *New York Times Book Review* (9 June 1985), *The Dangerous Summer* is "one of the best sports books that I have ever read," even though he, like most other Americans, does not care for bullfighting. Among the many new things unearthed by Peter Griffin for his biography, *Along with Youth: Hemingway, the Early Years* (New York, 1985), are five previously unpublished short stories—"Crossroads," "The Mercenaries," "The Ash-Heel's Tendon," "The Current," and "Portrait of the Idealist in Love"—that Griffin places within Hemingway's steady growth as an artist and comments on with a good deal of insight.

Hemingway's latest novel, *The Garden of Eden* (New York, 1986), edited out of 1,500 pages of manuscript by Tom Jenks of Scribner's, has stimulated a good deal of controversy. In spite of John Updike's view that "the book, as finally presented, is something of a miracle, a fresh slant on the old magic" that "adds to the canon not merely another volume but a new reading of Hemingway's sensibility" (*NYer*, 30 June 1986), many have found the book badly wanting. In her much-quoted *Rolling Stone* review (5 June 1986) Lorian Hemingway, Gregory's daughter, boldly asserts that "the novel is as dead as the man. It is not just bad, but god-awful" because the story is boring, the details repetitive, and the characters "mucked up," i.e., poor blends of several different people. Much less quoted but more interesting are her claims that the book is not about bisexuality but is "a writer's last grasping after his former powers over the distractions and indulgences life offers" and that the character of Catherine owes a lot to Zelda Fitzgerald. After comparing Jenks's edition to Hemingway's manuscripts, Barbara Probst Solomon concludes (*NR*, 9 Mar. 1987) that "Hemingway's publisher has committed a literary crime" by playing up youth, blonding, and bisexuality, by radically simplifying the plot, and by excising allusions to Rodin, Bosch, and Proust that added layers of meaning that are lost in Jenks's version. Like Lorian Hemingway, Solomon finds hints of Zelda in Catherine but unlike her contends that the novel "was to have been nothing less than Ernest Hemingway's final summation on art and literature, on the nature of love and the body, on the possibilities of human life." High praise indeed for writing that Carlos Baker found "emptily hedonistic."

Unlike Scribner's, which publishes and markets his fiction, those who teach and study Hemingway want revised, if not annotated, editions of his works because they have found numerous errors in them. Some of these are quite trivial, some rather important, and some have achieved the lofty status of cruxes. Among the nonsubstantive accidentals are two misprints, later corrected, found by William White in *Winner Take Nothing* (*PBSA*, Third Quarter 1978) and in *A Farewell to Arms* (*PBSA*, Fourth Quarter 1979); among the more important substantives are two found in "Summer People" by Peter M. Griffin: the omission of about eleven lines of manuscript from the printed text and the important misprint of "slut" for the manuscript's "Stut," one of the recognized nicknames of Kate, and a play on "Butstein," another one (*AL*, Nov. 1978).

Another kind of textual problem, which has stimulated two articles and mention in two German Ph.D. dissertations, concerns two anachronisms and the confused internal time scheme in *The Sun Also Rises*. In his careful review of the problem and its literature, Wayne Kvam argues that the three days left out between the Paris and Pamplona sections of the novel are not so much a "flaw" in its structure, as Kermit Vanderbilt would have it (*TCL*, Oct. 1969), but rather an oversight that could be corrected, if one chose to do so, with "three one-word corrections" (*PLL*, Spring 1979). Although important enough to attract the attention of two Germans, the chronology of *Sun* does not rank as The Great Crux of Hemingway Studies. This honor belongs to the attribution of the waiters' speeches in "A Clean, Well-Lighted Place," a problem that has by now stimulated well over a score of articles. The best place to begin is with George H. Thomson's "'A Clean, Well-Lighted Place': Interpreting the Original Text" (*HR*, Spring 1983). The clarity and calm with which Thomson surveys the history of the controversy, sorting out the opposing sides in his very full documentation, indicates that one should begin with him and then work backwards through the maze of arguments. Before doing that, however, one should carefully note Thomson's own conclusion: "The evidence is not sufficient to make a conclusive determination. It is possible, however, to entertain a preference based on one's general interpretation of the story."

We may conclude this section on editions with two papers that favor revision and one that does not. After surveying a number of the textual problems in *Farewell* and several short stories, Scott Donaldson calls for "a definitive edition of Hemingway's prose" that would use "the manuscripts at the Kennedy Library as an invaluable source of information" (*HN*, Spring 1981). In the same year, Michael S. Reynolds examines the textual problems in *Sun* and *Farewell*, and then takes the more extreme position that "the question is not *should* there be a standard Hemingway text, but *when* will it be edited" (*HN*, Spring 1981; the emphasis is Reynolds's). In response to Donaldson's and Reynolds's call for a corrected, standard text, free of errors, Robert E. Gajdusek stoutly defends most of the so-called errors as aesthetically justifiable (*HR*, Fall 1981). Gajdusek, who apparently believes the Master never nodded, advances some very clever arguments for the aesthetic value of certain errors, e.g., his discussion of *Sun*'s bothersome time scheme is particularly inventive, but not very convincing. His objections are well taken, however, since cleaning up Hemingway's texts with a view to establishing a critically acceptable standard text is by no means as simple as it may seem at first glance.

III   MANUSCRIPTS AND LETTERS

Two important moves were made in the late 1970s that changed the basic direction of Hemingway Studies. They were Mary Hemingway's decisions to open her husband's collected papers to the public and to allow his letters to be published. Although both of these courageous and generous decisions are equally important, the first has probably had more impact on the field since it played a great part in the move away from exegesis to background studies that has recently characterized the academic study of Ernest Hemingway's works.

Although the Hemingway Collection was opened to the public in 1975, its official beginning is dated 18 July 1980, with the establishment of its permanent home in the John F. Kennedy Library. This opening was the occasion for two other events of some importance: the unofficial beginning of the Hemingway Society and the organization of a three-day conference devoted to Hemingway's papers. The papers presented at the conference, whose theme was "The Papers of a Writer: Ernest Hemingway," were first published in a special issue of *College Literature* (Fall 1980), a journal edited by Bernard Oldsey, and then again in a book with the same title and editor (New York, 1981). Oldsey's book is a faithful reproduction of the journal issue except for the addition of an introduction by the editor and one small title change.

As Jo August tells us in her brief history of the Hemingway Collection (Oldsey), its nucleus was the papers Mary Hemingway had stored in her bank vault in New York. It was these papers that Philip Young and Charles W. Mann described in *The Hemingway Manuscripts: An Inventory* (1969), and that Philip Young discussed in "Locked in the Vault" (1972). The ever-growing collection was shipped "in boxes, trunks, filing cabinets, and shopping bags" to the Federal Archives and Records Center in Waltham, Massachusetts, where it was opened to the public in January 1975. It was, however, just barely usable there because of the center's inaccessibility and the sorry condition of the papers. Aaron Latham has given us a vivid description of what it was like in Waltham in his rather sensationally titled article "A Farewell to Machismo: Revelations from Hemingway's Unpublished Novels and Notebooks" (*NYTM*, 16 Oct. 1977). Finally, the collection, now carefully preserved and catalogued, reached its present home in the Hemingway Room of the Kennedy Library at Crown Point, a slightly more accessible location than Waltham. But, as Michael S. Reynolds pointed out in his conference paper, the Hemingway collection with "its drafts, typescripts, fragments, letters, and pictures" was still by no means easy to get at and use (Oldsey). One needed a map. Such a map was supplied in 1982 by Jo August who compiled and edited a two-volume *Catalog of the Ernest Hemingway Collection at the John F. Kennedy Library* (Boston). Volume 1 of the *Catalog* inventories the collection's manuscripts, outgoing correspondence, and incoming correspondence A-L; volume 2 catalogues incoming correspondence M-Z, photographs, newspaper clippings, and other materials. The *Catalog* lists everything that was acquired up to September 1981 and will be updated with supplements (there was one dated 5 Jan. 1982); it is an invaluable guide to an extremely complex collection.

Among the more important articles making use of the Hemingway papers is Charles W. Mann's publication of F. Scott Fitzgerald's critique of *Farewell* with extensive notes and commentary (*FHA*, 1976). This critique, which Hemingway very emphatically rejected, complements the one Fitzgerald made of *Sun* (in a letter) that he willingly accepted, as his excision of the original beginning of that novel indicates. Both Hemingway's original beginning and Fitzgerald's letter were published in *Antaeus* (Spring 1979). The letter was also published with valuable background material by Matthew Bruccoli in his *Scott and Ernest: The Authority of Failure and the Authority of Success* (New York, 1978) and by Philip Young and Charles Mann (*FHA*, 1970). Another article making excellent critical use of unpublished material is Scott Donaldson's careful examination of the drafts for "A Canary for One" (*SAF*, Autumn 1978). One year after Donaldson's article, Warren Bennett tried to use the manuscripts to crack the famous "Clean, Well-Lighted Place" crux (*AL*, Jan. 1979), but then David Kerner looked at the way Hemingway typically pointed his dialogue to come up with data that cast serious doubt on Bennett's conclusions (*FHA*, 1979). What this suggests is that while the study of early drafts may be useful in some cases, it is not the universal panacea for the really hard problems.

As one might expect, Oldsey's collection celebrating the opening of the Hemingway Collection includes several essays which make use of that collection. Oldsey himself analyzes the ways in which "Big Two-Hearted River" ends and "Indian Camp" and "Macomber" begin by comparing the versions that were rejected to those that were accepted. In the same collection, Scott Donaldson makes skillful use of the papers to study Hemingway's work at the *Toronto Daily Star*. Of particular interest are two unpublished items: a Hemingway interview with Clemenceau the *Star* refused to publish because of the Old Tiger's views on Canada and a typescript fragment in which Hemingway compared a "'real reporter' to a photographic plate." Jacqueline Tavernier-Courbin casts a very skeptical Gallic eye on the well-publicized but poorly documented "discovery" of the Ritz Hotel Papers. In another essay she discusses the manuscripts of *A Moveable Feast* to find that they support her earlier skepticism (*HN*, Spring 1981); and then, on yet another occasion, she makes an exhaustive description of all the Paris notebooks housed in the Kennedy Library (*HR*, Fall 1981).

One of the more unique and well-publicized items to come out of the Hemingway Collection was the discovery by William B. Watson of the English original of a news story about Spain that had appeared in *Pravda* on 1 August 1938. The English original appeared for the first time in the *Chicago Tribune* (29 Nov. 1982) as well as in several other newspapers around the country. In 1983, Kathryn Derounian examined four different drafts of *In Our Time*'s all-important "Chapter VI," showing how Hemingway gradually achieved clarity and compression as he moved from the earliest draft to the printed version (*PBSA*, First Quarter 1983; reprinted in *Critical Essays on Ernest Hemingway's "In Our Time"* [CEAmL, ed.

Michael S. Reynolds, Boston, 1983; hereinafter referred to as Reynolds]). The reprint omits the facsimiles of the four drafts. Derounian's article is carefully done but lacks the critical interest of Donaldson's "Canary" study because no interpretation of "Chapter VI" is offered; as a result, we see the revisions but not their point. Much the same thing could be said of Robert W. Lewis's careful study of "The Making of *Death in the Afternoon*," in *Ernest Hemingway: The Writer in Context* (ed. James Nagel, Madison, Wis., 1984: hereinafter referred to as Nagel). After giving us an excellent account of the text's evolution as well as the history of the manuscript, Lewis describes in some detail the many layers of revisions, additions, and deletions that produced the printed text. One misses, however, any statement as to what it all means beyond the not unexpected conclusion that "tracing this book's growth is tracing a part of Hemingway's esthetic process."

It is the presence of such an informing idea, i.e., of a hypothesis, that makes three recent articles by Paul Smith so critically interesting. In a paper written especially for Reynolds's collection, Smith uses a careful analysis of the structure, background, and revisions of "Out of Season" to argue that much more is left out of that story than Peduzzi's suicide. Also omitted is the imminent break-up of the young couple which in turn hints at the break-up of Ernest and Hadley. In his contribution to Nagel's volume, Smith again uses a structural analysis combined with the study of three versions of the conclusion of "Ten Indians" to establish a link between Nick and his father as men without women so that Nick's father is, as much as Nick, a man with "a broken heart," one of the rejected titles of the story. Lying behind these two specific analyses is a general interest in Hemingway's theory of omission, an interest that surfaces in Smith's third article, "Hemingway's Early Manuscripts: The Theory and Practice of Omission" (*JML*, June 1983). He first surveys Hemingway's explicit discussions of his theory of omission and then studies its practice in the way he revised "The Killers," "Big Two-Hearted River," and "Up in Michigan." What Hemingway's revisions indicate, not surprisingly, is that he was a better practitioner than theoretician so that if we want to know what he really meant by omission, we need to analyze the ways he revised those crucial stories written between 1922 and 1926.

We conclude our survey of the uses made of Hemingway's papers at about the same place where it began, with the work of Michael S. Reynolds. In "Looking Backward," the introduction to his collection of essays on *In Our Time*, Reynolds produces a real *tour de force* of basic research. Surveying Hemingway's earliest writing, Reynolds draws almost exclusively on unpublished letters and manuscripts housed for the most part in the Kennedy Library. It is a fascinating account of Hemingway's progress from a callow young man who wrote well-made stories with "WOW" endings to the artist who wrote stories in which "Much was left out, much implied," stories that changed our conception of the genre itself.

In addition to having the pluck to open her husband's unpublished papers to the public, Mary Hemingway also had the strength to have his letters published against his clear and unambiguous wishes. As Carlos Baker points out in his edition of Hemingway's *Selected Letters: 1917–1961* (New York, 1981), Mary Hemingway decided in May 1979 to go against her husband's wishes (expressed in 1958) because she could not recall the letters that had already been published nor police attempts at new publication. Accordingly, she called upon Carlos Baker, Hemingway's biographer, to select and edit Hemingway's letters. Baker's edition is a selection of six hundred of the estimated six or seven thousand that Hemingway wrote during the sixty-two years of his lifetime. The criterion of selection used was simply "the interest and value of the contents." Baker's *Selected Letters* is an invaluable addition to Hemingway scholarship, since, as Robert W. Lewis points out in his review (*HR*, Fall 1981), it is, in effect, not only Hemingway's autobiography but also the longest book that he ever wrote. Lewis's idea was shared by several other reviewers, as Delbert E. Wylder indicates in his excellent survey of the critical reaction to Baker's book (*HR*, Fall 1983).

One reason the publication of the letters was generally greeted with enthusiasm is that before it was done, scholars had to search them out in all sorts of odd corners and then, when they were found, they could not be quoted directly but had to be paraphrased. Among these odd places were auction catalogues and exhibitions. As Jackson R. Bryer pointed out in his review (*AmLS*, 1973), such an apparently unpromising book as *Hemingway at Auction 1930–1973*, compiled by Matthew J. Bruccoli and C. E. Frazer Clark, Jr. (Detroit, 1973), a collection of pages reproduced from sixty auction sales and fifty-nine dealers' catalogues, was actually "a mine of information for future scholars" because it provided "the most extensive detailed information we will ever have about Hemingway letters." Fortunately, that is no longer the case even though the book's reproductions of letters, original covers, and signed dedications still make it a fascinating volume for even the noncollector to look at. Just as fascinating for its excellent facsimiles of letters, manuscripts, and inscriptions is the catalogue of an exhibition held at the University of Virginia Library, December 1977–March 1978, that is syncretistically entitled *Fiestas, Moveable Feasts and "Many Fêtes" in their Time: 1920–1940* (Bloomfield Hills, Mich., and Columbia, S.C., 1977). An even more out-of-the-way discovery was the letter, translated into German, that Hans-Joachim Kann found published in the East German journal *Heute und Morgen* (3 Aug. 1948). Kann reproduced the German text and then translated it into English with some annotations (*FHA*, 1976). Luckily, we no longer have to be satisfied with Kann's translation since Wayne

Kvam was able to acquire a transcript of the original English text written in late August 1940, which he published with an extensive commentary on Hans Kahle, its recipient (*HR*, Spring 1983).

Just as the opening of Hemingway's papers initiated a new wave of scholarly research, so the possibility of quoting his letters directly, with the permission of Mrs. Hemingway or her lawyer, stimulated a number of studies based on his correspondence. For example, at the Kennedy Library conference in 1980, E. R. Hagemann (Oldsey) discussed two batches of letters; one, from Hemingway to his family, covered the period from 6 December 1917 to 11 December 1918; the other, between Hemingway and Ezra Pound, covered the period 1922–24. What strikes Hagemann most about the letters to his family from Italy is their carefree attitudes toward war as a kind of exciting game and the complete lack of those negative attitudes that so animate his fiction. As for the letters exchanged with Ezra Pound, they indicate that he was the first and perhaps only man that Hemingway could ever confide in. Hagemann appends a useful "Calendar of Letters" to his article that enumerates the history of each letter as completely as possible. In a similar fashion, Scott Donaldson uses the published and unpublished letters exchanged between John Dos Passos and Hemingway to chart the ups and downs of that literary friendship (Waldmeir).

The tide of studies based on letters crested in 1982 when one article in the *Hemingway Review* and three papers given at a conference in Boston derived their findings almost exclusively from unpublished letters. In his study of the letters Hemingway wrote to his sister Madelaine "Sunny" Hemingway Miller, Michael Culver discovers evidence for attributing two articles published in the *Kansas City Star* and *Times* to Hemingway. The two pieces, published 5 December 1917 and 26 January 1918, are included in Culver's essay (*HR*, Fall 1982). The Boston Conference, "Ernest Hemingway: The Writer in Context," was organized by James Nagel, who edited the papers into a book with the same title (Madison, Wis., 1984; hereinafter referred to as Nagel). In one paper, Max Westbrook uses the extensive collection of letters exchanged among the members of Hemingway's family (none of them, however, to or from Ernest) that is now owned by the University of Texas to examine the crucial events that lead to Ernest being "kicked out" of the family. What Westbrook finds is that the whole matter is much more complex than Hemingway chose to present it, and that Ernest's father comes off as rather weak, wavering, and self-pitying. Westbrook, who is preparing a book on the Hemingway papers at Texas, clearly is at ease with his material and uses it to very good effect. James Brasch, another scholar who knows the correspondence well and is preparing a book of the letters exchanged between Hemingway and Malcolm Cowley, discusses that correspondence under the heading "Invention from Knowledge" (Nagel). Focusing primarily, but not exclusively, on that theme, Brasch tried to determine what Hemingway meant by "invention" and by "knowledge." Perhaps more interesting than this weighty problem are the side issues that emerge from the letters, such as why Hemingway disliked biography, the role Cowley played in the editing of Philip Young's book, and Hemingway's attitude toward F. Scott Fitzgerald. In her paper on Hemingway and Pound (Nagel), Jacqueline Tavernier-Courbin provides one of the reasons why the two had the long and close relationship that Hagemann noted in his study of the two men's letters. It was because of Pound's humorous tact in dealing with the younger man's very large ego; only Pound could criticize Hemingway's work and still survive as Ernest's "pore ole uncle."

IV BIOGRAPHY

More than twenty years after his death, the name and face of Ernest Hemingway still command attention. One consequence of this lasting appeal is a mass of books and articles focusing on Hemingway the man and the legend rather than on what he wrote. In this survey of biographical work we shall begin with what those who knew him have to report and conclude with those books and articles that try to interpret what it all means.

The immediate family has been very busy supplying us with information about its famous kinsman. Three of Hemingway's five siblings have written books about him, all of his three children have discussed him, and three of his four wives have said something about him in print. To these family reports we must also add two others: the extended comments made by Agnes Von Kurowsky, his nurse and fantasy mistress, and the book written by Adriana Ivancich, the Venetian girl who became his favorite, but by no means last, adopted "daughter."

Of the "Sibling Biographies" (Philip Young's term in *Three Bags Full* [1972]), the first and best is *At the Hemingways: A Family Portrait* (1962) by Marcelline Hemingway Sanford, his oldest sister and pseudo-twin; the second is *My Brother, Ernest Hemingway* (1962) by Leicester Hemingway, his younger brother by some sixteen years who committed suicide on 14 September 1982 at the age of sixty-seven; the third and least is *Ernie: Hemingway's Sister "Sunny" Remembers* (New York, 1975) by Madelaine Hemingway Miller, his third sister and favorite family member. Mrs. Miller, who is probably the model for Helen, Harold Krebs's favorite sister in "Soldier's Home," and for Littless, Nick's favorite sister in "The Last Good Country," has written a very anecdotal and rather unfactual book that requires one to know a great deal about the Hemingway family before he can get very much out of it. It is, in fact, little more than "an illustrated literary valentine" that has been "lovingly contrived" by a "worshipful little sister," as Robert Traver very cagily suggests in his preface to the book. Traver quite correctly puts the emphasis on "illustrated" since the pictures of Ernest's early days, up to his wedding to Hadley (which Sunny did not attend because she "had been sent to camp in Minnesota"), are by far the most informative and accurate parts of the book. To keep all of these siblings apart and in order, one may want to consult the brief "Hemingway Genealogy" compiled by Sterling S. Sanford (*FHA*, 1978).

Hemingway's three sons have all had something to say about their famous father. The first contribution was made by Dr. Gregory (Gigi) Hemingway, the youngest son by Pauline Pfeiffer, his second wife. Gregory Hemingway's *Papa: A Personal Memoir* (New York, 1976) reveals how difficult it was to be the son of an overwhelming personality like Ernest Hemingway, but tells us little new about his father as a man or a writer. Gregory's book is much more about his troubled life and difficult relationship with his father than it is about Ernest Hemingway; viewed that way, it is a very honest, if not very important book. The memories of Patrick Hemingway (Nagel), the older of his two sons by Pauline, are quite different from his brother's. Recalling his days as a crewman on the Pilar during its sub-hunting days, a period dubbed "Don Quixote vs the Wolf Pack" by Gregory, Patrick remembers them as an endless round of fun with a good deal of time spent shooting flying-fish with a .22 and blowing up sea turtles with hand grenades. Concerned with the difference between fact and fiction, Patrick points out that Gregory never hooked a huge marlin nor was he ever menaced by a shark, as Hemingway told it in *Islands in the Stream*; on the contrary, Patrick believes that the shark incident was based on a children's story by Tolstoy, the title of which he does not reveal. (For more information about Patrick, see Scott Eyman's interview in *Sunshine*, 3 Mar. 1985.)

The latest and longest filial memoir is by Papa's eldest, John Hadley Nicanor Hemingway, also known as Bumby and Schatz, but who calls himself Jack. Jack, the father of the two actresses Mariel and Margaux (known to him as Margot), recounts his life in *Misadventures of a Fly Fisherman* (Dallas, 1986), a pleasant book that is quite accurately subtitled "My Life With and Without Papa" because he does indeed devote much more space to his own wayward life than to his rather infrequent encounters with his father. Accordingly, Jack tells us little new about his old man and only gets interesting in the afterword where he is against Mary Hemingway and Carlos Baker's biography but strongly for A. E. Hotchner's picture of his father and Tom Jenks's version of *The Garden of Eden*. It is no surprise that the fun-loving Jack, who has failed in a number of ill-conceived business ventures, should favor Hotchner and Jenks because, according to the *Wall Street Journal* (18 July 1986), he has recently formed "Hemingway Ltd., which will market the family name for use on products including shotguns, fishing rods, jogging suits and sunglasses. The first item is a $975 English-style double-barreled shotgun. Given this line of goods, it is little wonder that Lorian Hemingway roundly condemned "the business of selling Hemingway 'product'—a business now bordering on necrophagia" (*Rolling Stone*, 5 June 1986).

As one might expect, Hemingway's wives have had more to say about their very demanding husband than his sons. His first and last wives have written books; his third wife broke her silence about him just once, and then quite unwillingly; and Pauline, his second and unluckiest wife, published nothing about the man who abandoned Hadley for her and then her for Martha Gellhorn. The book that Alice Sokoloff wrote with Hadley Richardson Hemingway's help, *Hadley: The First Mrs. Hemingway* (New York, 1973), reminds one of Sunny's book. Full of rather loosely connected anecdotes and undigested details about her very sheltered upbringing, her wooing in Chicago, and her early married life in Paris, the book tells us very little about Hadley, her husband, or their rather complex relationship. As Gertrude M. White put it in her review, "Mrs. Sokoloff had a splendid chance to produce something memorable, and muffed it" (*HN*, Fall 1973).

Far more substantial is Mary Hemingway's *How It Was* (New York, 1976), the autobiography of Hemingway's fourth and last wife. Mary Welsh Hemingway was a clever, capable, and hard-working journalist who left an excellent career and exciting life to become Hemingway's rather badly treated housekeeper, typist, hostess, and nursemaid in such backwaters as San Francisco de Paula and Ketchum, Idaho. Perhaps in an effort to recapture her lost identity, Mrs. Hemingway does not begin with their meeting in London in 1944 nor end it with his death; instead, she goes back to her own happy days with her father as a girl in Minnesota and concludes in 1975, several years after her husband's suicide. The picture we get of Hemingway from her book is of a very difficult and rather spoiled man who became much worse as he grew older. So over-whelmed was Mrs. Hemingway by her husband's difficult ways and by her household chores that we hear very little about his writing or his work routine. It is a book full of details about their everyday, outer life, but has little insight into their inner life of feelings and emotions.

Unlike Mary Hemingway, who says a lot about the man but very little about the writer, Martha Gellhorn, his third and probably most mal-treated wife, had nothing to say at all until she finally broke her silence in response to certain "apocryphal" stories that Stephen Spender and Lillian Hellman had written about her, stories they had almost certainly gotten from Ernest himself. Gellhorn's response to Spender (*ParR*, Spring 1981) is so vehement that one is startled to find that his rather offhand remarks amount to only two pages in a very long interview (*ParR*, Winter–Spring 1980). Gellhorn is certainly overreacting and doing it in so much detail that one quickly loses track of the principal issues. In her extended peroration she does, however, make quite clear what she was reacting against. As she says, Hemingway "was a genius, that un-easy word, not so much in what he wrote . . . as in how he wrote; he liberated our written language. All writers, after him, owe Hemingway a debt for their freedom whether the debt is acknowledged or not. It is sad that the man's handmade falsehoods—worthless junk, demeaning to the writer's reputation—survive him." This is remarkably generous and perceptive from a woman who had suffered enormously at the hands of a man who she notes had "a fair amount of hyena in him."

We cannot leave Hemingway's wives without noting what two of his "other women" said about him. In preparation for *Hemingway's First War* (Princeton, N.J., 1976), Michael S. Reynolds conducted a six-hour taped interview with Mrs. William Stanfield, née Agnes Von Kurowsky, the woman whom many believe to be the model for Catherine Barkley in *A Farewell to Arms*. Reynolds's edited transcript of the interview (*FHA*, 1979) shows him to be a good questioner who pursues a topic with tactful persistence so that the transcript, along with several pictures not included in his book, give us a fairly complete picture of who Agnes was, that is, a very capable, self-possessed woman who bears little resemblance to Hemingway's fantasy mistress.

Like several of Hemingway's wives, Agnes was several years older than Ernest and so had enough maturity to survive her brush with him. Adriana Ivancich, on the other hand, was many years younger than Hemingway when they met in December 1948 (she was eighteen, he forty-nine), and so was less able to deal with his ambivalent attentions and the publicity that made her the model of Renata, the nineteen-year-old mistress of the fifty-year-old Colonel Cantwell in *Across the River and into the Trees* (1950; but not published until 1964 in Italy): Adriana hung herself in April 1983 at the age of fifty-three (*Hn*, July 1983). In 1980, however, she was still flattered enough by the attention she had gotten to record the story of her relationship with Hemingway in *La Torre Bianca* (Milan). Her book has not yet been translated into English; but, as Valerie Meyers informs us in her very knowledgeable review (*HR*, Fall 1983), Adriana's book traces her acquaintance with Ernest from December 1948 to April 1954 and is a "self-regarding, impressionistic book" that is an expanded version of an article she wrote for *Epoca*, an Italian photo-news magazine, in July 1965 under the provocative title "La Renata di Hemingway sono io" (I am Hemingway's Renata). In spite of these defects, the book is biographically important, Meyers concludes, for the self-portrait it gives of Hemingway's "last and true love" and for its picture of the author as he crossed into his fifties. Those two pictures are neither very happy nor exciting since the letters from Hemingway that Adriana publishes, extracts in Italian and undated, make, we are told, "boring and embarrassing reading"; as for Adriana, her ambivalent relationship with Hemingway and Renata left her feeling guilty, ill-at-ease in her own society, and, in the end, estranged from the man who had thrust her into the limelight.

In addition to these relatives, wives, and women who knew Hemingway quite well, many others who crossed his path have felt it worthwhile to report what happened when their lives were touched by Papa. It is staggering to realize that anyone who had the slightest contact with Hemingway felt it worth recording: like Harold Krebs Friend who told Fred Bliss in 1943 that Hemingway owed him money (*FHA*, 1975); like Eduardo Zayas-Bazan who interviewed three of his Cuban friends (*FHA*, 1975); like the distinguished South American novelist Gabriel García Márquez who wrote a brief essay about his three-word exchange with Hemingway in 1957 (*NYTBR*, 26 July 1981); and like his high school friends and teachers who went over yet again their well-worn souvenirs in *Ernest Hemingway: As Recalled by His High School Contemporaries* (Oak Park, Ill., 1973).

Of more value than these brief and fading encounters are the accounts of those who met him in Paris in the 1920s. Hemingway's tempestuous friendship with F. Scott Fitzgerald is the subject of *Scott and Ernest: The Authority of Failure and the Authority of Success* (New York, 1978) by Matthew J. Bruccoli, Fitzgerald's biographer, editor, and collector. As one might expect from a scholar so devoted to Fitzgerald, Bruccoli spends a good deal of time debunking Hemingway's many fabrications about his friend. As with all of Bruccoli's books, this one is overflowing with chronologically arranged facts but is rather thin on interpretation. Perhaps the most surprising of Bruccoli's very rare general observations is that "Neither Hemingway nor Fitzgerald influenced the other's writing." Given the intensity of the relationship between these two very gifted and competitive men, one would be surprised if this were the case, and two articles have suggested that it may not be. In "Hemingway and Fitzgerald" (Astro and Benson), Peter L. Hays adduces very specific evidence that T. S. Eliot's *The Waste Land* (1922) influenced *The Great Gatsby* (1925) and that both of them influenced *The Sun Also Rises* (1926). Somewhat less convincing is T. Jeff Evans's argument that Fitzgerald parodied the earth-moved love scene of *Bell* in *The Last Tycoon* (*AN&Q*, Apr. 1979).

Another writer who met Hemingway in Paris was Nathan Asch. Reviewing Asch's memoirs and letters, Eva Mills concludes that he, like many others, "loved, hated, envied, admired, and respected Ernest Hemingway" (*HR*, Spring 1983). Even though Henry (Mike) Strater's remarks about Hemingway were made some time ago (*Art in America*, No. 6, 1961), they are worth mentioning because not only does he comment on the origins of his three portraits (two in Paris, one in Key West), he also makes several very perceptive remarks about their subject's tough-guy persona that made him dislike his own fair skin: Hemingway wanted to be dark-skinned and so kept himself deeply tanned. A similar interest in the smallest facts about Hemingway's life in Paris encouraged Robert Crozier to locate the church where Pauline and Ernest were married by searching out their marriage registration form (*PLL*, Winter 1979).

Several other people besides Stephen Spender had vivid encounters with Hemingway in Spain. In *Distant Obligations: Modern Writers and Foreign Causes* (New York, 1983), David C. Duke carefully reviews the friendship between Hemingway and John Dos Passos that fell apart because of Hemingway's brutal attitude toward the killing of Dos Passos's friend José Robles. Strangely enough, Duke does not mention the admittedly very sly allusion to Dos Passos in the last section of *A Moveable Feast*; fortunately, Scott Donaldson discusses the allusion and its maliciousness in the paper mentioned above (Waldmeir). Edward F. Stanton tells us about a less famous Spanish friend, Dr. Juan Madinaveitia, who met Ernest in 1937 and then treated his various ailments for several years afterwards (*HR*, Fall 1981). The very length of José Luis Castillo-Puche's *Hemingway in Spain* (New York, 1974) argues that he was one of Hemingway's most intimate Spanish friends; and, in fact, he apparently knew him fairly well from 1953 to 1960. But the highly personal, very anecdotal, and rather unfactual style of his book suggests that his intimacy may well be inflated. Anglo-Saxon attitudes toward Latin writing come out very clearly in Kenneth Rosen's report on the reactions of ten Spanish writers to Hemingway's death. Rosen finds their reactions "eulogistic, of course, but expressed in a very romantic, personal and often mythic manner" that saw Hemingway's suicide as "existential" and "macho" (*BNYPL*, Spring 1974).

As he grew older and sicker, Hemingway became more subject to violent changes in mood, as two generally sympathetic observers report. While in Cuba to interview Hemingway about the craft of writing, George Plimpton recalls that in the midst of telling the Hemingways at lunch about his very brief bout with Archie Moore, Ernest got up and challenged him to fight "while Miss Mary picked at her salad" (Oldsey). Charles Scribner, Jr., another very sympathetic witness, recalls that while Hemingway was always very serious, practical, and professional in his letters, he could become quite boorish in public (Nagel). On one occasion, as Scribner and his wife were waiting to see him off on an ocean trip, Hemingway suddenly burst into the cabin with a crowd of people "and the air turned blue with four-letter words and Hemingwayisms."

This sharp contrast between the serious writer and the foul-mouthed performer that so clearly upset Charles Scribner helps explain the radically differing pictures we get of this very changeable man. The Hemingway who discoursed so seriously on the craft of writing with Malcolm Cowley in the letters discussed by Brasch (Nagel) is sharply at odds with the one presented in A. E. Hotchner's memoir of Hemingway's later years. Hotchner's original book *Papa Hemingway: A Personal Memoir* (1966) was reissued as a 1983 paperback with a new title, *Papa Heming-*

way: The Ecstasy and Sorrow (New York), and with the promise that it was a "New Edition with previously unpublished material." There is, in fact, nothing new about Hemingway in the book; the only addition is a "Postscript" that continues Hotchner's feud with Mary Hemingway and tries to pay back Philip Young for his wittily devastating review, "On Dismembering Hemingway" (*AtM*, Aug. 1966; reprinted in his *Three Bags Full* [1972]). Privy to Papa's "true gen," Hotchner clearly believes that he, rather than "Younger dunger," as Hemingway called Young, should be "The Great Hemingway Authority." Quite the opposite is the case with Arnold Samuelson, the author of *With Hemingway: A Year in Key West and Cuba* (New York, 1984). Even though he spent only about one year (1935) as Hemingway's factotum, Samuelson composed a three-hundred-page manuscript about his experience that his daughter, Diane Samuelson Darby, discovered after his death in 1981 and published. Of the many reminiscences about Hemingway, Samuelson's is one of the few that captures the man, as a person and as a writer. The latter is particularly striking since Hemingway actually talked to Samuelson about writing, something he rarely did with anyone else, as we see all too well in Norberto Fuentes's *Hemingway in Cuba* (Secaucus, N.J., 1984). In his attempt to discover "what the Hemingway of Cuba was really like," Fuentes relies mostly on interviews with the Cubans who knew him, a technique that produces a lot of rather trivial gossip about the great man—he kept a lucky stone in his pocket, wore no underwear, was always combing his hair, etc. Although such stuff is fascinating in its own small way, of much more value are the excellent pictures of the Finca, an inventory of its contents, and the sixty-one letters reproduced in "Appendix I: The Finca Vigía Papers." The book is a fascinating collection of trivia that fails to capture a sense of the man as a writer.

All the people mentioned above, except Fuentes, had met Hemingway and come, therefore, under the spell of his forceful personality; all the writers we shall consider next never met him and had, therefore, a better chance to achieve some perspective on the man and his deeds. Carlos Baker never met Ernest Hemingway, but assembled so many facts about him in *Ernest Hemingway: A Life Story* (1969) that we probably know more about "Ernie" than we do about our own friends. But this virtue also contributes to the book's often-noted defect—the absence of an interpretation to organize the facts into a narrative that would engage the reader's interest. (For a fairly recent discussion of his book that also surveys its reviews, see Dennis W. Petrie, *Ultimately Fiction: Design in Modern American Literary Biography*, West Lafayette, Ind., 1981.) And, perhaps, even Baker felt this defect since he offers an interpretation in *Individual and Community* (ed. Kenneth H. Baldwin and David Kirby, Durham, N.C., 1975). According to Baker, Hemingway's strong point was his "empirical imagination," that is, the external factual basis of his fiction, but starting in 1954, he began turning away from this external, factual base, and started producing softened and sentimentalized works in which he tried to justify himself to the world. One appreciates the dangers of making such general statements about a man's life when we are told by James T. McCartin (*ArQ*, Summer 1983) that what prevented Hemingway from maturing was his lack of introspection and disinterest in criticism.

Another attempt at interpretation is made by Scott Donaldson in *By Force of Will: The Life and Art of Ernest Hemingway* (New York, 1977). Donaldson wants to find out "what Ernest Hemingway thought on a variety of subjects" in order "to construct a mosaic of his mind and personality, of the sort of man he was." The division of his subject into thirteen chapters labeled "Fame, Money, Sex, Art, Mastery, Death," etc., certainly does create a "mosaic," but, unfortunately, the thirteen discrete pieces never completely jell into a unified picture of this very complex man. Even though he does produce a number of striking insights absent in Baker, Donaldson's topical approach tends to fragment the object it seeks to describe. In the same year that Donaldson's book appeared, Richard E. Hardy and John G. Cull, two psychological counselors, provided us with "a transactional analysis" in *Hemingway: A Psychological Portrait* (Sherman Oaks, Calif., 1977). Although one might shrug off the absence of footnotes, bibliography, or index in a paperback clearly intended for a popular audience, one cannot forgive the string of errors that mar its opening pages. All of this tempts one to dismiss the book without a second thought; nevertheless, the "Psychological Evaluation" that concludes it is worth looking at for some of its very basic but still rather perceptive comments.

The year 1978 produced two interesting picture biographies. Peter Buckley, dubbed "our dear semi-giant friend" by Mary Hemingway, had access to her collection of over 10,000 photographs while assembling his big picture book, *Ernest* (New York, 1978). Buckley, who also used many of his own pictures, has an extremely keen eye and has selected some of the most evocative pictures ever published. His seventy-five-page summary of Hemingway's life is, however, much less original. The second of the two 1978 picture books, *Ernest Hemingway and His World* (New York), is certainly as interesting for its text as for its pictures, since the former is written with great verve and insight by the British writer Anthony Burgess. Burgess is especially sharp about small but very telling details, and this, plus his extremely able survey of Hemingway's life, as well as the excellent pictures (many never published before), make Burgess's book the best short introduction to the American writer's life.

The years 1985–86 produced three very long accounts of Hemingway's life. Jeffrey Meyers's *Hemingway: A Biography* (New York, 1985) adds a number of small new facts as well as noting some interesting recurrent patterns, whereas Peter Griffin's *Along with Youth: Hemingway, the Early*

Years (New York, 1985) not only produces a lot of new material—letters by Hadley and his friend Bill Horne, five new short stories, and very strong evidence that Ernest's affair with Agnes Von Kurowsky was much more than a fantasy—but also attempts to create the atmosphere of Hemingway's early years as well as a sympathetic portrayal of the man. In a similar way, Michael Reynolds in *The Young Hemingway* (New York, 1986) makes extensive use of letters and contemporary newspaper accounts to recreate the feel of Hemingway's life up to 1921. For a perspective on these three biographies, one should read Jackson R. Bryer's review (*Novel*, Spring 1986) and then compare it to James Campbell's (*TLS*, 1 Aug. 1986) and Wilfrid Sheed's (*NYRB*, 12 June 1986).

It is a pleasure to conclude this survey of books about Hemingway's life with two that make a genuine contribution to our understanding of the man and his legend. The first is Bernice Kert's *The Hemingway Women* (New York, 1983); the second is John Raeburn's *Fame Became of Him: Hemingway as Public Writer* (Bloomington, Ind., 1984). Kert has written a well-researched book (she makes great use of unpublished letters and papers) that gives us the perspective and understanding of Hemingway's women that is so notably lacking in their own accounts. When we compare their first-hand reports to Kert's book, we find that her treatment of the same material is usually more complete and informative; moreover, she provides accounts of several women, Pauline Pfeiffer, Martha Gellhorn, and Jane Mason, that are quite new. We learn that there was much more to Ernest's relationship with Pauline than his interest in her money or her desire for a famous husband. And we hear, for the first time, about Hemingway's affair with Jane Mason, a beautiful but suicidal and accident-prone socialite who contributed a great deal to his portrayals of Margot Macomber and Helène Bradley. Kert is also very informative about Martha Gellhorn who was, before she met Hemingway in Sloppy Joe's, a distinguished writer, an intimate of Mrs. Eleanor Roosevelt, and the author of a book, *The Trouble I've Seen* (1936), that had made her something of a celebrity. We can easily assess just how good Kert's book is by comparing it to the section on Hemingway's wives in Jeffrey Meyers's *Married to Genius* (London, 1977). There, all of Baker's facts are simply rehashed with a strong anti-Hemingway bias that produces no new insights or observations—for example, Pauline is, as usual, "predatory."

Although not strictly speaking a biography, Raeburn's *Fame Became of Him* is another important contribution to our understanding of Hemingway's life. Raeburn's subject is Hemingway the public writer, the celebrity, and the media culture hero, not his real life or his work; accordingly, he draws upon a mass of popular journalism, from photo-quizzes and squibs in gossip columns to features in magazines like *Sports Illustrated*, *Astrology: Your Daily Horoscope*, *Wisdom*, etc., that most of us ignore, in order to describe the way Hemingway was pictured in the popular imagination. Raeburn concludes with the observation that "there seems to have been an inverse relationship between the growth of Hemingway's celebrity and the quality and quantity of his fiction" and that the turning point appeared in "The Snows of Kilimanjaro." Like Harry in that story, Hemingway "'traded' on his talent and 'sold vitality' without maintaining an emotional connection with its product"; after this story, Hemingway never again faced in his fiction "the consequences for a writer of pursuing ends other than his art."

In addition to the kind of popular journalism Raeburn studied, the movies have also played an enormous role in nurturing the Hemingway myth. As Robert W. Lewis puts it, "Hollywood has interposed between the literature of a writer and his work rather monstrously" (*HN*, Spring 1981). The precise nature of this interposition, among other things, is the subject of two books about Hemingway and the movies, Gene D. Phillips's *Hemingway and Film* (New York, 1980) and Frank M. Laurence's *Hemingway and the Movies* (Jackson, Miss., 1981). While both authors systematically study the differences between Hemingway's works and the fifteen movies made of them, Laurence emphasizes the mythologizing process in his chapters, "The Hemingway Hero as a Hollywood Star" and "The Ernest Hemingway Story" (as retold by Hollywood). The problem of translating Hemingway's work into films is the subject of three essays in *The Modern American Novel and the Movies*, edited by Gerald Peary and Roger Shatzkin (New York, 1978): by William Rothman, about *To Have and Have Not*; by Constance Pohl, about *Bell*; and by Robert Nadeau, about *The Old Man and the Sea*. The same two editors produced a similar book, *The Classic American Novel and the Movies* (New York, 1977), in which William Horrigan discusses the differences between *Farewell* and Frank Borzage's 1932 film version of it.

Having discussed the books and articles that attempt a general interpretation of Hemingway's life and times, we may now turn to those more specialized works that concentrate on a specific period or aspect of his life. In preparation for his "larger study of Hemingway's quarrel with androgyny" (*Hn*, Jan. 1984), Mark Spilka has published two studies on "Victorian Keys to the Early Hemingway" that attempt a revised view of Grace Hall Hemingway by taking a feminist viewpoint on the values of the post-Victorian genteel tradition. Spilka's first Victorian key (*JML*, Mar. 1983) is Dinah Mulock Craik's novel, *John Halifax, Gentleman* (1856), which helped crystallize Grace Hemingway's notion of manliness as that of a financially successful Christian gentleman, qualities she admired in her very British father, Ernest (Abba) Hall, and discovered, in its more muscular American form, in her husband Clarence Edmonds (Ed) Hemingway.

Spilka's second Victorian key is another bestselling novel by a woman, *Little Lord Fauntleroy*, written by Frances Hodgson Burnett in 1886. Again, this novel defines genteel British values that Grace actualized by dressing her two oldest children in Fauntleroy outfits, values that were again counterbalanced by American frontier attitudes that surfaced in pictures of Ernest dressed up like Huck Finn—barefoot, ragged pants, and straw hat. Spilka concludes that the true golden age of Hemingway's imagination, the one that he tried to recapture in his later fiction, was that "androgynous happiness of the Fauntleroy phase of childhood . . . when Grace and Clarence and their children lived with 'Abba' Hall in genteel harmony" (*JML*, June 1983).

After graduating from high school, Hemingway did not go to college but to Kansas City where his paternal Uncle Tyler Hemingway used his friendship with Henry J. Haskell to get him a job on the *Kansas City Star*, as Dale Wilson tells us (*FHA*, 1976). As for Uncle Tyler, Martin Staples Shockley discovered that he married into wealth and then wrote a short success manual with a very long title, *How to Make Good . . .* (1915), that preached, among other things, the evils of tobacco and alcohol (*FHA*, 1977).

In addition to Michael S. Reynolds's book on *Farewell* that includes biographical information, most of it on Agnes Von Kurowsky, Peter Stine has surveyed the impact of World War I on Hemingway, using insights from Paul Fussell's *The Great War and Modern Memory* (New York, 1975), to make what is essentially a Youngian analysis of his life and fiction (*FHA*, 1979). Two less ambitious works have searched out and republished original material about Hemingway's war experiences. C. E. Frazer Clark, Jr. reprints with some discussion four documents that report Hemingway's wounding. The first two, dated 1918, are from Red Cross records; the third is an article published in Hemingway's hometown newspaper the *Oak Parker*, dated 1 February 1919; the fourth is from his high school newspaper the *Trapeze*, dated 21 March 1919 (*FHA*, 1974). After a rather long lead-in discussing his own stay in Italy and the difficulties of sorting out fact from fiction, Robert W. Lewis eventually produces two new documents: the official Italian citations authorizing Hemingway's two medals: he got *la Croce al Merito di Guerra* ("the War Cross of Merit") for being in action and *la Medaglia D'Argento al V.M.* ("the Silver Medal of Military Valor") for being wounded. Lewis also presents evidence that G. M. Trevelyan's *Scenes from Italy's War* (1919) was a source for *Farewell* (*JML*, May 1982).

In addition to the paper by Donaldson mentioned above (Oldsey), two others have discussed Hemingway's life in Toronto. Relying for the most part on the recollections of Gregory Clark, a former feature editor for the *Toronto Star Weekly*, Richard Winslow summarizes the details of Hemingway's stay from the invitation by the Ralph Connables to take care of their son to his quick departure from an apartment on which he still owed three months' rent (*FHA*, 1977). Winslow also provides a very complete bibliography of Hemingway's Toronto period. Quite a bit longer but much less informative is David Donnell's *Hemingway in*

Toronto: A Post-Modern Tribute (Windsor, Canada, 1982). As Donnell's title suggests, his sixty-one-page booklet is a very impressionistic tour of the well-known facts without benefit of footnotes or bibliography. There are, however, some evocative pictures of Toronto in the 1920s. Hemingway's skills as a reporter are reviewed with a very cold eye by William E. Coté who reminds us that Ernest had no formal training as a journalist and that his full-time experience amounted to about three years before he went to Spain (Waldmeir). Turning to his Spanish Civil War reporting, Coté finds, with a good deal of support from Phillip Knightley's *The First Casualty: From the Crimea to Vietnam: The War Correspondent as Hero, Propagandist, and Myth Maker* (New York, 1975), that Hemingway was a very poor reporter. He made things up, suppressed certain others, and, in the final analysis, used the Spanish Civil War, as Knightley saw it, "to gain a new lease on his life as a writer," an act that "for a novelist, . . . was understandable. For a war correspondent, it was unforgiveable."

Hemingway's early days in Europe have generally attracted more attention than his rather brief stays in Kansas City and Toronto. Robert E. Gajdusek's *Hemingway in Paris* (New York, 1978) collects pictures of the Paris places mentioned in Hemingway's works and associated with his life. George Wickes, a man who knows Paris and the 1920s very well, exposes many of the distortions Hemingway made about himself and others in *A Moveable Feast*. Wickes concludes that Hemingway had essentially "Rotarian" values that clashed with the bohemian style of life he encountered in Paris (Astro and Benson). The evidence that Wickes provides for his conclusion is far more convincing than Zvonimir Radeljkovic's unsupported assertion that Hemingway's European experience turned him away from the "post-Puritan, neo-Victorian" values of his homeland (Oldsey). Still in Paris, Richard Layman (*FHA*, 1975) and Noel Fitch (*FHA*, 1977) discuss Hemingway's reading by analyzing the library cards he used at Sylvia Beach's Shakespeare and Company (Brasch and Sigman do not include these titles in *Hemingway's Library* because he never owned them; Reynolds does include them in *Hemingway's Reading*). Lawrence Martin ponders what Gertrude Stein meant when she declared "Up in Michigan" to be *inaccrochable* and discovers that what she meant was that the story was "unpublishable" (*HN*, Spring 1981).

Even though we associate Ernest Hemingway the author most closely with Paris because of *The Sun Also Rises* and *A Moveable Feast*, Hemingway the man actually travelled all over Europe. He went quite regularly to Switzerland as Hans Schmid reminds us in an article with some excellent pictures (*FHA*, 1978), and at least once to Berlin in 1931, we are told by Wayne Kvam, to attend the opening of *Kat*, a play by Carl Zuckmayer and Heinz Hilpert based on *A Farewell to Arms*. Hemingway arrived drunk, fell asleep during the performance and acted like an "American hillbilly" (*PMLA*, Jan. 1976).

Hemingway's associations with the American West have been documented by Lloyd Arnold in *Hemingway: High on the Wild* (New York, 1977). As Carlos Baker points out in his review (*FHA*, 1978), this book, a reset and reduced issue of Arnold's *High on the Wild with Hemingway: A Pictoral Recollection* (1968), is "the most authoritative account of the time Hemingway spent in and around Ketchum and Sun Valley in the period 1939–1961." Those who open Arnold's book will find excellent, sometimes embarrassingly candid pictures, and a text that is almost unreadable. In 1975, Richard Winslow took a sentimental journey back to Lawrence Nordquist's L-T ranch where Hemingway worked in the 1930s (*FHA*), and John Unrue interviewed Forrest (Duke) MacMullen, one of Hemingway's hunting companions, who declared many of Hotchner's stories "distorted" (*FHA*, 1978).

Although this concludes our survey of the biographical work on Hemingway, it is by no means the end of the unquenchable interest in the story of his life. In addition to books forthcoming on the early Hemingway by Mark Spilka and Frank Scafella, James R. Mellow is preparing a popular biography, Peter Griffin and Michael Reynolds are planning second volumes, and Kenneth S. Lynn's *Hemingway: The Life and the Work* is announced for July 1987. Is this Hemingophilia or necrophagia?

V CRITICISM

1 Full-length Studies

Among the twenty-three critical books written between 1973 and 1986, there are three general surveys of the traditional sort, fifteen that take a definable critical stance on several of Hemingway's works, and five that concentrate on one specific work. Samuel Shaw's *Ernest Hemingway* (MLM, New York, 1973; reprinted 1982) is the traditional kind of popular survey that rarely wins much praise because it has to retell all the well-known facts in an uncomplicated way. And, while few of Shaw's facts are misleading and none of his interpretations very new or exciting, he does make several perceptive comments about Hemingway's style, arguing that the oft-quoted steamed-ants speech sounds more like Hemingway than Frederic Henry. This is a very perceptive remark since Hemingway apparently lifted this image from Harold Loeb's *The Professors Like Vodka* (New York, 1927), as Arthur Waldhorn discovered (*HR*, Fall 1982). If Shaw's book just passes muster, then James Barger's *Ernest Hemingway: American Literary Giant* (Charlottesville, N.Y., 1975) fails. It is a superficial and inaccurate addition to a series on "Outstanding Personalities" that numbered some eighty-four titles in 1975 and included studies of such worthies as James Hoffa, Spiro Agnew, and Wanda Gag. Just as bad is the survey chapter that Stewart F. Sanderson contributed to *20th Century American Literature* (ed. Warren French, London, 1980).

According to Sanderson, who wrote the short survey book *Ernest Hemingway* (1961), Hemingway was a member of the Italian Arditi and a reporter for the Hearst papers in Paris. Far and away the most solid new general survey is Scott Donaldson's *By Force of Will* (1977), already mentioned under Biography. As Earl Rovit noted in his review (*FHA*, 1978), Donaldson's book is a "vaguely old-fashioned literary biography" because interspersed among anecdotes, gossip, and the hard facts about Hemingway's life are "illustrative explications of most of Hemingway's significant stories."

Turning to books that organize their facts and insights around an argument, we may begin with Lawrence R. Broer's *Hemingway's Spanish Tragedy* (University, Ala., 1973). This short book continues an interest in the Hemingway hero, the code, and the fusion of his life and fiction that goes back to Philip Young's influential 1952 book. Broer's new wrinkle is to divide Hemingway's heroes into two groups based on their relationship to Spanish values. The early pre-Spanish heroes, like Nick Adams and Jake Barnes, were passive, trapped, and frustrated men who ran away from trouble; the later heroes, like Harry Morgan and Richard Cantwell, were aggressive, rebellious men who had been influenced by such uniquely Spanish values as *particularismo*, an intense individualism that rejects authority and the rights of others; *senequismo*, a belief in one's own will to power; and *pundonor*, pride, dignity, courage, defiance, and honor. Broer concludes that while these values may well have contributed to Hemingway's art, his idealization of these "forces of extreme, anarchistic individualism and primitive aggression" that disrupted Spanish culture also caused "a similar disintegration in both his person and in his art." In the same year that Broer published his book, Sheldon N. Grebstein reacted against its Youngian approach in *Hemingway's Craft* (Carbondale, Ill., 1973), a book that concentrates on Hemingway's craftsmanship, saying nothing at all about his life, the hero, or the code. In a very carefully defined approach, Grebstein surveys the stylistic devices and structural patterns that reappear throughout Hemingway's works rather than analyzing each work as a whole. Grebstein's section on style and method is exceptional because it discusses style in a precise but nontechnical way that linguistic analyses are quite incapable of doing. His analyses of "Chapter IX" of *In Our Time*, El Sordo's shooting of the Fascist captain, and the influence of Cézanne are full of insight and are fascinating. The book ends with a discussion of the manuscripts of *Farewell* and *Bell* that was way ahead of its time. For all of its virtues, Grebstein's formalistic approach does not seem to have had much direct influence; Young's biographical approach has had much more, perhaps because Grebstein's insights all seem so obvious and universal, as Robert W. Lewis suggests in his review (*HN*, Spring 1973), but such fundamental patterns always do seem obvious after someone has had the eyes to see them and the wit to bring them to our attention.

Two important books published by Linda W. Wagner in the mid-1970s continue the interest in technique that animated Grebstein. The first, *Ernest Hemingway: Five Decades of Criticism* (noticed below), is a collection of reprinted essays by others that focuses on Hemingway's craftsmanship; the second, *Hemingway and Faulkner: Inventors/Masters* (Metuchen, N.J., 1975), assembles several of her own essays on the same topic; one of these, "The Place of *To Have and Have Not*," had not been published elsewhere. The point of view that unites her own essays is Wagner's overriding concern with Hemingway as an Imagist: from her first chapter that discusses Pound's influence to her last one that analyzes *The Old Man and The Sea* as a prose poem, Wagner argues that Hemingway is fundamentally a prose Imagist. This basic concern has by no means slackened since, in a second collection of her essays, *American Modern: Essays in Fiction and Poetry* (Port Washington, N.Y., 1980), she selects one, "The Poetry in American Fiction," that discusses the Imagistic devices in the styles of Faulkner, Dos Passos, and Hemingway. Although Wagner herself would certainly agree that there is more to Hemingway's style than Imagism, her single-minded dedication to this particular feature of his work, as well as the theory underlying it, has made an invaluable contribution to our understanding of his craftsmanship.

Similarly, J. F. Kobler's *Ernest Hemingway: Journalist and Artist* (Ann Arbor, Mich., 1985), a revision of his 1968 dissertation, is a serious analysis of Hemingway's fiction, nonfiction, and journalism that seeks "to determine precisely where and how the three kinds of writing are different or similar in three basic areas: content, ideas, and style." Under content, Kobler analyzes the ways in which such thematic areas as "manly sports, including war," luck, art, love, etc. are handled in the factual writing and fiction; under ideas he considers the ways in which Hemingway's politics appear in the two kinds of writing; and, under style, clearly the factual heart of the book, he makes very detailed comparisons of the ways such things as different ethnic speech styles, punctuation, grammar, and word selection are handled.

The vices and virtues of a simple thesis reveal themselves in Sarah P. Unfried's *Man's Place in the Natural Order: A Study of Hemingway's Major Works* (New York, 1976). Depending on a large number of direct quotations from other critics and rather simple plot summaries, Unfried organizes her book around a very neat little scheme: *The Nick Adams Stories* showed their author's growing awareness of chaos and order in the world, *Sun* revealed an increasing tension between them, *Farewell* was a descent into chaos, but there was a sharp upturn in *Bell* where we see the integration of the ideal man into the cosmic order of universal brotherhood. If Unfried's thesis is too narrow, Raymond Nelson's key notion in *Hemingway: Expressionist Artist* (Ames, Iowa, 1979) is stretched too far. Nelson takes the position that Hemingway's basic themes, images, and stylistic elements are "Expressionistic"; but one must note that

Nelson has extended this term to mean all the modernist modes—
"fauvism, cubism, dadaism, surrealism, futurism, abstractionism, and
many others." Nelson's analysis of Hemingway's Expressionism includes anything and everything modernist and thus loses its power to
discriminate or classify in a meaningful way. Moreover, none of these
characteristics is necessarily or peculiarly modern since every one of
these so-called "modernist" themes, images, and stylistic elements appear, to give just one example, in the family sagas of medieval Icelandic
literature.

A similar problem weakens the analytical power of "tragic" in Wirt
Williams's *The Tragic Art of Ernest Hemingway* (Baton Rouge, La., 1981).
Williams first defines tragedy rather loosely as a "field" or range of
possibilities that have "the tragic philosophy, the irreversible catastrophe, the stunning impact," but not necessarily transcendence and
reconciliation since "they are not indispensable to all tragedy. The irreversible catastrophe is." He then proceeds to locate all of Hemingway's
work within this field. For example, *In Our Time* is deemed "subtragic"
because its stories are too small for "the stunning impact"; but since
Williams feels this impact in *Sun*, well aware that most others do not,
he classifies it as tragic. Although *Farewell* has neither transcendence
nor reconciliation, it too is tragic because it is all catastrophe and thus
has impact. Part of this impact comes from the use of rain as a "king
image" of doom in "a massive war." As for *Bell*, it is one of Hemingway's
greatest tragedies because its hero wins a spiritual victory "in his terminal
catastrophe"; the bridge is the nemesis. Discussing all of the works in
this special way, Williams concludes that Hemingway's "real novels are
all tragedies. So are a few of the stories" and that "when critical vision
is no longer even partially blocked by his public persona . . . another
generation may decide he was one of the century's greatest makers of
tragedy." Few would agree.

Gerry Brenner's *Concealments in Hemingway's Works* (Columbus, Ohio,
1983) is a dedicated Freudian analysis of Hemingway's novels whose
systematic point of view conceals Brenner's true critical skills. Starting
from the fundamental assumption that Hemingway was concealing the
ambivalent desire to kill/save his father, Brenner's analyses are generally
suggestive and effective until he lets Freud loose on the later works and
we enter a dream world where things lose their shape. At one point in
the discussion of *The Old Man and the Sea*, the marlin becomes a father
figure, a phallus, and *la belle dame sans merci*. In spite of his polymorphous
marlin and dubious hovering presence Brenner makes a real contribution
when he unearths unlikely influences and makes generic analyses; unfortunately, the book's strong points have been subverted by an extreme
commitment to Freud, a rather outdated and overly Anglo-Saxon Freud
at that. For a much subtler, if rather covert use of the new Freud, see
Millicent Bell's paper, "*A Farewell to Arms*: Pseudoautobiography and

Personal Metaphor" (Nagel), which will be discussed below. Brenner also has collaborated with Earl Rovit to produce a revised edition of Rovit's 1963 study of Hemingway in the Twayne's United States Authors Series (Boston, 1986).

The first of three books that turn out to be more interesting than their titles suggest is Roger Whitlow's *Cassandra's Daughters: The Women in Hemingway* (Westport, Conn., 1984) which takes a pro-Hemingway stance in the debate over Hemingway's treatment of female characters in his fiction. Responding to those critics who dichotomize his female characters into "passive sex kittens" and "bitches," Whitlow analyzes the several examples of the first group, Marie Morgan, Maria, Renata, to find that they "reject the death-seeking mentality" of their heroes, men who give "their energies—and often their lives—for inflated or manufactured causes," to offer instead "life-affirming" alternatives. Whitlow also finds a lot of good in such famous bitches as Brett, Mrs. Macomber, Harry's wife in "Snows," and Dorothy Bridges. After a similar kind of redemptive analysis of Hemingway's minor female characters, Whitlow concludes that our fascination with his violence has lured us away from considering each work on its own merits and attempting to see his women for what they really are in each work. Just as interesting in a different way is Larry E. Grimes's *The Religious Design of Hemingway's Early Fiction* (Ann Arbor, Mich., 1985), because it discusses how Hemingway's early fiction is patterned by its relationship to the fifth dimension of sacred time. Grimes's notion of time and its role in Hemingway's work may usefully be compared to Wilma Garcia's chapter in her *Mothers and Others: Myths of the Female in the Works of Melville, Twain, and Hemingway* (New York, 1984). And, finally, Gregory S. Sojka analyzes "Hemingway's angling aesthetic as a moral philosophy" in his *Ernest Hemingway: The Angler as Artist* (New York, 1985).

UMI Research Press of Ann Arbor, Michigan, has published, or will soon publish, no fewer than seven full-length critical studies on Hemingway's work. In addition to Kobler's and Grimes's books mentioned above, they have issued Harriet Fellner's *Hemingway as Playwright: "The Fifth Column"* (1986), a well-researched study of Hemingway's only play that carefully distinguishes the printed text from the produced play and evaluates the critical reaction to both; Myler Wilkinson's *Hemingway and Turgenev: The Nature of Literary Influence* (1986), which uses Harold Bloom's model of influence to evaluate the Russian's influence on the American; and Angel Capellán's *Hemingway and the Hispanic World* (1985), a wide-ranging and solidly researched book that uses both Spanish and English sources to discuss the influence of Spanish landscape, notions of the hero and his quest, bullfighting, tragic sense of life, and language and literature on Hemingway's work. Scheduled to appear are Susan F. Beegel's *Hemingway's Craft of Omission: Four Manuscript Examples* (1988), a study of what he left out of "Fifty Grand," "A Natural History of the Dead," "After the Storm," and *Death in the Afternoon*; and Stephen Cooper's *The Politics of Ernest Hemingway* (1987), an analysis of how his lifelong interest in politics relates to several of his recurrent themes. Also scheduled to appear in 1987 under another imprint is Kenneth G. Johnston's *The Tip of the Iceberg: Hemingway and the Short Story* (Greenwood, Fla.).

Even though only works in English are discussed in this report, an exception must be made for Geneviève Hily-Mane's *Le Style de Ernest Hemingway: La Plume et le Masque* (Paris, 1983), because it addresses what most agree to be the essence of Hemingway's achievement—his style. As Valerie Meyers points out in her review (*MFS*, Winter 1983), this 350-page revision of a seven hundred-page thesis for the Doctorat d'État is "virtually a compendium of previous scholarship on Hemingway's style." Meyers goes on to note that the book marshals all of its analytical devices and linguistic insights "to arrive at a conventional interpretation of 'The Short Happy Life of Francis Macomber.'" Meyers's last comment suggests that this book is another one of those complex linguistic analyses that construct an elaborate machine which then produces nothing very new. But this is not really the case since there are no elaborate charts, no tree diagrams, and no tables of statistics in the book; moreover, linguistic analyses are not designed to produce new insights, but rather to verify in a systematic and detailed way those of critics. The book deserves and requires careful study.

There are five new critical books on specific works of Hemingway's fiction: two on *Farewell*, one each on *Sun* and *The Nick Adams Stories*, and a collection of essays on *In Our Time*. Joseph Flora's *Hemingway's Nick Adams* (Baton Rouge, La., 1982) is the most traditional of the five, providing straightforward readings of the stories divided into six groups according to Nick Adams's growth from "Boyhood" to "Father and Son." And while this may sound like Philip Young's *Reconsideration* revisited, Flora sees Nick Adams as an artist whose stories compose a fragmented "work in progress" that moves "from loss or trauma to recovery and fortification." Flora's Nick Adams is therefore not a permanently traumatized Hemingway hero whose problems directly reflect those of his creator. This unusually positive attitude, one that invariably chooses to put "the best interpretation" on a character's actions, has several strong points and some weak ones. Flora's readings often lapse into simple retellings that generally ignore imagery, symbolic implications, and, above all, the dark, ironic depths of the stories. On the other hand, he is very alert to the subtle links between the stories, to Hemingway's name play (which may be derived from Sheridan Baker's 1967 book), and to such external echoes as the Gaby Delys/Gatsby allusions in "A Way You'll Never Be" and the A. E. Housman echoes in "Big Two-Hearted River."

Even though it is something of an embarrassment to have two books on *Farewell* published within three years of one another, they actually complement one another fairly well. As noted above, Michael S. Reynolds has an almost evangelical commitment to background and manuscript studies that eschews with some scorn the "exegetical game," "imposed patterns" versus "inherent" ones, and "the misleading thesis that Hemingway is always his own protagonist." All of these attitudes, repeated many times again, appear for the first time in *Hemingway's First War: The Making of "A Farewell to Arms"* (Princeton, N.J., 1976). In a concerted effort to put his principles into practice, Reynolds divides his book into three sections that move systematically from data and facts to interpretation. Reynolds's unflagging commitment to facts provides us with several excellent maps and pictures (he worked out the routes of Frederic Henry's retreat from Caporetto and the long row from Stresa to Switzerland), but it also lures him into awkward and illogical critical positions. When his researches into the early drafts of *Farewell* indicate that its five-book division was not Hemingway's but written into the galleys by someone else, Reynolds concludes that "the book divisions were not a controlling factor in the structure of the novel"; but then in his own analysis of *Farewell*'s structure, he argues that "not only has each of the five books its own piece of action, but each book takes place in the season most appropriate to the action." More examples of this kind of odd logic could be given, but what they would demonstrate is what most reviewers of *Hemingway's First War* have already seen: that, as Jeffrey Meyers puts it, "Reynolds' scholarship is superior to his criticism" (*Criticism*, Summer 1977); see also Charles L. Nolan's valuable summary of critical reactions in *Review* (1980).

Like Reynolds, Bernard Oldsey spent a great deal of time in the Kennedy Library's Hemingway Collection looking at early drafts of *Farewell*, but the main concern of *Hemingway's Hidden Craft: The Writing of "A Farewell to Arms"* (University Park, Pa., 1979) centers on how beginnings, endings, and titles function in a work of fiction. Oldsey discusses the narrative implications of the novel's several beginnings (among them a fourteen-page manuscript in the Hemingway Collection that Reynolds missed) and its forty-one conclusions. Both discussions are excellent because Oldsey does not seek one true answer but explores instead the critical implications of a range of possible answers.

Read the subtitle of Frederic Svoboda's *Hemingway and "The Sun Also Rises": The Crafting of a Style* (Lawrence, Kans., 1983) carefully because it means just exactly what it says. The book analyzes in great detail how Hemingway transformed the first draft of *Sun* into "a completely realized fictional whole"; it does not, however, offer a description of that whole nor an interpretation of its meaning. Svoboda's book is a very capable discussion of the crafting of Hemingway's style. Its weak points are very casual documentation and an outdated bibliography.

2 Collections

Michael S. Reynolds has edited *Critical Essays on Ernest Hemingway's "In Our Time"* (CEAmL, Boston, 1983), a collection of ten reviews, twenty-seven reprints, and three original essays on *in our time* (1924) and *In Our Time* (1925). The customary essay on Hemingway's life is supplied by Reynolds's introduction, "Looking Backward," but there is no bibliographical checklist. Including Reynolds's book, we now have eight collections of essays on six works by Hemingway: two on *Farewell*, two on *Sun*, and one each on *Old Man, Bell, In Our Time,* and the two African stories.

Of the four books using reviews to assess Hemingway's immediate critical reputation, only two will interest most readers. Frank L. Ryan's brief monograph, *The Immediate Critical Reception of Ernest Hemingway* (Washington, D.C., 1980), eliminates itself immediately because it summarizes reviews and is full of errors (see Scott Donaldson's review in *AmLS*, 1980, and Donald Daiker's in *HR*, Spring 1983). Much more substantial, but still of less interest to most American readers, is Wayne Kvam's *Hemingway in Germany: The Fiction, the Legend, and the Critics* (Athens, Ohio, 1973). After two fascinating chapters on American literature in Germany, the book becomes, in Jackson R. Bryer's words, a series of "summaries of German reviews and articles . . . with little or no effort at weeding out redundancy or providing interpretation" (*AmLS*, 1973). This is particularly true of Kvam's "Epilogue" that summarizes German criticism from 1965 to 1971, but less so of the very brief concluding chapter that tries to determine why Hemingway's German reputation is so different from what it is here—the big three novels in Germany are *Old Man, Bell,* and *Across* in that order (for a review that attempts to assess the value of such cross-cultural reputation studies, see Ward L. Miner [*HN*, Spring 1974]).

Of the two most important review collections, *Ernest Hemingway: The Critical Reception* (ed. Robert O. Stephens, New York, 1977) acknowledges the inspiration of Roger Asselineau's 1965 collection, *The Literary Reputation of Hemingway in Europe*, "as a model," whereas the second, *Hemingway: The Critical Heritage* (ed. Jeffrey Meyers, London, 1982), makes only passing mention of Asselineau and none at all of Stephens. The focus of Stephens's book is on shorter reviews in American newspapers and middle-brow periodicals that he treats in three ways: some are listed, a few are summarized, but the majority are reprinted in their entirety. Using this method and narrow double columns, Stephens is able to reprint 380 reviews of Hemingway's twenty-four major books; in contrast, Meyers reprints longer, more ambitious reviews in both British and American journals so that his collection includes only 122 reviews. Meyers does, however, give a brief sketch of each reviewer, annotates his reviews, and provides a handy analytical table of contents that gives, under each book reviewed, the author of the review, its source, and its date. Both editors precede their collections with long introductory essays. In his twenty-seven-page introduction, Stephens attempts to chart the ups and downs of Hemingway's career, a map that is also a mirror of the critics' preoccupations. Meyers's sixty-two-page introduction is somewhat more complicated. Preceding his survey of the reviews with a sketch of Hemingway's life, a brief discussion of his career, and a few remarks on his influence, Meyers summarizes the reviews of each book rather than attempting the kind of synoptic overview of Hemingway's career that Stephens provides. The two books complement one another because the selection and the approach of each is significantly different from the other, and different in ways that tend to reflect the differing critical values of the editors.

The differences between the critical attitudes of British and Americans and the effect they had on Hemingway's reputation in the two countries has been the subject of a valuable essay and the primary theme of two collections of essays. One year before his book of reviews was published, Stephens gave a paper at the 1976 Tuscaloosa Hemingway conference (Noble) on the differences between American and British responses to Hemingway. What he found was that American critics saw Hemingway as "the white hope in American eyes" who wrote in a tough, new style that was authentically American. Given this attitude, Americans tended to concentrate on his success, or lack of it, as a novelist rather than looking at his entire body of work. British critics, having no such patriotic stake in his career, accepted all of his work *in toto* and saw him, instead, as a man of letters who wrote in many different genres. In a "Special British Issue" of the *Hemingway Review* (Spring 1982), three items present the British attitude toward Hemingway quite explicitly. As noted above, Graham Clarke compiled a bibliography of Hemingway's publications in Britain, reviews of them, and critical articles, books, and essays devoted to them. Looking at this material and then back to D. S. R. Welland's "Hemingway's English Reputation" (1965), Moira Monteith surveys the changes that took place in British criticism between that essay and Clarke's bibliography. Returning the compliment with a twist, Andrew Gibson discusses Hemingway's attitudes toward the British in both his fiction and nonfiction, with particular emphasis on the generally neglected *Colliers* dispatches that were written while he was in England.

The second collection of essays exemplifies rather than analyzes the fundamental differences between American and British critical attitudes. It is A. Robert Lee's *Ernest Hemingway: New Critical Essays* (Totowa, N.J., 1983; hereinafter referred to as Lee), a collection of ten new essays, seven by British scholars and three by Americans. David Seed sorts out the links between the stories and vignettes of *In Our Time* very effectively, compares the techniques of the Adrianople vignette to Goya, and connects the six cabinet ministers vignette to Ezra Pound's poem "Liu Ch'e."

Turning to the later stories, Colin E. Nicholson maps "their literary contours" to find the old familiar landscape of fear, angst, pain, and the refusal to think and reflect. Andrew Hook's essay on *Sun* is not only just as lackluster (Paris is bad/Burguete good), it is also eccentric, arguing that Jake is just as much a hero as Pedro Romero when he goes back to Madrid to collect Brett. Even less effective is William Wasserstrom's self-indulgent effusion about himself and his friends that was apparently supposed to say something about *Farewell* but did not. After this low point, Lee's essay on *Bell* is a relief. Taking the kind of British stance that Stephens defines, he argues that this novel does not have to be an unalloyed success—the Big Novel in the American sense—in order to take its rightful place among others on the Spanish Civil War. After a balanced survey of critical attitudes toward *Bell*, Lee establishes the bridge as its narrative center and then discusses the outer ring of stories that surround and interact with it. It is one of the best essays in the collection.

As one of the American contributors to the Lee collection, James H. Justus bears out another of Stephens's observations: we are more committed to biography than the British. Looking at three of Hemingway's later novels, *Old Man*, *Across*, and *Islands*, Justus rediscovers what Philip Young found out many years ago—that their basic scene is the Papa figure being interviewed by adoring straight men like Hotchner or Renata. This, in turn, explains why Hemingway wanted no biographies or publication of his letters: his life was his only material, and he did not want anyone else to use it. Eric Mottram's essay, "Suicide and Nostalgia," is a real bravura piece that requires the reader to know his Hemingway extremely well since everything is alluded to, nothing discussed. After this second low point, there is another big bounce up with Brian Way's discussion of Hemingway as one kind of modernist intellectual. Unlike the familiar analytical kind, like Thomas Mann, Hemingway was the intuitive, nonverbal type, like dancers, musicians, and artists, who let memories and associative fantasies well up into their work. When such intuitive types realize the importance of their own memories, they become artists; but when they become self-conscious and start looking at their work critically, as Hemingway began to do in several letters to Maxwell Perkins, their work falls apart as Hemingway's showed signs of doing in parts of *Farewell* and then did completely in *Bell*. In other words, Way does not attribute Hemingway's decline to biographical factors, as an American critic might, but to an artistic failure, just what one would expect, after having read Stephens, a British critic to do.

Another low point in the Lee collection is Faith Pullin's narrow feminist attack on Hemingway. Her essay is the kind of strident, cliché-ridden and unintelligent criticism that plays into the hands of Pullin's macho adversaries. Even though Frank McConnell's subtitle, "Hemingway's Presence in Contemporary American Writing," suggests another drab influence study, his essay is in reality a very witty, rather wise-guy discussion of how Hemingway's "writerly persona" was assimilated by writers ranging from Mickey Spillane through Norman Mailer to Thomas Pynchon. McConnell's big surprise is that this influential persona was not tough, old Papa but rather a Byronesque and "dandified stylist of chaos" who, once everything was seen to be *nada*, spent the rest of his time showing off his love of life and disdain of death, thus setting his personal style against the *nada*. The extreme position of this gay little *jeu d'esprit* has enough truth in it to provoke serious consideration. Lee's collection is, therefore, a rather uneven one that clearly highlights some of the principal differences between American and British critical values.

Three books published in the early 1970s follow the pattern for multi-topic collections set by Baker and Weeks in 1961–62. Like those two books, Arthur Waldhorn's *Ernest Hemingway: A Collection of Criticism* (New York, 1973) begins with a biographical essay, reprints eight essays by various hands published elsewhere, and concludes with a bibliography. Waldhorn also continues something started by Weeks: he reprints an essay by Philip Young. A contribution by Young becomes an essential component of every collection; only one of the three is without one. The eight essays Waldhorn reprints take "an overview" of such matters as style (John Graham), symbolism and irony (E. M. Halliday and Bernard Oldsey), Hemingway's time sense, i.e., his "fifth dimension" (F. I. Carpenter), and the general shape of his work (Fuchs, Evans, and Young). There are no readings of individual works. If Waldhorn's book is conventional, our awareness of its conventions allows us to see just how unique Linda W. Wagner's collection of twenty-two reprinted essays, *Ernest Hemingway: Five Decades of Criticism* (East Lansing, Mich., 1974) really is. The primary concern of Wagner's collection, as her introduction declares and her section titles insist, is not the man but "the Work": there are five essays on "the Work as a Whole," five on "Studies of Method and Language," and eight on "Studies of Individual Novels," among them Edmund Wilson's famous "Dry Points" review. Wagner's introduction does what an introduction should do: it surveys the essays selected and places them in the context of previous work.

In Jackson J. Benson's *The Short Stories of Ernest Hemingway: Critical Essays* (Durham, N.C., 1975), as in Wagner's book, the emphasis is on technique and interpretation of individual works; and here, as in Wagner, there is no essay on Hemingway's life. Otherwise, Benson's volume follows the conventions of such collections: it reprints thirty-one essays by different authors; it provides the important checklist of criticism that was discussed above; and it prints Philip Young's introduction to *The Nick Adams Stories*. All thirty-one essays are worthwhile and touch on many different aspects of Hemingway's work; nevertheless, the three contributions by Benson stand out. In addition to his factual introduction and exceptional checklist, Benson's concluding overview of the stories is the book's capstone and in many ways still one of the best essays ever written on Hemingway's work. In this wide-ranging effort, Benson discusses in a precise and detailed way (right down to word-choice and syntax) exactly how Hemingway's early teachers influenced his prose. Along the way he defines Hemingway's tragic world view, a fundamental attitude that underlay the narrative pattern of his stories and became fully realized in his style as it evolved from his mentors. While considering these fundamental and subtle issues, Benson also analyzes two of Hemingway's most challenging stories—"Now I Lay Me" and "A Way You'll Never Be." He concludes with a fine discussion of Pound's role in developing Hemingway's style. The essay is a tour de force not only for its fluid ability to move from the smallest details of style to the largest issues of interpretation but also for its keen sense of those inherent imaginative patterns that inform all of Hemingway's work, fiction as well as nonfiction.

We conclude with the five collections of original essays based on papers delivered at conferences. The first one is the "published record of a literary conference devoted to a study of the work of Ernest Hemingway held at Oregon State University on April 26–27, 1973," *Hemingway In Our Time* (ed. Richard Astro and Jackson J. Benson, Corvallis, Oreg., 1974). This anthology of twelve original papers that Astro claims represents "a new approach to Hemingway studies" because it raises "provocative new theories, new perspectives" looks, from the present perspective, quite conventional. The Youngian interest in biographical analysis is provided by Young himself and George Wickes. Two essays enlarge on familiar themes in Hemingway criticism: John Griffith discusses with insight and clarity Hemingway's use of ritual, and Richard Lehan argues that his rejection of history and literary tradition required him to create his own mythology from such outré sources as hunting, fishing, and bullfighting. Although Lehan's first premise should be modified to read "appeared" to reject history and culture, and the second was suggested by Baker in 1952, it is still one of the best essays in the book. Nevertheless, the greatest number of essays argue against Lehan's thesis by attempting either to establish a literary influence or to place Hemingway in some familiar cultural tradition. Peter L. Hays argues for the influence of T. S. Eliot by way of *The Great Gatsby* on *Sun*; Faith G. Norris takes the surprising position that *Feast* is like Proust's *Remembrance of Things Past*, which it is, of course, but only in the most general way; John Pratt discusses Hemingway's ambivalent relationship to Catholicism as shown in *Old Man*; Michael Friedberg tries to place him in the metaphysical/mystical tradition of D. H. Lawrence, T. S. Eliot, and Huxley; and Robert W. Lewis approaches his sense of place from the angle of exiles looking for a place to settle down, a slant that recalls Baker's "Home/Not Home" theme. And even Jackson J. Benson, who usually comes up with something new, follows the trend by placing Hemingway in the midwestern WASP tradition that he was, however, able to transcend because he completely assimilated the lessons of his European mentors.

As for the essays in the Astro and Benson collection which concentrate on particular works, Joseph DeFalco claims to find "a major shift to the affirmative mode in the realism" in *Across, Old Man,* and *Islands;* Delbert E. Wylder offers an extremely able reading of "Two Tales of Darkness"; and Gerry Brenner offers a rare and well-handled analysis of *To Have and Have Not* as a classical tragedy that became one of the best chapters in his *Concealments* book. Thus, while all of these efforts are very worthy, none of them, with the possible exception of Benson and Brenner, could be said to "raise provocative new theories, new perspectives," as Richard Astro had hoped.

Although it is by no means easy to establish this fact, *Hemingway: A Revaluation* (ed. Donald R. Noble, Troy, N.Y., 1983) is really much older than its date of publication indicates, since most of its thirteen papers were presented at the Third Alabama Symposium on English and American Literature held in Tuscaloosa, Alabama, on 14–16 October 1976. As a consequence of this and the editor's decision to publish papers by well-established names, most of the essays are not only not new but strike one as being distinctly old-fashioned. Alfred Kazin, Leo Gurko, Richard B. Hovey, Scott Donaldson, Michael S. Reynolds, and Philip Young gave just the kind of papers one would expect from their published works. Even Jackson J. Benson and Robert Stephens offered the expected: Benson's paper is an excellent survey of Hemingway criticism from 1971 to 1974 that asks the really "Hard Questions," questions that still remain to be answered; and Stephens uses his knowledge of reviews to define several fundamental differences between American and British critical attitudes, as we have seen. The papers by less-established scholars are also rather mixed. Using a very slight reference to Ronceveaux in *Sun* as his springboard, H. R. Stoneback argues that Hemingway was a serious Catholic, a Medievalist, an influence on Faulkner, and that *Sun* is a spiritual quest. The chief virtue of W. Craig Turner's rather fragmented discussion of the narrative technique and motifs in *Across* is that, unlike Hovey or Young, he takes the novel seriously as a fiction.

Among the other essays in the Noble collection, Gregory S. Sojka pushes hard at the idea of order in *Islands,* but his argument goes flat with its unvarying insistence and overuse of paraphrases unrelieved by analysis. Much better is Charles and A. C. Hoffmann's fine discussion of the interconnections between the stories and chapters in *In Our Time.* The Hoffmanns are particularly good at relating the neglected sketches and non-Nick Adams stories to the book's overall pattern, a pattern that culminates in the telescoping of all times and places into one moment and place in "Big Two-Hearted River." The real critical bombshell is Allen Josephs's paper on the bad Spanish in *Bell.* Most of the errors could have been cleaned up by a good Spanish-speaking proofreader, but the real problem is that Hemingway seems so ignorant of Spanish slang that he calls Maria "rabbit," a name whose Spanish equivalent, *conejo*, is *not* a euphemism for "female sexual organ." Josephs argues his case for Hemingway's ignorance, or insensitivity, in a variety of very convincing ways. Because of its late publication date and the large number of papers that start from well-entrenched critical positions, Noble's collection seems flat and old-fashioned now except for Benson's farewell, Reynolds's emergence, and Josephs's rabbit.

As noted above, *Ernest Hemingway: The Papers of a Writer* (ed. Bernard Oldsey, New York, 1981) assembles twelve papers that were given at the 17–19 July 1980 conference celebrating the opening of the Hemingway Collection in the Kennedy Library. Since most of the innovative essays, those using the library's papers and letters, have already been discussed, we may review the others now. Linda W. Wagner takes the surprising position that the female characters in Hemingway's early fiction are treated sympathetically, including, even more surprisingly, Brett. The change came with "the catastrophe of his father's death" that turned Hemingway away from this sympathetic treatment and made *Farewell* into a novel about loss, "the loss . . . of his father, not of Catherine or a child." Nicholas Gerogiannis, the editor of Hemingway's poems, argues that Nietzsche and Gabriele D'Annunzio were influences on Hemingway. Although the latter's influence sounds the more unlikely, Gerogiannis offers some very striking evidence for his case. Bernard Oldsey continues his examination of Hemingway's starts and stops with his keen writerly eye. Two papers that complement one another in their contrasting attitudes are those by Michael S. Reynolds and Philip Young: Young looks backward to find an ever-increasing flow of less interesting work; Reynolds looks forward to the next ten years and calls for a turn away from the kind of work Young's book inspired to a new focus on background and manuscript studies making use of computers and data bases.

In almost all ways, *Up in Michigan: Proceedings of the First National Conference of the Hemingway Society* (ed. Joseph J. Waldmeir, Traverse City, Mich., 1983) appears the true eccentric among the five conference collections. Instead of the usual twelve papers it published eighteen of the twenty given; instead of an introduction by the editor, Waldmeir appended a Hemingwayesque short story to the collection; there are no notes on contributors; and there is no paper by Philip Young (perhaps his appearance in Oldsey's collection really was his last farewell). In spite of this apparent eccentricity, the collection as a whole is much more conservative than Oldsey's, published before it (1981), and Nagel's, published after it (1984). There are, for example, five readings of specific works: E. R. Hagemann and Bickford Sylvester on *In Our Time*, Lawrence H. Martin and Howard L. Hannum on "Big Two-Hearted

River," and Bruce Stark on "The End of Something." The two biographical papers, Scott Donaldson on John Dos Passos and William Coté on
Hemingway's reporting, have been reviewed above. Among the papers
on general themes are Douglas E. LaPrade's on the parallels between
Picasso and Hemingway, Kim Moreland's and Robert M. Hogge's on
the hot topic of Hemingway's medievalism, Patrick W. Shaw's on animal
references that seems to have created a new word, *zooerast*, for an old
pastime, Robert E. Gajdusek's on all kinds of somatic, psychic, and
material connectors that he gathers under the term "bridge," and Frank
Kersnowski's Jungian approach to several works that could have profited
from a close study of Gajdusek's more exciting use of "amplification."
Two papers claim to be about Hemingway's humor but are really about
something else: Marianne H. Knowlton's paper on "Comic Stance" is
really about the absurdist dilemma of the isolated man, and James
Hinkle's commentary on "sixty submerged jokes" in *Sun* is really about
Hemingway's use of figurative language and metaphors. Only two of
the eighteen published papers take new approaches. Frederic Joseph
Svoboda's essay on the background of "The Battler," which makes use
of an unpublished notebook, is not very successful because Svoboda
does not deal with the crafting of the story's style, as he did in his book
on *Sun*; by contrast, James Seaton's excellent feminist approach to
Farewell is very successful.

In sharp contrast to these Traverse City papers, *Ernest Hemingway: The
Writer in Context* (ed. James Nagel, Madison, Wis., 1984), the published
record of a conference held in Boston on 21–23 May 1982, makes extensive use of the papers located in nearby Crown Point. The personal
comment papers by Charles Scribner, Jr. and Patrick Hemingway have
already been discussed; Tom Stoppard discusses several striking passages, among them the generally ignored opening paragraph of "A Pursuit Race." In his study of Faulkner's influence on Hemingway, Peter
L. Hays gathers together all the possible links between the two writers
before presenting evidence that "The Bear" (1942) almost certainly influenced *The Old Man and The Sea* (1952).

Perhaps the most striking papers in Nagel's collection are by women.
Expanding on the influence of Henry James on Hemingway, mentioned
somewhat earlier by James D. Brasch and Jackson J. Benson, Adeline
R. Tintner finds that Hemingway tended "to realize and actualize"
James's imagery "so that his metaphors of feeding become actual meals
in Hemingway." In her study of five female characters, Carol H. Smith
finds that Hemingway generally subscribed to the old male myth that
all women, starting with Eve, are desirable and dangerous, innocent
helpmates and evil temptresses, but that his best work presented the
valiant struggle of complex personalities against the rigid dichotomies
of this predominant but by no means universal myth. Of all the papers
in Nagel's book perhaps the most interesting one is Millicent Bell's dis-

cussion of "Pseudoautobiography and Personal Metaphor" in *Farewell*. It catches the eye not so much for its findings, which turn out to be quite familiar, but rather for its approach. With no hint of what she is doing, Bell has made what appears to be a deconstructionist analysis of *Farewell*, using many of the insights of the French Freud. Averring that the novel is about neither love nor war but "a state of mind, and that state of mind is the author's," Bell defines it as "apathy" and "ennui" caused by several clashing dichotomies: Hemingway's feeling that death as much as life was the consequence of sexuality; his hostility and guilt toward his parents; his feeling of being orphaned after his father's suicide; and his "need to reject as well as the need to be wanted again." Bell's paper is important because it marks the encroachment of a new critical trend into the rather conservative world of Hemingway Studies. Just how strongly conservative that world is may be seen in Harold Bloom's edition of essays, *Ernest Hemingway*, for his Modern Critical Views series (New York, 1985): he reprints old favorites by such venerables as Trilling, Wilson, Baker, Spilka, Cowley, etc., adding only two new items, his fascinating introduction and John Hollander's rather arch but interesting reading of "Hills Like White Elephants." And, finally, a special issue of the *Clockwatch Review* (No. 2, 1986) includes a long interview with Patrick Hemingway, an article by Lorian Hemingway about her uncle Leicester, several poems by Philip Schultz and Anne Hemingway, Leicester's daughter, and an article by Bruce Stark that offers an overview of Hemingway's career and its place in the American myth.

3 Articles

This survey of critical articles will begin with general studies that cover several works and end with those concentrating on single works.

a. General Studies. The general studies fall into four groups: analyses of single well-defined motifs that shade in larger themes, attempts to place Hemingway in a particular intellectual or cultural tradition, essays that discuss his relationships with other authors, and stylistic approaches.

Among the single-motif studies are E. Nageswara Rao's collection of all the references to luck in Hemingway's work (*JAmS*, Apr. 1979); Peter L. Hays's study of bicycles as symbols of death (*NMAL*, Fall 1981); and Melvin Backman's very complete survey of birth/death imagery in the canon, in *The Stoic Strain in American Literature: Essays in Honour of Marston La France* (ed. Duane MacMillan, Toronto, 1979). Two authors have investigated the animal motif in Hemingway's works: Patrick Shaw (Waldmeir) and Mary Allen in her *Animals in American Literature* (Urbana, Ill., 1983). Allen's chapter is a fascinating study of such things as the rules for killing, the nobility of the animals hunted, the association of women with smaller domesticated animals like cats and canaries, and the varying colors of Santiago's marlin. All this hunting apparently gave Gerald Locklin and Charles Stetler the idea that Hemingway was a despoiler of nature, so they came to his defense with some help from Mary Hemingway who wrote them that Papa saved an injured owl once (*HN*, Spring 1981). Steven Phillips fits Hemingway's hunting interest into a stylized pattern of combat between men and animals that is best exemplified in the "tragic" ritual of the bullfight (*ArQ*, Spring 1973).

Against the strong tendency for motif studies to become collections of undigested data, David M. Wyatt offers an explanation of why Hemingway's heroes suffered wounds to their hands after 1940 rather than to their legs, as they had before then; their wounded hands reflect Hemingway's growing concern for his declining creative potency as a writer (*VQR*, Spring 1980). Another critic who makes intelligent use of what could be a pedestrian motif is Nancy Comley who analyzes how money is used to represent complex exchanges in values and emotions between the sexes (*Novel*, Spring 1979).

A number of general studies have been made of Hemingway's concepts of time and space. Wesley A. Kort argues that Hemingway's use of time is not simple and linear but cyclical, as in *Bell* and *Old Man*, and paradigmatic, as in *Sun* and *Across* where a tripartite Dantean model is used to organize the action (*MFS*, Winter 1980–81). Six authors have tried to map Hemingway's spaces. David McClellan analyzes his use of the battle of the Little Big Horn in three of his later novels (*FHA*, 1976) in an article that complements his earlier claim that El Sordo's last stand in *Bell* reflects General Custer's at the Little Big Horn (*FHA*, 1974); William C. Slattery investigates how the San Siro race track outside of Milan reflects Baker's mountain/plain paradigm (*PLL*, Fall 1980); Robert W. Lewis distinguishes three generic places in Hemingway's short stories: dislocations of people on the run, home places, and good places that have been corrupted (Astro and Benson); and, in the same collection of essays, Joseph M. DeFalco argues that the shift from bullfights to fishing and islands as central metaphors in Hemingway's later novels reveals a corresponding movement to a more affirmative attitude toward life. Raymond Benoit would certainly agree with DeFalco about fishing since not only does he see Nick's camp in "Big Two-Hearted River" as a place where *nada* is kept at bay, he also interprets the big trout that got away as a Christian symbol since the Greek word for fish, ICHTHUS, is an acronym for "Jesus Christ, son of God, savior" (*Prospects*, 1980). And, finally, Donald Monk finds a motivation for Hemingway's locophilia in the "territorial imperative," a basic urge that caused alienated outsiders, like Nick Adams and Frederic Henry, to search for safe places but then created megalomanic boors, like Colonel Cantwell and Thomas Hudson, when these places were found and occupied (*YES*, 1978).

In addition to places, dis-place-ments play an important thematic role in Hemingway's works; accordingly, Leo Gurko describes several characteristics of what he dubs Hemingway's "magic journey" (Noble), and Gary D. Elliott examines the spiritual aspects of his heroes' quest for faith that climaxes with Santiago in *Old Man* (*McNR*, 1977–78). Jacqueline Tavernier-Courbin reaches much the same conclusion for Hemingway himself when she argues that Santiago represents the kind of man that he would have liked to have been but was not (*JGE*, Fall 1978). Instead of a quest for the self, John R. Cooley views several of Nick Adams's journeys as searches for certain "good places" (like the pine island in "Big Two-Hearted River") where he could feel secure (*SHR*, Winter 1980). Nick's "good places" turn out to be the "secret places" that John Leland discovers to be the goal of all Hemingway heroes (*HR*, Fall 1983). As to why Hemingway sent his heroes out on these "magic journeys," Allen Josephs suggests that they may have had their source in the "out of body experience" he had when wounded (*HR*, Spring 1983), but note that for Josephs this experience was not a crippling trauma in the Youngian way but archetypal in the Jungian. Much closer to Young's position is Kenneth G. Johnston's view that Hemingway's heroes always chose the outer quest, like Mungo Park, over the inner one, like Thoreau, because the journey inward was always a nightmare-filled Conradian trip into the heart of one's own darkness, something to be avoided at all costs (*ForumH*, Summer–Fall 1972). The traumatic interpretation of Hemingway's wounding popularized by Philip Young is subjected to a sharp critical analysis by Kenneth Lynn who traces it back through Young to bad readings made by Malcolm Cowley and Edmund Wilson for their own ideological purposes (*Commentary*, July 1981). Lynn's essay is a fascinating revisionist effort that has much in its favor.

More apparent to the casual reader than these inner and outer quests is Hemingway's interest in war and sport. Peter Stine takes a biographical angle on Hemingway's war experience much like Young's (*FHA*, 1979), whereas Jeffrey Walsh views it more as a theme in two closely related studies: in a 1982 article, Walsh follows the war theme through the major works, uncovering as he goes their underlying myth and style (*HR*, Spring 1982); in his *American War Literature: 1914 to Vietnam* (London, 1982), Walsh compares *Farewell* to E. E. Cummings's *The Enormous Room* and *Bell* to Alvah Bessie's account of the Spanish Civil War, concluding that in both cases Hemingway's approach is reductive and Imagistic.

Two excellent articles have examined Hemingway's use of the closely related themes of sport, work, and play. In *Sport and the Spirit of Play in American Fiction* (New York, 1981), Christian K. Messenger discusses Hemingway's satire of the school sports hero in Robert Cohn, his rejection of the popular sports hero in his boxers, and his exaltation of the ritual sports hero in Pedro Romero. Related to Messenger's book is Leverett T. Smith's *The American Dream and the National Game* (Bowling Green, Ohio, 1975), which covers much the same material but from the more abstract point of view of Hemingway's shift from a "work ethic" to a "play ethic" in *Sun* and finally to a fusion of the two in *Old Man*. Like Messenger, Smith finds that boxing, which was urban and dominated by Jewish gamblers, destroys its practitioners.

In addition to the tutor and tyro figures, critics have noted several other general types among Hemingway's characters. Among the males there are the tough western stoic who "dares danger—laughs at pain—challenges death," a character who dominates the westerns of Ernest Haycox and the detective fiction of Raymond Chandler, two of Hemingway's favorite authors, according to Philip Durham (*Pacific Hist. Rev.*, Aug. 1976); the disabled old professional discussed by George Monteiro (*FHA*, 1979); and the middle-aged man who appears in *Across* as well as in the works of Joyce, James, Eliot, and Dreiser, as Sam Bluefarb tells us (*CLAJ*, Sept. 1976).

When it comes to Hemingway's female characters, some see him as completely hostile, others as partly sympathetic. The older, majority opinion that Hemingway was uniformly hostile to women in his work is admirably presented by John W. Presley, who wisely argues that the problem is not just sexual but involves rather a risky encounter with "the Other" (*HN*, Spring 1973). James W. Tuttleton finds much the same thing in "Combat in the Erogenous Zones," in *What Manner of Woman: Essays on English and American Life and Literature* (ed. Marlene Springer, New York, 1977); while Carol H. Smith places Hemingway's hostility in a Western tradition that goes back to Eve's betrayal of Adam (Nagel). Alan Lebowitz insists quite reasonably that women are seen as traps that keep the men from having fun with other men, but then falls into some rather odd traps of his own when he claims that Brett is a castrating bull in *Sun*, that George in "Cross-Country Snow" is the husband in "Cat in the Rain," and that the trap in *Farewell* snaps shut on Catherine Barkley rather than Frederic Henry (in *Uses of Literature*, ed. Monroe Engel, Cambridge, Mass., 1973). Even less successful is Faith Pullin's rehearsal of all the old anti-female clichés in Hemingway's work that leads nowhere (Lee).

The newer and still minority view that Hemingway could be sympathetic to women is presented in three articles published during the 1980s. Mona G. Rosenman makes a spirited defense of his sympathetic treatment of women in five short stories that have become central to this line of argument—"Up in Michigan," "Cat," "Hills," "The Sea Change," and, under the revisionist interpretation, "Macomber" (*CCR*, No. 1, 1977). Linda W. Wagner argues, as we have seen, that Hemingway was sympathetic to women until the suicide of his father (Oldsey). And, finally, Charles J. Nolan, Jr. surveys the same material, adding "Out of Season," "The End of Something," and "Snows" to the pro-women argument (*HR*, Spring 1984). Besides this new data, Nolan's chief contribution is his excellent bibliography of the sympathetic argument that goes all the way back, through several dissertations, to Alan Holder's 1963 article "The Other Hemingway" (reprinted in Wagner). The distorting effect of the majority opinion has been ably demonstrated by Roger Whitlow, who argues that Helen in "Snows" has unjustly been seen as a "bitch" because Margot Macomber was one (*Frontiers*, Fall 1978).

Hemingway's deeply ambivalent attitude toward women almost certainly influences the way families are treated in his fiction. With the notable exception of Santiago who enters the universal family of God, Roger Whitlow concludes that families in Hemingway are either never allowed to form, by the death of a child, or are destroyed, by infidelity or divorce (*LitR*, Fall 1976). As for the Adams family, Frank Shelton believes that Nick's bond to his sister Littless is a substitute for family relations (*SSF*, Summer 1974). Just exactly what kind of family may have contributed to Hemingway's ambivalence is explored by Earl Rovit, who outlines what white upper-middle-class families were like at the turn of the century (*MissQ*, Fall 1976).

We conclude this survey of thematic studies with seven essays that discover a simple theme unifying Hemingway's canon and career. After sampling several recurring themes in Hemingway's fiction, Herbie Butterfield concludes that their common feature is courage, both active and passive, in *American Fiction: New Readings* (ed. Richard Gray, New York, 1983). But two other articles argue from radically differing points of view that there really is no unifying theme in Hemingway's work: based on teaching experiences, Philip K. Jason concludes that there is no "code" in Hemingway (*Indirections*, Nos. 3–4, 1976); based on a sharp critical examination of Philip Young's *Reconsideration*, Charles Stetler and Gerald Locklin conclude that there is no pattern in Hemingway's canon so that each work must be read as a separate entity (*HN*, Fall 1979). Undeterred by such caveats, critics have gone on looking for unifying themes. William Adair finds that the romantic theme of loss, fear of it and its consequences, is more central to Hemingway's work than death and dying (*CollL*, Fall 1983); Stephen L. Tanner insists that nostalgia is not just an artistic device, i.e., nostalgic flashbacks appear when the heroes are under stress, but is at the very center of Hemingway's creative process (*FHA*, 1974); and James H. Justus uncovers the source of this nostalgia in another more basic theme—doomed characters (Lee). The most ambitious single-theme study is David M. Wyatt's analysis of five novels that attempts to formulate the "governing paradigm" of Hemingway's "career," i.e., "canon" (*GaR*, Summer 1977). Wyatt attacks the problem using the three-part metaphor of beginnings (Nick's life is all beginning with no middle), middles (Jake's life is all middle with no beginning or end), and ends (Robert Jordan's life is filled and fulfilled with an end that creates a liberating epiphany).

Even though Hemingway was not a thinker who tried to formulate his values in abstract terms, much less into a coherent system, his more thoughtful critics have tried to place him and his work into various intellectual and cultural traditions. Some of these critics view him as a conservative American while others see him as a radical European modernist. Among the Americanists are Nancy L. Bunge who discovers in Hemingway certain "Populist values," derived from Walt Whitman, that place him in a tradition of midwestern novelists that includes Sinclair Lewis, Saul Bellow, and Sherwood Anderson (*ON*, Sept. 1977); Viola Hopkins Winner, who discusses his "American literary pictorialism," a tradition that is quite distinct from British modes of seeing (*SAF*, Spring 1977); and, similarly but somewhat more specifically, William E. Meyer, Jr., who relates Hemingway's "prose-imagism" to America's "eye-oriented" culture with its Puritan emphasis on order and cleanliness which holds that since seeing is the ideal, saying must always fall short (*ArQ*, Summer 1983). As to why Hemingway was so traditionally American and midwestern, C. W. E. Bigsby believes that in his recoil from history, Hemingway retreated into a world "perpetually frozen in the youthful Mid-Western all-male society of his own past." Bigsby's essay appears in *The Twenties: Fiction, Poetry, Drama* (ed. Warren French, Deland, Fla., 1975).

Opposed to these heartlanders are the internationalists who place Hemingway in the tradition of European modernism. Roger Asselineau, the distinguished French Americanist, believes that Hemingway's values were those of a British sportsman and that love had a mystical, almost transcendent, value in his work (*The Transcendentalist Constant in American Literature*, New York, 1980). As eccentric as Asselineau's position may seem, it is strongly seconded by Joseph M. DeFalco, who traces Hemingway's changing values from the nihilism of his early works through the animalism of Harry Morgan to an apolitical humanism that climaxes in the last scene of *Bell* where Maria, the child of a Catholic mother and a Republican father, rides off with the band led by a regenerated Pablo because Robert Jordan sacrifices himself (in *Renaissance and Modern Essays in Honor of Edwin M. Moseley*, ed. Murray J. Levith, Saratoga Springs, N.Y., 1976). What DeFalco finds in Hemingway's work Leo Schneiderman finds in his life because it is, he feels, one of the basic conflicts of our times (*ConnR*, Apr. 1973).

Any sign of romanticism or transcendental love is completely ignored by Richard Godden, who attempts a commodity theory analysis of Hemingway's work in an essay whose heavy clouds of theory are relieved by only a few bright flashes on style (*Essays in Poetics*, Apr. 1983). Kenneth G. Johnston compares Hemingway's iceberg theory to Freud's theory of the mind by linking the revealed tip of the iceberg to the conscious and its hidden depths to the unconscious (*JNT*, Winter 1984). This rather simplistic correlation is almost certainly far off the mark, as Nina Schwartz's comments quite clearly indicate (*Criticism*, Winter 1984).

As for Hemingway's religion, most critics have concentrated more on his Catholicism, acquired in Europe, than on his native American Protestantism. Bates Hoffer searches out several religious themes in his stories, among them the descent into hell motif (*LNL*, Spring–Summer 1979); John C. Pratt discusses his ambivalence to Catholicism (Astro and Benson); William E. Meyer, Jr. traces a shifting balance between pagan and Christian symbolism in his works that began in 1937 when the heroes became more pagan as their female companions became more Christian (*ArQ*, Summer 1977); and Ben Stoltzfus studies the same mix of values in *Old Man* in his *Gide and Hemingway: Rebels against God* (Port Washington, N.Y., 1978). Sergio H. Bocaz, on the other hand, completely ignores the Christian symbolism that pervades Hemingway's work in order to see him as a pure Senecan stoic in *Studies in Language and Literature* (ed. Charles Nelson, Richmond, Ky., 1976).

Three related articles take a completely different approach to Hemingway's values by placing him in the existentialist tradition. Reviewing all the theories about why death was Hemingway's main theme, Mark Scheel concludes that it is best explained by a system of "positive existentialism" (*ESRS*, Summer 1979). Wayne C. Holcombe argues that while Hemingway shows the traits of Sartre's and Camus's "atheistic existentialism," he also shares many of the attitudes of the logical positivists and stoics (*HR*, Fall 1983); and Richard C. Gebhardt carefully sorts through the various ways in which Hemingway's values are discussed to find, on one hand, that they are very complex because he had the "dual drive to deny and affirm values simultaneously," but, on the other, that they are essentially Nietzschean, nihilistic, and existential (*HR*, Fall 1981). Finally, Moorhead Wright fuses the Americanist and internationalist stances when he argues that Frederic Henry is an "existential adventurer," like Crane's Henry Fleming and Vonnegut's Billy Pilgrim, because he is a rootless American expatriate with no tradition to sustain him (in *American Thinking about Peace and War*, ed. Ken Booth and Moorhead Wright, New York, 1978).

In the following survey of Hemingway's complex relations with other authors, the word "influence" is used in the broadest sense possible to include everything from direct influence, allusions, tags, unconscious paraphrases, affinities, feuds, reminiscences, to vague resemblances. With this qualification in mind, we shall first consider the "influence" of Europeans on Hemingway in more or less chronological order and then turn to the Americans that helped form him.

Certainly the most remote affinity yet found is Richard E. Braun's contention that Homer's catalogue of Greek ships is parodied in *To Have and Have Not*'s list of yachts; Helène Bradley is his Helen of Troy, and Richard Gordon is his Paris (*FHA*, 1974). Just as remote are the influence of the *Epistle of James* on "The Sea Change" that Robin Elaine Atherton

452

proposes because the bartender's name in that story is James (*LNL*, Spring–Summer 1979) and the association that Robert E. Jungman makes between Matt. 7:13–14 and the end of *Sun* because Jake rides down the Gran Via in Madrid which means "big street, large path, a great way" (*FHA*, 1977). Several critics have proposed medieval affinities: Arthur Coleman finds parallels between *Sir Gawain and the Green Knight* and "Macomber" (*AN&Q*, Jan.–Feb. 1981), Arnold E. Davidson discovers a complex Dantean perspective in the way Frederic Henry retells what happened to him in *Farewell* (*JNT*, May 1973), and Gerry Brenner insists that *Across* is a direct imitation of Dante (*FHA*, 1976). Just as insistent is Robert O. Johnson who believes that the source of Hemingway's tag "How do you like it now, Gentlemen" is George Villiers's 1671 play *The Rehearsal* (*AL*, Mar. 1973). Much less remote than these is the influence of Stendhal on *Farewell* proposed by Robert O. Stephens (*PMLA*, Mar. 1973) and by Carolina Donadio Lawson who covers much the same ground with no mention of Stephens (*HN*, Spring 1981). According to Edward Engelberg, another French influence on *Farewell* is Flaubert's *L'Education sentimentale*; he also believes that both novels are about "nothing" (*CLS*, Sept. 1979). A smaller but more substantial influence is argued for by Donald A. Daiker who finds an allusion to Robert Browning's "The Pied Piper of Hamelin" in chapter 15 of *Sun* (*FHA*, 1975).

Between 1978 and 1981 three articles unearthed Nietzschean influences. Using Hemingway's Shakespeare and Company library cards as evidence, Gregory Green argues that *Also Sprach Zarathustra* influenced *The Old Man and The Sea* (*HN*, Fall 1979); Charles Taylor finds the same influence but argues from the wider perspective of Nietzsche's "tragic vision" (*DR*, Winter 1981); and Nicholas Gerogiannis traces Nietzsche's influence on Hemingway by way of Gabriele D'Annunzio (Oldsey). The Nietzschean image of the egotistical hero alone in nature reappears in the influence of Arthur Rimbaud's *Le Bateau ivre* that Francis S. Heck finds in *The Old Man and The Sea* (*NDQ*, Winter 1981). Harbour Winn detects the influence of Tolstoy's "The Death of Ivan Illich" on Hemingway's two African stories: direct and detailed in "Snows" but only thematic in "Macomber" (*SSF*, Fall 1981). Two more very specific influences are Faith G. Norris's claim that Proust's *Remembrance* influenced *A Moveable Feast* (Astro and Benson) and Scott Donaldson's that Anatole France contributed the "Irony and Pity" phrase to *Sun* (*FHA*, 1978).

More general but still essential is the influence of Conrad, argued for by Peter L. Hays (*AN&Q*, Jan. 1976), and of Kipling, argued for by Jeffrey Meyers (*AL*, Mar. 1984). Two English writers who provoked Hemingway's enmity were Ford Madox Ford, who helped him, as Jeffrey Meyers points out (*CritQ*, Winter 1983), and Virginia Woolf, who criticized him, as Scott Donaldson indicates (*JML*, June 1983). Although Michael Garrety claims to be discussing the similarities between R. H. Mottram's *Spanish Farm Trilogy* and *Farewell*, his chapter in Holger Klein's

The First World War in Fiction: A Collection of Critical Essays (London, 1976) is really about Hemingway's Imagistic and ironic style. Another rather misleading essay is James Schroeter's study of James Joyce's influence on *Green Hills of Africa*, because the most striking thing in it is a pattern that he detects in Hemingway's career: discovering that his early works were overly subtle treatments of love and war, Hemingway produced a simplified treatment in *Bell*; discovering the same to be true of his treatment of what it is to be a writer in "Snows" and *Green Hills*, he again produced another simplified version in *The Old Man and the Sea* (*SoR*, Winter 1974). In an important essay that really does discuss Joyce's influence on Hemingway, Robert E. Gajdusek works out a number of parallels between *Dubliners* and *In Our Time* (*HR*, Fall 1982). Hugh Kenner sums up all of the modern European influences on Hemingway in his *A Homemade World: The American Modernist* (New York, 1975) in a way that looks new but whose allusive substance recalls the vague belletristic generalities of late nineteenth-century essayists.

The last non-American influence to consider is the much-vexed question of how Cézanne's painting is related to Hemingway's writing. Three articles circle the problem: Charles H. Cagle surveys the relationship between Hemingway, Cézanne, and Stein, who introduced the former to the latter (*MQ*, Spring 1982); Hans-Joachim Kann lists the ninety-one books on art and artists that Hemingway owned in Cuba (*FHA*, 1974); and Kenneth G. Johnston repeats the usual kind of general remarks about the two men (*AL*, Mar. 1984). A fourth article by Meyly Chin Hagemann attacks the question directly in a very ambitious essay that attempts to show exactly how Hemingway made his landscapes like Cézanne's and how specific pictures influenced particular stories (*JML*, Feb. 1979). Although Hagemann's conclusions are by no means always convincing, her analytical method is almost certainly the only way that any precise determination can be made of how Cézanne's paintings influenced Hemingway's writing.

Speculation about the American "influences" on Hemingway begin with Edgar Allan Poe, whose closest direct link to the younger author, according to Burton R. Pollin, is the shared theme of hanging (*ES*, Apr. 1976). More engaging is Donald M. Murray's claim for the influence of Thoreau on Hemingway, particularly after 1941 in *Green Hills of Africa* (*TJQ*, July and Oct. 1979). In Paul McCarthy's comparison of Melville's *Redburn* and *The Nick Adams Stories*, more differences than similarities appear (*KanQ*, Fall 1975). Such is definitely not the case when Jesse Bier examines the stylistic similarities between *Huckleberry Finn* and *Sun* to demonstrate the influence of Twain on Hemingway (*MQ*, Winter 1980) and when Glen W. Singer argues that "The Battler" is a debased version of the same white man with a man of color alone in the wilderness myth that underlies *Huck Finn* (*NMAL*, Winter 1978). Less convincing are Martin Light's comparisons between Robert Cohn, Tom Sawyer, and

Don Quixote and between Jake Barnes, Huck Finn, and Sancho Panza (*MTJ*, Winter 1974) and George Monteiro's arguments for the influence of Henry Adams on Hemingway (*JAmS*, Apr. 1974).

Six critics have traced the effect of Henry James on Hemingway: Charles W. Mayer presents a rather general discussion of their similarities (*ArQ*, Winter 1979), as does Adeline R. Tintner (Nagel); whereas Lois P. Rudnick argues for the direct influence of *Daisy Miller* on "A Canary for One" (*MSE*, No. 1, 1978); W. R. McNaughton for *What Maisie Knew* on *Sun* (*MFS*, Summer 1976); Stanley Wertheim for *The Portrait of A Lady* on the same novel (*HN*, Fall 1979); and Fred D. Crawford and Bruce Morton sort out the complex influences compressed into the "Henry's bicycle" remark made by Bill Gorton in *Sun* (*SAF*, Spring 1978).

George Monteiro makes a fascinating comparison between O. Henry's "The Last Leaf" and Hemingway's "A Day's Wait" to demonstrate the differences between their handling of surprise endings (*PrS*, Winter 1973–74); he also tracks down Oliver Wendell Holmes's reactions to Hemingway's early works, read when he was in his late eighties (*MarkhamR*, Fall 1978). Edward R. Stephenson begins by suggesting that Stephen Crane and Hemingway only shared "an angle of vision" but then stumps for a "clear affinity" between "The Open Boat" and *The Old Man and The Sea* (*HR*, Fall 1981). Nicholas Joost and Alan Brown make a long, detailed, and very convincing survey of Eliot's pervasive influence on all aspects of Hemingway's fiction and theorizing about literature (*PLL*, Fall 1978).

Three scholars have attempted to assess the precise effect of Sherwood Anderson on Hemingway. Paul P. Somers, Jr. discusses the characters in both writers who are permanently damaged (Anderson's "Twisted Apples," Hemingway's "crips") by failed initiations (*Midamerica*, 1974) and then carefully explores the stylistic and verbal resemblances between *Dark Laughter* and *The Torrents of Spring* (*SAQ*, Fall 1974). Anderson's reaction to Hemingway's parody is examined by Ray Lewis White in the exchange of letters that followed the publication of *Torrents* (*MFS*, Winter 1980–81). In addition to being a parody of Anderson, *Torrents* also made use of several popular sources, among them two jokes: one is Diana's loss of her mother in a Paris hotel, another is Yogi's story of the beautiful Parisienne who picked him up and used him for her own multifarious purposes, as Daniel R. Barnes informs us (*SSF*, Spring 1982). Another popular source that crept into *Torrents* was Madison Grant's *The Passing of a Great Race* (1916), which Taylor Alderman believes Hemingway heard about from F. Scott Fitzgerald (*FHA*, 1977). Scott Donaldson examines in some detail several other ways in which Fitzgerald influenced Hemingway's career; in addition to his editorial advice, Fitzgerald played an important role in helping Max Perkins woo Hemingway into the Scribner's camp (*AL*, Jan. 1982).

Passing on to the complex relations between William Faulkner, Hemingway, and Thomas Wolfe, we may begin with Faulkner's bear. On one hand, John H. Howell (*AL*, Mar. 1980) argues that *Bell* (1940) influenced "The Bear" (1942); on the other, Peter L. Hays contends that it influenced *The Old Man and The Sea*, written in 1952 (Nagel). Then there is Faulkner's completely offhand ranking of Thomas Wolfe ahead of Hemingway that got blown out of proportion by the eager press and the anxious Papa, as we are told by Richard Walser (*SAQ*, Spring 1979), because, as both Lex Gaither (*TWN*, Fall 1978) and John L. Idol, Jr. (*SCR*, Fall 1982) show, Hemingway had no use whatsoever for Wolfe. Even though John O'Hara tried to ingratiate himself with Hemingway by comparing him to Shakespeare in a review of *Across*, Carlos Baker points out that he was completely ignored (*JOHJ*, Fall/Winter 1980). Three critics discuss the affinities between John Steinbeck and Hemingway: Richard Astro compares Steinbeck's *Cup of Gold* (1929) to *To Have and Have Not* in *The Twenties: Fiction, Poetry, Drama* (ed. Warren French, Deland, Fla., 1975); Edward E. Waldron compares *The Pearl* to *The Old Man and The Sea* (*StQ*, Summer–Fall 1980); and Mimi R. Gladstein compares Ma Joad to Pilar (*StQ*, Summer–Fall 1981).

A handful of articles compare Hemingway's works to novels written after his death. Roger Sharrock's comparison of John Updike's *Couples* to *Farewell* (*ArielE*, Oct. 1973) and Adam J. Sorkin's of Joseph Heller's *Catch-22* to the same novel (*SAB*, Nov. 1979) dramatically highlight our changing attitudes toward love and war. A direct but rather superficial similarity between Heller and Hemingway underlies Andrew Crosland's supposition that Yossarian's trick of identifying himself as Washington Irving/Irving Washington while censoring letters goes back to one of Hemingway's *Esquire* letters (*AN&Q*, Jan. 1978). A more directly relevant comparison is made by Sandra Whipple Spanier between J. D. Salinger's *Catcher in the Rye* (1951) and "The Last Good Country," begun on 23 July 1952, because she suggests that when Hemingway realized how close the two novels had become, he stopped work on his manuscript (*SSF*, Winter 1982). Cynthia M. Barron, on the other hand, believes that "Soldier's Home" exerted an influence on *Catcher* (*HR*, Fall 1982). Finally, John Seelye spins out at some length a comparison between Erich Segal's *Love Story* and *Farewell* that might have been more interesting if he had been able to pin down what the differences between the two novels were (*CL*, Fall 1983). In a similar fashion, James Hinkle shows just how complex and slippery the whole question of "influence" can become when he produces sixty examples from *Sun* of Hemingway playing around with literary and not-so-literary sources, echoes, and allusions (*HR*, Fall 1982).

In addition to being influenced by others, Hemingway was an influence in his own right. Although Ernest S. Falbo uses the influence of

Hemingway on the Italian writer Carlo Linati as an opportunity to discuss Hemingway's role in Italian letters from 1929 to 1950 (*FHA*, 1975), American critics tend to concentrate on man-to-man influences. Frederick Busch, for example, detects the general influence of "After the Storm" on John Hawkes's imagery (in *A John Hawkes Symposium*, ed. Anthony C. Santore and Michael Pocalyko, New York, 1978); Donald M. Murray notes similarities between *Sun* and Nathanael West's *The Day of the Locust* (*FHA*, 1975); Sara Lennox finds traces of the same novel in Uwe Johnson's *Mutmassungen über Jakob* (*MLS*, Spring 1977); Frank Laurence uncovers Hemingway's trace in the works of Russell Hoban, a writer of children's stories (*HN*, Fall, 1980); and Myles Hurd believes that "Cat in the Rain" influenced Ed Bullins's play "Clara's Ole Man" (*NConL*, May 1981). More complex than these influences is Saul Bellow's very ambivalent attitude toward Hemingway that caused him to react toward Papa like a rebellious son, as Allan Chavkin tells us (*PLL*, Fall 1983). Two recent examples of completely conscious uses of Hemingway are Joseph J. Waldmeir's short story about a father and son following Hemingway's footsteps in Paris (Waldmeir) and James R. Giles's attempt to merge fiction and literary criticism in a story that depicts Nick Adams as a forty-year-old creative writing teacher (*ArQ*, Summer 1983).

William F. Nolan surveys seven authors, among them John Dos Passos, Leicester Hemingway, and Carlos Baker, who created characters based on Hemingway (*FHA*, 1974); Janet Lewis discusses Hemingway's part in the conception of Phillippe, the hero of Fitzgerald's "Phillippe, Count of Darkness" stories (*FHA*, 1975); Clinton S. Burhans, Jr. does the same for Kurt Vonnegut's use of him as the model for Harold Ryan in *Happy Birthday, Wanda June* (*MFS*, Summer 1975), as does Wayne Kvam for Rolf Hochhuth's play *Tod eines Jägers* (1977), in which Hemingway appears as "himself" just before committing suicide (*MSE*, Feb. 1981). Woody Allen uses the same device in "A Twenties Memory" that describes the good times he had with Hemingway, Gertrude Stein, and all the gang in France (in *Getting Even*, New York, 1971). Much more personal are Leonard Kriegel's long essay on Hemingway's influence on the American conception of manhood (*PR*, No. 3, 1977) and Jerry Underwood's imaginary conversation between several writers on why creative writing students sound like Hemingway (*CE*, Mar. 1976). More *au courant* is Irene Thompson's thought-provoking comparison between the careers of Jean Rhys and Hemingway (*GaR*, Spring 1981) that asks why he entered the canon whereas she was not only excluded but virtually forgotten.

Attempts to define Hemingway's deceptively simple style fall into two groups: linguistic analyses that concentrate on theory and formal elements versus literary discussions that ignore theory and concentrate on the function and significance of the formal devices. Waldemar Gutwinski displays the characteristic linguistic slant in his *Cohesion in Literary Texts:*

A Study of Some Grammatical and Lexical Features of English Discourse (The Hague, 1976) when he uses a stratificational model to compare the cohesive devices in Henry James's *The Portrait of a Lady* with those in Hemingway's "Big Two-Hearted River." What he discovers is that Hemingway uses lexical devices instead of syntactical ones to unify his text, i.e., proper nouns instead of pronouns, lots of redundancy (repetitions), pairs of nouns, and numerous "free sentences," like "it is . . ." and "there is/are. . . ." In another comparative study, Ahmad K. Ardat makes a statistical comparison of the styles of Gertrude Stein, Sherwood Anderson, and Hemingway to discover that the first is the most unique and the latter two the most alike (*Style*, Winter 1980). More theoretical is Walter A. Cook's case grammar analysis of state and process clauses in *Old Man* that presents the theoretical model, collects a lot of data under its tenets, but then makes no explicit comments about the stylistic function of the clauses (in *Meaning: A Common Ground of Linguistics and Literature*, ed. Don L. F. Nilsen, Cedar Falls, Iowa, 1973).

In the same volume, C. R. Stratton applies the traditional form/function model plus a rhetorical analysis to the three opening paragraphs of "Big Two-Hearted River" to discover that the hotel and saloon clauses are somehow subordinate to the rhetorical shape of the whole passage, but he cannot say exactly how. In yet another study of the same story, Richard L. McLain makes some very perceptive remarks about the active/causative versus the passive/noncausative characteristics of three passages, but almost all of them could have been, and, in fact, were made without recourse to the generative semantics model that was explained at great length in the first part of his article (*Lang&S*, Spring 1979). In much the same way, Olga K. Garnica compares real dialogue to its literary analogue in the last scene of "Indian Camp" to argue that Nick's questions display strong emotion in contrast to his father's evasive replies (*Poetics*, Sept. 1977). In a valuable study of Hemingway's use of Spanish in *Bell*, which should be compared to Allen Josephs's essay (Noble), Gary D. Keller sorts out the many ways in which Hemingway plays off Spanish against English and vice-versa in *The Analysis of Hispanic Texts: Current Trends in Methodology* (ed. Mary Ann Beck *et al.*, Jamaica, N.Y., 1976).

Standing somewhere between these theoretically motivated linguistic analyses and the empirically inclined literary discussions are language-based analyses of style like those employed by Bates Hoffer and his colleagues in a special edition of *Linguistics in Literature* (Spring 1976). Using the very basic inductive and lexically oriented model outlined by Hoffer, seven of the nine essays in the collection are essentially very brief image and symbol analyses of Hemingway's short stories. Ray Lanford offers a close reading of "My Old Man" that concludes that Joe's father wanted to go straight in Paris; Donna Pearson analyzes the number imagery of "The Gambler, the Nun, and the Radio" to find that the Nun's way is the preferred one; Trisha Ingman examines the symbolic motifs of "A Canary for One" to make an interesting link between the dark station in Paris and the one at the end of the line in *Sun*; Lois Brackenridge provides a close reading of "Today is Friday"; Barbara Maloy sees "The Light of the World" as a descent into the underworld with parallels to *Alice in Wonderland*; Leslie Miller's study of the imagery of "Cat in the Rain" belabors the obvious; whereas Mary Kay Willis provides an excellent analysis of the imagery in "The Battler." In the two most language-oriented essays of the collection, Jessie C. Gunn makes very dubious use of not very good sound-symbolism to reach a very questionable conclusion about "The End of Something," while Barbara Sanders offers an excellent analysis of the symbolic uses of some verb features in "Cross-Country Snow."

Much more substantial than these *Linguistics in Literature* essays is the inductive analysis of the language in *Sun* and "Soldier's Home" that allows Larzer Ziff to state, first, that Hemingway's style is a way of talking about private experiences without sacrificing them to the falsehoods of public ideals and, second, that when Hemingway's attitude about these ideals changes, he starts making bad imitations of his earlier style (*Poetics*, Dec. 1978). Two British linguists have used "Cat in the Rain" for their own purposes. Michael Stubbs uses it to investigate how competent readers summarize, generate propositions, and make implications about literary texts in *Literary Text and Language Study* (ed. Ronald Carter and Deirdre Burton, London, 1982); and Ronald Carter employs a fairly traditional model to investigate its style, examine his literary intuitions about it, and attempt an interpretation: for example, the cat is symbolic but its meaning is indeterminate (in *Language and Literature: An Introductory Reader in Stylistics*, ed. Ronald Carter, London, 1982).

Among the literary discussions of Hemingway's style are three articles by David Kerner that anatomize Hemingway's "Anti-Metronomic Dialogue," by which he means dialogue that "juxtaposes end and opening quotes in a single speaker's two consecutive speeches, or at least one of the speeches is presented without attribution" (*MFS*, Summer 1982). With a definition like that, one understands why Kerner presents examples without any definition in his first article (*FHA*, 1979); in his third article (*AL*, Oct. 1982), Kerner examines the manuscript evidence for Hemingway's use of this confusing device in order to shed some light on the "Clean, Well-Lighted Place" crux (for some comment refer, again, to George H. Thomson's article in the *Hemingway Review* [Spring 1983]). In another analysis of dialogue, Stephen R. Portch computes its absence down to the minute in "Hills" (thirty-one minutes of silence) and in "Killers" (the dialogue requires only a fraction of the hour and fifty minutes that Al and Max are in Henry's) to conclude that "the apparent simplicity of the unspoken" is an important aspect of Hemingway's style (*HR*, Fall 1982). The high percentage of dialogue in "Killers," "Hills,"

"Sea Change," and "A Clean, Well-Lighted Place" leads J. F. Kobler to conclude that these four stories are really more like plays (*FHA*, 1975); and John V. Hagopian finds the source of this pared-down, stoical style in the fact that Hemingway was a frozen exile from himself (*Mosaic*, Spring 1975).

In a more philosophical approach, Phillip D. Adams analyzes several passages in *Farewell* that exhibit the vagueness and impressionism that he associates with Husserl's "eidetic reduction," a notion that views simple concepts as "essentially and not accidentally inexact" (in *Images and Innovations: Update '70's*, ed. Malinda R. Maxfield, Spartanburg, S.C., 1979). In two separate essays, David Lodge places Hemingway in the tradition of one kind of modernist writing because his work shows "an essentially metonymic style [that] is made to serve the purposes of metaphor" (in *Modernism*, ed. Malcolm Bradbury and J. MacFarlane, Baltimore, Md., 1976), and, he continues, it was this way because his essentially materialistic and antimetaphysical turn of mind caused him to reject the metaphorical style of modernists like Joyce who used metaphor and myth to replace the dead God (*The Modes of Modern Writing: Metaphor, Metonymy, and the Typology of Modern Literature*, Ithaca, N.Y., 1977).

b. Individual Works. The critical articles on Hemingway's individual works will be discussed in chronological order, with the notable exception that articles on the short stories, except for those on *In Our Time*, will be gathered together at the end of this report.

After *Three Stories & Ten Poems* (1923), Hemingway's second book was *in our time* (1924), a collection of eighteen chapters that have been carefully analyzed by Keith Carabine (*FHA*, 1979); but since all of these chapters were assimilated into his third book, *In Our Time* (1925; revised 1930), critics have generally discussed them in this later form. In the collection of essays on *In Our Time* edited by Michael S. Reynolds (CEAmL, Boston, 1983), E. R. Hagemann analyzes both the textual history of the chapters and their historical background in two separate reprinted articles. Reynolds also reprints David J. Leigh's investigation of the shifting relationships between the chapters and stories that reveals to him an underlying pattern of "existential neurosis" that is similar to Young's trauma hypothesis (*SSF*, Winter 1975) and Linda W. Wagner's study of how the book's parts are related to óne another by "juxtaposition" (*SSF*, Summer 1975). E. D. Lowry sees the same relationship, dubs it "collage," and relates it to the chaotic aspects of the book while greatly overemphasizing its orderly and positive aspects (*L&P*, No. 3, 1976). Gilbert H. Muller adds very little to the discussion with his Janovian analysis of the "primal screams" in the book (*Renascence*, Summer 1977); but David Seed spells out the linkages between the parts very ably, connecting some of the chapters to Goya and Pound (Lee). The influence of Joyce on *In Our Time* is discussed by Robert E. Gajdusek, who relates it to *Dubliners* (*HR*, Fall 1982), whereas Charles G. and A. C. Hoffmann see a kind of Joycean epiphany as one of the collection's unifying themes (Noble).

Turning to the individual stories of *In Our Time*, Louis H. Leiter discusses the seven episodes within "On the Quai at Smyrna" and the narrator's ironic reactions to them (*SSF*, Summer 1968; reprinted in Reynolds), while Paul Witherington analyzes its narrative devices well but then makes rather dubious inferences from them (*NMAL*, Summer 1978). One of the great critical issues about "Indian Camp" involves Nick's enigmatic Uncle George: Larry Grimes argues very convincingly that Uncle George's paternity ties up several loose ends in the story (*SSF*, Fall 1975). Other critics have been concerned with different issues: using the deleted beginning of "Indian Camp" that Philip Young entitled "Three Shots," Dick Penner makes the familiar point that the story is about a lack of communication between Nick and his father (*FHA*, 1977), just as Kenneth G. Johnston takes the equally familiar stance that it reveals Nick's incapacity to deal with the demands of manhood (*SSF*, Winter 1978).

In addition to two notes on "The Doctor and the Doctor's Wife" from *The Explicator*, Reynolds includes a longer article by Richard Fulkerson who argues very reasonably that the story is not about Nick, as Young would have it, but about Doctor Adams (*SSF*, Winter 1979), a view to which Joseph M. Flora would assent (*SSF*, Winter 1977), as does Stephen D. Fox, who exposes all of the Doctor's evasions to conclude that the story is about "civilized half-truths" (*ArQ*, Spring 1973).

Several critics during the 1970s tried to date "The Three-Day Blow" on the basis of its baseball references: reacting to some errors in Roger Asselineau's Pléiade edition of Hemingway (1966, 1969), George Monteiro dates the story in 1916 (*FHA*, 1973), which is disputed by James Barbour and Robert Sattelmeyer, who place it after the 1917 World Series (*FHA*, 1975); in his reply, Monteiro revises his date to "1917, late in the season," averring that Hemingway may have adjusted the facts to fit his story (*FHA*, 1977; reprinted in Reynolds). After that exchange, Matthew O'Brien also places the story in 1917 but concentrates much more on its defensive adolescent male chit-chat (*AN&Q*, Sept. 1977), as does Kenneth G. Johnston, who reviews the story's historical background and dates it to postwar 1919 (*HR*, Fall 1982).

In one of the articles written especially for Reynolds's collection, Nicholas Gerogiannis adduces several Henry Fielding and Jack London parallels for "The Battler" and argues from "The Last Good Country" and other unpublished material that Nick, like Ad Francis, was strongly attracted to his sister. In the same vein, Frank B. Kyle notes several of the similarities between Ad and Nick, relating the story's images of chaos and cosmos to similar ones in "Big Two-Hearted River," for example, the cosmic campfire versus the chaotic swamp (*SSF*, Fall 1979). The only article of note on "Chapter VI," where Nick lies wounded, is Kathryn Zabelle Derounian's very detailed examination of its three early drafts that also includes several comments on its style and structure (*PBSA*, First Quarter 1983; reprinted in Reynolds).

Five articles were written about "Soldier's Home." Both Earl Rovit, in *The American Short Story* (ed. Calvin Skaggs, New York, 1977) and John J. Roberts (*SSF*, Fall 1976; reprinted in Reynolds) believe that the town's lies about the war hurt Harold Krebs more than the war itself. Horace P. Jones provokes two quick responses when he points out that although Krebs was a marine, he is referred to as a "soldier" and that he got back home only a few months after the war rather than "years after the war was over" (*Expl*, Summer 1979). George Monteiro's response is in terms of irony and literary effects (*Expl*, Fall 1981); and John D. Boyd's (*Expl*, Fall 1981) is similar.

Discovering no factual basis for "The Revolutionist," Anthony Hunt discusses the symbolic values of Montegna's association with Milan, a city of losses, and the role that Hemingway's own experiences played in the story's genesis (*FHA*, 1977; reprinted in Reynolds). In another essay written expressly for Reynolds's collection, Jim Steinke infers the compositional history of "The Revolutionist" and "A Very Short Story," notes their differing tones, and discusses their historical background as well as the critical work on them. After reviewing the criticism on "Cat in the Rain," Gertrude M. White argues that the wife's childish language and insistent demands indicate that she has not grown up so that the story is about alienation rather than a brief for either the girl or her husband (*FHA*, 1978).

In one of the four pieces on "Out of Season," Dix McComas charts the story's factual geography very well but then pushes too hard for its symbolic implications (*HR*, Spring 1984). Both Paul R. Jackson (*HR*, Fall 1981) and Paul Smith (Reynolds) believe that there is more below the story's surface than Peduzzi's implied suicide—it is the tension between the young couple that may lead to their eventual breakup. Jackson makes a particularly astute analysis of how the story's blurred point of view fails to focus the reader's attention properly. In the fourth paper the Italian Hemingway scholar, Giovanni Cecchin, adduces the factual prototype of Peduzzi (*HR*, Spring 1985). Kenneth G. Johnston speculates that the use of "Mike" for Nick Adams in "Cross-Country Snow" may be either an error or a code name like "Gidge" for George (*AN&Q*, Sept.–Oct. 1981).

All of the critical articles but one on "Big Two-Hearted River" accept what Keith Carabine calls the "dark reading" that goes back to Malcolm Cowley's "nightmares at noonday" comment; Carabine, however, proposes that the story captures the joy of fishing and is about euphoria (*HR*, Spring 1982). Against Carabine's eccentric "light reading" are the more usual dark readings of Lewis E. Weeks, Jr., who observes that

Nick's poor campcraft, for example, pulling his tent too taut, reflects his abnormally tense state of mind (*SSF*, Fall 1974), of Theo Vijgen, who claims that the switch to interior monologue after the big trout gets away indicates Nick's temporary loss of self-control (*NMAL*, Spring–Summer 1982), of Gregory S. Sojka, who suggests that "Chapter XV" about Sam Cardinella's loss of control is placed between the two parts of "Big Two-Hearted River" to highlight Nick's struggle to retain his (*FHA*, 1976), and of Howard L. Hannum, who not only discusses the lyric and ode-like aspects of the story but also unearths many of its buried war allusions (*HR*, Spring 1984; reprinted in Waldmeir). Rather different than these readings are B. J. Smith's contention that, in addition to referring to the war, the story is also about writing, so that the loss of the big trout reflects the theft of Hemingway's manuscripts, the big catches the big stories, and the little ones the little stories (*SSF*, Spring–Summer 1983); Jack F. Stewart's discussion of the Christian allusions which claims Nick had to reject the coffee according to Hopkins as a sentimental dependence in order to work out his own salvation (*SSF*, Spring 1978); and two articles on the story's landscape reprinted by Reynolds. In contrast to Robert Gibbs's rather vague discussion of the story's "interior landscape" (*HN*, Fall 1979; reprinted in Reynolds), William Adair carefully works out its dreamscape by adducing analogues from works like *Farewell*, "A Way You'll Never Be," and "Now I Lay Me" (*CE*, Spring 1977; reprinted in Reynolds).

Since all the articles on Hemingway's fourth book, *The Torrents of Spring*, have already been discussed, we may go on to the second book that he published in 1926, *The Sun Also Rises*. Two scholars have shown an interest in the novel's textual history. One is Frederic Joseph Svoboda in his 1983 book on the crafting of the novel's style, the other Michael S. Reynolds, who concludes from his study of the manuscripts that, even though Hemingway intended *Sun* to be about a bullfighter's corruption, what came out was the corruption of Jake Barnes (in *A Fair Day in the Affections: Literary Essays in Honor of Robert B. White, Jr.*, ed. Jack M. Durant and M. Thomas Hester, Raleigh, N.C., 1980; also in Noble). Svoboda's and Reynolds's interest in textual history is unique because most of the work on *Sun* has approached its meaning through its characters. Cathy N. Davidson believes that the death of Vincente Girones indicates that Brett does not change in a novel whose theme is death-in-life and life-in-death (*HN*, Fall 1979). Two critics have examined Count Mippipopolous and concluded that he too is impotent: William Kerrigan also argues that Jake becomes like the Count in the final scene of the book (*AL*, Mar. 1974); Leon Seltzer agrees but claims that Jake transcends the condition of his older counterpart (*Renascence*, Fall 1978). Two other pairs of critics have discussed Robert Cohn and Bill Gorton. Jesse Bier believes that Cohn is modeled on F. Scott Fitzgerald because of the similarity between a wisecrack in *Sun* to the famous "poor Scott/Julian" remark in "Snows" (AN&Q, May 1980); and Robert McIllvaine reads Cohn's favorite book, W. H. Hudson's *The Purple Land that England Lost* (1885), in order better to understand him as a misguided knight errant (NMAL, Spring 1981).

As for Bill Gorton, Morton L. Ross supposes that he plays the role of an Ecclesiastes-like preacher to Jake at Burguete (MFS, Winter 1972–73); by contrast, H. R. Stoneback, after pointing out the anachronism in the date of Bryan's death, argues that Jake is a believer like Bryan, whereas Bill is a mocking unbeliever like Mencken and Darrow (C&L, Winter 1983). Sam S. Baskett would certainly agree with Ross's notion of Bill the preacher since, in his survey of six men's reactions to Brett, only Jake absorbs Bill's preaching well enough to be "undaunted" by her as he "utilizes" food and drink at the end of the novel (CentR, Winter 1978). Charles C. Walcutt, on the other hand, believes that "utilize," in contrast to "use," represents a "phony" value (Expl, Apr. 1974).

Of all the characters in the novel, Jake Barnes has attracted the most critical attention. Jake's impotence is commented on by James Ellis, who tells us the British Distinguished Service Order was said to stand for "dick shot off," which implies the nature of Jake's injury (Expl, Spring 1978), and by three critics who relate it to the way he fished in Burguete: Charles B. Harris contends that Jake's still fishing with worms in contrast to Bill's fly fishing is a violation of the fisherman's code that foreshadows his later violation of the *aficionado*'s code when he introduces Brett to Romero (NMAL, Summer 1977); Warren Wedin makes the same point about Jake's fishing but relates it to his later self-betrayal with Brett in Madrid (ArQ, Spring 1981); and Jesse Bier says it all again, adding that Jake's narrative style, which mixes precision and vagueness, reflects his spriritual impotence (ArQ, Summer 1983). As for Jake's style, Terrence Doody uses the description of Bocanegra's ear to argue that Jake's narration is a function of Hemingway's own style of exorcism (JNT, Sept. 1974). Not everyone is hung up on Jake's DSO: David Henry Lowenkron, for example, emphasizes his pragmatism over his impotence and stoicism (TQ, Spring 1976), an interpretation that Ronald Lajoie and Sally Lentz would second since they use Jake's reading of A. E. W. Mason's "The Crystal Trench" to infer that he will no longer wait stoically for Brett but will be more pragmatically concerned with himself (FHA, 1975). Brett's offhand remark about Jake's "hell of a biblical name" has stimulated a good deal of onomastic ingenuity. Manuel Schonhorn uses the biblical Jacob allusion to emphasize Jake's manly struggles instead of his withered limb (BSUF, Spring 1975); Robert D. Crozier assents to this, bringing his own passion for St. John of the Cross to bear on the discussion (PLL, Summer 1975); and, in a similar leap of the imagination, Eben Bass uses the "In another country" allusion to explore the connections between the novel and Marlowe's *Jew of Malta*, proposing that one of the friar's names, Jacomo Barnadine, abbreviated "Jac." in the stage directions, may be the source of Jake's name (*MarkhamR*, Fall 1976). Even more surprising is Joseph M. Flora's attempt to relate Jake's name to the British slang word *jakes* (privy) and to *barn* (*EngR*, Fall 1973).

In contrast to these mostly negative views of Jake, several critics have tried to emphasize his more positive traits. Starting with the novel's opening in Paris, David Morgan Zehr examines Hemingway's critique of the expatriate mystique to conclude that Jake is the most balanced member of that crowd (*ArQ*, Summer 1977). Moving on to Spain, Kathleen L. Nichols contends that Jake becomes a realist when he very unromantically introduces Brett to Romero (*FHA*, 1978); and, turning to the finale in Madrid, Donald A. Daiker argues that Jake defeats Brett just as Romero defeats bulls (*McNR*, 1974–75). Andrew Hook draws a similar parallel when he insists that Jake gets up from his defeats in Pamplona just as Romero got up from his knockdowns by Cohn (Lee). Gerry Brenner, on the other hand, believes that Brett grows in awareness at Botin's whereas Jake does not, as his drunkenness and sarcasm clearly indicate (*ArQ*, Summer 1977).

Turning from the novel's characters to its themes, W. J. Stuckey rejects the familiar *Waste Land* parallels to insist that *Sun* is about male pleasure, which requires that passion, as represented by Brett, must be rigorously controlled (*JNT*, Fall 1976). As for the bullfighting, Mary Kathryn Grant views it as a kind of sacred dance that contrasts with the novel's secularized dancing (*ArQ*, Summer 1977); while Nina Elyot Schwartz, with characteristically Lacanian paradox, sees the bull as the male figure who is seduced to his destruction by the seductively feminine "secrets" of the matador, which further suggests that Jake controls Brett by his secret impotence, and the reader by his omissions (*Criticism*, Winter 1984). Using a different approach, Jane P. Tompkins comes to a similar conclusion when she makes a reader-response analysis of Hemingway's "repressive form," that is, one that mocks intellect and feeling in a very pared down style (*CE*, Oct. 1977). More conventional than these slippery paradoxes and readerly responses is Patrick D. Morrow's analysis of the novel's money theme that collects the 142 direct and 71 indirect references to it before sifting through its metaphorical values (in *Money Talks: Language and Lucre in American Fiction*, ed. Roy R. Male, Norman, Okla., 1980).

Since all of Hemingway's stories will be discussed together, we shall bypass his sixth book, the collection of short stories entitled *Men Without Women* (1927), in favor of his second novel, *A Farewell to Arms* (1929). In addition to the four books on *Farewell* already in print, two collections of critical articles by Jay Gellens (1970) and John Graham (1971) and two critical works by Michael S. Reynolds (1976) and Bernard Oldsey (1979), the many critical articles may be divided very roughly into background studies, character analyses, and thematic discussions. While in Italy, Robert W. Lewis unearthed the official Italian citations for Hemingway's two medals (*JML*, May 1982), and four critics have looked into the literary backgrounds of the novel. George Dekker and Joseph Harris collaborate in an investigation of its folkloristic supernatural elements, for example, revenants and second sight (*PMLA*, Mar. 1979); John Unrue goes against the critical grain by suggesting that Psalm 84, which mentions the valley of Baca, that is, "of weeping," should serve as the motto for the so-called Swiss "idyll" of Catherine and Frederic (*FHA*, 1974); Terry Box sees Catherine's death as an ironic reversal of the Pygmalion-Galatea myth because she turns into a statue when she dies (*Expl*, Summer 1979); and Kingsley Widmer interprets Frederic's ant-cooking memory as a kind of "insect fable" that lacks, however, the tragic reach of King Lear's speech about flies and wanton boys (in *Edges of Extremity*, University of Tulsa Monograph series, No. 17, Tulsa, Okla., 1980). The discussion of the novel's trial titles, begun by Reynolds and Oldsey, has been continued by Paul Smith, who produces a composite list of some thirty-one titles that Hemingway considered before selecting the one that now seems so natural and appropriate (*HR*, Fall 1982), by William Gargan, who proposes a Shakespearean source for one of the rejected titles, "Death once Dead" (*NMAL*, 1980), and by Robert Fleming, who feels that George Peele's poem contributes much more to the novel than its title (*SAF*, Spring 1983).

Even though most critics focus their attention on Catherine Barkley and Frederic Henry, Colin S. Cass uses Miss Van Campen to discuss the careful timing used to get Frederic back to the front in time for the retreat from Caporetto (*FHA*, 1978). Among those concerned with Frederic Henry, Scott Donaldson views him as a wily fox who pretends to be innocent and passive in order to shirk the responsibility for his actions (Noble); Linda C. Parton suggests that what he learns is that knowing how to die has a value of its own (*FHA*, 1979); J. F. Kobler examines three of the reasons Frederic gives for Catherine's death to conclude that none of them make any sense to him (*FHA*, 1978); Dale Edmonds reckons that Frederic writes his account of what happened ten years after Catherine died in the spring of 1918 (*NMAL*, Spring 1980); and Robert Merrill concludes that Frederic's story is a tragedy because he suffers for doing the right thing—falling in love with Catherine (*AL*, Jan. 1974).

Discussions of Catherine Barkley are pretty evenly divided between the masculinists who like her and the feminists who do not. Representing the pro-Catherine male view are Jim Steinke, who points out that Catherine takes Frederic away from the "war brotherhood" of whoring and war mongering that he shares with Rinaldi (*Spectrum*, Nos. 1–2, 1979); Jean Wyrick, who views her as a romantic symbol of an idyllic life separate from war so that her death initiates Frederic into the harsh realities of war, death, and disease (*MSE*, Fall 1973); and Roger Whitlow, who, in much the same way, believes that Catherine is so upset by the loss of her fiancé at the Somme and by her guilt at not having had sex with him that she takes a strong antiwar stance that is shared by neither Henry nor Hemingway (*MarkhamR*, Fall 1978). In contrast to these generally positive views of Catherine, the feminist critic Judith Fetterley argues very forcefully that there is a very strong latent hostility toward her that is revealed in the long drawn-out death scene (*The Resisting Reader: A Feminist Approach to American Fiction*, Bloomington, Ind., 1978). The defense against this very persuasive position, set forth by William K. Spofford, is that Frederic and Catherine are really mutually dependent so that their love elevates both of them (*FHA*, 1978). This line is continued by Peter Balbert, who agrees that both lovers grow from their affair (*HR*, Fall 1983), by Joyce Wexler, who contends that Catherine is Frederic's "counterpart," so that her death teaches him the limits of love (*GaR*, Spring 1981), and by Mark Spilka, who, in a wide-ranging essay on the rise and fall of androgyny in Hemingway's life and work, gives the counterpart idea its final extension by arguing that Catherine's death represents Hemingway's farewell to any serious attempt at a mature androgynous love (in *American Novelists Revisited: Essays in Feminist Criticism*, ed. Fritz Fleischmann, Boston, 1982).

Taking a wider view of the novel's themes and structure are Eugene B. Cantelupe, who feels that the meeting at Catherine's villa in Gorizia foreshadows her death in Lausanne so that the novel is "a study of doom" (*FHA*, 1977) and William Adair, who charts out the interaction in the novel between a dark, nightmarish Goya-like aspect representing thanatos, and a light, daytime Cézannesque aspect representing eros (*JNT*, Jan. 1975). In a second article, Adair explores the interaction of active temporal time (more thanatos) with attempts to contain its movement in stylized settings that reflect Hemingway's interior landscapes more than real places (*SDR*, Spring 1975).

Since most critics believe that Hemingway's work during the 1930s was of low quality, very little attention has been paid to the seven books he published during the Depression. In addition to Robert W. Lewis's study of the composition of *Death in the Afternoon* (Nagel) and a Yale dissertation by Susan Beegel, only Allen Josephs has looked at Hemingway's eighth book, finding it an excellent study of *torrero* that also reflects Hemingway's nostalgia for a lost Spain as well as his overriding interest in the ritualization of the monster-battle myth (*HR*, Fall 1982). We may pass by Hemingway's two 1933 publications, *God Rest You Merry Gentlemen* and *Winner Take Nothing*, which will be discussed with the short stories, to *Green Hills of Africa* (1935) and *To Have and Have Not* (1937). Barbara Lounsberry provides a serious literary analysis of the former when she interprets "pursuit" as a metaphor for life, the kudus as *kudos* "glory, fame," and the title as a recollection of Whittier's "Snowbound" (*HR*, Spring 1983). John Cobbs believes that *To Have and Have Not* was butchered when the social satire material was added to the otherwise excellent story of Harry Morgan (*SAB*, Nov. 1979).

Hemingway's interest in the Spanish Civil War surfaced in the commentary he wrote for Joris Ivens's film *The Spanish Earth*, published for the first time in 1938 by Jasper Wood, a Cleveland high school boy. This information, as well as a careful review of the film's script, is passed on to us by Arthur Coleman (*HR*, Fall 1982). Much more important for his career was *For Whom the Bell Tolls* (1940), the novel that pulled his reputation out of the doldrums of the Depression. In addition to the essays on *Bell*'s language already mentioned, R. H. Miller has reviewed the various texts of its John Donne epigraph (*FHA*, 1978), and Carole Moses has noted the "Elizabethan" quality of its language that makes the reader feel that he is an outsider looking in, like all men in this world (*FHA*, 1978). Digging much deeper into the verbal structure of the novel, Robert D. Crozier, S.J., gives a completely spiritualized reading of Maria's orgasm, what she refers to as "time in *la gloria*," which draws heavily upon the works of St. John of the Cross (*PLL*, Winter 1974). In a similar turn of mind, Robert G. Walker believes that St. Anselm of Canterbury (1033–1109) and his work *Cur Deus Homo* inform the portrayal of Anselmo (*NConL*, Mar. 1977), just as H. Keith Monroe supposes that Greta Garbo, as she appears in the film *Queen Christina* (1933), somehow aids Robert Jordan in his guerilla work (*FHA*, 1978).

As for *Bell*'s themes, David E. Zehr insists that Hemingway was a very conservative, bourgeois humanist and never a Communist sympathizer even though he was strongly anti-Fascist (*MQ*, Spring 1976); Walter J. Slatoff explores the complex theme of killing that culminates in Robert Jordan's shooting of the good Fascist Lt. Berrendo in order to cover the band's escape (*JNT*, Spring 1977); and Paul R. Jackson analyzes the theme of pompous seriousness versus fear-chasing joking to argue that Jordan finally achieves a delicate balance between the two as he waits for Berrendo (*HN*, Fall 1980). Herman Nibbelink, on the other hand, views Jordan's death as a union with nature whose antithesis is embodied in the very urbanized Pilar (*ArQ*, Summer 1977), and Robert E. Fleming compares the suicide theme in *Bell* with "Fathers and Sons" to conclude that Jordan's death, which is more like El Sordo's heroic last stand than Kashkin's cowardly end, compensates for the suicide of Hemingway's father (*ArQ*, Summer 1977).

One of the more striking aspects of the work on *Bell* is that much more attention has been paid to the novel's overall structure than to the analysis of its characters. John J. Teunissen analyzes the novel's "Topocosmic" structure that fuses its Spanish setting with the American west as well as such other mythic themes as the hierogamos of Maria and Robert, the death/rebirth aspects in Pilar's massacre story, and the wise old woman traits of Pilar herself (*DR*, Spring 1976). More conventionally,

Creath S. Thorne views the novel as a "narrative tragedy" set in motion by Golz's fateful order to blow the bridge at a specific moment (*AL*, Jan. 1980); and Gerry Brenner sorts out the novel's epic features in an article (*MFS*, Winter 1970–71) that became one of the better chapters in *Concealments*.

Since no one has bothered with *Men at War*, the anthology that Hemingway edited with an introduction in 1942, we may now look at the two novels he published in the 1950s, *Across the River and Into the Trees* (1950) and *The Old Man and the Sea* (1952). Criticism of *Across* is divided between biographical analyses and literary discussions. Among those who see Colonel Cantwell as a direct reflection of Ernest Hemingway à la Philip Young are James L. McDonald, who totals up the Colonel's drinks to conclude that Cantwell is "not really a character at all; he is an idealization, a fantasized projection of Hemingway himself, a caricature of the author" (*NMAL*, Winter 1977); A. Sidney Kowles, Jr., who comes to much the same conclusion after a review of the similarities between Cantwell and his creator and adds that the novel is a weary one that looks forward to death (*ELWIU*, Fall 1978); and Joan Crane, who suggests that Hemingway's long infatuation with Andrea del Sarto's "Portrait of a Woman" may have contributed to Cantwell's infatuation with Renata and her portrait (*ABC*, Sept.–Oct. 1980). In the minority are those who emphasize the novel's literary value. Since Gerry Brenner's discussion of its Dantean elements (*FHA*, 1976; reprinted in his *Concealments*) and W. Craig Turner's analysis of its motifs (Noble) have been discussed, we need only mention William Adair's view of Baron Alvarito as a Jungian shadow figure with an aristocratic and Jacobean lineage (*NConL*, Jan. 1977) and William Wirt's analysis of the novel's tragic pattern (*FHA*, 1979).

Much less concerned with autobiographical revelations, criticism of *The Old Man and the Sea* has concentrated on several well-defined motifs and Christian allusions. One of the motifs is the lions that Stephen D. Warner believes create an ironic dissonance between Santiago's happy recollections and the reader's response to fishing as work (*Expl*, Oct. 1974). After reviewing the case for three as an important Hemingway number, William Adair argues that eighty-five is lucky because $8 - 5 = 3$, $8 + 5 = 13$, and $8 \times 5 = 40$, but since the significance of neither the sum nor the product is ever established, the argument falls flat (*NConL*, Jan. 1978). The importance of lions and numbers pales in comparison to the critical attention devoted to the novella's baseball references. George Monteiro defends Hemingway's assignment of the Cincinnati Reds to the National League against an attack by Richard A. Davison (*NConL*, Jan. 1971) by claiming that Santiago was teasing and testing Manolin (*NConL*, May 1974), and then explores the relevance of Joe DiMaggio's career to *Old Man* in great detail with very informative footnotes (*FHA*, 1975). Shooting somewhat higher, James Barbour and

Robert Sattelmeyer review several of the interrelated functions of the baseball talk (*FHA*, 1975), while Sam S. Baskett argues that baseball is not as positive and heroic as it may seem because it is, like Mr. Frazer's radio listening, an opiate that Santiago transcends in his vision of the lions, a vision that unites many of the tale's clashing opposites (*FHA*, 1976). Baskett also believes that Santiago is dying at the end of the story, a minority opinion that Bickford Sylvester argued for very convincingly some time ago (*MFS*, Winter 1966–67).

As for the novella's style, Linda W. Wagner sees it as Hemingway's greatest achievement in the Imagistic prose poem form (*MFS*, Winter 1973–74), but something odd about it has so convinced Darrel Mansell that it was written much earlier (1935–36) than its 1952 publication date that he makes a very elaborate comparative study of its style using a computer (*CHum*, July 1974). Since his results would only convince a believer, he supplements them with other arguments (*FHA*, 1975) that no one has paid any attention to. But Mansell's intuition of a 1935–36 composition has recently been strengthened, if not confirmed, by Bruce Morton's discovery, made with no reference to Mansell's work, that while writing *Old Man*, Hemingway made extensive use of several articles that he had written in the 1930s, most notably "Marlin off Cuba," an article published in a very rare book (only six libraries have copies of it) in 1935 (*HR*, Spring 1983). Only one critic has discussed any other character besides Santiago or Manolin: Fordyce Richard Bennett has worked out the opposition between Manolin's father as his physical, mundane, and unheroic ancestor versus Santiago as his spiritual, exceptional, and heroic parent (*FHA*, 1979).

As Yuri Prizel points out in his useful survey of the critical work on *Old Man*, the larger critical issues are not so much biographical as ideological with the Christian interpretations set against the pagan, existential, Freudian, and archetypal approaches (*RS*, Sept. 1973). And, with the exception of S. David Price, who analyzes the details of the Santiago/ writer, marlin/work, sharks/critics allegory (*Expl*, Spring 1980) first suggested by Philip Young, most critics of *Old Man* have taken a Christian slant on it. G. R. Wilson, Jr. tries to align its events with the liturgical calendar of the Catholic church, claiming that Santiago becomes, like Christ, a mythic hero incarnate (*SSF*, Fall 1977). Joseph M. Flora, on the other hand, believes that while Santiago is neither an orthodox Christian nor a sinner, his story illustrates "discipleship" and does it in Christian terms (*SSF*, Spring 1973); but Sam S. Baskett finds only loose allusions to Christ and St. James in the "radical intensification" that Hemingway uses in the creation of the story (*CentR*, Fall 1975). Perhaps the most careful investigation of the Christian element in *Old Man* is made by Wolfgang Wittkowski who systematically goes over all of Santiago's apparent Christian virtues as well as the critics' arguments for them to conclude that his fighter-in-the-ring aspects subsume the Christ-on-the-cross aspects in an antithetical fashion (*HR*, Fall 1983, a translation of a German article written in 1967).

Bruce Morton's discovery of a 1930s source for a work that Hemingway claimed to have written with great ease and speed in the 1950s lends weight to Jacqueline Tavernier-Courbin's deep skepticism about the genesis of *A Moveable Feast* (Oldsey). Great support has been given to her skepticism by Gerry Brenner, who concludes from a careful investigation of the book's early versions in the Kennedy Library that Mary Hemingway wrote certain chapters, made deep and important cuts, reordered it in places, and even wrote the conclusion so that what we have is a bastardized text of Hemingway's last book (*AL*, Dec. 1982). Out of all the nonfiction that Hemingway wrote, Carroll Grimes chooses his "Defense of Dirty Words" as a pretext to review certain journalistic attitudes of the 1930s and to discuss Hemingway's feelings about Ring Lardner, a man whose sports writing he considered "phoney." This article is extremely well-researched, as Grimes's long footnote on the famous *Mot de Cambronne* demonstrates (*FHA*, 1975).

Unlike his nonfiction and Paris memoir, Hemingway's unfinished novel, *Islands in the Stream* (1970), has attracted a good deal of critical attention. As with *Across*, the critics divide into those who see *Islands* as directly autobiographical and those who do not. Richard B. Hovey very emphatically espouses the autobiographical approach (*HSL*, No. 3, 1980; reprinted in Noble), as does Stephen L. Tanner, who views *Islands* as a typical Hemingway study in isolation that reflects the many other psychological "islands" in his own life and other work (*SWR*, Winter 1976). Among those who see the novel as literature, Jesse Bier notes two problems in the lineation of the dialogue (*HR*, Fall 1983); Gregory S. Sojka discusses the theme of art and cosmos (Noble); and two critics try to figure out what went wrong with Thomas Hudson. Allen Shepherd suggests that he is an overly passive observer whose men admire him for reasons that are not apparent to the reader (*AntigR*, Spring 1972); similarly, Joseph M. DeFalco argues that Hudson has a "defective vision" morally and artistically that is revealed in the "Bimini" section of the novel (*Topic*, Fall 1977). In his analysis of the same section, Francis E. Skipp views David's long fishing scene as a crucifixion that redeems Roger Davis's guilt (*FHA*, 1974).

Ever since Philip Young decided to place all the published and unpublished stories, sketches, and fragments about Nick Adams into a sequence that matched what he supposed to be the chronology of Nick's life, others have been finding fault with various aspects of *The Nick Adams Stories* (1972). As noted above, Peter Griffin has found several errors in "Summer People" (*AL*, Nov. 1978), for which Paul J. Lindholdt provides an extenuating circumstance but then discovers several new errors (*SSF*, Fall 1983). A much larger bone of contention has been Young's ordering of the stories, which Bernard F. Rodgers, Jr. calls into question by trying to discover its hidden genesis (*FHA*, 1974), while Stuart L. Burns argues that thematic coherence based on Nick's desire to return to an Eden of lost sex with Trudy and good conversation with Simon Green is more important than the ordering problem (*ArQ*, Summer 1977). Ann Edwards Boutelle takes a similar tack but concludes that the hidden center of the stories is not a lost Eden but the fantasized parricide of knife-wielding and therefore castrating fathers (*JML*, No. 1, 1981–82). Frank Scafella analyzes several of the stories, taking issue with Young's contention that the war wound is the crucial event in Nick's life (*HR*, Spring 1983); and finally, after speculating about why Hemingway did not finish "The Last Good Country" and how it might have developed, David R. Johnson suggests that Hemingway may have started the story to refute Young's thesis of a passive Nick Adams but then stopped when he realized that he was going to wound Nick again in a way that would support Young (*FHA*, 1979).

In one of the rare attempts to establish a perspective on the stories written after *In Our Time*, Colin E. Nicholson searches out their recurrent features to conclude that the individual is so threatened by outside forces that the hero is reduced to the immediate "now" in them (Lee). Turning to the specific stories in *Men Without Women*, only Colin S. Cass chooses to look at *The Jew of Malta* allusion as well as at some of the other imagery in the cryptic "In Another Country" (*SSF*, Summer 1981), whereas nine critics have been attracted to "Hills Like White Elephants." Kenneth G. Johnston looks at the manuscript to discover that Jig had been called Hadley, the couple had gotten off at Caseta to wait for another train, and that absinthe, considered to be an aphrodisiac, was only sold in Spain (*SAF*, Fall 1982). Robert E. Fleming uncovers four distinct sources for the story, two of which involved Hadley, and concludes that speculation "about a single source for a given story . . . is a disservice to the reader as well as to the reputation of the artist" (*NMAL*, Spring–Summer 1983). Three articles explore the tension created in the story. George Monteiro notes several things left out, for example, the abortion and the girl's fear of death (*FHA*, 1976); Mary Dell Fletcher concentrates on the symbolic function of the setting, is puzzled by the meaning of "white elephant" because she does not bother to look it up in a dictionary, and calls the girl "Jill" (*Expl*, Summer 1980); Lewis E. Weeks, Jr., on the other hand, is so taken by the elephant that in addition to reminding us of its usual meaning, he also tells us that it is very rare and that Buddha's mother dreamed of one before the birth of her famous son (*SSF*, Winter 1980).

However interesting such white elephants may be, the great critical issue in "Hills" has been the beaded curtain in the doorway of the station. Gary D. Elliott starts it all when he suggests that the beads represent the rosary and that since the girl is Catholic (?), they remind her of her religion which, therefore, makes her resist the abortion (*Expl*, Summer

1977); and Dennis Organ responds by suggesting that the curtain represents children's playthings, which is just as dubious as Elliott's rosary, but goes on to say that it also stands for a literal and emotional barrier between the couple (*Expl*, Summer 1979). J. F. Kobler rediscovers the whole thing again with no reference to Elliott or Organ but does add the new point that when Jig says, "I feel fine," what she'll do is keep the child (*Expl*, Summer 1980); and finally, David R. Gilmour extends Kobler's idea by suggesting that after Jig decides to keep the child, she will get rid of her lover who becomes thereby another one of the story's "white elephants" (*Expl*, Summer 1983).

Four critics have had something to say about "The Killers." W. J. Stuckey considers the old problem of whether Nick or Ole is the story's hero; he chooses Nick, and then writes an excellent essay on the story's peculiar intensity based on "the experienced reality of the irrational" (*JNT*, May 1975). William V. Davis gets off to a shaky start by asserting that the story is set "in winter" and then adds little new about the way time is handled (*SSF*, Summer 1978); Paul Marx, by contrast, makes an excellent review of the ethnic attitudes prevailing during Hemingway's youth, emphasizing the role of Jewish gamblers in sports, which adds a whole new dimension to the tension between the Jewish hitmen and George (in *Seasoned Authors For a New Season: The Search for Standards in Popular Writing*, ed. Louis Filler, Bowling Green, Ohio, 1980). And Kenneth G. Johnston makes a very complete survey of the story's growth from its beginnings in a Madrid hotel room to its first publication in *Scribner's Magazine* (*SSF*, Summer 1982). With the exception of "Hills" and "Killers," only a handful of articles have been written about the other stories in *Men Without Women*. Robert P. Weeks demonstrates that "Fifty Grand" is a sophisticated retelling of a high school story called "A Matter of Colour" (*SAF*, Spring 1982); and Robert E. Fleming looks at Doctor Adams in "Ten Indians" and concludes, with the help of certain excised passages, that he is not a threatening figure but a deeply flawed individual (*ArQ*, Summer 1983), an argument that should be compared to Paul Smith's discussion (Nagel). We may note a pair of articles on "An Alpine Idyll" and "Banal Story." Herbert Ruhm interviews an Alpine family who knew Hemingway at Schruns and speculates that he may have heard the story, a familiar one in those parts, there (*Commonweal*, 28 Dec. 1973); Myra Armistead notes the same thing about such Alpine tall tales and goes on to suggest that the sexton falsely attributes such a story to Olz because he hates peasants (*SSF*, Summer 1977). As for "Banal Story," two articles on it appear in the 1974 *Fitzgerald/Hemingway Annual*: one, by Philip R. Yannella, reviews the genesis of the story, concluding that Hemingway's use of the *Forum* showed his interest in pastiche and parody before he wrote *Torrents*; the other, by Wayne Kvam, analyzes the connections between the *Forum* and the story in much greater detail, showing how they make up the story's basic structure. Robert D. Arner speculates that "Today is Friday" is influenced by the York mystery play about Christ's crucifixion (*MarkhamR*, Oct. 1973).

Hemingway's third major collection of short stories, *Winner Take Nothing* (1933), has not attracted as much critical attention as the first two because most of its stories are ignored in favor of a few very popular ones. Among those usually ignored is "After the Storm," in which Robert G. Walker finds a Platonic allusion that suggests to him that Hemingway's moral perspective goes beyond that of the scavengers (*SSF*, Summer 1976). Looking at "A Way You'll Never Be," Paul Witherington makes a very loose stylistic analysis of Nick's precarious balance between rest and movement (*Style*, Winter 1973); and E. R. Hagemann supplies us with a lot of invaluable information about Gaby Delys, i.e., Gaby Deslys, and her partner Harry Pilcer without considering their function in the story (*HN*, Spring 1981). Three critics have discussed the unattractive "A Natural History of the Dead." George Monteiro groups it with several other stories about physicians and professionals (*FHA*, 1978); Kenneth G. Johnston provides the passage from Mungo Park's *Travels* that is mocked (*ForumH*, Summer–Fall 1972); and Susan Beegel discusses a coda that was cut off at the last minute (delivered at the Up in Michigan Conference, 20–22 Oct. 1983, but not available for publication in Waldmeir). Only Kenneth G. Johnston has looked at "Wine of Wyoming," one of the two western stories in the collection, to find that it expresses a disillusionment with America through a mountain (illusion)/valley (reality) dichotomy (*WAL*, Fall 1974).

Among those stories in *Winner Take Nothing* that have received a good deal of critical attention are, not surprisingly, "A Clean, Well-Lighted Place" but, quite surprisingly, "The Gambler, the Nun, and the Radio" and "The Light of the World." Since most of the articles on the first have already been discussed, we need only add that George Monteiro noted in 1974 that "cleaning up the 'messy' dialogue in 'A Clean, Well-Lighted Place' has become a promising light industry in Hemingway Studies" (*FHA*, 1974) and that Annette Benert examines certain antitheses in the story to conclude that it is "totally affirmative" because the older waiter is a true human being who has an ironic vision of things as they are and yet feels for others (*SSF*, Spring 1974). Three critics have been interested in the very low-keyed "Gambler" story. George Monteiro provides a very complete survey of its factual background, reprinting a recollection of Hemingway by the nun who was the model for Sister Cecilia (*RS*, Mar. 1978); Amberys R. Whittle reviews its parabolic method (*ArQ*, Summer 1977); and Bruce Morton discusses the role of music in it (*SSF*, Spring–Summer 1983).

Even more surprising than the interest in Mr. Frazer's listening habit is the curious attraction that "The Light of the World" has had for eight critics. James F. Barbour believes that it has been neglected because the reader needs to know the story of Steve/Stan Ketchel to understand it;

accordingly, he, as Matthew J. Bruccoli has done before him (*FHA*, 1975), reviews the history of this boxer to conclude that Peroxide makes him into a cheap Christ figure whereas Alice exposes those illusions when she presents him in a realistic and clean way (*SSF*, Winter 1976). Gregory Green supplies another history of Ketchel and his fight with the black champion Jack Johnson when he reviews the racial tensions underlying the story (*HR*, Fall 1981). Among the other problems that have attracted attention are the sudden loss of one Indian that James F. Barbour suggests was done as a private joke (*NConL*, Dec. 1977); the "C. and M." reference that Richard Layman finds out means "cocaine and morphine" (*FHA*, 1976); and the title, which Michael S. Reynolds relates to Holman Hunt's famous picture, a copy of which Grace Hemingway gave to the Third Congregational Church to commemorate the death of her father Ernest Hall (*SSF*, Fall 1983). Gary D. Elliott argues that the title refers to neither Christ nor Hunt's picture but alludes to "Nick's inability to fulfill what he thinks should be his role: a light in a place of darkness" (*Expl*, Fall 1981).

After Hemingway's death, four stories about the Spanish Civil War were published with *The Fifth Column*, his only play, in 1969. Of these four, only one, "The Butterfly and the Tank," has been completely ignored, whereas Kenneth G. Johnston looks at "Night Before Battle" to conclude that Al Wagner is modeled on Don Quixote (*HN*, Fall 1980). As for "Under the Ridge," Christopher Knight finds a passage left out of the printed text (*NMAL*, Winter 1983) and Wayne Kvam makes a very detailed survey of its factual background, supporting nonfiction, and previous critical work (*FHA*, 1978). Two critics have written excellent articles on "The Denunciation" in 1979 and come up with two completely different interpretations. Jay A. Gertzman sees the story's basic theme as a condemnation of the writer who gets involved too soon in the action which produces a confused and unsatisfactory result (*RS*, Dec. 1979), while Kenneth G. Johnston concentrates more on the story's themes and symbols to conclude that it stands for the writer's and America's political aloofness (*FHA*, 1979).

Among the stories never collected are "Nobody Ever Dies" (1939), two fables for children (1951), and "Two Tales of Darkness" (1957); we shall also consider here the *inaccrochable* "Up in Michigan." Kenneth G. Johnston recounts the factual background and plot line of "Nobody Ever Dies," noting that many of its themes and images reappear in *Bell* (*KanQ*, Spring 1977); he then goes on to do much the same thing for the two children's fables, "The Faithful Bull" and "The Good Lion," published in *Holiday* (Mar., 1951), finding in them an allegory of the author's state of mind during the 1950s, that is, Hemingway is the bull who attacks his early critics, whereas the evil lioness may represent Martha Gellhorn, or Diana Trilling, or Gertrude Stein (*FHA*, 1977). Jayne A. Widmayer, on the other hand, sees the two fables as self-parodies of the Hemingway hero—the good lion—and of his motivations—the faithful bull (*SSF*, Fall 1981). Radically different from these children's fables are the Two Tales of Darkness, "A Man of the World" and "Get a Seeing-Eyed Dog," which Hemingway published in *Atlantic* in 1957. Delbert E. Wylder reviews both tales very carefully, finding the same haunted world that other American romantics have explored (Astro and Benson), whereas J. M. Ferguson, Jr. interprets "A Man of the World" as a latter day Valhalla because the action takes place on Wednesday, that is, "Woden's day" (*ArQ*, Summer 1977). Even though it is one of Hemingway's earliest stories, "Up in Michigan" (1921) never made it into his early single-volume collections because of its explicit and rather forceful sex, a feature discussed by James Leo Spenko, who argues that Liz's repeated "She liked it" foreshadows her exclamation "Oh, it's so big and hurts so" (*ArQ*, Summer 1983) and by Alice Hall Petry, who writes a model article on Liz's latent sexuality and its subtle expression in the story's imagery (*HR*, Spring 1984).

Turning from these minor stories, we conclude with two of Hemingway's best known and most studied works, "The Snows of Kilimanjaro" and "The Short Happy Life of Francis Macomber." The less popular of the two is "Snows," for which there are only three articles to consider. Neill R. Joy believes that F. Scott Fitzgerald responded to the famous "poor Scott/Julian" slur by making Stahr's fight with Brimmer in *The Last Tycoon* a parody of Hemingway's well-publicized scuffle with Max Eastman, that is, he makes Stahr temporarily like Hemingway and Brimmer like Max Eastman (*NMAL*, Spring 1978). The italicized versus the nonitalicized sections of "Snows" are scrutinized by Scott MacDonald, who concludes that the final ascent to Kilimanjaro and the frozen leopard represent Harry's failure, but they are such brilliantly conceived and executed failures that they show off Hemingway's success as a writer (*SSF*, Winter 1974). Much more elaborate is Alfred Kolb's analysis of two sets of cultural values in the story: the primitive, eastern Afro-Arabian values symbolized by the leopard and the hyena represent two sides of Harry's character—his physical side (hyena) and his frozen idealism (leopard)—whereas the enlightened, western Judeo-Christian values, symbolized by the mimosa tree and the airplane, represent a renewal and regeneration that fails (the tree) and a mechanical and unreliable transcendence (the plane); taken together, these two sets of symbols indicate that in the hopeless struggle between man and nature only the struggle is admirable (*NMAL*, Winter 1976).

Far and away the more popular of the two African stories is "The Short Happy Life of Francis Macomber." It is the subject of a special issue of *Hemingway Notes* (Spring 1980) that includes a special "'Macomber' Bibliography" of 101 items compiled by William White. Besides this honor, "Macomber" has the added distinction of being the subject of a controversy that has, for some, drastically revised the fundamental interpretation of a story that has become, along with "The Killers" and its African partner, "as famous as any of the Hemingway novels" (Benson). Warren Beck's very popular 1955 article, which claimed that Margot was trying to save her husband, was reprinted by *Modern Fiction Studies* twenty years later with some new pages added in reply (*MFS*, Fall 1975). Mark Spilka counters with an interesting article that says little about "Macomber" but explores with great skill the whole question of how to validate Beck's textual readings versus Spilka's contextual ones (*MFS*, Summer 1976); Beck replies immediately, arguing that each work has an "occasional quality" that makes it unique as to its place, locale, and coloration and cannot, therefore, be measured by abstractions derived from the author's life and other works (*MFS*, Summer 1976). And there things stood, to be picked up and carried on by others, until Spilka tried to get in the last word with the far-fetched proposal that Frederick Marryat's *Percival Keene* (1898) is a "Source for the Macomber 'Accident'" (*HR*, Spring 1984).

A few critics have carried on one aspect or another of Beck's "revisionist" reading of "Macomber." James Nagel makes a very careful analysis of the story's point of view and structure to conclude that Wilson is hypocritical and that Margot, fearing the change in her husband, shoots him but does it accidentally (*RS*, Mar. 1973). Robert R. Hellenga reviews the controversy about Wilson to find that in contrast to Francis, who is very open and wants to share his thoughts and feelings with everyone, including Margot, Wilson is hard bitten, cynical, world weary, and completely incapable of sharing his feelings and thoughts; as a result, Macomber transcends his flawed guide figure (*NMAL*, Spring 1979).

As we move into the 1980s, the attacks on Wilson increase: C. Harold Hurley uses a pun on *topping* as "domination" and "copulation," which is mentioned in passing by James Watson (*FHA*, 1974), to expose Wilson as a tyrant who wants to dominate both Macombers but especially Margot (*Expl*, Spring 1980). The same pun is also noted by Robert F. Fleissner, who pursues its Shakespearean sources as far as Iago's *tupping* (*Expl*, Summer 1983). Barbara Lounsberry extends and complicates the assault on Wilson by reviewing all of his misapprehensions and errors and then claiming that he is so corrupted by sex and money that he and Margot are "mutually tainted survivors" (*HN*, Spring 1980). Much less subtle is John J. Seydow's attack: he finds Wilson to be racist, sexist, an Ameriphobe, and a rationalizer who stunts Macomber's growth by providing him with a false model of manhood (*HR*, Fall 1981). And Kenneth G. Johnston goes over it all again, with no mention of previous work, to insist that Margot tries to save her husband (*HR*, Spring 1983).

Among the traditionalists who agree with Carlos Baker's positive assessment of Wilson and negative view of Margot and thus side with Spilka against Beck are James Gray Watson who studies the story's imagery and shifting relationships before making himself the eleventh critic in 1974 who favored the traditionalist reading versus three who did not (*FHA*, 1974). In the same year, H. H. Bell, Jr. argues that Wilson views Margot as a wounded lioness in the bush after she shoots Macomber and so, like the good hunter he is, kills her spiritually in order to make the world a safer place for other men (*Expl*, May 1974). Taking off from Nagel's close analysis of the story's point of view, Paul R. Jackson ends up pro-Wilson, agreeing with Watson that Margot wants neither to kill Macomber nor to save him but to save herself (*HN*, Spring 1980). Although he approaches the problem from the opposition of two contrasting worlds, the mechanized metropolitan world of the sporting set versus the traditional male world of the hunter and his men, and argues that Macomber moves from the first to the second, Robert O. Stephens ends up with an essentially code-hero interpretation of Wilson (*FHA*, 1977). Evidently rather fed up with the whole business, James M. Cahalan takes the compromise stance that the shooting of Macomber is "ambiguous" (*HN*, Spring 1980), just as Jerry A. Herndon argues that the flat, factual description of the shooting suggests an inquest that seeks only facts with no motivations, so that both Margot and Wilson will come out of the whole thing unharmed (*NMAL*, Fall 1981).

In addition to the revisionists and traditionalists, a third group of critics have concentrated on the story's background and motifs without paying much attention to its overall interpretation or to the controversy surrounding it. Above all, one should certainly not fail to look at John M. Howell's and Charles A. Lawler's fascinating description of the story's textual history and of the *Cosmopolitan* issue in which it first appeared. The picture of the magazine's cover is particularly striking (*Proof*, 1972). As for Macomber's identity, Jeffrey Meyers reports a fight Hemingway had with Wallace Stevens on 19 February 1936 in Key West that he believes influenced "Macomber" (finished on 19 Apr. 1936) because Stevens, like Macomber, asked Hemingway not to mention the fight (*AN&Q*, Nov.–Dec., 1982). Bruce Morton feels that F. Scott Fitzgerald is the model for Macomber because his "Crack-Up" articles in *Esquire* triggered Hemingway's animus against his former friend (*Expl*, Fall 1982). Michael S. Reynolds, on the other hand, believes that two prominent Oak Parkers went into the making of Macomber—his name is from Frank B. Macomber and his hunting exploits from Dale Bumstead (*HR*, Fall 1983); but Joseph H. Harkey suggests another source for his name in the Swahili word *mkubwa* meaning "leader, manager, superior, employer" and written *M'kumba* in *Green Hills of Africa* (*SSF*, Summer 1980); and John J. McKenna ponders what a "four letter man" would be, rejecting the lower-middle-class *shit* in favor of the upper-middle-class *jerk*, which accords with what Hemingway called Macomber's "factual" prototype (*AN&Q*, Jan. 1979). This kind of word-play and the by now familiar *topping* pun lead Bert Bender to conclude that Hemingway's "primitive sexist values . . . are embodied in the story from beginning to end" (*CollL*, Winter 1981). Still concerned with the factual background of the story, Jerry A. Herndon notes that Margot's 6.5 Mannlicher is considered a little rifle because of its mild recoil (*FHA*, 1975); but Robert E. Fleming points to several errors about Wilson's .505 Gibbs to argue that Hemingway is not a factual realist but an expressionist for whom the fiction is far more important than the facts (*NMAL*, Summer 1981). Hemingway creates another problem for critics when he puts the words of Shakespeare's Francis Feeble (2 Henry IV, III.2. 250–55), a palpable fool, into Wilson's mouth. Quoting a fool's words about owing God a death would seem to deflate Wilson and his wisdom but since, as John J. McKenna tells us, Hemingway got Feeble's words from his valued friend Chink Dorman and used them himself on several occasions, it would seem that he had no inkling of their precise source and was not, therefore, trying to undercut Wilson (*SSF*, Winter 1981). After a look at the story's themes, J. F. Kobler takes the eccentric position that Macomber is under the illusion of courage and would have bolted from the buffalo if Margot had not accidentally killed him (*Quartet*, Winter–Spring 1974). Eugene R. Kanjo believes the story to be a kind of "beast fable" that depicts all humans as "morally obtuse" and corrupt (*NMAL*, Summer 1981).

VI SUPPLEMENT

Two important recent additions to the Hemingway canon are a new edition of his short stories and a second edition of his Spanish dispatches. *The Complete Short Stories of Ernest Hemingway* (New York, 1987), subtitled "The Finca Vigía Edition" because he lived there "on and off during the last two decades of his life," adds twenty-one stories to *The First Forty-nine Stories* (1938), i.e., fourteen stories published in books and magazines after 1938 plus seven previously unpublished pieces of fiction. (Not included are the five stories slipped into Peter Griffin's 1985 biography.) The thirty dispatches that Hemingway wrote for the North American News Alliance (NANA) about the Spanish Civil War were edited for a second time by William Braasch Watson for a special edition of the *Hemingway Review* (Spring 1988). This new edition provides a brief introduction to NANA and the dispatches, clean, readable texts accompanied by good maps and photographs, and a detailed illustration of how field notes were transformed into cables, releases, and reprints. Serious students will still want to consult the first edition of the dispatches made by Margaret Calien Lewis in 1968 because her well-researched notes reveal how Hemingway reshaped and inflated what he saw.

Biography still remains a hot Hemingway item with four new efforts added to the many biographical volumes now in print. Two of the four are basically collections of interviews. Matthew J. Bruccoli's *Conversations with Ernest Hemingway* (Jackson, Miss., 1986) simply reprints forty interviews with Hemingway plus two of his speeches without any commentary, whereas Denis Brian's *The True Gen: An Intimate Portrait of Hemingway By Those Who Knew Him* (New York, 1988) weaves interviews, snippets from published accounts, and his own comments into an intermittently interesting but still rather thin attempt at biography *verité*. (For the meaning of *gen* and its many fascinating spin-offs, see Eric Partridge's spirited comments in *A Dictionary of Forces' Slang 1939–1949* [1970].) In spite of Brian's dogged pursuit of Hemingway and even of "The Hemingway Hunters" in his *Murderers and Other Friendly People: The Public and Private Worlds of Interviewers* (1973), he reveals much less about the man than does Kenneth S. Lynn in his substantial and insightful biography *Hemingway* (New York, 1987). As Frederick Crews makes clear in his valuable review (*NYRB*, 13 Aug. 1987), Lynn has shifted the ground for understanding Hemingway's life from Italy and his father to Oak Park and his mother, thereby opening up a more complex way for reading his works.

Two of the three new book-length critical studies bring UMI Research Press's list of books on Hemingway up to nine: John Gaggin's *Hemingway and Nineteenth-Century Aestheticism* (Ann Arbor, Mich., 1988) quite convincingly emphasizes his debt to the Aesthetic movement of the 1890s without even mentioning Gabriele D'Annunzio, one of the most flamboyant decadents of them all; and Deborah Schnitzer's *The Pictorial in Modernist Fiction from Stephen Crane to Ernest Hemingway* (Ann Arbor, Mich., 1988) attacks the *ut pictura poesis* problem once again by attempting to define the verbal strategies that create the visual effects of Impressionism, Post-Impressionism, and Cubism in prose. The third book is Michael S. Reynolds's *"The Sun Also Rises": A Novel of the Twenties* (Boston, 1988), a study of that novel's background, themes, and structure. Two new collections of critical essays are both by Linda Wagner even though she appears as Linda W. Wagner on the title page of *Ernest Hemingway: Six Decades of Criticism* (East Lansing, Mich., 1987), a complete revision of her *Five Decades of Criticism* (1974), but as Linda Wagner-Martin on the title page of *New Essays on "The Sun Also Rises"* (New York, 1987), a collection of six essays. In the introduction to the former book she promises us a revised edition of her very useful *Reference Guide to Ernest Hemingway*. And, finally, Norberto Fuentes reexplores the ground he opened with *Hemingway in Cuba* (1984) in *Ernest Hemingway Rediscovered* (New York, 1988), a collection of more than 150 previously unseen photographs taken by Roberto Herrera Sotolongo, the manager of the Finca Vigía for twenty years.

Eugene O'Neill

John Henry Raleigh

I BIBLIOGRAPHY

Jennifer McCabe Atkinson's *Eugene O'Neill: A Descriptive Bibliography* (Pittsburgh, 1974) supersedes the Sanborn and Clark bibliography of 1931: it covers O'Neill's whole career and is much more extensive and detailed than was the earlier one. The Atkinson bibliography is divided into six sections:

A. Works by O'Neill—full descriptions of all first printings of American first editions and of important later printings and listings of republications or reprints. First printings of English first editions are also described. A subsection lists, in alphabetical order, published acting scripts, which are often different from the published versions.

B. O'Neill material, letters, interviews, conversations, appearing in other authors' books.

C. A chronological list of plays, poems, essays, a short story, letters, interviews and conversations by O'Neill which were published in newspapers, periodicals, and occasional publications.

D. Blurbs by O'Neill on works by other authors.

E. Inscriptions and letters by O'Neill quoted in auction or book-dealer catalogues.

F. An enumeration of O'Neill's plays in collections and anthologies. An appendix lists adaptations of the plays into other mediums: films, radio, musicals, and one opera (*The Emperor Jones*).

Atkinson says that her bibliography is only a beginning and that a "prodigious" amount of textual work is needed: collating manuscript material with both English and American editions and, above all, the printed versions with the published acting scripts; and there is no complete record of O'Neill's dealings with his publishers, involving contracts, numbers of sales of the plays, and so on, although Atkinson has also looked into these realms. Her book is a most welcome addition to O'Neill studies.

Jordan Y. Miller has updated his 1962 volume, *Eugene O'Neill and the*

American Critic (Hamden, Conn., 1973). The original prologue is cut out, and the chronology of O'Neill's life has been completely recast, with help from Sheaffer's definitive biography. The nondramatic O'Neill section has been the most significantly altered because of the great amount of biographical material on O'Neill that has appeared since the first edition of Miller's book. The critical bibliography has been considerably expanded (by some ninety-eight pages). Whereas in 1962 seventeen graduate research projects were mentioned, the 1973 edition lists seventy. As an indication of the continued vitality of O'Neill studies, Miller is already planning another updating of this work.

Eugene O'Neill: Research Opportunities and Dissertation Abstracts (ed. Tetsumaro Hayashi, Jefferson, N.C., 1983) contains an eighteen-page summary of O'Neill scholarship, both dissertations and published books, concluding with suggestions for further areas of research by Robert T. Tener. The bulk of the book is a compilation of abstracts of dissertations done on O'Neill from the 1920s to 1980, all told 139 dissertations. James Martine's collection, *Critical Essays on Eugene O'Neill* (CEAmL, Boston, 1984; hereinafter referred to as Martine), includes a thirty-one-page bibliographical essay on O'Neill compiled by the editor and subdivided as follows: bibliography, editions, biography, criticism—general estimates in books and articles and studies of individual works.

A major event in O'Neill studies has been the inauguration and subsequent flourishing of the *Eugene O'Neill Newsletter*, beginning in January 1977, under the editorship of Frederick Wilkins of Suffolk University. This thrice-yearly publication is aimed not only at O'Neill scholars and critics but at actors, producers, directors, in short anyone interested in O'Neill plays and their performances. Critical essays, reviews of books, bibliographical notices, reviews of produced plays, interviews, personal reminiscences about O'Neill, anecdotes, and so on, are all included. It is a lively, interesting, and informative journal. The *Eugene O'Neill Newsletter* is the best single source for both extensive and detailed reviews of books and shorter items about O'Neill and for ongoing bibliographical listings. Periodically, Charles Carpenter's magisterial bibliographies for O'Neill are published in the pages of the *Eugene O'Neill Newsletter*.

II EDITIONS

In 1979 *Selected Plays of O'Neill* (New York) was published with an introduction by José Quintero. The plays are: *"Anna Christie," The Emperor Jones, The Hairy Ape, Desire Under the Elms, Strange Interlude, Mourning Becomes Electra, The Iceman Cometh, A Touch of the Poet,* and *A Moon for the Misbegotten*. Quintero's introduction consists mostly of reminiscences of directing some of these plays—*A Moon for the Misbegotten* in Norway with Liv Ullmann (the two of them once talked about *"Anna Christie"*), *Desire Under the Elms* with George Scott and Colleen Dewhurst, *Strange Interlude* with Geraldine Page as Nina, *The Iceman Cometh* with Jason

Robards, *A Moon for the Misbegotten* with Dewhurst and Robards, and *A Touch of the Poet* with Robards. Quintero concludes by saying he would like to do *Mourning Becomes Electra*, *The Hairy Ape*, and *The Emperor Jones*. The heart of O'Neill's plays, says Quintero, resides in two kinds of "realities": the commonplace, photographic one and the "interior reality of fantasy." Random House, in its Modern Library imprint, reissued in 1982 the three-volume *The Plays of Eugene O'Neill* (New York).

James Milton Highsmith's "'The Personal Equation': Eugene O'Neill's Abandoned Play" (*SHR*, Spring 1974) gives a plot summary, with quotations, of this autobiographical play that O'Neill abandoned. Winifred Frazer published in the *Eugene O'Neill Newsletter* (May 1979) a lost O'Neill poem, "The American Sovereign," a three-stanza parody of *The Rubáiyát* which had been published anonymously in Emma Goldman's *Mother Earth* in 1911. In 1980 *Eugene O'Neill, Poems, 1912–1944* (New York and New Haven) appeared, edited by Donald Gallup, including all known published and unpublished poems in the Yale collection and elsewhere. Many of them are parodies written in O'Neill's newspaper days for the *New London Telegraph*. The best parodies, according to Gallup, take off from Walt Mason, Robert Burns, and Robert Service; Kipling and Villon are also present, as are Longfellow, James Whitcomb Riley, and others. His serious poems were composed in 1915–17, 1925, and 1942. He wrote love poems for Maibelle Scott and more passionate and more numerous ones for Beatrice Ashe. The saddest and bleakest poems were written by the ailing man at Tao House in 1942. Despite the fact that most of the verse is ephemeral, one can discern in them right from the start emergent O'Neillian themes and subjects: politics, love, pop music, swimming, election campaigns, shipboard life (both idealized and real), the weather, T.B., economic injustice, hatred of war, the lure of exotic places, and being alone and desolate in a city. For example, one of the early parodies, à la James Whitcomb Riley, is called "Hitting the Pipe," and has for its refrain, "When my dreams come true."

Chris Christophersen (New York, 1982) is the only surviving produced O'Neill play that had never been previously printed. This forerunner to *"Anna Christie"* is much inferior to the final version. In *Chris*, Anna is a stunning English woman, from Leeds, and a typist. Burke is Andersen, of Swedish heritage, tall, broad-shouldered, blue-eyed, intelligent, good-humored, and the second-mate of a steamer, the *Londonderry*. As in *"Anna"* itself, Chris hates the sea and calls it that "Ole Davil," and his daughter falls in love with it and makes a mystique of it. Anna and Andersen fall in love, and Chris opposes the marriage of his daughter to a man of the sea. There is a sensationally happy ending, much more improbable than the much criticized happy ending of *"Anna Christie,"* which, as a play, is a good deal more realistic, unified, somber, and convincing than this Ur-*"Anna Christie."*

In 1982 Donald Gallup edited and published O'Neill's *The Calms of*

Capricorn (New Haven, Conn.). This is a scenario for what was to have been the first play of the American cycle; O'Neill began making notes on a "Clipper Ship-around-Horn" play at Le Plessis when working on *Mourning Becomes Electra*. There are notations for 1931, 1932, 1933, and 1934, although the scenario itself is dated 9 June 1935, Casa Genotta. Gallup prints both the scenario itself and a version of it translated into direct discourse. The root urge for this play came from O'Neill's mystique of the clipper ship, which he had celebrated in *Mourning*. The time is 1857, after the end of the later-composed *More Stately Mansions*. The widowed Sarah Harford, with her four sons, sets off at the time of the Gold Rush in a clipper ship to go around the Horn to San Francisco. The ship is becalmed off South America for a time but is approaching the Golden Gate at the end. At this stage in his plans for the cycle, O'Neill was to give each of the sons a separate play. Ethan, a sailor and First Mate, is the protagonist of *The Calms* and commits suicide at its end. Wolfe, a bank clerk, was to be the protagonist, as a gambler, of "The Earth is the Limit"; Honey, a tin peddler, as a politician in "Nothing Is Lost Save Honor"; and Jonathan, a clerk in a railroad office, as a railroad and shipping magnate, in "The Man on Iron Horseback." But before that O'Neill went backward in time through the histories of the Harfords and Melodys to create *More Stately Mansions* and *A Touch Of the Poet*. In *The Calms*, Sarah says she has been the daughter, wife, and mother of men with "a touch of the poet." (An earlier edition of *The Calms* in two volumes was published privately by the Yale University Library in 1981.) There are other characters, many themes, many of them familiar ones, but it is all very much in a preliminary stage. There is the usual great O'Neillian concern for exact settings, this time in terms of the inside of a clipper ship. *The Calms* is, so we are told, *the* last extant part of the cycle.

The most extensive new compilation of O'Neilliana is Virginia Floyd's *Eugene O'Neill At Work: Newly Released Ideas for Plays* (New York, 1981). Floyd was given access to the vast amount of O'Neill manuscript material—that on the American cycle excepted—at the Beinecke Library at Yale, and has published much of this with extensive commentary: O'Neill's notebooks, scenarios, and drafts of plays and a work diary. Four notebooks (1918–38), published in their entirety, contain over one hundred ideas for plays. The two poles of interest in this mass of material are the "might-have-beens," the numerous ideas for plays, some of them gigantic in concept and spectacularly innovative in dramatic technique, that O'Neill contemplated but never executed; and the "actuality," the creative evolution of some, not all, of his major plays. There are stretches of minimum interest—the agonized evolution of the unfortunate *Days Without End*; of moderate interest—the respective developments of *Mourning Becomes Electra* and *Lazarus Laughed*; and stretches of great interest—the genesis and elaboration of *The Iceman* and *Long Day's*

Journey. What it all underlines is how ambitious a playwright O'Neill was and how restless was his dramatic genius, never satisfied with what he had done and always on the alert for the new and the original, both in subject matter and technique. O'Neill scholars are in Floyd's debt for her victorious wrestle with O'Neill's notoriously miniscule handwriting, for her helpful ordering of the material, and her commentary on it.

The *Eugene O'Neill Newsletter* (Winter 1983) republished "Tomorrow," O'Neill's only short story, originally published in the June 1917 issue of *Seven Arts.* It has a memorable opening sentence: "It was back in my sailor days, in the winter of my great down-and-outness, that all this happened." Art, the narrator, is a down-and-outer living in a broken-down saloon, "Tommy the Priest's" in New York. His roommate is Jimmy Anderson, an alcoholic ex-newspaperman of very respectable Scotch ancestry, so he says, a correspondent in the Boer War, who is always vowing to straighten out and go back to work. He finally does go back to work, fails, returns to Tommy the Priest's, where he finally jumps out of the window and kills himself. The story both looks back to an experience O'Neill had actually had and, of course, looks forward to *The Iceman.*

Judith E. Barlow's *Final Acts: The Creation of Three Late O'Neill Plays* (Athens, Ga., 1985) is a detailed study of the evolution, from first notes to finished play, of *The Iceman, Long Day's Journey,* and *A Moon for the Misbegotten.* The initial sources for each play were threefold: O'Neill's early work, his personal experiences, and occasionally plays by other dramatists. What this interesting study shows is that in the evolution of each play the playwright successively diminished the focus on minor characters and emphasized major ones, demonstrated increasing compassion for his characters, cut down on repetitions, by imaginative touches transmuted the autobiographical bases of his fable, and made his characters gain more empathy for one another, with his own empathy growing for all of them.

For publication in 1988, the centennial of O'Neill's birth, Travis Bogard is preparing two editions of material. The first, a complete O'Neill—all the published plays, including the so-called "lost plays"—will be published in three volumes by the Library of America. The other book, to be issued by Yale University Press, will contain *The Personal Equation* (O'Neill's hitherto unpublished full-length play written in 1915 for George Pierce Baker's English 47 class at Harvard), the full eight-act version of *Marco Millions,* "Tomorrow," *The Ancient Mariner,* and a variety of critical pieces by O'Neill.

III LETTERS

There is as yet no full-scale volume of O'Neill's letters, although a selected edition is in preparation under the combined editorship of

Jackson R. Bryer and Travis Bogard, who expect their book will be published by Yale in 1988. So far some 3,000 pieces of correspondence have turned up, and they are still being discovered. However, letters continue to appear in print, either individually or in collections. James Milton Highsmith's "A Description of the Cornell Collection of Eugene O'Neill's Letters to George Jean Nathan" (*MD*, Feb. 1972) lists 130 items, written in the period from May 1919 to August 1949. In *Resources for American Literary Study* (Spring 1978), William J. Scheick published two O'Neill letters, one to Lawrence Langner, dated 5 April 1927, one to Philip Moeller of 19 August 1933. The letter to Langner indicates his readiness to scale down *Marco Millions* for a stage production; the one to Moeller is about the casting for the production of *Ah, Wilderness!* and makes some interesting comments on the sociology of the play.

Dorothy Commins's *What Is an Editor* (Chicago, 1978) is a memoir of her husband, the late, great editor, Saxe Commins. Since O'Neill bulked large in the life of the Comminses from 1916 on, he bulks large in this memoir, substantial sections of which are in Commins's own words. The book prints some eight O'Neill letters or parts of letters to Commins, all of considerable interest either biographically or dramatically. Three of O'Neill's letters to Commins are reproduced as illustrations. There is also a harrowing account of O'Neill's last years, about which Dorothy Commins concludes, "Far more tragic than any novel [the word "novel" is used here because Hamilton Basso's *The View from Pompey's Head* was based on O'Neill's last years] Gene might have written was the tragedy of his own life." In 1986 Duke University Press (Durham, N.C.) published, edited by Dorothy Commins, *"Love and Admiration and Respect": The O'Neill-Commins Correspondence*, which contains all of O'Neill's letters, postcards, and telegrams to Saxe and Dorothy Commins, along with a generous selection of Carlotta O'Neill's letters to the Comminses, some of Saxe's letters to the O'Neills, and long excerpts from Saxe's memoir of O'Neill, all prefaced with an introduction by Travis Bogard.

Traian Filip's "Relative editoriale cu Romania" (*Manuscriptum*, No. 1, 1980) prints a letter to Petru Comarnesco, translated into Rumanian, from O'Neill, 19 December 1939, settling an argument concerning who is his Rumanian translator: Petru Comarnesco is. S. S. Apseloff's "Eugene O'Neill—An Early Letter" (*RALS*, Spring 1981) prints a letter from O'Neill to Pierre Loving revealing his attitude toward his early one-act sea plays: *Moon of the Caribbees* is "my pet"; for *In the Zone* he cares not at all.

"The Theatre We Worked For": The Letters of Eugene O'Neill to Kenneth Macgowan (ed. Jackson R. Bryer, with introductory essays by Travis Bogard, New Haven, Conn., 1982) is the largest collection of O'Neill letters yet published, some 164 drawn from the correspondence between O'Neill and Macgowan, who along with Robert Edmond Jones and O'Neill made up the famous Triumvirate. Most of the letters are by

O'Neill but some are by Carlotta and some by Macgowan, most of whose correspondence with O'Neill has disappeared. The book is divided into four parts, each part taking as its symbol an O'Neill residence: Peaked Hill Bar, 1920–24; Spithead, 1925–27; Le Plessis, 1928–34; and Tao House, 1936–51. The letters are interesting both biographically—O'Neill's stormy married lives—and dramatically—for example, extensive commentary on *Lazarus Laughed* and a long letter on *The Iceman*. Bogard's introductions are very full and very helpful.

In James J. Martine's edition, *Critical Essays on Eugene O'Neill* (CEAmL, Boston, 1984), are published some nineteen letters and telegrams edited by Jackson R. Bryer, from O'Neill to Dudley Nichols, the screen writer who collaborated with John Ford on the celebrated film of *The Long Voyage Home* and who also did the script for the movie of *Mourning Becomes Electra*. O'Neill was notably enthusiastic about Nichols's film script for *The Long Voyage Home* and equally enthusiastic about the movie itself.

IV   BIOGRAPHY

The same year, 1973, saw the publication of Arthur and Barbara Gelb's new and enlarged edition of their *O'Neill* (New York) and Louis Sheaffer's *O'Neill: Son and Artist* (Boston). The Gelbs' biography is actually the same book that was published in 1962 but with the addition of a nineteen-page epilogue on the post-O'Neill life of Carlotta O'Neill, who survived the playwright by seventeen years. Beginning her widowhood with great gusto, THE widow (always dressed in black) and the official executor of her husband's literary estate, Mrs. O'Neill became progressively more erratic mentally, finally senile, and spent her last years in rest homes and psychiatric wards, finally dying 18 November 1970, aged eighty-one.

The second volume of the massive and meticulously researched Sheaffer biography is quite up to the high standards and consuming interest of the first volume, *O'Neill: Son and Playwright* (1968). This is certainly one of the preeminent literary biographies of our time and an immense mine of information for all those interested in its subject.

In *Comparative Drama* (Fall 1983), Sheaffer published "Correcting Some Errors in Annals of O'Neill." Here Sheaffer corrects errors of fact about the lives of O'Neill and his family, some of which were perpetrated by O'Neill himself, others by his biographers, which in turn were then perpetuated by other books on O'Neill. Sheaffer sets in order such matters as the real story of O'Neill's forebears, the exact date of Mrs. O'Neill's mastectomy (late in her life), the true story of O'Neill's sea-going days, Jamie's "love life," O'Neill's drinking problem, and so on. Sheaffer's statements appear to be definitive. The first half of the Sheaffer article has been reprinted in the *Eugene O'Neill Newsletter* (Winter 1983), and the second half was published in the *Eugene O'Neill Newsletter* for Spring 1984.

Paul D. Voelker's "Eugene O'Neill and George Pierce Baker: A Reconsideration" (*AL*, May 1977) argues against Bogard's dismissal of Baker as a noninfluence on O'Neill the fledgling playwright, claiming that even the weakest of O'Neill's early plays are strong in characterization, the dramatic quality most prized by Baker. There is an abstract of Voelker's dissertation, from which the above article was taken, in the *Eugene O'Neill Newsletter* (Sept. 1977).

Egil Törnqvist's "O'Neill's Work Method" (*SN*, No. 1, 1977) is a detailed and interesting reconstruction of how O'Neill actually composed his plays and concludes, "To overcome his stammering—this, in essence, is what O'Neill's lifelong struggle as a playwright was about." Le Roy Robinson's "John Howard Lawson on Eugene O'Neill" (*EON*, Sept. 1979) republishes those sections on O'Neill from the autobiography of John Howard Lawson, who contrasts O'Neill's *Dynamo* and his own *Nirvana* and recounts the cold reception he got from O'Neill when he visited him. "The Culture of the Provincetown Players," by Arnold Goldman (*JAmS*, Dec. 1978), projects the thesis that the American Progressivist movement which floundered in World War I lived on, in spirit, in the creation of the Provincetown Players, whose various constituencies are described, as is O'Neill's interaction with them. Goldman concludes that no previous American playwright had such a school to learn in as had O'Neill with the Players. Michael Hinden's "'Splendid Twaddle': O'Neill and Richard Middleton" (*EON*, Jan. 1979) describes O'Neill's one-time passion for an obscure English versifier. Robert K. Sarlós's "Nina Moise Directs Eugene O'Neill's *The Rope*" (*EON*, Winter 1982) tells how Moise judiciously, and over the author's protest, edited and cut the script of *The Rope* to good advantage for the successful production of the play. "Susan Glaspell and Eugene O'Neill" (*EON*, Summer–Fall 1982) by Linda Ben-Zvi describes the relationship between O'Neill and Glaspell, Jig Cook's wife. For the Provincetown Players Glaspell was, after O'Neill (fifteen plays), the most prolific playwright (eleven plays). In 1931 she was to win a Pulitzer Prize for her drama, *Alison's House*. *Jig Cook and the Provincetown Players* (Amherst, Mass., 1982), by Robert Karoly Sarlós, describes the formation, growth, and final disintegration of the Provincetown Players, with Cook as the catalyst and O'Neill as the most potent dramatist, from 1915 to 1922. Its climax comes when Cook builds the famous "dome" for *The Emperor Jones*; the play is a stunning success; the Players fall apart; O'Neill goes on to Broadway; and Cook departs for Greece.

V CRITICISM

1 Full-length Studies

Ulrich Halfmann's *Unreal Realism: O'Neill's dramatisches Werk im Spiegel seiner szenischen Kunst* (Bern and Munich, 1969) is a systematic and detailed study of O'Neill's scenic stagecraft: indoors, concerned with configurations in rooms, furnishings, books, pictures; and outdoors, dealing with nature, cities, and so on. A second section concerns itself with the uses of sound and light. Horst Frenz's *Eugene O'Neill*, originally published in German in Berlin in 1965, has been translated, was published in New York in 1971, and constitutes a brief general picture of O'Neill, emphasizing the theme of human suffering in the plays. Winifred L. Frazer's *E.G. and E.G.O.: Emma Goldman and "The Iceman Cometh"* (Gainesville, Fla., 1974) is a monograph dealing with the life and times of Emma Goldman and her relationship to O'Neill, and it offers convincing proof that O'Neill's Rosa Parritt in *The Iceman* was based on Emma. Bhagwat S. Goyal's *The Strategy of Survival: Human Significance of O'Neill Plays* (Ghaziabad, India, 1975) covers all of O'Neill's important plays, traces the evolution of his dramatic career, and argues the thesis that the playwright was, although a determinist, not a misanthrope but "deeply in love with life." *Eugene O'Neill: Irish and American* (New York, 1976) by Harry Cronin takes off from some of the categories about the nature of the American Irish Catholic suggested by Raleigh's "O'Neill's *Long Day's Journey Into Night* and New England Irish Catholicism" (*PR*, Fall 1959) and applies them more widely to other O'Neill plays, concluding that in many respects O'Neill never really abandoned his Catholicism.

Leonard Chabrow's *Ritual and Pathos: The Theatre of O'Neill* (Cranbury, N.J., 1976) stresses the religious aspects of O'Neill's plays, not only by a study of some of the prime ideologues—Buddha, Christ, Nietzsche, Freud, and Jung—of O'Neill but by stressing the vital elements in the plays themselves, rhythms of word, action, singing, dancing, by which the dramatist tried to establish a relation between actors and spectators and draw the spectators into the play itself. The final effect of O'Neill's great tragedy, *Long Day's Journey*, Chabrow asserts, is "pathos." Gunter Ahrend's *Traumwelt und Wirklichkeit im Spätwerk Eugene O'Neills* (Heidelberg, 1978) is a close examination of the form and meaning of "dreamworld" and "reality" in O'Neill's late plays. The examination demonstrates how complex these matters have become in the late plays where there is both "real reality" and "lying reality," "pipe dreams" and "lying pipe dreams." Thus the familiar reality-illusion theme of O'Neill, rather clear in the earlier plays, becomes in the late plays blurred, with the two sides of the dichotomy often overlapping one another, and it has become as difficult and problematical for the characters to exist in the dreamworld as it is to exist in either of the realities, real or lying.

Jean Chothia's *Forging a Language: A Study of the Plays of Eugene O'Neill*

(Cambridge, England, 1979) is a major contribution to O'Neill studies. It is ironic, in view of the well-known antipathy of the English to O'Neill, especially to his dialogue, that the first complete scholarly study of O'Neill's dramatic language should have been done by an English woman and that it demonstrates that in both his early and late plays, although not the middle, he was a master of the great varieties and riches of the American vernacular; thus in the American drama he played the same seminal role that Twain played in fiction and Whitman in poetry. The study culminates in a detailed and sensitive analysis of the dramatic dialogue of *The Iceman Cometh* and *Long Day's Journey Into Night*. At the same time O'Neill is solidly anchored in both his American and European cultural contexts. In 1979 Frederic I. Carpenter published a revised edition of his *Eugene O'Neill* (TUSAS; Boston; originally New York, 1964), with a rewritten bibliography, a revised text incorporating new information and new critical insights on O'Neill, and a new, and quite original, critique of *Hughie*, saying that the play is both a parable of the creative imagination and a reenactment of the evolution of O'Neill's dramatic career: like his protagonist, Erie Smith, O'Neill was also, through this play and other late plays, getting "in touch" once more with his audience. C. P. Sinha's *Eugene O'Neill's Tragic Vision* (New Delhi, 1981) is a brief survey of O'Neill's life and work, the various influences upon him, and an analysis of his tragic vision. The thesis is that for O'Neill emotion was much more real and powerful than thought and that his final vision of human life was affirmative rather than negative.

Four interesting books on O'Neill, each from a different angle, were all published in 1982. Normand Berlin's *Eugene O'Neill* (New York), part of the Grove Press Modern Dramatists series, emphasizes the importance of *Long Day's Journey* and also *The Hairy Ape* and *Desire Under the Elms* and concludes that O'Neill's accomplishments were fourfold: he made American drama serious; he stretched the bounds of the medium with his technical inventiveness; he belongs both to the American and the European dramatic tradition; and, most important, he was "primarily emotional," with a single tragic vision and elemental subjects, love, death, fate, freedom, and so on. Michael Manheim's *Eugene O'Neill's New Language of Kinship* (Syracuse, N.Y., 1982) argues twin theses: that all the plays, from first to last, are autobiographical, disguised or unconscious in the earlier career and explicit at the end, and that O'Neill's most effective dialogue is what Manheim calls the "language of kinship," that contrapuntal rhythm in the dialogue between hurt and forgiveness, split and reconciliation, love and hate, that is heard in both the early and late plays. The autobiographical thesis is perhaps overdone (Nina Leeds's experiences are those of O'Neill), but the "language of kinship" theme is quite tenable and reaches its culminating and concluding analysis, as does the autobiographical theme, in the discussion of *Long Day's Journey* and *A Moon for the Misbegotten*.

James A. Robinson's *Eugene O'Neill and Oriental Thought* (Carbondale, Ill., 1982) is the most complete study of O'Neill's absorption of and use of Oriental monism and mysticism, much of which he derived from Western sources such as Emerson and Nietzsche. This mysticism announced itself in his first works, peaked in the religious plays of the middle period, especially *Lazarus Laughed*, virtually disappeared between *Dynamo* and the cycle plays, and reappeared tangentially in *The Iceman* and *Long Day's Journey*. It is suggested that "his trans-cultural popularity may lie precisely in the peculiar combinations of East and West evident in these late tragedies." John Orlando's *O'Neill on Film* (Rutherford, N.J., 1982) is a critical analysis of some thirteen screen versions or adaptations of O'Neill's plays done over a fifty-year period, from *"Anna Christie"* (two versions, 1923 and 1930) to *The Iceman Cometh* (1973). The greatest cinematic failure was probably *Strange Interlude* (1932); the great successes were John Ford's *The Long Voyage Home* (1940), about which O'Neill himself was very enthusiastic, Sidney Lumet's *Long Day's Journey*, and John Frankenheimer's *The Iceman Cometh*. The book addresses itself throughout to the problems of transfering with success a play to the screen and concludes that artistically valid changes tend toward good screen effects and that changes based only on a compromise tend toward bad effects. The single most "memorable" movie, according to Orlando, is *Long Day's Journey*, which, he stresses, is not just a "filmed play." Orlando's book should be compared with the O'Neill chapter in Edward Murray's *The Cinematic Imagination* (see below).

Ward B. Lewis's *Eugene O'Neill: The German Reception of America's First Dramatist* (Bern, 1984) is a description and analysis of the productions and the reception of O'Neill's plays in Germany, which fall into four periods: 1923–24: *"Anna Christie," The Emperor Jones*, and *The Hairy Ape*; 1924–31: *Desire Under the Elms, All God's Chillun Got Wings, The Great God Brown*, and *Strange Interlude* (in which Elizabeth Bergner was a sensational success); 1932–45, a complete hiatus during the Hitler era; early post-World War II: *Mourning Becomes Electra* and *Ah, Wilderness!*; and finally the triumphant period of the 1950s and 1960s: *The Iceman Cometh, A Moon for the Misbegotten, Long Day's Journey*, and *A Touch of the Poet*. O'Neill's popularity in Germany has diminished somewhat since then, but he continues to outstrip all English-language playwrights except Shakespeare; he is "a classic author with a permanent place in the German repertoire."

2 Book Chapters

This is a selective list given in chronological order. In "Focus on Eugene O'Neill's *The Iceman Cometh*: The Iceman Hath Come," in *American Dreams, American Nightmares* (ed. David Madden, Carbondale, Ill., 1970), Frederic I. Carpenter attempts to answer the question of why *The Iceman* "will not stand still" but keeps growing in significance, and explains how he accounts for this protean process. Allen Lewis's *American Plays and Playwrights of the Contemporary Theatre* (New York, 1970) contains an extravagantly enthusiastic appreciation of O'Neill. Jackson R. Bryer's "'Hell is Other People': *Long Day's Journey Into Night*," in *The Fifties: Fiction, Poetry, Drama* (ed. Warren French, Deland, Fla., 1970), places O'Neill's play in the context of serious modern tragedy, from Ibsen and Chekhov, and shows how it is even more complex than most other modern tragedies. Ruby Cohn's *Dialogue in American Drama* (Bloomington, Ind., 1971) traces the evolution of O'Neill's dialogue from the stilted rhetoric of melodrama and the ungrammatical colloquialism of the early plays to the masterly handling of the various levels of the American vernacular in *The Iceman, Long Day's Journey*, and *Hughie*. Morris Freedman's *American Drama in Social Context* (Carbondale, Ill., 1971) argues that O'Neill remains the premier American dramatist because of his moral energy and because he "haunts" us.

Catherine Mournier's "L'espressionnisme dans l'oeuvre d'Eugene O'Neill," in *L'Expressionnisme dans le theatre européen* (ed. Denis Bablet and Jean Jacquot, Paris, 1971), describes the expressionistic elements of O'Neill's plays, where appropriate, from *The Emperor Jones* to *Dynamo*, stresses the influence of Strindberg, and defines expressionism as a spiritual movement whose end is the regeneration of man. Walter Stein's "Drama," in *The Twentieth-Century Mind* (ed. C. B. Cox and A. E. Dyson, New York, 1972), is an intelligent discussion of serious modern drama in Europe and America and calls O'Neill, although flawed, the most important of the "basically naturalistic" dramatists, whose highest achievements are *The Emperor Jones* and *Long Day's Journey*: the "catastrophic fusion of past and present elements." *Accelerated Grimace: Expressionism in the American Drama of the 1920's* (Carbondale, Ill., 1972) by Mardi Valgemae argues that *The Emperor Jones, The Hairy Ape*, and *The Great God Brown* are O'Neill's primary expressionist plays and that their techniques derive not from Strindberg but from the Germans, particularly Kaiser. Edward Murray's *The Cinematic Imagination: Writers and the Motion Pictures* (New York, 1972) says in its chapter on O'Neill that *The Emperor Jones* was one of the most "successful examples of the cinematic imagination on the stage," but that the film made from it was a failure. Murray calls *Long Day's Journey* the best film of O'Neill but adds that it is "another photographed stage play."

Robert Bechtold Heilman's *The Iceman, the Arsonist, and the Troubled Agent* (Seattle, Wash., 1973) asserts that O'Neill's characters cannot bear the truth about themselves and lack the strength to encounter either life or themselves (*The Iceman* being his key example). Thus O'Neill was not tragic, but anti-tragic, although possessing "integrity of feeling" and "great power" in portraying the melodrama of disaster. Albert Bermel's *Contradictory Characters* (New York, 1973) has a chapter on *Long Day's Journey*, "The Family as Villain," and examines in detail the various guilts real or asserted, of the Tyrones, concluding that Mary is the central character and that one could make a case for calling the play "Mary's tragedy." James Schevill's *Break Out!* (Chicago, 1973), in a chapter entitled "Eugene O'Neill: The Isolation and Endurance of an American Playwright," stresses O'Neill's great courage in his last years, the moving "compassion" of the late plays, and their senses of "fate" and "pity." Every American playwright, Schevill concludes, "must still measure himself against the depth and ambition of O'Neill." Dan Vogel's *The Three Masks of American Tragedy* (Baton Rouge, La., 1974) argues that the masks of American tragic heroes in American literature are Oedipus Tyrannos, Christ, and Satan. In *Desire Under the Elms*, Ephraim Cabot is described as "Ephraim Rex" and we feel for him pity and terror, as well as admiration for his steadfastness. In *Mourning Becomes Electra*, both Lavinia and Orin are the "tyrannos," but neither evokes full pity and terror, although Orin generates more than Lavinia.

Families Under Stress by Tony Manocchio and William Petitt (London, 1975) examines the Tyrone family of *Long Day's Journey* as an example of "the closed family," whose family rule is described as "you must not make anyone suffer unless they allow it." All are enclosed in a "blame frame." This is a Laing-ish book and concludes that more open communication would have helped the Tyrones. Jordan Miller's "The Other O'Neill," in *The Twenties: Fiction, Poetry, Drama* (ed. Warren French, Deland, Fla., 1975), views the O'Neill plays of the 1920s—failures and minor masterpieces—as O'Neill's proving ground, showing that he had the "makings" but that the real artist had not yet arrived. *The Psychology of Tragic Drama* (London, 1975) by Patrick Roberts examines *Mourning Becomes Electra* in the context of its attempt to translate Greek tragedy into modern terms; *Mourning* is seen as "a strange compound of strength and weakness." Gareth Lloyd Evans's *The Language of Modern Drama* (London, 1977) discusses *Mourning* in terms of its language and concludes, as did O'Neill, that it was not adequate to the task that the playwright set for himself. *The "Revels" History of Drama in English, Vol. VIII, American Drama* (London, 1977) includes Travis Bogard's "The American Drama: Its Range of Contexts," which terms O'Neill the "lens, a central reflector," of the American drama, enumerates some of his primordial themes—the land, the mother, the lost dream—and lists his many similarities to Shaw.

William R. Brashear's *The Gorgon's Head: A Study in Tragedy and Despair* (Athens, Ga., 1977) discusses O'Neill in various contexts and in terms of influences: Conrad, Schopenhauer (*Strange Interlude*), and Spengler (*Dynamo*); he also asserts that O'Neill, the voice of will and intuition, was a Dionysiac artist in Nietzsche's terms. N. S. Pradhan's chapter in *Modern American Drama* (New Delhi, 1978) concludes that O'Neill's greatness arises from the tragic tension between dream and reality. Tom Scanlan's *Family, Drama, and American Dreams* (Westport, Conn., 1978) has as its thesis the proposition that the family is the crucial subject of American drama, that O'Neill "established our family drama," and that he was "the last great playwright of bourgeois family life." Scanlan provides complex and intelligent discussions of, among others, *Desire Under the Elms* and, of course, *Long Day's Journey*. A. D. Choudhuri's *The Face of Illusion in American Drama* (Atlantic Highlands, N.J., 1979) takes *The Iceman* as O'Neill's key play and says it is "an affirmation of the defeat of the human will and spirit." *The Onstage Christ: Studies in the Persistence of a Theme* (London, 1980) by John Ditsky studies the Christ figure in modern drama, from Ibsen to Arden. *The Iceman* is the center-piece for O'Neill, with Hickey as the false Messiah, Larry Slade as a better one, and a message: that "the truth kills, and that only death frees." Richard B. Sewall's *The Vision of Tragedy* (New Haven, Conn., 1980) analyzes *Long Day's Journey* with Job and the Karamazov family as background archetypes. The "journey," according to Sewall, is toward a deeper understanding of one another by the Tyrones, and that last tableau at the end of the play evokes "pity" touched with "awe."

Vicki C. H. Ool's "Transcending Culture: A Cantonese Translation and Production of O'Neill's *Long Day's Journey Into Night*," in *The Languages of Theatre* (ed. Ortum Zuber, Elmsford, N.Y., 1980), says that the dramatic conventions and the dramatic language used in Chinese plays about families contain no such subtleties of language—nuances of love and hate, recrimination and acceptance, accusation and forgiveness—as *Long Day's Journey, par excellence*, exhibits. Thus a translator of O'Neill's play into Cantonese would have to teach himself how to extract these resources from the Chinese language itself. Robert J. Higgs's *Laurel & Thorn: The Athlete in American Fiction* (Lexington, Ky., 1981), a study of the representation of athletes in American literature, says that no other American writer has examined the milieu and the métier of the athletic hero as thoroughly as O'Neill did with Gordon Shaw in *Strange Interlude*. Taking Lord Raglan's paradigm for the hero, twenty-two aspects, Higgs claims that Gordon scores very high, with twelve of those aspects. Normand Berlin's *The Secret Cause* (Amherst, Mass., 1981) contains a comparison and contrast of Euripides's *Hippolytus*, Racine's *Phaedra*, and *Desire Under the Elms*, wherein the Elms (the Mother principle) and stones (the Father principle) control the play: "His [O'Neill's] plays touch the over-riding mystery, and the cause remains secret and haunting." *Tragic Drama and Modern Society* (London, 1981) by John Orr contains two chapters on O'Neill, making many high claims for him—among others, the full-scale dramatological destruction of the American dream and a breakthrough into lower-class life such as no other modern dramatist has made. There are interesting discussions of *The Emperor Jones, All God's Chillun, Desire Under the Elms, Mourning Becomes Electra* and, of course, *The Iceman* and *Long Day's Journey*: "The night of O'Neill's play is the darkness of the twentieth century fully brought to life," and the play explodes outward "to embrace the whole of modern civilization."

Winston Weathers's *The Broken Word: Communication Pathos in Modern Literature* (New York, 1981) includes a study of noncommunication in O'Neill's world, how characters for one reason or another fail to communicate, and points out how often in the plays the characters express the sense of futility of communication, each locked in his or her own cell. J. L. Styan's *Modern Drama in Theory and Practice, Vol. I* (Cambridge, England, and New York, 1980), a history of realism and naturalism in the European and American theatre, describes briefly *The Iceman, Long Day's Journey,* and *A Moon for the Misbegotten,* with emphasis on the actual stage performance. Volume 3 of Styan's *Modern Drama in Theory and Practice* (Cambridge, England, 1981), concerned with expressionism, does the same with *The Emperor Jones, The Hairy Ape,* and other expressionist plays by O'Neill. John R. Cooley's *Savages and Naturals: Black Portraits by White Writers in American Literature* (Newark, Del., 1982) argues that when white writers portray blacks, they turn them either into "Noble Savages" or "Savages" and that in *The Emperor Jones* O'Neill had taken the latter course.

C. W. E. Bigsby's *A Critical Introduction To Twentieth-Century American Drama, 1900–1940* (Cambridge, England, 1982) contains an eighty-three-page chapter on O'Neill which should be considered a monograph in itself, with a rich and complex discussion of the playwright and his plays from first to last. O'Neill's plays are seen as adumbrating the chief theme of twentieth-century American drama: man's alienation from God, from his environment, from his fellows, and from himself. Much is made of Schopenhauer's influence on O'Neill, along with that of Nietzsche and Freud, as well as his similarities to nineteenth-century American writers, the American writers of the 1920s, and twentieth-century absurd- ists like Beckett and Camus, although it is always O'Neill's own experiences, and its various antimonies, that the playwright is writing about: "They [his plays] constitute the history, or a metaphor for the history, of his life."

3 Collections

There have been five collections of O'Neill criticism in the past twelve years. In Hans Itschert's edition of *Das Amerikanische Drama* (Damrstadt, 1972; hereinafter referred to as Itschert), a section devoted to O'Neill includes six articles. *Eugene O'Neill* (ed. Ernest R. Griffin, New York, 1976; hereinafter referred to as Griffin) publishes twelve pieces, either sections from books or previously published articles. The most extensive collection is Virginia Floyd's *Eugene O'Neill: A World View* (New York, 1979; hereinafter referred to as Floyd). The book is divided into three parts, each with an extensive introduction by the editor: part 1, "A European Perspective," with nine essays; part 2, "An American Perspective," with six essays; and part 3, "Performers on O'Neill," taped recordings of Florence Eldridge, Arvin Brown, Geraldine Fitzgerald, and Ingrid Bergman talking of their experiences with O'Neill and his plays. Horst Frenz and Susan Tuck's *Eugene O'Neill's Critics: Voices From Abroad* (Carbondale, Ill., 1984) will be discussed elsewhere in this essay, as will the individual pieces in James J. Martine's *Critical Essays on Eugene O'Neill* (CEAmL, Boston, 1984).

4 Articles

a. Influences and Parallels. Winifred Frazer's "Chris and Poseidon: Man versus God in *Anna Christie*" (*MD*, Dec. 1969), reviewing O'Neill's lifelong attraction to the sea (his "grand opus" was to be called "Sea-Mother's son"), concludes that Poseidon presided over his psyche more than any other God and that *"Anna Christie"* was the clearest example of that fact. Fred Sochatoff's "Two Modern Treatments of the Phaedra Legend," in *In Honor of Austin Wright* (ed. Joseph Baim, et al., Pittsburgh, 1972), offers a three-way comparison of the Phaedra myth in Euripides's *Hippolytus*, T. C. Murray's *Autumn Fire* (1924), and *Desire Under the Elms*. Egil Törnqvist's "Platonic Love in O'Neill's *Welded*" (Floyd) demonstrates how the three views of love enunciated in Plato's *Symposium* all show up in *Welded*. James H. Dee's "Orestes and Electra in the Twentieth Century" (*CB*, Apr. 1979) contrasts the treatments of these myths in Hofmannsthal, Giraudoux, Sartre, Richardson, and O'Neill's *Mourning* in its "single-minded concentration," "unsurpassed in depicting fierce emotion." Manfred Fuhrman's "Myth as a Recurrent Theme in Greek Tragedy and Twentieth-Century Drama," in *New Perspectives In German Literary Criticism* (ed. Richard Amacher and Victor Lang, Princeton, N.J., 1979), mentions the indebtedness of *Mourning* to Aeschylus' *Oresteia*. John Chioles's "Aeschylus and O'Neill: A Phenomenological View" (*CompD*, Summer 1980) contains a three-way contrast of Aeschylus, Artaud, and *Mourning Becomes Electra*. "Phenomenological" means that man is at the center of things, and O'Neill is called "a far greater dramatic genius than his critics would allow," as the significances of the trilogy form, the functions of the chorus, and the "masked" faces of the Mannons are discussed.

Egil Törnqvist's "O'Neill's Lazarus: Dionysus and Christ" (*AL*, Jan. 1970) argues that O'Neill was a syncretist and that in *Lazarus Laughed*, with his Catholic mind turned Nietzschean, Lazarus is primarily pagan while Miriam is primarily Christian. Törnqvist's "Jesus and Judas: On Biblical Allusions in O'Neill's Plays" (*EA*, Jan.–Mar. 1971) surveys O'Neill's plays as a whole and their biblical echoes, arguing that the point is to show man's failure to achieve true Christianity, especially in America. On a much smaller scale is Patrick Bowles's "Another Biblical Parallel in *Desire Under the Elms*" (*EON*, Jan. 1979), which speculates on the biblical names of the play and their possible meaning in their biblical context. Sheng-chuang Lai's "Mysticism and Noh in O'Neill" (*TJ*, Mar. 1983) suggests that the early "mysticism" of O'Neill, as in *The Fountain* or *Lazarus*, was in part bogus and not true to Oriental thought but that the structures of the late plays are remarkably like the structure of the Japanese Noh play: time and dramatic action in the present are suspended and the past is recollected.

O'Neill's relationship to Scandinavia continues to be explored. "Strindberg and O'Neill" by Frederic Fleisher (Itschert) claims that Strindberg's expressionistic and "supernatural" plays most heavily influenced O'Neill's plays, especially those of the first part of the 1920s. Egil Törnqvist's "*Miss Julie* and O'Neill" (*MD*, Jan. 1976) mentions the affinities between *Miss Julie* and some of O'Neill's early works and emphasizes the many similarities between the Strindberg play and *Mourning Becomes Electra*. T. R. Ellis's "The Materiality of *Ghosts* in *Strange Interlude*: Influence of Henrik Ibsen on Eugene O'Neill" (*AN&Q*, Mar.–Apr. 1981) points out the several resemblances between the two plays. Törnqvist's "Strindberg and O'Neill," in *Structures of Influence* (ed. Marilyn Johns Blackwell, Chapel Hill, N.C., 1981), shows how six of Strindberg's plays impacted on twelve of O'Neill's at all stages of his career. The influence of Ibsen and Nietzsche are combined in Reinhold Grimm's "A Note on O'Neill, Nietzsche, and Naturalism: *Long Day's Journey into Night* in European Perspective" (*MD*, Sept. 1983), which suggests that although both Ibsen and Nietzsche are presences in the play, the more powerful, and bleaker, presences are Strindberg and Schopenhauer.

Studies of O'Neill and his favorite philosopher likewise persist. "Dionysus and Despair: The Influence of Nietzsche upon O'Neill's Drama" (*ETJ*, Dec. 1973) by Maurice M. LaBelle traces the Nietzschean influence on *The Hairy Ape*, *Desire Under the Elms*, *Mourning Becomes Electra*, *The Iceman Cometh*, and *Long Day's Journey Into Night*. Michael Hinden's "*The Birth of Tragedy* and *The Great God Brown*" (*MD*, Sept. 1973) claims, among other things, that, in the symbolic epic *The Great God Brown*, O'Neill takes Dion Anthony through the Nietzschean cycle and that the play asserts that the source of modern suffering is dualism and disharmony. The same author's "*The Emperor Jones*: O'Neill, Nietzsche and the American Past" (*EON*, Jan. 1980) argues that the play represents O'Neill's attempt to fuse a Nietzschean perspective with the myth of an American Eden, exploring the nature of the American past and slavery, the crime that destroyed the Eden. Linda Ben-Zvi's "*Exiles*, *The Great God Brown*, and the Specter of Nietzsche" (*MD*, Sept. 1981) exhibits the many parallels between Joyce's play and O'Neill's and the many parallels of both to the philosophical speculations of *Thus Spake Zarathustra*.

Influences, parallels, affinities to European, including Russian, writers and creators continue to be pointed out, both to those who preceded and to those who succeeded O'Neill. John H. Stroupe's "The Abandonment of Ritual: Jean Anouilh and Eugene O'Neill" (*Renascence*, Spring 1976) sees both playwrights as concerned with the relationship of characters to ritual and life as inextricably connected to acceptance of ritual. Zoltan Szilassy's "The Stanislavsky Heritage in the American Theatre" (*SEA*, 1978) attempts to make a connection between the autobiographical strain in O'Neill's plays and Stanislavsky's interest in "the individualization of theatrical roles." Peter Egri's "The Short Story in the Drama: Chekhov and O'Neill" (*ALitASH*, Nos. 1 and 2, 1978) cites Lukács's dictum that O'Neill was not an Ibsenite but a tragicomedian schooled by Chekhov and argues that in O'Neill's plays there is a "short story-like additive sequence in the dramatic plot," illustrated very comprehensively in *A Moon for the Misbegotten*. "Conrad and O'Neill as Playwrights of the Sea" by Kristin Morrison (*EON*, May 1978) discusses the possible influence of Conrad's one-act sea play "One Day More" on O'Neill's early sea plays. Winifred Frazer's "'Revolution' in *The Iceman Cometh*" (*MD*, Mar. 1979) identifies the source, in the German poem *Die Revolution* by Ferdinand Freilgrath, of Hugo Kalmar's favorite quotation, "The days grow hot, O Babylon! 'Tis cool beneath thy willow trees!" Frazer says that Freilgrath was of "both camps, the romantic and the revolutionary," and that O'Neill's play is also of both camps.

Peter Egri's "The Use of the Short Story in O'Neill's and Chekhov's One-Act Plays: A Hungarian View of O'Neill" (Floyd) shows the parallels between the short story and the one-act play in Chekhov and O'Neill and gives a list of O'Neill productions in Hungary from 1928 to 1978, from *The Hairy Ape* to *Long Day's Journey*. Egri's "The Reinterpretation of the Chekhovian Mosaic Design in O'Neill's *Long Day's Journey Into Night*" (*ALitASH*, Nos. 1 and 2, 1980) points out that the short-story-like elements integrated into the play by O'Neill and the play's basic oppositions are very similar to those same elements in Chekhov's plays, although these propositions are not advanced as a matter of influence but rather of convergence. Egri's three-part "*The Iceman Cometh*: European Origins and American Originality" (*EON*, Winter 1981; Spring 1982; Summer–Fall 1982) traces the significant parallels to, as well as divergences from, the works of Ibsen, Gorky, Synge, Chekhov, and Conrad in O'Neill's plays in the treatment of illusion and reality; he particularly remarks on the imprint of Chekhov and Conrad; but also stresses what an "original drama" *The Iceman* is. Michael Manheim's "Dialogue Between Son and Mother in Chekhov's *The Sea Gull* and O'Neill's *Long Day's Journey Into Night*" (*EON*, Spring 1982) asserts that O'Neill and Chekhov are unique in modern drama in that they both can invoke the greatest despair and yet generate some hope and illustrates the love-hate relationship of families by comparing the mother-son dialogues of *The Sea Gull* and *Long Day's Journey*.

"O'Neill and Frank Wedekind" by Susan Tuck (*EON*, Spring 1982; Summer–Fall 1982) shows the similarities between Wedekind's *Frühlings*

Erwachen and *Ah, Wilderness!*, and *Erdgeist* and *Strange Interlude*, with Nina as a kind of Lulu and with other character parallels between the two plays as well. Edward Strickland's "Baudelaire's 'Portraits de maîtresses' and O'Neill's *The Iceman Cometh*" (*RomN*, Spring 1982) points out that the Baudelaire that Edmund quotes in *Long Day's Journey* is taken from *Le Spleen de Paris* (1869), fifty prose poems by Baudelaire. The forty-second one, says Strickland, is very much like the climax of *The Iceman Cometh*, with one man telling three others of an excruciatingly perfect mistress whom he finally murdered and with the other three men reacting in much the same manner as Harry Hope's denizens do to Hickey's story. Michael Hinden's "When Playwrights Talk to God: Peter Shaffer and the Legacy of O'Neill" (*CompD*, Spring 1982) places Shaffer squarely in the O'Neill tradition, especially the O'Neill of the 1920s: the legacy of "robust expressiveness" and experimental devices, along with similarity of themes; *Equus* and *The Great God Brown*, and *Amadeus* and *The Iceman Cometh* are specifically compared and are shown to be quite similar. "Eugene O'Neill's *Days Without End* and The Tradition of the Split Character in Modern American and British Drama" (*EON*, Winter 1982) by Albert Wertheim points out that the device of the split character was not invented by O'Neill but that his use of it in *Days Without End* has exercised a powerful influence on modern British-American drama, as exemplified by plays by Kennedy, Leonard, Nichols, and Norman. Peter Egri, in "Beneath *The Calms of Capricorn*: O'Neill's Adoption and Naturalization of European Models" (*EON*, Spring–Summer 1983), sees twelve (!) European playwrights (Shakespeare, Ibsen, etc.) and modes of drama (Expressionist, well-made, farce, etc.) behind *The Calms*, which, says Egri, pulls the play in twelve different directions, making it tend toward the epic.

Some specifically English parallels from the past have been looked at. Winifred L. Frazer's "*King Lear* and Hickey: Bridegroom and Iceman" (*MD*, Dec. 1972) discusses, among other things, the dark subjects of sex, death, and incest in *King Lear* and compares them to the pessimism about women and love in *The Iceman*. Normand Berlin's "Ghosts of the Past: O'Neill and *Hamlet*" (*MR*, Summer 1979) describes the many relationships and resemblances between *Hamlet* and *Long Day's Journey* and *A Moon for the Misbegotten*: Oedipal relations, "ghosts," familial tangles, death wishes, sea voyages, excessive drinking, the past controlling the present, and so on. Susan Tuck's "'Electricity is God Now': D. H. Lawrence and O'Neill" (*EON*, Summer–Fall 1981) points out the parallels between O'Neill's *Dynamo* and "The Industrial Magnate" chapter of *Women in Love*, as well as the resemblances between O'Neill's Reuben Fife and Lawrence's Gerald Crich.

Two essays on Jung and O'Neill have been offered by Patrick J. Nolan. "*The Emperor Jones*: A Jungian View of the Origin of Fear in the Black Race" (*EON*, May–Sept. 1980) argues that the black unconscious seeks an internal or spiritual power, which in Jones is both repressed and deflected to pursue the white man's materialism. "*Desire Under the Elms*: Characters by Jung" (*EON*, Summer–Fall 1981) discusses the characters in terms of Jung's animus (the male, hard, possessive force) and anima (the female, loving, soft force). Abbie and Eben have a tragic victory and briefly harmonize the polarity, but by the end of the play the animus has reasserted itself.

Irene Przymecka's "Eugene O'Neill and The Irish Drama" (*KN*, No. 1, 1971) compares O'Neill to Yeats, Synge, and O'Casey with respect to the contest between the principles of life and death, and concludes there is no ambiguity in Synge and O'Casey; they praise love and life, but in O'Neill the contest is "catastrophic" and eventuates in nihilism. Micha̋el O hAodha's "O'Neill and the Anatomy of the Stage Irishman" (*EON*, Sept. 1977) touches on O'Neill's relation to the Irish theatre and his use of Irish themes, especially the conflict of life and dream and the notion of a land of youth beyond the horizon and beyond present memory. John Henry Raleigh's "The Last Confession: O'Neill and the Catholic Confessional" (Floyd) describes the history of the evolution of the Catholic confessional, which was really invented by medieval Irish monks, argues that the two great modern artistic representations of the process are by Joyce and O'Neill, and shows how a secular equivalent to the confessional operates in O'Neill's plays, especially his last ones. The same writer's "The Irish Atavism of *A Moon for the Misbegotten*" (Floyd) asserts that *A Moon* offers a miniature dramatic version of the Irish diaspora to America and that Josie Hogan is a reincarnation of several atayistic Irish female archetypes: the warrior-leader-confessor-virgin-queen.

Another center of interest for O'Neill studies is O'Neill's relationship to other American writers, both those coming before him and those after him. Guy Gey's "*Dynamo* de Eugene O'Neill: la maladie contemporaine et l'exploitation d'un mythe moderne" (*Caliban*, No. 1, 1970) notes the remarkable attention paid the dynamo by Henry Adams, H. G. Wells (in *The Lord of the Dynamos*), and O'Neill. For all three the dynamo was the "objective correlative" for a world without gods, although O'Neill's dynamo is much more sexualized than those of the other two. Lucina P. Gabbard's "At the Zoo: From O'Neill to Albee" (*MD*, Dec. 1976) argues that both *The Hairy Ape* and *The Zoo Story* are based on the same metaphor, man as a caged animal, but that O'Neill's play contains a touch of optimism—a hero strong enough to seek revenge—while Albee's figure is an antihero, ironic and absurd. Alan Ehrlich's "A Streetcar Named Desire under the Elms: A Study of Dramatic Space in *A Streetcar Named Desire* and *Desire Under the Elms*," in *Tennessee Williams: A Tribute* (ed. Jac Thorpe, Jackson, Miss., 1977), compares and contrasts the uses of space in both plays, arguing that the confined and claustrophobic space of each play is a crucial determinant of each tragedy. "Notes on Electricity: Henry Adams and Eugene O'Neill" (*PsychocultR*, Spring 1977) by William Wasserstrom constitutes the most passionate defense of *Dynamo* yet mounted: "phantasmagoric and visionary, hallucinatory and prophetic"; "prodigious"; "seminal," dealing with the principal myth of our era of industry, power, and with human treachery, O'Neill's real last theme. Henry Adams's "Prayer to the Virgin of Chartres" and D. H. Lawrence's *Studies in Classic American Literature* are the proper and magisterial companion texts.

Joyce Deveau Kennedy's "O'Neill's Lavinia Mannon and the Dickinson Legend" (*AL*, Mar. 1977), noting that while writing *Mourning Becomes Electra* O'Neill acquired both Emily Dickinson's *Complete Poems* and Genevieve Taggard's biography of her, points out the resemblances between O'Neill's Lavinia and Emily's sister Lavinia and Emily herself. The same writer's "*Pierre*'s Progeny: O'Neill and the Melville Revival" (*ESC*, Spring 1977) points out a remarkable series of parallels between Melville's dark novel and O'Neill's *Mourning Becomes Electra*. "The Salesman On the Stage: A Study In the Social Influence of Drama" by Christopher Innes (*ESC*, Fall 1977) contrasts three pictures of the psychology of selling: O'Neill's *The Iceman*, Miller's *Death of a Salesman*, and Gelber's *The Connection*, arguing that O'Neill paved the way and that in the other two dramas the picture of the psychology of selling became progressively more negative and mordant. Charmian Green's "Wolfe, O'Neill, and the Mask of Illusion" (*PLL*, Winter 1978) describes the points of resemblance between O'Neill's *The Great God Brown* and Wolfe's *Mannerhouse* and stresses the expressionistic ending of *Look Homeward, Angel* as a possible O'Neillian influence on the novelist.

The many parallels and resemblances between the lives, careers, and plays of O'Neill and Albee are demonstrated by James A. Robinson in "O'Neill and Albee" (*WVUPP*, Feb. 1979). Similarities between the style and substance of Crane's *Maggie* and *The Hairy Ape* are exhibited in Robert McIlvaine's "Crane's *Maggie*: A Source for *The Hairy Ape*" (*EON*, Jan. 1979). Le Roy Robinson's "John Howard Lawson's *Souls!*: A Harbinger of *Strange Interlude*" (*EON*, Winter 1980) shows how Lawson's play, unproduced and unpublished, used soliloquies to reveal the inmost "souls" of the characters. Judith Bryant Wittenberg's "Faulkner and Eugene O'Neill" (*MissQ*, Summer 1980) demonstrates that Faulkner knew O'Neill's plays very well and, noting that O'Neill broke the ground on such subjects as incest, miscegenation, infanticide, blacks as human beings, Freudianism, and intense family relationships, features the resemblances between *Mourning Becomes Electra* and *Absalom, Absalom!*, especially in the combination of Greek dramatic principles, American history, and modern psychology, along with other distinctive similarities. Joseph Jurich's "Jack London and *The Hairy Ape*" (*EON*, Jan. 1980) shows the parallels between *Martin Eden* and *The Hairy Ape*. "House of Compson, House of Tyrone: Faulkner's Influence on O'Neill" by

Susan Tuck juxtaposes *The Sound and the Fury* and *Long Day's Journey* and lists the considerable points of resemblance between the two works (*EON*, Winter 1981). Tuck's "The O'Neill-Faulkner Connection" (Martine) says that the most extended parallels in the works of the two authors are between *All God's Chillun* and *Light in August*.

O'Neill and American cultural history continue to be explored. Otis W. Winchester's "Eugene O'Neill's *Strange Interlude* as a Transcript of America in the 1920's" (*Literature and History*, ed. I. E. Cadenhead, Jr., Tulsa, Okla., 1970; reprinted in Griffin) shows how O'Neill's play embodies many of the consuming interests of the American 1920s: psychoanalysis, theological and ethical controversy, hedonism, hero worship, business, science, and art. "Eugene O'Neill and the Death of the 'Covenant'" (*QJS*, Oct. 1970) by Orley T. Holtan applies to O'Neill's cycle plays the ideas about American historical culture explored by historians such as Henry Nash Smith, R. W. B. Lewis, Leslie Fiedler, Leo Marx, and David Noble, and shows that, like the historians, O'Neill was dramatizing the contradictions of the American experience, especially the clash between the dream of pastoral bliss and the reality of materialism. William T. Going's "Eugene O'Neill, American" (*PLL*, Fall 1976) is a wide-ranging and ambitious attempt to place O'Neill and his plays at the center of American cultural history, "drama that speaks toward the future while defining the past," making its creator a great national dramatist like Chekhov, Ibsen, Strindberg, Shaw and Shakespeare. "*Desire Under the Elms*: O'Neill and the American Romance" (*ForumH*, Spring 1977) by Michael Hinden is an equally ambitious attempt to relate *Desire Under the Elms* to the writers of the American Renaissance, to Emerson, Hawthorne, Melville, pursuing, for example, the many analogies between Captain Ahab and Ephraim Cabot, plus other similar themes.

"The Idea of Puritanism in the Plays of Eugene O'Neill" (*Renascence*, Spring 1978) by Steven L. Fluckiger notes O'Neill's fondness for the New England setting and its concomitants, "denial and repression" and the idea of the conversion experience, and gives a close reading of *Desire Under the Elms*. Frederick Wilkins's "The Pressure of Puritanism in Eugene O'Neill's New England Plays" (Floyd) stresses O'Neill's critique of Puritanism as a creed gone hard, stony, and repressive, especially in *Desire Under the Elms* and *Mourning Becomes Electra*. Carol Billman's "Language as Theme in Eugene O'Neill's *Hughie*" (*NMAL*, Fall 1979) compares *Hughie* to Albee's *The Zoo Story* and LeRoi Jones's *Dutchman*, all dealing with the problem of communication in crowded urban space, but asserts that O'Neill's metier is "communication" and optimism, not violence, as in Albee and Jones. Another full-scale attempt to "place" O'Neill in American historical culture is John Gatta, Jr.'s "The American Subject: Moral History as Tragedy in the Plays of Eugene O'Neill" (*ELWIU*, Fall 1979). Emphasizing O'Neill's kinship to the American Renaissance, Gatta says, among other things, that the tragedy of the American dream became O'Neill's paradigm for the human tragedy and comments upon other aspects of the American romantic/realistic polarity.

Timothy J. Wiles's "Tammanyite, Progressivist and Anarchist: Political Communities in *The Iceman Cometh*" (*Clio*, Winter 1980) outlines a politico-social allegory behind *The Iceman*, with McGloin and others representing the Tammany legacy, "The Community of Illusions"; Hickey as a form of Progressivism; and Hugo, Rosa Parritt, and Slade representing revolution, both European communism and American anarchism. "The Community of Illusions" prevails. John Henry Raleigh's "Strindberg in Andrew Jackson's America: O'Neill's *More Stately Mansions*" (*Clio*, Fall 1983) contains the twofold thesis that in this cycle play O'Neill's treatment of familial-sexual relations became even more wild and tortured than in most previous plays and that his considerable knowledge of economics in America in the 1830s made it possible for him to integrate the processes of this economic system into the dramatic fable and the characterizations of the play.

On a somewhat wider scale, Frank Cunningham has attempted to relate O'Neill to historical Romanticism in three essays. "*The Great God Brown* and O'Neill's Romantic Vision" (*BSUF*, Summer 1973) argues that *Brown* embodies many of the central ideas of Romanticism: dynamic organicism, the apotheosis of the creative imagination, the cyclical nature of existence, the timelessness of Edenic time, and so on. Nietzsche and Jung are seen as the primary influences. "*The Ancient Mariner* and The Genesis of O'Neill's Romanticism" (*EON*, May 1979), taking off from the production of O'Neill's dramatization of *The Ancient Mariner* in Provincetown in 1924, stresses O'Neill's Romantic, nonpessimistic side, "the imaginative act of celebrating life," which he never lost. Cunningham's "Romantic Elements in Early O'Neill" (Martine) asserts that the familiar themes of historical Romanticism pervade some of the early plays, from *Beyond the Horizon* to *Desire Under the Elms*, wherein the final hero is "Nature, the ultimate Romantic value."

Studies in the psychology and pathology of O'Neill's characters and plays continue to invite examination. "The Defense of Psychoanalysis in Literature: *Long Day's Journey Into Night* and *A View from the Bridge*" by Albert Rothenberg and Eugene D. Shapiro (*CompD*, Spring 1973) is a lengthy, detailed, and complex analysis of the individual characters and their relationships in O'Neill's play, written to show that clinical psychoanalysis is not reductive but is fully aware of "form, flux and language," lending itself "directly to literary criticism." Arthur H. Nethercot's "The Psychoanalyzing of Eugene O'Neill: P.P.S" (*MD*, June 1973), updating two of his previous articles on O'Neill and psychoanalysis, tries to track down the missing psychoanalytical text of the four that O'Neill claims to have read (the other three are Freud's *Totem and Taboo* and *Beyond the Pleasure Principle* and Jung's *Psychology of the Unconscious*) and concludes it might have been Edward J. Kempf's

Psychopathology; there follows a good discussion of O'Neill's proper relation to psychoanalysis.

"High Hopes: Eugene O'Neill and Alcohol" by Stephen R. Grecco (*YFS*, 1974) argues that O'Neill's prolific "wet" period (when he was drinking heavily) from 1919 to 1933 was inferior in substance, though innovative in technique, to his "dry" period, 1933 to his death, and that in *The Iceman Cometh* he had learned to use his escapist drinking past as a theme essential to his play's structure. Nethercot's "Madness in the Plays of Eugene O'Neill" (*MD*, Sept. 1975) notes a preoccupation with madness in forty-two of the forty-five printed plays and lists some causes for it in O'Neill's dramatological world: heredity, hostile circumstances, drink, obsessions, and, most important, sex. The same author's "O'Neill's *More Stately Mansions*" (*ETJ*, May 1975) says that the play is about fairy tales, ghosts, dreams, and madness, especially about dreams and ghosts, and most especially about madness. Robert Feldman's "The Longing for Death in O'Neill's *Strange Interlude* and *Mourning Becomes Electra*" (*L&P*, No. 1, 1981) contrasts the "death wish" in Freud's *Beyond the Pleasure Principle* and O'Neill's plays: Freud's wish is instinctive, while O'Neill's is a conscious choice to escape the torture of living. The retreat into a house at the end of each O'Neill play mentioned in the title signifies the retreat to "the womb-tomb shelter of the past." Steven F. Bloom's "Empty Bottles, Empty Dreams: O'Neill's Use of Drinking and Alcoholism in *Long Day's Journey Into Night*" (Martine) is a detailed examination, with reference to the medical literature on the subject, of the respective chemical dependencies of the four Tyrones.

As the Frenz and Tuck collection demonstrates, almost more than any other American writer O'Neill is a world figure, literally spanning the globe, and there is ample critical-scholarly testimony to this fact. Lewis W. Falb's "The Critical Reception of Eugene O'Neill on the French Stage" (*ETJ*, Dec. 1970) says that French critics have praised O'Neill for his originality and lamented his naturalistic, primitivistic, and melodramatic tendencies, that the plays have met with critical but not popular acclaim in France, and that *Long Day's Journey* has been the most successful in both critical and popular realms. James P. Pettegrove's "Einiges über O'Neill—Übersetzungen ins Deutsche" (*MuK*, No. 1, 1971) describes the difficulties of making precise translations into German of O'Neill's dialogue, but says that if delicacy of characterization is lost, common humanity stands out and that what the translator must sacrifice in conveying a sense of individuality he can win back in a sense of universality. Horst Frenz, in "Notes on O'Neill in France," in *Texte Und Contexte* (ed. Manfred Durzak, Eberhard Reichmann, and Ulrich Weisstein, Bern, 1973), says that, from the first production of *The Emperor Jones* in 1923, O'Neill's plays have not been a great success in France, two of the great obstacles being the difficulties of translation and the radical differences between American and French dramatic modes and expectations. *Long*

Voyage vers la nuit (1957, 1959–60) was a success, and thirty-four of O'Neill's plays in ten volumes (1963–65) have been published in good translations.

Marián Gálik's *"Chao—The King of Hell* and *The Emperor Jones*: Two Plays by Hung Shen and O'Neill" (*Asian and African Studies XII*, Bratislavia, 1976) tells us that Hung Shen (1894–1955), China's foremost playwright of his time, studied with Baker at Harvard and adapted many of the Expressionist devices of *The Emperor Jones* for his *Chao Yen-wang* (*Chao—The King of Hell*, 1923), of which his audience did not approve. "O'Neill in Hungary: A Letter" by Peter Egri (*EON*, May 1977) describes the great interest and the many translations of O'Neill in Hungary. George Quimby's "O'Neill in Iran" (*EON*, Sept. 1977) describes lecturing on O'Neill in Teheran in 1956 and producing, in 1962, with some degree of success, *Ah, Wilderness!, Long Day's Journey*, and *The Straw*, alternating American and English actors in English and Iranians in Farsi.

"Three European Productions of *The Hairy Ape*" by Horst Frenz (*EON*, Jan. 1978) describes successful productions of O'Neill's play in small theatres in London, Berlin, and Paris, which helped O'Neill's European reputation. Peter Egri's "O'Neill Productions In Hungary: A Chronological Record" (*EON*, Sept. 1978; reprinted in Floyd) lists some twenty-six translations and/or productions of O'Neill's plays from 1928 to 1977. Halina Filipowicz-Findlay's "O'Neill's Plays in Poland" (*EON*, May 1978) says that although Polish theatre historians consider O'Neill important, productions of his plays beginning in the 1930s and continuing on after the interruption of World War II into the 1970s have never been very popular, one of the difficulties being that the Poles are never quite sure how to play him (favorites are *Desire Under the Elms, A Moon for the Misbegotten*, and *Long Day's Journey*).

An extensive collection of European assessments of O'Neill's plays is contained in Floyd's 1979 collection, from which all the following are taken. Marta Sienicka's "O'Neill in Poland" notes thirty productions of O'Neill plays in Poland and sixteen translations of separate plays, with an immense gamut of reactions, from extreme detestation, to middle-of-the-road appreciation, to enthusiasm, the conclusion being that he will never influence Polish drama but will remain permanently on the Polish stage. "The Lasting Challenge of Eugene O'Neill: A Czechoslovak View" by Josef Jařab says that from the early 1920s O'Neill has been considered "a major world dramatist," from the productions of *Desire Under the Elms* in 1925 to those of *"Anna Christie"* and *Long Day's Journey*, considered his great masterpiece, in 1979. There is also a considerable scholarly literature on O'Neill in Czechoslovakia. Maya Koreneva's "One Hundred Percent American Tragedy: A Soviet View" has as its thesis that the early sea plays were "universal tragedy," the middle plays "individual" tragedy, and *The Iceman* and *Long Day's Journey* both universal and individual tragedy. The author also discusses the brilliant productions by

Alexander Taïrov in the Kamerny Theatre of *The Hairy Ape, Desire Under the Elms*, and *All God's Chillun*, and concludes that *Long Day's Journey* is O'Neill's greatest work because of its "beauty and subtlety of characterization."

Horst Frenz's "Eugene O'Neill and Georg Kaiser" argues that, despite O'Neill's claim that he was unacquainted at the time with Kaiser, there are very close resemblances between *The Emperor Jones* and *From Morn to Midnight*; likewise with *The Hairy Ape* and *The Coral*, and *Dynamo* and *Gas I*. Timo Tiusanen's "O'Neill's Significance: A Scandinavian and European View" argues that O'Neill's great significance was, first, that he created his own personal or stage language and that he conveyed by that language significant statements about the condition of modern man. Americans, says Tiusanen, should set up an O'Neill Theatre and Institute and "classicize" him, as Europeans do their writers. Tom Olsson's "O'Neill and The Royal Dramatic" describes the rich relationship between O'Neill and the Swedish Royal Dramatic Theatre—over a period of forty years some fourteen of O'Neill's plays were staged—and the immense success of *Long Day's Journey*, the greatest success in the history of the Royal Dramatic, playing, with intervals, for six years, and constituting the key play in "a concept known as the Royal Dramatic's O'Neill tradition." Finally, there is Clifford Leech's "O'Neill in England—From *Anna Christie* to *Long Day's Journey Into Night*," describing his and his contemporaries' enthusiasm—"We went to see every O'Neill play we could"—in his younger days in England where O'Neill was popular in the experimental theatre, especially the Gate Theatre. This enthusiasm was finally to be extended to *Long Day's Journey* and *The Iceman*.

J. P. Pettegrove's "'Snuff'd out by an Article': '*Anna Christie*' in Berlin" (*MuK*, No. 4, 1981) unravels the considerable intricacies about the translation (who? how?) of the German version of "*Anna Christie*" and its production on 9 October 1923 in Berlin, which was a failure and was called such by the well-known German critic Rudolph Kommer. Horst Frenz's "*Marco Millions*, O'Neill's Chinese Experience and Chinese Drama" (*CLS*, Sept. 1981) says that O'Neill was the only American playwright to make a decisive impact on Chinese drama, inspiring the transplantation of Western expressionistic devices onto the Chinese stage, because he was admired by two influential playwrights, Hung Shen and Ts'ao Yü. Shen's *The King of Hell* is modeled on *The Emperor Jones* and Yü's *Thunderstorm* (1934), *The Wilderness* (1937), and *Sunrise* (1936) are all indebted to O'Neill for both character and stagecraft.

Eugene O'Neill's Critics: Voices from Abroad (ed. Horst Frenz and Susan Tuck, Carbondale and Edwardsville, Ill., 1984) contains twenty-six essays on O'Neill by foreign writers. Seventeen countries in Europe, Asia, and South America covering a period from 1922 to 1980 are represented. Included are the early classic analysis by Hugo von Hofmannsthal (1922) and the classic denunciation by St. John Irvine in the *Times Literary*

Supplement (1948). A good balance is struck between favorable assessments of O'Neill (the majority) and unfavorable. Most of the essays are reprints, but two were written expressly for this book: An Min Hsia's (Republic of China) "Cycle of Return: O'Neill and the Tao" (1978); and Timo Tiusanen's "O'Neill and Wuolijoki: A Counter-Sketch to *Electra*" (1980), concerned with how *Mourning Becomes Electra* influenced the *Justiina* of Finnish playwright Hella Wuolijoki, almost an exact contemporary of O'Neill. There is also a three-part bibliography to this volume: first, a standard list of the standard biographies and critical books on O'Neill; second, an extensive list of books and articles dealing with O'Neill's plays abroad; and third, a list of translations of O'Neill's plays in thirty-two countries, the only unrepresented continent being Africa. And, as the editors say, the list is not complete. This book constitutes the most comprehensive picture of O'Neill's worldwide reputation.

b. *General Studies.* Emil Roy's "The Archetypal Unity of Eugene O'Neill's Drama" (*CompD*, Winter 1969–70) sees in O'Neill's plays repeated dramatizations of the archetypal journey of the exiled son who ends his dark journey in "a blissful Liebestod with the long-sought mother breast." Rudolph Haas's "Eugene O'Neill" (Itschert) provides an introductory life-and-work summary of O'Neill, concluding that while O'Neill is interesting he is never great. Bruce I. Granger's "Illusion and Reality in Eugene O'Neill" (Itschert) argues that in O'Neill's world illusion brings order for men out of chaos but incapacitates them for meaningful action, that life without illusion is intolerable except for the few strong, like Lavinia Mannon and Larry Slade, and that meaningful action is only possible when man strips off his illusion, confronts terror, and acts in obedience to a secret impulse of character. "Liking O'Neill" (*ForumH*, Summer–Fall 1973 and Winter 1974) by Michael Hinden is a broad defense of O'Neill against his detractors, arguing among other things that his strengths were in his talent for characterization and structure; that his tragic structure is Nietzschean and involves the "ritual of self-purgation" and self-discovery; that, while opposed to the "theatre of ideas," he was an "imaginative" thinker in whose plays "the structure *is* the idea"; and that his social criticism is made through the intensity of the dramatic experience of the plays.

Willard Booth's "Haunting Fragment from Eugene O'Neill" (*Adam*, Nos. 376–78, 1973) is part a general survey of O'Neill's career and concerns and part a speculation on what the plays of the unfinished cycle would have been like. "Auffassungsweisen und Gestaltungskategorien der Wirklickeit im Drama: Zum Tragischen, Komischen, Satirischen und Grotesken bei O'Neill," in *Amerikanisches Drama Und Theatre Im 20 Jahrhundert* (ed. Alfred Weber and Siegfried Neuweiler, Gottingen, 1975) by Gerhart Hoffmann, tries to define and correlate with the structure of the plays O'Neill's senses of the tragic, the mystic, the comic, the satiric, the grotesque, and the absurd, under the aegis of the absolute (the religious, mystical, tragic, absurd) and society (the adjusted, comic, satiric, grotesque), with *The Iceman* considered as the fullest embodiment of the themes. In this same German volume is Peter Baulard's "Expressionism In Modern American Drama," with O'Neill as the most important example. Baulard suggests, among other things, that by *The Hairy Ape* O'Neill had begun to modify expressionism by bringing in palpably realistic details, thereby elevating the ordinary to the symbolic and imbuing the symbolic with plausibility, and itemizes the great number of devices of this modified expressionism that appear in the late "realistic" plays.

Thomas P. Adler, in "'Through a Glass Darkly': O'Neill's Esthetic Theory as Seen Through His Writer Characters" (*ArQ*, Summer 1976), says that O'Neill's writer figures reveal O'Neill's interest in the following: the writer's need for supportive love from outside himself; the relationship between life and art; the difficulty of finding an adequate language; the artistic vision as a mystical revelation; and, noting the persistence of fog in O'Neill's plays, says that for his writer characters "the poet's vision" is "a parting the veil of fog" (as it was for Nietzsche, Emerson, and Shelley). "O'Neill's Grotesque Dancers" by James A. Robinson (*MD*, Dec. 1976) asserts that in his experimental plays grotesque movements, "distorted dances," and mechanistic group movements demonstrate individual alienation in a grotesque universe ruled by mysterious forces. James R. Scrimgeour's "From Loving to the Misbegotten: Despair in the Drama of Eugene O'Neill" (*MD*, Mar. 1977) traces O'Neill's treatment of despairing human consciousness throughout his career, focusing both on the unchanging characteristics of human beings in despair and O'Neill's changing treatment of these despairing individuals; the title of the article gives rise to its conclusion: that *Days* is the same story as *A Moon*, but that in his last play O'Neill "leapt from an abstract theoretical treatment of this exorcism [of despair] to a concrete, existential treatment of the same subject."

The preview issue of the *Eugene O'Neill Newsletter* (Jan. 1977) was wholly given over to talks, which were tape-recorded, given at the O'Neill section of the Modern Language Association meeting held in San Francisco in December 1975. The theme was "The Enduring O'Neill: Which Plays Will Survive"; the organizer of the program and the introducer to the talks at the meeting was Frederick Wilkins. The participants were, in the order of their presentations, John Henry Raleigh, Doris Falk, Virginia Floyd, and Esther M. Jackson. Suffice it to say that although there were many disagreements, there was a general agreement that the late plays are the great plays and the enduring ones. Ironically, in the first regular issue of the *Newsletter* (May 1977), Frederick I. Carpenter published "The Enduring O'Neill: The Early Plays," invoking the emotional power of *Desire Under the Elms, Strange Interlude,* and others among the earlier plays; O'Neill's real gift was the "dramatization of irrational elements," *Strange Interlude* and *The Iceman Cometh* both being mentioned as examples of this. Paul Voelker's "Eugene O'Neill's Aesthetic of the Drama" (*MD*, Mar. 1978) pieces together, from various statements made on various subjects by O'Neill, an aesthetic rationale for the playwright which encompasses O'Neill's conception of the proper relationship between written play and acting play; his concern with a "main idea," a "central truth" for a play; the functioning of symbols; the emphasis on plot and rhythm; the totality of conception and execution (characters, setting, dialogue, sounds, etc.); and the notion that drama is "inherently a mode of mixed media," but always with recognizable humans at the center. Esther M. Jackson's "O'Neill the Humanist" (Floyd) stresses O'Neill's search for religious principles, compares him to the New Humanists and to Whitman, and considers *The Iceman* and *Long Day's Journey* as examples of O'Neill's tragic humanism.

"Poetry and Mysticism in O'Neill" by Albert Bermel (Floyd) shows mysticism in O'Neill as a longing of characters for some kind of mystical union and as the influence on the characters of the setting and the audience; in *Long Day's Journey* he notes the yearning for oblivion on the part of the characters and speculates on how the realistic setting of the play might be poeticized and the characters might be masked. J. Dennis Rich's "Exile Without Remedy: The Late Plays of Eugene O'Neill" (Floyd) sees *The Iceman, Long Day's Journey*, and *Hughie* as the world of the absurd, as defined by Camus: depicted both comically and tragically, survivors and casualties, all alone with no God and exiled without remedy, "but not the defeat of man." Hari Mohan Prasad's "The Tragic Mode: A Study in Eugene O'Neill's *Beyond the Horizon, The Emperor Jones* and *The Hairy Ape*" (*OJES*, No. 1, 1979) argues that O'Neill's tragedies feature "the common man," even "anti-heroes," generating intense emotional response in readers and audience and making "a triumphant assertion of human dignity." Joseph J. Moleski's "Eugene O'Neill and the Cruelty of Theater" (*CompD*, Winter 1981–82) takes off from Artaud's objection to the dominance of speech in the theatre (with a running parallel to Schoenberg's attempts to emancipate music from speech patterns) and argues, among other things, that O'Neill's early plays sacrifice thought to poetry, while the later plays sacrifice poetry to thought; O'Neill's cruelty consists in respecting "the limits of the possible" and "the factuality of the subjugation of writing to speech, of difference to identity."

"Concrete Images of the Vague in the Plays of Eugene O'Neill" by B. S. Field, Jr. (Martine) is an off-beat and original series of speculations on the various uses of the "vague" in O'Neill and argues that each play for O'Neill was a struggle "to find a method by which the great enemy of the plastic power of art, the formless and unformable, may be conquered by being embodied in art." Steven E. Colburn's "*The Long Voyage Home*: Illusion and the Tragic Patterns of Fate in O'Neill's *S.S. Glencairn*"

(Martine) argues that the early sea plays have a single theme—human illusion—and a single structure, the tragic struggle of the individual with fate.

c. *Individual Plays*. Alex Scarbrough's "O'Neill's use of the Displaced Archetype in *The Moon of the Caribbees*" (*WVUPP*, July 1972) lists the plays's ironies—a Blessed Isle which is tainted, a sailor who is not a sailor (Smitty), and so on. Frederick Wilkins (*EON*, Winter 1980) reports on an operatic version of *Before Breakfast*, music by Thomas Pasateri, libretto by Frank Cosaro, performed on 9 October 1980 in New York; generally, the critics were not enthusiastic. Gerald Lee Ratcliffe's "*Fog*: An O'Neill Theological Miscellany" (*EON*, Winter 1982) says the play is like a medieval morality play, with a divine pattern behind it. Robert Perrin's "O'Neill's Use of Language in *Where The Cross Is Made*" (*EON*, Winter 1982) is a study of Nat Bartlett's syntax: under the pressure of fear it becomes more incoherent. "The Ending of O'Neill's *Beyond the Horizon*" (*MD*, Sept. 1977) by William J. Scheick tries to demonstrate that the conclusion of the play is perfectly just and appropriate. Lisa M. Schwerdt, in "Blueprint for the Future: *The Emperor Jones*" (Martine), argues that the themes and patterns of the eight scenes of *The Emperor Jones* spell out configurations that are to appear in later plays.

P. N. Das's "The Alienated Ape" (*LHY*, No. 1, 1970) explores the idea of "belonging" in the play. In the *Eugene O'Neill Newsletter*'s January 1973 issue three articles appeared: Michael Hinden's "Ironic Use of Myth in *The Hairy Ape*"—it is an ironic, upside-down version of Nietzsche's Dionysian myth; Virginia Floyd's "The Search for Self in *The Hairy Ape*: An Exercise in Futility"—is it the stoker or ourselves we see in the play today?; and Ann D. Hughes's "Biblical Allusions in *The Hairy Ape*"—as its title indicates. Patrick Bowles's "The Hairy Ape as Existential Allegory" (*EON*, May 1979) sees Yank as "an existential Everyman . . . spreadeagled between ape and essence." "'Belonging' Lost: Alienation and Dramatic Form in Eugene O'Neill's *The Hairy Ape*" by Peter Egri (Martine) sees two overlapping antitheses generating the "alienation" of Yank: the conflict of haves and have-nots and the abstract opposition of civilization and nature.

James A. Robinson's "Christianity and *All God's Chillun Got Wings*" (*EON*, May 1978) says the meaning of the ending is that Jim is a dupe of Christianity. Michael Hinden's "The Transitional Nature of *All God's Chillun Got Wings*" (*EON*, May–Sept. 1979) claims the play is O'Neill's most successful effort to depict a psychologically complex sexual relationship and thus looks forward to the late plays. Mara Lemanis's "*Desire Under the Elms* and Tragic Form: A Study in Misalliance" (*SDR*, Autumn 1978) finds that Ephraim is close to tragic stature, Eben and Abbie less so. June Schlueter and Arthur Lewis, in "Cabot's Conflict: The Stones and the Cows" (Martine), describe the inner conflict in Ephraim Cabot's mind between the respective attractions of the cold stones and the warm cows and how the stones finally win out. Joseph S. Tedesco's "Dion Brown and His Problems" (Martine) is a Jungian, as opposed to a Nietzschean, analysis of *The Great God Brown*. "Eugene O'Neill: The Drama of Self-Transcendence" by Carl E. Rollyson, Jr. (Martine) concerns itself principally with *Lazarus Laughed* and is about the problem of transcending history.

Ronald T. Curran's "Insular Types: Puritanism and Primitivism in *Mourning Becomes Electra*" (*RLV*, No. 4, 1975) views the play as a vehicle for O'Neill's reinterpretation of naive Rousseauistic primitivism in the light of psychoanalytic insight and for his investigation of the failure of primitivism, in the tradition of Melville and Hawthorne, and the repressions of Puritanism. "Mother and Daughter in *Mourning Becomes Electra*" by William Young (*EON*, Summer–Fall 1982) argues that Christine, not Lavinia, is the "central tragic figure." Ben Lucow's "O'Neill's Use of Realism in '*Ah, Wilderness!*'" (*NMAL*, Spring 1977) says the language shows how the characters "remain true to a 'realistic' view of life." "Singing in the Wilderness: The Dark Vision of Eugene O'Neill's Only Mature Comedy" (*MD*, Mar. 1979) by Thomas F. Van Laan argues that the play examines three clichés of American life: Americans as Norman Rockwell figures, the July 4th myth, and the ideal of family life. Ellen Kimbel's "Eugene O'Neill as Social Historian: Manners and Morals in *Ah, Wilderness!*" (Martine) asserts that the play is a clear and convincing representation of the cultural milieu of middle-class small-town America in the early twentieth century and therefore shows us "what we have lost."

The Iceman Cometh continues to be the most sibylline utterance of O'Neill and attracts the greatest number of seekers to unravel its mysteries and ambiguities and reveal its meaning. Delma Eugene Presley's "O'Neill's Iceman: Another Meaning" (*AL*, Nov. 1970) points out that an "ice-man," in underworld slang, is a giver of worthless gifts and an undependable person (hence Hickey). Winifred L. Frazer's "O'Neill's Iceman—Not Ice Man" (*AL*, Jan. 1973) contests Presley's assertion in the name of the complexity of the themes of the play. James P. Quinn's "*The Iceman Cometh*: O'Neill's Long Day's Journey into Adolescence" (*JPC*, Summer 1972) says the play constitutes a "fatalistic existential dialectic," with mankind's choice being either an acceptance of objective reality or a return to the womb/death. "Formal Patterns in *The Iceman Cometh*" (*MD*, Sept. 1973) by Nancy Reinhardt is a close study of significant patterns, aural, visual, spatial, of the play and of its cyclic structure.

"The Theatre In *The Iceman Cometh*: Some Modernist Implications" by James G. Watson (*ArQ*, Autumn 1978) contends that, as modern literature is about literature, so *The Iceman* is a play about plays, with each character both an actor and a member of the audience. Denis M. Welch's "Hickey As Satanic Force In *The Iceman Cometh*" (*ArQ*, Autumn 1978) sees Harry Hope's saloon as a little Eden and Hickey as anti-Christ,

Satan, Lucifer. Edward Shaughnessy's "The Iceman Melteth: O'Neill's Return to Cultural Origins" (*EON*, Sept. 1979) sees the *psychology*, especially that of Larry Slade, as Catholic; O'Neill's "resentment" at his origins had "melted" away. Robert Butler's "Artifice and Art-Words In *The Iceman Cometh* and *Hughie*" (*EON*, Spring 1981) says that O'Neill's characters have a choice in their use of words: to devise illusions, which are debilitating (*The Iceman*) or to create sustaining fictions (*Hughie*). Brenda Murphy's "O'Neill's Realism: A Structural Approach" (*EON*, Summer–Fall 1983) analyzes the cyclicity of the play as a whole and the similarity of the structure of each act, "a drama of characters revealed through conflict, with each other and within themselves." "The Transcendence of Melodrama in O'Neill's *The Iceman Cometh*" by Michael Manheim (Martine) argues that melodrama simplifies things, that we look at the past melodramatically, and that the only reality is the complex present, as *The Iceman* demonstrates.

Albert Wertheim's "Gaspard the Miser in O'Neill's *Long Day's Journey Into Night*" (*AN&Q*, Nov. 1979) looks at the resonances given by Jamie Tyrone in describing his father as "Old Gaspard," the miser of *Les Cloches de Corneville* (*The Bells of Corneville*), a nineteenth-century comic opera, a pot-boiler much like James O'Neill-Tyrone's *Count of Monte Cristo*.

Hughie also continues to attract attention. Rolf Scheibler's "*Hughie*: a One=Act Play for the Imaginary Theatre" (*ES*, June 1973) provides an admirably detailed analysis of the play, especially the interplay between Erie's monologue and the silent thoughts of the desk clerk. D. V. K. Raghavacharyulu's "Waiting for Hughie," in *Studies in American Literature* (ed. Jagdish Chander and Narindar S. Pradhan, Delhi, 1976), is a standard analysis of the play. Robert Mayberry's "Sterile Wedding: The Comic Structure of O'Neill's *Hughie*" (*MSE*, No. 3, 1980) shows that *Hughie* contains all or most of the aspects of comic form enunciated by Suzanne Langer, Benjamin Lehman, Wylie Sypher, and Northrop Frye. Edward Shaughnessy's "Question and Answer in *Hughie*" (*EON*, Sept. 1978) shows the appearance of primordial O'Neill themes in the play. "Film and Fiction in O'Neill's *Hughie*" by Marcelline Krafchick (*ArQ*, Spring 1983) proposes that the play be fully staged, using film and tape, as O'Neill once suggested. Laurin Roland Porter's "*Hughie*: Pipe Dream for Two" (Martine) describes the relationship between *The Iceman* and *Hughie* and argues that the two are companion pieces.

Jordan Y. Miller's "Murky Moon" (*KanQ*, Fall 1975) sees *A Moon for the Misbegotten* as a failure. Michael Hinden's "Desire and Forgiveness: O'Neill's Diptych" (*CompD*, Fall 1980) points out the many parallels, in mothers, fathers, sons, familial relationships, between *Desire Under the Elms* and *A Moon for the Misbegotten* and argues that the themes of *Desire* are exorcized and self-forgiven in *A Moon*, at whose conclusion there are blessings everywhere. Michael Manheim's "O'Neill's Transcendence of Melodrama in *A Touch of the Poet* and *A Moon for the Misbegotten*"

(*CompD*, Fall 1982) takes off from John Henry Raleigh's "The Escape from the Chateau d'If" (1964), showing O'Neill's melodramatic heritage, carries the argument further on the essential melodramatic base of much of O'Neill's work, and describes the transcendence of that form at the end of *A Touch* and *A Moon*.

Jere Real's "The Brothel In O'Neill's *Mansions*" (*MD*, Feb. 1970) says that the prostitution motif of always "selling out" pervades the action and dialogue of *More Stately Mansions*. Edward Mullaly's "O'Neill and the Perfect Pattern" (*DR*, Winter 1972–73) describes, among other things, how "the perfect pattern" (as described in a letter from O'Neill to Clark) operates in *More Stately Mansions*: the idealist gets power; he uses it; and then he misuses it. The result is tragedy. Esther M. Jackson's "Eugene O'Neill's *More Stately Mansions*: Studies In Dramatic Form At The University of Wisconsin–Madison" (*EON*, Summer–Fall 1981) describes the study of and presentation of *More Stately Mansions* by a group at the University of Wisconsin and calls the play "a vision of American history which borrows from the past in order to create images of the present and future." Accompanying Jackson's description is Ronald R. Miller's "History as Image: Approaches To the Staging of Eugene O'Neill's *More Stately Mansions*," describing the ways of staging the play devised by the Wisconsin group. "The Paradox of Power in *More Stately Mansions*" (*EON*, Winter 1981) by Joseph Petite says that the goal of the characters is to get power, with money as the means of doing it, and to build walls around themselves.

d. Special Topics. In the decade of the 1970s, there have been five emergent centers of interest for O'Neill studies: blacks, film, women, manuscript studies, and special studies of specific dramatic aspects of O'Neill's plays.

Peter J. Gillett's "O'Neill and the Racial Myths" (*TCL*, Apr. 1972; reprinted in Griffin) discusses the five plays of O'Neill that contain black characters and focuses particularly on *All God's Chillun* as the height of O'Neill's achievement in treating black themes. Although Joe Mott of *The Iceman* is more finely-realized than any of O'Neill's earlier black characters, the playwright shows "courage and insight" in all his pictures of blacks. John R. Cooley's "*The Emperor Jones* and the Harlem Renaissance" (*SLitI*, Fall 1974) is a negative picture of its subject, as in the chapter in his book (see above); *Jones* exhibits O'Neill's "racial ambivalence" and is a play of racial stereotypes, as blacks recognized, even though it was a major breakthrough in the American theatre, with black actors playing black parts. James Corey's "O'Neill's *The Emperor Jones*" (*AN&Q*, May/June 1974) suggests that the Witch Doctor in scene 7 of the play was created by a composite of five African natives described by Conrad in chapter 3 of *The Heart of Darkness*. Roger Oliver's "From the Exotic to the Real: The Evolution of Black Characterization in Three Plays by Eugene O'Neill" (*ForumH*, Winter 1976) argues that O'Neill's evolution in black characterization parallels his artistic development: beginning with exotic theatricality and notions of a racial unconscious in *Jones*, he moved toward realism and character complexity in *All God's Chillun* and achieved it with Joe Mott in *The Iceman*. Joe Weixlmann's "Staged Segregation: Baldwin's *Blues for Mr. Charlie* and O'Neill's *All God's Chillun Got Wings*" (*BALF*, Spring 1977) claims that Baldwin borrowed his most effective staging device for his play (segregation by the separation of "Blacktown" and "Whitetown") from O'Neill's play.

The categories of "Black" and "Film" coincide in the movie made of *The Emperor Jones* (treated in the books of both Orlando and Murray already discussed). Norman Kagan's "The Return of *The Emperor Jones*" (*Negro Hist. Bull.*, Nov. 1971), noting that the Paul Robeson film was being redistributed in 1971, describes the history of the making of the film and its initial reception and concludes that *Jones* marked a departure from black self-hatred and hopelessness, that Jones was "civilized," and that "the way was clear to the now-emergent black cinema art of today." "*The Emperor Jones*—Robeson and O'Neill on Film" by John Krimsky (*ConnR*, Apr. 1974) is a reminiscence about the film by its producer, expressing pride in the choice of the black as protagonist and the choice of Robeson to play the role. Gordon Bordewyck's and Michael McGowan's "Another Source of Eugene O'Neill's *The Emperor Jones*" (*NMAL*, Autumn 1982) points out that the composition of *The Emperor Jones* coincided with the immense parade in August 1920 in Harlem and the mass meeting in Madison Square Garden organized by Marcus Garvey for his Universal Negro Improvement Association and spells out the many similarities, both in character and fate, between Garvey and Jones.

Linda Ben-Zvi's "Eugene O'Neill and Film" (*EON*, Spring 1983) gives a history of O'Neill's relationship to film and describes the scripts for *Before Breakfast* and *The Emperor Jones*, the mishmash of acting styles and scenic effects in *Mourning*, and concludes that O'Neill films capture only his "commonplace" reality, not his "fantasy" reality. William L. Sipple's "From Stage to Screen: *The Long Voyage Home* and *Long Day's Journey Into Night*" (*EON*, Spring 1983) discusses what are generally regarded as the two best filmic treatments of O'Neill, stressing that John Ford for *The Long Voyage Home* "opens" up and expanded the four one-act plays, while Sidney Lumet for *Long Day's Journey* maintained the closed structure of the stage, making the point that there is no single way to transfer a play to film.

Lois S. Joseph's "The Women of Eugene O'Neill" (*BSUF*, Summer 1973) concludes that O'Neill never goes outside traditional stereotyped roles for women. "O'Neill's Women" by Doris Nelson (*EON*, Summer–Fall 1982) says that O'Neill's women are always just *women*, never having an occupation, except the whores, and always defined only by their biological roles. Trudy Drucker's "Sexuality as Destiny: The Shadow

Lives of O'Neill's Women" (*EON*, Summer–Fall 1982) argues that O'Neill possessed a narrowly sexual view of the behavior and destiny of women, that they hardly ever have legitimate jobs, that the bodies of women have a mystical ability to save or destroy a man, and that a favorite O'Neill theme is a woman married to the wrong man. Bette Mandl's "Absence as Presence: The Second Sex in *The Iceman Cometh*" (*EON*, Summer–Fall 1982) says that the theme is woman's "otherness," that she is indicted as mother, wife, sister, mistress, and prostitute, and that a consistent hostility is directed at the women in the play, both those present on the stage and those absent, like Rosa Parritt and Evelyn Hickey.

Claude R. Flory's "Notes on the Antecedents of *Anna Christie*" (*PMLA*, Jan. 1971) is a very detailed examination of the three versions of "*Anna Christie*" (first, "Chris Christophersen," and second, "The Ole Davil"), concluding that "at least 95% of the text" of "The Ole Davil" is identical to the text published as "*Anna Christie*," the differences being primarily verbal (deletions from the earlier text); their common origin, "Chris," is also analyzed in great detail. Paul Voelker's "The Uncertain Origins of Eugene O'Neill's 'Bound East for Cardiff'" (*SB*, 1979) contrasts "Bound East" to its original, "Children of the Sea," in meticulous detail and attempts to determine its date of composition, probably the fall or winter of 1915–16.

Detailed studies of specific aspects of O'Neill's plays are more common among Europeans (see Ulrich Halfmann's *Unreal Realism*, described above; Törnqvist's *The Drama of Souls* [1969]; and Tiusanen's *Scenic Images* [1968]) than it is by Americans. Egil Törnqvist's "Personal Addresses in the Plays of O'Neill" (*QJS*, Apr. 1969) says that alterations in personal addresses (what characters call each other) are "pregnant telltale signs" in indicating psychological relations; for example, in *A Touch of the Poet* the protagonist is both "Con" and "the Major," and he addresses his wife variously as "Nora," "darlihnt" and "woman." Ilse Brugger's "Verwendung und Bedeutung der Maske bei O'Neill" (Itschert) examines the use and meaning of masks, not only actual masks but faces that are described as looking "masked" like the Mannons, concluding that a good part of modern life-anguish is conveyed by O'Neill in his use of masks. Gustav H. Blank's "Die Dramenschlusse Bei O'Neill" (Itschert) examines the significance of the endings, in all their dark variety, of eighteen O'Neill plays, from *Beyond the Horizon* to *Hughie*. Rudolph Haas's *Theorie und Praxis der Interpretation* (Berlin, 1977) has a section on the significance of stage directions, analyzing O'Neill's among others, specifically how the introductory stage directions to *Homecoming*, up to and including Seth's opening speech, forecast so much of *Mourning Becomes Electra*.

Ernest O. Fink's "Audience Aids for Non-Literary Allusions? Observation on the Transposition of Essential Technicalities in the Sea Plays of Eugene O'Neill," in *The Languages of Theatre* (ed. Ortum Zuber, Elmsford,

N.Y., 1980), suggests how certain visual and sound effects could update for a contemporary audience the now dated aspects of O'Neill's sea plays, observing that there is "no playwright to match O'Neill as shipwright." "The Mirror as Stage Prop in Modern Drama" (*CompD*, Winter 1980–81) by Thomas P. Adler examines Pirandello's *It is So! (If You Think So)*, O'Neill's *A Touch of the Poet*, Camus's *Caligula*, and Genet's *The Balcony*, with respect to their relativism, skepticism, existentialism, and absurdism, and notes that each makes use of mirrors, whereby the protagonist becomes his own audience. For Con Melody the mirror image is illusion, but not entirely, and when he changes from aristocrat to peasant, he is merely changing masks. Peter Egri's "The Dramatic Role of the Fog/Foghorn Leitmotif in Eugene O'Neill's *Long Day's Journey Into Night*" (*Amst*, No. 4, 1982) argues that the fog/foghorn serves as a leitmotif for the four principal themes of the play: collision between material gain and spiritual loss, antithesis of illusion and reality, opposition of love and hate, and confrontation of human aspirations and the workings of fate.

VI SUPPLEMENT

Eugene O'Neill's *Work Diary, 1921–1943*, edited and transcribed by Donald Gallup, "Preliminary Edition" (New Haven, Conn., 1981), is in two volumes: vol. I, 1924–1933; vol. II, 1934–1943. There is also a "Scribbling Diary" for 1925 with fuller entries than in the *Work Diary* as a whole. The *Work Diary* is essentially a calendar and indicates for each day, month by month, January 1924–May 4, 1943, what play O'Neill was working on; the information is given briefly, often in abbreviations, with occasional references to other matters, as, for example, swimming or a social occasion.

Ulrich Halfmann's *Eugene O'Neill: Comments on the Drama and the Theatre* (Tübingen, 1987) is an attempt to put together between two covers all of O'Neill's comments on drama and theater scattered throughout his life in letters, interviews, playbills, and so on. Halfmann sets forth 153 items drawn from 110 different sources. Part I consists of material published during O'Neill's lifetime (1888–1953). Part II is posthumously published material and consists of excerpts from letters, inscriptions, MS. notes, and other miscellaneous sources. This is a very useful compilation and has two indexes: Names and Titles and Analytic Subject.

Travis Bogard's *The Unknown O'Neill: Unpublished or Unfamiliar Writings of Eugene O'Neill* (New Haven, Conn., 1988) reprints "The Personal Equation," the four-act play written at Harvard for Professor Baker; a scenario of "The Reckoning," a projected four-act play conceived by O'Neill in 1917, and the completed play, by Agnes Bolton, called "The Guilty One," which O'Neill's wife fashioned out of her husband's scenario in 1924; act 4 of "The Ole Davil"—substantially the same play as *"Anna Christie"*—which gives a much happier ending to the play than does *"Anna Christie"* itself; O'Neill's 1923 theater adaptation of Coleridge's *The Rime of the Ancient Mariner*; the original eight-act version of *Marco Millions*, entitled first "Marco's Millions"; two short stories, "Tomorrow" and "S.O.S."; a late love poem; and miscellaneous critical and prose pieces. Bogard's commentary is full and to the point.

Virginia Floyd's *Eugene O'Neill, the Unfinished Plays* (New York, 1988) prints the notes, often extensive, for three ambitious plays that O'Neill worked on from 1940 to 1943 but never finished: "The Visit of Malatesta," "The Last Conquest," and "Blind Alley Guy." Floyd's own commentary on this material is detailed and helpful. What unites the three quite disparate plays is that they are all antitotalitarian, reflecting O'Neill's own very real concerns during World War II over such political phenomena as Hitler and Stalin and what they might represent for the future of mankind.

There are two other important new editions: the complete text of *More Stately Mansions*, edited and with an introduction by Martha Bower (New York, 1988); and the Library of America's three-volume edition of the collected plays of Eugene O'Neill, edited by Travis Bogard.

Finally, and to the delight of all lovers of song, there is forthcoming in 1989 *The Eugene O'Neill Songbook*, edited by Travis Bogard (Ann Arbor, Mich.), reprinting the complete words and music for all the songs sung, in whole or in part, in O'Neill's plays.

"As Ever, Gene": The Letters of Eugene O'Neill to George Jean Nathan consists of 130 letters from O'Neill to George Jean Nathan (Nathan's letters to O'Neill have been lost), edited by Nancy L. Roberts and Arthur W. Roberts (Rutherford, N.J., 1987). The collection is divided into four parts: I. Letters from May 1919 to December 1925; II. April 1926 to April 1931; III. June 1932 to August 1949; and IV. January 1937 to August 1949. O'Neill and Nathan genuinely liked and respected one another; so there is much warmth and camaraderie in the letters, as well as much information about O'Neill's struggles with composing his plays, as, for example, his monumental bout with *Mourning Becomes Electra*. Nathan appears to have been an O'Neill admirer from first to last, from the early sea plays to *The Iceman Cometh*. But he could also tell O'Neill when a play was a botch, as he did with *Dynamo*.

Selected Letters of Eugene O'Neill (New Haven, Conn., 1988) reprints 560 letters out of a total available of over 3,000. The collection is expertly edited by Travis Bogard and Jackson R. Bryer, with annotations that are clear and concise. Besides being a capsule life of the writer in his own words, the letters also contain interesting comments by O'Neill on his craft.

In 1985 Virginia Floyd published her *The Plays of Eugene O'Neill: A New Assessment* (New York). This is a chronological survey of O'Neill's life and works, heavily emphasizing the autobiographical elements in the plays. The author describes her work as an "introductory study" for "contemporary students and general readers." Fifty plays are considered, each given a plot summary and some critical commentary. The book is divided into four periods, and each of the four parts has at its conclusion a list of the plays that O'Neill contemplated writing but did not during the period just considered. Part I: The Sea-Mother's Son: Early Plays and Beginnings (up through *The Straw*); Part II: The Mariner's Horizon: Experimental Plays and Maturation (through *Dynamo*); Part III: Lost Horizons—Interrupted Journey: "Self" Plays and the Cycle (through "The Calms of Capricorn"); and Part IV: Homecoming—The Last Harbor: The Late Great Plays. There is an epilogue on the three contemplated plays of the 1940–43 period which have been described above.

Peter Egri's *Chekhov and O'Neill* (Budapest, 1986) has as its subtitle "The Uses of the Short Story in Chekhov's and O'Neill's Plays." The thesis is that O'Neill was well acquainted with Chekhov from his youth and that, especially in his later works, he showed Chekhovian affinities in his use of structural elements, generic traits, symbols, atmosphere, and moods. At the thematic center of this study is the problem of genre, namely, the relationship between the short story and the drama in Chekhov's and O'Neill's plays, how short story-oriented elements function in the plays, and how compositional and generic relationships develop between short story pattern and dramatic structure. The study concludes with a lengthy and detailed study of *Long Day's Journey* from the perspectives that have been outlined above.

Four books have appeared in 1988. Travis Bogard published a revised edition of *Contour In Time: The Plays of Eugene O'Neill* (New York; first ed., 1972). The chief revision is concerned with the composition of the cycle plays, based upon an examination of the cycle manuscripts previously unavailable. In the first edition of *Contour In Time*, Bogard said that O'Neill's Bessie Bowen was based upon the famous Mrs. Stephen Jumel, consort of Aaron Burr. This identification was incorrect and the real archetype for O'Neill's "Bowen" was one Kate Gleason (d. 1933), an immensely successful industrial leader from Rochester, New York.

John Stroupe has edited *Critical Approaches to O'Neill* (New York), with contributions from Emil Roy, Stephen Watt, Joseph Maleski, John Chioles, Louis Sheaffer, John Stroupe, James A. Robinson, Michael Manheim, Thomas P. Adler, Albert Rothenberg, Eugene D. Shapiro, and Michael Hinden. One of the raisons d'être for this collection is its diversity of critical approaches: "archetypal, psychoanalytical, philosophical, textual, biographical, phenomenological, cultural and through deconstructionist criticism, genre criticism and traditional comparative methods." Most of the articles were first published in *Comparative Drama* and have been mentioned above in the section on Critical Articles.

Gary Vena's *O'Neill's "The Iceman Cometh": Reconstructing the Premiere* (Ann Arbor, Mich.) is just what its title says: a complete recreation of the 1946 premiere of O'Neill's play. By dint of interviews with some of the original personnel, and access to prompt books, ground plans, rehearsal texts, set drawings, the staging plans of Robert Edmond Jones, the lighting, photographs of costumes, letters, and other materials pertaining to the intricate interrelations of O'Neill, producer Lawrence Langner, director Eddie Dowling, the Theatre Guild, and the other members of the cast, Vena provides an "intimate reconstruction" of *The Iceman*'s first night. Two appendixes document the modifications to the play during the long rehearsal period and print extracts from forty-five opening night reviews.

Edward Shaughnessy, in *Eugene O'Neill in Ireland: The Critical Reception* (Westport, Conn., 1988), describes the lengthy and complex relationship of the Irish to their most famous American dramatic descendant. Drawing on the published reactions of Irish critics, scholars, theater professionals, reviews of plays and personal interviews and questionnaires, Shaughnessy examines the following matters: O'Neill's American "Irishness" and its effects upon his plays; his various contacts with native Irish art, such as the Abbey Players; the productions of O'Neill's plays in Ireland (in sixty-five years more than fifty premieres or revivals); and, most important, Irish reactions to O'Neill's plays, which were complex and various, both pro and con. The most notorious "con" was St. John Irvine (reprinted here); on the positive side are two fine essays by Denis Donoghue and Christopher Murray (also reprinted here). An appendix lists all O'Neill productions in Ireland from 1922–87. This book is the definitive treatment of relations between O'Neill and his ancestral homeland.

Ezra Pound

John Espey

I BIBLIOGRAPHY

Donald Gallup's *A Bibliography of Ezra Pound* (1963) has been greatly expanded and, as *Ezra Pound: A Bibliography* (Charlottesville, Va., 1983), "describes in detail American, English, and Italian first editions of 106 books by Pound, with descriptions of some 130 first editions of books edited or translated by him or with his contributions. It lists more than 2,000 contributions by him to periodicals and more than 500 translations of his writings." Additional entries appear in every section, including the ephemera, and an altogether new section is included: "Books Contracted for but not Published."

But as all bibliographers know, their work is never done and already *Paideuma* (Spring 1983) has published "Additions and Corrections to the Revised Edition of the Pound Bibliography" by Gallup and Archie Henderson. This includes seventy-four entries (four of which are deletions) scattered throughout almost all the major classifications. So long as the Pound Archive at the Beinecke Library at Yale is being mined and other collections become available to scholars, this kind of supplementation will continue, but Gallup's work will remain every Pound scholar's *vade mecum*.

The first volume of Carroll F. Terrell's *A Companion to the Cantos of Ezra Pound* (Berkeley, Calif., 1980) has incorporated and expanded the entries of the *Annotated Index* (1957) for *Cantos I–LXXI*. Whereas the *Index* is arranged in alphabetical order, the *Companion* is arranged canto by canto, with sources, background reading, and exegeses listed before the glossary itself. Though the final responsibility is Terrell's for the entire work, certain sections and entries are based on the work of various individuals: Eva Hesse (*Cantos I–XI*); Ben Kimpel and T. Duncan Eaves (*Cantos XLII–XLIV, L*); John Nolde (*Cantos LII–LXI*); James Wilhelm (Italian and Provençal, passim); John Espey (passim), and to the user familiar with the work of these contributors personal tones will be recognizable. The second volume (*Cantos LXXIV–CXVIII*) (Berkeley, Calif.,

1985) shows the importance of the *Index*, which included *The Pisan Cantos*. Although Terrell has ignored to some extent the correct original glosses, in the main this section provides a dependable guide. The remainder is also largely reliable, but somewhat uneven in its proofing and more personally idiosyncratic in a number of readings. Nevertheless, the *Companion* will stand for this generation and the next as the standard work. As the slips and errors are corrected in successive printings, it will increase in value. It is already a monument to one man's endurance, energy, and devotion. Both volumes contain cross-references, and the second a four-part index. Terrell has also published two stimulating and highly personal collections of his own cantos, "versified footnotes to *The Cantos* of Ezra Pound": *Smoke and Fire* and *Rod and Lightning* (Orono, Maine, 1984; 1985).

A Catalogue of the Poetry Notebooks of Ezra Pound (New Haven, Conn., 1980), edited by Mary de Rachewiltz, offers a preliminary classification of the bound notebooks in the Beinecke Library, without making any pretense of exhausting the necessary listing of that vast archive. *A Concordance to "Personae: The Shorter Poems of Ezra Pound"* (New York, 1972), edited by Gary Lane, provides a useful aide-mémoire, as does *A Concordance to Ezra Pound's "Cantos"* (New York, 1981), compiled by Robert J. Dilligan, James W. Parins, and Todd K. Bender.

A Student's Guide to the Selected Poems of Ezra Pound by Peter Brooker (London, 1979) has been followed by *A Guide to Ezra Pound's "Selected Poems"* by Christine Froula (New York, 1983). A good bit of repetition occurs here, especially in the light of K. K. Ruthven's earlier *A Guide to Ezra Pound's "Personae"* (1969), but enough differences appear, particularly in their treatments of the longer poems (*Near Perigord, Propertius,* and *Mauberley*) to justify this, though for the greater part the information is purely factual.

II EDITIONS

Selected Prose 1909–1965 (ed. William Cookson, New York, 1973) contains a representative gathering from Pound's lively polemic and critical prose, including a brief and characteristic introductory note by Pound himself in which he refers to these works as "the scrapings from the cracker-barrel" and makes his retraction concerning Usury: "re USURY: / I was out of focus, taking a symptom for a cause. / The cause is AVARICE. / Venice, 4th July, 1972." (Always the American patriot.)

Two later volumes from New Directions have added substantially to making large sections of Pound's prose more easily available to the reader who is disinclined or unable to track down the originals in a variety of journals. The first, R. Murray Shafer's *Ezra Pound and Music* (New York, 1977), gathers almost all of Pound's writing on music and musicians, including his reviews from the *New Age* and other sources, and contains as well an engaging discussion of Pound's aims by a qualified expert in music and an attempt to define Pound's ideas of "absolute rhythm" and "the Great Bass." Shafer draws some suggestive, if not altogether convincing, parallels between Pound's theories and the movement of *The Cantos*. The promised companion volume, which is to be made up of Pound's own compositions, will probably not appear for some time, because several original scores remain in private hands and permission to reproduce them has not as yet been granted in a number of instances. "'Townsman' and Music: Ezra Pound's Letters to Ronald Duncan" by Archie Henderson (*LCUT*, 1984) provides a record both of Pound's correspondence with the British poet and playwright and of the problems Pound had in getting his writing specifically centered in music and music theory published. The new journal that he and Duncan planned for the inclusion of his articles published much of his theoretical material, and this record provides a useful compendium of Pound's practice, his plans for the Rapallo concerts, his use of the Münch-Janequin music, his conviction of a continuing tradition of musical line from the troubadours on down through Villon and Cavalcanti to the English lutenists and Vivaldi. Henderson's article is a well-articulated exposition of all this and is an excellent introduction for those wishing to learn of Pound and his music as well as an informative summary for the specialist. Henderson's unpublished dissertation, "Pound and Music: The Paris and Early Rapallo Years" (Univ. of California, Los Angeles, 1983), contains valuable material on Pound's aesthetic as it developed through contacts with Rummel, Dolmetsch, and Antheil. Appendixes include heretofore unavailable letters of Antheil as well as a listing of his published work on music theory.

The second collection, *Ezra Pound and the Visual Arts* (ed. Harriet Zinnes, New York, 1980), is somewhat less even than the gathering on music. The largest individual division within the book is given to Pound's contributions to the *New Age*, and the volume includes letters to John Quinn published here for the first time, as well as material held by the libraries at Chicago, Cornell, Harvard, and Yale. Contributions to other journals are included, but a sense of the chronology of Pound's shifting theories is difficult to put together because the individual items are reprinted according to the alphabetical order of the journals' titles.

One of the most significant volumes to appear is Leonard W. Doob's *"Ezra Pound Speaking": Radio Speeches of World War II* (Westport, Conn., 1978). It enjoys the great advantage of offering "the speeches as Pound wrote them" as well as in the order in which he wished to have them broadcast. The text is far more accurate than the transcriptions made by the Federal Communications Commission. Ten speeches "written before the FCC monitoring unit had been established" are included as well as several speeches either not used or not monitored. Appendixes analyze the content in a variety of ways. To anyone coming to Pound unprepared, a number of passages will be distasteful, but the reader who is familiar with Pound's personal vocabulary—such as his private meaning of "Jew," which is not the standard one—will not be surprised though he may be dismayed. The folksiness becomes as tiresome at times as it does in the fake Hoosier argot of certain passages in *The Cantos*, but there it is, and one is not (alas!) being chauvinistic in claiming that only an American born in a certain time and into a certain segment of American society can really "understand" everything that Pound was saying.

Pound's Cavalcanti: An Edition of the Translations, Notes, and Essays by David Anderson (Princeton, N.J., 1983) draws together all of Pound's work on the Italian poet who was as central to his theories of poetry and language as any other writer and includes unpublished work originally intended for the 1912 and 1927–29 editions. The editor's introduction is comprehensive. The text itself is a face-to-face presentation of Cavalcanti's original and Pound's "traduction," the variants in major texts of each noted below each poem. This edition represents a valuable consolidation of scholarship and could become the model for similar additions to Pound's complete text if such a thing ever becomes possible.

A minor, but attractive, addition to the history of the full text is contained in *From Syria: The Worksheets, Proofs, and Text* (ed. with an introduction by Robin Skelton, Port Townsend, Wash., 1981), which presents the publishing history of one of Pound's earliest translations from Provençal, the only known poem of Peire Bremon Le Tort's to survive, dropped by Pound very early from his first few collections of verse.

So long as the mass of material at the Beinecke Library remains in part unsorted and unpublished, the text of Pound's work will continue to grow, turning up in a variety of places. For examples, *Sulfur* (No. 1, 1981) contains 121 lines from an unpublished draft of *Canto LXXXIV*, with a reproduction of the last page of Pound's typescript and an introductory note by Matthew Jennett; and Sotheby's *Sale Catalogue* for 21 and 22 July 1980 (London) lists as Item 545 all of the typed versions of many passages from *The Cantos* sent over the years by Pound to Agnes Bedford and prints lines 160–98 from *Canto CXIII* as well as a reproduction of fifteen lines of typescript from *Canto XLII*. In the same catalogue, Item 546 is a typed letter signed to Margaret Widdemer (29 Oct. 1913) giving advice on French poetry, from which a couple of sentences have been reprinted. Catalogue Number Six of Maurice F. Neville's Rare Books (Santa Barbara, Calif., 1981) contains quotations from a number of unpublished letters of Pound (and Eliot) to a variety of correspondents including Harold Monro, Kate Buss, Babette Deutsch, and C. K. Ogden, covering a considerable range of dates. No doubt similar "publication" has occurred in the catalogues of many dealers during the period.

New Directions (New York) published Pound's translation of Paul Morand's *Fancy Goods/Open All Night*, edited by Breon Mitchell with an introduction by Proust in 1984. A collection of Pound's writings from the Paris period, *Pound in Paris*, edited by Richard Sieburth, is in preparation but as yet unscheduled by New Directions.

III   MANUSCRIPTS AND LETTERS

Although the archive at the Beinecke Library remains central to research on Pound, additions have been made to manuscript and Pound-related material at almost all major research libraries in America. The largest recent acquisition (over 12,500 items) is that of the Lilly Library of Indiana University (Bloomington). The range and importance of this collection are summarized by E. R. Hagemann in "Incoming Correspondence to Dorothy and Ezra Pound at The Lilly Library" (*Paideuma*, Spring 1983).

The prospect of a "Complete Letters of Ezra Pound" remains daunting. But a number of new collections, usually consisting of Pound's correspondence with a particular individual, have been published and more are either scheduled for future publication or in preparation. *Dk/Some Letters of Ezra Pound* (ed. Louis Dudek, Montreal, 1974) "covers the years from 1949 to very nearly the end of his life. It began as an offer to help, in his difficult days at St. Elizabeths . . . and it grew into a whirlwind of paper and communication for a few years; then it diminished after 1953." Pound's letters are reproduced as written, and Pound himself "marked a Xerox copy of the letters to indicate a few deletions." *Ezra Pound: Letters to Ibbotson, 1935–1952* (ed. Vittoria I. Mondolfo and Margaret Hurley, with an introduction by Walter Pilkington, Orono, Maine, 1979) contains the record of Pound's contacts with one of his favorite teachers at Hamilton College. The original letters are reproduced together with transcriptions.

Ezra Pound/John Theobald Letters, with a foreword by Theobald, and an introduction and interspersed commentary and notes by the editors, Donald Pearce and Herbert Schneidau (Redding Ridge, Conn., 1984), contains seventy-six heretofore unpublished letters dating from Pound's stay at St. Elizabeths. Pound's comments range "from the nature of education, *paideia* and *virtu*, to the goal of literature." *Letters to Tom Carter* (ed. Andrew Kappel, Redding Ridge, Conn., 1985) offers Pound's exchange with a particular correspondent. Black Swan Books announced, but without specific publication dates, *Ezra Pound/Sen. William Borah Letters*, edited by Daniel Pearlman, and *Ezra Pound and Japan*, edited by Sanehide Kodama.

Pound/Ford Madox Ford Letters: The Story of a Literary Friendship (ed. Brita Lindberg-Seyersted, New York, 1982) is a New Directions volume that provides a spirited account of the two writers' agreements and disagreements. New Directions has projected a number of additional exchanges, two of which have already appeared: *Ezra Pound and Dorothy Shakespear: Their Letters: 1909–1914* (ed. Omar Pound and A. Walton

Litz, New York, 1984) provides an engrossing account of their courtship and is particularly useful in the reading of many of Pound's earlier poems. *Pound/Lewis: The Letters of Ezra Pound and Wyndham Lewis* (ed. Timothy Materer, New York, 1985) is another lively exchange between two highly opinionated writers which also provides comments on a number of passages in *The Cantos*. The Pound-Aldington letters, edited by Ian MacNiven (begun by Harry T. Moore), and the Pound-William Carlos Williams correspondence, edited by Emily M. Wallace, are both already scheduled for publication. Due to appear soon is the Pound/ Zukofsky correspondence, to be edited by Barry Ahearn. Other collections projected somewhat less certainly by New Directions are the Pound/ Mary Moore Cross letters, the Pound/T. S. Eliot letters (presumably being prepared by Faber and Faber), and the Pound family letters (to be edited by Mary de Rachewiltz).

James Laughlin's *Gists and Piths: A Memoir of Ezra Pound* (Iowa City, 1982), adapted from a talk given at the University of Pennsylvania on 25 April 1981, presents a refreshingly lighthearted account of Pound and his chief American publisher. Drawing on a voluminous correspondence (over 1,500 letters from Pound over the years), Laughlin tells of his own education at the "Ezuversity" in Rapallo and Pound's final decision that, though Laughlin would probably never be a poet, he could at least go back to Harvard, get his degree, and, if he was "a good boy," use his family's money to found a press. The passages quoted from the letters, many of them impromptu satirical verses by Pound, are full of fun. Laughlin hopes eventually to put into shape a volume based on various lectures he has delivered on Pound and Williams to be published by the Brown University Press, which he describes (no doubt too modestly) as "a kind of elementary text book and anthology volume."

Mary Barnard's *Assault on Mount Helicon* (Berkeley, Calif., 1984) offers not only a number of hitherto unpublished letters from Pound, as well as several from her other two mentors (Marianne Moore and William Carlos Williams), but a revealing memoir of her own development, leading to her brilliant *Sappho: A New Translation* (1958) and a record of Pound's generosity in offering encouragement to one of *les jeunes*. The Pound letters show precisely what kinds of suggestions he made, most of them leading to either condensation or more natural speech. The entire book provides a dispassionate account of what it was like for a single woman, relying largely on her own resources, to support herself and to publish poetry during the central third of this century.

Drawing on a substantial acquisition by Simon Fraser University of letters written between 1946 and 1959 by Dorothy and Ezra Pound, James Laughlin, and Willis Hawley, Tom Grieve, in "The Ezra Pound/ Hawley Correspondence" (*Line: A Journal of the Contemporary Literature Collection* [Simon Fraser University], Spring 1983), uses several letters to indicate their importance as a source for Pound's use of Chinese characters, especially in the later *Cantos*, as well as his translations of Confucius, though Hawley's qualifications as a self-taught Sinologist are somewhat overstated.

"Eight Letters from Ezra Pound to Parker Tyler in the 1930s," introduced and edited by George Bornstein (*MQR*, Winter 1984), gives an interesting account of Pound's connection with the now pretty much forgotten avant-garde poet and defender of homosexuality, the latter part of whose career shifted to film and art criticism. Pound translated Tyler's poem "Nome" into Italian for *L'Indice* in 1931 during the height of their mutual promotion, and the letters are vintage Ezra with all the usual names dropped and opinions declared.

Some of Pound's editorial exchanges are printed in "*The Hound & Horn" Letters* (ed. Mitzi Berger Hamovitch, with a foreword by Lincoln Kirstein, New York, 1982), where Pound finds himself in the company of Eliot, Cummings, Blackmur, Williams, and others. In "Ezra Pound's Contributions to New Mexican Periodicals and His Relationship with Senator Bronson Cutting" (*Paideuma*, Winter 1980), E. P. Walkiewicz and Hugh Witemeyer treat Pound's contributions to the *Santa Fe New Mexican, Morada*, and *Front* from 1929 to 1935, emphasizing Pound's inheritance of American grassroots populism.

IV BIOGRAPHY

In 1932, Pound sent an outline of his life to date to Louis Untermeyer in the hope of providing an accurate history of his earlier days and his various domiciles in England and Europe. This has now been published in an edition of 226 copies as *An Autobiographical Outline* (New York, 1980). Pound is rather cryptic about his Wabash College contretemps, but he makes an occasional tart and typical comment on his youth and education.

Noel Stock's *The Life of Ezra Pound* (1970) was published in a paperback edition in both London and New York in 1974 that included some "minor changes" and "a handful of additions" worked into the text. Now reissued (San Francisco, 1982) in an "Expanded Edition," the original text remains virtually unaltered, but in a second preface Stock covers the alterations. Following his original research, Stock began gathering "new details on Pound's early life," and, using much of the material gathered by Carl Gatter of Philadelphia, he published *Ezra Pound's Pennsylvania* (*Poetry Australia*, 1973), which was expanded and reissued under the same title in 1976 by the Friends of the University of Toledo Libraries in an edition of 1,000 copies. Both the text and the illustrations communicate an intimate sense of the world of Pound's youth and that of his parents, who became active members in the social work of their local Presbyterian church. Pictures of William Carlos Williams as a member of the University of Pennsylvania's fencing team and of Mary Moore of

Trenton are two of the more than fifty illustrations, the most engaging of which is a picture of Pound costumed as a captive Greek maiden for a production of *Iphigenia among the Taurians*, staged in 1903.

James J. Wilhelm has also made use of the Gatter collection in an expansion of the same theme in *The American Roots of Ezra Pound* (New York, 1985). Wilhelm has tracked down family histories in detail, collected personal portraits, photographs of buildings that figured importantly in Pound's life, town plats of significant areas in which Pound lived, making clear the geography of cities and towns that played more than a casual part in Pound's work. Wilhelm has finally settled the (quite distant) family relationship with Longfellow, and he presents the first complete account of Pound's troubles at Wabash that have been passed on in a variety of accounts, showing that some of the "accepted" versions are conflations of two or more incidents. In essence, Wilhelm is illustrating what Pound himself claimed in *Indiscretions*: that almost any American family of six or seven generations could produce a Jamesian pattern. (Michael Martone has metamorphosed the Wabash incident into an interpretive tale, "The Greek Letter in the Bed," in *Alive and Dead in Indiana*, New York, 1984).

Another generously illustrated, largely biographical, treatment of Pound is *Ezra Pound and His World* by Peter Ackroyd (London, 1980; New York, 1980). The illustrations, which include photographs drawn from all periods of Pound's life, contain a number of familiar ones, but taken together they provide a full record, and Ackroyd's critical comments are balanced and largely uncontroversial. Like more than one Briton, Ackroyd believes that Idaho is part of the "folksy Midwest," and he calls the hospital in which Pound was confined "St. Elizabeth's"— common errors that should not be taken seriously as measures of the work's overall accuracy.

In spite of the doubt cast on the authenticity of certain interviews and conversations in C. David Heymann's *Ezra Pound: The Last Rower, A Political Profile* (New York, 1976), this limited biography contains much valuable and otherwise unavailable material. It is especially useful in connection with the courtroom proceedings that led to Pound's confinement in St. Elizabeths and Pound's letters to Mussolini, Ciano, and Fernando Mezzasoma (Minister of Popular Culture for the Republican Government at Salò), most of them translated from Pound's eccentric Italian into reasonably coherent English by Robert Connolly.

Almost all of the additional biographical information published during the period has shown the same kind of precise and limited focus. Thus, the details of Pound's lifelong concern with H.D. are set forth in characteristic style by H.D. herself in *End to Torment: A Memoir of Ezra Pound* (ed. Norman Holmes Pearson and Michael King, New York, 1979), which includes the poems from *Hilda's Book*, housed at the Houghton. King remarks in his foreword: "H.D.'s version of the past and present is characteristically enigmatic and emotionally transcendent." More straightforward information is provided in two recent biographies of Hilda Doolittle herself: Janice S. Robinson's *H.D.: The Life and Work of An American Poet* (New York, 1982) and Barbara Guest's *Herself Defined: The Poet H.D. and Her World* (New York, 1984). Much material that was restricted during Robinson's research was made available to Guest, so Guest's account is the fuller, but both deserve the attention of anyone interested in this aspect of Pound's personal life and the history of Imagism. Charles Tomlinson, in his 1982 Clark Lectures, *Poetry and Metamorphosis* (Cambridge, England, 1983), makes use of the connection between Pound and H.D. (as "Dryad" in the later cantos) in his third lecture: "Ezra Pound: Between Myth and Life."

A different kind of limited focus is used by Alan Levy in *Ezra Pound: The Voice of Silence* (Sag Harbor, N.Y., 1982). Concentrating on the closing years of Pound's life—Pound, who died at the age of eighty-seven, was eighty-six when Levy first met him—Levy's particular claim to importance lies in the explanation he gives for Pound's remaining in Italy following America's entry into World War II, when many Americans were taking advantage of their final chance to leave. Levy insists that it was the legal position in which Pound and Olga Rudge's daughter Mary found herself, unable to obtain an American passport, and her appeal to her father that led him to remain. Levy also reports Olga Rudge's reactions to her daughter's book, *Discretions* (1971), which is now available in paperback from New Directions under the title *Ezra Pound, Father and Teacher: Discretions*. Levy's monograph contains a bibliography that demonstrates the complex ramifications into which Pound studies lead. Though it is hardly a biography, Richard Stern's novel *Stritch* (New York, 1965) provides a fictionalized version of Pound's later years in Venice. A new biography of Pound by Humphrey Carpenter is reported to be in preparation for Faber and Faber, with the date of publication not yet announced. Irving Marder is also working on a full-length biography.

Alan Durant's *Ezra Pound, Identity in Crisis* (Totowa, N.J., 1981) provides an eccentric reading of Pound's life and works, his involvements in poetry and politics, from the point of view of Jacques Lacan's redefinition of orthodox Freudian psychoanalysis, with particular reference to Lacan's "four fundamental concepts of psychoanalysis." Some of the foci are predictable, though why it should be seen as particularly significant that anyone writing about the Chinese imperial court would consider the power of the palace eunuchs (hence discussions of castration and penile power in connection with Pound's efforts) strikes at least one reader as innocent almost beyond belief. As Durant remarks, his method depends upon "Lacanian psychoanalysis, in which the synchronic linguistic effects of the unconscious, rather than the dispensations of the Logos, may be explored." Like much Freudian work, some of the most significant revelations are the choices made by the critic and the particular stemma of the laying on of hands of which he is the inheritor.

Another work that leans heavily on Lacanian theory is Paul Smith's *Pound Revised* (London, 1983). Recording his debt to Durant, Smith states that he hopes to fill a gap in Pound scholarship by attempting to "relate the poetry to the politics—a task which I think necessarily involves some theoretical notion of what happens between a body and its language." As with Durant, the result appears predictable, but also instructive, as much in Lacanian theory as in understanding Pound's work. The bibliography is useful for anyone wishing to pursue this approach further, leading one to similar discussions.

V CRITICISM

1 Early Reactions

Norman Holmes Pearson of Yale was responsible for much of the earliest and most illuminating critical and textual work on Pound. As "keeper of the text" of *The Cantos* and as H.D.'s literary agent and executor, he remained throughout his life in close touch with these instigators of the "new poetry." Because he himself published almost nothing on the subject, it is gratifying to have a statement from him, and it is typical of the personal and bibliographical complexities of the subject that his words should appear obscurely both in their physical form and place of publication. Pearson's *The Escape from Time: Poetry, Language and Symbol: Stein, Pound, Eliot* (Portree, Isle of Skye, 1982) gives no date for its composition or provenance, though one would suppose that it came early in the record. Pearson notes that the twentieth-century displacement of Aristotelian logic and Newtonian physics demanded a new language from writers and that the three figures he discusses are best understood in light of their quest for an adequate response. Specifically for Pound, he comments on the importance of the Confucian requirement of calling "people and things by their true and proper names."

Pound's first literary focus came from his studies in Provençal at Hamilton College. The comment and criticism stemming from this interest has always been hazardous; for the study of Provençal even in Pound's graduate days was already on the decline for generalists. The first explorers trying to assess Pound's work in this area were not, and never pretended to be, specialists. That age has passed, but the specialists have moved in to carry on the kind of disagreement characteristic of nineteenth- and early twentieth-century Continental scholarly disputes, with attack, counterattack, parry, and thrust.

In 1972, Princeton University Press published Stuart Y. McDougal's *Ezra Pound and the Troubadour Tradition*, an informative study confined to Pound's early lyrics based on Provençal sources and those that led into echoing, resonant passages in *The Cantos*. Some of these themes had been dealt with, though not directly in connection with Pound, in James J. Wilhelm's *The Cruelest Month: Spring, Nature and Love in Classical Lyrics* (1965). Wilhelm discusses Pound's specific uses of the troubadours in his *Dante and Pound: The Epic of Judgement* (Orono, Maine, 1974).

A more ambitious undertaking appeared in 1978: Peter Makin's *Provence and Pound* (Berkeley, Calif.). The precedence of "Provence" is clearly deliberate. The reader is going to learn the truth about Provence and whatever uses or misuses Pound had made of it. One difficulty becomes apparent very early in Makin's hopes for his work. He wishes "to present the Provençal culture to those who know Pound, and Pound to those who know Provençal culture, and both, if possible, to those who know neither." Pound is always a temptation to other overreachers. Makin's study is most useful "to those who know neither." Even the amateur Pound scholar knows by this time most of what Makin has to say in that connection and may even feel a need to challenge his interpretations of some of Pound's uses of his sources; for Pound early made clear that he was letting his imagination run free over the known and the unknown and was aware of the unreliability of the "lives" of the troubadours. Nevertheless, Makin's attempt to give a full picture is challenging in its own right. Anyone wishing to pursue the ongoing controversies will find some entertainment in reviews of Makin by Stuart Y. McDougal (*ConL*, Spring 1980) and by James J. Wilhelm (*CRCL*, Winter 1981).

2 Pisa and St. Elizabeths

The Roots of Treason: Ezra Pound and the Secret of St. Elizabeths by E. Fuller Torrey (New York, 1984) is a full biography of Pound, but because it opens with Pound's imprisonment in Pisa in 1954 and the most controversial part of it is centered in Pound's indictment for treason, it seems only fair to consider it in connection with the emphasis of its subtitle. Before commenting on this, one should note that Torrey has made excellent use of John H. Edwards's unpublished dissertation, "A Critical Biography of Ezra Pound: 1885–1922" (Univ. of California-Berkeley, 1952), the materials for which were gathered at a time when Edwards, Pound's first bibliographer and founder of the *Pound Newsletter*, was still smiled upon by Pound, who told his friends to speak freely to Edwards. Precisely why this approval was later withdrawn is not clear, except that Pound apparently felt the *Newsletter* was not serving the functions he felt it should, and he was unhappy over some of the material in the *Annotated Index*, edited by Edwards and Vasse. In any event, Edwards gathered a great deal of information about Pound's earlier years, and it is gratifying to see it put to use.

The particular strains in Pound's life that Torrey traces are his anti-English, anti-Jewish, and profascist attitudes, leading ultimately to his broadcasts from Rome both before and after the Japanese attack on Pearl Harbor. Torrey wishes to prove that Pound was never insane in any legal sense and that once he had been judged incompetent to stand trial and was moved to St. Elizabeths from Gallinger Hospital, to which he had been transferred from the District of Columbia Jail, he enjoyed the protection of Dr. Winfred Overholser, superintendent of St. Elizabeths, was given special privileges, and was protected from all threats of being brought to trial. Many of the younger psychiatrists (and Torrey is himself now a member of the staff) judged Pound to be, however bigoted and eccentric, sane, but were unwilling to challenge their superior. Torrey also believes, and presents evidence through quoting from letters, that an entire group of Pound's friends were in varying degrees privy to this "conspiracy." Many will be surprised by the evidence presented to show that the Bollingen Award was planned as a prize to be given to Pound in order to embarrass the Department of Justice. If this is so, it simply demonstrates that Pound's friends were somewhat less effective politicians than his enemies. Only the most partisan of Pound's supporters and defenders can ignore these charges, though behind parts of the account one senses the kind of in-house jockeying for power found in any vertically structured organization. Both Pound and Overholser are dead, but for many this will not be an adequate reason for dismissing the issues raised.

Torrey's references supply a complete record of all the commentary surrounding the case, including the vivid picture of what the St. Elizabeths years meant to more than one person as presented in Catherine Seelye's edition of *Charles Olson & Ezra Pound: An Encounter at St. Elizabeths* (New York, 1975). Torrey also gives a slightly speculative account of Pound's relations with Sheri Martinelli, who was replaced by Marcella Spann. (Oddly, from a medical man, Torrey makes no mention of the fact that the reserpine with which Pound was treated for his later depression in Italy has by now been proved a depressant itself and must have added to Pound's withdrawal.) Torrey was preceded in almost all of his points by Stanley I. Kutler in "This Notorious Patient" (*Helix* [Ivanhoe, Australia], Nos. 13/14, 1983). His ultimate contention is that there was no conspiracy between the doctors and the Department of Justice, but there was one between Overholser and Pound himself.

For an amateur to pass judgment on questions such as the legal definition of "treason" and "insanity" would be presumptuous, and to say this is not an evasion. Anyone who has seen Pound's earliest Washington prison letters, with a few painfully written words taking up a full sheet, must feel they were written under severe stress—but insanity? It may be of interest to some readers to record that in the course of a long exchange between Pound and John Espey held during the afternoon of 25 June 1958 in Craig LaDrière's Washington apartment, Pound at one point, after failing to reply to a question, leaned his head back slowly for a time (almost as if he were a victim of petit mal) before he assumed his earlier posture and went on to another topic, remarking without any provocation, "You know, they were right when they said I couldn't stand the strain of a trial, because every now and then I have to lean my head back like that and rest." [Taken verbatim from notes made immediately after the interview: a fact that does not guarantee complete literal accuracy.]

L'Italia di Ezra Pound by Niccolo Zapponi (Rome, 1976) provides a survey of Pound's relations with Italian fascism as well as of his importance to the younger generation of Italian poets and his general influence. Zapponi's full documentation in footnotes suggests many avenues open to exploration, and the bibliography contains a section devoted to the works and comments of Italian critics on Pound running to over eighty titles. Another Italian work should be mentioned here—Piero Sanavío's *Ezra Pound* (Venice, 1977)—as an indication of Pound's placing in his never-quite-adopted country. Sanavio briefly surveys the entire run of Pound's work, with the primary emphasis on his poetry. Sanavio visited Pound in St. Elizabeths and is knowledgeable about many aspects of his life and work; but at times the sheer compression of his discussions appears misleading, as when he deals with *Mauberley* in five pages, citing only Ronsard and Corbière in connection with that much-debated sequence. A third Italian item, Felice Chilanti's *Ezra Pound fra i Sediziosi degli Anni Quaranta* (Milan, 1972), was triggered by a passage in *Canto LXXVII*. Unlike the two works mentioned above, this pamphlet has been translated by David Anderson and appears in *Paideuma* (Fall 1977). Chilanti is at pains to place himself and Pound at some distance from the truly fascistic fascists, and, though one smiles on occasion at his over-insistence, he provides valuable information on Pound during those years as well as giving specific information on a few references in *The Pisan Cantos*.

Because the issues here are Pound's political and economic beliefs and his conduct during World War II rising out of them, many critics have skirted them, not necessarily out of caution or cowardice, but from an awareness of their own limitations in dealing with monetary and social theories. Because of this, one of the most important books to be added to the critical canon is William M. Chace's *The Political Identities of Ezra Pound & T. S. Eliot* (Stanford, Calif., 1973). Chace presents a lucid summary of Pound's shifting beliefs, tracing the influence of his "old American" origins and the mythos created in his imagination by his birth in the Western Mountain Empire, together with the feeling of many of his generation of being threatened by the new wave of European (Jewish) immigrants. Chace is excellent throughout: on the theories of C. H. Douglas, the appeal of "order," the reasons for Pound's attraction to Mussolini, and Pound's distinction between "good" and "bad" banking. More than this, Chace is sensitively responsive to the movement of

Pound's language and shows how certain cantos are centos, montages of favorite echoing themes. Pound's attraction to "the real" is set off against the distinctly religious aura of his visionary worldly paradise. Though Chace includes no bibliography, his scrupulous footnoting covers the entire field of controversy up to the time of publication and guides both beginner and concerned scholar to all the pertinent sources. Many of the same issues are discussed by Peter Nicholls in *Ezra Pound: Politics, Economics, and Writing* (New York, 1984). Nicholls, less sympathetic and detailed than Chace, finds a steady progress toward fascism in *The Cantos*.

3 Later Criticism

The most salutary piece of writing on both the historical and critical aspects of the period is Marjorie Perloff's "Pound/Stevens: Whose Era?" (*NLH*, Spring 1982). Taking her title from Kenner's self-indulgent *The Pound Era* (1971), Perloff points out that whereas little love may have been lost between Pound and Stevens themselves, at least the critics who were their contemporaries felt no difficulty in discussing them both dispassionately, whereas many of the current generation have placed themselves exclusively in one camp or the other. Fortunately, though this is true of several leading figures, the division is not absolute. Perloff herself treats the division with an even hand and is equally at home with both Pound and Stevens; and her example is followed by many in the classroom if not in print.

Though specialization has become the hallmark of Pound scholars, there are still critics courageous enough to undertake full surveys and offer their concluding judgments. That a good bit of factual information is repetitious is inevitable, but it is usually interpreted in the light of the individual critic's theoretical center. These works tend to be of either monographic length or considerable bulk. In what follows, chronology is the control.

Max Nänny's *Ezra Pound: Poetics for an Electric Age* (Bern, 1973, though actually completed in 1969) is based on the familiar distinction to be drawn between linear and nonlinear patterns in literature. Nänny relies heavily on Marshall McLuhan's writing and discusses Pound's poetry as part of an "auditory or electric field" and, possibly more profitably, as an act of "co-creation" demanding the reader's involvement. (The study is altogether conventionally printed, with page following page in standard order.)

George Bornstein's *The Postromantic Consciousness of Ezra Pound* (Victoria, Canada, 1977) deals directly with selected passages taken from Pound's poetry and prose in order to demonstrate the revolutionary quality of his work. Bornstein feels that in spite of Pound's rebellion against Romanticism (itself a somewhat difficult term to define with any confidence) he never completely solved the problems of form involved in his longer sequences leading up to *The Cantos*.

William Harmon, in *Time in Ezra Pound's Work* (Chapel Hill, N.C., 1977), takes a different tack from Pearlman's in *The Barb of Time* (1969) and steers a consistent course through the never-to-be-completely-charted waters of Pound's voyage that finally broke up into drafts and fragments. Harmon finds "that the primary impulse of *The Cantos* is mystical. Gods exist for Pound because he has undergone certain experiences and because certain mythic correlatives enable him to harmonize his experiences with those of others. He is practical, and the basis of his mysticism is empirical."

The Poetic Achievement of Ezra Pound by Michael Alexander (Berkeley, Calif., 1979) is a thorough treatment of most of Pound's poetry, strategically arranged to lead into a reading of *The Cantos*. Unlike a number of other critics, Alexander believes that Pound's sensibility did not greatly change throughout his career and that although he refined his techniques and broadened his range as he continued to publish, it is still possible to offer a coherent interpretation of the entire body of verse and prose. Alexander is especially helpful for readers who have been satisfied to stop their reading with *Mauberley* and a brief sampling of *The Cantos*, and he presents a cogent case for their venturing further.

In *Critic as Scientist: The Modernist Poetics of Ezra Pound* (London, 1981), Ian F. A. Bell writes with an authoritarian tone that he may have picked up from his subject of largely late nineteenth-century and early twentieth-century scientists and their unified-field theories and their efforts to solve the equation that defeated Einstein even before he had tried to formulate it. Agassiz is called up as a latter-day Tiresias, and one is off on the old familiar gallop. Bell leans heavily on Stephen Fender's "Ezra Pound and the Words off the Page: Historical Allusions in Some American Long Poems" (*YES*, 1978) and Richard Sieburth's "*Instigations*" (see below).

As editor of *Ezra Pound: Tactics for Reading* (London and Totowa, N.J., 1982), Bell has drawn together a collection that further illustrates this yearning for a total view. Peter Brooker, in "The Lesson of Ezra Pound: An Essay in Poetry, Literary Ideology and Politics," finds his unity in "open-field poetry." David Murray, in "Pound-signs: Money and Representation in Ezra Pound," deals with misreadings of Marx and with money theory, classifying Pound's ideas as "a diversion of Populism." Martin A. Kayman, in "A Model for Pound's Use of 'Science,'" writes of science as the important "signifier" and connects it with the supernatural. H. N. Schneidau, in "Pound's Poetics of Loss," sees *The Cantos* in one sense as "a vast elaboration on Pound's advice about translation." Eric Mottram, in "Pound, Merleau-Ponty and the Phenomenology of Poetry," is concerned with the poet's "participating in the totality." The editor, in "'Speaking in Figures': The Mechanical Thomas Jefferson of Canto 31," is off with Agassiz again and his "discovery of an entire structure on the basis of a few remains." Joseph N. Riddel's "'Neo-Nietzschean Clatter'—Speculation and/on Pound's Poetic Image," a shortened version of an essay that originally appeared in *Boundary 2* (Spring 1981), taken together with Riddel's "Pound and the Decentered Image" (*GaR*, Fall 1965) and his "Decentering the Image: The 'Project' of 'American Poetics'" (*Boundary 2*, Fall 1979), suggests a number of strategies for "erasing rhetoricity." And Richard Godden, in "Icons, Etymologies, Origins and Monkey Puzzles in the Languages of Upward and Fenollosa," stresses "Upward's arguments as a diagrammatic sequence inclining to a universal figure." The most remarkable achievement of all these reachings after a critical totalitarianism is their uniform success, with the exception of Schneidau, in totally obliterating Pound's personal voice, which some might feel to be of primary importance.

Georg M. Gugelberger's *Ezra Pound's Medievalism* (Frankfurt am Main, 1983) suffers from a delay in appearance (it has a 1978 copyright date) that means that it has been preceded by a number of other works which Gugelberger could make no use of, particularly those of McDougal, Wilhelm, and Makin, covering much of the same ground. Though definition may be the last refuge of the scholar, something is required in using so general a term as "medievalism," and Gugelberger, like everyone before him, never quite succeeds in a persuasive overview. The most valuable part of his study is his emphasis on Chaucer as important to Pound, an influence largely neglected.

Two general, deliberately introductory, studies are of special value to the reader who comes to Pound without special preparation. Jeannette Lander's *Ezra Pound* (MLM, New York, 1971) is translated and revised from its original German appearance. Arranged chronologically, it is somewhat outdated and misleading, especially in the earlier biographical sections. James F. Knapp's *Ezra Pound* (TUSAS, Boston, 1979) presents an overview of Pound's life and work in greater detail and more accurately as to the biographical information than Lander's. Within the stringent limits of the series, it offers an excellent introduction and goes well beyond elementary material and interpretation, setting out an even-handed presentation of conflicting views on Pound's life and works, together with a broadly representative select bibliography.

Though Burton Raffel's *Ezra Pound: The Prime Minister of Poetry* (Hamden, Conn., 1984) is more ambitious than an introductory study, in many ways it resembles one. Raffel, though he takes occasional dips in the sea of scholarship, has had the courage to steer his own course for the greater part and record his personal reactions. The result is a mixture of the familiar with the unfamiliar, involving what appears to be an inevitable degree of repetition in such works; for, hardly surprisingly, on many issues he has been preceded by others. Nevertheless, the study provides an individual overview of the literary (though not the musical) achievement. A companion volume gathered by Raffel, *Possum and Ole Ez* (Hamden, Conn., 1985), is made up of short passages chronologically arranged that record individual reactions to the works and personalities of Eliot and Pound, set down by other writers (as distinct from critics). As for Ole Ez, almost all the entries come from published sources and offer the specialist few surprises. But for the beginner and the general reader they provide a lively running commentary on the man and his career.

In spite of the subtitle, *The Forméd Trace: The Later Poetry of Ezra Pound* (New York, 1980), its author, Massimo Bacigalupo, goes back to the London days, exploring their implications for the future, before he writes in some detail of *The Pisan Cantos* and the following sections. Centering his comments in Pound's "peculiar brand of Neoplatonism," he sets out an interesting reading. As one who knew Pound personally, Bacigalupo's comments, especially in connection with specific passages discussed, are invaluable. For what must be reasons of his own, he drops, at almost regular intervals, comments on Wagner's claim, prior to Pound's, to the use of *leitmotiv*, enabling him to mention in his own key a composer Pound—like Henry Adams—thought to be overinflated, both in reputation and in his own work. (Though of minor importance, it should be pointed out that Bacigalupo corrects a mistranslation of Italian by Espey that had ridden through printing after printing unnoticed.)

In *The Poetics of Indeterminacy* (Princeton, N.J., 1981), Marjorie Perloff discusses Pound's work as part of what "we loosely call 'Modernism' in Anglo-American poetry," pointing out that this poetry is made up of two different, though often intersecting, strands: the Symbolist inheritance and the anti-Symbolist mode of "indeterminacy." Using this approach, she presents a sensitive reading of Pound's development, with particular emphasis on interpreting the Malatestan cantos and by tracing what Kenner has called "the rhythms of recurrence." Perloff is, in addition to several other articles, the author of a chapter, "The Contemporary of Our Grandchildren," in *Ezra Pound Among the Poets* (ed. George Bornstein, Chicago, 1985). In it, she demonstrates the Poundian inheritance even among poets who felt negatively about the irritating instigator and suggests that *The Cantos* have become, either directly or indirectly, a shaping force in the structure of all modernist and postmodernist writing. Through examining Pound's theories of translation, she adds meaning to the concept of a "poem that contains history," and provides an effective summary of Pound as central not only to his own age but to the age—even ages—following. This is the concluding chapter of *Ezra Pound Among the Poets*. The other contributors are Hugh Kenner ("Pound and Homer"), Lillian Feder ("Pound and Ovid"), Ronald Bush ("Pound and Li Po: What Becomes a Man"), Stuart Y. McDougal ("Dreaming a Renaissance: Pound's Dantean Inheritance"), Hugh

Witemeyer ("Clothing the American Adam: Ezra Pound's Tailoring of Walt Whitman"), George Bornstein ("Pound's Parleyings with Robert Browning"), A. Walton Litz ("Pound and Yeats: The Road to Stone Cottage"), Thomas Parkinson ("Pound and Williams"), and Robert Langbaum ("Pound and Eliot").

Marianne Korn's *Ezra Pound: Purpose/Form/Meaning* (London, 1983) is a severely compact survey of Pound's poetry that discusses it in terms of his own catch-words ("melopoeia," "phanopoeia," and "logopeia," by now a somewhat tiresome trinity) and points out "a strategy for starting to read the *Cantos*." Even though she offers few precise examples, Korn writes clearly and without equivocation, providing the reader at what one might call (and with no intention of condescension) an intermediate stage in dealing with Pound, an excellent guide.

Scott Eastham's *Paradise & Ezra Pound: The Poet as Shaman* (Lanham, Md., 1983) is a study of Pound's "religion" shaped by the theories of Eliade and Heidegger. As such, it is an interesting exercise in combining a degree of learning with a degree of innocence. Pound would have been delighted to be saluted as a "psychopomp," but his Philadelphia Presbyterian boyhood manners might have been put under some strain by a number of readings. In a maundering discussion of "In a Station of the Metro," Eastham quotes as if it were private information Kenner's account of the two lines' genesis clearly drawn from one of Pound's *Fortnightly* essays, and later reprinted in *Gaudier-Brzeska*. Similar slips occur, but the overall attempt to fit Pound into a schematic structure will interest many, and all must stand in awe of a critic who, according to the biographical note, was "born in Chicago, 1949, with a Ph.D. in Religious Studies from the University of California."

The two chapters devoted to Pound in *The Modern Poetic Sequence: The Genius of Modern Poetry* by M. L. Rosenthal and Sally M. Gall (New York, 1983) present a curious contrast. The first of them, on the early sequences, takes as model in miniature Pound's repeatedly praised "The Return," discussing it as a prefiguring in all senses of Pound's more lengthily sustained later work, and speculates on Pound's possibly using Mallarmé's "Un Coup de Dès" as a model. It is difficult to believe that Rosenthal and Gall have forgotten Pound's own claims concerning the poem's genesis and his boast of how in a matter of fifteen minutes or so after reading Henri de Régnier's prefatory poem to *Les Médailles d'Argile* he was able to condense and reproduce the French rhythms. (Pound certainly turned a few more pages, probably spending more time on the freer patterns than the regular, though he picks up phrases from both.) This lapse should not keep the reader from going on to the next chapter; for the section titled "The Pisan Cantos in Retrospect" is responsive to that series' unity and ultimate success as Pound reassembled his materials through sheer force of memory in his confined surroundings.

Richard Sieburth's *"Instigations": Ezra Pound and Rémy de Gourmont* (Cambridge, Mass., 1978) is an exemplary study of the influence of one of the most neglected critics in his own country on British and American letters. Generously acknowledging Espey's references to Gourmont in connection with *Mauberley* and Glenn Burne's later studies, Sieburth traces Gourmont's importance for James Gibbons Huneker (himself largely neglected now), Eliot, and Pound. He demonstrates the importance of Gourmont for Eliot's theories of "impersonality" and Pound's "dissociation of ideas." He notes lightly that "Pound's 1922 version of Gourmont's *Physique de l'amour, The Natural Philosophy of Love,* went into its second mass paperback printing with an appropriately prurient cover to catch the commuter's tired eye."

A provocative survey of what an earlier generation of scholars might be satisfied to call an influence on Pound is handled in Kathryne V. Lindberg's dissertation, "Reading, Writing, and Rhetoric: Nietzschean Traces in the Later Criticism of Ezra Pound" (Univ. of California-Los Angeles, 1984). Lindberg has made excellent use of the Beinecke Library archive, citing a number of unpublished passages that show unexplored areas in the corpus of Pound's criticism. Lindberg's dissertation was published early in 1987 by Oxford University Press as *Reading Pound Reading: Modernism After Nietzsche.* In part derived from this text, but expanding aspects of the original, are Lindberg's articles: "Tradition and Heresy: Pound's Dissociation from Eliot" (*Paideuma,* Spring 1985) and "Writing 'Frankly': "Pound's Rhetoric Against Science" (*Boundary 2,* Spring–Fall 1984).

Pound has been a fructive influence in both the theory and practice of translation during the twentieth century. A variety of points of view concerning his achievements can be found in *The Craft and Context of Translation: A Symposium* (ed. William Arrowsmith and Roger Shattuck, Austin, Tex., 1961). Burton Raffel, in *The Forked Tongue: A Study of the Translation Process* (The Hague, 1971), pays tribute to Pound's influence. Ronnie Apter's *Digging for the Treasure: Translation After Pound* (New York, 1984) provides a history of Pound's own development as translator and theoretician together with a discussion of his influence on later generations of poets. Apter offers a useful guide to translation theory and is at her best in discussing Pound's growth and influence in connection with classical and French texts. She makes no mention of William Shepard's influence on Pound's Provençal and relies solely on Wai Lim Yip for Chinese. These are not serious flaws, though they tend to give Pound an exclusive, rather than a central, position.

4 To Imagism and Beyond

In *Ezra Pounds frühe Poetik und Kulturkritik zwischen Aufklärung und Avantgarde* (Stuttgart, 1979), Miriam Hansen explores the background of Pound's earliest practice and theory, tracing the shift from Imagism to Vorticism as a genuine refocusing of Pound's technique. Her most telling passages deal with Pound's admiration of Alvin Langdon Coburn's experimental photography when Coburn moved from his static prints, which Pound had already praised in connection with Henry James's suggestions to Coburn for the frontispieces of the New York Edition, to his "vortographs," and the parallel forces of active interpretation in the motion pictures of Charlie Chaplin.

Timothy Materer's *Vortex: Pound, Eliot, and Lewis* (Ithaca, N.Y., 1979) ably presents "the artistic crosscurrents in the careers of Ezra Pound, T. S. Eliot, and Wyndham Lewis" as they converged in the early days of Vorticism, with the founding of *Blast* by Lewis and the use made of Gaudier's sculpture. The exclusion of Joyce because of Lewis's reaction to his work is discussed, as well as the importance to many writers and artists of the movement. Materer supports his argument with a skillful use of illustrations drawn from the creations of both Lewis and Gaudier. Anyone wishing to pursue the history of Vorticism and its entanglements with Futurism in the work of Pound and others should consult Richard Cork's *Vorticism and Abstract Art in the First Machine Age* (Berkeley, Calif., 1976). Another study centered in Vorticism, Reed Way Dasenbrook's *The Literary Vorticism of Ezra Pound and Wyndham Lewis* (Baltimore, Md., 1985), examines Lewis's later novels and *The Cantos* as examples of "literary Vorticism" that demonstrate the movement's intended influence across all the arts.

5 China and Japan

Two dissertations should have been mentioned long before this. The first is Achilles Fang's unpublished "Materials for the Study of Pound's Cantos" (Harvard Univ., 1958), which has been mined by several scholars, especially for its Oriental references. In addition, Fang is the author of many articles and notes on Pound, most of which have appeared in *Paideuma* and can be found in the standard bibliographies. The second is Angela Jung (Palandri)'s 1955 University of Washington dissertation, *Ezra Pound and China* (Ann Arbor, Mich., 1979), which provides an early summary of Pound's use of Chinese sources and his vision of what Confucian China stood for in her patterns of discipline and values. Jung presents an amusing account of her interview with Pound, a politely Oriental exchange on her part with a somewhat cantankerous admirer of what used to be called "things Chinese" and caustic critic of the American university's failure to provide an adequate education for the modern world drawn from the enduring past.

Girolamo Mancuso's *Pound e la Cina* (Milan, 1974) presents a trenchant summary of Pound's use of Chinese themes from his first contact, through Giles, and his use of the Fenollosa papers. Mancuso, himself an accomplished Sinologist and the translator into Italian of the poetry of Mao Tse-tung (with an introduction by Alberto Moravia), points out the distinctively Confucian stress of Pound's assimilation of Chinese history, after the publication of *Cathay*, and its dynastic emphasis. Mancuso is particularly helpful in placing Confucius in the general history of China, pointing out that the great sage was both a reactionary and a utopian, living in a period of disorder, and relates this, as well as the "imagist" aspect of the written character, to Pound's attraction to Chinese and his influence on succeeding generations of poets.

Another discussion of the importance of China to Pound is Monika Motsch's *Ezra Pound und China* (Heidelberg, 1976), which systematically covers the ground from Pound's introduction (through Victor Plarr) to Japan and China by way of Giles and the Fenollosa papers, through the Confucian ethos, especially in the Chinese cantos, though the coverage here is not as detailed as Nolde's work, to be mentioned later in connection with *The Cantos* themselves. Motsch is especially skillful in avoiding the trap of what the "best" texts of various sources are as she concentrates on Pound's actual use of the material.

Nobuko Tsukui's *Ezra Pound and Japanese Noh Plays* (Washington, D.C., 1983) provides a few helpful observations on Pound's use of the Fenollosa papers, centering in the quality of the texts used and providing a glossary of Japanese words and phrases connected with the "translations."

David Gordon has in progress two works: an intensive study of two cantos, to be taken up later, and a more general one centered in the Confucian ethic as continuing control for a reading of *The Cantos* throughout and at least a partial explanation of Pound's discouragement near the end of his life over his total achievement.

In *The Great Circle: American Writers and the Orient* (Detroit, 1983), Beongcheon Yu devotes a chapter to Pound, placing him and his work in the larger pattern of Orientalism as a part of the American connections with the East from Transcendentalism (Emerson and Thoreau) on through Whitman, Fenollosa, and Hearn, and, for the twentieth century, Babbitt, O'Neill, Eliot, and Pound, closing with the Beats. With a refreshing lack of pretension, Yu summarizes Pound's introduction to the Orient and the importance to him of the Fenollosa papers, showing how Pound was ultimately to find a center in Confucius. Yu draws perceptively from the earlier studies of Miner, Dembo, Kenner, and others. The one surprising omission is the lack of any reference to the seminal effect on Pound of Giles's *Short History of Chinese Literature*, which presented him with his first raw material in the form of Victorian verse translations of Chinese poems which he promptly proceeded to turn into modern verse.

6 Individual Works

a. Homage to Sextus Propertius. J. P. Sullivan's *Ezra Pound and Sextus Propertius* (1964) has gone largely unchallenged as the standard comment on Pound's first extensive denunciation of Empire. Ron Thomas, in *The*

Latin Masks of Ezra Pound (Ann Arbor, Mich., 1983), a revision of his 1977 doctoral thesis, takes issue with some of Sullivan's assumptions and reads more autobiographical implications in the poem than have been claimed by most other critics, seeing it as self-criticism and a prelude in some senses to *The Cantos*. Thomas is at pains to distinguish between Pound's text and the "true" intentions of Propertius and thus, like most of us, flaunts his own special knowledge to extend his commentary. His summary of Pound's use of the major Latin poets is easily indicated by the titles of his chapters: "Virgil as Antimask," "Catullus as Lyric Mask," "Propertius as Dramatic Mask," "Ovid as Epic Mask," and "Horace as Demimask." This is all just a little too tidy to be entirely acceptable, but Thomas is persuasive. One wishes that in his revision he had included the poets of the Silver Age that distinguish Pound's Latin studies from the standard academic pattern of both his and our day, with discussions of, say, figures like Nemesianus or the polyglot Church fathers; but Thomas nevertheless provides a helpful guide.

b. *Hugh Selwyn Mauberley*. This suite, Pound's "poor man's *Propertius*," continues to provoke controversy and to yield a variety of readings. Virtually all of them can be found in Jo Brantley Berryman's *Circe's Craft: Ezra Pound's "Hugh Selwyn Mauberley"* (Ann Arbor, Mich., 1983), a revision of her 1973 doctoral thesis. Berryman reads the first section as being spoken in Mauberley's own voice as the testimony of an untrustworthy critic. She is most effective in demonstrating the importance of Raymonde Collignon's role both as the *diseuse* who gave Pound and Rummel's adaptations from Provençal their premiere performances in London and as Pound's acknowledged model for the singer in *Mauberley's* "Medallion." The study is especially helpful in its illustrations, which include a reproduction of Pound's final typescript, presented by Omar Shakespear Pound to the Hamilton College Library collection. In the publisher's listing, an anonymous Pound expert "comments that Berryman's study provides an encyclopedic compendium of facts and allusions concerning *Mauberley* and reaches well beyond John Espey's earlier [1955] work on the topic" (to which she gives over-generous acknowledgement). This statement should delight those in disagreement with Espey—even Espey himself?—and dismay those who felt that Espey had already gone much too far to begin with.

A further warning against being taken in by "Espey's fundamental distinction" (of the suite's two sections) is contained in *Ezra Pound: The London Years: 1908–1920* (ed. Philip Grover, New York, 1978), with Ian F. A. Bell's "Mauberley's Barrier of Style." The volume is an outgrowth of the April 1977 Pound Conference held at Sheffield. Most of the other articles have been absorbed by their authors or other critics in later works.

A new reading of the line "Even the Christian beauty defects—after Samothrace" is offered by Laurence W. Mazzeno in "A Note on 'Hugh Selwyn Mauberley'" (*Paideuma*, Spring 1975). He argues that it refers to Pauline interpretations of the new religion rather than the famous statue of Nike.

An attractive bilingual edition of *Mauberley*, edited by Massimo Bacigalupo, using a new translation into Italian by Giovanni Giudici (Milan, 1982), draws on the published scholarship and the editor's own readings, providing detailed notes on the rhythmic and sound patterns of the original as well as the poem's various interpretations.

With all this controversy still stirring, it is fit that Hugh Selwyn Mauberley "himself"—whoever that may be—is the central character in Timothy Findley's novel *Famous Last Words* (New York, 1982), its (in)action taking place during the fall of Nazi Germany.

A sensitive exploration of Pound's experimental subjects and techniques leading up to *The Cantos*, with particular emphasis on *Near Perigord*, *Propertius*, and *Mauberley*, Terri Brint Joseph's *Ezra Pound's Epic Variations: "The Cantos" and Major Long Poems* is in press without a fixed publication date for The National Poetry Foundation (Orono). Joseph is especially valuable in her use of a variety of critical approaches controlled by the works under discussion rather than a single doctrinaire theory.

c. Women of Trachis. Pound's translation of Sophocles's drama has attracted relatively little comment in recent years. Irvin Ehrenpreis, in a review-article, "Love, Hate and Ezra Pound" (*NYRB*, 27 May 1976), speculates on the possibility of Pound's making this particular choice for translation because his involvement with women at the time was not dissimilar to Hercules's in the play, with Hercules asking his wife's approval of his taking a mistress and even accepting her as a member of the household.

d. The Cantos. The Genesis of Ezra Pound's Cantos by Ronald Bush (Princeton, N.J., 1976) remains one of the most useful introductions to Pound's major work. In an entertaining opening chapter titled "Red Herrings" Bush takes care of all the "simple solutions" offered for that at once complex and simple and single- and multi-minded work and posits a functional "set of structural terms" arising from Pound's growth and practice in the following chapter. Bush deals with the *Ur-Cantos* in terms of a critic viewing the entire work as a whole rather than those of a poet who discovers that he is using up his material at far too fast a rate to sustain all his themes and his as yet somewhat vague grand design. In this, Bush sides with the majority of scholars. He then deals with the narrative voices that Pound had developed and discusses the stages of revision that *The Cantos* as well as Pound's general thinking underwent. Bush bravely runs the risk of taking positions that may be threatened by later discoveries in the mass of unpublished material, and he fits *The Cantos* possibly a little too neatly into the standard school-book definition of the epic on which most of us were suckled; but his exposition in all its variety remains solidly based.

Barbara Eastman's *Ezra Pound's Cantos: The Story of the Text* (Orono,

Maine, 1985), with an introduction by Kenner, contains "all the textual variants in all the Faber and the New Directions editions" and is a necessity for any scholar hoping for entire accuracy. The difficulties of establishing anything like a *Compleat Cantos* is made clear and becomes increasingly complex (and unlikely?) in view of all the unpublished and varying fragments that survive in a variety of forms but have never been incorporated in a fully printed version.

Dante and Pound: The Epic of Judgement by James J. Wilhelm (Orono, Maine, 1974) draws on Pound's expressed and unexpressed parallels between the *Commedia* and *The Cantos*, and has become by now a standard opening work for studies in the nature not only of the traditional and modern epic but also of the importance of Dante's influence on the shaping of Pound's attitudes as a voice of protest and reform for his own age. The same critic's *Il Miglior Fabbro* (Orono, Maine, 1982) is, as its subtitle indicates, a discussion of "The Cult of the Difficult in Daniel, Dante, and Pound," concentrating in each chapter on a specific text. It is a work of particular value to those of us whose Provençal, medieval Latin, Chinese, and Greek are not letter-perfect, for Wilhelm provides full translations of everything that he calls into question for examination.

Kay Davis's *The Structure of "The Cantos"* (Orono, Maine, 1984) is modestly presented as a book "to provide readers with an approach to *The Cantos* through Ezra Pound's own terminology." Actually, Davis does not only this but much more, taking up such terms as *fugue, fresco,* and *ideogram* and not only defining them in both standard and Poundian terms but also demonstrating through specific passages just how they function in the poem and how the larger pattern of the poem is affected by them. Without ever raising her voice, Davis takes on a number of explicators, such as Makin, and suggests that they may not have uttered the final word. Though intended primarily for the classroom as an introduction, and already tested as such, this is a refreshingly sane and unpretentious reading of *The Cantos* that readers at all levels can learn from.

Another treatment, both general and particular, is Christine Froula's *To Write Paradise: Style and Error in Pound's Cantos* (New Haven, Conn., 1984). Here Froula both establishes a definitive text of *Canto IV*, using the classic attack of textual scholars and also suggests, in the second half of her meaty study, strategies for the editing of a complete text of the poem. Her discussion is particularly valuable in its analysis of the kinds of "error" to be found throughout Pound's work and solutions for handling them. Her approach combines traditional methods of analysis and editing with postmodernist theory, and all students of Pound will find throughout both Froula's text and its full documentation provocative comments and judgments. The study is in many ways a turning-point for both textual and structural analysis of *The Cantos* as

Froula sets forth the problems involved and, without being dogmatic, suggests tactics for dealing with them in an evenhanded way.

Full treatments of *The Cantos* have become relatively rare, but some scholars are still willing to go the course. Leon Surette's *A Light from Eleusis: A Study of Ezra Pound's Cantos* (New York, 1979) is one of the most illuminating. He follows the general pattern derived from Dante, dealing patiently with Pound's American aberrations on his climb to Paradise. He remarks that if we take Pound's own description of *Thrones* at face value, Pound's "paradiso would be some sort of account of people 'who have been responsible for good government,' and of people 'who have some part of the divine vision.'" Surette is excellent on the success of *The Pisan Cantos*, but he runs into problems in the later units, for which his ear is not attuned: "Here the subjective lyric voice once again comes into its own because its subject is appropriate to its rhetoric, as the subject of the principles of good government is not." Even so, he gives an acceptable reading within the terms of a closed form, and one should not be put off by the fact that "St. Elizabeths Hospital" and "Mauberley" are misspelled throughout. There are, after all, greater sins than these in the crystal design of Eleusinian initiation.

Another full survey is Michael André Bernstein's *The Tale of the Tribe: Ezra Pound and the Modern Verse Epic* (Princeton, N.J., 1980). Bernstein points out a number of seeming contradictions in connection with *The Cantos* and goes on to say that most of them stem "directly from a stance that combined a very modern technique with a determinedly conservative aesthetics." He has earlier insisted that "one can isolate two fundamental structures upon which Pound relied throughout *The Cantos*. The first of these might be called the 'Inductive or Ideogrammic Method' and the second 'Confucian Historiography.' Traditionally, critics have followed Pound's own arguments and seen these two structures as essentially interdependent. However, a careful analysis reveals that each one receives its justification from a quite different conception of history and narration; each contains its own distinct advantages and limitations, constituting certain domains for textual inclusion while, at the same time, precluding others. Moreover, the two structures are by no means always mutually reinforcing. . . ." From time to time one forgets the common origin of German and English, but on the basis of this analysis Bernstein gives *The Cantos* a reading based on generous acknowledgement of previous scholars' work and a somewhat equivocal judgment of the entire poem as a "modern epic": "To see *The Cantos* entirely as a heroic achievement would distort the work as much as any claim for its unity. . . . As an epic, that is, *The Cantos* rightly express their ultimate inability to fashion a new synthesis for the tribe as a bitter defeat. However, if one considers *The Cantos* as one man's *attempt* to write a modern verse epic, it is perfectly legitimate to applaud Pound's fidelity to the imperatives of his initial project, and to acknowledge that only the poem's 'incoherence' saved the integrity of its historical foundation."

Wendy Stallard Flory, in *Ezra Pound and "The Cantos": A Record of Struggle* (New Haven, Conn., 1980), successfully skirts the somewhat outmoded nineteenth-century popular philosophical oppositions echoed in the two previous works by the simple strategy of approaching the work as a record, direct and indirect, of Pound's personal experience, not only as a writer altering his views as he matures but as something approaching autobiography, especially in connection with the women in his life: "Where D. H. Lawrence, for example, emphasizes the physical particularity of sexual experience, Pound mythologizes, aetherializes, and depersonalizes it." Setting aside Lawrence's "particularity"—about as vague as one could possibly find—the reader of Flory's study responds to the roles played either directly or behind masks by Dorothy Pound, Olga Rudge, Sheri Martinelli, and Marcella Spann. Flory feels that, as against this personal theme, Pound plays off the iniquities of usury, the opposite of human love, and that in the end he fuses all in the troubadour theme of "the unattainable lady." In addition to this overall interpretation Flory repeats a good bit of familiar scholarly detail but almost always adds a particularity of her own.

Another sustained review is Philip Furia's *Pound's Cantos Declassified* (University Park, Pa., 1984). Covering the major range of *The Cantos* in a text of little more than monographic length, Furia takes the poem on Pound's own terms—or at least one of Pound's terms—when he called his poem a "palimpsest." By taking this approach, Furia avoids all the familiar efforts to "classify" *The Cantos*. (Was Pound attempting an epic? If he was, what were the models: dear old blind Homer, Dante, Camoëns? Or is there really a new genre, "the long twentieth-century poem"? If this *is* a poem including history, what is history?) Furia sidesteps these—and other—slanted questions by presenting *The Cantos* as layers upon layers of the documents, codes, and precepts that Pound believed had either been blacked out by special interests or were in danger of being blacked out—records that in his opinion give directions for right living, right government, right use of money. (That all these documents are quite accessible in any major research library in the Western world is not pertinent.) Thus Furia does not have to pause and decide if Thomas Hart Benton is a completely reliable witness; he need only indicate Pound's use of Benton's memoirs. And Furia takes what he thinks of as "puns" in a large sense—such as the keeping of water flowing—and relates them to all the early American canals, the Venetian waterways, the draining of marshes, and connects them to the larger theme of keeping lines of communication open within a just society.

Eugene Paul Nassar's *"The Cantos" of Ezra Pound: The Lyric Mode* (Baltimore, Md., 1975) is not quite as limited a study as its subtitle implies. Nassar is more interested in the poem's tonalities than the strictly didactic and historical passages, and he traces them in all their variations through-out the entire sequence, providing at the same time a relatively full and dispassionate reading.

'76: One World and "The Cantos" of Ezra Pound by Forrest Read (Chapel Hill, N.C., 1981) is an example of a valuable reading that is warped by the critic's discovery of the one necessary clue to the entire work. Read fixes upon the half-playful "Revolutionary Calendar" first published in the Little Review, which declared the new age as opening on 30 October 1921 (Pound's thirty-sixth birthday) and the Great Seal of the United States of America as symbolic of the form of the long poem, and proceeds to elucidate from this base. Many of Read's expositions are both original and helpful, but the insistence with which he hammers away at these central symbols, "sealing" one canto after another, shows the individual obsession, parallel with, but never as clearly defined as Pound's "Usura."

A similar, but quite different, reading, based on a larger theme—the Confucian Ethos—is offered by David Gordon in a work originally titled Confucius and "The Cantos." It is announced as "in process" at Orono, with what revisions one cannot say. Gordon, however, finds the neces-sary clue in Pound's concentration on Confucius, reading both forward and backward from the Chinese cantos, with Pound's growing realization of his personal failure to live up to the Confucian ideal as explanation of the poem's irresolution. Here again, the individual readings are of great value, no matter what one thinks of the central, obsessive thesis.

In The Form of the Unfinished: English Poetics from Spenser to Pound (Prince-ton, N.J., 1985), Balachandra Rajan has at least offered us a classification under which to enter The Cantos. The varieties of "the unfinished poem," however, appear to be as varied as their authors. Nevertheless, Rajan's chapter titled "Ezra Pound and the Logocentric Survival" is a provocative reading, centered in the difficulties of writing a poem "including history" while history itself is being made and is in a very personal way shaping both the poem and the poet.

Peter Makin's Pound's Cantos (Winchester, Mass., 1985) devotes as much space to introductory material familiar to most serious readers of Pound as he does to the long poem itself. He emphasizes the importance of the Eleusinian mysteries as Pound's base and proposes a "secret cult of sexual delay" as an essential clue. Though written ostensibly as an introduction to Pound and The Cantos, the study's most valuable parts are Makin's occasional detailed analyses of particular passages and his support of the possibility of direct knowledge as apart from reasoned learning. Uneven and repetitive of published material as Makin's analysis is, it is stimulating and shares with Pound himself a vatic confidence of personal perceptions.

Using from time to time the Lacanian reduction of orthodox Freudian theory, Jean-Michel Rabaté, in his Language, Sexuality and Ideology in Ezra Pound's Cantos (London, 1986), provides a general overview of the poem preceded by a moderately interesting comparison of Pound and Heidegger. More closely tied to the text itself than much postmodernist criticism, Rabaté's discussion for the most part concentrates on passages that have already received possibly more than their due. Nevertheless, his classifications of Pound's various voices and paradoxical contradictions are rewarding in spite of the unnecessarily stilted critical vocabulary he employs. Throughout, Rabaté assumes in his reader at least a general knowledge of the sections and movements of the poem.

Margaret Dickie, writing *On the Modernist Long Poem* (Iowa City, 1986), concludes her discussion of *The Waste Land, The Bridge,* and *Paterson* with an analysis of *The Cantos,* tracing Pound's experimental openings and the development of a method that appears on the surface to destroy the assumptions of coherence and unity that Pound strove for. In her revealing conclusion, Dickie demonstrates how Pound became, as much through outer circumstance as through his published work, "the public poet of his generation."

In addition to the two volumes of the *Companion,* in which Terrell has wisely made every effort to remain objective, a number of volumes concentrating on individual sections of *The Cantos* have appeared.

Guy Davenport's *Cities on Hills: A Study of I–XXX of Ezra Pound's Cantos* (Ann Arbor, Mich., 1983), a revision of his 1961 doctoral thesis, centers in explicating the first large group of cantos as examples of Pound's use of "the ideogram," by which Davenport means "a pattern of images, as we shall see . . . which is read as the sum of its components, as in the Chinese written character which is built up of radicals." That no Chinese or Sinologists read characters in this way is not relevant here, for Pound himself did try to read them thus. The revision of the original thesis would appear to be minimal, but that hardly deprives it of originality or priority. ("William Carlos Williams' *Paterson* and Pound's *Cantos* are the only long poems to grow from the Imagist movement," Davenport writes. Whether or not they actually grew from Imagism might be challenged, but if they did, so at least did H.D.'s *Helen in Egypt*.) Davenport gives a persuasive reading of the first thirty cantos and is an excellent guide for the reader who feels the need of something more extended and coherent than the *Companion*'s entries.

Anyone wishing to consider the lasting effect of Pound's "ideogrammatic method" on the course of American poetry will find a sympathetic presentation in Laszlo K. Géfin's *Ideogram: History of a Poetic Method* (Austin, Tex., 1983).

The Malatesta cantos are part of the first larger group, and an intensive study of their development is given in Peter D'Epiro's *A Touch of Rhetoric: Ezra Pound's Malatesta Cantos* (Ann Arbor, Mich., 1983), a revision of his 1981 doctoral thesis. His analysis is especially valuable in his tracing of the beginnings of this group to their first form in the typescript Pound sent to James Sibley Watson of *The Dial*, and the "few revisions" he undertook to make, which, as D'Epiro points out, "eventually amounted to a rewriting of a substantial part of these cantos" through Pound's discovery of new materials supplementing the work of Yriarte, on whom he had largely relied up to that time. D'Epiro discusses the style of these cantos and relates the figure of Sigismundo to other "outsiders," tracing allusions to the Malatestan themes in the later cantos.

Michael North's "The Architecture of Memory: Pound and The Tempio Malatestiano" (*AL*, Oct. 1983), a discerning discussion of Pound's attraction to architecture and its meaning to him, has become one of three chapters on Pound (the others being "The Sculpture of Rhyme" and "A Trace in the Manifest") in *The Final Sculpture: Public Monuments and Modern Poetry* (Ithaca, N.Y., 1984). (The first section is centered in Yeats, and the third, "The American Monument," treats Stevens, Berryman, and Robert Lowell.) All three chapters on Pound are stimulating as North reviews Pound's interest in sculpture as one of the bases for Imagism, just as the cinema was one of the bases for Vorticism. He sees the Tempio, as Pound himself saw it, as both a success and a failure, and he admires St. Hilaire for its proportion, thus leading into a discussion of Brancusi "surrounded by the calm of his own creations," and Gourmont's *"Je sculpte une hypothèse dans le marbre de la logigue éternelle."*

Basic to an understanding of the Chinese cantos is John J. Nolde's *Blossoms from the East: The China Cantos of Ezra Pound* (Orono, Maine, 1983). Nolde gives both Pound's original sources—most of which come from Mailla's *Histoire Générale de la Chine*—and his own Englishing of them. Nolde also reproduces the Chinese characters that both adorn and enlarge the text even for the reader with no, or only an elementary, knowledge of the language. As Nolde observes, contemporary scholarship has challenged many of the interpretations of Mailla's source, showing its distinctly Confucian slant, but Nolde has sensibly refused to enter into these controversies and gives the reader the sources themselves. That the Confucian slant made Mailla's translation particularly appealing to Pound has long been known, and whatever distortions of the record—"history"—still under dispute are not germane to Pound's Chinese cantos. The only criticism to be made of Nolde's work is that by using it, the (ideal) reader of *The Cantos* is deprived of the pleasure of discovering what Pound omitted from his sources and the fun of tracking him through his quickly (and sometimes inaccurately) assimilated pursuit— a thoroughly Chinese criticism based on praise.

Almost simultaneously with Nolde's work, John Driscoll's *The China Cantos of Ezra Pound* (Uppsala, 1983) appeared. Though not as exhaustive as Nolde, Driscoll maintains some of Pound's own briskness of pace in analyzing this section of *The Cantos*, and his treatment should not be ignored. He provides perceptive readings, a summary of Pound's treatment of historical sources, and a lively commentary. In addition, he acknowledges the presence of a number of unpublished dissertations dealing with the same theme. Those not already mentioned here include studies by Woon-Ping Chin Holaday (Univ. of Toledo, 1977), Akiko Miyake (Duke Univ., 1970) and William W. Vasse, Jr. (Univ. of California-Berkeley, 1969).

As noted earlier, David Gordon has in progress a detailed study of *Cantos XCVIII and XCIX*, based on *The Sacred Edict* in Baller's edition used by Pound, which will presumably supply the same kind of information as Nolde's work on the whole unit. And, also as noted, Gordon hopes to complete a full review of the Confucian ethos through the entire run of *The Cantos*.

A facsimile reprint of F. W. Baller's 1921 *The Sacred Edict of K'ang Hsi* (Orono, Maine, 1984) offers the student of Pound's Oriental sources an opportunity of following him in his selectivity, pointing up what he omitted as being often as revealing as what he chose to include. One should not take too seriously Kenner's characterization of it as involving "personages in an international comedy reminiscent of Pound's old mentor Henry James." (Mentor?)

John Adams Speaking: The Sources of the Adams Cantos by Frederick Sanders (Orono, Maine, 1982) performs the same task for the Adams cantos as does Nolde for the Chinese and with the same thoroughness and accuracy.

Though *Canto XLV*, the first of the Usury Cantos, is the putative subject of Christine Brooke-Rose's *A Structural Analysis of Pound's "Usura Canto"* (The Hague, 1976), the real intent of this dense study is stated in its subtitle: "Jakobson's Method Extended and Applied to Free Verse." Not altogether surprisingly, Roman Jakobson is found wanting in certain respects, and Brooke-Rose makes heavy going of what many readers have found relatively direct statement. Some of these would question her assertion that *Canto XLV* can be adequately handled with little reference to *Canto LI*, except as a repetition "in more summary form, and modern." The treacherousness of working with the text in this way is accented by Pound's later addition to the Usury theme in *Drafts and Fragments*. But the notes here are valuable to anyone interested in the more trendy fashions of recent linguistic and structuralist studies as well as their beginnings, though one misses at one extreme the name of Otto Jespersen and at the other the splendid pioneering of Lord Monboddo.

The Pisan Cantos, from the time of their publication and the entire controversy over the awarding of the Bollingen Prize, have held a special place. Kenner, in his pioneer work on Pound (1951), opened his study with a discussion of them as being perhaps the most available section in every sense to the interested reader. Since then, more and more critics have seen their unity not only in Pound's personal terms, but as a reprise of the poem to date and a record of the poet's reassembling under the pressure of circumstances and almost entirely through (sometimes inaccurate) recall of the past, the foci of his intent. *Ezra Pound and the Pisan Cantos* by Anthony Woodward (London, 1980) gives a sensitive and personal reading of these cantos that appear to be the most accessible to all readers of Pound. After a general discussion of Pound's links with Romanticism and his delight in following guru-like figures somewhat out of the mainstream, Woodward discusses the persistent images of light and water throughout *The Cantos*, leading into the section on which he is concentrating, showing how personal it was for Pound and how he reconstituted his individual center.

In "Ezra Pound and the *Pisan Cantos*," a chapter of *At Last, the Real Distinguished Thing: The Late Poems of Eliot, Pound, Stevens, and Williams* (Columbus, Ohio, 1980), Kathleen Woodward finds this unit to be Pound's ultimate and effective merging of his "two paths to wholeness—the ascetic and the chivalric," resulting in genuine wisdom, a twentieth-century Confucian balance. Admittedly selective in her choice of references—the unifying variants of Micah 4.5 and other biblical passages are not mentioned—Woodward presents a persuasive and sympathetic reading, comparing Pound's final synthesis with the solutions that Stevens, Williams, and Eliot reached in their latter works. Though it is clearly outside her purpose, a reading of the later cantos in these terms would be welcome and possibly somewhat contradictory.

The title of Carlos Baker's chapter, "Pound's Prison Graffiti: *The Pisan Cantos*," in *The Echoing Green: Romanticism, Modernism, and the Phenomena of Transference in Poetry* (Princeton, N.J., 1984), is largely self-explanatory as Baker considers this section controlled by the poet's rather haphazard memories. The chapter does include an amusing letter from Pound concerning Baker on Hemingway as well as an entertaining reminiscence of Pound at table during his period of silence. For the rest, the tacit axiom of Pound students—"Never trust the American scholar who writes 'St. Elizabeth's.'"—would seem to apply. Baker's most hilariously distorted echo metamorphoses Spears's *Pocket Book of Verse* into a reference to "Richard Lovelace, a battered copy of whose poems Pound one day picked up in the latrine."

Ezra Pound in Italy: From the Pisan Cantos, with photographs by Vittorugo Contino and edited by Gianfranco Ivancich (New York, 1978), is a quite different, but equally effective, study, with an introduction written by Pound himself and a foreword by Contino. It is a brilliant collection of photographs, many of them including Pound, the first group centering in the Venice of his youth and then moving on to Pisa and Pound's return. For many of them, with the quoted text from a particular canto, Pound copied in his characteristically assertive, but never regular or beautiful handwriting, the pertinent passage. Many of the accompanying notes solve particularly knotty passages, such as "the hidden nest,

Tami's dream, the great Ovid / bound in thick boards, the bas relief of Ixotta" (*Canto LXXVI*).

The two "lost" cantos (LXXII and LXXIII), written in Italian, are still not generally accessible, though they have been privately issued and copyrighted by the Pound Estate: *Cantos LXXII and LXIII* (Washington, D.C., 1973). The first full discussion of them, by Barbara C. Eastman (*Paideuma*, Winter 1979), "The Gap in *The Cantos*: 72 and 73," gives an able survey of their content. In a comment on this paper as well as a useful discussion of the background of the two cantos' composition and particular references, Massimo Bacigalupo ("The Poet at War: Ezra Pound's Suppressed Italian Cantos" [*SAQ*, Winter, 1984]) suggests that Eastman has greatly overrated Pound's proficiency as a writer of Italian, but finds her paper "instructive." Bacigalupo gives the reference to the partial publication of these cantos in two issues of *Marina Repubblicana* (15 Jan. 1945 and 1 Feb. 1945) with corrections and editorial matter by Ubaldo degli Uberti. Bacigalupo states that Pound wanted these cantos to be read by Mussolini, thus accounting for several references and aspects of style. If these cantos are indeed, as Bacigalupo claims, a "telling consummation of Pound's long-standing commerce with things Italian," it is absurd that they are not available for anyone to read. Even if they are not quite this, it remains unfortunate that they have not been printed in their proper place.

Even with the publication of the second volume of the *Companion*, a reader of the highly condensed and increasingly fragmented passages of the poem without an ending should consult James J. Wilhelm's *The Later Cantos of Ezra Pound* (New York, 1977) in which he handles the theses, the reprises, and the effort to realize "a forging of a paradise as a political entity." Another learned guide is Eva Hesse, specifically for *Cantos CX–CXX* in her *Ezra Pound, Letzte Texte* (Zurich, 1975), where she prints a bilingual edition attesting to her skill in translation and the range of her knowledge of Pound and his life in the precision of the notes. In his *Guide to Ezra Pound's Selected Cantos* (New Brunswick, N.J., 1980), George Kearns provides both standard and original readings, following Pound himself in emphasizing *The Cantos* as a palimpsest, though he fails to make clear why, in his opinion, this means that *Drafts and Fragments* prove that *The Cantos* "is no longer a poem at all."

7 International Reputation

As should be clear by now, Pound's reputation is an international one. The references given in this essay, especially to studies in German and Italian, are placed where they are because they contribute to the entire corpus of scholarly writing about him. The few that follow are not really "drafts and fragments" but are cited chiefly to indicate the kind of international attention Pound, and especially *The Cantos*, have attracted.

Gerardo Cesar Hurtado's *Ezra Pound: Prologo, Seleccion y Notas* (San José, Costa Rica, 1978) is a critical anthology that includes representative passages from both Pound's poetry and critical prose and contains a listing of translations into Spanish and Portuguese up to the time of its publication.

Metamorphoseis tou Elpenora: Apo ton Paount ston Sinopoula by George Savidis (Athens, 1981) shows an interesting line of Poundian influence, tracing his handling of Homer's Elpenor as a partial self-identification, which is taken up by other writers in a variety of ways. He charts a descent from Pound to Giraudoux, Joyce, MacLeish, Sinopoulos, Seferis, and Ritsos, with side references to Eliot and Yeats and Forster. Though his dating of "Prufrock" in 1917 puts it closer to *Mauberley* than it actually was in composition (and first publication), the relation is suggestive even if that aspect of the Eliot/Pound interaction may appear to most as a result of Pound's late discovery of Laforgue and more closely connected to Pierrot than to Elpenor.

One of the most valuable Italian studies is also one of the earliest: Vittorio Vettori's *Ezra Pound e il Senso dell'America* (Rome, 1975). In addition to including Vettori's translations of selected passages from Pound and his own poems inspired by Pound, it also provides the record of an Italian man of letters exploring the United States, traveling from New York to California and back, relating his impressions to aspects of Pound's work. Vettori is a sensitive and perceptive commentator, quick to see how distinctly "American" many of Pound's attitudes remained throughout his life. *Italian Images of Ezra Pound: Twelve Critical Essays* (ed. and translated by Angela Jung and Guido Palandri, Taipei, 1979), is a gathering of representative essays on Pound appearing through the years from some of Italy's most distinguished critics.

An important example of Pound's reception in Spain is offered in a series of pieces collected by Jose Miguel Ibanez Langlois in *Rilke, Pound, Neruda: Tres Claves de la Poesia Contemporanea* (Madrid, 1978), which presents Pound as one of the unchallenged founders of twentieth-century poetry. ¡Arriba Ezra!

8 General Studies with Mention of Pound

By now few can question Pound's claim for major consideration as a twentieth-century figure for his poetry and as an influential, if erratic, theorist and critic, as well as a composer whose place is still to be established. Without fretting over the "placing" of Pound, some attention should be given to his handling in general histories of the period. One of the earliest in recent years, as well as one of the most balanced, is that contained in Louis Simpson's *Three on the Tower: The Lives and Works of Ezra Pound, T. S. Eliot, and William Carlos Williams* (New York, 1975). "Ezra Pound, or Art" is a skillful weaving of biography and interpretation, acknowledging as well as going forward with the work of individual scholars.

The latest estimate of this sort by a critic of general reputation occurs in Alfred Kazin's *American Procession: The Major American Writers From 1830 to 1930—The Crucial Century* (New York, 1984). Kazin disappoints as he follows a cautious, traditional line that consists almost entirely of summary. He frets over the definition of "epic" and suggests that *The Cantos* are actually Pound's "diary." Beyond this, he echoes the standard view of the reality of any sort of "Europe" existing only in the mind of the American artist.

A far more rewarding approach is put forward in *Einstein as Myth and Muse*, by Alan Friedman and Carol Donley (Cambridge, England, 1985). Here the authors devote a long paragraph to Pound, discussing his understanding of how modern scientific thought must affect the twentieth-century mind. Pound is not the only American poet discussed, and the handling of Frost, Williams, and Eliot offers points of view the contemporary critic cannot afford to ignore.

As any reader of this survey must have observed, just as in the first supplement (1973), "books tend to be stressed, especially when earlier work has been assimilated and made available in them; thus, some pioneer studies may appear to be ignored, but the later, more accessible works will lead the student to them." Everyone interested in Pound must be familiar with *Paideuma: A Journal Devoted to Ezra Pound* (Orono, Maine). If several seminal essays in it have not been mentioned here it is only because they have been absorbed in later works. Individual reactions to every article in *Paideuma* and other journals—including particular issues devoted to Pound, such as *Helix*, No. 13/14 (Ivanhoe, Australia, 1983) and the *South Atlantic Quarterly* (Winter 1984)—would have proved impossible to offer in light of the volume involved and the limits of this essay.

During the dozen years covered here, postmodernist criticism has burgeoned in all its variety. That Pound, not to mention William James and Charles Sanders Peirce, may have anticipated much of this is rarely mentioned, but at least old avenues of approach have been reopened and a few new trails hacked out. The only principle of choice here has been to attempt to single out work directed primarily toward clarifying Pound rather than substantiating a particular critical theory attempting to establish a total view—again an aim anticipated by Pound with his desperate striving after "coherence."

VI SUPPLEMENT

Bibliography. Ezra Pound, a Bibliography of Secondary Works, compiled by Beatrice Ricks (Metuchen, N.J., 1986), is a useful guide, especially for anyone starting on Pound studies.

Editions. Cantos LXXII and *LXXIII*, written in Italian and originally published in 1983 by Scheiwiller (Milan) and by New Directions (New York) in 1984 in limited editions, were incorporated in Mary de Rachewiltz's *I Cantos* (Milan, 1985) and have finally taken their rightful place in the 1986 New Directions printing of *The Cantos* (New York).

Forked Branches: Translations of Medieval Poems by Ezra Pound, edited by Charlotte Ward and with an introduction by James Laughlin (Iowa City, 1985), is made up largely of hitherto unpublished work—translated by Pound between 1905 and 1943—ranging from Anglo-Saxon through the early Italian poets, with the major portion drawn from the Troubadors and early Italians; the original texts face the translations.

New Directions plans the publication of the Pound/Fleming translation of *Elektra* at an unspecified date.

Manuscripts and Letters. Dear Ez: Letters from William Carlos Williams to Ezra Pound, commentary and notes by Mary Ellen Solt (Bloomington, Ind., 1985), provides an important record of one side of a long-standing friendship. *Pound/Zukofsky: Selected Letters of Ezra Pound and Louis Zukofsky*, edited by Barry Ahearn (New York, 1987), shows the importance of Pound to the younger poet, who even imitates Pound's epistolary style at times. Ahearn has provided full annotation and a convenient list of the principal figures involved with brief biographies. *Pound/"The Little Review": The Letters of Ezra Pound to Margaret Anderson: The "Little Review" Correspondence*, edited by Thomas L. Scott and Melvin J. Friedman (New York, 1988), shows the importance of Pound's editorial judgment and demonstrates the significance of the journal in the history of the "new" poetry and prose.

Brancusi, by Pontus Hulten, Natalia Dumitresco, and Alexandre Istrati (New York, 1986), contains two letters by Pound that indicate he was at one time contemplating a book on the artist. One of these is reproduced in facsimile, demonstrating his personal demotic French and providing a rare example of humility; for in it he labels himself both *bête* and *stupide*.

Over 200 of Pound's letters are described in the *Location Register of Twentieth-Century English Literary Manuscripts and Letters* (London, 1988), an enormously valuable resource for scholars working in the period with access to British libraries and collections.

Biography. James Laughlin has drawn together several of his essays and remarks on Pound in *Pound as Wuz* (St. Paul, 1987), absorbing and slightly rearranging the two memoirs contained in *The Master of Those Who Know* (San Francisco, 1986) in which he judged Guy Davenport's "Persephone's Ezra" in *The Geography of the Imagination* (San Francisco, 1981) to be "one of the great pieces on Pound." Laughlin's book gives considerable biographical information, drawing on the voluminous correspondence Pound kept up with his chief publisher, and includes extracts from Pound's improvised light verse contained in many of the letters. Written by a man who takes his subject seriously enough but handles it with a light touch, *Pound as Wuz* is a welcome corrective to more formal and solemn studies, and Laughlin's personal recollections of Pound as mentor, critic, and author are fresh and rewarding, making this one of the few books that succeed in offering a convincing individual portrait of Pound in his many aspects.

John Tytell's *Ezra Pound: The Solitary Volcano* (New York, 1987) was written as the result of an interview with Laughlin. In response to Tytell's inquiry as to the possibility of a new biography, Laughlin expressed his feeling about the failure of Pound's biographers to render their subject accurately. The result adds some new and detailed information, but Tytell is himself inaccurate from time to time. He refers to Pound's chief source for the Chinese cantos as "a French history of China by Mozriac [sic] de Mailla," whereas Mailla was actually the translator of a well-known history written in Chinese with a Confucian, anti-Buddhist slant. Tytell's legend, "Pound and two companions," beneath a photograph taken in Paris on the reopening of the Jockey Club in 1923 under Hilaire Hiler's management indicates that he does not recognize Jane Heap and Mina Loy. Nevertheless, his comments on Pound as an oversimplifier are apt, and a reader forewarned will often find Tytell a useful, if opinionated, guide.

The Genealogy of Demons: Anti-Semitism, Fascism, and the Myths of Ezra Pound by Robert Casillo (Evanston, Ill., 1988) offers a sustained reading of Pound's life and work as dependent on fascism and assumptions rising from Pound's anti-Semitism. Casillo traces this to the opposition Pound met early on in his "mission" to reform American and British culture and cogently observes that in Pound's earlier years the opposition that he met came from "enemies" in the Gentile world, and that he deflected "hostile impulses from many groups to a single group." The discussion is a much needed one, even if one finds oneself in frequent disagreement with Casillo's interpretations and his dependence on certain clusters—"filth, disease, castration, sterility, the feminine"—which he reads as Freudian equivalents of deeper fears. Casillo may overemphasize the importance to Pound of a European figure like Maurras and neglect the automatic American inheritance, but at the same time he concedes the effectiveness and frequent contradictions inherent in Pound's poetry. On the one hand over-ingenious, as in his reading of Pound's "translation" of Laforgue's "Salomé," and on the other overcredulous, as in his uncritical acceptance of many of Torrey's secondhand conclusions, Casillo has faced directly a central aspect of Pound and treated it in such a way as to arouse useful further discussion.

Jean-Michel Rabaté (see above), while taking up the issue of anti-Semitism in *The Cantos* and recognizing the economic issues involved, at the same time gives a reading that avoids much of Casillo's dogmatism and places Pound's admiration of Confucian society (which never existed in the terms used by Pound) in a possibly better balanced context. The sexual implications of many of these issues, made a part of Casillo's basic argument, are discussed deftly by Kevin Oderman in *Ezra Pound and the Erotic Medium* (Durham, N.C., 1986), with no reference to anti-Semitism whatsoever as he examines the visionary implications of eroticism throughout the body of Pound's work. None of this is written to minimize the importance of Casillo's massive survey, but to suggest that he may himself have become a Poundian victim in pursuit of a single cause.

Humphrey Carpenter's *Geniuses Together: American Writers in Paris in the 1920s* (London, 1987; New York, 1988) is an interesting collection of photographs and text in which Pound figures largely. All of it appears to be drawn from published sources, and possibly it served Carpenter as a warm-up and clearing house for his full-length, massive (1005-page) *A Serious Character: Ezra Pound* (London, 1988). The successive lives of Pound lead to a good bit of repetition. In spite of a recent declaration by Carpenter to the effect that when he reads or writes "a biography, I always try to skip the stuff about ancestry" (*NYTBR*, 31 July 1988), he provides a full review of forebears here and is at pains to trace the distant relationship of Pound's mother to the Wadsworths and Longfellows. The assertion in the body of this essay that only an American can hope to understand certain aspects of Pound is borne out in the early pages here, though not in quite the ways expected. A knowledge of baseball is hardly prerequisite to such analysis, but Carpenter provides unintentional entertainment in his one reference to it as well as in his reference to "Philadelphia English" as if it were a half-savage dialect; not to mention the "Midwestern drawl" (twang, perhaps?) and a quaint belief that St. Elizabeths "spells its name without an apostrophe, pedantically reproducing an early error." This last may have betrayed him into writing "Brer [sic] Fox" and "Brer [sic] Rabbit" when mentioning Joel Chandler Harris's *Uncle Remus*, though here he may be taking on faith a faulty entry in *The Oxford Companion to American Literature*.

These are unimportant details; what is important is how seriously Carpenter takes his "serious" character. That Pound was a deliberate poseur, especially in his earlier years, affecting eccentric dress and abrupt social manners, would be granted by even his most uncritical admirers. But the poetry and the critical essays and the translations are something else again. By and large Carpenter is fairly traditional in his readings of the major works. His real strength lies not in his account of Pound's literary life but in the detailed examination of Pound's daily life and contacts, which he documents with scrupulous detail. It may be this that leads him to treat in just as great fullness the later, less productive years after Pound's return to Italy following his release from imprisonment.

A healthy skepticism remains any biographer's best qualification in dealing with a figure like Pound, who naturally attracted and did little to deny myths about himself. But Carpenter at times carries his questioning too far. After quoting Pound on *The Cantos* as "the tale of the tribe—give Rudyard the credit for his use of the phrase," Carpenter continues: "(Ezra did not say where in Kipling's works he found this expression, which resembles Eliot's 'purify the dialect of the tribe' in *Little Gidding*, though that was a rough translation from Mallarmé.)" But there is no mystery here; Kipling used the phrase in his address entitled "Literature," delivered at the May 1906 Royal Academy dinner. Other examples could be cited, but this is too negative a note on which to end a description of this work. It will stand every scholar in good stead for its definitive tracking down of Pound's restless pilgrimage, which took him from place to place and brought him into contact with such half-forgotten figures as Victor Plarr, whom he probably admired more than Carpenter allows.

Criticism. Marjorie Perloff's essay, mentioned above, is now more easily available as part of her *Dance of the Intellect: Studies in the Poetry of the Pound Tradition* (New York, 1985), an excellent treatment of the pervasive influence of Pound on many of his successors.

A number of critics have chosen to treat Pound together with one or more of his contemporaries in an evaluation of twentieth-century literature. Thus Doris Eder in *Three Writers in Exile: Pound, Eliot, and Joyce* (Troy, N.Y., 1984) discusses the differing aspects and effects of expatriation in the work of her subjects. And in *The Matrix of Modernism: Pound, Eliot, and Early Twentieth-Century Thought* (Princeton, N.J., 1985), Sanford Schwartz accounts for Pound's return to the past for his models as the result of his rebellion against what he felt was an almost dictated uniformity in contemporary life. James Longenbach, in *Modernist Poetics of History: Pound, Eliot, and the Sense of the Past* (Princeton, N.J., 1987), analyzes Pound's "historical sense" in relation to both its philosophical implications and the reading of Eliot and Pound during the London period (1910–22), relating this to Romantic sources echoed in Pater and Yeats. Longenbach continues his analysis, in a sense, with *Stone Cottage: Pound, Yeats, and Modernism* (New York, 1988), dealing with the crucial seasons during which Pound acted as Yeats's informal secretary. Unfortunately, George Bornstein's forthcoming *Poetic Remaking: The Art of Browning, Yeats, and Pound* (University Park, Pa., 1988) was unavailable at the time of writing.

Though the greater part of Maud Ellmann's *The Poetics of Impersonality: T. S. Eliot and Ezra Pound* (Cambridge, Mass., 1987) deals with Eliot, the latter third handles issues raised by Pound's views of the persona and the contemporaneousness of "history." Ellmann would seem to be somewhat late in entering this field, with many of her conclusions foregone, but her use of poststructuralist theory is interesting as she discusses the difficulty of determining impersonality without examining antitheses, and the ultimate impossibility of altogether separating creation from creator, providing on the way original readings of many passages in *Mauberley* as well as *The Cantos*.

A general review of Pound's development provides the base for Bruce Fogelman's *Shapes of Power: The Development of Ezra Pound's Poetic Sequences* (Ann Arbor, Mich., 1988). Fogelman discusses the successive volumes of Pound's work by examining each collection as "the book-as-a-whole," using one of Pound's own phrases. The result is a novel revaluation of Pound's sense of organization from the beginning of his work. Though at times one feels that Fogelman is forcing the issue (in connection with the earliest volumes especially), the result is well worth the effort of suspending one's skepticism, if not altogether surrendering it, as the poet's progress "toward the long poem" advances into *Mauberley* and *The Cantos*.

Alan Robinson's *Symbol to Vortex: Poetry, Painting, and Ideas, 1885–1914* (New York, 1985) contains primary material and penetrating analysis of Pound's work in relation to his developing technique and links his work to largely unexplored origins.

Ezra Pound & Japan, edited by Sanehide Kodama (Redding Ridge, Conn., 1987), provides an overview of Pound's reactions to many aspects of Japanese culture as well as reproducing most of his correspondence with individual Japanese and other persons concerned with Japanese themes. These include Mary Fenollosa, the widow of Ernest Fenollosa, whose notebooks formed the base for much of Pound's early work in connection with the Orient, leading him ultimately to concentrate on Confucian China. Letters from and to the poet Noguchi open the collection, followed by those of Michio Ito and Tami Koumé. The core of the volume consists of the Katue Kitasono ("Kit Kat")/Pound correspondence, followed by letters exchanged with Japanese writers after the end of World War II and a reprinting of Pound's contributions to Japanese periodicals appearing in 1939–40. Appendixes by several hands close this important work, essential to anyone wishing to understand Pound's treatment of Oriental themes, providing the scholar as well as the general reader with basic information and primary documents. Anyone personally familiar with the Orient will smile at some of Pound's reactions, but at the same time will come to respect his consistent originality and frequent shrewdness during his assimilation of two often alien cultures.

In *The Classics in Paraphrase: Ezra Pound and Modern Translators of Latin Poetry* (Selinsgrove, Pa., 1988), Daniel M. Hooley reopens the discussion of Pound's *Homage to Sextus Propertius* and other work, particularly his Horatian pieces. Hooley is particularly valuable in indicating critical comment that has appeared since the publication of Sullivan's study. In his own detailed readings of key units Hooley both widens and deepens one's understanding of the relationship of translator and translated, primary text and derivation therefrom, to conclude with a classical trope.

Edwin Arlington Robinson

Ellsworth Barnard

I BIBLIOGRAPHY

The period since the last version of this essay has produced two notable additions to Robinson bibliography. In *Early Reception of Edwin Arlington Robinson: The First Twenty Years* (Waterville, Maine, 1974), Richard Cary continues his indefatigable effort to unearth and make available hitherto unnoted comments about Robinson's work. It reprints all known published materials—reviews, notices, or comments—dealing with Robinson's poetry before 1916 and more than doubles the number of items listed by Hogan (1936). These are accompanied by exhaustive and exemplary notes. In addition, an essay entitled "Preliminary Vistas" undertakes to answer the question of why Robinson was "consistently rebuffed by editors, disdained by critics, and virtually ignored by the reading public." The suggested answer is the almost universal prevalence of conventional, sentimental standards of taste.

An even more impressive achievement is Nancy Carol Joyner's *Edwin Arlington Robinson: A Reference Guide* (Boston, 1978). The stated purpose is "to help future scholars avoid redundancy and to identify those areas of Robinson scholarship that merit further attention." After listing "representative selections" of Cary's work, it expands the coverage by Hogan and White (1971), especially by the inclusion of newspaper as well as magazine reviews and comments on Robinson's work, and carries it through 1976. The arrangement is chronological, with a section for each year, which in turn is divided into "Books" and "Shorter Writings." (For some reason not apparent to this reader, some unpublished Ph.D. theses are listed in one group and some in the other.) Reviews of writings *about* Robinson, as distinguished from those about his own work, are as a rule not included. A particularly valuable feature is that important entries are accompanied by brief objective summaries of the contents; although of course readers will sometimes differ as to the main points of a piece of writing, and therefore as to what should go into a short summary.

Nevertheless, these summaries offer the reader an overview of the attitudes and judgments of critics, among whom, it is evident, there was never a consensus, even during the years of the poet's greatest fame, as to the merit either of particular works or of his achievement as a whole. One is tempted, viewing the irreconcilable interpretations and evaluations, to apply to literary criticism the wry definition of "metaphysics" by the British philosopher F. H. Bradley: "the finding of bad reasons for what we believe on instinct."

A similar response is evoked by Richard Crowder's "Robinson's *Tristram* and the American Reviewers" (*CLQ*, June 1980), which summarizes "39 reviews from Savannah to Seattle, from Chicago to Dallas, and from New York and Boston to San Francisco." Three newspaper reviews are added to those listed by Joyner.

II EDITIONS

There has been only one significant new publication of Robinson's work, but an extremely useful one: *Uncollected Poems and Prose of Edwin Arlington Robinson* (ed. Richard Cary, Waterville, Maine, 1975). There are three sections. The first consists of poems previously published but omitted from the *Collected Poems* (1937). Most of these, from *The Torrent and The Night Before* (1896), were made available in Charles T. Davis's *Selected Early Poems and Letters* (1960), but this is now, unfortunately, out of print. The second section, devoted to prose, aims "to make accessible to devotees and scholars, under one convenient cover, a conclusive record of Robinson's writings in this genre." The twenty-six items include essays, obituaries, introductions, and autobiographical sketches. Although these writings are relatively slight in volume and sometimes self-conscious in style, the content is often significant, and "devotees and scholars" will be grateful. The third section, headed "Briefs," includes "noteworthy comments made by Robinson and recorded by friends or interviewers" (or excerpted from letters). They come from a wide variety of sources, often not readily available, and not only offer a remarkable character portrait but also shed much light on the poetry. Scholars will find them useful, and the "general reader" who wishes an introduction to Robinson cannot do better than start here. Cary has also rescued from oblivion Robinson's earliest published sonnet in "'The Clam-digger of Capital Island': A Robinson Sonnet Recovered" (*CLQ*, Dec. 1974).

This is perhaps the place to record the melancholy fact that no volume of Robinson's poetry—neither the *Collected Poems* nor any volume of selections—is listed in the latest issue of *Books in Print*. Although this may be due in part to a conglomerate appetite for profits, to which nothing could be less relevant than poetry, it must be recognized that if enough people wanted his poetry badly enough to pay the current price of a book, an edition would be made available.

III MANUSCRIPTS AND LETTERS

Wallace Anderson, who had worked for many years on an edition of Robinson's collected letters, died in the spring of 1984, and the present status of the project is uncertain. Anderson did offer an enticing preview in "The Letters of E. A. Robinson: A Sampler" (*CLQ*, Mar. 1980).

In "Edwin Arlington Robinson's *Antigone*: Surviving Fragments" (*CML*, Winter 1984), Lewis E. Weeks, Jr. brings together the surviving passages of Robinson's translation of Sophocles's *Antigone*, a project on which he collaborated with his friend Harry de Forest Smith between 1894 and 1896. Smith supplied a literal prose translation, and Robinson turned it into blank verse. Many references in the letters to Smith show the depth of Robinson's engagement, but though he completed a tentative version, into which he obviously put much hard work, and later revised several hundred lines, he apparently made no serious attempt to get it published and left the manuscript behind in Gardiner when he went to New York. A later attempt to retrieve it was unsuccessful. Most of the surviving fragments are in letters to Smith, but two passages have been added from the manuscript of Smith's translation, which has been preserved. Weeks places the fragments in context, gives samples of Smith's translation, and offers for comparison some of the passages as rendered by other translators—Jebb, Plumptre, Palmer, and Fitts and Fitzgerald. Weeks's judgment that Robinson's version is in general "far superior" may not be shared by all readers, but all students of Robinson will agree that the loss of the complete version is greatly to be regretted.

Further information about the composition of the work is given by Weeks in "Edwin Arlington Robinson's *Antigone*" (*CLQ*, Sept. 1984). The article deals with Robinson's relations with Smith; it gives many details, often painful, about Robinson's personal and family affairs during this time, and records Robinson's varying feelings about the undertaking. Included are passages of unpublished letters from Robinson to his friend George Latham.

IV BIOGRAPHY

Brief glimpses of the poet, hitherto unrecorded, may be found in several articles in the *Colby Library Quarterly*. Richard Cary, in "Mowry Saben About Edwin Arlington Robinson" (Mar. 1972), adds substantially to the account in Hagedorn's 1938 biography. Saben, a friend from Robinson's days at Harvard, was almost the antithesis of the poet—a person of unbounded self-assurance, immense appetites, and uninhibited contempt for convention, who was nevertheless attracted both by Robinson's poetry and by his character. Though he was given to verbal extravagance, his judgments are sometimes sound and incisive (for example, Robinson "hated Puritanism but could never quite break away from it").

Cary has also, in "Robinson's Friend Arthur Davis Variell" (*CLQ*, June 1974), given an account of a previously unnoted friendship between Robinson and a boyhood friend with whom he became reacquainted in 1922. His letters to Variell, who had a varied career as a physician, a successful industrialist, an international medical authority, and a world traveler, show that both men enjoyed the association, which, however, gradually declined after 1929.

In "The Shadowed Years: Mrs. Richards, Mr. Stedman, and Robinson" (*CLQ*, June 1972), Robert J. Skolnick recounts Mrs. Richards's efforts to enlist the aid of the former stockbroker turned man of letters in getting a hearing for Robinson's poetry. Stedman was more than agreeable and did include several of Robinson's poems in his popular anthology. The article offers new information about the relations among the three persons, all of whom appear in a most attractive light.

Another article, by Louis J. Budd, "E. A. Robinson Unbends for Academe" (*CLQ*, Dec. 1980), describes Robinson's friendly relations with J. B. Hubbell in connection with the use of his poems in Hubbell and Beaty's *An Introduction to Poetry* (1922), and a visit to Robinson by a young Columbia graduate student, A. Gayle Waldrop, and Albert S. Pegues, head of the English Department at Southern Methodist University. In a letter to Hubbell, Waldrop tells of Robinson's cordial and outgoing reception of his guests and his comments on a number of contemporary poets.

Under this heading, also, may be mentioned Louis Untermeyer's recollections in "Edwin Arlington Robinson: A Reappraisal," reprinted in *Literary Lectures Presented at the House of Congress* (Washington, D.C., 1973). Many of these discursive comments on Robinson's life and character are already familiar, but the reader is struck by Untermeyer's emphasis, perhaps excessive, on Robinson as a "loner."

V CRITICISM

Contemporary trends in literary criticism and poetic taste, moving far from the nineteenth-century tradition to which Robinson belonged, have increasingly led critics to ignore his work. Since the flurry of interest following the centenary of his birth in 1969, no major critical studies have been published, and even periodical articles have been relatively rare. Except for the hospitality of the editors of the *Colby Library Quarterly*, even his name would be missing from some of the annual bibliographies; and in fact, it did not appear in the *MLA Bibliography* for 1982. An exception to the general trend is that his poetry has continued to supply topics for Ph.D. dissertations, of which about one a year, on the average, has been devoted in whole or in part to his work. Since published criticism of his work has been limited in volume during the past decade, it seems appropriate to discuss these dissertations briefly along with the published material related to the topics with which they deal. One which may be mentioned here, and which can only have been a labor of love, is a concordance, based on the *Collected Poems*, compiled by Michael W. Sundermeier (Univ. of Nebraska, 1972).

Robinson is still included, however, in the revised edition of the *Encyclopedia of World Literature in the 20th Century* (New York, 1984). And Ellsworth Barnard's brief and necessarily general account of Robinson's life and work concludes optimistically: "When a final verdict is rendered, uninfluenced by temporary trends in taste, R.'s psychological insight, his scrupulous and sometimes inspired verbal artistry, and his clear-eyed but compassionate observance of the human drama will make secure his standing as a major American poet."

What may be called the literary establishment does indeed accord merit, and occasionally high praise, to a number of the short dramatic poems, and is even willing to accept some of the middle-length character studies. But it confidently assigns to oblivion the long blank verse narratives, as well as the "philosophical" (always in quotation marks) pieces. Representative of this view are the essays in Donald B. Stauffer's *A Short History of American Poetry* (New York, 1974), David Perkins's *A History of Modern Poetry: From the 1890s to the High Modernist Mode* (Cambridge, Mass., 1976), and William H. Pritchard's *Lives of the Modern Poets* (New York, 1980). Stauffer finds the Arthurian poems "largely unreadable" and the other long narratives even less approachable but admires some of the short dramatic pieces and middle-length character portraits, and on the strength of these assigns Robinson to "a place among the major American poets of the twentieth century." Similarly, Perkins thinks that "about forty pages" of the 1,488 in the *Collected Poems* are "likely to last." He offers a brilliant analysis of "Richard Cory" (often viewed with condescension) as "exhibiting in flawless performance what was innovative in his art," and has some good things to say about others among the shorter pieces, but judges the long narratives to be uniformly unsuccessful, partly because of "the nineteenth century pursuit of strict metrical form" and partly because the long narrative poem as a literary genre has long been obsolete. "The didactic and 'philosophical' poems" represent Robinson's "weakest side."

Pritchard likewise condemns the long works as "on the whole prolix, fussy, and somehow terribly misguided," and finds "The Man Against the Sky" "virtually unreadable, to be admired neither for its ideas nor for its eloquence." He considers that "the life and the challenge of Robinson's poetry lie rather in the way of saying than in the truth or relevance or wisdom of the idea communicated." His special gift was in "using words that always hinted that there was something beyond them . . .

incapable of being at all adequately rendered by language, by 'mere words.'" It is this quality that gives luster to such poems as "Luke Havergal," "Miniver Cheevy," "Mr. Flood's Party," "For a Dead Lady," "Eros Turannos," and "The Sheaves." It is of interest that the poems he mentions have for the most part been exceptional in winning wide critical approval, transcending contrarieties of taste and interpretation.

Another general appraisal, though brief and cursory, is I. D. MacKillop's "Robinson's Accomplishment" (*EIC*, July 1971), a belated review of the volumes of selections edited by Davis (1960) and Zabel (1965), along with Murphy's anthology of critical essays (1970). He joins in the conventional disparagement of the "didactic" poems and praises those that deal concretely with common persons.

A more inclusive survey of Robinson's poetic achievement is David C. Downing's unpublished dissertation, "The Poetry of E. A. Robinson: A Critical Reappraisal" (Univ. of California-Los Angeles, 1977). The critic finds Robinson attempting to steer "a middle course" between the "Genteel Tradition" and the more innovative poets among his contemporaries. Stress is laid on his relation to New England, his creation in his character poems of "a *comedie humaine* of the early twentieth century," and his psychological treatment of materials from the Arthurian legend and the Bible.

An essay dealing with various phases of Robinson's early work is "Tilbury Town as Region: A Study in the Poetry of E. A. Robinson" by G. P. Thakur (*IJAS*, Jan. 1977). Tilbury Town (possible origins of the name suggest that it is satirical) is identified specifically with Gardiner, Maine, but is more generally viewed as "a fairly realistic imaginative portrait of the New England small town in transition during Robinson's creative poetic career." Noting that the town is defined not by its physical appearance but by its characters, the critic finds in the Tilbury poems, especially "Isaac and Archibald" and "Captain Craig," traits of character supposed to be typical of New England. Incidental to this theme are several novel interpretations of particular poems.

A seemingly universal impulse of students of literature is to search for sources, and Robinson's readers are not exempt. Among the studies of the substantive origins of his poetry, several contain a common emphasis on his relation to Emerson. One is Harold Bloom's "Bacchus and Merlin: The Dialectic of Romantic Poetry in America," in *The Ringers in the Tower* (Chicago, 1971; first published in *SR*, Jan. 1971), which discusses *The Torrent and The Night Before* in terms of Emerson's poems "Merlin" and "Bacchus," showing the darker and brighter sides of Emerson's concept of Fate. Though praising the poems, Bloom judges that "Robinson yielded too much to Necessity and too rapidly assimilated himself to the tendency I have named Merlin." Robinson is "an Emerson incapable of transport."

Emerson is also the focus of a section on Robinson in Annette Insdorf's unpublished dissertation, "An American Strain: Connecting Art and Experience" (Yale Univ., 1975). Robinson is one of six American writers who are discussed; the critic concludes that his "sources, methods and goals are intimately connected to Emerson's essay 'The Poet.'"

Emerson also appears as a progenitor of Robinson in another dissertation, Earl W. Booth's "New England Quartet: E. A. Robinson, Robert Frost, Charles Ives, and Carl Ruggles" (Univ. of Utah, 1974). The four artists have in common their revolt against traditional forms of expression and their adherence to the Emersonian doctrine of Transcendentalism, which they reinterpreted for their own century: "The pioneer efforts of Robinson and Frost in bringing the sound of the human voice to poetry and abandoning traditional poetic diction paved the way for the vigorous experimental nature of modern poetry." And in the substance of their work, both poets "reached for the momentary glimpse beyond the temporal to experience the Emersonian eternal." Both Robinson's nearness to Emerson and his divergence are obvious, and a comprehensive study of their relationship is a project much to be desired.

Robinson's use of the Bible was discussed by Edwin Fussell in 1954 (*Edwin Arlington Robinson: The Literary Background of a Traditional Poet*), but is examined further in Elizabeth J. McGregor's dissertation, "The Poet's Bible: Biblical Elements in the Poetry of Emily Dickinson, Stephen Crane, Edwin Arlington Robinson and Robert Frost" (Brown Univ., 1978). The "Biblical elements" involve both "language and content," and the thesis in regard to Frost and Robinson is that they "still quarreled with the Bible," but nevertheless tried "to salvage something of the spiritual values and tradition it represented, which seemed threatened with extinction. Robinson both retold its stories, emphasizing their relevance to modern problems, and tried with limited success to use its language to support and define his own confused religious hopes." Though it is evident that both poets knew the Bible well and used it naturally for their own purposes, there is no evidence that they needed it to "support" their religious beliefs, or that these beliefs were "confused"— though Frost liked to tease his readers.

Sources of a very different kind are the subject of another dissertation, William A. Yasinski's "Robinson, Frost, and Estheticism: The Imagination of Survival" (Indiana Univ., 1978). The critic contends that the "late nineteenth-century cultural tradition of estheticism was profoundly important to the poetic development" of both poets. For Robinson, the two most important "estheticists" were Schopenhauer and Swinburne, and his failure to "free himself" from the estheticist influence, as Frost was able to do, made him the lesser poet. It is interesting to speculate on how Robinson himself, though he would have acknowledged his indebtedness in his early poems to the French Symbolists, who one supposes were also "estheticists," would have responded to this analysis.

Aside from the subject matter of Robinson's poems, there has been a continuing, if limited, interest in his methods and techniques. One important study is Ulf Lie's analysis, in "A Poetry of Attitudes: The Speaker Personae in E. A. Robinson's Early Dramatic Poetry," in *Contributions to American Studies Dedicated to Sigmund Skard* (ed. Brita Seyersted, Oslo, 1973), of the role of the speaker or narrator in the short narrative-dramatic poems. The attitude of this person is crucial to the interpretation of the poem, but this attitude is sometimes left unclear because of Robinson's view that truth is subjective, and his reluctance to allow the speaker to pass "any judgment on any other character without at the same time assuring the reader that this is a subjective view." This is a just insight, and the implications are pursued at some length.

They are pursued further in Joan Manheimer's essay, "Edwin Arlington Robinson's 'Eros Turannos': Narrative Reconsidered" (*LitR*, Spring 1977), and are applied to the poem that has most consistently fascinated the critics. The premise is that narrative, by definition and in essence, excludes all but one series of events, imposes a single pattern on the almost infinite possibilities offered by actual experience: "In listening to a narrative voice we grant what we know is impossible in order to experience, if only temporarily, the fulfillment of a deep hunger. It is Robinson's achievement that he reminds us how much is lost in that fulfillment." Specifically, the first four stanzas are straight narrative; but then the narrator enters the poem as a character ("we") with a limited point of view, admits his ignorance of the main character, and thus presents new possibilities to the reader's imagination. This fresh and seminal idea, however, is linked to the questionable view that the central character, in this and many other Robinson poems, is isolated by a "hostile" community, "whose refusal of membership to the outcast in 'Eros Turannos' is the fact that completes her story." Still more dubious, and of doubtful relevance, is the suggestion that these characters are "outcasts" because they have contributed nothing to the community, and that "the community's capacity to include the individual is a function of the economy." The general ideas in this essay are developed in greater detail in Manheimer's unpublished dissertation, "A Study of the Speaker's Voice in the Poetry of Edwin Arlington Robinson" (Brandeis Univ., 1974).

The same general topic is dealt with in a brief piece by Richard Haas, "Oral Interpretation As Discovery Through Persona" (*OralEng*, Spring 1972). Two lines from "Richard Cory" are used to show how different emphases on certain words when read aloud suggest varying possibilities as to the character and attitude of the persona.

A minor matter concerning Robinson's technique is discussed by Nancy Joyner in "E. A. Robinson's Concessions to the Critics" (*RS*, Mar. 1972). Challenging the general assumption that Robinson was indifferent to public criticism, she contends "that there is evidence to suggest that his dependence on critical acceptance was a determining factor in his career." The evidence follows two lines: first, that he made textual changes in some poems, notably "Captain Craig" and *Avon's Harvest* (first published in a separate volume) in response to criticism; and second, that "many of [his] short poems were written because critics would not accept his long poems." The second statement is hard to prove, but the general thesis deserves attention.

Allied to technique is form, and passing mention may here be made of Oliver H. Evans's unpublished dissertation, "The Sonnet in America" (Purdue Univ., 1972). Robinson's distinctive contribution is that he "expanded the sonnet's subject matter and tone." This is true, and a full account of Robinson's use of the sonnet needs to be published.

Returning to "Eros Turannos," Benjamin Griffith, in "A Note on Robinson's Use of 'Turannos'" (*CP*, Spring 1971), objects to Laurence Perrine's interpretation of the title, according to which "Love is a tyrant who blinds, maddens, and whips." Citing the classical Greek meaning of "an unconstitutional leader who has seized power," he comments: "Perhaps Robinson means for the reader to see the husband as a *turannos*, an outsider who seized the love of a New England lady falsely, without rights either of birth or kindred love. Perhaps he posed as a lover, but was a *turannos* in the sense that he could not give love, due to impotence or homosexuality." Aside from the fact that there is nothing in the text to support the last suggestion, it may be noted that in the title it is *Love*, and not the husband, that is the "tyrant."

A different approach to this poem is Jeffrey L. Spear's "Robinson, Hardy, and a Literary Source of 'Eros Turannos'" (*CLQ*, Mar. 1979). The suggested source is Hardy's poem "Wives in the Sere," and Spear cites parallels in both meter and theme, which are plausible but not conclusive.

Despite the dismissal of the long poems by the establishment, they have continued to claim a measure of critical attention. The Arthurian poems, especially, have not been found unreadable by all critics, or unworthy of comment. The exploration of sources, to be sure, seems largely finished, and the findings are well-summarized in Laurence Perrine's "The Sources of Robinson's Arthurian Poems and His Opinion of Other Treatments" (*CLQ*, June 1974). The upshot is a strengthening of Robinson's claim to originality.

As for substantive issues, however, a number of other essays show that these are far from exhausted. Nathan C. Starr, in "Robinson's Arthurian Heroines: Vivian, Guinevere, and the Two Isolts" (*PQ*, Spring 1977), still finds these characters appealing human beings and stresses their credibility, their modernity, and their strength; they are "more confident, more resilient than the men." Robinson's originality in the portrayal of Vivian and Isolt of Brittany wins particular praise.

Further perceptive comments on Robinson's female characters can be found in Sybil Korff Vincent's too brief essay "Flat-breasted Miracles:

Realistic Treatment of the Woman's Problem in the Poetry of E. A. Robinson" (*MarkhamR*, Fall 1976). Robinson shows women as "real human beings" for whom he has a "far-ranging" sympathy. He is "not concerned with the superficial position of women in society. . . . Her need was first to be recognized as a human being—not angel, demon, toy, tool or possession. The beginning of women's liberation, and man's, would be in the recognition of each other as unique individuals, to be dealt with honestly, and not to be exploited." Still valid is a statement made in the original edition of this work that a comprehensive study of Robinson's treatment of the women characters in his poems and his conception of the rightful and proper place of women in society is overdue.

A study of Robinson's principal *male* characters was undertaken by Thomas W. Koontz in an unpublished dissertation, "The Master of the Moment: The Gentleman in the Poetry of E. A. Robinson" (Indiana Univ., 1970). The characters are analyzed according to type, with reference to the "Robinsonian model" of the gentleman.

Although the relation between the sexes is a constant theme in Robinson's poems, it is perhaps in the Arthurian stories, again, that the theme is developed most fully. In this connection, one naturally thinks first of *Tristram*, and in "Time Is a Casket: Love and Temporality in *Tristram*" (*CLQ*, June 1982), L. L. Clark and Julian Wasserman advance the thesis that while the other characters, even Isolt of Brittany, live in time and think of love in terms of time, the love between Tristram and Isolt of Ireland is not subject to time and even when their life in time is ended by death, their love somehow transcends the event.

The love between Tristram and Isolt of Ireland is approached from a different angle in Louise Mulligan's unpublished dissertation, "Mythology and Autobiography in Robinson's *Tristram*" (Univ. of Massachusetts, 1975). The author emphasizes the numerous departures from the traditional story and theorizes that these changes are due in large part to Robinson's frustrated love for Emma, the wife of his brother Herman. She concludes that "Robinson was, consciously or unconsciously, writing his own life-long love story when he composed *Tristram*." This of course rests on the acceptance of Chard Powers Smith's undocumented thesis in *Where the Light Falls* (1965). This may also be the place to mention Nancy Joyner's "What Ever Happened to *Tristram*?" (*CLQ*, June 1980), which gives an account of the extraordinary popularity of the poem on its appearance and its subsequent treatment, generally less enthusiastic, by the critics.

In *Lancelot* and *Merlin*, of course, Robinson is concerned less exclusively with the theme of love between the sexes, and it is these other themes, or love in relation to other themes, that critics have usually chosen to deal with. In "Robinson's Camelot: Renunciation As Drama" (*CLQ*, Mar. 1972), Celia Morris discusses both the general theme—"the Arthurian stories are not mainly about the end of the world; they are primarily about the world itself and the people who rule it"—and the importance of the legend as supplying a story element that Robinson did not have to invent, so that he could devote most of his energy to *interpreting* it. Of course, as other critics have pointed out, his reinterpretation involves not a little invention.

Later, concentrating on *Lancelot*, Morris presents a forceful argument, in "E. A. Robinson and the Golden Horoscope of Imperfection" (*CLQ*, June 1975), for the convincingness and appeal of the characters in the poem and notes the kinship with other poems that "exploit his characters' awareness that their needs and passions on the one hand and their obligations and rationality on the other basically conflict and that there can be no satisfactory resolution."

How this conflict in individuals affects society is the theme of "Wreck and Yesterday: The Meaning of Failure in *Lancelot*" (*CLQ*, Sept. 1971), in which N. E. Dunn argues plausibly that "by dramatizing the causes of failure in the medieval society of Arthur's Round Table, the poet intended to reveal some of the reasons for failure in the modern ideal of twentieth century American democracy." One cause is that the leading characters "are psychologically unable to meet the demands of the ideal society," but a second lies in the faulty social structure of Arthur's world, which rests on the flawed institution of chivalry, with its tolerance of adultery, and absolute monarchy, which has no provision for human fallibility.

"Ideal" is a word that often seems to find its way into critical comment on the Arthurian poems, and Don Richard Cox's "The Vision of Robinson's *Merlin*" (*CLQ*, Dec. 1974) is no exception. Here the critic studies the relation between Merlin and Vivian and that between Merlin and Arthur, and suggests that each member of each pair at first sees the other as embodying his or her ideal, only to be at last inevitably disillusioned.

A brief general discussion of the Arthurian poems is Ruth Berman's "E. A. Robinson and Merlin's Gleam" (*Eildon Tree*, No. 2, 1976). *Tristram* is dismissed on the ground that Tristram and Isolt of Ireland are too conventional as lovers and that their story is essentially the same as that of Lancelot and Guinevere, which is more imaginatively and movingly treated. *Lancelot* and *Merlin* are judged to be "worth the reading—and the rereading." This worth lies especially in the delineation of the characters, although it is suggested that for Robinson the Arthurian world as presented in these poems is "a symbol of his own world." The legend of the Grail also gets some attention, and Robinson's treatment of it is compared to Eliot's in *The Waste Land*.

The Arthurian poems also supply illustrations for Arthur M. Sampley's thoughtful essay, "The Power or the Glory: The Dilemma of Edwin Arlington Robinson" (*CLQ*, Sept. 1971): "Robinson appears to vacillate between value determined by self and that determined by society." Merlin and Lancelot choose the first, although not without a feeling of guilt. Tristram and Isolt, however, trust their own feelings completely. This is a reversion to the poet's stance in "Captain Craig," in which the Captain successfully resists society's pressure to conform. But in several of the late long poems the protagonist's initial self-trust leads to tragedy, for others if not for himself. And in *Amaranth* the dwellers in the "wrong world" are there because their self-assurance has deluded them; and when it withers under the eyes of Amaranth (who "seems to represent the totality of society . . . judging the work of the artist"), they are destroyed. As for the shorter poems, they are about "evenly divided" between those in which self-trust leads to salvation and those in which it leads to destruction: "Keenly aware that both the individual and society are subject to error, Robinson seems gradually inclined to place his hope for both in the individual who through the batterings of fate and the waverings of human frailty has achieved a measure of wisdom."

The relation between society and the self is also the general subject of John H. Miller's unpublished dissertation, "E. A. Robinson's Changing Beliefs about Living in the World" (Indiana Univ., 1970). In the early poems (e.g., "Captain Craig") the values and rewards of human life are to be found on earth, in society. In the middle period, however, salvation is to be sought in self-knowledge rather than in social involvement, and this trend continues. Of course, no genuine poet's work can be fitted into a formula, but there is certainly a change of emphasis as Robinson grows older, and this article helps to define the change.

Critics have generally agreed that *Amaranth* is unique among Robinson's poems, and W. R. Thompson's "The Identity of E. A. Robinson's Amaranth" (*RMR*, No. 4, 1981) is an especially thoughtful analysis of its "meaning." Pointing out that Amaranth repeatedly denies that he is "God" or "the Law," or that he *compels* the characters to see the devastating truth about themselves, Thompson argues that "Amaranth cannot be regarded as a personification of truth, reality, or reason," but that he is the *agent* of reason—"a semidivine figure charged with making men mindful of their potentiality for engaging in rational thought and endeavor." His "foil," the crazed inventor Ipswich, is the agent of unreason. Although not all readers will accept every detail of Thompson's interpretation, they will find rewarding insights into what the writer correctly regards as one of Robinson's richest poems.

A theme similar to that of *Amaranth*, namely the choice between reality and illusion, is treated by R. Meredith Bedell in "Perception, Action, and Life in *The Man Against the Sky*" (*CLQ*, Mar. 1976). Bedell reads the title poem as an affirmation of the possibility of salvation for those willing to face reality. For a dramatic illustration he turns to the hero (and he *is* a hero) of "Llewellyn and the Tree." On the other hand, the self-deluded mother in "The Gift of God" is condemned with a harshness strangely at odds with Robinson's own ironic but compassionate treatment. Bedell is probably correct, however, in his summary of the poet's general view: "Once reality is confronted and recognized, man lives by asserting his acceptance of life through deliberate willed actions."

That not everybody finds the late long poems unreadable and that they are even thought worthy of serious discussion is again demonstrated by Thelma J. Shinn's "The Art of a Verse Novelist: Approaching Robinson's Late Narratives through James's *The Art of the Novel*" (*CLQ*, June 1976). The contention is that "in subject matter, characterization and style, Robinson's verse novels achieve the intentions of the novelist as James describes them quite as clearly as the novels on which these prefaces are based." This is a bold assertion, but Shinn adduces many apt examples to support it.

Robinson's views on his own craft have always been of interest, and Nancy Joyner in "Robinson's Poets" (*CLQ*, Mar. 1972) offers a systematic inquiry into what is said or implied concerning the topic in the poems themselves: "His explicit subject matter for an unusually large number of poems is poets and the writing of poetry. These poems may be divided into three groups: those that celebrate the work of an actual poet, those that deal with the work of the generic poet, and those that have to do with a specific fictional poet." Perhaps the most interesting in the third group is Pink in *Amaranth*, who under close scrutiny turns out to be an extremely complex character. In summary, Robinson's view is that the poet's function is to communicate truth, and that to be successful he must both possess an "inner fire" and be a "conscious craftsman," but that the final effect defies analysis in that it "transcends the meaning and syntax of the words." (This recalls Pritchard's comment noted above.) A novel suggestion, which at first may seem whimsical, but is worth thinking about, is that Robinson's use of the phrase "the wrong world" in *Amaranth* may sometimes be ironic.

The relation of Robinson's life and poetry to another art, namely music, has often been noted, mostly in regard to the life; but Scott Donaldson's "Robinson and Music" (*CLQ*, Mar. 1980) stresses the importance of music in the poetry, both as a frequent theme and as a pervasive metaphor.

Of interest in connection with Robinson's general view of life (a topic that continues to find expositors) is John H. Miller's "The Structure of E. A. Robinson's *The Torrent and the Night Before*" (*CLQ*, June 1974). The writer notes that in Robinson's first volume the poems are arranged according to theme rather than (as in *The Children of the Night*) according to form and suggests that this arrangement shows "what Robinson himself thought his major themes were at this early stage." Miller finds "four major sections," dealing with "art, death, light, and living in the physical world." Despite the frequently somber themes and tone, the poet's attitude is judged to be generally affirmative. The topic is developed in greater detail in the author's unpublished dissertation noted above.

Though much recent criticism has disparaged "The Man Against the Sky," two writers during the 1970s chose to make it the subject of critical articles. Robert S. Fish, in "The Tempering of Faith in E. A. Robinson's 'The Man Against the Sky'" (CLQ, Mar. 1972), argues that "the poem should be considered dramatic rather than didactic." The "'I' addresses himself in an attempt to strengthen his faith" and in the process confronts and overcomes a series of temptations. Somewhat similar is the interpretation of John N. Sanborn, in "Juxtaposition as Structure in 'The Man Against the Sky'" (CLQ, Dec. 1974). The poem should not be read as the linear statement of a single theme but as an intellectual drama created by the juxtaposition of the problems and questions we have about both faith and reason: "Robinson confronts each starkly, and in the resultant play of one against the other, the reader may—in fact, must—construct his own 'Chaos stop.'" Both critics find that, at least by implication, the poem counsels to courage rather than despair.

The old issue of pessimism versus optimism is treated once more in Carlos Baker's "Robinson's Stoical Optimism" (NEQ, Mar. 1973), but the interest lies not in the threadbare theme but in the evidence of Robinson's familiarity with Wordsworth and Keats.

One still finds, however, that some critics persist in viewing Robinson as a pessimist; and William J. Wilson, in an unpublished dissertation, "Existentialist Implications in Edwin Arlington Robinson's Pessimism" (Univ. of Nebraska-Lincoln, 1973), carries this view to its extreme in arguing that Robinson is an "agnostic existentialist." Acknowledging that some poems are optimistic, the critic asserts that the great majority show that "Robinson regards the world as a cosmic joke played upon mankind," and that "attitudes of agnosticism, loneliness, alienation, failure, despair, futility" ally him to the existentialists. Evidently Wilson did not encounter Robinson's remark, "apropos of Hardy's pessimism, that Hardy's blunder, both philosophical and artistic, was his reiteration of the idea of God jesting with mankind." And of course Robinson himself always vehemently denied the allegation of pessimism.

Turning aside from general issues, we find that critics continue to comment on Robinson's short narrative-dramatic poems. One not hitherto studied in detail is shown to be worthy of such study in Donald E. Stanford's "Edwin Arlington Robinson's 'The Wandering Jew'" (TSE, 1978). The first part of the essay offers a close reading of the text, concludes that the "major moral and psychological theme is pride," and accords deserved praise to the style. The latter part attempts to identify the main character with Alfred H. Louis, who had previously sat for the portrait of Captain Craig. Stanford asserts that the poem contains an "exact and precise description of Louis," though this is hardly consistent with Robinson's own statement (which is quoted) that the poem was "perhaps suggested by a learned old Hebrew that I met in New York, but it is mostly fancy."

Another poem hitherto neglected by the critics is analyzed in G. E. Slethaug's "The King in Robinson's 'Old King Cole'" (*EngR*, Feb. 1971). On the basis of a comparison with *King Jasper*, along with a concept of "King" derived from a passage in Hawthorne, the critic views the central character as "the patronizing, proud, and arrogant head of the old order," who "ignores his responsibilities to his family and community." No "ripe old age" awaits him but "the kind of nemesis that ultimately destroys King Jasper and his mythical kingdom." This interpretation involves a certain measure of ingenuity, but one might argue for the simpler view that the poem is an admiring though humorous portrait of a man able to rise above misfortunes over which he has no control.

A footnote to one of Robinson's most admired poems is Ronald E. McFarland's "Some Observations on Carew's 'Song' and Robinson's 'For a Dead Lady'" (*MarkhamR*, Fall–Winter 1980–81). Asserting that the comparison aims not at demonstrating an influence but rather defining the quality of each poem, he comments: "What gives Robinson's lyric its particular appeal . . . is its mixture of the mundane with the profound." He adds that both pieces are "poems concerning an idea, not celebrations of personalities."

A crucial factor in the interpretation of many of Robinson's poems, especially those concerned with the delineation of character, is the ambiguity, dwelt on by Lie and Manheimer, of the attitude of the speaker or narrator—the persona—to the central character. Thus, Mordecai Marcus asks, in "E. A. Robinson's 'Flammonde': Some Essential Clarifications" (*MarkhamR*, Oct. 1971), "how reliable are the narrator and the point of view he represents?" His answer is that the narrator is "deeply involved" and generally to be trusted, and he attacks vehemently the view of William J. Free (in *Edwin Arlington Robinson: Centenary Essays* [1969]) that the narrator's understanding is limited. The critics agree, however, in finding Flammonde to be an essentially heroic figure.

Often, however, as in the case of "Old King Cole," different interpretations are totally incompatible; and in considering conflicting opinions, one should keep in mind two of the poet's own comments. Acutely aware of, yet unable to comprehend, readers' difficulty in understanding his poems, he once remarked about "Twilight Song": "I am bothered by the certainty that everyone who reads it will try to read a thousand things into it that I never dreamed of putting there." And elsewhere he more than half seriously regrets "having been born to such an ornery lot as that of an 'intellectual poet'—when, as a matter of fact, anything like a proper comprehension of his product was, and is . . . a matter of feeling, not of cerebration."

These remarks are certainly relevant to "Luke Havergal," a long-standing challenge to readers who, unlike Theodore Roosevelt, must "understand" it in order to "like" it. Bertrand F. Richards, in "No There Is Not a Dawn" (*CLQ*, Sept. 1971), after offering such outrageous (tongue-in-cheek?) suggestions as that Luke's last name is a pun ("Havergal" equals "have a gal"), offers three more rational, if speculative, interpretations: that the poem deals with "lost love and suicide," either with reference to an individual (this is of course a common view) or to mankind in general; or that it is a "personal expression of a poet's despair over the real or fancied loss of his creative ability." Less imaginative and more academic is the approach of Ronald McFarland in "Robinson's 'Luke Havergal'" (*CLQ*, June 1974), which presents a number of more or less plausible parallels with Dante's *Divine Comedy*.

A seemingly simpler poem, and one which for the better part of a century has perhaps been Robinson's most popular, still offers critics a chance to test their ingenuity. Charles A. Sweet, Jr., in "A Re-examination of 'Richard Cory'" (*CLQ*, Sept. 1972), contends that the central character, contrary to the conventional view that he commits suicide because of some unspecified inner flaw, is in fact a heroic figure, driven to self-destruction by the stupidity and envy of a community that forces upon him an undesired and undeserved isolation.

On the other hand, in "Richard Cory's Suicide: A Psychoanalyst's View" (*CLQ*, Sept. 1975), Jerome Kavka argues that Cory is a narcissist, who was "neither able to join the townsmen or to lead them," so that his life was "useless." This is followed by a brief article, "An Artist Without an Art" (*CLQ*, Sept. 1975), in which Lawrence Kart generally concurs but suggests a supplementary conclusion: Richard Cory's work of art is himself, but he fails as an artist because he cuts himself off from his audience.

An unexpected parallel with the character of Richard Cory is suggested in Giles Zimmer's "Grangerford and Cory: Similar Creations" (*MTJ*, Spring 1983), which notes similarities between the language used in Robinson's poem and that used by Huckleberry Finn in describing Colonel Grangerford, and in the character traits of the two, especially an inner weakness which leads to a violent death. The critic does not argue for a direct influence, but a comment in a letter to Josephine Preston Peabody reveals Robinson's unbounded admiration for *Huckleberry Finn*.

"Miniver Cheevy" always accompanies "Richard Cory" in anthologies, and even more arresting than any of the interpretations of the latter is that of the former offered by Michael G. Miller in "Miniver Grows Lean" (*CLQ*, Sept. 1976). Miniver's problem, it is argued, is not alcoholism but tuberculosis.

Eben Flood in "Mr. Flood's Party" is another Robinson character who has usually been viewed as too reliant on alcohol for escape from the harshness of reality, though presented with sympathy as well as humor. But this view is challenged by Joseph H. Harkey in "Mr. Flood's Two

Moons" (*MTJ*, Summer 1971), in which it is argued that the two moons seen by Mr. Flood are not the result of drink-induced double vision, but that the second is "a past harvest moon conjured up by him" in a pathetic, or even tragic, "attempt to escape from loneliness." The critic is certainly right in saying that Mr. Flood is not a "comic drunkard," but perhaps the "feeling" of most readers will still be that the two moons are contemporary.

Readers interested in possible sources of this poem will find suggestions in Carlos Baker's "The Jug Makes the Paradise: New Light on 'Eben Flood'" (*CLQ*, June 1974), which notes a possible indebtedness to James Kirke Paulding's "The Old Man's Carousal"; and Thomas L. Brasher's "Robinson's 'Mr. Flood's Party'" (*Expl*, Feb. 1971), where it is argued that the reference to Roland's horn is more probably a recollection of Browning's "Childe Roland to the Dark Tower Came" than of the medieval *Chanson de Roland*. It is noted that "enduring to the end" echoes Browning's answer to a question as to the theme of the poem. One may think that both works contributed; which is judged more important depends, again, on one's "feeling" about the mood of Robinson's poem.

Unfortunately, neither feeling nor cerebration helps much with "Lost Anchors," a poem that to this reader remains impenetrable despite ingenious efforts to fathom Robinson's intent. One of the most imaginative is James Grimshaw's "Robinson's 'Lost Anchors'" (*Expl*, Dec. 1971), in which it is suggested that "the anchors . . . represent the tenets of Judeo-Christian faith. . . . The sailor is a personification of Christ . . . the harbor-drowned vessel is the defunct (i.e., not operating) religion . . . the divers are ministers, priests, religious men who descend in the sense of diving into the exaltation of religious experience . . . the legend, of course, is Christ's legend that had lived its way around the world of religious denominations."

Slightly less implausible is the proposal of Richard Tuerk in "Robinson's 'Lost Anchors'" (*Expl*, Jan. 1974). After noting a number of biblical echoes in the phrasing, he concludes that the "lost anchors represent lost hope, especially the hope of salvation"; "the world of ships equals the world in which we live, and the anchorless ships [of which the sailor is one], equal men without hope." The trouble with this is that the text says nothing about "anchorless ships," and the sailor is compared not to a ship but to a fish.

With no wish to deter future adventurers, one may perhaps apply to "Lost Anchors" Robinson's half-apologetic comment about "The Whip": "In this poem—not to mention a few others—I may have gone a little too far and given the reader too much to carry. . . . I am inclined to believe that this particular poem is not altogether satisfactory or very important."

"Veteran Sirens" is another poem that has received conflicting interpretations, beginning with Yvor Winters's comment (*Edwin Arlington Robin-*

son [1946]) that it is "an expression of pity for old prostitutes." Laurence Perrine took issue with this view (*Expl*, Nov. 1947), advancing the notion, shared by Ellsworth Barnard (1952), that the "sirens" are, in the words of the latter, "superannuated flirts." Winters's interpretation is revived, however, by Ronald Moran in "Lorraine and the Sirens: Courtesans in Two Poems of E. A. Robinson," in *Essays in Honor of Esmond Linworth Marilla* (ed. Thomas A. Kirby and William J. Olive, Baton Rouge, La., 1970). Moran insists that "the compelling evidence [for this view] is in the poem itself." Much is made of the reference to "Ninon" (Ninon de l'Enclos, mistress of Louis XV of France). In addition, he suggests that in "anguish has no eye for grace," "'anguish' refers to the forces that prompt men to go to brothels"; that in the lines "While time's malicious mercy cautions them / To think a while of number and of space," "'number' refers literally to the number of men the prostitutes must entertain; 'space' refers to the time interval between each appointment"; "'the burning hope' is what men approaching the experience are looking for; 'the worn expectancy' is all the women really have to offer"; and so on. If this is not a deliberate parody of the misdirected "cerebration" to which many of Robinson's poems have been subjected, it misses two significant points: first, that the tone of the poem is playfully humorous (Ninon's fame is not as a mere courtesan but a great lady admired for her beauty and intelligence); and second, that, granting the lightness and humor, it is inconceivable that Robinson would have treated prostitution in this manner.

As for Lorraine, in "The Growth of 'Lorraine,'" she obviously *is* a prostitute. But Moran's suggested motive for her suicide—"some girls, because of their mental and physical natures, are able to endure (and probably enjoy) a promiscuous life; but Lorraine is simply unable to take the demands exacted upon her"—involves a bluntness of perception that takes no account of Robinson's subtlety, and ignores the more plausible interpretation that "the love that flings" is her love, once denied but now acknowledged, for the narrator. Equally questionable is the assumption of "the speaker's obvious lack of understanding and compassion"; one might argue, rather, that he is not "surprised," because he *does* understand her character, and he is not "grieved," because her decision to end a life of degradation bears witness to the better self in which he had always believed.

Moran's assumption, however, is accepted by Leon Satterfield, who in "Robinson's 'Leonora'" (*Expl*, Nov. 1971) comments that "the reader condemns the speaker, not Lorraine, for his blindness and subsequent indifference." He draws a parallel with "Leonora," in which he finds Robinson condemning the "monstrously presumptuous and sanctimonious" attitude of the townspeople, who "see her death as a blessing which will keep Leonora from a life of sin." This interpretation, at least, is persuasive.

Satterfield has also commented on "An Evangelist's Wife" (*Expl*, Spring 1983), pointing out the allusion in the last two lines to the story of David and one of his wives, Michal, in II Samuel 6.14–23. In this curiously unpleasant episode, Michal scolds David for dancing "before the Lord"— and, according to her, before the "Maidservants"—clad only in an ephod (a linen apron). David, angered, vows to "be more vile than thus" and to "be had in honor" by the maidservants, while rejecting *her* (apparently, since she "had no child unto the day of her death"). Pushing the parallel, Satterfield suggests that the minister has been having affairs with *several* women in the congregation—not just with "Her"—thus earning his wife's reproaches. One difficulty is that in the biblical story the narrator implies that Michal is initially to blame because of her jealousy, whereas in Robinson's poem the reader's sympathy seems to this observer to be clearly with the wife. But this does not necessarily invalidate Satterfield's conclusion.

Satterfield has also rehearsed, in "Bubble-Work in Gardiner, Maine: The Poetry War of 1924" (*NEQ*, March 1984), the long-running argument as to the interpretation of Robinson's sonnet "New England," first published in the London *Outlook* toward the end of 1923 and reprinted in the *Literary Digest* and the *New Republic* in December of that year. It stirred a small tempest in the *Gardiner Journal*, beginning with an attack on Robinson by a local patriot named Darling for publishing (and in *England*!) what he takes to be a condemnation of the New England character. Robinson's friend Laura E. Richards responded by quoting from a letter to her in which the poet said, "It was supposed to be aimed at those who patronize New England." Later Robinson himself wrote a letter to the *Journal* stating his inability to see how the sonnet made sense "if read in any other way than as an attack on all those who are forever throwing dead cats at New England for its emotional and moral frigidity." He also, when he collected the piece, made several changes in the text which were intended to clarify the meaning. Satterfield notes, however, that serious critics have continued to question whether the piece *actually* gives the impression that the poet says he intended; and he concludes that the poem shows "a rare failure in Robinson's irony."

Lengthening the list of explications of particular poems is Laurence Perrine's analysis of "The Tree in Pamela's Garden" (*Expl*, Nov. 1971). This sonnet has usually been taken as the portrait of a woman (like Aunt Imogen) resigned to a life of spinsterhood; but Perrine suggests, not implausibly, that Pamela "has had, or more likely is having, a secret love affair," and "smiles" at her success in deceiving the townspeople; the tree is the Tree of Knowledge.

The latest effort to supply a novel interpretation to a particular poem is "Allusion and Symbol in Robinson's 'Eros Turannos'" (*CLQ*, March 1984), by C. Hines Edwards, Jr. Here Freud supplies the light that dispels for this critic the ambiguities perceived by many previous readers.

Trees and ocean, for instance, are taken as sex symbols; the crisis occurs because the husband's increasing impotence as age advances leaves the wife's unabated sexual desires unsatisfied. "Clearly, the tragedy of the woman stems from extreme sexual frustration . . . [and] driven insane or nearly insane," she drowns herself. This reading has the virtue of being simple and definite. But some persons may question whether Edwards's "symbols" are really more than metaphors or descriptive details and may feel that much of the poem's effectiveness lies in the aura of uncertainty that surrounds the action—"As if the story of a house / Were told, or ever could be."

It is appropriate, in ending this discussion of the varying interpretations of many Robinson poems, to quote the poet's now famous answer to the earnest lady admirer who asked for an "easy way" to understand his poetry: "I don't know that there is any, except just to read it, one word after another." Still, the commonsense approach implied in this statement does not always work, and (as Falstaff opines, perhaps more wisely than he intends) "thought is free." As Richards says at the end of his essay on "Luke Havergal," "however meager the results [or, he might have added, how seemingly far-fetched], a thorough examination of the poem itself can engender an experience which is its own reward."

VI SUPPLEMENT

Bibliography. The editors of the Scarecrow Press evidently think that there is still some interest in Robinson, since that firm has recently issued *Edwin Arlington Robinson and the Critics: A Bibliography of Secondary Sources with Selective Annotations*, by Jeanetta Boswell (Metuchen, N.J., 1988). Unfortunately, the author does not make clear how or by whom the 276-page list of 1,383 published writings is intended to be used. The scope of the project, the arrangement of the materials, and the content of the annotations all present problems. The author's bibliographic broom has swept up a huge mass of heterogeneous material, ranging from full-length books to brief newspaper reviews of these books, arranged alphabetically according to authors' names, beginning with "Anonymous." It does not claim to be exhaustive, yet there seems to be no other reason for some of the listings.

Most of the items are annotated, often with a single quotation from the work itself but sometimes with an editorial summary; and, since quotation marks are usually dispensed with, the reader must often guess which is which. Moreover, there seems to be no rule governing the length of the annotations; a review of a book may be given as much space as the book itself. And the selection of quotations is also eccentric. For instance, a 300-page critical study is represented by a ten-line quotation concerning the allegorical significance of one character in one of the long poems. And there is at least one careless error: an article by

Wallace Anderson is listed as being by Newton Arvin. A vast amount of work obviously went into this volume, and even specialists may run across items that they were previously unaware of. It is a matter of regret that the presentation of the material is seriously flawed.

A more modest undertaking is A. Carl Bredahl's "A Descriptive Catalogue of the Edwin Arlington Robinson Collection," in *The Parkman Dexter Howe Library, Part IV* (Gainesville, Fla., 1986). This collection, as the foreword notes, "offers scholars the opportunity to work with an almost complete collection of first editions of Robinson's works." It also contains the various editions of *Collected Poems*, beginning in 1921, and the volume of selections titled *Tilbury Town*, edited by Lawrance Thompson, published in 1953. Included are the rare first volume *The Torrent and The Night Before* and the still rarer pirated *Three Poems*; also, besides the "trade editions" of the later volumes, there are copies of the limited editions that Robinson's fame made profitable. The only significant omissions are the *Selected Poems*, with a preface by Bliss Perry, bound in one volume with Cestre's *Introduction to Edwin Arlington Robinson* (1931), and the essay "The First Seven Years," in *Colophon* (Dec. 1930).

Criticism. Interest in Robinson's work, which, judging by the amount of published material, was almost nonexistent during the 1980s, has experienced a tentative revival. It is noteworthy that recent writings, in contrast to the comments of the previous generation of critics, are concerned mainly with the content of the poet's work rather than the form, the substance rather than the style, the thought rather than the art. What may loosely be called his philosophy, dismissed if not derided by most critics in recent decades, is now considered worthy of comment. And even the long poems, thrust aside as "unreadable," now apparently find readers.

A major work is David H. Burton's *Edwin Arlington Robinson: Stages in a New England Poet's Search* (Lewiston, N.Y., 1988). The critic's aim here is to present Robinson's poetry in relation to cultural trends in America during the four decades of his writing career. The general theme is the tension between his temperamental bent toward the traditional in art, ethics, and religion and the contemporary changes in these areas that his realistic vision compelled him to confront. Although this "dilemma," as Burton notes, has been a standard topic in Robinson criticism, it has never before been treated so fully and systematically. The work is also significant as illustrating the trends noted above, in the undivided attention directed toward the intellectual content of the poetry and in its unabashed interest in the long poems, not only the early "Captain Craig" and the *Merlin* and *Lancelot* of the middle period but in what may be called the novels in verse to which he devoted himself almost exclusively in his last years. Through the protagonists in these poems, it is contended, Robinson offered penetrating comments on prevailing cultural trends. The critic's main concerns are suggested by the titles of the last three chapters: "War and Democracy," "Soul and Psyche," and "An Idea of God."

Contrasting with the noncontroversial tone of Burton's work is Robert McDowell's "Recovering E. A. R. and the Narrative of Talk" (*NER*, Autumn 1985), which offers a vehement defense of Robinson against "contemporary arrogance and impatience." The writer stresses the poet's dramatic method, his rejection of the "thrill of confession" in favor of the "story told truthfully." He praises the "narratives of talk," with their "linguistic flexibility," "which, at their best, represent some of the finest American dramatic moments ever written." In the same vein, he says of the long poems, specifically *Merlin* and *Lancelot*, "In dramatic scope they have no rivals in our literature."

Not unsympathetic but more detached, and offering a different response, is George S. Lensing's "E. A. Robinson: The Sad, Wry Poet" (in *American Poetry between Tradition and Modernism*, ed. Roland Hagenbüchle, Regensburg, 1984). Asserting Robinson's "legitimate claim to the company of the modernists, both in his use of language and his attitude toward his subjects," the critic notes affinities with T. S. Eliot, Robert Frost, and Robert Lowell, but at the same time stresses his isolation from any school or group. This is related, in Lensing's view, to the personal isolation and loneliness that marked much of the poet's life. The unique quality of his work lies in "a wry and barely audible voice that would parry and thrust discreetly at Life's inescapable reversals." This attitude and its accompanying technique are illustrated by analyses of a number of the short poems. Lensing agrees with many earlier critics that it is "only on the basis" of such poems that "Robinson will survive."

Robinson is also discussed at some length by Hagenbüchle in his introduction to the same volume as "the only indisputably pivotal figure between tradition and modernism." The critic sees the poet as completely rejecting traditional certainties and speaks of "his redefinition of heroism as the gradual surrender of self-deception," elaborating the thought by stating that man's ability to achieve "complete self-knowledge" and still retain "a modicum of self-respect engaged his admiration and sympathy." It may be pointed out that if, as Hagenbüchle seems to say, "complete self-knowledge" involves the recognition "that man's search for a self-image is illusory," "that something cannot be grasped because it simply is not there," this is a view that Robinson himself consistently and vehemently rejected. But one may still agree that "Robinson—at his best—in utter honesty gave voice to the deepest perplexities and fears of his time."

The same general theme is treated by Ronald Primeau in "Robinson and Browning Revisited: 'Man Against the Sky' and 'Childe Roland'" (*CollL*, Fall 1985): "Read alongside 'Childe Roland,' 'The Man Against the Sky' reveals a tough and paradoxically triumphant futility," and both poems "take their place in literature as peculiarly modern renditions of the ancient quest motif." In both the quest is "internalized," and in both the ending is ambiguous, making possible a reading of them as pessimistic. But Primeau argues persuasively that in both poems the conclusion is positive, both in intention and in effect.

Another comparison between a work by Robinson and that of a nineteenth-century poet is found in "*Merlin*: E. A. Robinson's Debt to Emerson," by Owen W. Gilman, Jr. (*CLQ*, Sept. 1985). The author points out that Robinson in *Merlin* not only repeats specific words used by Emerson in "Merlin I" and "Merlin II," but also advances similar concepts. In Robinson's poem the despairing Arthur sees Merlin as a person "Whose Nemesis had made of him a slave, / A man of dalliance and a sybarite"; in "Merlin I" Emerson speaks of the sage as "By Sybarites beguiled" (though not enslaved), and in "Merlin II" describes "Nemesis" as a governing force in the universe. But, beyond this, "each poet's vision of Merlin is centered on Merlin's mediating capacity, his role as one who 'reconciles' or brings together conflicting elements in the world." In developing this theme Gilman offers a number of new insights into Robinson's characterization of Merlin. He fails to point out, however, a basic difference in the poets' treatment of the character: whereas Emerson's Merlin is a purely mythic and heroic character, Robinson's is one in which the mythic elements, though still present, are subordinated to the human and fallible.

The theme of tradition versus modernism in Robinson, prominent in the writings so far mentioned, is given further treatment by Dorothy Schuchman McCoy in "The Arthurian Strain in Early Twentieth-Century Literature: Cabell, T. S. Eliot, and E. A. Robinson" (*WVUPP*, 1982), which analyzes the role played by Merlin in Cabell's *Jurgen*, Eliot's *The Waste Land* (where Merlin is identified with the observer-seer-speaker), and Robinson's *Merlin*. All three works show a "modern suspicion of romance" and pose the question of "how much unvarnished reality mankind can accept," of how to resolve "the conflict of the seer's perceptions and his reason." Cabell is "the comic realist of acceptance"; Eliot is "the tragic realist of waste"; Robinson is "the psychological realist, studying the possibility of finding a new code for man's struggles to produce stimuli to accomplishment which are not entirely self-regarding."

Descending from the realm of philosophical inquiry to that of everyday existence, we find Winifred H. Sullivan exploring "The Double-Edged Irony of E. A. Robinson's 'Miniver Cheevy'" (*CLQ*, Sept. 1986). Even in this light-hearted portrait, however, in which the poet appears to be indulging in cheerful self-mockery, we find also the issue of realism versus romance and modernism versus antimodernism: "More than a clever spoof of Robinson, as Miniver, the poem satirizes the age and, especially, its literary taste." Miniver's yearning for the imagined glories of the past is a jab at the popular appetite, around the turn of the century, for romantic fiction set in an unreal past. Miniver's "scorn" of "the gold he sought" is an oblique comment on the gap between the professed moral ideals and the obsessive pursuit of wealth that the poet observed in many of his countrymen. Sullivan concludes, "This poem, popular and enjoyable in any reading, warrants reflection, after all, and by the demands and rewards of reflection proves the richer."

Besides the published material, there has been a recent dissertation on Robinson, Irwin Robert Blacker's "Primal Conflict and Modern American Long Narrative Poetry" (Case Western Reserve Univ., 1984). "Primal conflict," defined as "that which takes place within the immediate family," is said to be "more intense" than other forms of conflict: "In the twin poems *Merlin* and *Lancelot*, Robinson used sex, adultery, incest, family hatred, patricide, matricide, and infanticide in ways that had not previously been done in long narrative poetry." This is "modernism" with a vengeance.

John Steinbeck

Warren French

I BIBLIOGRAPHY

Since the last revision of this work, Tetsumaro Hayashi has published both *A New Steinbeck Bibliography (1929–1971)* (Metuchen, N.J., 1973) that updates and completely reorganizes his pioneering work in 1967 and *A New Steinbeck Bibliography: 1971–1981* (Metuchen, N.J., 1983), which completes—in an even further improved fashion—the record of what may be designated as the first period of Steinbeck scholarship. Hayashi's two volumes list both works by and about Steinbeck and are described in the more recent volume as "selective rather than exhaustive" (including only unannotated titles). Only "important critical sources, published or reprinted in English," mostly in the United States, are mentioned, though some foreign material of special interest is included. Hayashi has also edited with the help of a competent group of collaborators *John Steinbeck: A Dictionary of His Fictional Characters* (Metuchen, N.J., 1976), which provides a finding list of the figures in his novels and short stories with some discussion of their significance.

Two shorter compilations provide a start toward the more detailed works eventually needed. Robert B. Harmon's *The First Editions of John Steinbeck* (Los Altos, Calif., 1978) describes these now valuable titles, and Roy S. Simmonds has compiled "John Steinbeck's World War II Dispatches: An Annotated Checklist" (*Serif*, Summer 1974). Of unique value is bookseller Bradford Morrow's *John Steinbeck: A Collection of Books and Manuscripts Formed by Harry Valentine of Pacific Grove, California* (Santa Barbara, Calif., 1980), which provides detailed descriptions of unique materials and rare publications.

Invaluable also are four guides to the holdings of libraries with important Steinbeck collections. Early Steinbeck enthusiast Adrian Goldstone collaborated with John R. Payne on *John Steinbeck: A Bibliographical Catalogue of the Adrian H. Goldstone Collection* (Austin, Tex., 1974), describing the holdings of the University of Texas Humanities Research Center. John Gross and Lee Richard Hayman have compiled *John Steinbeck:*

A Guide to the Collection of the Salinas Public Library (Salinas, Calif., 1979), now named in honor of the hometown boy, and Susan F. Riggs followed with *A Catalogue of the John Steinbeck Collection at Stanford* (Stanford, Calif., 1980), the university Steinbeck intermittently attended without graduating.

The most recent addition to this group of guides is the late Robert H. Woodward's *The Steinbeck Research Center at San Jose State University: A Descriptive Catalogue* (San Jose, Calif., 1985), which was also published as the Winter 1985 issue of *San Jose Studies*. A special feature, "Steinbeck Research Libraries in the United States" (*StQ*, Summer–Fall 1978), also supplements these with descriptions of the Texas and Stanford holdings by Payne and Riggs, an account of the collection at San Jose State by Martha Heasley Cox, and "The Steinbeck Collection in Honor of Elizabeth R. Otis at the Alexander M. Bracken Library, Ball State University" by Juanita Smith. A controversial library holding is discussed in Robert S. Hughes, Jr.'s "Steinbeck Stories at the Houghton Library" (*HLB*, Jan. 1982), which argues that four unpublished manuscripts there are, despite earlier disputes, authentically Steinbeck's work.

Tetsumaro Hayashi has followed up his early guide to doctoral dissertations on Steinbeck (1971) with *Steinbeck and Hemingway: Dissertation Abstracts and Research Opportunities* (Metuchen, N.J., 1980), which reprints abstracts through 1977. Related to this work, which contains an article by Richard F. Peterson on "Research Opportunities in John Steinbeck," is a series, "Advice to a Graduate Student" (*StQ*, Spring 1973), by Richard Astro, Martha Cox, John Ditsky, Warren French, and Reloy Garcia. This project led to *A Handbook for Steinbeck Collectors, Librarians, and Scholars* (SMS No. 11, Muncie, Ind., 1981), edited by Tetsumaro Hayashi, which reviews at greater length many of the bibliographical works already mentioned.

II MANUSCRIPTS AND LETTERS

The special bibliographies of collections mentioned above describe archives of Steinbeck manuscripts. Additional material is in the Library of Congress, the Annie Laurie Williams collection at Columbia University, and the Pierpont Morgan Library in New York. The Bancroft Library at the University of California at Berkeley also has a substantial collection of letters, and the University of Minnesota library has acquired an impressive collection of first editions.

During his lifetime, Steinbeck disliked seeing himself rather than his work discussed, so he resented publication from his private papers. The kind of introduction needed to a writer of this complexity was not provided until a selection from his correspondence was made by his widow and a close friend for *Steinbeck: A Life in Letters* (ed. Elaine Steinbeck and Robert Wallsten, New York, 1975). Although this selection of a small portion of his voluminous correspondence, with only excerpts from individual letters sometimes included, was prepared for a commercial rather than a scholarly audience, it is an obvious labor of perhaps unnecessarily overprotective love by those close to him that does provide insights into his activities and into his relationships with the perhaps neurotically closed group whose friendships he valued.

Other letters to many of them, again with cuts, were published in an appendix to *The Acts of King Arthur and His Noble Knights* (New York, 1976), concerning his intention to create a modernized version of Malory's *Morte d'Arthur*. These include many excerpts from his voluminous correspondence with his longtime agent Elizabeth Otis. Another forty-four pieces from this correspondence have been published in a limited edition that is already commanding record prices from collectors as *Letters to Elizabeth: A Selection of Letters from John Steinbeck to Elizabeth Otis* (ed. Florian J. Shasky and Susan F. Riggs, San Francisco, 1978).

Illuminating material from Steinbeck's particularly important correspondence with his longtime, devoted editor Pascal Covici also turns up in Thomas Fensch's *Steinbeck and Covici: The Story of a Friendship* (Middlebury, Vt., 1979), a very uneven work derived from a 1977 doctoral dissertation. The book is valuable because Fensch went back to the original letters to check errors in *A Life in Letters* and to restore full texts of many excised there, but it fails to do justice to these materials because of the limited scholarship demonstrated by the minimal annotations and obvious comments.

III BIOGRAPHY

Steinbeck's reticence, usually expressed with vehement displeasure, prevented the publication during his lifetime of any detailed, authoritative biography. Shortly after the novelist's death, however, Jackson J. Benson began assembling materials for such a book with Elaine Steinbeck's cooperation. This ambitious effort preoccupied Benson for thirteen difficult years, but in January 1984 he could hold in his hand the eleven-hundred-page record. The appearance of *The True Adventures of John Steinbeck, Writer* (New York, 1984) is an event of such magnitude in Steinbeck studies that it necessitates a fresh beginning for the study of the man and his works. All Steinbeck study is going to be henceforth labeled as before-or-after January 1984.

Benson in his brief preface explains, "My first job in writing this book has been to get the facts straight. But beyond that, my most important task has been to try to bring a man alive, a very complicated man who led a very vivid and eventful life." The facts are certainly here, more than one would have thought could be unearthed, more than can be assimilated in any single reading, yet definitely no more than the little girl wanted to know about penguins. Benson's labors deserve highest honors; and he has even made a start toward achieving that difficult second purpose he assigned himself, though it will require the insights of many speculative minds before the evidence that Benson painstakingly has assembled begins to give us a comprehension of how the man behind the books could have been the man behind the books.

Wisely, Benson has avoided the trap into which many doorstop biographers have stepped of attempting to get the facts straight and evaluating the writer's achievements in the same work. After a sound assessment of the criticisms of Steinbeck's obscure first novel *Cup of Gold*, Benson, as space alone would have necessitated, does not attempt to arbitrate critical disputes. The remarkable thing is that through what must have proved exasperating labors that could well have induced the Mark Schorer syndrome, Benson manages to remain throughout his long account open-minded, sympathetic, so that if we do not quite get the unlikely evocation of Steinbeck alive, we do get a warm, compassionate picture of a man not having been prepared to face his destiny (like many fine recent American writers). Part of the success of the book must be attributed to Benson's own California background; he writes as a native son about a native son, who in a provincial sense went wrong, and this is the kind of a book that we need about a California artist. The finest chapters in the book are those in which Benson deals with Steinbeck's slowly growing realization after World War II of Thomas Wolfe's discovery that "you can't go home again."

The earlier attempts at biography that Steinbeck himself proscribed are almost completely superseded by Benson's work. Budd Schulberg's sob-brother account of Steinbeck's dying days in *The Four Seasons of Success* (New York, 1972) is too embarrassing even to discuss at this late date. As for Thomas Kiernan's attempt to beat Benson to the market with *The Intricate Music: A Biography of John Steinbeck* (Boston, 1979), one can only share the consensus opinion of long-time Steinbeck scholars expressed in Robert DeMott's review (*JML*, Annual Review Number, 1980–81) that "Kiernan's book is so unreliable that it should be used with extreme caution or avoided altogether." Troubles begin with the introduction; Kiernan calls this the "first full-scale biography of John Steinbeck to be written," yet it devotes only fifty of some three hundred pages to the crowded years after 1945, a third of the author's lifetime during which he produced a dozen works. Even more irresponsible is that in explaining the inspiration for his book in a conversation in which Steinbeck is *quoted* as having said, "if somebody wanted to write my biography with a view to showing me exactly how my storytelling imagination developed, I might be interested in reading it," Kiernan also comments, "I do not quote him verbatim, rather, I give the sense of what he said based on notes I took afterward." Anyone requiring a full bill of particulars for avoiding Kiernan's book, as well as Thomas Fensch's (except for the letters quoted), should consult Robert DeMott's review cited above.

Much more to be valued, though still trivial, is Nelson Valjean's *John Steinbeck: The Errant Knight* (San Francisco, 1975), an account by a former California newspaperman of Steinbeck's life in California through 1941 that details many personal incidents and suggests the sources of many of Steinbeck's works; but the lack of any documentation makes the book only a gossipy, old-buddy account of little scholarly value. Of more permanent worth, despite its unattractive form as a photocopied edition of corrected, typed sheets, is Carlton "Dook" Sheffield's *Steinbeck: The Good Companion* (Portola Valley, Calif., 1983), a warm and affectionate account of the author by the lifelong friend that he met at Stanford during one of his early stays there. Also of permanent value is Joel W. Hedgpeth's *The Outer Shores* (Eureka, Calif., 1978), a two-volume study that principally concerns Ed Ricketts's life and writings, but that chronicles in the first volume Ricketts's and Steinbeck's explorations of the Pacific coast. One account of significance not mentioned by Benson is Sherwood Anderson's diary entry about his meeting with Steinbeck, with whom he developed an immediate rapport, on 14 November 1939, as reported in Ray Lewis White's "Sherwood Anderson Meets John Steinbeck, 1939" (*StQ*, Winter 1978). There are also valuable informal photographs of Steinbeck at an outdoor party at Big Sur on 31 July 1935 in John D. Short, Jr.'s "John Steinbeck: A 1930's Photo-Recollection" (*SJS*, May 1976).

A most interesting comparison with part of Benson's comprehensive biography is afforded by Roy S. Simmonds's "Steinbeck and World War II: The Moon Goes Down" (*StQ*, Winter–Spring 1984), an account of Steinbeck's literary activities between May 1940 and May 1945, written in England by a British scholar, working entirely independently. The article appeared only a few weeks after Benson's book, but there are no noticeable discrepancies between them. Benson's approximately 125 pages covering the same five years contain, of course, far more personal detail than Simmonds's twenty pages. The briefer piece has the advantage, though, for readers entirely unfamiliar with the subject, of focusing on only one strand of interrelated events and leading to a testimonial to *The Moon Is Down*—which has always been more greatly admired in Europe than in the United States—as "one of the mere handful" of propagandist war fictions that have survived.

The perfect complement to Benson's monumental book appeared at almost the same time. The modest format of Robert DeMott's *Steinbeck's Reading: A Catalogue of Books Owned and Borrowed* (New York, 1984) belies the prodigious labor involved in preparing an account of the books that Steinbeck is known to have owned and read and its value in understanding both the writings and the literary tastes of this shy, secretive genius. Jackson J. Benson is quite scrupulous about documenting influences on Steinbeck's work, but his book could not delve into the history of Steinbeck as reader. DeMott begins his study with a brief account of what is known about the changes in Steinbeck's preferences over the years and follows this with a catalogue of titles—illustrated with Steinbeck's comments about the books—and an extensive and illuminating series of footnotes. The book is further enriched with photographs of the novelist, a list of books mentioned, selected letters, and a most valuable short bibliography of books by and about Steinbeck. If Benson has given us more of Steinbeck's life than we expected we might learn, DeMott has given us more of the elusive secrets of his mind.

Another approach to biography that has become popular since the rage two decades ago for "casebooks" is the compilation of documents that provide readers with the start towards a do-it-yourself biography. The *Dictionary of Literary Biography* has recently begun the publication of such material on a large scale with its "Documentary Series, an Illustrated Guide," volume 2 of which (Detroit, 1982) contains a more than fifty-page compilation of materials relating to John Steinbeck by Martha Heasley Cox. The collection consists largely of letters and reviews of the novels by prominent critics like Stark Young, Malcolm Cowley, and Bernard DeVoto, arranged in chronological order; and there are also interesting early articles about Steinbeck by Ella Winter and William Rose Benét, as well as numerous illustrations.

Since Steinbeck's death in 1968, he has also been twice honored by the government. His portrait appeared on a fifteen-cent postage stamp issued at Salinas, California, his birthplace, on the seventy-seventh anniversary of his birth, 27 February 1979. In 1984 he was pictured on a half-ounce gold medal struck as the last of a five-year series honoring two famous Americans annually. The relationship of the stamp to others honoring American writers is explained in Warren French's "The Political Context of the John Steinbeck Stamp," and the first-day-of-issue ceremonies are described by Lee Richard Hayman in an accompanying "Report from Salinas" (*StQ*, Summer–Fall 1979).

Finally, it should be noted that a number of recent books about Cannery Row and the Monterey peninsula, trading on Steinbeck's reputation, are generally tourism promotions without scholarly value. Of more than routine interest, however, is Ann-Marie Schmitz's *In Search of Steinbeck* (Los Altos, Calif., 1983), which contains a description and photographs of Steinbeck's five residences in California from 1930 through 1949.

IV CRITICISM

1 General Estimates

a. Full-length Studies. A steady flow of monographs about Steinbeck's work has continued to appear during the past decade, and we may expect it to speed up as the vast amount of material from the recent biographical and bibliographical works is assimilated.

The most important contribution to Steinbeck studies during the 1970s was Richard Astro's *John Steinbeck and Edward F. Ricketts: The Shaping of a Novelist* (Minneapolis, 1973), which discusses at length the complicated question of the influence on Steinbeck of Ricketts, a marine biologist who served as a model for the principal character in six Steinbeck novels, most importantly *In Dubious Battle* and *Cannery Row*, and shared and helped develop the novelist's interest in "non-teleological thinking." Astro analyzes the two men's contributions to "The Log" from *The Sea of Cortez*, an account of an expedition to the Gulf of California in 1940, and concludes that Steinbeck is at his best when he "integrates the marine biologist's way of seeing with his own commitment to human progress." (Astro's work now needs to be reexamined in comparison with Jackson J. Benson's long discussion of the same issues in chapters 14 and 15 of his Steinbeck biography.)

Also in 1973, Tetsumaro Hayashi's *Steinbeck's Literary Dimension: A Guide to Comparative Studies* (Metuchen, N.J.) collected nine essays from the *Steinbeck Quarterly* comparing Steinbeck with other novelists and one about his relationship with Adlai Stevenson. In a new essay commissioned for the collection, Richard F. Peterson, in "The God in Darkness: Steinbeck and D. H. Lawrence," continues a subject originated by Reloy Garcia and finds that the British novelist only briefly provided a model for Steinbeck in the early 1930s. In another essay commissioned for the collection, "Steinbeck and Salinger: Messiah-Moulders for a Sick Society," Warren French argues that both popular authors refreshed "the American literary idiom" by conjuring up "colloquial Messiahs" out of the "American myth of the perpetual frontier."

Fresh approaches to Steinbeck studies were also encouraged by the eleven numbers of the Steinbeck Monograph Series (SMS) issued by the Steinbeck Society of America between 1971 and 1981. In 1973 Lawrence William Jones's posthumous *John Steinbeck as Fabulist* (ed. Marston La France, SMS, No. 3, Muncie, Ind.) provided one of the most important analyses available of the failure of much of Steinbeck's later fiction, attributing it to the novelist's never developing "a compelling vision of evil to match his vision of good." In 1974 Tetsumaro Hayashi provided a building-block for future monographs by compiling *Steinbeck Criticism: A Review of Book-Length Studies (1939–1973)* (SMS, No. 4, Muncie, Ind.), reprinting some reviews from the *Steinbeck Quarterly* and commissioning new evaluations of earlier books. Hayashi also edited the first of two volumes comprising *A Study Guide to Steinbeck: A Handbook to His Major Works* (Metuchen, N.J., 1974; part 2 appeared from the same source in 1979). The first presents background information, plot synopsis, commentary, and an annotated bibliography for each of what Hayashi considered Steinbeck's twelve most important works, each by a different established Steinbeck scholar. In the second volume, ten more of Steinbeck's books are considered in five essays designed as an introduction for beginning students of the author.

The first new full-length close reading of Steinbeck's fiction in five years was Howard Levant's *The Novels of John Steinbeck: A Critical Study* (Columbia, Mo., 1974). Concerned like Jones with the comparative failure of Steinbeck's later fiction that many reviewers had simply attributed to events in his private life, Levant found an objective framework for analyzing the causes by studying all the works in terms of "structure" and "materials." His theory is that these were well balanced in the works written before 1945, but seriously out of balance after that.

The next year saw the appearance of a revised version of Warren French's *John Steinbeck* (TUSAS, Boston, 1975), in a revision that did not simply update the original 1961 edition, but constituted a complete rewriting of the book, except for the chapters on *The Grapes of Wrath* and *Cannery Row*, from an entirely new point of view. The first edition called attention to Steinbeck's allegory, his "non-teleological thinking," and the resemblance of his "theology" to the Transcendentalists. The new edition attempts to synthesize Donald Pizer's speculations on "late nineteenth-century Naturalism" with Jerry H. Bryant's critique in *The Open Decision* of "the drama of consciousness" (a term adopted from Henry James's preface to the New York Edition of *Roderick Hudson*) to produce "a viable concept of Naturalism." This concept is then used to reconsider Steinbeck's fiction in groups that reflect changes in his underlying philosophy and that suggest reasons for his uneven success when he abandons naturalistic writing for "dramas of consciousness," beginning at the time of his rewriting of the original version of *The Grapes of Wrath*.

Although this section is devoted to books exclusively about Steinbeck, French's article "John Steinbeck: A Usable Concept of Naturalism," in *American Literary Naturalism: A Reassessment* (ed. Yoshinobu Hakutani and Lewis Fried, Heidelberg, 1975), should be mentioned here because it is essentially a condensation of the main thesis of his revised book for a more professional audience, citing the short story "Flight" as Steinbeck's most prototypically naturalistic work and showing how it provides the basic structure for most of his novels from *The Pastures of Heaven* to *Of Mice and Men*.

French's search for an encompassing pattern to explain the surprising variety of Steinbeck's writing and his fluctuating success did not end with this revision of his initial study. The next year, he contributed "John Steinbeck and Modernism" to *Steinbeck's Prophetic Vision of America* (ed. Tetsumaro Hayashi and Kenneth D. Swan, Muncie, Ind., 1976), in which after discussing the problems of defining modernism, he treats Steinbeck's early novels as examples of the alienation most characteristic of the modernist sensibility. "In reshaping *L'Affaire Lettuceberg* into *The Grapes of Wrath*," however, French argues, the novelist "transcended the ironic detachment of Modernism with a new affirmative conception of individual regeneration" that associates him not so much with the recent postmodernist writers as it marks his "re-embracing of a Pre-Modernist,

Victorian compromise with traditional establishments." The author plans to use this preliminary sketch as the basis for a final revision of his basic work placing Steinbeck's work in the context of that of his distinguished contemporaries.

This bicentennial tribute to Steinbeck's "prophetic vision" contains also Kenneth D. Swan's "John Steinbeck: In Search of America," which portrays *The Grapes of Wrath* as concerning the memory of America as the promise of the realization of the Jeffersonian agrarian ideal, of the grim realities of the destruction of the dream by the Great Depression, and of the promise of what America might be if others, like the Joads, "learn hard lessons in the necessity of unity, love, and human co-operation"—a vision repeated in other Steinbeck novels. The book includes as well a chronology and bibliography by Tetsumaro Hayashi and a review of the critical debate over Steinbeck by coeditor Swan.

Meanwhile in 1975, Hayashi had also edited a collection of essays on *Steinbeck and the Arthurian Theme* (SMS, No. 5, Muncie, Ind.) introduced by Joseph Fontenrose and containing an expansion of his comments on the Arthurian motif in *Tortilla Flat* by Warren French. Renaissance scholar Arthur F. Kinney also updates an earlier study in *"Tortilla Flat* Re-Visited," but the major value of the collection lies in Roy S. Simmonds's two discussions of Steinbeck's then unfinished modernization of Malory's *Morte d'Arthur*, based on an examination of the typescript.

Simmonds is also responsible for the far too little-known work that should serve not as an introduction to Steinbeck criticism, but to the serious reading and understanding of his fiction, *Steinbeck's Literary Achievement* (SMS, No. 6, Muncie, Ind., 1976). It is an example of a work properly called an "appreciation" (which the *OED* defines as "the action of estimating qualities"), a traditional genre now rarely produced in the United States, but still very much alive in England, from which the finest examples have steadily emerged. Its author's message is best summed up in his own concluding sentence, following his tribute to Steinbeck's "immense artistic courage": "his work will date neither as rapidly nor with such finality as the work of some of his more stylistically daring and currently more highly regarded contemporaries." To arrive at this point, Simmonds examines "Steinbeck's Major Themes," stressing especially "the nationwide yearning of the American people for the better life, a paradise on earth," his often underappreciated humor, his style, and his sources and influences. This last matter needs reinvestigation in the light of Benson's and DeMott's findings, but the other chapters can stand as perhaps the best explanations of Steinbeck's continuing appeal as perhaps they could only be most objectively perceived from across the seas.

Another task of the utmost importance, in view of Steinbeck's novels (especially *Of Mice and Men*) being reputedly and credibly those most used in American high schools today, is to introduce young readers to his work. Happily this has been undertaken by Peter Lisca, author of the pioneering monograph *The Wide World of John Steinbeck* (1956; reprinted 1981). Lisca's succinct *John Steinbeck: Nature and Myth* (New York, 1978) dwells upon the importance of Steinbeck's work on the two vast subjects specified in his title, which is summarized in his conclusion that it is Steinbeck's "ability to bring together in his novels and in his image of man both the scientifically described world and that of the intuition and imagination, nature and myth, without distorting either, that is Steinbeck's own unique genius." While such a statement needs the extensive qualification for mature readers that keeps Steinbeck criticism flourishing, it is a magical introduction for young readers to the way in which Steinbeck's work can help them look out on the surrounding world and into themselves.

Also in 1978, Tetsumaro Hayashi, Yasuo Hashiguchi, and Richard F. Peterson edited with the title of *John Steinbeck: East and West* (SMS, No. 8, Muncie, Ind.; hereinafter referred to as *East and West*) the proceedings of the First International Steinbeck Congress, held at Kyushu University in Japan in August 1976. Seven Japanese and five American scholars contributed texts of their presentations, several of which are discussed in connection with the works with which they deal. With the publication of Lisca's second book and this international collection of commentaries, the cycle that had begun in 1956 with the publication of Lisca's *The Wide World of John Steinbeck* appropriately came full circle and seemed to close for the moment the subject of, as Roy Simmonds had put it, Steinbeck's literary achievement. None of the five volumes in the monograph series after Simmonds's provided a new perspective on the author's whole career, but rather concentrated on providing materials that might be used in working toward syntheses on specialized topics.

Steinbeck's Women: Essays in Criticism (ed. Tetsumaro Hayashi, SMS, No. 9, Muncie, Ind., 1979), for example, brings together some essays from the *Steinbeck Quarterly* with papers read at the Steinbeck Society meeting at the MLA in 1977 and Marilyn L. Mitchell's "Steinbeck's Strong Women: Feminine Identity in the Short Stories" (previously published in *SWR*, Summer 1976), which is discussed with individual works on *The Long Valley*. Sandra Beatty contributes two of the more general essays: "A Study of Female Characterization in Steinbeck's Fiction," which concludes that his women, "because of their closeness to Nature and to the Creator Himself, instinctively understand both human nature and life, which make the need to comprehend their implications and complexities unnecessary"; and "Steinbeck's Play-Women: A Study of the Female Presence in *Of Mice and Men, Burning Bright, The Moon Is Down*, and *Viva Zapata!*" which describes the women in the theatrical works as "powerful and dynamic characters, both in themselves and as evidenced by their actions in the plays." Mimi Reisel Gladstein asks the question "Female Characters in Steinbeck: Minor Characters of Major

Importance?" and answers that in his creation of the "indestructible woman," a figure who serves as a positive symbol for human endurance, "Steinbeck the sentimentalist edges out Steinbeck the scientist." (Another article by Gladstein is discussed below with essays on *The Pearl*.) Finally, Robert E. Morsberger's "Steinbeck's Happy Hookers" (reprinted from *StQ*, Summer–Fall 1976) concludes that "Prostitution may be casually accepted in the world of Steinbeck's fiction, but its ultimate name is loneliness."

Paul McCarthy's *John Steinbeck* (MLM, New York, 1980) also provides an intelligent synthesis of what had previously been said about Steinbeck rather than a new approach to his writings. McCarthy deals with the novelist's symbols and themes, his regionalism and social protest, and his literary craftsmanship, but stresses especially the underlying moral vision that Steinbeck clarified in his Nobel Prize acceptance speech. The book thus provides a quick introduction to the writer's reputation for those who have been attracted to Steinbeck's work but need a guide to the extensive body of criticism that has already been written about him. Another brief introduction by one of the most devoted Steinbeck specialists is John Ditsky's *John Steinbeck: Life, Work, and Criticism* (Fredericton, Canada, 1985), a contribution to a Canadian series of "Authoritative Studies in World Literature," Ditsky provides biographical and bibliographical information along with a summary of critical approaches to Steinbeck's fiction that make this an ideal introduction for high school and college students.

Longer but less useful than Ditsky's survey is John H. Timmerman's *John Steinbeck's Fiction: The Aesthetics of the Road Taken* (Norman, Okla., 1986), a traditional critical appraisal with the "twofold aim" of considering Steinbeck's "artistic premises and guiding beliefs" and appraising "the artistic product in the light of these beliefs and according to aesthetic standards of excellence." Timmerman returns to the tired view that "the philosophy of Naturalism constitutes Steinbeck's essential view of humanity" and that the novelist "operates solidly within the framework of his literary precursors" to reach the conclusion that his "greatest strengths" are "his genius for character, story and language" that "hardly distinguish him from any other major author." Behind these, however, Timmerman finds "something unique" that "does not derive from the work itself so much as from a sense of the author behind the work." Such a lapse back to the biographical criticism that the New Criticism replaced seems hardly the road that Steinbeck criticism should be taking.

The fresh beginning of Steinbeck studies called for by Benson's biography may be provided by Louis Owens's *John Steinbeck's Re-Vision of America* (Athens, Ga., 1985), which limits itself to thorough analyses of the novels and stories set in Steinbeck's native California. Owens argues, in challenging close readings, that the novelist used this promised New

World Eden that might fulfill the American Dream to explore the moral bankruptcy of our national society.

b. *Parts of Books and Articles.* Since Steinbeck's death, because of the extent and variety of his work, it has been difficult to undertake any significant kind of overview of his accomplishment in a work of less than book length. Such generalized studies as have been attempted have appeared most often in printed reports of the proceedings of meetings devoted to thematic considerations of the novelist's work.

One such gathering was held at the Marine Science Center at Newport, Oregon, on 4 May 1974, and the proceedings were subsequently edited in a pamphlet, *Steinbeck and the Sea* (Corvallis, Oreg., 1975), by Richard Astro and Joel W. Hedgpeth. Hedgpeth led off with "Steinbeck as Man and Artist," which discusses the powerful influence of marine biological studies on the development of his imagination from early childhood. Jackson J. Benson followed in "John Steinbeck: Novelist as Scientist" with questions about the possibility of combining these interests, which Steinbeck may have carried as far as one can. After some short remarks about Steinbeck's relationship with Ed Ricketts by Fred Tarp and Arthur W. Martin, William S. Williams, in "Steinbeck and the Spirit of the Thirties," presented Steinbeck as the spokesman for a social reform movement that failed, while Peter Copek concluded the program with "John Steinbeck and Feeling in Fiction," in which he attributes Steinbeck's popularity to his realistic approach to life and art in an age in which writers' concerns with technique often left little room for an adequate expression of human feelings.

San Jose Studies for November 1975 is a "Special Steinbeck Issue" that contains, besides articles on individual works to be mentioned below, Robert E. Work's "Steinbeck and the *Spartan Daily*," about a national furor that Work stirred up in 1939 when he found none of Steinbeck's novels in the San Jose library; recollections by Steinbeck's friend Webster Street; remarks on collecting Steinbeck's work by Adrian H. Goldstone; and reviews of recent books about Steinbeck. There are also four general articles. The gathering opens with Warren French's "The 'California Quality' of Steinbeck's Best Fiction," which expands an earlier statement that "Steinbeck unquestionably started downhill when he left California" by pointing out that his immediate contact with "the extraordinarily beautiful rural California landscape" provided the inspiration for its use as a "devastatingly ironic backdrop for his haunting tales of man's stupidity, sadism, and frustration." The article further argues that a similar "California quality" is found in much other fiction from the state beginning with Helen Hunt Jackson's *Ramona* and that Steinbeck never again found an equal inspiration elsewhere.

Martha Heasley Cox also investigates Steinbeck's relationship to "the long valley" of the Salinas River in "In Search of John Steinbeck: His People and His Land" and provides a detailed account, illustrated by quotations from the fiction, of the places that he used in the fiction, sometimes with their proper names, sometimes rechristened with symbolic fictional ones. Jaclyn Caselli contributes "John Steinbeck and the American Patchwork Quilt," a delightful account of the scattered references to homemade quilts and "comforts" in Steinbeck's works that "consciously or unconsciously" reinforce his "theme of community spirit as opposed to the aloneness of the individual."

Finally, Richard Astro makes an ambitious effort in "John Steinbeck and the Tragic Miracle of Consciousness" to present his understanding of "the main reason why John Steinbeck is among the most significant writers of our age." His complex reasoning, drawing on many of Steinbeck's works, reaches the conclusion that because "Steinbeck believed in people," "he treated their fumbling and only occasionally successful efforts . . . with sympathy, and with compassion" and that his thesis was that "humans are rarely satisfied," but their dissatisfaction is "the source of their greatness." Such a conclusion does not distinguish Steinbeck from contemporaries like William Faulkner and Thornton Wilder, but it may serve to clarify the company in which he belongs and to suggest why he won the Nobel Prize.

Astro addresses another ambitious inquiry into the underpinnings of Steinbeck's art in "From the Tidepool to the Stars: Steinbeck's Sense of Place" (*East and West*; reprinted from *StQ*, Winter 1977), beginning with the observation that this "'sense of place' reflects a thorough interpenetration of consciousness and environment." At the core of this "ecological perspective," Astro finds a "pastoral impulse" that "comes through as holism, an awareness of the environmental whole which affects the perception of each separate thing, each separate idea, each separate event." This sense, furthermore, led Steinbeck "to develop a meaningful response to the gathering ecological crisis" that led to the conclusion that "human beings must rechannel their energies, . . . locating their desires not in power and profit, but in the more elemental prior need to sustain life itself."

The papers from the MLA Steinbeck Society meeting in New York City in December 1976, appear under the collective title "New Directions in Steinbeck Studies" (*StQ*, Summer–Fall 1977) with an introduction by program chairman Robert DeMott. Except for Robin C. Mitchell's "Steinbeck and Malory: A Correspondence with Eugène Vinaver" about the exchange that brought the Malory enthusiast and Malory scholar together, the papers deal with broad issues that had not previously been sufficiently examined. Pascal Covici, Jr.'s "Steinbeck's Quest for Magnanimity" deals also with Malory and Steinbeck's *The Acts of King Arthur and His Noble Knights*, but raises the larger question of whether "close study of similarities and differences between Steinbeck's *Acts* and Malory's *Morte*" might not "provide insight into the structural problems in Steinbeck's other books." Clifford Lewis, in an effort to isolate elements of "Jungian Psychology and the Artistic Design of John Steinbeck," gives special emphasis to an early unpublished manuscript, "Murder at Full Moon," and goes on to argue that, as evidenced by Steinbeck's continuing use of folk tales, symbols, talismans, and religious drives, "Jung's ideas remained a part of Steinbeck's artistic design up to the very end of his career." Marcia D. Yarmus's "John Steinbeck and the Hispanic Influence" introduces her broad thesis that certain aspects of Steinbeck's fiction require an understanding of the influence of "underlying important Hispanic cultural, geographical, literary, and linguistic elements."

The most challenging general speculation on Steinbeck's art in recent years, however, is Robert DeMott's "The Interior Distances of John Steinbeck" (*StQ*, Summer–Fall 1979), which calls for a new era in Steinbeck studies by charging that his work and his "literary intentions" have been misread "by accepting too easily his position as a Realist." DeMott's thesis is rather that "Steinbeck is primarily a Romantic, occasionally a Romantic ironist, who experimented tirelessly with varying formal and technical elements in his fiction, and maintained an intense lifelong interest in psychology." He supports his position with an examination of four elements—"symbolic landscape, images of enclosure, dreams, and creativity"—that "spring from a linked generative point in the writer's unconscious," drawing copious illustrations, especially from such later works as *East of Eden, The Winter of Our Discontent*, and *The Acts of King Arthur*.

One analysis that could have greatly benefited by considering the material in Benson's biography is Stoddard Martin's long, three-part essay in *California Writers* (New York, 1983). Martin attempts "to define what has never been defined adequately: a California tradition," but he doesn't succeed. Objecting to Lawrence Ferlinghetti's *Literary San Francisco* (New York, 1980), with good reason, as "a coffee table book" that "ends by being dilettantish," he leaves his own work open to the same objection. His first section on radicalism misses the implications of that term in the 1930s, and the second about "the creations of a man disappointed in marriage" is premature. The essay remains worth reading, at least in part, however, for the judgment in the third part of *East of Eden*, which provides the most penetrating account yet of the undeniable failures of that novel, which Martin observes, "as befits a novel half-dead," has concerns that are "morbid and perverse." "Art based on unresolved confusions," he concludes, "is rarely satisfying."

2 Individual Works of Fiction

a. Cup of Gold. Discussions of individual novels still focus most frequently on *The Grapes of Wrath*, but almost every work has received some attention, with the later works mentioned above frequently cited for a less quick dismissal than early critics proposed. Steinbeck's first pub-

lished novel, *Cup of Gold*, is frequently overlooked as apprentice romanticizing, but Richard Astro, in "Phlebas Sails the Caribbean: Steinbeck,
Hemingway, and the American Waste Land," in *The Twenties: Fiction,
Poetry, Drama* (ed. Warren French, Deland, Fla., 1975), examining its
place in the modernist tradition of T. S. Eliot, reads it not only as "Steinbeck's critique of the solipsistic pursuit of wealth and empire," but finds
the author's vision grimmer even than Hemingway's in *To Have and Have
Not*. Although Darlene Eddy, in "To Go A-Buccaneering and Take a
Spanish Town: Some Seventeenth-Century Aspects of *Cup of Gold*" (*StQ*,
Winter 1975), acknowledges the dubious artistic value of the novel, she
documents Steinbeck's use of diverse historic, literary, and dramatic
contexts in fashioning his tale.

b. *To a God Unknown*. *To a God Unknown* also receives attention from
rising Steinbeck scholar Louis Owens, who insists that the novel has
usually been misread in teleological terms of cause-and-effect. His "John
Steinbeck's Mystical Outcrying: *To a God Unknown* and *The Log from the
Sea of Cortez*" (*SJS*, May 1979) argues rather that, even this early, Steinbeck sets the religious gropings in the novel against the background of
the nonteleological thinking discussed in *The Sea of Cortez*.

c. *The Pastures of Heaven*. New respect should certainly be accorded
The Pastures of Heaven as a result of the elegant privately printed *Steinbeck's
Unhappy Valley* (Berkeley, Calif., 1981), Joseph Fontenrose's final word
on a book to which this distinguished classicist has devoted some of his
finest efforts. It is impossible to summarize the wealth of erudition and
informed speculation that characterize this densely written, fifty-page
pamphlet, intended originally for a collection of essays on short story
cycles that failed to materialize, but Fontenrose's conclusion is that "there
is no curse." Rather he sees the novel as "a conflict of the contemporary
world with the evasion of it," so that the "curse" the Munroes bring
upon the beautiful valley results from their representing "'progress' and
conformity, the outside world coming in."

Two other interpretations of the novel, published earlier, are entirely
compatible with Fontenrose's conclusions. Melanie Mortlock's "The
Eden Myth as Paradox: An Allegorical Reading of *The Pastures of Heaven*"
(*StQ*, Winter 1978) also rejects the idea of a "curse" and argues that
Steinbeck's ironic use of it "carries the novel's thematic message" that
man must "acknowledge the paradoxical nature of his attempts to create
and sustain heaven on earth." Randall R. Mawer's "Takashi Kato, 'Good
American': The Central Episode in Steinbeck's *The Pastures of Heaven*"
(*StQ*, Winter–Spring 1980) focuses on a minor character in the Julius
Maltby episode to produce the kind of close reading one usually expects
to find only in a New Critical explication of a lyric poem, demonstrating
that "curse" or not, the likes of the Munroes and Takashi Kato are "great
losers" in exiling from the valley "everyone who is something other than
a total conformist."

d. Tortilla Flat. Although *Tortilla Flat* is one of Steinbeck's more complex works still in need of further analysis, its deceptively simple comic surface has attracted few commentators beyond those involved with the *Morte d'Arthur* parallels discussed elsewhere, and Louis Owens, who, in an article later incorporated into his book on Steinbeck's California fiction, "Camelot East of Eden: John Steinbeck's *Tortilla Flat*" (*ArQ*, Autumn 1982), argues that, contrary to much previous criticism, the novel is remarkably well unified.

e. In Dubious Battle. In Dubious Battle, on the other hand, attracts increasing attention, as the parochial quarrels over the accuracy of the treatment of the Communist field organizers fades into insignificance and new readers become intrigued by the fundamentally modernist sensibility of its cryptic conclusion. A series of articles in the *Steinbeck Quarterly* have attempted to refocus the emphasis from the tragic figures of Jim Nolan and Doc Burton as the central figures in the novel to the strike organizer Mac. Linda Ray Pratt leads off with "In Defense of Mac's Dubious Battle" (*StQ*, Spring 1977), observing that, "although imperfect," "Mac incorporates the strengths of both Doc and Jim," but she soon undermines this approach by summoning up the fashionable doctrine of "misreading": "Mac's humanity, let alone his moral integrity, is not always readily apparent in the novel." If her thesis is right, Steinbeck did a poor job. Jerry W. Wilson's "*In Dubious Battle*: Engagement in Collectivity" (*StQ*, Spring 1980) goes on to argue that in the novel the "self-character" that Steinbeck said could be found in each of his works is Mac. Barry W. Sarchett's "*In Dubious Battle*: A Revaluation" (*StQ*, Summer–Fall 1980) finds in Mac an analogue to Satan in Milton's *Paradise Lost.*

Readers must decide between the merits of this argument and Allen Shepherd's in "On the Dubiousness of Steinbeck's *In Dubious Battle*" (*NMAL*, Summer 1978) that Jim Nolan is not, as Peter Lisca claims, an imitation of Christ, but of Milton's Satan. More valuable than any of these, however, especially in relating the novel to *Tortilla Flat* and *Of Mice and Men*, is Alan Henry Rose's "Steinbeck and the Complexity of the Self in *In Dubious Battle*" (*StQ*, Winter 1976), which contends that Jim is moving steadily in the book "toward madness" and that his "momentary strength is largely the manic outburst of a radically unbalanced personality." (The article is part of a report on "The John Steinbeck Society Meeting at the 1974 MLA Convention" that also includes brief notes about Steinbeck's relationship to American naturalism by Donald Pizer and Peter Copek.)

f. Of Mice and Men. Although it is reportedly the most widely read novel in American high schools and recently the subject of an opera, the timeless *Of Mice and Men* has also received relatively little separate criticism, but a few articles about it are among the most provocative studies of Steinbeck's work. Hitherto overlooked, William Goldhurst's

"*Of Mice and Men*: John Steinbeck's Parable of the Curse of Cain" (*WAL*, Summer 1971) can prove one of the most useful in examining this work. Goldhurst examines the religious sources and "mythical-allegorical" implications of the short novel. Its theme of the "nature of man's fate in a fallen world" he finds analogous to chapter 4 of Genesis, in which Cain asks, "Am I my brother's keeper?" On the allegorical level, Goldhurst argues that George and Lennie's plan of establishing a ranch home for themselves is "doomed, not only because human fellowship cannot survive in the post-Cain world," but also because the image of the farm is "overly idealized" and suggests "the futility of human attempts to recapture Eden."

From a psychoanalytic viewpoint, Mark Spilka finds quite a different reason for the frustration of the partners' dream in "Of George and Lennie and Curley's Wife: Sweet Violence in Steinbeck's Eden" (*MFS*, Summer 1974). Spilka contends that George really creates the troubles for which Lennie suffers, because George uses Lennie to punish the people that George dislikes, like Curley and his straying wife. In selecting his characters, Spilka concludes, Steinbeck "has chosen aggressive sexuality as the force, in migrant life, which undermines the friendship dream."

Most recently, Michael W. Shurgot's detailed analysis in "A Game of Cards in Steinbeck's *Of Mice and Men*" (*StQ*, Winter–Spring 1982) seeks to prove that the games of solitaire George plays in the bunkhouse provide "an exact symbol of the unpredictable, often merciless world in which [Steinbeck's] characters vainly strive to maintain their dignity and fulfill their dreams."

g. The Long Valley. The individual analyses of the stories in *The Long Valley* mentioned in the earlier version of this essay as appearing in the *Steinbeck Quarterly* were subsequently collected in *A Study Guide to Steinbeck's "The Long Valley"* (ed. Tetsumaro Hayashi, Ann Arbor, Mich., 1976), along with newly commissioned essays on "The Murder" by Katherine M. and Robert E. Morsberger and on the sketch "Breakfast" by Robert Benton. The augmented collection concludes with the previously unpublished "Steinbeck as a Short Story Writer," in which Brian Barbour argues that Steinbeck "never reached artistic maturity in the short story," because "at the time his development should have been taking place, other interests had pre-empted the artistic."

Scholars continue, nonetheless, to find intriguing problems in the individual stories, especially "The Chrysanthemums," which leads off *The Long Valley*. In "The Original Manuscripts of Steinbeck's 'The Chrysanthemums'" (*StQ*, Summer–Fall 1974), Roy S. Simmonds makes a detailed study of changes in the printed versions to "suggest that the long-accepted view of Elisa as a wholly sympathetic character" could be open to question and that "Steinbeck was obliged to tone down some of the sexual implications in the story to mollify the editors of *Harper's Magazine*."

William Osborne continues the examination of the story in two related articles in *Interpretations*, "The Education of Elisa Allen: Another Reading of John Steinbeck's 'The Chrysanthemums'" (No. 8, 1978) and "The Texts of 'The Chrysanthemums'" (No. 9, 1979), which propose that the final irony in the story is "that Elisa comes into full, if painful knowledge of her identity—she is a romantic in a utilitarian society," and the tinker, "who might have redeemed other members of the society by being a notable exception, was in truth no different."

Even earlier, Charles Sweet's "Ms. Elisa Allen and Steinbeck's 'The Chrysanthemums'" (*MFS*, Summer 1974) had proposed that in her effort to make a business deal in a man's world, Elisa is not only less successful than her husband, but is also stripped "of her dignity and dreams of equality" by the tinker. Ernest W. Sullivan, II's "Cur in 'The Chrysanthemums'" (*SSF*, Summer 1979) goes along with this reading, but points out also the parallels between her behavior and that of the tinker's dog when it moves out of its accustomed role.

Marilyn L. Mitchell's "Steinbeck's Strong Women: Feminine Identity in the Short Stories," in *Steinbeck's Women* (ed. Tetsumaro Hayashi, SMS, No. 9, Muncie, Ind., 1979) pairs this story with "The White Quail" to point out also how "both examine the psychology and sexuality of strong women who must somehow express themselves meaningfully within the narrow possibilities open to women in a man's world," though in neither does he propose a solution for "the psychological conflicts which plague human interactions." Drawing upon our recently expanded knowledge of Steinbeck's reading, Stanley Renner argues in "Mary Teller and Sue Bridehead: Birds of a Feather in 'The White Quail' and *Jude the Obscure*" (*StQ*, Winter–Spring 1985) that Steinbeck's and Hardy's characters are "uncannily alike—in detailed resemblance, in attitude, and in the havoc they wreak in their relationships with men."

The controversy over the interpretation of "The Leader of the People," the final story in the *Red Pony* cycle, continues. Max L. Autrey contributes a further refinement with his observation in "Men, Mice and Moths: Gradations in Steinbeck's 'The Leader of the People'" (*WAL*, Fall 1975) that Jody's maturation in the story is suggested by his recognition in his microcosmic world of farm and field creatures of a "little chain of being," patterned after the universal system described in Arthur O. Lovejoy's *The Great Chain of Being*. Far more striking as one of the most provocative readings of the story, however, is James C. Work's later contribution to the same journal, "Coordinate Forces in 'The Leader of the People'" (*WAL*, Winter 1982), which examines the whole *Long Valley* collection to indicate that each story deals with an unchanging character in a closed-in setting, intruded upon by a vital outside force that does not change the situation, but does change the original character's interpretation of it. Jody has been such a character, but Grandfather's appearance in "The Leader of the People" brings out that Jody will "not be stifled by disciplined routine" and "will one day be an adult of more strength than his father."

Meanwhile, Roy S. Simmonds had reported, in "The First Publication of 'The Leader of the People'" (*StQ*, Winter 1975), that the story, long thought to have been first published in *The Long Valley*, appeared in the British magazine *Argosy* in August 1936. Simmonds also tabulates more than a hundred minor variants between the two versions, most largely attributable to British editing in order to anglicize the text.

Simmonds's "Steinbeck's 'The Murder': A Critical and Bibliographical Study" (*StQ*, Spring 1976) also provides additional information about the publishing history of this story that may have originally been a rejected chapter for *The Pastures of Heaven*. Simmonds examines the manuscript and three variant texts that appeared in the *North American Review*, the British *Lovat Dickson's Magazine*, and *The Long Valley* to make the point that none of the three is wholly reliable, which may in part account for the story's generally being regarded as one of Steinbeck's least successful.

Admitting that "The Murder" is "undoubtedly the most difficult and perplexing" of the stories in *The Long Valley*, Louis D. Owens finds, in "Steinbeck's 'The Murder': Illusions of Chivalry" (*StQ*, Winter–Spring 1984), that it uses, nevertheless, like other stories in the volume, "the theme of illusion to suggest man's failure to grasp a reality that conflicts with what he desires to believe." While the heavily ironic tale is concerned mainly with the destruction of Jim Moore's chivalric illusions, Owens concedes it is finally confused by Steinbeck's apparent difficulty in developing consistently the character of Jelka.

Maureen Girard also studies the alterations from the manuscript in the published version of "The Snake" in "Steinbeck's Frightful Story: The Conception and Evolution of 'The Snake'" (*SJS*, Spring 1982), pointing out that Steinbeck seemed to have decided in revising the story "to eliminate any emotional content in the relationship between the two main characters."

James Delgado takes us back not to the manuscript but the original sources in "The Facts Behind John Steinbeck's 'The Lonesome Vigilante'" (*StQ*, Summer–Fall 1983), explaining that the story was suggested by a lynching in Carol Steinbeck's home town of San Jose in 1933. Delgado uses the original title of the story when it appeared in *Esquire*; it was changed to simply "The Vigilante" in *The Long Valley*. In Edward J. Piacentino's purely critical "Patterns of Animal Imagery in Steinbeck's 'Flight'" (*SSF*, Fall 1980), he points out the ways in which man's relation to the natural order is established by the pattern of animal references in the published story.

Although "How Edith McGillcuddy Met R. L. Stevenson" did not appear in *The Long Valley*, Roy S. Simmonds's "John Steinbeck, Robert Louis Stevenson, and Edith McGillcuddy" (*SJS*, Nov. 1975), the only recent study of a short story not included in the collection, is most appropriately discussed here. Simmonds provides both a full account of the historical background of the story and of its publishing history, beginning with the changes made in the 1932–33 manuscript when the story was at last published in *Harper's* in August 1941.

h. *The Grapes of Wrath*. *The Grapes of Wrath* remains the central focus of Steinbeck study. Two of the most exciting pieces of recent Steinbeck scholarship offer new perspectives on its value by placing it in contexts beyond Steinbeck's oeuvre. Sylvia Jenkins Cook, in *From Tobacco Road to Route 66: The Southern Poor White in Fiction* (Chapel Hill, N.C., 1976), which the author describes as an attempt to trace the attractions and problems of the "paradoxical poor white stereotype" for writers in the 1930s, describes Steinbeck's novel as "the most popularly successful poor white novel of the decade," though it was neither by a southerner nor set in the south. The novel, she argues, "represents the final de-politicizing and remythologizing of the poor white social novel," for instead of challenging real economic conditions with political solutions, Steinbeck draws characters able to deal with the situation "by returning to them traditions of courage and generosity and philosophies of optimism and endurance."

Humanistic Geography and Literature: Essays on the Experience of Place (ed. Douglas C. D. Pocock, London, 1981) is a symposium by "a growing band of geographers seeking alternative perspectives and insights in the study of man-environment relationships" through "rediscovering the literary heritage of geography." Christopher L. Salter, in one of the twelve essays, "John Steinbeck's *The Grapes of Wrath* as a Primer for Cultural Geography," uses the novel to show how rereading classics "with an eye focused upon the themes of cultural geography" produces new insights; he then, through the use of extensive quotations, illustrates how the novel can "provide focus for instruction in migration, settlement forms, economic systems, cultural dualism, agricultural land use patterns, transportation technology, and social change."

These essays would seem to answer John Ditsky's request, in *"The Grapes of Wrath*: A Reconsideration" (*SHR*, Summer 1979), for reconsiderations of the reasons why the novel has attained "classic" status. Most other recent efforts, however, have elaborated upon Ditsky's familiar position that this *bildungsroman* is "fundamentally a romantic epic of the U.S. highway." Reloy Garcia's "The Rocky Road to Eldorado: The Journey Motif in John Steinbeck's *The Grapes of Wrath*" (*StQ*, Summer–Fall 1981), for example, reads the novel as a recapitulation of the myth of a fabled paradise, the quest for which proves a failure, though he contends that Steinbeck's pattern is richer and more complex than this since along the way Ma Joad, Casy, Tom and Rose of Sharon have learned something about the possibility of reordering the universe.

Patrick Shaw pushes Garcia's last point somewhat further, in "Tom's Other Trip: Psycho-Physical Questing in *The Grapes of Wrath*" (*StQ*, Winter–Spring 1983), by focusing on Tom Joad's "spiritual migration," which he finds most revealing of "Steinbeck's holistic design and moral intent." Shaw then traces Tom's movement through five states of psychological development until he reaches "the enlightened state of awareness that is his salvation." Sylvia Cook returns to the novel in "Steinbeck, the People, and the Party" (*StQ*, Winter–Spring 1982) to trace a similar transformation in both Casy and Tom and to place this motif against a background of Steinbeck's other early works and the literary-political situation in the 1930s to arrive at the conclusion that Steinbeck achieved a synthesis that "none of the genuine proletarian novelists, more closely engaged in the throes of the literary class war, was ever able to achieve." (A longer version of this article appears in *Literature at the Barricades: The American Writer in the 1930s* [ed. Ralph F. Bogardus and Fred Hobson, University, Ala., 1982].)

Horst Groene's "Agrarianism and Technology in Steinbeck's *The Grapes of Wrath*" (*SoRA*, Jan. 1976) returns to the question of the futility of traditional agrarian thinking in the twentieth century raised in Warren French's *The Social Novel at the End of an Era* (1966) to point out that, despite Steinbeck's resentment of the mechanization of agriculture, he praises the achievements of modern technology in chapter 25 and makes Tom Joad's successor as leader of the family his younger brother Al, "who has no interest in agriculture and dreams of working in a garage in the city."

The once problematical structural questions about the novel seem to have been resolved, since no further discussion of the relationship between the chapters and interchapters outlined by Peter Lisca and Warren French have appeared since Mary Ellen Caldwell's "A New Consideration of the Intercalary Chapters in *The Grapes of Wrath*" (*MarkhamR*, May 1973), which makes a detailed analysis of the central chapter 15, the sentimental fable about the rewards of goodness at a truck stop as "not only a microcosm of *The Grapes of Wrath* but also a microcosm of the United States."

As these interpretations suggest, the symbolism in the novel proves endlessly fascinating. James D. Brasch's "*The Grapes of Wrath* and Old Testament Skepticism" (*SJS*, May 1977) brings up again the shared initials of Jesus Christ and Jim Casy, but this time to argue that Casy is more nearly like the skeptical author of Ecclesiastes than the messianic savior. Helen Lojek's "Jim Casy: Politico of the New Jerusalem" (*StQ*, Winter–Spring 1982) takes an entirely opposite tack, however, and places Casy in the tradition deeply rooted in American literature that

Sacvan Bercovitch expounds in *The American Jeremiad* (Madison, Wis., 1978). She goes on, however, to observe that if Casy's career illustrates this tradition, "it also seems initially to indicate that an American dream in which the sacred and the secular were once mingled is now almost entirely secular."

A. Carl Bredahl, Jr.'s "The Drinking Metaphor in *The Grapes of Wrath*" (*StQ*, Fall 1973) discusses the successive roles that liquor, water, and milk play in the novel as it moves from sickness toward growth. While not dealing with a symbol, Kathleen Farr Elliott's "Steinbeck's 'IITYWYBAD'" (*StQ*, Summer 1973) is most appropriately mentioned in connection with problematic readings, since Elliott proposes that this abbreviation that has frustrated so many readers of the novel is a variant on a familiar riddle of the Depression, "If I tell you, will you buy a drink."

The ending of the novel also continues to need decoding. Lewis F. Cobb's "Maupassant's 'Idylle': A Source for Steinbeck's *The Grapes of Wrath*" (*NMAL*, Winter 1978) suggests that Steinbeck may have borrowed his final tableau from the French writer's story, but this seems doubtful in view of the totally different purposes the scenes serve. Ignoring the tableau altogether in "The Turtle or the Gopher: Another Look at the Ending of *The Grapes of Wrath*" (*WAL*, Spring 1974), Stuart L. Burns argues that the novel's ending would be better symbolized by the security-seeking gopher from *Cannery Row* than by the turtle in chapter 3 of *The Grapes of Wrath*, ignoring the way in which the turtle's odyssey foreshadows microcosmically the whole pattern of the migrants' quest in the novel, a matter explored in detail in Joyce Compton Brown's "Steinbeck's *The Grapes of Wrath*" (*Expl*, Summer 1983).

The whole controversy should by now have been stilled by Martha Heasley Cox's "The Conclusion of *The Grapes of Wrath*: Steinbeck's Conception and Execution" (*SJS*, Nov. 1975), one of the most illuminating Steinbeck criticisms published anywhere, although the author's claims for her discoveries are too modestly stated. After reviewing the continuing controversy over the suitability of the ending, Cox quotes from Steinbeck's unpublished "Diary of a Book," which he kept as he wrote *The Grapes of Wrath*, to prove that the ending was "not merely hastily contrived melodrama replete with false symbolism," but a scene that "Steinbeck carefully planned and prepared for the conclusion from the time he wrote the initial chapter of the novel." Steinbeck forbade publication of this diary during his lifetime, so most critics were unaware of its existence. We are deeply indebted to Martha Cox for making its importance known, and it is gratifying to report that it is at last being edited for publication by Robert DeMott. While this "Diary" sheds no light on Steinbeck's abandoned original version, "L'Affaire Lettuceberg," it is a remarkable account of the composition of one of our major novels that establishes exactly how carefully designed the work was and the great suffering that its production caused the author.

Most of the background material concerning Tom Collins, one of the persons to whom Steinbeck dedicated the novel and the manager of the original federal Weedpatch Camp, contained in Jackson J. Benson's "'To Tom, Who Lived It': John Steinbeck and the Man from Weedpatch" (*JML*, Apr. 1974), is incorporated into Benson's biography; but an appendix, with an introduction by Benson, "From Bringing in the Sheaves, by 'Windsor Drake,' with a Foreword by John Steinbeck," not reprinted in Benson's book, remains uniquely valuable, as it contains excerpts from an unpublished account of the migrant camps, written by Collins under a pseudonym. Martha Heasley Cox also discusses the relationship between Collins and Steinbeck in "Fact into Fiction in *The Grapes of Wrath*: The Weedpatch and Arvin Camps" (*East and West*), drawing extensively both upon the unpublished diary that Steinbeck kept while writing the novel and Collins's official reports from the camp, which bear such striking similarities to parts of the novel that there can be no doubt that Steinbeck "drew characters, episodes, motifs, themes, and settings directly" from them.

Three comparative studies of the novel, setting it beside distinguished contemporary works, provide particularly provocative insights into Steinbeck's stature as an American writer. Stanley Trachtenberg's "West's Locusts: Laughing at the Laugh" (*MQR*, Spring 1975) suggests reasons for Steinbeck's dismissal by the literary establishment in the late 1930s as sentimental by pointing out that *The Grapes of Wrath* affirms the possibility of social progress, while West's doomsday novel *The Day of the Locust* simply pokes fun at the concept. Linda Ray Pratt goes much further in parting company with other theorists of the period in "Imagining Existence: Form and History in Steinbeck and Agee" (*SoR*, Jan. 1975) by finding that while both authors sought to make readers aware of the miseries of a segment of the American poor, Steinbeck accentuated traditional American values that distorted history into literary myth (a much more self-conscious process than sentimentalizing). Agee, on the other hand, essentially opposed his society's values and demanded that art give way to "actuality" in order to create the consciousness that demands a revolution, although he did not advocate social violence. Finally, taking a close look at the often neglected female characters in *The Grapes of Wrath* and Hemingway's *For Whom the Bell Tolls*, Mimi Gladstein argues, in "Ma Joad and Pilar: Significantly Similar" (*StQ*, Summer–Fall 1981), that ultimately the optimistic possibilities inherent in both stories "are embodied in Maria and Rose of Sharon, who function as extensions of Pilar and Ma."

This theory of the centrality of Ma and Rose of Sharon in the novel is elaborated upon in the most radically revisionist interpretation of the novel to have so far appeared, Warren Motley's "From Patriarchy to Matriarchy: Ma Joad's Role in *The Grapes of Wrath*" (*AL*, Oct. 1982). Drawing upon anthropologist Robert Briffault's theories on the matriarchal organization of society, Motley argues that "as the older Joad men sink into ineffectiveness and despair, authority shifts to Ma Joad." Motley feels, however, that Steinbeck doubted that Americans would accept matriarchy as a governing principle. While this assumption would have been quite sound in 1939, it may be doubted that Steinbeck calculated the matter consciously. If works of art cannot be reinterpreted to meet changing times, they become museum pieces; and *The Grapes of Wrath* remains, to the surprise of many, a still lively work. Motley's reading may suggest wherein may be found a special appeal it has for the 1980s.

The essays discussed above by Stuart L. Burns, Mary Ellen Caldwell, and Horst Groene, along with chapters from Warren French's and Peter Lisca's recent books, have been brought together with earlier essays by George Bluestone, Edwin T. Bowden, Robert J. Griffin and William A. Freedman, J. Paul Hunter, R. W. B. Lewis, and Leonard Lutwack in *"The Grapes of Wrath": A Collection of Critical Essays* (ed. Robert Con Davis, TCI, Englewood Cliffs, N.J., 1982), which like the Benson and DeMott books and Hayashi bibliography may have arrived at the appropriate time to round out the first era in Steinbeck criticism. Davis's introduction intelligently traces three periods in the criticism of the novel, with turning points in 1954, when critics began to examine the novel's structure, and 1971, when they began to analyze it as "a development of the epic and romance traditions." He also includes Joan Hedrick's previously unpublished "Mother Earth and the Earth Mother: The Recasting of Myth in Steinbeck's *The Grapes of Wrath*," which like other recent criticisms emphasizes the primacy of Ma Joad in the novel, concluding that "men can grow up . . . only by leaving women alone and ascending to a higher 'spiritual' plane" and maintaining that the novel "could be read as the story of the reunion of a mother and son, and their forced separation at the end."

i. The Moon Is Down and *Bombs Away*. Because of their deceptive, apparent simplicity, the short, highly personal works between *The Grapes of Wrath* and *East of Eden* continue to receive minimal critical attention. Warren French's "*The Moon Is Down*: John Steinbeck's 'Times'" (*StQ*, Summer 1978) concerns the theatrical version of this curious work which is still revered in Europe and derided in the United States. The article examines, however, not so much the play itself as the taste-making *New York Times*'s efforts to promote Steinbeck's dramatic career, in which its staff's assessments proved "almost unexceptionably wrong." John Ditsky, however, takes Steinbeck himself to task in the only recent article about his early nonfiction novel (though Ditsky does not use this appropriate term), "Steinbeck's *Bombs Away*: The Group-man in the Wild Blue Yonder" (*StQ*, Winter 1979). Proceeding from the debatable premise that this is the author's weakest book, Ditsky argues that it does "provide the student of Steinbeck with an unintended self-portrait of the artist in the midst of a collapsing theory," referring to the idea of the group-man that he had embraced as late as *The Grapes of Wrath*.

j. Cannery Row. Even *Cannery Row*, Steinbeck's "poisoned cream-puff" lately traduced by tourism boards and Hollywood, has been little examined in recent years. The late Lawrence William Jones's "Poison in the Cream Puff: The Human Condition in *Cannery Row*" (*StQ*, Spring 1974) illuminates the novel's profound insights into the human condition—that both communal and individual elements are necessary in a total personality, that love and understanding are necessary for communal life, and that death, a lonely, individual thing, yet "implies final connection with nature." Peter Lisca's "*Cannery Row* and *Tao Teh Ching*" (*SJS*, Nov. 1975; revised and slightly condensed in *Nature and Myth*) demonstrates that "the novel's informing spirit" is the work of the sixth century B.C. Chinese philosopher Lao Tzu from which develops the twin themes of "the escape from Western material values (the necessity to 'succeed' in the world) and the escape from Western activism (the necessity to impose order or direction)."

Jackson J. Benson also interrupted his long work on the Steinbeck biography to publish "John Steinbeck's *Cannery Row*: A Reconsideration" (*WAL*, Spring 1977), the most important sections of which do not appear in the long book from which Benson had to omit most critical analyses. Like the biography, however, this extended example of Benson's critical technique is markedly "Californian" in its approach. Benson sees Steinbeck as a successor to Mark Twain as spokesman for the "folk tradition" opposed to "creeping gentility," the principal target of his humor. The book advocates "life as a form of art," and Steinbeck makes Doc the metaphor for this spirit that he so much admired. Benson also insists that interpreting the novel "depends upon adjusting our perspective rather than discovering an elaborate literary apparatus," but this comment, arising from Benson's feeling that the novel grows out of its environment that he knows quite well, may not do justice to Steinbeck's artful planning of a novel that appears quite exotic to readers elsewhere.

k. The Wayward Bus. Recent criticism has not done much to advance the status of *The Wayward Bus*, the postwar novel for which Steinbeck himself had high hopes that failed to materialize. After taking to task the inadequacy of previous criticism of the novel, John Ditsky's "*The Wayward Bus*: Love and Time in America" (*SJS*, Nov. 1975) argues that the narrative has been "a movement from talk, dreams, and cravings to communication, however limited, and satisfaction, however temporary and incomplete—and the restoration of realistically revised dreams." Louis Owens's "*The Wayward Bus*: A Triumph of Nature" (*SJS*, Feb. 1980) draws on Ditsky and goes on to argue that this novel is "perhaps the most positive statement in all of Steinbeck's fiction," since "nothing has changed" and "Steinbeck is saying that this is the way things are." Whatever the merits of these positions, both critics fail to overcome the objection that good intentions mean little if the writer fails to get them across to his reader.

l. The Pearl. Despite the continuing popularity of *The Pearl* as one of the few satisfactory works to introduce American high schoolers to moral fiction, the only supporting analyses recently have appeared in the *Steinbeck Quarterly* and have been largely directed at Warren French's argument that the contrived tale is a sellout to American commercial sentimentalism. Sidney J. Krause's *"The Pearl* and 'Hadleyburg': From Desire to Renunciation" (*StQ*, Winter 1974) is part of an overall comparison of Steinbeck with Mark Twain. Starting from the questionable observation that Steinbeck's fable "traces a pattern of moral deterioration closely resembling" that in "The Man Who Corrupted Hadleyburg," Krause concludes that the principals in both stories "return to the condition from which they had started, poorer the one way and richer the other" (that is, financially and spiritually, respectively).

Tetsumaro Hayashi's *"The Pearl* as a Novel of Disengagement" (*StQ*, Fall 1974) is a far more subtle essay that provides us with an oriental perspective on this colonialist fable. Briefly, Hayashi explains that it takes *Gedatsu*, the Zen Buddhist concept of total disengagement, to save Kino from the "moral bankruptcy" that is the "curse of the Pearl of the World." The article does a great deal to explain the international appeal of Steinbeck's work, especially in the Orient; but it must be read with the enlightened understanding that *Gedatsu* has never played any substantial role in Hispano-Anglo/American culture.

Edward E. Waldron's *"The Pearl* and *The Old Man of the Sea*: A Comparative Analysis" (*StQ*, Summer–Fall 1980) does a good job of making the inevitable comparison between these two short fables from Hispano-American sources and reaches the unsurprising conclusion that, in both, the authors "present portraits of triumph in the face of overwhelming adversity, perhaps the most basic of American themes from William Bradford on." The evocation of Bradford reminds us that these are perhaps the only two works by these Nobel laureates that please the Sunday school trade. Also uplifting is Mimi Reisel Gladstein's "Steinbeck's Juana: A Woman of Worth," in *Steinbeck's Women* (SMS, No. 9, Muncie, Ind., 1979), which describes the wife and mother in *The Pearl* as "a composite of all the best qualities of the archetypal feminine."

m. Burning Bright. John M. Ditsky's "Steinbeck's *Burning Bright*: Homage to Astarte" (*StQ*, Summer–Fall 1974) acknowledges that this novelette-play, which is arguably Steinbeck's weakest work, is "seldom discussed critically," but he proceeds to deliver a detailed and unexceptionable explication leading to the conclusion that the wife-mother Mordeen, "as Astarte-Ishtar, lover and destroyer, becomes the Great Mother who exploits sacrificed youth so that mankind may progress."

n. East of Eden. Ditsky has also emerged as the principal champion of Steinbeck's often-berated magnum opus in *Essays on "East of Eden"* (SMS, No. 7, Muncie, Ind., 1977). In the first of the three essays, "Towards a Narrational Self," Ditsky describes the long planning of this novel about the author's native region and his own family and concludes that it "dramatizes the conflict existent within the author himself" and is "a kind of confessional novel." The longest of the three interrelated pieces, "Outside of Paradise: Men and the Land in *East of Eden*," summarizes the entire action of this complex narrative to arrive at the conclusion that "The direct involvement of the Hamiltons—however unsuccessful in worldly terms—and the metaphorical involvement of the Trasks— based upon dreaming . . . of an unrealistic Eden—are both consistently related to their ground and basis, Nature itself, the Salinas Valley, which was the germ for the entire novel." Ditsky's most challenging thesis in the final "The 'East' in *East of Eden*" is that Steinbeck's interest in the geographical East (the Orient) "was by way of setting up a straw man meant for knocking down." If he came at last to feel that "*yin* and *yang* in balance made no human progress possible," he betrayed unremittingly Western ideas and was perhaps "American at heart beyond his knowing." (The identical essay appears in *East and West*.)

Ditsky has not been alone in his defense of the novel, but several short later pieces have added little to his interpretation of the origins of the novel and its relationship to those origins. Karen J. Hopkins's "Steinbeck's *East of Eden*: A Defense," in *Essays on California Writers* (ed. Charles L. Crow, Bowling Green, Ohio, 1978), advances the extraordinary argument that Steinbeck created this epic work in order to annoy critics, because there are so "few 'hidden' meanings" that require ingenious explication. Joyce C. Brown, taking a postmodernist tack, in "Steinbeck's *East of Eden*" (*Expl*, Fall 1979), suggests that Cathy Trask is not a figure of evil, but of "amorality."

The second ambitious reconsideration of the novel is a set of papers presented at the John Steinbeck Society meeting at the 1979 MLA meeting in San Francisco, which was appropriately devoted to "Mapping *East of Eden*." These appeared as a special section, edited by Robert DeMott in the *Steinbeck Quarterly* (Winter–Spring 1981). Daniel Buerger leads off with "'History' and 'Fiction' in *East of Eden* Criticism," which summarizes the generally negative early reaction to the book and evidences of a slowly growing appreciation of the novel still inadequate to do justice to its complexities. Mark Govoni's "'Symbols for the Wordlessness': The Original Manuscript of *East of Eden*" examines the differences between the first draft and published novel and reports that Steinbeck eliminated himself as narrator and many of his original speculations, while seeking throughout his revisions to maintain the personal effect and speculative nature of the work. Martha Heasley Cox's "Steinbeck's Family Portraits: The Hamiltons" discusses a photograph of the family taken at Samuel and Elizabeth's golden wedding anniversary celebration in 1900 and documents how closely Steinbeck reported the truth and to what extent he exercised his "novelist's prerogative to order his material to suit his purposes."

Barbara McDaniel's "Alienation in *East of Eden*: The 'Chart of the Soul'" refutes earlier thematic and structural criticism of the novel, arguing that the "basic structure is sound" and that the book is not just "vaguely about morality." Rather she depicts Steinbeck as finding in the Cain and Abel story "the basis of all neuroses." The weaknesses of the novel she attributes plausibly to "too much planning" rather than too little. The organizer of the session and editor of the papers, Robert DeMott, winds up the program with "'Culling All Books': Steinbeck's Reading and *East of Eden*," in which he anticipates his recent *Steinbeck's Reading*, described earlier, by commenting on the books cited and used in *East of Eden*, especially *Gunn's New Family Physician*, a late nineteenth-century "home book of health."

DeMott explores Steinbeck's reliance on Dr. John C. Gunn's work in much greater detail in "'A Great Black Book': *East of Eden* and *Gunn's New Family Physician*" (*AmerS*, Fall 1981); and he draws again upon the material collected during the research for his book in "Cathy Ames and Lady Godiva: A Contribution to *East of Eden*'s Background" (*StQ*, Summer–Fall 1981), which indicates that Steinbeck was prompted in his creation of Cathy Ames by "the secular and antimythic example of Raoul Faure's novel *Lady Godiva and Master Tom* (1948)."

o. Sweet Thursday and The Short Reign of Pippin IV. Recent critics have avoided *Sweet Thursday*; even Peter Lisca, grouping it with other short fiction in *Nature and Myth*, observes only that it was "written expressly as the source for a musical comedy," but that its "anti-intellectualism . . . goes beyond the needs of musical comedy, and is symptomatic of Steinbeck's own predicament" following the completion of *East of Eden*. Lisca finds that "stagnation of ideas" continued into the next novel, *The Short Reign of Pippin IV*, but John Ditsky comes to the defense of this dated satire in "Some Sense of Mission: Steinbeck's Pippin Reconsidered" (*StQ*, Summer–Fall 1983), claiming that it is "a distinctly American book in theme," despite its French setting, written out of Steinbeck's distaste for modern American and French politics and presenting in Pippin himself the kind of person who is responsible for "whatever progress as a race we make."

p. The Winter of Our Discontent. Lisca also finds *The Winter of Our Discontent* one of Steinbeck's weakest serious novels because the balance that has been "alive and active" in his best work between scientific thinking and a mystical view of human life is here static; an increasing number of analysts are becoming intrigued, however, with Steinbeck's attempt to make a fresh start, despite his earlier observation that "there is nothing beyond *East of Eden*."

Charles J. Clancy's "Light in *The Winter of Our Discontent*" (*StQ*, Summer–Fall 1976) is a complicated tracing of the light-dark imagery in the novel, especially in relation to two garbled quotations from the Anglo-Saxon of Caedmon's *Genesis* and Boethius's *Consolation of Philosophy*, to demonstrate that light in the novel stands for love and life itself and that Ethan Hawley, if not yet a hero in the story, could now develop into one. Donal Stone's "Steinbeck, Jung, and *The Winter of Our Discontent*" (*StQ*, Summer–Fall 1978) establishes many parallels in the novel to Jung's psychological theories but cautions that we lack evidence about the extent to which Steinbeck consciously employed mythic and symbolic motifs, despite his being remarkably "in tune" with ideas about man's collective unconscious. (Both Benson's and DeMott's recent books establish that Steinbeck had been reading Jung with serious interest off and on since the 1930s.)

Two tributes to the novel appear in the Summer–Fall 1979 issue of *Steinbeck Quarterly*. Tetsumaro Hayashi, in "Steinbeck's *Winter* as Shakespearean Fiction," points out the numerous Shakespearean analogies and allusions in the novel to conclude that while "Steinbeck fails to summon up the equivalent of Shakespeare's poetry to serve his end," he does go strongly against the current of much literature of his time by trying to rise above the squalor and suggest that "the situation might still be redeemed." Louis K. MacKendrick's "The Popular Art of Discontent: Steinbeck's Masterful *Winter*" finds virtue in Steinbeck's coming "in close touch with the transparency and simplicity which underscores popular literature" and powerfully mastering his "chosen mode" of telling "an old story in contemporary terms."

Occult elements in the novel also continue to attract attention. Kevin M. McCarthy's "Witchcraft and Superstition in *The Winter of Our Discontent*" (*NYFQ*, Sept. 1974) catalogues the numerous references to traditional folklore in the novel. Douglas L. Verdier's "Ethan Allen Hawley and the Hanged Man: Free Will and Fate in *The Winter of Our Discontent*" (*StQ*, Summer–Fall 1982) focuses on Margie Young-Hunt's reading of the tarot cards to prophesy Ethan's future, which foretells a final outcome much different from what she had hoped. McCarthy argues, however, that Ethan's salvation ultimately comes not from the tarot or even his talismans, "but from the realization that his moral choices, freely made and for which he alone is responsible, ultimately shape the future."

The critical response to Steinbeck's last novel has been chronicled with painstaking thoroughness in the late Carol A. Kasparek's "*The Winter of Our Discontent*: A Critical Survey," edited by John Ditsky, after the author's macabre death (*StQ*, Winter–Spring 1985). Kasparek traces the way in which the initially negative response to the novel "has become more positive as critics have begun to discover its complexities and sources in Shakespeare, Jung, and myth"; but she is not able to adduce evidence that it has attracted favorable attention from critics beyond those generally concerned with Steinbeck's work.

q. The Acts of King Arthur and His Noble Knights. The posthumous *The Acts of King Arthur and His Noble Knights*, which can only properly be grouped with Steinbeck's fiction, has begun to generate some commentaries—especially necessary since it has not yet received detailed attention in any full-length critical study of Steinbeck's work. Although John Ditsky's "The Friend at the Round Table: A Note on Steinbeck's *Acts*" (*AL*, Jan. 1978) appears only to identify an example of Steinbeck's often undervalued subtle wit in his reference to his old friend Webster F. Street as one of Arthur's company, it also advances but does not develop the theory that this modernization "provides the missing link, in terms of Steinbeck's developing fictional rhetoric on the subject of individual moral responsibility, between *East of Eden* and *The Winter of Our Discontent*."

Earlier, Robin C. Mitchell's "Steinbeck and Malory: A Correspondence with Eugène Vinaver" (*StQ*, Summer–Fall 1977) had established from the letters between Steinbeck and the distinguished Malory scholar the way that friends and publishers discouraged the Malory venture and Steinbeck's own reasons for pursuing it, crystallized in his question to Vinaver in July 1959, "Could you accept, at least as a working hypothesis, the thought that Arthur is a subjective figure and that every man carries the cycle in his soul?"

The most valuable work on the controversial book has been provided by Laura F. Hodges in two related articles. "The Personae of *Acts*: Symbolic Repetition and Variation" (*StQ*, Winter–Spring 1979) opens with the illuminating observation that while Malory's work is a Christian allegory, Steinbeck's is "not Christian," but "humanistic and psychological" and concludes that "true heroism lies in meeting the challenge of one's own individual personality," as mature characters like Lancelot do, while immature characters like Gawain and Arthur do not. Hodges develops this last point in "Arthur, Lancelot, and the Psychodrama of Steinbeck" (*StQ*, Summer–Fall 1980), which summarizes her brilliant thesis about the book in the observation that "Under the guise of translating Malory's story of Arthur and his knights for twentieth-century readers, Steinbeck in fact writes his own new version, a modern psychodrama [defined as 'a form of drama' employed by psychiatrists in which a patient experiences a cathartic relief through an enactment of an internal 'conflict'] which dramatizes through symbolic characters the universal conflict within each individual of the desires for power, for peace, for love, and for perfection." One hopes that this perceptive critic will go on to write an account of the way in which Steinbeck in his original works has also served up old theological wine in new psychological bottles. One could scarcely end this account of the recent critical treatment of the most important part of Steinbeck's work on a note that offered more promise for future criticism.

3 Nonfiction

Attention is belatedly turning to Steinbeck's nonfiction, especially accounts of his travels; but the only book so far to be devoted to these is *Steinbeck's Travel Literature: Essays in Criticism* (ed. Tetsumaro Hayashi, SMS, No. 10, Muncie, Ind., 1980). Seven of the eight pieces are reprinted—five from the *Steinbeck Quarterly*. Three of them are discussed below. Darlene Eddy's "Some Seventeenth-Century Aspects of *Cup of Gold*" and John Ditsky's "*The Wayward Bus*: Love and Time in America" are discussed above along with other criticisms of the novels named. Richard F. Peterson's "Mythology of American Life: *America and Americans*" is from *A Study Guide to Steinbeck* (ed. Tetsumaro Hayashi, Metuchen, N.J., 1974), and Charles J. Clancy's "Steinbeck's *A Russian Journal*" is from the same editor's *A Study Guide to Steinbeck, Part II* (Metuchen, N.J., 1979). There is nothing about the uncollected pieces from Europe in the 1950s or the later "Letters to Alicia."

The only overview in the group is Richard Astro's "Travels with Steinbeck: The Laws of Thought and the Laws of Things" (reprinted from *StQ*, Spring, 1975). Astro begins by distinguishing between those American travelers who seek to impose our beliefs on others and those who have "identified themselves with what they have seen" and have tried to transform American chauvinism. He sorts Steinbeck's books into three categories without any common denominator. *Once There Was a War* and the uncollected reports from Viet Nam show a distinctly pro-American bias; *A Russian Journal* is preoccupied with facts to such an extent that the significance of them is diminished; but *The Log from the Sea of Cortez* and *Travels with Charley* "are the record of a man who was not simply a visitor, but . . . wanted to join in."

Sanford Marovitz expands his subject beyond just the travel books in a two-part article, "The Expository Prose of John Steinbeck" (*StQ*, Spring, Summer–Fall 1974), which reviews the whole body of Steinbeck's nonfiction, again except for the unjustly neglected "Letters to Alicia" from the Long Island newspaper *Newsday* between 1965 and Steinbeck's death. Marovitz takes an even dimmer view of the author's later years than some critics of his fiction, observing that his "most estimable journalism" is from the early years, *Their Blood Is Strong* and *The Sea of Cortez*, "which in some way or other corresponds to his creative work," but going on to say that the later journalism "seldom illuminates the novels contemporaneous with it" and that when he did raise social or moral questions, "he was not as convincing as he had once been when the imagination of Steinbeck the novelist and the observations of Steinbeck the journalist synthesized."

Marovitz's temporizing account has not been adequately filled out by other discussions of individual books. The early books that Marovitz praises have not received much further attention except in the full-length studies by Richard Astro and Jackson J. Benson. The only original contribution to *Steinbeck's Travel Literature* is Betty L. Perez's "The Form of the Narrative Section of *Sea of Cortez*: A Specimen Collected from Reality," which traces the way in which each chapter of the narrative log of this account of the 1940 expedition to collect marine life moves subtly and suggestively "from factual narrative to mythical saga" about the acceptance of the brotherhood of man and the other animals he collects and studies.

A Russian Journal remains a book that has been too much ignored, especially in view of continued confrontations between the superpowers. While John F. Slater's statement in "American Past and Soviet Present: The Double Consciousness of Steinbeck's *A Russian Journal*" (*StQ*, Summer–Fall 1975) that the book "often resembles a partially inhibited debate between immobilizing bureaucracy and subversive, deadpan irony" is most accurate, the article largely relates the book to American genteel traditions rather than to the philosophy underlying Steinbeck's other works. John Ditsky's conclusion in "Between Acrobats and Seals: Steinbeck in the U.S.S.R." (*StQ*, Winter–Spring 1982) that the author's conclusions "are vapid in the extreme" serves only to justify the general dismissal of the book.

It is scarcely surprising that Louis D. Owens's "The Threshold of War: Steinbeck's Quest in *Once There Was a War*" (*StQ*, Summer–Fall 1980), which views this collection of dispatches from the African-Italian front in World War II as an attempt "to find a mythical structure for an otherwise uneven and disparate collection," must conclude that it is not "easily read as a totally unified work." The conditions of composition would have made such a work unlikely even from a writer with the kind of preconceived plan that Steinbeck lacked.

Travels with Charley is one of Steinbeck's most popular works, but one would never guess this from what has been written about it. John Ditsky's "Steinbeck's *Travels with Charley*: The Quest that Failed" (*StQ*, Spring 1975; reprinted in *Steinbeck's Travel Literature*) finds "ambivalence" the keynote to the book and concludes that the author never got "home" at all. Barbara Reitt's "I Never Returned as I Went In" (*SWR*, Spring 1981) describes the book as a potboiler, but yet says it reveals much about Steinbeck as a writer, though just what, as Jack Salzman points out in *American Literary Scholarship* (1981), is "never made very clear."

It is a relief to turn from these vaporizings to one of the most insightful pieces written about Steinbeck by an observer from abroad. Roy S. Simmonds's "Our land . . . incredibly dear and beautiful: Steinbeck's *America and Americans*" (*StQ*, Summer–Fall, 1975; reprinted in *Steinbeck's Travel Literature*), commenting on Steinbeck as an artist of international significance who merited the Nobel Prize, makes the point that "No citizen of any other country reading this book by one of the most American of Americans can fail to be impressed by the almost unbelievable honesty with which the American nation is prepared to parade its faults before the rest of the world."

4 Films

One of the most conspicuous gaps in Steinbeck criticism has been filled by Joseph Millichap's *Steinbeck and Film* (New York, 1983), which provides thorough analyses in chronological order of all the films derived from Steinbeck's fiction, along with a chapter on television adaptations. The work of a dependable film scholar, this useful history complements Benson's and DeMott's books in providing a comprehensive base for future studies.

Like most critics, Millichap finds the early film versions of Steinbeck's work superior, calling Lewis Milestone's *Of Mice and Men* the best, because while "John Ford's *The Grapes of Wrath* remains a more important film . . . it fails to capture the power of Steinbeck's original, while Milestone's film proves at least the equal of Steinbeck's fictional and dramatic versions." Millichap believes that, by 1945, "the really important part of [Steinbeck's] career was finished," with "the most artistically successful . . . occasioned by film projects involving Mexico" (*The Pearl* and Elia Kazan's *Viva Zapata!*). (The one major omission from Millichap's book, incidentally, is an account of the differences between the English-language version of *The Pearl* and the slightly longer Spanish-language version, in which some of the artificialities Millichap objects to are less distracting.) Millichap even provocatively concludes that involvement with the movies may have accounted for Steinbeck's much discussed post-World War II decline: "When he abandoned the realistic and documentary modes for a sentimental and meretricious imitation of the silver screen, film began to have an adverse and eventually fatal influence on his fiction."

Earlier writings by Millichap on Steinbeck's films have been superseded by the book, but additional approaches are suggested by Robert Morsberger's overview, "Steinbeck on Screen," in *A Study Guide to John Steinbeck* (Metuchen, N.J., 1974).

Nunnally Johnson's film adaptation of *The Grapes of Wrath*, directed by John Ford, which was chosen as one of the ten greatest American films of all time in a poll by the American Film Institute, is the subject of a separate monograph by Warren French, *Filmguide to "The Grapes of Wrath"* (Bloomington, Ind., 1973), which contains extensive comments about the differences between the novel and the film and an appended chart tabulating these variations chapter by chapter. While the film must ultimately be judged on its own merits, French points out that "the effect of Ford's direction . . . was to distance and universalize Steinbeck's intensely timely story," particularly by shifting the emphasis at the end from Tom Joad's rebellion to Ma Joad's faith that "woman can change better'n a man" and that the rich die out while the poor are "the people that live."

Vivian C. Sobchak's *"The Grapes of Wrath* (1940): Thematic Emphasis through Visual Style" (*AQ*, Winter 1979) supplements French's book and George Bluestone's earlier *Novels into Films* (1957) by exploring the visual image that had hardly been mapped. After spending too much time putting down the inadequacies of earlier analyses that were prompted by other considerations, she focuses on the effect of director John Ford's concentrating on static, tableau-like images on a cluttered screen to make the point that "the film projects the images of a ritualized world in which change is neither possible nor desirable." The article is extremely helpful as a guide to looking at this film (or any film) and to understanding cinematic technique, but even Sobchak admits that "the same conclusions can be arrived at through" other methods of analysis.

The only filmscript by Steinbeck to be published as a separate book is *Viva Zapata!* (New York, 1975), edited by Robert E. Morsberger and containing also a revised version of his "Steinbeck's Zapata: Rebel versus Revolutionary," discussed in the earlier version of this essay. John Ditsky's "Words and Deeds in *Viva Zapata!*" (*DR*, Spring 1976) attempts to extend Morsberger's insights by explaining that "Steinbeck's central means of discerning character is profoundly cinematic, and essentially non-literary," casting suspicion "on verbal, especially written," communication and reinforcing the value of physical contact, especially with the eyes. Tetsumaro Hayashi also contributes a provocative comparative study, "The Theme of Revolution in *Julius Caesar* and *Viva Zapata!*" to *East and West*, arguing that in both Shakespeare's play and Steinbeck's script, the martyred title characters "remain the masters of their own destiny" whose spirits survive in the followers who will push forward their causes even more forcefully.

In perhaps the most intriguing tribute to the literary qualities of Steinbeck's film script, Jerry W. Wilson, in "Steinbeck, Fuentes, and the Mexican Revolution" (*SWR*, Autumn 1982), compares *Viva Zapata!* to Mexican novelist Carlos Fuentes's celebrated *The Death of Artemio Cruz*, pointing out that although both works are pervaded by a sense of frustration about the failure of revolution to bring about progressive change, "Steinbeck fictionalizes and romanticizes Zapata partly in support of his own increasingly individualistic view of reality in general, and of revolution in particular," while "Fuentes focuses on the fictional Cruz [whose story unfolds from his deathbed in 1959] to epitomize the perversion of revolution."

Moving back to the wartime *Lifeboat*, Steven J. Federle revives the old story about the falling out between John Steinbeck and Alfred Hitchcock over the script in *"Lifeboat* as Allegory: Steinbeck and the Demon of Wars" (*StQ*, Winter–Spring 1979) in order to provide further details about the changes made from what Hitchcock called Steinbeck's "incomplete" treatment for the film. Federle maintains that Steinbeck's original script was "based on much broader humanitarian values" than the film and "ends on a profoundly ironic note in contrast to Hitchcock's suspensefully dramatic but morally empty conclusion."

For analysis of other Steinbeck scripts and films based upon his work, it is generally necessary to turn to Millichap's book, although some brief reports are in on the results of the long and troubled effort to film *Cannery Row*. After narrating the many problems that plagued the longtime project, Robert E. Morsberger reports in "*Cannery Row* Revisited" (*StQ*, Summer–Fall 1983) that the film, incorporating material also from *Sweet Thursday*, "has been made with loving care, and most of it works." Professional film critics and the general public disagreed violently, and the film was a box-office disaster. Closer to the mark as an evaluation of it is John C. Tibbetts's "It Happened in Monterey: *Cannery Row*" (*LFQ*, No. 2, 1982), a brief note explaining that the film was shot largely in a studio, since the original Cannery Row has become too fashionable to serve as an appropriate setting, with the result that the film "does not have the bristling energy and high speed of Steinbeck's original conception."

5 Foreign Reputation

Steinbeck's reputation has grown even faster abroad, especially in Asia, than at home, so that again any comprehensive overview of foreign criticisms would require a lengthy, separate study, contributions toward which are available elsewhere. Mitsuaki Yamashita's "A Survey of John Steinbeck Bibliographies in Japan" appears in *Persica* (Jan. 1978) and Takahiko Sugiyama's "Steinbeck Criticism: Present and Future" is included in *East and West*, which also includes papers presented at an International Steinbeck Congress held in Fukuoka City, Japan, in 1976. The *Steinbeck Quarterly* has also published accounts of "Japanese Steinbeck Criticism in 1971" (Fall 1973), in 1972–73 (Spring 1975), and in 1975 (Spring 1977) by Hidekazu Hirose, followed up by Kiyoshi Nakayama's several accounts of "Steinbeck Criticism in Japan" (Summer–Fall 1979, 1981, and 1983). So far the journal has carried only a single survey of "Steinbeck Criticism in India: 1968–1978," by M. R. Satyanarayana (Winter–Spring 1981).

Brief mention must be made here, however, of a limited number of books in English that make Asian writers' views of Steinbeck especially accessible to American readers. Sunita Jain's *Steinbeck's Concept of Man* (New Delhi, 1979) surveys all of Steinbeck's fiction with the ambitious aim of demonstrating that his concept of man remains the same throughout his fiction as he depicts man "struggling to attain dignity by imposing order on his dual existence as an individual and a group animal." In another eloquently written Indian survey of Steinbeck's work, *John Steinbeck: A Study in the Theme of Compassion* (Hyderabad, 1977), M. R. Satyanarayana concludes that although the novelist is unhappy at man's inhumanity to man, he does not despair, because "he believes that the evil of violence and hatred can be cured by love and understanding." The most ambitious book to appear so far from India is *Indian Response to Steinbeck: Essays Presented to Warren French* (ed. R. K. Sharma, Jaipur, 1984), a collection of seven overviews of Steinbeck and his works and eighteen essays on individual novels, concluding with summaries of eight doctoral dissertations about Steinbeck written in India between 1968 and 1984. The wide scope of the writings by Indian specialists in Steinbeck is a remarkable testimony to the international influence of his work.

The title of Noboru Shimomura's *A Study of John Steinbeck: Mysticism in His Novels* (Tokyo, 1982) identifies the subject of this ambitious effort to point out and comment upon the use of both Christian and Oriental mystical doctrines in all of his novels in chronological order. Steinbeck's "acceptance of God does not change," Shimomura concludes, "but his idea of God shifts from a pagan to a Christian conception," moving through animistic mysticism in *To a God Unknown*, nature mysticism in *The Grapes of Wrath*, and Eastern mysticism in *Cannery Row* to "a personal, conventional Christian mysticism in *The Winter of Our Discontent*."

Finally, an extraordinarily interesting book for Americans familiar with Steinbeck's work is Shigeharu Yano's *The Current of Steinbeck's World* (Tokyo, 1978–82), which collects in four fascicles that are continuously paginated a group of essays that Yano wrote between 1971 and 1977 about separate Steinbeck works. It is impossible to summarize the collection, because Yano has so far provided no synthesis of his views about Steinbeck or his work and the essays were neither written nor published in the order of the publication of the books they treat individually. The emphasis throughout, however, is on man's spiritual awakening. The general tenor of Yano's viewpoint is suggested by his comment that Steinbeck's "soul was elevated to the religious stage and sublimed, which led to *East of Eden*. Consequently, I value *East of Eden* above *The Grapes of Wrath*." (This is a view that, despite recent defenses of *East of Eden*, is not likely to be shared by American readers.) What is particularly interesting about Yano's work, in fact, is that it provides the opportunity to study a sensitive reading of Steinbeck that is little affected by the influence of American society and politics, American literature and folklore, or the tradition of the "American Dream." Yano looks beyond these parochial aspects of the novels to see how Steinbeck has dealt with the fundamental human mysteries of love and death, right and wrong, good and evil, freedom and spiritual enlightenment, the qualities that probably account for the unusual international success of Steinbeck's fiction that has puzzled many condescending American critics.

A most fitting observance of the conclusion of the first major phase of Steinbeck scholarship with the publication of Jackson J. Benson's biography and the meeting of the Second International Steinbeck Congress at the novelist's birthplace, Salinas, California, 1–8 August 1984, is the publication of the proceedings of this gathering of scholars from the United States and Asia, *John Steinbeck: From Salinas to the World* (Tokyo, 1985), edited by an international committee of Shigeharu Yano, Tetsumaro Hayashi, Richard F. Peterson, and Yasuo Hashiguchi.

The five American papers included serve to review the highlights of the first fifty years of Steinbeck scholarship. Warren French's keynote address, "John Steinbeck: From Salinas to the World," singles out, from the great mass of international scholarship reviewed in his three contributions to this present collection, the most lastingly important contributions by Frederic I. Carpenter, Richard Astro, Robert DeMott, Roy Simmonds, Jackson J. Benson, Shigeharu Yano, and Tetsumaro Hayashi, to suggest how a boy from a small California agricultural community could have become a Nobel Prize winner and a force for international good will.

John Ditsky's "Steinbeck as Dramatist: A Preliminary Account" outlines the considerations needing further attention in a still relatively neglected but influential phase of Steinbeck's work. Mimi R. Gladstein's "From Lady Brett to Ma Joad: A Singular Scarcity" reviews the female characters in Steinbeck's most highly regarded early work against a background of the stereotyping of women in the major American fiction between the two world wars. Robert E. Morsberger's "Steinbeck's Films" evaluates the quite uneven body of motion pictures derived from Steinbeck's works, suggesting reasons for the successes and the failures and citing especially Steinbeck's powerful writing for the screen in *Viva Zapata!* Tetsumaro Hayashi's "John Steinbeck: His Concept of Writing" approaches the delicate task of developing from this shy author's own statements the reasons for his dedication to the work that at last brought him international recognition.

Seven of the group of papers presented by Asian scholars also appear here, all published in English, as they were delivered. Several undertake broad subjects that are indicated by their titles: Kingo Hanamoto's "Steinbeck, Faulkner and Buddhism," Noboru Shimomura's "Steinbeck and Monterey: Theme and Humor in the 'Monterey Trilogy' [*Tortilla Flat, Cannery Row, Sweet Thursday*]," and M. R. Satyanarayana's illumination of the subject of much recent Steinbeck study, "Indian Thought in Steinbeck's Works." Kiyoshi Nakayama's "John Steinbeck and Yasunari Kawabata" opens up an area of great future promise in the comparison of Steinbeck's works with those of writers from other cultures, while Kiyohiko Tsuboi contributes to the many comparisons of Steinbeck with fellow Americans in "Two Jodys: Steinbeck and Rawlings," interrelating *The Red Pony* with Marjorie Kinnan Rawlings's popular novel *The Yearling* (1938).

The group concludes with two essays calling for further appraisal of two individual works that may have been too lightly regarded: Mrs. Rajul Bhargava's "*Tortilla Flat*: A Revaluation" and Takahiko Sugiyama's

"Camille Oaks, A Heroine of Nonsense—A Revaluation of *The Wayward Bus*."

With this volume, nearly as much scholarship about John Steinbeck has appeared during the first half of the 1980s as had appeared during the preceding forty years, calling attention particularly to Steinbeck's status as a world-class writer. A period of assimilation lies ahead during which the often previously provincial conception of Steinbeck as a literary artist may undergo considerable revision.

V SUPPLEMENT

Bibliography. The celebration of the fiftieth anniversary of the publication of *The Grapes of Wrath* in 1989 saw an unprecedented increase in Steinbeck studies. No comprehensive international bibliography is as yet in print or under way; but Robert B. Harmon has already superseded his *The First Editions of John Steinbeck* (1978) with *The Collectible John Steinbeck: A Practical Guide* (Jefferson, N.C., 1986), which includes information about prices and sources; and he has followed this up with *Steinbeck Bibliographies: An Annotated Guide* (Metuchen, N.J., 1987), which lists 202 publications containing information about writings by or about the writer. Before relying on this guide, however, one should read Robert DeMott's review (*BB*, Dec. 1987), which explains why Harmon's listing does not answer the need for a comprehensive catalogue. DeMott has also compiled *John Steinbeck: A Checklist of Books By and About* (Bradenton, Fla., 1987), an expensive but beautifully produced book that students and occasional teachers and readers of Steinbeck may find most useful.

Biography. The most interesting and useful supplement so far to Jackson J. Benson's 1984 biography is Benson's own *Looking for Steinbeck's Ghost* (Norman, Okla., 1988), the personal account of this "scholar-adventurer's" (to borrow Richard Altick's memorable term) fourteen-year quest for the materials for *The True Adventures of John Steinbeck, Writer*, which Benson declares he "enjoyed writing." This should be essential reading for anyone who aspires to a similar career.

Similarly of great value is *"Your Only Weapon Is Your Work"* (San Jose, Calif., 1985), which, with a long biographical introduction by Robert DeMott, reprints a letter from Steinbeck to Dennis Murphy, encouraging the promising young writer after the acceptance of his first novel (*The Sergeant*), which reveals Steinbeck's conception of the rewards and pitfalls of his craft. Tetsumaro Hayashi has collected other statements by Steinbeck on this inspiring but frustrating calling in *John Steinbeck on Writing* (SES, No. 2, Muncie, Ind., 1989). Hayashi's *John Steinbeck and the Vietnam War, Part 1* (SMS, No. 12, Muncie, Ind., 1986) also presents from a sympathetic viewpoint Steinbeck's growing pessimism about the conflict that he came to regard as a personal as well as a national tragedy.

Other items should prove ephemeral. Brian St. Pierre's *John Steinbeck: The California Years* (San Francisco, 1983) was completed before Benson's book, which supersedes it, but contains some interesting early photographs and debunkings of local rumors. The chapter on John and Elaine Steinbeck in J. Bryan III's tasteless *Merry Gentlemen (and One Lady)* (New York, 1985), recounting the author's intrusive travels with the couple, supplants Budd Schulberg's lugubrious memoir (1972) as the most embarrassing exploitation to date of such an acquaintance.

Criticism. Louis Owens's *John Steinbeck's Re-Vision of America* (1985) marks indeed a fresh beginning for Steinbeck studies with its complex effort to affirm that the novelist is "a craftsman and artist of the first rank in American literature." Owens's argument that Steinbeck has been "consistently ignored" as "illuminating the way out of the American wasteland" receives support from an unexpected quarter in Yale critic Harold Bloom's *Modern Critical Views: John Steinbeck* (New York, 1987), one building block in the stupendous edifice that Bloom labors to erect at the moment when academic criticism appears to be throwing off the halters of deconstruction in a quest for an as yet undetermined new guide to the placement of every major writer in the Anglo-American canon.

Breaking with the eastern establishment's half-century dismissal of Steinbeck as a popular sentimentalist, Bloom summons out of a surrounding sea of misreadings eleven artfully chosen but unhackneyed critiques published between 1947 and 1987 to document his concentration on *The Grapes of Wrath* in seeking to "define both its limitations and its abiding value." In his introduction Bloom confesses that he remains "uneasy about my own experience of rereading" the novel, since Steinbeck, who "aspired beyond his aesthetic means," is not "one of the inescapable American novelists of our century." Yet, Bloom concedes, "there are no canonical standards worthy of human respect that could exclude *The Grapes of Wrath* from a serious reader's esteem." Bloom thus graciously apologizes for the shortcomings of his forebears and colleagues without conceding too much; but even his inclusion of the novel in his program acknowledges that he does find that "a human strength, however generously worked through, is also an aesthetic value, in a literary narrative."

A related earlier charge that "critics have seemed to expect more from Steinbeck than he was willing to provide" keynotes another hitherto unnoted reservation about Steinbeck in a special issue of *American Examiner* (Fall/Winter 1978–79), honoring the fortieth anniversary of the publication of *The Grapes of Wrath*. It concludes with Cliff Lewis's "Critical Perspectives on *The Grapes of Wrath*," in which Lewis finds that as the 1980s began, "the challenge remains to identify [Steinbeck's] aesthetic intentions"—a difficult task indeed if, as Harold Bloom maintains, they exceeded his means.

Major parts of books devoted to Steinbeck, however, continue to emphasize sociological or psychological problems rather than face the more challenging questions of their relationships to wrestling with what Herman Melville called "the angel Art." Mimi Reisel Gladstein extends her earlier comments in *Steinbeck's Women* to his entire oeuvre in *The Indestructible Women in Faulkner, Hemingway, and Steinbeck* (Ann Arbor, Mich., 1986), but arrives at no synthesis beyond her earlier one about the indestructibility of women like Ma Joad in Steinbeck's best works during the years that he could depend on his first wife Carol's assistance.

A provocative new thesis is introduced in "John Steinbeck and Dorothea Lange" in Carol Shloss's *Photography and the American Writer: 1840–1940* (New York, 1987). Although Lange and Steinbeck never worked together, both were greeted with similar praise and hostility for their portrayal of California's migrant workers. Shloss claims that Steinbeck studied Lange's photographs during his research for *The Grapes of Wrath* and assumed "the ideological positions of the Taylor-Lange Reports on farm labor conditions," but that he failed "to understand or to emulate" her working methods, with the consequence that he "turned the experiences of the unwilling poor into private capital." While this argument reinforces the case against Steinbeck as a "sentimentalist," Shloss ignores Steinbeck's intention to fictionalize and universalize the California situation rather than to document it as he had in *Their Blood Is Strong*.

David Wyatt also relies principally on biography when, in "Steinbeck's Lost Gardens" in his *The Fall into Eden: Landscape and Imagination in California* (Cambridge, England, 1986), he traces Steinbeck's recurrent quest for "happiness in the garden" that he many times found and lost and arrives at the conclusion that *The Grapes of Wrath* "marks the end of Steinbeck's conception of home as a place," since he subsequently decided that "living is people, not places."

Probably the last major work by Steinbeck to be published—and one of his most important—is *Working Days: The Journals of "The Grapes of Wrath"* (New York, 1989), a transcription of the handwritten diary that he kept in 1938 while he was desperately pushing himself to complete the third version of his most famous novel (previously mentioned above as "Diary of a Book"). It is at last in print as part of the celebration of the fiftieth anniversary of the publication of the novel, with a prefatory essay by Robert DeMott placing this extraordinary document against the background of the writer's troubled life and times. Its revelation of his inner turmoil greatly revises understanding of his personality and artistic techniques.

This semicentennial is also marked with two new collections of essays devoted to the novel. John Ditsky's *Critical Essays on "The Grapes of Wrath"* (CEAmL, Boston, 1989) contains, along with reprinted pieces, new essays by Jackson J. Benson (on Steinbeck's coming to write the novel), Roy

Simmonds (on its early reception in war-torn England), Carroll Britch, Cliff Lewis, and Louis Owens, besides a large collection of early reviews of the novel. David Wyatt's forthcoming collection in Cambridge's new American Novel Series features writers not previously usually associated with Steinbeck—William Howarth, Nellie McKay, Stephen Railton, Kevin Starr, and Leslie Gossage on John Ford's film version. Harold Bloom's rehabilitation of the novel is apparently effecting quick reactions.

Other books have not yet benefited. Most new attention to them has been afforded by Tetsumaro Hayashi, veteran editor of the *Steinbeck Quarterly*. He offers three interpretations of the usually neglected *The Moon Is Down* in the first volume of a new Steinbeck Essay Series (Muncie, Ind., 1986). Two of these are detailed accounts of the play-novelette's parallels with Shakespeare's *Macbeth* as studies of men's "indomitable will to preserve their traditional democratic values against totalitarianism, oppression and slavery."

Hayashi and Thomas J. Moore have also edited *Steinbeck's "The Red Pony": Essays in Criticism* (SMS, No. 13, Muncie, Ind., 1988), which presents new readings of the four stories comprising the cycle in the order in which they are customarily printed by Thomas M. Tammaro, Robert S. Hughes, Jr., Roy S. Simmonds, and Mimi R. Gladstein. Warren French introduces the essays as "a variety of provocative new approaches not just to the particular subjects of these early stories, but to Steinbeck's fiction as a whole."

More traditional in approach is Hughes's *Beyond "The Red Pony": A Reader's Companion to Steinbeck's Complete Short Stories* (Metuchen, N.J., 1987), which provides a useful pedagogical tool for discussing not only the familiar stories from *The Long Valley*, but also a surprising number of lesser-known pieces ranging from unpublished tales from the 1920s to uncollected publications from the 1930s and 1940s, as well as interchapters from *The Grapes of Wrath* and dispatches from *Once There Was a War* that can be read as autonomous stories.

Hughes has followed this up with the even more useful *John Steinbeck: A Study of the Short Fiction* (Boston, 1988), which includes further material about the works mentioned above, along with an analysis of the short story cycle *The Pastures of Heaven* and previous critiques of the short stories by Charles May ("The Snake"), Marilyn H. Mitchell (female characters), Arnold L. Goldsmith (*The Red Pony*), and M. R. Satyanarayana (initiation stories).

Wallace Stevens

Joseph N. Riddel

I BIBLIOGRAPHY

There have been two most substantial additions and a solid number of smaller but no less important contributions to the Stevens bibliography over the past decade. First, J. M. Edelstein's *Wallace Stevens: A Descriptive Bibliography* (Pittsburgh, 1972) provided the nearly definitive listing and description of Stevens's publications up to that time, as well as a very complete but unannotated checklist of Stevens criticism, including reviews of his work. Scrupulous in its attention to detail and nearly exhaustive in its coverage, Edelstein's bibliography updates, amends, and supplements the Morse-Bryer-Riddel *Checklist* (1963), and therefore concludes the sixty years of criticism covered by the previous version of this essay. It terminates, however, at the onset of the decade this essay surveys and could now be usefully updated, to take account of the few new materials that have been uncovered, collected, and published along with the ever increasing volumes of criticism that no bibliography can ever quite catch up to.

A second important book, Abbie Willard's *Wallace Stevens: The Poet and His Critics* (Chicago, 1978), almost does for Stevens criticism what Edelstein does for his writings. It too updates, complements, and supplements previous essays by Riddel and others, but unlike those, its length allows for ample, thorough description of the various critical positions and categories. Willard's essay is an honest and objective, if not definitive or exhaustive, survey of the varieties of Stevens criticism. Her approach is generally detached and uncritical, as well as nonideological, though she is not without judgment of what is unsound, eccentric, or self-indulgent. Rather than treating the criticism historically, Willard divides it into a number of categories, the logic for which is not always evident, but the method allows her to discuss the major books not only at length but in different places and thus with different emphases.

Three other "events" also contribute substantially to bibliography during this period: the acquisition of the main body of Stevens's manuscripts and other materials by the Huntington Library at San Marino, California, in 1975–76; the establishment of the *Wallace Stevens Journal (WSJour)* in 1977, under the general editorship of Robert Deutsch at California State University, Northridge, assisted in the beginning by W. T. Ford who had edited the now-defunct *Stevens Newsletter* at Northwestern in the late 1960s; and the centennial year of Stevens's birth, 1979, which saw the publication of one book, *Wallace Stevens: A Celebration* (ed. Robert Buttel and Frank Doggett, Princeton, N.J., 1980; hereinafter referred to as Buttel and Doggett), and a few commemorative issues in serials, most notably the *Southern Review* (Autumn 1979) and the *Wallace Stevens Journal* (Fall 1979). The *Celebration* is essentially a collection of critical essays, which will be recounted in a later section in this essay, but it does include new material and bibliographical descriptions of it: these include the legendary but previously unpublished "From the Journal of Crispin," an early version of "The Comedian as the Letter C," edited with introductory commentary by Louis Martz; some unpublished "Adagia," introduced and edited by A. Walton Litz; and a working version of the essay, "A Collect of Philosophy," edited with commentary by Peter Brazeau.

The Huntington collection now contains only a small amount of significant unpublished material, especially since Holly Stevens's important edition/reminiscence, *Souvenirs and Prophecies: The Young Wallace Stevens* (New York, 1977), which presents substantial amounts of the juvenilia and pre-*Harmonium* poetry, most importantly a "journal" Stevens began in 1898 while at Harvard and continued through the first decade of the new century, and the "book of poems" which he wrote for his fiancée Elsie Moll during their courtship. *Souvenirs and Prophecies,* then, offers the first publication of some interesting if not accomplished early writing and provides something like a combined biography and autobiography of Stevens's early years. The collection at San Marino has proved to be the focal point for a good deal of research leading to a renewal of interest in a Stevens biography. Other collections have been of peripheral importance.

The *Wallace Stevens Journal* sustains an ongoing bibliography of criticism, though not in every issue, as well as updating the checklist of new Stevens material. It also periodically lists the availability of Stevens editions. Useful bibliographical essays and lists from its archives would include the following: William Ingoldsby, "The Wallace Stevens Manuscript Collection at the Huntington Library" (Spring 1977); Milton J. Bates, "Stevens' Books at the Huntington: An Annotated Checklist" (Fall 1978, Spring 1979); Michael O. Stegman, "Wallace Stevens and Music: A Discography of Stevens' Phonograph Record Collection" (Fall 1979); George Hendrick, "Wallace Stevens' Manuscripts at the University of Illinois" (Fall 1978); Peter Brazeau, "Wallace Stevens at the University of Massachusetts: Checklist of an Archive" (Spring 1978); and Ray Lewis White, "Wallace Stevens: A Collection of Reviews of His Works, 1931–

1967" (Spring 1980). To which need be added: Louis L. Martz, "Manuscripts of Wallace Stevens" (*YULG*, Oct. 1979); and J. M. Edelstein, "The Poet as Reader: Wallace Stevens and His Books" (*BC*, Spring 1974).

II EDITIONS

There have been several re-editions but in the strictest sense no new editions of the poet's writings since Holly Stevens's *The Palm at the End of the Mind* offered a slightly modified canon in 1971. His daughter's edition dissolved the "book" divisions of *The Collected Poems* and added some of the poems of *Opus Posthumous* and a few unpublished pieces like the play, "Bowl, Cat, and Broomstick." It also tended to produce a new effect of closure by displacing "Not Ideas about the Thing but the Thing Itself" as a concluding utterance which seemed to indicate that the poet had arrived at or achieved an unmediated and nonlinguistic moment of vision. Now, Knopf has reissued *The Collected Poems* (1954) in its Vintage paperback series, along with *Opus Posthumous* (New York, 1957, 1972, 1982), thereby offering the student and teacher a choice of ways to approach the canon, albeit there is not a great difference. *Opus Posthumous* was first reissued in hardback in 1972, with a note acknowledging that the essay "On Poetic Truth" was not Stevens's but a collection of sentences he had taken from an essay by the English aesthetician H. D. Lewis and had indeed used in an essay on Marianne Moore. The 1982 Vintage paperback silently omits the essay.

Both Holly Stevens's *Souvenirs and Prophecies* and the centennial essays, *Wallace Stevens: Celebration*, might be considered in part new editions, especially the former, which contains ample new material, as noted above, from Stevens's juvenilia. The *Wallace Stevens Journal* continues to turn up items, like the brief note "Insurance and Social Change" (Fall 1980). In the Spring 1978 issue, Samuel French Morse adds "A Note on 'Bowl, Cat, and Broomstick'" along with a photocopy of previously unpublished page ten of the play. And George S. Lensing provides us with an edition of Stevens's "Notebook," tentatively entitled *From Pieces of Paper*, now in the Huntington collection, in the *Southern Review* centennial issue (Autumn 1979), a listing of lines, metaphors, potential titles, and so on, that Stevens collected over a period of years and from which he occasionally drew for his poems. Lensing annotates the notebook entries with indexes of where the entries are eventually used.

All in all, however, there has been precious little added to the Stevens canon since the 1950s, excepting the *Letters* (1967). Even *Souvenirs and Prophecies* is more biography than anything else. And one wonders, given Knopf's reissues of the old collected editions, whether anything like a scholarly edition of the works will be possible; or even, given Stevens's reluctance to leave working papers that might solve textual cruxes, whether one is necessary. It is difficult to believe, given the paucity of holographs, etc., that a scholarly edition would radically alter the printed texts, though some kind of annotated work which underscored the range of Stevens's allusions, references, plays upon linguistic etymology and sound, etc., would certainly be helpful.

III MANUSCRIPTS AND LETTERS

As expected, new letters continue to turn up, especially personal correspondence, and to be published in serials like the *Wallace Stevens Journal* and *Antaeus* (see, for example, number 36 of the latter [Winter 1980] where there are letters from Williams as well as "Two Letters to a Friend," C. L. Daugherty). See also the listing of manuscripts and letters in the Bibliography section of this essay, which includes references to Stevens manuscripts at Yale University, the University of Massachusetts, the University of Illinois, as well as those housed at the Huntington.

The *Wallace Stevens Journal* continues to update information on the availability of manuscripts and new discoveries. Edelstein's bibliography offers an exhaustive listing up to 1972, but an updating is needed. The Huntington continues to be the main repository of unpublished materials, but with *Souvenirs and Prophecies* and other editions of pieces such as Lensing's of the "Notebook" (see above), the most important of the manuscripts are now in print. A publication of the holograph of "The Man with the Blue Guitar," long held by the Lockwood Library at SUNY/Buffalo, would be an important event, not only for its discarded sections of the poems but for Stevens's annotations. But the manuscript remains confined by the edict of Stevens's gift, that it not be "studied." Most recently (and too late for extended discussion in this essay), Beverly Coyle and Alan Filreis have edited *Secretaries of the Moon: The Letters of Wallace Stevens and José Rodríguez-Feo* (Durham, N.C., 1986).

IV BIOGRAPHY

Perhaps the most extensive, and in a sense least rewarding, efforts of scholarship during the past decade have been directed upon the "life." The renowned separation of vocation and avocation that lent such a mystery to the early discussions of Stevens's poetry is no longer the cliché about which biography turns. It is now acknowledged that Stevens the poet was not unknown to his fellow insurance brokers, nor was he an unreadable enigma to his peers, both artists and actuaries, as anecdotal essays like William York Tindall's perpetuated the legend of private and public man. Though a shy and reticent man and one not given to personal openness about the office or in artsy circles, except when on holiday with certain intimate friends or when indulging the grape or berry, Stevens was by no means the shade of Hartford he was made to appear. Nevertheless, the recent spate of inquiries into Stevens's "life" cannot escape the question. More significantly, biographical accounts cannot transcend the increasingly evident fact that Stevens's "life," thought of as a social, sexual, business, or even cultural series of events, was unaccountably ordinary, and that his "life" was essentially that of an "interior paramour," a life of the senses and of the act of the mind.

Efforts or notes toward a biography continue to proliferate nevertheless—and the most extraordinary continue to be those glimpses or shadows drawn by and out of his performance with and within language; the most forbidding, those which try to make out of the everyday facts some afflatus or inspirational source, even if that source only works to activate defense mechanisms and provoke a poetic substitution. The most suggestive and useful biography continues to be the Stevens *Letters*, and the reminiscences of *Souvenirs and Prophecies*, both books being the issue of his issue, Holly, who fortunately shies away from interpretation while providing a narrative to tie together the fragmentary journals and juvenilia. This crossing of biography and autobiography, of history and a literary life, produces an interesting hybrid and provides a reservoir for critics to bring some "facts" of life to bear upon the "life of poetry."

No one has yet attempted a formal biography, like Paul Mariani's massive life of Williams, let alone anything like a psychobiography. The unexceptional outward quality of the bourgeois life remains dispersed, if not sublated, in the "vast repetitions" of the poetry. The first major effort at biography arrives as a useful but marginal portrait, somewhat out of focus because it is refracted through too many lenses, or too many opaque memories. Peter Brazeau's *Parts of a World—Wallace Stevens Remembered: An Oral Biography* (New York, 1983) defines itself in the concluding phrase. It is a collection of reminiscences by people—relatives, fellow workers at the company, neighbors, friends acquired through business connections, and fellow poets—whose memories are recorded long after the fact and in the wake of the poet's critical fame. The oral record adds up to a series of fragmentary glimpses, occasionally detailing happenings that turn up, or seem to turn up, in poetic figures as if untransformed, but most often as enriched or disfigured. Brazeau ties together the almost random group of recollections with a narrative of his own, but his neutrality and his resistance to anything like a critical stance or thesis enforces an even further division between the life and the work, leaving for the critic the job of making imaginative connections. For example, Brazeau carefully documents, from numerous sources, Stevens's well-known preoccupation during the last decade and a half of his life with his own family history and his efforts, often at considerable expense, to acquire the genealogy of a family from which he had earlier been distanced if not alienated. Brazeau's kind of oral portrait, however, cannot connect the dots between Stevens's almost Mormon-like belief that a genealogy can return one to origins and thus substantiate one's spiritual identity, and the often ironic effect evident in poems like "Dutch

Graves . . ." or, more intensely, in "The Rock" and "The Sail of Ulysses,"
where the very question of ground, origin, and so on, are relentlessly
exposed as fictions less than supreme. Stevens's poems would seem to
expose the very dream of a regressive quest for origins, ground, or even
a theory of poetic expression itself and open up for criticism something
like Harold Bloom's reading of Stevens's "anxiety of influence."

Brazeau's book characterizes very well the unrewarding task of the
Stevens biographer. Once one has identified some relation between
"fact" and its subsequent refiguration, the only thing of significance is
linguistic, the poet's "tropic of resemblance." Yet, a great amount of
energy continues to be invested in the ordinary details of the Hartford
actuary, the walker of Westerly Terrace whose itinerary took him by
local parks where, sitting upon a bench, he would reflect upon the
reflections in a lake as if in a "Theatre of Trope," or would lead him
asymptotically by a dump where the solitary caretaker would supply
him with one of his figures of the modern poet's impoverishment.

One might, for example, point to Michel Benamou's "Displacements
of Parental Space: American Poetry and French Symbolism" (*Boundary
2*, Winter 1977), and to his study in the *Symbolisme* of Stevens reviewed
in an earlier version of this essay, as well as his Sorbonne thesis (to be
discussed later), as instances of a critical rather than a biographical de-
ployment of Stevens's concern with genealogy; and contrast this with
such interpretations as Milton J. Bates's in essays like "To Realize the
Past: Wallace Stevens' Genealogical Study" (*AL*, Jan. 1981) and "Selecting One's Parents: Wallace Stevens and Some Early Influences" (*JML*,
May 1982), each of which rehearses the history of Stevens's preoccupation with a family history and his own indulgence in genealogical research, before applying this to the thematics of certain poems. Also see
Joseph G. Kronick's essay, "Of Parents, Children, and Rabbis—Wallace
Stevens and the Question of the Book" (*Boundary 2*, Spring 1983), which
reads Stevens's concern with genealogy in its relation to both a Bloomian
and a poststructuralist critical questioning of the notion of origins and
the notion of poetic tradition, indicating that the question of genealogy
and all that it implied was a provocation to the Stevensian imagination
and a metaphor indeed for his poetics, not a benign task of recovering
the historical past or, in Bates's words, of indicating the "past's legacy
to the present." Bates's *Wallace Stevens: A Mythology of Self* (Berkeley,
Calif., 1985), which claims not to be a biography but a "fable of identity"
or a kind of spiritual biography, appeared just as this essay was going
to press.

Nevertheless, biographical projects, whether archivist or memorializa-
tions, continue to add to the Stevensian enigma: Brazeau has been the
most persistent; parts of his *Oral Biography* had appeared in the *Wallace
Stevens Journal* (Spring 1977), in *Antaeus* (Winter 1980), and in *The Motive
for Metaphor: Essays in Modern Poetry*, edited by Francis Blessington and

Guy Rotella (Boston, 1983; hereinafter referred to as Blessington and Rotella), a collection in honor of Samuel French Morse that contains five essays on Stevens. Brazeau has also explored Stevens's relations, mostly epistolary, with other artists, in essays like "The Irish Connection: Wallace Stevens and Thomas McGreevey" (*SoR*, July 1981). Glen MacLeod has made the most significant examination of Stevens's literary contacts and relations, especially those that left a mark on his early formative years. MacLeod's *Wallace Stevens and Company: The "Harmonium" Years, 1913–1923* (Ann Arbor, Mich., 1983), has recently been published in the UMI Research Press series which reproduces certain dissertations on modern writers. MacLeod's study confines itself to an exploration of Stevens's relations, socially and artistically, with certain members of the New York avant-garde scene, like Donald Evans, Carl Van Vechten, Walter Arensberg, Marcel Duchamp, and especially William Carlos Williams, among several others. It explores their possible influence on the development of Stevens's early style—the impact, say, of Dada and American surrealism on the mannerist exercises of some of the *Harmonium* poems or, to cite a specific instance, the effect of such a notion of Arensberg's, that poetry was a kind of encoded or cryptic language, on Stevens's manipulation of this anagrammatology into a play with sounds or with the shapes of written letters. MacLeod's study has its interest and use, even though it employs a rather literal sense of influence. The anagrammatic Stevens awaits its cryptic critic.

Thomas F. Lombardi, George S. Lensing, and Milton J. Bates, among others, have been almost as committed as Brazeau to the project of a Stevens biography, though the long-rumored major project by Richard Ellmann now is rumored to be on a side-burner if not altogether abandoned. Lombardi has been particularly interested in the Bucks County connection and Stevens's family heritage: see his "Wallace Stevens: At Home in Pennsylvania" (*WSJour*, Spring 1978) and "Wallace Stevens and the Haunts of Unimportant Ghosts" (*WSJour*, Spring 1983), as well as "Pennsylvania: a Keystone to Wallace Stevens" (*Historical Review of Bucks County*, Summer 1976). Bates, along with his bibliographical work, has tended to use biography as an instrument of criticism, in essays like "Stevens in Love: The Woman Won, the Woman Lost" (*ELH*, Spring 1981) and "Stevens as Regional Poet" (*WSJour*, Spring 1981), along with the essays on genealogy noted above; and Lensing has explored "The Early Years of Wallace Stevens" (*SoR*, Jan. 1978), more in the spirit of the criticism of Buttel and Litz that makes the poetry expressive if not representative of a personal history. (Lensing has other essays in this mode, ranging back into the 1960s and surveyed elsewhere.) William J. Hartigan has added little to Brazeau's investigations in his "Wallace Stevens at the Hartford" (*WSJour*, Summer 1977). More interesting are such reflections of poets like Theodore Weiss ("Lunching with Hoon," *APR*, Sept./Oct. 1978). But on the whole, a criticism oriented in the "life" renders increasingly fewer results, unless accompanied by some daring speculative departure that is likely to leave the empiricist evidence troped into "chits" that even the "stiffest realist," let alone a "fatalist," cannot jig upon his knee, "chits," to extend the figures of "The Comedian as the Letter C," which exact as great a price as the pleasure they give. Stevens turned his life into a text, or in Mallarmé's words on Poe, "Such as into himself eternity's changed him . . . ," and it is there, encrypted in his canon, that the "interior paramour" is best revealed.

V CRITICISM

There is a temptation to describe the difference between Stevens criticism in the 1960s and the 1970s simply as quantitative. Except for one major "turn," the recent work has not been revisionary but an extension and refinement of the canonical approaches which precede it: commentary on individual poems, worrying the question of whether Stevens was idealist or realist, modernist or Romantic, American or internationalist, skeptic/ironist/nihilist or visionary and prophetic poet, or some combination of the above, perhaps even some curious mixture of the American pragmatist and postmodern performer in the "Theatre of Trope." A large amount of the criticism is still devoted to interpretation or commentary upon the individual poems in a fashion more or less familiar to the New Critical practice *entre quatre guerres*, to stretch an old phrase into its larger historical form. In the past decade and a half, the New Criticism has been displaced by a heterogeneous group of critical *isms*, but Stevens's poetry and position has tended to remain, in his metaphor, "central." The modernist Stevens has become postmodernist, no matter the dubious nature of the categories. Recent Stevens criticism reflects a certain history of literary criticism in general.

A bibliographical essay should not be cryptic in this way, that is, in the way criticism has come to claim it must be—not straight or circular but parabolic. And a balanced or straight history of recent criticism would have first to say that the "parabolic" turn or trope that occurred in Stevens criticism in the 1970s was at most a minor aberration to the continuing work that never wavered from its devotion to getting Stevens right. An historian of Stevens criticism could not help noting one indelible pattern and one *almost* unchallenged value judgment—since he came to the attention of academic critics in the 1950s, Stevens has become an exemplary poet for almost every school or movement of criticism, whatever its ideology. Except for his notable exclusion from Hugh Kenner's "Pound Era" (Kenner's metonym for modernism) and that same critic's nomination of him as the "American Edward Lear" in *A Homemade World* (New York, 1975)—the title is also Kenner's metaphor for the American or parochial "tradition" that mimics by a kind of *bricolage* the Pound-Eliot great "tradition"—almost no authoritative critic, school, or theoretical ideology has failed to acknowledge Stevens as a "central man" in the multi-centered scene of modernist writing. Ironically, the one "ideology" which has decried his power and centrality otherwise establishes it, by negation, heaping upon Stevens much of the blame for the decadence, skepticism, and nihilism that has come to pervade, in a certain view, the discourse of postmodern criticism.

Briefly—Kenner in *A Homemade World* excludes Stevens from modernist seriousness which he identifies as an "objectivist" poetics, or the poet's achievement of a language of "accuracy" and "attention" to the world, the poet's creation of a "map" of reality rather than indulgence of a Bloomian "map of misreading"; Frank Lentricchia, in *After the New Criticism* (Chicago, 1980), a book surveying the developments of literary theory and critical practice over the last two decades, nominates Stevens as the metonymical figure for the most radical or negative developments of modernist thought, which like Kenner he associates with the frivolousness of (Romantic) subjectivity, and which he from the Left, like Kenner from the Right, indicts for being the soft underbelly if not the abyss that threatens all that gives expression to man and society in a reasonable and clear discourse. Little matter if Kenner thinks this the discourse of an intellectually cosmopolitan literati, and Lentricchia thinks of it as a discourse of the masses. For both Stevens is not only bourgeois, but he is not serious; and yet he is prototypically American and modern because of his abandonment of community for a retreat into self, his contamination of "natural" language, and his general self-indulgence of fuzzy pleasures, otherwise played out in linguistic games. Into this bourgeois middle ground, this great margin of the irrational, are tossed the avatars of modernism, poets and critics alike, the textualists who have separated art from life and retreated from reality into nonreferential language. Truth gives way to play, or more frighteningly, "freeplay," and all the interdisciplinary terror it implies. Yet this Stevens, for better or worse, remains both monument and enigma, model and metonym of a literature and a criticism that lives most richly in its "anxiety."

1 Reading Stevens "Otherwise"

Lentricchia's orienting of the crises and impasses of contemporary criticism in the epistemological skepticism of Stevens's poetics makes an interesting if very questionable point. While it is true that Stevens has been a central poet—or a source of basic metaphors—for the literary critics most active in the imbroglios of a so-called postmodern or poststructuralist "scene" of criticism (or as Harold Bloom would have it, Scene of Instruction), it has been this way with his poetry since the 1950s. The remarkable, and indeed marketable, fact about Stevens's poetry and the criticism it has instigated over the past quarter century is that it sketches out the contours of our generation's intellectual history. This is in part because Stevens's own reflective and self-reflexive poems were always posing critical questions to themselves (rather than advancing an argument toward some cognitive solution), but also primarily because the poems were such a fount of tropes that they offered up almost every possibility for a discourse on the question of metaphoricity, figurality, representation, and so on, all of those questions that philosophy, literature, and attendant discourses have marked as the signature of contemporary thought, the "turn toward language."

Harold Bloom's *Wallace Stevens: The Poems of Our Climate* (Ithaca, N.Y., 1977) is inarguably the most significant, because at the same time the most controversial, single text of Stevens criticism in the past decade, if not the past three. Its pertinence stems in part from the irritations it aggressively delivered upon a community of Stevens admirers who thought they had already found every humanistic value to admire in the poet's affirmations. As such it has become a motive force, producing by reaction ever more criticism. Bloom's study positions itself between what otherwise seems the monumental polarities of contemporary thought, or at least criticism's debates over the determinant and indeterminant. At first reading, Bloom's strategy would not appear an exception to the usual critical mode of reading the poet's canon exhaustively on its own terms and doing it more intensely than most. Once through an opening chapter that situates the poet in an American tradition, the critic proceeds poem by poem in a more or less chronological sequence that at first appears no more than a paraphrase of each poem's developing argument, though Bloom stresses a kind of incremental repetition rather than a development of Stevens's thematics. Moreover, his way of reading particular poems is to proceed from beginning to end and to comment by a kind of paraphrastic translation into his own heuristic terms on what he considers to be the crucial moments or crossing points, the tropisms or figural changes that he calls "revisionary ratios."

Bloom's reading, then, involves a subtle "translation" of the poet's rhetorical mapping (not quite expression) of his own psychic performance into the critic's own performance or *agon*. Performance, understood as a metaphor for rhetoric or suasion, defines Bloom's notion of poetry. Poetry is a "reading" or "misreading" performance, and so is criticism. Performance is intertextual and transformative, a misprision of one text (for Bloom the name of an "act" and not a literal thing, nor even a figure for a play of signifiers) by another which signifies a psychic conflict or "scene" that can provide us the topology of a human and a culture's history.

Bloom's Stevens might at first appear to be no more than the occasion for the elaboration of a theory which had previously been developed through a series of short books in which Stevens's poetry had prominently served as example. But Stevens is the exceptional example for Bloom, particularly since for him "theory" is only one's map of the marks left by an individual act of mind, and the poet in his Emersonian sense is both an individual who makes his act/mark in a specific rhetorical performance and a representative hero or universal figure whose repetition upon a previous hero/figure reveals for us a kind of human truth and a general "map" of the history of consciousness. Stevens is at once a modern, a contemporary, and a reviser of his master/father/precursor Emerson, each father and ephebe being at once individual writers and metonymic figures who represent an entire culture and tradition. Beginning with *The Anxiety of Influence* (New York, 1973) and continuing through *A Map of Misreading* (New York, 1975) and *Poetry and Repression* (New Haven, Conn., 1976), the last two of which include essays on Stevens which set the stage for *The Poems of Our Climate* and anticipate another theoretical revision in two more recent books, *Agon* (New York, 1982) and *The Breaking of the Vessels* (Chicago, 1982), Stevens remains the exemplary figure, now defined as the American "pragmatist." Bloom's "book" on Stevens continues to be written and the clearest sign of its consistency and its changes is a transforming vocabulary, so like those of Stevens's own variations.

Suffice it here to repeat that Bloom's theoretical texts elaborate a notion of poetry as psychic performance, for which the essential vocabulary is rhetoric, or more precisely, "trope," understood as an interrelated series of terms that account for or map a conflict. Criticism translates this psychic event into a generalized economy, or into "ratios." Bloom's "map" not only includes his own personally coined or borrowed series of tropes (see those of *The Anxiety of Influence*, for example, *kenosis* or a repetition that is also a discontinuity), but parallels that sequence with putatively isomorphic sequences drawn from, respectively, traditional rhetoric (*kenosis* is metonymy), Jewish Gnosticism or Kabbalah, and Freudian terminology (*kenosis* is undoing, isolation, and regression). Nevertheless, it is the critic's heuristic terminology, along with the ad hoc character of its reinscription into the discipline (if that is the word) of literary criticism, that brought down all kinds of wrath upon Bloom who, on the one hand, was identified with the "alien corn" of continental obscurantism being imported in yet another language by his colleagues at Yale and, on the other, with a kind of private prophetic critical voice, narcissistic and self-indulgent, which claimed that criticism was the equal of poetry, or also a poetry.

Bloom's Stevens book, because it brought the critic's almost obsessive concern for "theory" to bear on a poet who had in his turn motivated the concern with theory, posed a heady problem for the Stevens regulars. What was not considered, or if it was, was thought unseemly, was that Bloom performed upon Stevensian rhetoric the same kind of tropic displacement, or "misprision," that Stevens had consistently performed upon received terminology.

Perhaps because his own rhetoric or poetic criticism seemed to rewrite rather than clarify the poet's "evasions," Bloom's rereading Stevens was rarely confronted (see the reviews and commentaries in *WSJour* [Fall/ Winter 1977]; or Guy Davenport's "Epicurus in New Haven," *Canto* [Winter 1977]). But the main confusion over what Bloom was about in his Stevens book stemmed from his close identification with the new wave of continental philosophical criticism known as "deconstruction" or poststructuralism, which from the late 1960s had been imported piecemeal into the American universities and grafted onto the critical styles of a number of American critics, the most notable in the early years being a group of Bloom's colleagues at Yale. Readers of his Stevens seemed to ignore Bloom's own efforts to resist that identification, which had been written into the putative "history" of an American criticism in the 1970s largely through the self-assessments and self-advertisements of those very colleagues and even Bloom himself. The last chapter of *The Poems of Our Climate* is a long debate with the deconstructors, especially Paul de Man, but even when Bloom performed his own theory of resistance his critical mode and stance allied him with what J. Hillis Miller, again using Stevens as a model poet, called "uncanny" criticism. Thus, the group of Newer Critics at Yale, variously dubbed by establishment opponents as a "hermeneutical mafia," a "deconstruction company," or a "gang of four," came to encapsulate the major critical dialogue of the 1970s. And Wallace Stevens became in a sense both their model and mentor.

Of that group, Geoffrey Hartman, of course, and J. Hillis Miller repeatedly took Stevens as a measure of this "uncanny" and rhetorical critical "stance," which Bloom tries heroically to resist, revise, and, in his terms, "transume," in the name of Emerson's affirmation of the poet's Power, which in his more recent *Agon* Bloom associates with American pragmatism. In two essays which first appeared in the *Georgia Review* (Spring 1976; Summer 1976) under the collective title, "Stevens' Rock and Criticism as Cure" and now collected and revised into a chapter of *The Linguistic Moment: From Wordsworth to Stevens* (Princeton, N.J., 1985), Miller first submitted a number of Stevens's late poems, particularly "The Rock," to what might be called a "deconstructive" or dialogical reading, focusing on the problematics inscribed in a single word, "cure," that functioned so crucially in the poem as if it were a theme affirming some corrective or clarifying achievement realized by the poetic act. Miller puts the putative theme of "cure" as redemption, restoration, recuperation (and thus the realization of meaning, self-identity, etc.) under what the French call "erasure." By marking its contradictory and alogical double function throughout the poem, Miller shows that far from being a grounding concept or resolutionary theme, the word/trope sets off at least two incompatible and contradictory readings of the poem, a double reading. For Miller, criticism's attempt to totalize or master literature can only unveil the *aporia* or abyssal play (the "uncanniness") of at least two incompatible discourses running through both the poem and the critical argument. This reflexive/translative effect that Miller finds opening up in Stevens's poem becomes for him the instance of poetic language in general, which he calls the "linguistic moment" that marks all discourse as "poetic," including the discourse of criticism. Stevens, therefore, becomes a model for a discourse, poetic language, that proves that we can never find a model or method, a "cure of the ground," either in or for poetry. Criticism in this view is not something that can be applied from the outside to the en-kerneled plenitude of a poem, its enclosed structure, but itself is always already inscribed in the discourse of the poem which is made up of at least two languages or is intertextual.

The thrust of Miller's essays is to advance at least one of the most important lines of inquiry that goes under the name of "deconstruction," the notion of an inevitable "dialogical" or double reading. He therefore underscores the impossibility of any determinant reading, whether of Stevens or of a literary work in general. Stevens's endless "And yet(s)" are repeated instances of criticism's dilemma of reading. Deconstruction, therefore, acknowledges what earlier criticism had recognized as the self-reflexivity and self-referentiality of a modernist or post-Romantic verse like Stevens's, but only to note again that such an ideal of self-reflexivity never quite works. The poem no more accounts for its own operations or evolves its own metapoetic language than a criticism can master the poem or close its argument by achieving a metalanguage. Stevens becomes what the criticism of the 1960s had recognized, his own major theorist. But now we are forced to acknowledge that the separation of theory and practice, like idea and image, can never be formalized, or grounded, and that a poetry like Stevens's, moving between ontological statement and rhetorical performance, displays the rhetorical conundrum that has always already haunted both poetry and philosophy.

This brief summary of Miller's *atheoretical* theory is too schematic, but something of this kind of argument is necessary to establish what is involved and at risk in a modern criticism that has turned so fully to Stevens's performative rhetoric, and what is implied in Lentricchia's indictment of Stevens as the father of modern critical decadence. The problem is that in the minds of many astonished critics, deconstruction is anathema (as well as being ana-thematic) because it is only understood as a purely negative discourse, intent on pointing up again the inevitable abysses, *Abgrunds*, gaps, and breaks in a poem, rather than being a search for meanings, beliefs, or values, even those consciously embraced as "fictions" or "negative theology." Bloom would save Stevens from this negation, or argue that Stevens, repeating Emerson, saves us from it. Bloom's Stevens is at once universal poet and the poet in history, the virtue that Lentricchia denies him by identifying him with the dour, negative "idealism" of modern skeptical thought. But deconstructive criticism, in all of its varieties, has only seemed to deny history or temporality to literature. This popular notion that deconstruction affirms only the negative results from a tendency to see this criticism as making ontological or conative statements, for example, "there is nothing beyond the text." And if the criticism is read this way, so is the poetry. For Lentricchia, Stevens's solipsism everywhere affirms only subjectivity and thus textuality (a "world of words to the end of it"), a position he shares with the "uncanny" critics even when he talks of the necessary "other," of "reality." But the only answer to this critical placing of Stevens is another reading of his canon which stresses, as does Miller, not the poet's epistemology but the disturbing and dismantling effects of his poetic self-questioning. In this latter view, Stevens does not argue either for the imaginative/subjective or the reality/other. To the contrary, by putting such either/or positions into play or by troping the philosophical tropes, he undoes such binary oppositions and unveils their irreducibly poetic nature.

In two different commentary/reviews of Bloom's study ("Bloom—A Commentary—Stevens" [*WSJour*, Fall/Winter 1977]; and "Juda Becomes New Haven" [*Diacritics*, Summer 1980]), Joseph N. Riddel focuses upon this quarrel between Bloom and deconstruction, and argues that it is not as wide a breach as it first appears, and moreover that Stevens may well be the author of the double reading and hence the most vigorous instigator, by indirection, of a modern affirmative criticism. (The *parti pris* of this section of this essay is therefore unavoidable.) In the second review, Riddel offers a counter-reading to Bloom's troping of "The Auroras of Autumn," not as an instance of a deconstructive reading in opposition to a pragmatic one, but as an instance of the inevitable "swerving," as Bloom calls it, in all critical argument, a dialogical play best exemplified in Stevens's own demolition of received philosophical concepts in that poem. In another piece, "The Climate of Our Poems" (*WSJour*, Fall 1983), Riddel rehearses the influence of Stevens upon the history of our recent criticism and offers as example a reading of "The Credences of Summer," again in relation to Bloom's recognition of the centrality of the tropes of "climate" and "weather" in Stevens. Yet neither antithetical reading can be called a programmatic instance of deconstruction, though each argues that Stevens's poems do indeed "deconstruct" an inherited terminology without offering a more stable "world of words" to replace it. Riddel argues that there is not, and cannot be, an institution, let alone a method, of deconstruction, even though Miller's essay on Stevens has become a model for those who demand an institutionalized method, either to embrace or decry. Deconstructive essays may indicate a tendency or mode of reading "otherwise," but they are more likely to be a questioning of method and determinant readings than a strategy for performing them.

If the "linguistic moment," or a notion of language as unmotivated or "anasemic," is the displaced theme that Stevens motivated, one can only classify the newer criticism inspired by, and about, Stevens as a criticism focused upon the motiveless motives for metaphor. The Wallace Stevens Society, under the direction of John Serio, organized a session at the 1982 MLA convention devoted to a "post-structural" assessment of Stevens. Riddel's "The Climate of Our Poems" was one essay offered there, but the symposium as a whole was published in the *Wallace Stevens Journal* (Fall 1983), a series of four essays of somewhat different rhetorics but with a common attention to these problematics in Stevens. Several of the critics, particularly Terrance J. King in a series of essays, have begun to refocus the question of Stevens's self-reflexive poetry in terms of a semiotic rather than a deconstructive criticism or a criticism that tries to account for the structural operations rather than the *aporias* of the poem's linguistic moment. King's approach belongs in the category of newer approaches, however, as does Bloom's, not because of its ideological presumptions but because of the stance it takes in regard to the functions of language in the poems: the contrast, for example, of semiotic to a traditional stylistic description, as in the essays of Marie Borroff, to be discussed in the next section.

In the *Wallace Stevens Journal* special issue, besides Riddel's survey of the issues for theory and practice, there are three other very different kinds of readings of Stevens which share in common an aggressive style of argument and an attention to the illusory self-reflexiveness in certain Stevensian metapoems. Patricia A. Parker's "The Motive for Metaphor: Stevens and Derrida" reads the poem of that title in terms of the "heliotrope," at once the poem's theme and its predominant metaphor, and shows how within different languages poet and philosopher worry out a common question of trying to account for metaphoricity by the use of the very metaphors being explored. Joseph G. Kronick's "Large White Man Reading: Stevens' Genealogy of the Giant" traces the thematics of self-reading as a probing rather than a thematizing of the metaphor of "genealogy," the privileged trope by which the poet strives to achieve a genetic link between his utterance and some ground, or between a proper and a figural meaning, and concludes that the question of genealogy is less the evidence of a psychic struggle, as in Bloom, than an inevitably failed effort to hypostatize one's language, and one's self, by finding in the ghostly echoes of past signs and monuments some "parental" ground or origin. And Michael Beehler's "Stevens' Boundaries" begins with the question of the relation of rational and irrational in Stevens; but rather than continue the familiar argument for the distinctness of one from the other or the priority of one to the other, Beehler remarks the way Stevens in both prose and poetry erases the illusion of an absolute demarcation and enforces the entanglement of the two in any poetic utterance. Stevens's poetic acts, he argues, breach and erase all boundaries, making everything boundary or margin. Thus the epistemological polarities of imagination and reality which dominate Stevens's own metapoetic reflections and also his criticism are revealed to be nothing more than philosophical oppositions which Stevens's rhetoric transfigures, not fixed concepts or names of distinct faculties. Stevens thus tropes a philosophical language into something else, producing what has been called an *anasemic* figuration. Rational and irrational become intertropic, doubled names for imaginative force and its images. The interest in such essays lies not in what meaning they claim for Stevens's poems, but in the way they re-mark the problematics which the poet makes indelible in his "anatomy of figuration." They also reveal why Stevens's prose or his own explicit theorizing must be "read" as his poems are read. They insist that his own critical prose, like the metapoetic language of his poems, cannot be simply applied to his poems as explanation or extracted as a set of comments on the nature of poetry.

Beehler's essay is an extension of the work he did on his dissertation (Univ. of California-Los Angeles, 1977) on Stevensian "decentering," earlier essays from which appeared in *Criticism* (Summer 1977) under the title "Meteoric Poetry: Wallace Stevens' 'Description without Place'" and in *Genre* (Winter 1978) as "Inversion/Subversion: Strategy in Stevens' 'The Auroras of Autumn.'" These essays have been reworked into Beehler's comparative study, *T. S. Eliot, Wallace Stevens, and the Discourses of Difference* (Baton Rouge, La., 1987). Kronick's essays, "Of Parents, Children, and Rabbis: Wallace Stevens and the Question of the Book" (*Boundary 2*, Spring 1982) and in the *Wallace Stevens Journal* (Fall 1983), noted above, are on the problematic metaphors of "reading" and "genealogy" which force us to reassess Stevens's Romanticism. The first of these is reprinted with some alteration as a chapter in Kronick's ambitious study of an *American Poetics of History, from Emerson to the Moderns* (Baton Rouge, La., 1984), under the title of "Wallace Stevens and the Question of the Book." It explores Stevens's obsession with his personal genealogy and family history in relation to his concern with producing, authoring, or fathering a totalized form like a "book of poems"—a preoccupation revealed as early as the famous letter to Williams partially reproduced in the "Prologue" to *Kora in Hell*. But Kronick's strategy is to examine this interest in genealogy and the "book" in regard to certain poststructuralist critical notions of the "book" as a metaphysical or total form, a Mallerméan *oeuvre*, and to show how Stevens at once advances and undermines this reification of a holistic or closed form.

Mary Arensberg's dissertation, "Muse Poetry: Wallace Stevens and the 'Interior Paramour'" (State Univ. of New York at Albany, 1980), written with a certain orientation toward what is called "French Freud," indicates some influence of the newer criticism. But this is increasingly a fact, and its ramifications are impossible to trace in a bibliographical essay. Terrance J. King's previously mentioned essays, "The Semiotic Poetry of Wallace Stevens" (*Semiotica*, Nos. 1 and 2, 1978) and "'Certain Phenomena of Sound': An Illustration of Wallace Stevens' Poetry of Words" (*TSLL*, Winter 1978), investigate what he calls "autonomy of language" in Stevens, and through the application of certain semiotic principles argue that Stevens's word play is not related to a private or solipsistic self but is a deliberate maneuvering of language in its communal and public role as a "synoptic" index of reality. His interpretation of Stevens's realism, of the poet's belief that language is a kind of "corporeal thought," differs sharply from the positions of the other critics here but does seem to share something with the pragmatist notion of language which has certain roots in the semiotics of C. S. Peirce, though King appeals primarily to Heidegger and makes a curious identification of semiotics and Heidegger's notion of language as the "house of Being."

There is a tendency to view all the criticism that relates Stevens to, or reads him through, the thought of certain modern philosophers to be by definition deconstructive. Thus a Heideggerean or Nietzschean reading would be avant-garde, while a Bergsonian or Kantian reading would be truer to a notion of historical influence and of the priority of thought to its expression. This is not only a misunderstanding of deconstruction; it is a misreading of Stevens criticism. One might compare, for example, Frank Kermode's discovery of Heideggerean echoes in Stevens (in his contribution to Buttel and Doggett) with Miller's and Riddel's essays in the same volume, or Patricia A. Parker's crossing of Derrida and Stevens in the *Wallace Stevens Journal* with King's use of Heidegger. Kermode's essay proceeds along the lines of a more traditional, but no less authoritative, application of philosophical notions to poetic performances, much in the way that earlier critics like Frank Doggett in *Stevens' Poetry of Thought* (1966) found numerous philosophical parallels and influences for many of the poems or for Stevens's metapoetic reflections. There are, to be sure, appropriations like those of Geoffrey Hartman, a member of Miller's "uncanny" Yale School, throughout his writing in the 1970s and in his latest survey of the critical climate buffeting us in that decade, *Criticism in the Wilderness* (New Haven, Conn., 1980). Hartman makes liberal use of Stevensian metaphors to forge his own argument for what one might call the *new heuristicism*. He argues that criticism lives its own performance, rewriting poetic metaphors into its own discourse. If we live as we do in a time when there are too many methods and masters and if we are to avoid the dastardly charge of pluralism without principle, it follows in Hartman's view that we must recognize the dream of a totally disengaged or uncommitted critical discourse as an illusion and must therefore get about reassessing the manner in which critical rhetoric at once contaminates and translates, reduces and animates, in its intercoursing with the texts of literature; just as it follows that the texts of literature are intertextual or self-discursive.

Michel Benamou, whose earlier series of essays on *Wallace Stevens and the Symbolist Imagination* (1972) was noted in a previous version of this essay, completed his massive Sorbonne *thèse*, entitled *L'Oeuvre → Monde de Wallace Stevens* (Paris, 1975), now published in photo-offset, which amplifies the American essays into a full-blown investigation of Stevens's affiliations with and his differences from the network of *Symboliste* thought that was imported into modern American poetry. Except that in this text, Benamou, whose philosophical orientation such as it was remained phenomenological and at times psychoanalytical (Jungian), had to take account of the reassessment in our understandings of Symbolism forced by critiques like those of Jacques Derrida and others. While in no sense a deconstructive criticism, Benamou's approach is revisionary precisely to the degree he recognizes that there are at least two *Symbolismes*.

If all philosophical criticism of Stevens is not deconstructive, still there is a major difference between that which *applies* philosophy to his criticism, reads him in terms of a history of ideas, or parallels him with one strong philosopher or another (whether Kant, Nietzsche, Santayana, or Heidegger), and a criticism that tries to create a dialogue between the poetry and certain philosophical conceptions of the poetic. The difference in one sense would be between Bloom's placing of Stevens in a Romantic tradition and M. H. Abrams's positioning of him as the consummation of a very different kind of Romanticism. A more precise example might be the difference between studies like Paul Bové's *Destructive Poetics: Heidegger and Modern American Poetry* (New York, 1980), which includes a substantial chapter on Stevens, and Thomas J. Hines's *The Later Poetry of Wallace Stevens: Phenomenological Parallels with Husserl and Heidegger* (Lewisburg, Pa., 1976). Bové's chapter, as his title indicates, is a selective reading of the Stevensian canon as a "poetics" that works itself out in performances, or verbal strategies, best described by the Heideggerean notion of destructuration (as contrasted with deconstruction), though Stevens's mode has to be understood as a particularly American variation on Heidegger and not as a poet's borrowing or even a philosopher's direct influence.

Bové does not *apply* Heidegger but takes from him certain notions about poetic language and a certain kind of interpretative posture. Where he finds a common preoccupation between poet and philosopher with similar metaphors, Bové interprets the metaphors as posing or staging the problem, rather than rendering a set of meanings that can be exchanged between figure and thought. Stevens is to Bové what Hölderlin was to Heidegger, an exemplary poet, a textual case—though Bové's conception of the poet and poetic language differs markedly from Heidegger's late mystical notions. He finds Stevens's playful troping of the sanctified and reified metaphors of the poetic (western) tradition, however, as something quite different from Bloom's "revisionary ratios."

But his argument nevertheless falls into the newer critical position of celebrating the poet as "thinking" (as in Emerson's "Man Thinking" or Heidegger's "Denken"), rather than delivering a thought, and thus as a performer who desedimentizes the dominant and received concepts of his culture, opening them to some new and as yet unformulated understanding.

Bové's Heidegger is not exactly the one understood by deconstruction, the one deconstructed by a Jacques Derrida, and his particular notion of poetic language and the hermeneutic act is not itself severely questioned, but neither is Bové's philosopher a maker of systems which guarantees some kind of metalinguistic language for decoding a poet. Nor is Thomas Hines's Heidegger. Yet Hines's study proceeds in the more normative way of presenting the philosopher's thought as a set of coherent concepts applicable to the understanding of poetic figuration. The book is useful in revealing parallels between poetry and philosophy and pointing up common questions which the two approach from widely divergent postures and in different languages. But Hines does not focus on the issue that most concerns those who stress the "turn toward language": the problem, and perhaps the impossibility, of an ideal transaction and/or translation between the discourse of philosophy and the discourse of poetry. Hines's study belongs, then, to a history of poetic ideas, like that of earlier critics who have explored such Stevensian precursors as Kant, Hegel, Schopenhauer, Bergson, Nietzsche, Santayana, James, or earlier thinkers ranging back to Plato. These kinds of studies continue, and some will be reviewed in the following section. They retain the virtue and the limitations of any criticism which tries to tie the formation of a poet's "mind" to a genetic center or *logos* that has determined or shaped the conditions to which he gives expression. They inevitably ignore the problems of Stevens's own insistence on the transformative performance and all that "performative" implies now that we are in a period in which the question of language is so highly charged.

One last variation: Helen Regueiro [Elam's] *The Limits of Imagination: Wordsworth, Yeats, and Stevens* (Ithaca, N.Y., 1976) would need to be reviewed under the category of a comparatist criticism, even though its focus remains nonideological. In a critical idiom that owes much to the revisionary Romanticism of Bloom and Hartman, especially to the latter's phenomenological interests, Regueiro [Elam] situates Stevens in the tradition of post-Cartesian skeptic which Lentricchia designates as modernist escapism and explores his poetry in terms of its struggle to approach and overcome those "limits" which are always signified by language, or figuration, and hence by a poetry of representation or expression. Her work belongs at this stage more to the continental mode called a "criticism of consciousness" in the 1960s, than to the newer rhetoric which at once employs and undermines the model of language or the "linguistic moment." But the important point of her sensitive thematic and figural readings of Stevens is nevertheless her focus on language and/as limit, and hence on the putative self-reflexiveness of his poems which breaks down at the limits of the sublime and undoes the very "self" which seems to be invented in the space of the poetic image. Her exploration of the absences and silences produced by a poetry that both celebrates language's "gaiety" and is haunted by its "poverty" is reminiscent of the thematics of the Geneva critics and a certain existentialist criticism, but it also shares something with Bloom's notion of the poet's heroic struggle to overcome or "transume" as well as overturn or "break" the tyranny of past forms and linguistic limits. She concludes, like Bloom, that Stevens eventually triumphs as master of the void, passes through the "mortal no" to a "pleasure" which if only a fiction is no less humanly sufficient.

And lastly, Jacqueline V. Brogan's *Stevens and Simile, A Theory of Language* (Princeton, N.J., 1986) explores the Stevens canon within the postmodernist problematics of the "linguistic turn."

2 The "Central Man"

a. Books. No other single book or collection of essays, however ideologically fashionable or ecumenical, has had the impact of Bloom's, for the very good reason that Bloom took his stance against both the dominant tradition of literary studies and what he saw as the rising tide of anti-humanism which threatened to "un-self" the poet and subordinate poetry (or Power) to the dead effigies of thought. With the exception of the few discussed above, the book-length studies of the past decade ascribe to a normative critical posture—thematic, organized around a subject or point of view that nevertheless claims to be synoptic or comprehensive, above all deferential to the ideal that a criticism should be in some way transparent or self-effacing and not ideological and should do its best to translate the poet's idiom into a commensurate discourse. This criticism searches for the correct, or at least "better" and more adequate, interpretation of "intentions" and "meanings" ("The *the*") or for some regional thematic focus: say, the predominant influence of this or that philosopher or mode of thought, the identifying "style," or perhaps the organizing categories of ideas that allow us to classify the poet by a generic, periodistic, or nationalistic tradition—to identify his exemplariness, like Emerson's Representative Men.

Yet this variety of apparently normative criticism indicates one consistent critical or ideological fiction: the Stevens canon is organized upon a center, whether his personal self or hypostatized imagination (and voice), that is best defined by his own epistemological terms "imagination" and "reality," but as these broad concepts are in turn systematized by certain philosophical or theological traditions: is Stevens Romantic or modern? is his imagination best defined by Kant, Coleridge, or William

James? In brief, this criticism ascribes to the two great principles of western poetics: representation and expression.

Diane Wood Middlebrook's *Walt Whitman and Wallace Stevens* (Ithaca, N.Y., 1974) shows some of the Bloomian impact in her effort to situate Stevens within an American Romanticist tradition. Though she begins from the position that Stevens's notion of imagination (and self) must be approached through Coleridgean principles as they were transcribed and Americanized by Emerson—a notion, by the way, that derives from Matthiessen and was rearticulated by Charles Feidelson—she is more in tune with Bloom's argument that poetry is an *agon*, an act or performance. For Middlebrook, however, poetry is not a matter of psychic defense which produces a self out of conflict; rather the poetic act refines a true self out of the ordinary or commonplace consciousness. She argues that Whitman and Stevens are allied, even in their different styles, by their mutual production of a "mythology of imagination" rather than because they are precursor and ephebe, caught up in the conflictual genealogy of the poetic tradition—Whitman's search for the "real me" being analogous with, not identical to, Stevens's more contemporary effort to construct a literary "self" that is self-consciously a fiction. Thus each poet also represents in a way the milieu of thought and struggle that make up our "periods" of literary history, Stevens belonging to the modern epoch of disbelief in contrast to Whitman's transcendental idealism. Middlebrook emphasizes, as did Bloom, the "decreative" or resistant force of Stevens's imaginative acts, their paring away of the self to produce the "iconic self" evident in the poems. This is her version of the poetry's "negative theology," and it does issue in a sensitively written group of readings which trace this unfolding self from early to late poems. Despite her definite critical stance, Middlebrook does not argue for it philosophically or ideologically. Her notion of the "self" is not psychological, nor is it tied to a notion of language, but is drawn from a received notion of Romanticism more like Abrams's than Bloom's.

This focus on the Stevensian theory of imagination, his search for a modernist "self," is by all odds the dominant thesis of recent criticism, though there are some rather striking differences among the critics about how this self is to be defined—whether, for example, in the language of philosophy, psychology, or theology. And this leads to a set of contradictions in the effort to define the poet's "thought" and "beliefs." Michael Sexson's *The Quest of Self in the Collected Poems of Wallace Stevens* (New York, 1981) is a limited case in point, which examines Stevens's thematics of self without asking the kinds of questions the criticism described in the previous section asks about such notions as the "subject" or the "imagination." Susan B. Weston's *Wallace Stevens: An Introduction to the Poetry* (New York, 1977), a contribution to the Columbia University Press Introductions to Twentieth-Century American Poetry series, suffers precisely from a kind of neutrality in the face of critical choices or critical positions. More synoptic than analytic, aware of the earlier arguments of Stevens criticism yet unwilling to take sides with any one of them, Weston's study is too self-effacing and noncontroversial to do more than "introduce" the poetry by a set of normative readings. It offers the student basic materials or information out of which the more aggressive critical dialogues have been, and will be, fashioned. Weston thus provides little in the way of new readings of Stevens, but does present us with what might be called consensus interpretations, largely paraphrastic, making her text most useful to students who are beginning to grapple with the complexities of a difficult modern poetry but who have little awareness of the modernist canon and its philosophical coordinates.

Frank Doggett's *Wallace Stevens: The Making of the Poem* (Baltimore, Md., 1980), on the other hand, manages another and more effective kind of introduction, if not to the entire Stevens canon, then to a way of reading that can be extended to the longer poems which Doggett does not engage. Doggett, like Weston, eschews thesis, though he argues that Stevens does have a coherent poetics and that the poetics can direct a reading of his lyrics. In Doggett's view, the best access to Stevens's poetics goes through the *Letters*, rather than the critical essays, since the letters provide so much *materia poetica* and the poems, as Doggett contends, are transformations of experience. Doggett's procedure is to re-gather from the letters remarks, suggestions, details, nuances and to explore how they are transfigured into poems. The book provides an interesting complement to Doggett's earlier masterful study, *Stevens' Poetry of Thought* (1966), which concentrated on the poet's appropriation and transformation of the ideas and conceptual images of a number of philosophers known to influence Stevens, or who, whether he had deliberately studied them or was only casually acquainted with their writings, provide cognitive structures that appear in Stevens's poetry as poetic ones. Doggett confines himself in this later book to a reading of Stevens's shorter, more lyrical and less reflective or philosophical poems and offers a series of sensitive but not overingenious interpretations. The modesty of the study belies its authority, so that it becomes, in relation to Weston's, a better "introduction" to Stevens than her more comprehensive survey.

In contrast to both Weston and Doggett, Alan Perlis, in his *Wallace Stevens: A World of Transforming Shapes* (Lewisburg, Pa., 1976), begins by claiming not only a "thesis" but a revolutionary opening into Stevens's poetry never before recognized. Perlis's thesis is recorded in the title, that Stevens's poetry has as its main theme "transformation" and that it presents that theme in a transformative style. According to Perlis, all previous criticism of Stevens—he cites J. Hillis Miller and Richard Blessing as examples opposed to his thesis—tends to reduce him to a theoretical niche or category and thus "denies the poet's ability to transform" himself. While a curious misreading of Miller's early work (since a "criticism of consciousness" is premised on the dialectical evolving of the poet's "world" or "interior distance"), Perlis argues that he alone has seized upon the clue to the Stevens canon, its repeated turning of its own figurations, its recurrent re-vision. Perlis's notion of "transformation" is reductively literal, unlike Harold Bloom's sense of the poet's conflictual troping not only of precursor poets but, within his own canon, precursor poems. Unlike Bloom, or Miller, Perlis does not make it clear whether the poet internally transforms his own self or only his own work or whether in some way he acts upon the external world. Lacking a theoretical sense of what is involved in something like Bloom's revisionary rhetoric and psychic engagement, or even a more literally pragmatic notion of what it means to say that poetry affects the physical world and not just our perception of it, as Stevens at times seems to claim, Perlis falls back on an even more elementary notion and recounts Stevens's transformations in terms of a theme. He proceeds mainly by quoting passages where transformation is literally stated or claimed. He does maintain that Stevens's "language provides an illusion of natural process" while its "ideas" attempt to overcome natural process and turn the world into meaning or abstraction, but this only brings him back to the classical metaphysical argument over whether poetry is mimetic or expressive. What Perlis is really talking about is Stevens's obsession with "change," a repeated concern of his critics which has been handled in a rich variety of ways, from such questionable approaches as that of John Enck's (1963), in a study which used the *I Ching* as a map of Stevens repetitions, to Bloom's more convincing rhetorical mapping of Stevens's tropology.

Three books, however, do depart rather strikingly from the main body of the criticism, not only of this decade but the previous ones. Whatever the ideological focus or critical point of view, few critics have deviated from the position that the Stevens canon, from its early aestheticism or even hedonism to its late reflectiveness, was the utterance of a secular as opposed a religious man, of a skeptic who ironically undermined and troped religious figurations and forms, and whose paradox of the modern's need to believe in a fiction s/he knows not to be true is at the very least a radical inversion of anything traditionally meant by belief, a "belief beyond belief." Certain of Stevens's early critics, like Sister Bernetta Quinn and Amos Wilder, did manage very perceptive and sensible readings of Stevens's particular way of moving within religious structures or transfiguring them without heresy, because these critics refused to subordinate poetry to religion or read it as a dogmatic vehicle for certain orthodoxies. For most critics, however, the self-styled "dried-up Presbyterian" or the modern hedonist, the meditative or the philosophical poet, was rarely considered more than a poet of "negative theology," whether in Bloom's and Lentricchia's different sense or in Louis Martz's understanding of how Stevens had adapted High Church forms of meditation for a secular humanist poetry.

Lucy Beckett's *Wallace Stevens* (London, 1974), Adelaide Kirby Morris's *Wallace Stevens: Imagination and Faith* (Princeton, N.J., 1975), and Leonora Woodman's *Stanza My Stone: Wallace Stevens and the Hermetic Tradition* (Ann Arbor, Mich., 1983) attempt to reverse this consensus of the poetic doubter and to reposition Stevens, somewhat like a modern Descartes who uses doubt to affirm both the finite and the infinite self/God, within a certain orthodoxy of western ontotheological poetics. But beyond their shared opinion that Stevens was a "religious" rather than a nihilistic poet, the three share little in common, either in their notions of the relation between poetry and religion or in what constitutes Stevens's particular "belief." The books, therefore, divide Stevens across very different kinds of theology, from a poet who worked out a secular religion by reworking orthodox Christian forms to a poet who was an unremitting visionary in the mystical or "alchemical tradition."

Beckett's study assumes an unproblematical relation between poetry and belief, and offers itself as a general introduction to a poet who thought likewise. After establishing her thesis that Stevens develops from a Keatsian poet of "negative capability" to one who overcomes modern "poverty" through an affirmation of Christian humanism, she proceeds to read the canon chronologically as examples of the poet's testing his faith and overcoming the negative. She does not particularly like Stevens's long, more reflective, and potentially skeptical or nihilist poems and finds that the critics' fondness for them is the result of their finding a private "system" of thought there which makes him one of a "contemplative minority." Stevens eschews system, she argues, and employs philosophical concepts only as a vehicle for a "search" that eventually leads him from questing and questioning back to an acceptance of things, an acceptance best described in terms of a theological orthodoxy. She rejects the notion that Stevens is a narcissistic modernist or even anything like Bloom's Gnostic visionary. This forces her, as Abbie Willard says, to "impose" an orthodoxy on Stevens that is the exact reversal of those who read him as a post-Cartesian skeptic. For example, she reads "To an Old Philosopher in Rome" not only as affirming Stevens's devotion to Santayana but as a parable of Stevens's own resolve: a poem though without "specifically Christian connotations" which nonetheless brings Stevens "very near to a spiritual centre, a point of rest, that could as well be described in the traditional terms of Christian theology." "Near" is close enough to allow Beckett to make a continual analogy between modern aestheticism, and even decadence, and the Christian search for a nonascetic or living transcendence. Here, Beckett reveals more about the dominant strain of our critical tradition than about any particular poet—the tradition of which M. H. Abrams is the most sophisticated proponent.

Morris's book concentrates on the relation between Stevens's "mythic" imagination and its religious roots; that is, she views the mythic as that which mediates between visible and invisible, temporal and eternal. But without any rigorous sense of mythical mediation, like that of René Girard, or of the intermediary role of language, either in Vico's or Heidegger's sense, Morris proceeds by simply assuming myth's regulating role in the spiritual and mental economy. Morris does not focus so much upon the orthodox nature of Stevens's belief as upon his poetic employment of religious, or more precisely, biblical, modes like parable, hymn, proverb, meditation, and so on. She notes that Stevens does not only use the forms to confront and resolve questions of doubt; he also uses them parodically and demystifies them and thus she associates this latter with his fiercely individualistic and even antinomian religious consciousness. Yet, the prevalence of religious images, figures, forms, and themes in Stevens affiliates him, in her view, with poets of mystical power, again in a sense quite different and more orthodoxly Christian than Bloom's notion of the Gnostic poet. Therefore, she argues, biblical structures and religious terminology provide the best vocabulary for the study of his poetics and a reading of his poems, even though she wants to agree with those critics who find Stevens's main concern is with living in a "real" or "physical" world rather than with visionary or revelatory ecstasies. Yet, she maintains that Stevens's "theory of poetry did in time become a mystical theology" and that he thus transumes the irony which he early on played with to religious forms. Unlike Bloom, however, she does not find crisis at the heart of his rhetorical *agon*.

Leonora Woodman altogether dispenses with any notion that Stevens's mystical bent is related either to Christian humanism or critical Gnosticism. At first glance, her argument may seem to derive from Bloom's discovery that the visionary poet can best be read through unlocking his kabbalistic tropes, but Woodman is not the least concerned with critical problematics. She places Stevens fully within the Rosicrucian and Hermetic mystical traditions and argues that his poetry is not simply inspired by a mystical fervor but can only be understood as an encoded series of privileged archetypes. Stevens, she insists, came by his mystical mode both historically and inspirationally: his eastern Pennsylvania Dutch culture would have exposed him to, and nurtured him in, the "alchemical tradition"; and any reading of his poems, she continues, reveals that he has been inspirationally seized by the truth of an archetypal unconscious. Woodman provides a brief history of the Rosicrucian or "alchemical tradition" and links it with the psychology of C. G. Jung and other myth critics. She then turns to Stevens's poetry as a fount of archetypes which she accepts as, at the same time, poetic images and cryptic revelations. Stevens, she says, was possessed by his belief in the "ultimate poem" through which could be revealed "transcendental man." Thus she reads his poems as successful if oblique revelations of that "ultimate poem." This revelation, however, may not be available to a reader not equally attuned to the secret code by which such truths must be read.

This poses somewhat of a problem for reading Stevens: for example, to claim that he is obsessed with the "ultimate poem," as in, for instance, "A Primitive Like an Orb," is to obscure the fact that he restricts any knowledge of the "ultimate" to the indirect utterances of "lesser poems," which like Emerson's are always "miswritten." The last stanza of "A Primitive . . ." consigns the revelation of the "ultimate" to an endlessly deferred and deferring writing or utterance, and the poem gives no indication that this repeated and never-ending utterance is some form of continuous revelation, let alone continuous creation. For all her passion and single-mindedness—and the critical blindness allows her to claim that she has finally got Stevens right because her "method" is the method of truth applicable to all poetry—Woodman has produced a curiosity of modern criticism which is unlikely to convert many readers.

None of these studies had the benefit, or perhaps distraction, of knowing about Stevens's deathbed conversion to Catholicism which, as Peter Brazeau reveals in his oral biography, was kept secret from his wife and daughter as from the scholarly world until recently. This "event" is bound to prompt a good deal of critical speculation and to spur no little controversy, though it is unlikely to instigate a revisionary reading of the canon. It could, however, tempt a theoretically inclined critic to examine the persistent relation between religious metaphors and poetic ones in most criticism and the privilege the former has to the latter even when the critic, like Abrams, or even Bloom, insists that the poetic has displaced the religious. The conversion is also unlikely to effect or affect the writing of a Stevens biography, since it came so late, when the poet knew his illness was terminal, and does not seem anticipated even in his very late poems. Could he have thought again of Santayana, yielding to the consolation of the forms? There is no evidence of his state of mind and none to confirm that it was an answer to all the intellectual conflicts he had worked to master in his poems. The larger question it poses for criticism, however, is what to make of a poet's belief.

The place of Stevens between Romantic and modern remains one of the major controversies of his criticism, a problem vexed by the efforts of recent theoretical critics like Paul de Man to revise the received notion of Romanticism and along with it the larger issue of literary periods and thus historicism in general. Stevens, as noted earlier, remained an exemplary poet in the increasingly contentious struggles to define the problem, which might be simplified by opposing Abrams's Romanticism to that of the newest Yale School. George Bornstein's *Transformations of*

Romanticism in Yeats, Eliot, and Stevens (Chicago, 1976) explores the question in more or less traditional terms, of how the twentieth century "transformed" Romantic epistemology into a modernism with a continuously unfolding complexity. Continuity, or the history of ideas, is the ordering principle. Bornstein is not troubled by what French critics might call the epistemic break; at least for him, as for M. H. Abrams, the nineteenth century does not constitute a rupture in the history of ideas, and it is only a problem of charting the evolution of how certain poets responded to and refined upon the epistemological problems they were asked to confront. It was never a problem of supplanting or transuming their precursors, as Bloom insists, but rather a problem of completing, refining, and self-consciously advancing the questions in the way philosophical discourse also had to do. A. Walton Litz's essay, "Wallace Stevens' Defense of Poetry: *La Poesie pure*, the New Romantic, and the Pressure of Reality," in Bornstein's edition of critical essays, *Romantic and Modern: Revaluations of Literary Tradition* (Pittsburgh, 1977), clearly affirms this historicist, progressive view of the notion of "revaluation," which one could oppose to the Nietzschean proposal of "transvaluation" that characterizes so much of the problematics of recent critical theory.

Litz's essay also touches upon a continuing area of Stevens study, his place in the post-Romantic break that is associated with the desire for a "pure poetry" and is otherwise called *Symboliste* and post-Symbolist and sometimes identified with avant-garde movements like surrealism. Michel Benamou's *Wallace Stevens and the Symbolist Imagination* (1972) may serve as a summary view of a long-term interest in Stevens's relations with the post-Romantic Symbolist movement in France, a critical history reviewed in earlier essays and very well documented in Abbie Willard's study of the criticism. Benamou extended his American essays into a full-fledged study in his Sorbonne thesis (1976) noted in the previous section, which reexplores not only Stevens's direct appropriations of the French but his American deviations. Benamou also takes account of the significance of recent theoretical developments on the reinterpretation of Symbolism, both as a poetic movement and as a theory.

Like his putative Romanticism, Stevens's post-Symbolist affections have been pursued by a number of recent critics. The main lines of inquiry were laid out in the 1960s by Haskell M. Block, Frederick J. Hoffman, and Benamou, who were more interested in distinguishing between Stevens's uniquely American translation of French modes than in what earlier critics like Hi Simons and H. R. Hays had found to be direct influences and unproblematic adaptations, in technique if not in philosophical commitment. Benamou's Sorbonne thesis is a discriminating reassessment of these issues, and it puts in question any historical approach to influence and appropriation; it opens up a field of further studies, based on rapidly changing theoretical developments, especially the way a poetics like Mallarmé's is now used to dismantle the ideal of a pure, self-reflexive poetics which it was once thought to advance and institutionalize.

At least four other books demand some particular notice at this point, even though three are not exclusively on Stevens and the fourth, Beverly Coyle's *A Thought to be Rehearsed: Aphorism in Wallace Stevens' Poetry* (Ann Arbor, Mich., 1983), has the sharply limited focus of a dissertation, a portion of which first appeared in *PMLA* (March 1976) under the title, "An Anchorage of Thought: Defining the Role of Aphorism in Wallace Stevens' Poetry." Coyle's text is a thorough and attentive study of one of Stevens's most interesting "habits" of mind, evident, as Coyle notes, not simply in the "Adagia." More importantly, it is a principal characteristic of the poetry. Coyle argues that Stevens's "aphoristic style" makes possible his stance of "detachment," thereby allowing him to explore ideas without being committed to their cognitive truth and thus to avoid absolute positions or a dogmatic voice. She confines herself, however, largely to close textual readings of the varieties of this style and avoids setting up a larger context for this mode or pursuing the question, for example, of how it may be related to Romantic irony or to such post-Romantic philosophical developments as Nietzsche's or to the literature of "marginalia," from Poe to Valéry. Like parable and fable, which despite Morris's assertion are not exclusively biblical modes, aphorism belongs to a literary and philosophical tradition that breaches such generic demarcations and produces hybrids. After Friedrich Schlegel, we have come to recognize it as a question of the "fragment." Coyle's study virtually ignores the theoretical implications of this kind of "thought" to focus on it as a kind of style; but despite the limits, she provides a most interesting and useful focus on what is certainly a dominant characteristic especially of Stevens's verse from midcareer to the end, a style that disallows our categorizing his poetry either as philosophical or as "nonsense."

Marie Borroff's *Language and the Poet: Verbal Artistry in Frost, Stevens, and Moore* (Chicago, 1979) includes the essays she first published in *Modern Philology* (Aug. 1976; Nov. 1976) under the title "Wallace Stevens' World of Words," a study of the poet's "uses of diction." (A subsequent essay, "Sound Symbolism as Drama in the Poetry of Wallace Stevens" appeared in *ELH* in the Winter of 1981.) In an age of criticism preoccupied with the "linguistic moment," Borroff's essays might at first seem à la mode. But her stress on "diction" and semantic play marks them as more traditional essays employing stylistics. Borroff not only describes a style but uses it for interpretative purposes. Moreover, she supports her readings with charts and tables cataloguing the frequency with which certain words, as opposed to "images," are used, and with "etymological categories" that trace the philological history of the poet's diction, in order to give her study a scientific, or at least philological, rigor. "The *exact repetition* in the present of the verbal and other forms of behaviour used on ceremonial occasions in the past has always been an important means of inducing or perpetuating reverence for authority" (my italics) is the first sentence of her second essay. Borroff eschews the "new rhetoric," though at least one of her formulations indicates that she has been touched by such theoretical distinctions as Paul de Man draws from the contradiction or *aporia* which falls between language thought of as bearing meaning (a rhetoric of tropes) and as a performance or speech act (a rhetoric of persuasion): she describes Stevens's "idiosyncratic version of the high style" as a split between a "scholarly and discursive and a sacred or hierophantic strain." In Borroff's terms, however, these two functions of language in poetry do not produce an unbridgeable gap or *aporia*, but to the contrary permit the poet to transcend the limitations of philosophy with his own enhanced and even "sacred strain." Thus Borroff celebrates what she calls the "prodigality of Stevens' inventiveness," his "always incipient cosmos" or poetic world that is in effect a "world of words." Linguistic science gives way to a reification of poetic language, and descriptive stylistics affirms a basically humanist poet.

Somewhat in contrast to Borroff, yet a complement, is Suzanne Juhasz's *Metaphor and the Poetry of Williams, Pound, and Stevens* (Lewisburg, Pa., 1974) whose thesis is stated in its title. Though relying on certain principles of structural linguistics, particularly the metaphor-metonymy opposition, Juhasz's study is not at all problematized by theoretical concerns. She begins with an elementary structuralist assumption about metaphor, that it produces meaning by the conjunction of two opposing terms or a binarism as opposed to a hierarchical difference or substitution, and proceeds to show how this work of resemblance functions in various Stevens poems. Ultimately, this interplay of balanced oppositions accounts for Stevens's basic dualism of imagination and reality or, in the instance of certain poems like "Notes toward a Supreme Fiction," the opposition between literal statement and figural enhancement or between cognitive abstractions and figural play (though she does not use this rhetorical notion). One problem with Juhasz's view of Stevens's "theory" of metaphor is that she derives it almost literally from Stevens's own prose, a discourse, as several critics have noted, which is itself so metaphorical or poetic that it demands the same kind of reading one must give to the poems. Juhasz takes a step toward the critics of Stevens's "linguistic moment," but her own orthodox structuralist position does not lead to an incisive investigation into the "motives for metaphor" that, for example, Patricia A. Parker's essay reviewed in the previous section underscores. Like Borroff's essentially philological method, Juhasz's structural approach offers a number of incisive openings into a poet's use of language, but always at the expense of closing others. Fortunately, one does not have to choose one approach over the other but may learn from each the possibilities of Stevens's extraordinary capacity for "varia-tion" and his capacity for "transforming" his own medium.

Kathleen Woodward's *At Last, the Real Distinguished Thing: The Late Poems of Eliot, Pound, Stevens, and Williams* (Columbus, Ohio, 1980) is essentially a thematic exploration of something that inevitably preoccu-pies long-lived poets, the one thing common to these major figures of American modernism. As her metaphorical title, taken from the reported death-bed words of Henry James, indicates, her subject is death, or more precisely, the reflections upon death from the perspective of its "near-ness" to the elderly poet. For Woodward, Stevens, whose early poems like "The Emperor of Ice-Cream" were filled with dark yet playful reflec-tions upon death, crafted his late style as a defense against death's reality, against "death" as a "thing" constantly pressing back against the imagination. But unlike a psychoanalytical critic, or in contrast to a Bloom, she is not concerned with poetry as resistance or defense; there is no theoretical preoccupation with language as such in this study or with the notion that "death" inhabits language in the disguise of figura-tion, substitution, displacement. Woodward focuses on Stevens's medi-tative efforts to comprehend and contain the blank, to transform a personal anxiety into a "mythology of modern death," as his line from "The Owl in the Sarcophagus" puts it. Since the theme is so pervasive in the later Stevens, as well as in her other poets, Woodward has an ample subject, and she treats it intelligently and sympathetically.

This interest in Stevensian geriatrics is by no means an isolated or thematically arbitrary issue, as witness recent essays by Betty Buchsbaum ("Wallace Stevens: The Wisdom of the Body in Old Age" [*SoR*, Oct. 1979]) and Robert Buttel ("The Incandescence of Old Age: Yeats and Stevens in Their Late Poems" [*APR*, Jan./Feb. 1983]). There is a question of whether this kind of essay belongs to literary criticism or to a sociolog-ical and/or biographical interest, or whether it is simply inevitable for any criticism that wants to consider the most universal of themes. The question remains whether Stevens has any more to tell us about death than any other writer who reflects upon it or whether his poetry of death, like any such meditations, is not a self-reflection upon limitation and hence on the revelatory power of poetry itself, another instance of poetry's being the subject of the poem, or at least of the poet's own power, or lack of it, being his "subject."

Along with the book-length studies, one should probably include two collections of essays. One, *Wallace Stevens: A Celebration*, the centenary collection reviewed in part earlier for its inclusion of new materials, biography, and certain essays in the newer criticism, includes several major statements. The essays are mainly by canonical Stevens critics trying their hand once more and include pieces by Helen Vendler on Keats and Stevens, Isabel G. MacCaffrey reading "Le Monocle de Mon Oncle," Irvin Ehrenpreis on "Stevens' Nonsense," John Hollander on

Stevens's verbal music, and Roy Harvey Pearce arguing that Stevens's notion of "decreation" is a humanist act that refutes all efforts of the deconstructionists to turn it into a philosophical nihilism. There are also essays by Miller and Riddel, each engaged in revising their earlier approach to Stevens as well as rereading him, and by Frank Kermode on the Heideggerean implications of "Dwelling Poetically in Connecticut." Each of these last three was briefly discussed above. As mentioned earlier, the first third of *The Motive for Metaphor* (Boston, 1983), essays dedicated to Samuel French Morse, is devoted to Stevens. Besides the essentially biographical pieces, it includes critical essays by Morse on Stevens's "Sense of Place" and by Frank Doggett and Dorothy Emerson.

Another "pair" of books might well exemplify the divisions, and the divisions within divisions, of current Stevens criticism. David Walker's *The Transparent Lyric: Reading and Meaning in the Poetry of Stevens and Williams* (Princeton, N.J., 1984) presumes to align itself with the newer theoretical approaches noted above, since Walker stresses the rhetorical/performative dimensions of style in opposition to the cognitive or epistemological. Still, Walker understands rhetoric as performance in a somewhat reductive or even literal sense, so that his reigning thesis of the "transparent lyric" really claims nothing more than that a poem, rather than being an object or a holistic symbol (autotelic), is a form of utterance that "invites a reader" to enter its "world." This is not quite reader-response criticism either, for the reader does not perform the poem to completion; nor is it Bloom's *agon* or de Man's persuasion. Walker's notion of the poem's "world" suggests to the contrary that a poem is a unique and total unit of discourse, and the reader is invited there to mime the poet's univocal experience. Transparency, therefore, remains the nominal term for a mimetic rather than performative aesthetics. Moreover, Walker's readings back off from theory, almost to the point of self-effacement, and if they seem to promise a new subgenre of lyric, his appeal to commonsense descriptions of lyric style must be said to belong to the traditional (even thematic) approaches to Stevens and modernism.

Helen Vendler's modest collection of four lectures presented at the University of Tennessee, on the other hand, is aggressively defensive of the old descriptive stylistics and a reactive bow to the New Critical impressionism of which she is the last passionate arbiter. Marked by her usually untroubled style, *Wallace Stevens: Words Chosen Out of Desire* (Knoxville, Tenn., 1984) is something like a footnote to *On Extended Wings*, but in this case focused on Stevens's shorter lyrics rather than the longer poems. (It is reprinted in paperback as *Wallace Stevens* [Cambridge, Mass., 1986].) The shorter poems provide her even more conclusive evidence for her argument with the philosophical critics that Stevens, and "good" poetry in general, is best when it is expressive and thoughtless rather than a worrying of abstractions or trapped in the self-reflective abyss of epistemological crises. Philosophical critics, she asserts in her lapidary way, are simply misunderstanders, of Stevens and poetry at large, for good poetry is the expression and, in its way, satisfaction of some desire. Vendler proclaims that she wishes to re-authorize "the" Stevens ("to present the Stevens I know to the public eye" as her unblinking metaphor has it) against the metaphysical nitpickers. Ironically, her chief claim is that she will deal with Stevens's primary and universal themes, all forms of what she calls "desire." Desire has nothing to do with the philosophical stuff explored by French criticism—say, René Girard—but is for Vendler a kind of unique American experience, of the self isolated from nature, from others, and from itself. Yet this isolation, and this notion of self, does not require any philosophical exploration, not even the question of whether "desire" undermines or empties out the self into a "ghost," as Stevens often suggests. So Vendler retreats into the curiously uninterrogated position of her earlier book to claim only that the poem is the measure and expression of a personal experience of some lack, experience raised to a general plateau. She does not have to ask herself whether this central question of a central self did not pose such a question, from Emerson to Stevens, whether, that is, it provoked the "experience" of poems rather than providing an occasional experience that the poem could represent. Vendler's linguistics continue to derive from her master, the psychologism of I. A. Richards, but her notion of lyric privilege and lyric style is now applied in a way to authenticate sense as feeling (not the "emotive") against sense as thought. Her model of the "lyric," then, is different from Walker's, but her sense of poetic language is no less "transparent."

One recent book does indicate the directions a future criticism might take. David M. LaGuardia's *Advance on Chaos: The Sanctifying Imagination of Wallace Stevens* (Hanover, N.H., 1983) provides, in its own words, "a context for an extensive consideration of the telling impact of Emerson and James on Wallace Stevens, a confluence of imaginations. . . ." LaGuardia's point of departure is the context of American pragmatism that has been recuperated for philosophy by Richard Rorty and for literary criticism by Bloom. But where Rorty sees in pragmatism a precursor of poststructuralist thought, or at least a kind of critical dialogue compatible with the more "destructive" European "conversation," and Bloom finds it a way of advancing beyond the gloom of deconstruction, LaGuardia hopes for the return to a full-fledged "'humanistic' posture which presumes that a reader's task consists of an attempt to interpolate an author's intention." LaGuardia, in other words, hopes that by returning to "intention"—a recent movement in theory, by the way—he can avoid the negative abysses opened up by concentration on the priority of language or the sign, whether the questionable status of figural language or the rhetoric which Bloom says is the "power" of the "self" to resist meaninglessness. If LaGuardia refuses to grant that pragmatism is a philosophy of performance rather than the assertion of the sufficiency of partial meanings, he nevertheless provides a sensible and balanced reading of Stevens within a clearly defined American tradition. Moreover, his disaffiliation of "humanism," which he places in quotation marks, from a "deconstruction" he thinks of as purely negative tends more to reveal that Rorty is correct to affine the two and to see American "humanism" as a critical discourse. LaGuardia, then, offers us a pertinent chapter of revisionary criticism, which will no doubt turn to the question of pragmatic "performance."

Charles Berger's *Forms of Farewell: The Late Poetry of Wallace Stevens* (Madison, Wis., 1985) offers a fitting titular conclusion if not a new critical departure to this section. Berger's reprise of the later Stevens is primarily a thematic study which begins with the unconvincing thesis that most of Stevens's great phase is a series of reflections on the catastrophe of World War II and hence ruminations on the apocalypse of modern civilization. While the thematics of war are everywhere evident in the poetry from the late 1930s on (as it was in the earlier poetry of World War I), the conflict is not necessarily there as the motivation of all Stevens's imagery in the very literal way Berger claims. Thus his study tends to become, to paraphrase Stevens from "Esthétique du Mal," a book of one idea in a world of possible ideas. Berger's readings make the late poems representations of the "real" rather than resistances to a "violence without," though he acknowledges Stevens's broader concern with poetry as a resistance, and this leads to a curious literalness in explaining, for example, the "applied enflashings" (said of reason in "Notes") of poems like "The Auroras of Autumn" where for Berger the images of the northern lights are barely figural displacements of the battlefield. One might argue to the contrary that Stevens confronted the realities of war as he did a Europe he never visited, tropically or figuratively, and that whatever the historical motivation of his images the war was no more than an "occasion" for his "cry."

Late entries in this survey, which have appeared too recently for full coverage here, include Veena Rani Prasad's *Wallace Stevens: Symbolic Dimensions in His Poetry* (Atlantic Highlands, N.J., 1986) and two books which combine biographical and critical readings: Joan Richardson's *Wallace Stevens: The Early Years, 1879–1923* (New York, 1986) and George S. Lensing's *Wallace Stevens: A Poet's Growth* (Baton Rouge, La., 1986), which reworks some of the essays he has been publishing over the last decade and a half, some of which are reviewed in the section on "Biography" and others in the following section surveying "Essays" of a non-theoretical kind.

b. The Short View—Some Essays. If the books on Stevens offer a garden variety of perspectives rather than a God's plenty of insight, the essays collectively can be said to do little more than exacerbate contending positions. There seems very little pattern to the collection, except that much of it is exegesis or the reconsideration of points and opinions made in earlier criticism. Even the canonical critics like Bloom have not been able to produce critical ephebes who do authoritative readings by the book. The challenge, of course, remains to produce "totalized" readings of individual poems; and if any trend is evident, it would seem to be the increasing interest in the longer and later poems and a turn away from the earlier, more anthologized lyrics. Most of the shorter pieces of criticism take up the poems and poetics within the old categories of Romantic and modern, or who influenced whom. A count of the entries in the critical bibliography since 1972, excluding minor commentaries and mentions, would number at least four hundred fifty entries. The heterogeneity of foci pretty well reflects the contemporary critical "scene" which is united only in its regard for the subject, not in what that subject means or what is the best way to approach it. If the critical variety seems to reveal what Henry Adams called the "law of chaos," the predominant concern is to keep the discourse on Stevens well within the decorums of traditional approaches.

One does not discern in the essays any particular development or advance beyond the issues set forth by Bloom and his antagonists. Several critics have published more than one piece, indicating perhaps a book in progress or that they are drafting sections from a dissertation. Mary Arensberg, whose work was briefly noted earlier, is one of the latter, as is John N. Serio, whose activity has been most influential on the development of the *Wallace Stevens Journal* (with Robert Deutsch's death, in 1983, Serio has become the editor). Robert J. Bertholf has contributed at least three pieces, each asserting a revisionary approach to the understanding of a long poem: "Parables and Wallace Stevens' 'Esthétique du Mal'" (*ELH*, Winter 1975); "Renewing the Set: Wallace Stevens' 'The Auroras of Autumn'" (*BSUF*, Spring 1976); and "The Revolving Toward Myth: Stevens' 'Credences of Summer'" (*BuR*, Fall 1976), in which he argues that Stevens's later work tries to regenerate a "mythic formula" for healing the "fall" into dualism, thereby recuperating in poetic utterance a realm of "innocence" that prehistorical man found promised in the seasonal cycles. Bertholf reads Stevens's obsession with seasonal imagery as if the poet were a modern Blake, fashioning a self-conscious fiction or personal myth. Thus "Credences" and "Auroras" advance beyond the earlier "Notes" and "Esthétique du Mal," which had respectively articulated the failure of mind "to account for the world's processes" and reduced the problem of evil from a "metaphysical to a human basis." Bertholf sees the two later poems as completing the imagination-reality dialectic and thus advancing beyond skepticism to a mythic resolution.

Serio's essays are more varied and less focused on a single thesis than Bertholf's, even though they derive from a dissertation. In at least six pieces he provides such various topics as "The Comedian as the Idea of

Order in *Harmonium*" (*PLL*, Winter 1976); "'A Hard Rain in Hartford': The Climate of Stevens' Poetics" (*RS*, Dec. 1979); and a piece on the relation of Stevens to Charles Ives's music (*BuR*, Fall 1978), among other essays which reveal both a biographical and a critical interest in the poet. And Kathleen A. Dale has published two sections from her University of Wisconsin-Milwaukee dissertation on Stevensian metaphorics: "Thesis and Antithesis in Wallace Stevens' Concept of Metaphor" (*GyS*, Spring 1977); and "Extensions: Beyond Resemblance and the Pleasure Principle in Wallace Stevens' Supreme Fiction" (*Boundary 2*, Fall 1975), each interesting and provocative because of Dale's aggressive attack upon those who had taken Stevens's own commentary rather literally, though her own theory of metaphor is disengaged from the technical and philosophical revaluations of trope underway in structural and post-structural criticism.

To the groups of essays by Arensberg, Bertholf, Serio, and Dale may be added those of Joseph G. Kronick, Michael Beehler, and Terrance J. King, all surveyed earlier, each of whom is working on a book that will be in part on Stevens. Likewise, the canonical Stevens critics of the 1960s and early 1970s have continued to add to, or revise, their own theoretical postures. Bloom, of course, and Doggett, Miller, Vendler, Donoghue, Morse, Riddel, and Litz have continued in different ways to increase the bibliography. Again, many of these positions have been reviewed above. But at least three of the more notable earlier critics demand mention here not simply for additions but for efforts which try to advert, or at least resist, the direction criticism seems to be taking. Roy Harvey Pearce, for example, whose essay in Buttel and Doggett argued that future criticism should be more scholarly and less speculative, has provided two brief essays, almost notes, on two short but well-known exercises: "'Anecdote of the Jar': an Iconological Note" (*WSJour*, Summer 1977), and "'The Emperor of Ice Cream': A Note on the Occasion" (*WSJour*, Fall 1979), each an attempt to verify an historical event or reference in which to ground the poems and thus to preclude the impressionistic, allegorical, or even parabolic readings to which they have regularly been submitted. Pearce's historicism is really an attempt to return attention to Stevens's concern with a commonsense or factitious "reality," even though the notes' only claim is that they are providing some discrete biographical and historical detail in which to ground Stevens's images: such as the old "mason jar" which moonshiners in Tennessee used to jug whisky or the details concerning the cigar factory in Tampa which Stevens no doubt knew. But the "facts" tend to trivialize the poetry, if not criticism.

Northrop Frye also returns to his earlier interest in Stevens for a contribution to *Literary Theory and Structure* (ed. Frank Brady, John Palmer, and Martin Price, New Haven, Conn., 1973), and makes a slight revision of his earlier praise for Stevens's mythic imagination. While his essay, "Wallace Stevens and the Variation Form," sticks pretty much to a discussion of the poetry in terms of Stevens's imagination-reality opposition, Frye's emphasis on Stevens's "variations" is intended, first, to reject the notion that he is a mystical or prophetic poet, and second, to indicate how the poet's reliance on something outside the mind helps him escape that narcissism and solipsism which other critics have isolated as his primary signature, whether to praise or to blame. And the late Isabel G. MacCaffrey, who also contributed to Buttel and Doggett a reading of "Le Monocle de Mon Oncle," adds a substantial piece on the later poetry, "A Point of Central Arrival: Stevens' *The Rock*" (*ELH*, Winter 1973), in which she explores Stevens's "historical" allusiveness—not the simple allusion to facts or events or even other poems, but references which, she argues, reimagine or transform the referent. Thus "'History' for Stevens," she writes, "is the history of imagining," through which he escapes from a dangerous solipsism by relating himself to the "power of the past," especially a past invested in literature. Unlike Bloom, MacCaffrey does not find Stevens's relations with the past a conflictual encounter with precursors but as part of his engagement with the literary tradition. If such a concern with the imagined past is part of the "natural solipsism of old age," it nevertheless spares the poet from a more dangerous withdrawal into self-pity by allowing him to identify himself with the immortality of art.

There is an increasing tendency in these essays to define Stevens as a post-Romantic and anti-Symbolist poet and to give added significance to his encounters with "reality," including the necessity it imposes or the price it exacts. This point of view coincides with other efforts, like Bloom's, to define a uniquely American Romantic tradition that is in effect pragmatic, or concerned with the enduring moment, and thus not hung up on the old epistemological dilemmas. Robert Alter, for instance, finds this anti-Symbolist Stevens to be wholly modern, or postmodern, and to be engaged in a poetics that is comparable to, however different from, that of Jorge Luis Borges. In his "Borges and Stevens: A Note on Post-Symbolist Writing" (*TriQ*, Fall 1972), Alter not only adds to the criticism which has attempted to distinguish Stevens's appropriations of Symbolism from that of other modern poets, but he argues that Stevens altogether rejects the Symbolist aesthetic and like Borges goes beyond it by submitting it to an ironic critique:"If the symbolist mode of literature conveys a sense of the unlimited powers of imagination—that is, of the image-making faculty of mind—the kind of writing practiced in different ways by Borges and Stevens makes us aware simultaneously of the power of imagination and its limit." By marking this "limit," however, Stevens does not necessarily reinvent the imagination's opposite and submit to "reality." Rather, he turns to the reality of "abstractions" and like Borges reveals "the kind of literature that can be created out of the most lucid recognition of literature's inherent limits."

Robert Greer Cohn, in his "Stevens and Mallarmé" (*CLS*, Dec. 1979), disagrees somewhat with this reading of Stevens, but only because he thinks that most American critics have misconstrued Symbolism. Cohn directs his attack at the newer criticism's "poetic nihilism," or the post-symbolist argument for linguistic nonreferentiality, and says that the attempts in recent criticism to define Symbolism as a search for some "pure ideal essence" is a misunderstanding. Thus, Cohn argues, Mallarmé is more of a "realist" or "poet of things," as Jean-Pierre Richard has called him, than is usually recognized. In this sense, it does not suffice for critics to align Stevens against Mallarmé as realist against idealist and makes it necessary to reconsider what the two very different poets do share.

In contrast to these efforts toward a corrective "realism," there remains the criticism which attempts to establish Stevens's "right to vatic stature," as Peter L. McNamara puts it in his "Wallace Stevens' Autumnal Doctrine" (*Renascence*, Winter 1974), an essay which proffers a reading of "The Auroras of Autumn" as the exemplum of Stevens's ability in his later poetry to establish "communication between vision and reality," that is, "to pierce the mystery of reality" and arrive at a "vision adequate to and capable of containing reality." McNamara is satisfied to use the concept "reality" unproblematically, and without admitting that in Stevens it means different things at different times, from "physical world" to something like ontological ground—at times, even trope. Stevens's probing of the relations between "reality" and language, and what it might mean to say that words penetrate to the real or that vision contains reality, is much more exacting than the criticism which turns his key terms into fixed concepts and then celebrates his achievement of visionary "truth." Janet McCann's "'Prologues to What Is Possible': Wallace Stevens and Jung" (*BSUF*, Spring 1976) performs a similar operation in reifying the Stevensian concept of "imagination" as a magical transforming power, using Jung very much as Leonora Woodman uses the analyst to show how Stevens drew from the "alchemical" tradition to affirm the priority of consciousness, even the modern estranged consciousness, to the world: "The resolution which Stevens finally achieves after great effort is an aesthetic in which the mind strives continually to recognize itself in the world, to encompass the world, in a sense to create it again." This aesthetics, she argues, is best described by the "dynamics" of analytical psychology (though the Jung evoked is more prophet than psychologist or analyst).

The debate continues, then, more or less in the terms Stevens supplied, with very little effort to explore his own changing sense of them or how that sense changes as they are employed. The criticism tends to ignore that they are tropes, and that their sense changes as they are troped, or as they change places in tropic sequences. At its best, as in Sharon Cameron's "'The Sense against Calamity': Ideas of a Self in Three Poems by Wallace Stevens" (*ELH*, Winter 1976), the criticism shifts its focus from an epistemological to a phenomenological register—recalling the critical stance of J. Hillis Miller's *Poets of Reality* (1965)—and in doing so underscores its recognition that such notions as "poetic self" are not referential but are workable concepts for treating such questions as images and their origin or figural language and its meaning. The "self" Cameron discusses is not a psychological self or personal "ego," but a literary construct one finds produced in a poetry that must reflect on the origin of its own images. Thus Cameron investigates Stevens's reflections upon this "fictive" self which becomes, under self-examination or in a self-reflexive poetry, an increasingly diminished power. This diminishment comes about, she argues, because of the progressive self-consciousness that leads the poet toward a dead-end of solipsism. The younger poet asserts the power of his own inventiveness in the figure of a generic "self," while the later one submits this power to an unremitting self-questioning. The strongest part of Cameron's essay, however, is not the thesis but her attentive reading of three poems which bear out the dialectical stripping away of this fiction of the self in Stevens's meditations.

One might compare this essay with Lawrence Kramer's "Ocean and Vision: Imaginative Dilemma in Wordsworth, Whitman, and Stevens" (*JEGP*, Apr. 1980). Kramer argues that, like his precursor Romantics, Stevens employed the Freudian figure of "ocean" or the "oceanic feeling" (a figure of cosmic energy) as a trope of that otherness which at once summons the self to resist and transform it and threatens that self with annihilation. (Kramer rightly acknowledges Freud's *Civilization and Its Discontents* as the source which explains the hold this image of ocean has on poets, though he forgets that Freud considered the figure problematical.) The "oceanic dilemma," as Kramer calls it, provides us a way of examining Stevens's epistemological crisis in psychological terms or, better, allows us, by tracing a common thematic from Romantic to post-Romantic or post-Freudian poet, to distinguish the latter's unique variation on the notion of an "interior paramour" or interiority in general. Kramer's critical model is structural psychoanalysis—Lacan's use of the metonymy-metaphor or linguistic model of mind as opposed to, say, a Jungian model—which permits him to move easily between a discussion of consciousness and poetic language. But his Lacanism is loosely defined and not rigorously applied.

Three essays in *Philosophy and Literature* reveal a slightly different approach to Stevensian dialectics by shifting the model of discourse from psychology to philosophy. R. D. Ackerman's "Believing in a Fiction: Wallace Stevens at the Limits of Phenomenology" (Spring 1979) employs Husserl's stated "paradox," that "the *element* which makes up the life of phenomenology . . . is *fiction*," to explain Stevens's similar paradox of modern "belief," a position Ackerman amplifies in a subsequent essay,

"Death and Fiction: Stevens' Mother of Beauty" (*ELH*, Summer 1983). Ackerman finds in Stevens's recurrent figure of the woman (the "mother of beauty" who is also "death") a doubled and opposing figure, offering us the promise that poetry is self-renewing, like nature, even as it "signals the fiction that breaks with nature" and suspends us in a "language bound discontinuity."

Stanley J. Scott's "Wallace Stevens and William James: The Poetics of Pure Experience" (*P&L*, Spring 1979) calls upon Jamesian "psychology" to interpret Stevens's theory of poetry as the pursuit of "pure experience" and thus as an overcoming of the metaphysical dualism which most critics find in his verse. "Pure experience" suggests an "agreement with reality," or something like a precognitive perception, in which is manifest the imagination's "power" to transcend all self-consciousness and arrive at what a Stevens poem names "moments of awakening . . . in which / We more than awaken." Scott calls the moments "revelation." This is not a mystical state, however, but a pragmatic one like that James called the "will to believe." Thus Scott limns a Stevensian theory that is related to the one Bloom advocates in *Agon* or LaGuardia examines in *Advance on Chaos*, the latter being a much more convincing study because it by and large eschews the mystical argument.

Richard Kuhns, in "Metaphor as Plausible Inference in Poetry and Philosophy" (*P&L*, Fall 1979), uses Stevens to explore the uneasy relationship between poetry and philosophy. He claims that "Notes," for example, is a poem that enacts a direct challenge to the "philosophical position of Descartes." Kuhns wishes to indicate how, regardless of philosophy's effort to purge itself of the metaphorical, one kind of philosophical argument progresses exclusively through metaphor. Thus he reads Stevens's poem in its philosophical posture, as establishing the metaphorical *Abgrund* of all argumentation, a position that allows the poet to express fiction's priority to truth, and poetry's to philosophy. This is another way of saying that Stevens, among other poets, anticipated the "deconstruction of metaphysics" evident in such contemporary transvaluations of the philosophy of language as Jacques Derrida's "White Mythology."

Much of the criticism which employs a philosophical model to read Stevens proceeds in the more conventional way of analogizing his thought with this or that system or by finding a common terminology. These critics may take the stance of Scott and uncover a common set of metaphors, or the mode of the late Richard P. Adams, in one of his yearly essays for the annual *TSE: Tulane Studies in English* (1972), who argues that Stevens's skepticism is essentially a restatement of Schopenhauer's. Frank Kermode's contribution to Buttel and Doggett makes a similar argument, though it insists less on direct or conscious influence, for Stevens's extrapolations from Heidegger. Kuhns's essay, which posits the poet as a "reader" or troper of philosophy, moves in the direction of a poststructuralist criticism which submits philosophical texts to the strategies of literary criticism rather than extracting their cognitive statements and applying them to figural ones as if they were a metalanguage.

Judith McDaniel's "Wallace Stevens and the Scientific Imagination" (*ConL*, Spring 1974) takes the more traditional way, but ends up making the latter point. McDaniel's point of departure is Stevens's abortive philosophical essay, "A Collect of Philosophy," in which he argues that philosophy, including the modern philosophy of science, is irreducibly poetic or imaginative and should be understood to substantiate the privilege of a poetic utterance which has in recent times been split off from science and made into a minority "culture." McDaniel, however, does not locate Stevens's argument in language or in metaphor, as does Kuhns, but in a history of ideas, appealing to the writing of Whitehead and Norbert Weiner, among others, who argue that science can no longer provide a picture of a universe pervaded by a "rational order," as Thomas Huxley thought. Rather, in an age of thermodynamics, relativity, quantum theory, and indeterminacy, it must find a way of giving an orderly account of an unruly universe. Thus the scientist's problem, like the poet's, is a search for a coherent discourse commensurate with the incoherent, or a representation for the unrepresentable, while the poet's mode has always had to face this challenge of making the invisible visible.

Beyond these loosely grouped approaches, the essays are difficult to classify, except in their heterogeneity. Most are revisionary or corrective readings of individual poems, which may or may not reveal the focus of a critic's particular theory or *parti pris*. For example, Richard P. Adams's "Pure Poetry: Wallace Stevens' 'Sea Surface Full of Clouds'" (*TSE*, 1974) might have taken up the question of Stevens's Symbolism or anti-Symbolism, or the difference between his notion of "pure poetry" and, say, Mallarmé's, but the essay eschews theory for the most part and proceeds to a close thematic and formalist reading of the poem. William Bevis's "Stevens' Toneless Poetry" (*ELH*, Summer 1974) chastises the readers of such enigmatic or parabolic verse as "The Snow Man" for discovering thematic or ideological complications that are more the critics' than the poet's. These essentially "simple" poems, says Bevis, evoke emotional states of consciousness that cannot be translated into familiar abstractions. Stevens, he goes on, is a poet who explores and projects new and different kinds of consciousness for which a philosophical or psychoanalytical language is inadequate. In certain poems, which Bevis calls "toneless," Stevens renders these states as "detached ecstasies." And while there are very few poems like "The Snow Man" which one can call "toneless," that is, poems which render a mood of emotional coldness and detachment, many others can be read as reflections pro and con on the condition of "detachment": "if few poems imitate detached ecstasies, many seem affected by the possibility, attracted or repelled by this way of looking at the world." Since the "detached" state is beyond intellectual description, being a mood of noncommitment rather than conscious indifference or nihilism, the critic's use of philosophical or analytical terminology to read the poems as arguments translates the "ecstatic" into a false language: "A detached ecstasy may not be described in dualistic terms," leaving us to look for something like a Zen criticism as the sufficient context for reading Stevens's atonal language which imitates "mystical states of consciousness." Bevis wants it both ways, especially for himself—he is intellectually anti-intellectual, though not Nietzschean.

Lewis Turco's "The Agonism and the Existentity: Stevens" (*CP*, Spring 1973) takes the opposite position, that the key to Stevens is his struggle or *agon* to "represent" his "ideas" or "abstractions," since the only meaning of the world is what the perceiver or artificer imposes on it. Stevens, Turco says, was a poet seeking "objective correlatives" for his thought, abstractions which were his substitute for modern intellectual and religious poverty. Turco offers in support of this struggle in Stevens a somewhat elliptical thematic reading of "An Ordinary Evening in New Haven," in which the effort to "blood" abstractions reveals the problems facing any self-conscious intellectual poet who can no longer articulate his thoughts in the terms of systematic philosophy. But Turco has trouble himself stating precisely what this new existential thought might be, especially in relation to the old ideas from which it turns. His essay is thus the precise antithesis of Bevis's and encounters a similar contradiction.

The chapter on Stevens in Carlos Baker's *The Echoing Green: Romanticism, Modernism, and the Phenomena of Transference in Poetry* (Princeton, N.J., 1984) reverts to a pre-Bloomian notion of both poetic influence and the poetics of Romanticism. Baker situates Stevens within the Romantic tradition which, following Abrams and others, he finds to be an historical prelude to a modernism that does not so much compete with as complete its precursors. Thus "transference" has little of the thrust that it might have in psychoanalytic or poststructural criticism. The "echoing" of Baker's title is to be taken almost literally, and, in the case of Stevens, the critic pursues the modern poet's almost homonymic if not literal borrowings from his elders as an influence easily accommodated to a change from Romantic subjectivism to a modern realism, and from an obsession with an unavailable past to a commitment to the limited pleasures of the present. The conflict between "nature" as object and "nature" as symbol is muted and overcome by the modern; it does not produce the dizzying abyss that recent studies of the Romantic, like Paul de Man's, find haunting our poetry and also our criticism, making any clear distinction between Romantic and modern questionable. For Baker, Stevens's appropriation of the Romantics—Keats, Shelley, and Wordsworth more than Coleridge or Byron—is unproblematic, and can be traced in Stevens's almost literal repetitions of the most famous of

Romantic utterances. In brief, Baker's sense of Romanticism as a mode of negotiating between "La Vie Anterieure" and "Le Bel Aujourd'hui," the titular phrases for his chapter on Stevens, recapitulates the Romanticist criticism that culminated in "natural supernaturalism." Baker does it, of course, with effortless grace, but it makes for an anachronistic commentary.

In "Wallace Stevens: The Romantic Imagist" (*BSUF*, Winter 1980), Allan Chavkin asserts that Stevens's style is a marrying of those renowned opposites, Romantic meditation and Imagist objectivity. And Sandy Cohen in the same journal (Spring 1976) provides "An Alternate View" to critics who see Stevens as a Romantic poet rewriting the "Wordsworthian myth of reciprocity between man and nature" in a modern mode. His alternative is provided in a counterreading to "Credences of Summer" which must be understood as an analytical poem, something like a cubist painting by Duchamp, that is structured by a kind of "calculus." Thus Stevens's maneuvering of the four seasons is not referential to reality or to the old myths but is a new reading of nature in terms of a kind of post-Newtonian mathematics of perception. Cohen does not, however, suggest that Cubism and Imagism have anything in common. Daniel P. Tompkins, in "'To Abstract Reality': Abstract Language and the Intrusion of Consciousness in Wallace Stevens" (*AL*, Mar. 1973), contrasts Stevens's style with Imagism, and especially with the Imagist (and ideogrammic) method of working in a visible yet verbal language that at once evokes and pictures the processes of "nature." Stevens's style, to the contrary, is a refining of abstract diction which emphasizes the relations and arrangements of things; that is, it explores resemblances rather than trying to mime natural process. Thus his aphoristic style (studied with a different emphasis by Beverly Coyle in a book reviewed above) is in intellectual counterpoint to Imagism.

Robert N. Mollinger, in "Wallace Stevens' Search for the Central Man" (*TSL*, 1976), returns to the question of Stevens's humanism which changes from the early denigration of naturalistic or fatalistic man in "The Comedian" into an affirmation of the "hero" or "central man" of the later verse, who signifies a "final belief to replace the obsolete fiction" of supernatural or transcendent man. This is by no means a new reading of Stevens, and seems the result of a very reductive thematism. In *American Poets in 1976* (ed. William Heyen, Indianapolis, 1976), the poet Robert Bly passes a negative judgment on Stevens's development. "Wallace Stevens and Dr. Jekyll" takes the position that American poetry is at its most powerful when it is releasing the darker, primitive instincts that civilization has managed to repress or suffocate. He finds that Stevens has achieved that power only in his earlier poetry and that the rest, especially the self-reflexive later poems, are evidence of the baleful repression of the "shadow" that haunts and motivates the most powerful of our poems. Stevens's submission to the restraints and formalisms of the bourgeois life goes hand in hand with the sacrifice of the true poetic life to intellectual abstraction. This is a typical reassertion of American primitivism, and it hardly squares with either the facts of Stevens's life or with the poetry, since he was fully engaged in his professional life during the writing of the early poetry. Yet Bly's position does mark an as yet unresolved debate in Stevens criticism—the division between aesthete or instinctive poet and philosophical poet and the counterclaims for the superiority of one kind of poetry to the other.

And finally, two very different essays take up the question of Stevens's politics which, as Bly suggests, seem to reflect his submission to the bourgeois reality and capitalist economy. David Howard's "Wallace Stevens and Politics" (*RMS*, 1977), in a special issue on "Literature and Ideology," begins by commenting on Stevens's situation in an "age of unbelief," speculating quite correctly from one point of view that he always seemed "on the point of conversion" in many of his poems but that his real faith was the modern heresy, shared by his critics, in accepting the "absolute" of "art itself" for religion. Howard cavalierly assesses Stevens's capitalist politics in the same terms: whatever is dominant you appropriate. Thus Stevens in the 1930s would counter both fascism and communism with aesthetics or "take on or take over the threat of modern psychology" by concocting his own notion of a "self before the self began." But when Howard turns to the poetry as example, he reads so eccentrically as to effect his own misappropriation. He quotes, and the quotations finally choke off his commentary and make his argument as intellectually specious as he claims Stevens's politics to be.

Jonathan Holden's "Poetry and Commitment" (*OhR*, No. 2, 1982) is even less discriminating and more *au courant*. It praises Stevens for his poetry and deplores his abominable use of racist language in some poems, like "The News and the Weather." But Holden's essay is really on the political crudity of the poetry of Carolyn Forché, and Stevens, who is barely mentioned, is merely an incidental example of a good poet with bad politics. Strangely enough, there have been no ground-breaking essays on Stevens's politics in recent years, which is surprising when one considers the resurgence of a Marxist criticism that is theoretically integrated with poststructuralist discourse. Frank Lentricchia's indictment of Stevens's bourgeois skepticism as a progenitor of that criticism in the United States stands as the most incisive though undeveloped reassessment of a Stevens who in this one sense at least joins with Pound and Eliot as exemplars of modern poetry's affiliation with the extreme right. Michael Sexson, in his "Wallace Stevens' Theatre of Clouds: Imaginal Reality and the Idea of the Postmodern" (*HSL*, No. 1, 1982), might have engaged this question of modernism's affiliation with the right, and postmodernism's turn left, but Sexson's essay falters on the very questionable notion that there is a postmodernism. In any event, Sexson's essay turns to old questions posed by a reactionary "myth criticism" and the Jungian drama of "individuation." What goes around comes around in this kind of critical argument.

Obviously, bibliographical essays do not conclude and are not summed up, since they recount a dialogue that dare not close. They must be selective even when promising to be inclusive. Commendable essays are no doubt overlooked, and deserving critics or, more importantly, critical points deserving emphasis slighted. Some positions are dimmed in faint praise, and others flower or bloom at the expense of irritating the ideological opposition or the ignored. But the "author" of this compilation of marginalia would be remiss if he did not conclude with the mention of one piece which he will refuse to read, a brief essay in a little-known journal, *Windlass Orchard*, in 1979. It will remain without further reference, except to its author, one A. U. Contraire. Contraire, or "Oh" as he will be phonemically known, may very well be the metonym of criticism, of its *agon* and its ecstasy, of its contrariety, its contrariness, and its claims of certain certainties. Of the last word it will never have.

VI SUPPLEMENT

There have been the usual number of books and articles, though the latter will not be accounted for here (one can appeal to the ongoing bibliography and reviews of the *Wallace Stevens Journal*, among other bibliographical supplements); but the discourse remains normative, with perhaps one slight ripple of exception.

Bibliography. Bibliography or bibliographical essay is perhaps not the proper term for Melita Schaum's welcome and thoughtful *Wallace Stevens and the Critical Schools* (Tuscaloosa, Ala., 1988), for it is neither competitive with Edelstein's listings nor a comprehensive essay on criticism like Abbie Willard's book noted earlier or Riddel's essay in the previous edition of this book. Schaum's focus is, as it should be, on questions of theory and critical practice as that theo-praxis appropriates Stevens as model and poetic exemplum. She argues, much as the earlier part of this essay has, that Stevens has been a "central" poet for a variety of critical schools and that while each of these groups, schools, ideologies, and individuals has in its way illuminated and obscured "Stevens," each has also revealed its own blindness and the defining limits of its practice in its use and abuse of "Stevens." Thus the book serves not only as an overview of Stevens criticism (a "history") but also as a kind of record of contemporary criticism. It seems fair to say that Schaum is more authoritative on Stevens and Stevens criticism than she is on the philosophical subtleties and strategies of contemporary theory, but since this writer has his own parti pris, and moreover plays a large part in Schaum's narrative, it is best at this point to abandon judgment for reference.

Biography. The ordinariness of a bourgeois life, however cultivated and aestheticized against the ascetic tendencies and demands and sublimations of an American existence, is not necessarily resistant to biography, as witness the spate of recent ones that continue to search for a "representative man" or woman (Emerson), and clearly not resistant to autobiography, which one might argue is the American genre par excellence, from Whitman's "Song" through Henry Adams to the reign of confessional poetics. Yet, Stevens's life, as mentioned previously, has not proved conducive to what has been called saturational biography, after the late Richard Ellmann's classical reconstruction of Joyce. Joan Richardson's *Wallace Stevens: The Early Years, 1879–1923* (New York, 1986) is evidence enough of why Ellmann, among others, shied away from the challenge. The problem, however, may not just be the "ordinary," even though studies which have focused criticism of the poems in the particulars of the life have proved less interesting and useful than works like Brazeau's oral biography and the autobiographical signatures of texts like the *Letters* and *Souvenirs and Prophecies.* Nevertheless, Richardson's is the first full-fledged attempt at a biography. Like most of the biographically oriented studies, it focuses on the life up through the *Harmonium* years, as if to prove that what followed and was most interesting about Stevens was that which is summed up by the old cliché, a "life of the mind," despite her argument that she is a new convert to history and to a belief that a poet's life is shaped by his early encounters in the "real" world.

Richardson's study offers little to the student of the poetry and provides only a few details of the life that were not already available, scattered through the manuscripts and the previously published journals, memoirs, and so on. What marks Richardson's work is its self-indulgence, from a long opening section that describes her own strategy of improvisation upon facts to the execution of a narrative account that shifts between unimaginative documentation and fanciful speculation. On the one hand, Richardson wants to record the poet's growth of mind and sensibility, through his reading and education, his socialization, and the usual conflicts and sublimations of what we have come to call the "family romance." On the other, she wants to account for a complex "inner" struggle, the shaping of a sensibility. To reconstruct the latter, she indulges in a great deal of amateur psychologism; and for some of the former, she recounts an intellectual history—say, the way his ideas were shaped by a reading of Kant and Bergson, among others, and by lesser votaries of philosophy and modernist aesthetics he encountered or read. Both strategies are more reductive than usual, especially her recounting of the ideas of Kantian epistemology and Bergsonian comedy, as well as the latter's notion of subjective time. When she deals with "fact," much of it gleaned from widely available journals, letters, and the like, she at once resists reading cryptic, allusive, and suggestive phrases in a critical way and yet indulges her own speculation on what kind of emotional or reflective turmoil the poet as consciousness and sensibility might have been undergoing. Two instances: at one point, she commits several pages to reflections on Stevens's inscrutable handwriting and his apparent attempts to correct it, though there is little attempt to make clear what this means for either person or poet, let alone critic; at another, she takes a casual remark in a letter concerning a friend's failure to meet an appointment, in which Stevens remarks that this event provoked him to read Bacon's essay "On Friendship," and extends the confession into a point-by-point reading of the Bacon essay as a representation of Stevens's struggle with identity. The study is laced with such indulgent speculations, especially about the mysterious relations of husband and wife, but in the end there is no way Richardson can make a case for the extraordinary sensibility, nor convincingly reproduce a conflictual scene of inner life that accounts for the poetry. Certainly one is often led to question her own judgment of what is central and what trivial.

Since Richardson uses the poetry to reflect the "life," she has little to say about the poetry, and while occasionally she links specific tropes with particular events or occasions, for the most part such associations are adventitious, to say the least. George S. Lensing's *Wallace Stevens, A Poet's Growth* (Baton Rouge, La., 1986), mentioned earlier along with several of his essays, is, though not strictly speaking a biography, a much more successful exercise in reading the poetry out of and against the "life." One may question Lensing's titular metaphor of "growth," and all that it implies of a metaphysical, organicist interpretation, but it is a study capable both of getting down selectively crucial details and reading out of them the imaginative tropings, despite its low key criticism.

Criticism. Although the books keep coming there is little enough advance in "Stevens criticism" to anticipate what it might eventually produce, let alone say what it adds to or completes of the past. As Schaum's book validates, the most notable critical discourse continues to make Stevens represent and answer for certain modalities of recent theory, and this in turn has become most provocative and contentious among those who want criticism to remain devoted to poet and poem rather than displace them in theoretical hyperbole. First, Harold Bloom's *Wallace Stevens: Modern Critical Views* (New York, 1985), the Chelsea House collection of previously published essays, continues Bloom's efforts to establish the Stevensian "position" and "era," though the problem here is that he must try to contextualize a number of diverse essays into something central. But it is valuable as a memory device, not only in recovering a certain Stevens but in recording how canonization both in literature and criticism operate. In contrast to Bloom and his advocacy of a Paterean Stevens, one would have to advert to the very different strategy of Frank Lentricchia, who reenters the lists of "theoretical" challenge with yet another version of Stevens's representative "bad faith." True enough, Stevens in Lentricchia's latest version, *Ariel and the Police: Michel Foucault, William James, Wallace Stevens* (Madison, Wis., 1988), is only the "cry of its occasion." In a text that "classly" reads Stevens (with close attention to parts of four texts, "Anecdote of the Jar," "Sunday Morning," "Owl's Clover," and "Notes"), Lentricchia attempts another disruption of what he thinks of as American formalist (and totalitarian) criticism with some version of a Marxist, neohistoricist reading, against "determination" or authoritarianism. The critical question of "domination" and "authority," as interpreted from a sociopolitical notion of literature's "role" in history, is Lentricchia's theme, and he pursues Stevens and his critics (formalists of the old New Criticism and aestheticists of the new *nouvelle critique* alike) as exemplars of some great antidemocratic and antisocial project. It would be unfair to Lentricchia and to the discourses of recent critical theory to discuss his argument further without elaborate critique, since it condenses, yet marginalizes, so much of what is crucial today for theory, and even more marginal for a specific (Stevensian) literary criticism. One might well point, instead, to what Lentricchia has effectively instigated.

Lentricchia's essays on Stevens, later integrated into the larger text on an "American" version of archeological, as opposed to genealogical, criticism, first appeared in the *South Atlantic Quarterly* (Fall 1987) and in *Critical Inquiry* (Summer 1987). They happened almost by deflection to set off a kind of theoretical brush fire with the feminist critics Sandra Gilbert and Susan Gubar, since Lentricchia used his readings of Stevens on "domination" as a way of critiquing the Gilbert-Gubar argument over "gender" theory. It also produced a Gilbert-Gubar reading of Stevens, something missing from their book *No Man's Land* (1987) and the earlier *Madwoman in the Attic* (1979). Suffice it to report here, the Gilbert-Gubar response (*CritI*, Winter 1988) makes some interesting passing comments on Stevens and some of his poems, as well as engaging with the Lentricchia argument; and Lentricchia's own response to his critics in that issue is refined and amplified in *Ariel and the Police*. The critical engagement, therefore, is more important than any fallout upon Stevens or literary criticism specifically and will be of more interest to theorists than to Stevens critics or readers. Nevertheless, this newest marginalized centralization of Stevens points back to the role(s) he has been made to play in the three decades since he was textualized and canonized as a central poet and points forward to something else: the place that the notion of "resentment" in the Nietzschean sense plays in contemporary criticism and, as well, in the modernism (not postmodernism) that categorizes so much of our literary production. For Lentricchia's theme is "resentment," the resentment that Stevens felt as an elitist yet alienated modern, conserver of old yet producer of new values, the "double bind" of the modern centralist. This is a theme that Lentricchia sees so clearly yet reflects and articulates so pathetically in his own resentment of the critic's frustrated desire to engage, influence, direct, effect, and otherwise eliticize him/her-self by acting in the institutional margins of his/her culture.

Poetry and criticism have always asked the more than pragmatic and more than ideological question of their own performance: to what effect, and affect, do their representations or simulacra work? The Lentricchia/ Gilbert-Gubar standoff represents one such instance of criticism appropriating literature for its rhetorical move of engagement. Stevens's (modernism's) own self-reflexivity, or self-reflections, have always been understood to stand as critiques and acts, advancing and questioning the "poem of the act of the mind." This has salvaged Stevens for a poetics of the postmodern, confirmed his role as exemplar of the modern, and allowed him to use criticism as criticism has been able to *use* him. The deconstructive Stevens and the aesthetic Stevens go hand in hand. If only to confirm the evident fact that Stevens continues to provide exempla for opposing schools of critical thought, note this instance, which hardly deserves to be considered as Stevens criticism but clearly reveals the inmixtures of literary analysis and general theory: in a book entitled *Criticism in Society: Interviews with Jacques Derrida, Northrop Frye, Harold Bloom, Frank Kermode, Edward Said, Barbara Johnson, Frank Lentricchia, and J. Hillis Miller*, conducted by Imre Salusinszky, edited by Terence Hawkes (New York, 1987), the theorists were asked to include, as part of their reflections on their own "positions," a few remarks on "Not Ideas about the Thing but the Thing Itself." Two observations: the group included several notable Stevens critics, each of whom has made the poet a focal metonym for larger theoretical emphasis; only Derrida declined to speak offhand of a poem as example, perhaps because he was unfamiliar with the poem, perhaps because his theory does not permit such a use or abuse of literary example.

Yet, the predominant critical trend remains an attempt at another kind of representation: poetry as redemptive value rather than poetry as transactive re-valuation. It should not be surprising that Stevens criticism persists in trying to retrieve *the* Stevens (or "The *the*."). If Bloom's collection of previously published canonical essays signifies also a canonical effort to make Stevens the representative of a "new" (or newly defined) Romanticism, Albert Gelpi's collection in the Cambridge Studies in American Literature and Culture Series, entitled *Wallace Stevens: The Poetics of Modernism* (New York, 1985), containing essays by Gelpi, Gerald L. Bruns, Marjorie Perloff, Bonnie Costello, and Charles Altieri, among others, fulfills its title by returning to the old argument about both the periodization and the philosophico-aesthetic difference between Romantic and modern. This entails, of course, a lot of arguing about criticism and theory in general and about the appropriation of Stevens by poststructural or deconstructive criticism (a common confusion), but it also leads to considerable rehashing of the old epistemological and historicist definitions of the Romantic and modern, a kind of critical *déja re-vue.*

Gelpi's essay on Stevens and Williams in this collection, later amplified into a chapter of his *A Coherent Splendor: The American Poetic Renaissance, 1910–1950* (New York, 1987), is an indicative product of this attempt to unite a universalist notion of literature with an account of its historicist production: the title, reflecting so clearly Matthiessen's own classical grappling with theoretical dualism (the work as both universal and local, even in Williams's sense), contains an ample amount of archetypal or even Jungian theory about Romanticist revelation and a modicum of particular or biographical detail about the "scene" out of which individual poets (Pound, Williams, Eliot, H.D., and others) fashioned a poetry as a kind of psychic conflict and resolution. Again, one is struck by the difference in interpretation of the very notion of "psychic" conflict between Gelpi and Bloom, and thus by the many possibilities of recent criticism to retreat by radical advance or advance by salutary retreat, for while both critics suggest the performative force of poetry, both deny the role of the performative that is so crucial for much recent theory.

Gelpi's story of modernist success, of a struggle of opposites dialectically overcome, even when individual and local circumstances have necessitated the abandonment of metaphysical paraphernalia (a refrain often heard from the "new historicists"), only confirms the deeply entrenched ontotheological substructures of a recent criticism that remains in thrall to the old New Criticism. That Stevens remains an issue in the debate between a certain Romanticism and a certain modernism, and thereby available to those committed to a certain postmodernism, is a revealing sign of the impasses of a "theoretical crisis" that Stevens, and poetry in general, annul in their own performances. Nevertheless, one must conclude the critical "history" of another decade and a half of Stevens criticism with a familiar account, or with a repetition of the "family romance." That is, the criticism still moves within the purview of the old uninterrogated discourses, which the poststructuralist critics claim Stevens's own performance dismantles, resists, overturns rather than dialectically or spiritually resolves.

The main recent books on Stevens, then, may be said to lie outside what Schaum's bibliographical essay calls the "Critical Schools." Even J. S. Leonard and C. E. Wharton's *The Fluent Mundo: Wallace Stevens and the Structure of Reality* (Athens, Ga., 1988), which conducts a long quarrel with "phenomenological" critics of Stevens like Miller and Paul Bové in the name of a certain phenomenology of its own, is not a theoretical but an antitheoretical study, in that it pushes the analogies between poetic and philosophical thought as an instance of how the poet exemplifies an essential self or consciousness. Thus, in resisting the negative phenomenology and nihilism it perceives in a "criticism of consciousness," the authors return to a certain intentionalist criticism represented by the Warburg School, which celebrates poetry as a kind of "symbolic" production of "figures of capable imagination," that is, fictive truths as forms of conflictual overcoming.

This celebration of Stevens as a poet of "coherence," of self-overcoming, and of "integrations" (one of his favorite words for the poetic production of a fictive unity), whether it is articulated in the epistemological figures of an imagination-reality synthesis or the more theological terms of some kind of "psychic" triumph—to be distinguished from Bloom's figure of incessant and endless conflict or resistance—perhaps tells us more about the struggles of modern criticism than about any particular poet. It is an attempt to save the metaphor that poetry can "save us," as I. A. Richards and the American New Critics claimed, whether from a psychological, philosophical, or theological point of view; and it is a criticism that clearly underscores a need to conserve the old humanist ethical values.

A strikingly comprehensive book like Joseph Carroll's *Wallace Stevens' Supreme Fiction: A New Romanticism* (Baton Rouge, La., 1987) and even B. J. Leggett's *Wallace Stevens and Poetic Theory: Conceiving the Supreme Fiction* (Chapel Hill, N.C., 1987) indicate in their titles, whether appealing to the old Romantic-modern distinction or to a figure of their dialectical overcoming, a resistance to theory and an affirmation of poetry as a triumphant form of belief. Carroll's patient working through of the old critical debates over the Stevens body or "corpus," and his effort to account for the canon both in the part and in the whole, to "read" *the* Stevens out of the conflictual readings of others, never vary from Carroll's project to show that the poetic self who is "finally human" (the last, and quoted, words of his book) is the issue of a poetic realization that marries the practical and pragmatic (reality) with the spiritual (imaginative), as the title of the poem from which the phrase is taken clearly reveals. By insisting that Stevens's "apotheosis of poetry" was not a rhetoric but a realization, Carroll diminishes the conflict that rhetorical critics like Bloom, or even the dialectical critics, find in the poet's darker moments. Even when his poetry fails to achieve the purity it at times rhetorically desires and thus fails to attain a "permanent integration with the essential poem," it still "succeeded in creating a mode of poetic experience in which religious awe and Romantic wonder are still possible." This "visionary mythology," a fiction known to be fiction, is other than Bloom's visionary hypothesis and marks a distinct difference between criticism and reification, however celebratory of poetic overcoming the former's theory proves to be.

Leggett's study, on the other hand, is not theoretical, even though it is an effort toward recounting Stevens's "theory." In a certain sense, this is a very literal book, operating on a premise, much like Lowes's study of Coleridge, that a poet's experience is in the (his/her) reading.

As a study of Stevens's derivative and improvised "ideas" about "poetics," Leggett's book resists thoughts about "anxiety of influence" and refuses to submit either Stevens's theoretical writing (which he properly notes is inscribed as much in the poems as in the essays) or the discourse of his precursors (philosophers and critics) to a rigorous reading of their own. As such, his argument seems to take as much away from Stevensian "originality" as it gives by way of recounting his transformations. Nevertheless, this is a useful study, for it convincingly follows out Stevens's reading of Coleridge, I. A. Richards, Charles Mauron, and Henri Focillon, among others. It provides a number of readings that show the way Stevens could be influenced by an essay or book, borrowing and mirroring and toying with its ideas in an effort to account *almost* rationally for a poetry that "resists the intelligence, almost successfully." The study of Mauron's influence on Stevens's notion of "supreme fiction" and Focillon's *The Life of Forms* on "The Auroras of Autumn" should be welcomed by any critic, even those like Bloom and the poststructuralists who are more intent on accounting for the laws of transformation or the poet's tropings and resistances and who do not think that a critic, let alone a poet, can read so innocently.

Jacqueline Brogan's *Stevens and Simile: A Theory of Language* (Princeton, N.J., 1986) is similarly less theoretical than its title might suggest, for the simple and obvious reason that it follows a good deal of contemporary discourse in confusing theoretical criticism with the application of one or more "theories" in opposition to other positions. Brogan's turn toward language, and to a certain notion of language, is thus more descriptive than theoretical; for while she works her way through much of the poststructural discourse on figural language, her basic notion of such figures as "metaphor" and "simili" is more normative or structural than critical or poststructural. And in using a notion of "fragmentation"—in contrast, say, to the notions of unity, coherence, or overcoming of difference that marks a position like Carroll's—as a thematic or even epistemological name for Stevens's particular strategy with metaphor, she actually reverses poststructuralist studies of Stevensian metaphor, such as those of Patricia A. Parker or Joseph G. Kronick, by claiming for the poet a unique appropriation or style. She implies, that is, that the poet is a master of metaphor, or in Stevens's case, the particular figure of simili, and thus a master of "disjunction" ("connoisseur of chaos"); hence, she repeats by inversion the very logocentrism to which she opposes Stevens's poetic theory. Beyond theory, however, Brogan's study is a useful contribution to examinations of style and goes along with other important works, like the study of his adages, in making up a library of Stevensian signatures.

Two other books appeared or were announced too late to be included in review here: Robert Rehder's *The Poetry of Wallace Stevens* (New York, 1987); Richard N. Sawaya's *The Skepticism and Animal Faith of Wallace*

Stevens (New York, 1987); and another collection of *Critical Essays on Wallace Stevens*, edited by Steven Gould Axelrod and Helen Deese (CEAmL, Boston, 1988), which includes previously published essays by Bloom, Frye, Kronick, Miller, and Riddel, and some new ones by the editors and others. And so it goes, and so one may choose: between a criticism that attempts to master the poet, to read him correctly, and a criticism that tends to appropriate him for the more general purpose of theory and critical practice itself. But even this latter remains split, or doubled, since it either makes Stevens into a radical theorist (of poetry and language), whether consciously or unconsciously, or reads him as a poet who, like Derrida's Mallarmé, best reveals the double bind of the poetic desire for purity, unmediated vision, or supreme fictions.

William Carlos Williams

Linda W. Wagner-Martin

I BIBLIOGRAPHY

Chief bibliographic activity connected with Williams during the 1970s was related to the ever-growing secondary criticism on his work and to library collections of his manuscripts. Two major books and two bibliographies, one included in the Williams issue of *Journal of Modern Literature* (May 1971), the other in Carroll F. Terrell's *William Carlos Williams: Man and Poet* (Orono, Maine, 1983; hereinafter referred to as Terrell), comprised the major offerings. In 1975 Paul L. Mariani's *William Carlos Williams: The Poet and His Critics* (Chicago) began the assessment of kinds of critical recognition Williams had received. Mariani's survey is divided into five chapters, arranged in roughly chronological order (early reception, 1910–30; 1930–45; 1946–61 [*Paterson*]; 1946–63 [reputation as a whole]; and 1963–73). Rather than find critical patterns and place essays and books into those thematic categories, Mariani's tactic is to summarize key essays and then speculate on what further work might be done in areas already represented. His own preferences for certain of Williams's writings color his observations on the criticism noted, but on the whole, his study is a useful and helpful map of the terrain up to the early 1970s. Linda W. Wagner's *William Carlos Williams: A Reference Guide* (Boston, 1978) follows the annotated entry format for secondary books and essays, with brevity being a noticeable characteristic. The *Guide* includes materials published from 1909 through 1976.

In 1979 Norma Procopiow published "The Early Critical Reception of William Carlos Williams" (*WCWN*, Spring), an analysis which built on Mariani and Wagner but included other kinds of assessments as well. As early as 1971, Jack Hardie had provided invaluable service to Williams scholars by compiling a checklist of over five hundred general studies and reviews, and as many commentaries on specific collections and individual poems. "'A Celebration of the Light': Selected Checklist of Writings about William Carlos Williams" (*JML*, May 1971) is particularly useful because of its arrangement and annotations. Then in 1983 the bibliography compiled by Joseph Brogunier (Terrell) added 231 annotated items to those already extant. Brogunier's citations are of material published between 1974 and 1982. Many of his annotations are taken from published reviews, an interesting method that has one difficulty. Only one review is cited and, on occasion, books that have been positively reviewed are represented here by negative comment. This bibliography, as well as the Terrell collection as a whole, is one of the most important publications of the Williams centennial year.

Emily Mitchell Wallace's primary bibliography of Williams (1968) remains the chief source of information about Williams's publications. Several notes of addenda have appeared since its publication, among them those by Craig A. Lahm (*Serif*, Summer 1974), Charles Doyle (*PBSA*, Third Quarter 1975), Clement E. Vose (*WCWN*, Fall 1977), and Christopher J. MacGowan (*WCWR*, Fall 1980). These citations suggest the importance of the *William Carlos Williams Newsletter*, begun in 1975 by Theodora R. Graham, currently titled the *William Carlos Williams Review* and edited by Peter Schmidt (the 1983 Centennial Issue was edited by Emily Wallace). A source of a wide range of material interesting to the Williams scholar, this publication was from the first a composite of letters, notes both bibliographical and biographical, reviews, and essays on Williams's work. It also carries descriptions of various libraries' holdings of Williams's papers and manuscripts, surveys of Williams's reputation abroad (Helmut Bonheim and Reinhard Nischik on Williams in Germany [Spring 1978] and Caterina Ricciardi, Italy, and Jacqueline Saunier-Ollier, France [Fall 1978]), and descriptions of play performances and museum exhibits.

II EDITIONS

New Directions Publishers has kept nearly all of Williams's work in print, many books in both hardcover and paperback editions. Available are *The Autobiography of William Carlos Williams; In the American Grain; The Collected Earlier Poems; The Collected Later Poems* (with "The Lost Poems, 1944–1950"); *Imaginations*, edited by Webster Schott; *I Wanted To Write a Poem: The Autobiography of the Works of a Poet*, edited by Edith Heal; *Many Loves and Other Plays; Paterson; Pictures from Brueghel and Other Poems* (includes *The Desert Music* and *Journey to Love*); *Selected Essays of William Carlos Williams; Selected Letters of William Carlos Williams*, edited by John C. Thirlwall; *A Voyage to Pagany* (includes "The Venus"); *The William Carlos Williams Reader*, edited by M. L. Rosenthal; *The Build-Up; The Farmers' Daughters; In the Money; White Mule; Selected Poems;* and *Yes, Mrs. Williams.*

In 1974 Ron Loewinsohn edited Williams's writings on epistemology (from the late 1920s), *The Embodiment of Knowledge* (New York). Not intended to be a systematic account of his philosophy, the essays are loosely connected with Williams's readings in science and philosophy (Whitehead, Dewey) during these years and touch on a variety of topics, from his respect for Shakespeare's achievements to his complaints about his children's educations. In 1976 New Directions published Linda W. Wagner's *Interviews with William Carlos Williams: "Speaking Straight Ahead"* (New York). The collection includes Wagner's introduction about Williams's vivacious speech patterns; three interviews entire (with John W. Gerber and Emily M. Wallace, Dorothy Tooker, and Walter Sutton) and a dozen more excerpted from; and various reprinted materials from Gael Turnbull as well as Williams himself. In 1978 Bram Dijkstra compiled a collection of Williams's writings on aesthetics as well as on specific artists, *A Recognizable Image: William Carlos Williams on Art and Artists* (New York). The strength of this book lies partly in the fact that the editor found essays previously unpublished, or parts of essays which had been omitted from published versions, so that the collection is much more than a reprinting of available texts. Williams often described his theories about writing in terms germane to graphic art, so any student of Williams's writing will find much of value here.

A similar compilation is James Breslin's *Something to Say: William Carlos Williams on Younger Poets* (New York, 1985), the first volume in "The William Carlos Williams Archive Series," with Emily Mitchell Wallace as general editor. Comprising letters, essays, reviews, prefaces, and introductions, this book is a rich collection of Williams's usually apt and always enthusiastic responses to innovative, untested writing. No poet was such a friend of the beginner, and Breslin's introduction catches some of that warmth (*APR* published the introduction in its Sept./Oct. 1985 issue). Because many of these items are either unpublished or unavailable today, the collection is a valuable publication.

Charles Tomlinson's new edition of *William Carlos Williams: Selected Poems* (New York, 1985) is also an interesting book, modeled on Tomlinson's earlier Penguin collection. His introduction will be useful to the reader coming to Williams for the first time. So too is Robert Coles's edition of *William Carlos Williams, The Doctor Stories* (New York, 1984). Reprinting many stories and a few poems, the collection also includes William Eric Williams's memoir, previously published in the *William Carlos Williams Review* and in the New Jersey Medical Society Williams issue, and a brief introduction by Coles, a fellow physician and sociologist. Most recently, New Directions has issued *The Collected Poems of William Carlos Williams: Volume I—1909–1939* (ed. A. Walton Litz and Christopher MacGowan, New York, 1986) and *Volume II—1939–1962* (ed. Christopher MacGowan, New York, 1988).

III MANUSCRIPTS AND LETTERS

Emily Mitchell Wallace continues work on the projected four-volume collected letters. A few letters have been published since the Thirlwall collection, most effectively in Richard E. Ziegfeld's "Dear God/Dear Bill: The William Carlos Williams-James Laughlin Correspondence" (*WCWN*, Fall 1979), in which Ziegfeld surveys more than nine hundred letters and also makes use of interviews with Laughlin about his relationship with Williams; in "Letters to Norman Macleod" (*Pembroke Magazine*, 1975); in Hugh Witemeyer and E. P. Walkiewicz's "Desert Music: Carlos Williams in the Great Southwest" (Terrell), which draws on unpublished correspondence between Williams and Winfield Townley Scott; in William Eric Williams's foreword to the 1982 paperback of Williams's *Yes, Mrs. Williams*; in Richard C. Zbornik's "On Stealing *Paterson I* and Other Poems for William Carlos Williams" (Terrell); in "Richard Eberhart and William Carlos Williams—Making Poetry a Continuum: Selected Correspondence," introduced by Stephen Corey and drawing on materials in the Dartmouth College Library Collection (*GaR*, Fall 1983); in "The Exiles' Letters," Emily Mitchell Wallace's excellent description of correspondence between Williams and Pound (*In'hui* [Picardie and Paris], Spring 1981); in James Laughlin's "A World of Books Gone Flat," another very different account of the same writers' letters (*Grand Street*, Winter 1984); and in "Gists and Piths: From the Letters of Pound and Williams" (in *Ezra Pound & William Carlos Williams: The University of Pennsylvania Conference Papers*, ed. Daniel Hoffman, Philadelphia, 1983). Until the complete edition of Williams's letters is available, the best summary of information about his letters is Paul L. Mariani's note ("Letters") in *William Carlos Williams: A New World Naked* (New York, 1981).

Williams's manuscripts have also begun to appear in published books and essays, though not yet to the extent that would be possible. In 1978 Neil E. Baldwin and Steven L. Meyers published *The Manuscripts and Letters of William Carlos Williams in the Poetry Collection of the Lockwood Memorial Library, State University of New York at Buffalo: A Descriptive Catalogue* (Boston), with a foreword by Robert Creeley. The catalogue describes more than twenty thousand pieces of Williams manuscripts. The *William Carlos Williams Newsletter* also has published descriptions of other library holdings (Dean H. Keller, Kent State University [Spring 1976]; Joseph Evans Slate, University of Texas at Austin [Fall 1976]; John Rhodehamel, the Lilly Library of Indiana University [Spring 1977]; Joan St. C. Crane, University of Virginia Library [Spring 1978]; Gladys Eckardt, Rutherford Library [Spring 1978]; Edith Heal, Fairleigh Dickinson University [Spring 1978]; Neda M. Westlake, University of Pennsylvania [Spring 1978]; Christopher MacGowan, Princeton University Library [Spring 1979]; and Donald Gallup, Yale—including Williams's correspondence with Norman Holmes Pearson [Spring 1981]).

The Centennial Issue of the *William Carlos Williams Review* (Fall 1983) includes a facsimile section of Williams's 1914 "little red notebook," edited by Emily Wallace, as well as facsimile copies of "Tribute to Neruda the poet collector of seashells," a letter from Williams to Mary Ellen Solt, and six versions of "He Has Beaten about the Bush Long Enough." *Sulfur* (No. 1, 1983) published Williams's "Sketch for a Primer of Present Day Poetic Practice," an hour's writing—aside from six phone calls—on 4 May 1933; and Paul Williams reprints a letter from his father in "A Letter to My Father on his 100th Birthday" (*WCWR*, Spring 1984).

IV BIOGRAPHY

The absence of biographical accounts commented upon in the first of these surveys has been remedied, with two works that, together, give us as complete a picture of Williams as any reader could want. Reed Whittemore's *William Carlos Williams: Poet from Jersey* (Boston, 1975) is a good beginning for the poet's biography; and the Mariani 1981 study— much longer, much more comprehensive—gives us a full measure of Williams the man, doctor, poet, and literary influence. Whittemore's book was generally well-received (the reading world seemed to be hungry for Williams's life story), but it was apparently written a bit too easily. Whittemore, in places, gives us more sense of the author than of his subject: there are relatively long discussions of the (unsatisfactory) place of the artist in America, spoken in a voice not that of Williams. There is a tone of petulance as Whittemore recalls Williams's hard breaks; and more troublesome, there is the tendency to make generalizations without offering readers proof for them, as when Whittemore says, "With his English-French-Spanish-Jewish blood and past he was a puritan on odd days, a libertine on even, but the puritanism was always strong enough in him to make him think he could not afford to be *too* happy." Much of the difficulty with this first biography is that it is comparatively short (358 pages of large-type text), with little room available for the kind of proof one would welcome.

The obverse could be said about the Mariani biography, *William Carlos Williams: A New World Naked* (New York, 1981). Running to 770 pages of text, each page containing nearly 30 percent more print than the pages of the Whittemore biography, it draws on hundreds of unpublished letters and manuscript pages, as well as interviews. Mariani presents the view of Williams that echoes Williams's own self-portrait—and that similarity is convincing in its own right—but he buttresses that portrait with detail after detail that only the diligent scholar could have found. His book deserves the praise it has received.

To illustrate the difference in tone between the Whittemore and Mariani biographies, one can compare their use of Williams's acquaintance with John Reed. Mariani notes briefly that Williams knew Reed, having met him at gatherings at Lola Ridge's. The entire discussion occurs in a section that delineates Williams's period of depression after *Others* fails, before he begins to edit *Contact* with Robert McAlmon, while his own conception of himself as an American poet—not an expatriate—is being formed. All the facts Mariani gives about Williams's friends early in the 1920s feeds into his portrait of Williams during these difficult years. Whittemore, on the other hand, makes an issue of Williams's criticism of Reed as a radical but then goes on to criticize Williams for what Whittemore sees as his own do-nothing attitude toward social involvement. (Whittemore points out that Reed participated in the Paterson strike and went to jail because of his involvement, "while there is no record of WCW having picketed anything, signed any petitions, gone to the meeting at the Garden, or contributed a penny. What WCW did about the strike was steal a poem out of it.") The language Whittemore uses makes us question his motives, and he then proceeds into a discussion of poetry vs. journalism, the remote poet vs. the involved, and winds his way eventually (in what must be a digression, but one that occupies more pages than the ostensible topic here) to a long discussion of the Horatio Alger dream. In Whittemore's view, elite poets shared that dream along with would-be millionaires, and the reader thus finds Williams being attacked because he never joined the Communist party, never participated in John Reed's way, and chose to dream about fine art—though the comparison between Pound and Williams as effete artists and people who believed in the Horatio Alger myth is difficult to understand, especially in this context. Unfortunately, the Whittemore book—short as it is—includes many such apparent digressions.

One of the changes between 1975 and 1981, when the biographies were published, was an increased critical interest in the art of biography (with a journal titled *Biography* and a decade of very sophisticated theory having passed). Mariani's own writing about the process of completing this book evinces some of that sophistication, as when he publishes "Reassembling the Dust: Notes on the Art of the Biographer" (*NER*, Spring 1983). In this essay, he describes the biographer as "the dustman reassembling the dust . . . the inventor, the maker . . . creating a life."

Neil Baldwin's children's biography, *To All Gentleness: William Carlos Williams, The Doctor-Poet* (New York, 1984) includes a foreword by William Eric Williams, tracing the relationship between Williams's medical career and his writing. That is also what Baldwin does in this book, recreating the energy and vitality of the seemingly tireless Williams as he went about his life, caring for children and expectant mothers (his degree was in pediatrics, but he delivered nearly three thousand babies) with the same attention he gave to his writing.

Other accounts that are biographical include the section on Williams in William H. Pritchard's *Lives of the Modern Poets* (New York, 1980). Pritchard's view of Williams is expressed in the title of his chapter, "In the American Grain" (he also includes Eliot, Hardy, Yeats, Robinson, Frost, Pound, Stevens, and Crane), stressing the Americanism of his life, even to his maintaining two separate careers. Williams as the pragmatist, the over-achiever, meets with Pritchard's somewhat divided enthusiasm. When he says, "Williams got so much done because he lived in tension," he is partly justifying those who never even attempt the kind of schedules Williams had to face daily. While the essay is a good composite of quotations from Williams's critical writings and poetry, there is a hesitation about Pritchard's endorsement that undercuts his text. And when he announces—against a great many secondary readings that prove otherwise—"My conviction is also that as a poet Williams shows less 'development' than any of his contemporaries," he comes across as just plain perverse.

Among other biographical studies are Geoffrey H. Movius's "Caviar and Bread: Ezra Pound and William Carlos Williams" (*JML*, Sept. 1976) on the years 1902–14 at the University of Pennsylvania and beyond; Noel Riley Fitch's "Voyage to Ithaca: William Carlos Williams in Paris" (*PULC*, Spring 1979); Thomas Cole's "Remembering Williams and Pound" (*WCWR*, Fall 1981); Donald C. Gallup's "The William Carlos Williams Collection at Yale" (*YULG*, Oct. 1981); James Laughlin's "For the Record: On New Directions & Others" (*Amer. Poetry*, Spring 1984), as well as his *Grand Street* essay; Mary Barnard's *Assault on Mount Helicon: A Literary Memoir* (Berkeley, Calif., 1984); Reed Whittemore's *William Carlos Williams: "The Happy Genius of the Household"* (Washington, DC, 1984); Helen Williamson Fall's "Remembering Dr. Williams" (*WCWR*, Spring 1984); William Caldwell's "William Carlos Williams: The Doctor" (*WCWR*, Spring 1984); Robert Creeley's "A Visit with Dr. Williams" (*Sagetrieb*, Fall 1984); M. L. Rosenthal's "A Memoir" (*WCWR*, Spring 1984); and Hugh Kenner's "Breaking the Line: The Bard of Newark's Department Stores" (*Harper's*, Dec. 1981), on Williams's persistence late in life.

William Eric Williams, the older son of the poet, has written six essays about his father. Four were originally published in the *William Carlos Williams Newsletter* from 1977 through 1982 and are reprinted under the title "Life with Father" in Terrell's collection. Two others, "The Doctor" and "Money," were published in the *William Carlos Williams Review* (Fall 1983). Written with verve and convincing detail, these pieces give us Williams the harried but energetic poet-physician moving through his daily life. Each is well worth reading.

The Terrell collection includes several reminiscences of visits to Williams's 9 Ridge Road address in Rutherford or accounts of early meetings and—almost always—encouragement. Robert Creeley ("A Visit to an Idol"); Hayden Carruth ("The Agony of Dr. Paterson," on Williams's letters after his strokes); Ralph Gustafson ("Meeting the Great Man"); Mary Barnard ("William Carlos Williams and the Poetry Archive at

Buffalo"); Edith Heal Berrien ("Memory is a Sort of Renewal"); John G. Dollar ("William Carlos Williams and the Polytopic Club"); Roberta Chester ("On Thinking About an Interview With William Carlos Williams on the Subject of the Aesthetic Philosophy in the Poetry of Wallace Stevens"); and the Zbornik essay all recapture elements of Williams as human being as well as poet. And in the *William Carlos Williams Review* (Fall 1983) several essays also convey the sense of Williams as person: Mary Ellen Solt's "The American Idiom," which begins with "Rutherford: A Visit with WCW—April 18–19, 1960" and includes accounts of the poet's readings at Indiana University. Cecelia Tichi emphasizes Williams as physician and scientist in "Twentieth Century Limited: WCW's Poetics of High-Speed America."

The most biographical of all the centennial publications is the "William Carlos Williams Commemorative Issue" of the *Journal of the Medical Society of New Jersey* (Sept. 1983). Essays by William Eric Williams, John Ciardi, Paul Mariani (a reprinted section from the biography), and Henry Niese all stress the biographical. The latter essay, "William Carlos Williams: A Remembrance," describes Williams as he related to painters and other artists, as well as his kindness toward younger aspiring writers and artists. It also recounts the visit Pound made in Rutherford as he was being released from St. Elizabeths, Williams's reading at Bucknell University, and other episodes of his later life. The essay concludes, "Until the very end, Williams kept his vision fresh and clear. It was a vision that came from the way he lived his life. He wrote about the tangled life of the city, but he was a suburban man, even a country man."

Essays in this collection written by fellow-physicians are also of importance. William A. Caldwell, in "William Carlos Williams: The Doctor," recounts his memories of Williams as a general practitioner who cared and describes the Rutherford Chamber of Commerce luncheon in honor of Williams's *Autobiography*—when Williams cried as did his townspeople. William B. Ober outlines "the influence of a medical practice" in his account of Williams; and Andrew Giarelli describes that blend of intense observation and great warmth that make the fine physician, as well as the fine poet. In "The Medical Nature of William Carlos Williams," Giarelli discusses Williams's relationship with Eleanora Monahan and the writing of the poem "For Eleanora and Bill Monahan," seeing his relationship with his patient as typical of "the giving, attentive observer who longed to observe even more closely" and typical as well of the ways medicine and poetry were connected in his life. The strongest case for the affinity between physician and poet is made by Avrum L. Katcher in "William Carlos Williams: Physician and Poet." Katcher aligns the physician's caring about his patients with the poet's capacity to understand the people being observed and quotes at length from conversations with one of Williams's patients, a Mrs. Fall. He also quotes at length from an essay by Joanne Trautmann, published in *Ethics in Science and*

Medicine (Nov. 1975) in which Trautmann uses Williams to illustrate the philosophy and practice of the best medical humanists.

Dr. John Stone wrote the retrospective on Williams which appeared in the *Journal of the American Medical Association* (16 Sept. 1983). In "A Lifetime of Careful Listening," Stone, himself a published poet, emphasizes that Williams was one of the most important writers of this century: "What is remarkable about William Carlos Williams is that he changed the face of American poetry, all the while practicing medicine." As a revolutionary, as the master of the avant-garde, Williams was somehow able to dovetail two more-than-full-time careers without slighting either.

Other essays on Williams as physician appear in William B. Ober's collection, *Boswell's Clap and Other Essays: Medical Analyses of Literary Men's Afflictions* (Carbondale, Ill., 1979) and *Medicine and Literature* (ed. Enid Rhodes Peschel, New York, 1980); the latter includes "William Carlos Williams: The Diagnostic Eye" by Marie Borroff, which notes that Williams did not often use his experiences as a physician in his poems, but he did consistently use what Borroff calls his "diagnostic" eye to give his work focus. An earlier assessment of Williams as physician appeared in *William Carlos Williams* (ed. Charles Angoff, Rutherford, N.J., 1974; hereinafter referred to as Angoff). A. M. Sullivan describes the combined careers of Williams in "Dr. William Carlos Williams, Poet and Humanist."

Other treatments of Williams from a biographical perspective are either very short (Reed Whittemore's "Sons" [*WCWR*, Fall 1983]) or occur in texts that are primarily critical studies (Mike Weaver, *William Carlos Williams, The American Background*, Cambridge, England, 1971; Robert Coles, *William Carlos Williams: The Knack of Survival in America*, New Brunswick, N.J., 1975; and F. Richard Thomas, *Literary Admirers of Alfred Stieglitz*, Carbondale, Ill., 1983).

V CRITICISM

The quantity of books and essays on Williams's work in the past fifteen years has been exceeded only by its quality. During the early and mid-1970s, significant critical studies appeared on either Williams's poetry (and sometimes his prose) or on *Paterson*. Later in the 1970s, more specialized studies dominated the scene. Into the 1980s, the published work has drawn increasingly on young, new scholars: in short, there are many previously unknown people writing on Williams, a tendency that suggests even more work to come in the future.

When the first essay in this series was prepared in 1971, it seemed appropriate to lament the relative critical neglect of Williams's work, though even at that time, signs that adequate redressing of that neglect was occurring existed. Now, 1988, just eighteen years after the beginning of Williams's critical reassessment, it seems clear that Yvor Winters's 1939 prediction was more astute than was recognized. As Winters said ("Poetry of Feeling," *KR*, Jan. 1939), "If I may venture . . . to make a prediction, it is this: that Williams will prove as nearly indestructible as Herrick; that the end of the present century will see him securely established, along with Stevens, as one of the two best poets of his generation." Winters goes on to say that critics were lulled into thinking they understood "modernism" because they could read Pound and Eliot, but that much of Williams's poetry was more sophisticated, even more difficult, than poetry by those two writers—and in the ways in which it was different from their work lay the key to much poetry that would be written in future years.

One indication that Williams's work does point the way toward recent developments in American poetry—that in some respects his writing is more postmodern than it is modern—is the continuing interest in his work expressed by contemporary poets themselves. There is a largesse of information—spiritual, technical, linguistic—to be found in Williams's poetry and prose, only now beginning to be explored. This essay will include comments by these younger poets as illustration of that kind of influence (given not with "anxiety," fortunately, but, more often, with admiration and love). Another indication is that Williams's work is increasingly found, when anthologized, in a postmodern classification, belying his birth date and the actual context for his writing. And critically, another very interesting indication has been that readers and critics have had to develop new terminology, different grids of reading methods, in order to do justice to Williams's accomplishments. An art that jars critical response into finding new directions must surely be a significant art.

1 Books, Essay Collections, and Special Journal Issues

Mike Weaver's *William Carlos Williams: The American Background* (Cambridge, England, 1971) was rightfully read as one of the most comprehensive studies of Williams to that time. Billed as "literary biography," it more accurately is a cultural-critical study, with the emphasis falling on Williams's American/New Jersey context rather than on Williams's biography. The insights Weaver brings to readings of Williams's texts are accurate and far-reaching. This has been a model study, and remains useful for any reader. In considering "personal, literary, aesthetic, intellectual, and social" factors, Weaver discussed such then-unremarked topics as Whitehead's influence on Williams, Vorticism, Kandinsky, Antheil, precisionists, communism, social credit, relativity, and Dewey. It includes a very important appendix describing the sources for approximately ninety passages in *Paterson* and spends much time on Williams's use of *Passaic: A Group of Poems Touching that River* (1942) by Thomas Ward in his creation of *Paterson*. There is much here that explains Williams's fanaticism about "American idiom" and perhaps a British critic is the best suited for finding key differences between Williams's kind of Americanism and the more traditional Anglo-American tendencies.

Benjamin Sankey's *A Companion to William Carlos Williams' "Paterson"* (Berkeley, Calif., 1971) provides much factual information about the genesis of Williams's long poem, as well as some insight available only through manuscript study. In general, however, Sankey's study is weakened because he does not include Book 5 as more than a peripheral part of the epic (his treatment of that very interesting book is only a "note") and because he relies almost entirely on his own readings of the text, with very little reference to already existing criticism. Instead of becoming a compendium of information about *Paterson*, this study remains Sankey's reading of *Paterson*. As his concluding paragraph of his introductory chapter states, "The next few chapters follow the action of the poem," an approach suitable for the first book on a topic, but not for one that follows several others.

Jerome Mazzaro edited *Profile of William Carlos Williams* (Columbus, Ohio, 1971), adding an original essay by Philip L. Gerber ("So Much Depends: The Williams Foreground") to reprinted essays by William Heyen, Charles Angoff, Eric Mottram, Randall Jarrell, Robert Lowell, Charles Olson, Powell Woods, Peter Meinke, Hugh Kenner, and Mazzaro himself. The booklet includes a chronology but no other scholarly aids. In 1973 Mazzaro's own study of Williams appeared (*William Carlos Williams: The Later Poems*, Ithaca, N.Y.), evincing his belief that Williams had evolved—partly through the process of creating *Paterson* and working with a longer, more inclusive line—into a major poet. Mazzaro sees Williams's development as a means of achieving his aim, to link the phenomenal world of the older writer with the dream world of the poet as youth. The book concentrates on Williams's last major writing, *Paterson*, "Asphodel, That Greeny Flower," and "Pictures from Breughel," but it draws as well on the author's thorough knowledge and understanding of Williams's earlier work. Mazzaro sees what has been referred to as Williams's limitations in these late poems—his narrowing of focus and of subject—as a necessary tactic, once the poet had broadened his aesthetic of subject matter to include "the world," as Williams had. He observes, "Sub-personalities must be formed. In *Paterson*, Williams creates Dr. Paterson for this purpose; in these volumes, he revives the weavers and Breughel. These creations and revivals, moreover, are clearly separate from the epical stances advocated by Joyce and Eliot."

Mazzaro's study served to prepare readers for the 1974 book that was to bring Williams out of the relatively sheltered covey of Williams-as-subject-for-readers-of-Williams-poems into the arena of contemporary critical theory. Joseph N. Riddel's *The Inverted Bell: Modernism and the Counterpoetics of William Carlos Williams* (Baton Rouge, La.) did much more than connect the poet with aesthetic issues, as Mazzaro's study had done; it made the poet and his work part of current aesthetic issues.

As Riddel says, "the Modern, or post-Modern, poem tends to be habitually a poem about poetry, a metapoetry" and as such, needs an interpreter who can deal with it as "an art forced to reflect on itself and thus on its own act of reflection." He describes his choice of Williams, and particularly of *Paterson*, as stemming from his belief that Williams is "a poet who combines in another degree that post-Romantic crisis of consciousness which is manifest in a self-reflexive poetry." Using Heidegger and Hölderlin, as well as Georges Bataille and Jacques Derrida, Riddel spins his arguments, his own aesthetic constructions and deconstructions, into—according to his own expression of his aim—"a theory of post-Modernism, anticipated by Williams but imagined variously in the whole variety of Modernist experimentation—in Imagism, Vorticism, Objectivism, the poetics of H.D. and Pound, Louis Zukofsky, and Charles Olson. But the larger design can only be a projection. Williams remains the locus; *his* poetics, the *subject*. I want to argue the radicality of Williams' poetics: how repetitively original he was, how anxious to destroy, as he said, 'the whole of poetry as it has been in the past.' How metaphysically anti-metaphysical. How 'American!'" Just as in the earlier version of this essay the importance of J. Hillis Miller's work was stressed, because readers not already conversant with Williams came to him through Miller, so Riddel's book opened Williams's writing to many critical theorists who were perhaps less interested in Williams as poet than they were in Riddel's use of his work as a basis for distinctions between modernism and postmodernism. A relatively wide current of criticism has grown from this point.

Also appearing in 1974 was the formerly mentioned slim collection of four essays, *William Carlos Williams*, edited by Charles Angoff. Emily Wallace discussed Williams's use of tree imagery; Kenneth Burke, Williams's fragmentation, contrasting his dissociative process with Aiken's *Ideenflucht* and comparing it to the effects of modern traffic; A. M. Sullivan, Williams as physician; and Norman Holmes Pearson, the Williams collection at Yale. Written in French, Laurette Veza's *William Carlos Williams* (Paris, 1974) surveys all the writing, especially *Paterson* and the late poems, and discusses themes of identity, sexuality, and the poet as representative of the counterculture. She includes Charles Olson's "Projective Verse" and Marcelin Playnet's "Notes on Projective Verse" as appendixes.

Before assessing 1975, one of the most important years in Williams criticism, special journal issues and parts of books concerning Williams which appeared from 1971 to 1974 will be considered. Often, the critical reputation of a writer depends as much on the context in which he or she is read, which other writers are connected with the writer in question, as on studies devoted specifically to primary work. In Williams's case, for Kenneth Rexroth to contend, in *American Poetry in the Twentieth Century* (New York, 1971), that Williams was the only great American poet, both because of his philosophy and his thoroughly individual prosody, certainly enhanced his growing critical reputation. When Rexroth criticizes both Pound and Eliot for an overuse of "rhetoric," he begins to chart a direction new for the early 1970s: "Williams never slips . . . he doesn't talk about experience; he reveals it with humility." Idiosyncratic as Rexroth can be, his opinion carries weight, and his provocative comparisons among writers open the established canon in unforeseen ways.

Walter Sutton's *American Free Verse: The Modern Revolution in Poetry* (Norfolk, Conn., 1973) does much the same thing, placing Williams beyond the company he once would have scrambled to be a part of. Seeing in Williams the desired "radical experimentation" of the greatest American poets, Sutton links him—along with Pound—to, first, Whitman, and then to more contemporary poets such as Levertov, Koch, Ginsberg, Kinnell, and Olson (skipping the generation of the "conservative counterrevolution"—Ransom, Eberhart, Shapiro, Wilbur), and concluding that these are the important figures in the development of American poetry because they are involved in assessing the realities of life, political as well as aesthetic.

An even stronger statement of Williams's importance occurs in Edwin Fussell's *Lucifer in Harness: American Meter, Metaphor, and Diction* (Princeton, N.J., 1973). For Fussell, Williams, with Whitman, becomes the greatest of America's poets because he forged his own language and rhythm. As he quotes repeatedly from Williams's poems, Fussell concludes, "American poetry seldom gets much better than that. The lines are new and ancient . . . the words are supple and alive. The voice is heard. The rhetoric is real." One might wish for a somewhat more substantial critical argument in Fussell's study, but his placing Williams at the peak of American poetry remains clear for any reader.

Contrary to these remarks of high praise, Ian Hamilton's views of Williams, and any poet who has been influenced by him, are distinctly negative. Hamilton treats any poetic language that could be described as "the American idiom" with scorn in *A Poetry Chronicle* (New York, 1974). For Todd Lieber (*Endless Experiments: Essays on the Heroic Experience in American Romanticism*, Columbus, Ohio, 1973), artistic experimentation is the mark of the true writer-as-romantic, and Williams's *Paterson*, one of the best examples of a product of that effort. For Suzanne Juhasz, Williams is the most proficient poet of metaphor of the modern writers she discusses in *Metaphor and the Poetry of Williams, Pound, and Stevens* (Lewisburg, Pa., 1974). She considers the short poems early in the study and then concludes with a chapter on *Paterson*, showing how consistent Williams was—both in his use of certain kinds of metaphor and in his accumulation of meanings for specific metaphors. By the time of *Paterson V* and "Asphodel," even a simple image had wide impact for Williams's readers.

Donald Barlow Stauffer places Williams with the experimental poets rather than with the Imagists in *A Short History of American Poetry* (New York, 1974). "Williams stood spiritually in the center of much that was and is new in American poetry," says Stauffer, pointing out that Williams rebelled consistently against Pound's prescriptions so that he could "fashion a tough, original, and elastic language of his own." Like Stauffer's acute discussion, Karl Malkoff writes well about Williams in his introduction to *Crowell's Handbook of Contemporary Poetry* (New York, 1973). Malkoff thinks *Paterson* a seminal poem in contemporary literature and discusses Williams accordingly.

Much of Williams's recent prominence stems from special journal issues and collections of reprinted essays. In May 1971 the *Journal of Modern Literature* published a special Williams issue (the Hardie checklist has already been mentioned), which contained essays by Louis L. Martz and Sister Bernetta Quinn on *Paterson*; by Joel Conarroe on aesthetics in "Pictures from Breughel"; by Paul Ramsey on Williams as metrist, a study of scansion in relation to the poet's own critical theory. Ramsey concludes, "Williams wrote almost exclusively by ear, and denied the possibility of free verse. The combination led to much confusion and some pretension in his theory. . . . He is, in his theory, a poor prosodist; in his verse, a superb prosodist. . . . For Williams has his range, a greater range than some of his own theories, taken stringently, would permit."

Other important essays in this special issue are Joseph Evans Slate on *Kora in Hell*, James K. Guimond assessing Williams's roots in past traditions of literature and culture ("Williams' theory of creativity is what I would call an autochthonous one, one which insists that artistic forms must be indigenous rather than imported. . . ."), and Neil Myers reading a single poem, "Two Pendants: for the Ears," so that one link in Williams's development from being an Imagist, particularly good with the short poem, to the creator of *Paterson* is made to appear. James C. Cowan's study of water imagery in *Paterson* is also useful, and Cary Nelson's "Suffused-Encircling Shapes of Mind: Inhabited Space in Williams" represents a reader-response criticism. Nelson's premise is that Williams's use of flowering as metaphor suffuses his poems and leads to a complex image pattern in *Paterson*. But the poet's control of the metaphor is less an intellectual exercise than a mark of the poet's identity: "things, in Williams, are more than the recovered pieces of a dismembered god. A spatial interpretation encourages a more naturalistic notion of Williams' perception. He views the world with definite innocence and ease: the texture of one thing may be exchanged poetically for the texture of another. But the vision is incomplete without both the shock and violation of contact and the stillness of inhabitation that follows"—a view at variance with J. Hillis Miller's, of which Nelson also speaks.

In 1972 Charles Tomlinson edited *William Carlos Williams: A Critical Anthology* (Baltimore, Md.). Reprinting essays by Pound, Moore, Burke, Lawrence, Paul Rosenfeld, Gorham B. Munson, Stevens, Zukofsky,

Kazin, Blackmur, and—frequently—Williams himself, Tomlinson attempts to recreate the reception of the early work (to 1940). For commentary about *Paterson*, he chooses essays by Jarrell, Parker Tyler, Lowell, Edwin Honig, Edward Dahlberg, Kenner, and Joseph Bennett. Essays about Williams's derivation from and interest in graphic art include commentary by Ruth Grogan; about the influence of French writing on Williams, essays by Rexroth and Harold Rosenberg; and on Williams's prose, selections by Kenner, Thomas Whitaker, Alan Holder, and Donald Davie. Other critics represented are Neil Myers, Albert Cook, Winifred Nowottny, Paul Fussell, A. Kingsley Weatherhead, Alan Stephens, William Empson, J. Hillis Miller, Yvor Winters, Denis Donoghue, and Tomlinson himself. The book is rich with both familiar and little-known pieces and deserves to have had wider circulation than it did.

In its Winter 1973 issue the *Massachusetts Review* included "A Garland for William Carlos Williams," edited by Paul L. Mariani. The issue printed for the first time "Man Orchid," a collaborative effort at writing a novel, never completed, by Williams, Fred Miller, and Lydia Carlin. According to the introduction by Mariani, Miller and Williams wanted to write about a black-white character (as they were also at the time—1945—planning to edit an interracial magazine). Both were intrigued by jazz, black literature, and the issues being black in America presented. Also included were two essays by Williams on Pound, "A Study of Ezra Pound's Present Position, January 21, 1947–January 23, 1947" and "The Later Pound," dated 13 January 1950, in which Williams praises Pound's language and "the fineness, the subtlety, the warmth and the strength of the *material*" in the *Cantos*. Emily Wallace's editing of the Gerber interview with Williams closes the issue. Except for this, all material is reprinted from the Beinecke Library at Yale.

In 1975 a wide range of books on Williams appeared. Already mentioned in this essay were Reed Whittemore's biography and Paul L. Mariani's survey of secondary criticism; added to these is Louis Simpson's *Three on the Tower: The Lives and Works of Ezra Pound, T. S. Eliot, and William Carlos Williams* (New York). While Simpson's anecdotal style will appeal to the general reader, the very presence of this book testifies to the importance of these poets in the lives of younger writers of our time. Simpson sees the lives of these poets as "symbolic," representing (Pound) art, (Eliot) religion, and (Williams) experience.

Another comparatively general approach is Robert Coles's *William Carlos Williams: The Knack of Survival in America* (New Brunswick, N.J., 1975). Coles's fascination with Williams as writer comes in part from the fiction, the way Williams insists on particularizing the common people he writes about, raising them through art to art, and from Coles's consideration of the short stories and the Stecher novels, he deals with important issues of determining what is American about modern art. This short book accomplishes a great many things: it makes perceptive comments about the work, gives us a wide scope for placing Williams and his writing in the real world, and suggests qualities that Williams shares with other writers—such as Dos Passos—that will make him central in our developing literary consciousness.

Rod Townley's study, *The Early Poetry of William Carlos Williams* (Ithaca, N.Y., 1975), sees the work as "somatic," pieces of a "fluid, imaginative world" rather than as separate masterpieces. Just as Williams had found his identity through sensual relationships with his world, so his poems grew from the same life rhythms. What is most important about this book is Townley's emphasis on the body of a writer's work as "living," as unfinished, uncaught at that moment of stasis that might create a masterpiece. He admits to this paradox: "the poems are inseparable, yet each is a shrapnel-like fragment." And what is more important is the recognition that to the poet, all work is in flux, is only a part of the ongoing creation. In short, Townley gives us valuable information about the process of being a poet.

The year 1975 had then presented the critical world with the first biography of Williams (and countless reviews of the Whittemore book, meaning increased visibility for Williams and his art), the first bibliographic study of secondary work (meaning some recognition of how many—hundreds—scholars were writing about the good doctor-poet), the first cross-cultural kind of book (Coles as physician and winner of the Pulitzer Prize for an anthropological study), the first critical study that documented the poet's process of coming to poetry, and the first study of Williams by another well-known poet—a testimony to the influence of the older poet on the next generation of serious writers. Future years would see further work in each area.

In 1976 David Perkins published the first volume of *A History of Modern Poetry: From the 1890s to the High Modernist Mode* (Cambridge, Mass., 1976), which dealt briefly with Williams (Perkins explained that Williams would be treated more extensively in the second volume). Interesting as this division is (Perkins feels Williams should be grouped with "the younger poets he strongly influenced"), what is more interesting in this period is the complacency with which Williams is treated: paired with Frost as a latter-day Georgian, he is considered an accessible and entertaining writer. Perkins deals with his work only to 1923, and perhaps the early use of traditional forms lends more of an aura of tradition to Williams's work than is obvious from the perspective of his later poetry.

Congruent with Perkins's study is the treatment given Williams by both Hugh Kenner (in both *A Homemade World: The American Modernist Writers*, New York, 1975, and *The Pound Era*, Berkeley, Calif., 1971) and Albert Gelpi (*The Tenth Muse: The Psyche of the American Poet*, Cambridge, Mass., 1975). In all these studies, Williams is an accepted part of literary modernism; no longer the outsider, the laughable doctor-poet, he is rather a touchstone of avant-garde and, more importantly, of progressive metric and linguistic tactics. For Kenner, Williams writes "fieldwork notes . . . the habit of listening to voices extended to his own voice, so that he could write down the way he heard himself phrasing things. . . . Process: growth and emergence: these were his themes: the effort of the new organism to define itself." And Gelpi echoes, connecting Williams with Emerson's Dionysian impulses: "Williams and such followers of his as Olson, Creeley, and Levertov might well have taken this statement of Emerson as their experimental point of departure: 'Metre begins with the pulse-beat. . . .'"

Bernard Duffey gives Williams a position of prominence as well in his *Poetry in America: Expression and Its Values in the Times of Bryant, Whitman, and Pound* (Durham, N.C., 1978). One of the last sections of the study is titled "The Permanent Present," and there Duffey considers Stevens and Williams, finding them alike in that they used their poetry to "help place themselves in relation to present affairs." Pragmatists, both poets participated in the avant-garde; but for Williams, innovation in visualization and technique served a more important use—it led him to new philosophical positions. Duffey sees Williams as, finally, a much more subjective poet than Stevens: even the "'world' was more often seen as a subjective process." Accordingly, rather than terming *Paterson* an epic, Duffey finds it "a book of lyric parables showing mind and will fallen from a sovereign place in the kingdom of experience." Duffey places Williams, alone, in the epilogue to his study, the most representative poet so far as the absorption of the contradictions of twentieth-century poetics, and life, is concerned. Williams, in Duffey's study, becomes Ignatow's "figure of the human."

Mutlu Konuk Blasing, in her chapter on Williams in *The Art of Life: Studies in American Autobiographical Literature* (Austin, Tex., 1977), approaches the poet's versatile attempts to create his own life, whether in prose or poetry, as a means of epistemologically relating to others. Blasing begins by contending that the autobiographical genre is particularly compatible to American artists and studies Thoreau, Whitman, Henry James, and Henry Adams before arriving at Williams's *Paterson* (and Frank O'Hara). Tied closely to the autobiographical impulse is, often, a tendency to experiment with craft—as all her examples also prove. Blasing sees *Paterson* as purposefully "dissipated," its form reflecting the poet's commentary on his culture, but never becoming "a suicidal avant-gardism." Williams welcomes change rather than lamenting it; he takes his art seriously as "social communication." In many ways Blasing's work, typical of the many good studies in autobiographical theory current on the critical scene, also complements A. D. Van Nostrand's *Every Man His Own Poet: Romantic Gospels in American Literature* (New York, 1968). Van Nostrand's consideration of *Paterson* (along with Poe, Emerson, Crane, Whitman, Thoreau, Melville, James, Adams, and Faulkner) stresses again the symmetry between original form and original con-

sciousness (each work explores "the drama of the author's consciousness") and concludes, "*Paterson* is the most developed of all the American
cosmologies. It builds a simple, comprehensive theory of events; it is
convincingly pragmatic . . . is both the statement of that strategy and
the example of its own statement. It is also the drama of its author's
own desperate enterprise."

For Karl Malkoff also, Williams's importance—crucial as it is to
younger poets—lies more directly in his sense of vision, his presentation
of the divided self, "a distinct consciousness, separate from the rest of
creation and acutely aware of that separation, and a harmonious part
of nature, at one with the universe"—"at war with the traditional self."
Favoring the sensual over the intellectual, Williams was able to break
with his fellow poets and create new directions for American art (*Escape
from the Self: A Study in Contemporary American Poetry and Poetics*, New
York, 1977). Arthur Oberg, too, in *Modern American Lyric: Lowell, Berryman, Creeley, and Plath* (New Brunswick, N.J., 1978), translates Williams's
role for younger poets as a pacesetter, giving Berryman the key word
Invent and giving Creeley a whole new process of using language: "in
reading Creeley, as in reading Williams, we must and can distinguish
between thinking as a limited, analytic activity and as some more elemental process which involves feeling of the most intense kind." The presence
of Williams in all these discussions of poets who are much more contemporary affirms that influence spoken of earlier in this essay. Louis
Simpson suggests much the same kind of correspondence in his introduction to *A Revolution in Taste: Studies of Dylan Thomas, Allen Ginsberg, Sylvia
Plath, and Robert Lowell* (New York, 1978).

Until the publication of Dickran Tashjian's *William Carlos Williams and
the American Scene, 1920–1940* (Berkeley, Calif., and New York, 1978),
few books on Williams had appeared during the mid-1970s, though
there were essays in quantity. Linda Wagner's *Interviews* and *Reference
Guide* (1976 and 1977) and Bram Dijkstra's *A Recognizable Image* (1978)
have been noted elsewhere, the latter in good conjunction with Tashjian's
reproduction of the Whitney Museum's exhibition of many of these
materials (12 Dec. 1978–4 Feb. 1979). Tashjian's text for the painting
and photo reproductions is comprehensive, insightful, and clear—a
model of interdisciplinary scholarship. The year 1979 also saw the publication of Audrey T. Rodgers's *The Universal Drum: Dance Imagery in the
Poetry of Eliot, Crane, Roethke, and Williams* (University Park, Pa.). Necessary as image studies are, this one attempts to cover too many kinds of
areas and ends as less than convincing. Rodgers's section on Williams,
however, is more complete and draws from the range of his poetry, not
only from the late poems where he himself identifies his sympathies
with dance, and uses the figure of the dancer as surrogate for the poet.

The year 1980 saw the beginning of what seems to have been another
flood of publications, perhaps leading to the centennial year of 1983 (a

year in which no fewer than six MLA sessions were devoted to Williams and his work). Charles Doyle's long-awaited *William Carlos Williams: The Critical Heritage* (London) includes reviews and essays published contemporary with the work considered, as well as a long introduction by Doyle, tracing the trends and currents in Williams criticism, and a very helpful bibliography of sources not included. Margaret Glynne Lloyd's *William Carlos Williams' "Paterson": A Critical Reappraisal* (Rutherford, N.J., 1980) includes two earlier essays (published under the name of Bollard). A comprehensive survey of *Paterson*, the study begins with distinctions from Frye, the demotic and the hieratic, and continues to supplement textual reading and some manuscript study, where possible, with critical embellishments. She also attends to the controversy over whether or not *Paterson* can be considered an epic per se, and gives her own views on so naming it. This is a solid study.

Kathleen Woodward's *At Last, The Real Distinguished Thing: The Late Poems of Eliot, Pound, Stevens, and Williams* (Columbus, Ohio, 1980) also deals with *Paterson*, but in the guise of its being representative of much of Williams's late writing. Woodward's premise, that a writer's late work will evince accrued wisdom, shapes her readings of all the work included and, in that self-defined context, Williams comes off badly: "If we compare the Williams of *Paterson V* with the Pound of the *Pisan Cantos*, the Eliot of the *Four Quartets*, and the Stevens of *The Rock*, we understand just how much his poem suffers in comparison." Woodward finds Williams unable to handle the conventions of the meditative poem, and therefore unable to express whatever wisdom he had accumulated. But she concludes, sounding a little like Faulkner in his praise of Thomas Wolfe, that because Williams did not achieve what he tried, his failure becomes a triumph: "The infirmities of age demanded that he do what he had not done before, and confronting those weaknesses, he invented something new." Using Gregory Bateson's *Steps Toward an Ecology of Mind* as a subtext for her study, Woodward manages to translate failure into a positive result.

In 1981 appeared the well-reviewed and well-received Mariani biography of Williams (reviews of this book were still appearing in 1984), as well as Benjamin T. Spencer's *Patterns of Nationality: Twentieth-Century Literary Versions of America* (New York). In his section on Williams (he also includes Stein, Pound, Anderson, Fitzgerald, Crane, Dahlberg, and Mailer), Spencer applies his definition of "American literature" to Williams's myths, subjects, and style, giving the reader helpful insights and confirming his own readings by expert selections of Williams's own comments. It seems clear from Spencer's presentation that Williams knew he was an American artist: "one must be at the advancing edge of the art: that's the American tradition."

Peter Revell, in *Quest in Modern American Poetry* (Totowa, N.J., 1981), focuses his attention on Williams's epic *Paterson* but considers the oeuvre as he defines Williams as separate from other poets contemporary with him, but motivated similarly—searching for answers to all life's important questions. Jay Cantor, in *The Space Between: Literature and Politics* (Baltimore, Md., 1981), uses titles from Williams to establish the thematic arrangement of this comprehensive text. He compares Williams's aesthetics and philosophy with those of Norman O. Brown, seeing him as seminal for the 1970s and 1980s. In Williams's work, the artist becomes a part of "a primary physics," the whole of modern life. In so doing, the artist is no longer alienated.

The year 1982 saw the publication of Charles Doyle's study of Williams, *William Carlos Williams and the American Poem* (New York), another book that had been in progress for some time. Perhaps its ideas seem a bit dated because of that time in transit, for what Doyle says about Williams is much the same thing critics in the early 1970s had been explaining: that Williams's poetry is part of an ongoing process and should be considered as a whole; that Williams learned from doing one kind of poem how to do another and that he was consistently interested in craft; that his subject matter remained firmly rooted in his American surroundings and related objects; and that *Paterson* was a culmination of many kinds and deserves to be treated in great detail (five of Doyle's fourteen chapters focus on the long poem). In his conclusion, Doyle compares Williams with Pound and finds Williams the greater poet, more insistent on the virtues and vitality of the imagination (and Doyle, accordingly, finds Williams's greatest work to be *Kora in Hell, In the American Grain*, and the poems).

William Marling's *William Carlos Williams and the Painters, 1909–1923* (Athens, Ohio, 1982) is a meatier, more informative approach to a study of Williams's development as a poet. Limiting his concern to the poet's early years, Marling stresses Williams's alliances with graphic artists during a period when he could find little support or solace from other writers. Marling discusses Williams's friendships and shared aesthetics with Marcel Duchamp, Marsden Hartley, Walter Arensberg, Charles Demuth, Charles Sheeler, and others, drawing from previously unpublished materials—not only of Williams but of the artists. The first half of his study traces the relationships, the second connects Williams's writing of these years with aesthetic movements as germane to art as they were to writing. Marling's readings of *Spring and All* and *Kora in Hell* are among the most informative these books have received. Laszlo Géfin's *Ideogram: History of a Poetic Method* (Austin, Tex., 1982) shows the centrality of Williams's "No ideas but in things" to all modern poetry.

American Visionary Poetry (Baton Rouge, La., 1982), Hyatt H. Waggoner's continuation of his major study *American Poets*, contains a key chapter, "William Carlos Williams: Naturalizing the Unearthly." As Waggoner defines the visionary poet, he or she is one who "sees us as participants in the world, part and parcel of it, neither objective observers of it nor homeless in it." It contrasts with the poetry of alienation and with that of poetic idealism. Thus, Williams, Hart Crane, Roethke, and— primarily—Whitman are visionary poets, whereas Dickinson, Eliot, and Stevens are not. About Williams, Waggoner concludes that "The Desert Music" is his finest visionary poem, that *Paterson* fails as a successful long poem because so many of the poet's theories warred with the very concept of a long poem, and that Williams wrote too much (or preserved too much) and therefore damned himself; but Waggoner also goes on to state that "Williams in his best work came closer to reclaiming Whitman's vision for a later age than Crane had": "For poetry to be about poetry meant for it to be about life, or at least about what's really important in life."

This critical concern with *Paterson* as a long poem, a representation of a new genre, tied to both autobiography and ontological discovery, came to fruition in 1983 with M. L. Rosenthal's and Sally M. Gall's *The Modern Poetic Sequence: The Genius of Modern Poetry* (New York). It had been anticipated, more particularly, by the work of James E. Miller, Jr. in *The American Quest for a Supreme Fiction: Whitman's Legacy in the Personal Epic* (Chicago, 1979) and by Paul Christensen's "The New American Romances" (*TCL*, Fall 1980), in which *The Cantos*, "The Waste Land," *Paterson*, and *The Maximus Poems* are placed in the tradition of the European verse romance. What Rosenthal and Gall attempt, in their monumental study of the long poem/poetic sequence, is to relate Whitman's *Song of Myself* and Dickinson's fascicles to the work of Shakespeare and Tennyson, seeing, accurately, correspondences among these series of works dominated by "a driving emotional pressure toward a balanced resolution," a pressure that also leads, eventually, to deviations from a standard technique. Shakespeare and Tennyson were not able to achieve the leap into innovation, and in that bravado lay Whitman and Dickinson's greatness. This is a monumental study, one to which not only years but several lifetimes of knowledge and caring about poetry have been brought. Rosenthal and Gall find Williams's most important contribution to have been his use of the ultimately subjective themes ("issues of sexual interaction and artistic imagination") in a context that seems to be dominated by geographical considerations: "The poem's full subjective import cannot be limited to the one locale. . . . all the five Books, in any case, plunge again and again into internal states having nothing to do with locale." The authors' praise continues for *Paterson* as the "most humanly available" of all the great modern sequences.

Stephen Fredman emphasizes Williams's innovations in prose, concentrating on what he calls Williams's "generative sentence" in "*Kora in Hell: Improvisations*," in *Poet's Prose: The Crisis in American Verse* (Cambridge, England, 1983). He considers Williams's prose to hold a crucial place in the development of American poetry. F. Richard Thomas's *Literary Admirers of Alfred Stieglitz* (Carbondale, Ill., 1983) includes a chapter on Williams, in addition to Stein, Crane, and Anderson. Besides tracing the personal relationship between Stieglitz and Williams, Thomas describes many of Williams's poems as instances of the influence of photography: "The visual was important for him. In fact in Williams' work . . . the many instances of the use of camera techniques compel one to look upon certain poems or sections within poems as photographic images." There are only brief references to Williams in Sue Davidson Lowe's *Stieglitz: A Memoir/Biography* (New York, 1983).

A more important critical study that complements Thomas's brief chapter is Henry M. Sayre's *The Visual Text of William Carlos Williams* (Champaign, Ill., 1983). Sayre's essays are well-known to Williams scholars, and in this book he brings together many of these well-considered insights. His premise is that, because Williams was so much a part of the graphic artistic movement of the century, his concept of form and organization, even of the relation between language and spatial imagination, was very different from a similar concept held by poets like Pound or Eliot. For Williams, a poem is both graphic design and the representation of an experience as visual as it is intellectual. Sayre illustrates the kind of comprehensive design Williams aimed for by discussing "The Red Wheelbarrow," and then relating it to the sections surrounding it in *Spring and All*. Like Duchamp, Williams insisted that only "new measures" could shape American experience, and Sayre's study is an informative, even passionate, account of the far-flung dimensions of Williams's search.

Three new studies of Williams were published in 1983 as part of the UMI Research Press Studies in Modern Literature. Selected after a survey of unpublished dissertations by Paul L. Mariani, these texts were then revised and updated (the premise of the series is that very good work has been done and never published, and these books suggest that the premise is accurate). David A. Fedo's *William Carlos Williams: A Poet in the American Theatre* (Ann Arbor, Mich.) studies both published and unpublished Williams plays, attempting to relate Williams's work in the drama to the rest of his oeuvre. Fedo sees strong thematic correspondences between Williams's drama and his other writing and suggests that his unconventional form (for the theatre of those years) parallels his innovation in other kinds of writing. This is a sound study, with Fedo having interviewed Mrs. Williams, James Laughlin, and others connected with Williams; he has also used the manuscript collections at Texas, Yale, and Buffalo. The appendix to the study includes information about plays as first performed.

Steven R. Loevy's *William Carlos Williams' "A Dream of Love"* (Ann Arbor, Mich.), in the same series, presents a close textual analysis of the play usually considered Williams's best (although some defense could be made for *Many Loves*). Loevy stresses Williams's common themes, his reliance on the use of natural speech, and his ability to choose themes and methods of presentation that appeal to audience/reader. Some use of linguistic theory enables Loevy to deal meaningfully with the text as a speech act, a process of affecting the audience through language effects and structures. *A Dream of Love* opens to this explication and proves at least that, as printed language, it is excellent.

Roy Miki's *The Prepoetics of William Carlos Williams: "Kora in Hell"* (Ann Arbor, Mich.), a third UMI Research Press book, is a study of the poet's theoretical concerns early in his career. Miki sees Williams as being at his best when he is operating in "contraries—many ways all at once—that are held in their unresolved condition. Such writing harbors the kind of consciousness that thrives on what is indeterminate, unknown, and in the play of change. Crisis is the very air it breathes." Miki sees that once Williams recognized his mode of operation, he tested it in *Kora in Hell*, working through his sense of destruction, slaughter, by posing opposites, driving through contraries, playing reality against dream, intellect against subconscious. Miki's method is close reading, but informed reading, a critical text almost biographical, as—to handle a book like *Kora*—is necessary.

Stephen Tapscott's *American Beauty: William Carlos Williams and the Modernist Whitman* (New York, 1984) compares and contrasts the two New Jersey poets in important and sophisticated ways. He defines Whitman's poetics as being dependent on the creation of an idealized image of himself, whereas Williams instead creates an "Elsie," an image to fuse the private and public, inner and outer forces. Whitman's art never quite solved the problems inherent in the conflicts between public and private, though his reliance on metaphor helped him bridge the dichotomy. Williams carefully uses Whitman's terms but works to arrive at the position Whitman somewhat naively assumed. In the final outcome, while the size of Whitman's "Self" may trouble the proportions of the single poem, Williams works to resolve that tension by starting with the individual citizen (Whitman's weakest concern) and by finding the largest collective implications of the "giant" within the range of the individual's experience. Williams accomplished this through metonymy: "a formal poetic ambition ('no ideas but in things'), a political ideal (democratic individuation within a federated whole), and a philosophical commitment (each thing is itself so completely, so 'objectively' presented, that it comes to represent a category of discrete things."

While Tapscott's book is crucial (and includes several essays published earlier), two others attempt to place Williams in a line of direct descent from Emerson with an eye to naming him a Romantic. Both Joseph G. Kronik (*American Poetics of History: From Emerson to the Moderns*, Baton Rouge, La., 1984) and Carl Rapp (*William Carlos Williams and Romantic Idealism*, Hanover, 1984) arrive at similar conclusions, but proceed differently. They share a similar weakness: little reference to earlier critics, most importantly to Hyatt H. Waggoner and his seminal study, *American*

Poets: From the Puritans to the Present (1968), the definitive treatment of Emerson's influence on Williams. They also use very few texts—Rapp chooses "The Wanderer" and several unpublished essays from the early 1900s as his primary texts, and Kronik focuses on "The Wanderer," *Spring and All*, and *Paterson*. While some sense of the critics' excitement at working with Williams does come through, for the knowledgeable reader the frustration of having to plow through analysis that is already available in earlier criticism (how many times do we have to read these same snippets of *Paterson*?) overcomes any appreciation of these books. (Kronik's chapter on Williams—he deals with Emerson, Thoreau, Whitman, Henry Adams, Pound, Hart Crane, and Stevens in addition— is titled "William Carlos Williams' Search for an 'American' Place," a thematic concern that has been dealt with frequently in the past twenty-five years.)

David Walker's *The Transparent Lyric: Reading and Meaning in the Poetry of Stevens and Williams* (Princeton, N.J., 1984) is a well-argued corrective to the notion that both poets were Romantics. By defining their poetics in terms of craft, which Walker rightly sees as central to their work, he proves that one of the reasons these two poets remain so interesting to the 1980s reader is that their art is transcendent. He cites parallels to graphic art, defines the poets' "strategies of objectification and anti-sentimentalism" which differed in obvious ways from the techniques of Eliot and Pound, and insists that both poets use a form of "the transparent lyric." This he defines as a more open, inclusive, and active poem, which has as its dramatic center not the lyric speaker but the reading experience itself.

Anthony Libby's *Mythologies of Nothing: Mystical Death in American Poetry 1940–70* (Urbana, Ill., 1984) places Williams's *Paterson* as a seminal text for the establishment of a "deliberate negative mysticism" which extended through the writings of Roethke, Lowell, Plath, Bly, Merwin, and many other younger poets. By daring to deal with the *via negativa* in its preoccupation with death and apocalypse (the latter often an entry to new beginnings, to immanence), Libby helps to place Williams in a more meaningful relationship to postmodern poets. He uses Jung, Heidegger, and Hölderlin, and the great Western mystics (Boehme, Juliana, St. Theresa, and St. John of the Cross) to explicate many of the troublesome poems in the work of the writers studied, and provides important insights into the role of pantheism rather than Christianity in these poets' work.

James E. B. Breslin, in *From Modern to Contemporary: American Poetry, 1945–1965* (Chicago, 1984), sees Williams's importance to the postmodern poets (he and Hart Crane, rather than Eliot and Frost), but focuses his attention on the younger writers rather than the moderns. In *Lyric Apocalypse: Reconstruction in Ancient and Modern Poetry* (Chico,

Calif., 1984), John W. Erwin chooses *Paterson* as proof that most poets find and portray community as a central theme, from the Book of Revelations to the present. Like Pindar, Williams dramatized the interchanges between poet and reader in *Paterson*, thus creating a "dialectic structure" like the *Odes*.

Daniel Hoffman has edited *Ezra Pound & William Carlos Williams: The University of Pennsylvania Conference Papers* (Philadelphia, 1983). Based on papers given in 1981, the collection has been extended so that it now includes work by Hugh Kenner, Emily Mitchell Wallace, Ronald Bush, Denise Levertov, Michael F. Harper, Wendy Stallard Flory, Paul Christensen, Theodora R. Graham, and James Laughlin. It contains a checklist of the University of Pennsylvania libraries' holdings of Williams and Pound materials, compiled by Neda M. Westlake and Francis James Dallet. The most informative essays are those by Paul Christensen ("William Carlos Williams in the Forties: Prelude to Postmodernism") and Theodora R. Graham ("'Her Heigh Compleynte': The Cress Letters of William Carlos Williams' *Paterson*"). Christensen does a thorough survey of what Williams was writing in the 1940s, the longer-lined poetry and the matrix of prose and poetry that became *Paterson*. He links these new shapes to Williams's activity during the 1930s, publishing *Collected Poems, 1921–31* from the Objectivist Press and *The Complete Collected Poems* (1938). As a result of taking stock in preparing these books, Williams was ready to "make it new." World War II also forced the poet to create a new art to reflect a new, more sober world. Graham's long essay details the relationships between Marcia Nardi and Williams and Harvey Breit, and the use Williams made of Nardi's letters in *Paterson*.

Many of the papers from the August 1983 Williams Conference at the University of Maine at Orono have now been published in *Sagetrieb* (Spring 1984), including work by Diane Wakoski, Hugh Kenner (whose essay was earlier published in the *New York Times Book Review* for 18 Sept. 1983), and Eleanor Berry, who discusses Williams and George Oppen. Williams as dramatist is the subject of Linda W. Wagner's essay on *Many Loves*, of Theodora Graham's on *A Dream of Love*, and of Thomas Kilroy's treatment of Brecht, Beckett, and Williams. Douglas Messerli discusses Williams's early criticism; Patricia C. Willis writes of Marianne Moore and *The Dial* in relation to Williams; and E. P. Walkiewicz comments on Williams's development as a writer, in relation to other papers given during the conference.

A collection still in press at this time is John Bauer's edition of the papers from the "Spring and All" Conference at Kean College of New Jersey (1979). Essays by Linda W. Wagner, James Guimond, and others will be included, as will Elizabeth Huberman's account of the performance of Williams's *The First President* (which was published in the Spring 1980 *William Carlos Williams Review* issue as "The First *First President*").

2 Other Parts of Books and Periodical Essays

Rather than treating the accumulation of materials in this category chronologically, a thematic and methodological division will be used.

a. Studies of Williams, Art, and Graphic Artists. The central book for this approach to Williams is Dickran Tashjian's *Skyscraper Primitives: Dada and the American Avant-Garde, 1910–1925* (Middletown, Conn., 1975). Tashjian finds Williams important for his early poems and his editorship of *Contact* (also his influence on both *Broom* and *Secession*) and for his "defiant innovation" in *Kora in Hell, Spring and All, In the American Grain,* and *The Great American Novel.* Tashjian's methodology creates a respectable and viable means of comparing written art with graphic and establishes Williams as a key figure in the development of a collective American art.

Joan Burbick's excellent essay, "Grimace of a New Age: The Postwar Poetry and Painting of William Carlos Williams and Jackson Pollock" (*Boundary* 2, Spring 1982), employs many of the same techniques to conclude that the two artists began "post-modernism, a rhetoric of 'immanence' rather than symbolism." As a result of the chaos of real life, both artists shifted "to the proportionately immense"—enlarged canvases, literally, just as they shifted from the fragmentation of their earlier visions to a belief in "kinesis, matter in motion without purposeful direction but the animating power of both death and delight." Using Jakobson as well as art historians, Burbick builds a convincing argument. James E. B. Breslin has written just as convincingly about the use of what he calls "cubist realism" in "William Carlos Williams and Charles Demuth: Cross-Fertilization in the Arts" (*JML,* Apr. 1977), as has Rob Fure in "The Design of Experience: William Carlos Williams and Juan Gris" (*WCWN,* Fall 1978). Bonnie Costello provides more of an overview in "William Carlos Williams in a World of Painters" (*NBR,* June/July 1979), and Philip Furia relates Williams's process toward *Paterson* with characteristics of Pollock, Gris, and Picasso ("*Paterson*'s Progress" [*Boundary* 2, Winter 1981]).

Mary Ann Caws's "A Double Reading by Design: Breughel, Auden, and Williams" (*JAAC,* Spring 1983) sees Williams's instructions for relating poems to paintings in his emphasis on selecting details, bordering, creating frames ("It teaches us how a design may create what is to be brought, by design, into existence." Caws's comments on word choice, ordering, and the structure of lines and kind of lines ("Each poem in the series about Breughel paintings has this type of initial firm line.") are persuasive. Wendy Steiner approaches Williams's Breughel poems from a more artistically sophisticated perspective in *The Colors of Rhetoric: Problems in the Relation between Modern Literature and Painting* (Chicago, 1982), in her chapter "Williams' Breughel: An Interartistic Analysis." Here she compares Breughel's "Return of the Hunters" with Williams's "Hunters in the Snow" and proves that the media do align in many more ways than subject. Steiner's discussion of the works, through what she terms "correspondence of technical properties," opens this approach to poetry far beyond any other study. She concludes by considering Williams "a cubist writer," comparing him with Stein. An earlier essay related to these is David M. Wyatt's "Completing the Picture: Williams, Berryman, and 'Spatial Form'" (*CLQ*, Dec. 1977), a discussion of Breughel's "The Hunters in the Snow" with the Williams poem and Berryman's "Winter Landscape."

Another interesting approach is that of Peter Schmidt, writing in "Some Versions of Modernist Pastoral: Williams and the Precisionists" (*ConL*, Summer 1980). Williams's lyrics share the precisionists' "Arcadian vision of modern industry" and enable the poet to produce a radically American art ("Spring and All" and "Burning the Christmas Greens" illustrate the method Schmidt locates). Schmidt continues Marjorie Perloff's line of thinking in "'Lines Converging and Crossing': The 'French' Phase of William Carlos Williams" (*MoR*, Fall 1978), as she finds that a knowledge of French painting only led Williams to reject *mimesis*. Instead, Williams turned to what Perloff calls "metonymic" art, and in this the chief influence was Rimbaud. Far-reaching in its intent, this essay reminds one of Bram Dijkstra's "Wallace Stevens and William Carlos Williams: Poetry, Painting, and the Function of Reality," in *Encounters: Essays on Literature and the Visual Arts* (ed. John Dixon Hunt, London, 1971), where Dijkstra cites the influence of the 1913 Armory Show in both poets' work (Duchamp, Delaunay, Matisse, Gauguin, Cézanne, Wouters, Rodriguez)—and in their formulation of aesthetic principles in the years to come. A special issue of *In'Hui* (1981), edited by Jacques Darras, includes two essays that deal with Williams and graphic art, Jacqueline Ollier's "William Carlos Williams et le Futurisme" and Gerard-Georges Lemaire's "La poetique picturale de William Carlos Williams."

b. Studies from a Linguistic Perspective. One of the first readings of a Williams poem from the linguistic point of view was Robert G. Lint's "The Structural Image in Williams' 'Young Sycamore'" (*Lang&S*, Summer 1974). John L. Simons's "The Lying Cinders: Patterns of Linguistic Unity in W. C. Williams' 'Between Walls'" (*ConP*, Spring 1977) focuses on word play rather than structure. Two recent explications seem to provide expert models of what is possible, working with the poem in a complete enough reading so that an audience can understand both method and results: Maria Anita Stefanelli's "A Stylistic Analysis of Williams' 'The Descent'" (*Lang&S*, Spring 1983) and Irene R. Fairley's "On Reading Poems: Visual & Verbal Icons in William Carlos Williams' 'Landscape with the Fall of Icarus'" (*StTCL*, Fall 1981–Spring 1982).

Stefanelli begins with an early version of "The Descent," studying "syntax, semantics, and metric structure—the problems of style. By examining the shifting of the focus or the understressing of ordinary constituents in syntax, by discovering associations hidden behind the choice of a particular word, by pointing out features in grammar that led to morphological changes consequent on a rethinking or redefinition, . . ." Stefanelli justifies her method. She then charts oppositional parallelism (descent/ascent, present/past); oblique use of words ("The words in this poem are common. . . . the way they are used is unconventional, indeed, peculiar"); nominals used in place of verbs; and the alternation of pauses with sound in this very useful reading.

Fairley attends more to "graphic design and verbal structure" in her reading and claims that Williams achieves a parallel to the actual painting through "manipulation of deictics, selection of syntactic structures, especially subordination, his parallelisms, even his choice of deviant items." Then Fairley continues to test the hypothesis her own reading has created, that the shape and structure of the poem does, in fact, recreate the painting. She describes her testing ninety-one students with six structures for the Williams poem, structures designed to prove which features and which arrangements achieve particular effects. Her findings prove her contention and also, more importantly, the efficacy of Williams's original poem structure.

Michael Riffaterre chooses to use Williams's red wheelbarrow poem (along with several other early texts) to illustrate what he calls "activating the intertext" ("Intertextual Representation: On Mimesis as Interpretive Discourse" [CritI, Sept. 1984]). In Riffaterre's analysis, the text "offers a representation, the literariness of which results from a conflict between the textual mimesis of the object and an intertextual mimesis of the same object that voids or contradicts one or more basic semantic features of the textual one." In this far-ranging discussion, the author brings a new dimension to Williams's most apparent aesthetic tactic.

c. Studies of Individual Collections or Books. Much attention has been given to *Kora in Hell: Improvisations*, particularly in criticism dealing with the issues of modernism and postmodernism and in that of Williams as graphic writer. Four other essays should be mentioned specifically: David Jauss's "The Descent, the Dance, and the Wheel: The Aesthetic Theory of William Carlos Williams' *Kora in Hell*" (*BUJ*, No. 1, 1977); Thomas P. Joswick's "Beginning with Loss: The Poetics of William Carlos Williams' *Kora in Hell: Improvisations*" (*TSLL*, Spring 1977); Ron Loewinsohn's "'Fools Have Big Wombs': William Carlos Williams' *Kora in Hell*" (*ELWIU*, Fall 1977); and Stephen Fredman's "American Poet's Prose and the Crisis of Verse" (*Amer. Poetry*, Fall 1983), which treats Ashbery's *Three Poems* and Creeley's *Presences: A Text for Marisol* as well as *Kora in Hell*. Each essay stresses the cyclic, nonlinear shape of the work, its dwelling on immediate experience but moving beyond immediacy into the arrested vision of achieved art, and the poet's fascination with theoretical exploration. The Fredman essay also stresses Williams's importance as the originator of the sentence as a generative form.

Spring and All has shared critics' attention. Besides the Kean College volume in press, other studies include Richard J. Morgan's "Chaos and Order: The Cycle of Life and Art in Williams' *Spring and All*" (*Interpreta-*

tions, No. 1, 1979); Audrey Rodgers's "'Spring and All': The Myth of Kore in the Poetry of William Carlos Williams" (*Mosaic,* Winter 1981); and Linda W. Wagner's "Damn it, Bill: They Still Haven't Listened!" in her *American Modern* (Port Washington, N.Y., 1980).

Alan Holder opens his book, *The Imagined Past: Portrayals of Our History in Modern American Literature* (Lewisburg, Pa., 1980), with a chapter on *In the American Grain.* To Holder, Williams seems inconsistent. He praises Indians as the "flower" of the country but fails to deal with them in any depth. And though he appears to be firmly for the sensual, "the precise significance of the sexual and matrimonial metaphors used to convey acceptance or rejection of the New World, personified as a woman, appears to shift." Therefore, Holder sees the text as less historical than "private." E. P. Bollier's "Against the American Grain: William Carlos Williams between Whitman and Poe" (*TSE,* 1978) asks why Williams pays so much attention to Poe and gives only one sentence to Whitman.

George Monteiro's "The Doctor's Black Bag: William Carlos Williams' Passaic River Stories" (*MLS,* Winter 1983) presents Williams as a divided observer, torn between being a sentient person and a scientific physician. The inherent tension in the persona of most of these stories helps to create the life, the duality, the complexity of the point of view. Monteiro reads "The Use of Force," "Jean Beicke," "A Night in June," and "Comedy Entombed: 1930" to illustrate his "complementary/conflicting identities," evident primarily in the "doctor" stories.

Norma Procopiow assesses "Tradition and Innovation in William Carlos Williams' *The Great American Novel*" (*MSLC,* 1982) but adds little to work already done on the book (prior studies do not appear in her notes). A much more informative essay is Linda Ray Pratt's "Williams's Stecher Trilogy: 'The Pure Products of America'" (*SAF,* Spring 1982). Pratt discusses Williams's three novels—*White Mule, In the Money,* and *The Build-Up*—from the perspective of the Americanization of the immigrant. She discusses evidence of his interest in behavioral patterns of assimilation, as well as psychological and moral patterns, but she admits the unevenness of the three books ("Williams's own shifting themes, the difficulty of writing about living people, and the changed historical climate between the start of the novels in 1927 and their completion in 1952 confuse the trilogy's thematic clarity").

Aside from the books already noted, only Kurt Heinzelman's "Staging the Poem: William Carlos Williams' *A Dream of Love*" (*ConL,* Autumn 1977) discusses Williams as playwright. Heinzelman synthesizes Williams's dramatic theory and then reads the poem from that theoretical point of view.

Several essays focus on Williams's late poems (in addition to many, many essays on *Paterson*): Marc Hofstadter describes his "gentle meditative, embracing quality" in "A Different Speech: William Carlos Williams' Later Poetry" (*TCL,* Dec. 1977); Neil Baldwin's "'The world as it opens':

William Carlos Williams' 'The Descent'" comprises the whole of *Ordinary*, No. 1, 1977; Ronald E. McFarland reads Williams's poem "Fish" in "The Variable Voice in William Carlos Williams' 'Fish'" (*Sagetrieb*, Summer–Fall 1983); Dawn Trouard centers on "Perceiving Gestalt in 'The Clouds'" (*ConL*, Spring 1981); and Rosalyn A. Bernsteen assesses the theme of the beautiful in "The Beautiful Unbeautiful: W. C. Williams' Legacy in *Pictures from Breughel*" (*CP*, Autumn 1977).

d. *Studies of "Paterson."* Peter Revell uses *Paterson* as one of his examples in *Quest in Modern American Poetry* (Totowa, N.J., 1981) and correctly relates the long poem to *In the American Grain*. He is also treating H.D.'s *Trilogy*, *The Cantos*, *Four Quartets* and Aiken's *The Divine Pilgrimage* and, partly because of this context, finds that Williams does not make full use of all mythic materials which would have been available to him. *Paterson* fares better in Laszlo Géfin's 1982 study *Ideogram: History of a Poetic Method* (Austin, Tex.). He describes the poetic transfer from metaphor to vortex, discussing Pound's creation of the ideogram, from Fenollosa, and moving to "the poem as object" in a chapter titled "Dr. Williams: Ideas in Things." Here he refers to Williams as "an uncompromising modernist, at times even a one-man avant-garde" and praises his "nontransitional, paratactic mode of poetic expression." He accurately sees *Paterson* growing more directly from *Kora in Hell* and *Spring and All* than from Pound's influence.

Michael André Bernstein's *The Tale of the Tribe: Ezra Pound and the Modern Verse Epic* (Princeton, N.J., 1980) includes three chapters on *Paterson*, in which he views the long poem as a "critique" of *The Cantos* and an exploration in Williams's attempt to tell his own tale of the tribe. He sees that Paterson is "a 'mythical' city, but largely in the sense of an imaginary site in which the poet's desires for coherence and meaning are tested." He faults the work on the grounds that Williams is attempting to create the sounds of the city, and one listener simply cannot hear enough "townspeople" to create a full picture. Bernstein also points out that *Paterson*, unlike traditional epics, "has no one narrative voice able to function as the unquestioned spokesman for values acknowledged as essential for the entire community's welfare"; accordingly, Williams ends up with a "network of voices."

Roger Asselineau considers the importance of the city in American literature, including *Paterson* ("From Whitman's 'Yawp' to Ginsberg's 'Howl' or the Poetry of Large Cities in American Literature" [*RLV*, U.S. Bicentennial Issue, 1976]); his discussion reminds one of that by Monroe K. Spears in his 1970 *Dionysus and the City: Modernism and Twentieth-Century Poetry* (New York). Spears describes Williams then as, "like Lawrence, a temperamental Futurist, who takes historical discontinuity as a basic postulate."

Generally, essays on *Paterson* became increasingly specialized during the 1970s and early 1980s. Alan Ostrom describes "The Function of Names in the Mythopoeic Process in William Carlos Williams' *Paterson*" (*LOS*, 1980). Milne Holton is one of several to consider manuscript materials in his "Prolegomenon to *Paterson*: William Carlos Williams' Introduction to *By the Rivers of Babylon*" (*Proof*, 1978). Douglas Fiero reads four versions of *Paterson* I, from various libraries, in "Williams Creates the First Book of *Paterson*" (*JML*, Apr. 1974); and G. Morris Donaldson uses the same approach in "William Carlos Williams: *Paterson*, Books I and II" (*WCR*, Spring 1970). Roger Ramsey's "*Paterson*: The Seminal Seed Imagery" (*CP*, Spring 1978); Billy T. Tracy's "The Phryne Figure in *Paterson*" (*NConL*, Mar. 1978); and Helen H. Roulston's "The Four Elements and Poetic Consciousness in William Carlos Williams' *Paterson*" (*SDR*, Spring 1979) (the Heraclitean elements, discussed in a theme-and-variation pattern) are examples of useful but rather limited approaches to the poem.

Scientific approaches to the poem are the basis for Carol Donley's "'A little touch of / Einstein in the night': Williams' Early Exposure to the Theories of Relativity" (*WCWN*, Spring 1977) and "Relativity and Radioactivity in William Carlos Williams' *Paterson*" (*WCWN*, Spring 1978). Two essays make connections between Williams and Freud: Andrew Hudgins's "*Paterson* and Its Discontents" (*ArQ*, Spring 1979), which draws on Freud's *Civilization and Its Discontents*, and David Hurry's "William Carlos Williams' *Paterson* and Freud's *Interpretation of Dreams*" (*L&P*, No. 3/4, 1978).

Among the most interesting of the essays on *Paterson* is Paul Bové's "The World and Earth of William Carlos Williams: *Paterson* as a 'Long Poem'" (*Genre*, Winter 1978). Using Heideggerian language, Bové creates the entity of the poem as a dynamic process of gathering images and then dispersing them in new formulations. A 1981 essay by Joseph N. Riddel parallels some of the concepts in Bové's: "'Keep Your Pecker Up': *Paterson Five* and The Question of Metapoetry" (*Glyph*). And Paul L. Mariani's 1978 essay on the genesis of the fifth book is also an expert piece ("Paterson 5: The Whore/Virgin and the Wounded One-Horned Beast" [*UDQ*, Summer 1978]). Mariani also uses *Paterson* to return to the poems of the 1940s, in "The Hard Core of Beauty" (*Sagetrieb*, Spring 1984). Gay Sibley's "Documents of Presumption: The Satiric Use of the Ginsberg Letters in William Carlos Williams' *Paterson*" (*AL*, Mar. 1983) is a marvel of scholarship plus perspective. Our tendency to deify literature we admire can stand the kind of puncturing Sibley manages in this astute commentary on one motive for quoting texts within texts. As Sibley directs, "a satiric reading of the first two letters compels one to look afresh at all of *Paterson*, Books I through V. Although Ginsberg's first letter does not appear until Book IV, 'presumption' provides much of the tension in the first three books as well."

Assessing the fame of *Paterson* abroad, Minoru Hirooka connects the long poem with aesthetics from painting in "An American Cubist Poem: William Carlos Williams' *Paterson*" (*SALit*, 1978).

e. Studies of Williams and Other Poets. Donald Hall asks, in "Poetry and Ambition" (*KR*, Fall 1983), "if Pound, H.D., and William Carlos Williams had not known each other when young, would they have become William Carlos Williams, H.D., and Pound? There have been some lone wolves but not many." Whether essays deal with early associations among poets, technical or thematic similarities, or influences, the quantity of comparative studies has increased noticeably.

Jessie D. Green studies thematic and verbal influences of Whitman in "Whitman's Voice in 'The Wanderer'" (*WCWN*, Fall, 1977). Jacqueline Saunier-Ollier traces similarities in poetic devices in "Whitman, Williams, Ginsberg: histoire d'une filiation" (*RFEA*, Apr. 1978); and Ronald Hayman describes a repelling-attracting pattern in *Arguing with Walt Whitman* (London, 1971) (Hayman also considers Pound, Eliot, Crane, and Stevens). Thomas H. Jackson compares Williams with Eliot and Pound and finds that the former does a better job of realizing the goals of both Yeats and Mallarmé ("Positivism and Modern Poetics: Yeats, Mallarmé, and William Carlos Williams" [*ELH*, Fall 1979]).

Kenneth Johnson describes Williams's reaction to Eliot's *The Waste Land* and resulting interaction between the two in "Eliot as Enemy: William Carlos Williams and *The Waste Land*" (in *The Twenties: Fiction, Poetry, Drama*, ed. Warren French, Deland, Fla., 1975), and John M. Slatin narrates Williams's move to win Marianne Moore's sympathy away from Eliot in "The War of the Roses: Williams, Eliot, Moore" (*WCWR*, Spring 1980). Linda W. Wagner compares Williams's and Eliot's practices of allusion in their poems in "Ohhhh, That Shakespherian Rag" (*CollL*, Spring 1976). Bonnie Costello writes a comprehensive and important study of Marianne Moore and Williams, "'Polished Garlands' of Agreeing Difference': William Carlos Williams and Marianne Moore, An Exchange," in *The Motive for Metaphor: Essays on Modern Poetry* (ed. Francis C. Blessington and Guy Rotella, Boston, 1983), their friendship, their reviews of each other's work, and their poetry. Stanley Lourdeaux traces Moore's phrase "imaginary gardens with real toads in them" to Williams's poem "Romance Moderne," which had appeared in *Others* 5 (1919) ("Toads in Gardens for Marianne Moore and William Carlos Williams" [*MP*, Nov. 1982]).

Leroy Searle studies Eliot and Williams in light of Blake's poetry and vision in "Blake, Eliot, and Williams: The Continuity of Imaginative Labor," in *William Blake and the Moderns* (ed. Robert J. Bertholf and Annette S. Levitt, Albany, N.Y., 1982), seeing his chief influence to be his "intimate, consistent understanding of imagination as a generative process." In this regard, Williams is a more apt pupil than Eliot, largely because "Williams followed an avowedly personal strategy in which the artist is answerable to an open society but responsible to the imperatives of his own perceptions of human needs. In the place of an elite, whether of creed or education, Williams appealed to the 'function of the imagination,' as an 'order' which is 'in its vigor the process of ordering'"—a process much like Blake's.

For Anne Paolucci and Henry Paolucci, the Eliot and Williams duality is joined by A. D. Hope of Australia. "Poet-Critics on the Frontiers of Literature: A. D. Hope, T. S. Eliot, and William Carlos Williams" (*RNL*, 1982) is a comparison of critical views about the role of poetry and an informative discussion of the interaction among the three poets. Some of this material is worn but is given new life in this fresh geographical context.

Vera M. Kutzinski, in "Sterling Brown and William Carlos Williams" (*BALF*, Spring 1982), parallels Brown's *Southern Road* with *Paterson* and finds that neither long poem has anything to do with "local color"; rather, both are means of creating an "imaginary reality." Kutzinski discusses the work from a thematic point of view and also concludes that the poets' aims were similar.

Stephen Tapscott finds great similarity in the use of language by Joyce and Williams ("Paterson A'Bloom: Williams, Joyce, and The Virtue of 'ABCEDMINDEDNESS'" [*ArQ*, Winter 1977]). Stuart Peterfreund's "Keats's Influence on William Carlos Williams" (*WCWN*, Spring 1977) claims that *Paterson* attempts to revise *Endymion*; and Del Ivan Janik sees likenesses among Lawrence, Roethke, Williams, and Snyder (in that they all have respect and concern for biocentric objects) in "Poetry in the Ecosphere" (*CentR*, Fall 1976).

James E. Miller, Jr. connects the protagonist of *Paterson* with the narrator of *The Great Gatsby* and Jim Burden, in that these characters are all unable to be content with the present ("*My Ántonia* and the American Dream" [*PrS*, Summer 1974]). Steven Weisenburger links Nathanael West with Williams in "Williams, West, and the Art of Regression" (*SARev*, Nov. 1982), seeing them as friends and colleagues (sharing firm aesthetic principles) but also seeing them as participants in the tactic of "demolishing the familiar, then reformulating it in dance-like, dialectical configurations." Working from Williams's principles in *Kora in Hell*, Weisenburger follows imagery of the dance, language, and characters' regression through West's writing. He makes interesting observations throughout: "So *Day of the Locust*, like *The Great American Novel*, is in its deepest sense about the paradox of artistic influence."

Other essays that might be mentioned, to give some sense of the wide range of topics only partly covered here, are W. S. Sewall's "Hans Magnus Enzenberger and William Carlos Williams: Economy, Detail and Suspicion of Doctrine" (*GL&L*, Jan. 1979); and a group dealing with Wallace Stevens and Williams: David L. Green's "*The Comedian as the Letter C*, Carlos, and *Contact*" (*TCL*, Fall 1981), an excellent study with

Green reading Stevens's 1922 "Comedian" as a "parody of the intense seriousness of Williams' campaign for a new American poetry based on the hard grit of American life"; Jack Hardie's "Hibiscus and the Spaniard of the Rose: Williams' Dialogue with Wallace Stevens" (*WCWN*, Fall 1978); and Donald Gutierrez's "Circular Art: Round Poems of Wallace Stevens and William Carlos Williams" (*CP*, Spring 1981). Linda W. Wagner discusses Plath and Williams in "Modern American Literature: The Poetics of the Individual Voice" (*CentR*, Fall 1977) and also continues the discussion in her introduction to *Critical Essays on Sylvia Plath* (CEAmL, Boston, 1984). M. L. Rosenthal caps this kind of essay with his "Is There a Pound-Williams Tradition?" (*SoR*, Apr. 1984). He answers "No," insisting that both poets were themselves part of a lyric tradition, "the large common heritage, the whole retrievable body of poetry that keeps singing away."

f. Theoretical Studies. Donald M. Kartiganer chooses to discuss *Paterson* as an example of what he terms "process literature" in "Process and Product: A Study of Modern Literary Form" (*MR*, Spring and Autumn, 1971). Among the qualities Kartiganer notes are the subject of the poem becoming the poet's effort to create art, and involvement of the reader. Such art is of necessity fragmentary. Kartiganer also discusses the Imagists, Eliot, Conrad, and Faulkner, and the parallel methods of Freud and Jung.

David Antin's "Modernism and Postmodernism: Approaching the Present in American Poetry" (*Boundary 2*, Fall 1972) gives important orientation to the notion of the postmodern. Correctly placing Pound and Williams at the beginning of that movement, along with Stein, John Cage, and the European Dadaists and Surrealists, Antin stresses the importance of psycholinguistics and of a collage structure to the postmodern work. More specific in his application of theory to Williams's work, Anthony Libby terms Williams's reliance on imagery—particularly on imagery of brightness, flame, and the radiance of precious metals—to a structure like Joyce's epiphany ("'Claritas': William Carlos Williams' Epiphanies" [*Criticism*, Winter 1972]). Milne Holton's 1970 essay "To Hit Love Aslant: Poetry and William Carlos Williams," in *Private Dealings: Eight Modern American Writers* (ed. David J. Burrows, Lewis M. Dabney, Milne Holton, and Grosvenor E. Powell, Stockholm), aligns Williams's short poems to "field composition" as he emphasizes the engagement between the poet's imagination and an object. And in *The Incarnate Word: Literature as Verbal Space* (Urbana, Ill., 1973), Cary Nelson determines that Williams's primary metaphoric image is of flower and of space and then proceeds to follow that metaphor through both his poetry and prose.

Robert Kern, in "Williams, Brautigan, and the Poetics of Primitivism" (*ChiR*, Summer 1975), contends that Williams and the younger poet attempt to go beyond "literary" forms to create their own shapes consonant with archetypal forms. Christine Rabin's "Williams' Autobiog-rapheme: The Inscriptional *I* in *Asphodel*" (*MPS*, Autumn 1975) glosses the late poem as a graphic construct, with reference to French struc-turalism. She accordingly finds Williams's use of the pronoun *I* (used 120 times in the poem) as his index.

Sherman Paul's essay on Williams ("An Introduction"), in his *Repos-sessing and Renewing: Essays in the Green American Tradition* (Baton Rouge, La., 1976), describes his writing as an "interior drama of imagination." Unlike Eliot's, Williams's "modernism incorporated organicism and ex-pressed again the American wonder." Jacob Korg's "Ritual and Experi-ment in Modern Poetry" (*JML*, Feb. 1979) surveys the work of many poets, but comes to Williams with the announcement that his poems "illustrate the modern experimental mode perfectly because they are composed of thrusts of the imagination against a resistant reality, ending in a kind of local revelation." Williams wrote the kind of "parables of process" that influenced Allen Ginsberg and other younger poets. Korg looks on modern and contemporary trends with some alarm, but con-cludes that the "coexistence of ritual and experimental modes within individual poems and lines of poems is . . . in its broadest dimensions, an effort to bring together the apparently irreconcilable attitudes that mark the opposing limits of the modern consciousness."

Charles Altieri's *Act and Quality: A Theory of Literary Meaning and Humanistic Understanding* (Amherst, Mass., 1981) reprints in changed form his controversial essay from *Critical Inquiry* (Spring 1979), "Presence and Reference in a Literary Text: The Example of Williams." In his dis-cussion of Wittgenstein, Gricean pragmatics, speech act theory ("the foundations of a dramatistic view of language"), and hermeneutic theory, Altieri reads Williams's "This is Just to Say" as a "test case" of his contention that poets create forms out of necessity: "Without God, or even a very coherent culture, Williams must root the terms for mutual recognition of actions in frail domestic contexts. . . . Williams' domestic context ultimately becomes for him a possible metaphor for an 'identity' that conquers 'partiality' and a condition of 'mutual understanding and tolerance' that attends upon imaginative measures of performance."

Marjorie Perloff, in a 1983 essay in the Terrell collection as well as in her 1981 *Poetics of Indeterminacy: Rimbaud to Cage* (Princeton, N.J.), stresses the unavailability of definitions, of "answers." Words are, finally, words, not symbols—or not primarily symbols; and for relation-ships, verbal mirrors might be a good image. Perloff's readings of sections from *Kora in Hell* and *Spring and All* are set against comparable readings from Eliot. Just as in her "'To Give a Design': Williams and the Visual-ization of Poetry" (Terrell), she proves the importance of the word—to Williams—in his concentration on the shape of the poem and also defines his various stages of scansion as she moves chronologically through his poetry. Of interest with this treatment might be Eleanor Berry's "Williams' Development of a New Prosodic Form—Not the 'Variable Foot,' but the 'Sight Stanza'" (*WCWR*, Fall 1981).

g. General Studies. In the Fall/Winter 1976 issue of *Parnassus*, R. W. Flint gives Williams a central place in modern poetics, chiefly because of his successful experimentation with language in *Paterson* ("America of Poets"). By using Williams's collection *An Early Martyr*, Robert von Hallberg describes the ways in which Williams's work changed, better to reflect changing social concerns, in "The Politics of Description: W. C. Williams in the 'Thirties" (*ELH*, Spring 1978). The notion of Williams as "political" occurs also in M. L. Rosenthal's "The Idea of Revolution in Poetry" (*Nation*, 14–21 Aug. 1976), a survey essay in which he reads "To Elsie" and sections of *Paterson* to prove how involved Williams was with the realities of life, a topic already broached in his *Poetry and the Common Life* (New York, 1974) when he uses *Paterson* as an example of the poet making "a straightforward assault" on what connections exist between poetry and "the common life."

Marianne Baruchaise describes Williams's political involvement in "Williams and the Bomb" (*APR*, July–Aug. 1985), stating that for all his pose of aesthetic distance, Williams was more concerned with real life issues of nuclear war than most writers and artists. History will find him one of the great spokesmen for the central quandary of our time.

Lois Bar-Yaacov's wide-ranging essay, "Driving into the Twentieth Century: A Study of Some William Carlos Williams' Poems" (*HUSL*, Autumn 1980), is one example of the interest in Williams abroad, as is Jacqueline Ollier's "The Poetic Dynamic of William Carlos Williams" (*EA*, Jan.–Mar. 1983).

A very good sense of Williams in his dual roles of physician and writer, and divided writer, comes through in Herbert Liebowitz's "'You Can't Beat Innocence': *The Autobiography of William Carlos Williams*" (*APR*, Mar./Apr. 1981). And one of the most fascinating essays covered in this review is that by Lysander Kemp (*HudR*, Autumn 1981), "The Sunday Morning Wheelbarrow." Kemp fabricates a dialogue between Williams and Stevens, relying on so-called excerpts from unpublished letters. After Stevens has given some early versions of "Sunday Morning," Williams says acidly, "'Never saw a green cockatoo: Cockatoos are pink. . . . Poem very good, really, one of yr. best.'" Later in the piece, Kemp includes the wheelbarrow poem as part of Stevens's "Sunday Morning" and Williams proceeds to correct it. This is a charming impressionistic recounting of our great poets, and we can learn a great deal from it.

h. Studies of Williams and Younger Poets. One might begin with Annie Dillard's remark, in "Contemporary Prose Styles" (*TCL*, Fall 1981), that the main tradition in prose today, "a new sort of beauty in prose," stems from William Carlos Williams's "no ideas but in things." One might open any collection of interviews with contemporary writers at random (as, for example, Stephen Berg's *In Praise of What Persists*, New York, 1983) and find countless references to Williams (as when Robert Coles remembers that Williams was "both a refuge and a reprimand" to him, and so he went to medical school with a book of Williams's poems in his pocket). One might speculate at the existence of journals like *Sagetrieb*, founded to honor poets writing in the Pound-Williams tradition. One might mention, in passing, books as different as James F. Mersmann's *Out of the Vietnam Vortex* (Lawrence, Kans., 1974); Charles Molesworth's *The Fierce Embrace: A Study of Contemporary Poetry* (Columbia, Mo., 1979); Richard Howard's *Alone with America: Essays on the Art of Poetry in the United States since 1950* (enlarged edition, New York, 1980); Cary Nelson's *Our Last First Poets: Vision and History in Contemporary American Poetry* (Urbana, Ill., 1981); Jerome Rothenberg's *Pre-Faces & Other Writings* (New York, 1981); and Richard Kostelanetz's *The Old Poetries and the New* (Ann Arbor, Mich., 1981). One might specifically look for studies of the older poet's influence, like that on David Ignatow in Ralph J. Mills, Jr.'s *Cry of the Human* (Urbana, Ill., 1975) and John Vernon's "A Crowd of Oneself" (*Nation*, 14–21 Aug. 1976). Whatever approach the critic takes, it will be partial, limiting, and ultimately frustrating. The quantity of materials is endless; the quality, surprisingly good; and the joy and love of the tributes from poets and critics alike collected in the Terrell *William Carlos Williams: Man and Poet* almost overwhelms the reader. As Philip Booth recalls in his "William Carlos Williams—An Open Thanksgiving": "I marvel and I am, in all senses, moved. What a joy Williams is, even in this poem's intense misery. He realizes it! Always beyond self-pity, he realizes emotion *through* the poem, realizes it and releases it for sharing. Not only is Williams more unself-consciously open to experience than most poets, he opens his poems to every possibility of letting a reader experience them. . . ."

VI SUPPLEMENT

Stephen Cushman's *William Carlos Williams and the Meanings of Measure* (New Haven, Conn., 1985) is a thorough study of the poet's practice in metrics, as well as his broad use of the term "measure" as an aesthetic principle. Cushman finds Williams more influenced by a visual basis than an oral one and discusses the importance of his use of counterpointing lines and sentences in the structure of his writing. Marilyn Kallet's *Honest Simplicity in William Carlos Williams' "Asphodel, That Greeny Flower"* (Baton Rouge, La., 1985) is an appreciative reading of one of Williams's most important poems. Although Kallet uses the manuscripts of the poem extensively, her correlation does not shed as much light on the ways Williams achieved his later work as might be expected.

Albert Cook's "William Carlos Williams: Ideas and Things," in his *Figural Choice in Poetry and Art* (Hanover, N.H., 1985), discusses what

Cook calls "delineation" and "figuration" in relation to Williams's poetics. J. Hillis Miller's chapter on Williams in his *The Linguistic Moment* (Princeton, N.J., 1985) posits Williams's *Spring and All* as essential to any understanding of the principles of Williams's art. Miller also uses this point as the basis of his discussion of Williams in the chapter "William Carlos Williams and Wallace Stevens," in *The Columbia Literary History of the United States* (ed. Emory Elliott, New York, 1988). By stressing Williams's attempt to come to terms with his own aesthetic, marking him a poet in the Emerson-Whitman tradition, Miller insists that Williams's work was of a piece—that his anecdotal and autobiographical writing was as important as his poetry and fiction.

Christopher J. MacGowan also uses *Spring and All* as the centerpiece of his book *William Carlos Williams' Early Poetry: The Visual Arts Background* (Ann Arbor, Mich., 1984). MacGowan studies Williams's writing from 1909 through the mid-1920s, finding the seeds of Williams's later work in his first half-dozen collections, both poetry and prose.

Paul L. Mariani would agree, to some extent, as he discusses various aspects of Williams's poetics, particularly those treating *Paterson*, in several chapters of his collected essays, *A Usable Past: Essays on Modern and Contemporary Poetry* (Amherst, Mass., 1984). Mariani emphasizes the role of the feminine and the feminine principle in Williams's aesthetic.

A collection of six essays (four 1983 Williams Centenary Lectures and two new pieces) appeared in 1985 from the Harry Ransom Humanities Research Center in Austin, Texas. *WCW & Others* (ed. Dave Oliphant and Thomas Zigal) includes an introduction by Joseph Evans Slate and essays by Michael King (on Williams, Pound, and H.D.), Dickran Tashjian (on Williams and Duchamp), John M. Slatin (on Moore and Williams), Kurt Heinzelman (on Stevens and Williams), and Neil Baldwin (on Louis Zukofsky and Williams, tracing their friendship through their letters).

Mary Ellen Solt has edited an interesting collection, *Dear Ez: Letters from William Carlos Williams to Ezra Pound* (Bloomington, Ind., 1985); and *William Carlos Williams-John Sanford, A Correspondence*, commentary by John Sanford (Julian Shapiro) (Santa Barbara, Calif., 1984), shows once again the kindness Williams offered younger writers. These letters from half a century ago are written from the early 1930s through the 1940s. Thomas Parkinson's essay on Williams and Pound in *Ezra Pound Among the Poets* (ed. George Bornstein, Chicago, 1985) makes further good use of unpublished materials. James Laughlin's collection, *Pound as Wuz: Essays and Lectures on Ezra Pound* (St. Paul, Minn., 1987), also includes references to Williams.

Bernard Duffey's *A Poetry of Presence: The Writing of William Carlos Williams* (Madison, Wis., 1986) is an important study. Duffey uses the critical perspective of Kenneth Burke, a longtime friend of Williams, to treat all Williams's writing, not only the poems. He draws vocabulary

from Burke's *A Grammar of Motives* ("scene," "agent," "purpose," "act")
in order to define Williams's art as kinetic rather than static. For example,
Duffey points out that Williams's use of scene is usually bound up with
act: "Williams makes the American scene the occasion either of act or
of act's denial or perversion, and act in turn becomes the retroactive
shaper of scene." By providing new and valid terms for the critic, along
with his customarily insightful reading of Williams's work, Duffey's
book makes a valuable contribution.

In addition to Harold Bloom's *William Carlos Williams*, one of the
Chelsea House collections of reprinted materials, the only other book
that dealt with Williams's writing in 1986 was Margaret Dickie's *On the
Modernist Long Poem* (Iowa City). In placing *Paterson* with the *Cantos, The
Bridge*, and *The Waste Land*, Dickie provides some useful parameters for
discussion. Her attention, however, does not yield much new information.

Whereas David Frail's *The Early Politics and Poetics of William Carlos
Williams* (Ann Arbor, Mich., 1987) builds on a less than complete foundation of earlier criticism and therefore draws some inaccurate conclusions,
Kerry Driscoll's *William Carlos Williams and the Maternal Muse* (Ann Arbor,
Mich., 1987) presents much fresh material to create an important new
angle of vision for the poet's main writings. Driscoll thinks that Williams's
relationship with his artistic, strong-willed Puerto Rican mother dominated his life, and the fact that Mrs. Williams lived with her son's family
for much of the last quarter of her life (she lived to be 102) meant that
the bond was not limited to Williams's childhood years. His concern
with androgynous impulses, with what he called "the female principle,"
and with the all-encompassing rationale for life's choices that shows so
clearly in the five books of *Paterson* can all be traced to the influence,
and the ambiguity, of his mother's hold on his psyche. Driscoll sees *Yes,
Mrs. Williams* as a key text in Williams's oeuvre.

One of the most important essays on Williams's work in the last few
years anticipates Driscoll's book. "Mrs. Williams's William Carlos" by
Julio Marzan (*Reinventing the Americas: Comparative Studies of Literature of
the United States and Spanish America*, ed. Bell Gale Chevigny and Gari
Laguardia, Cambridge, England, 1986) points out Williams's uneasiness
with his mother's Puerto Rican origin. Although Spanish was the language spoken in the Williams home when the boys were small, Williams
pretended in retrospect that they spoke French, and he often attributed
much of his rearing to his English grandmother. His avoidance of his
mother's language and nationality was more than ambivalence. Marzan
asserts that "Williams gives signs of being psychologically blocked from
writing about Elena's life in a manner that does not hint of either the
historical persona's shame or the poet's condescension." Williams's
privileging of the Anglo-American over the Spanish could not disguise
his interest in Latin American writers, his Spanish past, and his language

affinity. But his writing about his mother, which Marzan calls sentimental and given to self-deception, shows the conflicts he felt about having to claim that culture.

Vera M. Kutzinski makes some of the same points in *Against the American Grain: Myth and History in William Carlos Williams, Jay Wright, and Nicolas Guillén* (Baltimore, Md., 1987). Her thesis is that "American" writing should more properly be called "New World" writing and that a text such as Williams's *In the American Grain* is seminal. Kutzinski notes that Williams was ever ready to broaden existing definitions of literature, of American experience, and of knowledge; and his example makes him one of the crucial modernists. Particularly in his role as creator of American myth, Williams has not yet been recognized sufficiently. Kutzinski's reading of Williams's work, and her placement of him within key contexts for future exploration of "New World" art, make this an important study.

Lisa M. Steinman's chapter on Williams in *Made in America: Science, Technology, and American Modernist Poets* (New Haven, Conn., 1987) also connects the poet with efforts to remake poetry in the light of developments in science and technology. She correctly places Williams in the forefront of those efforts—witness many of his metaphors for imagination and creation—and her chief contribution is seeing the way his efforts dovetailed with those of Marianne Moore, Wallace Stevens, and others.

Other recent studies of Williams include Geoffrey H. Movius's *The Early Prose of William Carlos Williams, 1917–1925* (New York, 1988), a perhaps overextended consideration of this early but significant work, and Peter Schmidt's *William Carlos Williams, The Arts, and Literary Tradition* (Baton Rouge, La., 1988), a survey of Williams's amalgam of sources for his verbal work and the way those sources either drew from, or broke with, existing aesthetic traditions during the five decades of Williams's active practice as a writer. Marjorie Perloff wrote the chapter on Williams for *Voices & Visions* (ed. Helen Vendler, New York, 1987), and David Perkins includes much material on Williams in the second volume of his *A History of Modern Poetry: Modernism and After* (Cambridge, Mass., 1987).

Audrey T. Rodgers's *Virgin and Whore: The Image of Women in the Poetry of William Carlos Williams* (Jefferson, N.C., 1987) is a good source study of Williams's use of female and feminist imagery, but the book does not go much beyond listing and classifying. Perhaps a more useful focus would have been on the ways the feminine principle activated Williams's imagination and the kinds of metaphor he chose to represent that all-significant principle. Of corollary interest is Theodora R. Graham's major essay, "Williams, Flossie, and the Others: The Aesthetics of Sexuality" (*ConL*, Summer 1987). Graham deals with some of the troubling critical problems that Rodgers's book does not mention—the various identities of the lover personae that Williams creates throughout his career, his need to maintain Flossie as stable figure in his existence while yet devaluing her role, and what possible force the ambivalence of his primary relationship gave to his artistic life.

Other valuable essays in these past few years of Williams criticism include James F. Knapp's "Not Wholeness but Multiplicity: The Primitivism of William Carlos Williams" (*Mosaic*, Winter 1987); Michel Oren's "Williams and Gris: A Borrowed Aesthetic" (*ConL*, Summer 1985); James Paul Gee's "The Structure of Perception in the Poetry of William Carlos Williams: A Stylistic Analysis" (*PoT*, 1985); Jay Rogoff's "Pound-Foolishness in *Paterson*" (*JML*, Summer 1987); Sandra M. Gilbert's "Purloined Letters: William Carlos Williams and 'Cress'" (*WCWR*, Fall 1985), as well as many other essays in the *William Carlos Williams Review*, which consistently includes work of high caliber.

Thomas Wolfe

Richard S. Kennedy

I BIBLIOGRAPHY

George R. Preston, Jr.'s *Thomas Wolfe: A Bibliography* (1943) remains the standard descriptive bibliography of Wolfe's works, but its section on criticism and reviews has been superseded by John S. Phillipson's excellent *Thomas Wolfe: A Reference Guide* (Boston, 1977), which provides full annotation for books and articles and lists doctoral dissertations and foreign publications. The arrangement of publications is year by year so that the rise of Wolfe's reputation and the shifts that it underwent over the decades may be observed. The work is supplemented by Phillipson's "Thomas Wolfe: A Reference Guide Updated" (*RALS*, Spring 1981), which brings the listing up to 1981, although many 1981 items are missing. Phillipson also offers a current bibliography, fully annotated, in each issue of the *Thomas Wolfe Review*. The bibliography of Wolfe's works in Preston's book will be superseded by Carol Johnston's *Thomas Wolfe: A Descriptive Bibliography* when it is published by the University of Pittsburgh Press in its Pittsburgh bibliographical series in 1987.

Aldo P. Magi, in "Thomas Wolfe: A Publishing Chronology" (*TWN*, Fall 1982), provides a list of Wolfe's publications from "A Field in Flanders" (1917) up to *The Mountains* (1970). *A Thomas Wolfe Collection* (An Exhibition of Books Held at the Ohio University Library, March 1–April 17, 1977) by Duane Schneider (Athens, Ohio) lists many variant editions of books by and about Wolfe. A checklist of scholarship and criticism, "Thomas Wolfe," by Richard S. Kennedy, appears in Louis D. Rubin, Jr.'s *A Bibliographical Guide to the Study of Southern Literature* (Baton Rouge, La., 1969) together with a brief treatment of Wolfe's reputation since 1950. Some evidence of the extent of that reputation is made clear in Morton I. Teicher's "A Bibliography of Books with Selections by Thomas Wolfe" (*BB*, Oct.–Dec. 1981). There are 339 items listed.

Theodore V. Theobald has supplied "Additions to Wolfe Bibliography" (*TWN*, Spring 1981), a clutter of items that do not appear in Phillipson's reference guide or in Elmer Johnson's "Thomas Wolfe: A Checklist" (1970), most of them reviews of books about Wolfe.

II EDITIONS

Three of Wolfe's four novels remain in print in their original trade editions by his two publishers, Charles Scribner's Sons and Harper and Row. *The Web and the Rock* is temporarily out of print in its hardcover edition. Reprints of *Look Homeward, Angel* and *You Can't Go Home Again* have also been issued in library binding. Inexpensive reprints, both in hardcover and paper, have come and gone over the years. At present, all the novels and his two collections of short fiction are available in paper.

The reprint of *Look Homeward, Angel* in the Modern Library Giant series is no longer available, nor is the deluxe edition illustrated by Douglas Gorsline. Scribner's launched the Hudson River edition (same plates as the trade edition) in 1979 to celebrate the fiftieth anniversary of *Look Homeward, Angel*. In 1977 the Franklin Library prepared a special edition with illustrations by Alan Reingold as a part of their series "The 100 Greatest Masterpieces of American Literature."

Most readers of *Look Homeward, Angel* come to it through the Contemporary Classics edition, a paperback which unfortunately omits the epigraph from the title page. Maxwell Perkins's essay "Thomas Wolfe," which serves as an introduction to this edition, contains a major factual error. This essay was the last piece of writing from Perkins's hand, and he was subject to failures of memory in his later years. He states, "and in truth the extent of cutting in [*Look Homeward, Angel*] has somehow come to be greatly exaggerated. Really, it was more a matter of reorganization." Examination of the manuscript shows that statement to be untrue. Perkins recommended that Wolfe shift only one episode, the account of Gant's return from California, now chapter 7. It had originally been a part of chapter 14, the awakening of Altamont on a spring morning. As for cutting, the eleven-hundred-page typescript was reduced to about eight hundred pages.

Duane Schneider, in "American Editions of *Look Homeward, Angel*" (*TWN*, Fall 1979), describes editions of the novel from 1929 to 1977 and gives the titles of other works that contain extensive selections from the book. Jean Michelet, in *L'Ange exilé* (Lausanne, 1982), has provided a complete translation of *Look Homeward, Angel* into French. Two earlier translations had omitted some material. For a review see Michel Braudeau's "Wolfe: le génie de univers" (*L'Express*, 24 Sept. 1982), which finds Wolfe resembling both Hugo and Rabelais.

Of Time and the River also appeared in a Hudson River edition and, together with *Look Homeward, Angel*, was a special offering of the Book-of-the-Month Club to its members in 1979. The former two-volume paperback edition has now been squeezed into a bulky Contemporary Classics edition. Also in 1979, *From Death to Morning* was published by the Franklin Library in a special edition, illustrated by Uldis Klavins, as part of their series "The Collected Stories of the World's Greatest Writers."

The University of Pittsburgh Press issued a paper edition of *A Western Journey* in 1968, but scholars will prefer to consult the more accurate transcription that was included in *The Notebooks of Thomas Wolfe* (1970). *The Story of a Novel*, Wolfe's account of his early career, and *Writing and Living*, his speech about his later career, have been published together under the title, *The Autobiography of a Novelist* (Cambridge, Mass., 1983), with a preface by Leslie Field. The text of *Writing and Living* has been prepared for the general reader. But scholars will still be wise to consult the original edition, *Thomas Wolfe's Purdue Speech: "Writing and Living,"* edited by William Braswell and Leslie Field (1964), which records Wolfe's revisions and deletions. Field's article, "A 'True Text' Experience: Thomas Wolfe and Posthumous Publication," in *Thomas Wolfe of North Carolina* (ed. H. G. Jones, Chapel Hill, N.C., 1982; hereinafter referred to as *TWNC*), describes the editorial problems that he and Braswell faced, as well as the search for and location of the pages missing from the manuscript. *Mannerhouse: A Play in a Prologue and Four Acts* (ed. Louis D. Rubin, Jr. and John L. Idol, Jr. Baton Rouge, La., 1985) is a new edition based on the "Bernstein" typescript that Wolfe submitted to dramatic producers in the mid-1920s. The excellent commentary on the text and background of the play by Idol points out the differences between this version and the one that Edward Aswell had revised, cut, and rearranged for publication in 1948. Aswell's changes may have improved the play for the production by New Stages that he was trying to bring about, but they went into print without any acknowledgment of Aswell's editorial presence. Rubin provides a critical introduction emphasizing the relation between the play and Wolfe's later work.

Welcome to Our City, A Play in Ten Scenes (ed. Richard S. Kennedy, Baton Rouge, La., 1983) is the version that was produced at Harvard in 1923. Wolfe's longer, final version had appeared in *Esquire* (Oct. 1957).

A number of short works, either unpublished or uncollected, have seen publication in recent years. *A Prologue to America*, with a foreword by Aldo P. Magi, was issued in a limited edition by Croissant (Athens, Ohio, 1978). "No More Rivers" appears in the appendix of *Beyond Love and Loyalty* (ed. Richard S. Kennedy, Chapel Hill, N.C., 1983). The Thomas Wolfe Society, an international organization founded in 1979 (membership about five hundred), has printed *London Tower*, with a prefatory note by Aldo P. Magi (Akron, Ohio, 1980), Wolfe's first publication aside from student work, a travel sketch he sent to the *Asheville Citizen* in 1925; *The Streets of Durham, or Dirty Work at the Crossroads* (Akron, Ohio, 1982), a topical farce written in doggerel verse, a product of Wolfe's undergraduate years; and *K-19: Salvaged Pieces* (Akron, Ohio, 1983), a reproduction of the proem and part of chapter 1, "The Station," that had been prepared as a book salesman's dummy for "K-19," Wolfe's abandoned second novel. John L. Idol, Jr. who supplied the foreword for this last item, explaining its background, also added the chapter "K-19," the nostalgic description of a pullman car.

The Train and the City, a 1933 short story which had never been reprinted, was published by the Society (Akron, Ohio, 1984). In the introduction, Richard S. Kennedy points out that "it is the first example of Wolfe's later practice of taking materials he had written for various other purposes and weaving them together, giving them another fictional existence." In 1986 the Society issued a major work, *The Hound of Darkness* (Akron, Ohio), a panorama of nighttime America in fourteen scenes, set on 18 June 1916. In his foreword, John L. Idol, Jr. finds that this experimental work gives "the total effect of something operatic." Wolfe's short novel, *The Good Child's River*, that was later partly incorporated into *The Web and the Rock*, is being edited by Suzanne Stutman and will be published by the University of North Carolina Press in 1990.

Two editions of Wolfe's prize-winning undergraduate essay, *The Crisis in Industry*, were issued in facsimile in 1978. The first one, with an attached "Prolegomena to Thomas Wolfe's A Crisis in Industry" by Richard Walser, was printed by the Loom Press, Chapel Hill, North Carolina, in a limited edition of three hundred numbered copies. Because it had not been authorized by the Estate of Thomas Wolfe, which held the copyright, this edition was ordered destroyed. (A few copies, however, are still extant in private hands.) The second facsimile issue was printed in an edition of two hundred copies by the Palaemon Press, Charlotte, North Carolina.

III MANUSCRIPTS AND LETTERS

1 Research Collections

The William B. Wisdom Collection of Thomas Wolfe at the Houghton Library, which holds the manuscripts of all of Wolfe's work, his notes and working drafts, galley proofs, letters, diaries, first editions, personal library, and miscellaneous papers, continues to be the essential research center for scholars. Over fifty collections have been added to it, including valuable files of the research materials of Elizabeth Nowell, the letters of Wolfe to Elaine Westall Gould, and the papers of Edward Aswell. The collections have now been amalgamated and indexed. Rodney Dennis, in "The William B. Wisdom Collection of Thomas Wolfe," in *Thomas Wolfe: A Harvard Perspective* (ed. Richard Kennedy, Athens, Ohio, 1983; hereinafter referred to as *TWHP*), describes how the collection was formed. To use the collection, scholars must obtain permission from the Estate of Thomas Wolfe, 7 West 51st St., New York 10019. Paul Gitlin, in "Problems and Policies of Administering the Estate of Thomas Wolfe"

(*TWHP*), explains his responsibilities as Administrator C.T.A. for the Wolfe heirs, how he differs from earlier administrators, why the material has restrictions, how one obtains permission to use the collection, and what some of the major projects are that have drawn upon the Wolfe papers at Harvard. A number of important items in the collection still remain unpublished, for example, "O Lost," the original version of *Look Homeward, Angel* and "Passage to England," Wolfe's first extended work of prose narrative.

The Thomas Wolfe Collection at the University of North Carolina, which holds valuable materials associated with Wolfe's Chapel Hill days, as well as letters and papers of Wolfe's mother, his sister Mabel Wolfe Wheaton, and his brother Fred Wolfe, has likewise continued to grow. Edward Aswell's letters to the Wolfe family about Wolfe's posthumous publications have been added, as well as further gifts from members of the Wolfe family. For a detailed description, see H. G. Jones's "I Have A Thing to Tell You—The Thomas Wolfe Collection" (*TWN*, Spring 1978); H. G. Jones's "The North Carolina Collection and Thomas Wolfe" (*TWNC*); and Francis Weaver's "The Thomas Wolfe Collection" (*TWNC*). For a description of the photograph collection, see Jerry Cotten's "The Thomas Wolfe Photographs: A Problem of Preservation and Accessibility," (*North Carolina Libraries*, Spring 1980). To consult the Wolfe manuscripts, one must obtain permission from the Estate of Thomas Wolfe.

The other major collections are open to researchers without restrictions. The Pack Memorial Library in Asheville, North Carolina, has built over the years an admirable collection of published materials by and about Wolfe. The collection is especially strong in foreign editions of Wolfe's work and in material about Wolfe's native town and its surroundings. A card catalogue of the collection is available for the researcher.

The Braden-Hachett Thomas Wolfe Collection at 834 Hudson Street, Memphis, Tennessee 38112, houses a rich collection of materials relating to the Wolfe family: letters of Wolfe's grandfather, father, mother, brothers, and sisters; documents about W. O. Wolfe's business affairs; Henry Westall's researches in the Westall genealogy; editions of Wolfe's books; photographs, legal papers, and miscellaneous Wolfeana. The bulk of the collection was formed from the Wolfe family papers in the possession of Fred Wolfe, the last surviving member of Wolfe's immediate family. A loose-leaf catalogue, *The Braden-Hatchett Thomas Wolfe Collection*, has been published by Croissant and Co., P.O. Box 282, Athens, Ohio 45701.

St. Mary's College Library in Raleigh, North Carolina, has developed a valuable Wolfe Collection in recent years. Building on Dr. John O. Fulenwider's collection of first editions and Wolfeana, the librarian, Andrea Brown, has recently acquired the papers of George McCoy, Edgar Wolf [sic] and Richard Walser, plus the Theodore Theobald collection of books and clippings. In "The McCoy Papers" (*TWN*, Spring 1981),

Richard Walser describes the letters from and about Wolfe and McCoy's research notes concerning Wolfe's ancestry and early life.

A private collection, especially strong in secondary sources and Wolfeana, has been developed by Aldo P. Magi, 415 Meigs St., Sandusky, Ohio 44870. Magi has been very helpful to researchers in answering queries. For a description of the collection, see John S. Phillipson's "A Collector Is Born" (*TWN*, Spring 1977).

2 Published Letters and Manuscripts

The most important Wolfe publication of the last decade is *My Other Loneliness: The Selected Letters of Thomas Wolfe and Aline Bernstein* (ed. Suzanne Stutman, Chapel Hill, N.C., 1983) with a helpful introduction by the editor that gives a full account of Aline Bernstein's life, the love affair between her and Wolfe from 1926 to the mid-1930s, and a discussion of the fictional works that each one based upon that relationship: Mrs. Bernstein's *Three Blue Suits* and *The Journey Down*, Wolfe's *The Web and the Rock* and *You Can't Go Home Again*. The letters themselves reveal Wolfe's passion and jealousy in love as well as his vigorous response to life during the years he was writing *Look Homeward, Angel*. They show Mrs. Bernstein tender and maternal in her care for the young genius whom she discovered and encouraged in the midsummer of her life. A group of Wolfe's letters in the middle of the book, written while he was in Europe in 1928, are marvelous travel reports as well as indications of Wolfe's anguish in trying to decide what to do with his life now that he had finished his first novel and could not find a publisher. The letters in the later part of the book record Wolfe's pain as he struggled, with paranoid hysteria, to free himself from this liaison. Mrs. Bernstein's letters show her distress as she doggedly persisted in pursuing him and accusing him of abandoning her. No documents from the Wolfe writings show quite so clearly that he was teetering at the edge of breakdown. This volume is supplemented by the Wolfe Society publication of *The Cablegrams and Postcards of Thomas Wolfe and Aline Bernstein* (Akron, Ohio, 1985), with a running commentary by Suzanne Stutman and illustrations of all the postcard scenes.

A very different picture of Wolfe emerges from *Beyond Love and Loyalty: The Letters of Thomas Wolfe and Elizabeth Nowell* (ed. Richard S. Kennedy, Chapel Hill, N.C., 1983). In this correspondence with his literary agent, Wolfe is seen to be the artist trying to support himself with his writing, striving to meet the demands of magazine editors, who always found his short fiction too long. In the stable personality and never-failing good sense of Miss Nowell, we see how fortunate Wolfe was in this literary relationship and how her help and guidance contributed to his success. Kennedy's introduction, which describes and assesses their professional friendship, had appeared earlier as "Thomas Wolfe and Elizabeth Nowell: A Unique Relationship" (*SAQ*, Spring 1982).

Charmian Green, in "Wolfe's Stonecutter Once Again: An Unpublished Episode" (*MissQ*, Fall 1977), prints a manuscript draft, found in the University of North Carolina Library, which shows that Wolfe was beginning to develop the character of W. O. Gant as early as the Harvard period. Rainer Lengeler's "Thomas Wolfe and S. T. Coleridge" (*N&Q*, Sept. 1973) points out that the manuscript fragment "Im Dunkeln Wald," which Hans Helmcke had published in *Die Familie im Romanwerk von Thomas Wolfe* (Heidelberg, 1967), was not by Wolfe but was Wolfe's transcript of Coleridge's "The Wanderings of Cain." Charles Scribner III, in "Crying Wolfe" (*Vanity Fair*, Oct. 1983), publishes Wolfe's verses, "Last Poem—Brooklyn 1934," a poet's cry for the return of his lyric powers, which was found in 1982 crammed in the back of a drawer of Maxwell Perkins's desk at Scribner's.

"Chronology" (*TWN*, Fall 1979) is an important find in the Wolfe Collection at the University of Minnesota. It begins "Jan 1—10—1900—I was conceived" and continues in autobiographical notes up to early July 1901. Although the editors do not say so, this is the missing page or pages from the beginning of Wolfe's so-called "Autobiographical Outline," his working notes for *Look Homeward, Angel*, in the Houghton Library.

Kathleen and Clayton Hoagland's "Terry, Wolfe, and the Biography that Never Was" (*TWN*, Fall 1977) gives an account of the manuscript materials found in the possession of John Terry, the official biographer of Wolfe, at the time of his death. These included a large selection of manuscripts he had taken from the Wolfe Estate fifteen years earlier and refused to return when the Wolfe papers were sold to William Wisdom. They have now been restored to the Houghton Library. Terry (the "Jerry Alsop" of *The Web and the Rock*) did not write a word of the biography during the fifteen years of his exclusive right to do so.

Jerry Cotten, who has recently organized the matchless collection of Wolfe photographs in the University of North Carolina Library, in "The Last Photographs of Thomas Wolfe" (*TWN*, Fall 1979) prints four group photographs taken in Seattle, July 1938, and identifies the people who appear with Wolfe in the pictures.

From time to time controversy has swirled around Wolfe—about his style, his methods of composition, his unflattering portraiture of living persons for his fictional characters, and about the editorial assistance that Perkins provided. In the last decade controversy has arisen about the editing of his posthumous novels. A minor skirmish began when Patrick Miehe, a Harvard bibliographer, in "The Outline of Thomas Wolfe's Last Book" (*HLB*, Oct. 1973; reprinted in Phillipson), asserted that the typescript which Richard Kennedy had published in an appendix to *The Window of Memory* (1962) and had given the title "Thomas Wolfe's Rough Outline of his Last Book" was the work of Edward Aswell. Kennedy replied in "Thomas Wolfe's Last Manuscript" (*HLB*, Apr. 1975;

nedy replied in "Thomas Wolfe's Last Manuscript" (*HLB*, Apr. 1975; reprinted in Phillipson), proving that it was composed by Wolfe and typewritten by his secretary.

A more serious controversy began with John Halberstadt's "The Making of Thomas Wolfe's Posthumous Novels" (*YR*, Autumn 1980), which restated some of the findings that Kennedy had published in *The Window of Memory* about Edward Aswell's shaping of Wolfe's later novels but went on to accuse Aswell of unethical editorial practices and to declare that Aswell was "the dominant contributor to the books that bore Wolfe's name." Halberstadt's next activities were more sensational. In a long letter to the *New York Review of Books* (19 Mar. 1981) published under the title "Who Wrote Thomas Wolfe's Last Novels?" he announced his "discovery" that the posthumous novels "were not written by Wolfe in the usual sense but were predominantly the work of an editor named Edward Aswell." Kennedy replied to Halberstadt (*NYRB*, 16 July 1981), declaring that the latter's assertions about Aswell's authorship were false, referring to evidence in *The Window of Memory*, *The Notebooks of Thomas Wolfe*, and in Aswell's description of his editorial duties in "A Note on Thomas Wolfe," appended to *The Hills Beyond*. Meanwhile, Eliot Fremont-Smith in the *Village Voice* (25 Feb. 1981) summarized an interview with Halberstadt, entitled "Wolfegate: Of Time, the River, and Fraud," and pointing to Halberstadt's published accounts, cried literary fraud. Since Halberstadt had published quotations from the Wolfe papers without permission, he was now barred from the Houghton Library for a year. Fremont-Smith thus further fulminated against the Houghton Library and the scholarly profession in general for not honoring Halberstadt's claims. A press release went out from the *Village Voice* entitled "Literary Fraud and Its Implications" and was picked up by several newspapers around the country.

Kennedy's article "The 'Wolfegate' Affair" (*Harvard Mag.*, Sept. 1981) met these charges in some detail, describing Wolfe's work on the manuscript during his last year, his compiling his draft, and Aswell's work as an editor. He concluded that Aswell "tried to the best of his understanding to fulfill Wolfe's intentions, those given him verbally and those discernible in the manuscript itself."

Much of the controversy was clouded by the argument over the Houghton Library's decision to forbid Halberstadt the use of its facilities for a year. Halberstadt's reply to Kennedy, "The 'Creative Editing' of Thomas Wolfe" (*Harvard Mag.*, Jan. 1982), repeats his accusations against Aswell but digresses into the question of his access to the Wolfe papers, which was now denied him by the Wolfe Estate. Halberstadt's complaint about his exclusion from Houghton Library is also voiced in "The Thomas Wolfe Controversy" (*WLB*, Dec. 1981). Eric Strange, in "Who Should Keep the Keys?" (*Chronicle of Higher Education*, May 1981), discusses the case and the general subject of manuscript restrictions in research libraries. Kennedy returned to the argument once more in "Editorial Influence and Authorial Intention" (*TWHP*), which deals with the exhibition in the Houghton Library for the May 1982 meeting of the Wolfe Society, a collection of Wolfe manuscripts that had been especially selected to show editorial changes made by Perkins and Aswell in dealing with Wolfe's work. Kennedy describes in detail the kinds of cuts, rearrangements, and changes Aswell made in Wolfe's final manuscript and why, illustrating his explanation with twelve plates of typescript pages from both *The Web and the Rock* and *You Can't Go Home Again*.

The controversy continued to reverberate in the letters column of the *Harvard Magazine*, the *New York Review of Books*, and the *Chronicle of Higher Education*. The question was frequently raised whether or not Wolfe's posthumous novels should be reedited, but those who advocated it were usually people who had never seen the Wolfe manuscript. The huge draft that Wolfe left behind contained so much material that he himself would have jettisoned—material already published in earlier volumes, fragments of aborted projects, variant versions of episodes—and so many episodes that were either incomplete or incongruent with the other parts that a new editor would have to make the same kinds of judgments that Aswell made—and without the benefit of conversations Aswell had with Maxwell Perkins, Elizabeth Nowell, and even with Wolfe himself. It might, however, be possible to reedit a portion of the manuscript in which the episodes were generally coherent one with another—for example, "The Party at Jack's" or parts of *You Can't Go Home Again* that received the most editorial attention—and thus to satisfy scholarly concerns about the effects of Aswell's editorial hand. Leslie Field's study of Wolfe's final manuscript will be published by the University of Oklahoma Press in 1987. About Wolfe's authorship of the posthumous work, he concludes that "Wolfe wrote, revised, and rewrote as he adhered to his overall plan; Aswell edited."

David Donald, in his afterword to *Look Homeward: A Life of Thomas Wolfe* (Boston, 1987), reports on his close study of every page of Wolfe's manuscript as well as drafts and carbon copies. He judges that "Except for the introductory passages linking the 'books' and for very occasional transitional sentences or paragraphs, Thomas Wolfe wrote these novels. . . . The structure of the novels is also Wolfe's; assisted by Miss Nowell, the editor followed Wolfe's outline for the books. Finally the theme of the books is Wolfe's not Aswell's." However, he finds Aswell's editorial interference "unacceptable": "Greatly exceeding the professional responsibilities of an editor, Aswell took impermissible liberties with Wolfe's manuscript, and his interference seriously eroded the integrity of Wolfe's text." Even so, Donald concedes that "it is not clear that another editor could have made better, or even considerably different, novels out of Wolfe's manuscripts."

IV BIOGRAPHY

1 Biography: Books and Monographs

Elizabeth Nowell's *Thomas Wolfe: A Biography* (1960) and Andrew Turnbull's *Thomas Wolfe* (1968), neither of which is wholly satisfactory, have been superseded by David Donald's *Look Homeward: A Life of Thomas Wolfe*. Donald's biography, carefully organized and beautifully written, is a product of thorough research in all the Wolfe collections and dogged pursuit of testimony from almost every living person who had known Wolfe. It presents Wolfe as a tortured genius, an egoistic personality who burned his energies expressing his responses to life in fiction but who was unable to function successfully as an author without the guidance of editors or mentors. A dark picture of Wolfe emerges, full of racial and ethnic prejudices, crude and selfish indulgences of appetite, and rages against imagined enemies. For judgment as to whether Donald has overemphasized the unpleasant side of Wolfe's personality or not, scholars may consult the two major biographical sources, *The Letters of Thomas Wolfe* (1956) and *The Notebooks of Thomas Wolfe* (1970).

Except for Donald's research, the best biographical work of the past decade has been done by Richard Walser in a book, two monographs, and two articles. His *Thomas Wolfe Undergraduate* (Durham, N.C., 1977) is an exemplary work of biographical research, based on interviews and documents in the Wolfe papers at Harvard and at the University of North Carolina. It is a full account of Wolfe's undergraduate years at Chapel Hill: his courses and textbooks, the friends he socialized with, and the teachers who affected his development, for better or worse. Reading this work, the critic can perceive the selection and emphasis that Wolfe carried out in transforming his experience into autobiographical fiction.

Walser's *Thomas Wolfe's Pennsylvania* (Athens, Ohio, 1978) deals with the ancestry and boyhood of Wolfe's father, W. O. Wolfe, in York Springs, Pennsylvania, as well as Wolfe's visits to his father's kin in the 1930s. Walser's *The Wolfe Family in Raleigh* (Raleigh, N.C., 1976) follows W. O. Wolfe to Raleigh, North Carolina, gives the details of his first two marriages, the story of his daughter Mabel's marriage and life with Ralph Wheaton, and accounts of Thomas Wolfe's visits to Raleigh during undergraduate days and in the 1930s. His articles, "Thomas Westall and His Son William" (*TWN*, Spring 1984) and "Major Thomas Casey Westall" (*TWN*, Fall 1984), provide a first-rate account of Wolfe's Westall ancestry, especially his eccentric grandfather Thomas Casey Westall, upon whom he drew for the characters Major Pentland in *Look Homeward, Angel* and Lafayette Joyner in *The Web and the Rock*.

Carole Klein's *Aline* (New York, 1979), a popular biography of Mrs. Bernstein, gives a lively account of her love affair with Wolfe. Unfortunately, she frequently uses dialogue from both Wolfe and Bernstein's fiction, as if the words had really been spoken. It is, nevertheless, the fullest treatment of Mrs. Bernstein that we are likely to have, and it is a sensitive and understanding appraisal of her relationship with Wolfe. Klein's "In Suffering, A Celebration: Aline Bernstein and Thomas Wolfe" (*TWN*, Spring 1979) offers a brief treatment of the same subject, but also corrects the notion (as stated in the Turnbull biography) that Aline's marriage to Theodore Bernstein was only a marriage of convenience and offers a picture of her warm, solid family life.

At this point it seems appropriate to note Suzanne Stutman's "The Wolfe-Bernstein Letters" (*TWN*, Fall 1982), a sensible overview of the Wolfe-Bernstein correspondence, adapted from her introduction to *My Other Loneliness*. Stutman feels that Wolfe's letters show him unable to love deeply and given to periods of erratic behavior that he called his "madness." He did not see Mrs. Bernstein "as she really was; she became for him almost instantly the composite of all his fantasies." But from this imaginative perspective arose the figure of "Esther Jack," the most fully developed character in Wolfe's later fiction.

A. Scott Berg's *Max Perkins: Editor of Genius* (New York, 1978) is a fully detailed picture of Maxwell Perkins's personal life and his editorial relations with Scribner's authors. Berg's narrative of the Wolfe-Perkins relationship is in broad outline satisfactory but is marred by his lack of understanding of Wolfe's methods and his obvious dislike of Wolfe as a person. The account of Perkins's work with Wolfe on *Of Time and the River* is badly muddled, giving the impression that Perkins's contribution was far greater than it was. For example, Berg quotes a series of revisions that Perkins suggested and dates them very late in the development of the book, whereas these suggestions were made early in 1933 and probably were directed toward the book publication of "No Door." Further, the book has no footnotes but only general references added as "Sources and Notes," thus giving a misleading impression of scholarly authority. The most accurate account of the development of *Of Time and the River* is still that in Kennedy's *The Window of Memory*, together with fuller details in *The Notebooks of Thomas Wolfe*. Two important reviews of Berg's book are C. Hugh Holman's (*SR*, Oct. 1978) and George Core's "Perkins, Commins and Editorial Transaction" (*SoR*, Apr. 1979). Both reviewers contend that Berg is blind to the fact that Perkins had a harmful effect on writers who lacked self-assurance and that he "may have hurt Wolfe almost as much as he helped him." Scholarly opinion, however, is divided on this matter.

Thomas Wolfe Interviewed (ed. Aldo Magi and Richard Walser, Baton Rouge, La., 1985) reprints the interviews that Wolfe gave to newspaper and magazine reporters. In this book, Wolfe, as the earnest, honest, struggling writer, appears in a more attractive light than that found in the biographies.

2 Biography: Shorter Studies

Mrs. Preston Thomas's *The Westall Family Genealogy* (Asheville, N.C., 1966) and William Hatchett's "Some Information to Assist Genealogists Concerning Thomas Wolfe's Maternal Ancestry and Collateral Relationships" (*TWN*, Fall 1983) provide helpful facts about Wolfe's Westall ancestry. Larry E. Tise's "The Thomas Wolfe State Memorial Site" (*TWN*, Spring 1978) gives a history of Julia Wolfe's boarding house, The Old Kentucky Home in Asheville. Wilson Angley's "Thomas Wolfe's *Other* House" (*TWN*, Fall 1981) offers a description of the house at 92 Woodfin Street where Wolfe was born and spent his early childhood.

Caroline North's "Thomas Wolfe in New Orleans: Letters of William H. Fitzpatrick to Andrew Turnbull" (*TWN*, Spring 1980) gives an account of Wolfe's visit to New Orleans in January 1937. Tristram Potter Coffin's "A Custom of Our Clan," in *The Old Ball Game: Baseball in Folklore* (New York, 1971), and Bob Terrell's "Wolfe, Baseball, and Nebraska Crane" (*TWN*, Spring 1980) both identify Jack Corbett, second baseman of the Asheville Tourists 1915–16, as the model for Nebraska Crane in *You Can't Go Home Again*. Terrell reveals that Wolfe was a "pseudo-batboy" for the team in those two years.

Wanda Stanard, in "Thomas Wolfe Called her 'Sheba'," (*The State* [Raleigh, N.C.], June 1979), gives an account of Hortense Roberts Pattison, who taught Wolfe German at the North State School. Mel Groth, in "The Education of Thomas Wolfe: Roberts, Greenlaw, Williams, Baker" (*StAR*, Spring 1974), assesses the influence of several of Wolfe's teachers, beginning with the North State School and going on to the University of North Carolina and Harvard. His discussion is weakened by the fact that he draws largely upon the work of other scholars and on Wolfe's fiction. Groth gives a lively characterization of Wolfe's drama teacher at Chapel Hill in "The Education of Thomas Wolfe II: Frederick Henry Koch, 'The Little Man with the Urge'" (*StAR*, Fall 1975), but he argues unconvincingly that Koch's uncritical enthusiasm was the basis of Wolfe's lack of critical judgment later in his career. Richard Walser's "Wolfe at the Di Society" (*The State* [Raleigh, N.C.], Mar. 1977) summarizes in full detail Wolfe's activities for four years as a member of the Dialectic Literary Society, an undergraduate oratorial and debating club, and lists speeches he gave and topics he debated.

Joseph M. Flora, in "Thomas Wolfe at New York University: His Friendship with Vardis Fisher" (*TWNC*), provides an excellent study of the two young novelists as fellow faculty members in the 1920s. Further, he identifies Wolfe as a fictional character in two of Fisher's novels. Richard S. Kennedy, in "Thomas Wolfe at New York University" (*TWN*, Fall 1981), publishes a chapter which had been cut from his critical study, *The Window of Memory*. Contrary to the implications in Oscar

Cargill's book, *Thomas Wolfe at Washington Square* (1954) that Wolfe was a poor teacher, Kennedy offers evidence that Wolfe was an effective teacher of both composition and literature, although he resented the time he had to take from his creative work. Kwak Hyo-suk's "A Case of East Meeting West" (*Korea Newsreview*, 9 Mar. 1980) describes the friendship between Wolfe and Younghill Kang when they were fellow instructors at New York University.

Guy Owen, in "A Rediscovery of Wolfe's England" (*The State* [Raleigh, N.C.], June 1976), follows Wolfe's footsteps during his four visits to London and offers a brief commentary on his use of English material in his fiction. John S. Phillipson's "Thomas Wolfe Visits Vermont: A Retrospect" (*TWN*, Spring 1977) retraces Wolfe's six-day tour of Vermont in 1933 with Robert Raynolds. Elizabeth Evans, in "Thomas Wolfe's 1937 Visits South: You Can Go Home Again" (*TWN*, Fall 1984), gives an excellent, well-researched account of Wolfe's two sojourns in North Carolina in 1937, showing that Wolfe was well-accepted but that he was so exhausted that he was on the brink of collapse. The article contains full details of the murder trial of Phillip Ray, at which Wolfe gave testimony.

Among the large body of publication about Asheville that mentions Wolfe and provides regional background for his life, three items seem especially worthwhile. Lou Harshaw, in "Someone to be Proud of," in *Asheville: Places of Discovery* (Asheville, N.C., 1980), discusses Wolfe and the members of his family in the Asheville context. Myra Champion's *A Literary Journey* (Asheville, N.C., 1983) is a guide to the principal places in Asheville associated with Wolfe. John L. Idol, Jr., in "Wealth in their Midst: Bill Nye and Thomas Wolfe on the Asheville Vanderbilts" (*TWN*, Fall 1983), describes the development of the Biltmore estate near Asheville and the impact of the Vanderbilt presence on the townspeople. He points out that Nye and Wolfe took a satirical view of the obsequious attitudes that Ashevilleans exhibited toward fabulous wealth.

3 Memoirs: Books and Pamphlets

Elaine Westall Gould, Wolfe's Boston cousin, daughter of Henry Westall, who stood as a model for Wolfe's character "Uncle Bascom," has provided a first-rate memoir in *Look Behind You, Thomas Wolfe: Ghosts of a Common Tribal Heritage* (Hicksville, N.Y., 1976), far superior to the rambling pieces of oral history from the Wolfe family: Hayden Norwood's *The Marble Man's Wife* (1947) and Mabel Wolfe Wheaton's *Thomas Wolfe and His Family* (1961). She gives a picture of the Wolfe and Westall families in the 1890s, of Wolfe at Harvard, and intermittent glimpses of him in later years.

Albert Coates's *Thomas Wolfe As I Knew Him* (Asheville, N.C., 1975) is an excéllent memoir by a lifelong friend who recalls Wolfe in college, at Harvard, and on his later visits to Chapel Hill in 1929 and 1937. Coates, in "Thomas Wolfe As I Remember Him" (*UNC Alumni Review*,

Nov. 1975), reminisces again about Wolfe. William J. Cocke's *Johnny Park Talks of Thomas Wolfe* (Asheville, N.C., 1973) is a detailed memoir by another friend, whom Wolfe depicted as Johnny Park in his fiction. He describes Wolfe at the North State School, at Oxford when Wolfe visited the Rhodes Scholars there in 1926, in New York in 1929, and in Asheville in 1937. Included is a reproduction of the program for the 1916 Shakespeare pageant in Asheville when Wolfe played Prince Hal.

Aldo Magi and Richard Walser have edited the Wolfe Society publication, *Wolfe and Belinda Jelliffe* (Akron, Ohio, 1987), a memoir by Mrs. Smith Ely Jelliffe, who was Wolfe's lover in his later years.

Samuel Marx, in *Thomas Wolfe and Hollywood* (Athens, Ohio 1980), gives an account of Wolfe's visit to the Metro-Goldwyn-Mayer studio in 1935 at the time he was offered a position as a script writer. This is the origin of the apocryphal story that Wolfe spent the night with Jean Harlow.

Clayton Hoagland, in *Thomas Wolfe, Our Friend, 1933–1938* (Athens, Ohio, 1979), draws on pocket and desk diaries and the reminiscences of his wife, Kathleen, for a series of accurate glimpses of Wolfe in the 1930s. Hoagland offers a few further remembrances of Wolfe and his warm and sociable manner in "Thomas Wolfe" (*Literary Sketches*, Sept. 1973 and Mar. 1978).

H. M. Ledig-Rowohlt's *Meeting Two American Giants* (Hamburg, 1965) reprints an earlier article (*ASch*, Spring 1953) in which he describes Wolfe's stays in Berlin in 1935 and 1936. He recalls his trepidation when Wolfe used him as the character "Franz Heilig," who was too critical of the Nazi regime.

4 Memoirs: Articles

There is an extensive list of short memoirs, mostly anecdotal, reflecting all stages of Wolfe's life. A series of four articles appeared in the issues of the *Thomas Wolfe Newsletter* in 1979 and 1980 under the title "Thomas Wolfe Remembered." Mary Louise Wolfe recalls Wolfe's visit to New Orleans when he was a child in 1909. James Howell and J. Y. Jordan have anecdotes of Wolfe's undergraduate years. Charles Tennant visited Wolfe's cabin in Oteen, North Carolina, in the summer of 1937.

Wolfe's nephew, Dr. R. Dietz Wolfe, recalls in "The 'Gants' Remembered" (*TWN*, Spring 1983) W. O. and Julia Wolfe in the early part of the century. Fred Wolfe, in "Christmas at The Old Kentucky Home" (*TWN*, Spring 1978), remembers several Christmases in the Wolfe home, especially one at which Tom, about sixteen years old, had his first encounter with whiskey. Louise Jackson Wright's "It Was in Paris That I Saw Thomas Wolfe" (*LGJ*, Spring 1984) is a memoir by a fellow Ashevillean that includes a remembrance of Tom at the Presbyterian Sunday School. Martha Abshire's "Thomas Wolfe . . . Adolescent" (*Arts Journal*, Oct. 1975) records a brief reminiscence by cousin Louise Wolfe of Tom rehearsing his valedictory address for the North State School. Edwin R. Andrews, in "'A Stranger and Alone,' Friends Reminisce about Thomas Wolfe" (*Mountain Living*, Oct. 1981), records anecdotal memories of Wolfe by several Ashevilleans: Rose and Sanford Brown, Ernest Briggs, James Howell, Harry Blomberg, and Francis Hulme.

M. A. Braswell, a college classmate who was also contemporary with Wolfe at Harvard, has a worthwhile memoir in "College Days with Tom Wolfe" (*The State* [Raleigh, N.C.], Nov. 1976). Phillip Hettleman, who worked on the college newspaper with Wolfe, has an amusing reminiscence in "Thomas Wolfe and the *Tar Heel*" (*TWNC*). Elizabeth Little, who was in the Chapel Hill playwriting group with Wolfe, recalls those days, as well as later evenings in Greenwich Village, in "A Brief Recollection of Thomas Wolfe" (*TWN*, Fall 1978). "Memories of Thomas Wolfe" (*TWNC*) is a valuable gathering of anecdotal reminiscences by fifteen of Wolfe's friends from his undergraduate days, describing him in the Carolina Playmakers, in Horace Williams's Philosophy class, at work on the college newspaper, and at friendly meetings in later years.

Guy Savino, in "Wolfe's First Interview" (*TWN*, Fall 1979), describes Wolfe's apartment at 263 West Eleventh Street in New York and records Wolfe's account of his work on his first novel at night in an unheated loft on Eighth Street. In *Boston's Elinor in Paris* (*TWN*, Fall 1982), Richard Walser interviews Marjorie Fairbanks, who gives her response to appearing as a character in *Of Time and the River* and also declares that Wolfe had rendered the character of Starwick in a way that was unfair to Kenneth Raisbeck. Melville Cane, Wolfe's New York lawyer, offers a clear and careful account of his reading the *Look Homeward, Angel* manuscript for Wolfe and his drawing up Wolfe's will two times, in "Thomas Wolfe: A Memoir" (*ASch*, Autumn, 1972). Louis Sheaffer, in "Memorable Nights in Brooklyn Heights" (*Confrontation*, No. 25–26, 1983) and again in "Tie up Them Loose Cables" and "Wolfe and Sheaffer" (*Brooklyn Bridge Bulletin*, July 1980), describes his chance acquaintance with Wolfe as a Brooklyn neighbor, Wolfe's reading Whitman's "Crossing Brooklyn Ferry" to him, and Wolfe's unpredictable and paranoid hostility when he had too much to drink. Frederic Prokosch, the novelist, recalls Wolfe's assertion that he wanted to be a force in American literature like Melville and Whitman, in "Lunch at Ruby Wang's" (*House and Garden*, Mar. 1983).

John B. Easley, in "Boulder Revisited" (*TWN*, Fall 1980), gives the fullest account of Wolfe's stay in Boulder, Colorado, in 1935. He points out that Wolfe's great success in his lecture at the Writer's Conference may have provoked Bernard DeVoto's spleen, for Wolfe was substituting for DeVoto on the program. Aldo Magi, in "A Visit with Jim Wolf" (*TWN*, Spring 1978), records Edgar (Jim) Wolf's memories of cousin Tom's visits in the 1930s, plus reminiscences of the earlier Wolfe generation. Addie Bradshaw Pegram tells a questionable story of overhearing

Wolfe on the telephone in Asheville in 1937 saying to his mother "You don't mean I can't come home?" in "Anecdote: Wolfe on the Telephone" (*TWN*, Spring 1980). Mary Aswell Doll's "Wolfe's Christmas with the Aswells" (*TWN*, Fall 1983) records her mother's memory of Wolfe at the Aswell home in Chappaqua in 1937 and a trip through Connecticut and upper New York State when Wolfe was thinking about renting a country retreat.

Jerry Cotten, in "Reminiscences of Thomas Wolfe: the KOAC Interviews" (*TWN*, Fall 1982), provides edited transcripts of interviews that were broadcast over station KOAC in Corvallis, Oregon, with Edward Miller and Ray Conway, who made the National Parks trip with Wolfe in 1938, and with James and Theresa Stevens about Wolfe's days in Seattle shortly before his death. Edward M. Miller, in "The Western Journey: Prelude and Aftermath" (*TWN*, Spring 1977), has his own memoir of Wolfe and the occasion that led to the two-week western trip. John Clark Hunt also has news about the National Parks trip that draws upon notes taken by Edward Miller, in "Thomas Wolfe Reflects upon the Big Gorgooby" (*Westways*, May 1974).

Jean Crawford, in "A Dying Giant" (*Vanderbilt Alumnus*, Spring 1974), interviews Annie Laurie Crawford, the Asheville nurse who had met Wolfe in the Seattle hospital and accompanied him on his train journey to Baltimore in his final illness. Elizabeth Evans, in "Wolfe's Final Days: The Correspondence of Elizabeth Nowell and Annie Laurie Crawford" (*TWN*, Fall 1980), published the letters from Crawford, about Wolfe's last days, to Nowell, who was completing her Wolfe biography.

Michael L. Furcolow, M.D., and R. Dietz Wolfe, M.D.'s "Thomas Wolfe: The Enigma of his Death" (*AppalH*, Fall 1975) is an undocumented article, not completely coherent, with a few errors of fact about Wolfe's life, in which Dr. Furcolow, a professor of medicine at the University of Kentucky, suggests that Wolfe may not have died of tuberculosis of the brain but that he may have contracted desert fever, a fungus disease (coccidioidomycosis) during his trip through the Southwest, where the disease is endemic. Furcolow's suspicions led him to check hospital records in Seattle and at Johns Hopkins, but he found most of the Hopkins records were missing. A report of the biopsy of a tissue from Wolfe's brain does still exist, however. It shows no evidence of either coccidioidomycosis or tuberculosis. Dr. Furcolow has not discussed his theory in any medical journal. James Meehan, in "Findings Suggest Another Cause of Tom Wolfe's Death" (*Raleigh News and Observer*, 29 July 1973) and in "Seed of Destruction: The Death of Thomas Wolfe" (*SAQ*, Sept. 1974), draws on Dr. Furcolow's information and reports his hypothesis as if it were a true diagnosis. Wolfe's hospital records have turned up in the Houghton Library, where they join X-rays from the Seattle Hospital. Donald's biography reports that the hospital records show the cause of death as tuberculosis of the brain.

Jane Mayhall, in "The Death of Thomas Wolfe" (*SoR*, Oct. 1982), presents a moving account of a young Wolfe's devotee's response to his death and funeral. Bryan Berger's short book, *Thomas Wolfe: The Final Journey* (West Linn, Oreg., 1984), focuses on Wolfe's sweep through the West on his National Parks trip. It includes a map of Wolfe's journey and eleven photographs of Wolfe during the trip. Edward Miller has contributed a memoir of Wolfe during that two-week period.

V CRITICISM

Despite a large increase in books and articles on Wolfe in the last decade, his work has not attracted major critics, with the notable exception of Malcolm Cowley. Even so, recent critical publication has been more perceptive and judicious than that of previous decades.

1 General Critical Studies

Three critical studies stand out above all others. Malcolm Cowley's "Thomas Wolfe: Homo Scribens," in his *A Second Flowering: Works and Days of the Lost Generation* (New York, 1973), the best short treatment of Wolfe's career, offers an illuminating examination of his creative process. After a sensitive scrutiny of *The Letters of Thomas Wolfe*, Cowley sees him as a man whose "mental operations were completely verbalized," a writer of unusually vivid memory who had an intense need to express his experiences. The result was Wolfe's presenting to the literary public the life of a different order of human beings and their interaction than had even been portrayed in literature. The extraordinary treatment of ordinary activities of life came about partly because of the emotional heights to which Wolfe raised them but also because in his obsessive desire for self-expression he wrote at such great length and in such great detail. What Wolfe admired in Joyce was not the structural and linguistic experiment but the precision and completeness with which he recorded life in Dublin. As a result, *Look Homeward, Angel*, his *Ulysses* book, had vibrancy of life as well as the excessive length that demanded editorial trimming. For his next books, Wolfe's attempts at thematic unity failed because his autobiographical episodes proliferated beyond any planned scheme. Cowley was the first to recognize, in earlier periodical articles, that Wolfe's natural unit of construction was the episode and that he had trouble connecting them for his novels. Thus he characterizes Wolfe as resembling an ancient bard who improvised from his store of materials, using stylistic formulations that frequently were repeated so that he often created, in his episodic narratives, "an epic movement with its surge and thunder."

C. Hugh Holman's *The Loneliness at the Core: Studies in Thomas Wolfe* (Baton Rouge, La., 1975), the best book-length critical study in recent years, is a series of critical meditations on how to account for the value of Wolfe's work without being blind to his limitations. Holman considers such questions as Wolfe and the problem of point of view, his use of autobiography, his developing mastery of the novella form, his contribution to the Southern Renaissance, his relationship to European literature, and his place in the epic tradition. The final chapter deals with the aesthetic questions that Wolfe poses. Holman sees the multivolume Wolfe narrative as an American epic whose plot may be described as "the experiences of Wolfe (under the guises of Eugene Gant and George Webber) as he moved from childhood and the 'meadows of sensation' through adolescence to maturity in his search for identity as an American." The plot is then bulked out by "episodes," many of them of novella length, which provide development and amplification. The appropriate epic treatment is carried out through elevated language and through characters and incidents of enlarged dimension. Holman's book incorporates all his previously published articles, plus "Thomas Wolfe, *Scribner's*, and the 'Blest Nouvelle'" from *Essays Mostly on Periodical Publishing in America: A Collection in Honor of Clarence Gohdes* (ed. James Woodress, Durham, N.C., 1973).

Monique Decaux, in *La création romanesque chez Thomas Wolfe* (Paris, 1977), has at last provided a worthwhile psychoanalytic approach to Wolfe's work. She examines his neurotic manifestations thoroughly and shows how he uses his neurosis creatively. In a neo-Freudian reading, she sees Wolfe as evoking "le sombre romantisme." At the heart of his work is the struggle with the mother figure: Eliza as the phallic mother, Aunt Maw as the evil mother, and Esther Jack in a dual role as both benign and demonic. Serving as a countervalue is the celebration of the father figure in full phallic vigor with the mythic power of the conqueror, whom the protagonist must emulate. It is a loss to Wolfe criticism that Decaux died before writing the final chapter, notes for which indicate that she planned to discuss the problem of the suitability of this conquering figure in democratic America. Wolfe solves it, she feels, by emphasizing the father as a working man, a craftsman who exercises power with his hands.

Elizabeth Evans's *Thomas Wolfe* (MLM, New York, 1984) is a well-documented, intelligent introduction to Wolfe's life and work. Although the commentary on the novels is largely a summary of their narratives, the treatment of the pieces of short fiction in chapter 4 is an excellent critical overview of Wolfe's total publication in short forms. The final chapter is a well-balanced evaluation of Wolfe's stylistic variety, his social attitudes, and his dedication to his vocation. Although Evans finds Wolfe "a failed artist," she acknowledges that he was "a man of great talent who, when subject matter, length, and style were harmonious, produced fiction of the first order."

Louis D. Rubin, Jr.'s *Thomas Wolfe: A Collection of Critical Essays* (TCV, Englewood Cliffs, N.J., 1973) gathers chapters and articles by W. M. Frohock, Alfred Kazin, John Peale Bishop, Bernard DeVoto, Maxwell Perkins, Wright Morris, William Styron, Pamela Hansford Johnson, Thomas Moser, Morris Beja, Richard S. Kennedy, and C. Hugh Holman, all of which were noticed in earlier editions of this book. Rubin's introduction, "The Sense of Being Young," is the best of a number of articles Rubin has written on Wolfe over the years. He recognizes that Wolfe provides a powerful appeal when he depicts the experiences of his youthful protagonists but that his rhetorical commentary attempting to validate those experiences as universal is only successful when the reader is convinced of its truth. Thus Rubin agrees with Holman that it was a mistake for Perkins to persuade Wolfe to change the narrative point of view in *Of Time and the River* from first to third person: the excessive valuation of Eugene's emotional responses is no longer that of a confessional voice but has become that of authorial opinion. A perceptive critic will recognize this difficulty but the general reader, especially the young reader, will respond indiscriminately to Wolfe's books because the variety and range of the fictional experience is compelling for him. Nevertheless, since Wolfe presents a "dramatized record of a talented and romantic young writer's experience of being an artist in America," his work succeeds in spite of its flaws, and the more we discover about Wolfe's methods of composition, especially as a writer of novellas, the more we need to offer new critical assessments of his achievement.

John Phillipson's edition, *Critical Essays on Thomas Wolfe* (CEAmL, Boston, 1985; hereinafter referred to as Phillipson), reprints twenty-one articles on Wolfe from the 1970s and 1980s, all of which receive comment in the present essay. The book includes work by many leading Wolfe scholars and critics: Richard Walser, John Hagan, Francis E. Skipp, Guy Owen, Leslie Field, James D. Boyer, and Richard S. Kennedy. Two original essays by Darlene H. Unrue and Webb Salmon are added to the collection. Phillipson has contributed an introduction that briefly summarizes Wolfe scholarship and criticism of the last fifty years.

Fritz Heinrich Ryssel's *Thomas Wolfe* (New York, 1972) is a translation from the German edition of 1963, slightly revised, of his perceptive critical introduction to Wolfe's writings, from the early plays down to the posthumous volumes. He concludes that Wolfe's "sense of self decreased as his sense of life grew. As he discovered the world, he turned to the humiliated and the reviled." Leo Gurko's *Thomas Wolfe: Beyond the Romantic Ego* (New York, 1975) is an undistinguished critical overview of Wolfe's work. After a sensible discussion of eight clichés about Wolfe's work, he offers the vague conclusion that Wolfe broke free of the novel form and "thus forged for himself an instrument by which the exploration of life . . . in terms of its ultimate possibilities could be sustained."

Paschal Reeves, in *Thomas Wolfe: The Critical Reception* (New York 1974), discusses Wolfe's reputation over a forty-year period and reprints the principal reviews of all of Wolfe's publications in book form, from *Look Homeward, Angel* (1929) to *The Notebooks of Thomas Wolfe* (1970). Title pages of each book are reproduced in facsimile. Reeves has also provided in the *Merrill Guide to Thomas Wolfe* (Columbus, Ohio, 1972) a brief but perceptive introduction, emphasizing "the polarization of response" to Wolfe's work.

John Hagan's "'The Whole Passionate Enigma of Life': Thomas Wolfe on Nature and the Youthful Quest" (*TWN*, Spring 1983) is an excellent consideration of Wolfe's ultimate theme. Hagan points out that in addition to the Romantic view of life, Wolfe balanced it with a naturalistic view that saw "man's insignificance in the cosmos," and conveyed it by means of natural symbols of earth, sky, river, and sea. This double vision presents the protagonist with "the whole passionate enigma of life." Further, the protagonist, living in such a world, pursues the archetypal pattern of the Youthful Quest in search of the Ultimate Answer or the Good Place, a quest which is always foiled. Yet, these failures are not to be regarded as futile, for these utopian dreams and strivings have value in themselves. Thus emerges the theme of the inevitable conflict between two species of good and a recognition that "to reject and accept the Youthful Quest itself" is to acknowledge "the complexity of reality."

Among several valuable studies by Japanese scholars, the most outstanding is Fumio Arahawa's *Thomas Wolfe: The Scheme of His Mind and His Novels* (Tokyo, 1965), an excellent, though sometimes oddly phrased, view of Wolfe's achievement. Since his work is autobiographical, Arahawa argues, Wolfe's insatiable hunger affects the characterization of his hero, making him an outsider doomed to wander and seek forever. Wolfe also tries to be the spokesman for the youth of America without losing that questing individuality. This represents "the romantic consciousness of provinciality," a cast of mind that seeks enrichment of experience in urban centers but in so doing must leave the province and continue to yearn for what has been given up. Dissatisfaction with the urban culture leads the hero to seek also for some universal absolute or some spiritual father. He finally comes to realize that to be victorious in his newer world he must be both an artist and a social critic of that world. Arahawa judges that Wolfe was not able to carry out his scheme completely, and it remains more an aspiration than a fulfillment.

Makiko Mitsushima's "A Study of Thomas Wolfe: Wolfe's Literary Works as a Record of his Ego" (*Essays and Studies in British and American Literature* [Tokyo], Spring 1975) is an admirable introduction to Wolfe's work, a treatment of the four-novel saga, emphasizing a "thematic development that reflects spiritual growth." Kayoko Miyauchi's "On Thomas Wolfe—Search for a Mother" (*Senzokuronso* [Senzoku Gakuen Univ. Junior College, Tokyo], 1974) is an exploration of Wolfe's characterizations of women and his handling of the experience of love. Miyauchi takes special interest in the hero's struggle to break away from the mother figure.

C. Hugh Holman, in "The Dwarf on Wolfe's Shoulder" (*SoR*, Apr. 1977), returns to his criticism of Perkins' editorial role in Wolfe's publications. He argues that Perkins damaged Wolfe as a writer by discouraging him from publishing "K-19" and other works and guiding him to continue the Eugene Gant story in *Of Time and the River*. Wolfe's talent lay in the short novel, not extended narrative.

John L. Idol, Jr., in "Thomas Wolfe and Painting" (*Arts and Letters*, Spring 1969), points out that Wolfe acknowledged he responded only to painters who have "a sense of life." He draws on the Wolfe letters and notebooks to identify those painters whom Wolfe admired. He describes Wolfe's self-education in art by visiting the great European art museums, his response to paintings that had gusto—especially those crowded with figures—and his use of this acquaintance with art in his fiction.

2 Wolfe and His Region

Wolfe is often placed in a regional context or compared with other southern writers—or even seen as an example of the uprooted southerner. Louis D. Rubin, Jr., in "Thomas Wolfe and the Place He Came From" (*VQR*, Spring 1976; reprinted in his *A Gallery of Southerners*, Baton Rouge, La., 1982), asserts that Wolfe was truly a "southern" writer in spite of the fact that he had working-class origins and thus did not display the formality and gentlemanly restraint that was expected of the southern man of letters. Although he had several of the "official characteristics of southern writing," his regional authenticity is shown in his rejection of an older mythology of the South and in his "agonizing need to define his own moral identity in terms of the relationship to time and place." Again, in *The Writer in the South* (Athens, Ga., 1972), Rubin includes Wolfe as one of the writers of the New South who was college-educated, an important feature of all the writers of the Southern Renaissance. They were the first generation of southern writers to confront the intellectual and artistic views of their time and not be distracted by a need to defend the pre- or post-Civil War situation of the South and its institutions.

Floyd Watkins's "Thomas Wolfe and Asheville Again and Again and Again . . ." (*SLJ*, Fall 1977) deals with the impact of the Asheville environment on Wolfe and his work. The mountains and their isolating influence lie behind the theme in Wolfe's books that a boy (and later "a man perpetually young") is "thrown out of a paradise and forced to live in a world which only provides inferior glimpses of the beauties formerly known." In his travels this character always sees with the perceptive eyes of a provincial and by this means social criticism emerges in the novels. C. Hugh Holman sees a similar awareness in "The Southern Provincial in the Metropolis," in his *Windows on the World: Essays on American Social Fiction* (Knoxville, Tenn., 1979). Wolfe is the exemplar of the southerner who becomes more conscious of his home ground when he is far from it. He was, Holman feels, able to record the experience of the southerner in the northern city more faithfully than any other writer. Anne Rowe, in "Thomas Wolfe in New York" (*TWN*, Spring 1981), agrees. Both the stimulation and the sense of isolation that Wolfe felt in New York City allowed him to contemplate his experience in the South and to bring to this material the energy drawn from city life that gave it creative expression.

Jack Weaver's "Why Only Thomas Wolfe? Some Questions and an Answer" (*AppalH*, Summer 1977) raises the question of why Wolfe is the only writer of national stature to emerge from the Appalachian region and suggests that his leaving home gave him the objectivity he needed in order to develop the materials of his home region. Weaver seems unaware of the Fugitive Group. Ruel E. Foster, in "Thomas Wolfe's Mountain Gloom and Glory" (*AL*, Jan. 1973), thinks that it was Wolfe's tragedy to leave the mountain region. In all his works from the early plays to the final manuscript, the mountains provide a "sense of joy, of euphoria, of majesty," but in *You Can't Go Home Again* when George Webber returns for a visit he is appalled by the commercial exploitation of the area. Wolfe was attempting then in *The Hills Beyond* to celebrate the past of the mountain men and was intending that it be a "book of affirmation."

Unlike all the other critics, Richard King in *A Southern Renaissance* (New York, 1980) finds Wolfe lacking a sense of southern tradition because he came from the hill country and his family had no status or wealth. His search for self-identification was really a search for a tradition. One result is that his settings, Altamont or Libya Hill, "could as well have been in the Midwest as the South." King's further comments on Wolfe's characteristics are similarly puzzling.

Richard Gray, in *The Literature of Memory: Modern Writers of the American South* (Baltimore, Md., 1977), his generally excellent study of southern writers, has approached Wolfe's novels as mythologized historical documents. Gray, a British historian, finds Wolfe "unsurpassed" in the accuracy with which he presents the old mountain ways, but he thinks him quite unique in that he is able to dramatize the transition from the traditional isolation to the newer urban culture of the region. He sees the thematic conflict between the desire for movement and the need for repose. finally resolved in *The Hills Beyond*, the work to which he gives his chief attention. This discussion incorporates Gray's article, "Signs of Kinship: Thomas Wolfe and His Appalachian Heritage" (*AppalJ*, Spring 1974).

James Meehan's "Thomas Wolfe as Regional Historian" (*TWN*, Spring 1977) supports the authenticity of Wolfe's fictional use of the western North Carolina scene and some of its historical characters—with special emphasis on *The Hills Beyond*. Wilma Dykeman and James Stokeley's "Voices of the Past and Present," in *The Border States* (New York, 1968), offers an appreciation of Wolfe for his sense of the past and his picture of region, although they acknowledge that he soared beyond the limitations of a regional writer. Ina Van Noppen, in *Western North Carolina Since the Civil War*" (Boone, N.C., 1973), recognizes Wolfe as North Carolina's greatest writer and comments with appreciation on *The Hills Beyond* as an important reflection of mountain life. James H. Justus's "On the Restlessness of Southerners" (*SoR*, Jan. 1975) cites Wolfe's character as exhibiting the itch to wander and explore that, strangely, he thinks is characteristic of southerners rather than of Americans in general.

3   Wolfe and America

No one since Whitman has been so widely acknowledged as Wolfe for his celebration of the American spirit. C. Hugh Holman, in "Thomas Wolfe and America" (*SLJ*, Fall 1977), points out that after 1930 Wolfe continued to ask himself what it meant to be an American. He was "obsessed by the vastness and complexity, the beauty and terror, the loneliness and the crowded manswarm," the contradictory characteristics of his nation, and he felt the need to express it all in his books. Like Whitman he was a great accepter, although he was aware of the evils that betrayed the promise of democracy in his native land. His last three novels, which "form a portrait of this continent, rest upon the assumption of human brotherhood." John S. Phillipson, in "Thomas Wolfe's Vision of America" (*Cresset*, Sept. 1976), focuses not on Wolfe's fiction but on his comments in his notebooks, in his speeches, and on his travels in the various regions of the country, and argues that Wolfe's feeling for the United States involves "not only the land but also the American people."

Paschal Reeves, in "Thomas Wolfe and the Family of Earth," in *The Poetry of Community* (ed. Lewis P. Simpson, Atlanta, 1972), notes that both Wolfe and Faulkner have a common view that the disruption of the family is at the heart of human ills. He offers an interesting view that Wolfe's suffering from the break-up of his family when he was a child was projected in his writing as a criticism of America's need to become a more cohesive brotherhood of all its peoples. Although in the early work, the Negroes and ethnic minorities are seen as "other" than real Americans, Wolfe's mature outlook emphasizes the need for human brotherhood both in the United States and the world at large. B. Ramachandra Rao, in *The American Fictional Hero* (Chandigarh, India, 1979), sees Wolfe's "artist-hero" in conflict with the outside world and in the process of defining himself. The quest for self leads to a discovery of the spirit of America and thus to his identity. The movement is from a personal vision to a social vision and a determined opposition to social evils that block "the fulfillment of the American promise."

In a comparison of Wolfe's attitudes in "Dark in the Forest, Strange as Time" with those in "I Have a Thing to Tell You," John Pleasant's "Two Train Rides of Thomas Wolfe" (*Innisfree* [Southeastern Louisiana Univ., Hammond, La.], 1977) argues that Wolfe demonstrates a maturity of outlook about human brotherhood and about death. Jesse C. Gatlin, Jr.'s "Thomas Wolfe: The Question of Value" (*TWN*, Spring 1980), a rather scattered essay, suggests that Wolfe, in drawing upon the literary heritage of the past, provides a rich sense of universal history because not only does he supply allusive images and phrases but also makes use of "the great mythic themes of Western civilization."

4 Themes, Characters, Technique

John Boone Trotti, in "Thomas Wolfe: The Presbyterian Connection" (*Journal of Presbyterian History*, Winter 1981; reprinted in Phillipson), offers the best discussion of Wolfe's religious outlook that has ever been written. This is a well-documented, sober assessment of Wolfe's association with the Presbyterian Church, although he was never baptized and never formally became a member, as his brothers and sister did. Trotti points out the many manifestations of Presbyterian belief that appear in Wolfe's fiction and other writings—the work ethic, the sense of guilt, the sense of destiny, and the belief in immortality. Although never an orthodox theist in later life, Wolfe still had a yearning for "the image of a strength and wisdom external to his need and superior to his hunger," as he expressed it in *The Story of a Novel*. Trotti's article, "On Divers Spirits: Theological Themes in Thomas Wolfe" (*Journal for Preachers*, No. 4, 1980), is a briefer treatment of the same topic.

Hari Singh's "Thomas Wolfe: The Idea of Eternity" (*SCR*, May 1969) is a philosophical consideration of Wolfe's concept of time. Wolfe has, according to Singh, an "unphilosophical view of eternity as an inordinate extension of time" and is thus not a mystic. Wolfe contrasts the ever-enduring natural elements such as mountains and rivers with the brevity and helplessness of man's life. Yet in his posthumous fiction, he puts aside this tragic view and sees eternity instead as a promise of "collective social progress transcending individual lives" and opening new possibilities. Larry Rubin, in "Thomas Wolfe: Halting the Flow of Time" (*AAus*, 1978; reprinted in Phillipson), concludes, after examining the many images of time passing and of transcendent time, that they help to convey Wolfe's sense of history and his recurrent awareness of the brevity of a human being's existence. Leroy Thomas's "Thomas Wolfe: 'A Stranger and Alone'" (*TWN*, Spring 1979) traces the theme of alienation through Wolfe's novels and stories and concludes that it is an organizing principle in his work. Stuart K. Dyck, in "Denial and Acceptance: Wolfe's Ambivalent Attitude Toward Death" (*TWN*, Spring 1982), confronts the contradiction about death found in Wolfe's work, although he continually confuses Wolfe with Eugene Gant. Even so, it appears that Wolfe's belief in immortality helps him to accept death as the final human experience.

John L. Idol, Jr.'s "Fame and the Athlete in Wolfe's Fiction" (*TWN*, Fall 1981; reprinted in Phillipson) shows how Wolfe used characters who were athletes as examples of how American life affected its people. Jim Randolph is seen seduced by fame and in his self-centered life becomes confused and lost; whereas Nebraska Crane, immune to the acclamation of his public life, remains his solid, unspoiled self—an ideal man of "simple faith and firm principles" and thus one of the hopes for a better America. Robert J. Higgs, in *Laurel & Thorn: The Athlete in American Fiction* (Lexington, Ky., 1981), admires Wolfe's treatment of Jim Randolph as the type of athlete who never matures beyond his college achievement and of Nebraska Crane as the athlete who sees his short career in its proper perspective.

Blanche Gelfant, in "Sister to Faust: The City's Hungry Woman as Heroine" (*Novel*, Fall 1981), sees Helen Gant among other characters from American fiction as vigorous and yearning for experience. Robert J. Willis, in "Thomas Wolfe's Hollow Men" (*TWN*, Fall 1981), examines Wolfe's handling of characters who are alienated figures or who are "smothered into stagnation" or who have lost touch with life because of their obsessive concerns with material things. He gives special attention to Judge Rumford Bland, C. Green, Frederick Jack, and Eliza Gant.

Anthony Bukowski, in "Wolfe's Questioning Intelligence," (*TWN*, Spring 1983), observes the pattern of "rhetorical episodes" in Wolfe's fiction that show questions and answers leading at length to another set of questions and answers and by this means exploring his world. In looking at the conclusion to *Look Homeward, Angel*, at "No Door" (the short version), and at "Chickamauga," he concludes that in his later work Wolfe was supplying more aesthetically satisfying answers at the conclusion of his works of short fiction. Elizabeth S. Bressan's "The Verbalization of Movement Forms: The Imagery of Thomas Wolfe" (*Quest*, Jan. 1975) points out that as he describes athletic participation or objections to team sports in *Look Homeward, Angel*, Wolfe shows how bodily movement can be expressed verbally in order to promote understanding of what the psyche feels about physical activity. Kenneth Seib, in "Thomas Wolfe in Miniature" (*TWN*, Fall 1978; reprinted in Phillipson), offers examples of Wolfe's technique of overview "like that of a cinema director."

5 Studies of Individual Novels

a. Look Homeward, Angel. Although *Look Homeward, Angel* has always drawn more critical attention than any of Wolfe's other works, it has received an increased amount of critical study in the last decade. John Hagan has written the two most important articles during this period. In "Structure, Theme, and Metaphor in Wolfe's *Look Homeward, Angel*" (*AL*, May 1981; reprinted in Phillipson), he argues that by means of an integration of theme, image, and symbol, the work achieves an organic unity and formal cohesion of a loose kind that is found in other classics of American literature. He demonstrates how Eugene, living in a world of chance and determinism, finally learns in his conversation with the ghost of Ben that he can break free of the confines of time and death in his vocation as a writer. Hagan takes another look at Eugene's attempts to escape from the presence of death and the confinements of a world of time in "Time, Death, and Art in *Look Homeward, Angel*" (*TWN*, Spring 1982). In this carefully weighed consideration of one of the principal thematic lines in the novel, he offers an especially full treatment of the images of the train, the angel, and the ghost (with reference to Eugene's preexistent self as well as to memories of the dead—Grover, Laura, and Ben). Eugene's development of his vocation is seen as the means of his liberation.

Leslie Field, in "*Look Homeward, Angel* and the Passage of Time" (*TWN*, Fall 1979), counters the argument that the novel is a book for reading in one's youth and offers an extended commentary on its complexities, its variety of attitude, and its rich texture of allusion. David O'Rourke's "The Lost Paradise of *Look Homeward, Angel*" (*TWN*, Spring 1983) is a reading that overhears religious references and thus sees an allegory of the South as a fallen world and Altamont as hell. Gant is unable to escape and return to the Eden of pre-Civil War America, but Eugene is able to take Ben's advice to get away and at the end is seen on his way north, which holds promise of his success. Elizabeth Evans, in "Music in *Look Homeward, Angel*" (*SLJ*, Spring 1976), is concerned with Wolfe's use of popular music as well as operatic arias "to evoke, to recall, and to reinforce emotion." Nancy Lenz Harvey, in "*Look Homeward, Angel*" (*BSUF*, Winter 1972), sees Ben as the tragic center of the novel. She approaches it from a reading of "Lycidas" to find all the standard features of the elegy form but also sees Ben as best representing "the basic theme of the buried life."

An important article, the first of three, is James Ray Blackwelder's "Literary Allusions in *Look Homeward, Angel*: The Narrator's Perspective" (*TWN*, Fall 1984), in which he argues that not only do the allusions enrich the hero's literary background but also the characters' use of poetic lines and fragments "provides the most subtle commentary on tone in the novel and helps define the main characters and their relations to the theme of escape and spiritual freedom." Darlene H. Unrue's overstated argument in "The Gothic Matrix of *Look Homeward, Angel*" (Phillipson) is that Eugene Gant, "trying to find his way in the spiritual landscape of terrors and horrors, confronts his world's absurdities in grotesque characters and nightmares."

Richard Steele's *Thomas Wolfe: A Study in Psychoanalytic Literary Criticism* (Philadelphia, 1976) is a critical failure in its treatment of *Look Homeward, Angel*, although it contains fascinating speculation about creativity and the relation of an author's life to his material. M. N. Smrchek's "Wolfe's Early Aesthetic and *Look Homeward, Angel*" (translated from the Russian; *TWN*, Spring 1981) is a strange philosophical article. Using references to Eugene Gant, the author argues that Wolfe "chose dialectical, causal dependence as a principle for selecting and presenting his factual material" and that the aesthetic reflected in the novel—that of Platonic idealism—was used only to explain Eugene's method of escaping from "the soullessness of a bourgeois society subject to the laws of material hoarding."

A. Carl Bredahl, Jr.'s intriguing article, "*Look Homeward, Angel*: Individuation and Articulation" (*SLJ*, Fall 1973), is concerned with the "true narrative voice" in the novel. What Bredahl sees taking place is "the discovery of language and its potential" that leads to the "birth of the narrator," who had only existed in embryo in Eugene. Joseph R. Millichap, in "Narrative Structure and Symbolic Imagery in *Look Homeward, Angel*" (*SHR*, Summer 1973), offers a pedestrian analysis of the novel but does make some interesting suggestions about the symbols of the leaf and the stone, relating them to Jung's theories.

Anthony Hilfer, in *The Revolt from the Village* (Chapel Hill, N.C., 1969), declares that Wolfe's "best writing came from his life-long quarrel with his home town" but that his attitude is ambivalent. It took a long time for him to discover that Asheville was a necessity. In *Look Homeward, Angel*, the attack on small-town philistinism is transcended by the expression of the sense of loss that human beings feel in their lives. John L. Idol, Jr., in "Angels and Demons: The Satire of *Look Homeward, Angel*" (*StCS*, Spring 1975), examines Wolfe's satiric handling of characters and situations, and he notes that the "narrator-confessor" even directs a satiric eye toward Eugene. John T. Hiers, in "The Graveyard Epiphany in Modern Southern Fiction: Transcendence of Selfhood" (*SHR*, Fall 1975), perceives that several southern writers, including Wolfe, use a graveyard scene for an episode in which the characters experience a "spiritual or imaginative rebirth." Robert T. Meyer's "Thomas Wolf [sic] and the Classics" (*CB*, Apr. 1980) is a largely worthless article that summarizes Eugene's classical studies. However, Meyer identifies the phoneticized Greek phrase in chapter 28 as *Iliad* 1.49, from J. R. S. Sitlington's 1907 textbook. Lawrence Clipper, in "Imperishable Verse and Perishable Criticism" (*CEA*, Mar. 1976), offers an odd discussion of versified sentimentality, which focuses on the tombstone verse chosen by W. O. Gant for the prostitute's epitaph.

H. B. Hassinger, in "Julia" (*TWN*, Fall 1980), gives an account of a visit with Julia Wolfe at the Old Kentucky Home, during which he observes the locutions and mannerisms that Wolfe used for his characterization of Eliza Gant. O. T. Powell's "Thomas Wolfe as Literary Predator" (*Antiquarian Bookman*, July 1978) describes a list drawn up by Mabel Wheaton in 1941, identifying 141 of the real-life models for characters in *Look Homeward, Angel*. Jack D. Wages, in "Names in *Look Homeward, Angel*" (*TWN*, Fall 1977; reprinted in Phillipson), discusses Wolfe's use of "Charactonyms" in choosing names for his characters. Robert McIlvaine, in "Thomas Wolfe's GarGANTuan Family" (*NConL*, Jan. 1976), observes that Wolfe's choice of the name Gant suggests both *giant* and *gargantuan* and is thus eminently suitable for his larger-than-life characters.

Mamoru Osawa, in "On Translating *Look Homeward, Angel*" (*TWN*, Fall 1979), describes his difficulties in making a Japanese translation in 1940–41, which was eventually published in two volumes in 1952 and 1954. Hiroshi Tsunemoto, in "Thomas Wolfe's *Look Homeward, Angel: A Story of an American Dream*" (*Studies in Cultural and Social Sciences* [Hiroshima], No. 12, 1982), discourses on the difficulties of Wolfe's style for a Japanese reader but goes on to say that the book offers a very full picture of American life in the early twentieth century. John Earl Bassett's "The Critical Reception of *Look Homeward, Angel*" (*TWN*, Spring 1982; reprinted in Phillipson) assesses the reviews from both northern and southern newspapers and periodicals. Although some North Carolina reviewers were harsh, other southern reviewers praised the book highly. But it was the approval of the northern reviewers that won success for the book.

Madeleine Boyd's *Thomas Wolfe: The Discovery of a Genius* (ed. Aldo P. Magi, Akron, Ohio, 1981) is a lively account by Wolfe's first literary agent of her enthusiasm for Wolfe's manuscript and her difficulties in placing it with a publisher until she discussed it personally with Maxwell Perkins at Scribner's. Richard S. Kennedy, in "Wolfe's *Look Homeward, Angel* in the Literary Marketplace" (*TWN*, Fall 1982), traces the sales figures of the novel in its ups and downs over a fifty-year period, pointing out that the 1960s saw an average annual sale of 43,730 copies, although no "mass market" paperbacks were published. The sales declined to about 20,000 copies per year for 1979 and 1980.

b. Of Time and the River. Louis D. Rubin, Jr.'s "In Search of the Country of Art: Thomas Wolfe's *Of Time and the River*," in *A Gallery of Southerners* (Baton Rouge, La., 1982), sees the novel as possessing a coherent development in spite of its unevenness: "What it involves is a young American writer's flight from . . . a middle-class southern community and his subsequent effort to discover a better place in which to live and write, and it culminates, not in the finding of such a Good Place but of a perspective from which, as an artist, he can write about his experience."

John Hagan, in "Thomas Wolfe's *Of Time and the River*: The Quest for Transcendence" (*TWHP*), concedes that the work does not have a perfectly achieved design but has a discernible and significant structure, tracing Eugene's attempt to escape from time and the inevitability of death through artistic achievement. The novel follows his desire to be a writer at Harvard, in New York, and in Europe until he discovers in Tours that what he must express is "America and the life he has already lived there."

Klaus Lansinger, in "Thomas Wolfe's Modern Hero—Goethe's Faust" (*TWHP*), identifies the performance of *Faust* that Wolfe attended in Vienna in 1928. He argues that Wolfe thereafter made his heroes be men who felt the tension between "the life of the withdrawn scholar and the man of the world who . . . wants to grasp and experience everything." Robert Fink's "Oswald Ten Eyck: Thomas Wolfe's Clown-hero" (*TWN*, Spring 1979) is a consideration of the starving, failed playwright in *Of Time and the River*, whose plays always involve the ingorging of food. Although Ten Eyck is the butt of Wolfe's humor, he is still presented as more sound and worthwhile than the pretentious Harvard aesthetes.

The *Thomas Wolfe Review* devoted a special issue (Spring 1985) to *Of Time and the River* that contains five articles of varying quality. John Hagan, in his sensible "'The Errant Muse': Anomalies in *Of Time and the River*," points out that although the book is "an imposing accomplishment," there are anomalous passages that seem to signal a significant change in Eugene's outlook, whereas his mood swings continue to take place throughout the book. It is important, he argues, that the reader recognize these as flaws in the composition of the book and look beyond them if the value of the book is to be appreciated. Richard Kane, in "The European-American Conflict in *Of Time and the River*: A Question of Form," recognizes that the novel develops a thematic construct posing American formlessness against European form. What is important for Eugene Gant is that he must experience the forms of an older way of life in Europe before he can perceive that "the torrential rivers of America" represent "the vital change that is the only guarantee of permanence and growth." Daniel Fruit, in "Of Time and Rhetoric: The Narrator in Thomas Wolfe's Second Novel," defends Wolfe's use of third-person narration against the criticism of Holman and others who, says Fruit, confuse Eugene Gant with the narrator. What is very clear is that "by putting himself in the third person, Wolfe purposely separates himself from his protagonist." Shelby Stephenson, in "Poetry, the Timeless Factor: *Of Time and the River* and *From Death to Morning*," is well-meaning in his appreciation of poetic passages in these works but is not clear in what he is trying to tell us about their significance for Wolfe as a novelist. M. N. Smrchek, a Russian critic whose article *"Of Time and the River*: Wolfe, Whitman, and America"* has been translated by Margaret Winchell, declares that Wolfe misuses the Whitman tradition because his celebration of Eugene Gant as an individual is in contradiction with Wolfe's narrator speaking as "the voice of the nation," although in Smrchek's erratic presentation it is not evident why this is supposed to be a problem.

The *Thomas Wolfe Review* brings its celebration of the fiftieth anniversary of the publication of *Of Time and the River* to a close in the Fall 1985 issue with Richard S. Kennedy's "What the Galley Proofs of *Of Time and the River* Tell Us." John Hall Wheelock's corrected galley proofs of the early portion of *Of Time and the River* have recently come to light, and they show that contrary to Perkins's statements, Wolfe worked correcting galley proofs too. But when Wolfe found that his additions to the text were not being accepted, he ceased cooperating. His early pattern of working with magazine editors and exercising his right to change, to add, to hesitate long over decisions was not possible with as complex a publication as *Of Time and the River*: hence, his later resentments, feeling that Perkins and Wheelock had taken his book away from him and rushed it into print.

c. The George Webber novels. Wolfe's single fictional work about George Webber was broken into three separate parts by his editor, Edward Aswell. But most readers, including critics, tend to think of the three parts as separate works. The first part about Webber's ancestors was published last, under the title *The Hills Beyond*. The story of George Webber in the next part, *The Web and the Rock*, separates itself easily from the third part, *You Can't Go Home Again*, which has less stylistic flourish and displays a more mature George Webber. Arthur Harris, in "A Tempestuous Romance" (*Williamstown Advocate*, 14 Sept. 1983), is dissatisfied with the division. He argues that the last half of *The Web and the Rock* and the first half of *You Can't Go Home Again* together make a more unified work than either of the novels and urges that the two halves be published together under the title "A Turbulent Affair."

Leslie Field's "*You Can't Go Home Again*: Wolfe's Germany and Social Consciousness" (*TWNC*; reprinted in Phillipson) ranges widely over Wolfe's final years and argues that the social awareness evident in Wolfe's fourth novel is especially involved with Wolfe's attitude toward Germany and the Jews. Field traces Wolfe's change in feeling about Germany from enthusiastic admiration to revulsion at Hitler's tyranny. The same argument is presented in Field's "Thomas Wolfe's Attitudes toward Germany and the Jews" (*JML*, March 1984). Livia E. Bitton, in "The Jewess as Fictional Sex Symbol" (*BuR*, Spring 1973), points out that such writers as Shakespeare, Marlowe, Scott, Hawthorne, and Flaubert, as well as Wolfe, have used the character of a beautiful Jewess to suggest a memory "of ancient Biblical past and of bygone innocence."

Sue Fields Ross, in "'The Wounded Faun': Wolfe's Reaction to Asheville's Rejection" (*Arts Journal*, Oct. 1979), suggests that the dialogue in *You Can't Go Home Again* between Randy Shepperton and George Webber represents a mature Wolfe looking back at the young Wolfe's attitudes toward Asheville's rejection of *Look Homeward, Angel*. Robert Fink, in "Thomas Wolfe's Parable of the Rich Fool" (*TWN*, Spring 1978), suggests that the section "The House that Jack Built" in *You Can't Go Home Again* had its origins in Luke 12.15–20, and offers an analysis of the episode, showing parallels. Lawrence Clayton, in "An Example of Ambiguous Imagery in *You Can't Go Home Again*" (*TWN*, Spring 1979), examines the chapter "The Hollow Men" about the suicide of C. Green and points to the paradox that there are suggestions of life and new growth associated with "green," as well as the unpleasant associations in the Brooklyn "jungle" where Green lived and died.

Frank J. D'Angelo's "Style as Structure" (*Style*, Spring 1974) is a linguistic and rhetorical analysis of the passage "Some things will never change" (chapter 4, *You Can't Go Home Again*), which demonstrates both the mean- ing and the appeal of Wolfe's style in his poetic meditations. John L. Idol, Jr., in "Thomas Wolfe Attends a Performance of Alexander Calder's Circus" (*TWHP*), points out that Wolfe's love of the circus as a child was in sharp contrast to the over-sophisticated travesty he witnessed in Aline Bernstein's apartment when Calder brought his puppet circus to her party. He suggests that this is why Wolfe used it for his cultural criticism in the episode about Piggy Logan's circus in *You Can't Go Home Again*.

6 Short Fiction

James Boyer, in "The Development of Form in Thomas Wolfe's Short Fiction" (*TWHP*), the best general discussion of Wolfe's treatment of short forms, shows the difference between Wolfe's early lyric form before 1935 and the gradual achievement of "dramatizing rather than telling, in careful plotting, in building characters with significant internal conflicts, and in using imagery to enforce theme." Boyer again examines the short stories in "Nowell and Wolfe: The Working Relationship" (*TWN*, Spring 1981), where he describes Nowell's work with Wolfe in getting his work published in magazines and concludes that she taught him "to compress material" and "to develop a clearer sense of plot and characterization." Elizabeth Evans also looks at that relationship in "Elizabeth Nowell: Thomas Wolfe's Agent and Friend" (*TWN*, Spring 1980), a first-rate account of Nowell and her value to Wolfe in helping him to shape his stories. Boyer returns to another aspect of Wolfe's stories in "The City in the Short Fiction of Thomas Wolfe" (*TWN*, Fall 1983; reprinted in Phillipson), which argues that in his early short fiction that showed city people as "abrasive, strident, reptilian, vulpine, and uncaring" Wolfe was really reflecting his own fear and isolation in New

York. Later, when his hostility to the city decreased, he displayed a compassion for the poor and the lower classes in their struggle to survive the deprivations and stresses of city life.

The best piece of research about any of Wolfe's short stories was carried out by John S. Phillipson for "Thomas Wolfe's 'Chickamauga': The Fact and the Fiction" (*TWN,* Fall 1982; reprinted in Phillipson). Phillipson investigated the correspondences between the events of the story and the exploits of the Twenty-ninth North Carolina Regiment in the Civil War. He demonstrates that, in manipulating his material, Wolfe "followed the precept of arranging and charging it with purpose to produce a romantic tale with a narrative center." Its theme is not that "war is hell," but rather a theme common to Wolfe's work that life is "stranger than a dream."

Sharon Doten, in "Thomas Wolfe's 'No Door': Some Textual Questions" (*PBSA,* First Quarter 1974), points to textual problems caused by the fact that Wolfe published pieces of short fiction only for financial reasons, that they were written as parts of his longer works. "No Door" has been published in three different versions, and the manuscript indicates that plans for a nine-section version existed before it was ever published. Her conclusion is that there is a need for a definitive text, but there are other implications too: that Holman, in creating his version in *The Short Novels of Thomas Wolfe,* made a mistake in adding material to the story without having consulted the manuscripts. One other point should be considered in connection with this article: at one time Wolfe and Scribner's planned a book publication of this work, and some of the notes and manuscripts may have been connected with an expanded version. More investigation of this problem is needed. Meanwhile, the *Scribner's Magazine* version is authoritative.

Guy Owen, in "'An Angel on the Porch' and *Look Homeward, Angel*" (*TWN,* Fall 1980; reprinted in Phillipson), calls attention to the skillful revisions Wolfe made when he lifted chapter 19 from his novel and converted it into a short story. Tim Elliott, in "Gant's Magnificent Obsession" (*TWN,* Spring 1982), interprets Gant's decision to sell the stone angel to Queen Elizabeth as an acknowledgment that he has failed in life.

William Domnarski, in "Thomas Wolfe's Success as Short Novelist: Structure and Theme in 'A Portrait of Bascom Hawke'" (*SLJ,* Fall 1980; reprinted in Phillipson), declares that Wolfe's work is best under control in short novels because the form imposed restrictions upon him, a judgment that gives the wrong reasons for a generally accepted idea. He goes on to examine the story, largely through summarizing its incidents and characterizations. Gloria Guzi, in "Weaving as Metaphor in Thomas Wolfe's *The Web of Earth*" (*TWN,* Fall 1983; reprinted in Phillipson), sees the narrator's procedure to be like that of a primitive weaver without a predetermined pattern, moving back and forth in time. But besides shaping the character of Eliza, Wolfe's device of weaving also provides a

748

structure for the narrative and develops a theme as her choices begin to make a design. Webb Salmon's "Thomas Wolfe's Search to Know Brooklyn" (Phillipson) regards the story "Only the Dead Know Brooklyn" as symptomatic of Wolfe's "attempts to solve the artistic problems that plagued and almost destroyed him."

Stephen Black's "Bloody Bones" (*TWN*, Fall 1978) is a short account of a happening already well known to Wolfe scholars, of a crazed man who ran amok in Asheville in 1906, shooting and killing at random: the origin of Wolfe's story "The Child by Tiger." David K. Hall, in "Contrast as Device in Wolfe's 'The Child by Tiger'" (*TWN*, Spring 1983), argues that the contrasts in imagery, action, and character in the story develop the theme of the duality of human nature. Albert E. Wilhelm, in "Borrowings from *Macbeth* in Wolfe's 'The Child by Tiger'" (*SSF*, Spring 1977), points out echoes of *Macbeth* that darken the atmosphere of a story about the end of childhood innocence.

John L. Idol, Jr.'s "Thomas Wolfe's 'A Note on Experts'" (*SSF*, Fall 1974) points out that the introductory material about the sports writer was influenced by Ring Lardner's "A Prize Fight" and it helps to establish the satiric theme of distrust for self-appointed experts like the aesthete Dexter Joyner. Marguerite Cohn's "*A Note on Experts*: How It Happened" (*TWN*, Fall 1977) tells how the House of Books came to publish the work. John L. Idol, Jr. turns next to "Wolfe's 'The Lion at Morning' and 'Old Man Rivers'" (*TWN*, Fall 1977), giving an account of the origins of these two stories (Wolfe's satiric sequence about The House of Rodney) and describing Perkins's demands for changes in the stories before publication.

James Boyer maintains that "For Wolfe the train remained a central metaphor of life" because of the chance encounters of strangers and the movement of the train past the unmoving, eternal earth, in "The Metaphorical Level in Wolfe's 'The Sun and the Rain'" (*SSF*, Fall 1982). He goes on to make a comparison between a note that Wolfe jotted in 1925 and the story he wrote in the 1930s, in order to show Wolfe's development in technique. Timothy Dow Adams's "The Ebb and Flow of Time and Place in 'The Lost Boy'" (*SoSt*, Winter 1980; reprinted in Phillipson) is a first-rate consideration of Wolfe's handling the theme of fixity and change, especially in his use of the fountain and the courthouse bell as symbols.

7 Plays

Ima H. Herron, in *The Small Town in American Drama* (Dallas, 1969), examines Wolfe's plays with special emphasis on *Welcome to Our City* and "its harsh and strident protest against the boom-town interests which were destroying the older and more peaceful relationship between the races in Altamont." She also includes a discussion of Ketti Frings's adaption of *Look Homeward, Angel* for the stage and Paul Baker and

Eugene McKinney's adaption of *Of Time and the River* at Baylor University and the Dallas Art Center.

Jerry L. Rice has turned out several useful articles on Wolfe and the drama. In "Thomas Wolfe and the Carolina Playmakers" (*TWN*, Spring 1981), he gives the background of Professor Frederick Koch, his interest in folk plays, and his establishment of the Carolina Playmakers. He goes on to discuss the four one-act plays that Wolfe wrote under Koch's guidance and concludes that this training "taught him to recognize the dramatic in the commonplace." In "Thomas Wolfe's *Mannerhouse*" (*TWN*, Spring 1982; reprinted in Phillipson), Rice concedes that, although some scenes have effective dialogue, the play is a failure because of wobbly symbols, uncertainty of thematic development, and overdependence on special effects in the conclusion. Takashi Kodaira, in "*Mannerhouse*, Eliza Gant, and *Look Homeward, Angel*: The Move Toward Autobiography" (*TWN*, Fall 1979), argues that the mother figure who was insufficiently developed in *Mannerhouse* was revived in *Look Homeward, Angel* as a vigorous antagonist in the conflict between Eliza and W. O. Gant because Wolfe was now ready to use autobiographical material.

Phyllis H. Lewis's "Thomas Wolfe's *Welcome to Our City*: An Angry Southerner Looks Back" (*TWN*, Spring 1984; reprinted in Phillipson) discusses Wolfe's themes in his play, especially his criticism of people "who worship material progress," but she misreads Wolfe's attitude toward Rutledge, the principal character: she thinks Wolfe satirizes him as one who romanticizes the South.

In "Thomas Wolfe's *Welcome to Our City*" (*TWN*, Fall 1981), Jerry L. Rice gives a full critical treatment of Wolfe's play, together with details of its production at Harvard in 1923, its reception, its later history, and its relationship to the Expressionist movement; but his otherwise excellent article is not documented. See also Richard S. Kennedy's introduction to *Welcome to Our City* (Baton Rouge, La., 1983) for additional details about the Harvard production and the appendix to this edition for two critiques written by members of that audience.

8 Relations with Other Writers

Leon W. Phillips, in "The Lost Boy and the Lost Girl" (*SLJ*, Fall 1976), points out that William Styron's *Lie Down in Darkness* had its origins in a short story that he wrote while a student at Duke University, "The Sun on the River," which derives from Wolfe's "The Lost Boy" and chapter 6 of *You Can't Go Home Again*. Monty Lowe Faltacosh's "Wolfe and *Sophie's Choice*" (*TWN*, Spring 1980) comments on the presence of Wolfe for Stingo, the hero of Styron's novel, and also on the satire directed at Edward Aswell in the character of Weasel, Stingo's editor at McGraw-Hill. For Styron's essay on Wolfe, see Rubin's *Thomas Wolfe: A Collection of Critical Essays* (New York, 1973).

James Henry, in "Thomas Wolfe, Jack Kerouac's Alter-Ego" (*TWN*,

Spring 1980), argues for the stylistic influence of Wolfe on Kerouac's novels and a travel article by listing in an unconvincing way some words and phrases that are found in both writers' works. Ladell Payne's "Look Homeward, Black Boy" in *Black Novelists and the Southern Literary Tradition* (Athens, Ga., 1981) is a somewhat strained comparison between Richard Wright's *Black Boy* and Wolfe's *Look Homeward, Angel*. Jack Sherting's "Echoes of *Look Homeward, Angel* in Dylan Thomas's 'A Child's Christmas in Wales'" (*SSF*, Fall 1972) suggests that Wolfe was an influence on Thomas's story.

Jerold J. Savoy's "Thomas Wolfe and the *Book of Job*" (*TWN*, Fall 1978) deals with Wolfe's use of *Job* from his Harvard play, *The Mountains*, through *You Can't Go Home Again*. John Satterfield, in "Thomas Wolfe's Reading of *Moby Dick*" (*MSEx*, Nov. 1981), describes Wolfe's markings in his copy of *Moby-Dick*. John L. Idol, Jr., in "Nathaniel Hawthorne and Thomas Wolfe" (*HSN*, Spring 1980), lists the various times that Wolfe mentions Hawthorne in his letters and notebooks and comments that Wolfe valued Hawthorne because of his handling of the dark side of human nature. Elizabeth Evans, in "Thomas Wolfe: Some Echoes from Mark Twain," (*MTJ*, Summer 1976), sees a likeness between Wolfe's and Twain's views of human nature and outrage at human cruelty.

John L. Idol, Jr.'s "Thomas Wolfe and Jonathan Swift" (*SCR*, Nov. 1975) is an examination of the influence of Swift on Wolfe's satirical method when he employs irony or satiric fantasy. But Idol also feels that Wolfe's desire to make *The Web and the Rock* a fable in the manner of Gulliver in modern life did not achieve that end, for he chose as satiric devices degrading portraiture and blunt social criticism, devices found more commonly in the naturalistic writer. Idol's "Hawthorne and Wolfe on New York University" (*HSN*, Spring 1982) is a note pointing out the contrast between Hawthorne's approval of New York University's goal that stresses practical education and Wolfe's satire on the institution as "The School for Utility Cultures." Idol's "Thomas Wolfe and T. S. Eliot: The Hippopotamus and the Old Possum" (*SLJ*, Spring 1981) is a perceptive consideration of Wolfe's early recognition of Eliot's position as a leader in the modernist school, his occasional use of Eliot's techniques in his work, and his attack on Eliot as an expatriate and one who was too given to despair about contemporary culture.

Idol has one more relationship to examine in "Ernest Hemingway and Thomas Wolfe" (*SCR*, Fall 1982), where he recounts each author's view of the other's work. He notes that Wolfe admired Hemingway's style and his skeptical view of patriotism, whereas Hemingway scorned Wolfe for his prolixity and resented the fact that Perkins spent more time with Wolfe than with him. Lex Gaither, in "Hemingway and Wolfe" (*TWN*, Fall 1978), records Hemingway's several disparaging remarks about Wolfe's work.

John L. Idol, Jr., in "Responses of Contemporary Novelists to *Look*

Homeward, Angel" (*TWN*, Fall 1979), gathers brief comments on Wolfe's first novel by Vance Bourjaily, John Cheever, R. V. Cassill, Nicholas Guild, Barry Hannah, William Harrison, Andrew Lytle, David Madden, Guy Owen, Mark Steadman, William Styron, Anne Tyler, Kurt Vonnegut, Sylvia Wilkinson, and Herman Wouk.

9 Reputation

Louis D. Rubin, Jr.'s "Two Books and Some Thoughts on Scholarship" (*SLJ*, Fall 1983) begins as a review of the two collections of Wolfe-Bernstein and Wolfe-Nowell letters, but goes on to a full consideration of the recent attention to Wolfe and becomes a call for further critical study of Wolfe's work, "a body of fiction of undeniable power, which yet contains a great deal of bad writing." He sees the need to account for why and in what way his fiction has cast its spell over so many readers for over fifty years. This is an important assessment of the current critical situation in Wolfe studies.

James Atlas, in a revisit to Wolfe's work on the fiftieth anniversary of the publication of *Look Homeward, Angel*, "The Case for Thomas Wolfe" (*NYTBR*, 2 Dec. 1979), notes that Wolfe does not occupy the place in American fiction that he once held—alongside Faulkner, Hemingway, and Fitzgerald. Moreover, major critics no longer discuss his work. Nevertheless, in spite of his overemotional indulgence and the gigantic narrative sprawl, his work has not lost its power to communicate a sense of life to the reader. A reappraisal on the same occasion by Alan Cheuse, "You Can Read Wolfe Again" (*Boston Sunday Globe*, 1 July 1979), sees the work declining in readership but on rereading is amazed how the novels speak anew to a person who read them as a young man. Francis Hulme, in "Thomas Wolfe . . . Adolescent?" (*Arts Journal*, Oct. 1975), offers a brief consideration of Wolfe's decline in the estimate of recent commentators and a reaffirmation of his impact on the common reader.

Richard Walser's "On Faulkner's Putting Wolfe First" (*SAQ*, Spring 1979) records that Faulkner in 1947 in a University of Mississippi classroom ranked Wolfe, Dos Passos, Hemingway, Cather (maybe it was Caldwell) and Steinbeck as the most important American novelists of his time. He frequently repeated it (including Caldwell, not Cather), saying that they all had failed "but Wolfe had made the best failure because he tried the hardest to say the most." Walser, in "The Angel in North Carolina" (*TWN*, Fall 1979; reprinted in Phillipson), gives a fully detailed description of the reviews that Wolfe's first novel received in his home state, including one by Howard Mumford Jones writing for the *Greensboro Daily News*. Betty Lynch Williams based her *Asheville and Thomas Wolfe: Changing Attitudes* (Asheville, N.C., 1972) on interviews and newspaper accounts to tell the story of the early angry response to Wolfe's first novel and then to trace how Asheville came to forgive Wolfe and finally to be proud of him. Nancy Joyner, in "Wolfe's Angel" (*Arts*

Journal, Oct. 1979), declares that the only reason Asheville finally accepted Wolfe is that he was a success—and one who brought recognition and thus became an economic resource for the city. Charles E. Chaffey, in "'Look Homeward, Angel'—to North Carolina" (*Boston Globe*, 14 Sept. 1981), records the views of some local Ashevilleans on Wolfe and his place in American literature.

Hiroshi Tsunemoto, in "*Look Homeward, Angel* and Japanese Readers" (*Studies in Cultural and Social Sciences*, Dec. 1981), explains why the novel is not widely known in Japan. The Japanese readers prefer "novels whose themes are obvious and current"; they prefer a plain style to a poetic one; and they do not respond to a novel that reflects the desire to escape the home region. But the main reason is that Wolfe is not well known among Japanese publishers. Richard Walser's "Wolfe in the Soviet Union" (*TWN*, Spring 1977) is a brief note about Wolfe's reputation in Russia, together with a bibliography of works in Russian about Wolfe, translations of his works into Russian, and dissertations (four) on Wolfe.

This flood of publication on Wolfe in the last twelve years seems to indicate that something of a revival is under way. Still there are scholarly needs and critical perspectives that have not come forth. A catalogue of the books from the Wolfe family library, presently stored in the Thomas Wolfe Memorial Home in Asheville, should be undertaken before some disaster befalls them. A Thomas Wolfe Miscellany drawing together uncollected items, or better still an edition of all of his short fiction, would be welcome. Other scholarly and critical projects come easily to mind: a study of Wolfe's reading based on the books in his personal library, a full-scale study of Wolfe as a teacher at New York University based on the textbooks and teaching materials now in the Houghton Library, a study of Wolfe and the Romantic poets, a study of Wolfe and the classics, a study of his impact on individual readers based on the letters he received from friends, acquaintances, and strangers, and finally a study of his creative process in relation to his unusual methods of composition. These are only a few obvious suggestions. The research collections hold magnificent material, much of it a thrill to examine. Its exploration awaits.

VI SUPPLEMENT

The flood of publication on Wolfe continued unabated in late 1987 and 1988. Two important reference works head the list. Carol Johnston's *Thomas Wolfe: A Descriptive Bibliography* (Pittsburgh, 1987) is an outstanding newcomer to the Pittsburgh Series in Bibliography. It goes far beyond Preston's bibliography in that all American and English editions are described in full, and photographs of title pages and dust jackets of the major editions are reproduced. The listing of variations between the

Scribner and Heinemann editions of *Look Homeward, Angel* and *Of Time and the River* is an important new feature. In addition, first appearances of Wolfe's writings, including individual letters and interviews, are given. A special section lists published appearances attributed to Wolfe, including quoted conversation.

John L. Idol, Jr.'s *A Thomas Wolfe Companion* (New York, 1988) far exceeds what its modest title promises. We expect plot summaries of the novels and stories, a directory that describes and locates all the characters in the fictional work, and genealogies of the fictional families. But the twenty-page life of Wolfe is the best short treatment now to be found, and the chapters on Wolfe's "Ideas and Attitudes" and "Major Themes in Wolfe's Works" constitute real contributions to Wolfe criticism. Appropriate for a book of basic information is the chapter "Wolfe and His Editors" that covers the effect on his work made by the editorial supervision of Maxwell Perkins, Edward Aswell, and Elizabeth Nowell and that goes on to summarize the controversies surrounding Wolfe's editorial dependency. A chapter on "Wolfe and His Critics" offers succinct treatment of the ups and downs of his literary reputation. Forthcoming in 1989, edited by Aldo Magi and John Phillipson, is *Thomas Wolfe: A Bibliography of Secondary Sources* from the Ohio University Press, a checklist (with annotation of major items) that will be more complete and more correct than Elmer Johnson's checklist.

In the Shadow of the Giant: Thomas Wolfe, Correspondence of Edward C. Aswell and Elizabeth Nowell, 1949–1958 (ed. Mary Aswell Doll and Clara Stites, Athens, Ohio, 1988) presents a vast body of information about Wolfe, about Perkins, about Scribner's, about Aswell and the editing of Wolfe's posthumous work, about Nowell and her editing of Wolfe's letters and writing his biography, and about the New York publishing scene in general. Of special interest is the overwhelming evidence of the laziness and deceit of John Terry, who stood as an obstacle to biographical work on Wolfe for fifteen years. In a way, this book is a sequel to Kennedy's *Beyond Love and Loyalty* because the emphasis is upon Nowell, her effervescent style, and her rock-solid character, but the ten-year sequence contains more letters and far more detail. The letter exchange reads like a narrative and moves toward a climax: Nowell struggles to complete her work as she succumbs to cancer.

Leslie Field's *Thomas Wolfe and His Editors* (Norman, Okla., 1987) provides what surely must be the last word on Aswell's editing of Wolfe's last manuscript. After a chapter summarizing the controversy launched when John Halberstadt charged that Aswell and not Wolfe was the real author of the three posthumous volumes of Wolfe's fiction, Field goes ahead to quote or to summarize in detail Wolfe's various plans for his book about Joe Doaks–George Webber, including eight early outlines, "A Statement of Purpose," and Wolfe's final outline, the list of "chapters" that he turned over to Aswell just before his death. Next, he summarizes the contents of each "chapter" that Aswell discarded, and he lists a further series of related manuscripts that were not included in Wolfe's final outline. (It is just possible that some of these items were the pieces that Wolfe threw out at the last minute, pieces then placed in a manila envelope separate from the huge manuscript and also given to Aswell.) Following this, Field gives a detailed scrutiny to Aswell's editorial process in four "Cameo Test Cases," each of which describes a chapter from one of the posthumous books just as Wolfe wrote it and points out every deletion, rearrangement, revision, or addition that Aswell made. Field's conclusion is this: "Inevitably the evidence reveals that Wolfe wrote, Aswell edited." An interesting addendum is "A Contemporary True Text," Field's account of the procedures he and William Braswell went through in editing "Writing and Living," Wolfe's speech at the Purdue literary banquet in May 1938. They faced similar but far less complex problems compared to those that confronted Aswell. In his conclusion, Field ponders carefully the literary and ethical questions raised by Aswell's work and comes down on the side of affirmation: "Despite our musings on what might have been and the questions that inevitably surface about this or that part of Wolfe's published writings, we are all richer now for having the posthumous publications written by Thomas Wolfe and edited by Edward Aswell."

The most important critical study of the last few years is the forthcoming book by Margaret Mills Harper, *The Aristocracy of Art: The Fiction of James Joyce and Thomas Wolfe* from the Louisiana State University Press. In a careful consideration of the work of both authors, Harper examines the question of authorial distance for successful autobiographical fiction. The introductory chapter that sets forth the critical problem is impressive for its theorizing and its readiness to make use of the critical theories of Wayne Booth, Northrop Frye, and several of the poststructuralist French critics. The chapters on Wolfe include a fresh treatment of *Look Homeward, Angel* that emphasizes the effects of Wolfe's sensitivity about his class position.

Another book on autobiographical fiction is John McCormick's *Wolfe, Malraux, and Hesse: A Study in Literary Vitality* (New York, 1987) issued in Garland's Harvard Dissertations in Comparative Literature Series. In this loosely conceived critical work written in 1951, McCormick sees all three writers as autobiographical novelists who reject their social milieu but who are representative of the political, social, and artistic climate of the period after World War I. He observes that Wolfe, who was hostile to European civilization, also reacted against the social and intellectual currents in his own nation: he yearned for an ideal "America the good," of "infinite possibility." Although McCormick draws fully upon the Wolfe papers in the Houghton Library, the picture that he presents seems dependent upon the incomplete impression of Wolfe and his attitudes that prevailed in the 1940s, and consequently, his study seems badly out of date in the 1980s.

Two collections of essays have been added to the five that already exist. The first, *Thomas Wolfe* (New York, 1987), edited by Harold Bloom for the Modern Critical Views Series, reprints recent articles by Clyde C. Clements, Jr., Leslie A. Field, Morris Beja, Richard S. Kennedy, Leo Gurko, C. Hugh Holman, and John Hagan, all of which have been noticed in the present book or its earlier edition. Bloom's introduction is worthless, a retread of a review attacking David Donald's biography and Wolfe himself. A reader will wonder why, if Bloom thinks Wolfe is not worth reading, does he pretend to be the editor of this volume, which was assembled by his assistant, Henry Finder.

The second, *Thomas Wolfe at Eighty-Seven* (Chapel Hill, N.C., 1987), edited by H. G. Jones, consists of papers presented at the 1987 meeting of the Thomas Wolfe Society. Those most worthy of notice are Robert Willis's "Thomas Wolfe and Catherine Brett," an account of Wolfe's relationship with the principal of a school for defective children; James W. Clark, Jr.'s "'The Lost Boy' and the Line of Life," which calls for the publication of Wolfe's original text of "The Lost Boy," after comparing it to the versions in *Redbook Magazine* and *The Hills Beyond*; and Elaine P. Jenkins's "The Gants in a Bottle," a study of the effect of W. O. Wolfe's alcoholism on his family.

Francis Skipp has answered a long-felt need in his collection of *The Complete Short Stories of Thomas Wolfe* (New York, 1987). Unfortunately, the book does not live up to its claim to print the texts of the stories as Wolfe wrote them rather than the cut or altered versions that appeared in periodicals. For example, Skipp does not use Wolfe's original version of "The Lost Boy"; he does not delete the headlines inserted by Frank Crowninshield into the middle of "A Prologue to America"; he includes eighteen stories that were not conceived of by Wolfe but were drawn from the mass of material Wolfe left behind by either Nowell or Aswell; and he resuscitates a fragment that he himself selected from the Wolfe papers ("A Spanish Letter") and calls it a short story. Nevertheless, it is good to have a large number of the early stories just as Wolfe developed them and in the state before Perkins or Nowell began cutting them down to the lengths that magazine editors demanded. James Dickey has contributed a foreword, a lively appreciation of Wolfe's fiction.

The Thomas Wolfe Society has continued its publication schedule. In 1988 John Phillipson edited William B. Wisdom's *The Table Talk of Thomas Wolfe* (Akron, Ohio), a memoir of Wolfe's visit to New Orleans in 1937. In 1989 the society will issue *The Starwick Episodes*, unpublished material about Francis Starwick that Perkins deleted from *Of Time and the River*. These works are obtainable only through the treasurer of the society, William P. Brown, 4302 Fordham Road, Richmond, Virginia 23236.

Notes on Contributors

ELLSWORTH BARNARD, Professor of English Emeritus at the University of Massachusetts at Amherst, was born in Shelburne, Massachusetts, in 1907. He holds his degrees from the University of Massachusetts (B.S.) and the University of Minnesota (M.A. and Ph.D.). He has taught at the University of Tampa, Williams College, the University of Wisconsin, Alfred University, the University of Chicago, Bowdoin College, and Northern Michigan University. He is the author of *Shelley's Religion* (1937), *Edwin Arlington Robinson: A Critical Study* (1952), *Wendell Willkie: Fighter for Freedom* (1966), and *English for Everybody* (1979). He has also edited *Shelley: Selected Poems, Essays, and Letters* (1944) and *Edwin Arlington Robinson: Centenary Essays* (1969), and has contributed articles to *Harper's*, the *New York Times Magazine*, and other periodicals. His current work-in-progress is an autobiography, *In Sunshine and in Shadow: A Teacher's Odyssey*, of which the first three volumes—*A Hill Farm Boyhood* (1983), *An Academic Apprenticeship* (1985), and *Life in the Ivory Tower* (1987)— have appeared.

JACKSON R. BRYER is Professor of English at the University of Maryland. Born in New York City in 1937, he received his B.A. from Amherst College, his M.A. from Columbia University, and his Ph.D. from the University of Wisconsin. The author of *The Critical Reputation of F. Scott Fitzgerald: A Bibliographical Study* (1967) and *Supplement* (1984), editor of *The Short Stories of F. Scott Fitzgerald: New Approaches in Criticism* (1982), and coeditor of *F. Scott Fitzgerald in His Own Time: A Miscellany* (1971) and *Dear Scott/Dear Max: The Fitzgerald-Perkins Correspondence* (1971), his work has also appeared in *Modern Fiction Studies, New Mexico Quarterly, Twentieth Century Literature, South Atlantic Quarterly, Critique, American Quarterly,* and *Modern Drama.* Between 1971 and 1978 and in 1983, he prepared the annual survey of Fitzgerald criticism for *American Literary Scholarship.* His current projects include an edition of the correspondence of Maxwell Perkins and Thomas Wolfe and a history of the American drama from 1940 to 1960.

PHILIP G. COHEN, Assistant Professor of English at the University of Texas at Arlington, was born in Easton, Pennsylvania, in 1954 and educated at American University (B.A.), the University of Southern California (M.A.), and the University of Delaware (Ph.D.). He has received NEH and SCMLA travel and research grants and contributed essays on Faulkner to *Mississippi Quarterly, Southern Literary Journal, Comparative Literature Studies, Journal of Modern Literature, Resources for American Literary Study, Southern Studies, Studies in American Fiction,* and other journals. He is currently completing a book on Faulkner's *Flags in the Dust* and beginning another on Faulkner's *Sanctuary.*

REGINALD L. COOK, Dana Professor of American Literature Emeritus at Middlebury College, was born in Mendon, Massachusetts, in 1903 and died in Middlebury, Vermont, on

August 5, 1984. He received his B.A. from Middlebury College and his M.A. from the Bread Loaf School of English. He then went to Oxford University as a Rhodes Scholar, returning to teach American Literature at Middlebury College, where he served as Chairman of the Department of American Literature for thirty-seven years, as Director of the Bread Loaf School of English from 1945 to 1964, and as Dana Professor of American Literature until his retirement in 1969. In 1960 Middlebury awarded him an honorary doctor of letters degree. He first met Robert Frost in 1924 and later wrote *The Dimensions of Robert Frost* (1968) and *Robert Frost: A Living Voice* (1974). He is also the author of *The Concord Saunterer* (1940) and *Passage to Walden* (1949), editor of *Selected Prose and Poetry of Ralph Waldo Emerson* (1950), and contributor of essays on Frost and other New England writers to *American Literature, College English, New England Quarterly, English Journal,* and *Western Review,* among other journals. At the time of his death, he was at work on a book on nature writing in the American tradition.

JOHN ESPEY, Professor of English Emeritus at the University of California at Los Angeles, was born in Shanghai in 1913. He was a Rhodes Scholar, received the Commonwealth Silver Medal for Literature (1945), was a Guggenheim Fellow, was appointed to the University of California Institute for Creative Arts, and taught at Occidental College. The author of volumes of fiction, poetry, and criticism, he wrote *Ezra Pound's "Mauberley": A Study in Composition* (1955; rev. ed., 1963). His first volume of verse, *The Empty Box Haiku* (1980), concludes with some lines entitled "Canto C Plus." At present he is one-third of a highly successful team of romance novelists, whose books are published under the name of Monica Highland.

WARREN FRENCH retired in 1986 as Professor of English at Indiana University (Indianapolis). He previously taught at the Universities of Mississippi, Kentucky, Florida, and Missouri-Kansas City, at Stetson University, and at Kansas State University. Born in Philadelphia in 1922, he received his B.A. from the University of Pennsylvania and his M.A. and Ph.D. from the University of Texas at Austin. His books include *John Steinbeck* (1961; rev. ed., 1975), *Frank Norris* (1962), *J. D. Salinger* (1963), *A Companion to "The Grapes of Wrath"* (1963), *The Social Novel at the End of an Era* (1966), *A Filmguide to "The Grapes of Wrath"* (1973), and *Jack Kerouac* (1986). He has edited *The Thirties: Fiction, Poetry, Drama* (1967), *The Forties: Fiction, Poetry, Drama* (1969), *The Fifties: Fiction, Poetry, Drama* (1971), *The Twenties: Fiction, Poetry, Drama* (1975), and, with Walter Kidd, *American Winners of the Nobel Prize in Literature* (1968). He contributed to *American Literary Scholarship* from 1966 to 1976 and edited the 1983 volume. He is now living in Swansea, Wales, where he is working on the promotion of American Studies programs in Europe.

RICHARD S. KENNEDY, Professor of English at Temple University, was born in St. Paul, Minnesota, in 1920 and was educated at the University of California at Los Angeles (B.A.), the University of Chicago (M.A.), and Harvard University (Ph.D.). He has taught at the University of Rochester and Wichita State University. He is the author of *The Window of Memory: The Literary Career of Thomas Wolfe* (1962), *Working Out Salvation with Diligence: The Plays of T. S. Eliot* (1964), and *Dreams in the Mirror: A Biography of E. E. Cummings* (1980), editor of *Beyond Love and Loyalty: The Letters of Thomas Wolfe and Elizabeth Nowell* (1983), *Welcome to Our City: A Play in Ten Scenes* by Thomas Wolfe (1983), *Thomas Wolfe: A Harvard Perspective* (1983), and *The Train and the City* by Thomas Wolfe (1984), and coeditor of *The Notebooks of Thomas Wolfe* (1970), *Tulips and Chimneys* by E. E. Cummings (1976), *The Enormous Room* by E. E. Cummings (1977), and *Etcetera: The Unpublished Poems of E. E. Cummings* (1983). He is presently at work on a critical study, "A Yankee Looks at Southern Fiction."

DAVID KRAUSE has taught American literature at Northwestern University since 1986. Born in 1951 in Hartford, Wisconsin, he received his Ph.D. in 1979 from Yale University, where he was a Danforth Fellow, a Yale College Prize Teaching Fellow, and studied Renaissance

758

literature, especially Shakespeare. He received his B.A. from Marquette University, where he later taught from 1977 to 1986. His essays and reviews on Faulkner have appeared in *PMLA, Centennial Review, Studies in American Fiction, Studies in the Novel, Modern Fiction Studies, Studies in Short Fiction,* and *Dictionary of Literary Biography.* He is currently completing a book to be called "Faulkner Reading: Fictions of Literacy and American Culture, 1935–1940."

STUART Y. McDOUGAL is Professor of English and Director of the Program in Comparative Literature at the University of Michigan. He was educated at Haverford College (B.A.) and the University of Pennsylvania (M.A., Ph.D.). He has served as secretary-treasurer of the American Comparative Literature Association. He has been a fellow of the American Council of Learned Societies and a senior Fulbright professor. His publications include *Ezra Pound and the Troubadour Tradition* (1973), *Made into Movies: From Literature to Film* (1985), and *Dante Among the Moderns* (editor, 1985), as well as review-essays on Pound and Eliot in *American Literary Scholarship.*

JOHN HENRY RALEIGH, Professor of English at the University of California at Berkeley, was born in Springfield, Massachusetts, in 1920. He received his B.A. from Wesleyan University and his Ph.D. from Princeton University. Since 1947 he has taught at the University of California at Berkeley, where he served as Chairman of the English Department in 1969 and as Vice-Chancellor for Academic Affairs from 1969 to 1972. He held a Guggenheim Fellowship in 1962–63. He is the author of *Matthew Arnold and American Culture* (1957), *The Plays of Eugene O'Neill* (1965), *Time, Place, and Idea: Essays on the Novel* (1968), *The Chronicle of Leopold and Molly Bloom: "Ulysses" as Narrative* (1977), and numerous essays and reviews on nineteenth- and twentieth-century English and American literature in English and American journals and book collections.

JOSEPH N. RIDDEL is Professor of English at the University of California at Los Angeles. A native of West Virginia, he holds M.S. and Ph.D. degrees from the University of Wisconsin at Madison and has taught at Duke University, the University of California at Riverside (visiting), the State University of New York at Buffalo, the University of Wisconsin at Milwaukee (visiting), and the School of Criticism and Theory, Northwestern University (summer 1981). He received a Guggenheim Fellowship in 1975–76 and in the fall of 1977 was a senior fellow at the Center for Twentieth-Century Studies of the University of Wisconsin at Milwaukee. His *The Clairvoyant Eye: The Poetry and Poetics of Wallace Stevens* (1965) won the Explicator Award. His two other book-length studies are *C. Day Lewis* (1971) and *The Inverted Bell: Modernism and the Counterpoetics of William Carlos Williams* (1974). He has published more than fifty critical essays on nineteenth- and twentieth-century American poetry and poetics and on the currents of recent critical theory in such journals as *PMLA, ELH, MLN, Modern Drama, Boundary 2, Modern Fiction Studies, New England Quarterly, Genre,* and *South Atlantic Quarterly,* and in such collections as *Textual Strategies* (1979), *Heidegger and the Question of Literature* (1979), *Wallace Stevens: A Celebration* (1980), *The Question of Textuality* (1980), and *Ezra Pound: Tactics for Reading* (1982). He is presently completing a book on American poetics from Poe to Postmodernism, tentatively titled "Purloined Letters."

WALTER B. RIDEOUT retired in 1986 as Harry Hayden Clark Professor of English at the University of Wisconsin at Madison, where he served as Chair of the English Department from 1965 to 1968. Born in 1917, he was educated at Colby College (B.A.) and Harvard University (M.A. and Ph.D.). From 1949 to 1963 he taught at Northwestern University. In 1951–52 he shared a Newberry Library Fellowship with Howard Mumford Jones, and in 1958–59 he held a Guggenheim Fellowship. He is the author of *The Radical Novel in the United States* (1956), editor of *The Experience of Prose* (1960), *Caesar's Column* by Ignatius Donnelly (1960), and *Sherwood Anderson: A Collection of Critical Essays* (1974), and coeditor of *Letters of Sherwood Anderson* (1953), *A College Book of Modern Verse* (1958), *A College Book of Modern Fiction* (1961), and *American Poetry* (1965). In 1968–69 he was Senior Visiting Professor, Institute for Research in the Humanities, University of Wisconsin at Madison, and in 1981 he was lecturer in English at the Kyoto (Japan) American Studies Summer Seminar. In 1983 he received the MidAmerica Award of the Society for the Study of Midwestern Literature. At present he is working on a critical biography of Sherwood Anderson and preparing a volume of Anderson's fiction for the Library of America.

BRUCE STARK is Associate Professor in the Departments of English and Comparative Literature at the University of Wisconsin at Milwaukee, where he teaches Old English, Old Norse, Norse mythology, Viking literature, history of the English language, structure of the English language, stylistics, and a course on Hemingway and Fitzgerald. He was educated at Beloit College (B.A.) and Columbia University (M.A. and Ph.D.) and has taught at Columbia University, Cornell University, and the University of Wisconsin at Madison. He was a Fulbright lecturer in linguistics at the University of Tel Aviv. He has published articles on Bloomfieldian linguistics, *The Great Gatsby*, *Heart of Darkness*, Norse mythology, contemporary Odinist cults in the United States, and Ernest Hemingway.

LINDA W. WAGNER-MARTIN is Hanes Professor of English at the University of North Carolina at Chapel Hill. She was born in 1936 in St. Marys, Ohio, and has a Ph.D. from Bowling Green State University. She has taught at Bowling Green State University, Wayne State University, and Michigan State University. She has received Guggenheim and Bunting Institute Fellowships as well as major grants from the American Council of Learned Societies and the National Endowment for the Humanities. Among her many books and essays on twentieth-century American writers are *The Poems of William Carlos Williams: A Critical Study* (1964), *The Prose of William Carlos Williams* (1970), *Denise Levertov* (1967), *Phyllis McGinley* (1971), *Dos Passos: Artist as American* (1979), *Ellen Glasgow: Beyond Convention* (1982), and *Sylvia Plath* (1987).

BROM WEBER retired as Professor of American Literature at the University of California at Davis in 1986. Born in New York City in 1917, he received his education at City College of New York (B.S.S.), the University of Wyoming (M.A.), and the University of Minnesota (Ph.D.). He has taught at City College, the New School for Social Research, Purdue University, DePauw University, and the Universities of Colorado, Minnesota, Washington, and Wyoming. He was Fulbright-Hays Professor in France (1966–67) and South Korea (1973) and has lectured on American literature in India, Turkey, Italy, England, Germany, and Taiwan. He is the author of *Hart Crane: A Biographical and Critical Study* (1948; rev. ed., 1970), *Sherwood Anderson* (1964), and *Our Multi-Ethnic Origins and American Literary Studies* (1975), editor of *The Letters of Hart Crane, 1916–1932* (1952; 1965), *Sut Lovingood* by G. W. Harris (1954), *An Anthology of American Humor* (1962; 1970), *The Story of a Country Town* by E. W. Howe (1964), *The Complete Poems and Selected Letters and Prose of Hart Crane* (1966), and *Sense and Sensibility in Twentieth-Century Writing* (1970), and coeditor of *American Vanguard* (1953) and *American Literature: Tradition and Innovation* (1969).

JAMES L. W. WEST III is Professor of English at Pennsylvania State University. He was born in Virginia in 1946 and received his B.A. and Ph.D. from the University of South Carolina. He previously taught at Virginia Polytechnic Institute and State University. He has held grants from the National Endowment for the Humanities, the American Council of Learned Societies, and the American Philosophical Society; he was a fellow at the National Humanities Center in 1981–82 and was Rosenbach Fellow at the University of Pennsylvania in 1983. He has published *William Styron: A Descriptive Bibliography* (1977), *The Making of "This Side of Paradise"* (1983), and *American Authors and the Literary Marketplace Since 1900* (1989), and serves as textual editor of the Pennsylvania Dreiser Edition and coeditor of the journal *Review*. His research has appeared in *Studies in Bibliography*, *PBSA*, *American Literature*, *Scholarly Publishing*, *Resources for American Literary Study*, *Mississippi Quarterly*, and other periodicals.

JAMES WOODRESS recently retired as Professor of English at the University of California at Davis. He was born in Webster Groves, Missouri, in 1916 and was educated at Amherst College (A.B.), New York University (M.A.), and Duke University (Ph.D.). He has held Ford Foundation and Guggenheim Foundation Fellowships, has been a Fulbright professor in France and Italy, and was a visiting professor at the Sorbonne. He has published book-length studies of William Dean Howells and biographies of Booth Tarkington, Joel Barlow, and Willa Cather. His revised and expanded edition of his Cather biography appeared in 1987. He was the founding editor of *American Literary Scholarship* and editor of many of the annual volumes in the series.

KARL F. ZENDER is Associate Professor of English at the University of California at Davis, where he has also served in several administrative capacities. He previously taught at Washington University in St. Louis and the University of Iowa. Born in Portsmouth, Ohio, in 1937, he holds degrees from Case Institute of Technology (B.S.), Case Western Reserve University (M.A.), and the University of Iowa (Ph.D.). He is the author of *The Crossing of the Ways: William Faulkner, the South, and the Modern World* (1989) as well as numerous essays on William Faulkner and other writers; he also contributed several chapters on Faulkner to *American Literary Scholarship*.

Index

This index includes the following: (1) authors of literary scholarship surveyed in this volume; if the author has published items under different names, for example, Linda Welshimer Wagner, Linda W. Wagner, and Linda Wagner-Martin, only the fullest version of the name is listed (Linda Welshimer Wagner-Martin); (2) literary or historical persons referred to throughout the volume; (3) works by the sixteen writers who are the subjects of the essays (these works are subentries under each writer's name); works by other authors are incorporated only under the author's name (e.g., *The Tempest* is not listed in the index by title; it appears under Shakespeare).

Library of Congress Cataloging-in-Publication Data
Sixteen modern American authors: volume 2, a survey of research and
criticism since 1972 / edited by Jackson R. Bryer
Bibliography.
Includes index.
ISBN 0-8223-0976-9 (alk. paper)   0-8223-1018-X (pbk.)
1. American literature—20th century—History and criticism.
I. Bryer, Jackson R.
PS221.S625   1989
810.9'0052—dc20   89-11789 CIP

Date Due